Lecture Notes in Computer Science　　10843

Commenced Publication in 1973
Founding and Former Series Editors:
Gerhard Goos, Juris Hartmanis, and Jan van Leeuwen

Editorial Board

David Hutchison
　Lancaster University, Lancaster, UK
Takeo Kanade
　Carnegie Mellon University, Pittsburgh, PA, USA
Josef Kittler
　University of Surrey, Guildford, UK
Jon M. Kleinberg
　Cornell University, Ithaca, NY, USA
Friedemann Mattern
　ETH Zurich, Zurich, Switzerland
John C. Mitchell
　Stanford University, Stanford, CA, USA
Moni Naor
　Weizmann Institute of Science, Rehovot, Israel
C. Pandu Rangan
　Indian Institute of Technology Madras, Chennai, India
Bernhard Steffen
　TU Dortmund University, Dortmund, Germany
Demetri Terzopoulos
　University of California, Los Angeles, CA, USA
Doug Tygar
　University of California, Berkeley, CA, USA
Gerhard Weikum
　Max Planck Institute for Informatics, Saarbrücken, Germany

More information about this series at http://www.springer.com/series/7409

Aldo Gangemi · Roberto Navigli
Maria-Esther Vidal · Pascal Hitzler
Raphaël Troncy · Laura Hollink
Anna Tordai · Mehwish Alam (Eds.)

The Semantic Web

15th International Conference, ESWC 2018
Heraklion, Crete, Greece, June 3–7, 2018
Proceedings

 Springer

Editors
Aldo Gangemi
University of Bologna
Bologna
Italy

Roberto Navigli (iD)
Sapienza University of Rome
Rome
Italy

Maria-Esther Vidal (iD)
Universidad Simón Bolívar
Caracas
Venezuela

Pascal Hitzler
Wright State University
Dayton, OH
USA

Raphaël Troncy (iD)
EURECOM
Biot
France

Laura Hollink
CWI
Amsterdam
The Netherlands

Anna Tordai (iD)
Elsevier B.V.
Amsterdam
The Netherlands

Mehwish Alam (iD)
CNR-ISTC
Rome
Italy

ISSN 0302-9743   ISSN 1611-3349   (electronic)
Lecture Notes in Computer Science
ISBN 978-3-319-93416-7   ISBN 978-3-319-93417-4   (eBook)
https://doi.org/10.1007/978-3-319-93417-4

Library of Congress Control Number: 2018946633

LNCS Sublibrary: SL3 – Information Systems and Applications, incl. Internet/Web, and HCI

© Springer International Publishing AG, part of Springer Nature 2018
This work is subject to copyright. All rights are reserved by the Publisher, whether the whole or part of the material is concerned, specifically the rights of translation, reprinting, reuse of illustrations, recitation, broadcasting, reproduction on microfilms or in any other physical way, and transmission or information storage and retrieval, electronic adaptation, computer software, or by similar or dissimilar methodology now known or hereafter developed.
The use of general descriptive names, registered names, trademarks, service marks, etc. in this publication does not imply, even in the absence of a specific statement, that such names are exempt from the relevant protective laws and regulations and therefore free for general use.
The publisher, the authors, and the editors are safe to assume that the advice and information in this book are believed to be true and accurate at the date of publication. Neither the publisher nor the authors or the editors give a warranty, express or implied, with respect to the material contained herein or for any errors or omissions that may have been made. The publisher remains neutral with regard to jurisdictional claims in published maps and institutional affiliations.

Printed on acid-free paper

This Springer imprint is published by the registered company Springer International Publishing AG
part of Springer Nature
The registered company address is: Gewerbestrasse 11, 6330 Cham, Switzerland

Preface

This volume contains the main proceedings of the 2018 edition of the Extended Semantic Web Conference (ESWC 2018). ESWC is established as a yearly major venue for discussing the latest scientific results and technology innovations related to the Semantic Web and linked data. At ESWC, international scientists, industry specialists, and practitioners meet to discuss the future of applicable, scalable, user-friendly, as well as potentially game-changing solutions. The 15th edition took place from June 3rd to June 7th, 2018, in Heraklion, Crete (Greece).

Building on its past success, ESWC is also a venue for broadening the focus of the Semantic Web community to span other relevant research areas in which semantics and Web technology play an important role, as well as for experimenting with innovative practices and topics that deliver extra value to the community and beyond.

This year's conference has introduced some novelties compared with the past: a new open reviewing policy (see later); three main tracks instead of two: the usual research and in-use tracks, plus a novel resource track; a new industry session dedicated to experiences and results by semantic technology companies.

The research track is organized into subtracks, and the chairs of ESWC 2018 organized two special subtracks putting particular emphasis on usage areas where Semantic Web technologies are facilitating a leap of progress, namely: "Benchmarking and Empirical Evaluations" and "Semantic Web for Science."

The other events keep the legacy of the past: a poster and demo session, workshops and tutorials, a PhD symposium, a challenges track, a project networking session. The regular subtracks include: vocabularies, schemas, ontologies, reasoning, linked data (including knowledge graphs), social Web and Web science, semantic data management, natural language processing and information retrieval, machine learning, mobile Web, sensors and semantic streams, services, APIs, processes and cloud computing.

Concerning the open reviewing policy, ESWC 2018 adopted a double-open reviewing schema, additionally placing all papers (either accepted or rejected) on the conference website, jointly with their reviews (rejected papers will be removed after the conference upon the authors' request) and the names of the reviewers (except when they decided to opt out). Two special chairs, Silvio Peroni and Sarven Capadisli, produced the website branch hosting papers and reviews, and enabled visitors to provide comments. The reviewing data have been processed in order to obtain insights over the multiple facets involved in the process and its argumentation. The overall policy is original for a conference, but we have inherited the experience of the successful open reviewing applied by the *Semantic Web Journal*, championed by one of its editors-in-chief, Pascal Hitzler, who was the resource chair at ESWC 2018. Data analytics and user feedback reports from this innovative process were discussed at the opening and closing sessions of ESWC 2018.

Emerging from its roots in AI and Web technology, the Semantic Web today is mainly a Web of linked data and a reference model for all sorts of knowledge graphs emerging in institutions, companies, and academia, upon which a plethora of services and applications for all possible domains are being proposed. Some of the core challenges that the Semantic Web aims at addressing are heterogeneity of content, and its volatile and rapidly changing nature, its uncertainty, provenance, and varying quality.

This, in combination with more traditional disciplines, such as logical modeling and reasoning, natural language processing, databases and data storage and access, machine learning, distributed systems, information retrieval and data mining, social networks, Web science and Web engineering, shows the span of topics covered by this conference. The nine regular research subtracks, in combination with resources and in-use tracks, and the two special research subtracks, constitute the main scientific program of ESWC 2018.

The main scientific program of the conference comprised 48 papers: 31 research, nine resources papers, eight in-use papers, selected out of 179 reviewed submissions, which corresponds to an acceptance rate of 23.5% for the research papers submitted, 41% for the resource papers, and 32% for the in-use papers. This program was completed by a demonstration and poster session (41 accepted out of 53 submissions), in which researchers had the chance to present their latest results and advances in the form of live demos or face-to-face presentations. In addition, the PhD symposium program included ten contributions, selected out of 17 submissions.

The conference program contained nine workshops, five tutorials, and an EU project networking session. This year, an open call also allowed us to select and support four challenges: Open Knowledge Extraction, Semantic Sentiment Analysis, Triple Store Performance, and Scalable Question-Answering over Linked Data. These associated events created an even more open, multidisciplinary, and cross-fertilizing environment at the conference, allowing for work-in progress and practical results to be discussed.

Workshops ranged from domain-focused topics, including the biomedical, scientific publishing, e-science, robotics, distributed ledgers, and scholarly fields, to more technology-focused topics ranging from RDF stream processing, query processing, data quality and data evolution, to sentiment analysis and semantic deep learning. Tutorial topics spanned NLP, ontology engineering, and linked data, including specific tutorials on knowledge graphs and rule-based processing of data. Proceedings from these satellite events are available in a separate volume.

The program also included three exciting invited keynotes, with topics ranging from the use of knowledge graphs in industrial applications, to traditional as well as novel Semantic Web topics.

The general and Program Committee chairs would like to thank the many people who were involved in making ESWC 2018 a success. First of all, our thanks go to the 24 co-chairs of the research track and the 360 reviewers for all tracks, including 49 external reviewers, for ensuring a rigorous and open review process that led to an excellent scientific program, and an average of four reviews per article. The scientific program was completed by an exciting selection of posters and demos chaired by Anna Lisa Gentile and Andrea Giovanni Nuzzolese.

Special thanks go to the PhD symposium chairs, Sebastian Rudolph and Maria Maleshkova, who managed one of the key events at ESWC. The brilliant PhD students will become the future leaders of our field, and deserve both encouragement and mentoring, which Maria and Sebastian made sure we could provide.

We also had a great selection of workshops and tutorials, as mentioned earlier, thanks to the commitment of our workshop and tutorial chairs, Heiko Paulheim and Jeff Pan.

Thanks to our EU project networking session chair, Maria Maleshkova, we had the opportunity to facilitate meetings and exciting discussions between leading European research projects. Networking and sharing ideas between projects is a crucial success factor for such large research projects.

We are additionally grateful for the work and commitment of Davide Buscaldi and Diego Reforgiato Recupero, and all the individual challenges chairs, who successfully established a challenge track.

Thanks to Andrea Conte for the organization of the industry track, which included six substantial presentations from companies that have started adopting Semantic Web technologies, and to York Sure for playing the ever-challenging sponsor chair role.

We thank STI International for supporting the conference organization, and particularly Dieter Fensel as the conference treasurer. YouVivo GmbH and Venja Lehmann in particular deserve special thanks for the professional support of the local conference organization and for solving all practical matters.

Further, we are very grateful to Mehwish Alam, our publicity and proceedings chair, who kept our community informed throughout the year and did an excellent job in preparing this volume with the kind support of Springer. We also thank Venislav Georgiev, who administered the website. We finally thank our sponsors, listed on the next pages, for their vital support of this edition of ESWC.

The general chair would like to close the preface with his warm thanks to the six program chairs for their relaxed but rigorous commitment in carrying out the novel open reviewing experiment, facing the thousands of questions and the few complaints from leading our peer community in an almost unknown territory, which will be a milestone for future events fostering openness in science.

June 2018

Aldo Gangemi
Maria-Esther Vidal
Roberto Navigli
Pascal Hitzler
Raphaël Troncy
Anna Tordai
Laura Hollink

Organization

General Chair

Aldo Gangemi — University of Bologna and CNR, Italy

Research Track Program Chairs

Roberto Navigli — Sapienza University of Rome, Italy
Maria-Esther Vidal — Leibniz Information Centre for Science and Technology University Library, Germany, and Universidad Simon Bolivar, Venezuela

Resource Track Program Chairs

Pascal Hitzler — Wright State University, USA
Raphael Troncy — Eurecom, France

In-Use Track Program Chairs

Laura Hollink — Centrum Wiskunde and Informatica, The Netherlands
Anna Tordai — Elsevier, The Netherlands

Workshop and Tutorial Chairs

Heiko Paulheim — University of Mannheim, Germany
Jeff Pan — The University of Aberdeen, UK

Poster and Demo Track Chairs

Anna Lisa Gentile — IBM Research Almaden, USA
Andrea Giovanni Nuzzolese — ISTC-CNR, Rome, Italy

Challenge Chairs

Davide Buscaldi — Université Paris 13, France
Diego Reforgiato Recupero — University of Cagliari, Italy

PhD Symposium Chairs

Sebastian Rudolph — Technische Universität Dresden, Germany
Maria Maleshkova — Karlsruhe Institute of Technology, Germany

EU Project Networking Chair

Maria Maleshkova   Karlsruhe Institute of Technology, Germany

Industry Session Chair

Andrea Conte   Reply Spa, Italy

Sponsoring Chair

York Sure-Vetter   Karlsruhe Institute of Technology, Germany

Open Conference Data Chairs

Sarven Capadisli   University of Bonn, Germany
Silvio Peroni   University of Bologna, Italy

Publicity Chairs

Mehwish Alam   ISTC-CNR, Rome, Italy

Web Presence

Venislav Georgiev   STI, Austria

Proceedings Chair

Mehwish Alam   ISTC-CNR, Rome, Italy

Treasurer

Dieter Fensel   STI, Austria

Local Conference Organization

Venja Lehmann   YouVivo GmbH, Germany

Subtrack Chairs

Vocabularies, Schemas, Ontologies

Helena Sofia Pinto   Universidade de Lisbon, Portugal
Christoph Lange   University of Bonn Fraunhofer IAIS, Germany

Reasoning

Jeff Pan	The University of Aberdeen, UK
Diego Calvanese	Free University of Bozen-Bolzano, Italy

Linked Data

Hala Skaf-Molli	University of Nantes, France
Jorge Gracia	University of Zaragoza, Spain

Social Web and Web Science

Harald Sack	Leibniz Institute for Information Infrastructure, Karlsruhe Institute of Technology, Germany
Stefan Dietze	L3S Research Center, Germany

Semantic Data Management, Big Data, Scalability

Maribel Acosta	Karlsruhe Institute of Technology, Germany
Olaf Hartig	Linköping University, Sweden

Natural Language Processing and Information Retrieval

John McCrae	National University of Ireland, Ireland
Valentina Presutti	Institute of Cognitive Sciences and Technologies, Italy

Machine Learning

Andreas Hotho	University of Würzburg, Germany
Achim Rettinger	Karlsruhe Institute of Technology, Germany

Mobile Web, Sensors, and Semantic Streams

Themis Palpanas	Paris Descartes University, France
Intizar Ali	National University of Ireland, Ireland

Services, APIs, Processes, and Cloud Computing

Amrapali Zaveri	Maastricht University, The Netherlands
Ruben Verborgh	Research Foundation Flanders Ghent University, Belgium

Benchmarking and Empirical Evaluation

Oscar Corcho	Universidad Politécnica de Madrid, Spain
Emanuele Della Valle	Politecnico di Milano, Italy

Scientific Semantic Web

Catia Pesquita	University of Lisbon, Portugal
Adrian Paschke	Freie Universität Berlin, Germany

Program Committee

Maribel Acosta	Karlsruhe Institute of Technology, Germany
Nitish Aggarwal	IBM, USA
Asan Agibetov	Medical University of Vienna, Austria
Henning Agt-Rickauer	HPI, Germany
Mehwish Alam	Consiglio Nazionale delle Ricerche, Italy
Céline Alec	Université Caen-Normandie, France
Intizar Ali	Insight Centre for Data Analytics, National University of Ireland
Vito Walter Anelli	Politecnico di Bari, Italy
Grigoris Antoniou	University of Huddersfield, UK
Mihael Arcan	Insight Centre for Data Analytics, National University of Ireland
Luigi Asprino	University of Bologna and STLab, Italy
Judie Attard	Trinity College Dublin, Ireland
Martin Atzmueller	Tilburg University, The Netherlands
Sören Auer	TIB Leibniz Information Center of Science and Technology and University of Hannover, Germany
Michele Barbera	SpazioDati SRL, Italy
Payam Barnaghi	University of Surrey, UK
Caroline Barriere	CRIM, Canada
Pierpaolo Basile	University of Bari, Italy
Valerio Basile	Inria, France
Hannah Bast	University of Freiburg, Germany
Martin Becker	University of Würzburg, Germany
Wouter Beek	Vrije Universiteit Amsterdam, The Netherlands
Khalid Belhajjame	Université Paris-Dauphine, France
Vito Bellini	Politecnico di Bari, Italy
Eva Blomqvist	Linköping University, Sweden
Carlos Bobed	University of Rennes 1, France
Shawn Bowers	Gonzaga University, USA
Loris Bozzato	Fondazione Bruno Kessler, Italy
Christopher Brewster	TNO, The Netherlands
Carlos Buil Aranda	Universidad Técnica Federico Santa María, Chile
Paul Buitelaar	Insight Centre for Data Analytics, National University of Ireland
Davide Buscaldi	LIPN, Université Paris 13, France
Elena Cabrio	Université Côte d'Azur, CNRS, Inria, France

Jean-Paul Calbimonte	University of Applied Sciences and Arts Western Switzerland, Switzerland
Diego Calvanese	Free University of Bozen-Bolzano, Italy
Mario Cannataro	University Magna Graecia of Catanzaro, Italy
Caterina Caracciolo	Food and Agriculture Organization of the United Nations, Italy
Irene Celino	CEFRIEL, Italy
Davide Ceolin	Vrije Universiteit Amsterdam, The Netherlands
Miguel Ceriani	Queen Mary University of London, UK
Michelle Cheatham	Wright State University, USA
Christian Chiarcos	Universität Frankfurt am Main, Germany
Key-Sun Choi	Korea Advanced Institute of Science and Technology, South Korea
Diego Collarana	Enterprise Information System
Pieter Colpaert	Ghent University, Belgium
Andrea Conte	Reply, Italy
Oscar Corcho	Universidad Politécnica de Madrid, Spain
Francesco Corcoglioniti	University of Trento, Italy
Melanie Courtot	European Bioinformatics Institute, UK
Francisco Couto	University of Lisbon, Portugal
Roberta Cuel	University of Trento, Italy
Edward Curry	Insight Centre for Data Analytics, National University of Ireland
Claudia d'Amato	University of Bari, Italy
Mathieu D'Aquin	Insight Centre for Data Analytics, National University of Ireland
Aba-Sah Dadzie	The Open University
Laura M. Daniele	TNO, Netherlands Organization for Applied Scientific Research, The Netherlands
Brian Davis	Insight Centre for Data Analytics, National University of Ireland
Victor de Boer	Vrije Universiteit Amsterdam, The Netherlands
Ernesto William De Luca	Georg Eckert Institute – Leibniz Institute for International Textbook Research, Germany
Jeremy Debattista	Trinity College Dublin, Ireland
Daniele Dell'Aglio	University of Zurich, Switzerland
Emanuele Dellavalle	Politecnico di Milano, Italy
Gianluca Demartini	University of Queensland, Australia
Tommaso Di Noia	Politecnico di Bari, Italy
Dennis Diefenbach	Jean Monet University, France
Stefan Dietze	L3S Research Center, Germany
Anastasia Dimou	Ghent University, Belgium
Christian Dirschl	Wolters Kluwer, Germany
Dejing Dou	University of Oregon, USA
Mauro Dragoni	Fondazione Bruno Kessler, Italy
Alistair Duke	BT, UK

Anca Dumitrache	Vrije Universiteit Amsterdam, The Netherlands
Michel Dumontier	Maastricht University
Floriana Esposito	Università degli Studi di Aldo Moro Bari, Italy
Ralph Ewerth	Leibniz Information Centre for Science and Technology, Germany
Nicola Fanizzi	Università degli Studi di Bari Aldo Moro, Italy
Stefano Faralli	University of Mannheim, Germany
Daniel Faria	Instituto Gulbenkian de Ciência, Portugal
Catherine Faron Zucker	Université Nice Sophia Antipolis, France
Anna Fensel	Semantic Technology Institute Innsbruck, University of Innsbruck, Austria
Miriam Fernandez	Knowledge Media Institute
Javier D. Fernández	Vienna University of Economics and Business, Austria
Agata Filipowska	Poznan University of Economics, Poland
Valeria Fionda	University of Calabria, Italy
George H. L. Fletcher	Eindhoven University of Technology, The Netherlands
Giorgos Flouris	FORTH-ICS, Greece
Flavius Frasincar	Erasmus University of Rotterdam, The Netherlands
Irini Fundulaki	FORTH-ICS, Greece
Luis Galárraga	Aalborg University, Denmark
Aldo Gangemi	Università di Bologna and CNR-ISTC, Italy
Daniel Garijo	Information Sciences Institute, USA
Anna Lisa Gentile	IBM, USA
Alain Giboin	Inria, France
Martin Giese	University of Oslo, Norway
Rafael S Gonçalves	Stanford University, USA
Jorge Gracia	University of Zaragoza, Spain
Irlan Grangel	University of Bonn, Germany
Michael Granitzer	University of Passau, Germany
Alasdair Gray	Heriot-Watt University, UK
Dagmar Gromann	TU Dresden, Germany
Paul Groth	Elsevier Labs
Giovanna Guerrini	University of Genoa, Italy
Alessio Gugliotta	Innova, Italy
Giancarlo Guizzardi	Ontology and Conceptual Modeling Research Group/Federal University of Espirito Santo, Brazil
Christophe Guéret	Accenture, Ireland
Amelie Gyrard	Ohio Center of Excellence in Knowledge-enabled Computing, USA
Peter Haase	metaphacts
Lavdim Halilaj	Fraunhofer, Germany
Siegfried Handschuh	University of Passau, Germany
Andreas Harth	Karlsruhe Institute of Technology, Germany
Olaf Hartig	Linköping University, Sweden
Oktie Hassanzadeh	IBM, USA
Jörn Hees	TU Kaiserslautern and DFKI, Germany

Sven Hertling	University of Mannheim, Germany
Daniel Hienert	GESIS, Leibniz Institute for the Social Sciences, Germany
Pascal Hitzler	Wright State University, USA
Robert Hoehndorf	King Abdullah University of Science and Technology, Saudi Arabia
Rinke Hoekstra	University of Amsterdam, The Netherlands
Aidan Hogan	Universidad de Chile, Chile
Laura Hollink	CWI, The Netherlands
Anett Hoppe	TIB, Leibniz Information Centre for Science and Technology, Germany
Matthew Horridge	Stanford University, USA
Tomas Horvath	Eötvös Loránd University, Hungary
Katja Hose	Aalborg University, Denmark
Andreas Hotho	University of Würzburg, Germany
Zhisheng Huang	Vrije Universiteit Amsterdam, The Netherlands
Antoine Isaac	Europeana and Vrije Universiteit Amsterdam, The Netherlands
Ashutosh Jadhav	IBM, USA
Valentina Janev	The Mihajlo Pupin Institute, Serbia
Krzysztof Janowicz	University of California, Santa Barbara, USA
Ernesto Jimenez-Ruiz	University of Oslo, Norway
Anna Jordanous	University of Kent, UK
Simon Jupp	European Bioinformatics Institute
Martin Kaltenböck	Semantic Web Company
Naouel Karam	Freie Universität Berlin, Germany
Anna Kaspzik	Technische Informationsbibliothek, Germany
Tomi Kauppinen	Aalto University School of Science, Finland
Takahiro Kawamura	Japan Science and Technology Agency, Japan
Ali Khalili	Vrije Universiteit Amsterdam, The Netherlands
Evgeny Kharlamov	University of Oxford, UK
Sabrina Kirrane	Vienna University of Economics and Business, Austria
Tomas Kliegr	University of Economics, Prague, Czech Republic
Roman Kontchakov	Birkbeck, University of London
Maria Koutraki	FIZ Karlsruhe, Germany
Kouji Kozaki	Osaka University, Japan
Adila A. Krisnadhi	Wright State University, USA and Universitas Indonesia
Sebastian Köhler	Institut für Medizinische Genetik, Charite Universitätsmedizin Berlin, Germany
Christoph Lange	University of Bonn and Fraunhofer IAIS, Germany
Mike Lauruhn	Elsevier
Agnieszka Lawrynowicz	Poznan University of Technology, Poland
Danh Le Phuoc	TU Berlin, Germany
Maxime Lefrançois	Mines Saint-Etienne, France
Jens Lehmann	University of Bonn, Germany

Steffen Lohmann	Fraunhofer, Germany
Vanessa Lopez	IBM, Ireland
Phillip Lord	Newcastle University, UK
Ismini Lourentzou	University of Illinois at Urbana - Champaign, USA
Bertram Ludaescher	University of Illinois at Urbana-Champaign, USA
Ioanna Lytra	University of Bonn, Germany
Valentina Maccatrozzo	Vrije Universiteit Amsterdam, The Netherlands
Christian Mader	Fraunhofer, Germany
Veronique Malaise	Elsevier BV
Maria Maleshkova	Karlsruhe Institute of Technology, Germany
Alessandro Margara	Politecnico di Milano, Italy
Nicolas Matentzoglu	EMBL-EBI, UK
Diana Maynard	The University of Sheffield, UK
John P. McCrae	National University of Ireland
Fiona McNeill	Heriot Watt University, UK
Edgar Meij	Bloomberg L.P., London
Albert Meroño-Peñuela	Vrije Universiteit Amsterdam, The Netherlands
Aditya Mogadala	Karlsruhe Institute of Technology, Germany
Pascal Molli	University of Nantes, France
Stefano Montanelli	University of Milan, Italy
Steven Moran	University of Zurich, Switzerland
Till Mossakowski	University of Magdeburg, Germany
Andreas Mueller	Schaeffler Technologies AG, Germany
Varish Mulwad	GE Global Research, USA
Raghava Mutharaju	GE Global Research, USA
Roberto Navigli	Sapienza University of Rome, Italy
Axel-Cyrille Ngonga Ngomo	Paderborn University, Germany
Vinh Nguyen	National Library of Medicine, NIH, USA
Andriy Nikolov	metaphacts GmbH, Germany
Lyndon Nixon	MODUL Technology GmbH
Vit Novacek	DERI, National University of Ireland, Ireland
Andrea Giovanni Nuzzolese	University of Bologna, Italy
Leo Obrst	MITRE, USA
Fabrizio Orlandi	University of Bonn, Germany
Francesco Osborne	The Open University
Petya Osenova	Sofia University and IICT-BAS, Bulgaria
Guillermo Palma	Universidad Simón Bolívar, Venezuela
Matteo Palmonari	University of Milano-Bicocca, Italy
Themis Palpanas	Paris Descartes University, France
Jeff Z. Pan	University of Aberdeen, UK
Adrian Paschke	Freie Universität Berlin, Germany
Michele Pasin	Nature Publishing Group
Tommaso Pasini	Sapienza University of Rome, Italy
Pankesh Patel	Fraunhofer CESE, Germany
Heiko Paulheim	University of Mannheim, Germany

Tassilo Pellegrini	University of Applied Sciences St. Pölten, Austria
Silvio Peroni	University of Bologna, Italy
Catia Pesquita	Universidade de Lisboa, Portugal
Rafael Peñaloza	Free University of Bozen-Bolzano, Italy
Hsofia Pinto	Algos, INESC-ID/IST, Portugal
Giuseppe Pirrò	Institute for High Performance Computing and Networking, ICAR-CNR, Italy
Antonella Poggi	Sapienza University of Rome, Italy
Axel Polleres	Vienna University of Economics and Business, Austria
Jedrzej Potoniec	Poznan University of Technology, Poland
María Poveda-Villalón	Universidad Politécnica de Madrid, Spain
Valentina Presutti	CNR, Institute of Cognitive Sciences and Tecnologies, Italy
Freddy Priyatna	Universidad Politécnica de Madrid, Spain
Gustavo Publio	Universität Leipzig, Germany
Dharmen Punjani	National and Kapodistrian University of Athens, Greece
Guilin Qi	Southeast University
Steffen Remus	University of Hamburg, Germany
Achim Rettinge	Karlsruhe Institute of Technology, Germany
Martin Rezk	Rakuten, Tokyo, Japan
Martin Riedl	University of Stuttgart, Germany
Petar Ristoski	University of Mannheim, Germany
Carlos R. Rivero	Rochester Institute of Technology, USA
Giuseppe Rizzo	ISMB, Italy
Víctor Rodríguez Doncel	Universidad Politécnica de Madrid, Spain
Mariano Rodríguez Muro	IBM, USA
Francesco Ronzano	Universitat Pompeu Fabra, Spain
Ana Roxin	University of Burgundy, France
Edna Ruckhaus	Universidad Politécnica de Madrid, Spain
Sebastian Rudolph	TU Dresden, Germany
Anisa Rula	University of Milano-Bicocca, Italy
Alessandro Russo	STLab, ISTC-CNR, Italy
Michele Ruta	Politecnico di Bari, Italy
Harald Sack	FIZ Karlsruhe, Leibniz Institute for Information Infrastructure and KIT Karlsruhe, Germany
Satya Sahoo	Case Western Reserve University, USA
Idafen Santana-Pérez	Universidad Politécnica de Madrid, Spain
Cristina Sarasua	University of Zurich, Switzerland
Felix Sasaki	Lambdawerk
Kai-Uwe Sattler	TU Ilmenau, Germany
Marco Luca Sbodio	IBM, Ireland
Ralf Schenkel	Trier University, Germany
Stefan Schlobach	Vrije Universiteit Amsterdam, The Netherlands
Michael Schmidt	Amazon, USA
Jodi Schneider	University of Illinois Urbana Champaign, USA

Juan F. Sequeda	Capsenta Labs
Barış Sertkaya	Frankfurt University of Applied Sciences, Germany
Nicolas Seydoux	LAAS-CNRS/IRIT, France
Hamed Shariat Yazdi	University of Bonn, Germany
Chaitanya Shivade	IBM, USA
Pavel Shvaiko	Informatica Trentina, Italy
Mantas Simkus	Vienna University of Technology, Austria
Kuldeep Singh	Fraunhofer, Germany
Hala Skaf	Nantes University, France
Jennifer Sleeman	University of Maryland Baltimore County, USA
Monika Solanki	University of Oxford, UK
Steffen Staab	University of Koblenz-Landau, Germany and University of Southampton, UK
Timo Stegemann	University of Duisburg-Essen, Germany
Thomas Steiner	Google, Germany
Armando Stellato	University of Rome Tor Vergata, Italy
Daria Stepanova	Max Planck Institute for Informatics, Germany
Markus Stocker	German National Library of Science and Technology, TIB, Germany
Umberto Straccia	ISTI-CNR, Italy
Olga Streibel	Bayer, Germany
York Sure-Vetter	Karlsruhe Institute of Technology, Germany
Mari Carmen Suárez-Figueroa	Universidad Politécnica de Madrid, Spain
Vojtěch Svátek	University of Economics, Prague, Czech Republic
Danai Symeonidou	INRA, France
Ruben Taelman	Ghent University, Belgium
Hideaki Takeda	National Institute of Informatics, Japan
Harsh Thakkar	University of Bonn, Germany
Krishnaprasad Thirunarayan	Wright State University, USA
Steffen Thoma	Karlsruhe Institute of Technology, Germany
Ilaria Tiddi	The Open University, UK
Tabea Tietz	FIZ Karlsruhe, Germany
Riccardo Tommasini	Politecnico di Milano, Italy
Anna Tordai	Elsevier
Ignacio Traverso-Rebon	Karlsruhe Institute of Technology, Germany
Cassia Trojahn	UT2J and IRIT, France
Raphael Troncy	EURECOM, France
Jürgen Umbrich	Vienna University of Economy and Business, Austria
Ricardo Usbeck	Paderborn University, Germany
Astrid van Aggelen	CWI, The Netherlands
Marieke van Erp	KNAW Humanities Cluster, The Netherlands
Jacco van Ossenbruggen	CWI and VU University Amsterdam, The Netherlands
Ruben Verborgh	Ghent University, Belgium
Maria Esther Vidal	Universidad Simon Bolivar, Venezuela
Maria-Esther Vidal	Leibniz Information Centre, Germany

Serena Villata	CNRS, Laboratoire d'Informatique,
	Signaux et Systèmes de Sophia-Antipolis, France
Simon Walk	Graz University of Technology, Austria
Sebastian Walter	Semalytix GmbH, Germany
Haofen Wang	Shenzhen Gowild Robotics Co. Ltd.
Kewen Wang	Griffith University, Australia
Krzysztof Wecel	Poznan University of Economics, Poland
Josiane Xavier Parreira	Siemens AG Österreich, Austria
Guohui Xiao	Free University of Bozen-Bolzano, Italy
Chenyan Xiong	Carnegie Mellon University, USA
Takahira Yamaguchi	Keio University, Japan
Ondřej Zamazal	University of Economics, Prague, Czech Republic
Amrapali Zaveri	Maastricht University, The Netherlands
Lei Zhang	Karlsruhe Institute of Technology, Germany
Ziqi Zhang	Sheffield University, UK
Jun Zhao	University of Oxford, UK
Antoine Zimmermann	École des Mines de Saint-Étienne, France
Daniel Zoller	University of Würzburg, Germany

Additional Reviewers

Agapito, Giuseppe
Arcan, Mihael
Bader, Sebastian
Bakkelund, Daniel
Barros, Márcia
Basile, Pierpaolo
Bin, Simon
Brosius, Dominik
Calabrese, Barbara
Chakravarthi, Bharathi Raja
Corman, Julien
d'Amato, Claudia
de Graaf, Klaas Andries
Ding, Linfang
Elias, Mirette
Fafalios, Pavlos
Ferreira, João
Fischl, Wolfgang
Gaignard, Alban
Galliani, Pietro
Galárraga, Luis
Ghiasnezhadomran, Pouya
Güzel, Elem

Ibrahim, Yusra
Idrissou, Al
Janke, Daniel
Jurgovsky, Johannes
Karlsen, Leif Harald
Klungre, Vidar
Lamurias, Andre
Lohr, Matthias
Malone, James
Matentzoglu, Nicolas
Milano, Marianna
Mireles, Victor
Monti, Diego
Montoya, Gabriela
Moodley, Kody
Mousavi Nejad, Najmeh
Müller-Budack, Eric
Nayyeri, Mojtaba
Neuhaus, Fabian
Neumaier, Sebastian
Nooralahzadeh, Farhad
Pandit, Harshvardhan Jitendra
Paudel, Bibek

Peñaloza, Rafael
Potoniec, Jedrzej
Revenko, Artem
Ringsquandl, Martin
Rizzo, Giuseppe
Rula, Anisa
Sadeghi, Afshin
Saha Roy, Rishiraj
Savkovic, Ognjen
Schlötterer, Jörg
Schmelzeisen, Lukas
Skjæveland, Martin G.
Sousa, Diana

Spahiu, Blerina
Springstein, Matthias
Steinmetz, Nadine
Sun, Chang
van Soest, Johan
Weller, Tobias
Westphal, Patrick
Wilke, Adrian
Zayed, Omnia
Zhou, Lu
Zhou, Qianru
Zhu, Rui
Zucco, Chiara

Sponsoring Institutions

Gold Sponsors

Silver Sponsors

Bronze Sponsors

Abstracts of Keynotes

How to Make, Grow, and Sell a Semantic Web Start-Up

Milan Stankovic

Sépage, Paris, France

Abstract. The Semantic Web broke down the boundaries of academia years ago, and started being used to solve more and more industry challenges. However, inducing the change toward embracing Semantic Web technologies in many domains remains a mystery. How to sell Semantic Web solutions, in competition with aggressively marketed legacy technologies? How to get old and stagnant industry players to invest in a Semantic Web future? What are the key advantages that make clients buy Semantic Web solutions? In his talk, Milan will address these questions from the perspective of his own experience in creating and growing a Semantic Web start-up in the travel market. He will share recipes for success and discuss the remaining potential for the Semantic Web to yet greatly impact the travel industry.

Knowledge Representation and the Semantic Web – An Ontologician's View

Sebastian Rudolph

TU Dresden, Germany

Abstract. With the rise of the Semantic Web and in the course of the standardization of ontology languages, logic-based knowledge representation (KR) has received great attention from academics and practitioners alike. This talk will present a – necessarily subjective – view on the role of KR in the context of the Semantic Web. It will make a case for rigid logical underpinnings with principled analyses of expressivity and computational properties (like decidability or complexity) of KR formalisms, but also discuss the challenges that the KR community has to address in order to ensure the ongoing uptake of modern KR technology by the wider Semantic Web public and IT business in general.

Structural Summarization of Semantic Graphs

Ioana Manolescu

Inria, Paris-Saclay, Paris, France

Abstract. RDF graphs comprise highly complex data, both from a structural and from a semantic perspective. This makes them hard to discover and learn, and hinders their usability.

An elegant basis for summarizing graphs is provided by the graph quotient formalism. In a nutshell, a graph quotient specifies a way to view some graph nodes as equivalent to each other, and represents a graph through its equivalence classes based on this equivalence. This talk presents work carried out over the past few years on quotient summarization of semantic-rich RDF graph. In particular, it introduces a set of summaries particularly suited to the heterogeneous structure of RDF graphs, and discusses novel results at the interplay of summarization and saturation with RDF schema rules.

Contents

Analyzing the Evolution of Vocabulary Terms and Their Impact on the LOD Cloud

Mohammad Abdel-Qader[1,2]([✉]) ⓘ, Ansgar Scherp[1,2] ⓘ, and Iacopo Vagliano[2] ⓘ

[1] Christian-Albrechts University, Kiel, Germany
{stu120798,asc}@informatik.uni-kiel.de
[2] ZBW – Leibniz Information Centre for Economics, Kiel, Germany
{m.abdel-qader,a.scherp,I.Vagliano}@zbw.eu

Abstract. Vocabularies are used for modeling data in Knowledge Graphs (KGs) like the Linked Open Data Cloud and Wikidata. During their lifetime, vocabularies are subject to changes. New terms are coined, while existing terms are modified or deprecated. We first quantify the amount and frequency of changes in vocabularies. Subsequently, we investigate to which extend and when the changes are adopted in the evolution of KGs. We conduct our experiments on three large-scale KGs: the Billion Triples Challenge datasets, the Dynamic Linked Data Observatory dataset, and Wikidata. Our results show that the change frequency of terms is rather low, but can have high impact due to the large amount of distributed graph data on the web. Furthermore, not all coined terms are used and most of the deprecated terms are still used by data publishers. The adoption time of terms coming from different vocabularies ranges from very fast (few days) to very slow (few years). Surprisingly, we could observe some adoptions before the vocabulary changes were published. Understanding the evolution of vocabulary terms is important to avoid wrong assumptions about the modeling status of data published on the web, which may result in difficulties when querying the data from distributed sources.

1 Introduction

Vocabulary terms define the schema of Knowledge Graphs (KGs) such as the Linked Open Data (LOD) cloud or Wikidata. After ontology engineers publish the first version of a vocabulary, the terms are subject to changes to reflect new requirements or shifts in the domains the vocabularies model. So far it is unknown how such vocabulary changes are reflected by the KGs that are using their terms. Data publishers may not be aware that changes in the vocabulary terms happened since it occurs rather rarely [7]. Explicitly triggering data publishers to update their model is also challenging due to the distributed nature of KGs such as the LOD cloud. Data publishers may be interested in being notified when certain vocabulary term changes happen, but they lack proper tools and

© Springer International Publishing AG, part of Springer Nature 2018
A. Gangemi et al. (Eds.): ESWC 2018, LNCS 10843, pp. 1–16, 2018.
https://doi.org/10.1007/978-3-319-93417-4_1

services to track whether and what kind of changes on vocabulary terms happened. Likewise, ontology engineers are not aware of who uses their vocabularies and lack a tool that reflects the adoption status of their ontologies and changes on the defined terms. In this paper, we study the evolution of vocabulary terms in KGs. We address three research questions: (1) *When are the newly created terms adopted in KGs?* (2) *What is the use rate of terms for a set of vocabularies in each dataset?* (3) *Are the deprecated terms still used in KGs?*

To address these questions, we analyzed various vocabularies to better understand by whom and how they are used, and how these changes are adopted in evolving KGs. Formally, we understand a vocabulary V as a set of terms T. A term T is either a class C or a property P. A set of terms relates to a vocabulary as $T(V) = C(V) \bigcup P(V)$. Changes in a vocabulary V are changes on its terms, i.e., classes and properties. Data that uses terms of a changed vocabulary should be updated accordingly. In a previous work [2], we manually conducted a qualitative analysis of vocabulary evolution on the LOD cloud. We analyzed the changes for a set of vocabularies by clarifying which terms changed, the type of change, and if those changes were done on terms defined in the vocabularies or on the classes and properties that were imported from other vocabularies. In this paper, we consider the two basic types of changes: addition and deletion. Any other change, e.g., a modification, can be expressed by these two basic changes. We use three well-known dataset: Dynamic Linked Data Observatory (DyLDO) [8], Billion Triples Challenge (BTC)[1], and Wikidata[2].

Our experiments showed that even if the frequency of vocabularies terms changes is rather low, they have a large impact on the real data. Most of the newly coined terms are adopted in less than one week after their publishing date.

Our work may help ontology engineers to select classes and properties that fit their needs when creating or updating ontologies. For example, we believe it can make ontology engineers more aware of who uses their terms and how. Furthermore, it may foster a better understanding what is the impact of their changes and how they are adopted, to possibly learn from previous experience what change is effective and what not. This study may also assists data publishers in updating their models by providing information about vocabulary changes.

The remainder is structured as follows. In Sect. 2, we review related work. We present our methodology in Sect. 3, and describe the datasets considered in Sect. 4. We outline our results in Sect. 5, we discuss them in Sect. 6 and conclude in Sect. 7.

2 Related Work

In terms of analyzing the use of structured data on the web, some works focused on *schema.org*. Meusel et al. [9] analyzed its evolution and adoption. They made a comparison of the use of *schema.org* terms over four years by extracting the

---

[1] http://challenge.semanticweb.org/, last accessed: 29/11/2017.

[2] https://www.wikidata.org, last accessed: 29/11/2017.

structured data from the web pages that use this vocabulary from *WebDataCommons* Microdata datasets[3]. They discovered that not all terms in *schema.org* are used and deprecated terms are still used, as it is also illustrated in this work. Furthermore, they found that publishing new types and properties is preferred over using *schema.org*'s extension mechanism. Guha et al. [6] investigated the use of the *schema.org* in the structured data of a set of web pages. They analyzed a sample of 10 billion web pages crawled from Google index and *WebDataCommons* and found that about 31% of those pages had some *schema.org* elements and estimated that around 12 million websites are using *schema.org* terms. In contrast to this work, they did not consider the changes in vocabulary terms. Additionally, we are not limited to one vocabulary only.

Mihindukulasooriya et al. [10] conducted a quantitative analysis for studying the evolution of DBpedia, *schema.org*, PROV-O, and FOAF ontologies. They proposed recommendations such as the need of dividing large ontologies into modules to avoid duplicates when adding new terms and adding provenance information beside the generic metadata when the change occurred. Papavassiliou et al. [11] proposed a framework that automatically identifies changes for both schema and data. They provide a formal language for identifying ontology changes and a change detection algorithm. Roussakis et al. [12] introduced a framework for analyzing the evolution of LOD datasets. Their framework allows users to identify changes in datasets versions and make a complex analysis on the evolved data.

Other works exploited DyLDO to study the use of vocabularies. Dividino et al. [4] analyzed how the use of RDF terms on the LOD cloud changed over time. They studied the combination of terms that describe a resource but did not investigate whether a vocabulary and its terms have changed. The authors applied their analysis on a dataset of 53 weekly snapshots from the DyLDO dataset, as it is also investigated in this work. Over six months, Käfer et al. [7] observed the documents retrieved from DyLDO. They analyzed those documents using different factors, their lifespan, the availability of those documents and their change rate. Also, they analyzed the RDF content that is frequently changed (triple added or removed). Additionally, they observed how links between documents are evolved over time. While their study is important for various areas such as smart caching, link maintenance, and versioning, it does not include information about adopting new and deprecated terms.

Gottron et al. [5] provided an analysis of the LOD schema information by analyzing the BTC 2012 dataset in three different levels. The first level concerns unique subject URIs by studying the dependency relations between the classes and their properties. They found a redundancy between classes and the attached properties. The second level addresses Pay-Level Domains (PLDs) by dividing the BTC 2012 dataset into individual PLDs. They found that 20% of the PLDs can be ignored without losing the graph explanation. The third level focuses on the vocabularies by analyzing how important a vocabulary is for describing the

---

[3] http://webdatacommons.org/, last accessed: 10/10/2017.

data. They stated that data publishers either made a strong schematic design, or apply a combination between a set of vocabularies to model their data.

Finally, some studies analyzed the use of vocabularies with other sources. Vandenbussche et al. [15] published a report that describes Linked Open Vocabularies (LOV). It provides statistics about LOV and its capabilities such as the total number of terms and the top-10 searched terms, but does not include information about adopting new terms and which PLD uses which vocabulary. Chawuthai et al. [3] proposed a model that facilitates the understanding of organisms. Their model presents the changes in taxonomic knowledge in RDF form. The proposed model acts as a history tracking system for changing terms but gives no information about how and when the terms are used, and which PLDs adopted the changed terms. Schaible et al. [13] published a survey of the most preferred strategies for reusing vocabulary terms. The participants, 79 Linked Data experts and practitioners, were asked to rank several LOD modeling strategies. The survey concluded that terms widely used are considered as a better approach. Furthermore, the use rate of vocabularies is a more important argument for reuse than the frequency of a single vocabulary term. Their survey can help to understand why there are some terms frequently used and why some of them are not used at all.

3   Analysis Method

Our analysis method consists of two steps. First, we determined vocabularies that have more than one published version on the web. Second, we investigated how the changed terms of vocabularies are adopted and used in the evolving KGs. For the first step, we relied on Schmachtenberg et al. [14] who published a report with detailed statistics about a large-scale snapshot of the LOD cloud. The snapshot comprises seed URIs from the datahub.io dataset[4], the BTC 2012 dataset[5], and the public-lod@w3.org mailing list[6]. We selected a set of vocabularies that satisfy the following set of conditions and characteristics. (1) The vocabulary have at least two versions published on the web to make a comparison between them. (2) These two versions are covered by the dataset that we investigate. For example, for the DyLDO dataset, there is to be one version of the vocabularies that have been published after May 6th, 2012. This is needed since at this date the first snapshot of the DyLDO dataset has been crawled. (3) The vocabulary terms are directly used for modeling some data, i.e., the vocabulary terms occur in at least one triple in the published dataset. In contrast, vocabularies could also be just linked from a data publisher, where changes of external vocabularies may not have any impact on the published data.

On the basis of these criteria, we examined 134 of the most used vocabularies listed in the state of the LOD cloud 2014 report by Schmachtenberg et al. [14]. We

---

[4] http://datahub.io/group/lodcloud, last accessed: 10/10/2017.

[5] http://km.aifb.kit.edu/projects/btc-2012/, last accessed: 10/10/2017.

[6] http://lists.w3.org/Archives/Public/public-lod/, last accessed: 10/10/2017.

found 18 vocabularies that have more than one version. From them, 13 vocabularies have changes (additions or deprecations) on terms created by the ontology engineers of those vocabularies in the timeframe of the considered datasets. We downloaded the different versions using the Linked Open Vocabularies (LOV) observatory[7]. Due to the low number of changes in the vocabulary, we did not use data mining techniques. Instead, we exploited the PromptDiff Protégé 4.3.0[8] plugin to identify the vocabulary changes. This plugin identifies simple as well as complex changes, and shows the difference between two versions. The vocabularies selected are listed in Table 1, which also provides the number of versions considered for each vocabulary and the total number of changes (additions and deletions) occurred. Considering all the vocabularies and all their versions the total number of terms studied is 936.

Table 1. Overview of the vocabularies and their changes.

Vocabulary	Versions	Changes
Asset Description Metadata Schema (ADMS)[a]	2	18
Citation Typing Ontology (CiTO)[b]	3	218
The data cube vocabulary (Cube)[c]	2	6
Data Catalog Vocabulary (DCAT)[d]	2	13
A vocabulary for jobs (emp)[e]	2	1
Ontology for geometry (geom)[f]	2	2
The Geonames ontology (GN)[g]	7	31
The music ontology (mo)[h]	2	46
Open Annotation Data Model (oa)[i]	2	31
Core organization ontology (org)[j]	2	8
W3C PROVenance Interchange (Prov)[k]	5	168
Vocabulary of a Friend (voaf)[l]	4	8
An extension of SKOS for representation of nomenclatures (xkos)[m]	2	1

[a] https://www.w3.org/TR/vocab-adms/, last accessed: 10/11/2017
[b] https://sparontologies.github.io/cito/current/cito.html, last accessed: 10/11/2017
[c] http://www.w3.org/TR/vocab-data-cube/, last accessed: 10/11/2017
[d] https://www.w3.org/TR/vocab-dcat/, last accessed: 10/11/2017
[e] http://lov.okfn.org/dataset/lov/vocabs/emp, last accessed: 10/11/2017
[f] http://data.ign.fr/def/geometrie/20160628.htm, last accessed: 10/11/2017
[g] http://www.geonames.org/ontology/documentation.html, last accessed: 10/11/2017
[h] http://www.geonames.org/ontology/documentation.html, last accessed: 10/11/2017
[i] http://www.openannotation.org/spec/core/, last accessed: 10/11/2017
[j] https://www.w3.org/TR/vocab-org/, last accessed: 10/11/2017
[k] https://www.w3.org/TR/prov-o/, last accessed: 10/11/2017
[l] http://lov.okfn.org/vocommons/voaf/v2.3/, last accessed: 10/11/2017
[m] http://rdf-vocabulary.ddialliance.org/xkos.html, last accessed: 10/11/2017

---

[7] http://lov.okfn.org/dataset/lov, last accessed: 10/10/2017.
[8] http://protege.stanford.edu, last accessed: 10/10/2017.

Subsequently, we investigated how the vocabulary terms changed are used in the evolving KGs. We extracted all PLDs from the subject of the crawled triples that use any of the terms from the 13 vocabularies above. Specifically, we relied on the Guava library[9], which returns the PLD from any given URL. Besides the date of the first appearance of a vocabulary term, we also recorded the number of triples which contain that term. This information is then used to compute the adoption time of terms over the dataset snapshots.

4 Datasets

We applied our analysis approach on three large-scale KGs. The first two are DyLDO and BTC, which are obtained from the Linked Open Data cloud, and the third is Wikidata. We analyzed the use, changes and adoption of vocabularies within each individual dataset. We did not compare any results across the datasets because the results cannot be meaningfully compared. Below, we briefly characterize the datasets.

DyLDO is a repository to store weekly snapshots from a subset of web data documents [8]. For our study, we parse 242 snapshots (from May 2012 until March 2017). BTC (See footnote 1) is yearly crawled from the LOD cloud from 2009 to 2012, as well as in 2014. We used all available versions to analyze the adoption of the extracted vocabularies in our study. Wikidata (See footnote 2) is a knowledge base to collaboratively store and edit structured data. To analyze the Wikidata vocabulary, we first extracted the terms introduced by this vocabulary. Specifically, through the RDF Exports from Wikidata page[10], we parsed the terms and properties from the RDF dump files that were generated using the Wikidata toolkit[11]. We assumed that the first snapshot of those files is the first version of the Wikidata vocabulary, and based on this assumption we parsed the next dump files to extract the changes to the first version, and so on. Relying on the 25 RDF dump files (from April 2014 until August 2016), we extracted the terms that are added or deprecated. Subsequently, we parsed those files to extract the adoption of terms to analyze the adoption behavior for the Wikidata vocabulary's terms.

5 Results

In this section, we summarize our findings based on the experiments conducted. Section 5.1 presents the results of vocabulary changes, use, and adoption in the LOD Cloud, while Sect. 5.2 outline the same findings for Wikidata.

---

[9] https://github.com/google/guava/, release 23.1.
[10] https://tools.wmflabs.org/wikidata-exports/rdf/, last accessed: 29/11/2017.
[11] https://github.com/Wikidata/Wikidata-Toolkit, last accessed: 29/11/2017.

5.1   The LOD Cloud

Changes in LOD Vocabularies. We studied the changes of terms in the vocabularies, focusing on creation and deprecation. Overall we observed 35% of newly created terms and 11% of deprecated ones. 85% of the vocabularies in this study have an increased number of terms. Two exceptions are *ADMS* and *CiTO*: the number of terms decreased for the former, while the latter vastly dropped in the number of classes.

During our analysis, we noticed that some of the deprecated properties were reintroduced later. These reintroduced terms belongs to the *CiTO* and *GN* vocabularies. The former deprecated 18 properties in May 2014 (introduced in March 2010), which reappeared in the version that was published in March 2015, i.e. after around ten months. The latter reintroduced three deprecated properties: `alternateName` (creation: October 2006, deprecation: September 2010, recreation: February 2012), `name` (creation: October 2006, deprecation: September 2010, recreation: October 2010), and `shortName` (creation: September 2010, deprecation: May 2010, recreation: February 2012). *GN* reintroduced two out of three deprecated terms after about 17 months and one shortly after (13 days).

Use of LOD Vocabularies. We analyzed the use of the selected vocabularies by considering triples which contains one of their terms in the predicate and/or the object position and a PLD in the subject. *Geonames.org* is the PLD that uses most terms of the selected vocabularies in the BTC 2009 and 2010 datasets (Table 2). In BTC 2011 and 2012, *zitgist.com* and *rdfize.com* are the most frequent PLDs, while in BTC 2014 and DyLDO, *dbtune.org* accounts for the highest use. However, the number of triples in BTC 2009, 2011, and 2012 is significantly lower than for the other datasets. The PLDs with the highest use of certain terms vary over time. For example, *geonames.org*'s triples did not disappear in BTC 2011. It still accounts for around 500,000 triples, i.e. much less than BTC 2009 and BTC 2010, but Table 2 only lists the PLD that has the highest amount of triples for each dataset (*zitgist.com* for BTC 2011). Please note that there are different crawling strategies for each BTC dataset and this may contribute to the variations in the number of triples.

Table 2. PLDs with the highest use of terms from the selected vocabularies for each of the datasets.

Dataset	PLD	Triples
BTC 2009	geonames.org	81M
BTC 2010	geonames.org	7M
BTC 2011	zitgist.com	2.6M
BTC 2012	rdfize.com	3.8M
BTC 2014	dbtune.org	81.5M
DyLDO	dbtune.org	160M

In DyLDO, the use of most vocabularies is steady. Figure 1 shows the vocabularies with a varying use. Notably, *mo* shows increasing and declining intervals, *Prov* is increasing in popularity despite some slight negative picks, while *ADMS* had a significant drop in 2015 after an initial increasing use, although it seems again slightly increasing from 2015 to 2017. Furthermore, *Cube* had a pick towards the end of 2015 to then come back to its initial use rate, while *emp* seems no more used from 2015.

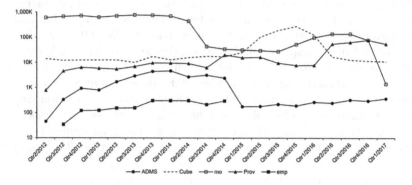

Fig. 1. The mean number of triples that use terms for a subset of the vocabularies considered by DyLDO snapshots aggregated in quarters.

The great majority of the deprecated terms (87%) are still used after deprecation. We found that *geonames.org* is the PLD that most frequently uses deprecated terms in the BTC and DyLDO datasets. For instance, Fig. 2 shows the use of the `gn:Country` class in DyLDO, which was deprecated in September 2010. Despite various fluctuations, its use increased until August 2015, then declined and increased again to reach a peak in August 2016.

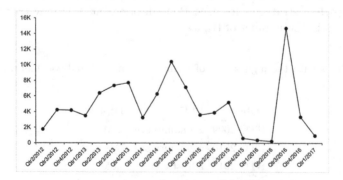

Fig. 2. The use of `gn:Country` class in the DyLDO dataset.

Adoption of LOD Vocabulary Changes. The majority of the newly created terms were adopted in less than 10 days, as showed in Table 3. The triples column represents the total number of triples in DyLDO that contains the adopted terms, while μ and σ are the average number of days before adoption and the standard deviation, respectively. Additionally, adopting *geom* and *GN* terms took long time.

Table 3. The adoption of newly created terms for each of the vocabularies.

Vocabulary	New terms	Adopted terms	Triples	μ	σ
ADMS	6	100%	31K	7	0
CiTO	80	100%	281K	7	0
Cube	5	100%	15K	7	0
DCAT	5	100%	104K	8.4	3.13
emp	1	100%	4K	7	0
geom	2	100%	16K	420	0
GN	21	100%	160M	127.76	255.33
mo	44	100%	45M	8.75	9.68
oa	21	0%	-	-	-
org	8	100%	173K	7	0
Prov	106	85%	121M	30.15	37.49
voaf	10	100%	75K	43.33	68.58
xkos	1	0%	-	-	-

After being adopted, 50% of the newly created terms decreased in use during the considered period, 47% showed a steady use, while 3% increased. For example, during its evolution, the *voaf* vocabulary created 10 new terms. All but one of those have a decline in the use. Figure 3 shows only six terms as the remaining are exploited in much fewer triples. In general, a similar trend holds for all the vocabularies. More details about the adoption time of other vocabularies are available in an extended technical report [1].

Not all terms are adopted. For example, the percentage of adoption for half of the vocabularies is less than 50% of terms in the BTC dataset (in total, 50% of all terms were not used). While in DyLDO, the percentage of unused terms of all vocabularies was 23%, and only one vocabulary (*CiTO*) adopted 60% of the terms, while the remaining vocabularies less than 40% (Table 4). Notably, the 21 new terms of the *oa* vocabulary and the only *xkos* term are never adopted.

5.2 Wikidata

After parsing the terms and properties from the RDF dump files for the period from April 2014 until August 2016, we have extracted the added and deprecated terms of the Wikidata vocabulary. Figure 4 presents the total number of classes and properties in each Wikidata snapshot, which grows to reach 11 classes and 27 properties in August 2017. Ontology engineers added 3 classes and 9 properties during the analyzed period. Notably, there are no terms that are deprecated during the ontology evolution.

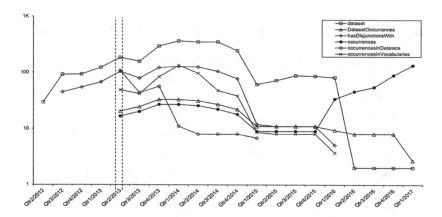

Fig. 3. The use (amount of triples in which a term occurs) of the *voaf's* newly created terms by quarters of DyLDO snapshots. The vertical dashed lines represent the publishing time of new versions of the vocabulary. Please note that two versions of *voaf* have been published before the first snapshot of DyLDO (i.e. `dataset` and `hasDisjunctionsWith` are newly created in versions released before the second quarter of 2012).

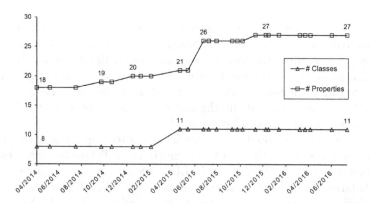

Fig. 4. Total number of terms of the Wikidata vocabulary per RDF dump file.

Figure 5 illustrates the use of newly created terms in Wikidata. Only 5 out of 12 terms are adopted. `NormalRank` and `rank` are much more used than the other new terms. Furthermore, the actually adopted terms among all the newly

Table 4. The percentage of unused terms in the BTC and DyLDO datasets.

Vocabulary	Total terms	BTC	DyLDO
ADMS	31	68%	3%
CiTO	220	72%	60%
Cube	37	35%	0%
DCAT	23	48%	9%
emp	31	87%	6%
geom	34	100%	3%
GN	43	26%	9%
mo	208	36%	2%
oa	63	83%	35%
org	44	20%	11%
Prov	143	22%	24%
voaf	24	33%	8%
xkos	35	63%	14%

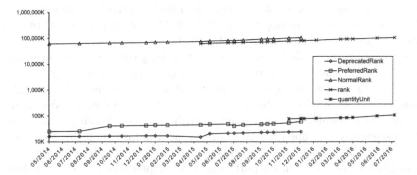

Fig. 5. The amount of triples that the adopted newly created classes and properties of the Wikidata vocabulary after parsing Wikidata RDF dump files.

created ones are adopted directly after their creation date (i.e., on the same day). One possible reason is that Wikidata is a more controlled and centralized environment than a distributed KG, such as the LOD cloud, as discussed in Sect. 6.2.

6 Discussion

We found that not all vocabulary changes are reflected in the data in KGs, and there is a need for a service to track vocabulary changes. Such service helps ontology engineers and data publishers in updating their ontologies and models. In Sect. 6.1, we discuss the results related to the LOD Cloud, and in Sect. 6.2 we discuss the results of changes and adoption of the Wikidata terms.

6.1   The LOD Cloud

Changes in LOD Vocabularies. The number of terms' changes is small. This is in line with existing studies [2,6,9]. However, those changes may have a large impact on the data of KGs. For example, the new version of the *oa* vocabulary caused a significant increased of its use: the triples containing its terms almost triplicates (from roughly 400 hundred to over 1100). In general, the changes impact on the use either in an increasing or decreasing way (6 and 5 out of 13 vocabularies, respectively), although with varying time. For *DCAT* there is an increase so delayed in time (3 years) which is probably not due to the new version. More details are available in our extended technical report [1].

Most of the vocabularies increased in the total number of terms. This suggests that more knowledge is represented in the LOD cloud, requiring new terms. One exception is *CiTO*, which consisted of 94 classes and 36 properties when initially published. The second version counted only one class and 50 properties. Specifically, all the 94 classes were replaced with the new class *CitationAct* and most of the 36 properties of the first version were substituted. The third version provided 91 properties, although 18 of the new properties were reintroduced from the first version (deprecated in the second and reintroduced in the third). In practice, almost a new ontology was built. This is particularly important since *CiTO* has grown much in popularity (BTC 2014 contained over 300 thousand triples compared to 40 thousand in BTC 2011).

New versions of vocabularies, together with the great variety of vocabularies already existing, and the new vocabularies may overwhelm ontology engineers, which need to choice among a vast amount of alternative terms when building or updating their ontologies. Similar issues may occur to data publishers when deciding which vocabularies to exploit in their datasets. Missing some changes and consequently not updating an ontology or a dataset is likely (see the following discussion on the use of terms), notably in a distributed environment as the LOD cloud. This holds particularly for deprecation. There is a lack of tools to notify ontology engineers and data publishers when there are changes in the vocabularies. Such tools may help ontology engineers to select classes and properties that they want to use by knowing the latest updates of terms, and help them in updating their vocabularies. They could also assist data publishers in updating their models by providing a history of changes for the terms they use. While these systems can ease the maintenance of vocabularies and datasets, more advanced one could also recommend terms and vocabularies according to the specific needs of their users. The insights provided in this study can be beneficial to build such tools.

Use of LOD Vocabularies. Cross-domain (*Prov*, *voaf*, and *ADMS*) and Geographic (*Cube* and *GN*) vocabularies were the most popular among data publishers. Some of them are exploited by few PLDs. For instance, *w3.org* widely used *ADMS* terms at the beginning of the investigated time-frame, while later *deri.de* accounted for the highest use of this vocabulary. On the other hand, some vocabularies have been used by various PLDs. For example, *Cube* has been employed by *ontologyCenter.com, esd.org.uk, linked-statistics.org,* and *linkedu.en.* This may suggest that some vocabularies are applicable in multiple domains, while others are more application-specific, but it should be further investigated.

Overall, *geonames.org* and *dbtune.org* are the most frequent PLDs. In the BTC 2009 and BTC 2010 datasets, *geonames.org* was the PLD that uses most of the terms. This is caused by the wide use of the *GN* vocabulary in those years. Later, *dbtune.org* accounted for the highest number of triples in the BTC 2014 and DyLDO snapshots from 2012 to 2014.

Although some terms are deprecated, 87% of them were still exploited. This is in line with [9]. *Geonames.org* is the PLD with the highest number of deprecated terms. For example, in the BTC 2011 dataset, *geonames.org* used six deprecated terms in about 522 thousand triples. That number declined to three terms and roughly 181 thousand triples in BTC 2012, but increased again to 49 terms in BTC 2014 (5.5 thousand triples). It seems is that data publishers did not update their data models. A possible reason of this is that they are not aware of changes in the vocabularies exploited. Thus, as previously discussed, they could benefit from tools to notify these changes.

In order to provide information about the status of a term, the Vocabulary Status ontology[12] can be used. This ontology consists of three properties: vs:term_status, vs:moreinfo, and vs:userdocs. Unfortunately, this ontology is not widely used. Only 7 out of the 134 vocabularies investigated in our paper rely on it.

Adoption of LOD Vocabulary Changes. Most of the newly coined terms are adopted rather quickly (in less than one week). Surprisingly, we even found some terms adopted before their official publishing date. We believe that some of the new versions of vocabularies are already online and can be used before their official announcement. In some cases, it may take time to finish the procedures to publish the new version of the vocabulary. Thus, data publishers can access the new terms before their formal release, simply because they are available online.

Although most of the terms have fast adoption time, some vocabularies, such as *GN*, took more than 120 days, in average, to adopt new terms. However, this average does not reflect the actual adoption behavior: the new version of *GN* provides 21 new terms, 17 terms are adopted within 7 days, while the remaining 4 terms are adopted in over 600 days. Therefore, the average result was affected by those few terms that have a vast adoption time.

Another interesting point is that some newly created terms are never adopted. For example, ontology engineers published a new version of the *oa* vocabulary in June 2016, with 21 new classes and properties. None of those terms have been adopted (at least until April 2017, the last DyLDO snapshot considered), while the first version of *oa* was published in February 2013 with 42 terms and all but one were adopted in less than 3 months. However, the reasons why those terms are unused likely depends on the specific application scenario. For instance,

---

[12] https://www.w3.org/2003/06/sw-vocab-status/note.html, last accessed: 27/02/2018.

not all terms need to be currently in use: some could be designed for future applications. Furthermore, although some terms are not used in the LOD cloud, they may be exploited in other forms. We do not mean that every term has to be adopted: we aim to raise awareness to ontology engineers that there are some of their terms that are never adopted. We also believe that raising awareness to data publishers about the existence of other terms in an ontology in use may further stimulate the reuse of ontologies.

6.2   Wikidata

We found that the Wikidata vocabulary showed no deprecated terms, although some were never adopted during the investigated time-frame (e.g., the `Article` class). Likewise most of the LOD vocabularies, the Wikidata vocabulary counts a small number of additions (3 classes and 9 properties) and no deprecation.

Three classes (`DeprecatedRank`, `NormalRank`, and `PreferredRank`) suddenly disappeared from Wikidata statements after the snapshot in December 2015, after about 8 months (they were created in May 2015). There is a huge difference in the number of triples in which the terms occur. For instance, the `NormalRank` and `Statement` classes have been used in about 106 and 81 million triples, respectively. The other classes (except `Item`) are used in less than 2.4 million triples. The same observation can be made for the properties: all but `rank` appeared in less than 2.7 million triples, while `rank` accounted for approximately 62 million triples when introduced in May 2015, then reached about 106 million triples in August 2016. The wide exploitation of these terms suggests a pressing necessity for adding them to the vocabulary.

Only 5 out of 12 of the newly created terms are adopted and their adoption occurs directly after their creation date. This was expected in Wikidata which is a more controlled and centralized environment than a distributed KG as the LOD cloud. Surprisingly, the majority of new terms (2 classes and 9 properties) seems not adopted in any statements of Wikidata. However a deeper analysis showed that these are used to define properties and their types, except the `Article` class, which needs further investigation.

7   Conclusion and Future Work

Even small changes of vocabulary terms can have a deep impact on the real data that use those terms. Most of newly coined terms are adopted immediately afterwards, while 50%, and 23% of the terms studied are never adopted in the BTC and DyLDO datasets, respectively. Unexpectedly, some deprecated terms have been recreated after some time by their deprecation. Deprecation is a critical operation, notably in a distributed KG as the LOD cloud. We are not surprised that most of the deprecated terms are still used, because data publishers may not be aware of the changes to the exploited vocabularies. We think that this study can help ontology engineers and data publishers in updating their ontologies and datasets. Providing a service to notify changes on ontologies can simplify the update of vocabulary and datasets, as well as foster the adoption of new terms. In order to reproduce our research and extend on them, we provide all results and datasets to the public[13]. As future work, we plan to study the impact of vocabulary changes on the ontology network and provide a service for tracking changes on vocabulary which incorporate the insights of this study. Furthermore, we plan to investigate the impact of similarity measures on the reuse of vocabulary terms on the LOD cloud.

Acknowledgment. This work was supported by the EU's Horizon 2020 programme under grant agreement H2020-693092 MOVING.

References

1. Abdel-Qader, M., Scherp, A.: Towards understanding the evolution of vocabulary terms in knowledge graphs. ArXiv e-prints, September 2017. https://arxiv.org/pdf/1710.00232.pdf
2. Abdel-Qader, M., Scherp, A.: Qualitative analysis of vocabulary evolution on the linked open data cloud. In: PROFILES Workshop Co-located with ESWC, vol. 1598. CEUR-WS.org (2016)
3. Chawuthai, R., Takeda, H., Wuwongse, V., Jinbo, U.: Presenting and preserving the change in taxonomic knowledge for linked data. Semant. Web **7**(6), 589–616 (2016)
4. Dividino, R., Scherp, A., Gröner, G., Grotton, T.: Change-a-LOD: does the schema on the linked data cloud change or not? In: Consuming Linked Data Workshop Co-located with ISWC, vol. 1034. pp. 87–98. CEUR-WS.org (2013)
5. Gottron, T., Knauf, M., Scherp, A.: Analysis of schema structures in the linked open data graph based on unique subject URIs, pay-level domains, and vocabulary usage. Distrib. Parallel Databases **33**(4), 515–553 (2015)
6. Guha, R.V., Brickley, D., Macbeth, S.: Schema.org: evolution of structured data on the web. Commun. ACM **59**(2), 44–51 (2016)
7. Käfer, T., Abdelrahman, A., Umbrich, J., O'Byrne, P., Hogan, A.: Observing linked data dynamics. In: Cimiano, P., Corcho, O., Presutti, V., Hollink, L., Rudolph, S. (eds.) ESWC 2013. LNCS, vol. 7882, pp. 213–227. Springer, Heidelberg (2013). https://doi.org/10.1007/978-3-642-38288-8_15
8. Käfer, T., Umbrich, J., Hogan, A., Polleres, A.: Towards a dynamic linked data observatory. In: LDOW Co-located with WWW (2012)
9. Meusel, R., Bizer, C., Paulheim, H.: A web-scale study of the adoption and evolution of the schema.org vocabulary over time. In: International Conference on Web Intelligence, Mining and Semantics, p. 15. ACM (2015)
10. Mihindukulasooriya, N., Poveda-Villalón, M., García-Castro, R., Gómez-Pérez, A.: Collaborative ontology evolution and data quality - an empirical analysis. In: Dragoni, M., Poveda-Villalón, M., Jimenez-Ruiz, E. (eds.) OWLED/ORE -2016. LNCS, vol. 10161, pp. 95–114. Springer, Cham (2017). https://doi.org/10.1007/978-3-319-54627-8_8
11. Papavassiliou, V., Flouris, G., Fundulaki, I., Kotzinos, D., Christophides, V.: On detecting high-level changes in RDF/S KBs. In: Bernstein, A., Karger, D.R., Heath, T., Feigenbaum, L., Maynard, D., Motta, E., Thirunarayan, K. (eds.) ISWC 2009. LNCS, vol. 5823, pp. 473–488. Springer, Heidelberg (2009). https://doi.org/10.1007/978-3-642-04930-9_30

---

[13] https://figshare.com/s/d5487f88a2bdfab4c2ee.

12. Roussakis, Y., Chrysakis, I., Stefanidis, K., Flouris, G., Stavrakas, Y.: A flexible framework for understanding the dynamics of evolving RDF datasets. In: Arenas, M., et al. (eds.) ISWC 2015. LNCS, vol. 9366, pp. 495–512. Springer, Cham (2015). https://doi.org/10.1007/978-3-319-25007-6_29
13. Schaible, J., Gottron, T., Scherp, A.: Survey on common strategies of vocabulary reuse in linked open data modeling. In: Presutti, V., d'Amato, C., Gandon, F., d'Aquin, M., Staab, S., Tordai, A. (eds.) ESWC 2014. LNCS, vol. 8465, pp. 457–472. Springer, Cham (2014). https://doi.org/10.1007/978-3-319-07443-6_31
14. Schmachtenberg, M., Bizer, C., Paulheim, H.: Adoption of the linked data best practices in different topical domains. In: Mika, P., et al. (eds.) ISWC 2014. LNCS, vol. 8796, pp. 245–260. Springer, Cham (2014). https://doi.org/10.1007/978-3-319-11964-9_16
15. Vandenbussche, P.Y., Atemezing, G.A., Poveda-Villalón, M., Vatant, B.: Linked open vocabularies (LOV): a gateway to reusable semantic vocabularies on the web. Semant. Web 8(3), 437–452 (2017)

GSP (Geo-Semantic-Parsing): Geoparsing and Geotagging with Machine Learning on Top of Linked Data

Marco Avvenuti[1] , Stefano Cresci[2](✉) , Leonardo Nizzoli[1,2],
and Maurizio Tesconi[2]

[1] Department of Information Engineering, University of Pisa, Pisa, Italy
marco.avvenuti@unipi.it
[2] Institute for Informatics and Telematics, IIT-CNR, Pisa, Italy
{stefano.cresci,leonardo.nizzoli,maurizio.tesconi}@iit.cnr.it

Abstract. Recently, user-generated content in social media opened up new alluring possibilities for understanding the geospatial aspects of many real-world phenomena. Yet, the vast majority of such content lacks explicit, structured geographic information. Here, we describe the design and implementation of a novel approach for associating geographic information to text documents. GSP exploits powerful machine learning algorithms on top of the rich, interconnected Linked Data in order to overcome limitations of previous state-of-the-art approaches. In detail, our technique performs semantic annotation to identify relevant tokens in the input document, traverses a sub-graph of Linked Data for extracting possible geographic information related to the identified tokens and optimizes its results by means of a Support Vector Machine classifier. We compare our results with those of 4 state-of-the-art techniques and baselines on ground-truth data from 2 evaluation datasets. Our GSP technique achieves excellent performances, with the best $F1 = 0.91$, sensibly outperforming benchmark techniques that achieve $F1 \leq 0.78$.

Keywords: Geoparsing · Machine learning · Linked data · Twitter

1 Introduction

The ever-growing amount of user-generated content in social networking and social media platforms has recently opened up new possibilities for studying and understanding the geospatial aspects of many real-world phenomena [14]. Yet, the vast majority of user-generated content lacks explicit and structured geographic information. For instance, only 1% to 4% of all Twitter posts (henceforth *tweets*) come with latitude and longitude coordinates [4]. This lack of geospatial information drastically limits the usefulness of social data for solving many important problems [2]. Indeed, having access to geotagged content could allow journalists to identify and cross-check the location of breaking news,

© Springer International Publishing AG, part of Springer Nature 2018
A. Gangemi et al. (Eds.): ESWC 2018, LNCS 10843, pp. 17–32, 2018.
https://doi.org/10.1007/978-3-319-93417-4_2

by corroborating multiple posts related to the same event [17]. Similarly, geo-tagged health-related posts could be exploited by epidemiologists to track the spread and diffusion of epidemics [9]. Furthermore, during mass emergencies, first responders could leverage crisis maps in order to track the unfolding situation and identify stricken locations that require prioritized intervention [1,3,17].

Given the importance of geospatial information in user-generated content, a large body of research has recently tackled the tasks of geoparsing and geotagging [11,14]. However, a number of challenges make these tasks extremely difficult, thus limiting the performance of current state-of-the-art techniques. Among such challenges is the problem of toponymic polysemy. Namely, a toponym might refer to different places according to the context in which it is used [1]. For example, the word "Washington" can refer to 30 different cities in the US[1]. Other challenges are the variable degree of granularity with which results should be returned (i.e., country-level, city-level, or even street- and building-level, depending on the application) [17], the time-evolving nature of geospatial information (e.g., new places and points-of-interest are continuously created, moved, and removed, especially in urban environments) [8,14], and the limited amount of context information typically available for social media content (e.g., tweets are limited to 280 characters).

Meanwhile, the Semantic Web has recently seen a flourishing of new datasets published as Linked Data, thus forming a rich and interconnected network of structured information. Indeed, such data already proved valuable in a number of practical domains, comprising health, journalism, and tourism [5,17]. A few preliminary works also investigated the usefulness of Linked Data from a geospatial perspective [12,17]. However, to date no working solution has ever been proposed to perform geoparsing and geotagging of text documents by exploiting Linked Data.

Contribution. We aim at demonstrating that previous state-of-the-art geoparsing and geotagging techniques can be outperformed by leveraging powerful machine learning algorithms on top of the rich and interconnected Linked Data. Our proof-of-concept is a context-agnostic *Geo-Semantic-Parsing* (GSP) technique for automatically associating geographic coordinates to text documents. GSP receives a text document as input and returns an enriched document, where all mentions of places/locations are associated to the corresponding geographic coordinates. To achieve this goal, in a first step GSP performs semantic annotation with the aim of identifying relevant parts of the input text, and to link them to pertinent resources (e.g., DBpedia entities) in the Linked Data cloud. Then, GSP exploits the rich and structured information associated to RDF resources to identify, via machine learning, geographic resources and to extract the right geographic coordinates for each resource.

Among the advantages that GSP has over previously proposed solutions are: (i) it does not require any explicit geographic information (e.g., GPS coordinates, location information, timezones), contrarily to [9]; (ii) it only exploits text data of input documents (e.g., it does not require any user information or social network

---

[1] https://en.wikipedia.org/wiki/Washington.

topology), contrarily to [15]; (iii) it processes only one text document at a time (e.g., it does not require all tweets from a user's timeline, or many documents on a given topic), contrarily to [4]; (iv) it does not require users to specify a target geographic region but, instead, it geoparses and geotags places all over the world, contrarily to [17]; (v) by leveraging Linked Data, GSP is capable of extracting fine-grained, structured geographic information (e.g., street/building → city → county/region → country) similarly to [9,13].

2 Related Work

The task of associating geographic information to social media content has been carried out mainly in 3 fashions: inferring (i) users home location [4,15], (ii) posts origin location [8,9], and (iii) locations of places mentioned within posts [11,13, 14,17]. In the following, we thoroughly survey relevant approaches to the latter task, since our work also falls in that category.

The majority of approaches to (iii) are either based on named entity recognition (NER), gazetteer lookup and matching, language models (LM), or on a combination of them. Among state-of-the-art systems, is the one proposed by Middleton *et al.* [17]. It is publicly accessible via the *geoparsepy* Python package[2] and it is based on a combination of NER and gazetteer matching. Input texts undergo token expansion and tokenization, before being matched against an in-memory cache of known location n-gram tokens. The pre-loaded cache of known locations is stored in a local planet-deployment of the OpenStreetMap's gazetteer. Possible locations matches are disambiguated via heuristics and then ranked by confidence. Highest confidence matches are then selected as the output of the algorithm. Similarly, also the *mordecai* system by Halterman [13] is distributed as the namesake Python package[3]. The system takes unstructured text as input and returns structured geographic information. It is based on *spaCy*'s NER to extract toponyms from text. Then, it leverages the Geonames gazetteer to find the potential coordinates of extracted toponyms. The final coordinates returned by *mordecai* are selected via deep learning by a neural network classifier. In [11] is described an algorithm for extracting fine-grained mentions of places (i.e., streets, buildings) from text. It is based on lexico-semantic pattern recognition to identify streets and abbreviations, lexico-semantic matching enriched with gazetteer for spell checking and toponym identification and machine learning for abbreviation disambiguation and identification of buildings.

Grounding on the assumption that NER and gazetteer approaches to geoparsing are intrinsically hard due to the informal nature of social media content, in [14] is proposed a solution based on LM. The system in [14] does not operate on top of an explicit toponym dictionary, but instead it is trained on a large corpora of geotagged images complemented with textual tags. Given the set of tags related to a non-geotagged image, the learned model provides an estimate of the likelihood that the image refers to a particular location. Although proving very

---

[2] https://pypi.python.org/pypi/geoparsepy.
[3] https://github.com/openeventdata/mordecai.

effective for geotagging images, [14] cannot directly operate on text documents, differently from our proposed approach.

In addition to the works briefly surveyed in this section, others have tackled the tasks of geoparsing and geocoding. However, we omitted a specific discussion of those works since they are largely overlapping with, or outperformed by, those already surveyed here.

3   The Geo-Semantic-Parsing Approach

We aim at developing a technique that, given a text document T_i, is capable of extracting the correct set C_i of geographic coordinates related to all and only the K places mentioned within T_i:

$$T_i \xrightarrow{\ ?\ } \{C_{i,1}, C_{i,2}, \ldots, C_{i,K}\}$$

To achieve this goal, our proposed *Geo-Semantic-Parsing* (GSP) technique employs machine learning on top of Linked Data, and combines the strengths of several state-of-the-art approaches introduced in Sect. 2. In detail, we firstly perform *semantic annotation* [10] in order to identify possible toponyms within the input document T_i. Semantic annotation is a process aimed at augmenting portions of a plain-text (i.e., tokens) with pertinent links to RDF resources ($\mathcal{E}$) contained in knowledge-bases, such as DBpedia. The result of this process is an enriched (annotated) text where mentions of knowledge-bases entities in T_i have been linked to the corresponding RDF resource. This annotation process is highly informative since it enables the exploitation of the rich information associated to the RDF resources $\mathcal{E}_{i,j}$ that have been linked to the j-th annotated portion of the i-th text. The resulting text enrichment effectively mitigates the drawbacks related to the limited amount of context. Semantic annotation also has the side effect of alleviating geoparsing mistakes caused by toponymic polysemy. In fact, some tokens of a plain-text can potentially be linked to multiple knowledge-bases entities. Semantic annotators automatically perform a disambiguating operation and only return the most likely reference to a knowledge-base entity for every annotated token [22]. Notably, this disambiguation operation is much more accurate than those carried out in previous works, such as those based on simple heuristics [17].

As a result of semantic annotation, each annotated token represents a relevant portion of T_i, and the entity to which it has been linked can potentially contain geographic information useful for geoparsing. Thus, after the semantic annotation step carried out by a given annotator An, we *parse* the metadata of each RDF resource $\mathcal{E}_{i,j}$ linked to T_i by An and we extract any geographic information it contains. In this way, every RDF resource with geographic information is automatically associated to a geographic coordinate $C_{i,j} = (\mathsf{lat}_{i,j}, \mathsf{lon}_{i,j})$:

$$T_i \xrightarrow[\text{annotation}]{\text{semantic}} \{\mathcal{E}_{i,1}, \mathcal{E}_{i,2}, \ldots, \mathcal{E}_{i,X}\}$$
$$\xrightarrow{\text{parsing}} \{C_{i,1}, C_{i,2}, \ldots, C_{i,Y}\}, \quad Y \leq X \tag{GSP}$$

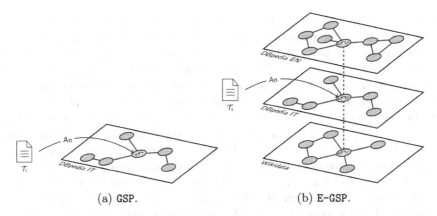

(a) GSP.   (b) E-GSP.

Fig. 1. The *expansion* step of E-GSP allows to extend the search for geographic information to all the $\mathcal{E}^0, \dots, \mathcal{E}^N$ resources of the $\mathcal{E}$ sameAs graph, thus exploiting all knowledge-bases in which $\mathcal{E}$ is described.

Given the basic GSP approach defined above, in the following we introduce two improvements that can be adopted in order to respectively (i) increase the number of geographic information retrieved (E-GSP) and (ii) optimize the output of the algorithm, thus limiting prediction errors (GSP-F). These two improvements can also be combined together, in the so-called E-GSP-F approach.

3.1 E-GSP: Extracting Additional Geographic Information

Given a resource $\mathcal{E}_{i,j}$ linked to a portion of document $\mathcal{T}_i$ by An, the basic GSP approach only exploits metadata of $\mathcal{E}_{i,j}$ in order to extract geographic information. However, the links between different semantic resources of the Linked Data graph open up the possibility to exploit metadata of many more nodes of the graph. Many different types of links exist between RDF resources, so as to express a broad range of different relations. Among them, `owl:sameAs` relations link the descriptions of equivalent RDF resources within and across knowledge-bases. Given an RDF resource $\mathcal{E}_{i,j}$, the graph of all $\mathcal{E}_{i,j}^0, \mathcal{E}_{i,j}^1, \dots, \mathcal{E}_{i,j}^N$ RDF resources directly or indirectly connected to $\mathcal{E}_{i,j}$ via `owl:sameAs` links is called the $\mathcal{E}_{i,j}$ *sameAs graph* [7]. Thus, in order to extract geographic information about a resource $\mathcal{E}_{i,j}$, the *Expanded Geo-Semantic-Parsing* (E-GSP) technique also exploits all semantically-equivalent resources $\mathcal{E}_{i,j}^0, \mathcal{E}_{i,j}^1, \dots, \mathcal{E}_{i,j}^N$ reachable by traversing the $\mathcal{E}_{i,j}$ sameAs graph:

$$\mathcal{T}_i \xrightarrow[\text{annotation}]{\text{semantic}} \{\mathcal{E}_{i,1}, \mathcal{E}_{i,2}, \dots, \mathcal{E}_{i,X}\}$$

$$\xrightarrow{\text{expansion}} \{\{\mathcal{E}_{i,1}^0, \dots, \mathcal{E}_{i,1}^{N_1}\}, \dots, \{\mathcal{E}_{i,X}^0, \dots, \mathcal{E}_{i,X}^{N_X}\}\}$$

$$\xrightarrow{\text{parsing}} \{\mathcal{C}_{i,1}, \mathcal{C}_{i,2}, \dots, \mathcal{C}_{i,Y}\}, \quad Y \leq X \qquad \text{(E-GSP)}$$

Figure 1 visually highlights the difference between the GSP and the E-GSP approaches, by leveraging the formalism of multilayer networks. The previously defined *expansion* step opens up the possibility to leverage the set of resources $\{\mathcal{E}_{i,j}^0, \mathcal{E}_{i,j}^1, \ldots, \mathcal{E}_{i,j}^{N_j}\}$ for extracting geographic information, instead of the single resource used in GSP. However, only one geographic coordinate $\mathcal{C}_{i,j}$ must be associated to each resource $\mathcal{E}_{i,j}$ linked to the input document $\mathcal{T}_i$. Thus, the E-GSP approach also includes a *voting mechanism* used to select one coordinate, when multiple resources of the $\mathcal{E}_{i,j}$ sameAs graph contain geographic information. In detail, geographic coordinates are extracted for each resource of the $\{\mathcal{E}_{i,j}^0, \mathcal{E}_{i,j}^1, \ldots, \mathcal{E}_{i,j}^{N_j}\}$ set. Then, a geospatial binning is applied in order to group and count coordinates that lay near to one another. This process acts pretty much like a geographic clustering step. The final $\mathcal{C}_{i,j}$ coordinate associated to $\mathcal{E}_{i,j}$ is the geographic centroid of the biggest cluster. When two or more clusters contain the same number of elements, the winning cluster is picked as the one containing the "best" resource $\hat{\mathcal{E}}_{i,j}$ (i.e., the most reliable one). In E-GSP, resources in $\{\mathcal{E}_{i,j}^0, \mathcal{E}_{i,j}^1, \ldots, \mathcal{E}_{i,j}^{N_j}\}$ are ranked by a score $S_{i,j}^n$, and the "best" resource is the one achieving the highest score: $\hat{\mathcal{E}}_{i,j} = \mathcal{E}_{i,j}^{\bar{n}} \mid \bar{n} = \arg\max_n S_{i,j}^n$. The score $S_{i,j}^n$ quantifying the goodness of a resource can be computed in many ways – e.g., by computing its Page Rank value, by employing one of the many ranking algorithms for Linked Data or by computing simple metrics of completeness, such as the number of predicates that describe the RDF resource.

Notably, the voting mechanism introduced in E-GSP also solves possible mistakes caused by spurious wrong metadata in the description of an RDF resource. For example, extracting the coordinates for the city of Milan (Italy) exclusively from the corresponding resource in the Italian DBpedia[4] results in a mistake, since such coordinates point (at the time of writing) to a place in Switzerland. Instead, by aggregating and counting the coordinates found in the sameAs graph of Milan, it is actually possible to infer the correct coordinates. Considering that our proposed technique grounds on data contained in collaboratively-curated knowledge-bases, the ability to automatically correct inconsistencies and mistakes represents a much desirable feature [20].

3.2   GSP-F: Filtering Results to Increase Correctness

As with any algorithm, not all results returned by the algorithm are correct. For our task, this means that some of the $\mathcal{C}_{i,j}$ coordinates found with the GSP approach, might have been erroneously identified. In order to reduce the occurrences of wrong predictions, many machine learning algorithms include an optimization phase where candidate results are evaluated before being returned to the users. In this way, only those results for which the algorithm is reasonably confident are actually returned. In order to enhance the correctness of the coordinates identified by our GSP technique, we devised the *Geo-Semantic-Parsing with Filtering* (GSP-F) approach, in which a binary machine learning classifier is trained to evaluate candidate results. The classifier takes as input a number of features and outputs a binary label defining whether a candidate result $\mathcal{C}_{i,j}$ should actually be returned ($\overline{\mathcal{C}}_{i,j}$), or whether it should rather be discarded, being probably

---

[4] http://it.dbpedia.org/resource/Milano.

incorrect:

$$T_i \xrightarrow[\text{annotation}]{\text{semantic}} \{\mathcal{E}_{i,1}, \mathcal{E}_{i,2}, \dots, \mathcal{E}_{i,X}\}$$

$$\xrightarrow{\text{parsing}} \{\mathcal{C}_{i,1}, \mathcal{C}_{i,2}, \dots, \mathcal{C}_{i,Y}\}, \quad Y \leq X$$

$$\xrightarrow{\text{filtering}} \{\overline{\mathcal{C}}_{i,1}, \overline{\mathcal{C}}_{i,2}, \dots, \overline{\mathcal{C}}_{i,Z}\}, \quad Z \leq Y \qquad \text{(GSP-F)}$$

The features used by the machine learning classifier, its training and its evaluation are described in detail in Sect. 4.3.

3.3   E-GSP-F: Expanded GSP with Filtering

The E-GSP and the GSP-F techniques previously described can be employed simultaneously, on top of the basic GSP approach, for optimized performances. Indeed, the E-GSP and the GSP-F improvements are orthogonal, since the former aims at increasing the set of candidate results, while the latter reduces actual results by filtering out those candidate results that are likely to be incorrect. The E-GSP-F technique resulting from the combination of E-GSP and GSP-F is defined in the following, and it is described by the pseudo-code in Algorithm 1:

$$T_i \xrightarrow[\text{annotation}]{\text{semantic}} \{\mathcal{E}_{i,1}, \mathcal{E}_{i,2}, \dots, \mathcal{E}_{i,X}\}$$

$$\xrightarrow{\text{expansion}} \{\{\mathcal{E}_{i,1}^0, \dots, \mathcal{E}_{i,1}^{N_1}\}, \dots, \{\mathcal{E}_{i,X}^0, \dots, \mathcal{E}_{i,X}^{N_X}\}\}$$

$$\xrightarrow{\text{parsing}} \{\mathcal{C}_{i,1}, \mathcal{C}_{i,2}, \dots, \mathcal{C}_{i,Y}\}, \quad Y \leq X$$

$$\xrightarrow{\text{filtering}} \{\overline{\mathcal{C}}_{i,1}, \overline{\mathcal{C}}_{i,2}, \dots, \overline{\mathcal{C}}_{i,Z}\}, \quad Z \leq Y \qquad \text{(E-GSP-F)}$$

4   System Implementation

4.1   Semantic Annotation

In recent years, the tasks of *semantic annotation*, *wikification* and *entity linking* have attracted a great interest from scholars of many disciplines [10]. This large body of work resulted in a number of readily available tools and Web APIs capable of effectively performing semantic annotation. Thus, when implementing the semantic annotation step of our system, we could rely on a number of well-known, state-of-the-art, off-the-shelf semantic annotators. In particular, we developed Python wrappers to DBpedia Spotlight [16], TagMe [10], Dexter 2.0 [21] and Dandelion[5]. All these systems provide Web applications[6,7,8,9] as

---

[5] https://dandelion.eu/.
[6] DBpedia Spotlight: http://demo.dbpedia-spotlight.org/.
[7] TagMe: https://tagme.d4science.org/tagme/.
[8] Dexter 2.0: http://dexter.isti.cnr.it/demo/.
[9] Dandelion: https://dandelion.eu/semantic-text/entity-extraction-demo/.

```
input  : T                                      // tweet to analyze
         An                                     // semantic annotator to use
output : C̄                                     // coordinates extracted from T
 1  C = ( );
 2  E = semanticAnnotation(An, T);
 3  for i = 1 to |E| do
 4  │   aliases = expansion(E_i);
 5  │   allCoords = ( );
 6  │   for n = 1 to |aliases| do
 7  │   │   coords_{i,n} = parsing(E_i^n);
 8  │   │   if coords_{i,n} ≠ null then
 9  │   │   │   allCoords.append(coords_{i,n});
10  │   │   end
11  │   end
12  │   bestCoord = votingMechanism(allCoords);
13  │   C.append(bestCoord);
14  end
15  C̄ = filter(C);
16  return C̄;
```

Algorithm 1. E-GSP-P algorithm for associating geographic coordinates $\bar{C}$ to document $\mathcal{T}$, by exploiting the semantic annotator An.

well as RESTful APIs for programmatic access. Each wrapper is capable of querying the Web APIs of the related semantic annotator, passing a textual document and returning URIs of the RDF resources found in the document by the semantic annotator. Despite the different inner functioning of the 4 supported semantic annotators, all wrappers expose a common interface to the rest of our system, so that the choice of the specific annotator to use is transparent to the users and to the other components of our system. Among the information returned by our wrappers for each found RDF resource, is the DBpedia URI of the resource and a confidence score ρ expressing how likely is a specific annotation (*token → resource*) to be correct. Notably, our proposed technique does not depend on any specific annotator, and indeed it can be implemented with any annotator currently available or with a combination of them.

4.2 Extraction of Geographic Information

Supported Knowledge-Bases. All proposed versions of our technique involve a *parsing* step, where RDF resources are associated to geographic coordinates, whenever possible. This step is performed by looking for geographic metadata among the predicates of RDF resources. Possibly relevant metadata is fetched in JSON format via SPARQL queries, and then it is parsed. As a result of the semantic annotation step, in GSP and GSP-F all the resources to parse belong to DBpedia (either the English DBpedia or a different one, depending on the language of the input document $\mathcal{T}_i$). However, as a consequence of the *expansion* step employed in E-GSP and E-GSP-F, the system may be required to parse other equivalent resources belonging to different knowledge-bases (e.g., YAGO, Freebase, Geonames, etc.). In order to query a knowledge-base for metadata of a resource, our system must necessarily know the SPARQL endpoint of the knowledge-base. However, it is not possible to know in advance all knowledge-bases that should be queried, since they depend on the resources linked to each specific input document, which is known only at runtime. Thus, in order to be able to parse the highest possible set of RDF resources, we provided support for all DBpedias deploying their SPARQL endpoint to the standard URL http://<$lang$>.dbpedia.org/sparql, as well as to 11 other well-known knowledge-bases for which we manually specified the SPARQL endpoint by means of a configuration file. Notably, our set of supported knowledge-bases leverages the results of previous studies on the distribution of geospatial information in Linked Open Data [12]. Furthermore, such set can be easily extended by adding additional SPARQL endpoints to the configuration file.

Geographic RDF Predicates. In Linked Data there exist many different RDF predicates designed to store geographic information (e.g., geo:lat and geo:long, georss:point, etc.). The capability of our system to associate a set of geographic coordinates to an RDF resource depends on its ability to parse as many as possible of such RDF predicates. In our implementation, we provided support for as many as 45 RDF predicates. Since the geographic information conveyed by the supported predicates can be represented in different formats (e.g., decimal degrees; degrees, minutes, seconds), we then implemented a set of simple formulas for converting the different input formats into *decimal latitude and longitude* coordinates. As a result, the output of the *parsing* step is represented, wherever available, by a geographic coordinate $\mathcal{C}_{i,j} = (\mathsf{lat}_{i,j}, \mathsf{lon}_{i,j})$ for each provided RDF resource $\mathcal{E}_{i,j}$, thus adhering to the specifications defined in Sect. 3.

Voting Mechanism. In the E-GSP and E-GSP-F approaches, multiple coordinates extracted from the sameAs graph of a resource are clustered by a voting mechanism. In our implementation, such coordinates are approximated to the third decimal place before being grouped and counted. This equals to performing a geographic binning, with bin width $\simeq$0.1 km ($\simeq$0.06 miles) at the equator. Then, the scoring metric used to resolve draws between geographic clusters containing the same number of resources, simply quantifies the number of predicates of each resource. In other words, in our implementation RDF resources described by a higher number of predicates are considered more reliable than those described by fewer predicates.

4.3   Machine Learning Filtering

The GSP-F and the E-GSP-F approaches involve a *filtering* step, where candidate results $\mathcal{C}_{i,j}$ are evaluated before being returned to the users. Candidate results that are likely to be incorrect $(\underline{\mathcal{C}}_{i,j})$ are discarded (pruned), while those for which the system is confident $(\overline{\mathcal{C}}_{i,j})$ are outputted. Within this context, a candidate result is represented by a resource $\mathcal{E}_{i,j}$ (associated to a geographic coordinate) that has been linked to a portion of the input document $\mathcal{T}_i$ by a semantic annotator An. This filtering operation is performed by a binary machine learning classifier, implemented with a Support Vector Machine (SVM). Once trained, the

SVM classifier takes as input a set of features describing one candidate result at a time, and it outputs the predicted class label for that candidate result (either $\underline{\mathcal{C}}_{i,j}$ or $\overline{\mathcal{C}}_{i,j}$).

Features. Features describing candidate results are divided into 3 classes, according to the information they convey. The first class of features describes the *textual* properties of the input document $\mathcal{T}_i$. We rely on a state-of-the-art natural language processing tool for Italian and English texts [6] for the analyses of input documents. Given a token (or a sequence of tokens) linked to a resource $\mathcal{E}_{i,j}$, we compute categorical features as its (i) coarse- and (ii) fine-grained part-of-speech (POS) tag, (iii) its morphosyntactic tag, (iv) its type of named entity (if any) and (v) a binary feature representing whether the token begins with a capital letter. Our *textual* features capture linguistic patterns correlated to the use of toponyms in texts and include information used by state-of-the-art NER approaches [11,13,17]. The second class of features evaluates the *link* established by the semantic annotator An between the token and the resource $\mathcal{E}_{i,j}$. Features of this class are (i) the ρ confidence of An for the link and the (ii) absolute and (iii) percentage edit distance between the token and the rdfs:label of $\mathcal{E}_{i,j}$. Notably, the confidence feature that we exploit is similar to that of [17]. The third class of features describes the properties of the $\mathcal{E}_{i,j}$ *resource*. Specifically, we define a (i) binary and an (ii) integer feature for representing if, and how many times, the token appears in the ontology:abstract of $\mathcal{E}_{i,j}$. Then, we devised 3 categorical features for modeling the structural properties of $\mathcal{E}_{i,j}$ as (iii) the RDF ontologies/vocabularies of the predicates of $\mathcal{E}_{i,j}$ (e.g., OWL, RDFS, FOAF, etc.), (iv) its RDF predicates and (v) its rdf:types. Indeed, structural properties of Linked Data have already proved useful for a number of ranking, clustering, and classification tasks [18,19].

Training Pipeline. The initial data for training the SVM classifier is represented by $\simeq 7,000$ manually-annotated candidate results. This dataset is almost balanced with 57% correct geo-predictions ($\overline{\mathcal{C}}_{i,j}$) and 43% incorrect ones ($\underline{\mathcal{C}}_{i,j}$). The training pipeline begins with a stratified sampling of the whole dataset into a training (80%) and a testing (20%) dataset. Then, preprocessing steps perform imputation of missing feature values and scaling, in order to improve results of the learning algorithm. Since some of our categorical features have high dimensionality (e.g., we have over 6,800 different rdf:types), we perform an L1-based feature selection step, which resulted in a reduced set of only 60 features. Next in the pipeline, a hyperparameters tuning process picks the best settings for the SVM classifier (RBF kernel, $C = 100$, $gamma = 0.001$), via cross-validation over the training dataset. We then learn our SVM models on the training dataset and evaluate their performances in classifying candidate results of the testing dataset. In detail, we learn 4 different models, one for each of the supported semantic annotators, plus one global model using all available training data.

Classification Results. Table 1 reports the performances of the SVM classifiers against testing data. In order to better evaluate the difficulty of the task and the results of our SVM classifiers, we also compared results with those of 2 simple

Table 1. Evaluation of the *filtering* step of GSP-F and E-GSP-F.

Model	Evaluation metrics					
	Precision	*Recall*	*Specificity*	*Accuracy*	*F1*	*MCC*
Baselines						
Majority class	0.569	1.000	0.000	0.569	0.725	–
Random classifier	0.475	0.499	0.512	0.506	0.487	0.012
SVM classifiers						
TagMe	0.916	0.932	0.928	0.930	0.924	0.858
DBpedia Spotlight	**0.968**	0.949	0.971	0.960	0.959	0.921
Dexter 2.0	0.966	**0.986**	**0.974**	**0.979**	**0.976**	**0.958**
Dandelion	0.903	0.940	0.911	0.924	0.921	0.849
Global	0.963	0.980	0.967	0.973	0.971	0.946

baseline classifiers that respectively (i) always predict the majority class and (ii) output random predictions. As shown, our best classifier achieves an excellent $F1 = 0.976$, way higher than the baselines and comparable with the other SVM classifiers. Since the global classifier achieved only slightly lower results with respect to the best one, in our system implementation we relied on it instead of using one different classifier for every semantic annotator.

5 Evaluation

Our evaluation metrics are those typically used in previous machine learning and entity linking tasks [14]. Specifically, we consider as a correct match a prediction by an algorithm/technique when the predicted coordinate falls within a certain distance threshold (e.g., a few kilometers/miles) from the ground-truth coordinate. This assumption is the same already made in recent machine learning challenges, such as the *MediaEval 2016 Placing Task*[10], where participants were asked to estimate the locations of multimedia items (i.e., photos or videos).

5.1 Datasets

Although capable of working with text documents of any kind, we benchmarked our proposed GSP technique with social media data, namely for geoparsing and geotagging tweets. Indeed, social media represent an environment where such techniques are most needed [4]. In addition, tweets are short documents filled with jargon and colloquial expressions, thus representing a challenging proving ground for our technique.

The first evaluation dataset (henceforth labeled ENG-NEEL) is composed of 9,289 English tweets. It is the official dataset of the *Named Entity rEcognition*

---

[10] http://www.multimediaeval.org/mediaeval2016/.

and Linking (*NEEL 2016*) challenge[11]. The dataset comprises tweets extracted from a collection of over 18 million documents including event-annotated tweets covering multiple noteworthy events from 2011 and 2013, and tweets extracted from Twitter's Firehose in 2014 and 2015 via a selection of hashtags. Annotated mentions of places/locations in tweets are provided by *NEEL 2016* organizers.

The second evaluation dataset (henceforth labeled ITA-DSTR) is composed of 1,807 Italian tweets that we collected in the aftermath of 2 major natural disasters in Italy, respectively the *Emilia 2012 earthquake* and the *Sardinia 2013 flood*. Such dataset has recently been used in a number of works related to crisis mapping and emergency management [1]. Mentions of places/locations in the dataset have been manually annotated by 2 graduate students.

The distance threshold for comparing the obtained results with the ground-truth was set equal to 50 Km for the ENG-NEEL dataset and to 20 Km for the ITA-DSTR dataset.

5.2   Benchmarks

To thoroughly evaluate our proposed technique, we compared our results to those of different state-of-the-art geoparsing and geotagging techniques, namely the geoparsing technique by Middleton *et al.* [17] and the geoparsing and geocoding technique by Halterman [13]. Such benchmark techniques are thoroughly described in Sect. 2. Since the technique by Middleton *et al.* only outputs location tokens extracted from the input text, we obtained coordinates for the tokens via queries to OpenStreetMap's APIs. Instead, the technique by Halterman already outputs coordinates of found locations. Thus, no further operations are needed in order to include [13] in our evaluation.

In addition to [13,17], we also compared our results to those of 2 baselines. The "geoparser" baseline leverages the *geopy* Python package[12] and employs the ArcGIS service to extract coordinates from tweets. The "NER + geocoder" baseline performs NER and then geocodes location NEs via queries to the Web APIs of Google Maps. The NER step is performed using the well-known *polyglot* natural language processing pipeline[13].

5.3   Results

Table 2 reports geoparsing results for all our techniques and all benchmarks, on the two evaluation datasets. As shown, the simplest of our proposed techniques (GSP) already achieves results that are in line with those of the best benchmarks. In fact, it achieves the second best $F1$ on the ITA-DSTR dataset and the best $F1$ on the ENG-NEEL dataset, when compared to the benchmarks. Results also show the effectiveness of our 2 improvements E-GSP and GSP-F. As hypothesized in Sect. 3, the *expansion* step of E-GSP increases the number of retrieved coordinates

---

[11] http://microposts2016.seas.upenn.edu/challenge.html.
[12] https://geopy.readthedocs.io/.
[13] https://polyglot.readthedocs.io/.

Table 2. Evaluation results of GSP-derived techniques and comparison with state-of-the-art techniques and baselines.

Technique	ENG-NEEL				ITA-DSTR			
	Precision	Recall	Accuracy	F1	Precision	Recall	Accuracy	F1
Benchmarks								
Geoparser	0.030	0.139	0.025	0.050	0.242	0.453	0.182	0.306
NER + geocoder	0.331	0.297	0.186	0.313	0.879	0.698	0.636	0.777
Halterman (mordecai) [13]	0.291	0.288	0.169	0.289	0.625	0.338	0.282	0.439
Middleton (geoparsepy) [17]	0.173	0.373	0.134	0.236	0.567	0.754	0.478	0.647
Our contributions								
GSP	0.335	0.403	0.217	0.356	0.686	0.664	0.506	0.668
E-GSP	0.398	0.574	0.295	0.455	0.671	0.769	0.559	0.693
GSP-F	0.655	0.449	0.363	0.531	0.894	0.692	0.640	0.779
E-GSP-F	**0.888**	**0.634**	**0.588**	**0.738**	**0.977**	**0.813**	**0.798**	**0.885**

Table 3. Detailed results of the E-GSP-F technique, when using different annotators for the *semantic annotation* step.

Technique	Annotator	ENG-NEEL				ITA-DSTR			
		Precision	Recall	Accuracy	F1	Precision	Recall	Accuracy	F1
E-GSP-F	TagMe	**0.905**	0.673	0.629	0.772	0.967	**0.853**	**0.831**	**0.906**
	DBpedia Spotlight	0.888	**0.697**	**0.640**	**0.781**	0.983	0.835	0.824	0.903
	Dexter 2.0	0.860	0.513	0.474	0.643	**0.992**	0.716	0.711	0.829
	Dandelion	0.901	0.652	0.608	0.756	0.965	0.847	0.824	0.902

allowing to boost *Recall* from 0.664 to 0.769 on ITA-DSTR and from 0.403 to 0.574 on ENG-NEEL, an average improvement of +37%. Similarly, the machine learning *filtering* step in GSP-F boosts *Precision* from 0.686 to 0.894 on ITA-DSTR and from 0.335 to 0.655 on ENG-NEEL, with an average improvement of +63%. As a result, the E-GSP-F technique, combining both E-GSP and GSP-F, largely outperforms all other techniques and benchmarks on both datasets. Indeed on ITA-DSTR, it achieves $F1 = 0.885$ versus $F1 = 0.777$ of the best benchmark. The performance gap is even more pronounced on the much more challenging ENG-NEEL dataset, where E-GSP-F achieves $F1 = 0.738$ versus $F1 = 0.313$. Furthermore, detailed results of E-GSP-F reported in Table 3 also show that our performances are consistent when using different semantic annotators, with no annotator clearly outperforming the others. The best results are obtained with DBpedia Spotlight on the ENG-NEEL dataset and with TagMe on ITA-DSTR, respectively with $F1 = 0.781$ and $F1 = 0.906$. Instead, Dexter 2.0 achieves slightly worse results than all other annotators on both datasets, mainly because of the lower *Recall*. As such, it is not recommended to use an implementation of our techniques solely based on Dexter 2.0.

In addition to an evaluation of the correctness of our geo-predictions, we also evaluated the geospatial granularity of our results. Table 4 shows the different types of places/locations extracted from tweets by E-GSP-F. As seen, E-GSP-F

Table 4. Types of places extracted
with **E-GSP-F**. Place types are
obtained from rdf:types.

Place types [#]
dbo:Airport
dbo:ArchitecturalStructure
dbo:Building
dbo:Castle
dbo:City
dbo:Country
dbo:Island
dbo:Mountain
dbo:Municipality
dbo:NaturalPlace
dbo:RailwayStation
dbo:Region
dbo:ReligiousBuilding
dbo:River
dbo:Settlement
dbo:Station

[#] dbo: PREFIX is http://dbpedia.
org/ontology/

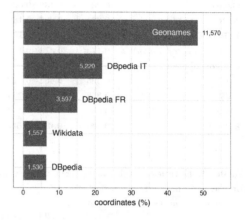

Fig. 2. Number of geographic coordinates
extracted from the different knowledge-
bases by **E-GSP-F**.

geoparsed both coarse- (e.g., countries, regions) and fine-grained (e.g., buildings)
locations, depending on the content of tweets. This result seems to favor the
application of our proposed technique in a broad range of different situations.
Finally, in Fig. 2 we reported the top 5 knowledge-bases from which **E-GSP-F**
extracted geographic coordinates. As shown in figure, the *expansion* step of
E-GSP-F allowed to retrieve geographic information from multiple knowledge-
bases, and indeed Geonames proved to be the richest source of geographic information, in our experiments.

6 Conclusions

We presented the novel *Geo-Semantic-Parsing* (GSP) technique for automatically
associating geographic coordinates to text documents. Furthermore, we improved
the basic GSP approach by introducing the *Expanded* GSP (E-GSP) and GSP *with
Filtering* (GSP-F), which we also combined together in the so-called **E-GSP-F**. The
excellent results obtained by **E-GSP-F** on 2 real-world evaluation datasets (best
$F1 = 0.91$) demonstrated that previous state-of-the-art approaches can be outperformed by leveraging powerful machine learning algorithms on top of Linked
Data. In particular, semantic annotation proved to be very effective in overcoming the drawbacks related to the language polysemy and the limited amount of
context, being able to brilliantly perform disambiguation and enrichment tasks

by leveraging on the Linked Data content and structural properties. Our results also showed that our technique is capable of extracting structured geographic information with variable degrees of granularity, ranging from country-level to building-level.

Future works along this direction should be focused on further improving the *expansion* step in E-GSP. Indeed, current results of E-GSP-F are mainly constrained by the moderate *Recall*. This calls for additional efforts aimed at increasing the set of geographic information extracted from RDF resources.

Acknowledgements. This research is supported in part by the EU H2020 Program under the schemes INFRAIA-1-2014-2015: Research Infrastructures grant agreement #654024 *SoBigData: Social Mining & Big Data Ecosystem*.

References

1. Avvenuti, M., Cresci, S., Del Vigna, F., Tesconi, M.: Impromptu crisis mapping to prioritize emergency response. Computer **49**(5), 28–37 (2016)
2. Avvenuti, M., Cresci, S., Marchetti, A., Meletti, C., Tesconi, M.: Predictability or early warning: using social media in modern emergency response. IEEE Internet Comput. **20**(6), 4–6 (2016)
3. Avvenuti, M., Del Vigna, F., Cresci, S., Marchetti, A., Tesconi, M.: Pulling information from social media in the aftermath of unpredictable disasters. In: ICT-DM 2015. IEEE (2015)
4. Cheng, Z., Caverlee, J., Lee, K.: You are where you tweet: a content-based approach to geo-locating Twitter users. In: CIKM 2010. ACM (2010)
5. Cresci, S., D'Errico, A., Gazzé, D., Duca, A.L., Marchetti, A., Tesconi, M.: Towards a DBpedia of tourism: the case of Tourpedia. In: 2014 International Semantic Web Conference (Posters & Demos), pp. 129–132, October 2014
6. Dell'Orletta, F., Venturi, G., Cimino, A., Montemagni, S.: T2K^2: a system for automatically extracting and organizing knowledge from texts. In: LREC 2014 (2014)
7. Ding, L., Shinavier, J., Shangguan, Z., McGuinness, D.L.: SameAs networks and beyond: analyzing deployment status and implications of owl:sameAs in linked data. In: Patel-Schneider, P.F., Pan, Y., Hitzler, P., Mika, P., Zhang, L., Pan, J.Z., Horrocks, I., Glimm, B. (eds.) ISWC 2010. LNCS, vol. 6496, pp. 145–160. Springer, Heidelberg (2010). https://doi.org/10.1007/978-3-642-17746-0_10
8. Dredze, M., Osborne, M., Kambadur, P.: Geolocation for Twitter: timing matters. In: HLT-NAACL 2016. ACL (2016)
9. Dredze, M., Paul, M.J., Bergsma, S., Tran, H.: Carmen: a Twitter geolocation system with applications to public health. In: AAAI 2013 Workshops. AAAI (2013)
10. Ferragina, P., Scaiella, U.: TagMe: on-the-fly annotation of short text fragments (by Wikipedia entities). In: CIKM 2010. ACM (2010)
11. Gelernter, J., Balaji, S.: An algorithm for local geoparsing of microtext. GeoInformatica **17**(4), 635–667 (2013)
12. Gottron, T., Schmitz, J., Middleton, S.: Focused exploration of geospatial context on linked open data. In: 2014 Workshop on Intelligent Exploration of Semantic Data (IESD 2014) at the 2014 International Semantic Web Conference, pp. 1–12, October 2014

13. Halterman, A.: Mordecai: full text geoparsing and event geocoding. J. Open Source Softw. **2**(9), 91 (2017). https://doi.org/10.21105/joss.00091
14. Kordopatis-Zilos, G., Papadopoulos, S., Kompatsiaris, I.: Geotagging text content with language models and feature mining. Proc. IEEE **105**(10), 1971–1986 (2017)
15. McGee, J., Caverlee, J., Cheng, Z.: Location prediction in social media based on tie strength. In: CIKM 2013. ACM (2013)
16. Mendes, P.N., Jakob, M., García-Silva, A., Bizer, C.: DBpedia spotlight: shedding light on the web of documents. In: I-Semantics 2011. ACM (2011)
17. Middleton, S.E., Middleton, L., Modafferi, S.: Real-time crisis mapping of natural disasters using social media. IEEE Intell. Syst. **29**(2), 9–17 (2014)
18. Paulheim, H., Fürnkranz, J.: Unsupervised feature generation from linked open data. In: WIMS 2012. ACM (2012)
19. Rietveld, L., Hoekstra, R., Schlobach, S., Guéret, C.: Structural properties as proxy for semantic relevance in RDF graph sampling. In: Mika, P., et al. (eds.) ISWC 2014. LNCS, vol. 8797, pp. 81–96. Springer, Cham (2014). https://doi.org/10.1007/978-3-319-11915-1_6
20. Töpper, G., Knuth, M., Sack, H.: DBpedia ontology enrichment for inconsistency detection. In: I-Semantics 2012. ACM (2012)
21. Trani, S., Ceccarelli, D., Lucchese, C., Orlando, S., Perego, R.: Dexter 2.0: an open source tool for semantically enriching data. In: 2014 International Semantic Web Conference (Posters & Demos), pp. 417–420, October 2014
22. Usbeck, R., Ngonga Ngomo, A.-C., Röder, M., Gerber, D., Coelho, S.A., Auer, S., Both, A.: AGDISTIS - graph-based disambiguation of named entities using linked data. In: Mika, P., et al. (eds.) ISWC 2014. LNCS, vol. 8796, pp. 457–471. Springer, Cham (2014). https://doi.org/10.1007/978-3-319-11964-9_29

LDP-DL: A Language to Define
the Design of Linked Data Platforms

Noorani Bakerally$^{(\boxtimes)}$, Antoine Zimmermann$^{(\boxtimes)}$ ⓘ, and Olivier Boissier$^{(\boxtimes)}$

Univ Lyon, IMT Mines, Saint-Étienne, CNRS,
Laboratoire Hubert Curien UMR 5516, 42023 Saint-Étienne, France
{noorani.bakerally,antoine.zimmermann,olivier.boissier}@emse.fr

Abstract. Linked Data Platform 1.0 (LDP) is the W3C Recommendation for exposing linked data in a RESTful manner. While several implementations of the LDP standard exist, deploying an LDP from existing data sources still involves much manual development. This is because there is currently no support for automatizing generation of LDP on these implementations. To this end, we propose an approach whose core is a language for specifying how existing data sources should be used to generate LDPs in a way that is independent of and compatible with any LDP implementation and deployable on any of them. We formally describe the syntax and semantics of the language and its implementation. We show that our approach (1) allows the reuse of the same design for multiple deployments, or (2) the same data with different designs, (3) is open to heterogeneous data sources, (4) can cope with hosting constraints and (5) significantly automatizes deployment of LDPs.

Keywords: RDF · Linked data · Linked data platform

1 Introduction

In the context of open data, data sets are made available through Web data portals with the intention to offer innovative third party developers the opportunity to provide new services to end users. In particular, today's smart cities usually publish urban data openly. However, exploitation of urban open data is made very difficult by the current heterogeneity of data sets. The problem becomes even more prominent when considering multiple data portals from several metropolises.

Semantic Web technologies are largely addressing heterogeneity issues, with a uniform identification mechanism (URIs), a uniform data model (RDF), and a standard ontology language (OWL). Recently, a new standard was added to provide a uniform data access mechanism for linked data, based on RESTful principles: the Linked Data Platform 1.0 standard (LDP [18]). Considering the alledged advantages of the Semantic Web and Linked Data, we believe that LDPs can ease the path towards achieving Tim Berners-Lee's 5-star[1] open data scheme.

---

[1] http://5stardata.info/en/, last accessed 23 March 2018.

© Springer International Publishing AG, part of Springer Nature 2018
A. Gangemi et al. (Eds.): ESWC 2018, LNCS 10843, pp. 33–49, 2018.
https://doi.org/10.1007/978-3-319-93417-4_3

Yet, while LDPs greatly simplify the work of data users (developers, analysts, journalists, etc.), it puts a heavy burden on the data publishers, who have to make use of these new, unfamiliar technologies. The move towards LDPs requires a redesign of how the data is organized and published. Moreover, current LDP implementations are in their early stage and provide no automatic support for deploying data whether it is static, dynamic or heterogeneous. This paper is an attempt to provide a solution targeted towards data publishers to facilitate the use and deployment of linked data platforms conforming with the LDP standard from existing data sources.

We start by identifying requirements that any solution to the problem should satisfy (Sect. 2.1), then show how the state of the art is failing to satisfy them (Sect. 2.2), and subsequently propose a general approach to more easily design and deploy LDPs (Sect. 2.3). An important and central part of the approach is to provide a language, LDP Design Language (LDP-DL), for declaratively defining the design of data organization and deployment. This paper is mostly focused on describing this language, with Sect. 3.3 dedicated to its abstract syntax and Sect. 3.4 to its semantics. Our implementation is explained in Sect. 4.1 followed by Sect. 4.2 that describes what experiments we conducted to highlight the requirements that the approach satisfies. Finally, immediate directions towards overcoming the limitations are presented in the concluding section (Sect. 5).

2 Foundations and Motivations

In order to better understand the problem that we consider, we start by listing the requirements that the automatic generation of LDP from existing data sources should satisfy (cf. Sect. 2.1). To that aim, we will use the motivating example of LDP deployment in smart cities that we are considering in the OpenSensingCity project[2]. However, let's keep in mind that these requirements are also relevant for other application domains as well. We analyze and point current limitations in the current approaches with respect to these requirements (cf. Sect. 2.2). We end this section then by presenting a global view of the approach that we propose in this paper (cf. Sect. 2.3).

2.1 Requirements

To better explain the requirements on automatic LDP generation, let's take the example of a city governmental institution that decides to expose the data (open or not) produced in the city, in order to enable their exploitation by smart city applications to support citizens in their activities in the city.

To that aim, it decides to deploy a data platform. In order to enhance interoperability and homogenize access, the choice has been made to use a data platform which is compliant with Semantics Web standards including the LDP standard. However, in order to deploy such a Linked Data Platform in this context, the following requirements must be satisfied:

---

[2] http://opensensingcity.emse.fr/.

- **Handling heterogeneous data sources (*Heterogeneity*).** A city is a decentralized and open ecosystem where data come from different organizations that are normally heterogeneous. As such, the city LDP may have to exploit and aggregate data from these sources and must be therefore open to heterogeneous data sources.
- **Handling hosting constraints (*Hosting Constraints*).** Smart city and open data consist of data sources whose exploitation can give rise to hosting constraints that prevent from hosting a copy of the data in a third-party environment. Such constraints can be on the data itself (e.g. license restrictions), or it can be a limitation of the third-party software environment (e.g. bandwidth or storage limitations to continuously verify and maintain fresh copies of dynamic or real-time data). Thus, the city LDP has to be able to cope with hosting constraints.
- **Reusable design (*Reusability*).** If LDPs are spreading in different cities, one can easily imagine that there may be a city wishing to reuse the design of another city LDP to expose their data in a similar way. One potential reason for doing so may be to enhance integration and access of their date to cross-city applications. Such applications may exploit any city LDP as long as the LDPs use both a design and vocabulary known by the application.
- **Automated LDP generation (*Automatization*).** Finally, the use of existing LDP implementations (discussed in next section) necessitates much manual development and thus requires time and expertise that the city may not want to invest when putting in place its LDP. Also, having automated solutions may help organizations wishing to open their data in conformance to Semantic Web standards via LDPs.

2.2   LDP Overview and Current Limitations of Existing Approaches

The LDP standard provides a model to organize data resources known as LDP resources and an interaction model to interact (read-write) with them. Two types of LDP resources exist: LDP RDF Sources (LDP-RS) and LDP Non-RDF Sources. These resources can be organized in LDP containers and as such are known as member resources. An LDP container is itself an LDP-RS. Three types of containers exist, but currently in our work, we only consider LDP Basic Containers (LDP-BC) in which members are limited to Web documents. Note that among current LDP implementations (discussed below), most support LDP-BCs and fewer support other types of containers. In this paper, we want facilitate the way LDP resources are organized in term of their IRIs, the content and organization in LDP containers and the content of LDP-RSs.

There are existing solutions for deploying linked data that do not conform with the LDP standard. Although we would like to take advantage of the homogeneous access mechanism of LDP, some non-LDP-conformant tools partially cover our requirements. Pubby[3], D2R Server [5], Virtuoso[4] and Triplify [2] are

---

[3] http://wifo5-03.informatik.uni-mannheim.de/pubby/ on 18 May 2017.
[4] https://virtuoso.openlinksw.com on 19 July 2017.

such examples. Triplify and D2R, have been designed to expose relational data as linked data and are focused on mappings. The final steps of publishing linked data only involves ensuring resources can be dereferenced with RDF. Virtuoso goes a step forward by doing the latter as well as providing a linked data interface to its triple store. Pubby can provide a linked data interface both to SPARQL endpoints and static RDF documents. Pubby and Virtuoso are the only tools for directly publishing RDF data as linked data in a highly automatized way. However, most design decisions are fixed and cannot be parameterized. Moreover, these solutions implement their own interpretation of the linked data principles, where data access and the content of RDF sources are neither standardized nor customizable. For instance, Pubby uses DESCRIBE queries to provide the content of RDF resources, which is a feature whose implementation varies from a SPARQL query engine to another. In summary, these tools offer the automatization that we require, but with little flexibility, and lacking the standard data access mechanism of LDP.

Concerning LDP implementations, they are mostly referenced in the standard conformance report[5] with the exception of Cavendish[6] which, to our knowledge, is the only one not referenced. We categorize them into *LDP resource management systems* (Cavendish, Callimachus, Carbon LDP, Fedora Commons, Apache Marmotta, Gold, rww-play, LDP.js) and *LDP frameworks* (Eclipse Lyo, LDP4j). LDP resource management systems can be seen as a repository for resources on top of which read and write operations conforming to the LDP standard are allowed. Currently, they do not satisfy our requirements because their deployment requires hardcoding most design decisions into appropriate write requests to an already deployed platform. On the other hand, LDP frameworks can be used to build custom applications which implement LDP interactions. While they are more flexible than management systems, they are not satisfying our requirements because their use involves much manual development. In summary, current LDP implementations are in their early stages as there is little to no support for automating the generation and deployment of LDPs from existing data, even if it is already in RDF.

Besides existing implementations, the current scientific literature about LDP is itself limited. To our knowledge four works [12,14–16] have a focus on LDP. Among them, only [16] provides an approach for automatizing generations of LDPs from relational data using simple R2RML mapping (no SQL view, no multiple mappings to a class/property). While it minimally address the *Heterogeneity* requirement, it is rigid as it is not possible to customize the design of the output LDP. Apart from this, we find no other work that attempts to automatize the generation of LDPs.

2.3   Our Approach: The LDP Generation Workflow

In order to satisfy the requirements listed in Sect. 2.1, we provide an approach based on model-driven engineering that involves using models as first-class

---

[5] https://www.w3.org/2012/ldp/hg/tests/reports/ldp.html on 19 July 2017.

[6] https://github.com/cavendish-ldp/cavendish on 07 July 2018.

entities and transforming them into running systems by using generators or by dynamically interpreting the models at run-time [9]. Doing so enables separation of concerns thus guaranteeing higher reusability of systems' models [20].

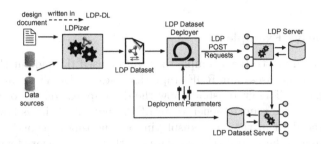

Fig. 1. General overview of our LDP generation workflow proposal

Figure 1 shows a general overview of the approach. The LDP generation work-flow includes two processes: LDPization and deployment. In the former process, the LDPizer consumes a design document written in our language, LDP-DL, that we use as a domain-specific language, a core component of model-driven engineering, to explicitly describe LDP design models. Doing so enables us to consider our *Reusability* requirement as the models are standalone, independent and separate from any implementation. The LDPizer interprets the model and exploits the data sources to generate what we call an LDP dataset (defined in Sect. 3), which is a structure to store LDP resources introduced to abstract ways from how current implementations store resources. The *Heterogeneity* require-ment is handled by the possibility to specify mappings between non-RDF data to RDF graphs. The deployment process involves configuring the LDP and load-ing the LDP dataset into it. It can be done in two ways based on the nature of the LDP server. First, if the LDP server accepts POST requests, an LDP Dataset Deployer can generate and send such requests for each resource contained in the LDP dataset. Second, using an LDP server that can directly consume the LDP dataset and expose resources from it. Such a server can generate the content of requested resources at query time thus enable considering the *Hosting Con-straint* requirement by avoiding the need for storing content of LDP resources. For now, our approach only requires the design document from which the entire LDP can be automatically generated (*Automatization* requirement).

In our approach, we exploit possibilities of model-driven engineering by per-forming model-to-model transformation when generating an LDP dataset from a design document in the LDPization process and by performing model-to-system transformation by generating an LDP from an LDP dataset in the deployment process.

3 LDP Design Language

In this section, we describe our language LDP-DL. We start with a general overview of its key concepts and provide its abstract syntax and formal semantics.

3.1 Illustrative Example

Figure 2 shows an illustrative example that will be used throughout this section and later on. It comprises of an RDF graph that uses the DCAT vocabulary [13], shown in Fig. 2(a). The graph shows how the data appear on the original data portal from which we want to generate an LDP. Figure 2(b) shows how we want to organize the data in the LDP, displaying the nesting of containers. In the DCAT vocabulary, data catalogs have datasets that are associated with themes and distributions. The organization of resources in the LDP in Fig. 2(b) uses a structure similar to DCAT where there are containers for describing catalogs that contains other containers for describing their datasets. The dataset containers in turn contain two containers for grouping non-containers that describe their distributions and themes. In this case, we want the resources identified under the namespace `ex:` to be described in an LDP available at the namespace `dex:`. On the LDP, we would like, e.g., that resources `dex:parking` and `dex:pJSON` be dereferenceable to obtain, respectively, the graphs shown in Fig. 2(c) and (d). Thus, `dex:parking` is an LDP resource that describes `ex:parking` with an graph that contains a subset of the original RDF graph in Fig. 2(a). What the design language must describe is how we can exploit the graph in Fig. 2(a) to generate the container hierarchy of Fig. 2(b), and make available the descriptions of the resources as RDF graphs found in Fig. 2(c) and (d).

3.2 Overview of the Language

As mentioned in Sect. 2.2, in this paper, we restrict ourselves only to LDPs where all containers are basic and exclude non-RDF sources. From an abstract point of view, the data in such an LDP can be described as an *LDP dataset*, a structure where each LDP resource is assigned a URL and has an associated RDF graph, and a set of members if it is a container. In it, pairs $(url, graph)$ representing a non-container, formalize the fact that accessing the URL on the LDP returns the graph, whereas triples $(url, graph, M)$ indicates that not only access to the URL returns the graph but the resource is a container whose members are in M. For example, in Fig. 2(b), `dex:parking` is the URL of a container associated with the graph in Fig. 2(c) and having members `dex:distributions` and `dex:themes`. Furthermore, `dex:pJSON` is the URL of a non-container in Fig. 2(b) with its graph in Fig. 2(d).

In a nutshell, LDP-DL provides constructs for describing the generation of an LDP dataset from existing data sources. In general, data sources may not be in RDF or may contain resources whose IRIs do not dereference to the LDP. Therefore, associated LDP resources within the LDP namespace may have to

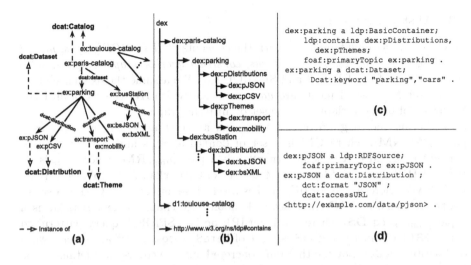

Fig. 2. Example of structure of an LDP with its data source and graphs

be generated to describe resources from the original data sources. For example, `dex:parking`, from Fig. 2(b), has been generated for the resource `ex:parking` from Fig. 2(a). `ex:parking` cannot be used directly as an LDP resource. Doing so may violate the LDP standard with respect to the lifecycle of the resource as the standard states that "a contained LDPR cannot be created (...) before its containing LDPC exists" [17, Sect. 2].[7] This is why in LDP-DL, to expose a resource from the data source via an LDP, a new LDP-RS is always generated to describe it. The resource for which an LDP-RS is generated is called the *related resource*. Thus, the related resource of the LDP-RS `dex:parking` is `ex:parking`. Let us note that an LDP-RS may not have a related resource, such as `dex:pDistributions` from Fig. 2(b). This is because it describes the set of distributions of `ex:parking` and such set is not itself identified as a proper resource in the data source. Figure 3 shows an overview of the language in UML that we further describes in the next section.

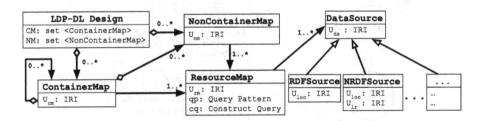

Fig. 3. Overview of the main constructs of LDP-DL in UML notation.

---

[7] "LDPR" means LDP resource and "LDPC" means LDP container in the standard.

3.3   Abstract Syntax

Hereafter, we assume familiarity with the concepts of *IRIs*, *RDF graphs*, *named graphs*, *query variables*, *query patterns*, *construct queries*, *graph template*, *solution mappings* from RDF [7] and SPARQL [10]. We assume the existence of an infinite set $\mathcal{D}$ whose elements are *documents* and write **IRI** the set of all IRIs, **V** the set of query variables, $\mathcal{G}$ the set of all RDF graphs.

Following the diagram of Fig. 3, we can abstract a *design document* as a pair $\langle \mathbf{CM}, \mathbf{NM} \rangle$, where **CM** is a set of ContainerMaps and **NM** is a set of NonContainerMaps. A NonContainerMap is a pair $\langle u_{\mathsf{nm}}, \mathbf{RM} \rangle$ where u_{nm} is an IRI and **RM** is a set of ResourceMaps. A ContainerMap is a tuple $\langle u_{\mathsf{cm}}, \mathbf{RM}, \mathbf{CM}, \mathbf{NM} \rangle$ where u_{cm} is an IRI, **RM** is a set of ResourceMaps, **CM** is a set of ContainerMaps, and **NM** is a set of NonContainerMaps. A ResourceMap is a tuple $\langle u_{\mathsf{rm}}, \mathsf{qp}, \mathsf{cq}, \mathbf{DS} \rangle$ where u_{rm} is an IRI, qp is a SPARQL query pattern, cq is a CONSTRUCT query, and **DS** is a set of DataSources. There are several ways of describing a DataSource that our concrete language covers (see details in the language specification [3]). Here, we only consider the cases of a pair $\langle u_{\mathsf{ds}}, u_{\mathsf{loc}} \rangle$ or a triple $\langle u_{\mathsf{ds}}, u_{\mathsf{loc}}, u_{\mathsf{lr}} \rangle$ where u_{ds}, u_{loc} and u_{lr} are IRIs that respectively refer to a data source, its location and an RDF lifting rule.

As we can see, all components of a design document in LDP-DL have an IRI. Given a *Map or DataSource x, we refer to the IRI of x as $\mathrm{iri}(x)$. In a ResourceMap, qp is used to extract a set of related resources from DataSources, and cq is used to generate the graph of the LDP-RSs associated with the related resources. In a DataSource, u_{loc} corresponds to the location of the source file,

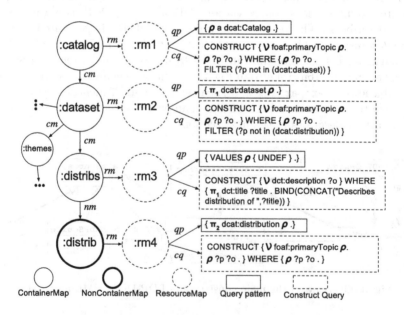

Fig. 4. Example of an LDP-DL document in the abstract syntax.

whereas u_{lr} is the location of what we call a *lifting rule*, used to generate an RDF graph from non-RDF data.

We assume the existence of an infinite set of variables $V_r = \{\rho, \nu, \pi_1, \ldots, \pi_i, \ldots\} \subseteq \mathbf{V}$ called the *reserved variables*, such that $\mathbf{V} \setminus V_r$ is infinite. ResourceMaps may use the reserved variables but these have a special semantics as explained in the next section. However, due to undesirable consequences, we forbid the use of variable ν in the WHERE clause of the CONSTRUCT query cq.

Figure 4 shows a simple example of a design document[8] in the abstract syntax of the language. An arrow with the label *cm*, *nm* or *rm* indicates that the construct has a ContainerMap, NonContainerMap or ResourceMap in its **CM**, **NM** or **RM** respectively. Also, though not shown in the figure, in the **DS** of all ResourceMaps, there is a DataSource (ex:ds, ex:paris) which is actually the RDF graph in Fig. 2(a).

3.4   Overview of the Formal Semantics

The aim of the formal semantics is to associate an LDP dataset (as described in Sect. 3.2) to a design document. To this end, we define a notion of interpretation and a notion of satisfaction in a model-theoretic way. Several interpretations may satisfy a given design document, leading to different evaluations of it. This approach allows developers to implement the language in different ways, leading to different results, depending on whether they implement optional or alternative parts of the standard, yet have a non-ambiguous way to check the correctness of an implementation output.

LDP-DL Interpretation. An LDP-DL interpretation determines which IRIs denote ContainerMaps, NonContainerMaps, ResourceMaps, DataSources, or something else. Then, each ContainerMap (resp. NonContainerMap) is interpreted as a set of triples $(url, graph, M)$ (resp., a set of pairs $(url, graph)$) wrt a list of ancestors. A list of ancestors is a finite sequence of elements that can be IRIs or a special value $\epsilon \notin \mathbf{IRI}$ that indicates an absence of related resource. Formally, an *ancestor list* is an element of $\mathbf{IRI}^* = \bigcup_{n>=0} (\mathbf{IRI} \cup \{\epsilon\})^n$ and $\emptyset$ being the empty list $(\mathbf{IRI} \cup \{\epsilon\})^0$. We use the notation $\vec{p}$ to denote an ancestor list and use $\text{len}(\vec{p})$ to denote the length of the list. Also $\vec{p}::r$ denotes appending element r to $\vec{p}$.

Definition 1 (LDP-DL Interpretation). *An LDP-DL interpretation $\mathcal{I}$ is a tuple $\langle \Delta^{\mathcal{I}}, \mathcal{C}, \mathcal{N}, \mathcal{R}, \mathcal{S}, \cdot^{\mathcal{I}}, \mathcal{I}_{\mathcal{C}}, \mathcal{I}_{\mathcal{N}}, \mathcal{I}_{\mathcal{R}}, \mathcal{I}_{\mathcal{S}} \rangle$ such that:*

- *$\Delta^{\mathcal{I}}$ is a non empty set (the domain of interpretation);*
- *$\mathcal{C}, \mathcal{N}, \mathcal{R}, \mathcal{S}$ are subsets of $\Delta^{\mathcal{I}}$;*
- *$\cdot^{\mathcal{I}} : \mathbf{IRI} \to \Delta^{\mathcal{I}}$ is the interpretation function;*
- *$\mathcal{I}_{\mathcal{C}} : \mathcal{C} \times \mathbf{IRI}^* \to 2^{\mathbf{IRI} \times \mathcal{G} \times 2^{\mathbf{IRI}}}$;*
- *$\mathcal{I}_{\mathcal{N}} : \mathcal{N} \times \mathbf{IRI}^* \to 2^{\mathbf{IRI} \times \mathcal{G}}$;*

---

[8] Design document in concrete syntax https://tinyurl.com/y8n9cls2.

- $\mathcal{I}_\mathcal{R} : \mathcal{R} \times \mathbf{IRI}^* \rightarrow 2^{\mathbf{IRI} \times \mathbf{IRI} \cup \{\epsilon\} \times \mathcal{G}}$ such that $(n, r_1, g_1) \in \mathcal{I}_\mathcal{R}(u_1, \overrightarrow{p_1}) \wedge$ $(n, r_2, g_2) \in \mathcal{I}_\mathcal{R}(u_2, \overrightarrow{p_2}) \implies r_1 = r_2 \wedge g_1 = g_2$ *(unicity constraint)*;
- $\mathcal{I}_\mathcal{S} : \mathcal{S} \rightarrow \mathcal{G}$.

$\mathcal{C}$ (resp. $\mathcal{N}$, $\mathcal{R}$, $\mathcal{S}$) represents the container maps (resp., non container maps, resource maps, data sources) according to the interpretation. That is, if the interpretation function $\mathcal{I}$ maps an IRI to an element of $\mathcal{C}$, it means that this interpretation considers that the IRI is the name of a container map. For a given ContainerMap $cm \in \mathcal{C}$ and an ancestor list $\overrightarrow{p}$, $\langle n, g, M \rangle \in \mathcal{I}_\mathcal{C}(cm, \overrightarrow{p})$ means that, in the context of $\overrightarrow{p}$, cm must map the data sources to containers where n is the IRI of a container, g is the RDF graph obtained from dereferencing n, and M is the set of IRIs referring to the members of the container. Similarly, for a NonContainerMap $nm \in \mathcal{N}$, $\langle n, g \rangle \in \mathcal{I}_\mathcal{N}(nm, \overrightarrow{p})$ means that nm must map to resources where n is the IRI of a non-container LDP-RS that provides g when dereferenced. For a DataSource $ds \in \mathcal{S}$, $\mathcal{I}_\mathcal{S}(ds)$ is an RDF graph representing what can be obtained from the data source.

Informal Description of the Satisfaction. We describe satisfaction $\models$ relating interpretations to syntactic constructs that they validate. Due to space restriction, we only provide an overview of the definitions, that are formally given in our technical report [4] with more explanations. The rest of this section informally explains the semantics of LDP-DL constructs. To do so, we use Fig. 4, which is a design in LDP-DL for building the LDP[9] having the structure shown in Fig. 2(b), using the data source in Fig. 2(a).

In principle, a DataSource provides information to retrieve an RDF graph, using parameters that can take several forms. Here, we define only two forms of DataSources, $ds = \langle u_{\mathsf{ds}}, u_{\mathsf{loc}} \rangle$ that provides a URL to an RDF document directly, and $ds = \langle u_{\mathsf{ds}}, u_{\mathsf{loc}}, u_{\mathsf{lr}} \rangle$ that provides an additional URL to an arbitrary document with a transformation script to generate an RDF graph. We call such a script a *lifting rule* and can be seen as a function $lr : \mathcal{D} \rightarrow \mathcal{G}$. Our semantics is flexible enough to be extended to more complex such as for access rights, content negotiation etc. For example, the retrieval of the RDF graph in Fig. 2(a) could be described by a DataSource $ds_1 = \langle u_{ds_1}, u_{loc_1} \rangle$ where $\mathcal{I}_\mathcal{S}(u_{ds_1}^\mathcal{I})$ is the RDF graph located at u_{loc_1}. Similarly, for a DataSource $ds_2 = \langle u_{ds_2}, u_{loc_2}, u_{lr_2} \rangle$, $\mathcal{I}_\mathcal{S}(u_{ds_1}^\mathcal{I})$ is the RDF graph obtained by executing the lifting rule found at u_{lr_2} on the document found at u_{loc_2}.

At the top level of the design document, the ContainerMap :catalog uses the ResourceMap :rm1 to generate the top level containers. The DataSource used by :rm1 is interpreted as the RDF graph of Fig. 2(a). At this level, :rm1 is evaluated with an empty ancestor list. Using its query pattern, related resources extracted from the source are DCAT catalogs ex:paris-catalog and ex:toulouse-catalog. For each of them, an IRI is generated, namely dex:paris-catalog and dex:toulouse-catalog. Also, to satisfy the map :rm1, the RDF graph associated with the container IRI is obtained using its CONSTRUCT

---

[9] http://opensensingcity.emse.fr/ldpdfend/catalogs/ldp.

query, where the variable ρ is bound to the related resource IRI, and ν to the IRI of the new LDP resource. For example, when doing so for dex:paris-catalog, ρ is bound to ex:paris-catalog, and ν to dex:paris-catalog. Finally, new containers generated from :catalog must define their members as well, and is thus satisfied only if its members correspond to the resources generated by their underlying ContainerMaps and NonContainerMaps (in this case, :dataset only).

The ContainerMap :dataset is used to generate members for containers generated from :catalog. Let us consider the case for dex:paris-catalog. Its related resource is ex:paris-catalog and its members must only have related resources that are DCAT datasets from this catalog. This is why the extraction of these resources is parameterized by the parent variable π_1 in the query pattern :rm2. π_1 is binded to the first element of the ancestor list which at this stage is ex:paris-catalog. The evaluation of :dataset generates two containers, dex:parking and dex:busStation, that are added to the members of dex:paris-catalog.

The map :distribs is used to generate members for containers generated by :dataset. Consider the case of doing so for dex:parking whose related resource is ex:parking. In this context, the aim of using :distribs is to generate a container to describe the set of distributions of ex:parking. Note that in the data source, there is no explicit resource to describe this set. This is why, in the ResourceMap :rm3, the query pattern returns a single result where ρ is unbound. Although the query pattern does not use any ancestor variable, it is evaluated using the ancestor list (ex:paris-catalog, ex:parking) and thus ancestor variables π_1 and π_2 are bound. The evaluation of :distribs in the context of dex:parking generates a single container dex:pDistributions. :distribs is satisfied when a single container is generated without a related resource.

Finally, the NonContainerMap :distrib is used to generate non-containers for each distribution of a DCAT dataset. Consider the case of doing so for dex:pDistributions with ancestor list (ex:paris-catalog, ex:parking, $\emptyset$). In this context, the proper related resource that must be used to extract the relevant distributions is associated with the grand parent container. This is why the query pattern of :rm4 uses π_2, bound to ex:parking, rather than π_1. Using the result (ex:pJSON and ex:pCSV) of this query pattern, two non-containers dex:pJSON and dex:pCSV in dex:pDistributions are generated using :distrib. In general, any ancestor's related resources can be referenced through the ancestor variables π_i simultaneously, even when they are unbound.

Evaluation of a Design Document Using an Interpretation. With an interpretation, we have a way of assigning an LDP dataset (as described in Sect. 3.2) to a design document, using the interpretations of the ContainerMaps and NonContainerMaps that appear in the document. We call this an *evaluation* of the document. Formally, it takes the form of a function that builds an LDP dataset given an LDP-DL interpretation and a document δ. We formalize the notion of LDP dataset as follows:

Definition 2 (LDP dataset). *An* LDP dataset *is a pair* $\langle \mathbf{NG}, \mathbf{NC} \rangle$ *where* $\mathbf{NG}$ *is a set of named graphs and* $\mathbf{NC}$ *is a set of* named container, *that is a set of triples* $\langle n, g, M \rangle$ *such that* $n \in \mathbf{IRI}$ *(called the container name),* $g \in \mathcal{G}$ *and* $M \in 2^{\mathbf{IRI}}$, *and such that:*

- *no IRI appears more than once as a (graph or container) name;*
- *for all* $\langle n, g, M \rangle \in \mathbf{NC}$, *and for all* $u \in M$, *there exists a named graph or container having the name* u.

Having the notion of LDP dataset, the maps of the design document are evaluated wrt an ancestor list as follows:

Definition 3 (Evaluation of a map). *The* evaluation *of a* ContainerMap *or* NonContainerMap m *wrt an interpretation* $\mathcal{I}$ *and an ancestor list* $\vec{p}$ *s.t.* $\mathcal{I}, \vec{p} \models m$ *is:*

$$
[\![m]\!]_{\mathcal{I}}^{\vec{p}} = \begin{cases} \mathcal{I}_{\mathcal{N}}(\mathsf{iri}(m)^{\mathcal{I}}, \vec{p}), & \text{if } m \text{ is a } \texttt{NonContainerMap} \\[2ex] \mathcal{I}_{\mathcal{C}}(\mathsf{iri}(m)^{\mathcal{I}}, \vec{p}) \cup \bigcup_{\substack{rm \in \mathbf{RM} \\ \langle n, r, g \rangle \in \mathcal{I}_{\mathcal{R}}(\mathsf{iri}(rm)^{\mathcal{I}}, \vec{p}) \\ m' \in \mathbf{NM} \cup \mathbf{CM}}} [\![m']\!]_{\mathcal{I}}^{\vec{p} :: r}, & \text{if } m = \langle u_{\mathsf{cm}}, \mathbf{RM}, \mathbf{CM}, \mathbf{NM} \rangle \text{ is a } \texttt{ContainerMap} \end{cases}
$$

The evaluation of a map yields an LDP dataset. Indeed, the first condition of Definition 2 is satisfied because of the unicity constraint from Definition 1, and the second condition is satisfied because $\mathcal{I}, \vec{p} \models m$. Now we can define the evaluation of a design document wrt an interpretation:

Definition 4 (Evaluation of a design document). *Let* $\mathcal{I}$ *be an interpretation and* $\delta = \langle \mathbf{CM}, \mathbf{NM} \rangle$ *a design document. The* evaluation *of* δ *wrt* $\mathcal{I}$ *is*

$$
[\![\delta]\!]_{\mathcal{I}} = \bigcup_{m \in \mathbf{CM} \cup \mathbf{NM}} [\![m]\!]_{\mathcal{I}}^{\emptyset}
$$

In practice, an LDP-DL processor will not define an explicit interpretation, but will build an LDP dataset from a design document. Hence, we want to define a notion of conformity of an algorithm wrt the language specification given above. To this aim, we first provide a definition of a valid LDP dataset for a design document.

Definition 5 (Valid). *An LDP dataset* D *is* valid *wrt a design document* δ *if there exists an interpretation* $\mathcal{I}$ *that satisfies* δ, *such that* $[\![\delta]\!]_{\mathcal{I}} = D$.

The validity of LDP dataset is an important property used in our implementation when generating and deploying LDPs. Finally, we can define the correctness of an algorithm that implements LDP-DL.

Definition 6 (Correct). *An algorithm that takes an LDP-DL document as input and returns an LDP dataset is* correct *if for all document* δ, *the output of the algorithm on* δ *is valid wrt* δ.

If an algorithm evaluates LDP-DL documents, the formal semantics given in [4] should be used to prove its correctness.

4   Implementation and Evaluation

This section describes the implementation of the tools participating in the LDP generation workflow described in Sect. 2.3. Then, we evaluate our approach with respect to our requirements outlined in Sect. 2.1 by performing experiments to deploy real datasets on LDPs. A detailed description of the tools and the experiments we conducted are available on GitHub[10] (Fig. 5).

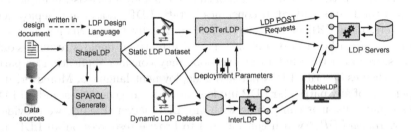

Fig. 5. Implementation of our LDP generation workflow proposal

4.1   Implementation of LDP Generation Workflow

ShapeLDP[11] is an LDPizer that interprets design documents and generate the LDP dataset from them. The concrete syntax in RDF is described in [3] and the algorithms we use are described in [4]. To enhance modularity, the design model may be split and written in different documents that are merged before processing. To exploit heterogeneous data sources, for now it can use lifting rules specified for `DataSources` in SPARQL-Generate [11]. Future versions may consider other languages such as RML [8], XSPARQL [1] and others. ShapeLDP can process design documents in two modes: *static evaluation* and *dynamic evaluation*. In both modes, the output uses relative IRIs without an explicit base and act only as an intermediary document from which the LDP dataset should be constructed. In *static evaluation* (resp. *dynamic evaluation*), a *static LDP dataset* (resp. *dynamic LDP dataset*) is generated in TriG format [6]. The final LDP dataset is obtained from a static LDP dataset by adding a base IRI at deployment time. The result stays valid wrt to the sources as long as the evaluation of the query patterns and CONSTRUCT queries of all `ResourceMaps` from the design document do not change. The LDP dataset obtained from a dynamic LDP dataset stays valid wrt the sources as long as the evaluation of the quert patterns of all `ResourceMaps` do not change, but the result of CONSTRUCT queries may change from one request to the next. A *dynamic LDP dataset* is a structure somewhat similar to the LDP dataset that store all containers and non-containers and a CONSTRUCT query to generate their RDF graphs at request

---

[10] https://github.com/noorbakerally/LDPDatasetExamples.
[11] https://github.com/noorbakerally/ShapeLDP.

time. The `CONSTRUCT` query is obtained when evaluating `ResourceMaps` by using the bindings of the reserved variables.

InterLDP[12] is an LDP server which can directly consume an LDP dataset (static or dynamic) and expose resources from it. It was validated against the conformance tests of the LDP read interactions.[13] To cater for hosting constraints, it uses the dynamic LDP dataset to generate the RDF graph of the requested resource at query time.

POSTerLDP[14] is the implementation of the LDP deployer on existing implementations of the LDP standard. It consumes a static LDP dataset and deployment parameters: base URL of LDP server and optionally the username and password for basic authentication on the server. Currently, it deploys resources only on one server at a time but future versions may consider replication or partitioning schemes described in a particular deployment language. Moreover, it is independent of any particular LDP implementations. It generates standard LDP requests and thus, it is compatible with any LDP server. Finally, we provide a browser, *HubbleLDP*[15] which can be used to browse resources on an LDP and view their content. An instance of it is running at http://bit.ly/2BGYl9X.

4.2   Evaluation

We evaluate our approach by performing the following five experiments, that show the main requirements they satisfy.

Experiment 1: The input data sources correspond to 22 RDF datasets from city data portals, structured per the DCAT vocabulary. Five design documents have been defined and used to automatize the generation of 110 LDPs from the 22 datasets. This demonstrate the *Reusability* requirement through the use of the same design document on all input data sources. It also shows the flexibility as we are able to generate different platforms by applying different design documents on the same data source.

Experiment 2: The aim is to show the compatibility of our approach with existing implementations. To that aim, an LDP dataset is automatically generated from one input data source and the design document from Experiment 1. We use POSTerLDP to automatize its deployment over LDP servers that are instances of Apache Marmotta and Gold, both of them being referenced implementation. This experiment shows also the loose coupling of our approach as we are able to reproduce the two platforms with the same design on different LDP servers.

---

[12] https://github.com/noorbakerally/InterLDP.

[13] The conformance report is available at https://w3id.org/ldpdl/InterLDP/execution-report.html.

[14] https://github.com/noorbakerally/POSTerLDP.

[15] https://github.com/noorbakerally/HubbleLDP.

Experiment 3: To show the ability of our approach to consider the *Heterogeneity* requirement, a design document is used with a lifting rule to deal with original data sources, one in CSV and the other in JSON format. ShapeLDP uses the embedded SPARQL-Generate engine and the lifting rules to automatically generate the respective RDF data that is then deployed via an LDP.

Experiment 4: To evaluate satisfaction of the *Hosting Constraints* requirement, we use ShapeLDP in dynamic evaluation mode: a dynamic LDP dataset is generated first, from which we can deploy an LDP that offers dynamic results generated at request time from real-time data sources. Generating responses from the platform takes more time because their content are generated at query time.

Experiment 5: For now, we do not automatically generate design models, but we provide 2 generic design documents that organize data according to the class hierarchy of an ontology. We believe that this is a typical design that many data providers would choose, such that they would not have to rewrite the design document. In this experiment, we deploy LDPs using the generic designs from all data sources used in Experiment 1. For now, the generic designs can be reused on all RDFS/OWL vocabularies that do not have cycles in the class hierarchy.

The results of the above experiments and the requirements they fulfilled is shown in the Table 1.

Table 1. Summary of experiments and requirements fulfilled

	Requirements			
	Heterogeneity	*Hosting Constraints*	*Reusability*	*Automatization*
Experiment 1			✓	✓
Experiment 2				✓
Experiment 3	✓			✓
Experiment 4	✓	✓		✓
Experiment 5			✓	✓

Contribution to Existing Implementations: Our approach benefits both categories of LDP implementation described in Sect. 2.2. Using our tools, an LDP dataset can be generated from static, dynamic or heterogenous data sources from a custom-written design or a generic design we provided. In the case of LDP management system, it is possible to deploy the LDP dataset via an existing LDP implementation using POSTerLDP. With LDP frameworks, it is possible to develop complex applications using the LDP dataset (static or dynamic) and thus avoiding boilerplate code for retrieving data resources from their sources and transforming them into LDP resources.

Performance Test: Finally, a simple performance test was carried on ShapeLDP using one design document in Experiment 1. Random DCAT datasets were generated with a maximum size of one million triples and were used as input data sources. We find that the performance is approximately linear[16]. However, more tests have to be made in this regard using different types of designs. The generation of the datasets, all scripts and the results are given on the GitHub page with all explanations.

5   Conclusion and Future Work

Linked Data Platforms can potentially ease the work of data consumers, but there is not much support from implementations to automate the generation and deployment of LDPs. Considering this, we proposed a language for describing parts of the design of an LDP. Such a description can be processed to generate and deploy LDPs from existing data sources regardless of the underlying implementation of the LDP server. We demonstrated the flexibility, effectiveness, and reusability of the approach to cope with heterogeneity and dynamicity of data sources.

For now, LDP-DL is restricted only to some design aspects. Yet, due to its flexibility and some original features, it can fulfill the requirements that we identified. We intend to consider other aspects in our future work. First, we want to support non-RDF sources and other types of LDP containers. Second, we want to generate LDPs that supports paging [19], which is a desired feature for large datasets. Third, we want to extend LDP-DL to allow the description of deployment design, security design, transaction model, etc. Our long term objective is to have a complete design language for LDPs. Finally, from a theoretical perspective, we want to analyze formal properties of the language, such as design compatibility, design containment, design merge, parallelizability, and so on, based on the formal semantics.

Acknowledgments. This work is supported by grant ANR-14-CE24-0029 from *Agence Nationale de la Recherche* for project OpenSensingCity. We are thankful to the reviewers who helped very much improving this paper.

References

1. Akhtar, W., Kopecký, J., Krennwallner, T., Polleres, A.: XSPARQL: traveling between the XML and RDF worlds – and avoiding the XSLT pilgrimage. In: Bechhofer, S., Hauswirth, M., Hoffmann, J., Koubarakis, M. (eds.) ESWC 2008. LNCS, vol. 5021, pp. 432–447. Springer, Heidelberg (2008). https://doi.org/10.1007/978-3-540-68234-9_33
2. Auer, S., Dietzold, S., Lehmann, J., Hellmann, S., Aumueller, D.: Triplify: lightweight linked data publication from relational databases. In: Proceedings of the 18th International Conference WWW. ACM (2009)

---

[16] https://github.com/noorbakerally/PerformanceTestShapeLDP.

3. Bakerally, N.: LDP-DL: RDF syntax and mapping to abstract syntax. Technical report, Mines Saint-Étienne (2018). https://w3id.org/ldpdl
4. Bakerally, N., Zimmermann, A., Boissier, O.: LDP-DL: a language to define the design of linked data platforms. Technical report, Mines Saint-Étienne (2018). http://w3id.org/ldpdl/technical_report.pdf
5. Bizer, C., Cyganiak, R.: D2R server-publishing relational databases on the semantic web. In: Poster at the 5th ISWC, vol. 175 (2006)
6. Carothers, G., Seaborne, A.: RDF 1.1 TriG, RDF dataset language, W3C recommendation, 25 February 2014. Technical report, W3C (2014)
7. Cyganiak, R., Wood, D., Lanthaler, M.: RDF 1.1 concepts and abstract syntax, W3C recommendation, 25 February 2014. Technical report, W3C (2014)
8. Dimou, A., Vander Sande, M., Colpaert, P., Verborgh, R., Mannens, E., Van de Walle, R.: RML: a generic language for integrated RDF mappings of heterogeneous data. In: LDOW (2014)
9. France, R.B., Rumpe, B.: Model-driven development of complex software: a research roadmap. In: FOSE (2007)
10. Harris, S., Seaborne, A.: SPARQL 1.1 query language, W3C recommendation, 21 March 2013. Technical report, W3C (2013)
11. Lefrançois, M., Zimmermann, A., Bakerally, N.: A SPARQL extension for generating RDF from heterogeneous formats. In: Blomqvist, E., Maynard, D., Gangemi, A., Hoekstra, R., Hitzler, P., Hartig, O. (eds.) ESWC 2017. LNCS, vol. 10249, pp. 35–50. Springer, Cham (2017). https://doi.org/10.1007/978-3-319-58068-5_3
12. Loseto, G., Ieva, S., Gramegna, F., Ruta, M., Scioscia, F., Sciascio, E.: Linking the Web of things: LDP-CoAP mapping. In: ANT/SEIT Workshops (2016)
13. Maali, F., Erickson, J.: Data catalog vocabulary (DCAT), W3C recommendation, 16 January 2014. Technical report, W3C (2014)
14. Mihindukulasooriya, N., Garcia-Castro, R., Gutiérrez, M.E.: Linked data platform as a novel approach for enterprise application integration. In: COLD (2013)
. 15. Mihindukulasooriya, N., Gutiérrez, M.E., García-Castro, R.: A linked data platform adapter for the Bugzilla issue tracker. In: ISWC Posters & Demo, pp. 89–92 (2014)
16. Mihindukulasooriya, N., Priyatna, F., Corcho, O., García-Castro, R., Esteban-Gutiérrez, M.: morph-LDP: an R2RML-based linked data platform implementation. In: Presutti, V., Blomqvist, E., Troncy, R., Sack, H., Papadakis, I., Tordai, A. (eds.) ESWC 2014. LNCS, vol. 8798, pp. 418–423. Springer, Cham (2014). https://doi.org/10.1007/978-3-319-11955-7_59
17. Speicher, S., Arwe, J., Malhotra, A.: Linked data platform 1.0. Technical report, W3C, 26 February 2015
18. Speicher, S., Arwe, J., Malhotra, A.: Linked data platform 1.0, W3C recommendation, 26 February 2015. Technical report, W3C (2015)
19. Speicher, S., Arwe, J., Malhotra, A.: Linked data platform paging 1.0 W3C working group note, 30 June 2015. Technical report, W3C (2015)
20. Stahl, T., Volter, M., Bettin, J., Haase, A., Helsen, S.: Model-driven software development: technology, engineering, management. Pitman (2006)

Empirical Analysis of Ranking Models
for an Adaptable Dataset Search

Angelo B. Neves[1]([✉]) [iD], Rodrigo G. G. de Oliveira[1] [iD],
Luiz André P. Paes Leme[1] [iD], Giseli Rabello Lopes[2] [iD],
Bernardo P. Nunes[3,4], and Marco A. Casanova[3] [iD]

[1] Fluminense Federal University, Niterói, RJ, Brazil
{nevesangelo,rodrigoguerra,lleme}@id.uff.br
[2] Federal University of Rio de Janeiro, Rio de Janeiro, RJ, Brazil
giseli@dcc.ufrj.br
[3] PUC-Rio, Rio de Janeiro, RJ, Brazil
{bnunes,casanova}@inf.puc-rio.br
[4] Federal University of the State of Rio de Janeiro, Rio de Janeiro, RJ, Brazil
bernardo.nunes@uniriotec.br

Abstract. Currently available datasets still have a large unexplored
potential for interlinking. Ranking techniques contribute to this task by
scoring datasets according to the likelihood of finding entities related
to those of a target dataset. Ranked datasets can be either manually
selected for standalone linking discovery tasks or automatically inspected
by programs that would go through the ranking looking for entity links.
This work presents empirical comparisons between different ranking
models and argues that different algorithms could be used depending
on whether the ranking is manually or automatically handled and, also,
depending on the available metadata of the datasets. Experiments indicate that ranking algorithms that performed best with nDCG do not
always have the best Recall at Position k, for high recall levels. The best
ranking model for the manual use case (with respect to nDCG) may need
13% more datasets for 90% of recall, i.e., instead of just a slice of 34%
of the datasets at the top of the ranking, reached by the best model for
the automatic use case (with respect to recall@k), it would need almost
47% of the ranking.

Keywords: Linked Data · Entity linking · Recommendation
Dataset · Ranking · Empirical evaluation

1 Introduction

The Web of Data (WoD) has been growing fast and is facing the challenge of
increasing the links between entities from distinct datasets. The more interlinked
they are, the greater intrinsic value of their underlying knowledge base will be,
which allows the development of more innovative applications.

© Springer International Publishing AG, part of Springer Nature 2018
A. Gangemi et al. (Eds.): ESWC 2018, LNCS 10843, pp. 50–64, 2018.
https://doi.org/10.1007/978-3-319-93417-4_4

The *entity linking* task with respect to the entities of a target dataset consists of: (1) selecting other so-called *relevant datasets* that would contain related entities; (2) inspecting their content to infer entity relationships, i.e., infer links; and (3) making the relationships explicit by adding new RDF statements to the target dataset. One of the most popular relationships is the equivalence relation (*owl:sameAs*) addressed in [13,15,16,18].

Statistics about the WoD [1] show that more than 70% of the datasets are linked with entities of at most two other datasets, and that the vast majority of them are linked only with popular ones, such as DBpedia, Geonames, W3C and Quitter. This scenario can be explained by at least two main reasons. First, the available datasets vary greatly in their quality. So developers have been choosing to search for links in more reliable and comprehensive datasets, such as DBpedia. This may be a safer strategy, but it narrows the potential of the WoD, as it avoids exploring less known, but more specialized datasets that could aggregate more detailed and important knowledge. The second reason refers to dataset selection, since selecting datasets with related entities is a very error-prone, arduous and time-consuming task. Several search techniques have been proposed in the literature [3,5–7,10,12] to reduce the effort and increase the selection accuracy, however none of them has been widely adopted by the WoD community.

Selecting the most relevant datasets can be cast as a ranking problem, i.e., the task of ranking existing datasets $d_i \in D$ according to the likelihood of finding entities in d_i that could be linked with the entities in d_t. Thus, it is at the user's discretion to decide which datasets to inspect or which slice of the ranking to automatically scan with a program in searching for entity links. More precisely, the problem we address is:

> Given a target dataset d_t, compute a rank score $score(d_t, d_i)$ for each dataset $d_i \in D$, which induces a ranking $(d_1, d_2, \ldots, d_{|D|})$ of the datasets in D such that $score(d_t, d_1) \geq score(d_t, d_2) \geq \ldots \geq score(d_t, d_{|D|})$. The rank score should favor those datasets with the highest probabilities of containing entities that could be linked with entities of d_t.

The two use cases are possible in the context of WoD, i.e., either the ranked datasets would be manually selected and sent as input for further entity linking tasks or automated processes would scan the content of each dataset in an upper slice of the rank to find links, and the experiments indicated that different algorithms better suits each case.

Indeed, it is reasonable to propose an adaptable dataset search application that would deal with the two use cases differently, using distinct ranking models. By means of content negotiation, like IRI dereferencing mechanisms, human users can be distinguished from automated processes by the preferred data formats (Accept field) sent in HTTP request headers.

One can come up with three different strategies for dataset ranking: similarity ranking [3,10]; using known dataset links and their metadata to learn linking rules [3,5–7,10,12]; and identifying relevant hubs [4]. Intuitively, the first strategy suggests that the more similar two dataset descriptions are, the more likely it will be that their contents will be similar as well. The second strategy, frequently used by recommender systems, is the collaborative filtering. It is assumed that similar groups of people share the same behavior. Of course, the similarity criterion interferes with the acknowledgement of such intuitions. For example, if two datasets are similar in their update metadata, it does not mean that they are similar in their content. The last strategy seeks highly referenced datasets, which then become authorities in certain information domains. If it is possible to identify to which information domains a dataset belongs to, hubs can be recommended as good opportunities of finding entity links. This paper examines the first two strategies, since the last one would not rank all existing datasets, but rather it would remove from the search results the non hub datasets, which implies that rankings generated with this strategy will be non comparable with the rankings of the first two strategies.

The metadata used by ranking strategies vary, but the most used are linksets, topic categories and vocabularies. They can be harvested from catalogs, such as DataHub, VoID descriptions and even from the datasets themselves. Some techniques use known linksets as features of target datasets for ranking. It can be a problem, however, if the target datasets are not yet interlinked with others. Deciding the best set of metadata for ranking is still an open problem. This paper argues that this choice will also influence the ranking model. Indeed, the experiments based on known linksets indicated that Bayesian models perform better; on the other hand, based on topic categories, rule-based classifiers would outperform Bayesian models. The performance gap can reach up to 10% at the accumulated gain (nDCG). An alternate ranking model, based on social networks, would have comparable performance to these two models, with the drawback of requiring the computation of dataset similarities. Moreover, if a dataset is already linked to others, it is better to use linksets instead of topic categories to rank them.

The contributions of this paper are an empirical analysis of five dataset ranking models, using three types of features, and a strategy to use different ranking models for the two use cases. For the first use case, the experiments indicated that the best models are those based on Bayesian and JRip classifiers and that one can use either linksets or topic categories as dataset features. Using at least 5 linksets of a dataset, the best model can improve nDCG by at least 5%, after 40% of top datasets, and even more before 40%. In the case of datasets for which no linkset is known, JRip with topic categories as dataset features would be the best choice. For the second use case, JRip would be the best model with a rank slice of 22%, 27%, and 34% at the recall levels of 70%, 80%, and 90%, respectively. The best ranking model for the first use case (with respect to nDCG) may need 13% more datasets for 90% of recall, i.e., instead of just a slice of 34% of the datasets at the top of the ranking, reached by the best model (with respect to recall@k), it would need almost 47% of the ranking.

The rest of this paper is organized as follows. Section 2 introduces the basic concepts used throughout the paper. Section 4 describes the ranking models. Section 5 addresses the preparation of the test data. Section 6 presents the experiments for assessing the ranking models. Section 3 discusses related work. Finally, Sect. 7 concludes the paper.

2 Background Knowledge

In this section we briefly present some background definitions used throughout this paper regarding entity linking, dataset search and ranking evaluation metrics.

RDF Dataset – An RDF dataset, or a *dataset* for short, is a set d of RDF triples of the form (s, p, o) maintained by a single provider. The *subject* s of the triple is a global identifier (IRI), which denotes an entity of the real world, the *predicate* p is an attribute of the entity and the *object* o is an attribute value of the entity. One says that the subject s *is an entity of* d, denoted $s \in d$. An object can be either a literal value or an entity IRI. Triples can be accessed on the Web through IRI dereferencing (Linked Data) or via SPARQL queries, and can be stored in triplestores, relational databases, data files, or even HTML pages, thanks to RDF serialization schemes, such as RDFa.

Linksets – A *linkset* ls of a dataset d is a subset of RDF triples of d that link entities from two distinct datasets through a particular predicate, i.e., it is a set of triples (s, p, o) that have the same predicate p, $s \in d$, $o \in d'$, and $d \neq d'$. One says that (s, p, o) is an *entity link*, ls is a *linkset of* d, d' is the *target of* ls, denoted $target(ls)$, and d is *linked with* d'. We denote the *set of all linkset targets of a dataset* d by L_d, and the *set of all linkset targets of a set of datasets* D by $L_D = \bigcup_{d_i \in D} L_{d_i}$. For the sake of simplicity, from here on, we refer to linkset targets simply as linksets.

Let ls be a linkset and $dfreq(ls)$ be the number of datasets in D that have ls as linkset. We define $tf\text{-}idf(ls)$ as follows.

$$tf\text{-}idf(ls) = \frac{|ls|}{max(\{|ls_i|/ls_i \in L_d\})} \cdot log\left(\frac{|D|}{dfreq(ls)}\right) \tag{1}$$

Topic categories – The *set of topic categories of a dataset* d, denoted C_d, is the set of topic IRIs from a particular knowledge base, e.g. DBpedia, that describe the information content of the dataset.

It can be inferred from literal values or extracted from VoID descriptions. In the case of inference, literal values are scanned with named entity recognition tools, such as DBpedia Spotlight, as proposed by Caraballo et al. [4], the recognized entities are matched with entities of a knowledge base and the topic categories associated with the entities are harvested. DBpedia, for example, associates a list of topic categories to entities through the predicate *dcterms:subject* and each category can be subsumed by others through the predicate *skos:broader*. We say that a category c is in C_d iff there exists a property path [8] {e *dcterms:subject/skos:broader** c.} from a named entity e to c in DBpedia. The *set of topic categories of a set of datasets* $d_i \in D$ is $C_D = \bigcup_{d_i \in D} C_{d_i}$.

Topic categories can also be extracted from VoID descriptions. According to the VoID vocabulary, datasets can be partitioned by subject such that one can describe subsets of triples whose subjects are associated with a given category. In the code snippet of an example VoID file of Fig. 1, the dataset d has 100 triples containing entities associated with the topic category *dbc:Information_retrieval*. The number of triples in each subset can be taken as an estimate of the occurrence frequency of the topic category for the sake of computing *tf-idf(c)* as follows.

```
@prefix dcterms: <http://purl.org/dc/terms/> .
@prefix void:    <http://rdfs.org/ns/void#> .
@prefix dbc:     <http://dbpedia.org/resource/Category:> .

<d> a void:Dataset;
      void:subset [a                 void:Dataset;
                   dcterms:subject dbc:Information_retrieval;
                   void:triples    100;].
```

Fig. 1. Code snippet of an example VoID file.

Let *occurr(D, c)* be the number of entity occurrences in D associated with a topic category c. We define C'_D and C'_d as follows.

$$C'_D = \{c | c \in C_D \wedge o1 \leq occurr(D, c) \leq o2\} \tag{2}$$
$$C'_d = (C_d \cap C'_D) \tag{3}$$

such that $\Delta = max(\{ocurr(D, c_i)/c_i \in C_D\}) - min(\{ocurr(D, c_i)/c_i \in C_D\})$, $o1 = min(\{ocurr(D, c_i)/c_i \in C_D\}) + 0.1\Delta$ and $o2 = max(\{ocurr(D, c_i)/c_i \in C_D\}) - 0.1\Delta$. Cutting limits were empirically chosen. The reason for narrowing category sets is that the very frequent or rare categories do not discriminate datasets appropriately, like indexing terms in traditional Information Retrieval.

Let *occurr(d,c)* be the number of entity occurrences in a dataset $d \in D$ associated with c, *dfreq(c)* be the number of datasets $d' \in D$ that have category c, $c \in C'_d$, $c_i \in C'_d$. We define *tf-idf(c)* of a dataset d as follows.

$$\textit{tf-idf(c)} = \frac{ocurr(d, c)}{max(\{ocurr(d, c_i)/c_i \in C_d\})} \cdot log\left(\frac{|D|}{dfreq(c)}\right) \tag{4}$$

Ranking evaluation – One of most commonly used metric for ranking evaluation is the normalized Discounted Cumulative Gain (nDCG). It is a user-centric measure which expresses the degree of novelty unveiled by rankings as users go through their elements. It is computed by ranking datasets $d_i \in D$ for a set of target datasets $d_{t_j} \in T$, for each of which it is known the relevance degree of d_i. Let *rel(i)* be the relevance degree of the *ith* dataset of the ranking for d_t and *relI(i)* be the relevance degree of an ideal ranking, which would arrange datasets decreasingly by relevance degree. nDCG is defined as follows [2].

$$DCG[i] = \frac{rel(i)}{log(i)} + DCG[i-1] \tag{5}$$

$$IDCG[i] = \frac{relI(i)}{log(i)} + IDCG[i-1] \tag{6}$$

$$nDCG[i] = \frac{\overline{DCG}[i]}{\overline{IDCG}[i]} \tag{7}$$

such that $\overline{DCG}[i]$ and $\overline{IDCG}[i]$ are averages over all $d_t \in T$ and $DCG[1] = rel[1]$ and $IDCG[1] = relI[1]$. Ranking computing models are compared by the area under the respective interpolated $nDCG[i]$ curves. The best model has the largest area.

A second metric is Recall at Position k (recall@k), intuitively defined as the usual recall measure at each rank position. Let $tp(i)$ be the number of relevant datasets to d_t in the first i rank positions and R be the total number of relevant datasets to d_t. Formally, recall@k is defined as follows.

$$recall[i] = \frac{tp(i)}{R} \tag{8}$$

$$recall@k[i] = \overline{recall}[i] \tag{9}$$

such that $\overline{recall}[i]$ is the average over all $d_t \in T$. Ranking computing models are compared at each recall level by the size of ranking slice, the smaller the i at the same recall level, the better the ranking will be.

In order to compare rankings with different sets D, we take $i' = i/|D|$ and compute $nDCG[i']$ and $recall@k[i']$.

3   Related Work

Liu et al. [10] get inspiration from methods of social network analysis by computing several network measures, such as PageRank and Preferential Attachment, and use them as features for the Random Forest algorithm to classify datasets as relevant or not with respect to a given dataset. The links between datasets are defined based on known linksets of each dataset that represent equivalence links (owl:sameAS).

Martins et al. [12] adopts a content-based filtering approach based on the tokens extracted from the labels of the entities. They define that if two datasets have similar sets of tokens then it is likely that they will have related entities.

Ellefi et al. [6] propose a technique based on known linksets and topic profiles to rank relevant datasets for a given target dataset. Topic profiles are generated with the Latent Dirichlet Allocation algorithm and serve as descriptors of the datasets. Two datasets are compared with a similarity measure proportional to the amount of common linksets normalized by the total number of linksets between them. Descriptors and similarities are combined such that to penalize datasets that resemble each other through very popular topics. Intuitively two datasets sharing very popular features would likely be less related than if it was through unpopular topics.

Emaldi et al. [7] propose a method based on comparing RDF subgraphs of two datasets. Those pairs of datasets with a greater amount of similar subgraphs were supposed to have a higher correlation of content and therefore a greater chance of containing more correlated entities.

Ellefi et al. [5] use an intentional approach that compares profiles of different datasets. The most similar profiles indicate that two datasets may contain similar entities. The profiles are obtained by representing datasets as text documents composed of words extracted from textual descriptions of the classes of their schemes (the objects of the predicates *rdf:type*) that are captured from Linked Open Vocabularies. Very common or rare classes are filtered out because they are little or very discriminatory. To reduce the set of comparisons between profiles, only profiles that have at least two classes in common are compared. The comparisons between classes are made with similarity functions applied to the class labels.

4   Ranking Models Used in the Experiments

This section briefly defines five ranking models and the variations used in the experiments. In what follows, let F_D be the set of distinct features of a dataset corpus D to be ranked and F_d be the set of distinct features of a single dataset, d.

4.1   Ranking by Cosine Similarity

The first ranking model scores datasets $d_i \in D$ according to their similarities with a target dataset d_t. Intuitively, the more similar d_i and d_t are, the greater the likelihood that they will contain related entities. The similarity is estimated by the cosine of the angle $\theta_{\vec{d_t}\vec{d_i}}$ between the vector representations of d_t and d_i denoted $\vec{d_t}$ and $\vec{d_i}$. Therefore, the $score(d_t, d_i)$ function is defined as follows

$$score(d_t, d_i) = cos(\theta_{\vec{d_t}\vec{d_i}}) \tag{10}$$

The vector coordinates correspond to the distinct features $f_i \in F_D$ and their values can be either *tf-idf*(f_i) or 0, if f_i does not belong to F_d. Recall that *tf-idf*$(\cdot)$ over linksets and topic categories were defined in Sect. 2. We tested three feature sets: $F_D = L_D$, $F_D = C'_D$ and $F_D = L_D \cup C'_D$. The number of features of d_i had no limit, since it depends only on the available metadata, while the number of features of d_t was limited to 5; i.e., five linksets (5L), five categories (5C) or five linksets and five categories (5L5C), as summarized in Table 1. Other similarity scores could have been used, but this was left for future work.

Table 1. List of similarity-based computing ranking models.

Ranking model label	F_D	$score(d_t, d_i)$
cos-5L	L_D	$cos(\theta_{\overrightarrow{d_t}\overrightarrow{d_i}})$
cos-5C	C'_D	
cos-5L5C	$L_D \bigcup C'_D$	

4.2   Ranking by Preferential Attachment

The second ranking model comes from the domain of social network analysis and it was previously proposed by Lopes et al. [11]. Taking friendship as dataset links, one may transpose this approach to the context of dataset ranking, as follows [11].

$$score(d_t, d_i) \doteq pa(d_t, d_i) = \frac{|P_{d_i}|}{|D|} \cdot \sum_{d_j \in S_{d_t} \cap P_{d_i}} \frac{1}{|P_{d_j}|} \tag{11}$$

where $pa(\cdot, \cdot)$ is the preferential attachment metric.

Equation 11 defines that the likelihood of d_i being relevant to d_t is directly proportional to the popularity of d_i and inversely proportional to the popularity of those datasets that have d_i as one of their linksets. In this work, we defined S_{d_t}, the *similarity set* of d_t, as the set of all datasets in D that have at least 10% of the features of d_t in common. This similarity filtering was empirically defined. P_{d_i}, the *popularity set* of $d_i \in D$, is the set of all datasets in D that have links to d_i, and similarly P_{d_j} is the popularity set of $d_j \in D$. A preprocessing step computes P_{d_i} from L_D, which must be given. We also tested different feature sets and limited the number of features for d_t to 5 or 12, as summarized in Table 2. Similarly to the first ranking model, 5L means that d_t has five linksets, 12C means that d_t has twelve categories and 5L12C means that d_t has five linksets and twelve categories.

Table 2. List of social-network-based computing ranking models.

Ranking model label	F_D	$score(d_i, d_t)$
sn-5L	L_D	$pa(d_i, d_t)$
sn-12C	C'_D	
sn-5L12C	$L_D \bigcup C'_D$	

4.3   Ranking by Bayesian Probabilities

The third ranking model is inspired by Bayesian classifiers and was previously proposed by Leme et al. [9]. It computes the probability that d_i is relevant to d_t

given that d_t has features $f_i \in F_d$. The naive assumption on the joint probability of having multiple features induces the following score function.

$$score(d_t, d_i) = P(d_i|d_t) = \left(\sum_{j=1..n} log(P(f_i|d_i)) \right) + log(P(d_i)) \qquad (12)$$

$P(f_i|d_i)$ is the probability that a dataset has feature f_i if it is linked to d_i, and $P(d_i)$ is the probability of d_i being a linkset. A preprocessing step computes probabilities from $L_D \cup C'_D$, which must be given. We also tested different feature sets as summarized in Table 3 with the same notation conventions used in previous models.

Table 3. List of Bayesian computing ranking models.

Ranking model label	F_D	$score(d_i, d_t)$
bayesian-5L	L_D	$prob(d_i, d_t)$
bayesian-12C	C'_D	
bayesian-5L12C	$L_D \bigcup C'_D$	

4.4   Ranking with Rule Classifiers

The last two ranking models use the machine learning algorithms C4.5 and RIP-PERk through their respective Java implementations J48 an JRip in the Weka Toolkit [19]. They are rule-based classification algorithms that learn conjunctive rules from vector representations of $d_i \in D$. The algorithms differ in the pruning heuristics of the decision tree, which may impact computing and classification performances. Each learned rule R_j^C for a class C has an associated probability $P_{R_j^C}$ which estimates the confidence of classifying an instance as being of the class C with R_j^C. We trained a set of binary classifiers for the classes d_i and $\neg d_i$, such that $d_i \in D$. Classifying a target dataset d_t as an instance of a class d_i means that d_t may have entity links to d_i, i.e., d_i may be a linkset of d_t, i.e., d_i is the target of a linkset of d_t. We defined $score(d_t, d_i)$ function as follows

$$score(d_t, d_i) = \begin{cases} P_{R_j^{d_i}} & \text{if } d_t \in d_i \\ 1 - P_{R_j^{\neg d_i}} & \text{if } d_t \in \neg d_i \end{cases} \qquad (13)$$

such that j is the rule index for which $R_j^{d_i}$ oR $R_j^{\neg d_i}$ applies to d_t and that has the biggest $P_{R_j^C}$. Classifiers were trained with sets of positive and negative examples of each class. Positive examples of the class d_i are datasets that have d_i as one of their linksets and negative examples are the opposite. The feature sets are summarized in Table 4 with the same notation conventions for model labels.

Table 4. List of rule-based computing ranking models.

Ranking model label	F_D	$score(d_i, d_t)$
j48-5L	L_D	
jrip-5L		
j48-12C	C'_D	$pRule(d_i, d_t)$
jrip-12C		
j48-5L12C	$L_D \bigcup C'_D$	
jrip-5L12C		

5   Data Preparation and Methodology

The data for the experiments [14] is a collection of VoID descriptions of the datasets in the LOD Cloud.

DataHub is a catalog of open data used by the Linked Data community to disseminate metadata about the datasets available in the LOD Cloud. This catalog is built on top of the Comprehensive Knowledge Archive Network (CKAN) platform that has a RESTful API through which one can browse the content of the catalog. Datasets that do not belong to the LOD Cloud have been disregarded in this paper. Among others, the available metadata on the catalog are linksets, SPARQL endpoints and dumps. The CKAN adopts DCAT as the standard metadata scheme, but some conventions allowed to record particularities of RDF datasets. The following example of an HTTP request returns a JSON document doc with metadata of the Association for Computing Machinery (ACM) dataset, where m = doc['result']['results'][0] is a dictionary with the metadata itself.

https://datahub.ckan.io/api/3/action/package_search?fq=name:rkb-explorer-acm

Linksets can be identified in m with two structures of different formats, but with similar contents, which are ls1 = m['relationships_as_subject'] and ls2 = m['extras']. In ls1, the target dataset of a linkset is identified by its local ID ls1[i]['id'], where i is an index of the linksets' vector, and the number of triples is ls1[i]['comment']. In ls2, the target dataset is ls2['key'] and the number of triples is ls2['value'].

The metadata of each dataset was enriched with topic categories as follows. Let e be a named entity recognized in literal values of the dataset. A topic category c should be associated with the dataset if and only if there exists a path $\{e\ dcterms:subject/skos:broader^*\ c.\}$ between e and c in DBpedia. Named entities recognition was performed with DBpedia Spotlight, which is also available through a RESTful API. Topic categories were annotated as subsets of the datasets according to the pattern in Fig. 1.

Datasets without available dumps were not annotated with topic categories. Both linksets and datasets were annotated with their respective number of triples.

There is a total of 1,113 datasets with at least one linkset, from which 348 datasets have more than 8 linksets and 153 have more than 8 linksets and some topic category. This filtering was necessary to select appropriate datasets for the ranking models. The usable sets of datasets were randomly partitioned into three groups for a 3-fold cross validation.

The set of 1,113 datasets was divided into three equal parts P_1, P_2 and P_3 and, in a 3-fold cross validation process, the datasets in two parts P_i and P_j were ranked for each dataset of the third part P_k, which was taken as the set T of target datasets. Recall from Sect. 2 that nDCG and recall@ can be computed for a set of target datasets P_k as the mean of these measures for the datasets in P_k. The consolidated cross-validation result is the mean of nDCG and recall@ for $k \in 1, 2, 3$. This process was repeated for each of the proposed ranking models.

For each dataset in P_k, it was created a representation based on its available characteristics which was used as input for the ranking algorithms. Remember from Sect. 4 that these representations can be based on linksets, categories, and a combination of the two.

Notice that DataHub stores a list of known linksets for each dataset in the LOD Cloud. The targets of these linksets (objectsTarget - VoID) are, by definition, datasets with which there are links and, therefore, are the datasets that one would wish to find in higher ranking positions, i.e., they are the set of relevant datasets, denoted R. Only when a representation of a target dataset (d_t) includes a linkset, the objectsTarget of that linkset must be removed from R.

6   Experiments

We refer the reader to Neves et al. [17] for the full set of ranking evaluations. This section presents results for the best ranking models.

Recall from Sect. 4 that we consider two use cases for dataset rankings. In the first use case, datasets are manually selected and users intuitively focus on the initial ranking positions. Comparing ranking models with nDCG would unveil models with the highest gain rate of relevance. In order to compute nDCG, it is necessary, however, to define the degree of relevance of each entry of the ranking. Let

- D be a dataset corpus to be ranked
- L_{d_t} the linksets of a target dataset as extracted from DataHub
- F_{d_t} the feature set of d_t
- $R = (D \cap L_{d_t}) - F_{d_t}$, be the datasets relevant to d_t in D
- $triples(r_i)$ be the number of triples of the linkset ls of d_t that has $target(ls) = r_i$
- $T_1 = min(triples(r_i)/r_i \in R)$
- $T_2 = max(\{triples(r_i)/r_i \in R\})$
- $\Delta = (T_2 - T_1)/3$

Notice that R is the set of datasets which are taken as unknown linksets and that must be better positioned in the ranking. The degree of relevance of $d_i \in D$ to d_t is defined as follows.

$$rel(d_i) = 0, d_i \notin R$$
$$rel(d_i) = 1, d_i \in R \wedge T_1 \leq triples(r_i) < T_1 + \Delta$$
$$rel(d_i) = 2, d_i \in R \wedge T_1 + \Delta \leq triples(r_i) < T_1 + 2\Delta$$
$$rel(d_i) = 3, d_i \in R \wedge T_1 + 2\Delta \leq triples(r_i) \leq T_2$$

In the second use case, programs would scan a slice of the ranking in search of entity links. In such cases, the best models would be those that would provide the best recall@k for the same ranking size.

The use of different feature sets causes D to have different sizes depending on the ranking model, that is, not all datasets have all possible feature sets. To compare rankings with different sizes we compute $nDCG(i')$ and $recall@k(i')$, where $i' = i/|D|$, we call i' as the normalized rank position.

Figure 2 shows that the best models for the first use case, based on nDCG. Traditional use of rankings are those based on Bayesian classifiers, Social Network and JRip classifiers. One can see that knowing at least 5 linksets of a dataset can improve at least 5%, after 40% of top datasets (normalized rank position = 0.4), and even more before 40%. In the case of datasets for which no linkset is known, the best it can be done is to use topic categories with JRip or Social Network ranking models. Ranking models with a mixed set of features (Linksets and Topic Categories) did not achieved comparable performances [17]. This is an important outcome of the experiments. Moreover, as Bayesian and JRip approaches have ranking performances very similar to that of the Social Network (SN), one can avoid computational cost of the similarity calculations needed for SN.

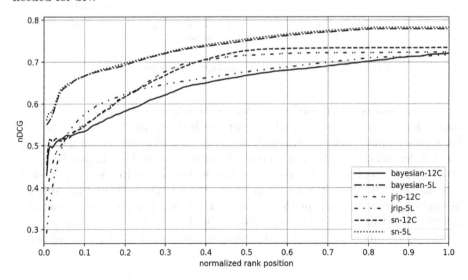

Fig. 2. nDCG of the best ranking computing models.

Figure 3 shows the best models for the second use case, based on recall@k. Note that, after 20% of the top datasets, the rankings start diverging in performance. As the average size of the ranking is 143, it means that the divergence starts at the 28th position, on average. For a recall of 70%, bayesian-12C would need 28% of the top datasets, while jrip-12C would need 22%. For a recall level of 80%, the bayesian-12C would need 40% of top datasets, while the jrip-12C would require just 27%. The difference would be even greater at 90% of recall: the bayesian-12C would need 65% of the top ranking, while jrip-12C would need just 34%. The best ranking model for the first use case (with respect to nDCG) may need 13% more datasets for 90% of recall, i.e., instead of just a slice of 34% of the datasets at the top of the ranking, reached by the best model (with respect to recall@k), it would need almost 47% of the ranking.

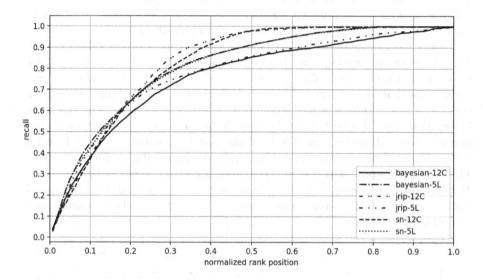

Fig. 3. Recall@k of the best ranking computing models.

We can then conclude that if one wants to exhaustively examine rankings looking for entity links, one would better use jrip-12C as the ranking model. Besides better performance, JRip with topic categories has the advantage that it does not depend on the assumption that all datasets would have known linksets, but only on the existence of topic categories, which can be frequently provided for a dataset. Moreover, the results pose empirical limits for sizing the slice of the ranking depending on the desired recall level, for example, if one wants to find 80% of the linksets of a target dataset, Fig. 3 shows that a program can be coded to scan only the top 27% of the ranking, for a recall of 70% it would scan just 22%, and so on.

7   Conclusions and Future Work

The growth of the Web of Data strongly depends on entity interlinking, as the traditional Web depends on hyperlinks. Current strategies, which focus only on well known datasets, although safe, overlook important opportunities for entity interlinking. The dataset ranking techniques discussed in this paper strongly facilitate this task, since they can reduce the computational effort of searching links and unveiling important datasets.

This paper presented an empirical comparison of several ranking models in order to identify the conditions in which they are best applied. The first conclusion is that, for human interactions with a dataset search tool, the best ranking models (with respect to nDCG) are based on Bayesian classifiers and JRip. Bayesian is preferable when one knows linksets, since it can have the nDCG at least 5% greater, otherwise JRip is the best choice. Secondly, the similarity computation of social network approach can be avoided, since Bayesian and JRip have similar performances. Thirdly, we can conclude that models with the JRip classifier and topic categories are always desirable, when one wants to automatically scan rankings. Besides better performance (with respect to recall@k), 13% less datasets for 90% of recall, JRip with topic categories has the advantage that it does not depend on the assumption that all datasets would have known linksets, but only on the existence of topic categories, which can be frequently provided a dataset. Finally, The experiments also indicated the ranking size to be traversed for each desired level of recall, which may be taken as input of the search. For a recall level of 70% scan 22% of the ranking, for a recall level of 80% scan 27%, for a recall level of 90% scan 34%, and so on.

One limitation of the experiments was the amount of data available. The lack of availability of dataset samples (dumps) did not allow the use of all data obtained from DataHub. Expanding this availability and comparing other proposed methods may bring new conclusions to the design of dataset ranking methods with the purpose of entity interlinking.

Acknowledgments. This work has been funded by FAPERJ/BR under grants E-26/010.000794/2016, E-26/201.000337/2014 and CNPq under grant 303332/2013-1.

References

1. Abele, A., McCrae, J.P., Buitelaar, P., Jentzsch, A., Cyganiak, R.: Linking open data cloud diagram 2017. Technical report, Insight Centre for Data Analytics at NUI Galway (2017). http://lod-cloud.net
2. Baeza-Yates, R.R., Ribeiro-Neto, B.: Modern Information Retrieval: The Concepts and Technology Behind Search, 2nd edn. ACM Press, New York (2011)
3. Caraballo, A.A.M., Arruda, N.M., Nunes, B.P., Lopes, G.R., Casanova, M.A.: TRTML - a tripleset recommendation tool based on supervised learning algorithms. In: Presutti, V., Blomqvist, E., Troncy, R., Sack, H., Papadakis, I., Tordai, A. (eds.) ESWC 2014. LNCS, vol. 8798, pp. 413–417. Springer, Cham (2014). https://doi.org/10.1007/978-3-319-11955-7_58
4. Caraballo, A.A.M., Nunes, B.P., Lopes, G.R., Leme, L.A.P.P., Casanova, M.A.: Automatic creation and analysis of a linked data cloud diagram. In: Cellary, W., Mokbel, M.F., Wang, J., Wang, H., Zhou, R., Zhang, Y. (eds.) WISE 2016. LNCS, vol. 10041, pp. 417–432. Springer, Cham (2016)

5. Ellefi, M.B., Bellahsene, Z., Dietze, S., Todorov, K.: Dataset recommendation for data linking: an intensional approach. In: Sack, H., Blomqvist, E., d'Aquin, M., Ghidini, C., Ponzetto, S.P., Lange, C. (eds.) ESWC 2016. LNCS, vol. 9678, pp. 36–51. Springer, Cham (2016). https://doi.org/10.1007/978-3-319-34129-3_3

6. Ellefi, M.B., Bellahsene, Z., Dietze, S., Todorov, K.: Beyond established knowledge graphs-recommending web datasets for data linking. In: Bozzon, A., Cudre-Maroux, P., Pautasso, C. (eds.) ICWE 2016. LNCS, vol. 9671, pp. 262–279. Springer, Cham (2016). https://doi.org/10.1007/978-3-319-38791-8_15

7. Emaldi, M., Corcho, O., López-De-Ipiña, D.: Detection of related semantic datasets based on frequent subgraph mining. In: Proceedings of the Intelligent Exploration of Semantic Data (IESD 2015) (2015)

8. Harris, S., Seaborne, A.: SPARQL 1.1 query language. Technical report, W3C (2013)

9. Leme, L.A.P.P., Lopes, G.R., Nunes, B.P., Casanova, M.A., Dietze, S.: Identifying candidate datasets for data interlinking. In: Daniel, F., Dolog, P., Li, Q. (eds.) ICWE 2013. LNCS, vol. 7977, pp. 354–366. Springer, Heidelberg (2013). https://doi.org/10.1007/978-3-642-39200-9_29

10. Liu, H., Wang, T., Tang, J., Ning, H., Wei, D.: Link prediction of datasets sameAS interlinking network on web of data. In: Proceedings of the 3rd International Conference on Information Management (ICIM 2017), pp. 346–352 (2017)

11. Lopes, G.R., Leme, L.A.P.P., Nunes, B.P., Casanova, M.A., Dietze, S.: Two approaches to the dataset interlinking recommendation problem. In: Proceedings of the 15th International Conference on Web Information Systems Engineering (WISE 2014), pp. 324–339 (2014)

12. Martins, Y.C., da Mota, F.F., Cavalcanti, M.C.: DSCrank: a method for selection and ranking of datasets. In: Garoufallou, E., Subirats Coll, I., Stellato, A., Greenberg, J. (eds.) MTSR 2016. CCIS, vol. 672, pp. 333–344. Springer, Cham (2016). https://doi.org/10.1007/978-3-319-49157-8_29

13. Nentwig, M., Hartung, M., Ngonga Ngomo, A.C., Rahm, E.: A survey of current link discovery frameworks. Semant. Web 8(3), 419–436 (2016)

14. Neves, A.B., Leme, L.A.P.P.: Dataset Descriptions. figshare (2017). https://doi.org/10.6084/m9.figshare.5211916

15. Ngomo, A.C.N., Auer, S.: LIMES - a time-efficient approach for large-scale link discovery on the web of data. In: Proceedings of the 22nd International Joint Conference on Artificial Intelligence (IJCAI 2011), pp. 2312–2317 (2011)

16. Nikolov, A., Uren, V., Motta, E.: KnoFuss: a comprehensive architecture for knowledge fusion. In: Proceedings of the 4th International Conference on Knowledge Capture (K-CAP 2007), pp. 185–186 (2007)

17. Oliveira, R.G.G., Neves, A.B., Leme, L.A.P.P., Lopes, G.R., Nunes, B.P., Casanova, M.A.: Empirical Analysis of Ranking Models for an Adaptable Dataset Search: Complementary Material. figshare (2017). https://doi.org/10.6084/m9.figshare.5620651

18. Volz, J., Bizer, C., Gaedke, M., Kobilarov, G.: Discovering and maintaining links on the web of data. In: Bernstein, A., Karger, D.R., Heath, T., Feigenbaum, L., Maynard, D., Motta, E., Thirunarayan, K. (eds.) ISWC 2009. LNCS, vol. 5823, pp. 650–665. Springer, Heidelberg (2009). https://doi.org/10.1007/978-3-642-04930-9_41

19. Witten, I.H., Frank, E., Hall, M.A., Pal, C.J.: Data Mining: Practical Machine Learning Tools and Techniques, 4th edn. Morgan Kaufmann Publishers Inc., Burlington (2016)

sameAs.cc: The Closure of 500M
`owl:sameAs` Statements

Wouter Beek[1]📷, Joe Raad[2,3(✉)]📷, Jan Wielemaker[1]📷,
and Frank van Harmelen[1]📷

[1] Department of Computer Science, VU University Amsterdam,
Amsterdam, The Netherlands
{w.g.j.beek,J.Wielemaker,Frank.van.Harmelen}@vu.nl
[2] UMR MIA-Paris, AgroParisTech, INRA, Paris-Saclay University, Paris, France
joe.raad@agroparistech.fr
[3] LRI, Paris-Sud University, CNRS 8623, Paris-Saclay University, Orsay, France

Abstract. The `owl:sameAs` predicate is an essential ingredient of the Semantic Web architecture. It allows parties to independently mint names, while at the same time ensuring that these parties are able to understand each other's data. An online resource that collects all `owl:sameAs` statements on the Linked Open Data Cloud has therefore both practical impact (it helps data users and providers to find different names for the same entity) as well as analytical value (it reveals important aspects of the connectivity of the LOD Cloud).

This paper presents sameAs.cc: the largest dataset of identity statements that has been gathered from the LOD Cloud to date. We describe an efficient approach for calculating and storing the full equivalence closure over this dataset. The dataset is published online, as well as a web service from which the data and its equivalence closure can be queried.

Keywords: Linked Open Data · Identity · Reasoning

1 Introduction and Related Work

The absence of a central naming authority for minting IRIs is essential to the architecture of the Semantic Web. Just as on the regular Web [13], allowing different organizations and individuals to mint their own IRIs, without the bottleneck of centralized coordination, is a precondition for the Semantic Web to scale, and has been a deliberate motivation in the design of OWL [1].

However, the absence of any central authority also makes it impossible to enforce the Unique Name Assumption on the Semantic Web. Despite attempts such as OKKAM to encourage the re-use of existing IRIs [3], the same thing is often denoted by many names on the Semantic Web. Because of this, the need arose to state that two names, possibly minted by different organizations or individuals, denote the same thing. For this purpose OWL introduced `owl:sameAs` [11]: the statement $\langle x, \texttt{owl:sameAs}, y \rangle$ asserts that x and y denote the same thing, formalized as follows (with I the interpretation function):

© Springer International Publishing AG, part of Springer Nature 2018
A. Gangemi et al. (Eds.): ESWC 2018, LNCS 10843, pp. 65–80, 2018.
https://doi.org/10.1007/978-3-319-93417-4_5

$$I(\langle x, \mathtt{owl:sameAs}, y \rangle) \text{ is true iff } I(x) = I(y)$$

Such identity management is not merely a luxury but is essential for the Semantic Web. It allows parties to independently mint names, while at the same time ensuring that these parties are able to understand each other's data. In other words, `owl:sameAs` statements are an important part of the glue that connects different datasets on the Semantic Web, and they are indeed the most often used linking predicate across many domains on the Semantic Web [15].

1.1   Related Work

The special status of `owl:sameAs` links has motivated earlier studies into the use of these links on the Semantic Web, as well as the construction of specialized services to harvest and publish these links. An early analysis of the use of `owl:sameAs` links was performed by Ding et al. [6] in 2010, which extracted 8.7M `owl:sameAs` links from the 2010 Billion Triple Challenge dataset, resulting in a graph of 2.9M weakly connected components, most of which are very small (average size 2.4), only 41 components with hundreds of IRIs, and only two components with thousands of IRIs, the largest of which has size 5,000.

In the same year, Halpin et al. [9], retrieved 58M `owl:sameAs` links from 1,202 domains in the 2010 Linked Open Data Cloud, and provided an aggregated analysis at the level of datasets.

A later analysis, by Schmachtenberg et al. [15] from 2014, crawled 1,014 datasets containing 8B resources, and again analyzed the use of `owl:sameAs` links at the aggregation level of datasets. The entire graph of datasets was found to consist of 9 weakly connected components, the largest one contained 297 datasets, with dbpedia.org having the largest in-degree, with 89 datasets containing `owl:sameAs` links to it. This work is similar in spirit to ours, but we advance over it by (i) using a bigger corpus, (ii) analyzing the `owl:sameAs` graph at the level of individual resources instead of datasets (a graph of over 500M `owl:sameAs` links), and most importantly, (iii) computing and publishing the closure of this massive graph. Also in 2014, Schlegel et al. [14] queried 200 SPARQL endpoints to obtain 17.6M `owl:sameAs` links over 2.4M IRIs for which they did compute the transitive closure, obtaining 8.4M equivalence classes. The dataset and analysis we present in this paper is an order of magnitude larger.

The largest collection of RDF links hosted to date is at http://sameas. org. It provides a Consistent Reference Service (CRS) [8] over an impressive number of 203M IRIs that are combined into 62.6M 'identity bundles' based on 345M triples[1]. As such, it is the main predecessor of the work presented in this paper. However, the sameas.org collection mixes identity pairs (linked with the `owl:sameAs` property) together with pairs that are not identity pairs (linked with other properties, such as `umbel:isLike`, `skos:exactMatch`, and `owl:inverseOf`). This means that the overall closure is not semantically sound. The crucial difference with our work is that the identity closure that we calculate is *semantically interpretable*, because it is exclusively based on `owl:sameAs`

---

[1] Up-to-date numbers obtained by personal communication from Hugh Glaser.

statements, and the computed closure adheres to the OWL semantics. As a result, our dataset can be used by a DL reasoner in order to infer new facts.

Finally, the Schema.org vocabulary[2] includes the `schema:sameAs` property. However, the semantics of this property is substantially different from that of `owl:sameAs`. It states that two terms "are two pages with the same topic" and does not express equality.

1.2 Contributions and Structure of this Paper

This paper makes the following three contributions:

1. It presents the largest downloadable dataset of identity statements that have been gathered from the LOD Cloud to date, including its equivalence closure. The dataset and its closure are also exposed through a web service.
2. It gives an in-depth analysis of this dataset, its closure, and its aggregation to datasets.
3. It presents an efficient approach for extracting, storing, and calculating the identity statements and their equivalence closure. Even though the dataset and closure are quite large, they can be stored on a USB stick and queried from a regular laptop.

In Sect. 2 we discuss the requirements that a semantically interpretable `owl:sameAs` dataset and web service must satisfy. Section 3 describes the algorithm and implementation for calculating and storing the explicit and implicit identity relations that fulfills the requirements. Section 4 gives an analysis of some of the key properties of our dataset. Section 5 describes the sameAs.cc dataset and web service, and Sect. 6 concludes.[3]

2 Requirements

2.1 Preliminaries

We distinguish between two identity relations. The *explicit identity relation* $(\sim_e)$ is the set of pairs (x, y) for which a statement $\langle x, \texttt{owl:sameAs}, y \rangle$ has been asserted in a publicly accessible dataset. The *implicit identity relation* $(\sim_i)$ is the explicit identity relation closed under equivalence (reflexivity, symmetry and transitivity).

---

[2] https://schema.org.

[3] This paper uses the following RDF prefixes for brevity:

`dbr`: http://dbpedia.org/resource/.
`owl`: http://www.w3.org/2002/07/owl#.
`rdf`: http://www.w3.org/1999/02/22-rdf-syntax-ns#.
`rdfs`: http://www.w3.org/2000/01/rdf-schema#.
`xsd`: http://www.w3.org/2001/XMLSchema#.

Let N denote the set of RDF nodes: the RDF terms that appear in the subject- or object position of at least one triple. A *partitioning* of N is a collection of non-empty and mutually disjoint subsets $N_k \subseteq N$ (called *partition members*) that together cover N. We leave it to the reader to verify that the relations $\sim_e$ and $\sim_i$ both induce a partitioning of N when taking their connected components as the partition members. Adopting terminology from [8], we call these partition members *equality sets*, and the partition members of $\sim_i$ *identity sets*. The equality set of a term x is denoted $[x]$. Each equality set of $\sim_e$ is a connected directed graph; each equality set of $\sim_i$ is a fully connected graph.

2.2 Requirements

In order to calculate $\sim_i$, we have to close $\sim_e$ under equivalence. Existing approaches do not scale, due to multiple dimensions of complexity:

$\sim_i$ **can be too large to store.** In Sect. 4, we will see that the LOD Cloud contains equality sets with cardinality well over 100K. It is not feasible to store the materialization of $\sim_i$, since the space consumption of that approach is quadratic in the size of the equality set. (E.g., the materialization of an equality set of 100K terms contains 10B identity pairs.)

We will not store the materialization, but the equality sets themselves, which is only linear in terms of the size of the universe of discourse (i.e., the set N of RDF nodes).

$|N_k|$ **can be too large to store.** Even the number of elements within one equality set can be too large to store in memory. The current version of the resource already contains equality sets that contain over 100K terms. Since our calculation of $\sim_i$ must have a low hardware footprint and must be future proof, we will not assume that every individual equality set will always be small enough to fit in memory.

sim_e **changes over time.** We calculate the identity closure for a large snapshot of the LOD Cloud. Since datasets in the LOD cloud are constantly changing, and datasets are constantly added, we want to update $\sim_i$ incrementally, allowing for both additions and deletions, without having to recompute the entire closure.

Even though applications of a LOD Cloud-wide identity service are beyond the scope of this paper, there are many use-cases for such a service:

Findability of backlinks. Since the Semantic Web does not allow backlinks to be followed (an architectural property it shares with the World Wide Web), it is only possible to follow outgoing `owl:sameAs` links but not incoming ones. An identity service retrieves all IRIs that are linked through `owl:sameAs` links, and thereby allows the full set of assertions about a given resource to be retrieved from across the LOD Cloud.

Query answering. A special case of the findability of links arises in distributed query answering over the LOD Cloud, which requires an overview of existing alignments between concepts and individuals [12].

Query answering under entailment. When a SPARQL query is evaluated under OWL entailment, the query engine must follow a large number of `owl:sameAs` links in order to retrieve the full result set. With an identity service, a query engine can translate the terms in the query to identity set identifiers (see Sect. 3.3), calculate the SPARQL query using these identifiers, and translate the identifiers to terms in the result set.

Ontology alignment. Existing algorithms for assessing whether or not two IRIs denote the same resource are currently evaluated on relatively small datasets [5]. The availability of a large dataset of real-world identity links can help quantify the utility of existing alignment algorithms such as [4].

3   Algorithms and Implementation

In this section we describe our approach for calculating and storing the identity relations $\sim_e$ and $\sim_i$ under the above requirements.

3.1   Explicit Identity Relation

The explicit identity relation ($\sim_e$) is obtained from the *LOD-a-lot* dataset[4] [7], a compressed data file that contains the unique triples from the 2015 LOD Laundromat corpus [2]. We use the HDT C++ library[5] to stream the result set of the following SPARQL query to a file, which takes $\sim$27 min:

```
select  distinct  ?s  ?p  ?o  {
   bind  (owl:sameAs  ?p)
   ?s  ?p  ?o  }
```

The results of this query are unique (keyword **distinct**) and the projection (**?s ?p ?o**) returns triples instead of pairs, so that regular RDF tools for storage and querying can be used.

The 558.9M triples that are the result of this SPARQL query are written to an N-Triples file, which is subsequently converted to an HDT file. The HDT creation process takes almost four hours using a single CPU core. The resulting HDT file is 4.5 GB in size, plus an additional 2.2 GB for the index file that is automatically generated upon first use.

3.2   Explicit Identity Relation: Compaction

Since the implicit identity relation is closed under reflexivity and symmetry, the size of the input data can be significantly reduced prior to calculating the identity closure. We call this preparation step *compaction*. Assuming an alphabetic order $\leq$ on RDF terms, we can reduce the input for the closure algorithm to: $\{(x, y) \mid x \sim_e y \wedge x \leq y\}$. For this we use GNU sort unique, which takes 35 min on an SSD disk.

---

[4] http://lod-a-lot.lod.labs.vu.nl.
[5] https://github.com/rdfhdt/hdt-cpp.

The impact of the compaction step is significant: from ~558.9M to ~331M identity pairs, leaving out ~2.8M reflexive and ~225M duplicate symmetric pairs. As a result, the input size for the identity closure algorithm has been reduced by over 40%.

3.3 Implicit Identity Relation: Closure

Now that we have a compacted version of $\sim_e$, we calculate the identity closure $\sim_i$. As before, let N denote the set of RDF nodes. The implicit identity relation $\sim_i$ consists of a map from nodes to identity sets $(N \mapsto \mathcal{P}(N))$. For space efficiency, we store each identity set only once by associating a key with each identity set: $key : ID \mapsto_k \mathcal{P}(N)$; and map each RDF term to the key of the unique identity set that it belongs to $val : N \mapsto_v ID$.[6] The composition $key(val(x))$ gives us the identity set of x. We built an efficient implementation of this key-value scheme using the RocksDB persistent key-value store through a SWI Prolog API that we designed for this purpose[7].

When computing $\sim_i$ we successively derive new pairs (x, y). To store these efficiently we distinguish three cases:

Neither x nor y occurs in any identity set. Then both x and y are assigned to the same new unique key for a new identity set: $x \mapsto_v id$, $y \mapsto_v id$, and $id \mapsto_k \{x, y\}$.

Only x already occurs in an identity set. In this case, the existing (key for the) identity set of x is extended to contain y as well: $y \mapsto_v val(x)$, and $val(x) \mapsto_k key(val(x)) \cup \{y\}$. (The case of only y occurring in an identity set is analogous.)

x and y already occur, but in different identity sets. In this case one of the two keys is chosen and assigned to represent the union of the two identity sets: $val(x) \mapsto_k key(val(x)) \cup key(val(y))$ and $y' \mapsto_v val(x))$ for every $y' \in key(val(y))$.

This is the most costly step, especially when both identity sets are large, but it is also relatively rare. Since the input pairs are sorted during the compacting stage, this case only occurs when there are pairs (a, x), (x, b) and (c, y) such that $a < x$, $c < x$ and $b < y$. A further speedup is obtained by choosing to merge the smaller of the two sets into the larger one. The merging of values is performed efficiently by RocksDB.

The calculation of the identity closure takes just under 5 h using 2 CPU cores on a regular laptop. The result is a 9.3 GB on-disk RocksDB database (2.7 GB for $\mapsto_v$, and 6.6 GB for $\mapsto_k$). RocksDB allows to simultaneously read from and write to the database. Since changes to the identity relation can be applied incrementally, the initial creation step only needs to be performed once.

---

[6] Note that each IRI in N does indeed belong to a unique identity set, because the identity sets of $\sim_i$ form a partitioning of N.

[7] See https://rocksdb.org and https://github.com/JanWielemaker/rocksdb.

3.4 Identity Schema

In addition to the explicit and implicit identity relation, which use `owl:sameAs` to say something about other resources, we also extract the schema statements about `owl:sameAs` itself. This is obtained by storing the result of the following SPARQL Query in an HDT file.

```
select distinct ?s ?p ?o {
  { bind(owl:sameAs as ?s) ?s ?p ?o } union
  { bind(owl:sameAs as ?o) ?s ?p ?o } }
```

4 Data Analytics

In this section we perform several analyses over the dataset created with the algorithm described in Sect. 3.

4.1 Explicit Identity Relation

Terms in $\sim_e$: In the LOD Laundromat corpus, 179,739,567 unique terms occur in `owl:sameAs` assertions. As to be expected, the vast majority of these are IRIs (175,078,015 or 97.41%). Only a few literals are involved in the identity relation (3,583,673 or 1.99%), and even fewer blank nodes (1,077,847 or 0.60%). The majority of IRIs contain the HTTP(S) scheme (174,995,686 or 97.36.). Figure 1 gives an overview.

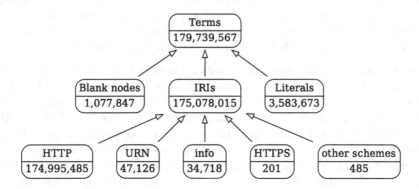

Fig. 1. Overview of the terms involved in the identity relation. Blank nodes, IRIs and literals do not sum to the number of terms exactly, because there are 32 terms that are neither (they are syntactically malformed IRIs).

Statements in $\sim_e$: The LOD Laundromat corpus contains a total of 558,943,116 `owl:sameAs` statements. Based on the 2011 Billion Triple Challenge dataset, the authors of [16] observed that the number of `owl:sameAs` statements

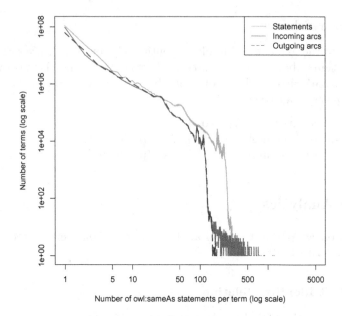

Fig. 2. The number of `owl:sameAs` statements per term.

per term approximated a power-law distribution with coefficient −2.528. In contrast to this, we find that in the 2015 LOD Laundromat corpus, although most terms do appear in a small number of statements, this distribution does not display a power-law distribution. The patterns for the distribution of **incoming arcs** (identity statements where the term appears in the object position) and the distribution of **outgoing arcs**, (identity statement where the term appears in the subject position) all follow a similar distribution pattern (Fig. 2).

Dataset links in $\sim_e$**:** Because `owl:sameAs` is the most frequently used predicate to link between datasets [15], we also analysed $\sim_e$ at the aggregation level of links between datasets[8]. Unfortunately, there is no formal definition of what a dataset is. Since most of the terms involved in `owl:sameAs` assertions are HTTP(S) IRIs (Sect. 4.1), the notion of a *namespace* is a good proxy. According to the RDF 1.1 standard, IRIs belong to the same namespace if they have "a common substring". Obviously not every common substring counts as a namespace, otherwise all IRIs would be in the same namespace. A good pragmatic choice for a namespace-denoting substring is to take the prefix of HTTP(S) IRIs that ends with the *host name*. The host name is part of every syntactically valid HTTP(S) IRI, and denotes a physical machine that is located on the Internet.

Using this interpretation, Fig. 3 shows that the number of terms occurring in `owl:sameAs` links is very unevenly distributed over namespaces (which we use as proxies of datasets). For each namespace we calculated the number of *incoming*

---

[8] In this section, a *link* is an `owl:sameAs` statement between terms that belong to different datasets.

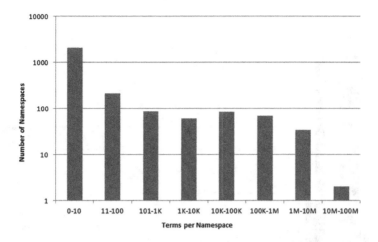

Fig. 3. The number of terms in identity links by namespace.

and *outgoing* links (statements whose subject, respectively object, term is in a different namespace.) The remaining statements are *internal edges* (they either have two HTTP(S) IRIs that belong to the same namespace, or they have at least one node that is not an HTTP(S) IRI (i.e., either a blank node or a literal).

Figure 4 shows the distribution of internal edges, incoming links, and outgoing links over namespaces. While the majority of namespaces have incoming links, far fewer namespaces have outgoing links. This means that a relatively small number of namespaces is linking to a relatively large number of them. These namespaces are responsible for interlinking in the LOD Cloud. Finally, an even smaller number of namespaces have internal `owl:sameAs` edges. This means that most namespaces only use identity statements for linking to other datasets, but not for equating dataset-internal resources. This is a strong indication that most datasets enforce the Unique Name Assumption internally.

To give a high level impression, we have visualised the entire identity-graph at namespace level in Fig. 5. This graph contains 2,618 host-based namespaces/datasets, that are connected through 10,791 edges, and consists of 142 components. The large black cluster at the bottom of the figure is the densely interconnected set of multilingual variants of dbpedia.org, with the two high centrality nodes for dbpedia.org and freebase.com clearly visible just above the black cluster.

The figure shows that there are high-centrality nodes that act as domain-specific naming authorities/hubs. For example, the central node in the large top cluster is www.bibsonomy.org, which links to a large number of bibliographic datasets. A similar role is fulfilled by geonames.org, for interlinking geographic datasets; bio2rdf.org, for interlinking biochemistry datasets; and revyu.com (appearing at the right hand-side of the figure), for interlinking datasets that contain online reviews. A high-resolution version of this figure, together with textual namespace labels, is available at https://sameas.cc/explicit/img.

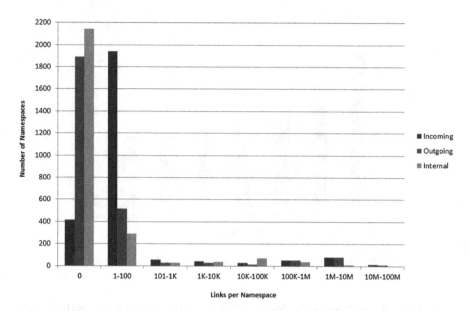

Fig. 4. The distribution of internal edges, incoming links, and outgoing links by namespaces.

4.2   Implicit Identity Relation

Terms in $\sim_i$: The number of unique terms in $\sim_i$ is 179,672,306. This is less than the number of unique terms in $\sim_e$ (179,739,567), because 67,261 terms (or 0.037%) *only* appear in reflexive `owl:sameAs` assertions.

Identity sets in $\sim_i$: For the identity closure, it makes sense to separate out singleton identity sets, i.e., terms x for which $[x]_\sim = \{x\}$. A term has a singleton identity set if it never appears in a `owl:sameAs` assertion, or if all its `owl:sameAs` assertions are reflexive. We will not include singleton identity sets in our figures because they are conceptually trivial and their inclusion sometimes makes it hard to discern interesting aspects about the rest of $\sim_i$.

   The number of non-singleton identity sets is 48,999,148. The LOD-a-lot file, from which we extract $\sim_e$, contains 5,093,948,017 unique terms. This means that there are 5,044,948,869 singleton identity sets in $\sim_i$. The distribution of identity set size (Fig. 6) is very uneven and fits a power law with exponent 3.3 ± 0.04. The majority of non-singleton identity sets (31,337,556 sets; 63.96%) has size 2. There are relatively few large identity sets, and the largest identity set has cardinality 177,794. It includes Albert Einstein, the countries of the world, and the empty string.

Edges in $\sim_i$. We calculate the number of directed edges (or arcs) in the identity closure. This is the number of `owl:sameAs` triples that would be needed in order to express the full materialization of $\sim_e$. This calculation requires

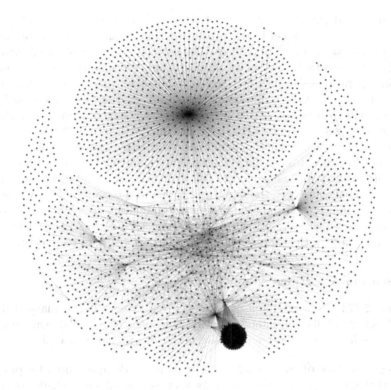

Fig. 5. All inter-dataset links in the LOD cloud. Thicker edges represent more identity links. The full diagram is available at https://sameas.cc/explicit/img.

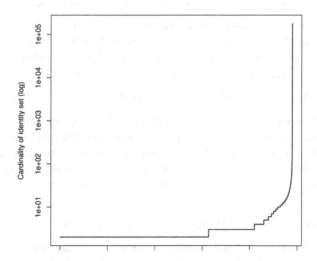

Fig. 6. The distribution of identity set cardinality in $\sim_i$. The x-axis lists all 48,999,148 non-singleton identity sets.

us to query and stream through the full RocksDB closure index, and there-fore gives a good indication of the processing time required for running large-scale jobs over the sameAs.cc dataset. The calculation (i) retrieves all identity sets, (ii) calculates their cardinality, and (iii) sums the squares of the cardinali-ties. This operation takes only 55.6 seconds and shows that the materialization consists of 35,201,120,188 `owl:sameAs` statements. Notice that almost 90% (or 31,610,706,436 statements) of the materialization is contributed by the single largest identity set (i.e., $[$`dbr:Albert_Einstein`$]_\sim$).

In addition to calculating the number of `owl:sameAs` statements in the iden-tity closure, we can also calculate the minimal number of identity statements that would result in the same closure. We call such a minimal identity relation *a kernel*, and calculate it as the number of terms whose equivalence set is not a singleton set, minus the number of non-singleton identity sets. The kernel iden-tity relation for $\sim_i$ consists of 130,673,158 statements (or 0.37% of $\sim_i$). This also means that 76.6% of the explicit identity statements ($\sim_e$) are redundant.

4.3   Schema Assertions About Identity

There are 2,773 assertions about `owl:sameAs` that extend the schema as defined in the OWL vocabulary in interesting ways. The dataset is available at https:// sameas.cc/schema. We observe the following kinds of schema extensions:

Super-properties of `owl:sameAs`. As [9] indicate, there is a need for proper-ties that are weaker than `owl:sameAs` that express different shades of simi-larity and relatedness:

owl:sameAs rdfs:subPropertyOf <http://lexvo.org/ontology#nearlySameAs>.

Some super-property assertions introduce semantic bugs. For instance, since identity is the strongest equivalence relation, it does not make sense to assert new *identity* relations that are superproperties of it. The following statement introduces the semantic bug that everything is an individual:

owl:sameAs rdfs:subPropertyOf owl:sameIndividualAs.

Sub-properties of `owl:sameAs`. Several datasets introduce sub-properties of `owl:sameAs`, i.e., strengthenings of the identity relation, without a clear use case. Our hypothesis is that these datasets intend to *weaken* the `owl:sameAs` property instead, since there are many use cases for weaker forms of similarity, relatedness, and context-dependent identity. For example:

bbc:sameAs rdfs:subPropertyOf owl:sameAs.

Other `rdfs:subPropertyOf` assertions cannot be easily corrected by swap-ping the subject and object term. For instance, from the fact that two things are the same link it does not follow that they are identical *sui generis* (since the same link may appear on different web pages):

```
<http://spitfire-project.eu/ontology/ns/sameAsLink>
rdfs:subPropertyOf owl:sameAs.
```

Domain/range declarations. As observed earlier by [10], the intersection-based semantics of `rdfs:domain` and `rdfs:range` is often not followed. The following classes are asserted as the domain of `owl:sameAs`, effectively stating that all resources are both legal entities, anniversaries, strings, etc.

```
owl:sameAs rdfs:domain <http://govwild.org/0.6/
GWOntology.rdf#LegalEntity>.
owl:sameAs rdfs:domain <http://s.opencalais.com/1/
type/em/e/Anniversary>.
owl:sameAs rdfs:range xsd:string.
```

Properties identical to `owl:sameAs`. Several datasets mint alternative names for `owl:sameAs`. This is mainly used in combination with the introduction of sub- and super-properties of `owl:sameAs`, e.g.:

```
<http://rhm.cdepot.net/xml/#is> owl:sameAs owl:sameAs.
<http://sw.opencyc.org/concept/Mx4robv6phbFQdiM86Z2
jmH52g> owl:sameAs owl:sameAs.
```

5 sameAs.cc: Dataset and Web Service

The sameAs.cc dataset consists of the following components:

sameAs.cc. The explicit identity relation ($\sim_e$) (https://sameas.cc/explicit) can be browsed online, queried for Triple Patterns, and downloaded as N-Triples and HDT.

sameAs.cc Closure. We publish the implicit identity relation ($\sim_i$) (https://sameas.cc) as a downloadable snapshot of the RocksDB index (instead of a materialized RDF file). When RocksDB is installed, this snapshot can be queried locally.

sameAs.cc Schema. The identity schema (https://sameas.cc/schema) can be browsed online, queried for Triple Patterns, and downloaded in N-Triples, and HDT.

The sameAs.cc web service[9] consists of the following components:

sameAs.cc Triple Pattern API. The explicit identity relation web service (https://sameas.cc/explicit/tp) allows all `owl:sameAs` assertions to be queried with Triple Patterns. Queries are expressed through (combinations of) the HTTP query parameters `subject`, `predicate`, and `object`.

sameAs.cc Closure API. The implicit identity relation ($\sim_i$) can be queried through the following URI paths:

    https://sameas.cc/id. Enumerates all identity set IDs. Each member of the identity closure is assigned such a unique ID.

---

[9] Code is available at https://github.com/wouterbeek/SameAs-Server.

Terms for identity set 44000248
- <http://rdf.muninn-project.org/ontologies/graves#Burial_mound> (↦ id) ⟨s, owl:sameAs , o⟩
- "#Tumulus"^^<http://www.w3.org/2001/XMLSchema#string> (↦ id) ⟨s, owl:sameAs , o⟩
- <http://rdf.muninn-project.org/ontologies/graves#Tumulus> (↦ id) ⟨s, owl:sameAs , o⟩

Previous   results 1 to 3 (of 3)   Next

Fig. 7. Screenshot of the *sameAs.cc Closure API*. The screenshot shows the little known fact that tumulus is a synonym for burial mound.

https://sameas.cc/id?term=dbr:Albert_Einstein. Returns the ID of the identity set to which the given RDF term belongs. This view is shown in Fig. 7.

https://sameas.cc/term. Enumerates all RDF terms that appear in the identity relation.

https://sameas.cc/term?id=44000248. Enumerates only the RDF terms that appear in the identity set with ID 44000248 as key.

We deliberately expose the internal key-value mechanism explained in Sect. 3.3 to the users of the sameAs.cc Closure API. The typical use case that we envision is one in which (i) terms are replaced by identity set identifiers, (ii) efficient computation is performed with the much more compact identifiers, and (iii) only when computation is done and end results need to be displayed are identifiers translated back to the potentially many terms that make up the respective identity sets.

6   Conclusion

In this paper we have presented *sameAs.cc*, the largest and most versatile dataset and web service of semantic identity links to date. The resource that we provide includes a large collection of `owl:sameAs` assertions and the closure calculated over it. The data can be freely downloaded and queried. Even though the datasets are large, our algorithms and data-structures ensure that the resources can be stored on and queried from a regular laptop.

In addition to the dataset and web services themselves, we have also presented several analytics over the data, including calculations of the size of the identity relation, its closure and its kernel, and various distributions. We hope that these resources will be used by other researchers in order to uncover aspects of identity that have not been studied before.

Acknowledgment. This work was partially conducted within the MaestroGraph project (612.001.553), funded by the Netherlands Organization for Scientific Research (NWO), and was partially supported by the Center for Data Science, funded by the IDEX Paris-Saclay, ANR-11-IDEX-0003-02.

References

1. Bechhofer, S., van Harmelen, F., Hendler, J., Horrocks, I., McGuinness, D.L., Patel-Schneider, P.F., Stein, A.L.: OWL web ontology language reference. Technical report, W3C, February 2004. http://www.w3.org/TR/owl-ref/
2. Beek, W., Rietveld, L., Schlobach, S.: LOD Laundromat (archival package 2016/06) (2016). https://doi.org/10.17026/dans-znh-bcg3
3. Bouquet, P., Stoermer, H., Bazzanella, B.: An entity name system (ENS) for the semantic web. In: Bechhofer, S., Hauswirth, M., Hoffmann, J., Koubarakis, M. (eds.) ESWC 2008. LNCS, vol. 5021, pp. 258–272. Springer, Heidelberg (2008). https://doi.org/10.1007/978-3-540-68234-9_21
4. Correndo, G., Penta, A., Gibbins, N., Shadbolt, N.: Statistical analysis of the owl:sameAs network for aligning concepts in the linking open data cloud. In: Liddle, S.W., Schewe, K.-D., Tjoa, A.M., Zhou, X. (eds.) DEXA 2012. LNCS, vol. 7447, pp. 215–230. Springer, Heidelberg (2012). https://doi.org/10.1007/978-3-642-32597-7_20
5. da Silva, J., Baiao, F.A., Revoredo, K.: ALIN results for OAEI 2017. In: Proceedings of the Twelfth International Workshop on Ontology Matching, OM-2017, p. 114 (2017)
6. Ding, L., Shinavier, J., Shangguan, Z., McGuinness, D.L.: SameAs networks and beyond: analyzing deployment status and implications of owl:sameAs in linked data. In: Patel-Schneider, P.F., Pan, Y., Hitzler, P., Mika, P., Zhang, L., Pan, J.Z., Horrocks, I., Glimm, B. (eds.) ISWC 2010. LNCS, vol. 6496, pp. 145–160. Springer, Heidelberg (2010). https://doi.org/10.1007/978-3-642-17746-0_10
7. Fernández, J.D., Beek, W., Martínez-Prieto, M.A., Arias, M.: LOD-a-lot. In: d'Amato, C., Fernandez, M., Tamma, V., Lecue, F., Cudré-Mauroux, P., Sequeda, J., Lange, C., Heflin, J. (eds.) ISWC 2017. LNCS, vol. 10588, pp. 75–83. Springer, Cham (2017). https://doi.org/10.1007/978-3-319-68204-4_7
8. Glaser, H., Jaffri, A., Millard, I.: Managing co-reference on the semantic web. In: WWW 2009 Workshop: Linked Data on the Web (LDOW 2009), April 2009
9. Halpin, H., Hayes, P.J., McCusker, J.P., McGuinness, D.L., Thompson, H.S.: When owl:sameAs isn't the same: an analysis of identity in linked data. In: Patel-Schneider, P.F., Pan, Y., Hitzler, P., Mika, P., Zhang, L., Pan, J.Z., Horrocks, I., Glimm, B. (eds.) ISWC 2010. LNCS, vol. 6496, pp. 305–320. Springer, Heidelberg (2010). https://doi.org/10.1007/978-3-642-17746-0_20
10. Hogan, A., Harth, A., Passant, A., Decker, S., Polleres, A.: Weaving the pedantic web. In: Linked Data on the Web Workshop (2010)
11. Horrocks, I., Patel-Schneider, P.F., van Harmelen, F.: From SHIQ and RDF to OWL: the making of a web ontology language. J. Web Semant. 1(1), 7–26 (2003)
12. Joshi, A.K., Jain, P., Hitzler, P., Yeh, P.Z., Verma, K., Sheth, A.P., Damova, M.: Alignment-based querying of linked open data. In: Meersman, R., et al. (eds.) OTM 2012. LNCS, vol. 7566, pp. 807–824. Springer, Heidelberg (2012). https://doi.org/10.1007/978-3-642-33615-7_25
13. Whitehead Jr., J.E.: Control choices and network effects in hypertext systems. In: HYPERTEXT 1999, pp. 75–82. ACM, New York (1999)
14. Schlegel, K., Stegmaier, F., Bayerl, S., Granitzer, M., Kosch, H.: Balloon fusion: SPARQL rewriting based on unified co-reference information. In: 30th International Conference on Data Engineering Workshops, pp. 254–259, March 2014

15. Schmachtenberg, M., Bizer, C., Paulheim, H.: Adoption of the linked data best practices in different topical domains. In: Mika, P., et al. (eds.) ISWC 2014. LNCS, vol. 8796, pp. 245–260. Springer, Cham (2014). https://doi.org/10.1007/978-3-319-11964-9_16

16. Wang, X., Tiropanis, T., Davis, H.C.: Optimising linked data queries in the presence of co-reference. In: Presutti, V., d'Amato, C., Gandon, F., d'Aquin, M., Staab, S., Tordai, A. (eds.) ESWC 2014. LNCS, vol. 8465, pp. 442–456. Springer, Cham (2014). https://doi.org/10.1007/978-3-319-07443-6_30

Modeling and Preserving Greek Government Decisions Using Semantic Web Technologies and Permissionless Blockchains

Themis Beris[(✉)] [ID] and Manolis Koubarakis[ID]

Department of Informatics and Telecommunications,
National and Kapodistrian University of Athens, Athens, Greece
{tberis,koubarak}@di.uoa.gr

Abstract. We present a re-engineering of Diavgeia, the Greek government portal for open and transparent public administration. We study how decisions of Greek government institutions can be modeled using ontologies expressed in OWL and queried using SPARQL. We also discuss how to use the bitcoin blockchain, to enable government decisions to remain immutable. We provide an open source implementation, called DiavgeiaRedefined, that generates and visualizes the decisions inside a web browser, offers a SPARQL endpoint for retrieving and querying these decisions and provides citizens an automated tool for verifying correctness and detecting possible foul play by an adversary. We conclude with experimental results illustrating that our scheme is efficient and feasible.

Keywords: Linked open data · Blockchain · Open government
Semantic Web · Bitcoin · Tamper-proof · Public services

1 Introduction

Government decisions which are made by public authorities and institutions, affect significantly the daily lives of ordinary citizens. Therefore, an important dimension of open government is making these government decisions open and easily accessible to the public.

Diavgeia (https://diavgeia.gov.gr/en, διαύγεια means transparency in Greek) is a Greek program introduced in 2010, enforcing transparency over the government and public administrations, by requiring that all government institutions have to upload their decisions on the Diavgeia Web portal. The portal is managed by the Ministry of Administrative Reform and E-Governance. Diavgeia is now fully implemented by public authorities. The current rate of uploads in the Diavgeia portal is 16.000 decisions per working day, summing up to a total of 26 million decisions up to now. However, decisions are currently uploaded as PDF files and follow no structuring of their textual content. As a consequence,

© Springer International Publishing AG, part of Springer Nature 2018
A. Gangemi et al. (Eds.): ESWC 2018, LNCS 10843, pp. 81–96, 2018.
https://doi.org/10.1007/978-3-319-93417-4_6

interested parties (the government, public authorities, ordinary citizens, non-government bodies, courts, the media, etc.) rely on keyword search over PDF files, in order to find decisions that might effect them in some way or verify that uploaded decisions have been taken according to the law. Also, despite the fact that these decisions are digitally signed, there is no integrity mechanism which ensures the immutability of all decisions over time.

In this work, we aim at revolutionizing the way that decisions of the Diavgeia program are made public, by following the footsteps of other successful efforts in Europe which publish legislative documents as open linked data [1]. By applying Semantic Web techniques, we envision a new state of affairs in which ordinary citizens have advanced search capabilities at their fingertips on the content of public sector decisions. In addition, through the use of the bitcoin blockchain, we enable decisions to remain immutable, introducing unprecedented levels of transparency to the Diavgeia program and ensuring the integrity of the published decisions as open linked data.

Contributions. Towards achieving the aforementioned goals, we provide an open source implementation, named DiavgeiaRedefined[1], which aims to replace the current production implementation of Diavgeia. The DiavgeiaRedefined project consists of the following modules:

1. **Diavgeia ontology.** We follow the latest Semantic Web standards and best practices and develop an OWL ontology, called *Diavgeia ontology*, for modeling the content of decisions uploaded by the Greek public authorities to the Diavgeia website. Using this ontology, decisions can be encoded in RDF and be interlinked with other Greek government data (e.g., legislation in the system Nomothesia [1]), empowering interested parties to pose rich queries over these data sources. The linking of Diavgeia with Nomothesia has the benefit of making sure that the references of public sector decisions refer to valid legislative documents (laws). We also interlink Diavgeia with a dataset encoding the administrative geography of Greece.

2. **Web editor and Visualizer.** DiavgeiaRedefined provides web applications to prove that Semantic Web technologies can be used by the Greek government in a user-friendly manner. We develop a Web editor that can be used by public authorities, for authoring their decisions. The result of this procedure is the creation of decisions expressed in RDF, compatible with the Diavgeia ontology. We also develop a Web tool that visualizes the aforementioned decisions.

3. **Blockchain tools.** By organizing and aggregating decisions into Merkle trees [2], we provide a way to store decisions expressed in RDF on the bitcoin blockchain with very low cost. We also develop a blockchain verifier that can be used by interested parties to verify the correctness and detect possible foul play by a participant in the process.

---

[1] The source code of the project can be found on https://github.com/ThemisB/diavgeiaRedefined and its landing page can be accessed on http://pyravlos-vm5.di.uoa.gr/diavgeia/.

4. **SPARQL Endpoint.** By employing Fuseki server, we empower interested parties to browse, search and pose interesting SPARQL queries to public sector decisions.
5. **Evaluation.** We evaluate DiavgeiaRedefined in two ways: (i) by calculating the blockchain validation time for a month's regular workload, and (ii) by comparing it with the current implementation of Diavgeia in terms of disk space usage.

Organization. The rest of the paper is organized as follows. Section 2 discusses related work in legislative knowledge representation using Semantic Web technologies and presents endeavors that combine linked data with blockchain technology. Section 3 presents Diavgeia. Section 4 discusses the Diavgeia ontology, presents the Web editor and Visualizer and some interesting SPARQL queries. Section 5 provides background information on the bitcoin blockchain. Section 6 describes the two blockchain tools developed for the preservation and verification of decisions. Section 7 presents the evaluation results. Last, Sect. 8 summarizes our contributions and discusses future work.

2 Related Work

Democratizing access to government and legislative documents has been a primary concern of many governments across the world. Many countries have a government portal where government data is made available free of charge, in some cases as linked data (https://data.gov.uk/). The development of information systems archiving the content of legislative documents as linked data has been a common practice towards making legislation easily accessible to public [3]. For example, the MetaLex Document Server [4] hosts all national regulations of the Netherlands, while [5] presents a service for publishing the Finnish legislation as linked open data. Nomothesia (http://legislation.di.uoa.gr/) [1] is a research project in our group, which publishes Greek legislation as linked open data and it also offers SPARQL endpoint and RESTful API to interested parties for search reasons. All of the above endeavors adopt different vocabularies and ontologies to express the particularities of each country's legislation. Recently, the European Council introduced the European Legislation Identifier (ELI) [6] as a common framework that can be adopted by the national legal publishing systems in order to unify and link national legislation with European legislation. ELI is partly based on the use of Uniform Resource Identifiers (URIs), and partly on a set of structured metadata for referencing European and domestic legislation. All of the aforementioned vocabularies and ontologies, are not a one-size-fit-all model but they have to be extended to capture the particularities of national legislation systems.

The Semantic Web community has just begun to consider applications which take advantage of the distributed, undeletable and immutable nature of the blockchain. Decentralized Semantic Identity [7] examines a semantic approach for W3C WebID, in which the Namecoin blockchain is used to register the user's WebID URI and domain names. In this endeavor, the proposed authentication scheme is outside the control of any single entity. Recently, [8] proposed a linked data based method of utilizing blockchain technology to create tamper-proof audit logs that provides proof of log manipulation and non-repudiation. Finally, [9] discusses what Semantic Web research and development can offer to blockchain research and development and vice versa.

The present work follows in the footsteps of the aforementioned efforts. DiavgeiaRedefined offers an OWL ontology which extends ELI and is linked with the Nomothesia ontology [1] and with the ontology of the administrative geography of Greece[2]. Similar to the blockchain enabled audit logs, we use bit-coin's transaction scripting language to store government data on the blockchain as metadata of a blockchain transaction.

3   Background on Diavgeia

In this section, we present Diavgeia in detail and point out the problems of the current implementation.

3.1   Greek Public Sector Decisions and Relevant Laws

Public sector decisions cover a broad spectrum of activities in Greece. The Greek government has enacted 34 different decision types that may be uploaded on Diavgeia. The decision type is chosen by the government institutions according to the context of the decision. Despite the many different decision types, we observed that the majority of them follow the same pattern. A decision starts by referring to a number of different Greek laws on which is based[3] and then gives the main text of the decision. The following figure illustrates an example of an *Appointment* decision type that adheres to the aforementioned pattern.

---

[2] The Greek Administrative Geography dataset and the ontology are available on: http://linkedopendata.gr/dataset/greek-administrative-geography.

[3] The following is a fun example. A recent decision, listing the proposals that will be funded under a particular research and innovation call, starts with references to 33 (!) Greek laws. The good news is that 176 proposals will be funded; one of them for our work extending Nomothesia [1].

Example of an *Appointment* decision type

Appointment of R.F. as Full Professor
In accordance with:

1. The provisions of Law 3549/2007, article 25, paragraph 1.
2. The provisions of Presidential Decree 2011/54.
3. The provisions of Law 4386/2016, article 70, paragraph 4.

We decide:

1. The appointment of R.F. as Full Professor at the X department, at the Y University, on the subject of "Semantic Web".

Despite the fact that this pattern can be used to define a common format for the different types of decisions, for the time being, public sector authorities upload their decisions as PDF files which follow no structuring of their textual content. Futhermore, citizens have no guarantee that the legislative references of a decision exist and are valid (such as *Laws* and *Presidential Decree* of the appointment example). By using the 5-star rating model for data [10], Greek public sector decisions are marked as 1-star.

In this work, we improve the current way of publishing Greek public sector decisions on the Web, by expressing them as 5-star open linked data. We take advantage of the aforementioned pattern and develop the Diavgeia ontology based on it. Technically, we view decisions as a collection of legal RDF documents with this standard structure.

We also employ the Nomothesia in order to ensure that the references to Greek legislation exist. Nomothesia has so far published 5 primary types of Greek legislation (*Constitution, Presidential Decrees, Laws, Acts of Ministerial Cabinet,* and *Ministerial Decisions*), as well as, 2 secondary ones (*Legislative Acts* and *Regulatory Provisions*). Nomothesia structures all legal documents, by using persistent URIs according to the template proposed by ELI http://www.legislation.di.uoa.gr/eli/{type}/{year}/{id}. For instance, for the first provision of the appointment example, a linking of Diavgeia with the Nomothesia URI http://legislation.di.uoa.gr/eli/law/2007/3549/article/25/paragraph/1 can be made. By integrating Nomothesia into Diavgeia, we also give citizens the ability to simply click to the legislative references of public sector decisions and see instantly the relevant passage of Greek legislation.

3.2 Metadata of Decisions

In addition to the uploading of the PDF file, public sector authorities also have to fill metadata information which describe the decision. The metadata used vary according to the type of decision. For instance, the metadata of the *ExpenditureApproval* decision type, holds important information about government's expenditure (such as the sender and receiver VAT registration numbers, the expense amount, etc.). Diavgeia offers an OpenDataAPI (https://diavgeia.gov.gr/api/help) that can be used as an endpoint to query over the metadata. Despite the fact that Open-DataAPI is a step towards promoting transparency, inconsistency between decision text and metadata information is possible[4]. In our work, we embed metadata information into the RDF document, eliminating the possibility of inconsistency.

3.3 Identifiers and Modifications of Decisions

Each decision is assigned a unique Internet Uploading Number (IUN), certifying that the decision has been uploaded on Diavgeia. IUN is of significant importance, since citizens and other public authorities can use decisions, by solely referring to their unique number. In addition to IUN, each decision is also assigned a unique version token. Government institutions can upload a new version of a decision by claiming a new version token, but maintaining the same IUN. Diavgeia functions in an **append-only** manner, as it maintains the original decision with all its subsequent modifications. This is exactly why Diavgeia is amenable to blockchain technologies as we discuss in Sect. 6.

4 Modeling Decisions Using Semantic Web Technologies

In this section, we develop an OWL ontology for modeling decisions of Diavgeia. We call our ontology *Diavgeia ontology* and we discuss its current version that adopts the ELI framework and the Nomothesia ontology. We present the Web editor and Visualizer components of DiavgeiaRedefined that generate and visualize the decisions expressed in RDF, respectively. Futhermore, we describe the linking of decisions with other datasets and we pose interesting SPARQL queries which take advantage of this interlinking.

4.1 The Diavgeia Ontology

The ontology of Diavgeia is based on the pattern followed by public sector decisions, as discussed in Sect. 3.1. It imports and uses properties that are defined in the ELI ontology and the Nomothesia ontology. The core[5] of Diavgeia ontology is shown on Fig. 1. The 34 different decision types can be viewed as legal documents (class `LegalResource` of the ELI ontology). A decision (`LegalResource`) `changes` itself, by generating a new `version` and maintaining its unique `iun`. A `LegalResource` is composed of multiple `Considerations` and `Conclusions`. The `Consideration` class models the passages that are used to prove the validity of the decision (e.g. the three provisions of the appointment example), while `Conclusion` models the passages that are used as conclusions of the decision (that is the final passage of the appointment example). Both `Consideration`

---

[4] An article about inconsistent metadata on Diavgeia website: https://eellak.ellak.gr/
2016/07/06/veltionontas-tin-piotita-dedomenon-stin-diavgia/.

[5] The full Diavgeia ontology is available on: https://github.com/ThemisB/diavgeia
Redefined/blob/master/rdf/diavgeia.owl.

and `Conclusion` classes, use the `cites` property of the ELI ontology, to make a reference either to Greek Legislation (Nomothesia) or to another decision of Diavgeia. The `has_text` property is used to describe the text body of either `Consideration` or `Conclusion`.

The Diavgeia ontology offers 121 properties to cover all the particularities of different decision types. In addition to `Consideration` and `Conclusion`, the ontology provides classes which describe important public sector activities. For instance the class `Expenses` links an expense of a public authority to an individual or business. For the time being, this crucial information is expressed as metadata of the PDF decision, underlying the possibility of metadata inconsistency as described in Sect. 3.2. By merging metadata and decision text in a single RDF file, this possibility is eliminated.

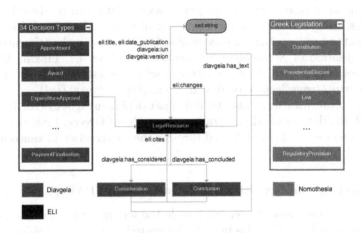

Fig. 1. The core of Diavgeia ontology

In order to identify legal resources, we also need appropriate URIs. Persistent URIs is a strongly recommended best practice [11], according to ELI. It is very important to have reliable means to identify the public sector decisions. Based on what is stated in Sect. 3.3, we can structure the persistent URIs of decisions according to the template http://www.diavgeia.gov.gr/eli/{iun}/{version}. Modifications of a decision result to the generation of a new URI which has the same `iun` and a new `version` number. Thus, the version of an enacted decision can be seen as the decision which has the most recent `date_publication` for a specific `iun`.

4.2 Web Editor and Visualizer

DiavgeiaRedefined offers two main Web components in order to transparently adopt Semantic Web technologies to the production implementation of Diavgeia. The first one is a web editor for decisions, used exclusively by public sector authorities. The Web editor is a well-structured HTML form that government institutions can use in order to write their decisions. The HTML elements of the form are associated with the properties and classes of Diavgeia ontology. By submitting the form, the decision is stored both as a compressed Notation3 file in the filesystem of Diavgeia and in Jena Apache's triple store.

The Visualizer is another component of DiavgeiaRedefined which can be used both by public authorities and citizens. Its purpose is to provide a visualization of the decisions expressed in RDF inside a Web browser. Users provide the persistent URI of the decision they want to visualize and the decision is displayed in the browser in a user-friendly manner.

4.3 Linking Decisions with Other Public Sector Data

The linking of decisions with other public sector data, can be done by public authorities, using the Web editor component of DiavgeiaRedefined. Firstly, the Consideration or Conclusion classes of a decision, may make reference to the Greek Legislation of Nomothesia, as mentioned in Sect. 4.1. Linking Diavgeia with Nomothesia is easy, since the latter provides persistent URIs according to template http://www.legislation.di.uoa.gr/eli/{type}/{year}/{id}.

Public authorities have also to link SpatialPlanningDecisions decision type, with the dataset of administrative geography of Greece. Linking decisions with it is also easy and it is achieved through the construction of constant mappings.

4.4 Querying the Resulting RDF Data Using SPARQL

By employing the Fuseki Server, we enable the formulation of complex queries over decisions of Diavgeia. This provides interested parties a mechanism to monitor the decisions of public sector organizations. We present some interesting queries one can pose.

```
SELECT ?decision WHERE {
  ?decision diavgeia:has_expense ?expense;
            eli:date_publication ?date.
  ?expense diavgeia:expense_amount ?amount.
  FILTER (?date >= "2017-01-01"^^xsd:date &&
  ?date <= "2017-12-31"^^xsd:date)
} ORDER BY DESC(?amount) LIMIT 5
```

Retrieve the decisions with the 5 highest government expenses of 2017.

```
SELECT DISTINCT ?decision WHERE {
  ?nomothesiaLegislation eli:passed_by ?signatory;
                         eli:date_publication ?date.
  ?signatory foaf:name "I.Stournaras".
  ?reference eli:cites ?nomothesiaLegislation.
  {?decision diavgeia:has_concluded ?reference} UNION
  {?decision diavgeia:has_considered ?reference}
}
```

Find decisions which make a reference to Greek legislative documents that have been signed by the ex-Greek Minister of Finance I. Stournaras.

5   Background on Bitcoin Blockchain

Bitcoin [12] is the first decentralized digital currency based on a distributed, peer-to-peer consensus network. Transactions propagate through the network in order to be verified and stored in a blockchain. Blockchain is the immutable public distributed ledger which records all bitcoin transactions, forming a chain of blocks. Each block in the blockchain is composed of the previous block in the chain and a payload of transactions.

Bitcoin uses a stack-based scripting system for modeling transactions, called Script [13]. Transactions consist of multiple inputs and multiple outputs. Bitcoins are transferred on a transaction input and output, where the input defines where bitcoins are coming from and the output defines the destination. OP_RETURN opcode is a special instruction of Script which allows to save metadata up to 80 bytes on a transaction output [14]. *Miners* are specialized nodes on the network that keep the blockchain consistent, complete, and unalterable. By solving a hard cryptographic problem, miners generate and add new blocks to blockchain. The rest nodes of the network can easily verify and mutually agree that the solution given by the miner is correct and accept the new block.

The consensus algorithm of bitcoin guarantees that, for an attacker to be able to alter an existing block, he must control the majority of the computational resources of the network [15]. As more transactions and blocks are generated, the difficulty of the cryptographic problem increases significantly, which makes the tampering of data written in the blocks very difficult. This security property is often rephrased by saying that the bitcoin blockchain can been seen as an immutable, permissionless data structure. Thus, even if the main goal of bitcoin is to transfer digital currency, there are certifying services which take advantage of the tamper-proof nature of blockchain, by providing users a way to certify existence or ownership of documents (such as *Proof of Existence*[6], *Open-Timestamps*[7] and *Stampery* [16]). In our work, we use the OP_RETURN opcode to embed government data as metadata of a bitcoin transaction, similar to the aforementioned certifying services.

6   Preserving Decisions Using Bitcoin Blockchain

In this section, we describe the use of the bitcoin blockchain on Diavgeia. We present in detail the two blockchain tools that DiavgeiaRedefined offers, called Stamper and Consistency Verifier.

6.1   Stamper

Stamper is the tool which should be used by the administrators of Diavgeia in order to store public sector decisions on the bitcoin blockchain. The stamping procedure is described as follows:

---

[6] Proof of Existence: https://poex.io/about.
[7] OpenTimestamps: https://opentimestamps.org/.

1. Government institutions upload their decisions on Diavgeia. The backend of Diavgeia stores decisions as compressed Notation3 files in its filesystem and in the triple store.
2. The administrator of Diavgeia has to decide that the stamping procedure should take place at predefined time intervals t, ensuring the integrity of decisions. Thus, the backend of Diavgeia starts a new stamping procedure every t time units.
3. At the start of the stamping procedure, we find all the compressed Notation3 decisions which have not been stamped yet. Stamper organizes and aggregates these decisions into a Merkle Tree [2], using the hash function SHA-256. The root of the Merkle tree represents the fingerprint of the decisions which will be included in the forthcoming bitcoin transaction. By applying the SHA-256 hash function on the Merkle tree construction, the resulting root has a constant size of 32 bytes.
4. The next step is to create a Bitcoin transaction and broadcast it to the rest of the network. DiavgeiaRedefined uses the bcoin library (http://bcoin.io/), offering Diavgeia an spv node[8], maintaining only a chain, a pool, and a *hierarchical deterministic (HD)* wallet [17] based on BIP44 [18].

   A stamping transaction in our model consists of two outputs and one input. The first output contains the OP_RETURN opcode followed by the Merkle root in the *scriptPubKey* output (*scriptPubKey* = OP_RETURN + Root). This output guarantees the immutability of decisions. The second output is a pay-to-pubkey-hash[9], having as *pubKey* the next derived public address of the HD wallet. The input *scriptSig* consists of Diavgeia's signature and the current *publicKey* derived from HD wallet (*scriptSig* = *signature* + *publicKey*). The size of a stamping transaction is 267 bytes. In order to have certain guarantees that our transaction will be written into the next block and confirmed nearly immediately, mining fees can cost up to 120,150 satoshi (0.00125 bitcoin), which at the time of writing roughly amounts to $16.84 (Fig. 2).

   After the end of each stamping transaction, Diavgeia publishes to its website the transaction identifier (Txid) and the order of decisions, as used for the Merkle tree construction. It also publishes once, the Master Public Key of its HD wallet. By publishing Diavgeia's master public key, interested parties are able to track the sequence of public keys and stamping transactions of Diavgeia. These publications are necessary to be made for the proper functionality of the Consistency Verifier (see Sect. 6.3).

---

[8] A method for verifying if particular transactions are included in a block without downloading the entire block (https://bitcoin.org/en/developer-guide#simplified-payment-verification-spv).

[9] https://en.bitcoin.it/wiki/Script#Standard_Transaction_to_Bitcoin_address_.28pay-to-pubkey-hash.29.

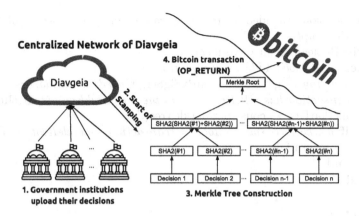

Fig. 2. The stamping procedure

6.2 Guarantees of Stamper

The Stamper tool provides high levels of immutability guarantees, especially when t value is configured to be small. Generally, the threat of a decision's modification or deletion appears on the time gap between two consecutive stampings. Small t values imply more stamping invocations and as a result Diavgeia creates more stamping transactions, but this comes at a higher cost. We consider a t value ranging from 3 h to 1 day, to be an affordable solution for the government, since the daily cost of the usage of the blockchain will range from 0.00125 to 0.005 bitcoin (\$16.84–\$134.72). The threshold for a decision's modification is also small, since an adversary (the administrators of Diavgeia, the government or other public authorities) are able to modify the decision in the next 3 h to 1 day after its publishment.

As mentioned in Sect. 6.1, Stamper uses the open source bitcoin library (bcoin) in order to create the stamping transactions and relay them to the network. DiavgeiaRedefined does not use existing blockchain timestamping services (such as Stampery or OpenTimeStamps) because, in case of a foul play by an adversary, these third-party services might be accused of having modified the Merkle root in the first place.

6.3 Consistency Verifier

Consistency Verifier is the tool which can be used by the interested parties in order to verify that decisions have remained immutable over time. Algorithm 1 formalizes the steps Consistency Verifier takes to verify the integrity of decisions.

Data: Decisions included in stamping transaction i: d_i, Master Public
       Key: mpk
Result: Boolean result of verification.
1 **foreach** *usedPublicAddress of mpk* **do**
2   *transaction* ← getTransactionBySigScript(*usedPublicAddress*);
3   **if** *transaction has OP_RETURN in the scriptPubKey output* **then**
4   merkleTree ← constructMerkleTree(d_i);
5   **if** *merkleTree→merkleRoot != transaction→merkleRoot* **then**
6   return false;
7   **end**
8   **end**
9 **end**
10 return true;

Algorithm 1. Consistency Verification procedure

The first step is to download the compressed Notation3 decisions which have
been included in stamping transactions. Afterwards, the verifier downloads in
ascending time order all bitcoin transactions (using the *chain.so* bitcoin block
reader, available at https://chain.so/), related to the used public addresses
derived from Diavgeia's master public key. In case of a stamping transaction,
the verifier constructs the Merkle tree using the decisions of the first step. If
the computed Merkle root is equal to the Merkle root found on the stamping
transaction, decisions have remained unmodified.

7   Experimental Evaluation

This section presents a scalability evaluation of the Consistency Verifier tool
and discusses the disk space reduction that gzip compression of Notation3 files
offer. Section 7.1 describes the synthetic dataset used in the Consistency Verifier
experiment. In Sect. 7.2, we illustrate the details of the test environment and in
Sect. 7.3. we discuss the results of the experiment. The disk space reduction is
presented in Sect. 7.4.

7.1   Dataset

To simulate the consistency verification process, we generated synthetic gzip
Notation3 decisions[10], according to the *Diavgeia ontology*. Firstly, synthetic decisions have 7–17 `Consideration` and `Conclusion` class entities, each one of them
has 150–350 random bytes as text part. Moreover, we have included several
common-used properties, such as protocol number and thematic categories of
a decision, as well as, information related to the departments of government
institutions which upload them (phone number, address, etc.).

We examine the time it takes an interested party to verify the consistency
of Diavgeia in a month's common workload. We consider the scenario in which

---

[10] Datasets are available in: https://doi.org/10.6084/m9.figshare.5729292.v1.

Diavgeia stores decisions on bitcoin blockchain, once a day. According to the Webpage of Diavgeia (https://diavgeia.gov.gr/en), the current rate of uploads is 16000 decisions per working day and assuming a month has 22 working days, we make 22 bitcoin stamping transactions. To examine the scalability of the verifier, we provide 3 different datasets, containing 8000, 16000 and 24000 decisions per day, summing up to 176000, 352000, 528000 compressed gzip N3 decisions, respectively.

7.2 Test Environment

The verification experiment was run on a MacBook Pro with a 2.9 GHz Intel Core i5 processor and 8 GB of memory, since this process may be executed by interested parties with a standard modern computer. The Javascript methods used to measure the elapsed verification time is *console.time - console.timeEnd*. The execution time measures the time needed to create the 22 Merkle trees and compare the computed roots with the roots extracted from the stamping transactions. The recorded time does not take into account any network time; the time needed to download synthetic decisions from our Web server or the time needed to gather bitcoin transactions, by making requests to *chain.so*. To account for variability in the testing environment, each reported elapsed time is the average of five independent executions.

7.3 Experimental Results

The experiment consisted of retrieving all synthetic decisions from our Web server and bitcoin transactions from *chain.so* and then compare the corresponding Merkle roots for validity, as presented in Algorithm 1. We use the 3 different datasets described in Sect. 7.1. The elapsed verification time is plotted in Fig. 3.

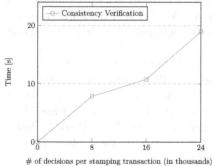

#of decisions per stamping tx	Verification Time (s)
8000	7.853
16000	10.780
24000	18.986

# of decisions per stamping transaction (in thousands)

Fig. 3. Evaluation of the Consistency Verifier

This experiment validates the linear time growth of the Consistency Verifier. The integrity check for a month's regular workload, consisting of 16000 decisions per day, takes about 11 s. Even for the extreme case of 24000 decisions per day, the verifier takes approximately 19 s to perform the integrity check. These results validate the scalability of our blockchain solution and demonstrate that interested parties can efficiently perform integrity checks over the data of Diavgeia.

7.4 Disk Space Reduction

Diavgeia currently hosts over 26 million decisions, leading to disk space limitations. The average size of a PDF-decision is about 2.5 MB, summing up to a total of 65 TB. We have created a sample, consisting of equivalent PDF and compressed gzip Notation3 files, for each different decision type of Diavgeia ontology[11]. For the aforementioned sample, we notice that compressed Notation3 decisions are about 86 times smaller, compared to the equivalent PDF files. Hence, encoding decisions in RDF not only allows for sophisticated SPARQL querying, but it also saves space.

8 Conclusions and Future Work

In this paper we presented how Greek public sector decisions can be published as linked open data using Semantic Web technologies. We also discussed how to use the bitcoin blockchain to guarantee decision immutability over time. The Diavgeia ontology we employed, is based on the latest European standards and captures the particularities of Greek public sector decisions. We highlighted the importance of interlinking Diavgeia with other publicly available open data, by posing interesting SPARQL queries. We implemented the Web editor and Visualizer components in order to transparently adopt Semantic Web technologies in a user-friendly manner. We also introduced two blockchain tools; Stamper is responsible for storing government data on the bitcoin blockchain and Consistency Verifier provides citizens an automated way to verify the integrity of decisions. Finally, we evaluated the Consistency Verifier and measured the disk space reduction which compressed Notation3 decisions offer over the current PDF-format.

As an initial step of our future work, we would like to proceed with a usability evaluation of DiavgeiaRedefined and study possible improvements. As a part of functional improvements, we would like to implement a question answering system which will translate natural language queries to SPARQL queries. This system will offer ordinary citizens a way to examine the legality and good administration of Diavgeia, without posing SPARQL queries by themselves. Futhermore, we plan to integrate the HDT mechanism [19] to store the decisions on the Apache Jena Fuseki as compressed data and pose SPARQL queries, without the need of decompressing the decisions.

We acknowledge bitcoin's limitations in terms of cost, speed, and scalability [20]. We would like to apply Stamper and Consistency Verifier to other

---

[11] The sample is available on: https://github.com/ThemisB/diavgeiaRedefined/tree/master/rdf/samples.

blockchain technologies, such as Ethereum [21]. In our future work, we will further develop Consistency Verifier. Firstly, we will offer a slower, but safer option of downloading the blockchain, in order to replace the requests made on *chain.so* explorer. We will also implement an inclusion mechanism, to verify that a given decision has remained unchanged. Moreover, the verifier does not take into account the data available through the SPARQL endpoint, meaning that a modification to this data will go unnoticed. We will extend the verifier with the option to perform a full verification procedure which will ensure that data offered through SPARQL endpoint is the same with the compressed Notation3 decisions and therefore same with the stamping transactions of bitcoin.

References

1. Chalkidis, I., Nikolaou, C., Soursos, P., Koubarakis, M.: Modeling and querying Greek legislation using semantic web technologies. In: Blomqvist, E., Maynard, D., Gangemi, A., Hoekstra, R., Hitzler, P., Hartig, O. (eds.) ESWC 2017. LNCS, vol. 10249, pp. 591–606. Springer, Cham (2017)
2. Cucurull, J., Puiggalí, J.: Distributed immutabilization of secure logs. In: Barthe, G., Markatos, E., Samarati, P. (eds.) STM 2016. LNCS, vol. 9871, pp. 122–137. Springer, Cham (2016). https://doi.org/10.1007/978-3-319-46598-2_9
3. Casanovas, P., Palmirani, M., Peroni, S., van Engers, T.M., Vitali, F.: Semantic web for the legal domain: the next step. Semant. Web 7(3), 213–227 (2016)
4. Hoekstra, R.: The MetaLex document server - legal documents as versioned linked data. In: Aroyo, L., Welty, C., Alani, H., Taylor, J., Bernstein, A., Kagal, L., Noy, N., Blomqvist, E. (eds.) ISWC 2011. LNCS, vol. 7032, pp. 128–143. Springer, Heidelberg (2011). https://doi.org/10.1007/978-3-642-25093-4_9
5. Frosterus, M., Tuominen, J., Wahlroos, M., Hyvönen, E.: The finnish law as a linked data service. In: Cimiano, P., Fernández, M., Lopez, V., Schlobach, S., Völker, J. (eds.) ESWC 2013. LNCS, vol. 7955, pp. 289–290. Springer, Heidelberg (2013). https://doi.org/10.1007/978-3-642-41242-4_46
6. ELI Task Force: ELI implementation methodology. http://data.europa.eu/doi/10.2830/813167
7. Faísca, J.G., Rogado, J.Q.: Decentralized semantic identity. In: Proceedings of the 12th International Conference on Semantic Systems, pp. 177–180. ACM (2016)
8. Sutton, A., Samavi, R.: Blockchain enabled privacy audit logs. In: d'Amato, C., Fernandez, M., Tamma, V., Lecue, F., Cudré-Mauroux, P., Sequeda, J., Lange, C., Heflin, J. (eds.) ISWC 2017. LNCS, vol. 10587, pp. 645–660. Springer, Cham (2017). https://doi.org/10.1007/978-3-319-68288-4_38
9. English, M., Auer, S., Domingue, J.: Block chain technologies & the semantic web: a framework for symbiotic development. In: Lehmann, J., Thakkar, H., Halilaj, L., Asmat, R. (eds) Computer Science Conference for University of Bonn Students, pp. 47–61 (2016)
10. Berners-Lee, T.: 5 star deployment scheme. https://www.w3.org/DesignIssues/LinkedData.html
11. Archer, P., Goedertier, S., Loutas, N.: Study on persistent URIs, with identification of best practices and recommendations on the topic for the MSs and the EC (2012). https://joinup.ec.europa.eu/sites/default/files/document/2013-02/D7.1.3-StudyonpersistentURIs.pdf

12. Nakamoto, S.: Bitcoin: A Peer-to-Peer Electronic Cash System (2008)
13. Bitcoin Wiki: Script Manual. https://en.bitcoin.it/wiki/Script
14. Bartoletti, M., Pompianu, L.: An analysis of Bitcoin OP_RETURN metadata. In: Brenner, M., et al. (eds.) FC 2017. LNCS, vol. 10323, pp. 218–230. Springer, Cham (2017). https://doi.org/10.1007/978-3-319-70278-0_14
15. Garay, J., Kiayias, A., Leonardos, N.: The Bitcoin backbone protocol: analysis and applications. In: Oswald, E., Fischlin, M. (eds.) EUROCRYPT 2015. LNCS, vol. 9057, pp. 281–310. Springer, Heidelberg (2015). https://doi.org/10.1007/978-3-662-46803-6_10
16. de Pedro Crespo, A.S., García, L.I.C.: Stampery Blockchain Timestamping Architecture (BTA) - Version 6. CoRR (2017)
17. Gutoski, G., Stebila, D.: Hierarchical deterministic Bitcoin wallets that tolerate key leakage. IACR Cryptology ePrint Archive: Report 2014/998 (2014)
18. Palatinus, M., Rusnak, P.: Multi-Account Hierarchy for Deterministic Wallets. https://github.com/bitcoin/bips/blob/master/bip-0044.mediawiki
19. Fernández, J.D., Martínez-Prieto, M.A., Gutiérrez, C., Polleres, A., Arias, M.: Binary RDF representation for publication and exchange (HDT). Web Semant.: Sci. Serv. Agents World Wide Web **19**, 22–41 (2013)
20. Sporny, M.: LD-DL'17 workshop keynote talk: building better blockchains via linked data. In: Proceedings of the 26th International Conference on World Wide Web, p. 1429. ACM (2017)
21. Buterin, V.: A Next-Generation Smart Contract and Decentralized Application Platform. https://github.com/ethereum/wiki/wiki/White-Paper

Towards a Binary Object Notation
for RDF

Victor Charpenay[1,2](✉) (iD), Sebastian Käbisch[1], and Harald Kosch[2]

[1] Corporate Technology, Siemens AG, Munich, Germany
{victor.charpenay,sebastian.kaebisch}@siemens.com
[2] Fakultät für Informatik und Mathematik, Universität Passau, Passau, Germany
harald.kosch@uni-passau.de

Abstract. The recent JSON-LD standard, that specifies an object notation for RDF, has been adopted by a number of data providers on the
Web. In this paper, we present a novel usage of JSON-LD, as a compact
format to exchange and query RDF data in constrained environments,
in the context of the Web of Things.

A typical exchange between Web of Things agents involves small
pieces of semantically described data (RDF data sets of less than hundred triples). In this context, we show how JSON-LD, serialized in binary
JSON formats like EXI4JSON and CBOR, outperforms the state-of-the-
art. Our experiments were performed on data sets provided by the literature, as well as a production data set exported from Siemens Desigo
CC.

We also provide a formalism for JSON-LD and show how it offers a
lightweight alternative to SPARQL via JSON-LD framing.

Keywords: Web of Things · Internet of Things · SPARQL · RDF
EXI · JSON-LD · HDT · CBOR

1 Introduction

The mismatch between the triple structure of RDF and the object-oriented
nature of most programming languages on the Web has probably hindered the
development of Semantic Web technologies. A standard object notation for RDF,
to e.g. manipulate RDF data directly in JavaScript, was a prerequisite for further adoption. Such a standard, JSON for Linked Data (JSON-LD), was recently
published by the W3C [26].

JSON-LD documents must link to a *context* that maps terms to Semantic
Web entities. Given a proper context, documents can be expanded, compacted or
flattened, as well as turned into RDF triples [18]. A JSON-based query language
to match and reshape JSON-LD documents was also requested by the community
but it has not been included in the official W3C standard. A new community
draft (JSON-LD 1.1) attempts to fill this gap by defining a procedure known as
JSON-LD *framing* [25].

© Springer International Publishing AG, part of Springer Nature 2018
A. Gangemi et al. (Eds.): ESWC 2018, LNCS 10843, pp. 97–111, 2018.
https://doi.org/10.1007/978-3-319-93417-4_7

JSON-LD has rapidly been adopted by a number of data providers, such as Open Data platforms, as well as by major browser vendors via schema.org[1]. It has also become the default exchange format for Linked Data Notifications, which are e.g. implemented by Mastodon, a successful decentralized micro-blogging platform[2].

Most reported usages of JSON-LD involve large-scale data exchange[3]. In this paper, we explore the usage of JSON-LD as a compact RDF serialization, in the context of the Internet of Things (IoT). It is envisioned that Web technologies will sustain the massive integration of embedded devices to the Internet, by using RESTful architectures, with JSON as a primary serialization format [8,27]. In what would then become a Web of 'Things', Semantic Web technologies would allow connected devices to be self-descriptive and autonomous [2]. Therefore, JSON-LD appears to be a good candidate as a serialization format for the Web of Things (WoT).

The major issues with using Semantic Web technologies in an embedded environment are (1) the verbosity of RDF and (2) the complexity of semantic processing. In this paper, we show how JSON-LD can address both issues. We first provide the theoretical foundations for JSON-LD compaction and framing (Sect. 3). In particular, we show how JSON-LD framing can be implemented in SPARQL, a language with well-known semantics. Then, we experimentally show how JSON-LD compaction using a global context can reduce the size of RDF documents (Sect. 4). Before introducing our work, we present a short overview of the state-of-the-art with respect to using RDF in constrained environments (Sect. 2).

2   Related Work

Until today, a large part of research towards storing and querying RDF has focused on very large, static data sets stored on powerful machines, sometimes involving parallel computation. In contrast, storage mechanisms for resource-constrained devices remain mostly unexplored. Until recently, no realistic use case could be found where computational devices had limited resources but still IP connectivity. The situation has changed with the coming of the IoT where RDF is predicted to play a significant role.

In our context, constrained devices correspond mostly to low-power micro-controllers (MCUs) with integrated IP communication stack [4]. Typically, such devices are too constrained to support standard Web technologies (HTTP, XML, JSON). A range of technologies were however developed in the last years as a substitute. The Constrained Application Protocol (CoAP), the Efficient XML Interchange format (EXI) and the Constrained Binary Object Representation (CBOR) are the counterpart of HTTP, XML and JSON in the so-called "Embedded Web" [23].

---

[1] http://schema.org.

[2] https://joinmastodon.org/.

[3] https://github.com/json-ld/json-ld.org/wiki/Users-of-JSON-LD.

The European project SPITFIRE [22] paved the way to the use of RDF on the Embedded Web, combining it with architectural principles of the Web of Things. Since then, several methods were proposed to serialize and process RDF data on constrained devices.

2.1 Serializing RDF Data

The first work that addressed constrained devices—and to the best of our knowledge, the only one—is part of SPITFIRE and is called the Wiselib TupleStore [12]. Built on top of Wiselib, a substitute to the C++ standard library designed for embedded systems, the Wiselib TupleStore internally stores RDF nodes in a tree-shaped data structure in order to compact them. In SPITFIRE, the Wiselib TupleStore was ported on wireless motes (iSense, MICAz, . . .) and the data was serialized in a binary format called SHDT [11], a streaming version of the Header-Dictionary-Triples format for RDF (HDT).

The original objective of HDT was to compact large RDF data sets. e.g. to fit in the main memory of a standard PC. But as a binary format, its compression scheme could reasonably be used on small data sets as well. An HDT document is divided into three sections containing respectively metadata (header), resource IRIs (dictionary) and the triples themselves, indexed by subject (triples). Although most RDF stores also implement a similar partitioning, HDT compresses each section separately with dedicated compression methods [7].

In the original proposal for HDT, all triples are merged in an single array while separations between them are stored in a bitmap, easily compressible. HDT achieves high compression ratios compared to classical compression schemes like gzip. An alternative triple indexing method was also proposed, performing vertical partitioning with k^2-tree compression (k^2-triples) [1]. k^2-triples achieves better compression ratios while efficiently processing predicate-bound triple pattern matching queries.

HDT and k^2-triples show excellent results in terms of compression and query processing speed. However, a recent study suggests that there exists a better alternative for small data sets, i.e. on embedded devices [15]. The study presents data sets of semantically annotated sensor measurements where an EXI serialization of RDF/XML data is more compact than HDT. The two approaches (EXI and HDT) have been combined in a proposal called Efficient RDF Interchange (ERI) [6], which, however, primarily addresses data streams (with time considerations).

2.2 Processing RDF Data

In most use cases of SPITFIRE, the RDF data exposed by IoT devices was crawled by a Web agent and put in a central RDF repository, which clients could query through a SPARQL endpoint. In practice, IoT networks can be very heterogeneous and complex. A more dynamic approach to querying might be preferable over static crawling.

Without any change on the SPITFIRE infrastructure, one possible approach is what is referred to in the literature as Linked Data (LD) queries [10]. To answer an LD query, Web clients follow links exposed by an RDF source according to a global strategy defined by the client (e.g. based on statistics from the Linked Open Data cloud). This type of processing might be encouraged by the recent standardization by the W3C of Linked Data Platforms (LDPs) [24]. A mapping of LDPs to CoAP has been proposed [19], which in theory makes LD queries a possible candidate for RDF data exchange on constrained environments.

In parallel with LDPs, another architecture has been proposed to expose RDF data sets at low cost: Triple Pattern Fragments (TPFs) [28]. TPFs try to provide an intermediary in terms of computational cost between a full SPARQL endpoint and an LDP that serves static data. In contrast to a SPARQL endpoint, a TPF endpoint restricts queries to triple patterns. As for LD queries, Web clients must define a strategy to order atomic triple patterns and reconstruct the result set from the received fragments. A TPF server must also expose metadata (statistics) to guide clients.

Both LD queries and TPFs have the drawback of generating many exchanges between the client and the (constrained) server. Given that low-power devices consume most of their energy on data exchange, especially with radio protocols, these approaches would considerably lower their overall lifetime. We addressed this issue in a previous work on a SPARQL engine for MCUs [5]. This engine, which we called the μRDF store, is capable of answering basic graph patterns (BGPs) and exposes a CoAP interface with RDF/EXI serialization. We implemented it for the ESP8266, a microcontroller with an integrated Wi-Fi chip (64 kB RAM, 80 MHz). Our experiments show that BGP processing, including EXI coding, is fast in comparison to sending and receiving the data over Wi-Fi, while significantly reducing the amount of data exchanged. In the present work, we show how the μRDF store could support SPARQL beyond BGPs, by implementing JSON-LD framing.

Another work on embedded systems reported similar observations: shifting SPARQL joins (AND operator) to the edges in a wireless sensor network results in 5 to 10 times faster query processing [3]. Although these results apply to exchanges based on non-IP radio protocols with restricted frame size—thus not directly comparable to our results, it is consistent with our results and encourages more experiments in this direction.

3   Theoretical Background

Although JSON-LD 1.0 officially became a W3C recommandation in 2014, it is still a moving standard. Its version 1.1 is currently under development. To the best of our knowledge, no formalim has been provided yet for either JSON-LD 1.0 or JSON-LD 1.1. In the following, we formalize parts of JSON-LD 1.1 (generic syntax, compaction and framing), without aiming at exhaustivity.

3.1   Definitions

Our formalism is based on the flattened representation of a JSON-LD document, i.e. an array of node objects without nesting. The notation we use is borrowed from F-logic, an extension of predicate logic for object-oriented programming [17]. Predicate logic defines terms and formulas. F-logic extends the definition of formulas to include class membership and object fields, where object identifiers, class identifiers and field names and values are constant terms.

Definition 1. *Let I, B, L be pairwise disjoint sets of IRIs, blank nodes and literals, respectively. A JSON-LD (node) object is the formula*

$$\mathsf{id}:\mathsf{t}_1,\ldots,\mathsf{t}_l\,[\mathsf{p}_1 \to \mathsf{id}_1,\ldots,\mathsf{p}_m \to \mathsf{id}_m, \mathsf{p}_{m+1} \to \mathsf{v}_1,\ldots,\mathsf{p}_n \to \mathsf{v}_{n-m}] \qquad (1)$$

where $\mathsf{id}, \mathsf{id}_i \in (I \cup B)$, $\mathsf{t}_i, \mathsf{p}_j \in I$ *and* $\mathsf{v}_k \in L$.

In the JSON-LD terminology, id is an object identifier, t a type, p a property and v a value. A JSON-LD graph is a set of JSON-LD objects. It can include several formulas with the same object identifier.

Example 1. The following graph represents a room equipped with a temperature sensor (IRI namespaces were omitted for the sake of conciseness):

> r46 : Thing, Room [hasDataPoint → temp21],
> r46 [hasName → 'Room 46 (conference room)'],
> device137 : Thing, Sensor [measures → temp21],
> temp21 : Property, Temperature [hasUnit → degreeCelsius]

We now define a straightforward transformation from JSON-LD to RDF, denoted σ_R. This transformation is based on the RDF deserialization algorithm of the JSON-LD processor. In the original JSON-LD syntax, properties are allowed to be blank nodes, in which case they should be ignored during RDF deserialization. We exclude blank node properties in the present work.

Definition 2. *Let F be the set of formulas as per Definition 1. Let $f \in F$ be a formula. We define σ_R, as follows:*

$$\sigma_R(f) = \{(\mathsf{id}, \mathit{type}, \mathsf{t}_1), \ldots, (\mathsf{id}, \mathsf{p}_1, \mathsf{id}_1), \ldots, (\mathsf{id}, \mathsf{p}_n, \mathsf{v}_{n-m})\} \qquad (2)$$

$\sigma_R(f)$ is an RDF graph (*type* being the RDF type predicate IRI). It is trivial to define the inverse transformation, from RDF to JSON-LD, along the lines of the serialization algorithm of the JSON-LD processor.

Example 2. By applying σ_R on all formulas of Example 1, we obtain the following merged graph:

> {(r46, type, Thing),   (r46, type, Room),
> (r46, hasDataPoint, temp21),   (r46, hasName, 'Room 46 (conference room)'),
> (device137, type, Thing),   (device137, type, Sensor),
> (device137, measures, temp21), (temp21, type, Property),
> (temp21, type, Temperature),   (temp21, hasUnit, degreeCelsius)}

Compaction. Compaction consists in mapping IRIs appearing in a JSON-LD object to arbitrary (short) UTF-8 character strings. The IRI map required to turn a compacted JSON-LD object into its original form is called a JSON-LD *context*. Compaction is one of the procedures defined by the JSON-LD processor [18].

Definition 3. *Let U be the set of UTF-8 character strings. A JSON-LD context is a map $c : U \mapsto I$. By abuse of notation, we denote $c(f)$ the result of applying c to all UTF-8 strings in the formula f.*

Definition 4. *Let c be a JSON-LD context. The formula f' is a compacted JSON-LD (node) object against c if $c(f')$ is a formula as per Definition 1 (i.e. if $c(f') \in F$).*

It is possible to define a global context c_g that would apply to any formula f, such that JSON-LD interchange and procedures like framing or RDF serialization can be done on the compacted form directly. The notion of global context is key in optimizing the exchange and processing of JSON-LD data.

Example 3. As an example, one can define a simple global context that removes all characters from an IRI but the first letter(s) of its local name (assuming it introduces no name collision). A compacted form of Example 1 would then look like the following:

r46 : T, R [hdp → temp21],
r46 [hn → 'Room 46 (conference room)'],
device137 : T, S [m → temp21],
temp21 : P, T [hu → dc]

In practice, the ontology for a given domain of application includes a finite set of concepts and properties. One can therefore build a context c_g by assigning the shortest possible UTF-8 string to all IRIs of this ontology (or set of ontologies). In Sect. 4, we present experimental results on the performances of this compaction technique.

Framing. JSON-LD framing is not part of the official W3C recommendation. The formalism we present in the following is based on the latest community draft for JSON-LD 1.1, as of December 2017 [25]. JSON-LD framing includes two aspects: frame matching and re-shaping, analogous to SPARQL's SELECT and CONSTRUCT clauses. In the following, we only consider frame matching.

Let V be the set of variables (equivalent to the set of SPARQL variables). Intuitively, a frame is a set of JSON-LD objects with variables.

Definition 5. *A JSON-LD frame object f^* is one of the following formulas:*

1. none, *which matches no JSON-LD node object;*
2. wildcard, *which matches any JSON-LD node object;*
3. $\text{id}^* : t_1, \ldots, t_l \, [p_1 \rightarrow \text{id}_1^*, \ldots, p_m \rightarrow \text{id}_m^*, p_{m+1} \rightarrow v_1, \ldots, p_n \rightarrow v_{n-m}]$;

where $\text{id}^*, \text{id}_i^* \in V \cup I \cup \{\text{none}, \text{wildcard}\}$. We denote the set of such formulas F^*.

A JSON-LD frame is a set of flagged JSON-LD frame objects, that is, of pairs $(f^*, b) \in F^* \times \{\text{true}, \text{false}\}$. The boolean flag b indicates that either all properties or at least one property of a frame object should match a node object. If b is *false*, any property can match. In the JSON-LD 1.1 specification, this flag is referred to as the 'require all' flag.

Example 4. The following frame should match any room that contains a sensor or an actuator (or both):

(room* : Room [hasDataPoint → dp*], *true*),
(device* : Sensor, Actuator [measures → dp*, actsOn → dp*], *false*),
(dp* [hasUnit → unit*], *true*)

The current JSON-LD 1.1 specification lacks clarity on how to match blank nodes. In the algorithm specification, as well in its reference implementation[4], a frame object identified by a blank node will only match node objects with the same blank node identifier. Yet, blank nodes are supposed to have a local scope, that is, they cannot be shared between RDF graphs. We therefore introduced variables, by analogy with SPARQL. In practice, when evaluating a frame against a graph, query variables can be defined as blank nodes that are disjoint with the set of blank nodes in the graph.

3.2   Semantics and Complexity

Given the transformation from Definition 2, it is straightforward to define JSON-LD entailment according to the well-defined RDF semantics [9,13]. We will focus here on the semantics of JSON-LD framing only. Although we borrowed aspects of F-logic in our formalism, F-structures and object semantics are not relevant in the present work.

Before defining the semantics of JSON-LD framing, we define the transformation σ_F from a JSON-LD frame ϕ to SPARQL. We use the algebraic syntax of Pérez et al. to express SPARQL graph patterns [21].

Definition 6. *Let ϕ be a frame, i.e. a set of pairs $(f_h^*, b_h), 1 \leq h \leq |\phi|$. The transformation function σ_F is defined as follows:*

$$\sigma_F(\phi) = P_1 \ AND \ \ldots \ AND \ P_{|\phi|} \tag{3}$$

where each P_h is the graph pattern

$$P_h = (((\text{id}^*, type, \text{t}_1) \ UNION \ \ldots \ UNION \ (\text{id}^*, type, \text{t}_\text{l})) \ AND \ P) \tag{4}$$

such that

$$P = \begin{cases} P_1 \ AND \ \ldots \ AND \ P_n, \text{ if } b_h \text{ is true} \\ P_1 \ UNION \ \ldots \ UNION \ P_n, \text{ otherwise} \end{cases} \tag{5}$$

---

[4] https://github.com/ruby-rdf/json-ld/.

where each $P_i, i \leq m$, is a graph pattern of the form

$$P_i = \begin{cases} (\text{id}^*, \text{p}_i, \text{id}_i^*), \text{ if id}_i^* \in (V \cup I) \\ (\text{id}^*, \text{p}_i, ?wildcard_i), \text{ if id}_i^* \text{ is wildcard} \\ (\text{id}^*, \text{p}_i, ?none_i) \text{ } FILTER \text{ } (\neg bound(?none_i)), \text{ if id}_i^* \text{ is none} \end{cases} \quad (6)$$

and each $P_i, i > m$ is the triple pattern $(\text{id}^*, \text{p}_i, \text{v}_{i-m})$.

Example 5. The frame of Example 4 maps to the following SPARQL query:

(((?room, type, Room) AND (?room, hasDataPoint, ?dp)) AND
(((?device, type, Sensor) UNION (?device, type, Actuator)) AND
((?device, measures, ?dp) UNION (?device, actsOn, ?dp))) AND
(dp?, hasUnit, ?unit))

The range of σ_F is comprised in the subset of SPARQL that includes three operators (UNION, AND, FILTER) and two filtering predicates ($\neg$, *bound*). However, the two are not equivalent. For instance, there is no frame ϕ such that $\sigma_F(\phi) = ((?s_1, ?p_1, ?o_1)$ UNION $(?s_2, ?p_2, ?o_2))$.

It is also interesting to note that, despite the existence of the frame object none which can exclude node objects, it is not necessary to include the operator NOT in the definition of σ_F.

The transformation σ_F allows us to base the semantics of JSON-LD framing on the semantics of SPARQL, which relies on the definition of a mapping μ and an evaluation function $[\![\cdot]\!]_G$ [21]. Here, we override the definition of μ as follows: a mapping $\mu : V \mapsto I \cup B$ is a partial function representing a match for a frame ϕ against a graph γ (a set of node objects). We also define the evaluation of ϕ against γ as a function, denoted *eval*.

Definition 6 translates the special formulas none and wildcard into SPARQL variables ($?none_i$, $?wildcard_i$) which are however irrelevant to define the semantics of framing. We therefore must define a projection of mappings on the set of variables only appearing in the original frame ϕ. We denote V_ϕ this set of variables and $\Pi_{V_\phi}(M)$ the projection on V_ϕ of every mapping $\mu \in M$ returned by the evaluation of $\sigma_F(\phi)$.

Definition 7. *Let ϕ be a frame, let γ be a graph.*

$$eval(\phi, \gamma) = \Pi_{V_\phi}([\![\sigma_F(\phi)]\!]_{\sigma_R(\gamma)}) \quad (7)$$

Example 6. Applying the room frame (Example 4) on the room graph (Example 1) should return the mapping μ, such that $\mu(\text{room}^*) = \text{r46}$, $\mu(\text{device}^*) = \text{device137}$, $\mu(\text{dp}^*) = \text{temp21}$ and $\mu(\text{unit}^*) = \text{degreeCelsius}$.

Proposition 1. *The semantics we define here is equivalent to the procedural semantics of the W3C JSON-LD 1.1 framing algorithm.*

Some elements exposed here differ from the JSON-LD 1.1 draft. For instance, we define the 'require all' flag on a per-object basis while the W3C algorithm defines it once for the whole frame. It is, however, possible to rewrite any frame as per Definition 5 as a (more verbose) frame ϕ such that all flags $b_h, 1 \le h \le |\phi|$, are set to the same value.

Similarly, for the sake of simplicity, we did not consider value pattern matching and identifier matching in our formalism. These aspects, however, are mostly syntactic sugar and do not influence the general semantics of framing.

To conclude with theoretical considerations, we give an insight into the complexity of JSON-LD framing evaluation. In particular, the next theorem shows that a SPARQL normal form can be computed in polynomial time for any JSON-LD frame. A normal form is a disjunction of UNION-free graph patterns.

Theorem 1. *Let ϕ be a frame. Let η be the number of frame objects in ϕ, such that the 'require all' flag is false, let l, n be the maximum number of types and properties (respectively) in a frame object of ϕ. A SPARQL normal form can be computed for $\sigma_F(\phi)$ in $O(\eta \cdot l \cdot n)$.*

Proof. As a preliminary, we recall that the AND and UNION operators are associative and commutative. Moreover, the following equivalence holds [21]: $(P_1 \text{ AND } (P_2 \text{ UNION } P_3)) \equiv ((P_1 \text{ AND } P_2) \text{ UNION } (P_1 \text{ AND } P_3))$.

More generally, one can observe that if P_1, P_2 are both normal forms with respectively i and j UNION-free patterns, then $(P_1 \text{ AND } P_2)$ has an equivalent normal form with $i \cdot j$ patterns. This applies in particular to any P_h as defined in Eq. 4 ($l \cdot n$ patterns).

$\sigma_F(\phi)$ can be rewritten by commuting AND clauses until there exists an index η, such that $\forall 1 \le h \le \eta, b_h$ is *false* and $\forall \eta < h \le |\phi|, b_h$ is *true*. Let $\overline{P_\eta}$ be the pattern $(P_{\eta+1} \text{ AND } \dots \text{ AND } P_{|\phi|})$. $\overline{P_\eta}$ is in normal form. Using the same observation as above, we can obtain a normal form NF_η for $(P_\eta \text{ AND } \overline{P_\eta})$. The same applies to $(P_{\eta-1} \text{ AND } \overline{P_{\eta-1}}) \equiv (P_{\eta-1} \text{ AND } \text{NF}_\eta)$, recursively. We can therefore obtain a normal form for $\sigma_F(\phi)$ in η iterations.

The UNION-free patterns we obtain from ϕ include only AND and FILTER operators (BGPs). Deciding whether a mapping is a solution to a BGP query is polynomial [21]. However, it becomes NP-complete if we include UNION patterns. JSON-LD framing is therefore equivalent to an intermediate subset of SPARQL that includes the UNION operator but for which the decision problem remains polynomial. In practice, this means that JSON-LD framing can be easily implemented on top of BGP processing.

3.3 Summary

Our primary motivation in the context of this paper is the exchange and processing of RDF data on embedded devices (MCUs). The main limitation of MCUs is the low amount of RAM available (8 to 64 kB). In this section, we highlighted two important aspects of JSON-LD that can be leveraged to reduce the memory footprint of RDF processing: (1) it is possible to process JSON-LD data in a compacted form, given a global context c_g and (2) JSON-LD framing is a lightweight alternative to SPARQL that can be reduced to BGP processing in polynomial time.

4   Experiments and Discussion

We implemented JSON-LD framing on the ESP8266. This implementation extends our previous work on the μRDF store, which already demonstrated the feasibility of processing BGPs on an MCU. As suggested in the previous section, frames are first pre-processed to obtain a normal form and then processed by the μRDF store. JSON-LD frames and graphs are processed in their compacted form, no transformation to RDF is required.

In the following, we concentrate on JSON-LD compaction. As underlined in Sect. 2, the state-of-the-art in binary formats for RDF includes two main approaches: HDT and RDF/EXI. JSON-LD compaction allows for a third alternative: encoding JSON-LD in its compacted form (using a global context) in a binary JSON format. The binary formats we selected for these experiments are EXI for JSON (EXI4JSON) and CBOR. EXI4JSON is an extension of EXI to represent JSON documents in binary XML [20].

Building a global context, as mentioned in Sect. 3.1, is somewhat arbitrary. For instance, one could either choose to include all ontological concepts exposed on the Semantic Web in a single context or tailor an application-specific context covering a limited set of ontologies. In our experiments, we generated two contexts for every test set. The first one acts as a 'minimal' context, for comparison purposes: for a test set with n distinct IRIs, the minimal context maps the n first UTF-8 characters to them. The second context acts as a more realistic one: for a test set with n distinct IRIs defined in m distinct vocabularies, the second context maps the $|vocab_1| + \ldots + |vocab_m|$ first UTF-8 characters to all IRIs found in the vocabularies. Compaction using this context will not perform as good as with the minimal context but it better estimates the performances one should expect in a production environment.

We compared the compaction performances of the three approaches on four data sets: a sample from the Billion Triples Challenge (BTCSAMPLE), a single sensor measurement (NODE), the output of a proxy service for sensor data (SSP) and an export of a building model from the Siemens Desigo CC platform (DESIGO). The first three data sets were provided by Hasemann et al. in the context of SPITFIRE. We added the last one to provide a comparison on real-world data, exported from a production environment. We provide statistics on these data sets on Table 1. For each of them, the set of ontologies we used to build a realistic JSON-LD context is as follows:

BTCSAMPLE – RDF, FOAF, DC, SIOC, SKOS, SWIVT;
NODE – RDF, RDFS, OWL, DC, SPITFIRE, SSNX, DUL, QUDT;
SSP – RDF, RDFS, OWL, DC, SPITFIRE, SSNX, DUL, SWEET;
DESIGO – RDF, CC, CCBA, SAREF, TD.

All data sets and context files can be found online[5].

---
[5] https://github.com/vcharpenay/urdf-store-exp/.

Table 1. Test set statistics

	BTCSAMPLE	NODE	SSP	DESIGO
Nb. of triples	174	73	4859	84908
Nb. of distinct subjects/nodes	174	26	1345	21527
Nb. of pieces	–	–	313	1843
Avg. nb. of triples (piecewise)	–	–	15	70
Min. nb. of triples (piecewise)	–	–	13	5
Max. nb. of triples (piecewise)	–	–	19	662

4.1 SPITFIRE Data Sets

The BTCSAMPLE data set includes 174 random triples from a large social network. All subject, predicate and object IRIs are disjoint. These IRIs come from a variety of vocabularies, such as FOAF[6], GeoNames[7] or SKOS[8]. The main purpose of BTCSAMPLE as a test set is to evaluate how the different approaches perform on IRI compaction, regardless of the data structure.

In contrast to BTCSAMPLE, NODE and SSP mostly use the SSNX vocabulary[9] to express the semantics of sensor measurements. The former is a small data set produced by one single sensor (73 triples) while the latter includes the measurements of hundreds of sensing devices (4859 triples). SSP shows many redundancies in the data. Both NODE and SSP are realistic WoT data sets.

4.2 Desigo CC Data Set

Our last data set, which we denote DESIGO, was generated from a simulated Siemens building managed by the Desigo CC platform, at a real scale. The data is exported from Desigo CC as a collection of WoT Thing Descriptions (TDs) [14]; the examples of Sect. 3 are taken from this data set. A TD is a document providing pointers to Web resources allowing a WoT client to interact with the server exposing them. These Web resources can e.g. encapsulate measurement values (room temperature reading), commands (start/stop ventilation) or events (fire alarm). The data set, which includes around ten thousand data points, is the sum of 1843 interlinked TDs.

In the Web of Things architecture, TD documents are not meant to be centralized in a unique data set. Instead, every IoT device should carry its own TD as a self-descriptive agent, so that machine-to-machine interaction is possible [16]. We therefore consider DESIGO both as a whole and as an aggregation of separate pieces of information, scattered across a network. Similarly, SSP

---

[6] http://xmlns.com/foaf/0.1/.
[7] http://www.geonames.org/ontology.
[8] http://www.w3.org/2004/02/skos/core.
[9] http://purl.oclc.org/NET/ssnx/ssn.

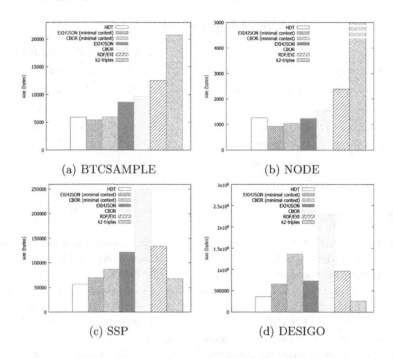

(a) BTCSAMPLE

(b) NODE

(c) SSP

(d) DESIGO

Fig. 1. Compaction results (whole data sets)

is an aggregation of sensor measurements, which could also be exchanged in a machine-to-machine fashion. This WoT principle drove our experiments, as later shown in Sect. 4.3.

Desigo CC includes a core object-oriented data model, which has been formalized in OWL (CC)[10]. The CCBA ontology[11] is a specialization of CC for building automation, with alignments with the SAREF ontology[12].

4.3   Results

We compared the following compaction methods: HDT with bitmap encoding, HDT with k^2-triples encoding, JSON-LD with minimal context (both with EXI4JSON and CBOR encoding), JSON-LD with ontology-based context (again with EXI4JSON and CBOR encoding) and RDF/EXI. The results are shown on Figs. 1a–d.

What our results first show is that k^2-triples, although highly efficient on large datasets, performs poorly on small ones: on NODE, the size for k^2-triples is 16 kB while all others remain under 3 kB. This observation consolidates our previous results on the μRDF store. Moreover, on all data sets, RDF/XML is outperformed by other approaches. In particular, it is outperformed by HDT,

---

[10] Currently in the process of being publicly released.

[11] Idem.

[12] https://w3id.org/saref.

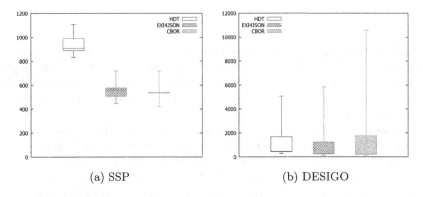

(a) SSP   (b) DESIGO

Fig. 2. Compaction result distributions (piecewise data sets)

contrary to what earlier results suggested [15]. The difference in performances most likely rests on the fact that EXI performs good on data sets with many non-string literals (e.g. numeric sensor values), which happens not to be the case in these data sets. It is interesting to note, however, that EXI performs better than CBOR on compressing structural patterns (as in SSP).

HDT was originally designed to compress very large datasets but it also performs good on medium size data sets, like SSP and DESIGO. It is more than twice as performant as EXI4JSON and by far better than CBOR (which is consistently outperformed by EXI4JSON). However, on the small NODE dataset, EXI4JSON and HDT have comparable results, regardless of the context used. The results on BTCSAMPLE illustrate the impact of choosing a context on the overall compaction performances: the minimal context allows for 37% compaction compared to the ontology-based context (5409 kB/8639 kB). Indeed, the higher the variety of IRIs used in an application, the more arduous it is to design a context that fits.

JSON-LD compaction shows best results on datasets of less than hundred triples, the typical size of a TD document carried by a constrained WoT agent. Figure 2a and b show how EXI4JSON and CBOR are more efficient than HDT on SSP and DESIGO, when pieces of data are serialized separately (using the same ontology-based context). For median results on DESIGO, EXI4JSON and CBOR achieve a compaction ratio of 58% and 50% compared to HDT (respectively). Compaction ratios on SSP are similar: 62% and 59%. Interestingly, CBOR performs better on median results but it shows a higher variance than EXI4JSON. One can also note that the DESIGO data set appears skewed towards small TDs. The reason is that many TDs in the data set are logical entities, without any Web resource attached (and thus relatively small TDs). It is the case for e.g. buildings, floors, rooms, etc.

The overhead of HDT on small data sets is due to the dictionary it embeds in all individual documents (mostly redundant). One could note that the principle of defining a global context for a set of documents could also apply to HDT dictionaries. However, splitting a dictionary into global and local parts would lower the compaction ratio and require decompression on the MCU before processing (e.g. a SPARQL or JSON-LD framing query).

5   Conclusion

Throughout this paper, we considered the use of JSON-LD as a serialization format for embedded devices (MCUs). Our formalization of JSON-LD highlights how compaction can address the verbosity of RDF, by defining a global JSON-LD context shared across agents in a network, and how framing extends SPARQL basic graph patterns.

This work follows on from of our development of the μRDF store, an RDF store for MCUs. We regard JSON-LD framing as an important building block for autonomous systems, a driver of machine-to-machine communication.

Experimentally, we found that JSON-LD compaction, coupled with EXI4-JSON or CBOR, can lead to compaction ratios around 50–60% compared to the state-of-the-art (HDT) for small WoT data sets (around hundred triples). JSON-LD has already been adopted by many providers in the Web of data but the results we presented in this paper suggest that it might as well become a reference in the Web of Things.

References

1. Álvarez-García, S., Brisaboa, N.R., Fernández, J.D., Martínez-Prieto, M.A.: Compressed k2-Triples for Full-In-Memory RDF Engines. CoRR abs/1105.4004 (2011)
2. Atzori, L., Iera, A., Morabito, G.: The internet of things: a survey. Comput. Netw. 54(15), 2787–2805 (2010)
3. Boldt, D., Hasemann, H., Karnstedt, M., Kroeller, A., von der Weth, C.: SPARQL for networks of embedded systems, pp. 93–100. IEEE, December 2015
4. Bormann, C., Ersue, M., Keranen, A.: Terminology for Constrained-Node Networks, May 2014. https://tools.ietf.org/html/rfc7228
5. Charpenay, V., Käbisch, S., Kosch, H.: μRDF store: towards extending the semantic web to embedded devices. In: Blomqvist, E., Hose, K., Paulheim, H., Lawrynowicz, A., Ciravegna, F., Hartig, O. (eds.) ESWC 2017. LNCS, vol. 10577, pp. 76–80. Springer, Cham (2017). https://doi.org/10.1007/978-3-319-70407-4_15
6. Fernández, J.D., Llaves, A., Corcho, O.: Efficient RDF interchange (ERI) format for RDF data streams. In: Mika, P., et al. (eds.) ISWC 2014. LNCS, vol. 8797, pp. 244–259. Springer, Cham (2014). https://doi.org/10.1007/978-3-319-11915-1_16
7. Fernández, J.D., Martínez-Prieto, M.A., Gutierrez, C.: Compact representation of large RDF data sets for publishing and exchange. In: Patel-Schneider, P.F., Pan, Y., Hitzler, P., Mika, P., Zhang, L., Pan, J.Z., Horrocks, I., Glimm, B. (eds.) ISWC 2010. LNCS, vol. 6496, pp. 193–208. Springer, Heidelberg (2010). https://doi.org/10.1007/978-3-642-17746-0_13
8. Guinard, D.: A web of things application architecture - integrating the real-world into the web. Ph.D. thesis, ETH Zurich, Zurich, Switzerland, August 2011
9. Gutierrez, C., Hurtado, C., Mendelzon, A.O.: Foundations of semantic web databases, p. 95. ACM Press (2004)
10. Hartig, O.: An overview on execution strategies for linked data queries. Datenbank-Spektrum 13(2), 89–99 (2013)
11. Hasemann, H., Kroller, A., Pagel, M.: RDF provisioning for the internet of things, pp. 143–150 (2012)

12. Hasemann, H., Kröller, A., Pagel, M.: The Wiselib TupleStore: a modular RDF database for the internet of things. CoRR, abs/1402.7228, March 2014
13. Hayes, P.J., Patel-Schneider, P.: RDF 1.1 Semantics. http://www.w3.org/TR/rdf11-mt/
14. Käbisch, S., Kamiya, T.: Web of Things (WoT) Thing Description. W3C First Public Working Draft, W3C, September 2017. https://www.w3.org/TR/wot-thing-description/
15. Käbisch, S., Peintner, D., Anicic, D.: Standardized and efficient RDF encoding for constrained embedded networks. In: Gandon, F., Sabou, M., Sack, H., d'Amato, C., Cudré-Mauroux, P., Zimmermann, A. (eds.) ESWC 2015. LNCS, vol. 9088, pp. 437–452. Springer, Cham (2015). https://doi.org/10.1007/978-3-319-18818-8_27
16. Kazuo, K., Kovatsch, M., Davuluru, U.: Web of Things (WoT) Architecture. W3C First Public Working Draft, W3C, September 2017. https://www.w3.org/TR/wot-architecture/
17. Kifer, M., Lausen, G., Wu, J.: Logical foundations of object-oriented and frame-based languages. J. ACM **42**(4), 741–843 (1995)
18. Longley, D., Kellogg, G., Lanthaler, M., Sporny, M.: JSON-LD 1.0 Processing Algorithms and API. W3C Recommendation, W3C, January 2014. https://www.w3.org/TR/json-ld-api/
19. Loseto, G., Ieva, S., Gramegna, F., Ruta, M., Scioscia, F., Di Sciascio, E.: Linked data (in low-resource) platforms: a mapping for constrained application protocol. In: Groth, P., Simperl, E., Gray, A., Sabou, M., Krötzsch, M., Lecue, F., Flöck, F., Gil, Y. (eds.) ISWC 2016. LNCS, vol. 9982, pp. 131–139. Springer, Cham (2016). https://doi.org/10.1007/978-3-319-46547-0_14
20. Peintner, D., Brutzman, D.: EXI for JSON (EXI4JSON). W3C Working Draft, W3C, August 2016. https://www.w3.org/TR/exi-for-json/
21. Pérez, J., Arenas, M., Gutierrez, C.: Semantics and complexity of SPARQL. In: Cruz, I., Decker, S., Allemang, D., Preist, C., Schwabe, D., Mika, P., Uschold, M., Aroyo, L.M. (eds.) ISWC 2006. LNCS, vol. 4273, pp. 30–43. Springer, Heidelberg (2006). https://doi.org/10.1007/11926078_3
22. Pfisterer, D., Romer, K., Bimschas, D., Kleine, O., Mietz, R., Truong, C., Hasemann, H., Kröller, A., Pagel, M., Hauswirth, M., Karnstedt, M., Leggieri, M., Passant, A., Richardson, R.: SPITFIRE: toward a semantic web of things. IEEE Commun. Mag. **49**(11), 40–48 (2011)
23. Shelby, Z.: Embedded web services. IEEE Wirel. Commun. **17**(6), 52–57 (2010)
24. Speicher, S., Arwe, J., Malhotra, A.: Linked Data Platform 1.0, February 2015. https://www.w3.org/TR/ldp/
25. Sporny, M., Kellogg, G., Longley, D., Lanthaler, M.: JSON-LD Framing 1.1. W3C Draft Community Group Report, October 2017. https://json-ld.org/spec/latest/json-ld-framing/
26. Sporny, M., Longley, D., Kellogg, G., Lanthaler, M., Lindström, N.: JSON-LD 1.0 - A JSON-based Serialization for Linked Data. W3C Recommendation, W3C, January 2014. http://www.w3.org/TR/json-ld/
27. Trifa, V.M.: Building blocks for a participatory web of things: devices, infrastructures, and programming frameworks. Ph.D. thesis, ETH Zurich, Zurich, Switzerland, August 2011
28. Verborgh, R., et al.: Querying datasets on the web with high availability. In: Mika, P., et al. (eds.) ISWC 2014. LNCS, vol. 8796, pp. 180–196. Springer, Cham (2014). https://doi.org/10.1007/978-3-319-11964-9_12

User-Centric Ontology Population

Kenneth Clarkson, Anna Lisa Gentile$^{(\boxtimes)}$ ⓘ, Daniel Gruhl, Petar Ristoski ⓘ,
Joseph Terdiman, and Steve Welch

IBM Research Almaden, San Jose, CA, USA
{klclarks,dgruhl,welchs}@us.ibm.com,
{annalisa.gentile,petar.ristoski,joseph.terdiman1}@ibm.com

Abstract. Ontologies are a basic tool to formalize and share knowledge. However, very often the conceptualization of a specific domain depends on the particular user's needs. We propose a methodology to perform user-centric ontology population that efficiently includes human-in-the-loop at each step. Given the existence of suitable target ontologies, our methodology supports the alignment of concepts in the user's conceptualization with concepts of the target ontologies, using a novel hierarchical classification approach. Our methodology also helps the user to build, alter and grow their initial conceptualization, exploiting both the target ontologies and new facts extracted from unstructured data. We evaluate our approach on a real-world example in the healthcare domain, in which adverse phrases for drug reactions, as extracted from user blogs, are aligned with MedDRA concepts. The evaluation shows that our approach has high efficacy in assisting the user to both build the initial ontology (*HITS@10* up to 99.5%) and to maintain it (*HITS@10* up to 99.1%).

1 Introduction

Maintaining data in a structured and machine-readable form allows easy data sharing between humans and software agents, and also enables other tasks related to data handling, including data analysis and data reuse to name a few. In some domains where the majority of data is only available as unstructured text, extracting such structured knowledge constitutes a crucial step.

Many available tools extract items of interest (mainly in the form of named entities) from free text. The extracted instances can be maintained at varying degrees of complexity: as simple as flat dictionaries, or as rich as a structured concept organization in the form of an ontology.

While ontologies are an excellent means to formalize and share knowledge, it is rare to have a single unique conceptualization of a domain: depending on the field, on the task at hand, and on the specific user, the best representation can vary, in some cases extensively. It is well known that human annotation tasks intrinsically carry a level of disagreement among annotators, regardless of their level of domain expertise [1,43]. While it is important to maintain the user conceptualization of the domain, connecting it to any existing and well-defined

© Springer International Publishing AG, part of Springer Nature 2018
A. Gangemi et al. (Eds.): ESWC 2018, LNCS 10843, pp. 112–127, 2018.
https://doi.org/10.1007/978-3-319-93417-4_8

ontology in the field is one of the paramount principles of the Semantic Web movement.

The challenge is to achieve the right balance between the user conceptualization and available knowledge, enabling the population and maintenance of the user ontology with both relevant facts already available in structured form (e.g. other ontologies), as well as the new extracted facts from unstructured data.

Most of the ontology population solutions proposed in the literature focus on solutions for open domain problems, where it is not crucial to achieve perfect performance. However, in many domains near-perfection is required. For example, many biomedical applications have near 0% error tolerance, despite datasets full of uncertainty, incompleteness and noise. Furthermore, some problems in the medical domain are quite challenging, making the application of fully automated models difficult, or at least raising questions on the quality of results. Consequently, efficiently including a domain expert as an integral part of the system not only greatly enhances the knowledge discovery process pipeline [14,15], but can in certain circumstances be legally or ethically required.

We propose a methodology to perform user-centric ontology population that efficiently includes human-in-the-loop at each step: the user is assisted in building, connecting and maintaining their conceptualization of the domain, while taking advantage of any already available ontology.

Given initial user data comprising a number of concepts and their initial instances, and assuming the existence of candidate ontologies for the alignment, available either publicly (the Linked Open Data cloud) or within the enterprise, our methodology supports three main steps: (i) selecting the relevant ones (*target ontologies*); (ii) aligning the concepts in the user's conceptualization with concepts of the target ontologies, using a novel hierarchical classification approach; (iii) assisting the user to build, change, and grow their initial ontology, by (respectively) creating new concepts, splitting or merging concepts, and adding new instances to each concept, all via exploitation of both target ontologies and new facts extracted from unstructured data. Each step includes human-in-the-loop. That is, the methodology is designed to efficiently assist the user rather than fully automate the process.

The contribution of this work is threefold. First, our approach does not require the user to have any expertise with the Semantic Web:[1] the input data is a set of coherent concepts defined with only some initial instances that can be provided as a simple populated taxonomy, or even as disconnected groups. These instances are used to identify available target ontologies. Second, we propose a novel hierarchical classification method that allows mapping the user data to the target ontology. To the best of our knowledge, this is the first method for ontology population that builds hierarchical classification models that are dynamically refined and based on user interaction. Finally, the method does not require any training material (since it only exploits the target ontology), nor any

---

[1] It is expected the user to be able to perform simple browsing and navigation through data, but no knowledge of Semantic Web Technologies is needed, e.g., RDF, SPARQL etc.

NLP processing or linguistic features. Therefore, the method is also potentially flexible with respect to different domains and languages.

The main advantage of our approach is that the user has full control of their level of involvement, with a trade-off on the accuracy of results, so that the more precise and granular the representation needs to be, the more they can be in the loop. We test the approach on a real-world example in the setting of Adverse Drug Reactions. Starting from a concepts representation extracted from user medical blogs,[2] we identify an available ontology, namely MedDRA [2], within the enterprise knowledge base, and map the user's initial concepts to the target ontology. In the experiment, a user concept is a group of coherent phrases, e.g. *teeth grinding, teeth clenching, clench my teeth, jaw clenching, clinching my jaw*, which we help to align to concepts in MedDRA, in this case "Bruxism". We show that we can assist the user with the alignment with $HITS@10 = 99.5\%$ on the most general level of the ontology and $HITS@10 = 86.5\%$ on the most granular level of the ontology. We also evaluate the approach for adding new instances, achieving $HITS@10 = 99.1\%$ on the most general level of the ontology and $HITS@10 = 91.27\%$ on the most granular level of the ontology.

In the following, we give an overview of related work in Sect. 2; we formally define the problem of user-centric ontology population and describe our solution in Sect. 3; and we test our solution in the medical domain, Sect. 4.

2   State of the Art

There is a vast literature devoted to ontology population from text, with many established initiatives to foster research on the topic, such as the Knowledge Base Population task at TAC,[3] the TREC Knowledge Base Acceleration track,[4] and the Open Knowledge Extraction Challenge [24]. In these initiatives, systems are compared on the basis of recognizing individuals belonging to a few selected ontology classes, spanning from the common Person, Place and Organization [36], to more specific classes such as Facility, Weapon, Vehicle [8], Role [24] or Drug [31], among others.

FRED and Framester [11] and [10] are an established example of a comprehensive solution to the problem. The tools transform text in an internal ontology representation and then attempt to align it with available Linked Data. FRED is a general purpose machine reader, mostly based on core NLP tools, which can potentially process text from any domain and in many different languages (bounded to the availability of NLP components). In the same direction, there is a plethora of tools for automatically detecting named entities in free text and aligning them to a predefined knowledge base, i.e., Spotlight [19], X-Lisa [44], Babelfy [21]. However, all these tools are able to identify only instances that already exist in a knowledge base.

---

[2] www.askapatient.com.

[3] http://www.nist.gov/tac/2015/KBP.

[4] http://trec-kba.org/.

Some of the earliest approaches for ontology population from text are based on pattern matching, string similarity functions, and external glossaries and knowledge bases. Velardi et al. [37,38] develop OntoLearn which is one of the first tools for learning and populating ontologies from text. The approach heavily uses NLP parsers, pattern matching, and external glossaries, in combination with human assistance. Similar approaches are presented in [3,18]. Cimiano and Völker [4] describe an unsupervised approach, called Class-Word, for ontology population based on vector-feature similarity between each concept and a term to be classified. The feature vectors are generated from the text corpus. The approach assumes that the entity and the concept usually appear together in the same sentences. The approach is extended in Tanev and Magnini [35], called Class-Example, which learns a classification model from a set of classified terms, exploiting lexico-syntactic features. They upgrade the previous approach by adding features extracted from dependency parse trees. Giuliano and Gliozzo [12] propose an approach that is based on the assumption that entities that occur in similar contexts belong to the same concept(s), and so it counts the shared n-grams in the context of the entities. An overview of pattern-based approaches is given in a survey by Petasise et al. [25].

Several works use machine learning for ontology population. HYENA [42] and FIGER [17] are two examples of fine-grained multi-label classifiers for named entity types based on hierarchical taxonomies derived from YAGO. Ling and Weld [17] also release the benchmark dataset annotated with 112 classes from YAGO. Typically, the models use standard NLP features extracted from text, or more sophisticated features such as type relational phrases: either their type signatures and disjointness constraints [23], or type correlation based on co-occurring entities [27].

Many approaches for ontology population are based on word and graph embedding models. WSABIE [41] adopts weighted approximate pairwise loss to learn embeddings of features and types in a common feature space. Entities that share the same type appear close to each other in the embedded space. Similarly, FIGMENT [40] proposes a combination of global and context model, where the global model performs global embedding over the whole corpus using multilayer perceptron, while the context model focuses on small context windows sizes. Ristoski et al. [29] use standard word embeddings and graph embeddings to align instances extracted from the Common Crawl[5] to the DBpedia ontology.

The use of deep learning models has also been explored for this task. Dong et al. [9] propose the first deep learning architecture for entity typing. The architecture consist of two models. The mention model uses recurrent neural networks to recursively obtain the vector representation of an entity mention from the words it contains. The context model, on the other hand, employs multilayer perceptrons to obtain the hidden representation for contextual information of a mention. The approach is evaluated on 22 general types from DBpedia. Shimoaka et al. [32,33] propose a very simple neural network, using averaging encoder, LSTM encoder, and attentive encoder, for computing context representations.

---

[5] http://webdatacommons.org/isadb/index.html.

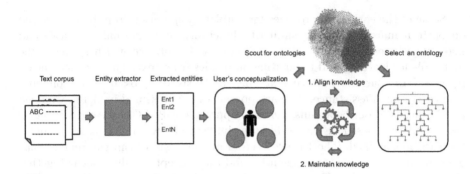

Fig. 1. System architecture. Complete workflow of the proposed methodology for ontology population.

Similarly, Yaghoobzadeh et al. [39] propose a convolutional neural network for entity typing. Both approaches are evaluated on 112 entity types. Murty et al. [22] present TypeNet, a dataset of entity types consisting of over 1941 types organized in a hierarchy, on which they train several neural models for entity typing.

None of these methods take into consideration the hierarchical structure of the ontology, and for all of them the number of types is relatively small and within a general open domain. In this paper, we present an approach that exploits such hierarchical structure, which we evaluate on an ontology with significantly more concepts than related work.

3   Approach

Input. The input of our approach is a set of example entities within a particular domain, usually extracted from a coherent textual corpus. Given a textual corpus, we assume there is a domain entity extractor (specifically we used SPOT [5]) that produces the set of relevant entities in the corpus $I_U = i_1, i_2, \ldots, i_n$. The user refines this set by organizing all instances in I_U in *concepts*. The result is a finite set of user-defined concepts $C_u = c_{u1}, c_{u2}, \ldots, c_{un}$ where each concept contains at least one instance. Using the user-defined conceptualization C_u, we scout for ontology candidates that can fit the user data.

Alignment. After a target ontology C_T is selected, our goal is to align C_u to C_T. The alignment can be performed at different granularity: given the depth L (or number of levels from root to leaves) of the target ontology, the user can specify the desired level for the alignment, and our method will use as target concepts all concepts $l_{CT} = c_{ct_1}, c_{ct_2}, \ldots, c_{ct_n}$ at level l.

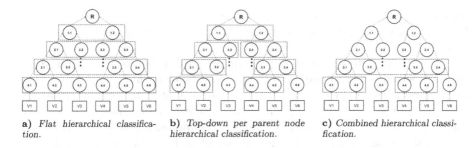

a) *Flat hierarchical classification.*

b) *Top-down per parent node hierarchical classification.*

c) *Combined hierarchical classification.*

Fig. 2. Hierarchical classification for ontology population.

Maintenance. Once the initial alignment is done, we support the maintenance of user knowledge by providing functions for adding new instances, splitting or merging concepts and creating new concepts.

Figure 1 illustrates the overall design of the proposed system.

3.1 Aligning User's Conceptualization with a Target Ontology

We identify available knowledge using simple collective instance matching between user data and a repository of ontologies. From the repository, either publicly available (such as the Linked Open Data cloud) or proprietary, the top N matching ontologies are presented to the user, who chooses a target ontology C_T. This step can be performed using many alternative state-of-the-art methods [19,28,30]; in this work we consider this step as given, and focus on the alignment.

Three novel machine learning approaches are proposed for hierarchical classification, inspired by existing top-down hierarchical classification methods [34]. Considering the user data as "new instances," the approaches try to identify the concepts in the target ontologies that represent the best match. To do so, we build machine learning models that use the instances of the target ontology as training data (completely unsupervised), and exploit domain-specific word embeddings as features.

In the first solution, we perform a flat hierarchical classification. Given C_u, and considering user-chosen level l of the ontology, we build one classifier with as many classes as concepts at level l, using the leaves of each concept as instances for training the classifier. The architecture is shown in Fig. 2a. This model is rather simple, and it achieves high performance in the upper levels of the hierarchy. However, in the lower levels of the ontology, when the number of classes rapidly increases, the complexity of the model rises, and the performance drops.

The second solution is a top-down model, where we build a local classifier for each parent node. Given C_u, and considering user-chosen level l of the ontology, the approach builds a classifier for each parent node, starting from the top of the hierarchy to level $l-1$, using all children nodes as classes, and their corresponding leaves as instances to train the model. The architecture is shown in Fig. 2b. This approach can easily cope with a large number of classes in the lower levels of the hierarchy; however, the errors are propagated from the top to the bottom of the ontology.

To circumvent this drawback, we propose a third hierarchical architecture (Fig. 2c), which is a combination of the previous two. Given C_u, and considering user-chosen level l of the ontology, the approach builds (i) a flat classifier for level $l-1$ of the ontology, and (ii) a classifier for each parent node at level $l-1$ using the concepts of the l level as classes. This approach is very effective when there is significant difference in the number of nodes between the l and $l-1$ level of the ontology, for two reasons: (i) the flat classifier performs well on level $l-1$, which has smaller number of classes; (ii) the per-parent node classifier will only be affected by the errors propagated from the previous level, rather than from the top of the hierarchy.

As classification methods we use standard machine-learning models, i.e., Support Vector Machines, Logistic Regression, and Random Forests, and state-of-the-art deep learning models, i.e., Convolutional Neural Networks.

To perform the final alignment for each user concept $c_u = i_{u1}, i_{u2}, \ldots, i_{un}$, we classify each instance of c_u into concepts at target level l of the ontology, and choose the final assignment by majority vote on all instances of c_u, weighting each of them by the class probability distribution returned by the classifier.

The user can define their level of involvement by defining a confidence threshold for each level in the hierarchy: whenever the confidence of the approach is below the given threshold, the system displays top-N candidates to the user who can manually select the desired alignment.

3.2   Ontology Maintenance

Once the alignment has been completed, we provide functions for maintaining the created knowledge base, such as adding instances, adding new concepts and merging/splitting concepts. These functions have been shown to be of a high importance, because of the continuous need to add new data as well as to take into account changes in the user conceptualization over time.

Adding New Instances. When new instances appear, we use the same approaches proposed in Sect. 3.1 to align them to the user's conceptualization. In this case, the models only consider the concepts defined by the user. When an instance doesn't fit any of the user-defined concepts, a new concept is added to the user's conceptualization (with the "Adding New Concepts" function), which is then aligned to the target ontology.

Adding New Concepts. To decide if there is a need for a new concept in the user representation, we follow an approach similar to the one presented in [7], i.e., using entropy as uncertainty measure for the classifier's predictions. Given the class probability distribution $[P(C_1|x) \ldots P(C_k|x)]$ of existing classes k, for a new instance x, for a given machine learning approach, we decide that we need to generate a new class if the class probabilities entropy is larger than 1.0:

$$E(x) = \sum_{i=0}^{k} P(C_i|x) * \log_2 P(C_i|x) > 1 \tag{1}$$

Whenever the entropy is high, we inform the user that there might be the need to introduce a new concept. Using the hierarchical classification models, we suggest potential new candidate concepts retrieved from the target ontology.

Merging Concepts. The action of merging concepts is trivial: if two user-defined concepts are aligned to the same target ontology concept, then the user concepts are merged.

Reassigning Instances. As the user conceptualization grows by adding new instances and new concepts, the user's view is also evolving, so reorganization of the instances might be needed. To assist the user in this step, we train the hierarchical classification model on all the instances in the user's conceptualization data, and then we use the model to classify all the instances. Analyzing the class prediction distribution, we can identify two types of candidates for reassigning: (i) Misclassifying an instance indicates that the instance might be an outlier in the currently assigned concept, implying that the instance is assigned in the current concept because of a user error; (ii) High entropy (see Eq. 1) indicates that the instance might fit better in a different concept than the current one. The system presents the suggestions to the user to decide if the instances need to be reassigned. When instances are reassigned, the model is retrained on the updated conceptualization. The stopping criterion for reassignment is that there are no more updates in the concepts.

4   Experiments

The goal of the experiments is to (i) test the performance of the novel alignment strategy (Sect. 4.1), and (ii) test the effectiveness of the ontology maintenance steps: adding new instances to existing user concepts (Sect. 4.2), detecting when a new concept should be added to the user model (Sect. 4.2), and suggesting when a concept should be split (Sect. 4.2).

All the experiments were carried out in the medical domain, specifically tackling the problem of Adverse Drug Reactions, for which we worked with a medical doctor to create a manually annotated gold standard dataset. Starting from user blogs extracted from http://www.askapatient.com (a forum where patients report their experience with medication drugs), we extracted all instances referring to adverse drug events, grouped the instances referring to the same adverse event into concepts, and aligned them to the MedDRA ontology [2]. MedDRA is a rich and standardized medical terminology organized in 5 levels, arranged from very general to very specific concepts: the fifth level contains 95, 061 leaf instances. The user data contains 203 concepts (adverse drug reactions), each of them containing several different phrases to refer to each concept, for a total of 3, 262 instances. The 203 concepts have been manually aligned to MedDRA, using a total of 169 concepts at the lowest level (some of the user concepts are aligned to the same MedDRA concept). The details for the user's dataset and the MedDRA dataset per level are shown in Table 1.

Table 1. Datasets statistics. Total number of concepts at each level of MedDRA and the portion used in the gold standard alignment.

	MedDRA	User's conceptualization
#level1	27	17
#level2	304	62
#level3	1,444	106
#level4	20,935	169
#Instances	95,061	3,262

4.1 Aligning User's Conceptualization with a Target Ontology

Given each user concept, the task is to identify, if it exists, a concept in the target ontology that identifies it. We assess the performance of our proposed methods against the gold standard dataset, and compare them against different baseline methods. To evaluate the approaches, we use the metric HITS@K, which measures if the correct alignment is in the top-K ranked results of the approach.

We implemented three baselines for comparison:

String-based average-link matching. Given a user concept c_u, we calculate the similarity to each concept c_t at a given level of the hierarchy (Eq. 2), using a Lucene[6] token-based similarity score with edit distance of 2 and tf-idf weighting. We then rank the results and select the top-N classes.

$$sim(c_u, c_t) = \frac{1}{|c_u||c_t|} \sum_{i=1}^{|c_u|} \sum_{j=1}^{|c_t|} sim(x_{ci}, x_{cj}) \tag{2}$$

Word embeddings. To build the word embedding we first collected a domain-specific text, i.e., patient reports about adverse drug reaction for more than 2,000 drugs, retrieved from www.askapatient.com, the ADE corpus [13], and the *EMEA* dataset[7] (European Medicines Agency documents). We use the corpora of sentences to build both CBOW and Skip-Gram models with the default parameters proposed in [20].[8] Given a user-defined group c_u, we calculate the similarity to each concept c_t on a given level of the hierarchy, using Eq. 2, where the similarity between two instances is calculated as a cosine similarity between the averaged vectors of all the words in the instances.

---

[6] https://lucene.apache.org/.

[7] http://opus.lingfil.uu.se/EMEA.php.

[8] Additionally we fix window size = 5; dimensions = 200; number of iterations = 15; negative sampling for optimization; negative samples = 25; average input vector for CBOW.

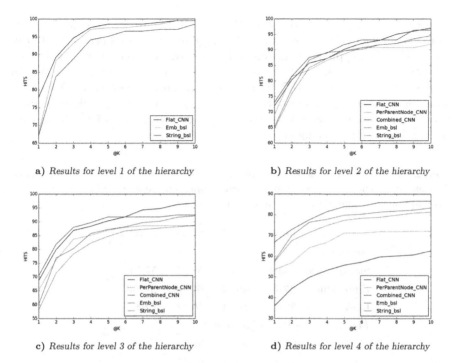

a) *Results for level 1 of the hierarchy*   **b)** *Results for level 2 of the hierarchy*

c) *Results for level 3 of the hierarchy*   **d)** *Results for level 4 of the hierarchy*

Fig. 3. Results per level of the hierarchy. Each plot shows the results for the two baselines, and the best performing models for the three hierarchical classification approaches.

LDA. We use the Stanford Labeled LDA tool [26] to build a supervised topic model, using the nodes in each level of the hierarchy as labels. To select the top-N classes for each user-defined group, we perform majority vote using the topic probabilities as weights.

Our three methods (Sect. 3.1) are not bound to the choice of the specific classifier. We use the instances of the target ontology to train each classifier, which is then used to classify the user's concepts. We report the performances for the following classifiers: Support Vector Machines (SVM) with RBF kernel, Random Forests (RF), Logistic Regression (LR), and Convolutional Neural Network (CNN). All classifiers use the domain-specific word2vec word embedding as features, the same as the baseline method. The architecture of the CNN model is inspired by Collobert et al. [6] and Kim [16], which has shown high performances in many NLP tasks.[9]

---

[9] We selected the following parameters for the CNN model: an input embedding layer, 4 convolutional layers followed by max-pooling layers, a fully connected softmax layer, rectified linear units, filter windows of 2, 3, 4, 5 with 100 feature maps each, dropout rate of 0.2 and mini-batch size of 50. For the embedding layer we use the word2vec embeddings used in the baseline approach to initialize the weighing matrix. We train 100 epochs with early stopping.

Figure 3 shows the results for HITS@1 to HITS@10 for each level of the hierarchy. For each of the three hierarchical approaches we report the best classifier.[10] The LDA approach performs rather poorly, therefore we exclude it from the plots. The HITS@1 results for all approaches are shown in Table 2. As the curves show (Fig. 3), while HITS@1 results (fully automated approach) are very encouraging, including human-in-the-loop (proposing the 10 most likely options) increases the performance up to 99.5% accuracy (on level 1 of the hierarchy) which is desirable in this domain.

Table 2. HITS@1 results for the baseline approaches and the three hierarchical classification approaches. The best results for each approach are marked in bold. The best overall approach is marked in bold and asterisk.

	Level 1	Level 2	Level 3	Level 4
Baselines				
String-based	66.99	64.53	58.12	57.14
Embeddings	**67.54**	**65.05**	**60.09**	**57.63**
LDA	33.52	28.23	10.83	7.64
Flat hierarchical classification				
SVM	68.47	60.59	56.15	/
RF	72.9	69.45	61.57	/
LR	71.92	70.44	68.47	/
CNN	**77.83**	**71.92**	**68.62**	35.96
Top-down per parent node hierarchical classification				
SVM	68.47	42.85	16.26	5.41
RF	72.9	38.37	22.16	12.31
LR	71.92	58.12	52.38	50
CNN	**77.83**	**69.07**	**65.22**	**53.46**
Combined hierarchical classification				
SVM	68.47	66.92	58.64	46.03
RF	72.9	5.9	32.5	18.43
LR	71.92	70.59	69.24	63.25
CNN	***77.83**	***73.05**	***70.39**	***66.78**

We can observe that all three approaches outperform the baseline methods, with a larger margin as we move down in the hierarchy. The word embeddings approach outperforms the string-based baseline approach on all levels. The CNN classifier outperforms the standard classifiers, although Logistic Regression

---

[10] Note that for the first level we report only the results for the flat hierarchical classification approach, because the results are the same for all three approaches.

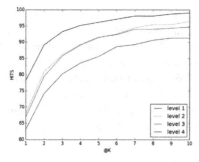

Fig. 4. HITS@10 results for adding new instances per level.

achieves comparable performance. It is noteworthy that the flat hierarchical classification approach performs rather well on the first 3 levels, however the performance drops at level 4, where the number of classes is significantly higher. Furthermore, we were not able to build flat SVM, RF and LR models for the lowest level of the hierarchy, as the number of class labels is rather high, the models ran out of memory. The top-down per parent node approach shows comparable results for HITS@1, however the propagation of errors from the previous levels leads to poor performances for HITS@10, i.e., if an instance is incorrectly classified in level $l - 1$, in level l the HITS will not increase when k increases because the model cannot find the correct concept in the ontology. The combined hierarchical classification approach outperforms all the others on all levels of the hierarchy.

4.2   Ontology Maintenance

Adding New Instances. In this experiment the goal was to add new instances to the user's knowledge base. To do so, we first built a CNN model for each level of the already aligned user hierarchy. Then we retrieved additional 298 instances of Adverse Drug Events from www.askapatient.com, which were not included in the initial data, and used the previously built model to assign each of them in the user's knowledge base.

The results for HITS@10 at each level of the hierarchy are shown in Fig. 4. The results show that we were able to classify the instances in the correct user concepts with HITS@10 = 99.1% on the most general level, and HITS@10 = 91.27% on the lowest level of the hierarchy.

Adding New Concepts. In this experiment we evaluated the model's ability to notify the user that a new concept should be introduced, i.e., a new instance doesn't fit in any of the defined concepts, therefore a new concept should be added. To do so, we selected 500 instances from the MedDRA ontology that don't belong to any of the user's concepts, i.e., positive instances for which the model is expected to create a new concept, and 500 instances that belonged to some of the user's concepts, i.e., negative instances for which the model shouldn't create a new concept.[11] Then we used the previously built CNN model for the last level of the hierarchy to classify the set of instances. We used the approach for adding new concepts (shown in Sect. 3.2) to decide if for each instance we need to add new concept. We expect the approach to notify the user that a new concept should be added for the first 500 instances.

For this task we measure precision (P), recall (R) and F-score(F). The approach achieved $P = 73.8\%$, $R = 84.6\%$ and $F = 78.83\%$.

Reassigning Instances. In this experiment we evaluated the model's ability to reassign instances to other concepts. We try to identify *(i)* mistakes made by the user in the conceptualization or *(ii)* alternative and potentially better concepts for a given instance (if any is found). Also, the user's view is evolving over time, so reorganization of the instances might be needed.

The model was able to identify 82 instances that needed to be reassigned. The instances were reviewed by a medical doctor, who accepted 67 instances to be reassigned, yielding precision $P = 81.7\%$. For those instances, we used the model to assign new concepts, achieving $HITS@1 = 76.11\%$ and $HITS@5 = 91.05\%$. Using our approach we were able to easily identify misclassifications caused by user error. For example, "stomach aches" was initially assigned in the "Emotional disorder" concept, which was identified by our model as a mistake and was reassigned to "Abdominal distension". Beside the trivial cases, the model proposes to the user to review instances that might fall in different concepts. For example, "sensitivity to light" was initially assigned in the "Visually impairment" concept, but after the growth of the concepts, the model suggested to move the instance to "Photophobia", which was accepted by the user.

5   Conclusions and Future Work

In this paper we introduce a methodology to perform user-centric ontology population that efficiently includes human-in-the-loop at each step: the user is assisted in building, connecting and maintaining their conceptualization of the domain, while taking advantage of already available ontologies. We design a novel hierarchical classification method for ontology population, which builds hierarchical classification models that are dynamically refined based on user interaction. Our main objective is not to fully automate the process but rather to assist the user in achieving their goals more efficiently and effectively. The experiments confirm that the approach supports the user to achieve nearly perfect performance. The user has full control on their level of involvement in the process, depending on the requirements for quality and precision of the data, and her time/cost limit.

As future work, we are performing experiments on a broader task in the medical domain and using $UMLS^{12}$ for the alignment. Furthermore, we will

---

[11] Note that these examples were not used in the training phase.
[12] https://www.nlm.nih.gov/research/umls/.

analyze to which extent our approach can be applied to different languages, and perform cross-lingual alignment.

Acknowledgement. We would like to thank Dr. Joseph Terdiman MD, a general practitioner with over 50 years of clinical experience, for the manual annotation of the gold standard.

References

1. Aroyo, L., Welty, C.: Crowd Truth: harnessing disagreement in crowdsourcing a relation extraction gold standard. Web Science 2013, 25371, pp. 1–6 (2013)
2. Brown, E.G., Wood, L., Wood, S.: The medical dictionary for regulatory activities (MedDRA). Drug Saf. **20**(2), 109–117 (1999)
3. Castano, S., Peraldi, I.S.E., Ferrara, A., Karkaletsis, V., Kaya, A., Möller, R., Montanelli, S., Petasis, G., Wessel, M.: Multimedia interpretation for dynamic ontology evolution. J. Log. Comput. **19**(5), 859–897 (2008)
4. Cimiano, P., Völker, J.: Towards large-scale, open-domain and ontology-based named entity classification. In: RANLP (2005)
5. Coden, A., Gruhl, D., Lewis, N., Tanenblatt, M., Terdiman, J.: SPOT the drug! An unsupervised pattern matching method to extract drug names from very large clinical corpora. In: Proceedings of the 2012 IEEE 2nd Conference on Healthcare Informatics, Imaging and Systems Biology, HISB 2012, pp. 33–39 (2012)
6. Collobert, R., Weston, J., Bottou, L., Karlen, M., Kavukcuoglu, K., Kuksa, P.: Natural language processing (almost) from scratch. J. Mach. Learn. Res. **12**(Aug), 2493–2537 (2011)
7. Dalvi, B., Mishra, A., Cohen, W.W.: Hierarchical semi-supervised classification with incomplete class hierarchies. In: Proceedings of the Ninth ACM International Conference on Web Search and Data Mining, pp. 193–202. ACM (2016)
8. Doddington, G.R., Mitchell, A., Przybocki, M.A., Ramshaw, L.A., Strassel, S., Weischedel, R.M.: The automatic content extraction (ACE) program-tasks, data, and evaluation. In: LREC (2004)
9. Dong, L., Wei, F., Sun, H., Zhou, M., Xu, K.: A hybrid neural model for type classification of entity mentions. In: IJCAI, pp. 1243–1249 (2015)
10. Gangemi, A., Alam, M., Asprino, L., Presutti, V., Recupero, D.R.: Framester: a wide coverage linguistic linked data hub. In: Blomqvist, E., Ciancarini, P., Poggi, F., Vitali, F. (eds.) EKAW 2016. LNCS (LNAI), vol. 10024, pp. 239–254. Springer, Cham (2016). https://doi.org/10.1007/978-3-319-49004-5_16
11. Gangemi, A., Presutti, V., Reforgiato Recupero, D., Nuzzolese, A.G., Draicchio, F., Mongiovì, M.: Semantic web machine reading with FRED. Semantic Web (Preprint), pp. 1–21 (2016)
12. Giuliano, C., Gliozzo, A.: Instance-based ontology population exploiting named-entity substitution. In: ACL 2008, pp. 265–272. ACL (2008)
13. Gurulingappa, H., Rajput, A.M., Roberts, A., Fluck, J., Hofmann-Apitius, M., Toldo, L.: Development of a benchmark corpus to support the automatic extraction of drug-related adverse effects from medical case reports. J. Biomed. Inform. **45**(5), 885–892 (2012)
14. Holzinger, A.: Interactive machine learning for health informatics: when do we need the human-in-the-loop? Brain Inform. **3**(2), 119–131 (2016)

15. Holzinger, A., Jurisica, I.: Knowledge discovery and data mining in biomedical informatics: the future is in integrative, interactive machine learning solutions. In: Holzinger, A., Jurisica, I. (eds.) Interactive Knowledge Discovery and Data Mining in Biomedical Informatics. LNCS, vol. 8401, pp. 1–18. Springer, Heidelberg (2014). https://doi.org/10.1007/978-3-662-43968-5_1

16. Kim, Y.: Convolutional neural networks for sentence classification. arXiv preprint arXiv:1408.5882 (2014)

17. Ling, X., Weld, D.S.: Fine-grained entity recognition. In: AAAI 2012, pp. 94–100. AAAI Press (2012). http://dl.acm.org/citation.cfm?id=2900728.2900742

18. McDowell, L.K., Cafarella, M.: Ontology-driven, unsupervised instance population. Web Semant. Sci. Serv. Agents World Wide Web **6**(3), 218–236 (2008)

19. Mendes, P.N., Jakob, M., García-Silva, A., Bizer, C.: DBpedia spotlight: shedding light on the web of documents. In: Proceedings of the 7th International Conference on Semantic Systems, pp. 1–8. ACM (2011)

20. Mikolov, T., Sutskever, I., Chen, K., Corrado, G.S., Dean, J.: Distributed representations of words and phrases and their compositionality. In: Advances in Neural Information Processing Systems, pp. 3111–3119 (2013)

21. Moro, A., Raganato, A., Navigli, R.: Entity linking meets word sense disambiguation: a unified approach. Trans. Assoc. Comput. Linguist. **2**, 231–244 (2014)

22. Murty, S., Verga, P., Vilnis, L., McCallum, A.: Finer grained entity typing with typenet. arXiv preprint arXiv:1711.05795 (2017)

23. Nakashole, N., Tylenda, T., Weikum, G.: Fine-grained semantic typing of emerging entities. In: ACL, vol. 1, pp. 1488–1497 (2013)

24. Nuzzolese, A.G., Gentile, A.L., Presutti, V., Gangemi, A., Garigliotti, D., Navigli, R.: Open knowledge extraction challenge. In: Gandon, F., Cabrio, E., Stankovic, M., Zimmermann, A. (eds.) SemWebEval 2015. CCIS, vol. 548, pp. 3–15. Springer, Cham (2015). https://doi.org/10.1007/978-3-319-25518-7_1

25. Petasis, G., Karkaletsis, V., Paliouras, G., Krithara, A., Zavitsanos, E.: Ontology population and enrichment: state of the art. In: Paliouras, G., Spyropoulos, C.D., Tsatsaronis, G. (eds.) Knowledge-Driven Multimedia Information Extraction and Ontology Evolution. LNCS (LNAI), vol. 6050, pp. 134–166. Springer, Heidelberg (2011). https://doi.org/10.1007/978-3-642-20795-2_6

26. Ramage, D., Hall, D., Nallapati, R., Manning, C.D.: Labeled LDA: a supervised topic model for credit attribution in multi-labeled corpora. In: Empirical Methods in Natural Language Processing (EMNLP), pp. 248–256. Association for Computational Linguistics, Singapore, August 2009

27. Ren, X., He, W., Qu, M., Huang, L., Ji, H., Han, J.: AFET: automatic fine-grained entity typing by hierarchical partial-label embedding. In: Proceedings of the Conference on Empirical Methods in Natural Language Processing (EMNLP) (2016)

28. Ristoski, P., Bizer, C., Paulheim, H.: Mining the web of linked data with rapidminer. Web Semant. Sci. Serv. Agents World Wide Web **35**, 142–151 (2015)

29. Ristoski, P., Faralli, S., Paolo Ponzetto, S., Paulheim, H.: Large-scale taxonomy induction using entity and word embeddings. In: Proceedings of the International Conference on Web Intelligence (2017)

30. Ristoski, P., Paulheim, H.: Semantic web in data mining and knowledge discovery: a comprehensive survey. Web Semant. Sci. Serv. Agents World Wide Web **36**, 1–22 (2016)

31. Segura-Bedmar, I., Martínez, P., Herrero Zazo, M.: Semeval-2013 task 9: extraction of drug-drug interactions from biomedical texts (DDIExtraction 2013). In: SemEval 2013, pp. 341–350. ACL, June 2013

32. Shimaoka, S., Stenetorp, P., Inui, K., Riedel, S.: An attentive neural architecture for fine-grained entity type classification. arXiv preprint arXiv:1604.05525 (2016)

33. Shimaoka, S., Stenetorp, P., Inui, K., Riedel, S.: Neural architectures for fine-grained entity type classification. arXiv preprint arXiv:1606.01341 (2016)

34. Silla Jr., C.N., Freitas, A.A.: A survey of hierarchical classification across different application domains. Data Min. Knowl. Discov. **22**(1–2), 31–72 (2011)

35. Tanev, H., Magnini, B.: Weakly supervised approaches for ontology population. Citeseer (2008)

36. Tjong Kim Sang, E.F., De Meulder, F.: Introduction to the CoNLL-2003 shared task: language-independent named entity recognition. In: HLT-NAACL 2003, pp. 142–147. CONLL, Stroudsburg (2003)

37. Velardi, P., Faralli, S., Navigli, R.: Ontolearn reloaded: a graph-based algorithm for taxonomy induction. Comput. Linguist. **39**(3), 665–707 (2013)

38. Velardi, P., Navigli, R., Cuchiarelli, A., Neri, R.: Evaluation of ontolearn, a methodology for automatic learning of domain ontologies. In: Ontology Learning from Text: Methods, Evaluation and Applications, vol. 123, p. 92 (2005)

39. Yaghoobzadeh, Y., Adel, H., Schütze, H.: Noise mitigation for neural entity typing and relation extraction. arXiv preprint arXiv:1612.07495 (2016)

40. Yaghoobzadeh, Y., Schütze, H.: Corpus-level fine-grained entity typing using contextual information. arXiv preprint arXiv:1606.07901 (2016)

41. Yogatama, D., Gillick, D., Lazic, N.: Embedding methods for fine grained entity type classification. In: ACL, vol. 2, pp. 291–296 (2015)

42. Yosef, A.M., Bauer, S., Hoffart, J., Spaniol, M., Weikum, G.: HYENA: hierarchical type classification for entity names. In: COLING 2012: Posters, pp. 1361–1370 (2012)

43. Zhai, H., Lingren, T., Deleger, L., Li, Q., Kaiser, M., Stoutenborough, L., Solti, I.: Web 2.0-based crowdsourcing for high-quality gold standard development in clinical natural language processing. J. Med. Int. Res. **15**(4), 1–17 (2013)

44. Zhang, L., Rettinger, A.: X-LiSA: cross-lingual semantic annotation. VLDB **7**(13), 1693–1696 (2014)

Using Ontology-Based Data Summarization to Develop Semantics-Aware Recommender Systems

Tommaso Di Noia[1]([✉])(iD), Corrado Magarelli[2], Andrea Maurino[2],
Matteo Palmonari[2](iD), and Anisa Rula[2,3](iD)

[1] Polytechnic University of Bari, Via Orabona, 4, 70125 Bari, Italy
tommaso.dinoia@poliba.it
[2] University of Milano-Bicocca, Piazza dell'Ateneo Nuovo, 1, 20126 Milan, Italy
{corrado.magarelli,andrea.maurino,matteo.palmonari,anisa.rula}@unimib.it
[3] University of Bonn, Endenicher Allee 19a, Bonn, Germany
rula@cs.uni-bonn.de

Abstract. In the current information-centric era, recommender systems are gaining momentum as tools able to assist users in daily decision-making tasks. They may exploit users' past behavior combined with side/contextual information to suggest them new items or pieces of knowledge they might be interested in. Within the recommendation process, Linked Data have been already proposed as a valuable source of information to enhance the predictive power of recommender systems not only in terms of accuracy but also of diversity and novelty of results. In this direction, one of the main open issues in using Linked Data to feed a recommendation engine is related to feature selection: how to select only the most relevant subset of the original Linked Data thus avoiding both useless processing of data and the so called "curse of dimensionality" problem. In this paper, we show how ontology-based (linked) data summarization can drive the selection of properties/features useful to a recommender system. In particular, we compare a fully automated feature selection method based on ontology-based data summaries with more classical ones, and we evaluate the performance of these methods in terms of accuracy and aggregate diversity of a recommender system exploiting the top-k selected features. We set up an experimental testbed relying on datasets related to different knowledge domains. Results show the feasibility of a feature selection process driven by ontology-based data summaries for Linked Data-enabled recommender systems.

1 Introduction

Semantics-aware Recommender Systems (RSs) exploiting information held in knowledge graphs (including any kind of RDF datasets) represent one of the most interesting and challenging application scenarios for Linked Data (LD). A high number of solutions and tools have been proposed in the last years showing the effectiveness of adopting LD as knowledge sources to feed a recommendation

© Springer International Publishing AG, part of Springer Nature 2018
A. Gangemi et al. (Eds.): ESWC 2018, LNCS 10843, pp. 128–144, 2018.
https://doi.org/10.1007/978-3-319-93417-4_9

engine (see [17] and references therein for an overview). Nevertheless, how to automatically select the "best" subset of a LD dataset to feed a LD-based RS without affecting the performance of the recommendation algorithm is still an open issue. In other words, is there any valuable criterion to automatically perform a feature selection (FS) over semantic data available in the Web? Notice that the selection of the top-k features to use in a RSs means to discover which properties in a LD-dataset (e.g., DBpedia) encode the knowledge useful in the recommendation task and which ones are just noise [16].

In most of the approaches proposed so far, usually, the FS process is performed by human experts that choose properties resulting in more "suitable" for a given scenario. For instance, in the movie domain, properties such as `dbo:starring` or `dbo:director` look more relevant than `dbo:releaseDate` or `dbo:runtime`. Analogously, for the book domain, properties such as `dbo:literaryGenre` and `dbo:author` seem more representative than `dbo:numberOfPages` or `dbp:releaseNumber`. Unfortunately, a manual selection of features is strongly grounded in the knowledge domain and is not easily executed automatically. Over the years, many algorithms and techniques for feature selection, e.g., Information Gain, Information Gain Ratio, Chi Squared Test and Principal Component Analysis, have been proposed with reference to machine learning tasks. Yet, they mainly rely on statistical distribution of data in the dataset and they do not consider a characteristic which makes unique LD: the semantics attached to data. Ontologies give meaning to data through the modeling of classes, properties and their mutual relations. Information encoded in the ontological schema is often under-exploited when developing RSs based on LD; thus, in a typical graph-based RS the exploration of the knowledge graph is driven exclusively by the data and it goes on by following the "fact" graph, without taking into account the knowledge lying in the ontology and then in its class hierarchy.

The main objective of this paper is thus to investigate how ontology-based data summarization [12,25] can be used as a new and semantic-oriented feature selection technique for LD-based RSs thus improving results over other non-semantic feature selection techniques. In particular, we define a feature selection method that automatically extracts the top-k properties that are deemed to be more important to evaluate the similarity between instances of a given class on top of data summaries built with the help of an ontology. The method uses frequency and cardinality descriptors computed over schema patterns such as ⟨`dbo:Film`, `dbo:starring`, `dbo:Actor`⟩ extracted from the data.

We perform an experimental evaluation on three well-known datasets in the RS domain (*Movielens, LastFM, LibraryThing*) in order to analyze how the choice of a particular FS technique may influence the performance of recommendation algorithms in terms of quality measures such as Precision, Mean Reciprocal Rank (MRR), Catalog Coverage and Aggregate Entropy which are typical in the field of RSs [6]. Experimental results show that information provided in ontology-based data summaries selects features that achieve comparable, or, in most of the cases, better performance than state-of-the-art, semantic-agnostic analytical methods such as Information Gain [14].

We believe that these results are interesting also because of practical reasons. The use of statistical measures like the ones mentioned above for FS requires that a user acquires an entire dataset beforehand and compute the measures on the whole dataset. Conversely, LD summaries are published online and summary-based FS can be performed even without acquiring the entire dataset and efficiently (on top of summary information). Thus, by using LD summaries for FS, a user could acquire and work with a subset of the dataset useful for him, without collecting and analyzing an entire dataset. Finally, these results provide further evidence for the usefulness of these kinds of summaries and the informativeness of the information they encode.

Some intuitions behind this work were published in previous work [21], where we tested the use of frequency associated with schema patterns in a FS approach that included a manual preprocessing step. The approach was evaluated only in the movie domain, using, for the recommendation, a similarity measure based on graph kernels. In this paper, we provide a fully automatic FS method, which leads us to extend the ontology-based data summarization framework to compute cardinality descriptors. In addition, for the recommendation, we use a different and well-known similarity measure and conduct experiments in three different domains.

The paper is organized as follows: in Sect. 2, we introduce the ontology-based data summarization approach used in this work, while in Sect. 3, we describe the feature selection and recommendation methods. Section 4 is devoted to the explanation and discussion of the experimental results. Section 5 briefly reviews related literature for schema and data summarization as well as on recommender systems while Sect. 6 discuss conclusions and future work.

2   Ontology-Driven Linked Data Summarization

While relevance-oriented data summarization approaches are aimed at finding subsets of a dataset or an ontology that are estimated to be more relevant for the users [26], vocabulary-oriented approaches are aimed at profiling a dataset, by describing the usage of vocabularies/ontologies used in the dataset. The summaries returned by these approaches are complete, i.e., they provide statistics about every element of the vocabulary/ontology used in the dataset [25]. Statistics captured by these summaries that can be useful for the feature selection process are the ones concerning the usage of properties for a certain class of items to recommend.

Patterns and Frequency. In our approach, we use pattern-based summaries extracted using the ABSTAT framework[1]. Pattern-based summaries describe the content of a dataset using schema patterns having the form $\langle C, P, D \rangle$, where C and D, are types (either classes or datatypes) and P is a property. For example, the pattern $\langle \texttt{dbo:Film}, \texttt{dbo:starring}, \texttt{dbo:Actor} \rangle$ tells that films exist in

---

[1] ABSTAT summaries for several datasets can be explored at http://abstat.disco. unimib.it.

the dataset, in which star some actors. These patterns are extracted from relational and typing assertions found in RDF datasets. Differently, from similar pattern-based summaries [12], ABSTAT uses the subclass relations in the data ontology, represented in a *Type Graph*, to extract only *minimal type patterns* from relational assertions, i.e., the patterns that are more type-wise specific according to the ontology[2]. A pattern $\langle C, P, D \rangle$ is a minimal type pattern for a relational assertion $\langle a, P, b \rangle$ according to a type graph $\mathcal{G}$ iff C and D are the types of a and b respectively, which are minimal in $\mathcal{G}$. In a pattern $\langle C, P, D \rangle$, C and D are referred to as *source* and *target* types respectively. A minimal type pattern $\langle$dbo:Film, dbo:starring, dbo:Actor$\rangle$ (simply referred to as *pattern* in the following) tells that there exist entities that have dbo:Film and dbo:Actor as minimal types which are connected through the property P. Non minimal patterns can be inferred from minimal patterns and the type graph. Therefore, they can be excluded as redundant without information loss, making summaries more compact [25]. Each pattern $\langle C, P, D \rangle$ is associated with a *frequency*, which reports the number of relational assertions $\langle a, P, b \rangle$ from which the pattern has been extracted.

Local Cardinality Descriptors. For this work, we have extended ABSTAT to extract *local cardinality descriptors*, i.e., cardinality descriptors of RDF properties, which are specific to the patterns in which the properties occur. To define these descriptors, we first introduce the concept of restricted property extensions. The *extension* of a property P restricted to a pattern $\langle C, P, D \rangle$ is the set of pairs $\langle x, y \rangle$ such that the relational assertion $\langle x, P, y \rangle$ is part of the dataset and $\langle C, P, D \rangle$ is a minimal-type pattern for $\langle x, P, y \rangle$. When referring to extensions, we keep the well-known terminology used in RDF triples, using subject and object to refer respectively to the first and the second element of each pair in the extension. Given a pattern π with a property P, we can define the functions:

- $minS(\pi)$, $maxS(\pi)$, $avgS(\pi)$, denoting respectively the minimum, maximum and average number of distinct subjects associated to unique objects in the extension of P restricted to π;
- $minO(\pi)$, $maxO(\pi)$, $avgO(\pi)$, denoting respectively the minimum, maximum and average number of distinct objects associated to unique subjects in the extension of P restricted to π.

All functions return integer values, and, in particular, $avgS$ and $avgO$ return the integer values closer to the real average values. ABSTAT can also compute global cardinality descriptors by adjusting the above mentioned definition so as to consider unrestricted property extensions. Local cardinality descriptors carry information about the semantics of properties as used with specific types of resources (in specific patterns) and can be helpful for selecting features used to compute the similarity between resources. For example, to compute similarity for movies, one would like to discard properties that occur in patterns π

---

[2] If no ontology is specified, all types are minimal and patterns are extracted like in frameworks that do not adopt minimalization.

with dbo:Film as source type and $avgS(\pi) = 1$, i.e., properties where different objects are linked to different subjects (e.g., movies). We remark that the values of local cardinality descriptors for patterns with a property P may differ from values of global cardinality descriptors for P. As an example, for the property dbo:cinematography we find as global cardinality descriptors $minS = 1$, $maxS = 249$, $avgS = 5$, $minO = 1$, $maxO = 13$, $avgO = 1$. For the pattern ⟨dbo:Film, dbo:cinematography, dbo:Person⟩, we find as local cardinality descriptors $minS = 1$, $maxS = 249$, $avgS = 14$, $minO = 1$, $maxO = 7$, $avgO = 1$. More examples of local cardinality descriptors can be found in the faceted-search interface (ABSTATBrowse)[3]. Observe that our definition of extensions (restricted and unrestricted) are de facto based on the Unique Name Assumption, as they consider that two subjects or two objects denoted by different constants (URIs or literals) are distinct. We consider this acceptable in relation to the descriptive purpose of the cardinality descriptors. Finally, observe that all measures used in ABSTAT are intended to be expressive for end users, can be easily explained and are based on integer values.

In conclusion, ABSTAT takes a linked dataset and - if specified - one or more ontologies as input, and returns a summary that consists of: a type graph, a set of patterns, their frequency, local an global cardinality descriptors.

3 Semantics-Aware Feature Selection

Feature selection is the process of selecting a subset of relevant attributes in a dataset, removing irrelevant or redundant attributes that can decrease the accuracy of the model at hand and increase the *overfitting* risk. Thanks to the feature selection process it is possible to improve the prediction performance, to provide faster and more cost-effective predictors and to give a better understanding of the process that generates the data [7]. A good feature selection technique should exclude features that give no, or little, information contribution, as low frequent features or, conversely, popular features assuming always different values. There are three typical measures of feature selection (i) **"filters"**, statistical measures to assign a score to each feature (here the feature selection process is a preprocessing step and can be independent from learning [5]); (ii) **"wrapper"** where the learning system is used as a black box to score subsets of features [9]; (iii) **embedded methods** that perform the selection within the process of training [7]. In the following, we discuss two approaches used for the feature selection task: the first operates on the summarization of the datasets and the second operates on the instances of the datasets.

3.1 Feature Selection with Ontology-Based Summaries

As described in Sect. 2, the ABSTAT framework provides two useful statistics: the pattern frequency and the cardinality descriptors that are used in the feature selection process as described in Fig. 1. The process starts by considering

---

[3] http://abstat.disco.unimib.it/browse.

all patterns $\Pi = \{\pi_1, \pi_2, \ldots, \pi_n\}$ of a given class C occurring as a source type. The example in Fig. 1 shows a subset of Π with `dbo:Film` as source type. The first step of our approach (*FILTERBY*) filters out properties based on the local cardinality descriptors. In particular, it filters only properties for which the average number of distinct subjects associated with unique objects is more than one ($avgS > 1$). The rationale behind this step is to consider only those properties connecting one target type with many source types. In the example, patterns π_4 and π_8 with `dbo:wikiPageExternalLink` and `owl:sameAs` property respectively are removed because there exists on average only one subject of type `dbo:Film` associated with a distinct object. The second step of the process (*SELECTDIS-TINCTP*) selects all properties of the patterns in Π by applying the maximum of the pattern frequency (# in the figure). Then, the properties are ranked (*ORDERBY*) in a descending order on pattern frequency and then k properties (*TOPK*) are selected (k = 2).

In some datasets, such as DBpedia, properties may use redundant information by using same properties with different namespaces, e.g., `dbo:starring` and `dbp:starring`. For this reason, in such case, a pre-processing step for removing replicated properties to avoid redundant ones is requested (see Sect. 4.1).

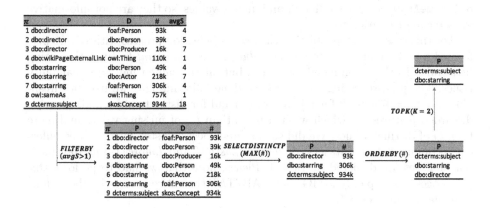

Fig. 1. Feature selection with ABSTAT with source type `dbo:Film`

3.2 Feature Selection with State-of-the-Art Techniques

In this work we consider RDF properties as features, so among the different feature selection techniques available in the literature, we initially selected *Information Gain, Information Gain Ratio, Chi-squared test* and *Principal Component Analysis* as their computation can be adapted to categorical features as LD and we then evaluated their effect over the recommendation results. The features selected from each technique have been used as an input of the recommendation algorithm that uses the Jaccard index as similarity measure. In order to identify the best technique among the one we selected, they have been evaluated by using Information Gain (IG), Gain Ration and Chi Squared Test. At the end, IG resulted as the best performing one[4]. In order to make the paper self-consistent, we report hereafter the definition of Information Gain. It computes the expected reduction in entropy occurring when a feature is *present* versus when it is *absent*. For a feature f_i, IG is defined as [14]:

$$IG(f_i) = E(I) - \sum_{v \in dom(f_i)} \frac{|I_v|}{|I|} * E(I_v)$$

where $E(I)$ is the entropy of the data, I_v is the number of items in which the feature f_i (e.g. *director* for movies) has a value equal to v (e.g. *F.F.Coppola* in the movie domain), and $E(I_v)$ is the entropy computed on data where the feature f_i assumes value v. The IG of a feature means that higher values of f_i are correlated with lower values of entropy $E(I_v)$. Then features are ranked according to their IG value and the top-k ones are returned.

Feature Pre-processing. LD datasets usually have a quite large feature set that can be, at the same time, very sparse depending on the knowledge domain. For instance, taking into account the movies available in *Movielens*, properties as `dbp:artDirection` or `dbp:precededBy` are very specific and have a lot of missing values. On the other hand, properties as `dbo:wikiPageExternalLink` or `owl:sameAs` always have different and unique values, so they are not informative for a recommendation task.

For this reason, before starting the feature selection process with IG, we performed a preliminary step to reduce *redundant* or *irrelevant* features that bring little value to the recommendation task, but, at the same time, pose scalability issues. The pre-processing step has been done following [20]: we fixed a threshold $t_m = t_d = 97\%$ both for missing values and for distinct values and, then, we discarded features for which we had more than t_m of missing values and more than t_d of distinct values. We did such a pre-processing step for the three different recommendation datasets *Movielens*, *LastFM* and *LibraryThing*. Results of our analyses are depicted in Table 1. Please, note that we had to perform this pre-processing step only for IG, as for ABSTAT the entire process has been done as explained in Sect. 3.1.

Table 1. Reduction on the number of features after the pre-processing step.

Dataset	# of features before pre-processing	# of features after pre-processing
Movielens	148	34
LastFM	271	25
LibraryThing	201	22

---

[4] For the sake of conciseness, we do not report all the results here. Results obtained with other FS techniques can be found at https://zenodo.org/record/1205712#. WrRCypPwa3U.

3.3   Recommendation Method

We implemented a content-based recommender system using an item-based nearest neighbors algorithm as in [16], where the similarity is computed by means of Jaccard's index. We use a Jaccard-based similarity because it is a straight and effective measure used in semantic recommendation for categorical features. Given two resources i and j in a LD dataset the metric calculates their similarity as:

$$jaccard(i,j) = \frac{|N(i)\bigcap N(j)|}{|N(i)\bigcup N(j)|} \tag{1}$$

where $N(i)$ and $N(j)$ are the neighbors of i and j in the RDF graph. In this work, the neighborhood of i (respectively j) includes all the nodes in the graph reachable starting from the resource i (respectively j) following the properties selected by the feature selection phase. The neighbors are thus one-hop features. Observe that considering values of frequent properties like dbo:wikiPageExternalLink or owl#sameAs, which have always different and unique values, would only bring noise when computing Jaccard similarity. In addition, computing Jaccard using the very large number of features that can be found in linked datasets (see Table 1) would not be efficient at runtime, considering that recommendations need to be computed almost at real time. These observations provide additional evidence for the need of a FS method before computing recommendations.

The similarity values are then used to recommend to each user the items which result most similar to the ones she has liked in the past. Given an item j and a user u, the following formula is used to predict the rating of items i which is unknown to the user:

$$r^*(u,i) = \frac{\sum_{j\in N(i)\cap r(u)} jaccard(i,j)\cdot r(u,j)}{\sum_{j\in N(i)\cap r(u)} jaccard(i,j)} \tag{2}$$

where $r(u)$ represents the items rated by the user u, and $r(u,j)$ the rating value given by the user u with respect to the item i. Therefore, the above equation takes into account the neighbors of i belonging to the user profile and computes an average of the user ratings to such neighbors weighted by the similarity values.

4   Experimental Evaluation

4.1   Experimental Setup

Datasets. The evaluation has been carried out on the three datasets belonging to three different domains, i.e. movies, books, and music. The first recommendation dataset we tested is based on the Movielens 1M. The original dataset contains 1,000,209 ratings (1–5 stars) given by 6,040 users to 3,883 movies. The second one, LibraryThing contains 7,112 users, 37,231 books and 626,000 ratings ranging from 1 to 10. The third dataset comes from recent initiatives on information heterogeneity and fusion in recommender systems[5] and has been built

---

[5] http://ir.ii.uam.es/hetrec2011/datasets.html.

on top of the `Last.fm` music system[6]. It originally contains 1,892 users, 17,632 artists and 92,834 relations between a user and a listened artist together with their corresponding listening counts.

Measures. While evaluating a recommendation algorithm we are interested in measuring its performances not just in terms of accuracy of the predicted results but also in terms of their diversity and novelty. Hence, depending on the adopted feature selection technique we are interested in evaluating the variations of different aspects (accuracy, diversity, novelty) in the final result. Indeed, some techniques may improve the accuracy of the recommendation, some improve diversity, others may provide a good trade-off between diversity and accuracy. Therefore, for evaluating the quality of our recommendation algorithm (given a particular feature selection technique) we used four different metrics. To evaluate recommendation **accuracy**, we used *Precision* (Precision@N) and *Mean Reciprocal Rank* (MRR). Precision@N is a metric denoting the fraction of relevant items in the Top-N recommendations. MRR computes the average reciprocal rank of the first relevant recommended item, and hence results particularly meaningful when users are provided with few but valuable recommendations (i.e., Top-1 to Top-10) [23]. **Aggregate diversity** is considered one of the other most important quality factors [1]. A good recommender system should provide a good balance between accuracy and diversity of results. For instance, recommendations not equally distributed among the items, even if accurate, indicate a low degree of personalization [1]. To evaluate aggregate diversity, we considered *catalog coverage* (the percentage of items in the catalog recommended at least once) and *aggregate entropy* [1]. The former is used to assess the ability of a system to cover the item catalog, namely to recommend as many items as possible. While the latter measures the distribution of the recommendations across all the items, showing whether the recommendations are concentrated on a few items or they have a better distribution.

Implementation. Summaries are expected to be computed for entire datasets by data publishers or third parties and then accessed via web interface efficiently. Extracting the summary and the cardinality descriptors on the full DBpedia takes 6 to 8 h on a single core (split in $\approx 1/4$ for pattern stats and $\approx 3/4$ for cardinality descriptors). Filtering and ranking using information in the summaries is then very efficient (a few milliseconds, on a base of more than 300K patterns extracted from DBpedia).

We tried different ranking and filtering functions by combining local cardinality descriptors and pattern frequency to study their effect on feature selection. For lack of space, we include the best three combinations from those proposed in Sect. 3.1:

- **AbsMaxS** considers as input of *SELECTDISTINCTP* the *maxS* instead of the frequency of patterns.
- **AbsOccAvgS** considers as input of *FILTERBY* the *avgS* and *SELECTDISTINCTP* the maximum of the pattern frequency.

---

[6] http://www.lastfm.com.

- **AbsOcc*MaxS** considers as input of *SELECTDISTINCTP* the product of *maxS* and pattern frequency.

Both for ABSTAT and IG we consider different configurations in the experimental settings:

- **noRep.** Here, we consider the first N features selected and if there are both dbo: and dbp: feature (e.g. dbo:starring and dbp:starring) we delete the feature that appears later in the ranking.
- **withRep.** Here, we take into account both dbo: and dbp: feature (e.g. if among the first N features there are either dbo:starring or dbp:starring we consider both features in the order in which they appear in the ranking).
- **Onlydbp.** Here, if among the first N features selected there are both dbo: and dbp: feature we consider only the dbp: one.
- **Onlydbo.** Conversely, here we take into account only the dbo: one. However, notice that in the experiments for *Movielens* and *Lastfm* datasets we never have this configuration as the features selected by such a configuration are exactly the same selected with the *noRep* configuration.

ABSTAT Baseline. As a baseline for ABSTAT-based feature selection we use TfIdf (short for term frequency-inverse document frequency). We use this as baseline for ABSTAT-based feature selection as TfIdf is a well-known measure to identify most relevant terms (properties in this case) for a document (a class in this case). We adopt *TfIdf* in our context where by document we refer to a set of patterns having the same subject-type and by term we refer to a property. *TfIdf* is based on the number of properties occurring in a document that corresponds to *Tf* and the logarithm of the ratio between the total number of documents and the number of documents containing the property that corresponds to *Idf*. While *TF* is proportional to the number of properties occurring in a document, *IDF* tries to penalize those properties that occur very frequently and those that rarely occur.

4.2   Results and Discussion

Tables 2, 3 and 4 show the experimental results obtained on, respectively, *Movielens*, *Last.FM* and *LibraryThing* datasets in terms of **Precision**, **MRR**, **catalogCoverage**, and **aggrEntropy**. Results are computed over lists of top-10 items recommended by the RS, which expresses the average number of items to be recommended in similar domains, using top-k features selected with different configurations. We conducted experiments using top-k selected features for different k, i.e., $k = 5, 10, 15, 20$, and all configurations but we report only results for $k = 5, 20$ and best configurations for lack of space[7]. We highlight in bold only the values for which there is a statistical significant difference. For *Lastfm* dataset the differences are not statistical significant so the two methods are equivalent in selecting features.

---

[7] The interested reader can find results for all values of k and configurations on GitHub: http://ow.ly/zAA530d0wu0.

Table 2. Experimental results on the Movielens dataset. Bold values indicates that the difference with the other methods are statistical significant (T-test with p-value < 0.0001).

	Precision@10		MRR@10		catalogCoverage @10		aggrEntropy @10	
Top K features	5	20	5	20	5	20	5	20
withrep.IG	.0658	.1078	.2192	.3417	.3829	.5280	7.56	8.50
withrep.AbsOccAvgS	**.1059**	**.1081**	**.3380**	.3477	.5398	.5253	8.70	8.53
withrep.AbsOcc*MaxS	.0967	.1074	.3274	**.3541**	.5962	.5247	8.87	8.54
withrep.AbsMaxS	.0919	.1030	.3065	.3400	**.6016**	**.5698**	**8.96**	**8.66**
withrep.TfIdf	.0565	.0851	.2267	.3326	.4347	.3360	8.36	7.80
norep.IG	.0841	.1076	.2961	.3390	.3372	.5226	7.94	8.44
norep.AbsOccAvgS	**.1066**	.1076	**.3388**	.3400	.5344	.5208	8.68	8.45
norep.AbsMaxS	.0885	.1063	.3075	**.3467**	**.6234**	**.5550**	**8.99**	**8.60**
norep.TfIdf	.0823	.0856	.2994	.3123	.3520	.3908	7.83	7.99
dbo.IG	.0841	.1076	.2961	.3390	.3372	.5226	7.94	8.44
dbo.AbsOccAvgS	**.1066**	.1067	**.3388**	.3402	.5344	.5208	8.68	8.51
dbo.AbsMaxS	.0885	.1059	.3075	**.3464**	**.6234**	**.5535**	**8.99**	**8.60**
dbo.TfIdf	.0823	.0856	.2994	.3123	.3520	.3908	7.83	7.99
dbp.IG	.0688	.1046	.2134	.3336	.2799	.5065	6.54	8.31
dbp.AbsOccAvgS	**.1065**	**.1059**	.3408	.3360	.5426	.5105	8.64	8.31
dbp.AbsMaxS	.0908	.1030	.3124	**.3396**	**.6219**	**.5395**	**8.98**	**8.52**
dbp.TfIdf	.0549	.0745	.1924	.2687	.2530	.3575	6.33	7.41

Discussion. As an overall result, ABSTAT-based FS leads to the best results in terms of accuracy and diversity for both the movie and books domains while IG leads to better results (although not statistically significant) for music. Specifically, considering the results on Movielens (Table 2), ABSTAT produces better accuracy with respect to IG in all the four configurations (noRep, withRep, Onlydbp, Onlydbo) both with 5 and 20 features. In terms of aggregate diversity, i.e. itemCoverage and aggrEntropy, ABSTAT is still the best choice, overcoming IG in almost all the situations. Interestingly, as for diversity we always obtain the best results with the AbsMaxS configuration. On Lastfm (Table 3) there are no particular differences, and hence the choice of the method seems irrelevant: both summarization-based and statistical methods are comparable. Eventually, on LibraryThing (Table 4), ABSTAT strongly beats IG in almost all the configurations. In particular, it gets more than twice of the precision and MRR respect to IG in top-5 features scenario. Also in this domain, ABSTAT is the best choice also in terms of catalog coverage on the AbsMaxS configuration, while the aggregate distribution is not particularly influenced by the two methods. Summing up, ABSTAT beats IG in almost all the configurations on the two datasets Movielens and LibraryThing, while they act in the same way on the Lastfm dataset.

Table 3. Experimental results on the LastFM dataset.

Top K features	Precision@10		MRR@10		catalogCoverage @10		aggrEntropy @10	
	5	20	5	20	5	20	5	20
withrep.IG	.0576	.0588	.2348	.2273	.3983	.4034	10.47	10.44
withrep.AbsOccAvgS	.0458	.0568	.2003	.2343	.3670	.4014	10.28	10.50
withrep.AbsOcc*MaxS	.0457	.0560	.2116	.2355	.3854	.3826	10.54	10.21
withrep.AbsMaxS	.0571	.0567	.2319	.2360	.3689	.4011	10.24	10.29
withrep.TfIdf	.0215	.0145	.1607	.1202	.1314	.2349	8.81	9.75
norep.IG	.0571	.0579	.2346	.2274	.3988	.4037	10.47	10.44
norep.AbsOccAvgS	.0561	.0593	.2328	.2329	.3982	.4030	10.54	10.48
norep.AbsOcc*MaxS	.0459	.0570	.2119	.2372	.3852	.3809	10.54	10.15
norep.AbsMaxS	.0541	.0567	.2301	.2365	.3653	.4008	10.24	10.29
norep.TfIdf	.0215	.0138	.1608	.1211	.1314	.2877	8.81	10.26
dbo.IG	.0571	.0579	.2346	.2274	.3988	.4037	10.47	10.44
dbo.AbsOccAvgS	.0561	.0593	.2328	.2329	.3982	.4030	10.54	10.48
dbo.AbsOcc*MaxS	.0459	.0570	.2119	.2372	.3852	.3809	10.54	10.15
dbo.AbsMaxS	.0541	.0567	.2301	.2365	.3653	.4008	10.24	10.29
dbo.TfIdf	.0579	.0605	.2374	.2477	.4086	.3991	10.55	10.20
dbp.IG	.0586	.0586	.2350	.2299	.4027	.4043	10.49	10.40
dbp.AbsOccAvgS	.0623	.0612	.2467	.2342	.3943	.4043	10.42	10.45
dbp.AbsOcc*MaxS	.0464	.0606	.2126	.2504	.3862	.3797	10.53	10.07
dbp.AbsMaxS	.0571	.0592	.2318	.2398	.3689	.4002	10.24	10.22
dbp.TfIdf	.0215	.0132	.1608	.1218	.1314	.2696	8.81	9.96

In order to investigate the reasons behind the different behaviors depending on the selected knowledge domain, we evaluated two orthogonal dimensions related to their corresponding sub-graphs. The two dimensions reflect the two different aspects related to the FS techniques. Indeed, while the ones based on ABSTAT are strongly grounded in the ontological nature of the knowledge graph, the others (IG, CHI and GR) mainly consider the triples representing data without taking into account the schema. Hence, for the three domains of movies, books and music we measured: (i) the number of minimal patterns and (ii) the average number of triples per resource and the corresponding variance. Regarding the former, we may say that a higher number of minimal patterns means a richer and more diverse ontological representation of the knowledge domain. As for the latter, a high variance in the number of triples associated to resources is a clue of an unbalanced representation of the items to recommend. Hence, items with a higher number of triples associated result "more popular" in the knowledge graph compared to those with only a few. This may reflect in the

Table 4. Experimental results on the LibraryThing dataset. Bold values indicates that the difference with the other methods are statistical significant (T-test with p-value < 0.0001).

	Precision@10		MRR@10		catalogCoverage @10		aggrEntropy @10	
Top K features	5	20	5	20	5	20	5	20
withrep.IG	.0501	.1325	.2283	.4102	.4290	.5051	11.00	11.18
withrep.AbsOccAvgS	**.1330**	.1320	**.4047**	.4105	.4812	.5036	11.10	11.18
withrep.AbsOcc*MaxS	.1102	.1227	.3649	.3749	**.5500**	.5332	11.40	11.36
withrep.AbsMaxS	.0371	.1156	.1249	.3691	.1680	**.5440**	9.79	11.39
withrep.TfIdf	.1017	.1158	.2960	.3584	.4210	.4602	10.86	10.97
norep.IG	.0501	.1311	.2283	.404	.4290	.5018	11.00	11.17
norep.AbsOccAvgS	**.1305**	**.1307**	**.3994**	**.4074**	.4890	.5019	11.11	11.15
norep.AbsOcc*MaxS	.1062	.1228	.3546	.3708	**.5362**	.5161	11.40	11.29
norep.AbsMaxS	.0392	.1227	.1952	.3715	.4520	**.5344**	11.09	11.34
norep.TfIdf	.1024	.1132	.3064	.3554	.4026	.4508	10.76	10.96
dbo.IG	.0411	.1319	.1989	.4083	.4425	.5053	11.06	11.20
dbo.AbsOccAvgS	.1283	.1292	.3986	.4063	.4915	.4949	11.14	11.14
dbo.AbsOcc*MaxS	.1062	.1214	.3546	.3710	.5362	.5109	11.40	11.27
dbo.AbsMaxS	.0381	.1211	.1927	.3727	.4291	.5222	10.97	11.31
dbo.TfIdf	.1024	.1132	.3064	.3554	.4026	.4508	10.76	10.96
dbp.IG	.0678	.1319	.2553	.4083	.4364	.5053	10.83	11.20
dbp.AbsOccAvgS	**.1319**	**.1316**	**.4026**	**.4113**	.4926	.5055	11.14	11.20
dbp.AbsOcc*MaxS	.1065	.1239	.3580	.3773	**.5444**	.5270	**11.42**	11.36
dbp.AbsMaxS	.0401	.1105	.1969	.3553	.4528	**.5447**	11.08	11.42
dbp.TfIdf	.0790	.1170	.2371	.3572	.3894	.4698	10.69	11.04

rising of a stronger content popularity bias while computing the recommendation results. If we look at the values represented in Table 5 we see that while the music domain is the one with the lowest number of minimal patterns and the highest variance, books have the lowest values in terms of variance and, eventually movies show intermediate values in terms of variance and the highest number of minimal patterns. Based on these values we may assert that a higher sparsity in the knowledge graph data may lead to statistical methods beat ontological ones. In other words, it seems that the higher the sparsity of the knowledge graph at the data level, the lower the influence of the ontological schema in the selection of the most informative features to build a pure content-based recommendation engine.

Table 5. Ontological and data dimensions of the three datasets

Domain	Number of minimal patterns	Average number of triples	Variance
Movies	57757	74,015	549,313
Books	41684	44,966	169,478
Music	40481	80,502	981,509

5 Related Work

Summarization. Different approaches have been proposed for schema and data summarization. Here we compare our work to approaches that provide vocabulary/ontology-based summaries (or profiles) of linked data that describe, even if in an abstract way, the whole content of a dataset. We refer to [25] for a more detailed comparison also with summarization approaches for ontologies or aimed at representing only the most relevant content of a dataset. Several data profiling approaches have been proposed to describe linked data by reporting statistics about the usage of the vocabularies, types and properties. SchemeEx extracts interesting theoretic measures for large datasets, by considering the co-occurrence of types and properties [10]. Linked Open Vocabularies[8], RDFStats [11] and LODStats [2] provide such statistics. In contrast, ABSTAT represents connections between types using schema patterns, for which it also provides cardinality descriptors (a contribution of this paper). Loupe [12], a framework to summarize and inspect LD, extracts schema patterns that are similar to the ones extracted by ABSTAT, but without our minimalization approach, and their frequency. The additional information it provides (e.g., about provenance) does not include cardinality descriptors for properties or patterns. TermPicker extracts [22] patterns consisting in triples $\langle S, E, O \rangle$, where S and O are *sets* of types and E is a set of predicates. Instead, ABSTAT and Loupe extract patterns each consisting in a triple $\langle C, P, D \rangle$ where C and D are types and P a property. TermPicker summaries do not describe cardinality and are extracted from RDF data without considering relationships between types. Only a few works have addressed the problem of extracting cardinality descriptors - related to mining cardinality constraints - as the ones introduced in this paper. According to a recent article [13], which proposes a method to define and discover classes of cardinality constraints with some preliminary results, current approaches focus only on mining keys or pseudo-keys (e.g., [24]). We discover richer statistics about property cardinality like the above mentioned work, but with a purely descriptive approach. In addition, we compute cardinality descriptors for properties occurring in specific schema patterns.

Recommender Systems. The world of recommender systems can be divided into two main classes: *Collaborative Filtering* and *Content-Based* systems. The former predicts users interests relying on the statistical information about the

---

[8] http://lov.okfn.org/.

users ratings. The underlying assumption is that users sharing similar scores may have similar preferences, and similarly scored items may be of interest to the same users. Collaborative filtering recommender systems suffer from the data sparsity problem; while, content-based recommender systems exploit the descriptive content of the item (tags, textual description, etc.) in order to recommend items similar to the ones the user liked in the past. The latter do not suffer from data sparsity, as they do not rely on the ratings of different users. Moreover, several times we miss descriptive content information about the items, by exploiting LD sources like `DBpedia` [3] we can overcome such a problem of missing content information. Several are the approaches proposed to exploit information extracted from LD in a recommendation scenario. One of the first approach for using LD in a recommender system was proposed by Heitmann and Hayes [8]. A system for recommending artists and music using DBpedia was presented in [19]. The task of cross-domain recommendation leveraging DBpedia as a knowledge-based framework was addressed in [4], while in [15] the authors present a content-based and context-aware method adopting a semantic representation based on a combination of distributional semantics and entity linking techniques. In [18] the authors use a hybrid graph-based algorithm based on the learning-to-rank method and path-based features extracted from networks built upon DBpedia and collaborative information [18]. To the best of our knowledge, the only approaches proposing an automatic selection of LD features are [14,21]. In [14] seven different techniques for automatic selection of LD-based features are compared. Differently from [14], we are not interested in the best performing techniques for feature selection. Here we want to investigate if the knowledge encoded at ontological level can be used to select the most significant properties in a LD for recommendation purposes. Differently from [21] here we have used a different recommendation algorithm, a new and fully automatic approach to pre-processing and to rank the features coming from the ABSTAT summarization tool and evaluated the approach on three different datasets. Finally, we observe that even approaches that do not perform automatic FS like [3,14,18] used (hand-crafted) FS to improve their performance.

6   Conclusions

In this work we investigated the role of ontology-based data summarization for feature selection in recommendation tasks. Having its roots in pure machine learning, feature selection techniques do not usually exploit the semantics associated to data while computing the importance of a set of features. Here we compare the results coming from ABSTAT, a schema summarization tool, with classical methods for feature selection and we show that the former are able to compute better predictions not just in terms of precision of the recommended items but also considering other dimensions such as diversity. Experiments have been carried out in three different knowledge domains namely movies, books and music thus showing the effectiveness of a feature selection based on schema summarization over classical techniques such as Information Gain.

In future work, we plan to use patterns and local cardinality descriptors provided by ABSTAT summaries to compute the most relevant paths to be used in multi-hop similarity measures used in RSs. As a result, more complex subgraphs that are estimated to be relevant for LD-based RSs could be extracted. In addition, based on the promising results obtained in the domain of LD-based RSs, we would like to extend our study to investigate the effectiveness of ontology-based schema summaries also in other application domains where semantic similarity measures are used, for example for semantic relatedness or entity co-resolution. Finally, the algorithm for feature selection used in this paper will be incorporated in a new more mature version of ABSTAT (built in two innovation projects), in which it will be exposed through an API that given a concept returns the set of top-k most salient properties (similarly to other APIs currently implemented like ABSTAT search and ABSTAT autocomplete).

Acknowledgments. This research has been supported in part by EU H2020 projects EW-Shopp - Grant n. 732590, and EuBusinessGraph - Grant n. 732003.

References

1. Adomavicius, G., Kwon, Y.: Improving aggregate recommendation diversity using ranking-based techniques. IEEE Trans. Knowl. Data Eng. **24**(5), 896–911 (2012)
2. Auer, S., Demter, J., Martin, M., Lehmann, J.: LODStats – an extensible framework for high-performance dataset analytics. In: ten Teije, A., Völker, J., Handschuh, S., Stuckenschmidt, H., d'Acquin, M., Nikolov, A., Aussenac-Gilles, N., Hernandez, N. (eds.) EKAW 2012. LNCS (LNAI), vol. 7603, pp. 353–362. Springer, Heidelberg (2012). https://doi.org/10.1007/978-3-642-33876-2_31
3. de Gemmis, M., Lops, P., Musto, C., Narducci, F., Semeraro, G.: Semantics-aware content-based recommender systems. In: Ricci, F., Rokach, L., Shapira, B. (eds.) Recommender Systems Handbook, pp. 119–159. Springer, Boston, MA (2015). https://doi.org/10.1007/978-1-4899-7637-6_4
4. Fernández-Tobías, I., Cantador, I., Kaminskas, M., Ricci, F.: A generic semantic-based framework for cross-domain recommendation. In: 2nd HetRec Workshop, RecSys (2011)
5. Geng, X., Liu, T.-Y., Qin, T., Li, H.: Feature selection for ranking. In: SIGIR. ACM (2007)
6. Gunawardana, A., Shani, G.: Evaluating recommender systems. In: Ricci, F., Rokach, L., Shapira, B. (eds.) Recommender Systems Handbook, pp. 265–308. Springer, Boston, MA (2015). https://doi.org/10.1007/978-1-4899-7637-6_8
7. Guyon, I., Elisseeff, A.: An introduction to variable and feature selection. JMLR **3**, 1157–1182 (2003)
8. Heitmann, B., Hayes, C.: Using linked data to build open, collaborative recommender systems. In: AAAI Spring Symposium: Linked Data Meets Artificial Intelligence (2010)
9. Kohavi, R., John, G.H.: Wrappers for feature subset selection. Artif. Intell. **97**(1–2), 273–324 (1997)
10. Konrath, M., Gottron, T., Staab, S., Scherp, A.: SchemEX - efficient construction of a data catalogue by stream-based indexing of linked data. Web Semant. **16**, 52–58 (2012)

11. Langegger, A., Wöß, W.: RDFStats - an extensible RDF statistics generator and library. In: 20th DEXA Workshop. IEEE (2009)
12. Mihindukulasooriya, N., Poveda Villalon, M., Garcia-Castro, R., Gomez-Perez, A.: Loupe - an online tool for inspecting datasets in the linked data cloud. In: ISWC Posters and Demonstrations (2015)
13. Muñoz, E.: On learnability of constraints from RDF data. In: Sack, H., Blomqvist, E., d'Aquin, M., Ghidini, C., Ponzetto, S.P., Lange, C. (eds.) ESWC 2016. LNCS, vol. 9678, pp. 834–844. Springer, Cham (2016). https://doi.org/10.1007/978-3-319-34129-3_52
14. Musto, C., Lops, P., Basile, P., de Gemmis, M., Semeraro, G.: Semantics-aware graph-based recommender systems exploiting linked open data. In: UMAP (2016)
15. Musto, C., Semeraro, G., Lops, P., de Gemmis, M.: Combining distributional semantics and entity linking for context-aware content-based recommendation. In: UMAP (2014)
16. Nguyen, P., Tomeo, P., Di Noia, T., Di Sciascio, E.: An evaluation of SimRank and Personalized PageRank to build a recommender system for the web of data. In: WWW. ACM (2015)
17. Di Noia, T.: Knowledge-enabled recommender systems: models, challenges, solutions. In: 3rd KDWEB Workshop (2017)
18. Di Noia, T., Ostuni, V.C., Tomeo, P., Sciascio, E.D.: SPrank: semantic path-based ranking for top-N recommendations using linked open data. Trans. Intell. Syst. Technol. 8(1), 9:1–9:34 (2016)
19. Passant, A.: dbrec—music recommendations using DBpedia. In: Patel-Schneider, P.F., Pan, Y., Hitzler, P., Mika, P., Zhang, L., Pan, J.Z., Horrocks, I., Glimm, B. (eds.) ISWC 2010. LNCS, vol. 6497, pp. 209–224. Springer, Heidelberg (2010). https://doi.org/10.1007/978-3-642-17749-1_14
20. Paulheim, H., Fümkranz, J.: Unsupervised generation of data mining features from linked open data. In: WIMS (2012)
21. Ragone, A., Tomeo, P., Magarelli, C., Di Noia, T., Palmonari, M., Maurino, A., Di Sciascio, E.: Schema-summarization in linked-data-based feature selection for recommender systems. In: SAC. ACM (2017)
22. Schaible, J., Gottron, T., Scherp, A.: *TermPicker*: enabling the reuse of vocabulary terms by exploiting data from the linked open data cloud. In: Sack, H., Blomqvist, E., d'Aquin, M., Ghidini, C., Ponzetto, S.P., Lange, C. (eds.) ESWC 2016. LNCS, vol. 9678, pp. 101–117. Springer, Cham (2016). https://doi.org/10.1007/978-3-319-34129-3_7
23. Shi, Y., Karatzoglou, A., Baltrunas, L., Larson, M., Oliver, N., Hanjalic, A.: CLiMF: learning to maximize reciprocal rank with collaborative less-is-more filtering. In: RecSys. ACM (2012)
24. Soru, T., Marx, E., Ngomo, A.N.: ROCKER: a refinement operator for key discovery. In: WWW. ACM (2015)
25. Spahiu, B., Porrini, R., Palmonari, M., Rula, A., Maurino, A.: ABSTAT: ontology-driven linked data summaries with pattern minimalization. In: Sack, H., Rizzo, G., Steinmetz, N., Mladenić, D., Auer, S., Lange, C. (eds.) ESWC 2016. LNCS, vol. 9989, pp. 381–395. Springer, Cham (2016). https://doi.org/10.1007/978-3-319-47602-5_51
26. Troullinou, G., Kondylakis, H., Daskalaki, E., Plexousakis, D.: RDF digest: efficient summarization of RDF/S KBs. In: Gandon, F., Sabou, M., Sack, H., d'Amato, C., Cudré-Mauroux, P., Zimmermann, A. (eds.) ESWC 2015. LNCS, vol. 9088, pp. 119–134. Springer, Cham (2015). https://doi.org/10.1007/978-3-319-18818-8_8

PageRank and Generic Entity Summarization for RDF Knowledge Bases

Dennis Diefenbach[1]([envelope])[iD] and Andreas Thalhammer[2][iD]

[1] Université de Lyon, CNRS UMR 5516 Laboratoire Hubert Curien, Lyon, France
dennis.diefenbach@univ-st-etienne.fr
[2] Roche Pharma Research and Early Development Informatics,
Roche Innovation Center Basel, Basel, Switzerland
andreas.thalhammer@roche.com

Abstract. Ranking and entity summarization are operations that are tightly connected and recurrent in many different domains. Possible application fields include information retrieval, question answering, named entity disambiguation, co-reference resolution, and natural language generation. Still, the use of these techniques is limited because there are few accessible resources. PageRank computations are resource-intensive and entity summarization is a complex research field in itself.

We present two generic and highly re-usable resources for RDF knowledge bases: a component for PageRank-based ranking and a component for entity summarization. The two components, namely PAGERANKRDF and SUMMASERVER, are provided in form of open source code along with example datasets and deployments. In addition, this work outlines the application of the components for PageRank-based RDF ranking and entity summarization in the question answering project WDAqua.

Keywords: RDF · Ranking · PageRank · Entity summarization
Question answering · Linked data

1 Introduction

PageRank scores and entity summaries are important tools in many applications that are relying on RDF data. We want to start with concrete examples in the question answering domain:

PageRank scores can be used as a feature to disambiguate between resources. Suppose a user asks just for "River". While there are many different meanings for "River" like a film or a village, the most probable one is the one referring to a natural watercourse. PageRank scores can be used in this context to rank the different meanings of "River" and to present the most probable one to the user. Another possible application of PageRank scores is the ranking of an answer set. Suppose a user asks "Which lakes are located in Italy?" Without any ranking, the resulting list could easily start with an unknown lake like "Lake Reschen". This is probably not very relevant information for the user. By ranking the

© Springer International Publishing AG, part of Springer Nature 2018
A. Gangemi et al. (Eds.): ESWC 2018, LNCS 10843, pp. 145–160, 2018.
https://doi.org/10.1007/978-3-319-93417-4_10

answer set properly, like in the information retrieval context, the usefulness of the answer for the user is increased.

Entity summarization [14] is the problem of identifying a limited number of ordered triples that summarize an entity in the best way—typically presented in knowledge panels. Those are then presented to the user together with the answer to a question (or search result) to enrich the current search context. Moreover they can also be useful for increasing the discoverability within the dataset (in the sense that the user can explore different aspects relating to the answer). Entity summarization and ranking algorithms (such as PageRank) are tightly related as the relevance of a triple given a specific entity needs to be estimated.

On one side, PageRank-based ranking and entity summaries can be essential tools in many domains like information retrieval, named entity disambiguation [20], entity linking [17], co-reference resolution, and natural language generation. On the other side, PageRank computations are resource-intensive and entity summarization is a research field in its own. So, while there are potentially many application areas the lack of easy access to re-usable resources is limiting the use of these technologies.

We present two highly re-usable resources for **(1)** **PageRank** [4] **on RDF graphs** (PAGERANKRDF) that can be combined to a **(2)** **generic framework for entity summarization** (SUMMASERVER). Both components are well documented and licensed under the MIT License (see Sect. 2). This enables extensibility and reusability without any types of restrictions. The framework has matured from earlier contributions [16,18,19] in the context of the WDAqua[1] research project with a focus on re-usable components for question answering [5–7].

This paper is organized as follows: In Sect. 2 we provide an overview of the presented resources. In Sect. 3 we first analyze the performance of PAGERANK-RDF with respect to scalability in time and memory which are the limiting resources during PageRank computations. Second we compare the PageRank scores when computed over the RDF graph and when computed over the corresponding link structure of Wikipedia. In Sect. 4 we describe the SUMMASERVER component. We also describe how to extend SUMMASERVER in order to generate summaries for new knowledge bases and its API. In Sect. 5 we describe how PAGERANKRDF and SUMMASERVER are used in an existing question answering system called WDAqua-core1. In Sect. 6 we compare this work to existing ones and we conclude with Sect. 7.

2   Resources

The main contribution of this work encompasses the following two resources.

> R1 A command line tool called PAGERANKRDF to compute PageRank scores over RDF graphs. The source code of PAGERANKRDF can be found at https://github.com/WDAqua/PageRankRDF with a complete documentation and usage instructions. It is released under the permissive MIT

---

[1] WDAqua (Answering Questions using Web Data) – http://wdaqua.eu/.

Licence. Moreover we deliver some derived resources with the PageRank scores for some known datasets in the LOD cloud, namely:

R 1.1 DBLP[2], using a dump provided by Jörg Diederich of the 22.07.2017, available under the DOI https://doi.org/10.6084/m9.figshare.5767008.v1.

R 1.2 DBpedia [1][3], using the dump of latest release of English DBpedia[4], available under the DOI https://doi.org/10.6084/m9.figshare.5769312.

R 1.3 Freebase [3][5], using the last Freebase dump before shutdown, available under the DOI https://doi.org/10.6084/m9.figshare.5767017.v1.

R 1.4 MusicBrainz[6], using the dump of December 2016 generated using MusicBainz-R2RML, available under the DOI https://doi.org/10.6084/m9.figshare.5769189. (https://github.com/LinkedBrainz/MusicBrainz-R2RML).

R 1.5 Scigraph[7], using the current release of February 2017 (http://scigraph.springernature.com/), available under the DOI https://doi.org/10.6084/m9.figshare.5769201.v1.

R 1.6 Wikidata [21][8], using the dump from the 28 September 2017, available under the DOI https://doi.org/10.6084/m9.figshare.5766432.v1.

The datasets are available at https://figshare.com/projects/PageRank_scores_of_some_RDF_graphs/28119.

R 2 An easily extensible framework for entity summarization called SUMMA-SERVER. It allows to generate entity summaries and currently supports the following knowledge bases: DBLP, DBpedia, Freebase, MusicBrainz, Scigraph, and Wikidata. Moreover it can be easily extended to support new knowledge bases. The source code of the SUMMASERVER can be accessed at https://github.com/WDAqua/SummaServer. It is released under the permissive MIT Licence. Moreover, we deliver a running service of the SummaServer. It can generate summaries for the above-mentioned knowledge bases that can be accessed at the following service endpoints:

R 2.1 https://wdaqua-summa-server.univ-st-etienne.fr/dblp/sum

R 2.2 https://wdaqua-summa-server.univ-st-etienne.fr/dbpedia/sum

R 2.3 https://wdaqua-summa-server.univ-st-etienne.fr/freebase/sum

R 2.4 https://wdaqua-summa-server.univ-st-etienne.fr/musicbrainz/sum

R 2.5 https://wdaqua-summa-server.univ-st-etienne.fr/scigraph/sum

R 2.6 https://wdaqua-summa-server.univ-st-etienne.fr/wikidata/sum

---

[2] http://dblp.l3s.de/dblp++.php.

[3] www.dbpedia.org.

[4] All files retrived by: wget -r -nc -nH –cut-dirs=1 -np -l1 -A '*ttl.bz2' -A '*.owl'-R '*unredirected*'–tries 2 http://downloads.dbpedia.org/2016-10/core-i18n/en/, i.e. all files published in the english DBpedia. We exclude the following files: nif_page_structure_en.ttl, raw_tables_en.ttl and page_links_en.ttl. The first two do not contain useful links, while, the last one contains the link structure of Wikipedia that was already used in previews works [18].

[5] http://freebase.com.

[6] https://musicbrainz.org.

[7] http://scigraph.springernature.com/.

[8] www.wikidata.org.

As a side note: From a previous contribution [19] there already exists the summaClient JavaScript component. It is a client of the SUMMASERVER that can be easily embedded in web pages. It is also licensed under the MIT License and can be accessed at https://github.com/athalhammer/summaClient.

3   Computation of PageRank on RDF Graphs

In the following we describe Resource ⟨R1⟩, namely PAGERANKRDF, a command line tool for computing PageRank scores over RDF graphs. In particular we analyze its scalability in terms of time and memory which are the limiting resources for PageRank computation. Then we analyze the quality of PageRank scores of Wikidata by comparing them with PageRank scores computed using untyped links between the corresponding Wikipedia articles.

3.1   Runtime Comparison: Non-HDT Version vs. HDT-Version

Implementing the Pagerank algorithm is a fairly easy task. The main problem is to make it scalable in terms of time and memory. We present two different ways to compute the PageRank scores over RDF graphs. Both implement the PageRank algorithm as presented by Brin and Page in [4]. The first implementation is a straight-forward implementation of the algorithm that takes as input an RDF dump in one of the current formats (like N-triples, Turtle) and computes the corresponding PageRank scores. The second implementation takes as input an RDF graph in HDT format [8]. HDT is a format for RDF that stores the graph in a very efficient way in terms of space. Generally, a factor ×10 between the space consumption of the original RDF dump in one of the usual formats and the corresponding HDT dump is realistic. Moreover at the same time the RDF graph remains queryable, in the sense that triple patterns can be resolved in milliseconds. An HDT file contains three sections: the **H**eader (which simply contains some metadata), the **D**ictionray (which is a compressed mapping between URIs and integers) and the **T**riples (which are also compressed using the Dictionary and additional compression techniques). The second implementation is based on two observations. First, only the graph structure is important for the computation of the PageRank scores, i.e. the last section of the HDT file. Second, the dictionary section, i.e. the URIs, are occupying most of the space. The implementation basically computes the PageRank scores on the third section of the HDT file and uses the dictionary only at the end to assign the scores to the different URIs. This makes the second implementation much more time and memory efficient.

In Fig. 1 the two implementations are compared by computing the PageRank scores for the Wikidata dump of the 28 September 2017 which has a size of 237 Gb and contains 2.2 billion triples. While the tool supports literals we ignore them in this experiment. It shows that when starting from an HDT dump of the graph the time consumption is reduced by a factor of ×19 and the memory consumption by a factor of ×5. In particular this last point is important since it allows the computation of PageRank scores of bigger datasets on affordable hardware. The time performance is increased for the following reason: When computing PageRank over an RDF file, most of the time is spent parsing and putting the data in a well-suited structure. The computation of the PageRank scores is rather short. With HDT the data is already in an optimal structure for the computation.

Note that HDT dumps of online available datasets can be found in the LOD laundromat [2][9] or under http://www.rdfhdt.org/datasets/. Moreover they can be easily created using the corresponding command line tools.[10]

3.2   Input Comparison: RDF Relations vs. Wikipedia Links

Next to the standard parameters "damping factor" and "number of iterations", PageRank [4] computations naturally depend most strongly on the input graph. Thalhammer and Rettinger showed in their work "PageRank on Wikipedia: Towards General Importance Scores for Entities" [18] that link filtering and weighting can have a strong influence on the output of PageRank calculations. In the same work it was indicated that the output of PageRank computations on the extracted RDF version of Wikipedia (i.e., DBpedia) could correlate less with page-view-based rankings than PageRank computations on the untyped Wikipedia link graph. However, the experiment was not performed and the following question is still open: "How do PageRank computations based on RDF relations compare to those based on Wikipedia links?" In order to answer this question, we start with the assumption that a higher ranking correlation (in our case Spearman's ρ and Kendall's τ)[11] to page-view-based rankings indicates a better ranking outcome.

The input data consists of three different ranking computations: PageRank on the Wikidata RDF graph (via PAGERANKRDF on a dump from September 28, 2017), PageRank on the Wikipedia link graph (computed with danker v0.1.0[12] on a Wikipedia dump from October 2, 2017 with option ALL[13]), and SubjectiveEye3D[14] by Paul Houle. The latter reflects the aggregated Wikipedia page view counts of the years 2008 to 2013 with different normalization factors (particularly considering the dimensions articles, language, and time). The datasets consist of different numbers of entities:

---

[9] http://lodlaundromat.org/.

[10] http://www.rdfhdt.org/manual-of-the-c-hdt-library/.

[11] Both correlation measures have a codomain of $[-1, 1]$ where -1 means fully anti-correlated and 1 means fully correlated. For computing Spearman's ρ we used the R cor.test function and for computing Kendall's τ we used the function cor.fk of the R package pcaPP https://cran.r-project.org/web/packages/pcaPP/.

[12] danker v0.1.0 – https://github.com/athalhammer/danker/releases/tag/v0.1.0.

[13] The option ALL uses the different language editions in a voting style using "bag of links semantics": if 200 languages cover the link $USA \rightarrow Barack\ Obama$ it is given more importance than 15 languages that cover the link $USA \rightarrow Donald\ Trump$. The PageRank algorithm supports multiple occurrences of the same link by default.

[14] SubjectiveEye3D – https://github.com/paulhoule/telepath/wiki/SubjectiveEye3D.

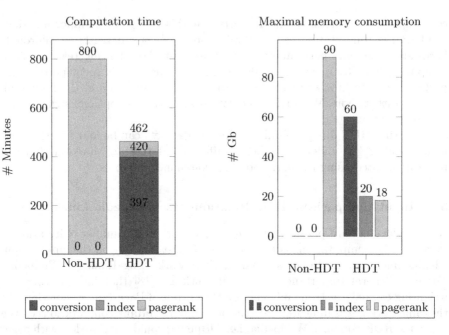

Fig. 1. This figure shows the time consumption and maximal memory consumption for the computation of the PageRank scores for Wikidata. We choose the dump of the 28 September 2017 which has a size of 237 Gb and 2.2 billion triples. The left figures shows the time consumption of the two implementation. The Non-HDT version takes 13 h. The HDT version takes 42 min when the HDT file is already computed and 8.8 h when the HDT file has to be generated from a different serialization. The right figure shows the memory consumption for the two implementation. The first implementation needs 90 Gb of RAM while the second 18 Gb if the HDT file is already computed and 60 Gb otherwise. The experiments were executed on a Server with Intel(R) Xeon(R) CPU E5-2667 v3 @ 3.20 GHz and 94 Gb of RAM.

- Wikidata, PAGERANKRDF : 38 433 113 Q-IDs (total 80 646 048 resources)
- Wikidata, danker (Wikipedia links): 17645575 Q-IDs
- SubjectiveEye3D: 6211 717 Q-IDs
- PAGERANKRDF ∩ danker ∩ SubjectiveEye3D: 4253 903 Q-IDs

danker only includes entities from the Wikipedia namespace 0 (Main/Article), which particularly excludes "File" (namespace 6) and "Category" (namespace 14). Both types of entities are included in the SubjectiveEye3D dataset which, in consequence, reduces the number of entities in the intersection set significantly. Another reduction factor were articles that have been deleted since 2013 (the upper limit of the SubjectiveEye3D input).

The result of the mutual correlation computations is outlined in Table 1. Both PageRank-based rankings have a positive correlation with the page-view-based ranking. The results show that danker correlates stronger with SubjectiveEye3D than PAGERANKRDF for both ranking correlation measures. Note that danker

Table 1. Spearman's ρ/Kendall's τ correlations of PageRank on RDF relations vs. Wikipedia links (via danker) and the comparison to SubjectiveEye3D.

	PAGERANKRDF	danker	SubjectiveEye3D
PAGERANKRDF	1.000/1.000	0.427/0.328	0.184/0.138
danker	0.427/0.328	1.000/1.000	0.400/0.276
SubjectiveEye3D	0.184/0.138	0.400/0.276	1.000/1.000

is tailored to the Wikipedia and/or Wikidata setting while PAGERANKRDF generalizes for all RDF graphs. Although there is no separation of A-Box and T-Box in Wikidata, terms like "Wikipedia Category" (wd:Q4167836), "scientific article" (wd:Q13442814), and "human" (wd:Q5) are prevalent in the top ten terms in the output of PAGERANKRDF. For specific applications it could make sense to pre-filter the input graph by certain predicates, such as rdfs:subClassOf, but this comes at the cost of generality and could impact the ranking output on other ends. Therefore, all datasets presented in [R1.x] were computed without such pre-filtering.

The correlation between danker and SubjectiveEye3D is weaker than expected from the more positive results of [18]. In that work, the PageRank experiments are based on page link datasets of English Wikipedia. In contrast, the danker ALL option factors in page links from all Wikipedia language editions and therefore reduces bias towards English Wikipedia. One possibility for the lower correlation could be that SubjectiveEye3D maintains a rather strong bias towards English Wikipedia (despite the mentioned normalization steps).

4 Re-usable API for Serving Summaries of Entities

In this section we present Resource [R2]—namely the SUMMASERVER—a service implementation that serves summaries of entities contained in RDF graphs. We first recapitulate the SUMMA API design [19] which is implemented by SUMMA-SERVER. Then, we sketch how a typical entity summarization service can be implemented using the SUMMASERVER code base.

4.1 The SUMMA API

The SUMMA API [19] is composed of two main components:

- SUMMA Vocabulary.[15]
- RESTful interaction mechanism.

This combination enables seamless integration with other Semantic Web components and a large degree of freedom with respect of the underlying entity summarization algorithm(s). When requesting a summary of an RDF entity only two parameters are mandatory:

---

[15] Available at http://purl.org/voc/summa.

entity the URI of the target resource (i.e., the resource to be summarized).
topK the number of triples the summary should contain.

The first interaction with the RESTful server is an HTTP `POST` request for creating a summary (see Listing 1). Note that the identifier of the summary in the summary request is a blank node (Turtle notation). The request basically says: "I would like the server to create a summary that complies with the given parameters." The server then responds with HTTP code 201 (`CREATED`). The `Location` header field denotes where we can find the newly created summary for future reference (i.e., to be accessed via `GET`): https://wdaqua-summa-server. univ-st-etienne.fr/wikidata/sum?entity=http://www.wikidata.org/entity/ Q42&topK=5&maxHops=1&language=en.

Listing 1. Example `POST` request for creating a new summary.

```
curl -d "[ a <http://purl.org/voc/summa/Summary> ; \
<http://purl.org/voc/summa/entity> \
<http://www.wikidata.org/entity/Q6414> ; \
<http://purl.org/voc/summa/topK> 5 ] ." \
-H "Content-type: text/turtle" \
-H "Accept: application/ld+json" \
https://wdaqua-summa-server.univ-st-etienne.fr/wikidata/sum
```

Different client applications can request summaries and interpret the returned content. For this, SUMMASERVER can parse and create output in all standard RDF serializations (in accordance to the provided `Content-type` and `Accept` header parameters). As a matter of fact, summaries do not necessarily need to be requested via `POST` requests but can also be directly accessed via `GET` (SUMMASERVER keeps the URL layout). However, the interaction mechanism could also return summaries identified by non-speaking URIs like https://wdaqua-summa-server.univ-st-etienne.fr/wikidata/sum/xyz. An example implementation of a client—the summaClient JavaScript component (https://github.com/athalhammer/summaClient)—can interact with any server that implements the SUMMA API layout (see for example Sect. 5.2).

For more details on SUMMA the reader is kindly referred to [19].

4.2   Implementation Guide

We briefly want to describe the idea used by the SUMMASERVER to generate summaries. Imagine one wants to generate the summary for an entity, like the Wikidata entity Q6414 corresponding to "Lake Garda", one of the biggest Italian lakes. The objective is to present to the user, between all facts that are known about this entity, the ones that best summarize it. An example of a summary for the "Lake Garda" is given in Fig. 2. The idea presented in [16] generates the summary for a target entity X using the following straight-forward strategy. First the knowledge base is explored around X in a breadth-first traversal up to a certain depth (typically only 1, i.e., the next neighbours). For all reached entities

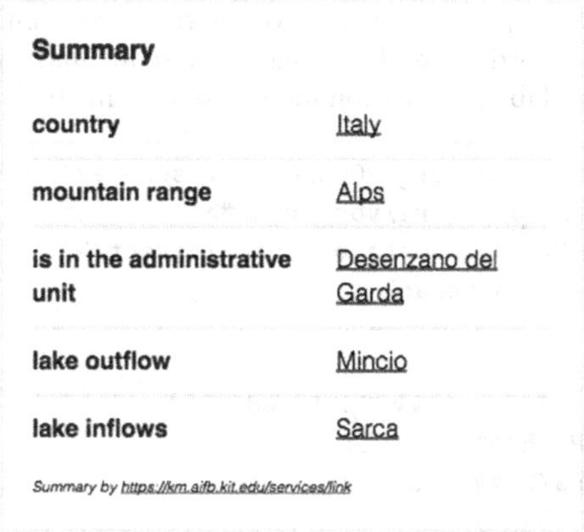

Summary

country	Italy
mountain range	Alps
is in the administrative unit	Desenzano del Garda
lake outflow	Mincio
lake inflows	Sarca

Summary by https://km.aifb.kit.edu/services/link

Fig. 2. Example of a summary for "Lake Garda".

the PageRank scores are considered and ranked in decreasing order. The entities corresponding to the first *topK* scores are shown in the summary. In the concrete example of "Lake Garda" the first 5 entities would be "Italy", "Alps", "Desenzano del Garda", "Mincio" and "Sarca". Note, during the breadth-first search the knowledge base can be either traversed in a directed or in an undirected way. In the following, we assume that the PageRank scores for all entities in the knowledge base were computed (for example using the command line tool in Sect. 3) and stored using the vRank vocabulary [13]. Moreover the PageRank scores are loaded in a SPARQL endpoint together with the original knowledge base. Setting up the SUMMASERVER to generate summaries for entities reduces to: indicate the address of the SPARQL endpoint and writing three SPARQL queries. We want to describe the three queries using as a concrete example the Wikidata knowledge base.

Listing 2. QUERY 1: This query retrives for an ENTITY the corresponding label in the language LANG. For Wikidata the query is

```
PREFIX rdfs: <http://www.w3.org/2000/01/rdf-schema#>
SELECT DISTINCT ?l
WHERE {
  <ENTITY> rdfs:label ?l .
  FILTER regex(lang(?l), "LANG", "i") .
}
```

(note that this information must be given since there are multiple ways to express the label of an entity. For example in MusicBrainz it is indicated with properties like <http://xmlns.com/foaf/0.1/name> and <http://purl.org/dc/elements/1.1/title>)

Listing 3. QUERY 2: This query must retrieve the resources connected to the resource ENTITY, order them according to the PageRank score and take the first TOPK. Moreover it retrieves the labels of the founded resources in the language LANG.

```
PREFIX rdf: <http://www.w3.org/2000/01/rdf-schema#>
PREFIX vrank: <http://purl.org/voc/vrank#>
PREFIX wdd: <http://www.wikidata.org/prop/direct/>
SELECT DISTINCT ?o ?l ?pageRank
WHERE {
  <ENTITY> ?p ?o .
    FILTER (?p != rdf:type && ?p != wdd:P31
    && ?p != wdd:P735 && wdd:P21
    && ?p != wdd:P972 && wdd:P421
    && ?p != wdd:P1343 )
  ?o rdfs:label ?l .
  regex(lang(?l), "LANG", "i") .
  graph <http://wikidata.com/pageRank> {
    ?o vrank:pagerank ?pageRank .
  }
}
ORDER BY DESC (?pageRank) LIMIT TOPK
```

(note that we do not traverse the edges with some labels like rdf:type and wdd:P31).

Listing 4. QUERY 3: This query must retrieve given two resource, ENTITY and OBJECT, the label of the property between them in the language LANG. For Wikidata we use the following query:

```
PREFIX rdf: <http://www.w3.org/2000/01/rdf-schema#>
PREFIX vrank:<http://purl.org/voc/vrank#>
SELECT ?p ?l
WHERE {
<ENTITY> ?p <OBJECT> .
OPTIONAL {
    ?o <http://wikiba.se/ontology-beta#directClaim> ?p .
    ?o rdfs:label ?l .
    FILTER regex(lang(?l), "LANG", "i")
}}
ORDER BY asc(?p) LIMIT 1
```

(note that in Wikidata the label of a direct property is not directly attached to it.)

We have implemented such queries for the following knowledge bases: Wikidata, DBpedia, DBLP, MusicBrainz, Freebase and the Scigraph. The implementations can be found at https://github.com/WDAqua/SummaServer/tree/master/src/main/java/edu/kit/aifb/summarizer/implemented. After indicating the endpoint and writing the three above queries the SUMMASERVER provides a

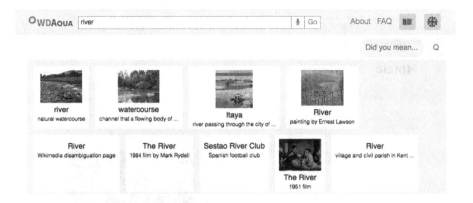

Fig. 3. Screenshot of WDAqua-Core1 for the question "River". The "did you mean" functionality shows other possible meanings of "River" that the user could have intended. The ranking, from left to right, from top to bottom, is based on PageRank scores.

summarization service for the corresponding knowledge base. For a more detailed instruction we refer to https://github.com/WDAqua/SummaServer#extending-to-a-new-knowledge-base-kb.

5   Use Case: Question Answering

In this section we show how the PageRank scores and the entity summarization services are used in the Quesiton Answering system WDAqua-Core1 [6,7].

5.1   PageRank for Question Answering

PageRank scores are used by WDAqua-core1 at two places. The first is for disambiguating entities. Suppose a user just asks for "River" and the question answering system uses Wikidata as an underlying knowledge bases. Multiple entities could be meant like Q4022 (a natural watercourse), Q2784912 (a village and civil parish in Kent) or Q7337056) (a studio album by Izzy Stradlin). The question is ambiguous but one still wants to present the most probable interpretation to the user. PageRanks are used here to identify the most probable intended interpretation by the user, i.e. the one with the highest PageRank between the possible candidates. A concrete usage is shown in Fig. 3.

A second application of PageRank scores relates to result set ordering. Imagine the following scenario. A user asks "Give me lakes in Italy." There are hundreds of lakes in Italy and currently there are 499 in Wikidata. Returning just a list will not be very useful for the user. Since the order is random the first presented lakes can be some unknown lake like the "Lago di Posta Fibreno". Ranking the answers according to PageRank will provide "Lago di Garda" and "Lago di Como" in the top ranks which is probably more relevant information for the user.

Fig. 4. Screenshot of WDAqua-Core1 for the question "What is the outflow of Lake Garda?". The entity summary is on the right-bottom part. Note that the links are discoverable, i.e. by clicking on "Po" information of "Po" are displayed (in the same way if the user asked directly for "Po").

The PageRank scores used in WDAqua-Core1 correspond to R1.1, R1.2, R1.3, R1.4, R1.5, R1.6 and are computed using the tool presented in Sect. 3.

5.2   Entity Summarization for Question Answering

Entity summaries are used in Trill [5], the front-end used by WDAqua-Core1. An example is given in Fig. 4. The summarization service is used mainly for two reasons: First, to add context to the retrieved answer. An expected result of this is that the confidence of the user in the answer is increased. Second, to increase discoverability within the dataset, i.e., offering a number of facts related to the answer entity the user. The facts are browse-able in the sense that the summary facts are clickable links that allow to easily explore other information in the graph that are connected to the original entities. WDAqua-Core1 currently uses the summarization services offered by SUMMASERVER corresponding to R2.1, R2.2, R2.3, R2.4, R2.5, R2.6. As explained in Sect. 3.2 the PageRank scores computed over the linked structure of Wikipedia express better the page views of the user. Since in DBpedia every entity corresponds to a Wikipedia article, for DBpedia we use the PageRank scores computed over the linked structure of Wikipedia.

A demo of WDAqua-Core1 can be found at www.wdaqua.eu/qa.

6 Related Work

We touch on two fields in this work, namely ranking for RDF knowledge bases and entity summarization. For a good survey on ranking for RDF knowledge bases we refer the reader to Roa-Valverde and Sicilia [12]. Recent work on this topic includes Ngomo et al. [10] which gives an alternative to traditional PageRank computation.[16] Also some vendors have included PageRank functionality in their products.[17] We presented an efficient implementation of PageRank that, when data is already provided in HDT format (as often already done; see LOD laundromat [2]), has a very high time and memory efficiency. For an overview on the field of entity summarization we kindly refer the reader to Sect. 2.2 of [14]. Recent work includes Pouriyeh et al. [11].

The presented work is intended to provide findable, accessible, interoperable, and re-usable (FAIR) baselines for ranking and entity summarization in RDF knowledge bases. It stands in the light of the FAIR guiding principles [22] that every modern researcher should try to adhere to. We build on [19] where the SUMMA API was originally presented. Next to the service endpoints presented in this work, this API definition has been implemented by [15] with the show case of DBpedia and is online available. We encourage other researchers in the field also to publish their research prototypes along the FAIR guiding principles by adhering to the SUMMA API definition. To the best of our knowledge, DBpedia/Wikidata PageRank[18] [18] is currently the only public source for pre-computed datasets of knowledge bases that can easily be loaded into triplestores. PAGERANKRDF builds on this work and provides general, affordable PageRank computation for RDF knowledge bases. An initial implementation of PAGERANKRDF was used for experiments by Andreas Harth that are documented at http://harth.org/andreas/2016/datenintelligenz/.

7 Summary

We have presented two important and tightly connected resources: a command line tool for computing PageRank scores called PAGERANKRDF [R1], and a framework for computing entity summaries called SUMMASERVER [R2]. The code is open source and available under an open licence. We have demonstrated that

---

[16] We tried to use the provided library to carry out the same experiments presented in this paper. The corresponding discussion with the authors can be found here: https://github.com/dice-group/HARE/issues/1.

[17] See for example https://wiki.blazegraph.com/wiki/index.php/RDF_GAS_API# PageRank or http://graphdb.ontotext.com/documentation/free/rdf-rank.html.

[18] DBpedia/Wikidata PageRank – http://people.aifb.kit.edu/ath/.

PAGERANKRDF can scale up to large datasets and we are publishing the computed scores for example knowledge bases. Moreover, we have described SUMMA-SERVER and shown how it can be extended to new knowledge bases. Finally, we have shown how the existing resources are used in a concrete scenario, namely in the existing question answering system WDAqua-Core1.

The presented resources will be maintained and used within the WDAqua ITN Project[19] [9]. Due to the popularity of the previously published PageRank scores [18] for DBpedia/Wikidata and the number of possible applications in different research areas, we believe that the presented resources are an important contribution for the Semantic Web community.

Acknowledgments. Parts of this work received funding from the European Union's Horizon 2020 research and innovation programme under the Marie Sksłodowska-Curie grant agreement No. 642795, project: Answering Questions using Web Data (WDAqua).

References

1. Auer, S., Bizer, C., Kobilarov, G., Lehmann, J., Cyganiak, R., Ives, Z.: DBpedia: a nucleus for a web of open data. In: Aberer, K., et al. (eds.) ASWC/ISWC -2007. LNCS, vol. 4825, pp. 722–735. Springer, Heidelberg (2007). https://doi.org/10.1007/978-3-540-76298-0_52

2. Beek, W., Rietveld, L., Bazoobandi, H.R., Wielemaker, J., Schlobach, S.: LOD laundromat: a uniform way of publishing other people's dirty data. In: Mika, P., et al. (eds.) ISWC 2014. LNCS, vol. 8796, pp. 213–228. Springer, Cham (2014). https://doi.org/10.1007/978-3-319-11964-9_14

3. Bollacker, K., Evans, C., Paritosh, P., Sturge, T., Taylor, J.: Freebase: a collaboratively created graph database for structuring human knowledge. In: Proceedings of the 2008 ACM SIGMOD International Conference on Management of Data, pp. 1247–1250. SIGMOD 2008. ACM, New York (2008). http://dx.doi.org/10.1145/1376616.1376746

4. Brin, S., Page, L.: The anatomy of a large-scale hypertextual web search engine. In: Proceedings of the Seventh International Conference on World Wide Web 7, WWW7, pp. 107–117. Elsevier Science Publishers B.V., Amsterdam (1998). http://dx.doi.org/10.1016/S0169-7552(98)00110-X

5. Diefenbach, D., Amjad, S., Both, A., Singh, K., Maret, P.: Trill: a reusable front-end for QA systems. In: Blomqvist, E., Hose, K., Paulheim, H., Lawrynowicz, A., Ciravegna, F., Hartig, O. (eds.) ESWC 2017. LNCS, vol. 10577, pp. 48–53. Springer, Cham (2017). https://doi.org/10.1007/978-3-319-70407-4_10

6. Diefenbach, D., Singh, K., Maret, P.: WDAqua-core0: a question answering component for the research community. In: Dragoni, M., Solanki, M., Blomqvist, E. (eds.) SemWebEval 2017. CCIS, vol. 769, pp. 84–89. Springer, Cham (2017). https://doi.org/10.1007/978-3-319-69146-6_8

7. Diefenbach, D., Both, A., Singh, K., Maret, P.: Towards a question answering system over the semantic web (2018). arXiv:1803.00832

---

8. Fernández, J.D., Martínez-Prieto, M.A., Gutiérrez, C., Polleres, A., Arias, M.: Binary RDF representation for publication and exchange (HDT). Web Semant.: Sci. Serv. Agents World Wide Web **19**, 22–41 (2013). http://dx.doi.org/10.1016/j.websem.2013.01.002

9. Lange, C., Shekarpour, S., Auer, S.: The WDAqua ITN: answering questions using web data. In: EU Project Networking Session at ESWC (2015)

10. Ngomo, A.C.N., Hoffmann, M., Usbeck, R., Jha, K.: Holistic and Scalable ranking of RDF data. In: 2017 IEEE International Conference on Big Data (2017). to appear

11. Pouriyeh, S., Allahyari, M., Kochut, K., Cheng, G., Arabnia, H.R.: ES-LDA: entity summarization using knowledge-based topic modeling. In: Proceedings of the Eighth International Joint Conference on Natural Language Processing (Volume 1: Long Papers), pp. 316–325. Asian Federation of Natural Language Processing (2017). http://aclweb.org/anthology/I17-1032

12. Roa-Valverde, A.J., Sicilia, M.A.: A survey of approaches for ranking on the web of data. Information Retrieval **17**(4), 295–325 (2014). http://dx.doi.org/10.1007/s10791-014-9240-0

13. Roa-Valverde, A.J., Thalhammer, A., Toma, I., Sicilia, M.A.: Towards a formal model for sharing and reusing ranking computations. In: Proceedings of the 6th International Workshop on Ranking in Databases (DBRank 2012) held in conjunction with the 38th Conference on Very Large Databases (VLDB 2012) (2012). http://www.aifb.kit.edu/web/Inproceedings3537

14. Thalhammer, A.: Linked data entity summarization. Ph.D. thesis, KIT, Fakultät für Wirtschaftswissenschaften, Karlsruhe (2016). http://dx.doi.org/10.5445/IR/1000065395

15. Thalhammer, A., Lasierra, N., Rettinger, A.: LinkSUM: using link analysis to summarize entity data. In: Bozzon, A., Cudre-Maroux, P., Pautasso, C. (eds.) ICWE 2016. LNCS, vol. 9671, pp. 244–261. Springer, Cham (2016). https://doi.org/10.1007/978-3-319-38791-8_14

16. Thalhammer, A., Rettinger, A.: Browsing DBpedia Entities with Summaries. In: Presutti, V., Blomqvist, E., Troncy, R., Sack, H., Papadakis, I., Tordai, A. (eds.) ESWC 2014. LNCS, vol. 8798, pp. 511–515. Springer, Cham (2014). https://doi.org/10.1007/978-3-319-11955-7_76

17. Thalhammer, A., Rettinger, A.: ELES: combining entity linking and entity summarization. In: Bozzon, A., Cudre-Maroux, P., Pautasso, C. (eds.) ICWE 2016. LNCS, vol. 9671, pp. 547–550. Springer, Cham (2016). https://doi.org/10.1007/978-3-319-38791-8_45

18. Thalhammer, A., Rettinger, A.: PageRank on Wikipedia: towards general importance scores for entities. In: Sack, H., Rizzo, G., Steinmetz, N., Mladenić, D., Auer, S., Lange, C. (eds.) ESWC 2016. LNCS, vol. 9989, pp. 227–240. Springer, Cham (2016). https://doi.org/10.1007/978-3-319-47602-5_41

19. Thalhammer, A., Stadtmüller, S.: SUMMA: a common API for linked data entity summaries. In: Cimiano, P., Frasincar, F., Houben, G.-J., Schwabe, D. (eds.) ICWE 2015. LNCS, vol. 9114, pp. 430–446. Springer, Cham (2015). https://doi.org/10.1007/978-3-319-19890-3_28

20. Tristram, F., Walter, S., Cimiano, P., Unger, C.: Weasel: a machine learning based approach to entity linking combining different features. In: Proceedings of 3th International Workshop on NLP and DBpedia, co-located with the 14th International Semantic Web Conference (ISWC 2015), October 11–15, USA (2015). http://nbn-resolving.de/urn:nbn:de:0070-pub-27755352
21. Vrandečić, D., Krötzsch, M.: Wikidata: a free collaborative knowledgebase. Commun. ACM **57**(10), 78–85 (2014). http://dx.doi.org/10.1145/2629489
22. Wilkinson, M.D., et al.: The FAIR Guiding Principles for scientific data management and stewardship. Sci. Data **3** (2016). http://dx.doi.org/10.1038/sdata.2016.18

Answering Multiple-Choice Questions in Geographical Gaokao with a Concept Graph

Jiwei Ding[iD], Yuan Wang[iD], Wei Hu[iD], Linfeng Shi[iD], and Yuzhong Qu$^{(\boxtimes)}$[iD]

National Key Laboratory for Novel Software Technology,
Nanjing University, Nanjing, China
jwdingnju@outlook.com, ywangnju@outlook.com, lfshinju@outlook.com,
{whu,yzqu}@nju.edu.cn

Abstract. Answering questions in Gaokao (the national college entrance examination in China) brings a great challenge for recent AI systems, where the difficulty of questions and the lack of formal knowledge are two main obstacles, among others. In this paper, we focus on answering multiple-choice questions in geographical Gaokao. Specifically, a concept graph is automatically constructed from textbook tables and Chinese wiki encyclopedia, to capture core concepts and relations in geography. Based on this concept graph, a graph search based question answering approach is designed to find explainable inference paths between questions and options. We developed an online system called CGQA and conducted experiments on two real datasets created from the last ten year geographical Gaokao. Our experimental results demonstrated that CGQA can generate accurate judgments and provide explainable solving procedures. Additionally, CGQA showed promising improvement by combining with existing approaches.

Keywords: Concept graph · Geographical Gaokao
Question answering · CGQA

1 Introduction

With the great development of Artificial Intelligence (AI) technologies, having machines to pass human examination is becoming a hot AI challenge. Similar to the Aristo project [5] and the Japanese Todai project [6], China has launched a National High-tech R&D Program [4] to promote AI systems to pass the national college entrance examination (commonly known as *Gaokao*). The goal of the project is to make AI systems not only answer complicated questions but also provide explainable solving procedures.

In recent years, a multitude of question answering (QA) approaches have been proposed for various application scenarios, such as reading comprehension [15], intelligent assistant [2], and community QA [12]. However, these approaches are not suitable for QA in Gaokao, due to the following three main difficulties:

© Springer International Publishing AG, part of Springer Nature 2018
A. Gangemi et al. (Eds.): ESWC 2018, LNCS 10843, pp. 161–176, 2018.
https://doi.org/10.1007/978-3-319-93417-4_11

- The difficulty in question understanding. Most multiple-choice questions in Gaokao use sentences as their options (answer choices) in order to test a student's ability in different topics. Figure 1 shows an example of multiple-choice questions in geographical Gaokao. In this example, option A is related to climate and vegetation in physical geography, while option B is related to agriculture in human geography. Also, there are multiple sentence structures in options, e.g., the first part of option C is factoid, while the second part contains a comparison. Traditional semantic parsing approaches [1, 19] may have difficulty in processing such sentences, due to the lack of question patterns and specific knowledge bases.
- The lack of formal knowledge. Concepts play an important role for students to learn knowledge in high school, and form testing points in Gaokao questions. In the example question, "temperate steppe zone", "crop farming", etc., are all geographical concepts in textbooks. These concepts involve different topics and form complex hierarchies. Currently, geographical databases such as GeoNames[1] and Clinga [8] cover a large number of geographical entities. However, they contain little knowledge for geographical concepts and their relations.
- The complexity of inference. Inference is a common task in answering scientific questions, but the inference procedures in Gaokao are more complex. For example, option A needs student to judge whether London is "warm and rainy all year round". It is possible to solve this question by adapting related rules if we have London's temperature and precipitation data. However, students solve this question in another way, because "warm and rainy all year round" is a characteristic for the concept "temperate oceanic climate", which is London's climate type. For the first solution, AI systems may have difficulty in mapping natural language phrases to predicates and constants in rules, and need a large amount of geographical data. For the second solution, we need to collect related natural language descriptions for geographical concepts.

Fig. 1. A multiple-choice question in geographical Gaokao. To help readers understanding, the examples in this paper are translated into English.

In this paper, we focus on answering multiple-choice questions in geographical Gaokao. To overcome the above difficulties, we construct a concept graph

---

[1] http://www.geonames.org/ontology.

automatically, which not only captures the relations between geographical concepts, but also contains concept descriptions in natural language extracted from textbook tables and Chinese wiki encyclopedia. Furthermore, we propose a graph search based QA approach, which finds explainable inference paths between questions and options. We developed an online system called CGQA and conducted experiments on two real datasets created from the last ten year geographical Gaokao. Our experiments showed that CGQA generated accurate judgments and provided explainable solving procedures. Additionally, CGQA showed promising improvement by combining with existing approaches.

2 Related Work

Information retrieval techniques are wildly used in QA systems for short factoid questions. By searching sentences in a large web corpus, Clark et al. [5] scored 60.6% for multiple-choice questions in the 4th Grade Science Test. Cheng et al. [4] studied answering multiple-choice questions in historical Gaokao by retrieving and filtering pages in Chinese Wikipedia. However, the facts appeared in geographical Gaokao questions are not explicitly stated in text or databases, thus inference is required for this problem.

Over the years, several studies have been conducted to solve questions with inference. As an early study, OntoNova [3] represents chemistry knowledge in F-Logic to answer formal queries via rule reasoning. Similar approaches were used for physics and biology questions. These approaches cannot be directly applied to geographical Gaokao, since it is difficult to map natural language phrases to predicates and constants in rules. Khashabi et al. [9] employed textual entailment and integer liner programming to answer elementary science questions with tables. However, this approach relies on many manually-constructed constraints, and cannot handle questions with sentences as options.

Recently, deep neural networks achieve promising performance in some QA tasks. Sukhbaatar et al. [17] exploited an end-to-end memory networks, which outperformed other methods like LSTM on the synthetic QA tasks from Facebook. Guo et al. [7] proposed a permanent-provisional memory network to answer multiple-choice history questions in Gaokao, which gained the best score (45.70%) compared to other memory-capable neural network models. However, these approaches cannot provide explainable solving procedures, and sometimes suffer from the lack of training data.

In addition to a few open-domain knowledge bases like DBpedia [10] and XLore [18], GeoNames is perhaps the most well-known database for geographical information, which contains data like place names, latitude and longitude coordinates. Clinga [8] is a Chinese linked geographical dataset, which contains a large number of entities extracted from Chinese wiki encyclopedia, and links them to other knowledge bases like DBpedia. All datasets mentioned above cover a large number of geographical entities such as cities and mountains, but contain little knowledge of geographical concepts, which wildly appear in geographical Gaokao questions.

With the rapid development of KBQA methods, users are able to query knowledge bases with natural language questions. Zou et al. [19] exploited semantic query graphs for question analysis. Abujabal et al. [1] mapped questions to automatically generated SPARQL templates. However, these approaches may have difficulty in processing Gaokao questions, due to the lack of question patterns and specific knowledge bases.

3   Concept Graph Construction

We first give the definition for the concept graph as follows:

Definition 1 (Concept Graph). *We define a concept graph as a 5-tuple* (S, C, D, R, T), *where* S, C, D *and* R *denote the sets of concept schemes (topics), concepts, descriptions and relations, respectively.* $T \subseteq (C \times R \times S) \cup (C \times R \times C) \cup (C \times R \times D)$ *denotes the set of triples.*

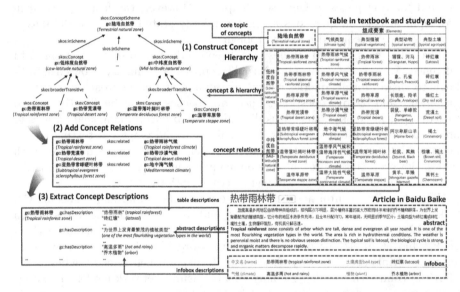

Fig. 2. General steps to construct concept graph for geographical Gaokao

We construct our geographical Gaokao concept graph according to Simple Knowledge Organization System (SKOS). Figure 2 depicts the general steps to construct the concept graph, including: (1) Construct Concept Hierarchy, (2) Add Concept Relations, and (3) Extract Concept Descriptions. The methodology that we use is largely automatic, with little manual amendment to ensure quality.

3.1 Construct Concept Hierarchy

We choose geography textbooks and study guides[2] as the main data sources due to their high quality and targetedness. These materials usually organize different concepts in the form of tables in addition to plain text descriptions, to help students to explicitly notice their commodities and differences. For a table in textbook, geographical concepts are often placed in the first column, with the concepts' topic name (e.g., Terrestrial natural zone) in the column header. For each concept, a unique ID is generated as URI (e.g., *gc:Tropical_rainforest_zone*) and *skos:Concept* is defined as its type. Similarly, a URI is generated for the concepts' topic name and is declared with type *skos:ConceptScheme*. *skos:inScheme* relation is used to connect concepts with their topics. The broader-narrower relations between concepts can also be extracted from the table cell hierarchy, and are represented using *skos:broaderTransitive* and *skos:narrowerTransitive* in concept graph. If two concepts in the same *skos:ConceptScheme* do not have the broader-narrower relation, a *gc:disjointWith* relation is added between them automatically. A few tables have empty column headers, or use common words such as "type" as their column headers. This issue is manually fixed by giving an appropriate topic name.

3.2 Add Concept Relations

Geographical concepts in different topics often relate to each other (e.g., *volcanic landform* is related to *magmatic rock, tropical rainforest zone* is related to *tropical rainforest climate*). We collect this kind of relations through the co-occurrence of concepts in the following sources and represent them using relation *skos:related*.

- Textbook. Concepts appearing in the same row of a table are considered as related. Also, if two concepts co-occur frequently in text, we consider them as related. In our construction process, this frequency threshold is set to 2 based on our experimental experience.
- Baidu Baike. Baidu Baike is the largest collaboratively-built Chinese wiki encyclopedia. The first few paragraphs are an overview of the geographical concept, called *abstract*. We consider two concepts as related if both of them appear in each other's Baidu Baike abstract.

It is worth noting that *skos:related* is only used between concepts in different concept schemes, as concepts in the same concept scheme only have *skos:broaderTransitive*, *skos:narrowerTransitive* or *gc:disjointWith* relation.

3.3 Extract Concept Descriptions

Many concepts have specific natural language phrases describing their characteristics of different aspects. For example, "hot and rainy" describes the climatic characteristic for *gc:Tropical_rainforest_zone*. We call these phrases *Descriptions*, and store them in plain text as the values of *gc:hasDescription*. Descriptions are automatically extracted from the following sources:

---

[2] We used electronic editions at http://kb.cs.tsinghua.edu.cn/res/index.

- Textbook tables. Table cells in the same row of a concept can be regarded as its descriptions if they do not contain any other concepts.
- Baidu Baike infobox and abstract. In a concept's Baidu Baike article, the key-value pairs in the infobox present some structural facets of the concept. We consider each value as a description, if it does not contain any other concepts. Especially, values of "alias" and "also known as" are described as the value of *skos:altLabel*. Also, each sentence in the abstract is considered as a description if it has proper length (less than 30 Chinese characters in our current setting) and does not contain any other concepts. We will consider the method in [16] to extract descriptions from tables in Baidu Baike in the future.

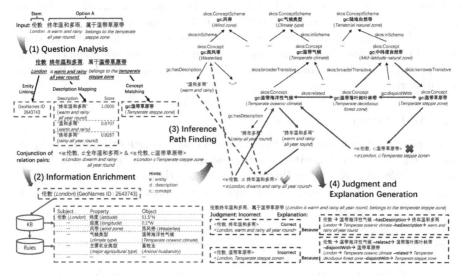

Fig. 3. Multiple-choice question answering with concept graph

4   Multiple-Choice Question Answering

A multiple-choice question in geographical Gaokao contains a string qs called *question stem* and four strings $O = \{o_1, o_2, \ldots, o_4\}$ called *options*. Some questions contain background text qb or diagrams qd as extra materials.

The framework of our QA approach is shown in Fig. 3. Given a multiple-choice question, we convert it to four statements by combining each option o_i with the question stem qs. Our approach takes each statement as input, and gives judgment and explanation with four stages: (1) Question Analysis, (2) Information Enrichment, (3) Inference Path Finding, and (4) Judgment and Explanation Generation. The statement with the highest score among the four is chosen as the answer.

4.1   Question Analysis

The question analysis stage in our approach contains three steps: (1) Entity Linking and Concept Matching, (2) Description Mapping, and (3) Relation Pairs Generation.

Entity Linking and Concept Matching. In geographical Gaokao, entities and concepts usually appear with their canonical names to ensure the rigor of the exam. This makes the linking process easy. We use a sliding window based approach to recognize concept and entity mentions, and link them to the concept graph and GeoNames, respectively. For entities with the same name in GeoNames, we select the one with the highest administrative division level and the latest update date. Furthermore, a few patterns are manually built to recognize anonymous entities such as "place A" and "area One", which are often used to refer to entities in figures or background materials. Our experiment over 200 multiple-choice questions shows that, by using the above method, the precision and recall reached 92% and 90%, respectively.

Description Mapping. Description mapping is to recognize the descriptive text in question stems and options, and map them to the descriptions (D) in the concept graph, which is quite similar with the semantic matching task [11]. Each question and option is split into several clauses according to conjunction and punctuation, and each clause is supposed to contain at most one continuous descriptive text, which might map to several descriptions in the concept graph. For example, the option A in Fig. 3 is split into two clauses, and the first one is mapped to description "warm and rainy all year round" and "warm and rainy". Since there are thousands of descriptions in the concept graph, we firstly tried a Lucene-based approach to ensure efficiency. However, this approach failed to achieve satisfactory mapping precision since Lucene only considers lexical similarity and TF-IDF value. In order to achieve higher mapping precision, a two-step mapping approach is developed.

Firstly, we use a comprehensive measurement which considers both Levenshtein distance and word embedding similarity to find candidate descriptions for each clause. The Levenshtein distance measures the lexical similarity, while the word embedding similarity measurement handles the problem of semantic heterogeneity. Each n words in the clause (n decreases from clause length to 1) is seen as a query q, and the mapping score between query q and description d is calculated as follows:

$$MScore(q, d) = \alpha\left(1 - \frac{LevenshteinDistance(q, d)}{\max(Length(q), Length(d))}\right) + (1 - \alpha)\cos(v(q), v(d)),$$

$$(1)$$

where $v(q)$ and $v(d)$ stand for the embedded word vectors for query and description, respectively. The training process of the word embedding model is introduced in Sect. 5.4. The longest query that has mapping score larger than θ with any description is seen as the descriptive text for the clause, and all descriptions having mapping scores larger than θ are seen as candidate descriptions.

Secondly, we find that adjectives usually play an important role when measuring semantic similarity. For example, "warm and rainy all year round" is similar to "cold and rainy all year round" in lexical similarity, but they refer to totally different climates in geography. In our approach, we exploit adjective relations in WordNet [14] to filter candidate descriptions. Suppose that candidate description d contains several adjectives $d_1, \ldots, d_i, \ldots, d_N$, and the query q contains adjectives $q_1, \ldots, q_j, \ldots, q_M$. If any pair of d_i and q_j have the antonym relation in WordNet, description d is removed from the candidates. After filtering, the top k candidate descriptions are selected as the output of our description mapping approach.

Relation Pairs Generation. In this step, entities, concepts and descriptions are reorganized as relation pairs according to their relationships in the dependency tree. Particularly, some relation pairs are ignored since both of their components are in the question stem. Then, the whole input statement is transformed into the conjunction of relation pairs. The disjunction of relation pairs is not considered in our work, since it never appears in real-life Gaokao questions. An example of the conjunction of relation pairs is as follows: $\langle e : London, d : warm\_and\_rainy\_all\_year\_round\rangle$ & $\langle e : London, c : Temperate\_ste\text{-}ppe\_zone\rangle$, where e: stands for entity, c: stands for concept, and d: stands for description.

4.2   Information Enrichment

Inferring concepts associated with a given geographical entity is an important ability for students, and is frequently tested in Gaokao (e.g., inferring the climatic zone of London). We implement two different methods to relate geographical entities to concepts and descriptions in the concept graph.

- **Structured Knowledge Acquisition.** Knowledge bases such as GeoNames (see footnote 1), Wikidata[3], Clinga [8] and Koppen[4] provide plenty of geographical information for entities, such as latitude, climate type and precipitation. Entities can be related to concepts directly by querying the knowledge bases, or indirectly by applying geographical rules. For example, "The latitude of westerlies is between 35 and 65°" is a simple geographical rule that links entity and wind belt in the concept graph using latitude information, which can be fetched in GeoNames and Wikidata for most of the entities.
- **Related Text Matching.** Some geographical concepts and descriptions occur in entities' related text, such as background materials in a test paper, or articles in Chinese wiki encyclopedia. We use the mapping approach described in the question analysis section to extract related concepts and descriptions from these materials. Also, the concepts having "examples" or "typical areas" as their descriptions may contain the entity names directly.

---

[3] https://www.wikidata.org/.
[4] http://hanschen.org/koppen/.

4.3   Inference Path Finding

Our approach infers *supporting paths* and *protesting paths* in the concept graph, which are defined as follows:

Definition 2 (Supporting Path). *A path is a supporting path if and only if no gc:disjointWith relation exists between any two vertices in this path. Formally, let G be a concept graph. Given a path P containing vertices $V(P) = \{v_1, v_2, \ldots, v_n\}$, P is a supporting path iff $\nexists v_i, v_j \in V(P)$, $v_i \xrightarrow{gc:disjointWith} v_j \in G$.*

Definition 3 (Protesting Path). *A path is a protesting path if and only if at least a gc:disjointWith relation exists between some of the vertices in this path. Formally, let G be a concept graph. Given a path P containing vertices $V(P) = \{v_1, v_2, \ldots, v_n\}$, P is a protesting path iff $\exists v_i, v_j \in V(P)$, $v_i \xrightarrow{gc:disjointWith} v_j \in G$.*

The following theorem is easy to be proved.

Theorem 1 *A path in the concept graph is either a supporting path or a protesting path.*

The procedure for making the judgment for a relation pair $\langle A, B \rangle$ is shown below:

1. Add nodes A and B to the concept graph, connect them with related concepts and descriptions.
2. Find a supporting path from A to B using Algorithm 1. If found, return **Correct**.
3. Otherwise, find a shortest path from A to B through the Breadth-First Search. If found, according to Theorem 1, this path must be a protesting path, return **Incorrect**.
4. If there is no path from A to B in the concept graph, return **Unknown**.

Algorithm 1. Supporting path finding

Input: Nodes in relation pair $\langle A, B \rangle$ and concept graph G
Output: A path from A to B, or null for no path found
1: **function** FINDSUPPORTPATH(A, B, G)
2:    **if** $A = B$ **then**
3:       **return** a path only containing B;
4:    $G' \leftarrow G - \{v | v \xrightarrow{gc:disjointWith} A, v \in G\}$;
5:    **for all** A's neighbour v_i in G' **do**
6:       $P \leftarrow$ FINDSUPPORTPATH($v_i, B, G' - \{A\}$);
7:       **if** $P \neq$ null **then**
8:          **return** append A to the head of path P;
9:    **return** null;

4.4 Judgment and Explanation Generation

Our approach generates the judgment for each statement by combining the judgment for each relation pair through the following method:

– If any relation pair in the statement is incorrect, the whole statement is incorrect, scores −1;
– If there are m correct relation pairs and n unknown relation pairs in the statement, the whole statement is partial correct, scores $\frac{m}{n+m}$;
– If all the relation pairs of the statement are unknown, the whole statement is not judged, scores 0;

Additionally, our approach combines the inference path for each relation pair to generate the explanation for the whole statement. For a correct relation pair, we display the supporting path found by Algorithm 1; while for an incorrect relation pair, we display the shortest protesting path. Relation pairs with no judgment are ignored to explain.

Table 1. Statistics of the geographical Gaokao concept graph

	Names	Count
Nodes	skos:Concept Scheme	57
	skos:Concept	588
	Plain literals	4,312
Edges	skos:inScheme	588
	skos:broader Transitive	373
	skos:narrower Transitive	373
	skos:related	142
	gc:disjointWith	12,602
	skos:prefLabel	645
	skos:altLabel	213
	gc:hasDescription	3,453

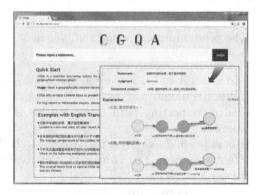

Fig. 4. Screenshot of CGQA

5 Experiments

5.1 Geographical Gaokao Datasets

We collected multiple-choice questions with expected answers from real-life geographical Gaokao all over the states in recent ten years (2008–2017). After removing duplicate questions, 4,305 multiple-choice questions were collected in total: 1,756 from 128 geography tests in Gaokao, and 2,549 from 116 geography tests in mock Gaokao. The average length for question stems and options are 19.65 and 8.44, respectively. About 87% of questions contain diagrams, which are currently difficult to be processed. To evaluate our approach, we constructed the following two datasets [5]:

- **Beijing Geographical Gaokao (BGG):** It contains all multiple-choice questions in Beijing Geography Gaokao from 2008 to 2017: six no-diagram questions and 104 questions with 60 different diagrams. All of these diagrams were annotated by geography majors in triples in advance. These labels only contain basic information for anonymous entities, such as longitude and latitude, which can only be fetched from diagrams.
- **No-Diagram Questions (NDQ):** It contains all no-diagram multiple-choice questions in Gaokao and mock Gaokao all over the states from 2008 to 2017. There are 545 questions in total.

5.2 Geographical Gaokao Concept Graph

Table 1 shows the numbers of nodes and edges of our concept graph [6]. In total, it contains 19,034 triples describing 588 concepts in 57 concept schemes.

To evaluate the accuracy of concept relations and descriptions, we manually judged the correctness of all *skos:related* relations and 500 randomly picked descriptions. The precisions are 93.66% and 90.60%, respectively. We observed that the precision of descriptions extracted from Baidu Baike infoboxes is not good, because some contain short common words such as "global" and "geography" as values.

5.3 Demo

The demo of our approach, called CGQA, is currently available at http://ws.nju.edu.cn/cgqa/. As shown in Fig. 4, the system will give out judgment and solving procedure after user input a geographically related statement.

5.4 Comparative Approaches

We compared our approach with three existing approaches. Each approach is required to provide a score for each option, and the options with the highest score are chosen as the answer. For our approach, the parameter α in Eq. (1) is set to 0.2, the mapping score threshold θ is set to 0.80, and k is set to 3 in description mapping.

IR-Based Approach. The information retrieval (IR) based approach [4] is to find out the confidence that the question stem qs along with an answer option o_i is explicitly stated in a corpus. For this purpose, a text corpus containing 14.8 million sentences was automatically built using geographical textbooks, study guides and Baidu Baike articles used in Clinga. We used $qs + o_i$ as the input for Lucene, and returns the Lucene's score for top retrieved sentence having at least one non-stopword overlap with qs and o_i. This is repeated several times to score all options.

---

[5] Both datasets are available at http://ws.nju.edu.cn/cgqa/datasets.zip.
[6] The concept graph is available at http://ws.nju.edu.cn/cgqa/cg.zip.

WE-Based Approach. The word embedding (WE) based approach [5] computes the semantic relevance between each answer option o_i and the question stem qs by exploiting word similarity. In our approach, a word embedding (150 dimensions) was learned using Skip-gram [13] over the corpus built for the IR-based approach. We defined the semantic relevance of qs and o_i as the cosine similarity between their composite vectors, which were computed by summing the vector for each word in qs and o_i, respectively.

NN-Based Approach. As neural network (NN) is widely used in QA, we designed an end-to-end NN-based approach according to [7,17]. All questions not included in the test set were treated as training data (3,650 questions in total). The design of our network is shown in Fig. 5, which includes:

- The input module maps the question stem, options, and the top 10 related sentences retrieved by Lucene into vectors using a pre-trained word2vec model (the same as the WE-based approach);
- The encoder module embeds the vectors from each input to a new vector space by a single Bi-GRU layer;
- The attention module combines the top 10 related vectors using weighted sum, and adds the combined vector with the question stem vector as the final question vector;
- The output module computes the match between the final question vector and option vectors by taking the inner product followed by a softmax.

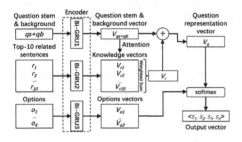

Fig. 5. Design of NN-based approach

Table 2. Results for accuracy of judgments and explanations

	BGG	NDQ
Number of statements	440	2,180
Answered percentage	11.36%	11.24%
Judgment precision	84.00%	90.61%
Explanation correctness	81.20%	88.52%
Average path length	3.76	3.05

5.5 Procedures and Metrics

We firstly evaluated the accuracy of judgments and explanations of our approach. For each multiple-choice question, four statements were generated by combining stem text with each option. The following metrics were used in this step:

- Answered percentage: percentage of judged statements in all statements;

- Judgment precision: percentage of correctly-judged statements in all judged statements;
- Explanation correctness: percentage of correct explanations in all the explanations, to avoid the statement being answered correct by accident.

To measure the explanation correctness, five undergraduate students of geography specialty were invited to score the explanations provided by our approach. An explanation is labeled correct only if it provides enough evidence to make the accurate judgment. Explanations for wrong judgments were labeled incorrect automatically.

Secondly, we compared the scores of our approach with several comparative approaches listed above. In addition, we combined our approach with each comparative approach using priority strategy to observe whether there are scores improvements. For scoring function, we followed the work in [5]. If the approach provides N answers including the correct one, it scores $1/N$. If no answer is produced, it scores $1/K$ for question with K options, equivalent to random guessing.

5.6 Results

Table 2 shows the accuracy of judgments and explanations for our approach. Our approach judged a part of statements (about 11%) with high precision (84.00% and 90.61% for BGG and NDQ, respectively). The reason of unsatisfactory answered percentage is that there are more than 60% statements that do not contain any concept or description in both two datasets. The average length of the inference paths is larger than 3, which indicates that these questions are quite difficult. Additionally, the mean value for explanation correctness reaches 81.20% and 88.52%, respectively, and the standard deviation between different assessors is approximately 1%. Repeated Measures ANOVA indicates that there is no divergence between different assessors ($p > 0.95$). Most assessors reported that the inference path proposed by our approach is reasonable and easy to be understood during the experiments.

Table 3 shows the test performance for each single approach. Our approach outperformed the IR-based and WE-based approaches, and achieved comparable results with the NN-based approach. When we took a look at the output for each approach, we found that our approach only answered a few part of the questions (22.73% of BGG and 16.88% of NDQ). The score of our approach on these answered questions is 68.00% and 83.33%, respectively. In contrast, all the comparative approaches answered nearly 100% of the questions, with scores lower than 38%.

In Table 4, comparative approaches gained an increment of approximately 6%–14% in test scores by combining with our approach. This indicates that our approach and existing approaches are complementary. CGQA + NN achieved the best performance on both datasets (43.41% and 45.50%, respectively).

Additionally, we allowed each comparative approaches to answer a part of questions according to the descending order of confidence value, where confidence

Table 3. Scores for single approaches

	CGQA	IR	WE	NN
BGG	**34.77%**	20.91%	22.73%	32.50%
NDQ	34.85%	28.99%	29.72%	**37.25%**

Table 4. Scores for combined approaches

	CGQA +IR	CGQA +WE	CGQA +NN
BGG	30.76%	36.36%	43.41%
NDQ	35.23%	39.45%	45.50%

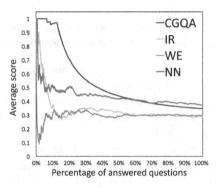

Fig. 6. Scores for single approaches

value is defined as the difference between the highest score and the second-highest score among the options. Figure 6 shows the average score on answered questions for these approaches on NDQ. It can be found that, the score of IR-based approach declined quickly when answered percentage becomes larger, which means only a few question-answer pairs can be directly found in corpus. Although the NN-based approach achieved highest overall precision, its average score on top 10% high confidence questions is lower than 50%, which indicates that the result might be unstable and inexplainable. Our CGQA approach achieved extremely high score (nearly 100%) on questions with high confidence value, and performed best when answering less than 60% questions.

6   Discussion

The experimental results allow us to make the following observations:

- CGQA achieved high scores on a part of the questions and provided explainable solving procedures. The average length of inference path is larger than 3, which proves the difficulty of these questions. However, the coverage of our approach is restricted to the scale and quality of the concept graph. Extracting knowledge from web tables and plain text in textbooks should be considered in the future.
- There are still some questions cannot be solved with our current CGQA architecture, such as questions with spatio-temporal reasoning and questions involving numerical calculation. A question classification stage will be needed to make better combination with upcoming QA approaches.
- CGQA can also be adapted to answer short answer questions by searching relevant concepts and descriptions in the concept graph. At the time of writing this paper, we are working on transforming inference paths in the concept graph to natural language question answers. A challenge that we are facing is analyzing background materials in short answer questions. There might

be some newly-defined concepts or introduced rules in the material, which may lead to dynamic adjustment of the concept graph and the path finding algorithm.

– At present, we only consider geographical Gaokao due to our project goal. In the future, we are going to apply CGQA to other subjects such as history. Most of the concepts in history can also be organized as tree hierarchies, such as "political system" and "school of thought", which indicates that our CGQA approach can still be feasible.

7 Conclusion

In this paper, we studied the problem of answering multiple-choice questions in geographical Gaokao. Our main contributions are summarized as follows:

– We constructed a concept graph of high quality from textbook tables and Chinese wiki encyclopedia, to capture core concepts and relations in geography. The largely-automated construction approach can be applied to other domains.
– We proposed a graph search based QA approach to find explainable inference paths between questions and answer choices.
– We developed an online system CGQA and conducted experiments on real datasets created from the last ten year geographical Gaokao. Our experiments showed that CGQA generated accurate judgments and provided explainable solving procedures. Also, CGQA gained promising improvement by combining with existing methods.

Acknowledgments. This work is funded by the National Natural Science Foundation of China (No. 61772264) and the National High-tech R&D Program of China (No. 2015AA015406). We thank all participants in the evaluation for their time and effort.

References

1. Abujabal, A., Yahya, M., Riedewald, M., Weikum, G.: Automated template generation for question answering over knowledge graphs. In: Proceedings of the 26th International Conference on World Wide Web, pp. 1191–1200. International World Wide Web Conferences Steering Committee (2017)
2. Agrawal, R., Golshan, B., Papalexakis, E.: Toward data-driven design of educational courses: a feasibility study. J. Educ. Data Min. 8(1), 1–21 (2016)
3. Angele, J., Moench, E., Oppermann, H., Staab, S., Wenke, D.: Ontology-based query and answering in chemistry: OntoNova Project Halo. In: Fensel, D., Sycara, K., Mylopoulos, J. (eds.) ISWC 2003. LNCS, vol. 2870, pp. 913–928. Springer, Heidelberg (2003). https://doi.org/10.1007/978-3-540-39718-2_58
4. Cheng, G., Zhu, W., Wang, Z., Chen, J., Qu, Y.: Taking up the Gaokao challenge: an information retrieval approach. In: Proceedings of the 25th International Joint Conference on Artificial Intelligence, pp. 2479–2485. AAAI (2016)
5. Clark, P., Etzioni, O., Khot, T., Sabharwal, A., Tafjord, O., Turney, P.D., Khashabi, D.: Combining retrieval, statistics, and inference to answer elementary science questions. In: Proceedings of the 30th AAAI Conference on Artificial Intelligence, pp. 2580–2586. AAAI (2016)

6. Fujita, A., Kameda, A., Kawazoe, A., Miyao, Y.: Overview of Todai robot project and evaluation framework of its NLP-based problem solving. In: Proceedings of the 9th International Conference on Language Resources and Evaluation, pp. 2590–2597 (2014)
7. Guo, S., Zeng, X., He, S., Liu, K., Zhao, J.: Which is the effective way for Gaokao: information retrieval or neural networks? In: Proceedings of the 15th Conference of the European Chapter of the Association for Computational Linguistics, pp. 111–120. ACL (2017)
8. Hu, W., Li, H., Sun, Z., Qian, X., Xue, L., Cao, E., Qu, Y.: Clinga: bringing Chinese physical and human geography in linked open data. In: Groth, P., Simperl, E., Gray, A., Sabou, M., Krötzsch, M., Lecue, F., Flöck, F., Gil, Y. (eds.) ISWC 2016. LNCS, vol. 9982, pp. 104–112. Springer, Cham (2016). https://doi.org/10.1007/978-3-319-46547-0_11
9. Khashabi, D., Khot, T., Sabharwal, A., Clark, P., Etzioni, O., Roth, D.: Question answering via integer programming over semi-structured knowledge. In: Proceedings of the 25th International Joint Conference on Artificial Intelligence, pp. 1145–1152. AAAI (2016)
10. Lehmann, J., Isele, R., Jakob, M., Jentzsch, A., Kontokostas, D., Mendes, P.N., Hellmann, S., Morsey, M., van Kleef, P., Auer, S., Bizer, C.: DBpedia - a large-scale, multilingual knowledge base extracted from Wikipedia. Semant. Web J. **6**(2), 167–195 (2015)
11. Li, H., Xu, J.: Semantic matching in search. Found. Trends Inf. Retr. **7**(5), 343–469 (2014)
12. Lu, H., Kong, M.: Community-based question answering via contextual ranking metric network learning. In: Proceedings of the 31st AAAI Conference on Artificial Intelligence, pp. 4963–4964. AAAI (2017)
13. Mikolov, T., Chen, K., Corrado, G., Dean, J.: Efficient estimation of word representations in vector space. In: Proceedings of the 1st International Conference on Learning Representations (2013)
14. Miller, G.A.: WordNet: an electronic lexical database. Commun. ACM **38**(11), 39–41 (1995)
15. Richardson, M., Burges, C.J.C., Renshaw, E.: MCTest: a challenge dataset for the open-domain machine comprehension of text. In: Proceedings of the 20th Conference on Empirical Methods in Natural Language Processing, pp. 193–203. ACL (2013)
16. Ritze, D., Lehmberg, O., Oulabi, Y., Bizer, C.: Profiling the potential of web tables for augmenting cross-domain knowledge bases. In: Proceedings of the 25th International World Wide Web Conference, pp. 251–261. ACM (2016)
17. Sukhbaatar, S., Szlam, A., Weston, J., Fergus, R.: End-to-end memory networks. In: Proceedings of the 29th International Conference on Neural Information Processing Systems, pp. 2440–2448. Curran Associates, Inc. (2015)
18. Wang, Z., Li, J., Wang, Z., Li, S., Li, M., Zhang, D., Shi, Y., Liu, Y., Zhang, P., Tang, J.: XLore: a large-scale English-Chinese bilingual knowledge graph. In: Proceedings of the 12th International Semantic Web Conference, pp. 121–124 (2013)
19. Zou, L., Huang, R., Wang, H., Yu, J.X., He, W., Zhao, D.: Natural language question answering over RDF: a graph data driven approach. In: Proceedings of the 2014 ACM SIGMOD International Conference on Management of Data, pp. 313–324. ACM (2014)

Tweetskb: A Public and Large-Scale RDF Corpus of Annotated Tweets

Pavlos Fafalios$^{(\boxtimes)}$ ⓘ, Vasileios Iosifidis ⓘ, Eirini Ntoutsi, and Stefan Dietze

L3S Research Center, University of Hannover, Hannover, Germany
{fafalios,iosifidis,ntoutsi,dietze}@L3S.de

Abstract. Publicly available social media archives facilitate research in a variety of fields, such as data science, sociology or the digital humanities, where Twitter has emerged as one of the most prominent sources. However, obtaining, archiving and annotating large amounts of tweets is costly. In this paper, we describe *TweetsKB*, a publicly available corpus of currently more than 1.5 billion tweets, spanning almost 5 years (Jan'13–Nov'17). Metadata information about the tweets as well as extracted entities, hashtags, user mentions and sentiment information are exposed using established RDF/S vocabularies. Next to a description of the extraction and annotation process, we present use cases to illustrate scenarios for entity-centric information exploration, data integration and knowledge discovery facilitated by *TweetsKB*.

Keywords: Twitter · RDF · Entity linking · Sentiment analysis
Social media archives

Resource type: Dataset
Permanent URL: https://doi.org/10.5281/zenodo.573852.

1 Introduction

Social microblogging services have emerged as a primary forum to discuss and comment on breaking news and events happening around the world. Such user-generated content can be seen as a comprehensive documentation of the society and is of immense historical value for future generations [4].

In particular, Twitter has been recognized as an important data source facilitating research in a variety of fields, such as data science, sociology, psychology or historical studies where researchers aim at understanding behavior, trends and opinions. While research usually focuses on particular topics or entities, such as persons, organizations, or products, entity-centric access and exploration methods are crucial [31].

However, despite initiatives aiming at collecting and preserving such user-generated content (e.g., the Twitter Archive at the Library of Congress [33]),

© Springer International Publishing AG, part of Springer Nature 2018
A. Gangemi et al. (Eds.): ESWC 2018, LNCS 10843, pp. 177–190, 2018.
https://doi.org/10.1007/978-3-319-93417-4_12

the absence of publicly accessible archives which enable entity-centric exploration remains a major obstacle for research and reuse [4], in particular for non-technical research disciplines lacking the skills and infrastructure for large-scale data harvesting and processing.

In this paper, we present *TweetsKB*, a public corpus of RDF data for a large collection of anonymized tweets. *TweetsKB* is unprecedented as it currently contains data for more than 1.5 billion tweets spanning almost 5 years, includes entity and sentiment annotations, and is exposed using established vocabularies in order to facilitate a variety of multi-aspect data exploration scenarios.

By providing a well-structured large-scale Twitter corpus using established W3C standards, we relieve data consumers from the computationally intensive process of extracting and processing tweets, and facilitate a number of data consumption and analytics scenarios including: (i) time-aware and entity-centric exploration of the Twitter archive [6], (ii) data integration by directly exploiting existing knowledge bases (like DBpedia) [6], (iii) multi-aspect entity-centric analysis and knowledge discovery w.r.t. features like entity popularity, attitude or relation with other entities [7]. In addition, the dataset can foster further research, for instance, in entity recommendation, event detection, topic evolution, and concept drift.

Next to describing the annotation process (entities, sentiments) and the access details (Sect. 2), we present the applied schema (Sect. 3) as well as use case scenarios and update and maintenance procedures (Sect. 4). Finally, we discuss related works (Sect. 5) and conclude the paper (Sect. 6).

2   Generating TweetsKB

TweetsKB is generated through the following steps: (i) tweet archival, filtering and processing, (ii) entity linking and sentiment extraction, and (iii) data lifting. This section summarizes the above steps while the corresponding schema for step (iii) is described in the next section.

2.1   Twitter Archival, Filtering and Processing

The archive is facilitated by continuously harvesting tweets through the public Twitter streaming API since January 2013, accumulating more than 6 billion tweets up to now (December 2017).

As part of the filtering step, we eliminate re-tweets and non-English tweets, which has reduced the number of tweets to about 1.8 billion tweets. In addition, we remove spam through a Multinomial Naive Bayes (MNB) classifier, trained on the HSpam dataset which has 94% precision on spam labels [25]. This removed about 10% of the tweets, resulting in a final corpus of 1,560,096,518 tweets. Figure 1 shows the number of tweets per month of the final dataset.

For each tweet, we exploit the following metadata: tweet id, post date, user who posted the tweet (username), favourite and retweet count (at the time of

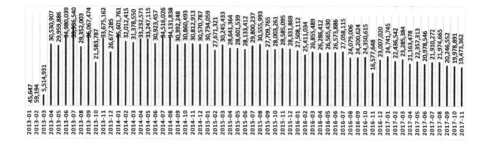

Fig. 1. Number of tweets per month of the *TweetsKB* dataset.

fetching the tweet[1]). We also extract hashtags (words starting with #) and user mentions (words starting with @). For the sake of privacy, we anonymize the usernames and we do not provide the text of the tweets (nevertheless, one can still apply user-based aggregation and analysis tasks). However, actual tweet content and further information can be fetched through the tweet IDs.

2.2 Entity Linking and Sentiment Extraction

For the *entity linking* task, we used Yahoo's FEL tool [1]. FEL is very fast and lightweight, and has been specially designed for linking entities from short texts to Wikipedia/DBpedia. We set a confidence threshold of −3 which has been shown empirically to provide annotations of good quality, while we also store the confidence score of each extracted entity. Depending on the specific requirements with respect to precision and recall, data consumers can select suitable confidence ranges to consider when querying the data.

In total, about 1.4 million distinct entities were extracted from the entire corpus, while the average number of entities per tweet is about 1.3. Figure 2 shows the distribution of the top-100,000 entities. There are around 15,000 entities with more than 10,000 occurrences, while there is a long tail of entities with less than 1,000 occurrences. Regarding their type, Table 1 shows the distribution of the top-100,000 entities in some popular DBpedia types (the sets are not disjoint). We notice that around 20% of the entities is of type *Person* and 15% of type *Organization*.

For *sentiment analysis*, we used SentiStrength, a robust tool for sentiment strength detection on social web data [28]. SentiStrength assigns both a positive and a negative score to a short text, to account for both types of sentiments expressed at the same time. The value of a positive sentiment ranges from +1 for no positive to +5 for extremely positive. Similarly, negative sentiment ranges from −1 (no negative) to −5 (extremely negative). We normalized both scores in the range $[0, 1]$ using the formula: $score = (|sentimentValue| - 1)/4)$. About

---

[1] By exploiting the tweet IDs, one can retrieve the latest favourite and retweet counts (however, only in case the corresponding tweets have not been deleted and are still publicly accessible).

Table 1. Overview of popular entity types of the top-100,000 entities.

DBpedia type	Number of distinct entities
http://dbpedia.org/ontology/Person	21,139 (21.1%)
http://dbpedia.org/ontology/Organisation	14,815 (14.8%)
http://dbpedia.org/ontology/Location	8,215 (8.2%)
http://dbpedia.org/ontology/Athlete	5,192 (5.2%)
http://dbpedia.org/ontology/Artist	3,737 (3.7%)
http://dbpedia.org/ontology/City	2,563 (2.6%)
http://dbpedia.org/ontology/Event	510 (0.5%)
http://dbpedia.org/ontology/Politician	208 (0.2%)

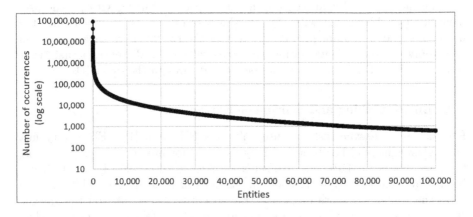

Fig. 2. Distribution of top-100,000 entities.

788 million tweets (50%) have no sentiment ($score = 0$ for both positive and negative sentiment).

Quality of Annotations. We evaluated the quality of the *entity annotations* produced by FEL using the ground truth dataset provided by the 2016 NEEL challenge of the 6th workshop on "Making Sense of Microposts" (#Microposts2016)[2] [16]. The dataset consists of 9,289 English tweets of 2011, 2013, 2014, and 2015. We considered all tweets from the provided training, dev and test files, without applying any training on FEL. The results are the following: *Precision* = 86%, *Recall* = 39%, *F1* = 54%. We notice that FEL achieves high precision, however recall is low. The reason is that FEL did not manage to recognize several difficult cases, like entities within hashtags and nicknames, which are common in Twitter due to the small number of allowed characters per tweet. Nevertheless, FEL's performance is comparable to existing approaches [15,16].

---

[2] http://microposts2016.seas.upenn.edu/.

Regarding *sentiment analysis*, we evaluated the accuracy of SentiStrength on tweets using two ground truth datasets: SemEval2017[3] (Task 4, Subtask A) [18], and TSentiment15[4] [8]. The SemEval2017 dataset consists of 61,853 English tweets of 2013–2017 labeled as positive, negative, or neutral. We run the evaluation on all the provided training files (of 2013–2016) and the 2017 test file. SentiStrength achieved the following scores: *AvgRec = 0.54* (recall averaged across the positive, negative, and neutral classes [24]), $F1^{PN} = 0.52$ (F1 averaged across the positive and negative classes), *Accuracy = 0.57*. The performance of SentiStrength is good considering that this is a multi-class classification problem. Moreover, the user can achieve higher precision by selecting only tweets with high positive or negative SentiStrength score. Regarding TSentiment15, this dataset contains 2,527,753 English tweets of 2015 labeled only with positive and negative classes (exploiting emoticons and a sentiment lexicon [8]). SentiStrength achieved the following scores: $F1^{PN} = 0.80$, *Accuracy = 0.91*. Here we notice that SentiStrength achieves very good performance.

2.3   Data Lifting and Availability

We generated RDF triples in the N3 format applying the RDF/S model described in the next section. The total number of triples is more than 48 billion. Table 2 summarizes the key statistics of the generated dataset. The source code used for triplifying the data is available as open source on GitHub[5].

Table 2. Key statistics of *TweeetsKB*.

Number of tweets	1,560,096,518
Number of distinct users	125,104,569
Number of distinct hashtags	40,815,854
Number of distinct user mentions	81,238,852
Number of distinct entities	1,428,236
Number of tweets with sentiment	772,044,599
Number of RDF triples	48,207,277,042

TweetsKB is available as N3 files (split by month) through the Zenodo data repository (DOI: 10.5281/zenodo.573852)[6], under a *Creative Commons Attribution 4.0* license. The dataset has been also registered at `datahub.ckan.io`[7].

---

[3] http://alt.qcri.org/semeval2017/task4/.
[4] https://l3s.de/~iosifidis/TSentiment15/.
[5] https://github.com/iosifidisvasileios/AnnotatedTweets2RDF.
[6] https://zenodo.org/record/573852.
[7] https://datahub.ckan.io/dataset/tweetskb.

Sample files, example queries and more information are available through *Tweet-sKB*'s home page[8]. For demonstration purposes, we have also set up a public SPARQL endpoint, currently containing a subset of about 5% of the dataset[9].

2.4   Runtime for Annotation and Triplification

The time for annotating the tweets and generating the RDF triples depends on several factors including the dataset volume, the used computing infrastructure as well as the available resources and the load of the cluster during the analysis time. The Hadoop cluster used for creating *TweetsKB* consists of 40 computer nodes with a total of 504 CPU cores and 6,784 GB RAM. The most time consuming task is entity linking where we annotated on average 4.8M tweets per minute using FEL, while SentiStrength annotated almost 6M tweets per minute. Finally, for the generation of the RDF triples we processed 14M tweets per minute on average.

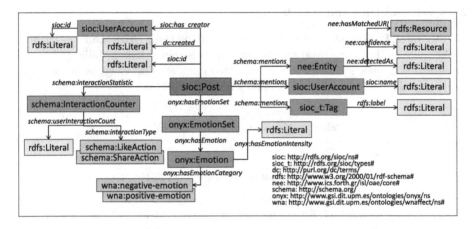

Fig. 3. An RDF/S model for describing metadata and annotation information for a collection of tweets.

3   RDF/S Model for Annotated Tweets

Our schema, depicted in Fig. 3, exploits terms from established vocabularies, most notably SIOC (Semantically-Interlinked Online Communities) core ontology [3] and schema.org [17]. The selection of the vocabularies was based on the following objectives: (i) avoiding schema violations, (ii) enabling data interoperability through term reuse, (iii) having dereferenceable URIs, (iv) extensibility. Next to modeling data in our corpus, the proposed schema can be applied over

---

any annotated social media archive (not only tweets), and can be easily extended for describing additional information related to archived social media data and extracted annotations.

A tweet is associated with six main types of elements: (1) *general tweet meta-data*, (2) *entity mentions*, (3) *user mentions*, (4) *hashtag mentions*, (5) *sentiment scores*, (6) *interaction statistics* (values expressing how users have interacted with the tweet, like favourite and retweet count). We use the property schema:mentions from schema.org[10] for associating a tweet with a mentioned entity, user or hashtag. We exploit schema.org due to its wide acceptance and less strict domain/range bindings which facilitate reuse and combination with other schemas, by avoiding schema violations.

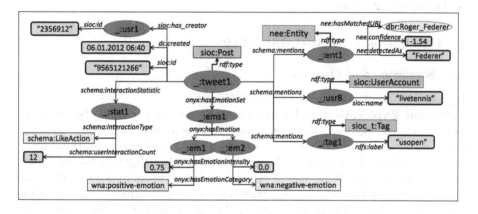

Fig. 4. Instantiation example of the RDF/S model.

For general *metadata*, we exploit SIOC as an established vocabulary for representing social Web data[11]. The class sioc:Post represents a tweet, while sioc:UserAccount a Twitter user.

An *entity mention* is represented through the Open NEE (Named Entity Extraction) model [5] which is an extension of the Open Annotation data model [23] and enables the representation of entity annotation results. For each recognized entity, we store its surface form, URI and confidence score. A *user mention* simply refers to a particular sioc:UserAccount, while for *hashtag mentions* we use the class sioc_t:Tag of the SIOC Types Ontology Module[12].

For expressing *sentiments*, we use the Onyx ontology[13] [22]. Through the class onyx:EmotionSet we associate a tweet with a set of emotions (onyx:Emotion). Note that the original domain of property onyx:hasEmotionSet is owl:Thing, which is

---

[10] http://schema.org/.

[11] Specification available at: http://rdfs.org/sioc/spec/.

[12] http://rdfs.org/sioc/types\#.

[13] https://www.gsi.dit.upm.es/ontologies/onyx/.

compatible with our use as property of sioc:Post. The property onyx:hasEmotion-Category defines the emotion type, which is either negative-emotion or positive-emotion as defined by the WordNet-Affect Taxonomy[14] and is quantified through onyx:hasEmotionIntensity.

Finally, for representing aggregated *interactions*, we use the class InteractionCounter of schema.org. We distinguish schema:LikeAction (for the favourite count) or schema:ShareAction (for the retweet count) as valid interaction types.

Figure 4 depicts a set of instances for a single tweet. In this example, the tweet mentions one user account (@livetennis) and one hashtag (#usopen), while the entity name *"Federer"* was detected, referring probably to the tennis player *Roger Federer* (with confidence score -1.54). Moreover, we see that the tweet has a positive sentiment of 0.75, no negative sentiment, while it has been marked as "favourite" 12 times.

4   Use Cases and Sustainability

4.1   Scenarios and Queries

Typical scenarios facilitated by *TweetsKB* include:
Advanced Exploration and Data Integration. By exploiting tweet metadata, extracted entities, sentiment values, and temporal information, one can run sophisticated queries that can also directly (at query-execution time) integrate information from external knowledge bases like DBpedia. For example, Listing 1 shows a SPARQL query obtaining popular tweets in 2016 (with more than 100 retweets) mentioning *German politicians* with strong negative sentiment (≥ 0.75). The query exploits extracted entities, sentiments, and interaction statistics, while it uses query federation to access DBpedia for retrieving the list of German politicians and their birth place.

```
1 SELECT DISTINCT ?tweetID ?sentNegScore ?retweetCount ?politician ?birthPlace WHERE {
2   SERVICE <http://dbpedia.org/sparql> {
3     ?politician dc:subject dbc:German_politicians ; dbo:birthPlace ?birthPlace }
4   ?tweet a sioc:Post ; dc:created ?date ; sioc:id ?tweetID FILTER(year(?date) = 2016) .
5   ?tweet schema:mentions ?entity . ?entity a nee:Entity ; nee:hasMatchedURI ?politician .
6   ?tweet schema:interactionStatistic ?stat . ?stat schema:interactionType schema:ShareAction .
7   ?stat schema:userInteractionCount ?retweetCount FILTER(?retweetCount > 100) .
8   ?tweet onyx:hasEmotionSet ?emotSet . ?emotSet onyx:hasEmotion ?emot .
9   ?emot onyx:hasEmotionCategory wna:negative-emotion ;
10         onyx:hasEmotionIntensity ?sentNegScore FILTER (?sentNegScore >= 0.75) }
```

Listing 1. SPARQL query for retrieving popular tweets in 2016 mentioning German politicians with strong negative sentiment.

Listing 2 shows a query that combines extracted entities with hashtags. The query requests the top-50 hashtags co-occurring with the entity *Refugee* (http://dbpedia.org/resource/Refugee) in tweets of 2016. The result contains, among others, the following hashtags: #auspol, #asylum, #Nauru, #Greece, #LetThemStay, #BringThemHere.

---

[14] http://www.gsi.dit.upm.es/ontologies/wnaffect/.

```
1 SELECT ?hastagLabel (count(distinct ?tweet) as ?num) WHERE {
2   ?tweet dc:created ?date FILTER(year(?date) = 2016) .
3   ?tweet schema:mentions ?entity .
4   ?entity a nee:Entity ; nee:hasMatchedURI dbr:Refugee .
5   ?tweet schema:mentions ?hashtag.
6   ?hashtag a sioc:Tag ; rdfs:label ?hastagLabel
7 } GROUP BY ?hastagLabel ORDER BY DESC(?num) LIMIT 50
```

Listing 2. SPARQL query for retrieving the top-50 hashtags co-occurring with the entity *Refugee* in tweets of 2016.

Temporal Entity Analytics. The work in [7] has proposed a set of measures that allow studying how entities are reflected in a social media archive and how entity-related information evolves over time. Given an entity and a time period, the proposed measures capture the following entity aspects: *popularity, attitude* (predominant sentiment), *sentimentality* (magnitude of sentiment), *controversiality,* and *connectedness* to other entities (entity-to-entity connectedness and k-network). Such time-series data can be easily computed by running SPARQL queries on *TweetsKB*. For example, the query in Listing 3 retrieves the monthly popularity of *Alexis Tsipras* (Greek prime minister) in Twitter in 2015 (using Formula 1 of [7]). The result of this query shows that the number of tweets increased significantly in June and July, likely to be caused by the Greek bailout referendum that was held in July 2015, following the bank holiday and capital controls of June 2015.

```
1 SELECT ?month xsd:double(?cEnt)/xsd:double(?cAll)
2 WHERE {
3 { SELECT (month(?date) AS ?month) (count(?tweet) AS ?cAll) WHERE {
4     ?tweet a sioc:Post ; dc:created ?date FILTER(year(?date) = 2015)
5   } GROUP BY month(?date) }
6 { SELECT (month(?date) AS ?month) (count(?tweet) AS ?cEnt) WHERE {
7     ?tweet a sioc:Post ; dc:created ?date FILTER(year(?date) = 2015) .
8     ?tweet schema:mentions ?entity .
9     ?entity a nee:Entity ; nee:hasMatchedURI dbr:Alexis_Tsipras
10  } GROUP BY month(?date) }
11 } ORDER BY ?month
```

Listing 3. SPARQL query for retrieving the monthly popularity of *Alexis Tsiprats* (Greek prime minister) in tweets in 2015 (using Formula 1 of [7]).

Time and Social Aware Entity Recommendations. Recent works have shown that entity recommendation is time-dependent, while the co-occurrence of entities in documents of a given time period is a strong indicator of their relatedness during that period and thus should be taken into consideration [29, 32]. By querying *TweetsKB*, we can find entities of a specific type, or having some specific characteristics, that co-occur frequently with a query entity in a specific time period, a useful indicator for temporal prior probabilities when implementing time- and social-aware entity recommendations. For example, the query in Listing 4 retrieves the top-5 politicians co-occurring with *Barack Obama* in tweets of summer 2016. Here one could also follow a more sophisticated approach, e.g., by also considering the inverse tweet frequency of the top co-occurred entities.

```
1 SELECT ?politician (count(distinct ?tweet) as ?num) WHERE {
2   SERVICE <http://dbpedia.org/sparql> {
3     ?politician a dbo:Politician }
4   ?tweet a sioc:Post ; dc:created ?date FILTER(?date >= "2016-06-01"^^xsd:date &&
5                                                 ?date <= "2016-08-30"^^xsd:date) .
6   ?tweet schema:mentions ?entity .
7   ?entity a nee:Entity ; nee:hasMatchedURI dbr:Barack_Obama .
8   ?tweet schema:mentions ?entityPolit.
9   ?entityPolit nee:hasMatchedURI ?politician FILTER (?politician != dbr:Barack_Obama)
10 } GROUP BY ?politician ORDER BY DESC(?num) LIMIT 5
```

Listing 4. SPARQL query for retrieving the top-5 politicians co-occurring with *Barack Obama* in tweets of summer 2016.

Data Mining and Information Discovery. Data mining techniques allow the extraction of useful and previously unknown information from raw data. By querying *TweetsKB* we can generate time series for a specific entity of interest modeling the temporal evolution of the entity w.r.t. different tracked dimensions like sentiment, popularity, or interactivity. Such multi-dimensional time-series can be used in a plethora of data mining tasks like entity forecasting (predicting entity-related features) [21], network-analysis (find communities and influential entities) [19], stream mining (sentiment analysis over data streams) [9,27], or change detection (e.g., detection of critical time-points) [11].

Thus, research in a range of fields is facilitated through the public availability of well-annotated Twitter data. Note also that the availability of publicly available datasets is a requirement for the data mining community and will allow not only the development of new methods but also for valid comparisons among existing methods, while existing repositories, e.g., UCI[15], lack of big, volatile and complex data.

4.2 Sustainability, Maintenance and Extensibility

The dataset has seen adoption and facilitated research in inter-disciplinary research projects such as ALEXANDRIA[16] and AFEL[17], involving researchers from a variety of organizations and research fields [6,7,10,30]. With respect to ensuring long-term sustainability, we anticipate that reuse and establishing of a user community for the corpus is crucial. While the aforementioned activities have already facilitated access and reuse, the corpus will be further advertised through interdisciplinary networks and events (like the Web Science Trust[18]). Besides, the use of Zenodo for depositing the dataset, as well as its registration at `datahub.ckan.io`, makes it citable and web findable.

Maintenance of the corpus will be facilitated through the continuous process of crawling 1% of all tweets (running since January 2013) through the public Twitter API and storing obtained data within the local Hadoop cluster at L3S Research Center. The annotation and triplification process (Sect. 2) will be

---

[15] http://archive.ics.uci.edu/ml/.
[16] http://alexandria-project.eu/.
[17] http://afel-project.eu/.
[18] http://www.webscience.org/.

periodically (quarterly) repeated in order to incrementally expand the corpus and ensure its currentness, one of the requirements for many of the envisaged use cases of the dataset. While this will permanently increase the population of the dataset, the schema itself is extensible and facilitates the enrichment of tweets with additional information, for instance, to add information about the users involved in particular interactions (retweets, likes) or additional information about involved entities or references/URLs. Depending on the investigated research questions, it is anticipated that this kind of enrichment is essential, at least for parts of the corpus, i.e. for specific time periods or topics.

Next to the reuse of *TweetsKB*, we also publish the source code used for triplifying the data (see Footnote 5), to enable third parties establishing and sharing similar corpora, for instance, focused Twitter crawls for certain topics.

5 Related Work

There is a plethora of works on modeling social media data as well as on semantic-based information access and mining semantics from social media streams (see [2] for a survey). There are also Twitter datasets provided by specific communities for research and experimentation in specific research problems, like the "Making Sense of Microposts" series of workshops [15,16], or the "Sentiment Analysis in Twitter" tasks of the International Workshop on Semantic Evaluation [13,18]. Below we discuss works that exploit Semantic Web technologies for representing and querying social media data.

Twarql [12] is an infrastructure which translates microblog posts from Twitter as Linked Data in real-time. Similar to our approach, Twarql extracts entity, hashtag and user mentions, and the extracted content is encoded in RDF. The authors tested their approach using a small collection of 511,147 tweets related to iPad[19]. SMOB [14] is a platform for distributed microblogging which combines Social Web principles and Semantic Web technologies. SMOB relies on ontologies for representing microblog posts, hubs for distributed exchanging information, and components for linking the posts with other resources. TwitLogic [26] is a semantic data aggregator which provides a set of syntax conventions for embedding various structured content in microblog posts. It also provides a schema for user-driven data and associated metadata which enables the translation of microblog streams into RDF streams. The work in [20] also discusses an approach to annotate and triplify tweets. However, none of the above works provides a large-scale and publicly available RDF corpus of annotated tweets.

6 Conclusion

We have presented a large-scale Twitter archive which includes entity and sentiment annotations and is exposed using established vocabularies and standards. Data includes more than 48 billion triples, describing metadata and annotation

---

[19] The dataset is not currently available (as of March 15, 2018).

information for more than 1.5 billion tweets spanning almost 5 years. Next to the corpus itself, the proposed schema facilitates further extension and the generation of similar, focused corpora, e.g. for specific geographic or temporal regions, or targeting selected topics.

We believe that this dataset can foster further research in a plethora of research problems, like event detection, topic evolution, concept drift, and prediction of entity-related features, while it can facilitate research in other communities and disciplines, like sociology and digital humanities.

Acknowledgements. The work was partially funded by the European Commission for the ERC Advanced Grant ALEXANDRIA under grant No. 339233 and the H2020 Grant No. 687916 (AFEL project), and by the German Research Foundation (DFG) project OSCAR (Opinion Stream Classification with Ensembles and Active leaRners).

References

1. Blanco, R., Ottaviano, G., Meij, E.: Fast and space-efficient entity linking for queries. In: Proceedings of the Eighth ACM International Conference on Web Search and Data Mining. ACM (2015)
2. Bontcheva, K., Rout, D.: Making sense of social media streams through semantics: a survey. Semant. Web **5**(5), 373–403 (2014)
3. Breslin, J.G., Decker, S., Harth, A., Bojars, U.: SIOC: an approach to connect web-based communities. Int. J. Web Based Commun. **2**(2), 133–142 (2006)
4. Bruns, A., Weller, K.: Twitter as a first draft of the present: and the challenges of preserving it for the future. In: 8th ACM Conference on Web Science (2016)
5. Fafalios, P., Baritakis, M., Tzitzikas, Y.: Exploiting linked data for open and configurable named entity extraction. Int. J. Artif. Intell. Tools **24**(02), 42 (2015)
6. Fafalios, P., Holzmann, H., Kasturia, V., Nejdl, W.: Building and querying semantic layers for web archives. In: ACM/IEEE-CS Joint Conference on Digital Libraries, JCDL 2017, Toronto, Ontario, Canada (2017)
7. Fafalios, P., Iosifidis, V., Stefanidis, K., Ntoutsi, E.: Multi-aspect entity-centric analysis of big social media archives. In: Kamps, J., Tsakonas, G., Manolopoulos, Y., Iliadis, L., Karydis, I. (eds.) TPDL 2017. LNCS, vol. 10450, pp. 261–273. Springer, Cham (2017). https://doi.org/10.1007/978-3-319-67008-9_21
8. Iosifidis, V., Ntoutsi, E.: Large scale sentiment learning with limited labels. In: Proceedings of the 23rd ACM SIGKDD International Conference on Knowledge Discovery and Data Mining, pp. 1823–1832. ACM (2017)
9. Iosifidis, V., Oelschlager, A., Ntoutsi, E.: Sentiment classification over opinionated data streams through informed model adaptation. In: Kamps, J., Tsakonas, G., Manolopoulos, Y., Iliadis, L., Karydis, I. (eds.) TPDL 2017. LNCS, vol. 10450, pp. 369–381. Springer, Cham (2017). https://doi.org/10.1007/978-3-319-67008-9_29
10. Kowald, D., Pujari, S.C., Lex, E.: Temporal effects on hashtag reuse in Twitter: a cognitive-inspired hashtag recommendation approach. In: Proceedings of the 26th International Conference on World Wide Web, pp. 1401–1410. International World Wide Web Conferences Steering Committee (2017)
11. Liu, S., Yamada, M., Collier, N., Sugiyama, M.: Change-point detection in time-series data by relative density-ratio estimation. Neural Netw. **43**, 72–83 (2013)

12. Mendes, P.N., Passant, A., Kapanipathi, P.: Twarql: tapping into the wisdom of the crowd. In: 6th International Conference on Semantic Systems. ACM (2010)
13. Nakov, P., Ritter, A., Rosenthal, S., Sebastiani, F., Stoyanov, V.: SemEval-2016 task 4: sentiment analysis in Twitter. In: SemEval@ NAACL-HLT, pp. 1–18 (2016)
14. Passant, A., Bojars, U., Breslin, J.G., Hastrup, T., Stankovic, M., Laublet, P., et al.: An overview of SMOB 2: open, semantic and distributed microblogging. In: ICWSM, pp. 303–306 (2010)
15. Rizzo, G.: Making sense of microposts (# Microposts2015) named entity rEcognition and linking (NEEL) challenge (2015)
16. Rizzo, G., van Erp, M., Plu, J., Troncy, R.: Making sense of microposts (#Microposts2016) named entity rEcognition and linking (NEEL) challenge (2016)
17. Ronallo, J.: HTML5 microdata and schema.org. Code4Lib J. (16) (2012)
18. Rosenthal, S., Farra, N., Nakov, P.: SemEval-2017 task 4: sentiment analysis in Twitter. In: Proceedings of the 11th International Workshop on Semantic Evaluation, SemEval 2017, pp. 502–518 (2017)
19. Rossi, M.-E.G., Malliaros, F.D., Vazirgiannis, M.: Spread it good, spread it fast: identification of influential nodes in social networks. In: Proceedings of the 24th International Conference on World Wide Web, pp. 101–102. ACM (2015)
20. Sahito, F., Latif, A., Slany, W.: Weaving Twitter stream into linked data a proof of concept framework. In: International Conference on Emerging Technologies (2011)
21. Saleiro, P., Soares, C.: Learning from the news: predicting entity popularity on Twitter. In: Boström, H., Knobbe, A., Soares, C., Papapetrou, P. (eds.) IDA 2016. LNCS, vol. 9897, pp. 171–182. Springer, Cham (2016). https://doi.org/10.1007/978-3-319-46349-0_15
22. Sánchez-Rada, J.F., Iglesias, C.A.: Onyx: a linked data approach to emotion representation. Inf. Process. Manag. **52**(1), 99–114 (2016)
23. Sanderson, R., Ciccarese, P., Van de Sompel, H., Bradshaw, S., Brickley, D., Castro, L.J.G., Clark, T., Cole, T., Desenne, P., Gerber, A., et al.: Open annotation data model. W3C Community Draft (2013)
24. Sebastiani, F.: An axiomatically derived measure for the evaluation of classification algorithms. In: Proceedings of the 2015 International Conference on The Theory of Information Retrieval, pp. 11–20. ACM (2015)
25. Sedhai, S., Sun, A.: HSpam14: a collection of 14 million tweets for hashtag-oriented spam research. In: SIGIR ACM (2015)
26. Shinavier, J.: Real-time #SemanticWeb in <= 140 chars. In: Proceedings of the Third Workshop on Linked Data on the Web, LDOW 2010 at WWW 2010 (2010)
27. Spiliopoulou, M., Ntoutsi, E., Zimmermann, M.: Opinion stream mining. Encycl. Mach. Learn. Data Min. 1–10 (2016)
28. Thelwall, M., Buckley, K., Paltoglou, G.: Sentiment strength detection for the social web. J. Am. Soc. Inf. Sci. Technol. **63**(1), 163–173 (2012)
29. Tran, N.K., Tran, T., Niederée, C.: Beyond time: dynamic context-aware entity recommendation. In: Blomqvist, E., Maynard, D., Gangemi, A., Hoekstra, R., Hitzler, P., Hartig, O. (eds.) ESWC 2017. LNCS, vol. 10249, pp. 353–368. Springer, Cham (2017). https://doi.org/10.1007/978-3-319-58068-5_22
30. Tran, T., Tran, N.K., Hadgu, A.T., Jäschke, R.: Semantic annotation for microblog topics using Wikipedia temporal information. In: Proceedings of the 2015 Conference on Empirical Methods in Natural Language Processing, pp. 97–106 (2015)
31. Weikum, G., Spaniol, M., Ntarmos, N., Triantafillou, P., Benczúr, A., Kirkpatrick, S., Rigaux, P., Williamson, M.: Longitudinal analytics on web archive data: it's about time! In: Biennial Conference on Innovative Data Systems Research (2011)

32. Zhang, L., Rettinger, A., Zhang, J.: A probabilistic model for time-aware entity recommendation. In: Groth, P., Simperl, E., Gray, A., Sabou, M., Krötzsch, M., Lecue, F., Flöck, F., Gil, Y. (eds.) ISWC 2016. LNCS, vol. 9981, pp. 598–614. Springer, Cham (2016). https://doi.org/10.1007/978-3-319-46523-4_36
33. Zimmer, M.: The Twitter archive at the library of congress: challenges for information practice and information policy. First Monday **20**(7) (2015)

HDTQ: Managing RDF Datasets in Compressed Space

Javier D. Fernández[1,2](✉) [iD], Miguel A. Martínez-Prieto[3] [iD],
Axel Polleres[1,2,4] [iD], and Julian Reindorf[1] [iD]

[1] Vienna University of Economics and Business, Vienna, Austria
{javier.fernandez,axel.polleres}@wu.ac.at, julian.reindorf@gmail.com
[2] Complexity Science Hub Vienna, Vienna, Austria
[3] Department of Computer Science, Universidad de Valladolid, Valladolid, Spain
migumar2@infor.uva.es
[4] Stanford University, Stanford, CA, USA

Abstract. HDT (Header-Dictionary-Triples) is a compressed representation of RDF data that supports retrieval features without prior decompression. Yet, RDF datasets often contain additional graph information, such as the origin, version or validity time of a triple. Traditional HDT is not capable of handling this additional parameter(s). This work introduces HDTQ (HDT Quads), an extension of HDT that is able to represent quadruples (or quads) while still being highly compact and queryable. Two HDTQ-based approaches are introduced: Annotated Triples and Annotated Graphs, and their performance is compared to the leading open-source RDF stores on the market. Results show that HDTQ achieves the best compression rates and is a competitive alternative to well-established systems.

1 Introduction

In little more than a decade, the *Resource Description Framework (RDF)* [17] and the *Linked Open Data (LOD) Cloud* [4] have significantly influenced the way people and machines share knowledge on the Web. The steady adoption of Linked Data, together with the support of key open projects (such as schema.org, DBpedia or Wikidata), have promoted RDF as a de-facto standard to represent facts about arbitrary knowledge in the Web, organized around the emerging notion of knowledge graphs. This impressive growth in the use of RDF has irremediably led to increasingly large RDF datasets and consequently to scalability challenges in *Big Semantic Data* management.

RDF is an extremely simple model where a graph is a set of *triples*, a ternary structure (subject, predicate, object), which does not impose any physical storage solution. RDF data management is traditionally based on human-readable serializations, which add unnecessary processing overheads in the context of a large-scale and machine-understandable Web. For instance, the latest DBpedia (2016–10) consists of more than 13 billion triples. Even though transmission

© Springer International Publishing AG, part of Springer Nature 2018
A. Gangemi et al. (Eds.): ESWC 2018, LNCS 10843, pp. 191–208, 2018.
https://doi.org/10.1007/978-3-319-93417-4_13

speeds and storage capacities grow, such graphs can quickly become cumbersome to share, index and consume.

HDT [7] tackles this issue by proposing a compact, self-indexed serialization of RDF. That is, HDT keeps big datasets compressed for RDF preservation and sharing and –at the same time– provides basic query functionality without prior decompression. HDT has been widely adopted by the community, (i) used as the main backend of Triple Pattern Fragments (TPF) [18] interface, which alleviates the traditional burden of LOD servers by moving part of the query processing onto clients, (ii) used as a storage backend for large-scale graph data [16], or (iii) as the store behind LOD Laundromat [3], serving a crawl of a very big subset of the LOD Cloud, to name but a few.

One of the main drawbacks of HDT so far is its inability to manage RDF datasets with multiple RDF graphs. HDT considers that all triples belong to the same graph, the *default graph*. However, triples in an RDF dataset can belong to different (named) graphs, hence the extension to the so-called RDF quadruples (subject, predicate, object, graph), or *quads*. The graph (also called context) is used to capture information such as trust, provenance, temporal information and other annotations [19]. Since RDF 1.1 [17] there exist standard RDF syntaxes (such as N-Quads or Trig) for representing RDF named graphs. SPARQL, with its *GRAPH* keyword, allows for querying and managing RDF named graphs, which most common triple stores have implemented. Interestingly, while RDF compression has been an active research topic for a while now, there is neither a compact RDF serialization nor a self-indexed RDF store for quads, to the best of our knowledge.

In this paper we extend HDT to cope with quads and keep its compact and queryable features. HDTQ extends the HDT format with (i) a dictionary that keeps track of all different graph names (or contexts) present in an RDF dataset and assigns a unique integer ID to each of them, and (ii) a compressed bit matrix (named Quad Information) that marks the presence (or absence) of a triple in the graphs. We propose two implementations for this matrix, Annotated Triples (HDT-AT) and Annotated Graphs (HDT-AG), based on indexing the matrix per triple or per graph. Then, we define efficient algorithms for the resolution of quad patterns, i.e. quads where each of the components can be a variable, on top of HDTQ. Our empirical results show that HDTQ keeps compression ratios close to general compression techniques (such as gzip), excels in space w.r.t state-of-the-art stores and remains competitive in quad pattern resolution, respecting the low-cost philosophy of HDT. All in all, HDTQ opens up HDT to a wider range of applications, since GRAPH querying is a key feature in triple stores and SPARQL.

The paper is organized as follows. Section 2 describes the related work and Sect. 3 provides preliminaries on RDF and HDT. HDTQ, the proposed extension of HDT to handle RDF quads, is presented in Sect. 4, and evaluated in Sect. 5. We conclude and devise future work in Sect. 6.

2   State of the Art

RDF datasets with named graphs are traditionally serialized in standard verbose formats such as N-Quads, Trig or JSON-LD [17]. Although they include some compact features (e.g. prefixes or lists), their human-readable focus still adds unnecessary overheads to store and transmit large RDF datasets. Instead, HDTQ proposes a compact, binary serialization that keeps retrieval features.

In turn, all major triple stores supporting SPARQL 1.1 also support named graphs. Regardless of the underneath model (based on a relational schema, implementing a native index or a NOSQL solution), RDF stores often speed up quad-based queries by indexing different combinations of the subject, predicate, object and graph elements in RDF [13]. Virtuoso [5] implements quads in a column-based relational store, with two full indexes over the RDF quads, with PSOG and POSG order, and 3 projections SP, OP and GS. The well-known Apache Jena TDB[1] stores RDF datasets using 6 B+Trees indexes, namely SPOG, POSG, OSPG, GSPO, GPOS and GOSP. A recent approach, RDF-4X [1] implements a cloud-based NOSQL solution using Apache Accumulo[2]. In this case, quads are organized in a distributed table where 6 indexes, SPOG, POG, OGS, GSP, GP and OS, are built to speed up all triple patterns. Blazegraph[3] (formerly BigData) follows a similar NOSQL approach making use of OGSP, SPOG, GSPO, PGSO, POGS, and SPOG indexes.

Finally, other approaches focus on extending current triple indexes to support quads, such as RQ-RDF-3X [14] or annotating triples with versions, such as v-RDFCSA [6]. HDTQ shares a similar annotation strategy as this latter, extending this concept to general named graphs on top of HDT in order to achieve, to the best of our knowledge, the first compact and queryable serialization of RDF datasets.

3   Preliminaries

This section introduces some terminology and basic concepts of RDF and HDT.

3.1   RDF and SPARQL

An *RDF graph* G is a finite set of triples (subject, predicate, object) from $(I \cup B) \times I \times (I \cup B \cup L)$, where I, B, L denote IRIs, blank nodes and RDF literals, respectively. RDF graphs can be grouped and managed together, conforming an *RDF dataset*, that is, a collection of RDF graphs [17]. Borrowing terminology from [10], an *RDF dataset* is a set $DS = \{G, (g_1, G_1), \ldots, (g_n, G_n)\}$ consisting of a (non-named) default graph G and *named graphs* s.t. $g_i \in I$ are graph names. Figure 1 represents a dataset DS consisting of two named graphs (*aka* subgraphs), graphWU and graphTU, coming from different sources

---

[1] http://jena.apache.org/documentation/tdb/index.html.
[2] https://accumulo.apache.org/.
[3] https://www.blazegraph.com/.

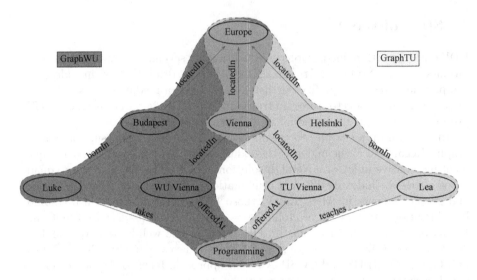

Fig. 1. An RDF dataset DS consisting of two graphs, `GraphWU` and `GraphTU`.

(e.g. from two universities). Note that terms[4] (i.e. subjects, predicates and objects) and triples can belong to different named graphs. For instance, the triple ($Vienna, locatedIn, Europe$) is shared among the two subgraphs.

An *RDF quad* can be seen as an extension of a triple with the graph name (*aka* context). Formally, an RDF quad q from an RDF dataset DS, is a quadruple (subject, predicate, object, g_i) from $(I \cup B) \times I \times (I \cup B \cup L) \times I$. Note that the graph name g_i can be used in other triples or quads to provide further meta-knowledge, e.g. the subgraph provenance. We also note that quads and datasets (with named graphs) are in principle interchangeable in terms of expressiveness, i.e. one can be represented by the other.

RDF graphs and datasets are traditionally queried using the well-known SPARQL [10] query language. SPARQL is based on graph pattern matching, where the core component is the concept of a triple pattern, i.e. a triple where each subject, predicate and object are RDF terms or SPARQL variables. Formally, assuming a set V of variables, disjoint from the aforementioned I, B and L, a triple pattern tp is a tuple from $(I \cup B \cup V) \times (I \cup V) \times (I \cup B \cup L \cup V)$. In turn, SPARQL defines ways of specifying and querying by graph names (or the default graph), using the GRAPH keyword. To capture this, following the same convention as the triple pattern, we define a quad pattern qp as an extension of a triple pattern where also the graph name can be provided or may be a variable to be matched. That is, a quad pattern qp is a pair $tp \times (I \cup V)$ where the last component denotes the graph of the pattern (an IRI or variable).

---

[4] All terms are IRIs whose prefix, http://example.org/, has been omitted for simplicity.

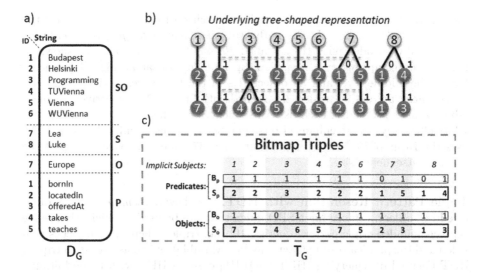

Fig. 2. HDT Dictionary and Triples for a graph G (merging all triples of Fig. 1).

3.2   HDT

HDT [7] is a compressed serialization format for single RDF graphs, which also allows for triple pattern retrieval over the compressed data. HDT encodes an RDF graph G into three components: the *Header* holds metadata (provenance, signatures, etc.) and relevant information for parsing; the *Dictionary* provides a catalog of all RDF terms in G and maps each of them to a unique identifier; and the *Triple* component encodes the structure of the graph after the ID replacement. Figure 2 shows the HDT dictionary and triples for all RDF triples in Fig. 1, i.e. disregarding the name graphs.

HDT Dictionary. The HDT dictionary of a graph G, denoted as D_G, organizes all terms in four sections, as shown in Fig. 2(a): SO includes terms occurring both as subject and object, mapped to the ID-range $[1, |SO|]$. Sections S and O comprise terms that only appear as subjects or objects, respectively. In order to optimize the range of IDs, they are both mapped from $|SO|+1$, ranging up to $|SO|+|S|$ and $|SO|+|O|$, respectively. Finally, section P stores all predicates, mapped to $[1, |P|]$. Note that (i) no ambiguity is possible once we know the role played by the term, and (ii) the HDT dictionary provides fast lookup conversions between IDs and terms.

HDT Triples. The Triples component of a graph G, denoted as T_G, encodes the *structure* of the RDF graph after ID replacement. Logically speaking, T organizes all triples into a forest of trees, one per different subject, as shown in Fig. 2(b): subjects are the roots of the trees, where the middle level comprises the ordered list of predicates associated with each subject, and the leaves list the objects related to each (subject, predicate) pair. This *underlying representation* is practically encoded with the so-called *BitmapTriples* approach [7], shown in Fig. 2(c). It comprises *two sequences*: Sp and So, concatenating all predicate IDs in the middle level and all object IDs in the leaves, respectively; and *two bitsequences*: Bp and Bo, which are aligned with Sp and So respectively, using a 1-bit to mark the end of each list. Bitsequences are then indexed to locate the 1-bits efficiently. These enhanced bitsequences are usually called *bitmaps*. HDT uses the Bitmap375 [11] technique that takes 37.5% extra space on top of the original bitsequence size.

Triple Pattern Resolution with HDT. As shown, *BitmapTriples* is organized by subject, conforming a SPO index that can be used to efficiently resolve subject-bounded triple pattern queries [10] (i.e. triples where the subject is provided and the predicate and object may be a variable) as well as listing all triples. HDT-Focused on Querying (HDT-FoQ) [16] extends HDT with two additional indexes (PSO and OPS) to speed up the resolution of all triple patterns.

4   HDTQ: Adding Graph Information to HDT

This section introduces HDTQ, an extension of HDT that involves managing RDF quads. We consider hereinafter that the original source is an RDF dataset as defined in Sect. 3, potentially consisting of several named graphs. For simplicity, we assume that graphs have no blank nodes in common, otherwise a re-labeling step would be possible as pre-processing.

4.1   Extending the HDT Components

HDT was originally designed as a flexible format that can be easily extended, e.g. to include different dictionary and triples components or to support domain-specific applications. In the following, we detail HDTQ and the main design decisions to extend HDT to cope with quads. Figure 3 shows the final HDTQ encoding for the dataset *DS* in Fig. 1. We omit the header information, as the HDTQ extension only adds implementation-specific metadata to parse the components.

Dictionary. In HDTQ, the previous four-section dictionary is extended by a fifth section to store all different graph names. The IDs of the graphs are then used to annotate the presence of the triples in each graph, further explained below. Figure 3(a) shows the new HDTQ dictionary encoding for the dataset *DS*. Compared to the dictionary shown in Fig. 2, i.e. the HDT conversion of all triples disregarding the named graphs, two comments are in order:

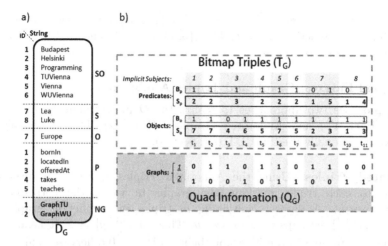

Fig. 3. HDTQ encoding of the dataset DS.

- The terms of all graphs are merged together in the traditional four dictionary sections, SO, S, O, P, as explained in Sect. 3. This decision can potentially increase the range of IDs w.r.t an individual mapping per graph, but it keeps the philosophy of storing terms once, when possible.
- The graph names are organized in an independent graph section, NG (named graphs), mapped from 1 to n_g, being n_g the number of graphs. Note that these terms might also play a different role in the dataset, and can then appear duplicated in SO, S, O or P. However, no ambiguity is possible with the IDs once we know the role of the term we are searching for. In turn, the storage overhead of the potential duplication is limited as we assume that the number of graphs is much less than the number of unique subjects and objects. An optimization for extreme corner cases is devoted to future work.

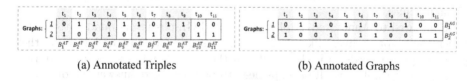

(a) Annotated Triples   (b) Annotated Graphs

Fig. 4. Annotated Triples and Annotated Graphs variants for the RDF dataset DS.

Triples. HDTQ respects the original *Bitmap Triples* encoding and extends it with an additional *Quad Information* (Q) component, shown in Fig. 3(b). Q represents a boolean matrix that includes (for every *triple - graph* combination) the information on whether a specific triple appears in a specific graph. Formally, having a triple-ID t_j (where $j \in \{1 \ldots m\}$, being m the total number of triples in the dataset DS), and a graph-ID k (where $k \in \{1 \ldots n_g\}$), the new Q component defines a boolean function $graph(t_j, k) = \{0, 1\}$, where 1 denotes that t_j appears in the graph k, or 0 otherwise.

4.2 Quad Indexes: Graph and Triples Annotators

HDTQ proposes two approaches to realize the Q matrix, namely Annotated Triples (HDT-AT) and Annotated Graphs (HDT-AG). They both rely on bitmaps, traditionally used in HDT (see Sect. 3).

Annotated Triples. Using the Annotated Triples approach, a bitmap is assigned to each triple, marking the graphs in which the corresponding triple is present. A dataset containing m triples in n different graphs has $\{B_1^{AT}, \cdots, B_m^{AT}\}$ bitmaps each of size n. Thus, if $B_j^{AT}[i] = 1$, it means that the triple t_j is present in the ith graph, being $B_j^{AT}[i] = 0$ otherwise. This can be seen in Fig. 4(a), where 11 bitmaps (one per triple) are created, each of them of two positions, corresponding to the two graphs. In this example, the bitmap for the first triple holds $\{0, 1\}$, meaning that the first triple, (1,2,7), only appears in the second graph, which is graphWU.

Intuitively, Annotated Triples favors quad patterns having the graph component as a variable, like SPO?, as only a single bitmap needs to be browsed. On the other hand, if the graph is given, like in the pattern ???G, all of the bitmaps need to be browsed.

Annotated Graphs. This approach is orthogonal to Annotated Triples: a bitmap is assigned to each graph, marking the triples present in the corresponding graph. Thus, a dataset containing m triples in n different graphs has $\{B_1^{AG}, \cdots, B_n^{AG}\}$ bitmaps each of size m. Thus, if $B_j^{AG}[i] = 1$, it means that the triple t_i is present in the jth graph, being $B_j^{AG}[i] = 0$ otherwise. This can be seen in Fig. 4(b), including 2 bitmaps, each of size 11. For instance, the bitmap for the first graph, graphTU, holds $\{0, 1, 1, 0, 1, 1, 0, 1, 1, 0, 0\}$ meaning that it consists of the triples $\{t_2, t_3, t_5, t_6, t_8, t_9\}$, which can be found in the respective positions in BitmapTriples.

Compared to Annotated Triples, Annotated Graphs favors quad patterns in which the graph is given, like ???G, as only a single bitmap (the bitmap of the given graph G) needs to be browsed. On the other hand it penalizes patterns with graph variables, as all bitmaps need to be browsed to answer the query.

Finally note that, both in HDT-AT and HDT-AG, depending on the data distribution, the bitmaps can be long and sparse. However, in practice, HDT-AT and HDT-AG can be implemented with compressed bitmaps [15] to minimize the size of the bitsequences.

4.3 Search Operations

The resolution of quad patterns in HDTQ builds on top of two operations inherently provided by the *BitmapTriples* component (BT):

Algorithm 1. SEARCHQUADS - *quad patterns with unbounded graphs*

Input: BitmapTriples BT, Quad Information Q, quad pattern q
Output: The quads matching the given pattern
1 $result \leftarrow ();\ graph \leftarrow 0$
2 $(triple, posTriple) \leftarrow BT.getNextSolution(q, 0)$
3 **while** $posTriple \neq null$ **do**
4 | $graph \leftarrow Q.nextGraph(posTriple, graph + 1)$
5 | **if** $graph \neq null$ **then**
6 | | $result.append(triple, graph)$
7 | **else**
8 | | $(triple, posTriple) \leftarrow BT.getNextSolution(q, posTriple)$
9 | | $graph \leftarrow 0$

10 **return** $result$

- **BT.getNextSolution(quad, startPosition).** Given a *quad* pattern, BT removes the last graph term and resolves the triple pattern, outputting a pair $(triple, posTriple)$ corresponding to the next triple solution and its position in BT. The search starts at the *startPosition* provided, in BT. For instance, in our example in Fig. 3, with a pattern $quad = 7???$, an operation `BT.getNextSolution(quad,8)` will jump the first 8 triples in BT, $\{t_1, \cdots, t_8\}$, hence the only solution is the pair $((7, 5, 3), 9)$ or, in other words, t_9.
- **BT.getSolutionPositions(quad).** This operation finds the set of triple positions where solution candidates appear. In subject-bounded queries, these positions are actually a consecutive range $\{t_x, \ldots, t_y\}$ of BT. Otherwise, in queries such as ?P?G, ??OG and ?POG, the positions are spread across BT. For instance, t_2 and t_5 are solutions for $quad = ?2?1$, but t_3 and t_4 do not match the pattern.

Note that we assume that the HDT-FoQ [16] indexes (PSO and OPS) are created, hence BT can provide these operations for all patterns. In the following, we detail the resolution depending on whether the graph term is given or it remains unbounded.

Quad Pattern Queries with Unbounded Graph. Algorithm 1 shows the resolution of quad patterns in which the graph term is not given, i.e. ????, S???, ?P??, ??O?, SP??, S?O?, ?PO? and SPO?. It is mainly based on iterating through the solutions of the traditional HDT and, for each triple solution, returning all the graphs associated to it. Thus, the algorithm starts by getting the first solution in BT (Line 2), using the aforementioned operation *getNextSolution*. While the end of BT is not reached (Line 3), we get the next graph associated with the current triple (Line 4), or *null* if it does not appear in any further graph. This is provided by the operation *nextGraph* of Q, explained below. If there is a graph associated with the triple (Line 5), both are appended to the results (Line 6). Otherwise, we look for the next triple solution (Line 8).

The auxiliary *nextGraph* operation of Q returns the next graph in which a given triple appears, or *null* if the end is reached. Algorithm 2 shows this operation for HDT-AT. First, the bitmap corresponding to the given triple is

Algorithm 2. NEXTGRAPH - AT	**Algorithm 3.** NEXTGRAPH - AG
Input: Quad Information Q, int posTriple, int graph	**Input**: Quad Information Q, int posTriple, int graph
Output: The position of the next graph	**Output**: The position of the next graph

```
Algorithm 2. NextGraph - AT
Input: Quad Information Q, int posTriple, int graph
Output: The position of the next graph
1  bitmap ← Q[posTriple]
2  return bitmap.getNext1(graph)
```

```
Algorithm 3. NextGraph - AG
Input: Quad Information Q, int posTriple, int graph
Output: The position of the next graph
1  do
2  │   bitmap ← Q[graph]
3  │   if bitmap[posTriple] = 1 then
4  │   │   return graph
5  │   else
6  │   └   graph ← graph + 1
7  while graph ≤ Q.size()
8  return null
```

Algorithm 4. SEARCHQUADSG - *quad patterns with bounded graphs*

```
Input: BitmapTriples BT, Quad Information Q, quad pattern q
Output: The quads matching the given pattern
1  graph ← getGraph(q); result ← ()
2  sol[] ← BT.getSolutionPositions(q)
3  while !sol.isEmpty() do
4  │   posTripleCandidateBT ← sol.pop()
5  │   posTripleCandidateQT ← Q.nextTriple(posTripleCandidateBT, graph)
6  │   if posTripleCandidateBT = posTripleCandidateQT then
7  │   │   (triple, posTriple) ← BT.getNextSolution(q, posTripleCandidateBT − 1)
8  │   │   result.append(triple, graph)
9  │   else
10 │   └   sol.removeLessThan(posTripleCandidateQT)
11 return result
```

retrieved from Q (Line 1). Then, within this bitmap, the location of the next 1 starting with the provided graph ID is retrieved (or null if the end is reached) and returned (Line 2). This latter is natively provided by the bitmap indexes.

Algorithm 3 shows the same process for HDT-AG. In this case, a bitmap is associated with each graph. Thus, we iterate on graphs and access one bitmap after the other (Line 1–7). The process ends when a 1-bit is found (Line 3), returning the graph (Line 4), or the maximum number of graphs is reached (Line 7), returning null (Line 8).

Quad Pattern Queries with Bounded Graph. Algorithm 4 resolves all quad patterns where the graph is provided. To do so, the graph ID is first retrieved from the quad pattern (Line 1). The aforementioned *getSolutionPositions* operation of BT finds the triple positions in which the solutions can appear (Line 2). Then, we iterate on this set of candidate positions until it is empty (Line 3). For each *posTripleCandidateBT* extracted from the set (Line 4), we check if this position is associated with the given graph (Line 5), using the operation *nextTriple* of the Q structure. This operation, omitted for the sake of concision as it is analogous to *nextGraph* (see Algorithms 2 and 3), starts from *posTripleCandidateBT* and returns the next triple position (*posTripleCandidateQT*) that is associated to the given graph. Thus, if this position is exactly the current candidate position (Line 6), the actual triple is obtained for that position (Line 7), and appended to the final resultset (Line 8). Otherwise, the candidate position was

Table 1. Statistical dataset description.

		Subjects	Predicates	Objects	Graphs	Triples	Quads
BEAR	A	74,908,887	41,209	64,215,355	58	378,476,570	2,071,287,964
	B day	100	1,725	69,650	89	82,401	3,460,896
	B hour	100	1,744	148,866	1,299	167,281	51,632,164
LUBM500	G1	10,847,183	17	8,072,358	1	66,731,200	66,731,200
	. . .	. . .	. . .	. . .	. . .	. . .	. . .
	G9998	10,847,183	17	8,072,358	9998	66,731,200	68,823,803
LDBC		668,711	16	2,743,645	190,961	5,000,197	5,000,197
LIDDI		392,344	23	981,928	392,340	1,952,822	2,051,959

not a valid solution (it was not related to the graph), and we can remove, from the set of candidate solutions, all positions lesser than *posTripleCandidateQT* (Line 10), given that none of them are associated to the given graph.

5   Evaluation

We evaluate the performance of HDTQ in terms of space and efficiency on quad pattern resolution. The HDTQ prototype[5], built on top of the existing HDT-Java library[6], implements both HDT-AG and HDT-AT approaches using existing compressed bitmaps (called Roaring Bitmaps [15]), which are optimal for sparse bitsequences.

Datasets. Experiments are carried out on heterogeneous RDF datasets[7], described in Table 1. BEAR-A [8], a benchmark for RDF archives, includes 58 weekly crawls of a set of domains in the LOD cloud. Each of the snapshots is considered to be a graph, resulting in a dataset of 58 graphs. BEAR-A is relatively dynamic as 31% of the data change between two versions, resulting in more than 2 billion quads. BEAR-B day and BEAR-B hour [9] extend BEAR-A to consider more dynamic information. They crawl the 100 most volatile resources in DBpedia Live over the course of three months, and consider a new version by day or hour, respectively. Each of the versions is seen as a graph, summing up 89 and 1,299 graphs, respectively. Given that most of the triples remain unchanged, most triples appear in multiple graphs.

The well-known LUBM data generator [12] is also considered as a way to generate several RDF datasets with increasing number of graphs: 1, 10, 20,. . . , 100, 1,000, 2,000,. . . , 9,000 and 9,998. We first set up the generator to produce synthetic data describing 500 universities (LUBM500), which results in 66 m

---

[5] HDTQ library: https://github.com/JulianRei/hdtq-java.

[6] HDT-Java library: https://github.com/rdfhdt/hdt-java.

[7] Datasets, queries, scripts, raw results and additional material is available at: https://aic.ai.wu.ac.at/qadlod/hdtq/eswc2018/.

triples. Given that the generator produces 9,998 files, $\{f_1, f_2 \cdots, f_{9998}\}$, we first consider an RDF dataset with a graph per file, $\{g_1, g_2 \cdots, g_{9998}\}$, named as LUBM500-G9998. Then, to generate a dataset with an arbitrary number of graphs n ($n <= 9998$), each file f_j was merged to a graph g_i, where $i = j$ mod n. For simplicity, Table 1 only shows LUBM500-G1 and LUBM500-G9998. In general, triples are rarely repeated across graphs.

LDBC[8] regards the Semantic Publishing Benchmark (SPB), which considers diverse media content. We use the default SPB 2.0 generator that generates more than 190k named graphs, where each triple appears only in one graph.

Finally, the Linked Drug-Drug Interactions (LIDDI) dataset [2] integrates multiple data collections, including provenance information. This results in an RDF dataset with an extremely large number of graphs, 392,340, as shown in Table 1.

Triple Stores. We compare HDTQ against two well-known triple stores in the state of the art, Apache Jena TDB 2.10 store[9] and Virtuoso 7.1 Open Source[10]. Following Virtuoso instructions, we also consider a variant, named as Virtuoso+, which includes an additional index (GPOS) that may speed up quad patterns where the subject is not given. Experiments were performed in a -commodity server- (Intel Xeon E5-2650v2 @ 2.6 GHz, 16 cores, RAM 180 GB, Debian 7.9). Reported (elapsed) times are the average of three independent executions. Transactions are disabled in all systems.

Table 2. Space requirements of different systems.

		Size (GB)	gzip	HDT-AG	HDT-AT	Jena	Virtuoso	Virtuoso+
BEAR	A	396.9	5.8%	**2.3%**	2.8%	96.8%	NA	NA
	B day	0.6	4.8%	**0.7%**	0.8%	97.7%	13.7%	33.7%
	B hour	9.7	4.8%	0.3%	**0.1%**	96.4%	4.3%	25.6%
LUBM500	G1	11.4	3.0%	**6.6%**	17.0%	118.8%	17.2%	21.0%
	G9998	11.6	3.0%	**6.6%**	16.7%	120.1%	17.5%	27.5%
LDBC		0.9	9.7%	**15.9%**	25.1%	126.3%	71.2%	80.8%
LIDDI		0.7	3.7%	**11.8%**	15.6%	78.1%	49.9%	53.4%

5.1   Space Requirements and Indexing Time

Table 2 lists the space requirements of the uncompressed RDF datasets in N-Quads notation (column "Size"), in gigabytes, the respective gzipped datasets (column "gzip") and the systems under review, as the ratio between the size for

---

[8] LDBC: http://ldbcouncil.org/developer/spb.

[9] Apache Jena: http://jena.apache.org.

[10] Virtuoso: http://virtuoso.openlinksw.com.

the required space and the uncompressed size. The numbers reported for HDT-AG and HDT-AT include the size of HDTQ and the additional HDT indexes (created with HDT-FoQ [16]) needed to resolve all quad patterns[11]. Note that Virtuoso was not capable of importing the BEAR-A dataset due to a persistent error when inserting large quad data. In fact, a similar bug in the current Java implementation of Roaring Bitmaps [15] made us use Bitmap375 [11] for this particular scenario, as the HDTQ prototype supports both implementations interchangeably, being transparent to users consuming/querying HDTQ.

As expected, gzip achieves large space savings that outperform the space needs of the RDF stores. However, HDTQ improves upon gzip in all BEAR datasets, where a large amount of (verbose) triples are shared across graphs. In this scenario, HDTQ is able to mitigate the repetitions thanks to the dictionary and Quad Information structures.

HDTQ outperforms Jena and Virtuoso in all datasets, being particularly noticeable in BEAR datasets (1–2 levels of magnitude smaller), with a limited number of graphs (58 to 1,299) and many shared triples across graphs. HDTQ gains are still noticeable in LDBC (3 to 5 times smaller than Virtuoso and Jena) with a very large number of graphs (190k) and no shared triples. Similar results are obtained in LIDDI, with 392k graphs.

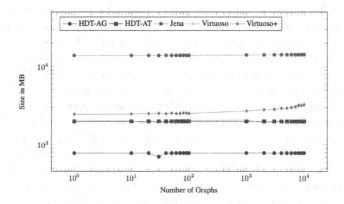

Fig. 5. Space requirements for the LUBM500 datasets with increasing number of graphs.

In turn, HDT-AG reports better compression ratios than HDT-AT (except for a small difference in BEAR-B hour). The main reason lies in the compressed implementation of the bitmaps [15] that exploits consecutive runs of 0's or 1's to achieve further compression. In most of the cases, longer runs are produced when annotating the triples per graph (HDT-AG), than viceversa (HDT-AT). In fact, HDT-AT largely outperforms all systems except for LUBM, where the compression is only slightly better than Virtuoso (without additional indexes) given that

---

[11] The HDTQ website additionally includes the size of each structure of HDT and HDTQ.

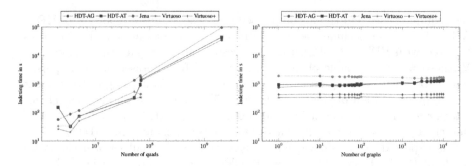

Fig. 6. Indexing times (in s) of the RDF datasets.

Fig. 7. Indexing times (in s) of LUBM500 datasets.

triples are mostly present in one single graph, hence HDT-AT needs to pay the price of storing multiple bitmaps (one per triple), each of them representing just a single value. In LDBC, with a similar scenario, the HDT-AT overhead is compensated by the overall compression of the dictionary and triples components, and HDTQ still excels in space.

Figure 5 shows the space requirements (in MB, and log log scale) of LUBM500 at increasing number of graphs (1, 10, 20,..., 100, 1,000, 2,000,..., 9,000 and 9,998), where few triples are shared across graphs. All systems, including HDTQ, demand close to constant size regardless of the number of graphs. The exception is Virtuoso+, as it pays the price of the additional index GPOS.

Figure 6 represents (in log log scale) the indexing times of the RDF datasets in Table 2, sorted by the number of quads of each dataset. For HDT-AG and HDT-AT, this includes the creation of all components (standard HDT and HDT-FoQ, and the novel graph dictionary and Quad Information structures). Virtuoso is the fastest system regarding creation time in all cases, except for the failed BEAR-A. In mostly all cases, Jena doubles the time required by HDTQ. As expected, the time in all systems shows a linear growth with an increasing number of quads. In turn, Fig. 7 focuses on LUBM500 at increasing number of graphs. In general, Jena and Virtuoso perfectly scale in this scenario, whereas HDTQ pays the overhead of the creation of increasing large bitmaps in HDT-AG and HDT-AT. Nonetheless, the overhead is limited and the creation can be seen as a one-off cost by the publisher.

5.2   Performance for Quad Pattern Resolution

To test the performance of the systems, we select, for each dataset, 100 random queries for each combination of quad patterns (except for the pattern ???? and those patterns such as ?P?? where the data distribution prevents from having 100 different queries). Each query is then executed in two scenarios: cold, where cache was first cleared, and warm, which considers a warmup by first querying ???? and taking 100 results.

Figures 8 and 9 show the averaged resolution times of the selected queries for two exemplary datasets, BEAR-B day with limited number of named graphs and

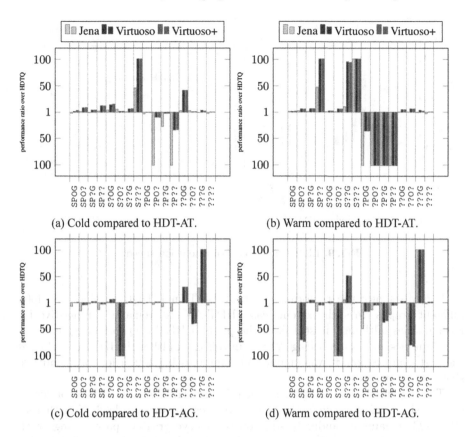

(a) Cold compared to HDT-AT.

(b) Warm compared to HDT-AT.

(c) Cold compared to HDT-AG.

(d) Warm compared to HDT-AG.

Fig. 8. BEAR-B day quad pattern resolution speed.

many repeated triples across graphs, and LIDDI, with opposite characteristics. In these figures, a k number above the x-axis means that HDTQ is k times faster than the compared system. A k number below shows that the system is k times faster than HDTQ.

Results for HDT-AT in BEAR-B day, Fig. 8a and b, show that HDT-AT, while taking 1–2 order of magnitude less in space, excels in subject-based queries (in special S??? and S??G), in cold and warm scenarios. In contrast, it is penalized in predicate-based queries (such as ?P?? and ?P?G). This result is in line with previous HDT-FoQ [16] remarks, which shows that adding the quad information as a triple annotation in HDT-AT keeps the retrieval features of HDT.

HDT-AG reports less promising numbers in Fig. 8c and d. As expected, listing the triples by graphs (???G) is extremely efficient. However, HDT-AG design penalizes most operations, in particular those with unbounded graphs, as results must be first found, and then all graph bitmaps have to be accessed to check the presence of the triple. In contrast HDT-AT allows for quickly jumping to the next solution (the next 1-bit annotation) of the triple.

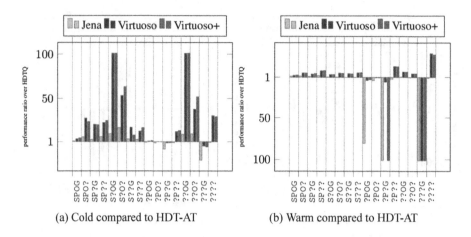

(a) Cold compared to HDT-AT   (b) Warm compared to HDT-AT

Fig. 9. LIDDI quad pattern resolution speed.

Figure 9 shows the performance of HDT-AT in LIDDI, with almost 400k different graphs. In such extreme case, HDT-AT still remains competitive for most queries, although it still pays the price of HDT-FoQ in some predicate-based queries and graph listing (???G). In this case, although HDT-AG achieves the best compression, it was unable to compete, being 1–2 orders of magnitude slower in most cases.

These results show that, in a general case, HDT-AT should be preferred over HDT-AG as it provides the best space/performance tradeoff. Nonetheless, HDT-AG remains a candidate solution to achieve greater space savings with reasonably performance if the number of graphs is limited. Given that HDT-AG excels when listing graphs, further inspection of a combined approach (AG-AT) is devoted to future work.

6   Conclusions and Future Work

This work presents HDTQ as an extension of HDT, a compact and queryable serialization of RDF, to support RDF datasets including named graphs (quads). HDTQ considers a new dictionary to uniquely store all different named graphs, and a new Quad Information component to annotate the presence of the triples in each graph of the RDF dataset. Two realizations of this component are proposed, HDT-AG and HDT-AT, and space/performance tradeoffs are evaluated against different datasets and state-of-the-art stores. Results show that HDTQ keeps the same HDT features, positioned itself as a highly compact serialization for RDF quads that remains competitive in quad pattern resolution. Our ongoing work focuses on inspecting an hybrid AT-AG strategy for the quad information and supporting full SPARQL 1.1. on top of HDTQ. To do so, we plan to use HDTQ as a backend store within existing frameworks, such as Jena.

Acknowledgements. Supported by the EU's Horizon 2020 research and innovation programme: grant 731601 (SPECIAL), the Austrian Research Promotion Agency's (FFG) program "ICT of the Future": grant 861213 (CitySpin), and MINECO-AEI/FEDER-UE ETOME-RDFD3: TIN2015-69951-R and TIN2016-78011-C4-1-R; Axel Polleres is supported under the Distinguished Visiting Austrian Chair Professors program hosted by The Europe Center of Stanford University. Thanks to Tobias Kuhn for the pointer to the LIDDI dataset.

References

1. Abbassi, S., Faiz, R.: RDF-4X: a scalable solution for RDF quads store in the cloud. In: Proceedings of MEDES, pp. 231–236 (2016)
2. Banda, J.M., Kuhn, T., Shah, N.H., Dumontier, M.: Provenance-centered dataset of drug-drug interactions. In: Arenas, M., et al. (eds.) ISWC 2015. LNCS, vol. 9367, pp. 293–300. Springer, Cham (2015). https://doi.org/10.1007/978-3-319-25010-6_18
3. Beek, W., Rietveld, L., Bazoobandi, H.R., Wielemaker, J., Schlobach, S.: LOD laundromat: a uniform way of publishing other people's dirty data. In: Mika, P., et al. (eds.) ISWC 2014. LNCS, vol. 8796, pp. 213–228. Springer, Cham (2014). https://doi.org/10.1007/978-3-319-11964-9_14
4. Bizer, C., Heath, T., Berners-Lee, T.: Linked data - the story so far. In: Semantic Services, Interoperability and Web Applications: Emerging Concepts, pp. 205–227 (2009)
5. Boncz, P., Erling, O., Pham, M.-D.: Advances in large-scale RDF data management. In: Auer, S., Bryl, V., Tramp, S. (eds.) Linked Open Data – Creating Knowledge Out of Interlinked Data. LNCS, vol. 8661, pp. 21–44. Springer, Cham (2014). https://doi.org/10.1007/978-3-319-09846-3_2
6. Cerdeira-Pena, A., Farina, A., Fernández, J.D., Martínez-Prieto, M.A.: Self-indexing RDF archives. In: Proceedings of DCC, pp. 526–535 (2016)
7. Fernández, J.D., Martínez-Prieto, M.A., Gutiérrez, C., Polleres, A., Arias, M.: Binary RDF representation for publication and exchange (HDT). JWS **19**, 22–41 (2013)
8. Fernández, J.D., Umbrich, J., Polleres, A., Knuth, M.: Evaluating query and storage strategies for RDF archives. In: Proceedings of SEMANTiCS, pp. 41–48 (2016)
9. Fernández, J.D., Umbrich, J., Polleres, A., Knuth, M.: Evaluating query and storage strategies for RDF archives. Semant. Web J. SWJ (2017, under review). http://www.semantic-web-journal.net/content/evaluating-query-and-storage-strategies-rdf-archives
10. Garlik, S.H., Seaborne, A., Prud'hommeaux, E.: SPARQL 1.1 Query Language, W3C Recommendation (2013)
11. González, R., Grabowski, S., Mäkinen, V., Navarro, G.: Practical implementation of rank and select queries. In: Proceedings of WEA, pp. 27–38 (2005)
12. Guo, Y., Pan, Z., Heflin, J.: LUBM: a benchmark for owl knowledge base systems. JWS **3**(2), 158–182 (2005)
13. Harth, A., Decker, S.: Optimized index structures for querying RDF from the web. In: Proceeding of LA-WEB, p. 10 (2005)
14. Leeka, J., Bedathur, S.: RQ-RDF-3X: going beyond triplestores. In: Proceedings of ICDEW, pp. 263–268 (2014)

15. Lemire, D., Kaser, O., Kurz, N., Deri, L., O'Hara, C., Saint-Jacques, F., Ssi-Yan-Kai, G.: Roaring bitmaps: implementation of an optimized software library. arXiv preprint arXiv:1709.07821 (2017)
16. Martínez-Prieto, M.A., Arias Gallego, M., Fernández, J.D.: Exchange and consumption of huge RDF data. In: Simperl, E., Cimiano, P., Polleres, A., Corcho, O., Presutti, V. (eds.) ESWC 2012. LNCS, vol. 7295, pp. 437–452. Springer, Heidelberg (2012). https://doi.org/10.1007/978-3-642-30284-8_36
17. Schreiber, G., Raimond, Y.: RDF 1.1 Primer. W3C Working Group Note (2014)
18. Verborgh, R., Vander Sande, M., Hartig, O., Van Herwegen, J., De Vocht, L., De Meester, B., Haesendonck, G., Colpaert, P.: Triple pattern fragments: a low-cost knowledge graph interface for the web. JWS **37–38**, 184–206 (2016)
19. Zimmermann, A., Lopes, N., Polleres, A., Straccia, U.: A general framework for representing, reasoning and querying with annotated semantic web data. JWS **11**, 72–95 (2012)

Answers Partitioning and Lazy Joins for Efficient Query Relaxation and Application to Similarity Search

Sébastien Ferré[(⊠)] [ID]

Univ Rennes, CNRS, IRISA, Campus de Beaulieu, 35042 Rennes, France
ferre@irisa.fr

Abstract. Query relaxation has been studied as a way to find approximate answers when user queries are too specific or do not align well with the data schema. We are here interested in the application of query relaxation to similarity search of RDF nodes based on their description. However, this is challenging because existing approaches have a complexity that grows in a combinatorial way with the size of the query and the number of relaxation steps. We introduce two algorithms, answers partitioning and lazy join, that together significantly improve the efficiency of query relaxation. Our experiments show that our approach scales much better with the size of queries and the number of relaxation steps, to the point where it becomes possible to relax large node descriptions in order to find similar nodes. Moreover, the relaxed descriptions provide explanations for their semantic similarity.

1 Introduction

Query relaxation has been proposed as a way to find *approximate answers* to user queries [10]. It consists in applying transformations to the user query in order to relax constraints, and make it more general so that it produces more answers. In previous work on SPARQL queries over RDF(S) graphs [5,6,9,14,15], typical relaxation steps consist in removing a query element or replacing a class by a superclass or a node by a variable. The major limitation of query relaxation is that the number of relaxed queries grows in a combinatorial way with the number of relaxation steps and the size of the query.

A potential application of query relaxation is *similarity search*, i.e. the search for the nodes most similar to a given query node in an RDF graph. We propose to start with the query node description as an overly specific query, and to relax it progressively in order to find similar nodes as approximate answers. The relaxed queries can then be used as *explanations* of the similarity with each node, and for *ranking* similar nodes. However, existing algorithms for query relaxation are not efficient enough for that purpose because node descriptions make up for

This research is supported by ANR project PEGASE (ANR-16-CE23-0011-08).

© Springer International Publishing AG, part of Springer Nature 2018
A. Gangemi et al. (Eds.): ESWC 2018, LNCS 10843, pp. 209–224, 2018.
https://doi.org/10.1007/978-3-319-93417-4_14

large queries, and many relaxation steps are necessary in order to find approximate answers. Various definitions of semantic distance/similarity have been proposed, especially between concepts in ontologies [17] but also between structural symbolic descriptions [7,13]. However, those distances/similarities are numerical measures, and the explanation of the similarity provided by the relaxed queries is lost. In this paper, we only consider symbolic forms of semantic similarity, i.e. similarities that can be represented with graph patterns [3,8]. A major drawback of those approaches is that the query node has to be compared to every other node in the RDF graph, and that each comparison is costly because it consists in finding the largest overlap between two rooted graphs.

In this paper, we introduce two algorithms, *answers partitioning* and *lazy join*, that together improve the efficiency of query relaxation to the point where it can be applied effectively to semantic similarity search. Despite the higher efficiency, our approach does not trade quality for efficiency as it produces the same results as query relaxation and symbolic semantic similarity. The contribution is that our partitioning algorithm is driven by both relaxed queries and similar nodes so as to prune the space of relaxed queries while avoiding individual comparison to each node. The set of nodes is partitioned into more and more fine-grained clusters, such that at the end of the process each cluster is a set of approximate answers produced by the same relaxed query. That relaxed query is the common subsumer between the query and each approximate answer. *Lazy join* is an essential optimization of our approach to address similarity search because multi-valued properties (e.g., hasActor) combined with high numbers of relaxation steps imply an explosion of the size of joins.

Section 2 discusses related work. Section 3 gives preliminary definitions. Section 4 defines query relaxation, and introduces its application to similarity search. Section 5 details our answers partitioning algorithm, and Sect. 6 details its optimization with lazy joins. Section 7 report experimental studies of efficiency and effectiveness. Finally, Sect. 8 concludes and draws perspectives.

2   Related Work

The existing approaches for query relaxation consist in enumerating relaxed queries up to some edit distance, and to evaluate each relaxed query, from the more specific to the more general, in order to get new approximate answers [9, 14,15]. The main problem is that the number of relaxed queries grows in a combinatorial way with the edit distance, and the size of the query. Moreover, many relaxed queries do not yield any new answer because they have the same answers as more specific relaxed queries. Huang *et al.* [14] use a similarity score in order to have a better ranking for the evaluation of relaxed queries. They also use a selectivity estimate to save the evaluation of some relaxed queries that are subsumed by a more general relaxed query. Hurtado *et al.* [15] optimize the evaluation of relaxed queries by directly computing their proper answer but the optimization only works for the relaxations that replace a triple pattern by a single other triple pattern. They also introduce new SPARQL clauses, RELAX and APPROX [9], to restrict relaxation to a small subset of the query. However, this requires from the user to anticipate where relaxation can be useful. The above approaches [14,15] put some limitations on the relaxation steps that can be applied. Triple patterns can be generalized by relaxation according to RDFS inference but generally can not be removed from the query. URI and literal nodes cannot always be replaced by variables, which may work in some querying use cases but is a dead-end for similarity search. Other approaches [5,6] present powerful relaxation frameworks but they do not evaluate their efficiency or only generate a few relaxed queries.

Among the numerous similarity/distance measures that have been proposed [4], only a few work on complex relational representations, and can be applied directly to RDF graphs. RIBL (Relational Instance-Based Learning) [13] defines a distance based on the exploration of a graph, starting from a given node and up to a given depth. Ferilli et al. [7] define a similarity between Horn clauses, which are analogous to SPARQL queries. However, although the input of those measures are symbolic, their output is numeric. The drawbacks are that they do not provide intelligible explanations for the measured similarity, and also that when two nodes are at the same distance/similarity to a query node, it is not possible to say whether this is by chance or because they share the same explanation. Proposals for a symbolic similarity between graph nodes include Least Common Subsumers (LCS) [3], and intersections of Projected Graph Patterns [8].

3 Preliminary Definitions

For ease of comparison with previous work, we largely reuse the notations in [15]. The only addition is the inclusion of filters in conjunctive queries. We here consider RDF graphs under RDFS inference, although our work can work with no schema at all, and can be extended to other kinds of knowledge graphs, like Conceptual Graphs [1] or Graph-FCA [8]. An *RDF triple* is a triple of *RDF nodes* $(s, p, o) \in (I \cup B) \times I \times (I \cup B \cup L)$, where I is the set of IRIs, B is the set of blank nodes, and L is the set of literals. An *RDF graph G* is a set of RDF triples. Its set of nodes is noted $nodes(G)$. Given an RDF(S) graph G, we note $cl(G)$ the closure of the graph with all triples that can be infered. A *triple pattern* is a triple $(t_1, t_2, t_3) \in (I \cup V) \times (I \cup V) \times (I \cup V \cup L)$, where V is an infinite set of variables. A *filter* is a Boolean expression on variables and RDF nodes. We here only consider equalities between a variable and a node: $x = n$. A *graph pattern P* is a set of triple patterns and filters, collectively called *query elements*. We note $var(P)$ the set of variables occuring in P. A *conjunctive query Q* is an expression $X \leftarrow P$, where P is a graph pattern, and $X = (x_1, \ldots, x_n)$ is a tuple of variables. X is called the *head*, and P the *body*. We define $var(Q) = X \cup var(P)$ the set of variables occuring in query Q. A query is said *connected* if its body is a connected graph pattern, and contains at least one head variable. A *matching* of pattern P on graph G is a mapping $\mu \in var(P) \rightarrow nodes(G)$ from pattern variables to graph nodes such that $\mu(t) \in cl(G)$ for every triple pattern $t \in P$, and $\mu(f)$ evaluates to true for every filter $f \in P$, where $\mu(t)$ and $\mu(f)$ are obtained from t and f by replacing every variable x by $\mu(x)$. The *match-set* $M(P,G)$ of pattern P on graph G is the set of all matchings of P on G. A match-set M can be seen as a relational table with $dom(M)$ as set of columns Relational operations such as natural join ($\bowtie$), selection (σ), and projection (π) can then be applied to match-sets [2]. The *answer set* of query $Q = X \leftarrow P$ on graph G is the match-set of the body projected on head variables: $ans(Q,G) = \pi_X M(P,G)$.

4 From Query Relaxation to Similarity Search

Query Relaxation. We propose a definition of query relaxation in the line of Hurtado *et al.* [15] but in a slightly more general form to allow for additional kinds of relaxations. We start from a partial ordering $\leq_e$ on query elements that is consistent with logical inference: e.g., $(x,\texttt{rdf:type},\texttt{:SciFiFilm}) \leq_e$ $(x,\texttt{rdf:type},\texttt{:Film})$. From there, we define the relaxation of query elements.

Definition 1 (element relaxation). *The set of relaxed elements of a query element e is the set of immediate $\leq_e$-successors of e: $relax(e) = \{e' \mid e \prec_e e'\}$.*

If there is no ontological definition, we have $relax(e) = \emptyset$ but queries can still be relaxed by removing query elements. In fact, element relaxation is handled as an optional refinement of element removal.

Definition 2 (query relaxation). *Let $Q = X \leftarrow P$ be a (conjunctive) query. Query relaxation defines a partial ordering $\leq_Q$ on queries. A relaxation step, noted $Q \prec_Q Q'$, transforms Q into a relaxed query Q' by replacing any element $e \in P$ by $relax(e)$: $Q' = X \leftarrow (P \setminus \{e\} \cup relax(e))$. Partial ordering $\leq_Q$ is defined as the reflexive and transitive closure of $\prec_Q$. The set of relaxed queries is defined as $RQ(Q) = \{Q' \mid Q <_Q Q'\}$. The relaxation distance of relaxed query $Q' \in RQ(Q)$ is the minimal number of relaxation steps to reach it.*

A novelty compared to previous work is that an element is not replaced by *one of* its immediate succesors but by its *set of* immediate successors. When that set is empty, it allows for the removal of a query element. When that set has several elements, it allows for a more fine-grained relaxation. For example, if class :FullProfessor is a subclass of :Researcher and :Teacher, then triple pattern $(x,\texttt{rdf:type},\texttt{FullProfessor:})$ will first be relaxed into pattern $\{(x,\texttt{rdf:type},\texttt{:Researcher}), (x,\texttt{rdf:type},\texttt{:Teacher})\}$, which can be further relaxed into either $\{(x,\texttt{rdf:type},\texttt{:Researcher})\}$ or $\{(x,\texttt{rdf:type},\texttt{:Teacher})\}$.

Another relaxation that is often missing is the replacement of a graph node (URI or literal) by a variable. The difficulty is that a graph node may occur in several query elements, and its relaxation into a variable is therefore not captured by element-wise relaxation. A solution is to normalize the original query in the following way. For each RDF node n occuring as subject/object in the graph pattern, replace its occurences by a fresh variable x_n, and add the filter $x_n = n$ to the query body. We note $Norm(P)$ the result of this normalization on pattern P. The node-to-variable relaxation then amounts to the removal of one query element, filter $x_n = n$. For the sake of simplicity, we do not include here the relaxation of property paths [9]. Another kind of relaxation that we let to future work is the gradual relaxation of equality filters.

We define the *proper answer* of a relaxed query with the same meaning as the "new answers" in [15], and extend this notion to *proper relaxed queries*.

Definition 3 (proper relaxed queries). *Let Q be a query, and $Q' \in RQ(Q)$ be a relaxed query, and G be a graph. The* proper answers *of Q' is the subset of answers of Q' that are not answers of more specific relaxed queries.*

$$properAns(Q', G) := ans(Q', G) \setminus \bigcup \{ans(Q'', G) \mid Q'' \in RQ(Q), Q'' < Q'\}$$

A proper relaxed query *Q' is a relaxed query whose proper answer is not empty. We note $PRQ(Q, G)$ the set of proper relaxed queries of Q in G:*

$$PRQ(Q, G) := \{Q' \in RQ(Q) \mid properAns(Q', G) \neq \emptyset\}.$$

The objective of query relaxation is to compute as efficiently as possible the proper relaxed queries, their proper answers, and their partial ordering.

Similarity Search. As a contribution to previous work, we lay a bridge from query relaxation to similarity search. Whereas Huang *et al.* [14] use a similarity measure to rank the relaxed queries, we propose to use proper relaxed queries to define a *semantic similarity* that is symbolic rather than numeric. Query relaxation is usually presented as a way to go from a query Q to approximate answers. However, it can in principle be applied to go from an RDF node n to *semantically similar nodes*. Simply build the original query $Q(n) = x \leftarrow Norm(P)$, where x abstracts over node n, and P is the description of node n, up to some depth in the graph, where n is replaced by x. For every $Q' \in PRQ(Q(n))$, $properAns(Q')$ is a set of similar nodes, and Q' describes the semantic similarity as a relaxed description. Compared to similarity (or distance) measures, similarity by query relaxation provides articulate and intelligible descriptions of the similarity. It also provides a more subtle ranking with a partial ordering instead of a total ordering, and the definition of clusters of nodes (proper answers) that share the same relaxed description. Furthermore, several numerical measures can be derived from proper relaxed queries, if desired:

- *extensional distance*: the number of answers in $ans(Q', G)$, i.e. the number of nodes that match what n has in common with nodes in $properAns(Q', G)$;
- *intensional similarity*: the proportion of elements in $cl(Q)$ that are in $cl(Q')$;
- *relaxation distance*: the number of relaxation steps from Q to Q'.

The latter two may be parameterized with weights on query elements [14] and relaxation steps [6], respectively. Note that those derived measures are total orderings that are compatible with partial ordering $\leq_Q$ on relaxed queries. Indeed, a relaxation step can only increase the relaxation distance, and produce a more general query: hence $Q_1 \leq_Q Q_2 \Rightarrow cl(Q_1) \supseteq cl(Q_2) \wedge ans(Q_1, G) \subseteq ans(Q_2, G)$.

Applying query relaxation to semantic similarity is very challenging to compute. The number of relaxed queries grows exponentially with the size of the original query. The description of nodes in real RDF graphs can easily reach 100 triples at depth 1, and grows exponentially with depth. Previous work on query relaxation has so far restricted its application in order to manage the complexity: (a) queries with a few triple patterns only, (b) a RELAX clause to limit relaxations to one or two chosen triple patterns, and (c) a maximum relaxation distance. Our objective is to lift those restrictions and limits to the point where query relaxation can be applied effectively on large queries like node descriptions. The expected benefits are to allow for parameter-free query relaxation, and for similarity search with explanations. We propose a solution that we demonstrate to be significantly more efficient, and that can behave as an anytime algorithm in the hard cases or when responsiveness is important.

5   Anytime Partitioning of Approximate Answers

We propose a novel approach of query relaxation and symbolic similarity that is based on the iterative partitioning of the set of possible approximate answers. The general idea is that, at any stage of the algorithm, the set of possible answers is partitioned in a set of clusters, where each cluster C is defined by a relaxed query Q', and the subset of $ans(Q')$ that are not answers of other clusters. Initially, there is a single cluster defined by the fully relaxed query – the query with an empty body – and the set of all possible answers. Each cluster may be split in two parts by using a query element as discriminating criteria. The algorithm stops when no cluster can be partitioned further. The resulting partition is the set of PRQs along with their (non-empty) proper answer.

Definition 4. *A cluster is a structure $C = (X, P', d, E, M, A)$, where:*

- *X is the head, and P' the body, of the relaxed query $Q'_C = X \leftarrow P'$;*
- *d is the relaxation distance of Q'_C;*
- *E is the set of elements that can be used to split the cluster;*
- *M is the match-set of P' over graph G;*
- *A is a subset of $ans(Q'_C, G) = \pi_X M$.*

A cluster represents a collection of relaxed queries, namely the subset of $RQ(X \leftarrow P' \cup E)$ whose body contains P'. Relaxed query $Q'_C = X \leftarrow P'$ is the most general in the collection, and d is its relaxation distance.

Algorithm 1 details the partitioning algorithm, and Fig. 1 shows its first steps on an example query about *Science-Fiction films directed by Spielberg*. Given a graph and an original query, it normalizes the query body, and initializes the partitioning with a single cluster C_{init} (C0 in Fig. 1) that represents the set of all relaxed queries, and covers all possible answers ({A1, A2, A3, A4} in Fig. 1). Every iteration picks a cluster C and an available query element $e \in E$ in order to split C into C_e, and $C_{\bar{e}}$. The picked element must be connected to the current relaxed query $X \leftarrow P'$ in order to avoid building disconnected queries (e.g. e3

Algorithm 1. *Partition*(G, Q)

Require: A graph G, and an original query $Q = X \leftarrow P$
Ensure: A partition $\mathcal{C}$ of approximate answers of Q on G, clustered by PRQ
1: $\mathcal{C} \leftarrow \{C_{init} := (X, \emptyset, 0, Norm(P), A_{init}, A_{init})\}$ where $A_{init} = ans(X \leftarrow \emptyset, G)$
2: **while** there are a cluster $C = (X, P', d, E, M, A) \in \mathcal{C}$
    and an element $e \in E$ connected with $X \leftarrow P'$ **do**
3:    $M_e \leftarrow ext(M, e, G) := \begin{cases} M \bowtie ans(var(e) \leftarrow \{e\}, G) & \text{if } e \text{ is a triple pattern} \\ \sigma_e M & \text{if } e \text{ is a filter} \end{cases}$
4:    $A_e = A \cap \pi_X M_e$
5:    $C_e = (X, P' \cup \{e\}, d, E \setminus \{e\}, M_e, A_e)$
6:    $C_{\overline{e}} = (X, P', d+1, E \setminus \{e\} \cup relax(e), M, A \setminus A_e)$
7:    $\mathcal{C} \leftarrow \mathcal{C} \setminus \{C\} \cup \{C_e \mid A_e \neq \emptyset\} \cup \{C_{\overline{e}} \mid (A \setminus A_e) \neq \emptyset\}$
8: **end while**

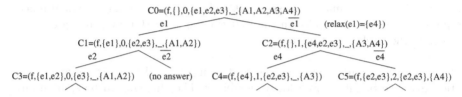

Fig. 1. First steps of the partitioning of query $Q = f \leftarrow \{e1, e2, e3\}$ where $e1 = (f,\texttt{rdf:type,:SciFiFilm})$, $e2 = (f,\texttt{:director},d), e3 = (d = \texttt{:Spielberg})$, and $relax(e1) = \{e4\}$ where $e4 = (f,\texttt{rdf:type,:Film})$.

is not eligible at C0). C_e selects the subset of answers $A_e \subseteq A$ where e holds. Element e is moved from available elements to the body, thus restricting the collection of relaxed queries to those containing e. Each matching $\mu \in M$ is *extended* to the new element if possible, and removed otherwise: $ext(M, e, G)$ is defined as a join if e is a triple pattern, and as a selection if e is a filter. The set of answers is restricted to those for which there is an extended matching. $C_{\overline{e}}$ is called the complement of C_e because both the collection of relaxed queries and the set of answers are the complement of the respective parts of C_e. The relaxed query remains the same, and so does the match-set. The relaxation distance is increased by 1, and element e is replaced by its immediate relaxations $relax(e)$, if any (e1 is replaced by e4 at C2 in Fig. 1), so that they are considered in further partitioning. Clusters C_e and $C_{\overline{e}}$ replace their parent cluster C in the partition $\mathcal{C}$, unless their answer set is empty (e.g. the right child of C1 in Fig. 1). The number of clusters can only grow, and therefore converges.

Impact of Ontology. Ontological definitions such as `rdfs:subClassOf` axioms allow for more fine-grained relaxations, e.g. replacing query element $e1 = (f,\texttt{rdf:type,:SciFiFilm})$ by $e4 = (f,\texttt{rdf:type,:Film})$, instead of simply removing e1. However, the main relaxation work is done by the replacement of URIs and literals by variables, through the removal of filters. For instance, the removal of $e3 = (f = \texttt{:Spielberg})$ allows to relax the query to *films by any director*. By including the description of Spielberg in the query, and by relaxing that description, the query can be relaxed to *films by similar directors*, e.g. *directors born in the same place and/or having directed similar films*. Note that the efficiency of our algorithms is essential to the effective relaxation of such descriptions. In comparison to description relaxation, ontology-based relaxation has a welcome but limited impact.

Complexity. The enumeration-based algorithm evaluates $O(2^n)$ relaxed queries, given an original query containing n elements, considering element removal only. This number can be lowered by setting a maximal relaxation distance d_{max}, but it grows very quickly with increasing d_{max}. In contrast, assuming p is the number of PRQs, the partitioning algorithm evaluates $O(p)$ queries (binary tree with p leaves). p is bounded by $min(N, 2^n)$, with N the number of nodes in the graph. As our experiments show (Sect. 7), p is much smaller than N in practice because many nodes match the same relaxed queries. Note that maximal relaxation distance can be applied in the partitioning algorithm by pruning clusters based on their relaxation distance.

Discussion. The partitioning algorithm does not find PRQs in increasing relaxation distance but it offers a lot of flexibility. The clusters can be split in any ordering, allowing for depth-first or breadth-first strategies or the use of heuristics [14]. The choice of the splitting element e is also free, and is independent from one cluster to another. Last but not least, the algorithm is *anytime* because a partition is defined at all time. If the algorithm is stopped before completion, the partition is simply coarser. Section 7.3 shows that the partitioning algorithm has less latency than enumeration-based algorithms for similarity search.

6   Optimization with Lazy Joins

The explicit computation of the match-set M of a relaxed query can be intractable, even in simple cases. For example, starting from the description of a film, the relaxed query $f \leftarrow (f, \texttt{rdf:type}, \texttt{:Film}), (f, \texttt{:actor}, p_1), \ldots, (f, \texttt{:actor}, p_n)$ will have in $O(Nn^n)$ matchings, assuming there are N films, and each film is related to n actors. For 1000 films related to 10 actors each, it amounts to 10^{13} matchings! It is possible to do better because the expected end result is the set of answers $A = \pi_X M$, whose size is bounded by the number of graph nodes in similarity search. We propose to represent M by a structure – called *match-tree* – containing several small local joins instead of one large global join.

Definition 5. *A* match-tree *is a rooted n-ary tree T where each node n is labeled by a tuple $l(n) = (e, D, M, \Delta)$ where:*

- *e is a query element, and $var(e)$ is its set of variables;*
- *$D \subseteq var(e)$ is the set of variables introduced by e;*
- *M is a match-set s.t. $dom(M) \supseteq var(e)$;*
- *$\Delta \subseteq dom(M)$ is the sub-domain that is useful to the node ancestors.*

Algorithm 2. $LazyJoin(T, n, n^*)$

Require: a match-tree T, a current node n in T labeled with (e, D, M, Δ),
and a new node n^* labeled with $(e^*, D^*, M^*, \Delta^*)$
Ensure: two sets of variables Δ^+, Δ^-
1: $\Delta^+ \leftarrow \emptyset;\quad \Delta^- \leftarrow \emptyset$
2: **for all** $n_c \in children(n)$, labeled with $(e_c, D_c, M_c, \Delta_c)$ **do**
3:     $\Delta_c^+, \Delta_c^- \leftarrow LazyJoin(T, n_c, n^*)$ // recursive call on each child node
4:     $\Delta^+ \leftarrow \Delta^+ \cup \Delta_c^+;\quad \Delta^- \leftarrow \Delta^- \cup \Delta_c^-$
5:     $M \leftarrow M \bowtie \pi_{\Delta_c} M_c$, if Δ_c or M_c was modified   // update of local join
6: **end for**
7: **if** $D \cap \Delta^* \neq \emptyset$ **then**   // if this node defines a variable of the new element
8:     **if** n^* not yet inserted in T **then**   // insert new node, unless already inserted
9:         $\Delta^- \leftarrow \Delta^- \cup (\Delta^* \setminus D);\quad M \leftarrow M \bowtie \pi_{\Delta^*} M^*;\quad parent(n^*) \leftarrow n$
10:     **else**
11:         $\Delta^+ \leftarrow \Delta^+ \cup (\Delta^* \cap D)$
12:     **end if**
13: **end if**
14: $\Delta^+, \Delta^- \leftarrow \Delta^+ \setminus \Delta^-, \ \Delta^- \setminus \Delta^+$
15: $\Delta \leftarrow \Delta \cup \Delta^+ \cup \Delta^-$ // update Δ
16: **return** Δ^+, Δ^-

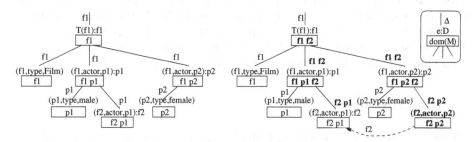

Fig. 2. Match-tree before and after lazy join with element $e^*=(f_2,\text{:actor},p_2)$.

We replace the match-set M of a cluster $C = (X, P', d, E, M, A)$ by an equivalent match-tree T. The match-tree has one node for each element $e \in P'$. M is equal to the join of the local match-set M_n of all nodes n in T. The *initial match-tree* is used for the initial cluster C_{init}, and is defined by match-tree T_{init} that has a single node labeled with $(\top(X), X, ans(X \leftarrow \emptyset, G), X)$, where $\top(X)$ is a void query element. During the split of C with a query element e^*, the match-set extension $ext(M, e^*, G)$ is replaced by $LazyJoin(T, root(T), n^*)$ (see Algorithm 2), where T plays the role of M, and n^* is a new node labeled with $(e^*, var(e^*) \setminus var(P'), ans(var(e^*) \leftarrow \{e^*\}, G), var(e^*) \cap var(P'))$. This "lazy" join consists in inserting n^* as a leaf node into T, and in updating local joins M_n only as much as necessary to compute A correctly. Figure 2 illustrates lazy join on a richer version of the above example on films. It starts with the match-tree of query $f_1 \leftarrow (f_1,\text{rdf:type},\text{:Film}), (f_1,\text{:actor},p_1), (p_1,\text{:sex},\text{:male}), (f_2,\text{:actor},p_1), (f_1,\text{:actor},p_2), (p_2,\text{:sex},\text{:female})$, and inserts element $e^* = (f_2,\text{:actor},p_2)$ that forms a cycle through f_1 and p_1. Changes (shown in bold) are propagated from the two nodes that define p_2 and f_2 (see D), and the new leaf is inserted under one of the two nodes as a child (here, under the node defining p_2). The insertions of other elements, which led to the first tree in Fig. 2, change only one path in the match-tree because they do not introduce a cycle. In Algorithm 2, the computation of Δ^+, Δ^- is used to correctly handle cycles. They are sets of variables of the new query element e^* that are not in the match-set of its parent (f_2 in the example), and hence need to be joined with distant nodes in the match-tree. Δ^- propagates up the tree branch of the parent (node $(f1, actor, p2)$ in Fig. 2), and Δ^+ propagates up the tree branch of distant nodes (node $(f2, actor, p1)$). When they meet at their common ancestor (node $\top(f1)$), the distant join can be done, and their propagation stops.

Complexity. The dominant factor is the project-and-join operation in lines 5, 9 of Algorithm 2. In the worst case, there is such an operation for each node of the match-tree, i.e. one for each element of the relaxed query (m). The cost of the project-and-join depends heavily on the topology of the relaxed query and of the RDF graph. Assuming a tree-shape graph pattern (no cycle) and R triples per predicate, the match-set at each node is a table with at most 2 columns and at most R rows. The space complexity of a match-tree is therefore in $O(mR)$, and the time complexity of each lazy join is in $O(mR \log R)$. In the simpler example on films, $m = n + 1$, $R = Nn$ for property :actor, and $R = N$ for class :Film. The total size is therefore in $O(Nn^2)$ local matchings instead of $O(Nn^n)$. For 1000 films related to 10 actors each, it amounts to 10^5 instead of 10^{13}!

7   Experiments

We have implemented Algorithms 1 and 2, and integrated them to SEWELIS[1] as an improvement of previous work on the guided edition of RDF graphs [12]. We here report extensive experiments to evaluate their efficiency, in the absolute and relative to other approaches, as well as their effectiveness.

7.1   Methodology

We ran all experiments on a Fedora 25 PC with i7-6600U CPU and 16 GB RAM.

Algorithms. We compare four algorithms: two baseline algorithms, and two variants of our algorithm. RELAXENUM is the classical approach that enumerates relaxed queries, and computes their answers. NODEENUM does the opposite by enumerating nodes, and computing the associated PRQ as the least common subsumer between the query and the node description [3]. PARTITION and PARTITIONLJ are our two variants, and differ in that only the latter uses lazy joins.

---

[1] Source code at https://bitbucket.org/sebferre/sewelis, branch **dev**, files **cnn***.

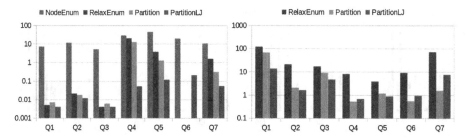

Fig. 3. Runtime (seconds, log scale) per algorithm and per query for MONDIAL (left) and LUBM10 (right).

Parameters. We consider three execution modes. In the NOLIMIT mode, all PRQs are computed. It is the best way to compare algorithms with different parameters. The MAXRELAX mode sets a limit to relaxation distance (not applicable to NODEENUM). The TIMEOUT mode sets a limit to computation time.

Datasets. We use three different datasets, MONDIAL, LUBM10, and LUBM100. MONDIAL is a simplification of the MONDIAL dataset [16] where numbers and reified nodes have been removed because they are not yet well handled by query relaxation. It contains a rich graph of real geographical entities (e.g., *countries containing mountains and rivers that flow into lakes*), and no ontological definitions. It contains 10k nodes and 12k triples. LUBM10 and LUBM100 are synthetic datasets about universities, and are based on an ontology introducing class and property hierarchies [11]. LUBM10 contains 315k nodes and 1.3M triples, and LUBM100 is 10 times bigger (3M nodes, 13M triples). Both datasets are interesting in our work because they are rich in multi-valued properties, and hence are a challenge for query relaxation.

Queries. For each dataset, we have two sets of queries. The first set is made of queries typically used in query relaxation, having less than 10 triple patterns and having different shapes. The second set is made of object descriptions, having up to hundreds of elements. More details are given below.

7.2 Efficiency of Query Relaxation

We here compare all algorithms with (small) queries[2]. On MONDIAL we defined 7 queries having different sizes and shapes. They have between 5 and 21 elements after normalization. On LUBM10/100 we reused the 7 queries of Huang *et al.* [14]. They have between 3 and 7 elements.

NoLimit Mode. Figure 3 compares the runtime (log scale) of all algorithms on all queries of MONDIAL and LUBM10 in NOLIMIT mode. A few runtimes are missing on Q6 of MONDIAL because they are much higher than other runtimes. RELAXENUM is sensitive to the query complexity, in particular to multi-valued

---

[2] Visit http://www.irisa.fr/LIS/ferre/pub/eswc2018/queries.txt.

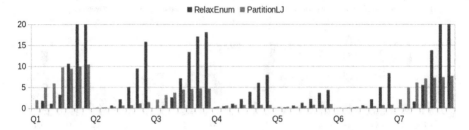

Fig. 4. Runtime (seconds) per algorithm and per LUBM10 query for increasing maximum relaxation distance (1 to 7). Full height bars represent runtimes over 20 s.

properties. NODEENUM looks unsensitive to the query complexity but does not scale well with the number of nodes. PARTITION and PARTITIONLJ are always more efficient – or equally efficient – and the use of lazy joins generally makes it even more efficient. On LUBM10, PARTITIONLJ is typically one order of magnitude more efficient than RELAXENUM. It can also be observed that PARTITIONLJ scales well with data size because from MONDIAL to LUBM10, a 100-fold increase in number of triples, the median runtime also follows a 100-fold increase, from 0.01–0.1 s to 1–10 s. This linear scaling is verified on LUBM100 (not shown) where the runtimes are all 10 times higher. We want to emphasize that it is encouraging that the full relaxation of a query over a 1.3M-triples dataset can be done in 4 s on average.

MaxRelax Mode. In practice, one is generally interested in the most similar approximate answers, and therefore in the relaxed queries with the smaller relaxation distances. It is therefore interesting to compare algorithms when the relaxation distance is bounded. Figure 4 compares RELAXENUM and PARTITIONLJ on LUBM10 queries for increasing values of maximal relaxation distance, here from 1 to 7 relaxations. As expected, the runtime of RELAXENUM grows in a combinatorial way, like the number of relaxed queries, with the relaxation distance. On the contrary, the runtime of PARTITIONLJ grows more quickly for 1–4 relaxations, and then almost flattens in most cases. The flattening can be explained by several factors. The main factor is that the relaxed queries that are not proper are pruned. Another factor is that query evaluation is partially shared between different queries. That sharing is also the cause for the higher cost with 1–4 relaxations. In summary, PARTITIONLJ scales very well with the number of relaxations, while RELAXENUM does not. This is a crucial property for similarity search where many relaxation steps are necessary.

Number of Relaxed Queries. The efficiency of PARTITION and PARTITIONLJ is better understood when comparing the number of PRQs to the number of relaxed queries (RQ). Over the 7 LUBM10 queries, there are in total 59 PRQs out of 2899 RQs, hence a 50-fold decrease.

7.3 Efficiency of Similarity Search

We now consider the large queries that are formed by node descriptions at depth 1 (including ingoing triples), and that include many multi-valued properties. On MONDIAL we used 10 nodes, one for each class: e.g., country *Peru*, language *Spanish*. The obtained queries have 5 to 248 elements (average = 61). On LUBM10 we used 12 nodes, one for each class: e.g., university, publication. The obtained queries have 5 to 1505 elements (average = 201). Main facts and measures are summarized in Table 1.

NoLimit Mode. PARTITIONLJ is the only algorithm that terminates under 600 s in NOLIMIT mode, and it does terminate for all queries of both datasets[3]. The full runtime has a high variance and a low median, between 0.03 s and 269 s (average = 30 s, median = 0.13 s) for MONDIAL, and between 0.13 s and 535 s (average = 179 s, median = 110 s) for LUBM10. The average number of PRQs is 32 (max = 117) for MONDIAL and 28 (max = 52) for LUBM10. It is noteworthy that both the runtime and the number of PRQs are relatively close for different datasets with very different sizes. It is also noteworthy that the number of PRQs is very small w.r.t. the size of queries and the number of nodes. It is therefore possible to manually inspect all PRQs, i.e. semantic similarities with all other nodes.

MaxRelax Mode. On LUBM10, RELAXENUM does not scale beyond 3 relaxations on node descriptions, except for the 3 smallest descriptions. Moreover, using PARTITIONLJ with a maximum of 10 relaxations, we have observed that only 75 PRQs are produced out of 340 over the 12 queries (0 PRQs for 3 queries), and computation takes 40 s on average. To limit the average runtime to 2 s, the maximum relaxation distance has to be 1, and then only 3 PRQs are produced out of 340. RELAXENUM and the MAXRELAX mode are therefore not effective for similarity search because of their high latency in generating the first PRQs.

TimeOut Mode. Although PARTITIONLJ can compute all PRQs in a reasonable time, it may still be too long in practice. Our anytime algorithm allows to control runtime by timeout. An important question is the latency of the generation of PRQs. Figure 5 shows that most PRQs are generated in a small fraction of the total runtime. For example, 50% PRQs are generated in 30 s, and 20% in 2 s. This superlinear production of PRQs is confirmed when looking at what happens when moving from LUBM10 to LUBM100. At timeout = 64 s, the number of computed PRQs is only divided by 2.6 although the data is 10 times bigger.

7.4 Effectiveness of Similarity Search

We assess the effectiveness of PRQs for similarity search with an empirical study that evaluates their use for the inference of property values. The null hypothesis

---

[3] The ranked list of PRQs and their proper answers is available for the 10 MONDIAL nodes at http://www.irisa.fr/LIS/ferre/pub/eswc2018/mondial_PRQs.txt.

Table 1. Measures about the relaxation of node descriptions. The measure are given in the form *min - max (average)*: number of query elements, number of PRQs, number of PRQs within maximum 3 relaxation steps, and runtime of PARTITIONLJ.

Dataset	MONDIAL	LUBM10
nb. elts	5–248 (61)	5–1505 (201)
nb. PRQs	2–117 (32)	7–52 (28)
nb. PRQs (1–3 steps)	0–9 (3.2)	0–7 (1.3)
Runtime	0.03–269 (30)	0.13–535 (179)

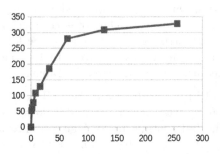

Fig. 5. Number of computed PRQs over lubm10 queries (out of 340 PRQs) as a function of timeout(s).

is that using the most similar nodes makes no difference compared to using random nodes. We do not claim here that this value inference method is better than other methods in machine learning, only that PRQs effectively capture semantic similarities. We do not compare our results to other query relaxation algorithms because we have shown in the previous section that they are not efficient enough for similarity search, and because, if given enough time, they would compute the same PRQs. Our experiment consisted in performing value inference for each property p (e.g., :continent) of each country c (e.g., *Peru*) of the MONDIAL dataset. Note that a property may have several values (e.g., :language). For each pair (c, p) we computed the PRQs starting with the description of c minus triples (c, p, v) for any value v. Then, we selected the 3 most similar nodes S (e.g., *Bolivia*, *Colombia*, and *Argentina* for *Peru*) as the proper answers of the most similar PRQs according to intensional similarity (size of the relaxed query). We used S to infer a set of values V for property p using a majority vote. V is compared to the actual set of values to determine precision and recall measures. Table 2 shows the obtained measures for each property and for all properties together, averaged over the countries. The baseline F1-score is obtained by using 3 random countries instead of the most similar nodes. It shows a significant improvement over the baseline, and good results for properties *continent* and *religion*. The result is poor for *government* because values are noisy strings, and for *dependentOf* because few countries have this property. Overall, 75% of infered values are correct, and 48% of correct values are infered. We obtained very close results when using extensional distance (number of answers) for ranking PRQs.

Table 2. Average precision/recall/F1-score over countries of value inference for each property and for all properties together. The last line gives the baseline F1-score.

	Continent	Religion	was Dependent Of	Language	Neighbor	Ethnic Group	Government	Dependent Of	All
Precision	0.97	0.80	0.77	0.75	0.43	0.65	0.82	0.50	0.75
Recall	0.93	0.76	0.47	0.34	0.33	0.25	0.19	0.00	0.48
F1-score	0.93	0.74	0.47	0.36	0.30	0.28	0.19	0.00	0.56
Baseline F1-score	0.12	0.07	0.00	0.00	0.00	0.00	0.00	0.00	0.05

8   Conclusion and Perspectives

We have proposed two algorithms that together significantly improve the efficiency of query relaxation and symbolic semantic similarity. In fact, they are efficient enough to tackle the challenging problem of applying many relaxation steps to large queries with hundreds of elements. For a 1M-triples dataset like LUBM10 it is possible to explore the entire relaxation space of queries having up to 1500 elements in a matter of minutes. The computation can be stopped at any time while still having a fair approximation of the final result.

Many perspectives can be drawn from this work. The partitioning algorithm offers opportunities for strategies and heuristics for choosing the cluster to split and the splitting element. New kinds of element relaxation can be explored, e.g. for the gradual relaxation of URIs and literals. There are potential applications in classification, case-based reasoning, concept discovery, or recommendation.

References

1. Chein, M., Mugnier, M.L.: Graph-Based Knowledge Representation: Computational Foundations of Conceptual Graphs. Advanced Information and Knowledge Processing. Springer, Heidelberg (2008). https://doi.org/10.1007/978-1-84800-286-9
2. Codd, E.F.: A relational model of data for large shared data banks. Commun. ACM **13**(6), 377–387 (1970)
3. Colucci, S., Donini, F.M., Di Sciascio, E.: Common subsumers in RDF. In: Baldoni, M., Baroglio, C., Boella, G., Micalizio, R. (eds.) AI*IA 2013. LNCS (LNAI), vol. 8249, pp. 348–359. Springer, Cham (2013). https://doi.org/10.1007/978-3-319-03524-6_30
4. Cunningham, P.: A taxonomy of similarity mechanisms for case-based reasoning. IEEE Trans. Knowl. Data Eng. **21**(11), 1532–1543 (2009)
5. Dolog, P., Stuckenschmidt, H., Wache, H., Diederich, J.: Relaxing RDF queries based on user and domain preferences. J. Intell. Inf. Syst. **33**(3), 239 (2009)
6. Elbassuoni, S., Ramanath, M., Weikum, G.: Query relaxation for entity-relationship search. In: Antoniou, G., Grobelnik, M., Simperl, E., Parsia, B., Plexousakis, D., De Leenheer, P., Pan, J. (eds.) ESWC 2011. LNCS, vol. 6644, pp. 62–76. Springer, Heidelberg (2011). https://doi.org/10.1007/978-3-642-21064-8_5

7. Ferilli, S., Basile, T.M.A., Biba, M., Di Mauro, N., Esposito, F.: A general similarity framework for horn clause logic. Fundamenta Informaticae **90**(1–2), 43–66 (2009)
8. Ferré, S., Cellier, P.: Graph-FCA in practice. In: Haemmerlé, O., Stapleton, G., Faron Zucker, C. (eds.) ICCS 2016. LNCS (LNAI), vol. 9717, pp. 107–121. Springer, Cham (2016). https://doi.org/10.1007/978-3-319-40985-6_9
9. Frosini, R., Calì, A., Poulovassilis, A., Wood, P.T.: Flexible query processing for SPARQL. Semant. Web **8**(4), 533–563 (2017)
10. Gaasterland, T.: Cooperative answering through controlled query relaxation. IEEE Expert **12**(5), 48–59 (1997)
11. Guo, Y., Pan, Z., Heflin, J.: LUBM: a benchmark for OWL knowledge base systems. J. Web Semant.: Sci. Serv. Agents **3**, 158–182 (2005)
12. Hermann, A., Ferré, S., Ducassé, M.: An interactive guidance process supporting consistent updates of RDFS graphs. In: ten Teije, A., Völker, J., Handschuh, S., Stuckenschmidt, H., d'Acquin, M., Nikolov, A., Aussenac-Gilles, N., Hernandez, N. (eds.) EKAW 2012. LNCS (LNAI), vol. 7603, pp. 185–199. Springer, Heidelberg (2012). https://doi.org/10.1007/978-3-642-33876-2_18
13. Horváth, T., Wrobel, S., Bohnebeck, U.: Relational instance-based learning with lists and terms. Mach. Learn. **43**(1–2), 53–80 (2001)
14. Huang, H., Liu, C., Zhou, X.: Approximating query answering on RDF databases. World Wide Web **15**(1), 89–114 (2012)
15. Hurtado, C.A., Poulovassilis, A., Wood, P.T.: Query relaxation in RDF. In: Spaccapietra, S. (ed.) Journal on Data Semantics X. LNCS, vol. 4900, pp. 31–61. Springer, Heidelberg (2008). https://doi.org/10.1007/978-3-540-77688-8_2
16. May, W.: Information extraction and integration with FLORID: the MONDIAL case study. Technical report 131, Universität Freiburg, Institut für Informatik (1999). http://dbis.informatik.uni-goettingen.de/Mondial
17. Rodríguez, M.A., Egenhofer, M.J.: Determining semantic similarity among entity classes from different ontologies. IEEE Trans. Knowl. Data Eng. **15**(2), 442–456 (2003)

Evaluation of Schema.org for Aggregation of Cultural Heritage Metadata

Nuno Freire[1]([⊠]) [iD], Valentine Charles[2] [iD], and Antoine Isaac[2,3] [iD]

[1] INESC-ID, Lisbon, Portugal
nuno.freire@tecnico.ulisboa.pt
[2] Europeana Foundation, The Hague, The Netherlands
valentine.charles@europeana.eu
[3] Vrije Universiteit Amsterdam, Amsterdam, The Netherlands
aisaac@few.vu.nl

Abstract. In the World Wide Web, a very large number of resources is made available through digital libraries. The existence of many individual digital libraries, maintained by different organizations, brings challenges to the discoverability, sharing and reuse of the resources. A widely-used approach is metadata aggregation, where centralized efforts like Europeana facilitate the discoverability and use of the resources by collecting their associated metadata. The cultural heritage domain embraced the aggregation approach while, at the same time, the technological landscape kept evolving. Nowadays, cultural heritage institutions are increasingly applying technologies designed for the wider interoperability on the Web. In this context, we have identified the Schema.org vocabulary as a potential technology for innovating metadata aggregation. We conducted two case studies that analysed Schema.org metadata from collections from cultural heritage institutions. We used the requirements of the Europeana Network as evaluation criteria. These include the recommendations of the Europeana Data Model, which is a collaborative effort from all the domains represented in Europeana: libraries, museums, archives, and galleries. We concluded that Schema.org poses no obstacle that cannot be overcome to allow data providers to deliver metadata in full compliance with Europeana requirements and with the desired semantic quality. However, Schema.org's cross-domain applicability raises the need for accompanying its adoption by recommendations and/or specifications regarding how data providers should create their Schema.org metadata, so that they can meet the specific requirements of Europeana or other cultural aggregation networks.

Keywords: Metadata · Cultural heritage · Metadata aggregation
Schema.org · Europeana Data Model · Digital libraries

1 Introduction

In the World Wide Web, a very large number of resources is made available through digital libraries. The existence of many individual digital libraries, maintained by different organizations, brings challenges to the discoverability and usage of the resources by potential audiences.

© Springer International Publishing AG, part of Springer Nature 2018
A. Gangemi et al. (Eds.): ESWC 2018, LNCS 10843, pp. 225–239, 2018.
https://doi.org/10.1007/978-3-319-93417-4_15

An often-used approach is metadata aggregation, where a central organization takes the role of facilitating the discovery and use of the resources by collecting their associated metadata. Based on these aggregated datasets of metadata, the central organization (often called aggregator) is in a position to further promote the usage of the resources by means that cannot be efficiently undertaken by each digital library in isolation. This scenario is widely applied in the domain of cultural heritage (CH), where the number of organizations with their own digital libraries is very large. In Europe, Europeana has the role of facilitating the usage of digitized CH resources from and about Europe [1]. It seeks to enable users to search and access knowledge in all the languages of Europe via the Europeana Collections portal[1] and applications to use cultural data through open APIs. Although many European CH institutions do not yet have a presence in Europeana, it already holds metadata from over 3,700 providers, mostly libraries, museums and archives [2].

In several contexts, the technological approach to metadata aggregation has been mostly based on the OAI-PMH protocol, a technology initially designed in 1999 [3]. OAI-PMH was meant to address shortcomings in scholarly communication by providing a technical interoperability solution for discovery of e-prints, via metadata aggregation. OAI-PMH allows metadata to be aggregated using any metadata schema, although its specification includes the use of the Dublin Core Element Set [4] as the minimal metadata schema for aggregation, to enable the widest metadata interoperability across domains.

The Cultural Heritage domain embraced the solution offered by OAI-PMH, however, the technological landscape around our domain changed. Nowadays, CH organizations are increasingly applying technologies designed for the wider interoperability on the Web. Particularly relevant for our work are those related to the social web, the web of data, and internet search engine optimization. In this context, we have identified the Schema.org vocabulary and its associated web-based dissemination channels [5] as a potential technology for metadata aggregation in the CH domain. Our interest in Schema.org for metadata aggregation originates from our earlier work in reviewing the state of the art and emerging Web technologies for their applicability in the context of CH [6], where the relevance of Schema.org was identified from its relation to other technologies used by Internet search engines.

Europeana has recently evaluated Schema.org as a means to publish CH data [7]. This paper presents our work on another application of Schema.org: we seek to test whether it can also bring usable data sources for CH aggregators like Europeana. We therefore aim to investigate whether more incentive can be provided for the (still infrequent) use of Schema.org in the CH sector, beyond its original goal of publishing data for search engines.

This paper starts by describing the motivation for evaluating Schema.org for applicability in metadata aggregation in the CH domain. It follows with a section about Schema.org, which provides a description of how it covers the representation of metadata about CH resources, the related technologies required for its processing, and the main requirements for its usage in metadata aggregation. We then present our case

---

[1] https://europeana.eu.

studies, the experimental setup and our observations and analysis on existing Schema. org metadata. The paper ends with our key conclusions regarding the impact of supporting Schema.org metadata in CH.

2 Motivation and Context

Schema.org is an activity for encouraging the publication and consumption of structured data in the Internet. Its main application is in web pages - for example, stating that a web page describes a culinary recipe, its ingredients and preparation method; or that it describes a movie, its actors, user reviews, etc. Web pages built according to the Schema.org principles (Schema.org data can be referenced or embedded in several different encodings, including RDFa[2], Microdata[3] and JSON-LD[4]) can be processed by search engines and other applications that use this structured data, in addition to text and links from the HTML body. The Schema.org website[5] reports usage in more than 10 million sites and Google, Microsoft, Pinterest, Yandex, among others, already provide services and applications that are based on the available Schema.org structured data.

Schema.org has applicability across a vast range of domains. Especially, it could allow CH institutions to reduce the overall effort on data conversion that they conduct for discovery purposes. From these institutions' point of view, Schema.org could indeed be a unified solution for allowing the discovery of their resources through both internet search engines and CH specific metadata aggregation efforts like Europeana.

In the CH metadata aggregation approaches, a common practice has been to aggregate metadata using an agreed data model that allows to deal with the data heterogeneity between organizations and countries in a sustainable way. These data models typically aim to address two main requirements:

- Retaining the semantics of the original data from the source providers.
- Supporting the information needs of the services provided by the aggregator.

Under the guidance of these requirements, we have conducted two case studies to assess the suitability of the Schema.org vocabulary to support the metadata aggregation approach in CH. The case studies were also guided by the existing aggregation network of Europeana, from where we identify more detailed requirements for data modeling in real metadata aggregation scenarios.

In the Europeana aggregation process, the Europeana Data Model (EDM) [8] is the data model that allows Europeana to be 'a big aggregation of digital representations of culture artefacts together with rich contextualization data and embedded in a linked Open Data architecture' [9]. EDM supports several of the core processes of Europeana's

---

[2] https://www.w3.org/TR/2015/NOTE-rdfa-primer-20150317/.

[3] https://www.w3.org/TR/microdata/.

[4] https://www.w3.org/TR/json-ld/.

[5] http://schema.org/docs/about.html.

operations and contributes to the access layer of the Europeana platform, supporting the sharing of data with third parties [10].

EDM has been a collaborative, community-based effort from the very start, involving representatives from all the domains represented in Europeana: libraries, museums, archives, and galleries. It was initially defined in 2010 and has been under continuous improvement since, under the coordination and maintenance of Europeana.

EDM also plays a key role in other parts of the Europeana Network[6] and elsewhere. Other organizations using approaches for aggregation similar to that of Europeana also apply EDM. In our work, we have explored the Digital Public Library of America[7] (DPLA), which operates within the USA and uses a model heavily based on EDM for its aggregation process [12].

An important aspect of EDM is that it does not impose any constraint in the choice of Web technologies for metadata exchange. This comes from EDM following the principles of the Web of Data [11], and that it can be serialized in various XML and RDF syntaxes (i.e., N-Triples[8], Turtle[9], JSON-LD, etc.). This flexibility gives the Europeana Network much choice for technological innovation of the aggregation network. The genericity of EDM's constructs (and of the systems built on top of them) also makes it easier to use other data models to aggregate metadata that, although not based on EDM, would match Europeana's information requirements.

Given our purpose of evaluating the suitability of Schema.org metadata for fulfilling the metadata aggregation in the specific domain of CH, we conducted case studies where we collected and analyzed Schema.org metadata from real collections and systems from CH institutions. We used cases of institutions that publish Schema.org metadata to make their resources better discoverable on the Web, and not for CH aggregation. Therefore, the extent to which this data could fulfill the requirements of CH aggregation was unknown at the start of our work. As a platform for evaluation, we performed our analysis of Schema.org CH metadata according to the specific requirements of Europeana [13].

The main premise behind our study is the following: if Schema.org metadata can express the information requirements of the Europeana Data Model and the main factors for data quality defined by Europeana, then Schema.org may be used to fulfil the requirements of many CH services that are based on a metadata aggregation approach. Conversely, if using Schema.org data as source of data for Europeana is impossible or would require specific efforts, then the same obstacles will probably hold in other CH contexts.

---

[6] The Europeana Network is a community of 1,700 experts with the shared mission to expand and improve access to Europe's digital cultural heritage, in the organization they work for and/or by contributing to shape Europeana's services.

[7] http://dp.la/.

[8] https://www.w3.org/TR/n-triples/.

[9] https://www.w3.org/TR/turtle/.

3   The Basic Principles for Applying Schema.org to the Cultural Heritage Domain

Schema.org covers the data modeling needs of a wide range of domains. Its level of development varies across domains, however. This section provides a description of how it covers the representation of metadata about CH resources, the related technologies required for its processing, and the main requirements for its usage in metadata aggregation.

3.1   (Digital) Cultural Heritage Objects Represented in Schema.org

Schema.org comes with a vocabulary that allows the description of entities of different types with subclasses, as well as attributes and relationships between entities, following the Semantic Web principles [14]. For CH digital libraries, Schema.org allows the description of books, maps, visual art, music recordings, and many other kinds of cultural resources.

The most relevant Schema.org classes to Europeana are *schema:CreativeWork*[10] and several of its refining subclasses, which we detail here with their connection to the main modeling constructs of EDM:

- Several types of *schema:CreativeWork*, such as *schema:VisualArtwork, schema: Book, schema:Painting, schema:Sculpture*, and *schema:Product*, can be matched to EDM's Provided Cultural Heritage Object (CHO) *edm:ProvidedCHO*, which represents the object that CH institutions provide metadata about (and a digitized representation of). Each of these subclasses may be used with more specific properties than the ones available for *schema:CreativeWork*, e.g., *schema:artMedium*[11] for *schema:VisualArtwork*.
- The subclass *schema:MediaObject* and its subclasses *schema:ImageObject, schema:VideoObject, schema:AudioObject* can be matched to what EDM defines as *edm:WebResource*, which represents a digital version (representation) of the CHO.
- The *schema:Person, schema:Place* and *schema:Organization* classes match the semantics of EDM contextual classes *edm:Agent, edm:Place* and *foaf:Organization*.

Schema.org can also be extended to cover cases requiring properties or terms currently not available in the model. These extensions are either approved as part of the core Schema.org or are managed externally. Two of the existing extensions are of relevance to the CH domain:

- The Bibliographic Extension[12] provides additional properties and types to describe bibliographic resources. For example, terms such as 'atlas', 'newspaper', 'work and translation', or relationships such as *schema:exampleOfWork* and *schema: workExample*[13].

---

[10] http://schema.org/CreativeWork.

[11] http://schema.org/artMedium.

[12] http://bib.0.3-2f.schemaorgae.appspot.com/.

[13] http://blog.schema.org/2014/09/schemaorg-support-for-bibliographic_2.html.

- The Architypes extension[14] currently works on identifying relevant types and properties to describe archives and their contents. The current proposal[15] defines three new classes: *Archive*, *ArchiveCollection* and *ArchiveItem*.

Schema.org is a collaborative and community-based activity and its main platform of collaboration is the W3C Schema.org Community Group[16]. The Community Group also serves as a hub for discussion with other related communities, at W3C and elsewhere. E.g., other W3C Community Groups exist that are focused on specific domains, such as health, sports, bibliography, etc. Representatives of the Europeana community may be involved this way, should a need to 'improve' Schema.org for CH aggregation be raised.

3.2 Aggregation Mechanisms for Schema.org Metadata

Originally, indexing of web pages is the main use case for the development of Schema. org, therefore, it is mostly found encoded within (or referred from) HTML pages. A process to aggregate Schema.org data can thus start the same way as for crawling ordinary web pages. The remainder of the aggregation can also rely on a process comparable to the one for ordinary web pages, which is based on following the hyperlinks within the HTML. Schema.org has been developed according to the Semantic Web and Linked Data principles: whatever encoding used for Schema.org data (RDFa, Microdata or JSON-LD), Schema.org data always consists of an RDF graph. Therefore, applications only interested in the Schema.org data, and not on the (HTML) textual content, can crawl the web pages in the same way as search engines, but simply discard the textual content, extract hyperlinks from the HTML, links from the Schema.org RDF graph, and continue the crawling by following (a selection of) these links.

Webmasters may aid the web crawling process (both for "regular" HTML pages and Schema.org-enabled ones) by providing Sitemaps[17] of their website. These inform search engines about which of the website URLs are available for crawling and some additional information, such as update frequency and importance within the website, that will enable the website to be crawled more effectively. In the case of digital library websites, Sitemaps help dealing with some typical discovery problems faced by CH institutions:

- They enable web crawlers to reach areas of the website that are not available through the browsable interface. For example, some pages for CH objects may be only reachable through searching via web forms.
- Often, CH digital libraries contain a very large number of objects, which varies in time as collections grow, and there are chances that the web crawlers will overlook some of the new or recently updated content.

---

[14] https://www.w3.org/community/architypes/.

[15] https://www.w3.org/community/architypes/wiki/Initial_model_proposal.

[16] http://www.w3.org/community/schemaorg.

[17] http://www.sitemaps.org/.

The combination of Schema.org and Sitemaps is also used in customized indexing services provided by search engines, such as Google's Custom Search Engine[18].

We attempted to identify cases of usage of Schema.org metadata in CH institutions (libraries, archives, museums) from the Europeana Network, Digital Public Library of America, and other communities. In those cases, we identified the use of the following encodings and mechanisms:

- Schema.org metadata encoded in HTML pages with JSON-LD and/or Microdata:
  - University of Illinois at Urbana-Champaign (UI) in the context of the Linked Data for Special Collections (LD4SC) project[19],
  - North Carolina State University Libraries (NCSU)[20]
  - OCLC's WorldCat[21],
  - data.bnf.fr[22] from the French National Library (BnF)
- Publication of linked data using Schema.org as the main vocabulary and HTTP content negotiation[23]:
  - OCLC's WorldCat,
  - BBC's Research and Education Space[24]
  - Schema.org referenced from IIIF[25] services, within the IIIF presentation layer (i.e. IIIF Manifests using a *seeAlso* property[26]):
  - North Carolina State University Libraries

4 Case Studies

To assess the suitability of Schema.org for carrying the necessary information for supporting the requirements of metadata aggregation in CH, we selected, among the CH cases of Schema.org usage identified above, the most relevant ones to the metadata acquisition scenario of Europeana. I.e., the cases where:

- The Schema.org data directly derives from the source data at a CH institution (i.e. directly from a digital library catalogue).
- The Schema.org data is created by the institution owning the data, not by a third party, such as an aggregator.
- The same dataset is also available in EDM.

---

[18] https://cse.google.com/cse/.

[19] http://publish.illinois.edu/linkedspcollections/.

[20] https://www.lib.ncsu.edu/.

[21] http://www.worldcat.org/.

[22] http://data.bnf.fr/.

[23] https://www.w3.org/Protocols/rfc2616/rfc2616-sec12.html.

[24] https://bbcarchdev.github.io/res/.

[25] The International Image Interoperability Framework (IIIF) is a family of specifications that facilitate publishing and reuse of image resources [15]. It specifies HTTP based web services covering access to images, the presentation and structure of complex digital objects, and searching within their content.

[26] http://iiif.io/api/presentation/2.1/#seealso.

This setting allowed us to do an unbiased comparison between Schema.org metadata and EDM metadata about the same CH objects and derived from the same source. Two datasets fulfill these requirements: these of NCSU and UI.

4.1   Experimental Setup

We have analyzed data from NCSU and UI. Both institutions use digital library management systems based on other metadata standards than EDM or Schema.org, from which the representation in EDM and Schema.org is always derived. The EDM metadata is created for the purposes of DPLA aggregation, and Schema.org is created for Internet discovery.

The activity of these data providers in working with both data models offered us a very suitable scenario to assess Schema.org data. Our idea is to combine the Schema. org available for these cases with a new iteration (actually, an inversion) of a mapping from EDM to Schema.org we have created earlier [7]. This allows us to compare EDM metadata resulting from two different data conversion paths: the EDM data available in DPLA, and EDM data obtained after the application of the new mapping of Schema. org to EDM. This experimental setting is illustrated in Fig. 1.

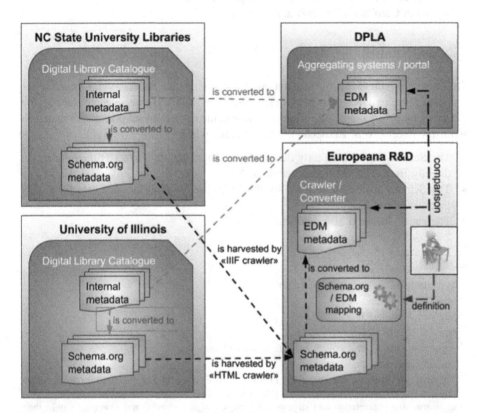

Fig. 1. The experimental process. Black lines indicate the steps performed for the experiment.

For each of the data providers, a subset of their digital library catalogue was selected. Selection of objects was made according to the following criteria:

- being part of a collection, for which Schema.org metadata is available.
- being aggregated by DPLA already (so that EDM metadata is available).

For the selected objects, Schema.org metadata was obtained from both providers with the appropriate crawling mechanism for each case: crawling of a IIIF service, for NCSU Libraries, and web page crawling via a Sitemap, for UI. Most of the crawling software required for the case studies was reused from our past work on data acquisition mechanisms [16]. We only needed to develop one software component to allow the parsing of data encoded within HTML pages[27].

The EDM metadata for the same set of objects was obtained from the DPLA downloadable data dump[28].

We initially collected a sample of 905 Schema.org objects from the UI and 1000 objects from NCSU Libraries, on which we did a preliminary analysis and data profiling to support the definition of the mapping. A listing was made of all Schema.org classes and properties used by both data providers (these listings can be consulted in appendices A and B[29]).

For the following steps of the experiment, we focused our analysis on a maximum of 100 digital objects selected from each provider, resulting in a sample of metadata for 193 objects[30] (each with one Schema.org record and one DPLA EDM record).

The definition of the Schema.org to EDM mapping used, as a starting point, Europeana's earlier work in mapping from the opposite direction, where EDM data was the input [7]. The mapping was further refined based on the documentation of the Schema.org profile defined by UI's LD4SC project[31].

For this study, since our intent was to evaluate Schema.org created by data providers, the mappings to EDM did not include any classes or properties from Europeana's internal EDM profile[32]. We focused instead on the EDM expected from providers within Europeana's regular aggregation flow [13].

A software implementation of the mapping was done[33]. It was then applied to the sample dataset, the resulting EDM metadata was analyzed, and a second revision of the mapping was done, before we performed the final analysis on the resulting EDM

---

[27] For this we have used the open source tool Apache Any23, https://any23.apache.org/.

[28] Digital Public Library of America website, bulk download section: https://dp.la/info/developers/download/. We used the dump from June 2017.

[29] Available at https://github.com/nfreire/Open-Data-Acquisition-Framework/tree/master/opaf-casestudies/eswc2018-paper.

[30] 7 objects ended up missing in the University of Illinois dataset because the Schema.org data (on which the selection of 100 objects was made) and the DPLA one had been produced based on different versions of the dataset.

[31] http://publish.illinois.edu/linkedspcollections/methods-outcomes/.

[32] https://github.com/europeana/corelib/wiki/EDMObjectTemplatesEuropeana.

[33] https://github.com/nfreire/Open-Data-Acquisition-Framework.

metadata (described in the next section). The full listing of the EDM classes and properties generated after the application of the mapping is available in appendix C (See footnote 29).

5 Analysis and Discussion

The metadata obtained after conversion from Schema.org to EDM was examined from two points of view:

- Analysis of the mapping from Schema.org to EDM, in terms of results achieved, potential for application in Europeana and potential improvement.
- Analysis of the obtained data using our experimental aggregation setup.

This section presents and discusses the outcomes of our work on these two aspects.

5.1 Results of the Mapping from Schema.org to EDM

We highlight three key aspects from our experience with mapping Schema.org data to EDM: requirements of the EDM model for aggregation [8, 13], overall data quality and comparative loss of information.

Basic EDM Requirements. Our first assessment consisted in making sure the different entities, defined in the Schema.org model, were matched with their corresponding EDM classes. *schema:CreativeWork* and its subclasses were mapped to *edm: ProvidedCHO* and *schema:MediaObject* and its subclasses mapped to *edm:WebResource*. Only the *ore:Aggregation* class required in EDM – a rather artificial construct associating the Provided CHO to Web Resources and administrative metadata specific to the aggregation process, such as the data provider (see below) – had to be created as part of the conversion of the data.

EDM also requires the presence of some properties to ensure a basic level of data quality, as for example, at least one title, or alternatively a description. In the context of this analysis, all the mandatory properties required by EDM can be mapped from the Schema.org metadata, except for *edm:type* and *edm:rights*, which are defined by Europeana under controlled vocabularies for enabling functionalities of its portal or its licensing policies.

The case of *edm:type* may be overcome by inferencing the correct value from the specific Schema.org class mapped to *edm:ProvidedCHO*. However, this won't be possible for the data simply defined as *schema:CreativeWork*.

Regarding *edm:rights*, in the metadata analyzed for this experiment we could not find data (literal or URI) that could be used for this property. Schema.org does contain properties (such as *schema:license*) that can be suitable vehicles for the values requested by EDM. However, while Schema.org does not restrict the values for schema:license, EDM expects rights statements from Creative Commons and RightsStatements.org[34]. In the future, providers expecting Europeana to harvest their

---

[34] http://pro.europeana.eu/available-rights-statements.

metadata via Schema.org would be expected to use these statements in an agreed Schema.org property. Nevertheless, since interoperable values like these are beneficial to other actors than Europeana, there should probably be more efforts to encourage their use in the wider Schema.org context.

Europeana requires also aggregation-specific EDM metadata, such as the name of the original data provider (*edm:dataProvider*) that is typically a CHI that holds the digital resources, and the direct provider (*edm:provider*) of the data to Europeana that is typically an organization fulfilling the role of data (sub-)aggregator within the Europeana Network. In the context of this experiment, we could find the relevant information to map a *schema:Organization* to *edm:dataProvider* and *edm:provider*. However, for other datasets, the Schema.org elements we mapped from (*schema: provider* and *schema:copyrightHolder*) may be used in a slightly different way.

In a Europeana aggregation scenario based on Schema.org data, for their records to be valid, data providers would be expected to provide the information mandatory for Europeana aggregation process. This was not the case for this experiment, as seen. The missing elements were very closely related to usage of Europeana, yet, and one must note the institutions we selected had prepared their Schema.org metadata with Internet discovery in mind, and not specifically for a CH aggregation scenario such as Europeana's. It could be relatively easy for them to add the required information.

Overall Data Quality: Getting Rich Data in EDM. The work on mapping from EDM to Schema.org that we started from had highlighted some limitations regarding the granularity of the mapping for the main CHO entity. The semantics of *schema: CreativeWork* match well the semantics of *edm:ProvidedCHO*, but it would be better to use its subclasses when possible, such as *schema:Book* or *schema:Newspaper*. Yet the initial mapping could not use these subclasses as the type would need to be deduced from the *dc:type* element in the EDM data, which is often not normalized. Unless Europeana data providers used controlled vocabularies in *dc:type* it is very difficult to define the precise type of a CHO in EDM. The same issue applies for the mapping between *edm:WebResource* and the subclasses of *schema:MediaObject*.

This issue does not happen in a mapping from Schema.org to EDM as the subclasses of *schema:CreativeWork* can directly be mapped onto *dc:type* and their URIs be preserved in the process. A mapping in this direction does not cause any information loss during data conversion.

Granularity Mismatches Between EDM and Schema.org and Resulting Information Loss. Schema.org covers an extensive range of entity types that can be used in the description of all the "things" mentioned in the metadata as entities with their own URIs. It is much more comprehensive than EDM. This results in entity descriptions that are more granular than the ones in EDM, e.g., using *schema:Collection* for a collection level description, *schema:Distance* to specify the type of values available as height and width of the *schema:CreativeWork*. Some of those entities cannot be directly mapped in EDM since a corresponding EDM entity (or a relevant superclass) does not exist.

In addition, one of the data providers in our experiment extended its Schema.org profile with properties from its own namespace (http://ns.library.illinois.edu/scp/). Considering this information would have required an additional mapping; which we decided not to do. Our experiment has been carried out in the context of investigations of alternative data acquisitions for Europeana. While mapping data to EDM from standard Schema.org data is an endeavor Europeana can afford, taking into account any extensions of it would not be a sustainable approach.

To address the absence of corresponding EDM classes for a given Schema.org or custom one, we could decide to map the data at a more generic level. For instance, UI uses a custom class *scp:StageWork*, which is a subclass of *schema:CreativeWork*. It does not have an exact equivalent in EDM but could be mapped to *edm:ProvidedCHO* as explained earlier. While this mapping would not retain the exact original semantics, it would retain all the data values.

Another approach would be to describe these resources as "contextual works", for which the current approach in EDM would be to use *skos:Concept*. This is actually similar to another case we encountered, where the granularity mismatch was in the opposite direction: NCSU had used over one thousand instances of *schema:Thing* as objects for the *schema:about* property. We made the decision to map them to *skos: Concept* in a way that is quite collection-specific and rather bold: *schema:Thing* is not equivalent to *skos:Concept* in absolute.

Again, such mappings allow to keep data resources in, which the Schema.org data show to be very useful to contextualize digital objects. They however require harder work, and the creators of the data may find it cumbersome to handle the semantic gap between the original type and the notion of 'concept'. Both obstacles may explain why the data could not be found in the EDM for UI in DPLA, either.

5.2   Analysis of Data Obtained in the Experimental Schema.org-Based Aggregation Setup

Both datasets used in this experiment allowed us to explore the potential of Schema.org data for data aggregation into Europeana.

The mapping from source data to EDM done in the process of the DPLA aggregation enables the (re)structuring of source data according to the main information entities defined by the EDM model: each resource (CHO, digital object, collection, additional contextual resources) is identified by its own URI and gathers all the data referring to a particular entity. But the new efforts – by providers – for mapping this source data to Schema.org has shown that the data can be even better structured. Schema.org is indeed slightly more granular in terms of classes and properties, and thus provides more motivation for data publishers to make a better mapping, and even enrich the data they have (a phenomenon that is already happening within the boundaries of EDM but can do with more encouragement[35]). In the particular cases we analyzed, we have especially noticed that the Schema.org data have been further enriched with links to external resources such as controlled vocabularies – the Library of Congress Subjects Headings[36] (LCSH), the Virtual International Authority File[37]

---

[35] https://pro.europeana.eu/page/europeana-semantic-enrichment.

[36] http://id.loc.gov/authorities/subjects.html.

[37] https://viaf.org/.

(VIAF) and the Art and Architecture Thesaurus[38] (AAT) – and other related resources –Wikipedia[39], WorldCat, IMDB[40].

In a way and like the class mappings discussed in Sect. 5.1, a mapping from Schema.org to EDM can retain these enrichments as long as a suitable property for representing them is found. Most of these links are indeed a way to get richer, authoritative data from external sources. For example the UI dataset defines no name for the persons it uses, but all are in fact VIAF resources (URIs) that are provided with names via the OCLC service. UI's efforts can instead be focused on defining 'job titles' (e.g., roles of actors in plays) in the Schema.org data for these persons, which is a key characteristic of their collection.

Note that EDM includes very generic properties such as *edm:hasType*[41] and *edm: isRelatedTo*, which can be used as fallback options in case EDM has no property that would keep the semantics of the Schema.org one being used for the enrichment. Although this approach results in loss of semantic grain, it would help to progressively improve the granularity of data in Europeana, nonetheless.

6 Conclusions

The experiments we have reported in this paper show that Schema.org is suitable for describing CH objects. The data providers in the study prepared Schema.org metadata for Internet discovery, not specifically for CH aggregation. In spite of this, the EDM metadata derived from Schema.org has been found to be close to being fully suitable for aggregation by Europeana.

There are still some issues with employing Schema.org metadata acquisition as a direct replacement to the current Europeana metadata aggregation workflow. EDM defines some properties with specific semantics for Europeana aggregation and requires the use of controlled vocabularies for which Schema.org provides no suitable solution by itself. In our case studies, we have identified several properties that would require particular attention at mapping time: *edm:rights*, *edm:type*, *edm:dataProvider* and *edm: provider*. Data providers expecting Europeana to harvest their metadata via Schema.org should provide the required information in agreed Schema.org properties. Yet, we can conclude that Schema.org poses no obstacle that cannot be overcome to allow data providers to deliver metadata in full compliance with EDM requirements and with the desired semantic quality.

We claim that these findings can be extended to CH aggregation services similar to Europeana, as EDM has been designed to meet very diverse CH cases and has indeed been re-used/extended in a number of CH data interchange scenarios[42]. In fact, Schema.org provides additional semantic granularity, which may allow the description

---

[38] http://www.getty.edu/research/tools/vocabularies/aat/.

[39] https://www.wikipedia.org/.

[40] http://www.imdb.com/.

[41] Note that edm:hasType is a different property from edm:type discussed earlier.

[42] https://pro.europeana.eu/page/edm-profiles.

of additional types and characteristics of CH objects found in specific metadata schemas but not (yet) implemented in EDM. For example, UI's theatre events can be represented using the class *schema:theaterEvent*. As it is backed – and consumed – by main web search engines, Schema.org brings further motivation to data owners for publishing richer data on the web.

With this combination of factors, we are convinced that Schema.org presents an opportunity for progressively improving the granularity of EDM data at Europeana and similar CH services, in a sustainable way. To ensure it, however, we must provide clear recommendations and/or specifications regarding how data providers should provide their Schema.org metadata.

Future work at Europeana will contribute to such support and try to motivate more CH institutions to publish Schema.org data. As a matter of fact, we plan to publish our complete dataset as Schema.org data in the second semester of 2018, based on our earlier work [7]. We will also investigate whether the handling of rights in Schema.org can be better aligned with CH practices. Europeana is involved in an initiative – RightsStatements.org – that provides a good framework for contributing to the Schema.org community-based extension process mentioned in Sect. 3, if appropriate.

Acknowledgements. We would like to acknowledge the support given by staff members of North Carolina State University Libraries, the University of Illinois at Urbana-Champaign and the Digital Public Library of America, for their support in access and analysis of the data sources for the case studies: Jason Ronallo, Timothy Cole, Jacob Jett, Gretchen Gueguen and Michael Della Bitta.

This work was partially supported by Portuguese national funds through Fundação para a Ciência e a Tecnologia (FCT) with reference UID/CEC/50021/2013, and by the European Commission under the Connecting Europe Facility, telecommunications sector, grant agreement number CEF-TC-2015-1-01, and under contract number 30-CE-0885387/00-80.

References

1. Verwayen, H.: Business Plan 2017: Spreading the Word. Europeana Foundation (2017). https://pro.europeana.eu/files/Europeana_Professional/Publications/europeana-business-plan-2017.pdf
2. Scholz, H., McCarthy, D., Gomez, P.U., Katrinaki, E., Herlt, K., Welter, J., Natale, M.T., Piccininno, M., Baumann, G., Fernie, K., Gavrilis, D., Rendina, M., Verbruggen, E., Ivacs, G., van Schaverbeke, N., Garvin, J.: Amount of Data Partners and Outeach to Major Institutions. Europeana Core Service Platform D1.2 (2017). https://pro.europeana.eu/files/Europeana_Professional/Projects/Project_list/Europeana_DSI/Deliverables/europeana-dsi-d1.2-amount-of-data-partners-and-outreach-to-major-institutions.pdf
3. Lagoze, C., Van de Sompel, H., Nelson, M., Warner, S.: The Open Archives Initiative Protocol for Metadata Harvesting, Version 2.0 (2002). http://www.openarchives.org/OAI/2.0/openarchivesprotocol.htm
4. Dublin Core Metadata Initiative. Dublin Core Metadata Element Set, Version 1.1: Reference Description. DCMI Recommendation (2012). http://www.dublincore.org/documents/dces/
5. Google Inc., Yahoo Inc., Microsoft Corporation and Yandex. About Schema.org. http://schema.org/docs/about.html

6. Freire, N., Manguinhas, H., Isaac, A., Robson, G., Howard, J.B.: Web technologies: a survey of their applicability to metadata aggregation in cultural heritage. In: 21st International Conference on Electronic Publishing (2017)

7. Wallis, R., Isaac, A., Charles, V., Manguinhas, H.: Recommendations for the application of Schema.org to aggregated Cultural Heritage metadata to increase relevance and visibility to search engines: the case of Europeana. Code4Lib J. (36) (2017). http://journal.code4lib.org/articles/12330. ISSN 1940-5758

8. Definition of the Europeana Data Model v5.2.8. Europeana Foundation (2017). http://pro.europeana.eu/edm-documentation

9. Gradmann, S.: Knowledge = Information in Context: on the Importance of Semantic Contextualisation in Europeana. Europeana Whitepaper (2010). http://pro.europeana.eu/publication/knowledgeinformation-in-context

10. Charles, V., Isaac, A.: Enhancing the Europeana Data Model (EDM). Europeana white paper (2015). http://pro.europeana.eu/files/Europeana_Professional/Publications/EDM_White Paper_17062015.pdf

11. Berners-Lee, T.: Linked Data. W3C Design Issues (2006). http://www.w3.org/DesignIssues/LinkedData.html

12. Digital Public Library of America. Metadata Application Profile, Version 4.0 (2015). https://dp.la/info/wp-content/uploads/2015/03/MAPv4.pdf

13. Europeana Data Model - Mapping Guidelines v2.4. Europeana Foundation (2017). http://pro.europeana.eu/edm-documentation

14. Berners-Lee, T., Hendler, J., Lassila, O.: The semantic web. Sci. Am. **284**(5), 29–37 (2001)

15. Snydman, S., Sanderson, R., Cramer, T.: The International Image Interoperability Framework (IIIF): a community & technology approach for web-based images. Archiving (2015). http://purl.stanford.edu/df650pk4327

16. Freire, N., Robson, G., Howard, J.B., Manguinhas, H., Isaac, A.: Metadata aggregation: assessing the application of IIIF and sitemaps within cultural heritage. In: Kamps, J., Tsakonas, G., Manolopoulos, Y., Iliadis, L., Karydis, I. (eds.) TPDL 2017. LNCS, vol. 10450, pp. 220–232. Springer, Cham (2017). https://doi.org/10.1007/978-3-319-67008-9_18

Dynamic Planning for Link Discovery

Kleanthi Georgala[1]($\boxtimes$), Daniel Obraczka[1],
and Axel-Cyrille Ngonga Ngomo[2]

[1] AKSW Research Group, University of Leipzig,
Augustusplatz 10, 04103 Leipzig, Germany
georgala@informatik.uni-leipzig.de, soz11ffe@studserv.uni-leipzig.de
[2] Data Science Group, Paderborn University,
Pohlweg 51, 33098 Paderborn, Germany
axel.ngonga@upb.de

Abstract. With the growth of the number and the size of RDF datasets
comes an increasing need for scalable solutions to support the linking of
resources. Most Link Discovery frameworks rely on complex link specifications for this purpose. We address the scalability of the execution of
link specifications by presenting the first dynamic planning approach for
Link Discovery dubbed CONDOR. In contrast to the state of the art, CON-
DOR can re-evaluate and reshape execution plans for link specifications
during their execution. Thus, it achieves significantly better runtimes
than existing planning solutions while retaining an F-measure of 100%.
We quantify our improvement by evaluating our approach on 7 datasets
and 700 link specifications. Our results suggest that CONDOR is up to
2 orders of magnitude faster than the state of the art and requires less
than 0.1% of the total runtime of a given specification to generate the
corresponding plan.

1 Introduction

The provision of links between knowledge bases is one of the core principles of
Linked Data.[1] Hence, the growth of knowledge bases on the Linked Data Web
in size and number has led to a significant body of work which addresses the
two key challenges of Link Discovery (LD): efficiency and accuracy (see [1] for a
survey). In this work, we focus on the first challenge, i.e., on the efficient computation of links between knowledge bases. Most LD frameworks use combinations
of atomic similarity measures by means of *specification operators* and *thresholds*
to compute link candidates. The combinations are often called linkage rules [2]
or link specifications (short LSs, see Fig. 1 for an example and Sect. 2 for a formal definition) to compute links [1]. So far, most approaches for improving the
execution of LSs have focused on reducing the runtime of the atomic similarity
measures used in LSs (see, e.g., [3–5]). While these algorithms have led to significant runtime improvements, they fail to exploit global knowledge about the
LSs to be executed. In CONDOR, we *build upon these solutions* and tackle the
problem of *executing link specifications efficiently*.

---

[1] http://www.w3.org/DesignIssues/LinkedData.html.

© Springer International Publishing AG, part of Springer Nature 2018
A. Gangemi et al. (Eds.): ESWC 2018, LNCS 10843, pp. 240–255, 2018.
https://doi.org/10.1007/978-3-319-93417-4_16

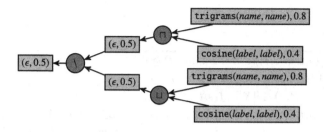

Fig. 1. Graphical representation of an example LS

CONDOR makes used of a minute but significant change in the planning and execution of LSs. So far, the execution of LSs has been modeled as a linear process (see [1]), where a LS is commonly rewritten, planned and finally executed.[2] While this architecture has its merits, it fails to use a critical piece of information: *the execution engine knows more about runtimes than the planner once it has executed a portion of the specification.* The core idea behind our work is to make use of the information generated by the execution engine at runtime to re-evaluate the plans generated by the planner. To this end, we introduce an architectural change to LD frameworks by enabling a flow of information from the execution engine back to the planner. While this change might appear negligible, it has a significant effect on the performance of LD systems as shown by our evaluation (see Sect. 4).

The contributions of this work are hence as follows: (1) We propose the first planner for link specification which is able to re-plan steps of an input LS L based on the outcome of partial executions of L. By virtue of this behavior, we dub CONDOR a *dynamic planner*. (2) In addition to being dynamic, CONDOR goes beyond the state of the art by ensuring that duplicated steps are executed exactly once. Moreover, our planner can also make use of subsumptions between result sets to further reuse previous results of the execution engine. (3) We evaluate our approach on 700 LSs and 7 datasets and show that we outperfom the state of the art significantly.

2   Preliminaries

The formal framework underlying our preliminaries is derived from [6,7]. LD frameworks aim to compute the set $M = \{(s,t) \in S \times T : R(s,t)\}$ where S and T are sets of RDF resources and R is a binary relation. Given that M is generally difficult to compute directly, declarative LD frameworks compute an approximation $M' \subseteq S \times T \times \mathbb{R}$ of M by executing a *link specification* (LS), which we define formally in the following.

An *atomic LS* L is a pair $L = (m, \theta)$, where m is a similarity measure that compares properties of pairs (s,t) from $S \times T$ and θ is a similarity threshold. LS

---

[2] Note that some systems implement the rewriting and planning in an implicit manner.

Table 1. Semantics of link specifications

L	$[[L]]$
(m, θ)	$\{(s, t, m(s, t)) \in S \times T : m(s, t) \geq \theta\}$
(f, τ, X)	$\begin{cases} \{(s, t, r) \in [[X]] : r \geq \tau\} \text{ if } f = \epsilon \\ \{(s, t, r) \in [[X]] : f(s, t) \geq \tau\} \text{ else.} \end{cases}$
$\sqcap(L_1, L_2)$	$\{(s, t, r) \mid (s, t, r_1) \in [[L_1]] \wedge (s, t, r_2) \in [[L_2]] \wedge r = \min(r_1, r_2)\}$
$\sqcup(L_1, L_2)$	$\left\{ (s, t, r) \mid \begin{cases} r = r_1 \text{ if } \exists(s, t, r_1) \in [[L_1]] \wedge \neg(\exists r_2 : (s, t, r_2) \in [[L_2]]), \\ r = r_2 \text{ if } \exists(s, t, r_2) \in [[L_2]] \wedge \neg(\exists r_1 : (s, t, r_1) \in [[L_1]]), \\ r = \max(r_1, r_2) \text{ if } (s, t, r_1) \in [[L_1]] \wedge (s, t, r_2) \in [[L_2]]. \end{cases} \right\}$
$\backslash(L_1, L_2)$	$\{(s, t, r) \mid (s, t, r) \in [[L_1]] \wedge \neg \exists r' : (s, t, r') \in [[L_2]]\}$
$\emptyset(L)$	$[[L]]$

can be combined by means of operators and filters. Here, we consider the binary operators $\sqcup$, $\sqcap$ and $\backslash$, which stand for the union, intersection and difference of specifications respectively. *Filters* are pairs (f, τ), where f is either empty (denoted ϵ), a similarity measure or a combination of similarity measures and τ is a threshold.

A *complex LS* L is a triple $(f, \tau, \omega(L_1, L_2))$ where ω is a specification operator and (f, τ) is a filter. An example of a LS is given in Fig. 1. Note that an atomic specification can be regarded as a filter (f, τ, X) with $X = S \times T$. Thus we will use the same graphical representation for filters and atomic specifications. We call (f, τ) the *filter of L* and denote it with $\varphi(L)$. For our example, $\varphi(L) = (\epsilon, 0.5)$. The *operator of a LS L* will be denoted $op(L)$. For $L = (f, \tau, \omega(L_1, L_2))$, $op(L) = \omega$. In our example the operator of the LS is $\backslash$. The *size of L*, denoted $|L|$, is defined as follows: If L is atomic, then $|L| = 1$. For complex LSs $L = (f, \tau, \omega(L_1, L_2))$, we set $L = |L_1| + |L_2| + 1$. The LS shown in Fig. 1 has a size of 7. For $L = (f, \tau, \omega(L_1, L_2))$, we call L_1 resp. L_2 the left resp. right direct child of L.

We denote the semantics (i.e., the results of a LS for given sets of resources S and T) of a LS L by $[[L]]$ and call it a *mapping*. We begin by assuming the natural semantics of the combinations of measures. The semantics of LSs are then as shown in Table 1. To compute the mapping $[[L]]$ (which corresponds to the output of L for a given pair (S, T)), LD frameworks implement (at least parts of) a generic architecture consisting of an execution engine, an optional rewriter and a planner (see [1] for more details). The *rewriter* performs algebraic operations to transform the input LS L into a LS L' (with $[[L]] = [[L']]$) that is potentially faster to execute. The most common planner is the *canonical planner* (dubbed CANONICAL), which simply traverses L in post-order and has its results computed in that order by the execution engine.[3] For the LS shown in Fig. 1, the execution plan returned by CANONICAL would thus first compute the mapping

---

[3] Note that the planner and engine are not necessarily distinct in existing implementations.

$M_1 = [[(\text{cosine}(label, label), 0.4)]]$ of pairs of resources whose property $\texttt{label}$ has a cosine similarity equal to, or greater than 0.4. The computation of $M_2 = [[(\text{trigrams}(name, name), 0.8)]]$ would follow. Step 3 would be to compute $M_3 = M_1 \sqcup M_2$ while abiding by the semantics described in Table 1. Step 4 would be to filter the results by only keeping pairs that have a similarity above 0.5 and so on. Given that there is a 1–1 correspondence between a LS and the plan generated by the canonical planner, we will reuse the representation of a LS devised above for plans. The sequence of steps for such a plan is then to be understood as the sequence of steps that would be derived by CANONICAL for the LS displayed.

3   CONDOR

The goal of CONDOR is to improve the overall execution time of LSs. To this end, CONDOR aims to derive a time-efficient execution plan for a given input LS L. The basic idea behind state-of-the-art planners for LD (see [7]) is to approximate the costs of possible plans for L, and to simply select the least costly (i.e., the presumable fastest) plan so as to improve the execution costs. The selected plan is then forwarded to the execution engine and executed. We call this type of planning *static planning* because the plan selected is never changed. CONDOR addresses the planning and execution of LSs differently: Given an input LS L, CONDOR's planner uses an initial cost function to generate initial plans P, of which each consists of a sequence of steps that are to be executed by CONDOR's execution engine to compute L. The planner chooses the least costly plan and forwards it to the engine. After the execution of each step, the execution engine overwrites the planner's cost function by replacing the estimated costs of the executed step with its real costs. The planner then re-evaluates the alternative plans generated afore and alters the remaining steps to be executed if the updated cost function suggests better expected runtimes for this alteration of the remaining steps. We call this novel paradigm for planning the execution of LSs *dynamic planning*.

3.1   Planning

Algorithm 1 summarizes the dynamic planning approach implemented by CONDOR. The algorithm (dubbed *plan*) takes a LS L as input and returns the plan $P(L)$ with the smallest expected runtime. The core of the approach consists of (1) a cost function r which computes expected runtimes and (2) a recursive cost evaluation scheme. CONDOR's planner begins by checking whether the input L has already been executed within the current run (Line 2). If L has already been executed, there is no need to re-plan the LS. Instead, *plan* returns the known plan $P(L)$. If L has not yet been executed, we proceed by first checking whether L is atomic. If L is atomic, we return $P = run(m, \theta)$ (line 6), which simply computes $[[L]]$ on $S \times T$. Here, we make use of existing scalable solutions for computing such mappings [1].

If $L = (f, \tau, \omega(L_1, L_2))$, *plan* derives a plan for L_1 and L_2 (lines 10 and 11), then computes possible plans given $op(L)$ and then decides for the least costly plan based on the cost function. The possible plans generated by CONDOR depend on the operator of L. For example, if $op(L) = \sqcap$, then *plan* evaluates three alternative plans: (1) The *canonical* plan (lines 21, 23, 27, 31), which consists of executing $P(L_1)$ and $P(L_2)$, performing an intersection between the resulting mappings and then filtering the final mapping using (f, τ); (2) The *filter-right* plan (lines 24, 32), where the best plan P_1 for L_1 is executed, followed by a run of a filtering operation on the results of P_1 using $(f_2, \tau_2) = \varphi(L_2)$ and then filtering the final mapping using (f, τ); (3) The *filter-left* plan (lines 28, 32), which is a *filter-right* plan with the roles of L_1 and L_2 reversed.

As mentioned in Sect. 1, CONDOR's planning function re-uses results of previously executed LSs and plans. Hence, if both P_1 and P_2 have already been executed $(r(P_1) = r(P_2) = 0)$, then the best plan is the *canonical* plan, where CONDOR will only need to retrieve the mappings of the two plans and then perform the intersection and the filtering operation (line 20). If P_1 resp. P_2 have already been executed (see Line 22 resp. 26), then the algorithm decides between the *canonical* and the *filter-right* resp. *filter-left* plan. If no information is available, then the costs of the different alternatives are calculated based on our cost function described in Sect. 3.2 and the least costly plan is chosen. Similar approaches are implemented for $op(L) = \setminus$ (lines 12–18). In particular, in line 17, the *plan* algorithm implements the *filter-right* plan by first executing the plan P_1 for the left child and then constructing a "reverse filter" from $(f_2, \tau_2) = \varphi(L_2)$ by calling the *getReverseFilter* function. The resulting filter is responsible for allowing only links of the retrieved mapping of L_1 that are not returned by L_2. For $op(L) = \sqcup$ (line 36) the plan always consists of merging the results of $P(L_1)$ and $P(L_2)$ by using the semantics described in Table 1.

3.2   Plan Evaluation

As explained in the first paragraphs of Sect. 2, one important component of CONDOR is the cost function required to estimate the costs of executing the corresponding plan. Based on [8], we used a linear plan evaluation schema as introduced in [7]. A plan P is characterized by one basic component, $r(P)$, the approximated runtime of executing P.

Approximation of $r(P)$ for Atomic LSs. We compute $r(P(L))$ by assuming that the runtime of $L = f(m, \theta)$ can be approximated in linear time for each metric m using the following equation:

$$r(P) = \gamma_0 + \gamma_1 |S| + \gamma_2 |T| + \gamma_3 \theta, \tag{1}$$

where $|S|$ is the size of the source KB, $|T|$ is the size of the target KB and θ is the threshold of the specification. We used a linear model with these parameters since the experiments in [7,8] suggested that they are sufficient to produce accurate approximations. The next step of our plan evaluation approach was to estimate the parameters $\gamma_0, \gamma_1, \gamma_2$ and γ_3. However, the size of the source and the target KBs is unknown prior to the linking task. Therefore, we used a sampling method, where we generated source and target datasets of sizes $1000, 2000, \ldots, 10000$ by sampling data from the English labels of DBpedia 3.8. and stored the runtime of the measures implemented by our framework for different thresholds θ between 0.5 and 1. Then, we computed the γ_i parameters by deriving the solution of the problem to the linear regression solution of $\Gamma = (R^T R)^{-1} R^T Y$, where $\Gamma = (\gamma_0, \gamma_1, \gamma_2, \gamma_3)^T$, Y is a vector in which the y_i-th row corresponds to the runtime retrieved by running ith experiment and R is a four-column matrix in which the corresponding experimental parameters $(1, |S|, |T|, \theta)$ are stored in the r_i-th row.

Approximation of $r(P)$ for Complex LSs. For the *canonical* plan, $r(P)$ is estimated by summing up the $r(P)$ of all plans that correspond to children specifications of the complex LS. For the *filter-right* and *filter-left* plans, $r(P)$ is estimated by summing the $r(P)$ of the child LS whose plan is going to be executed along with the approximation of the runtime of the filtering function performed by the other child LS. To estimate the runtime of a filtering function, we compute the approximation analogously to the computation of the runtime of an atomic LS.

Additionally, we define a set of rules if $\omega = \sqcap$ or $\omega = \backslash$: (1) $r(P)$ includes only the sums of the children LSs that have not yet been executed. (2) If both children of the LS are executed then $r(P)$ is set to 0. Therefore, we force the algorithm to choose *canonical* over the other two options, since it will create a smaller overhead in total runtime of CONDOR.

3.3   Execution

Algorithm 2 describes the execution of the plan that Algorithm 1 returned. The *execute* algorithm takes as input a LS L and returns the corresponding mapping M once all steps of $P(L)$ have been executed. The algorithm begins in line 2, where *execute* returns the mapping M of L, if L has already been executed and its result cached. If L has not been executed before, we proceed by checking whether a LS L' with $[[L]] \subseteq [[L]]'$ has already been executed (line 7). If such a L' exists, then *execute* retrieves $M' = [[L]]'$ and runs $(f, \tau, [[L]]')$ where $(f, \tau) = \varphi(L)$ (line 9). If $\nexists L'$, the algorithm checks whether L is atomic. If this is the case, then $P(L) = run(m, \theta)$ computes $[[L]]$. If $L = (f, \tau, \omega(L_1, L_2))$, *execute* calls the *plan* function described previously.

3.4   Example Run

To elucidate the workings of CONDOR further, we use the LS described in Fig. 1 as a running example. Table 2 shows the cost function $r(P)$ of each possible plan that can be produced for the specifications included in L, for the different calls of the *plan* function for L. The runtime value of a plan for a complex LS additionally includes a value for the filtering or set operations, wherever present. Recall that *plan* is a recursive function (lines 10, 11) and plans L in post-order (bottom-up, left-to-right). CONDOR produces a plan equivalent to the *canonical* plan for the left child due to the $\sqcup$ operator. Then, it proceeds in finding the least costly plan for the right child. For the right child, *plan* has to choose between the three

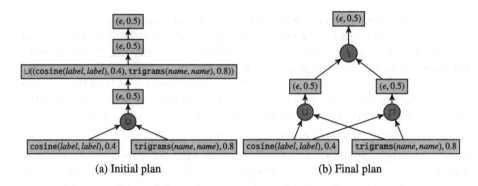

(a) Initial plan   (b) Final plan

Fig. 2. Initial and final plans returned by CONDOR for the LS in Fig. 1

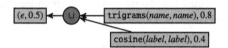

Fig. 3. Plan of the left child for the LS in Fig. 1

alternatives described in Sect. 3.1. Table 2 shows the approximation $r(P)$ of each plan for $(\sqcap((\text{cosine}(label, label), 0.4), (\text{trigrams}(name, name), 0.8)), 0.5)$. The least costly plan for the right child is the *filter-left* plan, where $L' = (\text{trigrams}(name, name), 0.8))$ is executed and $[[L']]$ is then filtered using $(\text{cosine}(label, label), 0.4))$ and $(\epsilon, 0.5)$. Before proceeding to discover the best plan for L, CONDOR assigns an approximate runtime $r(P)$ to each child plan of L: 3.5 s for the left child and 1.5 s for the right child.

Once CONDOR has identified the best plans for both children of L, it proceeds to find the most efficient plan for L. Since both children have not been executed previously, *plan* goes to line 15. There, it has to chose between two alternative plans, i.e., the *canonical* plan with $r(P) = 6.2$ s and the *filter-right* plan with $r(P) = 5.2$ s. It is obvious that *plan* is going to assign the *filter-right* plan as the least costly plan for L. Note that this plan overwrites the right child *filter-left* plan, and it will instead use the right child as a filter.

Once the plan is finalized, the *plan* function returns and assigns the plan shown in Fig. 2a to $P(L)$ in line 14. For the next step, *execute* retrieves the left child $(\sqcup((\text{cosine}(label, label), 0.4), (\text{trigrams}(name, name), 0.8)), 0.5)$ and assigns it to L_1 (line 15). Then, the algorithm calls *execute* for L_1. *execute* repeats the plan procedure for L_1 recursively and returns the plan illustrated in Fig. 3. The plan is executed and finally (line 16) the resulting mapping is assigned to M_1. Remember that all intermediate mappings as well as the final mapping along with the corresponding LSs are stored for future use (line 29). Additionally, we replace the cost value estimations of each executed plan by their real values in line 28. Now, the cost value of $(\text{cosine}(label, label), 0.4)$ is assigned to 2.0 s, the cost value of $(\text{trigrams}(name, name), 0.8)$ is assigned to 1.0 s and finally, the cost value of the left child will be replaced by 4.0 s.

Now, given the runtimes from the execution engine, the algorithm re-plans the further steps of L. Within this second call of *plan* (line 17), CONDOR does not re-plan the sub-specification that corresponds to L_1, since its plan (Fig. 3) has been executed previously. Initially, *plan* had decided to use the right child as a filter. However, both $(\text{cosine}(label, label), 0.4)$ and $(\text{trigrams}(name, name), 0.8)$ have already been executed. Hence, the new total cost of executing the right child is set to 0.0. Consequently, *plan* changes the remaining steps of the initial plan of L, since the cost of executing the *canonical* plan is now set to 0.0. The final plan is illustrated in Fig. 2b.

Once the new plan $P(L)$ is constructed, *execute* checks if $P(L)$ includes any operators. In our example, $op(L) = \backslash$. Thus, we execute the second direct child of L as described in $P(L)$, $L_2 = (\sqcap((\text{cosine}(label, label), 0.4), (\text{trigrams}(name, name), 0.8)), 0.5)$. Algorithm 2 calls the *execute* function for L_2, which calls *plan*. CONDOR's planning algorithm then returns a plan for L_2, which is similar to the plan for the left child illustrated in Fig. 3 by replacing the $\sqcup$ operator with the $\sqcap$ operator, with $r(P(L_2)) = 0$ s.

When the algorithm proceeds to executing $P(L_2)$, it discovers that the atomic LSs of L_2 have already executed. Thus, it retrieves the corresponding mappings, performs the intersection between the results of $(\text{cosine}(label, label), 0.4)$ and $(\text{trigrams}(name, name), 0.8)$, filters the resulting mapping of the intersection with $(\epsilon, 0.5)$ and stores the resulting mapping for future use (line 29). Returning to our initial LS L, the algorithm has now retrieved results for both L_1 and L_2 and proceeds to perform the steps described in line 21 and 27. The final plan constructed by CONDOR is presented in Fig. 2b.

If the second call of the *plan* function for L in line 17 had resulted in not altering the initial $P(L)$, then *execute* would have proceeded in applying a reverse filter (i.e., the implementation of the difference of mappings) on M_1 by using $(\sqcap((\text{cosine}(label, label), 0.4), (\text{trigrams}(name, name), 0.8)), 0.5)$ (line 24). Similarly operations would have been carried out if $op(L) = \sqcap$ in line 26.

Overall, the complexity of CONDOR can be derived as follows: For each node of a LS L, CONDOR generates a constant number of possible plans. Hence, the complexity of each iteration of CONDOR is $O(|L|)$. The execution engine executes at least one node in each iteration, meaning that it needs at most $O(|L|)$ iterations to execute L completely. Hence, CONDOR's worst-case runtime complexity is $O(|L|^2)$.

4   Evaluation

4.1   Experimental Setup

The aim of our evaluation was to address the following questions: (Q_1) Does CONDOR achieve better runtimes for LSs? (Q_2) How much time does CONDOR spend planning? (Q_3) How do the different sizes of LSs affect CONDOR's runtime? To address these questions, we evaluated our approach against seven data sets. The first four are the benchmark data sets for LD dubbed Abt-Buy, Amazon-Google Products, DBLP-ACM and DBLP-Scholar described in [9]. These are manually curated benchmark data sets collected from real data sources such as the publication sites DBLP and ACM as well as the Amazon and Google product websites. To assess the scalability of CONDOR, we created three additional data sets (MOVIES, TOWNS and VILLAGES, see Table 3) from the data sets DBpedia, LinkedGeodata and LinkedMDB.[4],[5] Table 3 describes their characteristics and presents the properties used when linking the retrieved resources. The mapping properties were provided to the link discovery algorithms underlying our results. We generated 100 LSs for each dataset by using the unsupervised version of EAGLE, a genetic programming approach for learning LSs [10]. We used this algorithm because it can detect LSs of high accuracy on the datasets at hand. We configured EAGLE by setting the number of generations and population size to 20, mutation and crossover rates were set to 0.6. All experiments were carried out on a 20-core Linux Server running *OpenJDK* 64-Bit Server 1.8.0.66 on Ubuntu 14.04.3 LTS on Intel Xeon CPU E5-2650 v3 processors clocked at 2.30 GHz. Each experiment was repeated three times. We report the average runtimes of each of the algorithms. Note that all three planners return the same set of links and that they hence all achieve 100% F-measure w.r.t. the LS to be executed.[6]

4.2   Results

We compared the execution time of CONDOR with that of the state-of-the-art algorithm for planning (HELIOS [7]) as well as with the canonical planner implemented in LIMES. We chose LIMES because it is a state-of-the-art declarative framework for link discovery which ensures result completeness. Figure 4 shows the runtimes achieved by the different algorithm in different settings. As shown in Fig. 4a, CONDOR outperforms CANONICAL and HELIOS on all datasets. A Wilcoxon signed-rank test on the cumulative runtimes of the approaches (significance level = 99%) confirms that the differences in performance between CONDOR and the other approaches are statistically significant on all datasets. This observation and the statistical test clearly answer question Q_1:

Answer to Q_1: CONDOR outperforms the state of the art in planning by being able to generate more time-efficient plans than HELIOS and CANONICAL.

Figure 4a shows that our approach performs best on AMAZON-GP, where it can reduce the average runtime of the set of specifications by 78% compared to CANONICAL, making CONDOR 4.6 times faster. Moreover, for the same dataset, dynamic planning is 8.04 times more efficient than HELIOS. Note that finding a better plan than the canonical plan on this particular dataset is non-trivial (as shown by the HELIOS results). Here, our dynamic planning approach pays

---

[4] http://www.linkedmdb.org/.

[5] The new data and a description of how they were constructed are available at http://titan.informatik.uni-leipzig.de/kgeorgala/DATA/.

[6] Our complete experimental results can be found at http://titan.informatik.uni-leipzig.de/kgeorgala/condor_results.zip. Our open source code can be found at http://limes.sf.net.

off by being able to revise the original and altering this plan at runtime early enough to achieve better results than the CANONICAL planner and HELIOS. The highest absolute difference is achieved on DBLP-Scholar, where CONDOR reduces the overall execution time of the CANONICAL planner on the 100 LSs by approximately 600 s per specification on average. On the same dataset, the difference between CONDOR and HELIOS is approximately 110 s per LS.

The answer to our second question is that the benefits of the dynamic planning strategy are far superior to the time required by the re-planning scheme (as showed by Fig. 4). CONDOR spends between 0.0005% (DBLP-SCHOLAR) and 0.1% (AMAZON-GP) of the overall runtime on planning. The specifications computed for the AMAZON-GP dataset have on average the largest size in contrast to the other datasets. On this particular dataset, CONDOR spends less than 10 ms planning. We regard this result as particularly good, as using CONDOR brings larger benefits with growing specifications.

Answer to Q_2: In our experiments, CONDOR invests less than 10 ms and out-performs planning and re-planning.

To answer Q_3, we also computed the runtime of LSs depending on their size t (see Figs. 4b and c). For LSs of size 1, the execution times achieved by all three planners are most commonly comparable (difference of average runtimes $= 0.02$ s) since the plans produced are straight-forward and leave no room for improvement. For specifications of size 3, CONDOR is already capable of generating plans that are 7.5% faster than the canonical plans on average. The gap between CONDOR and the state of the art increases with the size of the specifications. For specifications of sizes 7 and more, CONDOR plans only necessitate 30.5% resp. 55.7% of the time required by the plans generated by CANONICAL resp. HELIOS. A careful study of the plan generated by CONDOR reveals that the re-use of previously executed portions of a LS and the use of subsumption are clearly beneficial to the execution runtime of large LSs. However, the study also shows that in a few cases, CONDOR creates a *filter-right* or *filter-left* plan where a *canonical* plan would have been better. This is due to some sub-optimal runtime approximations produced by the $r(P)$ function. We can summarize our result as follows.

Answer to Q_3: CONDOR's performance gain over the state of the art grows with the size of the specifications.

5 Related Work

This paper addresses the creation of better plans for scalable link discovery. A large number of frameworks such as SILK [2], LIMES [11] and KnoFuss [12] were developed to support the link discovery process. These frameworks commonly rely on scalable approaches for computing simple and complex specifications. For example, a lossless framework that uses blocking is *SILK* [2], a tool relying on rough index pre-matching. KnoFuss [12] on the other hand implements classical

---

Algorithm 1. *plan* Algorithm for CONDOR

Input: a link specification L;
Mapping of executed LS to plans $specToPlanMap$
Output: Least costly plan P of L

1 $P \longleftarrow \emptyset$
2 **if** $specToPlanMap.contains(L)$ **then**
3 $\quad$ $P \longleftarrow specToPlanMap.get(L)$ //return plan stored in buffer for L
4 **else**
5 $\quad$ **if** $(L == (m, \theta))$ **then**
6 $\quad\quad$ $P \longleftarrow run(m, \theta)$
7 $\quad$ **else**
8 $\quad\quad$ $L_1 = L.leftChild$
9 $\quad\quad$ $L_2 = L.rightChild$
10 $\quad\quad$ $P_1 \longleftarrow plan(L_1)$
11 $\quad\quad$ $P_2 \longleftarrow plan(L_2)$
12 $\quad\quad$ **if** $(L.operator == \backslash)$ **then**
13 $\quad\quad\quad$ **if** $specToPlanMap.contains(L_2)$ **then**
14 $\quad\quad\quad\quad$ $P \longleftarrow merge(minus, P_1, P_2)$
15 $\quad\quad\quad$ **else**
16 $\quad\quad\quad\quad$ $Q_0 \longleftarrow merge(minus, P_1, P_2)$
17 $\quad\quad\quad\quad$ $Q_1 \longleftarrow merge(getReverseFilter(\varphi(L_2)), P_1)$
18 $\quad\quad\quad\quad$ $P \longleftarrow getLeastCostly(Q_0, Q_1)$

19 $\quad\quad$ **else if** $(L.operator == \sqcap)$ **then**
20 $\quad\quad\quad$ **if** $(specToPlanMap.contains(L_1) \wedge specToPlanMap.contains(L_2))$ **then**
21 $\quad\quad\quad\quad$ $P \longleftarrow merge(intersection, P_1, P_2)$
22 $\quad\quad\quad$ **else if** $(specToPlanMap.contains(L_1) \wedge \neg specToPlanMap.contains(L_2))$
$\quad\quad\quad$ **then**
23 $\quad\quad\quad\quad$ $Q_0 \longleftarrow merge(intersection, P_1, P_2)$
24 $\quad\quad\quad\quad$ $Q_1 \longleftarrow merge(\varphi(L_2), P_1)$
25 $\quad\quad\quad\quad$ $P \longleftarrow getLeastCostly(Q_0, Q_1)$
26 $\quad\quad\quad$ **else if** $(\neg specToPlanMap.contains(L_1) \wedge specToPlanMap.contains(L_2))$
$\quad\quad\quad$ **then**
27 $\quad\quad\quad\quad$ $Q_0 \longleftarrow merge(intersection, P_1, P_2)$
28 $\quad\quad\quad\quad$ $Q_1 \longleftarrow merge(\varphi(L_1), P_2)$
29 $\quad\quad\quad\quad$ $P \longleftarrow getLeastCostly(Q_0, Q_1)$
30 $\quad\quad\quad$ **else**
31 $\quad\quad\quad\quad$ $Q_0 \longleftarrow merge(intersection, P_1, P_2)$
32 $\quad\quad\quad\quad$ $Q_1 \longleftarrow merge(\varphi(L_2), P_1)$
33 $\quad\quad\quad\quad$ $Q_2 \longleftarrow merge(\varphi(L_1), P_2)$
34 $\quad\quad\quad\quad$ $P \longleftarrow getLeastCostly(Q_0, Q_1, Q_2)$

35 $\quad\quad$ **else**
36 $\quad\quad\quad$ $P \longleftarrow merge(union, P_1, P_2)$ //last possible operator is $\sqcup$
37 $\quad\quad$ $specToPlanMap.put(L, P)$

38 Return P

---

blocking approaches derived from databases. These approaches are not guaranteed to achieve result completeness. Zhishi.links [13] is another framework that scales (through an indexing-based approach) but is not guaranteed to retrieve all links. The completeness of results is guaranteed by the LIMES framework, which combines time-efficient algorithms such as Ed-Join and PPJoin+ with a

---

Algorithm 2. *execute* Algorithm

Input: a link specification L; mapping *specToPlanMap*; result buffer *results*

Output: Mapping M of L

1 $M \longleftarrow \emptyset$

2 **if** *(specToPlanMap.contains(L)* **then**

3 $\quad$ $M \longleftarrow results.get(L)$

4 $\quad$ get the value for the key L

5 **else**

6 $\quad$ $L' = checkDependencies(L, results)$

7 $\quad$ **if** $L' \neq null$ **then**

8 $\quad\quad$ $M' \longleftarrow results.get(L')$

9 $\quad\quad$ $M = filter(\varphi(L), M')$

10 $\quad$ **else**

11 $\quad\quad$ **if** $L = (m, \theta)$ **then**

12 $\quad\quad\quad$ $M \longleftarrow run(m, \theta)$

13 $\quad\quad$ **else**

14 $\quad\quad\quad$ $P \longleftarrow plan(L)$

15 $\quad\quad\quad$ $L_1 \longleftarrow P.getSubSpec(0)$

16 $\quad\quad\quad$ $M_1 \longleftarrow execute(L_1)$

17 $\quad\quad\quad$ $P \longleftarrow plan(L)$

18 $\quad\quad\quad$ **if** $op(P) \neq \emptyset$ **then**

19 $\quad\quad\quad\quad$ $L_2 \longleftarrow P(L).getSubSpec(1)$

20 $\quad\quad\quad\quad$ $M_2 \longleftarrow execute(L_2)$

21 $\quad\quad\quad\quad$ $M \longleftarrow runOperator(op(P), M_1, M_2)$

22 $\quad\quad\quad$ **else**

23 $\quad\quad\quad\quad$ **if** $L = (f, \tau, \backslash(L_1, L_2))$ **then**

24 $\quad\quad\quad\quad\quad$ $M \longleftarrow filter(getReverseFilter(\varphi(L_2)), M_1)$

25 $\quad\quad\quad\quad$ **else**

26 $\quad\quad\quad\quad\quad$ $M \longleftarrow filter(\varphi(L_2), M_1)$

27 $\quad\quad\quad$ $M \longleftarrow filter(\varphi(L), M)$

28 $\quad$ $update()$

29 $\quad$ $results \longleftarrow results.put(L, M)$

30 Return M

---

set-theoretical combination strategy. The execution of LSs in LIMES is carried out by means of the CANONICAL [11] and HELIOS [7] planners. Given that LIMES was shown to outperform SILK in [7], we chose to compare our approach with LIMES. The survey of Nentwig et al. [1] and the results of the Ontology Alignment and Evaluation Initiative for 2017 of the OAEI [14],[7] provide an overview of further link discovery systems.

CONDOR is the first dynamic planner for link discovery. The problem we tackled in this work bears some resemblance to the task of query optimization in

---

[7] Ontology Alignment Evaluation Initiative: http://ontologymatching.org.

Table 2. Runtime costs for the plans computed for the specification in (Fig. 1) by the two calls of the *plan* in lines 14 and 17. All runtimes are presented in seconds. The 1st column includes the initial runtime approximations of plans. The 2nd column includes (1) a real runtime value of a plan, if the plan has been executed ($^\circ$), (2) a 0.0 value if all the subsequent plans of that plan have been executed previously ($^\bullet$) or have an estimation of zero cost in the current call of *plan* (*), (3) a runtime approximation value, that includes only runtimes of subsequent plans that have not been executed yet ($^\square$).

P	$r(P)$	
	1st	2nd
($\mathbf{cosine}(label, label), 0.4$)	1.8	2.0°
($\mathbf{trigrams}(name, name), 0.8$)	0.5	1.0°
$\varphi(\mathbf{cosine}(label, label), 0.4$)	0.8	0.8$^\square$
$\varphi(\mathbf{trigrams}(name, name), 0.8$)	0.6	0.6$^\square$
canonical plan: $merge(\sqcap, (\mathbf{cosine}(label, label), 0.4), (\mathbf{trigrams}(name, name), 0.8))$	3.5	0.0$^\bullet$
filter-right plan: $merge(\varphi(\mathbf{trigrams}(name, name), 0.8), (\mathbf{cosine}(label, label), 0.4))$	2.6	0.8$^\square$
filter-left plan: $merge(\varphi(\mathbf{cosine}(label, label), 0.4), (\mathbf{trigrams}(name, name), 0.8))$	1.5	1.0$^\square$
canonical plan: $merge(\sqcup, (\mathbf{cosine}(label, label), 0.4), (\mathbf{trigrams}(name, name), 0.8))$	3.5	4.0°
canonical plan for L	6.2	0.0*
filter-right plan for L (see Fig. 2a)	5.2	1.7$^\square$

Table 3. Characteristics of data sets

Data set	Source (S)	Target (T)	$\|S\| \times \|T\|$	Source property	Target property
Abt-Buy	Abt	Buy	1.20×10^6	product name, description manufacturer, price	product name, description manufacturer, price
Amazon-GP	Amazon	Google products	4.40×10^6	product name, description manufacturer, price	product name, description manufacturer, price
DBLP-ACM	ACM	DBLP	6.00×10^6	title, authors venue, year	title, authors venue, year
DBLP-Scholar	DBLP	Google scholar	0.17×10^9	title, authors venue, year	title, authors venue, year
MOVIES	DBpedia	LinkedMDB	0.17×10^9	dbp:name dbo:director/dbp:name dbo:producer/dbp:name dbp:writer/dbp:name rdfs:label	dc2:title movie:director/movie:director_name movie:producer/movie:producer_name movie:writer/movie:writer_name rdfs:label
TOWNS	DBpedia	LGD	0.34×10^9	rdfs:label dbo:country/rdfs:label dbo:populationTotal geo:geometry	rdfs:label lgdo:isIn lgdo:population geom:geometry/agc:asWKT
VILLAGES	DBpedia	LGD	6.88×10^9	rdfs:label dbo:populationTotal geo:geometry	rdfs:label lgdo:population geom:geometry/agc:asWKT

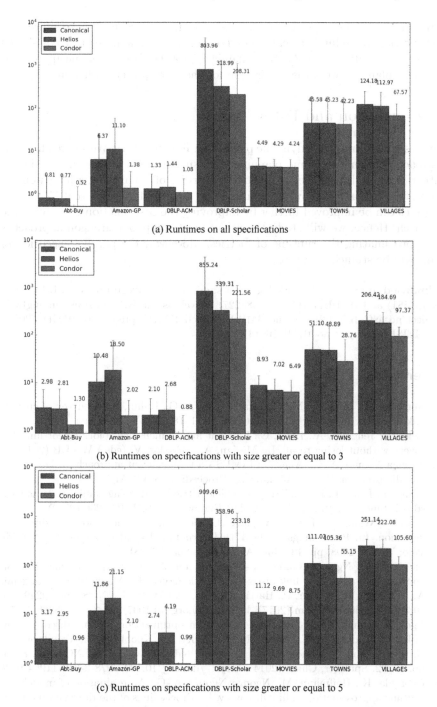

(a) Runtimes on all specifications

(b) Runtimes on specifications with size greater or equal to 3

(c) Runtimes on specifications with size greater or equal to 5

Fig. 4. Mean and standard deviation of runtimes of CANONICAL, HELIOS and CONDOR. The y-axis shows runtimes in seconds on a logarithmic scale. The numbers on top of the bars are the average runtimes.

databases [15]. There have been numerous advances which pertain to addressing this question, including strategies based on genetic programming [16], cost-based and heuristic optimizers [17], and dynamic approaches [18]. Dynamic approaches for query planning were the inspiration for the work presented herein.

6   Conclusion and Future Work

We presented CONDOR, a dynamic planner for link discovery. We showed how our approach combines dynamic planning with subsumption and result caching to outperform the state of the art by up to two orders of magnitude. A large number of questions are unveiled by our results. First, our results suggest that CONDOR's runtimes can be improved further by improving the cost function underlying the approach. Hence, we will study the use of most complex regression approaches for approximating the runtime of metrics. Moreover, the parallel execution of plans will be studied in future.

Acknowledgments. This work has been supported by H2020 projects SLIPO (GA no. 731581) and HOBBIT (GA no. 688227) as well as the DFG project LinkingLOD (project no. NG 105/3-2) and the BMWI Projects SAKE (project no. 01MD15006E) and GEISER (project no. 01MD16014).

References

1. Nentwig, M., Hartung, M., Ngonga Ngomo, A.-C., Rahm, E.: A survey of current link discovery frameworks. Semant. Web **8**, 1–18 (2015). (Preprint)
2. Isele, R., Jentzsch, A., Bizer, C.: Efficient multidimensional blocking for link discovery without losing recall. In: Marian, A., Vassalos, V. (eds.) WebDB (2011)
3. Ngonga Ngomo, A.-C., Auer, S.: LIMES - a time-efficient approach for large-scale link discovery on the web of data. In: Proceedings of IJCAI (2011)
4. Wang, J., Feng, J., Li, G.: Trie-join: efficient trie-based string similarity joins with edit-distance constraints. Proc. VLDB Endow. **3**(1–2), 1219–1230 (2010)
5. Xiao, C., Wang, W., Lin, X., Yu, J.X.: Efficient similarity joins for near duplicate detection. In: Proceedings of the 17th International Conference on World Wide Web, WWW 2008, pp. 131–140. ACM, New York (2008)
6. Sherif, M.A., Ngonga Ngomo, A.-C., Lehmann, J.: WOMBAT – a generalization approach for automatic link discovery. In: Blomqvist, E., Maynard, D., Gangemi, A., Hoekstra, R., Hitzler, P., Hartig, O. (eds.) ESWC 2017. LNCS, vol. 10249, pp. 103–119. Springer, Cham (2017). https://doi.org/10.1007/978-3-319-58068-5_7
7. Ngonga Ngomo, A.-C.: HELIOS – execution optimization for link discovery. In: Mika, P., Tudorache, T., Bernstein, A., Welty, C., Knoblock, C., Vrandečić, D., Groth, P., Noy, N., Janowicz, K., Goble, C. (eds.) ISWC 2014. LNCS, vol. 8796, pp. 17–32. Springer, Cham (2014). https://doi.org/10.1007/978-3-319-11964-9_2
8. Georgala, K., Hoffmann, M., Ngonga Ngomo, A.-C.: An evaluation of models for runtime approximation in link discovery. In: Proceedings of the International Conference on Web Intelligence, WI 2017, pp. 57–64. ACM, New York (2017)
9. Köpcke, H., Thor, A., Rahm, E.: Evaluation of entity resolution approaches on real-world match problems. Proc. VLDB Endow. **3**(1–2), 484–493 (2010)

10. Ngonga Ngomo, A.-C., Lyko, K.: EAGLE: efficient active learning of link specifications using genetic programming. In: Simperl, E., Cimiano, P., Polleres, A., Corcho, O., Presutti, V. (eds.) ESWC 2012. LNCS, vol. 7295, pp. 149–163. Springer, Heidelberg (2012). https://doi.org/10.1007/978-3-642-30284-8_17

11. Ngonga Ngomo, A.-C.: On link discovery using a hybrid approach. J. Data Semant. **1**(4), 203–217 (2012)

12. Nikolov, A., d'Aquin, M., Motta, E.: Unsupervised learning of link discovery configuration. In: Simperl, E., Cimiano, P., Polleres, A., Corcho, O., Presutti, V. (eds.) ESWC 2012. LNCS, vol. 7295, pp. 119–133. Springer, Heidelberg (2012). https://doi.org/10.1007/978-3-642-30284-8_15

13. Niu, X., Rong, S., Zhang, Y., Wang, H.: Zhishi.links results for OAEI 2011. Ontol. Matching **184**, 220 (2011)

14. Achichi, M., Cheatham, M., Dragisic, Z., Euzenat, J., Faria, D., Ferrara, A., Flouris, G., Fundulaki, I., Harrow, I., Ivanova, V., Jiménez-Ruiz, E., Kuss, E., Lambrix, P., Leopold, H., Li, H., Meilicke, C., Montanelli, S., Pesquita, C., Saveta, T., Shvaiko, P., Splendiani, A., Stuckenschmidt, H., Todorov, K., Trojahn, C., Zamazal, O.: Results of the ontology alignment evaluation initiative 2016. In: Proceedings of the 11th International Workshop on Ontology Matching, OM 2016, Co-located with the 15th International Semantic Web Conference (ISWC 2016) Kobe, Japan, 18 October 2016, vol. 1766, pp. 73–129. RWTH, Aachen (2016)

15. Silberschatz, A., Korth, H., Sudarshan, S.: Database Systems Concepts, 5th edn. McGraw-Hill Inc., New York (2006)

16. Bennett, K., Ferris, M.C., Ioannidis, Y.E.: A genetic algorithm for database query optimization. In: Proceedings of the fourth International Conference on Genetic Algorithms, pp. 400–407 (1991)

17. Kanne, C.C., Moerkotte, G.: Histograms reloaded: the merits of bucket diversity. In: Proceedings of the 2010 ACM SIGMOD International Conference on Management of Data, SIGMOD 2010, pp. 663–674. ACM, New York (2010)

18. Ng, K.W., Wang, Z., Muntz, R.R., Nittel, S.: Dynamic query re-optimization. In: Eleventh International Conference on Scientific and Statistical Database Management, pp. 264–273. IEEE (1999)

A Dataset for Web-Scale Knowledge Base Population

Michael Glass[(✉)] and Alfio Gliozzo[iD]

Knowledge Induction and Reasoning Group, IBM Research AI, New York, USA
mrglass@us.ibm.com

Abstract. For many domains, structured knowledge is in short supply, while unstructured text is plentiful. Knowledge Base Population (KBP) is the task of building or extending a knowledge base from text, and systems for KBP have grown in capability and scope. However, existing datasets for KBP are all limited by multiple issues: small in size, not open or accessible, only capable of benchmarking a fraction of the KBP process, or only suitable for extracting knowledge from title-oriented documents (documents that describe a particular entity, such as Wikipedia pages). We introduce and release CC-DBP, a web-scale dataset for training and benchmarking KBP systems. The dataset is based on Common Crawl as the corpus and DBpedia as the target knowledge base. Critically, by releasing the tools to build the dataset, we enable the dataset to remain current as new crawls and DBpedia dumps are released. Also, the modularity of the released tool set resolves a crucial tension between the ease that a dataset can be used for a particular subtask in KBP and the number of different subtasks it can be used to train or benchmark.

1 Introduction

Populating knowledge bases from text is an important element in resolving the knowledge acquisition bottleneck. However, a shortage of open, large scale and broadly scoped datasets has limited development and comparison of approaches for this task. This paper explains the creation and use of a new resource for training and benchmarking knowledge base population systems. The dataset can be used as training data for a system to expand the DBpedia ontology from text or used as a benchmark for developing new approaches for extending knowledge bases in general.

In Sect. 2 we define the task of Knowledge Base Population (KBP). In Sect. 3 we consider existing datasets for this task, and examine the differences between these datasets and the new dataset created in this work. Section 4 explains how the dataset was created, and what variations of the dataset can be created using the modular tool set we distribute. Finally, in Sect. 5 we provide some statistics on this dataset to provide a picture of its properties.

© Springer International Publishing AG, part of Springer Nature 2018
A. Gangemi et al. (Eds.): ESWC 2018, LNCS 10843, pp. 256–271, 2018.
https://doi.org/10.1007/978-3-319-93417-4_17

2   Knowledge Base Population

We define Knowledge Base Population (KBP) as extending a knowledge base with information extracted from text. In this view, there is already a substantial amount of knowledge. The goal may be to update it, keeping it current with new information. Also, the knowledge base is likely incomplete, even with respect to just the current knowledge. Fortunately, a large volume of the missing knowledge is in unstructured text. We do not assume the existence of any annotated text, nor of any process for writing rules. Although the task of KBP does not prohibit those approaches.

To be clear, it is not our true goal to label mentions of relations. KBP is not typically focused on using populating a knowledge base as a task to help train a relation extractor. KBP is fundamentally not an attempt to label any particular sentence with anything at all, neither in training nor when applying the model.

What we call KBP is also referred to by other terms in the literature. Automatic Knowledge Base Construction (AKBC) is often used to refer to this task, although often it is the case that there is no existing knowledge base in AKBC. Slot filling is a version of KBP where specific missing information for certain query entities is desired. Knowledge base validation or refinement is a related task where evidence for or against triples in the knowledge base is gathered from text and used to estimate a confidence for existing triples.

It is important to clarify some core concepts for this type of task. The knowledge in the knowledge base is in the form of *triples*. Triples connect two entities - or more generally *nodes* - by a *relation*. A node may be an entity (such as a person, place, creative work, etc) or a literal (such as a date, number, or string), or a type (such as Person, Sporting Event, etc). The relation for each triple is drawn from a fixed set of relations. Example relations include: is-a, born-on, member-of, and instance-of.

In KBP, the new knowledge added is in the form of triples with confidence. The nodes in the added triples could be existing nodes in the knowledge base or totally new entities or literals. The relation in the added triple is drawn from the fixed set of relations. Note that attaching a probability to a triple is not only motivated by the relation prediction's imperfections in its ability to interpret the textual evidence. The textual evidence itself is often inconclusive. In this view of KBP, the relation prediction should provide a probability well above zero for ⟨Samuel Smith born-in New York⟩ from the sentence "Samuel Smith went to school in New York".

2.1   Knowledge Graph View

We can also view the knowledge in a knowledge base as a knowledge graph. In this view, the result of a KBP system is to add both nodes and edges to our knowledge graph. The edges are labeled with the name of the relation, as well as the confidence from the relation prediction, a probability. Figure 1 shows a diagram of a knowledge graph with nodes and edges. New edges and nodes created from textual evidence are displayed with a dotted line.

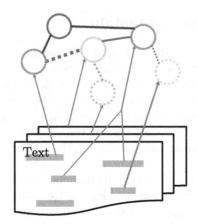

Fig. 1. Knowledge graph from text

Formally, there is a set of relation types R. There is a multigraph G with nodes N and edges E. The multigraph is directed and edge labeled. Each directed edge is labeled with a relation type from R and confidence in the range $[0, 1]$. We extend the knowledge graph by adding to N and E, while R remains fixed.

2.2 Subtasks of Knowledge Base Population

The process of KBP can be divided into a number of subtasks. We do not suggest that these are necessarily trained independently; there could be a single end-to-end deep architecture to perform all of these subtasks. Nor do we suggest that the decisions from earlier subtasks cannot be adjusted by information present in later subtasks. Rather, these are logically distinct steps. And, crucially for the introduction of a new dataset, these are subtasks that are carved along the boundaries of existing research programs.

These subtasks include Entity Detection and Linking (EDL), Context Set Construction (CSC), relation prediction and reasoning. Figure 2 illustrates the interaction of these components.

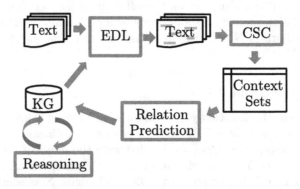

Fig. 2. Subtasks of knowledge base population

The subtask of Entity Detection and Linking (EDL) itself can be viewed as up to three subtasks: entity detection, co-reference and entity linking. A system for EDL finds mentions of the nodes that are, or should be, in the knowledge base. A mention is a span in text that refers to a specific node. Although we refer to the task as *Entity* Detection and Linking, we are concerned with nodes in general. For example, the term 'quarterly' is not an entity. But there are knowledge bases that contain information about magazines and journals including the frequency that they are published. So an appropriate EDL system would locate mentions of terms like 'quarterly' in text, as well as mentions of the magazines and journals. These mentions are also linked. In the case of nodes that are in the knowledge base, their mentions (which may be pro-nominal mentions) are linked to the node. For mentions of nodes that should be, but are not, in the knowledge graph, a new node is first created and then the mentions of it are all linked to that new node. This could also be seen as clustering mentions for nodes not present in the knowledge base.

In Fig. 3 we see three node mentions: 'The Pub Corp', 'magazine' and 'every month'. 'The Pub Corp' is a mention of a new entity, while 'magazine' is a mention of a type node that matches the label exactly, and 'every month' is a mention of a literal node that does not exactly match the label of the node.

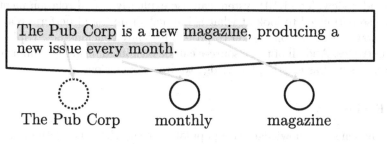

Fig. 3. Example of EDL

Context Set Construction (CSC) is the next step. A CSC system is responsible for gathering textual evidence for the relation prediction phase by identifying contexts in documents where two node mentions occur together. For a simple case, consider contexts defined as two node mentions in the same sentence. We refer to a context identified by the CSC system as a node-pair context. The CSC system is also responsible for grouping the contexts by node-pair to gather a context set for each node-pair. A node-pair context set is the direct textual evidence for the relationship (if any) between two nodes.

From this textual evidence KBP proceeds to the subtask of relation prediction. Training on sets of contexts for node-pairs is often called distantly supervised relation extraction [9]. Although, that term is also sometimes used to describe noisy supervision created by labeling each context for a node-pair by the set of relations that hold between them. Additional textual evidence may also be used to predict relations, such as the contexts of each node independently. We exclude from this logical subtask the use of other triples from the knowledge base as evidence.

The final subtask, which we call reasoning, encompasses any use of structured knowledge to predict, or adjust the confidence of, new triples. So Knowledge Base Completion (KBC) approaches based on tensor factorization such as TransE [3] qualify, as well as approaches based on induction and application of probabilistic logic [14].

2.3 Variant Definitions

A typical variation of KBP expects explicit provenance for each predicted triple. In this case the goal is still to populate a knowledge base, but with the constraint that each new triple must point to a specific sentence or passage that justifies it. Unlike our formulation of KBP, this version sharply limits the role of reasoning and extraction of implicit evidence. There is more knowledge that can be gathered from text and an existing knowledge base than just what is explicitly stated in text. So the task of knowledge base population as we have defined it, is a broader view. The KBP system can use explicitly stated relation mentions, but is also permitted to look at what is implicit in text, and perform reasoning or do knowledge base completion to probabilistically conclude new triples from existing triples. And all of these sources can be combined, using new information from text as well as existing knowledge to draw conclusions.

2.4 Evaluation

A key challenge of knowledge base population research is the method of evaluation. Three types of evaluation are commonly applied: Held-Out, Exhaustive Annotation, and Pooled Response. The first two types, Held-Out and Exhaustive Annotation are automatic evaluations, while Pooled Response requires manual judgements for any new triples produced by a system.

In a held-out evaluation, some triples of the knowledge base are removed from the training for the KBP system and must be predicted. Triples predicted by the system that match this held-out set are correct, while triples that do not match are wrong. One important advantage of this type of evaluation is that it can be applied whenever a substantial knowledge base exists, without an additional large manual effort. In exhaustive annotation, all triples that are stated in the corpus are annotated, though not necessarily with a specific location in text. Pooled response is a type of retrospective evaluation, where the ground truth is built in response to the outputs of a set of systems. The triples predicted by all systems are pooled and each distinct triple is manually judged. Figure 4 summarizes the way each approach to evaluation tabulates the true positives, false positives and false negatives.

Method	True Positives	False Positives	False Negatives
Held-Out	System triples in KB	System triples *not* in KB	KB triples not in system triples
Exhaustive Annotation	System triples in annotation	System triples *not* in annotation	Annotated triples not in system triples
Pooled Response	System triples verified to be true	System triples verified to be false	Triples verified to be true, produced by a different system

Fig. 4. Evaluation style comparison

We can see that in all evaluation approaches there is a difficulty with the tabulation of false negatives. Even in 'exhaustive' annotation, the recall basis is formed by what is explicitly stated in text - limiting both the relation prediction and especially the reasoning. However, for a benchmark used to compare different approaches, the absolute recall, or area under the precision/recall curve is not needed. Judging the relative value is enough. Figure 5 shows that determining the number of false negatives not produced by either system is not needed to compare the P/R curves of two approaches. Whether we choose a recall basis of a, b, or c the relative area of the two curves is unchanged.

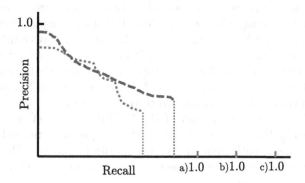

Fig. 5. Irrelevance of shared false negatives for relative precision/recall curve

3   Related Datasets

With the background information established, and the task clearly defined, we can catalog the existing datasets that are suitable for some or all of the subtasks in KBP. The most relevant existing datasets are: NYT-FB, TAC-KBP, FB15K-237, WikiReading and T-REx.

NYT-FB [10] is a dataset based on a subset of Freebase [2] relations: 56 relations in total, but some with a negligible amount of training and test data. NYT-FB was built using an NER system and a simple entity linker to locate the node-pair-contexts in the New York Times news corpus [11]. The unit of context used is a sentence. The data is prepared to the point of providing the node-pair context sets and also providing extracted features, such as dependency path information, on each of the contexts (sentences). So NYT-FB is immediately suitable for benchmarking the relation prediction subtask. However, the ease of use for relation prediction comes at the price of flexibility in benchmarking variations on EDL or CSC. The unit of context is fixed at a single sentence, and the EDL system is fixed as well, with no co-reference. The dataset can be combined with the rest of Freebase to benchmark approaches to combined relation prediction and reasoning.

There are a number of datasets from different TAC-KBP[1] competitions. TAC-KBP is organized by NIST and covers many parts of the knowledge base population task: EDL, CSC and relation prediction. All of these subtasks can be addressed with varied approaches to determine how they impact the final score. Unfortunately, a few serious practical issues limit its effectiveness. TAC-KBP is not an automatic evaluation. Many researchers have, regardless, used the pooled evaluation judgements from past TAC-KBP as a ground truth for an automatic evaluation. This is known to introduce a serious bias, favoring systems that were used to construct the pooled evaluation [4]. Furthermore, the TAC-KBP datasets are subject to considerable constraints. The data must be specifically requested and is not available under any form of open source license.

KBP Online[2] is working to adapt TAC-KBP data to an open evaluation and to accelerate the scoring based on pooled evaluation with crowd sourcing. But even with crowd sourcing, it is not a benchmark that can support dozens of rapid experiments. The task itself is also slightly different. In TAC-KBP slot filling, the fillers are not new or existing nodes, instead they are regarded simply as strings. Provenance - a justifying sentence - must be provided. This constraint naturally limits the types of approaches that can be applied. Information from multiple sentences can not be combined through reasoning.

FB15K-237 [12] is an extension of the FB15K dataset [3] with additional textual evidence gathered from ClueWeb12[3]. The provided textual evidence is the dependency parse path from one Freebase entity to another. The dataset has been used to combine textual relations with the structured relations when doing knowledge base completion.

Of the datasets we list, FB15K-237 has the most heavily processed text data. The textual mention files have lines with two entities connected by a lexicalized dependency path, along with a count of the number of times such a path connected the two entities. So it is very limited in what approaches can be explored even for relation prediction. Figure 6 shows an example of a lexicalized dependency path.

$X :\leftarrow nn : fact :\leftarrow pobj : in :\leftarrow prep : game :\leftarrow nsubj :' s : ccomp \rightarrow: pivot : nsubj \rightarrow: Y$

Fig. 6. Lexicalized dependency path from FB15K-237

---

[1] https://tac.nist.gov/.

[2] https://kbpo.stanford.edu/.

[3] http://lemurproject.org/clueweb12/FACC1/.

WikiReading [7] is also suitable for some kinds of knowledge base population research. In this dataset, the knowledge base of WikiData [13] is aligned with English Wikipedia[4]. The DBpedia URI for WikiData resources is mapped to its Wikipedia page, for those WikiData resources that have them. The task is to predict the slot fillers for the WikiData node using the text of the Wikipedia page. Unlike most other datasets, this dataset relies on what are sometimes called title-oriented-documents (TODs). A TOD is a document that describes a single node in a knowledge graph. TODs are not a very typical format for documents, although they are also not rare, Wikipedia is one example, but there are others as well such as Mayo Clinic[5] articles in the medical domain. The focus on TODs limits the EDL to finding nodes that are slot fillers. Like FB15K-237, the evaluation is at the knowledge base level so approaches to relation predictions based on implicit textual evidence, as well as or reasoning, can be evaluated. The data is distributed in a custom JSON format or TensorFlow data format.

A new dataset called T-REx[6] has also been created. This dataset aligns DBpedia triples with Wikipedia text. The EDL system employs DBpedia Spotlight [5] and co-reference. The CSC system is somewhat sophisticated, using paragraph and sentence boundaries. However, only cases where two entities occur together, when those two entities have a relation are annotated. So it is suitable for relation classification, but not relation prediction, since there are no unrelated node-pair contexts. Like our approach, T-REx supplies the code used to create the dataset, so variations are possible, but it is not designed as a modular benchmark where different components can be cleanly substituted.

Across several of these datasets we see a tradeoff between data that is immediately useable for at least one subtask and data that is flexible enough to allow for different approaches to many subtasks. By providing baseline - but replaceable - implementations for subtasks in the early pipeline, we can meet the goal of a dataset that is immediately useable while also flexible enough to explore the full scope of the KBP task. The tools allow for the creation of an immediately usable relation prediction dataset, but also allow for the creation of very different versions.

Dataset	Corpus	Relation Types	Node-Pair Contexts	Available
NYT-FB	1.8M sent.	56	157K	partially
TAC-KBP	90K sent.	41	122K	closed
FB15K-237	2.7M dep.-paths	237	2.7M	public
WikiReading	4.7M articles	884	N/A	public
T-REx	6.2M sent.	642	11M	public
CC-DBP	173M sent.	298	3M	public

Fig. 7. Dataset size comparison

---

[4] https://en.wikipedia.org.
[5] https://www.mayoclinic.org.
[6] https://hadyelsahar.github.io/t-rex/.

The size of the dataset, and the diversity of relations present are also important considerations. Figure 7 compares the size and availability of the different datasets to CC-DBP.

4   Dataset Creation

The CC-DBP[7] dataset creation process begins by filtering both Common Crawl and DBpedia to a useful subset. In the case of DBpedia, the useful subset is the set of triples that can be supported with textual evidence. The useful subset of Common Crawl is the text in the same language as the version of DBpedia used, in this case English. Baseline systems for EDL and CSC are also provided to enable the dataset to be immediately useable for relation prediction or combined relation prediction and reasoning. Figure 8 shows the pipeline to produce the base dataset as well as more processed forms.

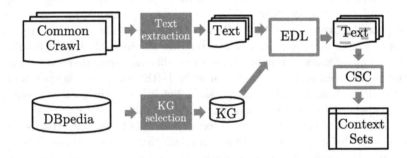

Fig. 8. CC-DBP construction

4.1   Common Crawl

Common Crawl[8] is a large, publicly available crawl of web pages. It is updated on a monthly basis to remain current and includes new seed URLs to expand the scope and size.

The dataset is available in Web ARChive (WARC) format, which stores the raw responses from the websites crawled. Although it is also available in WET format, providing the HTML stripped text, we use the WARC format so that we can apply Boilerpipe to discard the boilerplate text from web pages. In its raw form it contains over three billion web pages and hundreds of terabytes of content (uncompressed).

In order to find the English content text that will be used as textual evidence for training and benchmarking KBP systems we execute the following pipeline:

– Obtain the list of WARC paths from the Common Crawl website

---

[7] https://github.com/IBM/cc-dbp.
[8] http://commoncrawl.org.

- Download the WARC files hosted on Amazon S3
- Filter the WARC entries to text or HTML response pages
- Remove the boilerplate, such as navigation menus and headers, extracting only the main textual content
- Remove web pages not in the desired language, selected to match the version of DBpedia used

The initial steps are straightforward. Filtering the boilerplate and removing the HTML formatting to retain only the text content is more challenging. We use the open source library Boilerpipe [8], configured with the KeepEverything-WithMinKWordsExtractor filter. This removes any text-blocks that have fewer than k (configured as 5) words. By inspection, this was effective in selecting the main textual content. Filtering the web pages, now text documents, by language was accomplished through another open source library: the Optimaize language-detector library[9]. This library supports 71 languages and detects the language by comparing the profile of N-grams to a reference profile.

The result of this processing on the June 2017 crawl was 4.6 million documents with 173 million sentences and 1.5 billion words.

4.2 DBpedia

DBpedia [1] is a mature knowledge base built from the infoboxes of Wikipedia. It is publicly available under a Creative Commons Attribution-ShareAlike 3.0 License as well as the GNU Free Documentation License.

We first downloaded the main portions of the most recent DBpedia English knowledge base (http://wiki.dbpedia.org/downloads-2016-10 as of this writing). These files are the mappingbased_objects_en.ttl.bz2, mapping-based_literals_en.ttl.bz2, labels_en.ttl.bz2, and dbpedia_2016-04.owl. The "mappingbased" files are the higher quality (but lower quantity) versions of triples involving two DBpedia resources, or a DBpedia resource and a literal. We collapse the distinction between resources and literals, considering both simply as nodes. The labels file provides, for each resource, a term or terms that can be used to refer to it in text. The dbpedia_2016-04.owl file provides the type and relation taxonomy.

To avoid having relations that have very few positive examples in either train or test, we limit our focus to the relations with a large number of triples. The relations were further filtered with the goal of finding relations where both arguments could be matched in text. We examined the most frequent 400 relations. From these we exclude relations based on the following criteria:

- We exclude all relations that connect a resource to a textual label for that resource. These are important for EDL, but are out of scope for relation prediction. Examples of these relations are: foaf:name, dbo:synonym or dbo:birthName.

---

[9] https://github.com/optimaize/language-detector.

- We excluded a relation (dbo:filename) where the filler did not have a textual label, instead referencing the URL for a file.
- We removed relations where the filler was often a long phrase or free-form text. Examples include dbo:description, dbo:identificationSymbol and dbo:otherServingLines.
- Relations were filtered when they have numeric fillers that are unlikely to be found in text exactly, especially floating point numbers or values where multiple units of measure may apply. This was a substantial category, with relations such as dbo:militaryUnitSize, dbo:topSpeed, dbo:mouthElevation and dbo:numberSold.
- Relations with date slot fillers were converted to years or discarded if there was already another relation for the year value. This was done to avoid the complexity of date detection, normalization and matching.
- We also removed all mediator relations. These are relations that connect to a blank node, often used to represent n-ary relations. These included dbo:careerStation, where the "career station" is a blank node used to represent a time period in a person's career, as well as several others.

The result of applying these filters is 298 relations, not including super-relations from the DBpedia relation taxonomy.

To address some of the mostly spurious ambiguity in EDL, we collapse nodes with only a case difference (or no difference) in preferred labels into one, where the preferred label for a literal is the string representation of the literal.

4.3 Baseline EDL

For a baseline Entity Detection and Linking (EDL) system we build a gazetteer from the DBpedia resource labels, and for literals the string representations. In cases where the same label could link to multiple resources we connected to only the more popular resource. To measure popularity our baseline EDL simply counts the number of triples in which the node appears.

To avoid annotating the corpus with mentions of extremely generic nodes, we filter out labels that occur more than a threshold frequency (300000) unless they are multi-words or numbers. This removes mappings for low value nodes such as "dbl:had" and "dbl:he".

The resulting gazetteer is used in a simple string matching annotator, serving as the baseline EDL.

4.4 Baseline CSC

For the baseline Context Set Construction (CSC) we use a sentence as the unit of context. Sentence detection was performed by the open source OpenNLP library[10]. In addition, we excluded node-pairs from CSC based on a type filter. To enable simple type based filtering, we constructed a shallow, coarse grained type system of 35 types. The type filter ignores node-pairs where there is no triple in the training set that has the same (unordered) pair of types.

---

[10] https://opennlp.apache.org/.

5   Dataset Statistics

In this section we present some statistics on the relations and nodes present in the dataset.

Figure 9 shows the distribution of entity frequency in the corpus. The most common number of times for an entity to be mentioned is 1, with over 200,000 entities having this count. While there are about 1000 entities with over a million mentions. Both axes are log scale and each bar groups together entities whose frequency is closest to the indicated value. This can be seen as a probability mass function plot in log-log space, with the near-linear relationship indicating a typical Zipfian distribution.

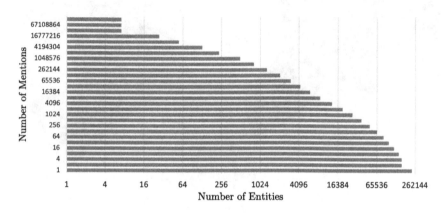

Fig. 9. Entity mention count distribution

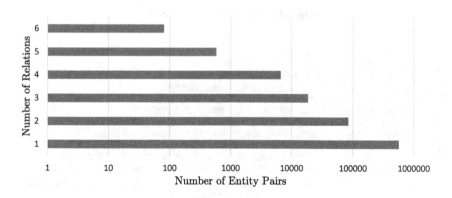

Fig. 10. Number of relations for an entity pair

Since a node-pair can be related by multiple relations, this is a multi-label task. Figure 10 shows how much the task is multi-label. Considering only leaf

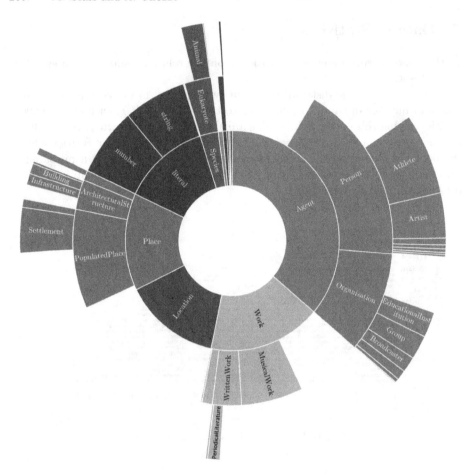

Fig. 11. Entity type distribution

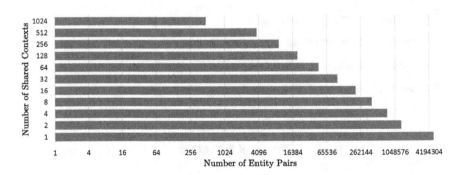

Fig. 12. Number of contexts for an entity pair

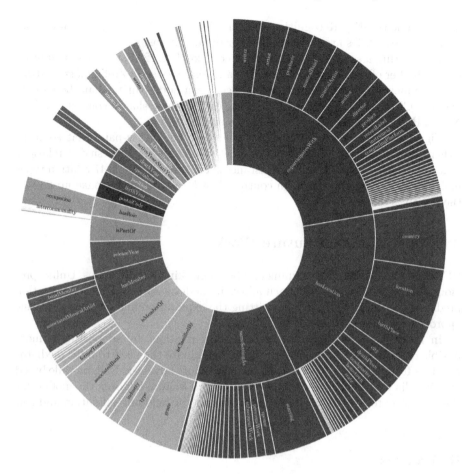

Fig. 13. Relation type distribution

relation types in the relation hierarchy, we see that the most frequent number of relations between a node-pair is one, with over five hundred thousand entity-pairs having a single relation type label. Fewer than one hundred node-pairs have six different labels. Highly related pairs are typically a person and a creative work, such as Peter Jackson and the movie *Bad Taste* related by: cinematography, director, editing, producer, starring, and writer. Figure 10 shows only the positive node-pairs. But by far the most common number of relation labels for a node-pair is zero. The negatives are typically downsampled when training relation prediction.

For the distinct entities mentioned in the corpus, Fig. 11 shows the distribution of different node types. Most of the nodes are entities of type person, place or organization with significant numbers of creative works, as well as string and number literals, and plants and animals. For comparison, the NYT-FB dataset uses a Named Entity Recognition (NER) system to locate mentions of entities so almost all entities are people, places or organizations.

Considering a sentence as the unit of context, Fig. 12 shows the distribution of the number of contexts for each node-pair. Again we see a Zipfian distribution, with the most frequent number of sentences for a node-pair to share being only one. For CC-DBP, 63% of node-pairs have only a single shared context, while in NYT-FB, 81% of entity-pairs have only a single context.

Figure 13 shows what relations hold between the entity-pairs that co-occur (when a relation does hold). Perhaps most striking is the diversity of relations that have a substantial fraction of instances. The most frequent 47 relation types make up 80% of the positives. In contrast just 5 relation types make up 83% of the positives for NYT-FB.

6   Conclusion and Future Work

CC-DBP[11] is a dataset for training and benchmarking KBP systems. Unlike previous efforts, its modular approach allows immediate application to the relation prediction subtask, while also permitting the exploration and evaluation of new approaches in the EDL and CSC subtasks.

In future work we hope to address n-ary relations by supporting a more flexible definition of a context set, this will eliminate the need to filter mediator relations from DBpedia. We also will include a more advanced EDL module based on DBpedia Spotlight [5] or Tagme [6]. This will require blinding the models for these systems to the subset of DBpedia used for the held-out validation and test data.

References

1. Auer, S., Bizer, C., Kobilarov, G., Lehmann, J., Cyganiak, R., Ives, Z.: DBpedia: a nucleus for a web of open data. In: Aberer, K., Choi, K.-S., Noy, N., Allemang, D., Lee, K.-I., Nixon, L., Golbeck, J., Mika, P., Maynard, D., Mizoguchi, R., Schreiber, G., Cudré-Mauroux, P. (eds.) ASWC/ISWC -2007. LNCS, vol. 4825, pp. 722–735. Springer, Heidelberg (2007). https://doi.org/10.1007/978-3-540-76298-0_52
2. Bollacker, K., Evans, C., Paritosh, P., Sturge, T., Taylor, J.: Freebase: a collaboratively created graph database for structuring human knowledge. In: Proceedings of the 2008 ACM SIGMOD International Conference on Management of data, pp. 1247–1250. ACM (2008)
3. Bordes, A., Usunier, N., Garcia-Duran, A., Weston, J., Yakhnenko, O.: Translating embeddings for modeling multi-relational data. In: Advances in Neural Information Processing Systems, pp. 2787–2795 (2013)
4. Chaganty, A., Paranjape, A., Liang, P., Manning, C.D.: Importance sampling for unbiased on-demand evaluation of knowledge base population. In: Proceedings of the 2017 Conference on Empirical Methods in Natural Language Processing, pp. 1049–1059 (2017)

---

[11] Available at: https://github.com/IBM/cc-dbp (Apache 2.0 License).

5. Daiber, J., Jakob, M., Hokamp, C., Mendes, P.N.: Improving efficiency and accuracy in multilingual entity extraction. In: Proceedings of the 9th International Conference on Semantic Systems (I-Semantics) (2013)
6. Ferragina, P., Scaiella, U.: Fast and accurate annotation of short texts with wikipedia pages. IEEE Softw. **29**(1), 70–75 (2012)
7. Hewlett, D., Lacoste, A., Jones, L., Polosukhin, I., Fandrianto, A., Han, J., Kelcey, M., Berthelot, D.: WikiReading: a novel large-scale language understanding task over Wikipedia. In: Proceedings of the Conference on Association for Computational Linguistics (2016)
8. Kohlschütter, C., Fankhauser, P., Nejdl, W.: Boilerplate detection using shallow text features. In: Proceedings of the Third ACM International Conference on Web Search and Data Mining, WSDM 2010, pp. 441–450. ACM, New York (2010). https://doi.org/10.1145/1718487.1718542
9. Mintz, M., Bills, S., Snow, R., Jurafsky, D.: Distant supervision for relation extraction without labeled data. In: Proceedings of the Joint Conference of the 47th Annual Meeting of the ACL and the 4th International Joint Conference on Natural Language Processing of the AFNLP: Volume 2 - Volume 2. ACL 2009, pp. 1003–1011. Association for Computational Linguistics, Stroudsburg (2009). http://dl.acm.org/citation.cfm?id=1690219.1690287
10. Riedel, S., Yao, L., McCallum, A.: Modeling relations and their mentions without labeled text. In: Machine learning and knowledge discovery in databases, pp. 148–163 (2010)
11. Sandhaus, E.: The new york times annotated corpus. Linguist. Data Consortium, Philadelphia **6**(12), e26752 (2008)
12. Toutanova, K., Chen, D., Pantel, P., Poon, H., Choudhury, P., Gamon, M.: Representing text for joint embedding of text and knowledge bases. EMNLP **15**, 1499–1509 (2015)
13. Vrandečić, D., Krötzsch, M.: Wikidata: a free collaborative knowledgebase. Commun. ACM **57**(10), 78–85 (2014)
14. Wang, W.Y., Cohen, W.W.: Learning first-order logic embeddings via matrix factorization. In: IJCAI, pp. 2132–2138 (2016)

EventKG: A Multilingual Event-Centric Temporal Knowledge Graph

Simon Gottschalk$^{(\boxtimes)}$ and Elena Demidova

L3S Research Center, Leibniz Universität Hannover, Hannover, Germany
{gottschalk,demidova}@L3S.de

Abstract. One of the key requirements to facilitate semantic analytics of information regarding contemporary and historical events on the Web, in the news and in social media is the availability of reference knowledge repositories containing comprehensive representations of events and temporal relations. Existing knowledge graphs, with popular examples including DBpedia, YAGO and Wikidata, focus mostly on entity-centric information and are insufficient in terms of their coverage and completeness with respect to events and temporal relations. EventKG presented in this paper is a multilingual event-centric temporal knowledge graph that addresses this gap. EventKG incorporates over 690 thousand contemporary and historical events and over 2.3 million temporal relations extracted from several large-scale knowledge graphs and semi-structured sources and makes them available through a canonical representation.

Resource type: Dataset
Permanent URL: http://eventkg.l3s.uni-hannover.de

1 Introduction

Motivation: The amount of event-centric information regarding contemporary and historical events of global importance, such as Brexit, the 2018 Winter Olympics and the Syrian Civil War, constantly grows on the Web, in the news sources and within social media. Efficiently accessing and analyzing large-scale event-centric and temporal information is crucial for a variety of real-world applications in the fields of Semantic Web, NLP and Digital Humanities. In Semantic Web and NLP, these applications include Question Answering [14] and timeline generation [1]. In Digital Humanities, multilingual event repositories can facilitate cross-cultural studies that aim to analyze language-specific and community-specific views on historical and contemporary events (examples of such studies can be seen in [11,18]). Furthermore, event-centric knowledge graphs can facilitate the reconstruction of histories as well as networks of people and organizations over time [19]. One of the pivotal pre-requisites to facilitate effective analytics of contemporary and historical events is the availability of knowledge repositories providing reference information regarding events, involved entities and their temporal relations (i.e. relations valid over a time period).

© Springer International Publishing AG, part of Springer Nature 2018
A. Gangemi et al. (Eds.): ESWC 2018, LNCS 10843, pp. 272–287, 2018.
https://doi.org/10.1007/978-3-319-93417-4_18

Limitations of the Existing Sources of Event-Centric and Temporal Information:
Currently, event representations and temporal relations are spread across heterogeneous sources. First, large-scale knowledge graphs (KGs) (i.e. graph-based
knowledge repositories [7] such as Wikidata [6], DBpedia [16], and YAGO [17])
typically focus on entity-centric knowledge. Event-centric information included
in these sources is often not clearly identified as such, can be incomplete and
is mostly restricted to named events and encyclopedic knowledge. For example,
as it will be discussed later in Sect. 5, of 322, 669 events included in EventKG,
only 18.70% are classified using the dbo:Event class in the English DBpedia.
Furthermore, event descriptions in the existing knowledge graphs often lack the
key properties such as times and locations. For example, only 33% of the events
in Wikidata provide temporal and 11.70% spatial information. Second, a variety of manually curated semi-structured sources (e.g. Wikipedia Current Events
Portal (WCEP) [22] and multilingual Wikipedia event lists) contain information on contemporary events. However, the lack of structured representations
of events and temporal relations in these sources hinders their direct use in
real-world applications through semantic technologies. Third, recently proposed
knowledge graphs containing contemporary events extracted from unstructured
news sources (such as [19]) are potentially highly noisy (e.g. [19] reports an
extraction accuracy of 0.55) and are not yet widely adopted. Finally, the sources
of event-centric information that can potentially be explored in future work are
Web markup [21] and event-centric Web crawls [8]. Overall, a comprehensive
integrated view on contemporary and historical events and their temporal relations usable for real-world applications is still missing. The provision of EventKG
will help to overcome these limitations.

EventKG and Advances to the State of the Art: EventKG presented in this
paper takes an important step to facilitate a global view on events and temporal relations currently spread across entity-centric knowledge graphs and manually curated semi-structured sources. EventKG extracts and integrates this
knowledge in an efficient light-weight fashion, enriches it with additional features, such as indications of relation strengths and event popularity, adds provenance information and makes all this information available through a canonical
representation. EventKG follows best practices in data publishing and reuses
existing data models and vocabularies (such as Simple Event Model [23] and
the DBpedia ontology) to facilitate its efficient reuse in real-world applications
through the application of semantic technologies and open standards (i.e. RDF
and SPARQL). EventKG currently includes data sources in five languages –
English (en), German (de), French (fr), Russian (ru) and Portuguese (pt) – and
is extensible. The main contributions of EventKG are as follows:

- A multilingual RDF knowledge graph incorporating over 690 thousand events
  and over 2.3 million temporal relations in V1.1 extracted from several large-
  scale entity-centric knowledge graphs (i.e. Wikidata, DBpedia in five language
  editions and YAGO), as well as WCEP and Wikipedia event lists in five languages. In the following, we refer to these sources used to populate EventKG
  as *the reference sources*. The key features of EventKG include:

- provision of event-centric information (including historical and contemporary events) and temporal relations using a canonical representation;
- light-weight integration and fusion of event representations and relations originating from heterogeneous reference sources;
- higher coverage and completeness of event representations compared to the individual reference sources (see Sect. 5);
- provision of interlinking information, to facilitate e.g. an assessment of relation strength and event popularity;
- provenance for all information contained in EventKG.
- An open source extraction framework to extract and maintain up-to-date versions of EventKG, extensible to further languages and reference sources.

Comparison to Other Existing Resources: To the best of our knowledge, currently there are no dedicated knowledge graphs aggregating event-centric information and temporal relations for historical and contemporary events directly comparable to EventKG. The heterogeneity of data models and vocabularies for event-centric and temporal information (e.g. [12,19,20,23]), the large scale of the existing knowledge graphs, in which events play only an insignificant role, and the lack of clear identification of event-centric information, makes it particularly challenging to identify, extract, fuse and efficiently analyze event-centric and temporal information and make it accessible to real-world applications in an intuitive and unified way. Through the light-weight integration and fusion of event-centric and temporal information from different sources, EventKG enables to increase coverage and completeness of this information. For example, EventKG increases the coverage of locations and dates for Wikidata events it contains by 14.43% and 17.82%, correspondingly (see Table 6 in Sect. 5 for more detail). Furthermore, existing sources lack structured information to judge event popularity and relation strength as provided by EventKG – the characteristic that gains the key relevance given the rapidly increasing amount of event-centric and temporal data on the Web and the information overload.

2   Relevance

Relevance to the Semantic Web Community and Society: Our society faces an unprecedented number of events that impact multiple communities across language and community borders. In this context, efficient access to, as well as effective disambiguation of, and analytics of event-centric multilingual information originating from different sources, as facilitated by EventKG, is of utmost importance for several scientific communities, including Semantic Web, NLP and Digital Humanities. In the context of the Semantic Web community, application areas of EventKG include event-centric Question Answering and ranking-based timeline generation that requires assessment of event popularity and relation strength. In Digital Humanities, EventKG as a multilingual event-centric repository can provide a unique source for cross-cultural and cross-lingual event-centric

Table 1. All sub-events of the World War II in EventKG that started between February 12 and February 28, 1941.

Start date	Sources	Description
Feb 12	Wikipedia event lists	Erwin Rommel arrives in Tripoli
Feb 17	YAGO, DBpedia	Battle of Trebeshina
Feb 25	YAGO, DBpedia	Operation Abstention
Feb 27	YAGO, DBpedia, Wikidata[†]	Action of 27 February 1941

[†]Wikidata misses the fact that this action is part of the World War II.

analytics (e.g. illustrated in [11,18]), while reducing barriers of data extraction, integration and fusion.

Relevance for Question Answering Applications: In the field of Question Answering (QA) [14], the current focus of research is on the generation of formal query expressions (e.g. in the SPARQL query language) from user queries posed in a natural language as well as interactive approaches for QA and semantic search [4,24]. Currently, research is mostly performed on questions that can be answered using popular entity-centric knowledge graphs such as DBpedia. With the provision of EventKG, it will become possible to train QA approaches for event-related questions, e.g. *"Which events related to Bill Clinton happened in Washington in 1980?"* and ranking-based questions, e.g. *"What are the most important events related to Syrian Civil War that took place in Aleppo?"*.

Relevance for Timeline Generation Applications: Timeline generation is an active research area [1], where the focus is to generate a timeline (i.e. a chronologically ordered selection) of events and temporal relations for entities from a knowledge graph. EventKG can facilitate the generation of detailed timelines containing complementary information originating from different sources, potentially resulting in more complete timelines and event representations. For example, Table 1 illustrates an excerpt from the timeline for the query *"What were the sub-events of the World War II between February 12 and February 28, 1941?"* generated using EventKG. The first event in the timeline in Table 1 ("Erwin Rommel arrives in Tripoli") extracted from an English Wikipedia event list ("1941 in Germany") is not contained in any of the reference knowledge graphs used to populate EventKG (Wikidata, DBpedia, and YAGO). The reference sources of the other three events include complementary information. For example, while the "Action of 27 February 1941" is assigned a start date in Wikidata, it is not connected to the World War II in that source.

Assessing Event Popularity and Relation Strength in Cross-Cultural Event-Centric Analytics: Event popularity and relation strength between events and entities vary across different cultural and linguistic contexts. For example, Table 2 presents the top-4 most popular events in the Russian vs. the English Wikipedia language editions as measured by how often these events are linked

Table 2. Most linked events in the English (en) and the Russian (ru) Wikipedia.

Rank	Event (en)	#Links (en)	Event (ru)	#Links (ru)
1	World War II	189,716	World War II	25,295
2	World War I	99,079	World War I	22,038
3	American Civil War	37,672	October Revolution	7,533
4	FA Cup	20,640	Russian Civil War	7,093

Table 3. Top-3 persons mentioned jointly with the World War II per language.

	fr	de	ru	pt
1	Adolf Hitler	Adolf Hitler	Adolf Hitler	Adolf Hitler
2	Charles de Gaulle	Winston Churchill	Franklin D. Roosevelt	Getúlio Vargas
3	Winston Churchill	Franklin D. Roosevelt	Joseph Stalin	Joseph Stalin

to in the respective Wikipedia edition. Whereas both Wikipedia language editions mention events of global importance, here the two World Wars, most frequently, other most popular events (e.g. "October Revolution" and "American Civil War") are language-specific. The relation strength between events and entities in specific language contexts can be induced by counting their joint mentions in Wikipedia. For example, Table 3 lists the persons most related to the World War II in different language editions. Information regarding event popularity and relation strength can enable the selection of the most relevant timeline entries given the layout constraints (e.g. EventKG contains 2, 816 sub-events of the World War II). An EventKG application to cross-lingual timeline generation is presented in [10]. EventKG-empowered interfaces can be used as a starting point to identify controversial events for more detailed analysis using tools such as MultiWiki [9].

Impact in Supporting the Adoption of Semantic Web Technologies: EventKG follows best practices in data publishing and relies on open data and W3C standards to make the data reusable for a variety of real-world applications. We believe that researchers using EventKG outside the Semantic Web community, e.g. in the fields of NLP and Digital Humanities, will profit from the adoption of the W3C standards such as RDF, SPARQL and re-use of established vocabularies, thus stimulating adoption of Semantic Web technologies, e.g. in the context of Information Extraction, media analytics and cross-cultural studies.

3   EventKG Data Model

The goal of the EventKG data model is to facilitate a light-weight integration and fusion of heterogeneous event representations and temporal relations extracted from the reference sources, and make this information available to real-world applications. The EventKG data model is driven by the following goals:

- Define the key properties of events through a canonical representation.
- Represent temporal relations between events and entities (including event-entity, entity-event and entity-entity relations).
- Include information quantifying and further describing these relations.
- Represent relations between events (e.g. in the context of event series).
- Support an efficient light-weight integration of event representations and temporal relations originating from heterogeneous sources.
- Provide provenance for the information included in EventKG.

EventKG Schema and the Simple Event Model: In EventKG, we build upon the Simple Event Model (SEM) [23] as a basis to model events. SEM is a flexible data model that provides a generic event-centric framework. Within the EvenKG schema (namespace eventKG-s[1]), we adopt additional properties and classes to adequately represent the information extracted from the reference sources, to model temporal relations and event relations as well as to provide provenance information. The schema of EventKG is presented in Fig. 1.

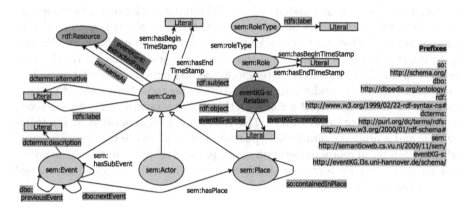

Fig. 1. The EventKG schema based on SEM. Arrows with an open head denote rdfs:subClassOf properties. Regular arrows visualize the rdfs:domain and rdfs:range restrictions on properties. Terms from other reused vocabularies are colored green. Classes and properties introduced in EventKG are colored orange. (Color figure online)

Events and Entities: SEM provides a generic event representation including topical, geographical and temporal dimensions of an event, as well as links to its actors (i.e. entities participating in the event). Such resources are identified within the namespace eventKG-r[2]. Thus, the key classes of SEM and of the

---

[1] http://eventkg.l3s.uni-hannover.de/schema/.
[2] http://eventkg.l3s.uni-hannover.de/resource/.

EventKG schema are **sem:Event** representing events, **sem:Place** representing locations and **sem:Actor** to represent entities participating in events. Each of these classes is a subclass of **sem:Core**, which is used to represent all entities in EventKG. (Note that entities in EventKG are not necessarily actors in the events; temporal relations between two entities are also possible). Events are connected to their locations through the **sem:hasPlace** property. A **sem:Core** instance can be assigned an existence time denoted via **sem:hasBeginTimeStamp** and **sem:hasEndTimeStamp**. In addition to the SEM representation, EventKG provides textual information regarding events and entities extracted from the reference sources including labels (**rdfs:label**), aliases (**dcterms:alternative**) and descriptions of events (**dcterms:description**).

Temporal relations are relations valid over a certain time period. In EventKG, they include event-entity, entity-event and entity-entity relations. Temporal relations between events and entities typically connect an event and its actors (as in SEM). A typical example of a temporal relation between two entities is a marriage. Temporal relations between entities can also indirectly capture information about events [19]. For example, the DBpedia property http://dbpedia.org/property/acquired can be used to represent an event of acquisition of one company by another. Temporal relations in SEM are limited to the situation where an actor plays a specific role in the context of an event. This yields two limitations: (i) there is no possibility to model temporal relations between events and entities where the entity acts as a subject. For example, it is not possible to directly model the fact that "Barack Obama" participated in the event "Second inauguration of Barack Obama", as the entity "Barack Obama" plays the subject role in this relation; and (ii) a temporal relation between two entities such as a marriage can not be modeled directly. To overcome these limitations, EventKG introduces the class **eventKG-s:Relation** that links two **sem:Core** instances (each representing an event or an entity). This relation can be annotated with a validity time and a property **sem:RoleType** that characterizes the relation. This way, arbitrary temporal relations between entity pairs or relations involving an entity and an event can be represented. Figure 2 visualizes the example mentioned above using the EventKG data model.

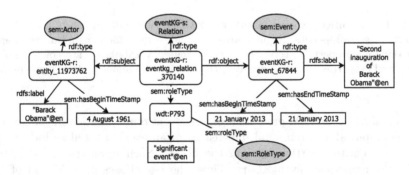

Fig. 2. Example of the event representing the participation of Barack Obama in his second inauguration as a US president in 2013 as modeled in EventKG.

Relations with Indirect Temporal Information: The temporal validity of a relation is not always explicitly provided, but can often be estimated based on the existence times of the participating entities or events. For example, the validity of a "mother" relation can be determined using the birth date of the child entity. Therefore, in addition to temporal relations with known validity times, EventKG also includes relations connected to events as well as relations connected to entities as long as the existence time of both entities is provided.

Other Event and Entity Relations: Relations between events (in particular sub-event, previous and next event relations) play an important role in the context of event series (e.g. "Summer Olympics"), seasons containing a number of related events (e.g. in sports), or events related to a certain topic (e.g. operations in a military conflict). Sub-event relations are modeled using the so:hasSubEvent property. To interlink events within an event series such as the sequence of Olympic Games, the properties dbo:previousEvent and dbo:nextEvent are used. A location hierarchy is provided through the property so:containedInPlace.

Towards Measuring Relation Strength and Event Popularity: Measuring relation strength between events and entities and event popularity enables answering question like *"Who was the most important participant of the event e ?"* or *"What are the most popular events related to e ?"*. We include two relevant factors in the EventKG schema:

1. *Links:* This factor represents how often the description of one entity refers to another entity. Intuitively, this factor can be used to estimate the popularity of the events and the strength of their relations. In EventKG the links factor is represented through the predicate eventKG-s:links in the domain of eventKG-s:Relation. eventKG-s:links denotes how often the Wikipedia article representing the relation subject links to the entity representing the object.

2. *Mentions:* eventKG-s:mentions represents the number of relation mentions in external sources. Intuitively, this factor can be used to estimate the relation strength. In EventKG, eventKG-s:mentions denotes the number of sentences in Wikipedia that mention both, the subject and the object of the relation.

Provenance Information: EventKG provides the following provenance information: (i) provenance of the individual resources; (ii) representation of the reference sources; and (iii) provenance of statements.

Provenance of the Individual Resources: EventKG resources typically directly correspond to the events and entities contained in the reference sources (e.g. an entity representing Barack Obama in EventKG corresponds to the DBpedia resource http://dbpedia.org/page/Barack_Obama). In this case, the owl:sameAs property is used to interlink both resources. EventKG resources can also be extracted from a resource collection. For example, philosophy events in 2007 can be extracted from the Wikipedia event list at https://en.wikipedia.org/wiki/2007_in_philosophy. In this case, the EventKG property

eventKG-s:extractedFrom is utilized to establish the link between the EventKG resource and the resource collection from which it was extracted. Through the provenance URIs, background knowledge contained in the reference sources can be accessed.

Representation of the Reference Sources: EventKG and each of the reference sources are represented through an instance of **void:Dataset**[3]. Such an instance in the namespace **eventKG-g**[4] includes specific properties of the source (e.g. its creation date).

Provenance Information of Statements: A statement in EventKG is represented as a quadruple, containing a triple and a URI of the named graph it belongs to. Through named graphs, EventKG offers an intuitive way to retrieve information extracted from the individual reference sources using SPARQL queries.

4   EventKG Generation Pipeline

The EventKG generation pipeline is shown in Fig. 3.

Fig. 3. EventKG generation pipeline.

Input: First, the dumps of the reference sources are collected.

Identification and Extraction of Events: Event instances are identified in the reference sources and extracted, as follows:

Step Ia: Identification and extraction of events.

- **Wikidata** [6]: We identify events as subclasses of Wikidata's "event" and "occurrence". The "occurrence" instances are added to increase recall. Some of the identified subclasses are blacklisted manually.
- **DBpedia** [16]: For each language edition, we identify DBpedia events as instances of **dbo:Event** or its subclasses.

---

[3] The VoID vocabulary https://www.w3.org/TR/void/.
[4] http://eventkg.l3s.uni-hannover.de/graph/.

- **YAGO** [17]: We do not use the YAGO ontology for event identification due to the noisy event subcategories (e.g. event > act > activity > protection > self-defense > martial_art). YAGO events are identified in Step Ib.
- **Wikipedia Event Lists:** For each language, we extract events from the Wikipedia event lists whose titles contain temporal expressions, such as "2007 in Science" and "August 11", using methods similar to [13].
- **WCEP**: In the Wikipedia Current Events Portal, events are represented through rather brief textual descriptions and refer to daily happenings. We extract WCEP events using the WikiTimes interface [22].

We manually evaluated a random sample of the events identified in this step in DBpedia and Wikidata including 100 events per KG and language edition, achieving precision of 98% on average.

Step Ib: Using Additional Event Identification Heuristics to Increase Recall: First, we propagate the information regarding the identified events across the reference sources using existing owl:sameAs links. Second, we use Wikipedia category names that match a manually defined language-dependent regular expression (e.g. English category names that end with "events") as an indication that a KG entry linked to such an article is an event. We manually evaluated this heuristic on a random sample of 100 events linked to the English and the Russian Wikipedia, respectively, achieving 94% and 88% precision.

In EventKG V1.1, we do not explicitly distinguish between single events such as "Solar eclipse of August 10, 1915", seasons with a number of related events such as "2008 Emperor's Cup" and event series like "Mario Marathon".

Extraction of Event and Entity Relations: We extract the following types of relations: (1) *Temporal relations* are identified based on the availability of temporal validity information. Temporal relations are extracted from YAGO and Wikidata, as DBpedia does not provide such information. (2) *Relations with indirect temporal information*: we extract all relations involving events as well as relations of entities with known existence time. (3) *Other event and entity relations*: we use a manually defined mapping table to identify predicates that represent event relations in EventKG such as so:hasSubEvent (e.g. we map Wikidata's part of property (P361) to so:hasSubEvent in cases where the property is used to connect events), dbo:previousEvent and dbo:nextEvent as well as so:containedInPlace to extract location hierarchies. We extract information that quantifies relation strength and event popularity based on the Wikipedia interlinking for each pair of interlinked entities containing at least one event. Entities are extracted only if they participate in an extracted relation.

Integration: The statements extracted from the reference sources are included in the named graphs, each named graph corresponding to a reference source. In addition, we create a named graph eventKG-g:event_kg. Each sem:Event and sem:Core instance in the eventKG-g:event_kg integrates event-centric and entity-centric information from the reference sources related to equivalent real-world instances. For the instances extracted from the KGs, known owl:sameAs links are used. Events extracted from the semi-structured sources are integrated using a rule-based approach based on descriptions, times and links.

Fusion: In the fusion step, we aggregate temporal, spatial and type information of eventKG-g:event_kg events using a rule-based approach. *Location fusion*: For each event in eventKG-g:event_kg, we take the union of its locations from the different reference sources and exploit the so:containedInPlace relations to reduce this set to the minimum (e.g. the set {Paris, France, Lyon} is reduced to {Paris, Lyon}). *Time fusion*: For each entity, event or relation with a known existence or a validity time stamp, the integration is done using the following rules: (i) ignore the dates at the beginning or end of a time unit (e.g. January, 1st), if alternative dates are available; (ii) apply a majority voting among the reference sources; (iii) take the time stamp from the trusted source (in order: Wikidata, DBpedia, Wikipedia, WCEP, YAGO).

Type fusion: We provide rdf:type information according to the DBpedia ontology (dbo), using types and owl:sameAs links in the reference sources.

Output: Finally, extracted instances and relations are represented in RDF according to the EventKG data model (see Sect. 3). As described above, the information extracted from each reference source and the results of the fusion step are provided in separate named graphs.

5   EventKG Characteristics

In EventKG V1.1, we extracted event representations and relations in five languages from the latest available versions of each reference source as of 12/2017. Table 4 summarizes selected statistics from the EventKG V1.1, released in 03/2018. Overall, this version provides information for over 690 thousand events and over 2.3 million temporal relations. Nearly half of the events (46.75%) originate from the existing KGs; the other half (53.25%) is extracted from semi-structured sources. The data quality in the individual named graphs directly corresponds to the quality of the reference sources. In eventKG-g:event_kg, the majority of the events (76.21%) possess a known start or end time. Locations are provided for 12.21% of the events. The coverage of locations can be further increased in the future work, e.g. using NLP techniques to extract locations from the event descriptions. Along with over 2.3 million temporal relations, EventKG V1.1 includes relations between events and entities for which the time is not available. This results in overall over 88 million relations. Approximately half of these relations possess interlinking information.

5.1   Comparison of EventKG to its Reference Sources

We compare EventKG to its reference sources in terms of the number of the identified events and completeness of their representation. The results of the event identification Step Ia are shown in Table 5. EventKG with 690, 247 events

Table 4. Number of events and relations in eventKG-g:event_kg.

	#Events	Known time	Known location
Events from KGs	322,669	163,977	84,304
Events from semi-structured sources	367,578	362,064	Not extracted
Relations	88,473,111	2,331,370	Not extracted

Table 5. Number of events extracted from the reference sources (Step Ia).

Wikidata	DBpedia					Wikipedia event lists					WCEP
	en	fr	de	ru	pt	en	fr	de	ru	pt	
266,198	60,307	43,495	9,383	5,730	14,641	131,774	110,879	21,191	44,025	18,792	61,382

contains a significantly higher number of events than any of its reference sources. This is especially due to the integration of KGs and semi-structured sources.

Table 6 presents a comparison of the event representations in EventKG and its reference knowledge graphs (Wikidata, YAGO, DBpedia). As we can observe, through the integration of event-centric information, EventKG: (1) enables better event identification (e.g. we can map $322,669$ events from EventKG to Wikidata, whereas only $266,198$ were identified as events in Wikidata initially - see Table 5), and (2) provides more complete event representations (i.e. EventKG provides a higher percentage of events with specified temporal and spatial information compared to Wikidata, that is the most complete reference sources). The most frequent event types are source-dependent (see Table 7).

5.2 Relation and Fusion Statistics

Over 2.3 million temporal relations are an essential part of EventKG. The majority of the frequent predicates in EventKG such as "member of sports team" (882,398 relations), "heritage designation" (221,472), "award received" (128,125), and "position held" (105,333) originate from Wikidata. The biggest fraction of YAGO's temporal relations have the predicate "plays for" (492,263), referring to football players. Other YAGO predicates such as "has won prize" are less frequent. Overall, about 93.62% of the temporal relations have a start time from 1900 to 2020. 81.75% of events extracted from KGs are covered by multiple sources. At the fusion step, we observed that 93.79% of the events that have a known start time agree on the start times across the different sources.

5.3 Textual Descriptions

EventKG V1.1 contains information in five languages. Overall, 87.65% of the events extracted from KGs provide an English label whereas only a small fraction (4.49%) provide labels in all languages. Among the 367,578 events extracted

Table 6. Comparison of the event representation completeness in the source-specific named graphs (after the Step Ib).

	EventKG	Wikidata	YAGO	DBpedia				
				en	fr	de	ru	pt
#Events with	322,669	322,669	222,325	214,556	78,527	62,971	47,304	35,682
Location (L)	26.13%	11.70%	26.61%	6.21%	8.32%	4.03%	10.60%	6.15%
Time (T)	50.82%	33.00%	39.02%	7.00%	17.21%	2.00%	1.35%	0.08%
L&T	21.97%	8.83%	19.02 %	4.29%	0.00%	4.84%	1.18%	0.08%

Table 7. The most frequent event types extracted from the references sources and the percentage of the events in that source with the respective type.

	Wikidata	DBpedia				
		en	fr	de	ru	pt
dbo:type	Season	Military conflict	Sports event	Tennis tournament	Military conflict	Soccer tournament
Events, %	11.37%	6.31%	21.86%	33.00%	11.87%	16.17%

from the semi-structured sources, just 115 provide a description in all five languages, e.g. the first launch of a Space Shuttle in 1981. This indicates potential for further enrichment of multilingual event descriptions in future work.

6   Reusability Aspects

In order to facilitate an efficient reuse of EventKG, we provide the resource for download, as well as through a SPARQL endpoint. The homepage of EventKG provides a comprehensive documentation of the resource including example queries. A schema diagram of EventKG is presented in Fig. 1. EventKG is modeled in RDF and is highly extensible. For example, it is possible to include further languages and customize the selection of the reference data sources. Recent studies indicate that interlinking is an important factor of dataset reuse [5]. To this extent, EventKG provides substantial interlinking with its reference sources.

At the moment, the intended use of EventKG includes collaboration with EU-projects such as ALEXANDRIA (for enrichment of Web Archives with event-centric data)[5], and WDAqua ITN[6], in the context of innovative event-centric Question Answering applications. We believe that due to its unique nature and general applicability, EventKG will be widely reused by third parties in a number of communities in the future, as also discussed in Sect. 2.

---

[5] http://alexandria-project.eu/.

[6] WDAqua (Answering Questions using Web Data) http://wdaqua.eu/.

EventKG follows best practices in data publishing. It uses RDF W3C standard to model and interlink the data it contains. EventKG adopts the open data and open source approach to make it available to a wide audience and facilitates data and software reuse. EventKG supports multilinguality of the data, provides dereferencable URIs and implements a persistent strategy to maintain its URIs across the versions, ensuring that the same URIs are consistently reused for the same real-world objects.

EventKG reuses and extends an established event model, which is SEM [23] to describe event-related information it includes, and reuses existing vocabularies (e.g. DBpedia ontology, Dublin Core). The EventKG metadata is provided using the VoID[7] vocabulary. EventKG follows FAIR principles[8] to make it findable, accessible, interoperable and reusable. The EventKG description is available in human and machine readable formats at the EventKG homepage.

7   Availability and Sustainability

Availability Aspects: EventKG uses open standards and is publicly available under a persistent URI[9] under the CC BY 4.0 license[10]. The EventKG homepage[11] provides information on citing the resource. Our extraction pipeline is available as open source software on GitHub[12] under the MIT License[13].

Sustainability Plan: The sustainability of EventKG is ensured though three building blocks: (1) *Open source architecture and software*: The software developed for the creation of EventKG is available as open source and can be re-used by the community to extract a new version of the knowledge graph, or extend the resource to include more reference sources, languages, or event properties. (2) *Integration of existing publicly available data*: The reference sources that serve as a basis for the data within the EventKG are publicly available and many of them are maintained by the community, so that it is possible to maintain a fresh version of the resource, in particular to include new events. (3) *Maintenance of EventKG*: The authors plan to perform regular EventKG updates. The URIs of EventKG resources will be maintained and remain stable across versions.

8   Related Work

Data Models and Vocabularies for Events: Several data models and the corresponding vocabularies (e.g. [12,19,20,23]) provide means to model events. For example, the ECKG model proposed by Rospocher et al. [19] enables fine-grained

---

[7] https://www.w3.org/TR/void/.
[8] https://www.force11.org/group/fairgroup/fairprinciples.
[9] https://doi.org/10.5281/zenodo.1112283.
[10] https://creativecommons.org/licenses/by/4.0/.
[11] http://eventKG.l3s.uni-hannover.de.
[12] https://github.com/sgottsch/eventkg.
[13] https://opensource.org/licenses/MIT.

textual annotations to model events extracted from news collections. The Simple Event Model (SEM) [23], schema.org [12] and the Linking Open Descriptions of Events (LODE) ontology [20] provide means to describe events and interlink them with actors, times and places. In EventKG, we build upon SEM and extend this model to represent a wider range of temporal relations and to provide additional information regarding events.

Extracting Event-Centric Information: Most approaches for automatic knowledge graph construction and integration focus on entities and related facts rather than events. Examples include DBpedia [16], Freebase [2], YAGO [17] and YAGO+F [3]. In contrast, EventKG is focused on events and temporal relations. In [22], the authors extract event information from WCEP. EventKG builds upon this work to include WCEP events.

Extraction of Events and Facts from News: Recently, the problem of building knowledge graphs directly from plain text news [19], and extraction of named events from news [15] have been addressed. These approaches apply Open Information Extraction methods and develop them further to address specific challenges in the event extraction in the news domain. State-of-the-art works that automatically extract events from news potentially obtain noisy and unreliable results (e.g. the state-of-the-art extraction approach in [19] reports an accuracy of only 0.551). In contrast, contemporary events included in EventKG originate from manually curated sources such as WCEP and Wikipedia event lists.

9   Conclusion

In this paper we presented EventKG – a multilingual knowledge graph that integrates and harmonizes event-centric and temporal information regarding historical and contemporary events. EventKG V1.1 includes over 690 thousand event resources and over 2.3 million temporal relations. Unique features of EventKG include light-weight integration and fusion of structured and semi-structured multilingual event representations and temporal relations in a single knowledge graph, as well as the provision of information to facilitate assessment of relation strength and event popularity, while providing provenance. The light-weight integration enables to significantly increase the coverage and completeness of the included event representations, in particular with respect to times and locations.

Acknowledgements. This work was partially funded by the ERC ("ALEXANDRIA", 339233) and BMBF ("Data4UrbanMobility", 02K15A040).

References

1. Althoff, T., Dong, X.L., Murphy, K., Alai, S., Dang, V., Zhang, W.: TimeMachine: timeline generation for knowledge-base entities. In: Proceedings of SIGKDD 2015 (2015)
2. Bollacker, K., et al.: Freebase: a collaboratively created graph database for structuring human knowledge. In: Proceedings of SIGMOD 2008, pp. 1247–1250 (2008)

3. Demidova, E., Oelze, I., Nejdl, W.: Aligning freebase with the YAGO ontology. In: Proceedings of CIKM 2013, pp. 579–588. ACM (2013)
4. Demidova, E., Zhou, X., Nejdl, W.: Efficient query construction for large scale data. In: Proceedings of SIGIR 2013, pp. 573–582 (2013)
5. Endris, K.M., Giménez-García, J.M., Thakkar, H., Demidova, E., Zimmermann, A., Lange, C., Simperl, E.: Dataset reuse: an analysis of references in community discussions, publications and data. In: Proceedings of the K-CAP 2017, pp. 5:1–5:4 (2017)
6. Erxleben, F., Günther, M., Krötzsch, M., Mendez, J., Vrandečić, D.: Introducing Wikidata to the linked data web. In: Mika, P., et al. (eds.) ISWC 2014. LNCS, vol. 8796, pp. 50–65. Springer, Cham (2014). https://doi.org/10.1007/978-3-319-11964-9_4
7. Färber, M., Bartscherer, F., Menne, C., Rettinger, A.: Linked data quality of DBpedia, Freebase, OpenCyc, Wikidata, and YAGO. Semant. Web 1–53 (2016)
8. Gossen, G., Demidova, E., Risse, T.: iCrawl: improving the freshness of web collections by integrating social web and focused web crawling. In: JCDL 2015 (2015)
9. Gottschalk, S., Demidova, E.: MultiWiki: interlingual text passage alignment in Wikipedia. TWEB 11(1), 6:1–6:30 (2017)
10. Gottschalk, S., Demidova, E.: EventKG+TL: creating cross-lingual timelines from an event-centric knowledge graph (2018, inpress)
11. Gottschalk, S., Demidova, E., Bernacchi, V., Rogers, R.: Ongoing events in Wikipedia: a cross-lingual case study. In: Proceedings of WebSci 2017, pp. 387–388 (2017)
12. Guha, R.: Introducing schema.org: Search engines come together for a richer web. Google Official Blog (2011)
13. Hienert, D., Wegener, D., Paulheim, H.: Automatic classification and relationship extraction for multi-lingual and multi-granular events from Wikipedia. In: Proceedings of DeRiVE 2012 (2012)
14. Höffner, K., et al.: Survey on challenges of question answering in the semantic web. Semant. Web 8(6), 895–920 (2017)
15. Kuzey, E., Vreeken, J., Weikum, G.: A fresh look on knowledge bases: distilling named events from news. In: Proceedings of CIKM 2014, pp. 1689–1698 (2014)
16. Lehmann, J., et al.: DBpedia - a large-scale, multilingual knowledge base extracted from Wikipedia. Semant. Web J. 6(2), 167–195 (2015)
17. Mahdisoltani, F., Biega, J., Suchanek, F.: YAGO3: a knowledge base from multilingual Wikipedias. In: Proceedings of CIDR 2014 (2014)
18. Rogers, R.: Digital Methods. MIT Press, Cambridge (2013)
19. Rospocher, M., et al.: Building event-centric knowledge graphs from news. Web Semant. 37, 132–151 (2016)
20. Shaw, R., Troncy, R., Hardman, L.: LODE: linking open descriptions of events. In: Gómez-Pérez, A., Yu, Y., Ding, Y. (eds.) ASWC 2009. LNCS, vol. 5926, pp. 153–167. Springer, Heidelberg (2009). https://doi.org/10.1007/978-3-642-10871-6_11
21. Tempelmeier, N., Demidova, E., Dietze, S.: Inferring missing categorical information in noisy and sparse web markup. In: Proceedings of WWW 2018 (2018)
22. Tran, G.B., Alrifai, M.: Indexing and analyzing Wikipedia's current events portal, the daily news summaries by the crowd. In: Proceedings of WWW 2014 (2014)
23. Van Hage, W.R., Malaisé, V., Segers, R., Hollink, L., Schreiber, G.: Design and use of the simple event model (SEM). Web Semant. 9(2), 128–136 (2011)
24. Zheng, W., Cheng, H., Zou, L., Yu, J.X., Zhao, K.: Natural language question/answering: let users talk with the knowledge graph. In: CIKM 2017 (2017)

Semantic Concept Discovery
over Event Databases

Oktie Hassanzadeh[(✉)] ⓘ, Shari Trewin ⓘ, and Alfio Gliozzo ⓘ

IBM Research, Yorktown Heights, NY, USA
hassanzadeh@us.ibm.com

Abstract. In this paper, we study the problem of identifying certain types of concept (e.g., persons, organizations, topics) for a given analysis question with the goal of assisting a human analyst in writing a deep analysis report. We consider a case where we have a large event database describing events and their associated news articles along with meta-data describing various event attributes such as people and organizations involved and the topic of the event. We describe the use of semantic technologies in question understanding and deep analysis of the event database, and show a detailed evaluation of our proposed concept discovery techniques using reports from Human Rights Watch organization and other sources. Our study finds that combining our neural network based semantic term embeddings over structured data with an index-based method can significantly outperform either method alone.

1 Introduction

Analysts are often tasked with preparing a comprehensive, accurate, and unbiased report on a given topic. The first step in preparing such a report is a daunting discovery task that requires researching through a massive amount of information. Information sources can have large volume, variety, varying veracity, and velocity - the common characteristics of the so-called Big Data sources. Many times the analysis requires a deep understanding of various kinds of historical and ongoing *events* that are reported in the media. To enable better analysis of events, there exist several *event databases* containing structured representations of events extracted from news articles. Examples include GDELT [17], ICEWS [11], and EventRegistry [16]. These event databases have been successfully used to perform various kinds of analysis tasks, e.g., forecasting societal events [22]. However, there has been little work on the discovery aspect of the analysis, that results in a gap between the information requirements and the available data, and potentially a biased view of the available information.

In this paper, we present a framework for concept discovery over event databases using semantic technologies. Unlike existing concept discovery solutions that perform discovery over text documents and in isolation from the remaining data analysis tasks [18,28], our goal is providing a unified solution that allows deep understanding of the same data that will be used to perform

ⓒ Springer International Publishing AG, part of Springer Nature 2018
A. Gangemi et al. (Eds.): ESWC 2018, LNCS 10843, pp. 288–303, 2018.
https://doi.org/10.1007/978-3-319-93417-4_19

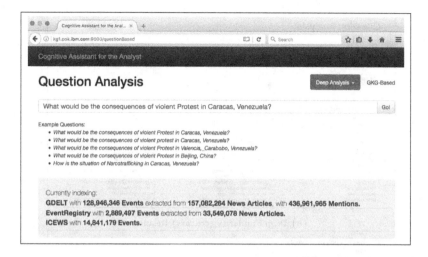

Fig. 1. Question analysis UI - main page

other analysis tasks (e.g., hypothesis generation [27], scenario planning [26], or building models for forecasting [15,22]). Figures 1 and 2 show different views of our system's UI that is built using our concept discovery framework APIs. The analyst can enter a natural language question or a set of concepts, and retrieve collections of relevant concepts identified and ranked using different discovery algorithms described in Sect. 3. Using this system provides a new starting point for an analyst's work. Instead of performing complex search queries and examining pages of results, the analyst reviews the related concepts, exploring what connects them to the analytical question. Unexpected concepts broaden the scope of their thinking, helping to overcome confirmation bias. A key aspect of our framework is the use of semantic technologies. In particular:

- A unified view over multiple event databases and a background RDF knowledge base is achieved through semantic link discovery and annotation.
- Natural language or keyword query understanding is performed through mapping of input terms to the concepts in the background knowledge base.
- Concept discovery and ranking is performed through neural network based semantic term embeddings.

In what follows, we first describe the overall framework and its various components. We then describe the algorithms used for concept discovery and ranking. In Sect. 4, we present the methodology and results of our evaluation using a ground truth built from a large corpus of reports written by human experts.

2   Concept Discovery Framework

Figure 3 shows the architecture of our system. The system takes in as input a set of event databases and RDF knowledge bases and provides as output a set of

(a) Deep Similarity (context) Results

(b) Index-Based (co-occur) Results

Fig. 2. Question analysis UI - concept discovery results

APIs that provide a unified retrieval mechanism over input data and knowledge bases, and an interface to a number of concept discovery algorithms. In what follows, we describe the input sources and each of the components in detail.

2.1 Event Data and Knowledge Sources

Event databases are structured records describing various kinds of societal, political, or economic events. While event extraction from text is a well-studied topic in the NLP literature [12,14] with a dedicated track at the annual Text Analysis Conference (TAC) [6], there are only a few publicly available large-scale event databases. The input of these event databases is a large corpus of news articles that are either gathered from various news sources (e.g., news agencies and other proprietary sources) or crawled from the Web. The output is structured records (i.e., relational data tables) describing various features of the identified events.

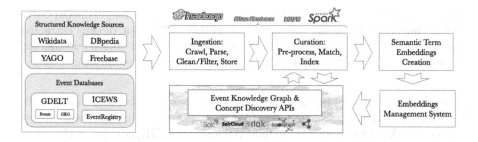

Fig. 3. System architecture

GDELT. The Global Data on Events, Location, and Tone (GDELT) project [17] claims to be "the largest, most comprehensive, and highest resolution open database of human society ever created". GDELT data contains three databases. GDELT Event database provides *coded* event data based on a popular scheme using the CAMEO (Conflict And Mediation Event Observations) coding framework [24] to code actors and actions. GDELT includes other features of the events such as the date of the event, information about the source articles, numerical scores reflecting the "tone" of the source articles and other similar features, and geographical coordinates. The second database provided by GDELT is the Global Knowledge Graph (GKG) and contains records describing the source articles of the events. Each record provides a comprehensive set of numerical features for the article, in addition to annotations with several dictionaries of persons, organizations, and "themes". The third database GDELT provides is the Mentions database which connects event records with GKG article records. The most recent version of GDELT data is updated daily and includes historical data since February 2015. At the time of this writing, we have ingested 128,946,346 Event records, 157,082,264 GKG records, and 436,961,965 Mention records.

ICEWS. Integrated Conflict Early Warning System [11,30] provides a coded event database similar to the GDELT Event database. ICEWS event records describe features of source and target actors including their name, "sector", and country, features of the action including date, source, a short text description, and geographical descriptions. A recent version of the data also includes CAMEO codes for actions. We have ingested the most recent publicly available data that has a coverage of historical events from 1995 to 2015, with 14,757,915 records.

EventRegistry. The EventRegistry [16] project takes a completely different approach than the coded event databases, and performs event extraction based on a clustering of news articles and event mentions. EventRegistry records contain a multilingual title and summary text, the number of articles reporting the event, the event date (when the event has happened or will happen and not the report date as in coded event databases), and a set of concepts along with the concept type (e.g. location, person, or "topic") and its Wikipedia URL. At the time of this writing, we have ingested 2,889,497 event records extracted from 33,549,078 news articles from the past two years, with 98,435,900 concept annotations, 42,006,079 similarity links, 772,553 location annotations.

Knowledge Sources. In addition to event data, our system also ingests publicly available RDF knowledge bases to use as a source of reference knowledge. Our current knowledge sources include Wikidata [29], DBpedia [8], YAGO [23], and Freebase [9]. At the time of this writing, we have ingested over 6.3 billion RDF triples, containing over 488 million entities (unique URIs) and over 83 million English label statements.

2.2 Ingestion

As shown in Fig. 3, we have a common ingestion pipeline for both the event databases and knowledge sources that is capable of crawling remote sources, parsing structured relational, semi-strcutured (JSON), and RDF (NTriples) data, cleaning invalid records or statements and applying basic filters (e.g., removing non-English labels), and finally storing the data. Our platform is implemented on top of Apache Hadoop and Spark, enabling efficient data processing on a cluster on public or private cloud.

2.3 Curation

We adopt a pay-as-you-go integration approach [13,19] and perform only a minimal curation by a lightweight mapping of known entities, linking them using a common URI when possible. To integrate the knowledge sources we use the existing Wikipedia URLs. We then index all the facts (RDF triples) in a key-value store (powered by Riak [4]) in addition to a document store (powered by SolrCloud [5]) that makes it possible to perform highly efficient fact-based or label-based lookups. We also create an auxiliary unified index of common entities using our mapping strategy that results in a collection of 16,108,676 entities with Wikipedia URLs, each linked with one or more of their Wikidata, DBpedia, YAGO, and Freebase URIs. All the event databases are indexed in a similar way in our key-value and document stores, with labels matched and linked with a Wikipedia URL when possible.

2.4 Semantic Embeddings Engine

Inspired by the idea of word embeddings in NLP [21], recent work has proposed the use of shallow neural networks to map values in structured tables to vectors (referred to as embeddings) [10]. This enables powerful semantic similarity queries even without a prior knowledge of the database schema and contents. We adopt a similar strategy and transform every value in the input event databases into an embeddings vector using a variation of the *continuous skip-gram model* of the original *word2vec* [7,20,21]. The first step in this process is a *virtual document* creation process in MapReduce, turning each row in the input database into a context in a corpus of text. We then feed the text corpus into a word2vec model construction modified to take into account the different characteristics of structured data:

- The order of columns in structured databases is of little importance. While distance between two words in a text document makes them farther in terms of context, the first column in a database table is as relevant to the second column as to the last column.
- In text documents, typically a random-sized window of words is selected. The length of each database record is fixed and so there is no need for a random window size.
- Most importantly, while all words in a text corpus are treated in the same way and do not have specific roles, values in different columns in structured sources describe different (event) features and may need to be grouped and queried differently. There is often a need to search over (or query using) the terms from specific attributes (columns).

Once attribute values are mapped into low-dimensional vectors, aggregate vectors can represent individual records (articles or events), and similarity queries over the vectors can be used for concept discovery and analysis as described in Sect. 3. These vectors represent the semantic context of every single value seen in the input data, enabling a powerful and extremely efficient method of performing similarity analysis over large amounts of data. As an example, the corpus size (number of words in the "virtual documents") for GDELT GKG is 23,901,358,498 while the size of the vocabulary (number of unique words) in our embeddings is 2,829,213. Still, a key requirement is efficient similarity queries over the vectors with milliseconds running time to enable real-time analysis queries through our UI (Figs. 1 and 2) as some analysis queries require several similarity queries each over millions of vectors. We achieve this using the efficient Annoy library [1] as the core of our embeddings management system.

2.5 Event Knowledge Graph and Concept Discovery APIs

The final outcome of all the components is a set of APIs to perform knowledge graph and concept discovery queries. In particular:

- **Lookup APIs.** These APIs provide access to the ingested and curated event data and knowledge. For example, one can perform search over knowledge base entity labels and subsequently retrieve human-readable facts as JSON objects. Using this API the user can retrieve infobox-style information about each of the concepts shown under the "Global Context" box in Fig. 2a. These APIs also enable queries across event databases, e.g., retrieve ICEWS, GDELT, and EventRegistry events in a given time range that is annotated with a particular concept.

- **Natural Language and Keyword Query Understanding APIs.** These APIs turn the user query into a set of knowledge base concepts and event database terms. In Fig. 2a, the concepts shown under the "Global Context" are extracted using the API that outputs knowledge base concepts, whereas the terms shown under "DeepSim Context" are terms found in GDELT GKG data used for the shown concept discovery results.
- **Concept Discovery and Ranking APIs.** These APIs take a set of concepts or terms and return as output a ranked list of concepts of different types (e.g., Persons, Organizations, Themes). Details of the concept ranking algorithms are described in the following section.

3   Concept Ranking Algorithms

In this section, we describe three classes of algorithms for concept discovery and ranking. These algorithms *identify* and *rank* a set of most relevant concepts of various types (e.g., persons or organizations) for a given set of concepts. An example use of these rankings is shown in Fig. 2 where sorted lists of ranked concepts relevant to the user's analysis question are shown. The end goal is providing the output either directly to an analyst or to other components of an analysis system. We first describe the algorithms, followed by an evaluation of their effectiveness in identifying relevant concepts.

3.1   Index-Based Method (`co-occur`)

The `co-occur` method relies on an efficient index to measure the level of co-occurrence of concepts in a collection of events and uses this as a measure of relevance. Using the index described in Sect. 2.3, we can search for (all or recent) event records annotated with a given set of concepts. By counting the concept annotations for every record in the output, a list of most frequently co-occurring concepts of various types is returned along with the percentage of co-occurrence of the annotations among all the retrieved event records. Figure 2b shows an example of ranked "Topic", "Key Player" (Person), and "Location" concepts over EventRegistry event records. The concepts extracted from the input question are "Caracas", "Protest", and "Venezuela". Obviously, these concepts themselves are on top of the lists as they appear in 100% of the event records containing them. The topic concept "Government" appears in 87% of the events and "Nicolás Maduro" appears in 69% of the events, indicating that these concepts are highly relevant to the input concepts in recent events.

3.2   Deep Similarity Method Using Semantic Embeddings (`context`)

The `context` method relies on the term embeddings built over an event database as described in Sect. 2.4. First, a vector is retrieved for each of the terms extracted from the input question (where there exists a vector representation in the embeddings space), and an average vector is constructed by summing the values in each dimension and normalizing the resulting vector. Using the embeddings management system, the most similar vectors of various kinds of terms are retrieved, ranked by their similarity to the average vector. Figure 2a shows an example of concept rankings with the same question. The API used in the following evaluation queries embeddings built over 157 million GDELT GKG records, with vectors of size 200 and cosine similarity as our choice of vector similarity measure. These rankings result in less-obvious and harder-to-explain but deeply relevant sets of concepts in the output.

3.3   Combination Methods

We implement two combination methods. In the co-occur_context method, we retrieve a set of 3*k results of an index-based method, re-rank the output using the embeddings-based similarity of the terms in the output, then select the top k terms. In the context_co-occur method, we retrieve 3*k results of the context retrieval and sort the output based on their position in the co-occur results before selecting the top k terms. In the following section in Table 1, we show an example of how these re-rankings improve the results.

4   Experiments

To evaluate the performance of the concept ranking algorithms, we use queries represented as sets of query terms that would be extracted from an analyst's question. We sought to identify a 'ground truth' of concepts related to each query, where a concept is a person or organization directly involved with the topic of the query.

As mentioned in Sect. 2, our framework enables real-time or near real-time response time for each of the algorithms and so we do not compare running times.

4.1   Evaluation Data

To our knowledge, there is no existing public data set that identifies key people and organizations for a set of analytical questions. To provide an objective basis for our evaluation, we used reports that summarize a political or social event or situation, making the assumption that these reports are a response to such a question, and will mention the most important key players. We did not use news articles because these are the source of GDELT events, so as not to bias the results. We identified three potential sources of reports:

- Declassified US Government intelligence reports. We were only able to identify one such report that relates to the time period covered by the GDELT GKG event database: 'Assessing Russian Activities and Intentions in Recent US Elections', released in January 2017.

- Wikipedia pages describing a newsworthy event or topic with relevance to social unrest. For example 'Impeachment of Dilma Rousseff' or 'Shortages in Venezuela'.
- Human Rights Watch reports. These are detailed descriptions of specific human rights situations around the world, for example 'Philippine Police Killings in Duterte's "War on Drugs"'. 1,091 such reports are available in HTML.

Using these sources we developed test queries consisting of a small set of query terms and 'ground truth' sets of people and organizations. The query terms can include a country, people, organizations, and themes (drawn from the GDELT GKG themes described earlier). The 'ground truth' items are selected from the people and organizations mentioned in the report, to represent the ideal response of the system to the query. Three query sets were developed: *Manual*, *Curated*, and *Auto*.

Manual. A small set of 12 hand-built queries derived from 6 Wikipedia pages, 5 Human Rights Watch Reports from 2014 or later; and 1 declassified intelligence report. All queries specified the country most strongly associated with the report, and 1–3 manually selected themes from GDELT GKG, in addition to any people or organizations mentioned in the report title. For example, the query terms for the Wikipedia page 'Impeachment of Dilma Rousseff' consisted of the country 'Brazil', the person 'Dilma Rousseff', and the theme 'IMPEACHMENT'.

The ground truth concepts were the people and organizations mentioned in each report as key players for the topic. We removed concepts that were found in the report but not in our embedding. Subsequently, each query had an average of 10 ground truth people and 7 ground truth organizations.

Curated. A set of 25 queries based on Wikipedia pages describing events from 2014–2016, where the query terms (country, people, organizations and themes) were selected manually, but the ground truth terms were automatically generated from the Wikipedia links within the page, and then curated to remove non-person and non-organization terms. Some people and organizations mentioned in the original report may be missed in this process.

Auto. A larger set of 179 queries derived from the Human Rights Watch reports, with fully automatic generation of both query terms and ground truth. To generate the query terms, the query builder used the document title, subtitle and teaser - a short paragraph of a few sentences describing the report. It used concept extraction software that combines output from ClearNLP [3] and OpenNLP [2] to identify noun phrases referring to named entities, and assigns types to them according to their linguistic context. We relied on these types to identify countries, people and organizations in the text. The ground truth people and organizations were generated by using the same concept extraction software, applied to the full text of the report. We removed people and organizations not found in our embedding. Finally, we selected the 179 queries that had a country, at least one other query term (person, organization or theme), and had ground truth terms that were not already present in the query. Of these, the majority (102) were queries consisting of a country and the single organization 'Human Rights Watch'. 26 contained a person, and 51 contained an organization other than Human Rights Watch. From these, we further selected only the usable queries with ground truth items that were not in the query (143 for people and 155 for organizations) These queries had, on average, 21 ground truth people and 32 ground truth organizations.

4.2   Example Results

Table 1 shows the set of ground truth people and the output of the algorithms for a query from the manual test set, based on the 2016 Human Rights Watch report "Venezuela's Humanitarian Crisis. Severe Medical and Food Shortages, Inadequate and Repressive Government Response"[1].

Of the 14 most relevant people identified in the report, only 7 were present in the embedding (indicated in column 1 with (*)). Two of the others were not found in the GKG data at all, and the remaining five were mentioned only 1–59 times - not enough to be included in the embedding. For organizations, 17 were mentioned in the report, and 9 of these were found in the embedding. The GKG data does not often include common acronyms like BBC or FBI, although there are some exceptions. This creates challenges for automated testing since the reports often use an acronym to refer to an organization.

The most relevant people mentioned in the report, 14 in all, are listed in the first column of Table 1, while the remaining columns show the top 14 results for each algorithm, given the query for the country "Venezuela" and the GKG theme "SELF_IDENTIFIED_HUMANITARIAN_CRISIS". The seven items from the ground truth that are potentially findable in the index and in the embedding are indicated with (*) in column one, while the found items are highlighted in bold in the subsequent columns, including alternate spellings of the same person's name.

The co-occur method finds only the Venezuelan leaders in the top 14. It also returns ten other world leaders, politicians and spokespeople. These people have either made statements about Venezuela's humanitarian crisis, or Venezuela has made comments about their own country's crisis (e.g. Bashar Assad). Although Donald Trump was not yet president of the United States during the period covered by the data, his opinions on foreign policy in Latin America were discussed in the news, and he made statements about the situation in Venezuela. Two journalists who write frequently about Venezuela are also suggested (Joshua Goodman, Gonzalo Solano).

In marked contrast, the context method's results do not include any foreign leaders and politicians. Instead, there are seven Venezuelan politicians, along

---

[1] https://www.hrw.org/report/2016/10/24/venezuelas-humanitarian-crisis/severe-medical-and-food-shortages-inadequate-and.

Table 1. Example results from each algorithm for the query "Venezuela", "SELF_IDENTIFIED_HUMANITARIAN_CRISIS". (*) indicates those candidates that were potentially findable in the GKG data.

Ground truth	co-occur	context	co-occur_context
Nicolás Maduro (*)	**Nicolás Maduro**	**Delcy Rodriguez**	**Delcy Rodriguez**
Hugo Chávez (*)	Barack Obama	**Nicholás Maduro**	**Nicholás Maduro**
Zeid Ra'ad Al Hussein (*)	Rafael Correa	Jesus Torrealba	Hannah Dreier
Ban Ki-moon	**Hugo Chávez**	Vladimir Padrino	**Luis Almagro**
Delcy Rodríguez (*)	Joshua Goodman	Henrique Capriles	Juan Manuel Santos
Luisana Melo (*)	John Kerry	**Nicolás Maduro**	Barack Obama
Luis Almagro (*)	Bashar Assad	Jorge Arreaza	Rafael Correa
Johan Gabriel Pinto Graterol	Donald Trump	Hannah Dreier	**Hugo Chávez**
Julio León Heredia	Juan Manuel Santos	Girish Gupta	Joshua Goodman
Carlos Zapa	Gonzalo Solano	Eyanir Chinea	John Kerry
Flor Sánchez	Vladimir Putin	Andrew Cawthorne	Bashar Assad
Diosdado Cabello (*)	David Granger	David Smilde	Donald Trump
Rafael Uzcátegui	John Kirby	Ernesto Villegas	Gonzalo Solano
Feliciano Reyna	Salva Kiir	**Luis Almagro**	Vladimir Putin

with four journalists and a human rights advocate and academic (David Smilde), and the secretary-general of the Organization of Latin American States (Luis Almagro). Some of these politicians are very closely associated with the humanitarian crisis in Venezuela, notably Vladimir Padrino, the Venezuelan Minister of Defense, who is responsible for food distribution, even though they were not mentioned by name in the report.

Combining these methods by ranking the first 90 co-occur results according to their context ranking moved five highly related candidates to the top of the list, including a new ground truth person: Luis Almagro. Similarly, the context_co-occur method (omitted from Table 1 for space constraints) moved four items to the top of the ranking, including the misspelling of Nicolás Maduro as Nicholás Maduro. Both combination methods slightly increased the number of ground truth items found in the top 10 ranked results from 2 or 3 to 4 out of a possible maximum of 7.

4.3 Evaluation Method

To evaluate and compare the methods of identifying key players, we applied each of the four methods (co-occur, context, co-occur_context and context_co-occur) to the test query data sets (manual, curated and auto), for both people and organizations. All methods were limited to 30 returned candidates. For each query, we calculated four classic information retrieval evaluation measures: precision (ratio of correct concepts in the output), recall (ratio of ground truth concepts returned in the output), F1 (harmonic mean of precision and recall), and average precision (average precision value at all the ranks where a correct concept is returned). Overall values for each test set are reported as the mean of the values for the individual queries in the set. Following the recommendation by Smucker et al. [25], we performed randomization test and two-tailed paired samples t-tests to test for statistical significance.

4.4   Evaluation Results

Manual. Table 2 shows the results for the manual data set. For person experiments, all measures showed better performance from the combination methods, with the `context` method performing the lowest. The `co-occur_context` method outperformed the `co-occur` method by 19%. However, pairwise comparisons of F1 scores between methods showed only the (`context`,`context_co-occur`) and (`co-occur`,`co-occur_context`) pairs to be statistically significantly different ($p < 0.05$). For the organization experiments, again the `co-occur_context` combination method performed best over all four measures, but only the (`context`,`context_co-occur`) pair was found to be statistically significant in terms of comparison by MAP or F1 scores. The lack of statistical significance is due to the high variance of the results for each query, and show in part the need for a larger data set for a proper comparison as our overall results described in Sect. 4.4 also confirm.

Table 2. Accuracy results over the manual data set.

	Person				Organization			
	co-occur	context	co-occur context	context co-occur	co-occur	context	co-occur context	context co-occur
MAP	0.233	0.199	0.251	0.233	0.179	0.143	0.184	0.189
F1	0.192	0.174	0.228	0.213	0.178	0.107	0.183	0.141
Pr.	0.133	0.121	0.158	0.149	0.117	0.066	0.119	0.089
Re.	0.372	0.328	0.437	0.388	0.436	0.304	0.459	0.374

Curated. Table 3 shows the results for the curated data set. For the person experiments, the overall pattern was very similar to the manual data set, with the `co-occur_context` method showing the best performance across all measures, including an 18% improvement for F1 over the `co-occur` method. For F1, the differences between the (`context`,`co-occur`), (`context`,`context_co-occur`) and (`co-occur`,`co-occur_context`) pairs were statistically significant. For the organization experiments the `co-occur` and `co-occur_context` methods performed the best, and their F1 scores were not significantly different, while all other pairwise comparisons were, except for the two lowest performing methods: `context` and `context_co-occur`.

Table 3. Accuracy results over the curated data set.

	Person				Organization			
	co-occur	context	co-occur context	context co-occur	co-occur	context	co-occur context	context co-occur
MAP	0.132	0.070	0.135	0.123	0.130	0.039	0.075	0.051
F1	0.140	0.104	0.165	0.143	0.142	0.058	0.142	0.058
Pr.	0.119	0.090	0.139	0.124	0.107	0.042	0.108	0.045
Re.	0.251	0.160	0.300	0.225	0.290	0.116	0.289	0.122

Auto. Table 4 shows the results for the auto data set. For these results, organizations followed a similar pattern to the two other datasets, and all pairwise comparisons were statistically significant for all metrics, with the only exception for MAP, where the two combination methods were not distinguishable. For person experiments, the results were lower, less than 0.1 for all metrics and methods, so that while the combination methods produced around 10% higher average scores, the differences were not statistically significant, with the exception of the (context,context_co-occur) and (co-occur,co-occur_context) pairs for F1 or MAP.

Table 4. Accuracy results over the auto data set.

	Person				Organization			
	co-occur	context	co-occur context	context co-occur	co-occur	context	co-occur context	context co-occur
MAP	0.041	0.046	0.050	0.051	0.132	0.073	0.117	0.116
F1	0.058	0.060	0.066	0.066	0.165	0.084	0.157	0.108
Pr.	0.051	0.056	0.059	0.061	0.173	0.088	0.163	0.112
Re.	0.090	0.086	0.099	0.094	0.224	0.114	0.217	0.150

Comparing Results Across the Data Sets. We also explored whether the different data sets provided similar results. Figure 4 shows F1 values for people (left) and organizations (right) as boxplots. Each box indicates the interquartile range of the data, the center line indicates the median value, the whiskers above and below give the 95% confidence intervals, and circles indicate outliers. Significant differences are indicated above with red brackets. For people, the less curated sets of queries produced lower results, but the pattern of results is very similar across all three datasets. Recall that the auto queries did not contain any themes, and so they often did not capture the topic of a report well, giving the system a low chance of success. Results were twice as good for organizations as for people in the auto data set, probably reflecting the large number of queries that included an organization. Again, the pattern of results remained similar across the data sets. We observed similar trends for other accuracy measures.

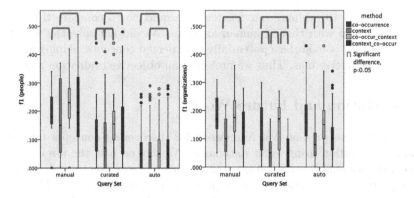

Fig. 4. Results for people and organizations across the data sets and four methods

4.5 Discussion

Overall, both the combination algorithms performed better than the individual co-occur and context algorithms. This suggests that combining methods did go some way towards addressing the individual weaknesses of the two approaches, with an effect size of up to 19% improvement over the best individual method.

Not surprisingly, the algorithms produced the best results on the manual test set, followed by the curated set, and the lowest values for the automatically generated set, which has less well constructed queries that do not capture the topic of the report as well. Importantly, the similarities between data set results when comparing the concept discovery algorithms increases confidence in the evaluation, and more generally in the use of automated methods as a valid and scalable way to approach the evaluation of concept discovery algorithms, despite the noise and loss of accuracy compared to hand-curated data.

Our approach to evaluation has some limitations. Our source reports do not mention all of the people and organizations relevant to the topic by name. We do not translate mentions like "The Minister for the Interior" into a named person, and nor do we attempt to resolve references to groups like "Brazilian steel companies." Our methods also draw from articles published after the publication of the report, when new concepts may be introduced. All people or organizations found by our methods but not named in the ground truth are treated as wrong answers, but some of these may be highly relevant to the topic. In the example shown in Table 1, the majority of the persons returned by the context method are in fact highly relevant despite the fact that our input report did not contain their names. This shows that a potential use case for our system is complementing analysts in finding concepts that are not already covered in their report. Also note that there is often a major difference between the number of candidates proposed (30) and the number of ground truth items provided (generally less than 30). Thus, our reported accuracy scores are very low and underestimate the overall quality of the responses.

Another way to evaluate our framework would be to compare the output of the algorithms with that of human analysts. We did not take this approach because our goal is to surface potentially unexpected concepts, helping analysts to mitigate cognitive bias. Thus we preferred an objective evaluation method.

5   Conclusion and Future Work

In this paper, we presented a framework for discovering concepts related to an analysis question using event databases. We showed how the use of semantic technologies enable a unified query mechanism across event databases using mappings to general-domain knowledge bases, and semantic embeddings. We then presented three classes of concept ranking algorithms and performed an evaluation of the quality of the rankings using a corpus of reports written by humans. We plan to extend our ground truth data sets for concept discovery, in part using crowd sourcing and human analysts, and make the outcome publicly available for future research. Our plan is to use our benchmark as a way to compare different event databases such as ICEWS, GDELT, and EventRegistry, and highlight their strengths and shortcomings. Finally, we are planning to analyze how the outcome of concept discovery affects other analysis tasks such as scenario planning [26] and building forecast models [15].

References

1. Annoy. https://github.com/spotify/annoy. Accessed 8 May 2017
2. Apache OpenNLP (v1.5.3). https://opennlp.apache.org/. Accessed 18 May 2017
3. ClearNLP (v3.2.0). https://github.com/clir/clearnlp. Accessed 18 May 2017
4. Riak. https://github.com/basho/riak. Accessed 8 May 2017
5. SolrCloud. https://wiki.apache.org/solr/SolrCloud. Accessed 8 May 2017
6. TAC KBP 2016 Event Track. https://tac.nist.gov/2016/KBP/Event/index.html. Accessed 8 May 2017
7. Word2vec: tool for computing continuous distributed representations of words. https://code.google.com/archive/p/word2vec/. Accessed 8 May 2017
8. Bizer, C., Lehmann, J., Kobilarov, G., Auer, S., Becker, C., Cyganiak, R., Hellmann, S.: DBpedia - a crystallization point for the web of data. JWS **7**(3), 154–165 (2009)
9. Bollacker, K.D., Evans, C., Paritosh, P., Sturge, T., Taylor, J.: Freebase: a collaboratively created graph database for structuring human knowledge. In: SIGMOD, pp. 1247–1250 (2008)
10. Bordawekar, R., Shmueli, O.: Enabling Cognitive Intelligence Queries in Relational Databases using Low-dimensional Word Embeddings. CoRR abs/1603.07185 (2016). http://arxiv.org/abs/1603.07185
11. Boschee, E., Lautenschlager, J., O'Brien, S., Shellman, S., Starz, J., Ward, M.: ICEWS Coded Event Data (2017). https://doi.org/10.7910/DVN/28075
12. Doddington, G., et al.: The automatic content extraction (ACE) program tasks, data, and evaluation. In: LREC, May 2004
13. Franklin, M.J., Halevy, A.Y., Maier, D.: From databases to dataspaces: a new abstraction for information management. SIGMOD Rec. **34**(4), 27–33 (2005)

14. Hogenboom, F., Frasincar, F., Kaymak, U., de Jong, F., Caron, E.: A survey of event extraction methods from text for decision support systems. Decis. Support Syst. **85**(C), 12–22 (2016). https://doi.org/10.1016/j.dss.2016.02.006

15. Korkmaz, G., Cadena, J., Kuhlman, C.J., Marathe, A., Vullikanti, A., Ramakrishnan, N.: Combining heterogeneous data sources for civil unrest forecasting. In: ASONAM, pp. 258–265 (2015). https://doi.org/10.1145/2808797.2808847

16. Leban, G., Fortuna, B., Brank, J., Grobelnik, M.: Event registry: learning about world events from news. In: WWW, pp. 107–110 (2014)

17. Leetaru, K., Schrodt, P.A.: GDELT: global data on events, location, and tone, 1979–2012. In: ISA Annual Convention (2013)

18. Lin, D., Pantel, P.: Concept discovery from text. In: COLING, pp. 1–7 (2002)

19. Madhavan, J., Jeffery, S.R., Cohen, S., Dong, X., Ko, D., Yu, C., Halevy, A.: Web-scale data integration: you can only afford to pay as you go. In: CIDR (2007)

20. Mikolov, T., Chen, K., Corrado, G., Dean, J.: Efficient estimation of word representations in vector space. arXiv preprint arXiv:1301.3781 (2013)

21. Mikolov, T., Sutskever, I., Chen, K., Corrado, G.S., Dean, J.: Distributed representations of words and phrases and their compositionality. In: NIPS (2013)

22. Muthiah, S., et al.: Embers at 4 years: Experiences operating an open source indicators forecasting system. In: KDD, pp. 205–214 (2016)

23. Rebele, T., Suchanek, F.M., Hoffart, J., Biega, J., Kuzey, E., Weikum, G.: YAGO: a multilingual knowledge base from Wikipedia, Wordnet, and Geonames. In: ISWC, pp. 177–185 (2016)

24. Schrodt, P.A., Yilmaz, O., Gerner, D.J., Hermreck, D.: The CAMEO (conflict and mediation event observations) actor coding framework. In: 2008 Annual Meeting of the International Studies Association (2008)

25. Smucker, M.D., Allan, J., Carterette, B.: A comparison of statistical significance tests for information retrieval evaluation. In: CIKM, pp. 623–632 (2007)

26. Sohrabi, S., Riabov, A., Katz, M., Udrea, O.: An AI planning solution to scenario generation for enterprise risk management. In: AAAI (2018)

27. Sohrabi, S., Udrea, O., Riabov, A.V., Hassanzadeh, O.: Interactive planning-based hypothesis generation with LTS++. In: IJCAI, pp. 4268–4269 (2016)

28. Tan, A.H.: Text mining: the state of the art and the challenges. In. In Proceedings of the PAKDD 1999 Workshop on Knowledge Disocovery from Advanced Databases, pp. 65–70 (1999)

29. Vrandecic, D., Krötzsch, M.: Wikidata: a free collaborative knowledgebase. Commun. ACM **57**(10), 78–85 (2014)

30. Ward, M.D., Beger, A., Cutler, J., Dickenson, M., Dorff, C., Radford, B.: Comparing GDELT and ICEWS event data. Analysis **21**, 267–297 (2013)

Smart Papers: Dynamic Publications on the Blockchain

Michał R. Hoffman$^{(\boxtimes)}$, Luis-Daniel Ibáñez⊙, Huw Fryer⊙, and Elena Simperl

University of Southampton, Southampton SO17 1BJ, UK
{M.R.Hoffman,L.D.Ibanez,H.Fryer,E.Simperl}@southampton.ac.uk

Abstract. Distributed Ledgers (DLs), also known as blockchains, provide decentralised, tamper-free registries of transactions among partners that distrust each other. For the scientific community, DLs have been proposed to decentralise and make more transparent each step of the scientific workflow. For the particular case of dissemination and peer-reviewing, DLs can provide the cornerstone to realise open decentralised publishing systems where social interactions between peers are tamper-free, enabling trustworthy computation of bibliometrics. In this paper, we propose the use of DL-backed *smart contracts* to track a subset of social interactions for scholarly publications in a decentralised and reliable way, yielding *Smart Papers*. We show how our Smart Papers approach complements current models for decentralised publishing, and analyse cost implications.

Keywords: Smart contracts · Blockchain · Dynamic publications
Ethereum · Open decentralised publishing · Collaborative processes
Trust

1 Introduction

With the advent of digitisation and Web technologies, dissemination of scientific research objects has become faster and less expensive. However, several authors (e.g. [7,11]) have pointed out that Web-based tools are currently mimicking the print-based format used in the past. The vast potential of the Web to separate dissemination, evaluation and retrieval aspects of publications is currently underused. More focus needs to be placed on the quality assessment aspect of both contributions and contributors, ensuring that proper credit is given to novel ideas and their proponents, and on avoiding the excessive concentration of power in the hands of the publishers and editors.

Conceptual models like Liquid Publications [7] and Dynamic Publication Formats [11] have been proposed to leverage Semantic Web technologies to transform research objects from static to *evolutionary* entities. In these models, authors collaborate on a *living* version of the research object that, upon the authors' agreement, has periodical snapshots or *releases* published on the Web. Releases can be open for comments and reviews from the members of

© Springer International Publishing AG, part of Springer Nature 2018
A. Gangemi et al. (Eds.): ESWC 2018, LNCS 10843, pp. 304–318, 2018.
https://doi.org/10.1007/978-3-319-93417-4_20

the public, or submitted to Calls for Contributions of conferences or journals. Authoring tools like Dokie.li [6] go one step further and provide *decentralised* implementations of living research objects that allow authors to retain the ownership of, and sovereignty over their data. This supplies an alternative to the current state of play, where scholarly publication processes are centralised in publishing houses and large technology providers. However, an under-explored aspect in these models is how to manage the interactions between authors and contributors of a research object in a trusted way, which is of utmost importance for computing bibliometrics transparently. Examples of these interactions are (i) Agreement between authors on which snapshot of a working version should be released (ii) Agreement between authors on the attribution due to each of them for each release of a living research object (iii) Public comments and reviews of public releases, both as a mean to complement bibliometrics - often overlooked, yet crucial labour in academia. From the point of view of a single scholar that co-authors several papers with different teams, receives reviews and comments from peers, and reviews and comments research made by others, data produced by these interactions, used to measure their performance, is not only controlled by her, or a single third party, but also by many other scholars (or their trustees). Any accidental or malicious change in a data store that is out of her control might have catastrophic impact on her performance measures.

Our work advances several Semantic Web research areas, including trust management for the Semantic Web and decentralised scholarly publication. By proposing a system that uses distributed ledgers and smart contracts to manage trust in a scenario which has been long understood as a critical showcase of semantic technologies, we provide a timely contribution to an ongoing discourse on the role and future of the Web as a (re-decentralised) platform for progress and social good. We aim at answering two research questions in the context of open decentralised publishing systems: RQ1. *How to manage releases and their attribution agreements in a trusted way?*; and RQ2. *How to avoid malicious/accidental modifications in remote data stores affecting the computation of bibliometrics?*

Recently, Distributed Ledger Technologies, commonly known as *Blockchains* [15], have emerged as a novel tool that provides a decentralised solution to the problem of managing transactions of digital assets among parties that do not necessarily trust each other, while guaranteeing the immutability and verifiability of records. Their record-keeping capabilities have been extended to user-defined programs that specify rules governing transactions, a concept known as *smart contracts*. Smart contracts offer guarantees of *security, tamper-resistance* and *absence of central control*.

In this paper, we introduce a system called *Smart Papers* to manage the attributions and annotations of scholar publications, filling the gap of existing open decentralised publishing models. In our approach, a suite of four smart contracts is deployed on top of the Ethereum platform, and reusability is achieved by an unbounded number of research objects calling those contracts, and storing publication metadata in a distributed ledger. The smart contracts take the place of a trusted third party in keeping records, with the critical difference being that of data and execution not being controlled by a single entity, but rather inheriting all the guarantees of the host blockchain platform. In our Motivating Example (Sect. 2), we highlight some of the most critical problems with current models - issues that directly affect the quality and trustworthiness of the existing approaches. In Sect. 3, we survey the existing models and implementations concerned with scientific authoring. We subsequently propose the Smart Papers model (Sect. 4) and its implementation in Ethereum, paying particular attention to the issues of trust, identity, and platform technological considerations. Our discussion then progresses to cost analysis (Sect. 5), after which our conclusions and future work recommendations are presented, in the final section of this paper.

2   Motivating Example

Bob and Alice are scholars from two separate institutions, who agree to collaborate on a publication. They begin by employing their collaborative authoring tool of choice to start a working version of their paper. After a few weeks of work, they decide to release a public version to receive open comments and reviews. Charlie is a scholar from a third institution that finds Bob and Alice's release through an aggregator or a search engine. He reads the article and leaves some comments on it that are stored in his personal data store and linked to the release, for instance, using the Web Annotation ontology[1].

Bob and Alice integrate Charlie's comments in their working version. They continue their work and eventually publish a second release. This time round, they submit it to the Call for Contributions of a conference that uses open reviewing. Diane is one of the assigned reviewers. Her review is linked to the release which she read, as stored in the conference's data store

When it is finally time for Bob, Diane and Charlie's appraisal meeting, their employers ask them for the dynamic publications that they have been involved in. Bob shows the full sequence of releases of the publication, while Charlie shows the comment he made on Bob and Alice's paper, and Diane shows the review she made for the conference. Employers apply their preferred credit models to assign weights to each type of attribution described in the attribution metadata, and quantify their values.

However, when reputation, credit, and ultimately, jobs are involved, social interactions can go wrong, with people trying to game the system in their favour, or to disfavour others. Below, we outline some examples of when things can go awry:

Example 1. Alice trusts Bob for creating the releases and their attribution metadata, as Bob controls the data store. However, Bob can publish a release with the metadata giving more attribution to himself. If using a Trusty URI mechanism, once the release is picked up by other agents, it is very hard to

---

[1] https://www.w3.org/TR/annotation-vocab/.

overwrite it. In a decentralised authoring tool like Dokie.li, each author would hold a copy of the working version, and they could independently generate the release, but if the attribution metadata differs between them, who solves this disagreement? How does an external agent know which copy to trust?

Example 2. Bob and Alice could collude to show different versions of the attribution metadata. For example, consider that employers use two different services to query dynamic publications linked to their faculty members. It is not hard to imagine a semantic store that returns a different version of the attribution metadata, depending on which agent is asking.

Example 3. Bob and Alice could collude to ignore Charlie's comment, in an attempt to not share part of the credit with him. In a decentralised model, a link to the comment and Charlie's identity should be stored in Bob and Alice's data store; however, if Bob and Alice control the data store, nothing prevents them from deleting the link. Charlie would have the copy of the comment and the link to the release, but he might have a hard time convincing a third party (his employer for example), that the comment was not forged.

Example 4. If Diane's review is considered unfair, the editors in control of the data store of the conference might be tempted to make it disappear. A third party agent querying the conference's data store would see nothing. An agent following links from Bob and Alice's data store would get a dereference failure (404). Even if Bob and Alice kept a copy of the review and a Trusty URI, how can they prove that they are not forging a review to damage Diane's reputation?

The common problem of these scenarios is that for all actors (Alice, Bob, Charlie, Diane and their employers), data that is crucial to show or measure performance is not entirely under their control, making it vulnerable to manipulation. Our approach addresses this problem by empowering all collaborators with the following:

- The notarisation of releases providing evidence that all the authors agreed to releasing a particular version of their paper.
- The notarisation of the attribution metadata linked to a release, ensuring that all authors have agreed on it, and guaranteeing to third parties that none of them can tamper with it.
- A mechanism that ensures that annotations made on releases by agents other than authors cannot be repudiated by annotators or their recipients, guaranteeing to both authors and third parties querying this data, that it was not tampered with.
- An index of links and data concerning a particular dynamic publication. This potentially facilitates the task of Web agents that compute bibliometrics, as there is no need to either trust the data store of the authors, or to crawl the Web in search of the comments and reviews to the publication.

3   Related Work

Several models have been proposed to take advantage of digital and Web tools to improve the way academic publications are produced and managed. Liquid Publications [7] proposes evolutionary, collaborative, and composable scientific contributions, based on a parallel between scientific knowledge artefacts and software artefacts, and leveraging lessons learned in collaborative software development. Their model is based on the interaction between Social Knowledge Objects, *i.e.*, digital counterparts of the traditional paper unit; people and roles, *i.e.*, agents involved in the scientific knowledge processes, playing various cooperating and competing roles (from traditional ones, like author, reviewer or publisher, to new ones derived from the model itself, like classifiers, quality certifiers, credit certifiers); and processes to manage its lifecycle, namely: authoring collaboration, access control, IPR and legal aspects, quality control and credit attribution and computation. The Living Document model [9] aims at creating documents that "live" on the Web by allowing them to interact with other papers and resources. It lets authors build social networks, with their interactions defined through the papers they write. Heller et al. [11] propose Dynamic Format Publications, where working versions are collaboratively edited by a small group of authors, that decide when a version or revision become widely available, following a formalised gate-keeping mechanism (e.g., consent among authors and/or peer-review). Only the Living Document approach provided a prototype (inactive at this time), and none of them discusses the security and trust implications of their models. Our work provides a foundation that can be used to track and manage credit attribution (and by extension, IPR and legal aspects) that can be easily plugged into a broader authoring model.

Concerning the decentralisation of scholarly communication, Dokie.li [6] is a fully decentralised, browser-based authoring and annotation platform with built-in support for social interactions, through which people retain the ownership of and sovereignty over their data. Dokie.li implements most of the functionalities described in the previously described conceptual models in a decoupled way. In a nutshell, a Dokie.li document is an HTML5 document enriched with RDFA, which is stored in the author's personal data store. The Linked Data Platform (LDP) protocol implementation enables the creation, update and deletion of documents. Interactions with documents are registered using the Web Annotations vocabulary. Documents are connected statically through links and dynamically through Linked Data Notifications [5], proving the viability of a decentralised authoring and annotation environment built according to Web standards. Authors consider that in a fully decentralised setting, each source is filterless and responsible for its own quality and reputation, whilst everyone is free to selectively distrust certain sources using any mechanism they desire. We argue that, although this assumption holds for trust in the *content* of the research object, stronger measures are needed for social interaction data on research objects that could be used to compute bibliometrics. Our approach also aims at solving some security issues that arise in decentralised environments, notably, the possibility of malicious deleting or updating of records to impact bibliometrics [14].

With respect to the application of blockchains for scholar processes, the Blockchain for Science association maintains a living document [3] that collects and proposes applications, use cases, visions and ventures that use blockchains for science and knowledge creation, providing an index of the potential impact of Distributed Ledger Technologies in all stages of the research workflow. For the particular case of publishing and archiving, timestamping and credit attribution of Dynamic Publications is mentioned as a promising use case. To the best of our knowledge, the open-source system that comes closest to ours is Manubot[2], a tool for writing scholarly manuscripts via GitHub. Manubot automates citations and references, versions manuscripts using git, and enables collaborative writing via GitHub. Data from Git related to commitment and authorship can be used to establish attribution. An innovation introduced by Manubot's authors [3] is the timestamping of manuscript versions on the Bitcoin blockchain, to prove the existence of the manuscript at a given point of time in a decentralised way. Our approach generalises Manubot's idea to further social interactions around publications.

Concerning the permanence and immutability of Web artefacts, Trusty URIs [13] propose to append to URIs the cryptographic hash of the Web artefact they represent, enabling the verification contain the content the URI is supposed to represent. Trusty URIs are immutable in the sense that any change in an artefact would change its URI as well, and permanent, under the assumption that Web archives and search engines that crawl them are permanent. Our approach implements functionality analogous to Trusty URIs, but also solves the further problem of conflicting metadata: if each author could publish metadata on the attribution about the research object, each one with its own Trusty URI, and both can be verified to not have been tampered with, then which one should an external agent use?

4   The Smart Papers Model

The Motivating Example (Sect. 2) illustrated the importance of trust management throughout the collaborative process. When reviewing related work (Sect. 3), we highlighted a strong need for making agreements and setting their outcomes in stone so that they cannot be later repudiated. Furthermore, all the essential artefacts associated with those agreements must be timestamped and securely stored in a truly permanent way. Currently available collaborative tools solve some trust issues, for example Dokie.li removes centralisation so that the authoring parties do not have to rely on an intermediary to publish and annotate their documents. This is a very welcome step towards removing the overhead associated with middleman activities (publishing house), albeit it merely shifts the trust towards the authoring parties (author, reviewer). It is easy to imagine

---

[2] https://github.com/greenelab/manubot-rootstock.
[3] https://github.com/greenelab/deep-review/pull/274.

a situation in which the authors destroy their data, the reviewers could do the same, and any track of their writing will be lost forever.

The purpose of our model is to provide trust where it has not existed before. Smart Papers provide a collaborative platform that preserves a single version of the truth throughout the collaborative process. This is somehow similar to employing a trusted third party (e.g. a notary public) to keep track of contracts signed by multiple parties, alongside with all the certified photocopies of all the evidence attached to the contracts as relevant appendices. An example of such notarised contract would be Alice and Bob signing an agreement specifying the ordering of their names on a paper (e.g. "Bob, Alice") and then attaching a certified photocopy of their paper in its current version as an appendix. We use smart contracts for maintaining all such signed agreements in order to implement Smart Papers. Table 1 summarises how smart contracts can provide the functionality analogous to that of a traditional trusted third party.

Table 1. Blockchain smart contracts as compared to a traditional trusted third party

Notary public function	Blockchain function
Authenticate parties using their legal identification	Identify parties cryptographically
Take statutory declarations, store them and certify photocopies	Store data permanently and securely and provide real time access
Prepare and certify contractual instruments	Store and execute smart contracts
Provide a trusted record for the above	Provide a trusted record for the above

4.1 Design

To design the Smart Papers model, we shall assume that all authors successfully identify through their ORCID (Open Researcher and Contributor ID [10]) which is a non-proprietary alphanumeric code to uniquely identify scientific and other academic authors and contributors. ORCIDs are mapped to authors' signing and encryption keys using a smart contract. The main functionality for our model is then designed using the separation of concerns (SoC) design principle [12], such that each contract file addresses a different concern, i.e. a different set of information that jointly affects the global state for the Smart Papers use case. We use UML to model the main classes corresponding to our smart contracts. It is important to note that smart contracts and OOP classes (as modelled by the UML) are not quite the same. The semantics are very similar in many cases, but some fundamental differences arise from the fact that smart contracts can store and send value and have a public address once deployed [16]. The UML diagram in Fig. 1 shows how we group these concerns into the following four categories: Paper, Version, Annotation and Contributor.

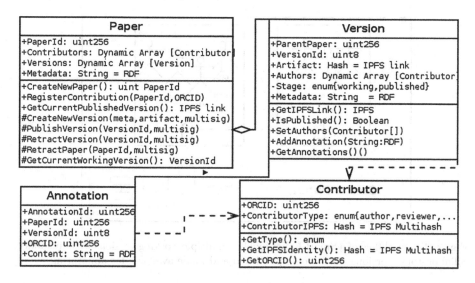

Fig. 1. The Smart Papers distributed application design

To begin with, an article and its metadata (e.g., attribution encoded in the ScoRO ontology[4]) is submitted by a writer (we shall refer to her as Alice, from our motivating example earlier), and stored in a distributed file store, all of which is recorded on the blockchain. Alice will have been set up in the system through the use of the *Contributor* smart contract. In our implementation, the *Contributor* contract requires Alice to have a valid ORCID as well as an IPFS node identity belonging to her. The default type for Alice is "author". Bob is also set up as an "author", but Diane uses a different argument for the *Contributor* contract, and so she becomes registered as a "reviewer".

Smart contracts often act as state machines, meaning that they have certain stages making them act differently, and in which different functions can be invoked. A function invocation often transitions the contract into the next stage which can be used to model work flows. We use this feature of smart contracts to model the Smart Paper workflow, as seen is Fig. 2, which allows the participants to release new versions of their paper and to publish versions when enough authors agree to do so.

Papers can also be retracted. As illustrated in Fig. 2, once instantiated, a Smart Paper becomes a dynamic list of versions, each of which can exist in a working state or become published. The number of contributors and their formal ordering is allowed to change on a per-version basis. Annotations can be left by reviewers on published versions.

To create a new Smart Paper, either Alice or Bob call *createNewPaper* in the *Paper* Contract which will return a valid *PaperId* that uniquely identifies their new publication. This also instantiates the workflow with an initial, blank,

---

[4] http://www.sparontologies.net/ontologies/scoro.

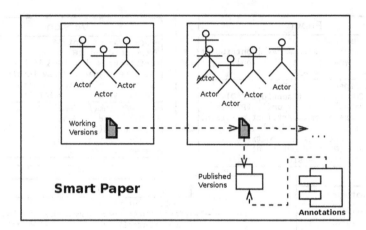

Fig. 2. The workflow of a Smart Paper involves multiple working versions with dynamic collaborators. Versions can become published and made available for annotating.

working version of this paper manufactured by the *Version* contract. Bob and Alice work on their preferred authoring tool to produce a first draft (e.g., to show to a trusted colleague), to register it in the Smart Paper, Bob calls *addNewVersion* in the Version contract, including the artefact, its metadata and his signature. Before committing the transaction, the Smart Paper will wait for Alice (marked as contributor of the paper) to also perform a call to *addNewVersion* using the same artefact, metadata and her signature.

The procedure is repeated each time Bob and Alice want to register a new version. For marking a version as public, Bob calls *publishVersion* in the *Paper* contract, providing the *versionID* and his signature. Similar to *addNewVersion*, Alice needs to issue her signature through a function call to *publishVersion* before the Smart Paper commits the transaction. The *getCurrentPublishedVersion* and *getCurrentWorkingVersion* return a versionID that can then become the input to the *getIPFSLink*. Up to this point, we have provided a solution for the issues between authors described in Example 1, the Smart Paper only commits a version (including metadata) if all authors sign their agreement to it. An external agent that gets a version from a Smart Paper instance has the assurance that it was approved by all authors, and that the Smart Contract consistently returns the correct version and metadata, solving the issue described in Example 2.

Interactions with external actors like reviewers or annotators, are abstracted as *Annotations*. When Charlie or Diane want to leave their comment or review, they call *addAnnotation* using the *versionID* of the version they want to comment on, and their signatures. Contrary to the *Version* functions, no approval from authors is needed. The annotation is registered in Ethereum's Blockchain and can be retrieved by calling *getAnnotation*. Looking back at Example 3, Charlie can now point to the Smart Paper to show that he made that comment. For the case of Example 4, the Smart Paper holds a register of the reviews. Alice and Bob can now prove that the annotation held by the Smart Paper was signed by Diane.

4.2   Implementation

Although in theory, the Smart Papers model could be implemented on any smart contract-enabled platform, the choice of the implementation framework dramatically impacts development time and costs. Whilst there are multiple distributed ledger technologies, such as Corda[5] or HyperLedger[6], that could be utilised to develop trusted smart contract code that runs on top of the blockchain, for this paper, we elect to develop on top of the Ethereum platform [16] which is the most commonly used technology of its kind [2]. We defer the feasibility and cost of development in other platforms for future analysis.

Background: Ethereum and IPFS. Ethereum is an open-source, public, blockchain-based distributed computing platform featuring smart contract functionality [16]. It plays the role of the trusted third party for all Smart Papers agreements in our model. Ethereum blockchain was designed to be deterministic. This means, that everyone should always end up with the same, correct state, if they try to replay the history of Ethereum transactions. In Ethereum, the code execution layer is provided by the Ethereum Virtual Machine (EVM), a Turing complete 256bit VM that allows anyone to execute code that references and stores blockchain data in a trust-less environment. Every contract on the Ethereum blockchain has its own storage which only it can write to; this is known as the contracts state and it can be seen as a flexible database albeit at a high cost. When deployed, Ethereum contracts get an *address*, that can be considered similar to an URI in Ethereum's namespace. Using this address, a client can call functions defined in a smart contract, in a similar fashion to a web service.

When implementing our model, we chose to store all the artefacts using IPFS [4]. The InterPlanetary File System is used for efficiently distributing and referencing hash-linked data in a way that is not centralised and does not necessarily involve blockchain transactions, thus avoiding the economic penalties associated with on-chain storage. In many ways, IPFS is similar to the World Wide Web, but it could be also seen as a single BitTorrent swarm for exchanging objects. Furthermore, the IPFS specification contains a special *commit* object which represents a particular snapshot in the version history of a file. This allows us to reference resources in an immutable way, akin to Trusty URI functionality. Using IPFS we can, therefore, limit the role of Ethereum, so that it only deals with the application logic; the data layer is provided by the InterPlanetary (IPFS) stack, and the two layers are integrated via hash references.

Reaching Agreements. One of the core requirements of the SmartPaper model is the ability to provide a tool for all collaborators to agree with the result of a certain interaction. Decision making can be implemented in different ways. In our implementation, the number of collaborators can be unbounded,

---

[5] https://github.com/corda/corda.
[6] https://www.hyperledger.org/.

but to make a decision, an agreement needs to be reached by all authors. We use the multiple signature scheme to enable the authors to jointly perform specific actions on a Smart Paper. The following Ethereum code snippet illustrates how multiple authors' signatures are verified by the *PublishVersion()* functionality of the Paper contract before the paper can be published, ensuring they've all agreed before committing to a change in their paper.

```
1    uint public threshold; //quorum needed to decide
2    mapping (address => bool) isCollaborator;
3    function PublishVersion(uint paperId, signature[] sigs){
         require(checkSignatures(sigs));
4        //Publishing code follows:...
5    }
6    function checkSignatures(signature[] signatures){
7        if (signatures.length < threshold) throw;
8        for (uint i = 0; i < signatures.length; i++) {
9            r = signatures[i].slice(0, 32)
10           s = signatures[i].slice(32, 64)
11           v = signatures[i].recovery + 27
12           checkSig(v, r, s);
13       }
14   }
15   function checkSig(uint8 sigV, bytes32 sigR, bytes32 sigS) {
16       //ERC191 signature: github.com/ethereum/EIPs/issues/191
17       bytes32 txHash = sha3(byte(0x19), byte(0), this);
18       address recovered = ecrecover(txHash, sigV, sigR, sigS);
19       if (!isCollaborator[recovered]) throw;
20   }
21   //The following code is called upon instantiating new paper
22   function SetUpCollabs(uint threshold_, address[] collabs_) {
23       if (threshold_ > collabs_.length || threshold_==0) throw;
24       for (uint i=0; i<collabs_.length; i++) {
25           isCollaborator[collabs_[i]] = true;
26       }
27       threshold = threshold_;
28   }
```

The *signatures* array acts as an accumulator waiting for enough signatures to be collected according to the threshold. The *PublishVersion* function on line 3 finally becomes triggered by an event (out of the scope of this snippet). The code example also shows how an elliptic curve signature can be parsed for every participant (*sigV, sigR and sigS* arguments) on line 15. To improve on the security of this code, a nonce should be used that is always incremented to prevent replay attacks. We make this pattern reusable, and reference it by all functions that require a quorum for a binding decision to be agreed upon. These functions include *RetractPaper(), PublishVersion(), RetractVersion() and SetContributions()*.

5   Discussion

5.1   Identity

Whereas most blockchain applications generally guarantee user anonymity, our use case calls for verifying collaborators' identities. Whilst different digital identity schemes exist, the most popular form seems to be digital certificates used to prove ownership of a public key associated with someone's private key. Even though public-private cryptography can exist in a decentralised environment, digital certificates are always issued by authorised entities.

There exist multiple such authorities which makes it difficult to implement a universal solution. Due to the complexity of this issue, the logic for liaising with different types of digital certificates to verify parties' identities is normally moved to the client's user interface, as it would be too costly to include in smart contracts.

5.2   Cost

Ethereum contracts are not free to execute. Currently, because of the complex nature of the Proof of Work consensus algorithm used by most blockchains including Ethereum, computations performed by blockchain based smart contracts are expensive compared to the same computations performed by a centralised entity.

Execution of a smart contract begins with a transaction that is sent to the blockchain. This transaction specifies the address for the contract, the arguments, and an amount of Ethereum's currency to pay for the execution. It is commonly observed in small-to-medium size contracts that most of the cost is taken up by a fixed "base fee". This base fee of 21,000 is expressed in "gas" which is an abstract unit. While gas is fixed per each transaction, it's additionally fixed for every operation called from within the smart contract. Each low level operation available in the EVM is called an OPCODE. These include operations such as *ADD* - adding two integers together, *BALANCE* - getting the balance of an account, and *CREATE* - creating a new contract with supplied code. Each of these OPCODEs has a fixed amount of gas that it costs to execute. The fixed amount of gas has been chosen by the designers of Ethereum for each OPCODE in a way that reflects the relative complexity of that OPCODE.

Whereas gas is fixed and predictable, the amount a user pays per gas, the *gas price*, is dynamic and dictated by market conditions. The price is usually given in units of *ether*, Ethereum's default currency. Miners receive ether fees based on the amount of gas multiplied by the gas price, which incentivises them to prioritise those transactions that attract higher fees. It also follows that the higher gas price you are willing to pay, the faster your transaction will be processed, and the sooner your contract will be allowed to execute. While offering a high gas price can speed things up, there is a limit to the acceleration. Finally, when discussing cost, it must be mentioned that Ethereum designers have planned mechanisms that will allow the owner of the contract to take all costs upon themselves, thus further incentivising the users of the contract to participate in it.[7]

6   Evaluation

We evaluate the cost of the Smart Papers system by simulating smart contract transactions in a local blockchain environment (Step 1) and then applying the live gas price (Step 2). We focus on the cost of the *Paper* contract functionality[8].

For Step 1, the Ethereum simulator **testrpc**[9] has been used, as it does not require payments for used gas when deploying or testing smart contracts locally. The testrpc utilty is a Node.js client that uses the **ethereumjs**[10] JavaScript library to simulate the blockchain ecosystem behavior and make developing Ethereum dapps (distributed applications) faster. For estimating gas consumption, we use the Web3.js library[11] is the Ethereum compatible JavaScript API that implements JSON remote procedure calls. After contract creation, we use the **estimateGas** call provided by Web3 to estimate the gas amount required to pay for our smart contracts' functions. We arrived at ~75,000 gas per typical Smart Paper transaction.

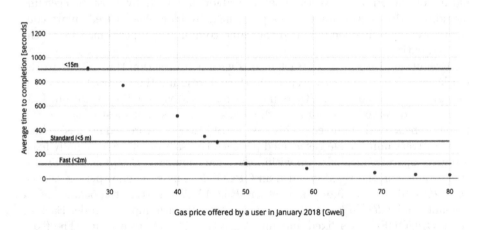

Fig. 3. Average wait times for Ethereum code execution on 11 January 2018

For Step 2, the gas price can be found with ETH Gas Station [1], the de-facto reference for understanding the current gas market conditions and miners' current policies. The "Recommended User Gas Prices" section of ETH Gas Station shows the range of gas prices you might pay for an expected transaction

---

[7] https://blog.ethereum.org/2015/12/24/understanding-serenity-part-i-abstraction/.
[8] https://github.com/mikehoff/SmartPapers.
[9] https://github.com/trufflesuite/ganache-cli.
[10] https://github.com/ethereumjs.
[11] https://github.com/ethereum/web3.js/.

commitment time. Typical time ranges are known as *SafeLow* (<30 min), *Standard* (<5 min) and *Fast* (<2m). Figure 3 illustrates this relationship for the 11th January 2018. Assuming the *Fast* (<2m) confirmation time, our graph suggests this would cost us 50 gwei per gas on this day (*gwei*, also known as *shannon*, is one billionth of one *ether*). On the same day, if we were happy to wait up to 15 min for a confirmation, gas price would have gone down to 26 gwei.

To put Steps 1 and 2 together, we use the following formula:

$$contractCost := baseFee + (gasUsed \times gasPrice)$$

which yields transaction cost in the *Fast* range to be around 3,750,000 *gwei*, i.e. *0.00375* ether per Smart Paper transaction. If we are happy to wait a bit longer (15 min), this goes down to 1,950,000 gwei.

This translates to a sterling cost of £1.7 ($2.3) per Smart Paper transaction such as publishing or retracting a paper if we want this transaction to be accepted in 15 min. Assuming that contributors have access to IPFS nodes, there is no extra cost, in terms of gas, associated with storing of the binary artefacts.

7 Conclusions and Future Work

There is an incentive to use blockchain technology for collaborative processes because it is inherently trustworthy. In Smart Papers, we used Ethereum to provide the framework for collaborative authoring, and IPFS for the storage of the papers.

We analysed a use case demonstrating how the nature of scientific publishing would benefit from storing agreements and artefacts in a verifiable distributed database that does not reside within the confines of a single point of failure, and also does not rely on a centralised party to provide proofs. We found that Distributed Ledger Technologies, by their design, are appropriate for this use case.

We have conducted initial testing to run simulations using a suite of Ethereum smart contracts that we have developed based on our Smart Paper model and workflow. Future development should be focused on implementing a robust web client, a working version contract, and the annotation functionality.

Further research work is needed to explore how the market conditions for transaction execution may impact our design, and how market volatility could impact user behaviour through the variable nature of gas pricing and transaction completion times. The stability and security of the Ethereum network is currently seeing novel research which needs to be constantly monitored. We would like to further explore the storage options for artefacts, metadata and reviews, to optimise for cost and flexibility.

We believe that distributed ledgers are key to decentralised trust in collaborative processes. In our case, these guarantees can be provided at a level of £1.7 ($2.3) per Smart Paper transaction. Future work needs to address the cost of more frequent operations like comments. We would also like to explore the mapping of the Smart Papers workflow to a relevant ontology (for example PWO [8]) to allow each paper to be traced in a semantically standardised way.

References

1. ETH Gas Station, accessed January 2018. https://ethgasstation.info/FAQpage. php
2. Alharby, M., van Moorsel, A.: Blockchain-based smart contracts: a systematic mapping study. CoRR abs/1710.06372 (2017). http://arxiv.org/abs/1710.06372
3. Bartling, S.: Blockchain for open science and knowledge creation. Technical report, Blockchain for Science. http://www.blockchainforscience.com/2017/02/23/blockchain-for-open-science-the-living-document/
4. Benet, J.: IPFS-content addressed, versioned, P2P file system. arXiv preprint arXiv:1407.3561 (2014)
5. Capadisli, S., Guy, A., Lange, C., Auer, S., Sambra, A., Berners-Lee, T.: Linked data notifications: a resource-centric communication protocol. In: Blomqvist, E., Maynard, D., Gangemi, A., Hoekstra, R., Hitzler, P., Hartig, O. (eds.) ESWC 2017. LNCS, vol. 10249, pp. 537–553. Springer, Cham (2017). https://doi.org/10.1007/978-3-319-58068-5_33
6. Capadisli, S., Guy, A., Verborgh, R., Lange, C., Auer, S., Berners-Lee, T.: Decentralised authoring, annotations and notifications for a read-write web with dokieli. In: Cabot, J., De Virgilio, R., Torlone, R. (eds.) ICWE 2017. LNCS, vol. 10360, pp. 469–481. Springer, Cham (2017). https://doi.org/10.1007/978-3-319-60131-1_33
7. Casati, F., Giunchiglia, F., Marchese, M.: Liquid publications: scientific publications meet the Web. Technical report 1313, University of Trento (2007)
8. Gangemi, A., Peroni, S., Shotton, D., Vitali, F.: The publishing workflow ontology (PWO). Semant. Web 8(5), 703–718 (2017)
9. Garcia-Castro, A., Labarga, A., Garcia, L., Giraldo, O., Montaña, C., Bateman, J.A.: Semantic web and social web heading towards living documents in the life sciences. Web Semant.: Sci. Serv. Agents World Wide Web 8(2–3), 155–162 (2010)
10. Haak, L.L., Fenner, M., Paglione, L., Pentz, E., Ratner, H.: Orcid: a system to uniquely identify researchers. Learn. Publish. 25(4), 259–264 (2012)
11. Heller, L., The, R., Bartling, S.: Dynamic publication formats and collaborative authoring. In: Bartling, S., Friesike, S. (eds.) Opening Science, pp. 191–211. Springer International Publishing, Cham (2014)
12. Hürsch, W.L., Lopes, C.V.: Separation of concerns. NorthEastern University, Technical report (1995)
13. Kuhn, T., Dumontier, M.: Making digital artifacts on the web verifiable and reliable. IEEE Trans. Knowl. Data Eng. 27(9), 2390–2400 (2015)
14. López-Cózar, E.D., Robinson-Garcia, N., Torres-Salinas, D.: Manipulating Google scholar citations and Google scholar metrics: simple, easy and tempting. arXiv preprint arXiv:1212.0638 (2012)
15. Wattenhofer, R.: The Science of the Blockchain, 1st edn. Inverted Forest Publishing, Erscheinungsort nicht ermittelbar (2016). oCLC: 952079386
16. Wood, G.: Ethereum: a secure decentralised generalised transaction ledger. Ethereum Project Yellow Paper 151 (2014). https://github.com/ethereum/yellowpaper

Mind the (Language) Gap: Generation of Multilingual Wikipedia Summaries from Wikidata for ArticlePlaceholders

Lucie-Aimée Kaffee[1]([✉]) [iD], Hady Elsahar[2] [iD], Pavlos Vougiouklis[1] [iD],
Christophe Gravier[2] [iD], Frédérique Laforest[2] [iD], Jonathon Hare[1] [iD],
and Elena Simperl[1]

[1] School of Electronics and Computer Science,
University of Southampton, Southampton, UK
{pv1e13,jsh2,e.simperl}@ecs.soton.ac.uk, kaffee@soton.ac.uk
[2] Laboratoire Hubert Curien, CNRS UJM-Saint-Étienne,
Université de Lyon, Lyon, France
{hady.elsahar,christophe.gravier,frederique.laforest}@univ-st-etienne.fr

Abstract. While Wikipedia exists in 287 languages, its content is unevenly distributed among them. It is therefore of utmost social and cultural importance to focus efforts on languages whose speakers only have access to limited Wikipedia content. We investigate supporting communities by generating summaries for Wikipedia articles in underserved languages, given structured data as an input.

We focus on an important support for such summaries: ArticlePlaceholders, a dynamically generated content pages in underserved Wikipedias. They enable native speakers to access existing information in Wikidata. To extend those ArticlePlaceholders, we provide a system, which processes the triples of the KB as they are provided by the ArticlePlaceholder, and generate a comprehensible textual summary. This data-driven approach is employed with the goal of understanding how well it matches the communities' needs on two underserved languages on the Web: Arabic, a language with a big community with disproportionate access to knowledge online, and Esperanto, an easily-acquainted, artificial language whose Wikipedia content is maintained by a small but devoted community. With the help of the Arabic and Esperanto Wikipedians, we conduct a study which evaluates not only the quality of the generated text, but also the usefulness of our end-system to any underserved Wikipedia version.

Keywords: Multilinguality · Wikipedia · Wikidata
Natural language generation · Esperanto · Arabic · Neural networks

---

L.-A. Kaffee, H. Elsahar and P. Vougiouklis—These authors contributed equally to this work.

© Springer International Publishing AG, part of Springer Nature 2018
A. Gangemi et al. (Eds.): ESWC 2018, LNCS 10843, pp. 319–334, 2018.
https://doi.org/10.1007/978-3-319-93417-4_21

1   Introduction

Despite the fact that Wikipedia exists in 287 languages, its content is unevenly distributed. The content of the most under-resourced Wikipedias is maintained by a limited number of editors – they cannot curate the same volume of articles as in the large Wikipedia communities. Part of this problem has been addressed by Wikidata, the KB supporting Wikipedia with structured data in a cross-lingual manner. Recently, Wikimedia introduced **ArticlePlaceholders** [12] in order to integrate Wikidata's knowledge into the Wikipedias of underserved languages and help in reducing the language gap. ArticlePlaceholders display Wikidata triples in a tabular-based way in the target Wikipedia language and are currently deployed to 11 underserved Wikipedias[1]. When a user searches for a topic on Wikipedia that has a Wikidata item, but no Wikipedia article yet, they are led to the ArticlePlaceholder[2] on the topic. Compared to stub articles[3], ArticlePlaceholders have the advantage of being dynamically updated in real time to accommodate information changes in Wikidata. This means less maintenance for small communities of editors. Since Wikidata is one central, language-independent place to edit information and each item or property has to be translated only once, any contribution in Wikidata has an impact on the ArticlePlaceholders. For example, an editor speaking only English can connect the existing items Q1299 (*The Beatles*) with the item Q145 (*United Kingdom*) via the property P495 (*country of origin*). This will automatically add the same triple with their Esperanto labels: *The Beatles – eldonit/ata en – Unuiĝinta Reĝlando*. Nonetheless, ArticlePlaceholders currently only display information in the form of tables.

In this paper, we propose an automatic approach to enrich ArticlePlaceholders with textual summaries that can serve as a starting point for the Wikipedia editors to write their article. The summaries resemble the first sentence of a Wikipedia article, that gives a reader an overview of the topic. We pose the following research questions:

RQ1. Given the challenges concerning underserved languages, can we generate textual summaries that match the quality and style of Wikipedia content?
RQ2. Can we generate summaries that are useful for Wikipedia editors of underserved language communities?

We adapt an end-to-end trainable model, which generates a monolingual textual summary (i.e. only in English) given a set of KB triples as input, for multilingual support. To this end, we introduce a new "property placeholders" feature and put them under distant supervision in order to enable our system to verbalise even rare or "unseen" entities. Since the summaries are generated explicitly based on

---

[1] cy, eo, lv, nn, ht, kn, nap, gu, or, sq, and bn.
[2] Example as of online now, without the integration of generated summaries: https:// gu.wikipedia.org/wiki/special:AboutTopic/Q7186.
[3] https://en.wikipedia.org/wiki/Wikipedia:Stub.

Table 1. Recent page statistics and number of unique words (vocab. size) of Esperanto, Arabic and English Wikipedias in comparison with Wikidata.

Page statistic	Esperanto	Arabic	English	Wikidata
Articles	241,901	541,166	5,483,928	37,703,807
Avg edits/page	11.48	8.94	21.11	14.66
Active users	2,849	7,818	129,237	17,583
Vocab. size	1.5M	2.2M	2.0M	–

the input triples, potential changes in the respective triples can manifest themselves immediately to the textual content of the summary without the inclusion of the translation loop. Furthermore, since we do not transfer any information from a source language, our model learns to generate Wikipedia content that captures the linguistic peculiarities of our target underserved Wikipedias.

We apply our model on two languages that have a severe lack of both editors and articles on Wikipedia: Esperanto and Arabic. Esperanto is an artificially created language, with an easy acquisition, which makes it a suitable starting point to explore challenges of our task. On the other hand, Arabic is a morphologically rich language with a significantly larger vocabulary. Arabic is the 5th most spoken language in the world [8], however as shown in Table 1 the Arabic Wikipedia suffers a severe lack of content compared to the English.

We propose a novel evaluation framework that assesses the usefulness of the summaries via a multitude of metrics, computed against strong baselines and involving readers and editors of underserved Wikipedias. We start our evaluation by measuring how close our synthesized summaries are to actual summaries in Wikipedia. We compare our model to two strong baselines of different natures: MT and a template-based solution. Our model substantially outperforms the baselines in all evaluation metrics in both Esperanto and Arabic. In addition, we developed three studies with the Wikipedia community, in which we ask for their feedback about the generated summaries, in terms of their fluency, appropriateness for Wikipedia, and engagement with editors. We believe that given the promising results achieved in the automatic and human evaluations, our approach along with the datasets, the baselines, and the experimental design of the human evaluation can serve as a starting point for the research community to further improve and assist in solving this critical task. Our code and experiments are available: https://github.com/pvougiou/Mind-the-Language-Gap.

2 Related Work

Multilingual Text Generation. Many existing techniques for text generation and RDF verbalization rely on templates. These templates are generated using linguistic features such as grammatical rules [26], or are hand-crafted [7]. These approaches face many challenges when scaling for a language-independent system, as templates need to be fine-tuned to any new languages they are ported to. This is especially difficult for the few editors of underserved Wikipedias since templates need extra attention. They would have to create and maintain templates while this time could be invested in the creation of an actual article. Recognizing this problem, the authors of [5,6] introduce a distant-supervised approach to verbalize triples. The templates are learned from existing Wikipedia articles. This makes the approach more suitable for language-independent tasks. However, templates always assume that items will always have the appropriate triples to fill the slots of the template. This assumption is not always necessarily true. In our experiments, we implement a template-learning baseline and we show that adapting to the varying triples available can achieve better performance.

Text Generation for Wikipedia. Pochampally et al. and Sauper et al. proposed the generation of Wikipedia summaries by harvesting sentences from the Internet [20,23]. Existing Wikipedia articles are used to automatically derive templates for the topic structure of the summaries and the templates are afterward filled using Web content. Such approaches are limited to only one or two domains and only in English. The lack of Web resources for underserved languages prevents these approaches to scale to undeserved languages in multiple domains [16]. Meanwhile, KBs have been used as a resource for NLG [2,5,19,25]. These techniques leverage linguistic information from KBs to build a dataset of triples aligned with equivalent sentences from Wikipedia. This alignment is used at subsequent steps to train NLG systems.

The most relevant work to our proposed model are the recent approaches by Lebret et al. [15], Chisholm et al. [2], and Vougiouklis et al. [25], who all propose adaptations of the general encoder-decoder neural network framework [3,24]. They use structured data from Wikidata and DBpedia as input and generate one sentence summaries that match the Wikipedia style in English in only a single domain. The first sentence of Wikipedia articles in a single domain exhibit a relatively narrow domain of language in comparison to other text generation tasks such as translation. However, Chisholm et al. [2] show that this task is still challenging and far from being solved. In contrast with these works, in our paper we extend those research work to include open-domain, multilingual summaries.

Evaluating Text Generation. Evaluating generated text is challenging and there have been different approaches proposed by the literature. Automatic scores [15], expert evaluation and crowdsourcing [2,14] have been employed. Additionally, similar to Sauper and Barzilay [23], we extend our evaluation to usefulness of the summaries for Wikipedia editors by measuring the amount of reuse of the generated summaries. This concept has been widely investigated in fields such as journalism [4] and plagiarism detection [21].

Table 2. The ArticlePlaceholder provides our system with a set of triples about *Floridia*, whose either subject or object is related to the item of Floridia. Subsequently, our system summarizes the input set of triples as text. We train our model using the summary with the extended vocabulary.

ArticlePlaceholder triples	f_1: Q490900 (Floridia)	P17 (ŝtato)	Q38 (Italio)
	f_2: Q490900 (Floridia)	P31 (estas)	Q747074 (komunumo de Italio)
	f_3: Q30025755 (Floridia)	P1376 (ĉefurbo de)	Q490900 (Floridia)
Textual summary	Floridia estas komunumo de Italio		
Vocab. extended summary	[[Q490900, Floridia]] estas komunumo de [[P17]]		

3 Methods

We use a neural network in order to understand the impact of adding automatically generated text to ArticlePlaceholders in underserved language Wikipedias.

3.1 Our System

Our system is adapted from our encoder-decoder architecture introduced in [25] that has already been used on a similar text generative task. The architecture of the generative model is displayed in Fig. 1. The encoder is a feed-forward architecture which encodes an input set of triples into a vector of fixed dimensionality. This is used at a later stage to initialise the decoder. The decoder is an RNN that uses Gated Recurrent Units (GRUs) [3] to generate the textual summary one token at a time.

An example is presented in Table 2. The ArticlePlaceholder provides our system with a set of triples about the Wikidata item of *Floridia* (i.e. Q490900 (Floridia) is either the subject or the object of the triples in the set). Figure 1 displays how our model generates a summary from those triples, f_1, f_2, and f_3. A vector representation h_{f_1}, h_{f_2}, and h_{f_3} for each of the input triples is computed by processing their subject, predicate and object. These vector representations are used to compute a vector representation for the whole input set h_{F_E}. h_{F_E}, along with the special start-of-summary <start> token, are used to initialise the decoder that sequentially predicts tokens ("[[Q490900, Floridia]]", "estas", "komunumo" etc.).

Formally, let F_E be the set of triples provided by the ArticlePlaceholder for the item E (i.e. item E is either the subject or the object of the triples in the set), our goal is to learn a model that generates a summary Y_E about E. We regard Y_E as a sequence of T tokens such that $Y_E = y_1, y_2, \ldots, y_T$ and compute the conditional probability $p(Y_E|F_E)$:

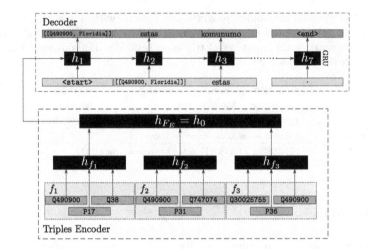

Fig. 1. The triple encoder computes a vector representation for each one of the three input triples from the ArticlePlaceholder, h_{f_1}, h_{f_2} and h_{f_3}. Subsequently, the decoder is initialized using the concatenation of the three vectors, $[h_{f_1}; h_{f_2}; h_{f_3}]$. The purple boxes represent the tokens of the generated summary. Each summary starts and ends with the respective start-of-summary <start> and end-of-summary <end> tokens. (Color figure online)

$$p(Y_E|F_E) = \prod_{t=1}^{T} p(y_t|y_1, \ldots y_{t-1}, F_E) \ . \tag{1}$$

3.1.1   Generating a Summary

Our model learns to make a prediction about the next token by using the negative cross-entropy criterion. We define a maximum number of triples per summary. Input sets with fewer triples are padded with zero vectors, which are consistently ignored by the encoder. During training our architecture predicts the sequence of tokens that make up the summary. During testing, the ArticlePlaceholder provides our model with a set of unknown triples. After the vector representation h_{F_E} for the unknown set of triples is computed, we initialize the decoder with a special start-of-sequence <start> token.

We adopt a beam-search decoder [15,24,25] which provides us with B-most-probable summaries for each triple set F_E.

3.1.2   Vocabulary Extensions

Each summary consist of words and mentions of named entities. Mapping those entities to words is hard since an entity can have several surface forms and the system may face rare/unseen entities at prediction time. We adopt the concept of *surface form tuples* to learn a number of different verbalisations of the same entity in the summary [25]. In Table 2, [[Q490900, Floridia]] in the vocabulary extended summary is an example of a surface form tuple where the entity Q490900 is associated with the surface form of "Floridia".

Additionally, we address the problem of learning embeddings for rare entities in text [17] by training our model to match the occurrence of rare entities in the text to the corresponding triple. To this end, we introduce *property placeholders*. The property placeholders are inspired by the *property-type placeholders* [25]. However, their applicability is much broader since they do not require any instance type-related information about the entities that appear in the triples. In the vocabulary extended summary of Table 2, [[P17]] is an example of property placeholder. In case it is generated by our model, it is replaced with the label of the object of the triple with which they share the same property (i.e. Q490900 (Floridia) P17 (stato) Q38 (Italio)).

Further details regarding the fundamental components of our neural architecture, such as the triples encoder and the surface form tuples, can be found in our previous work [25].

4 Training and Automatic Evaluation

In this section, we describe the dataset that we built for our experiments along with the results of the automatic evaluation of our neural network architecture against the baselines.

4.1 Dataset

In order to train and evaluate our system, we created a new dataset for text generation from KB triples in a multilingual setting. We wish to explore the robustness of our approach to variable datasets with respect to language complexity and size of available training data. Consequently, we worked with two linguistically distinct Wikipedias of different sizes (see Table 1) and different language support in Wikidata [13].

This dataset aligns Wikidata triples with the first, introductory sentence of its corresponding Wikipedia articles. For each Wikipedia article, we extracted and tokenized the first sentence using a multilingual Regex tokenizer from the NLTK toolkit [1]. Afterwards, we retrieved the corresponding Wikidata item to the article and queried all triples where the item appeared as a subject or an object in the Wikidata truthy dump[4].

In order to create the *surface form tuples* (i.e. Sect. 3.1.2), we identify occurrences of entities in the text along with their verbalisations. We rely on keyword matching against labels from Wikidata from the corresponding language, due to the lack of reliable entity linking tools for underserved languages.

For the *property placeholders* (described in more detail in Sect. 3.1.2), we use the distant-supervision assumption for relation extraction [18]. After identifying the rare entities that participate in relations with the main entity of the article, they are replaced from the introductory sentence with their corresponding

---

[4] https://dumps.wikimedia.org/wikidatawiki/entities/.

property placeholder tag (e.g. [[P17]] in Table 2). During testing, any property placeholder token that is generated by our system is replaced by the label of the entity of the relevant triple (i.e. triple with the same property as the generated token).

4.2   Automatic Evaluation

To evaluate how well our system generates textual summaries for Wikipedia, we evaluated the generated summaries against two baselines on their original counterparts from Wikipedia. We use a set of evaluation metrics for text generation BLEU 1, BLEU 2, BLEU 3, BLEU 4, METEOR and ROUGE$_L$. BLEU calculates n-gram precision multiplied by a brevity penalty which penalizes short sentences to account for word recall. METEOR is based on the combination of uni-gram precision and recall, with recall weighted over precision. It extends BLEU by including stemming, synonyms and paraphrasing. ROUGE$_L$ is a recall-based metric which calculates the length of the most common subsequence between the generated summary and the reference.

4.3   Baselines for Automatic Evaluation

Due to the variety of approaches for text generation, we demonstrate the effectiveness of our system by comparing it against two baselines of different nature. Both baselines are reproducible and the code is provided in the GitHub repo.

Machine Translation (MT). For the MT baseline, we used Google Translate on English Wikipedia summaries. Those translations are compared to the actual target language's Wikipedia entry. This limits us to articles that exist in both English and the target language. In our dataset, the concepts in Esperanto and Arabic that are not covered by English Wikipedia account for 4.3% and 30.5% respectively. This indicates the content coverage gap between different Wikipedia languages [10].

Template Retrieval (TP). Similar to template-based approaches for text generation [6, 22], we build a template-based baseline that retrieves an output summary from the training data based on the input triples. First, the baseline encodes the list of input triples that corresponds to each summary in the training/test sets into a sparse vector of TF-IDF weights [11]. Afterwards, it performs LSA [9] to reduce the dimensionality of that vector. Finally, for each item in the test set, we employ the K-nearest neighbors algorithm to retrieve the vector from the training set that is the closest to this item. The summary that corresponds to the retrieved vector is used as the output summary for this item in the test set. We provide two versions of this baseline. The first one (TP) retrieves the raw summaries from the training dataset. The second one (TP$_{ext}$) retrieves summaries with the special tokens for vocabulary extension. A summary can act as a template after replacing its entities with their corresponding *Property Placeholders* (see Table 2).

Table 3. Participation numbers: total number of participants (P), total number of sentences (S), number of P that evaluated at least 50% of S, and average number of S evaluated per P.

		#P	#S	#P: S > 50%	Avg. #S/P	All ann.
Arabic	Fluency	27	60	5	15.03	406
	Approp	27	60	5	14.78	399
	Editors	7	30	2	4	33
Esper.	Fluency	27	60	3	8.7	235
	Approp	27	60	3	8.63	233
	Editors	8	30	2	4.75	38

5 Community Study

Automatic measures of text quality such as BLEU can give an indication of how close a generated text is to the source of a summary. Complementary, working with humans is generally more trusted when it comes to quality evaluation of generated text, and captures the direct response of the community. We ran a community study for a total of 15 days to answer our research questions. To address the question whether the textual summaries can match the quality of Wikipedia (RQ1), we define text quality as fluency and appropriateness. Fluency describes the quality in terms of understandability and grammatical correctness. Appropriateness describes how well a summary fits into Wikipedia, i.e. whether a reader can identify it as part of a Wikipedia article. We assess editors reuse to answer whether we can generate summaries that are useful for Wikipedia editors (RQ2). Our evaluation targets two different communities: (1) *readers*: Any speaker of Arabic and Esperanto, that reads Wikipedia, independent of their activity on Wikipedia, and (2) *editors*: any active contributor to Arabic and Esperanto Wikipedia. Readers were asked to fill one survey combining fluency and appropriateness. Editors were also asked to fill an additional survey[5]. To sample only participants with previous activity on Wikipedia, we asked them for their reading and editing activity on Wikipedia. The survey instructions[6] and announcements[7] were translated in Arabic and Esperanto.

Recruitment. For the recruitment of readers, we wanted to reach fluent speakers of the language. For Arabic, we got in contact with Arabic speaking researchers from research groups working on Wikipedia related topics. For Esperanto, as there are fewer speakers and they are harder to reach, we promoted the survey

---

[5] Example questions: https://github.com/pvougiou/Mind-the-Language-Gap/tree/master/crowdevaluation/Examples.

[6] All instructions for the surveys: https://tinyurl.com/y7cgmesk.

[7] https://github.com/luciekaffee/Announcements.

Table 4. Automatic evaluation of our model against all other baselines using BLEU 1–4, ROUGE and METEOR on the validation and the test set for both Arabic and Esperanto.

	Model	BLEU 1		BLEU 2		BLEU 3		BLEU 4		ROUGE$_L$		METEOR	
		Valid.	Test	Valid.	Test	Valid.	Test	Valid.	Test	Valid.	Test	Valid.	Test
Arabic	MT	31.12	33.48	19.31	21.12	12.69	13.89	8.49	9.11	29.96	30.51	31.05	30.1
	TP	41.39	41.73	34.18	34.58	29.36	29.72	25.68	25.98	43.26	43.58	32.99	33.33
	TP$_{ext}$	49.87	48.96	42.44	41.5	37.29	36.41	33.27	32.51	51.66	50.57	34.39	34.25
	Ours	**53.18**	**52.94**	**45.86**	**45.64**	**40.38**	**40.21**	**35.7**	**35.55**	**57.9**	**57.99**	**39.22**	**39.37**
Esperanto	MT	5.35	5.47	1.62	1.62	0.59	0.56	0.26	0.23	4.67	4.79	0.66	0.68
	TP	43.01	42.61	33.67	33.46	28.16	28.07	24.35	24.3	46.75	45.92	20.71	20.46
	TP$_{ext}$	52.75	51.66	43.57	42.53	37.53	36.54	33.35	32.41	58.15	57.62	**31.21**	**31.04**
	Ours	**56.51**	**56.96**	**47.72**	**48.1**	**41.8**	**42.13**	**37.24**	**37.52**	**64.36**	**64.69**	28.35	28.76

on social media such as Twitter and Reddit[8] using the researchers' accounts. For the recruitment of editors, we posted on the editors' mailing-lists[9]. Additionally, for Esperanto we posted on the Wikipedia discussion page[10]. The Arabic editors survey was also promoted at WikiArabia, the conference for the Arabic speaking Wikipedia community. The numbers of participation in all surveys can be found in Table 3.

Fluency. We answer whether we can generate summaries that match the quality and style of Wikipedia content in a study with 54 Wikipedia readers from two different Wikipedia languages. We created a corpus consisting of 60 summaries of which 30 are generated through our approach, 15 are from news, 15 from Wikipedia summaries of the training dataset. For news in Esperanto, we chose introduction sentences of articles in the Esperanto version of Le Monde Diplomatique[11]. For news in Arabic, we chose introduction sentences of the RSS feed of BBC Arabic[12]. Each participant was asked to assess the fluency of the text. We employ a scale from 0 to 6, where: **(6) Excellent**: the given sentence has no grammatical flaws and the content can be understood with ease; **(3) Moderate**: the given sentence is understandable, but has minor grammatical issues; **(0) Non-understandable**: the given sentence cannot be understood. For each sentence, we calculate the mean quality given by all participants and then averaging over all summaries in each corpus.

Appropriateness. As we used the same survey for both fluency and appropriateness, participants answered questions regarding the appropriateness over the same set of sentences. They were asked to assess whether the displayed sentence

---

[8] https://www.reddit.com/r/Esperanto/comments/75rytb/help_in_a_study_using_ai_to_create_esperanto/.

[9] Esperanto: eliso@lists.wikimedia.org, Arabic: wikiar-l@lists.wikimedia.org.

[10] https://eo.wikipedia.org/wiki/Vikipedio:Diskutejo/Diversejo#Help_in_a_study_imp roving_Esperanto_text_for_Editors.

[11] http://eo.mondediplo.com/, accessed 28. September 2017.

[12] http://feeds.bbci.co.uk/arabic/middleeast/rss.xml, accessed 28 Sep 2017.

Table 5. Results for fluency and appropriateness.

		Fluency		Appropriateness
		Mean	SD	Part of Wikipedia
Arabic	Ours	4.7	1.2	77%
	Wikipedia	4.6	0.9	74%
	News	5.3	0.4	35%
Esper.	Ours	4.5	1.5	69%
	Wikipedia	4.9	1.2	84%
	News	4.2	1.2	52%

could be part of a Wikipedia article. We test whether a reader can tell the difference from just one sentence whether a text is appropriate for Wikipedia, using the news sentences as a baseline. This gives us an insight on whether the text produced by the neural network "feels" like Wikipedia text (appropriateness). Participants were asked not to use any external tools for this task. Readers have just two options to choose from (Yes and No).

Editors Reuse. We randomly choose 30 items from our test set. For each item, each editor was offered the generated summary and its corresponding set of triples and was asked to write a paragraph of 2 or 3 sentences. Editors had the freedom to copy from the generated summary, or completely work from scratch. We assessed how editors used our generated summaries in their work by measuring the amount of text reuse. To quantify the amount of reuse in text we use the Greedy String-Tiling (GST) algorithm [27]. GST is a substring matching algorithm that computes the degree of reuse or copy from a source text and a dependent one. GST is able to deal with cases when a whole block is transposed, unlike other algorithms such as the Levenshtein distance, which calculates it as a sequence of single insertions or deletions rather than a single block move. Given a generated summary $S = s_1, s_2, \ldots$ and an edited one $D = d_1, d_2, \ldots$, each consisting of a sequence of tokens, GST will identify a set of disjoint longest sequences of tokens in the edited text that exist in the source text (called ***tiles***) $T = \{t_1, t_2, \ldots\}$. It is expected that there will be common stop words appearing in both the source and the edited text. However, we are rather interested in knowing how much of real structure of the generated summary is being copied. Thus, we set minimum match length factor $mml = 3$ when calculating the tiles, s.t. $\forall t_i \in T : t_i \subseteq S \wedge t_i \subseteq D \wedge |t_i| \geq mml$ and $\forall t_i, t_j \in T | i \neq j : t_i \cap t_j = \emptyset$. This means that copied sequences of single or double words will not count in the calculation of reuse. We calculate a reuse score *gstscore* by counting the lengths of the detected tiles, and normalize by the length of the generated summary.

$$gstscore(S, D) = \frac{\sum_{t_i \in T} |t_i|}{|S|} \tag{2}$$

Table 6. Percentage of summaries in each category of reuse. A generated summary (top) and after it is was edited (bottom). Solid lines represent reused tiles, while dashed lines represent overlapping sub-sequences not contributing to the *gstscore*.

Category		Examples	%
Arabic	WD	خماسي كلوريد الزرنيخ مركب كيميائي له الصيفة(كلمة ناقصة)، ويكون على شكل بلورات بيضاء. خماسي كلوريد الزرنيخ هو مُركب كيميائي له الصيفة(AtClu2085)، ويكون على شكل بلورات بيضاء.	45.45%
	PD	يبتش باتوم أوهايو (بالإنجليزية (كلمة ناقصة) Ohio)هي منطقة سكنية تقع في الولايات المتحدة في(كلمة ناقصة.) يبتش باتوم (بالإنجليزية:Beach Batom)هي قرية تقع في الولايات المتحدة الامريكية في برووك كاونتي.	33.33%
	ND	دير علا هي بلدة تقع في جنوب غرب إيران. دير علا، أو بيثر، هي قرية أردنية	21.21%
Esperanto	WD	Zederik estas komunumo en la nederlanda provinco Zuid-Holland. Zederik estas komunumo en la nederlanda provinco Zuid-Hooland kaj estas ĉirkaŭata de la municipoj Lopik kaj Zederik.	78.98%
	PD	Nova Pádua estas municipo en la brazila subŝtato Suda Rio-Grando, kiu havis (manka nombro) loĝantojn en (jaro). Nova Pádua estas municipo en la brazila subŝtato Suda Rio-Grando.	15.79%
	ND	Ibiúna estas municipo de la brazila subŝtato San-Paŭlio, kiu taksis (manka nombro) enloĝantojn en (jaro). Ibiúna estas brazila [[municipo]] kiu troviĝas en la administra unuo [[San-Paŭlio]].	5.26%

We classify each of the edits into three groups according to the *gstscore* as proposed by [4]: (1) **Wholly Derived (WD):** the summary structure has been fully reused in the composition of the editor's text (*gstscore* ≥ 0.66); (2) **Partially Derived (PD):** the summary has been partially used ($0.66 > gstscore \geq 0.33$); (3) **Non Derived (ND):** The summary has been changed completely ($0.33 > gstscore$).

6   Results and Discussions

In this section, we will report and discuss our experimental findings with respect to the two research questions.

6.1   Automatic Evaluation

As displayed in Table 4, our model shows a significant enhancement compared to our baselines across the majority of the evaluation metrics in both languages. We achieve a **3.01** and **5.11** enhancement in BLEU 4 score in Arabic and Esperanto respectively over TP$_{ext}$, the strongest baseline. MT of English summaries is not competitive. We attribute this result to the differences in the way of writing across different Wikipedia languages – this inhibits MT from being sufficient for Wikipedia document generation. The results show that generating language directly from the knowledge base triples is a much more suitable approach.

6.2 Community Study

We present the results of the community study in order to find whether we could generate textual summaries that match the quality and style of Wikipedia (RQ1) and can support editors (RQ2).

Fluency (Table 5). Overall, the quality of our generated summaries is high (4.7 points in average in Arabic, 4.5 in Esperanto). In Arabic, 63.3% of the summaries were evaluated to have at least 5 (out of 6) in average. In Esperanto, 50% of the summaries have at least a quality of 5 (out of 6) in average, with 33% of all summaries given a score of 6 by all participants. This means the majority of our summaries is highly understandable and grammatically correct. Furthermore, our generated summaries are also considered by participants to have a similar average quality as Wikipedia summaries and news from widely read media organizations.

Appropriateness (Table 5). 77% (resp. 69%) of the generated Arabic (resp. Esperanto) summaries were categorized as being part of Wikipedia. In comparison, news sentences were identified more likely to not fit. In only 35% (Arabic) and 52% (Esperanto) of cases, readers have mistaken them for Wikipedia sentences. Wikipedia sentences were clearly recognized as such (77% and 84%) with scores that are closely matching the one from the generated summaries from our model. Wikipedia has a certain writing style, that seems to differ clearly from news. Our summaries are able to reflect this writing style, being more likely evaluated as Wikipedia sentences than the news baseline – we can expect the generated summaries to melt seamlessly with other Wikipedia content.

Editors Reuse (Table 6). Our summaries were highly reused. **79%** of the Arabic generated summaries and **93%** of the Esperanto generated summaries were either wholly (**WD**) or partially (**PD**) reused by editors. For the wholly derived edits, editors tended to copy the generated summary with minimal modifications such as Table 6 subsequences A and B in Arabic or subsequence G in Esperanto. One of the common things that hampers the full reusability are "rare" tokens, (كلمة ناقصة) in Arabic and *(mankas vorto)* in Esperanto. Usually, these tokens are yielded when the output word is not in the model vocabulary, it has not been seen frequently by our model such as names in different languages. As it can be seen in tiles E and D in the Arabic examples in Table 6, editors prefer in those cases to adapt the generated sentences. This can also go as far as making the editor to delete the whole subsentence if it contains a high number of such tokens (subsequence H in Table 6). By examining our generated summaries we find that such missing tokens are more likely to appear in Arabic than in Esperanto (2.2 times more). The observed reusability by editors of the Esperanto generated summaries (78.98% **WD**) in comparison to Arabic (45.45% **WD**) can be attributed to this. This can be explained as follows. First, the significant larger vocabulary size of Arabic, which lowers the probability of a word to be seen by the Arabic model. Second, since the majority of rare tokens are named entities mentioned in foreign languages and since the Latin script of Esperanto is similar to many other languages, the Esperanto model has an advantage over the Arabic one when capturing words representing named entities.

7 Conclusions

We introduce a system that extends Wikipedia's ArticlePlaceholder with multilingual summaries automatically generated from Wikidata triples for underserved language on Wikipedia. We show that with the encoder-decoder architecture that we propose is able to perform better than strong baselines of different natures, including MT and a template-based baseline. We ran a community evaluation study to measure to what extent our summaries match the quality and style of Wikipedia articles, and whether they are useful in terms of reuse by Wikipedia editors. We show that members of the targeted language communities rank our text close to the expected quality standards of Wikipedia, and are likely to consider the generated text as part of Wikipedia. Lastly, we found that the editors are likely to reuse a large portion of the generated summaries, thus emphasizing the usefulness of our approach to its intended audience.

Acknowledgements. This research is partially supported by the Answering Questions using Web Data (WDAqua) project, a Marie Skłodowska-Curie Innovative Training Network under grant agreement No 642795, part of the Horizon 2020 programme.

References

1. Bird, S.: NLTK: the natural language toolkit. In: ACL 2006, 21st International Conference on Computational Linguistics and 44th Annual Meeting of the Association for Computational Linguistics, Proceedings of the Conference, 17–21 July 2006, Sydney, Australia (2006)
2. Chisholm, A., Radford, W., Hachey, B.: Learning to generate one-sentence biographies from Wikidata. In: Proceedings of the 15th Conference of the European Chapter of the Association for Computational Linguistics, Long Papers, vol. 1, pp. 633–642. Association for Computational Linguistics, Valencia, April 2017
3. Cho, K., van Merrienboer, B., Gülçehre, Ç., Bougares, F., Schwenk, H., Bengio, Y.: Learning phrase representations using RNN encoder-decoder for statistical machine translation. CoRR abs/1406.1078 (2014)
4. Clough, P.D., Gaizauskas, R.J., Piao, S.S.L., Wilks, Y.: METER: MEasuring TExt reuse. In: Proceedings of the 40th Annual Meeting of the Association for Computational Linguistics, 6–12 July 2002, Philadelphia, PA, USA, pp. 152–159 (2002)
5. Duma, D., Klein, E.: Generating natural language from linked data: unsupervised template extraction. In: IWCS, pp. 83–94 (2013)
6. Ell, B., Harth, A.: A language-independent method for the extraction of RDF verbalization templates. In: INLG 2014 - Proceedings of the Eighth International Natural Language Generation Conference, Including Proceedings of the INLG and SIGDIAL 2014 Joint Session, 19–21 June 2014, Philadelphia, PA, USA, pp. 26–34 (2014)

7. Galanis, D., Androutsopoulos, I.: Generating multilingual descriptions from linguistically annotated OWL ontologies: the NaturalOWL system. In: Proceedings of the Eleventh European Workshop on Natural Language Generation, pp. 143–146. Association for Computational Linguistics (2007)

8. Gordon, R.G., Grimes, B.F., et al.: Ethnologue: Languages of the world, vol. 15. SIL International, Dallas (2005)

9. Halko, N., Martinsson, P., Tropp, J.A.: Finding structure with randomness: probabilistic algorithms for constructing approximate matrix decompositions. SIAM Rev. **53**(2), 217–288 (2011)

10. Hecht, B., Gergle, D.: The tower of Babel meets web 2.0: user-generated content and its applications in a multilingual context. In: Proceedings of the SIGCHI Conference on Human Factors in Computing Systems, pp. 291–300. ACM (2010)

11. Joachims, T.: A probabilistic analysis of the Rocchio algorithm with TFIDF for text categorization. In: Proceedings of the Fourteenth International Conference on Machine Learning (ICML 1997), Nashville, Tennessee, USA, 8–12 July 1997, pp. 143–151 (1997)

12. Kaffee, L.A.: Generating article placeholders from Wikidata for Wikipedia: increasing access to free and open knowledge. Bachelor's thesis, HTW Berlin (2016)

13. Kaffee, L.A., Piscopo, A., Vougiouklis, P., Simperl, E., Carr, L., Pintscher, L.: A glimpse into Babel: an analysis of multilinguality in Wikidata. In: Proceedings of the 13th International Symposium on Open Collaboration, p. 14. ACM (2017)

14. Kondadadi, R., Howald, B., Schilder, F.: A statistical NLG framework for aggregated planning and realization. In: Proceedings of the 51st Annual Meeting of the Association for Computational Linguistics, ACL 2013, 4–9 August 2013, Sofia, Bulgaria, Long Papers, vol. 1, pp. 1406–1415 (2013)

15. Lebret, R., Grangier, D., Auli, M.: Neural text generation from structured data with application to the biography domain. In: Proceedings of the 2016 Conference on Empirical Methods in Natural Language Processing, EMNLP 2016, Austin, Texas, USA, 1–4 November 2016, pp. 1203–1213 (2016)

16. Lewis, W.D., Yang, P.: Building MT for a severely under-resourced language: white hmong. In: Association for Machine Translation in the Americas, October 2012

17. Luong, T., Sutskever, I., Le, Q.V., Vinyals, O., Zaremba, W.: Addressing the rare word problem in neural machine translation. In: Proceedings of the 53rd Annual Meeting of the Association for Computational Linguistics and the 7th International Joint Conference on Natural Language Processing of the Asian Federation of Natural Language Processing, ACL 2015, 26–31 July 2015, Beijing, China, Long Papers, vol. 1, pp. 11–19 (2015)

18. Mintz, M., Bills, S., Snow, R., Jurafsky, D.: Distant supervision for relation extraction without labeled data. In: ACL 2009, Proceedings of the 47th Annual Meeting of the Association for Computational Linguistics and the 4th International Joint Conference on Natural Language Processing of the AFNLP, 2–7 August 2009, Singapore, pp. 1003–1011 (2009)

19. Mrabet, Y., Vougiouklis, P., Kilicoglu, H., Gardent, C., Demner-Fushman, D., Hare, J., Simperl, E.: Aligning texts and knowledge bases with semantic sentence simplification (2016)

20. Pochampally, Y., Karlapalem, K., Yarrabelly, N.: Semi-supervised automatic generation of Wikipedia articles for named entities. In: Wiki@ ICWSM (2016)

21. Potthast, M., Gollub, T., Hagen, M., Kiesel, J., Michel, M., Oberländer, A., Tippmann, M., Barrón-Cedeño, A., Gupta, P., Rosso, P., Stein, B.: Overview of the 4th international competition on plagiarism detection. In: CLEF 2012 Evaluation Labs and Workshop, Online Working Notes, Rome, Italy, 17–20 September 2012 (2012)
22. Rush, A.M., Chopra, S., Weston, J.: A neural attention model for abstractive sentence summarization. In: Proceedings of the 2015 Conference on Empirical Methods in Natural Language Processing, EMNLP 2015, Lisbon, Portugal, 17–21 September 2015, pp. 379–389 (2015)
23. Sauper, C., Barzilay, R.: Automatically generating Wikipedia articles: a structure-aware approach. In: Proceedings of the Joint Conference of the 47th Annual Meeting of the ACL and the 4th International Joint Conference on Natural Language Processing of the AFNLP, ACL 2009, vol. 1, pp. 208–216. Association for Computational Linguistics, Stroudsburg (2009)
24. Sutskever, I., Vinyals, O., Le, Q.V.: Sequence to sequence learning with neural networks. In: Ghahramani, Z., Welling, M., Cortes, C., Lawrence, N.D., Weinberger, K.Q. (eds.) Advances in Neural Information Processing Systems, vol. 27, pp. 3104–3112. Curran Associates, Inc. (2014)
25. Vougiouklis, P., ElSahar, H., Kaffee, L., Gravier, C., Laforest, F., Hare, J.S., Simperl, E.: Neural Wikipedian: generating textual summaries from knowledge base triples. CoRR abs/1711.00155 (2017). http://arxiv.org/abs/1711.00155
26. Wanner, L., Bohnet, B., Bouayad-Agha, N., Lareau, F., Nicklaß, D.: MARQUIS: generation of user-tailored multilingual air quality bulletins. Appl. Artif. Intell. 24(10), 914–952 (2010)
27. Wise, M.J.: YAP 3: improved detection of similarities in computer program and other texts. ACM SIGCSE Bull. 28(1), 130–134 (1996)

What Does an Ontology Engineering Community Look Like? A Systematic Analysis of the schema.org Community

Samantha Kanza[1](✉), Alex Stolz[2], Martin Hepp[2]®, and Elena Simperl[1]

[1] University of Southampton, Southampton, UK
{sk11g08,e.simperl}@soton.ac.uk
[2] Universitaet der Bundeswehr Munich, Munich, Germany
alex.stolz@unibw.de, mhepp@computer.org

Abstract. We present a systematic analysis of participation and inter-actions within the community behind schema.org, one of the largest and most relevant ontology engineering projects in recent times. Previous work conducted in this space has focused on ontology collaboration tools, and the roles that different contributors play within these projects. This paper takes a broader view and looks at the entire life cycle of the collaborative process to gain insights into how new functionality is proposed and accepted, and how contributors engage with one another based on real-world data. The analysis resulted in several findings. First, the collaborative ontology engineering roles identified in previous studies with a much stronger link to ontology editors apply to community interaction contexts as well. In the same time, the participation inequality is less pronounced than the 90-9-1 rule for Internet communities. In addition, schema.org seems to facilitate a form of collaboration that is friendly towards newcomers, whose concerns receive as much attention from the community as those of their longer-serving peers.

Keywords: Collaborative ontology engineering · GitHub
schema.org · Community analysis · Social computing · Mixed methods

1 Introduction

Creating an ontology is a complex process. It requires an understanding of the relevant domain, the technicalities of ontology engineering, and an ability and willingness to collaborate with others, often across disciplinary boundaries, to agree on what the ontology should cover and how. The Semantic Web community has built an impressive repertoire of methodologies, methods and tools to assist in this process [22]. Over a decade after the first influential papers in collaborative ontology engineering were published [18,24], it is broadly acknowledged that, for ontologies to unfold their benefits and be economically feasible, they must be developed and maintained by a community, using systems that support

© Springer International Publishing AG, part of Springer Nature 2018
A. Gangemi et al. (Eds.): ESWC 2018, LNCS 10843, pp. 335–350, 2018.
https://doi.org/10.1007/978-3-319-93417-4_22

the technical, social and participatory aspects of the process. Groupwork plat-forms such as MediaWiki, GitHub and Quora are broadly used for similar tasks in software development and are increasingly adopted for ontology engineering projects. They enable ontology stakeholders to ask questions, exchange ideas, and discuss modelling decisions; helping the community to form and thrive.

Analysing ontology engineering communities helps us understand how ontologies are built; whom they represent (and whom not); whether the community follows specific processes and if proposed methodologies work; how to improve group performance; and what tool support is needed in specific situations. Several studies in the ontology engineering literature illustrate this, including aspects such as: users collaborative roles [15,30]; how people use collaborative ontology editors [6,21,31]; or what tool features enable collaboration [5,22]. Our paper contributes to this field of research by analysing the activities and inter-actions of the schema.org community. Many consider schema.org [8] as one of the most successful collaborative Semantic Web projects of all times, alongside DBpedia, Wikidata and the Linked open Data Cloud. Founded by the four major Web search engines, it is home to a large community that follows an open par-ticipatory approach to develop and maintain Web vocabularies used by over 10 million websites[1]. The community is supported by two main tools: a GitHub repository (tracking issues, making vocabulary versions publicly available), and a public mailing list (for day-to-day discussions). The aim of this study is to gain an understanding of the community make-up in terms of topics, contribu-tion types, and engagement levels, using publicly available data from these two platforms.[2] We broke down the analysis into the following aspects:

Topic prevalence: The topics discussed across GitHub and the community-group public mailing-list help us understand whether the platforms are used as the community managers intended and whether additional tools are needed to support specific topic-centric community activities [34].

Popular topics: We define popularity by the level of engagement a topic attracts from the community via comments and replies. These metrics signal areas of interest, which may require better documentation, process and tool support, or the intervention of community managers [9].

Participation distribution: Online communities tend to be governed by the "90-9-1" rule, meaning that around 10% of the users contribute 90% of the work [16]; schema.org will be tested to see if it conforms to this pattern.

Typical user profiles: We aim to identify common user behavior patterns based on participation characteristics. They can be used to tailor commu-nity management towards certain sub-communities to improve participation inequality and improve group performance [11].

Our actual understanding of building and maintaining successful ontology engineering communities remains limited. schema.org seems to have some of the

---

[1] http://schema.org/.

[2] Whilst many other social channels host schema.org-related discussions (e.g. Quora or StackExchange), this paper focuses on the platforms that offer designated collab-oration and community support. See also http://schema.org/ [Accessed on 4/1/18].

answers and our analysis tries to translate them into observable characteristics, which can be applied to other ontology engineering projects. While our methods cannot claim to establish a causal link between any of them and schema.org's success; theory and studies in the broader space of online communities, e.g. [25], support our approach, and our study sheds light on how GitHub is used as a tool to facilitate the evolution of Web vocabularies, complementing previous works such as [1,17]. The paper is structured as follows. We give a brief overview of collaborative ontology engineering and discuss the main findings of related studies, including previous empirical work on collaboration with respect to ontologies and GitHub (Sect. 2). We then describe our methodology and data sources in Sect. 3, followed by our main results of the four analysis areas (Sect. 4), and a discussion of their implications and the study limitations (Sect. 4.5). We finish with interim conclusions and proposed future work (Sect. 5).

2   Related Work

The process of people using technology to work collaboratively, otherwise known as Computer Supported Cooperative Work (CSCW) [20], has been extensively studied. In this section, we focus on previous research on two specific areas in this vast literature space: (i) collaboration around ontologies (or related artifacts e.g. schemas, vocabularies, knowledge bases); and (ii) collaboration via GitHub.

2.1   Ontology Collaboration

Collaborative ontology engineering involves multiple individuals or organisations communicating, often remotely, to create an ontology. A significant amount of the early literature in this area looked at the steps that need to be carried out collaboratively [22], and at the tool support required in each step [21]. Several tools have been developed over the years for this purpose, from OntoEdit [24], Swoop [10] and Semantic MediaWiki [12] to WebProtégé [27] and Neologism [2]. Directly relevant to our study, several newer ontology editors specifically link to GitHub to leverage its teamwork and version control features [1,17].

As more ontology projects have been set up, researchers have begun to investigate collaborative ontology engineering empirically [23]. Initially, most work involved small user or case studies that aimed to validate or collect feedback on a specific methodology or tool [18]. As the field advanced, researchers had access to growing amounts of experimental and observational data, allowing them to expand their research questions. Walk et al. [32] analysed change log patterns of four collaborative ontology engineering projects, concluding that participants played different roles in the collaborative process. They identified four roles: administrators; moderators; gardeners (who focus on syntax errors and maintaining the ontology); and users (who frequently interact either to collaborate or revert each others changes over the same set of classes). They also concluded that the way people approach these edits depends on the hierarchical structure of the ontology. These findings align with Falconer et al's earlier study [5], who distinguished among the following roles: administrators; domain experts; and content editors (who typically make the most edits). Wang et al. [33] also investigated ontology editor change logs to try and predict user changes based on previous contributions, concluding that further work was needed to factor in different ontology life-cycle stages and participant roles, despite some prediction success. Gil et al. looked at contributions and editing patterns in 230 semantic wikis [7], noting that only a small subset of users create properties and that further work is needed in order to understand how and if editing restrictions in the wikis may have affected the observed editing patterns. Also related to MediaWiki, Müller-Birn et al. [15] clustered editing activities and determined that Wikidata has a stronger focus on peer production rather than ontology engineering, with a large share of editors specializing on specific types of contributions.

Studies like these offer valuable insights into typologies of ontology engineering contributions, levels of engagement with specific technical features, common tool usage or ontology editing patterns. Our work complements them by taking an overarching view of the collaborative process, focusing more on how interactions within the ontology community are instigated. Our main data sources are interactions of community members carried out via emails and GitHub, rather than system logs, which capture less immediate forms of collaboration. Our work thus aligns with earlier efforts such as DILIGENT [18], which annotated structured discussions using Rhetorical Structure Theory (RST) concepts to automatically detect inconsistencies and resolve conflicts, and Cicero [3], a Semantic MediaWiki extension focusing on decision support through discussions. While these previous works have not been extensively tested, they share similar aims to our study. Comparatively, we use observational data from emails and GitHub discussions from a real-world, successful ontology community, schema.org.

2.2   Collaborative Coding with GitHub

GitHub[3] is an open-source code repository that facilitates collaboration and revision control in technical projects. Developers can create project branches to work on different functionality, push and pull code updates, and clone repositories for direct usage or re-purposing. GitHub is more than a distributed version control system (DVCS). It contains advanced functionality of a social network platform: users have public profiles detailing their involvements in GitHub projects. Developers can have discussions about project progress and raise and comment on project issues; which can be branched into different threads [14]. As GitHub-style platforms entered the mainstream, researchers started analysing how they are used and which factors make projects and communities successful. Earlier work by Duncheneaut [4] hypothesized that group open-source projects involve complex social structures. Forums like GitHub with developer profiles mean that users can view other users' profiles and judge their coding abilities from their

---

[3] https://github.com/.

publicly available code before working with them. Similarly, new developers looking to join collaborative projects can assess the skills and contributions of other members from previous releases to estimate expected contribution [26]. Behavior and expectations adapt as newcomers become more familiar with a project. They may start by joining group discussions or building up a presence for themselves [28]. Their involvement evolves, both in volume and type of contribution and similar to other participatory platforms, a share of the community is made of "lurkers", people who observe projects without actively participating [26].

2.3 Collaborative Ontology Engineering Using GitHub

In recent years, ontology engineers have started to use DVCS in general, and GitHub in particular to collaborate. Related research mostly focuses on new GitHub-enabled ontology tools [1,17]. To the best of our knowledge, studies evaluating the use of GitHub in collaborative ontology engineering projects have yet to emerge. Additionally, schema.org is a broader collaborative venture than the case studies from the literature, with multiple ontologies being edited, documented and discussed. This paper focuses on analysing these discussions.

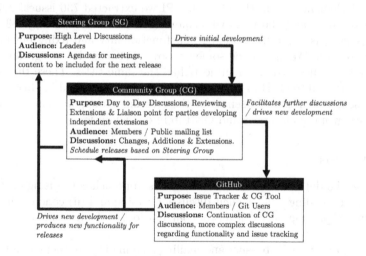

Fig. 1. Collaborative workflow of schema.org

3   Data and Methods

In our analysis we started from the three collaboration tools that were mentioned on the schema.org website: (i) the steering group;[4] (ii) the community group;[5] and (iii) the GitHub repository.[6] The collaborative workflow of

---

[4] https://groups.google.com/forum/#!forum/schema-org-sg.
[5] https://www.w3.org/community/schemaorg/.
[6] https://github.com/schemaorg/schemaorg.

schema.org, based on the details given on the project website, is illustrated in Fig. 1. Anonymised data and analysis code are available on GitHub at https://github.com/samikanza/schema-datasets.

3.1   Data

The steering group is a small group of individuals, appointed by the sponsors of schema.org, in order to coordinate the development of the vocabulary. Most of its discussions are public. The respective Google group is a forum for high-level discussions and is not meant for "heavy traffic"[7]. Unsurprisingly, it has the least content, totaling 32 group discussion topics that make up 112 posts overall. A bulk of the topics (28 topics with 81 posts) were made in 2015, with one post in 2016 and two in 2017. Emails tend to focus on planning and scheduling releases.

The community group is a W3C forum for day-to-day discussions[8]. The group promotes GitHub as main community platform, especially for bug reports, and details how to raise and manage issues. Nevertheless, discussions also happen on the @public-schemaorg mailing list, with 1506 messages and 313 email threads from 263 different authors recorded thus far. GitHub is used to organize technical project elements. From the GitHub API we extracted 736 issues, 227 users who raised issues, and 406 users who commented on issues, totaling 483 unique users. Discussions range from adding new functionality and fixing bugs to general organization. We also noted some crossover between the two groups, where some GitHub issues and email subjects had the same titles. These threads had either been moved to GitHub for further discussion, or resulted in GitHub issues being raised. Given the sparseness of the steering group, we mainly used the community group mailing list and GitHub in our analysis.

3.2   Methods

To analyse the data we used a mixed-methods approach comprising of: (i) iterative thematic coding [19], to elicit discussion topics; and (ii) concrete methods, to compute topic popularity, levels of contribution, and engagement.

Topic Prevalence: GitHub issues and mailing list emails were thematically coded to assess **topic prevalence**. Python scripts were written using PyGithub[9] to extract schema.org issues and issue comments from the GitHub API, which were manually coded to identify topics. We started from the list of categories from Walk et al. [32] that highlighted four ontology-centric activities: editing, adding, organizing and fixing content and formalized them into these topics: **Modification**; **Extension**; **Organization**; and **Bug**. Additionally, for issues that did not fit into these topics, or were considered off topic, we added an **Other/Off Topic** category. During coding, we identified six new topics (listed below).

---

[7] https://groups.google.com/forum/#!forum/schema-org-sg.

[8] https://www.w3.org/community/schemaorg/how-we-work/.

[9] https://github.com/PyGithub/PyGithub.

The topic descriptions were formalized to ensure consistency, and subsequently used to code the community group emails. Emails were inspected by thread, and each thread was coded according to its overall theme; for any that did not fit into the existing categories, they were inspected for common themes to form new topics, or were deemed **Other/Off Topic**. After coding the emails, we added a **Release** category; as noted earlier, the community group is also used to plan and schedule releases. Finally, completely random samples of 10% of both corpora were re-coded and checked for consistency reasons after ensuring agreement between the authors of the defined categories. The final topic list consists of:

- **Release** - Discussing new release versions.
- **Extension** - Proposing additional functionality.
- **Clarification** - How something should be used/implemented or if it exists.
- **Modification** - Proposing a change to existing functionality.
- **Bug** - Detailing a bug or a fix for a bug.
- **Use by consumers** - How the schemas could be used by consumers.
- **schema.org website** - About the schema.org website.
- **Github use** - About how GitHub should be used in this project.
- **Organisation** - About general organisation.
- **Investigate Technology** - About investigating a new technology.
- **Documentation** - Adding or improving or editing documentation.
- **Other/Off Topic** - Irrelevant or didn't fit into the other categories.

Topic Popularity: We computed several descriptive statistics: number of replies in relevant email threads; number of comments on GitHub issues; mean/median number of responses on the mailing list and on GitHub; and percentage of topical conversations with no comments. We also inspected a random sample of 10% of unanswered and off topic messages (emails, issues) to identify common themes.

Participation Distribution: Participation is defined as number of emails sent and replied to, or number of issues raised and commented on. We sorted participants by participation level and assessed the overlap among the top 10 participants in the community group and on GitHub. We compared email addresses and GitHub usernames to determine when a participant on the mailing list was the same as a GitHub user (email addresses were inspected manually, and GitHub user ids were extracted using PyGithub). There were some instances in the community group where users were sending emails using different email addresses, in these cases we merged the user totals.

Typical User Profiles: Participants were categorised into profiles according to several dimensions: how active they are in the community, whether they initiate new conversations (by raising new issues or starting a new email thread) or whether they contribute to existing conversations (through replies and comments).

4   Results and Discussion

In this section we aim to answer the four research questions by presenting the results and discussing the main themes that emerged from the analysis.

4.1   Topic Prevalence

Table 1 illustrates how the 313 community group email threads and the 736 GitHub issues were categorised via thematic coding.

Table 1. Topics discussed by the schema.org community

Topic	Community group	GitHub
Extension	21.9%	38.9%
Clarification	41.7%	19.8%
Modification	1.8%	16.2%
Bug	5.5%	10.3%
Documentation	0.6%	4.6%
Organisation	8.5%	3.5%
schema.org website	0.9%	2.6%
Use by consumers	2.4%	2.5%
GitHub use	0.6%	0.5%
Investigate technology	2.1%	0.1%
Other/Off Topic	9.7%	1.0%
Release	4.3%	0.0%

The community group focuses on clarifications and extension-based discussions (41.6% and 21.8%). Additionally, it hosts some organisational messages (8.5%), which is in line with the aims of the group. On GitHub, the community focuses mostly on extensions (38.8%), followed in roughly equal measure by modification or clarification issues (19.8% and 16.1%). This suggests that GitHub is used more to propose new functionality or changes to existing functionality, whereas the mailing list is used for clarifications of existing work.

We note that participants require an account to raise issues on GitHub, and might be hence more willing to make initial queries via a public mailing list. Further on, GitHub has stronger focus towards raising bugs (10.3% vs. 5.4% at almost double the number of posts), which fits with its purpose. The GitHub corpus also has much fewer off topic messages than the community group, where some of these messages involve unsubscription requests or irrelevant questions, both of which also lend themselves more to a public mailing list discussion. Finally, the community group is clearly the place to talk about scheduling and organisation of new releases, as intended by the community managers.

4.2 Topic Popularity

Figure 2 shows how many responses emails and issues in each topic category received. The types of topics the community engages with most via email are: extensions, clarifications, and releases; as well as organisational and off topic matters. Extensions and clarifications are also popular on GitHub, alongside modifications and bugs. The remaining topics, which are to a certain extent peripheral to the use of a revision control system, receive considerably less attention from the community on this platform. However, topic prevalence seems to have a bearing on the topic popularity; to refer back to Table 1, the most popular topics in both instances are the ones that also showed the highest prevalence.

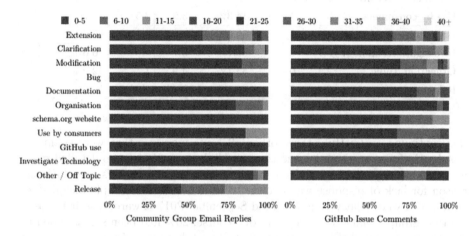

Fig. 2. Share of responses to community group emails and GitHub issues per topic

The difference between some topics' mean and median values (Table 2) shows that although some topics receive more engagement than others, the response level varies significantly. The median is mostly similar or lower for the community group, and consistently lower for GitHub, meaning that over 50% of these topics receive two or less responses (the results show that GitHub issues typically receive more comments than community group emails receive replies). It is also worth noting that, even popular topics typically receive between 0–5 responses and as many as 43% of bug issues and 32% of clarification issues remained unanswered. This may point to lack of resources or incentives, or other deficiencies in the community organisation. Of 313 email threads, 33% received no replies, while on GitHub of 736 issues 7% received no comments. Overall 40% of interactions received minimal engagement. The lack of engagement with **GitHub use** is less concerning, as this category only contains four issues.

We then looked in more detail at a random sample of 10% of the emails and issues that received no responses. The email sample had 10 emails: three extension emails that seemingly did not receive a response because the conversation

Table 2. Mean/median averages of responses per topic, and % of no responses

Topic	Community group			GitHub		
	Mean	Median	No replies	Mean	Median	No comments
Extension	6.4	4	27.1%	8.0	3	23.4%
Clarification	3.5	2	22.8%	4.3	2	32.2%
Modification	1	0	83.3%	5.2	2	24.4%
Bug	2.3	1	27.8%	2.4	1	43.4%
Documentation	2	2	0.0%	3.7	2	26.5%
Organisation	2.7	2	44.8%	3.0	2	19.2%
schema.org website	2	1	0.0%	4.1	2	15.8%
Use by consumers	3	1	14.3%	3.9	3.5	16.7%
GitHub use	1	1	50.0%	0.8	0	75.0%
Investigate technology	0.7	0	66.7%	6.7	0	0.0%
Other/Off Topic	2.1	0	53.1%	4.9	1	42.9%
Release	6.4	7	9.1%	N/A	N/A	N/A

was continued on GitHub; three other/off topic messages that were spam, an unsubscription request and a questionnaire link respectively; two detailed modifications which we believe did not merit replies; and two others for which the reason for lack of response was unclear to us. The GitHub sample included 20 issues: 55% were relatively new (dated September 2017 onwards), so it is possible that group members will reply in due course; 20% had been self assigned to the user who created the issue in the first place (all by two of the main GitHub users), therefore may not have necessitated a response. A further 15% were referenced in other, more descriptive issues which the community commented upon, suggesting that participants may have moved any potential discussion to those issues elsewhere; the final 10% of issues detailed how a certain fix had been made and linked to the appropriate commit, which could also justify a lack of response, as they did not include questions or other elements for discussion.

With respect to the off topic subjects, we were interested in learning more about which interactions attracted community participation despite their nature. 60% of the relevant emails were roughly equally split into: unsubscription requests (which would not occur in GitHub as users have control over leaving groups) and emails promoting surveys or courses which arguably did not merit a response. There were also two off topic political emails, and the rest were questions relating to schema.org that were more 'other' than 'off topic' and subsequently received responses. On GitHub, only 7 issues were classified as **Other/Off Topic**: three were uncommented (one had a blank issue body and a one word title, and the other had a one word title and issue body); the other four that were attended to either asked for advice about similar areas to schema.org or made suggestions regarding other technologies.

4.3   Participation Distribution

Figure 3 shows the participation level between the community group and GitHub. The group had 264 unique active users: 73 participants who only started email threads; 100 who only replied to them; and 91 who did both. The GitHub repository had 483 unique active users, which included 77 users who just raised issues, 256 who just commented on issues, and 150 who did both. The four graphs show similar contribution patterns, with 10% of users responsible for 80% of all contributions, which is a more balanced than the Nielsen norm [16], suggesting that there must be a higher proportion of users who contribute on a minimal, but significant enough level to influence these metrics. Finally, we note that in each case, there is one member that participates on a significantly higher level than other users; this will be elaborated on further when we analyse the most prolific members of the community (Table 3).

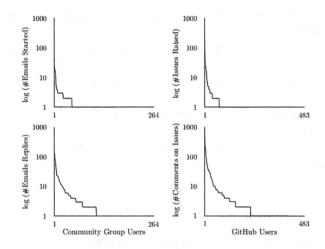

Fig. 3. Participation in the community group and GitHub

We then analysed the top 10 contributors on each platform (community group: users who sent/replied to the most emails, GitHub: users who raised/ commented on the most issues) to establish any overlap. The top contributor on both platforms is the same. In the community group, nine users achieve top 10 ranks regarding starting or contributing to threads. on GitHub, top participation is less concentrated, with only five users being very active in both raising and commenting on issues. Seven individuals appear across all four leaderboards, illustrating the inequality in participation. In Sect. 4.4, we will dig deeper into the types of contributions different categories of users are responsible for.

Table 3. Number of contributions of top 10 users, anonymised

Highest contributor	Community group		GitHub	
	Emails sent	Email replies	Issues raised	Comments
1st contributor	User #1 (26)	User #1 (135)	User #1 (193)	User #1 (949)
2nd contributor	User #2 (19)	User #2 (124)	User #10 (41)	User #2 (309)
3rd contributor	User #3 (18)	User #10 (81)	User #12 (30)	User #9 (245)
4th contributor	User #4 (14)	User #3 (64)	User #2 (25)	User #10 (227)
5th contributor	User #5 (7)	User #9 (44)	User #13 (23)	User #12 (173)
6th contributor	User #6 (5)	User #4 (37)	User #14 (21)	User #11 (118)
7th contributor	User #7 (4)	User #11 (24)	User #15 (18)	User #16 (99)
8th contributor	User #8 (4)	User #7 (23)	User #9 (17)	User #17 (98)
9th contributor	User #9 (4)	User #8 (23)	User #5 (15)	User #18 (81)
10th contributor	User #10 (3)	User #5 (22)	User #7 (13)	User #19 (60)

4.4   Typical User Profiles

From our analysis so far, we have identified several roles:

- **Leaders:** Actively start and engage in discussions.
- **Broadcasters:** Actively start discussions, but rarely reply to them.
- **Followers:** Rarely start discussions, but actively reply to them.
- **Lurkers:** Rarely start or reply to discussions.

To categorise users we averaged the number of emails sent, emails replied to, issues raised, and issue comments. In the community group, active users have started at least one email thread and replied to at least four emails; and GitHub raised at least three issues, and commented on at least 15 issues. About 10% of the community group members and 9% of GitHub users fall into the leaders category; including one user who is top of each category, suggesting high interest and commitment. Roughly 2% of the mailing list contributors, and 8% of GitHub users are broadcasters, suggesting that community group members are less likely to initiate new discussions than GitHub users. This is somewhat unexpected, as public mailing lists have lower entry barriers than

GitHub, as noted earlier. It does, however, fit with users preferring to hold lengthier discussions on GitHub, evidenced by some conversations beginning via email and then continuing on GitHub. Approximately 7% of both user bases are followers; showing a level of reactive engagement, where users are happy to discuss and express opinions on existing issues, but are less likely to or less comfortable in raising their own. In some instances, there are several followers who engage more with some issues than the leaders. The most common users are lurkers (community group: 75%, GitHub: 82%), suggesting either lurking until certain issue come to their attention to raise or discuss; or engaging episodically.

4.5   Discussion

Studying collaboration cross-sectionally reveals interesting differences. Both community channels appear to function under their intended purposes. However, this does not mean that certain areas could not still be improved. The unanswered topic sample suggested that engaging less with some topics is practical, due to conversations moving from the mailing list to GitHub, or because the topics do not necessitate a reply. However, both groups feature a fairly large share of unattended posts on core topics; and while our manual inspection shed some light into why they were left unanswered, further analysis is needed to understand the effects of this lack of engagement on participation, especially for newcomers [13], and across the four profiles discussed earlier. The popular GitHub topics map well to the ontology editing roles identified by Walk et al. [30] (administrators; moderators; gardeners; fixing content). Longitudinal studies should explore these parallels to establish how participation levels and discussions on community platforms impact ontology-centric activities. The participation distribution is less unequal than elsewhere, though a clear group of top contributors could be identified across the two corpora. Meanwhile, a fair share of activity seems to be generated by people outside the core of the initiative; contacting the community via the mailing list, or to a lesser extent via GitHub. The percentage of lurkers on GitHub is higher than reported in literature [29]. Overall, this speaks for an attractive community, with a more egalitarian participation of distribution, that could do more to onboard some members of the community, for example in the follower and broadcasting categories introduced earlier, in particular to resolve clarification or bug questions. Additionally, a more in-depth analysis is required to assess the importance of posts in each topic category; the current study considers them all equal, but the small samples we inspected painted a much more reassuring picture than the initial metrics suggested. So far, all metrics we calculated can be meaningfully interpreted only in the context of related literature. They prompt discussions around what makes a successful ontology engineering community, which requires exploration. Collaborative ontology engineering literature sometimes touches upon the quality of the created ontology, but appears to lack an understanding of healthy, purposeful participation in ontology projects.

4.6 Limitations and Threats to Validity

Our data is subject to the following limitations. Matching users between the two datasets was not an exact science and we did not always have enough information to confidently disambiguate between the different accounts. Furthermore, the PyGithub scripts used to analyse the GitHub data do not facilitate extracting all engagement types: one can extract the number of comments per issue, but not necessarily other types of engagement such as user assignment history. We have also not considered other activities such as watching issues. Finally, our analysis could include other data sources, such as Quora or StackExchange to enrich the findings and employ methods that dig deeper into content of the posts.

5 Conclusions and Future Work

Our main conclusions for the analysed areas are: Topic prevalence shows that GitHub is used more to propose creating or editing functionality, whereas the mailing list is used more for clarifications. We found that topic popularity reflects topic prevalence, in that the most popular topics are typically ones that initiated the most new discussions. Overall, participation distribution is less unequal than expected with 10% of the users performing 80% of the work. A majority of the users across both platforms were lurkers, who rarely started new discussions or engaged with others in the group, and around 10% of the users can be classified as leaders, where a small core rank very highly in any form of participation.

There are a number of avenues for future work such as calculating how many of the extensions suggested by new users are developed and included in releases, and to what degree a user's social standing within schema.org influences this. Other avenues could include performing further qualitative analysis of emails and issues to understand the different social dynamics within these groups to see if they differ across groups. It would also be valuable to study how engagement adapts over time such that recommendations can be made to improve engagement and understand where it peaks and dips. Finally, we could look at how issues get assigned and solved on GitHub; who is in charge of the assigning; how many are self assigned, and how long any issues take to get solved (if at all).

Acknowledgements. This work has been conducted in the context of the Data Stories Project: EPSRC (EP/P025676/1) and the WDAqua Project: (Marie Skłodowska-Curie Grant Agreement No 642795).

References

1. Alobaid, A., Garijo, D., Poveda-Villalón, M., Pérez, I.S., Corcho, O.: OnToology, a tool for collaborative development of ontologies. In: ICBO (2015)
2. Basca, C., Corlosquet, S., Cyganiak, R., Fernández, S., Schandl, T.: Neologism: easy vocabulary publishing (2008)

3. Dellschaft, K., Engelbrecht, H., Barreto, J.M., Rutenbeck, S., Staab, S.: Cicero: tracking design rationale in collaborative ontology engineering. In: Bechhofer, S., Hauswirth, M., Hoffmann, J., Koubarakis, M. (eds.) ESWC 2008. LNCS, vol. 5021, pp. 782–786. Springer, Heidelberg (2008). https://doi.org/10.1007/978-3-540-68234-9_58

4. Ducheneaut, N.: Socialization in an open source software community: a sociotechnical analysis. Comput. Support. Coop. Work (CSCW) 14(4), 323–368 (2005)

5. Falconer, S., Tudorache, T., Noy, N.F.: An analysis of collaborative patterns in large-scale ontology development projects. In: Proceedings of the 6th International Conference on Knowledge Capture, pp. 25–32. ACM (2011)

6. Gil, Y., Knight, A., Zhang, K., Zhang, L., Sethi, R.: An initial analysis of semantic wikis. In: Proceedings of the Companion Publication of the 2013 International Conference on Intelligent User Interfaces Companion, IUI 2013 Companion, pp. 109–110. ACM (2013)

7. Gil, Y., Ratnakar, V.: Knowledge capture in the wild: a perspective from semantic wiki communities. In: Proceedings of the Seventh International Conference on Knowledge Capture, K-CAP 2013, pp. 49–56. ACM (2013)

8. Guha, R.V., Brickley, D., Macbeth, S.: schema.org: evolution of structured data on the web. Commun. ACM 59(2), 44–51 (2016)

9. Jamali, S., Rangwala, H.: Digging Digg: comment mining, popularity prediction, and social network analysis. In: 2009 International Conference on Web Information Systems and Mining, WISM 2009, pp. 32–38. IEEE (2009)

10. Kalyanpur, A., Parsia, B., Sirin, E., Grau, B.C., Hendler, J.: Swoop: a web ontology editing browser. Web Semant. Sci. Serv. Agents World Wide Web 4(2), 144–153 (2006)

11. Kraut, R.E., Resnick, P., Kiesler, S., Burke, M., Chen, Y., Kittur, N., Konstan, J., Ren, Y., Riedl, J.: Building Successful Online Communities: Evidence-Based Social Design. Mit Press, Cambridge (2012)

12. Krötzsch, M., Vrandečić, D., Völkel, M.: Semantic MediaWiki. In: Cruz, I., Decker, S., Allemang, D., Preist, C., Schwabe, D., Mika, P., Uschold, M., Aroyo, L.M. (eds.) ISWC 2006. LNCS, vol. 4273, pp. 935–942. Springer, Heidelberg (2006). https://doi.org/10.1007/11926078_68

13. Lave, J., Wenger, E.: Legitimate peripheral participation in communities of practice. In: Supporting Lifelong Learning, vol. 1, pp. 111–126 (2002)

14. Lima, A., Rossi, L., Musolesi, M.: Coding together at scale: GitHub as a collaborative social network. In: ICWSM (2014)

15. Müller-Birn, C., Karran, B., Lehmann, J., Luczak-Rösch, M.: Peer-production system or collaborative ontology engineering effort: what is wikidata? In: Proceedings of the 11th International Symposium on Open Collaboration, p. 20. ACM (2015)

16. Nielsen, J.: Participation inequality: encouraging more users to contribute (2006)

17. Petersen, N., Coskun, G., Lange, C.: TurtleEditor: an ontology-aware web-editor for collaborative ontology development. In: 2016 IEEE Tenth International Conference on Semantic Computing (ICSC), pp. 183–186. IEEE (2016)

18. Pinto, H.S., Staab, S., Tempich, C.: DILIGENT: towards a fine-grained methodology for DIstributed, Loosely-controlled and evolvInG engineering of oNTologies. In: Proceedings of the 16th European Conference on Artificial Intelligence, pp. 393–397. IOS Press (2004)

19. Pope, C., Ziebland, S., Mays, N., et al.: Analysing qualitative data. Bmj 320(7227), 114–116 (2000)

20. Schmidt, K., Bannon, L.: Taking CSCW seriously. Comput. Support. Coop. Work (CSCW) 1(1), 7–40 (1992)

21. Schober, D., Malone, J., Stevens, R.: Practical experiences in concurrent, collaborative ontology building using collaborative Protégé. In: ICBO, p. 147 (2009)
22. Simperl, E., Luczak-Rösch, M.: Collaborative ontology engineering: a survey. Knowl. Eng. Rev. **29**(1), 101–131 (2014)
23. Strohmaier, M., Walk, S., Pöschko, J., Lamprecht, D., Tudorache, T., Nyulas, C., Musen, M.A., Noy, N.F.: How ontologies are made: studying the hidden social dynamics behind collaborative ontology engineering projects. Web Semant. Sci. Serv. Agents World Wide Web **20**, 18–34 (2013)
24. Sure, Y., Erdmann, M., Angele, J., Staab, S., Studer, R., Wenke, D.: OntoEdit: collaborative ontology development for the semantic web. In: Horrocks, I., Hendler, J. (eds.) ISWC 2002. LNCS, vol. 2342, pp. 221–235. Springer, Heidelberg (2002). https://doi.org/10.1007/3-540-48005-6_18
25. Tinati, R., Van Kleek, M., Simperl, E., Luczak-Rösch, M., Simpson, R., Shadbolt, N.: Designing for citizen data analysis: a cross-sectional case study of a multi-domain citizen science platform. In: Proceedings of the 33rd Annual ACM Conference on Human Factors in Computing Systems, CHI 2015, pp. 4069–4078. ACM (2015)
26. Tsay, J., Dabbish, L., Herbsleb, J.: Influence of social and technical factors for evaluating contribution in GitHub. In: Proceedings of the 36th International Conference on Software Engineering, pp. 356–366. ACM (2014)
27. Tudorache, T., Nyulas, C., Noy, N.F., Musen, M.A.: WebProtégé: a collaborative ontology editor and knowledge acquisition tool for the web. Semant. Web **4**(1), 89–99 (2013)
28. Von Krogh, G., Spaeth, S., Lakhani, K.R.: Community, joining, and specialization in open source software innovation: a case study. Res. Policy **32**(7), 1217–1241 (2003)
29. Wagstrom, P., Jergensen, C., Sarma, A.: Roles in a networked software development ecosystem: a case study in GitHub (2012)
30. Walk, S., Esín-Noboa, L., Helic, D., Strohmaier, M., Musen, M.A.: How users explore ontologies on the web: a study of NCBO's BioPortal usage logs. In: Proceedings of the 26th International Conference on World Wide Web, pp. 775–784. International World Wide Web Conferences Steering Committee (2017)
31. Walk, S., Singer, P., Noboa, L.E., Tudorache, T., Musen, M.A., Strohmaier, M.: Understanding how users edit ontologies: comparing hypotheses about four real-world projects. In: Arenas, M., et al. (eds.) ISWC 2015. LNCS, vol. 9366, pp. 551–568. Springer, Cham (2015). https://doi.org/10.1007/978-3-319-25007-6_32
32. Walk, S., Singer, P., Strohmaier, M., Tudorache, T., Musen, M.A., Noy, N.F.: Discovering beaten paths in collaborative ontology-engineering projects using Markov chains. J. Biomed. Inform. **51**, 254–271 (2014)
33. Wang, H., Tudorache, T., Dou, D., Noy, N.F., Musen, M.A.: Analysis of user editing patterns in ontology development projects. In: Meersman, R., Panetto, H., Dillon, T., Eder, J., Bellahsene, Z., Ritter, N., De Leenheer, P., Dou, D. (eds.) OTM 2013. LNCS, vol. 8185, pp. 470–487. Springer, Heidelberg (2013). https://doi.org/10.1007/978-3-642-41030-7_34
34. Yang, M.C., Rim, H.C.: Identifying interesting twitter contents using topical analysis. Expert Syst. Appl. **41**(9), 4330–4336 (2014)

FERASAT: A Serendipity-Fostering Faceted Browser for Linked Data

Ali Khalili[1]([✉])[iD], Peter van den Besselaar[2][iD], and Klaas Andries de Graaf[1][iD]

[1] Department of Computer Science, Faculty of Science,
Vrije Universiteit Amsterdam, Amsterdam, The Netherlands
{a.khalili,ka.de.graaf}@vu.nl
[2] Department of Organization Science, Faculty of Social Sciences,
Vrije Universiteit Amsterdam, Amsterdam, The Netherlands
p.a.a.vanden.besselaar@vu.nl

Abstract. Accidental knowledge discoveries occur most frequently during capricious and unplanned search and browsing of data. This type of undirected, random, and exploratory search and browsing of data results in Serendipity – the art of unsought finding. In our previous work we extracted a set of serendipity-fostering design features for developing intelligent user interfaces on Semantic Web and Linked Data browsing environments. The features facilitate the discovery of interesting and valuable facts in (linked) data which were not initially sought for. In this work, we present an implementation of those features called FERASAT. FERASAT provides an adaptive multigraph-based faceted browsing interface to catalyze serendipity while browsing Linked Data. FERASAT is already in use within the domain of science, technology & innovation (STI) studies to allow researchers who are not familiar with Linked Data technologies to explore heterogeneous interlinked datasets in order to observe and interpret surprising facts from the data relevant to policy and innovation studies. In addition to an analysis of the related work, we describe two STI use cases in the paper and demonstrate how different serendipity design features are addressed in those use cases.

1 Introduction

"Unless you expect the unexpected you will never find [truth], for it is hard to discover and hard to attain." -*Heraclitus*[1]

Serendipity (known as the art of unsought finding [19]) plays an important role in the emerging field of data science, allowing the discovery of interesting and valuable facts not initially sought for. Serendipity consists of two main steps: a *surprising observation* and then a *correct interpretation*. In our previous work [13], we extracted a set of serendipity-fostering design features (cf. Table 1) which help designers and developers of Semantic Web and Linked Data browsing environments to facilitate discovery and interpretation of new, useful, and interesting facts. For example, design Feature F_{10} (in Table 1) suggests sharing of

---

[1] According to secondary sources.

© Springer International Publishing AG, part of Springer Nature 2018
A. Gangemi et al. (Eds.): ESWC 2018, LNCS 10843, pp. 351–366, 2018.
https://doi.org/10.1007/978-3-319-93417-4_23

Table 1. List of the proposed serendipity-fostering design features [13].

Design features related to observations	
F_1	Make surprising observations more noticeable
F_2	Make errors in data more visible in order to detect successful errors easier
F_3	Allow inversion and contrast
F_4	Support randomization and disturbance
F_5	Allow monitoring of side-effects when interacting with data
F_6	Support detection and investigation of by-products
F_7	Support background knowledge and user contextualization
F_8	Support both convergent and divergent information behavior
Design features related to explanation of the observations	
F_9	Facilitate the explanation of surprising observations
F_{10}	Allow sharing of surprising observations among multiple users
F_{11}	Enable reasoning by analogy
F_{12}	Support extending the memory of user by invoking provocative reminders and relevance feedback

surprising observations among multiple users to increase the chance encounter. A surprising observation done by user A, when correctly explained by user B, can result in positive serendipity.

In this work, we present an implementation of those serendipity-fostering features called "FERASAT"[2] (FacEted bRowser And Serendipity cATalyzer). FERASAT provides an adaptive multigraph-based faceted browsing interface to catalyze serendipity while browsing Linked Data. It is important to mention that serendipitous discovery may be facilitated but it is by definition an emergent process. With our work we aim to facilitate the process of serendipity by providing an incubator-like environment for serendipity. In other words, the FERASAT environment will increase the likelihood of serendipity, without guaranteeing it.

FERASAT is built on top of the LD-R framework [11] to support the following serendipity-fostering principles:

- *Skeuomorphic Design.* "One way of overcoming the fear of new is to make it look like the old", said Don Norman to describe the process of skeuomorphic design [15]. Skeuomorphism in the context of UI design, refers to the practice of incorporating recognizable objects which are familiar to users to decrease the cognitive load of users and to hide complexity of the underlying technology. Most of the current Linked Data browsing interfaces fall into the *Pathetic Fallacy of RDF* [9] trap where they display RDF data to the users as a graph because the underlying data model is a graph. Abstracting the complexity of RDF and graph-based data representation provides more easily-discoverable

---

[2] In Persian, the term 'Ferasat' refers to the ability of intuitive knowledge acquisition.

and usable interactions (i.e. more affordances) for non-Semantic Web users to serendipitously browse data scattered over multiple knowledge graphs.

– *Adaptive Design.* In order to support serendipity-fostering features, the browser UI needs to act in a proactive way to persistently customize and personalize user interfaces based on the type of data and the information needs of the end-users. Intelligent UI adaptation allows the application to act more like a human and consequently, more intelligently.

– *Component-based Design.* Component-based design is a prerequisite to realize intelligent UI adaptation. A component-based environment consists of a set of structured UI components as building blocks, that can dynamically get injected to system, replaced and customized while user is interacting with the system.

The contributions of this work are in particular:

– Design and implementation of an open-source faceted browser to facilitate serendipity while browsing Linked Data.
– An analysis of the related work in terms of the serendipity design features.
– Discussing two use cases in the domain of science, technology and innovation (STI) studies to demonstrate the capabilities of our implemented solution.

The rest of this paper is organized as following: In Sect. 2 we elaborate on the design and architecture of the FERASAT environment and indicate how it addresses the proposed serendipity-fostering features. Implementation details are described in Sect. 3. Section 4 presents two use cases on serendipitous knowledge discovery when FERASAT was used in the STI domain. In Sect. 5, we review the related work in the area of serendipity on Linked Data and compare FERASAT to existing Linked Data-based faceted browsers. Finally in Sect. 6 we conclude and briefly mention the future directions of this work.

2 FERASAT: A Trigger and Facilitator for Serendipity on Linked Data

Figure 1 depicts the architecture of FERASAT where related elements are color coded. The system provides three main modes of interaction with data namely

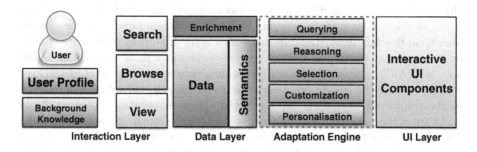

Fig. 1. Architecture of the FERASAT adaptive faceted browser. (Color figure online)

search, browse and view. During the user interactions, based on the semantics of data and the given user context, the system adapts its behavior by rendering appropriate interactive UI components. In the following sections we describe the main architectural building blocks of the FERASAT environment together with how they support the serendipity-fostering features shown in Table 1.

2.1 Interaction Layer

According to the theory of "Seven Stages of Action" [15], which explains the psychology of a person while executing a task, user interactions with a system occur in two gulfs namely a *gulf of execution* and a *gulf of evaluation*. The gulf of execution focuses on allowable interactions (i.e., *affordances* – clues about how an object should be used, typically provided by the object itself or its context) in the system, whereas the gulf of evaluation reflects the amount of effort that the person must exert to interpret the state of the system after an interaction. Within the FERASAT environment, interactions in the gulf of execution (e.g. interacting to invert a selected facet) are used as triggers for serendipity and interactions in the gulf of evaluation (e.g. visualization & in-detail browsing of the properties of a resource) are used to support the process of abduction – the process of guessing, interpreting, creating and testing hypotheses in order to find a correct explanation, one that is evidence-based.

Figure 2 shows a mock-up of the design we devised for the FERASAT faceted browser (Fig. 5 depicts the actual implementation). When browsing a set of linked data which is scattered over multiple knowledge graphs (e.g. Figure 3), the first step is to identify properties of interest as semantic links to move forward and backward in the data space. The index facet lists these designated RDF properties grouped by the aspect they are addressing. In the initial state, all the RDF resources are displayed without any constraints. When a user selects a property, a new facet is generated to display the object values of the selected property together with the number of resources containing those values. The facet can be configured to employ different interactive UI components (e.g. charts, maps, etc. in Fig. 2) to render the values of a selected property.

Flexible UI components support the serendipity-fostering features F_1, F_2 and F_4 (see Table 1) by allowing users to exploit multiple interactive visualizations to do surprising observations and also discover successful errors in data together with the possible explanations for their occurrence. The list of values in a facet can be shuffled to change the ordering based on a random factor or some criteria other than the default sorting criterion which is the frequency of the corresponding resources (supporting F_7). When a user selects one or more values of an active facet, a SPARQL query with the corresponding constraints is generated and executed to update the results list. Users can invert the selected values in a facet to see the results which exclude those selected values (supporting F_6). If multiple facets are active, any change to a facet will affect the remaining active facets to take into account the constraint imposed by that change (supporting F_9). Users can focus on each facet, search within its values and view in-detail characteristics of each object value (supporting both convergent and divergent information

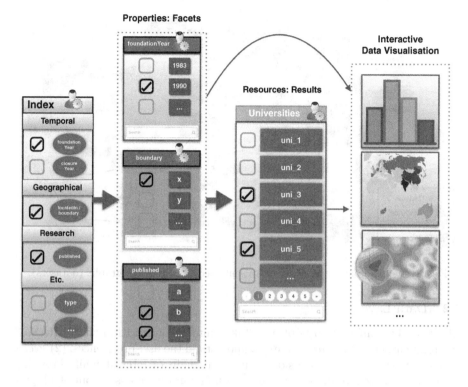

Fig. 2. A mock-up of the FERASAT adaptive faceted browser.

behavior presented by F_{12}). When a user is browsing a facet which was browsed before, the UI provides some reminders as pop-ups about the previous usage of that facet (supporting F_8).

The result list is the terminal facet in the system which shows the final result of the generated SPARQL query as a set of RDF resources constrained by the selected RDF properties and values. Clicking on a resource reveals the detailed characteristics of that resource (supporting F_2 to study a particular surprising observation). To further investigate the results, a user can select multiple resources and ask for the potential correlations between them (supporting F_9 to investigate by-products). For example, given the linked data in Fig. 3, a user might want to browse and find the relation between entities of type universities which are founded in certain years AND are located in certain administrative boundaries AND have published on certain research topics. Using the faceted browser, such a query is generated in a progressive way where users can investigate the effect of each selected facet on other facets and on the results list, while traversing multiple distributed knowledge graphs (in this case, graphs that provide data about universities connected to graphs that provide values related to publications and administrative boundaries), until the full query is answered.

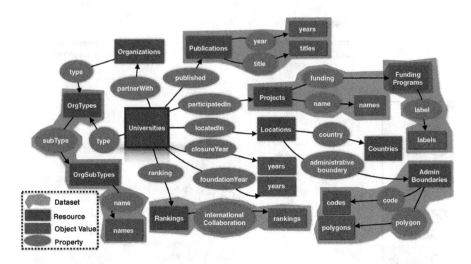

Fig. 3. An example of the linked data scattered over multiple graphs (datasets).

2.2   Data Layer

There are five different sorts of data taken into account within the FERASAT environment: (1) *user's profile data* to understand the user preferences, (2) *user's background knowledge* to consider a user's domain of interest while browsing data, (3) *original data* to be browsed, (4) *configuration data* as output of adaptation process to customize and personalize both data and UIs, (5) *complementary data* added as enrichment to original data for richer contextualization. All the above datasets are represented as single or multiple RDF graphs (e.g., Fig. 3) to be ready for integration (using federated SPARQL queries) and analysis.

FERASAT supports resource annotation to interlink the original data with the user's background knowledge and to generate complementary data connected to the original data to be browsed (supporting F_{11} for user contextualization by giving users additional contextual facets to complement their browsing experience). At the moment, two types of annotation are supported within the system: *Named Entity Recognition* (NER) using DBpedia Spotlight[3] and *Geo-boundary-tagging* supported by open geo boundaries from OpenStreetMap and GADM[4]. There are interactive UIs embedded in the FERASAT system to interactively annotate a dataset before the browsing activity starts. Above semi-automatic annotation supports F_6 and F_8, as information diverges (by adding annotations) with possible by-products resulting from the annotations.

2.3   UI Layer

As depicted in Fig. 4, there are four core component levels in an FERASAT Web application. Each core component abstracts the actions required for retrieving

---

[3] http://www.dbpedia-spotlight.org.

[4] http://gadm.org.

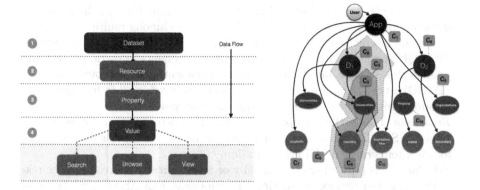

Fig. 4. (Left) core reactor components, (right) example configuration hypergraph.

and updating the graph-based data and provides a basis for user-defined components to interact with Linked Data in three modes: search, browse and view. The data-flow in the system starts from the Dataset component which handles all the events related to a set of resources under a named graph identified by a URI. The next level is the Resource component which is identified by a URI and indicates the RDF resource to be described in the application. A resource includes a set of properties which are handled by the Property component. Properties can be either individual or aggregate when combining multiple features of a resource (e.g. a component that combines longitude and latitude properties; start date and end date properties for a date range, etc.). Each property is instantiated by an individual value or multiple values in case of an aggregate object. The value(s) of properties are controlled by the Value component. In turn, Value components invoke different components to search, browse and view the property values. Value components are terminals in the FERASAT single directional data flow where customized user-generated components (e.g. charts, maps, diagrams, etc.) can be plugged into the system.

2.4 Adaptation Engine

An adaptive UI[5] is a UI which adapts, that is, changes its layout and elements to the needs of the user or context and is similarly alterable by each user. In the context of FERASAT, we devised a particular type of adaptive UI called a *data-aware UI* [10] that (a) can understand users' data and (b) can interact with users accordingly. As depicted in Fig. 1, FERASAT incorporates an adaptation engine to realize data-aware UIs when users interact with data. The task of adaptation engine is to make a bridge between data (enriched by semantics) and existing UI components suitable to render data. The adaptation engine includes the following core components:

– *Querying.* This part is responsible for composing, sharing and running of SPARQL queries within the FERASAT environment. FERASAT exploits the

---

[5] http://en.wikipedia.org/wiki/Adaptive_user_interface.

WYSIWYQ (What You See Is What You Query) model [12] to allow sharing, modification and repurposing of SPARQL queries among multiple users in a visual and interactive way (supporting F_3). The WYSIWYQ mode translates SPARQL queries to a set of user interface components in certain states and renders this set as a faceted browsing environment. It also provides a set of SPARQL query templates similar to the one discussed in [3] to find analogous resources within the same domain (partially supporting F_5).

- *Reasoning.* This is the core part of the engine where different datasets mentioned in Sect. 2.2 are analyzed in an integrative way to find the best strategy for data rendering and UI augmentation.
- *Selection.* This part allows to manually or automatically (as result of the reasoning) select or replace an existing UI component. FERASAT employs a specific notation to identify a chain of facet properties using RDF property path and federated SPARQL queries. For example, `ex:address->geo:geo` selects a property path, `ex:orcidID->[http://orcid.org]rdfs:label` allows using a property path which ends up in a named graph, and `ex:orcidID->[http://myendpoint.com>>http://orcid.org]rdfs:label` refers to a property path which is on a named graph located in a different SPARQL endpoint.[6]
- *Customization.* This part allows to manually or automatically customize an existing UI component.
- *Personalization.* This part allows to manually or automatically personalize an existing UI component. Personalization will overwrite the configurations used for customization to consider the user's context.

Figure 4 shows that the configuration process is done by traversing the hypergraph generated either manually by a user or automatically as result of the reasoning. FERASAT exploits a hierarchical permutation of the Dataset, Resource, Property, and Value components as *scopes* to select specific parts of the UI to be customized or personalized. Each scope conveys a certain level of specificity on a given context ranging from 1 (most specific: DRPV) to 15 (least specific: D). Scopes are defined by using either the URIs of named graphs, resources, and properties, or by identifying the resource types and data types. A configuration is defined as a setting which affects the way the UI components are interpreted and rendered (e.g. render a specific component for a specific RDF property or a specific RDF resource within a specific RDF graph). UI adaptation is handled by traversing the configurations for scopes, populating the configurations and overwriting the configurations when a more specific applicable scope is found.

3   Implementation

FERASAT is implemented as a ReactJS component (backed by NodeJS) within the open-source Linked Data Reactor[7] (LD-R) framework and is available to

---

[6] More details are available at http://ld-r.org/docs/configFacets.html.

[7] https://github.com/ali1k/ld-r.

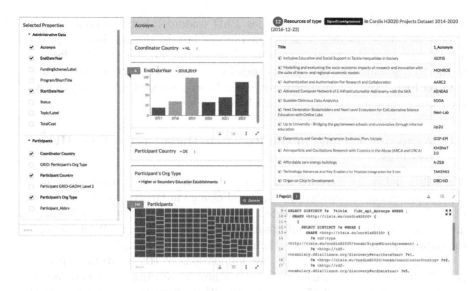

Fig. 5. An screenshot of the implemented FERASAT adaptive faceted browser.

download at http://ferasat.ld-r.org together with its documentation and demos (see Fig. 5 for an screenshot of the FERASAT environment). FERASAT supports two strategies for creating UI configurations:

- *Dynamic Configurations*: This option (that is necessary for reasoning and automatic UI adaptation) uses a SPARQL endpoint to store user configurations dynamically as RDF. This is a flexible approach that allows updating user configurations on-the-fly without the need to restart or rebuild the entire application. It also facilitates sharing and querying of the user configurations.
- *Static Configuration*: For this option, users do not require to provide a read/write SPARQL endpoint to store their configurations and can enter and store all their configurations locally on the application server as JSON. This options is faster than the static method (since it removes the overhead of using a triple store) and more secure, however the cost of this option is that users need to restart their application server anytime they modify the configurations. Users can combine this method with the dynamic method where the static configurations always have a higher priority in UI configuration.

4   Use Cases

FERASAT is integrated into the SMS[8] (Semantically Mapping Science) platform as the technical core within the RISIS.eu project. It is actively used to browse data related to Science, Technology & Innovation (STI) studies. The SMS platform has already 388 registered users varying from senior and experienced to

---

[8] http://sms.risis.eu.

junior researchers (professors, postdocs, PhD students), but also policy makers, librarians, project managers, scientific officers, etc. In this section, we provide a brief summary of two use cases related to serendipitous knowledge discovery in the STI domain written by two social scientists who experienced browsing data on FERASAT environment while conducting research. A complete list of use cases is available at http://sms.risis.eu/usecases.

4.1 Analyzing Change in the Research/Higher Education (HE) Systems

The RISIS datastore contains many datasets with information about organizations. I was mainly interested in structural change in HE systems by navigating through those datasets. The faceted browser was of great help, as it enabled me to explore the available information in a graphical form. While browsing the datasets, I found a property "foundation year". Selecting that property for a country, I got the frequency of new foundations of HE institutions per year (see Fig. 5), and I saw immediately (F_1) a high concentration in two consecutive years: in 1986 and 1987 some 21 new HE institutions were founded in the Netherlands, on a total of 114: So some substantial changes in the HE system seem to have taken place! By selecting these two years, the list of organizations shows the names of the institutions that were founded in these two years. I could inspect the list, but also select a single institution and inspect the available information in the datastore, but also more broadly on the web, as all the organizations are also linked to their website and their Wikipedia page (F_7, F_8, F_9). So, I did not only have much numerical data in the data network, such as numbers of students and staff, but also qualitative (textual) data for further inspection. Looking at the various newly founded schools showed that these are all Universities of Applied Sciences, so the "second layer" Dutch HE institutions. By reading the historical information on their Websites, one would find out that the new founded institutions in fact are conglomerations of smaller schools into very large new institutions (F_7, F_9). This indeed can be considered as a major reform of the Dutch HE system.

A follow-up question would be whether this is a typical Dutch phenomenon, or whether similar changes have taken place in other countries (F_{11}). Belgium could be a second case to inspect, and I followed the same steps. Indeed, as the browser shows, also here we find concentrations of foundations of new HE institutions, but now in the year 1995 when 32 new HE institutions were founded in Belgium. If I select the year 1995, I get a list with the names of the newly founded institutions and can further inspect the available information on those institutions. I did not have any prior knowledge on the Belgian system (F_7), but inspecting the list of names in the results, one immediately sees that the changes probably took place in the French speaking part of Belgium, as all institution names are French, and not in the Flemish speaking part (F_6). Indeed, the two language regions have their own HE system, so this could clearly be the case.

The third example I tried was Austria, and indeed also there I detected a concentration of new institutions in 2007 - a decade after the changes in Belgium

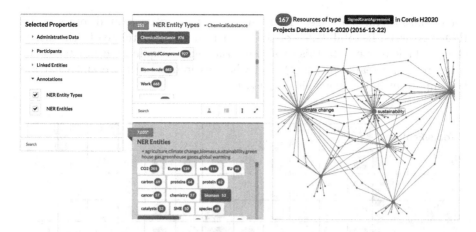

Fig. 6. Employing background knowledge to facilitate browsing of data.

and two decades after the changes in the Netherlands. Of the total of 102 HE institutions in Austria, 15 were created in 2007 - again a percentage suggesting some form of structural change. Even if one is completely unknowledgeable about the Austrian HE system, selecting the entity type in the browser tells us (F_5) that the changes have taken place in the sector of teacher education: the newly founded HE institutions are all of type "University of Education", "University College of Teacher Education", and "Pedagogical University". Without further investigation, one already can conclude that the changes in the Austrian system are less broad than in the Netherlands or in Belgium, where the changes seem to cover a much larger part of the HE system.

4.2 Evaluating Research Portfolios with Regards to Current Societal Challenges

I used the faceted browser to browse CORDIS open dataset on H2020 EU projects to evaluate research portfolios. The browser showed the relevant characteristics of the projects, such as organizations involved, the organization type, and the program the project belongs to. The CORDIS dataset contains among others a text summarizing the content of the projects. Using the annotator tool helped me to extract general encyclopedic concepts from these textual descriptions and enabled me to browse data using two new facets (F_7), one for extracted terms and one for categories these terms belong to (see Fig. 6). Combining extracted terms has a great advantage, as we can combine technical research terms and policy related terms to retrieve the relevant projects (F_1). This may solve the problem of finding how research links to the grand societal challenges. This is a core problem in assessing relevance of research (described in technical terms and policy related terms). Because the resulting set for a very specific topic is generally not too large, I could even manually inspect the policy-science link. As an example, I looked at chemical research in H2020 projects, related to one of the societal challenges. There are quite some water related topics in the H2020 projects. In total 22.5% of the water projects seem related to chemistry. Going a little deeper into this case shows the multidisciplinary character of the water related research in H2020, and what disciplines are more and what are less important in this portfolio (F_5, F_8, F_9).

Tools/Features	F1	F2	F3	F4	F5	F6	F7	F8	F9	F10	F11	F12
FERASAT	●	◐	●	●	●	●	●	●	●	●	○	○
SemFacet	○	◐	○	○	◐	○	○	◐	○	○	○	○
VisiNav	●	○	○	○	○	●	○	●	●	○	○	○
/facet	●	○	○	○	●	●	○	●	◐	○	○	○
LD Query Wizard	○	○	○	○	◐	○	○	○	○	◐	○	○
gFacet	○	○	○	◐	●	○	○	○	◐	○	◐	○
Sparklis	○	○	●	○	●	○	○	◐	○	◐	○	○

● supported   ◐ partly supported   ○ not supported

Fig. 7. Comparing existing RDF faceted browsers based on the proposed serendipity design features.

5 Related Work

Path-finding on semantic graphs such as RDF graphs, where semantics of the relations between resources are explicitly defined, leads to discovering meaningful and insightful connections between multiple resources. That is the reason why most of the current research work which investigates serendipity on Linked Data is focused on novel approaches for semantic traversal of RDF graphs and thereby serendipitous discovery of new related nodes.

Tools such as Everything_Is_Connected_Engine [2] and DBpedia RelFinder[9] allow serendipitous *storytelling* and *relation extraction* which benefit from path-finding on general knowledge graphs. In addition to that, domain-specific knowledge graphs enable experts to reveal *unsuspected connections* and/or *hidden analogies*. For instance, the Linked Data version of the TCGA (The Cancer Genome Atlas Database) [18] allows bio-medical experts to discover how cancer types tend to metastasize into other cancer types and to serendipitously explore linked data to see how the rheology of certain cancer types affects this metastasis. Furthermore, serendipitous recommendation realized by LOD paths-based techniques has been incorporated into the design of many personalized systems to

---

[9] http://www.visualdataweb.org/relfinder.php.

minimize blind spots in information delivery. For example, in [14], a serendipity-powered TV recommender using BBC programs dataset is presented.

There are also several frameworks, tools and related works in the area of browsing (semi) structured data which do not claim explicitly for a contribution in terms of serendipity (cf. Figure 7):

In [16] a generic guideline is proposed for designing expressive exploration environments over semi-structured data which organizes the design space of exploration tools in a three-layer architecture: Data Access, Functional, and Interaction/Interface. Except for the adaptation engine, their proposed architecture fits very well with the technical architecture of the FERASAT.

SemFacet [1] is a faceted search tool enhanced by the Semantic Web technologies to allow browsing of interlinked documents. SemFacet is implemented on top of a fragment of Yago and DBpedia abstracts. Similar to the pivot change feature in FERASAT, SemFacet allows refocusing results to support F_8. Although SemFacet exploits ontology-based reasoning for generation of facets and queries, no user-contextualization is supported. The main advantages of FERASAT over SemFacet are supports for customized interactive facet visualizations and enabling federated SPARQL queries over multiple knowledge graphs tailored based on the user context. *VisiNav* [5] is another linked data navigation system which combines features such as keyword search, object focus, path traversal and facet selection to browse web of data with a large variance. Although VisiNav provides some mechanisms to address the issue of *naked objects* (i.e. objects that are displayed without type-specific styling), it does not provide any personalized integrated view on distributed knowledge graphs. In our opinion, VisiNav acts more as a tool for traversing web of data rather than a direct knowledge discovery tool. \facet [7] is a linked data faceted browser very similar to FERASAT but with limited capabilities to share the generated queries, adapt the results based on user context and to invert and randomize the facets for increasing the chance encounter. \facet enables multi-type browsing experience and allows adapting the dynamically generated facets based on their RDF relations. It also allows users to create facet specifications and build facet dependent visualizations and interactions to make surprising observations more noticeable. *Linked Data Query Wizard* [8] is a linked data browsing UI, heavily dependent on RDF Data Cube standard, which turns graph-based data into a tabular interface with support for search and filtering to facilitate exploring linked data. Although converting graphs to interactive spreadsheet tables increases the learnability of UI for users, it also results in limited capabilities for serendipity by limiting the flexibility of information visualization related to certain dimensions of data. *gFacet* [6] is a graph-based faceted browser which allows users to build their facets of interest on the fly. It enable users to perform a pivot operation and switch a facet to a result list. Color coded facets and their relationships facilitate explaining the surprising observations. However, no mechanism for sharing the query results, inverting and randomizing values is offered. *Sparklis* [4] is a query-based faceted search UI that uses the expressivity of natural language to facilitate browsing Linked Data and understanding the generated query. It does not exploit any interactive visualizations in the facets to make surprising observations more noticeable. Also using only a single facet on a single knowledge graph, to browse data, makes the divergent information behavior difficult to achieve, though it increases the expressiveness and scalability of the traversed paths.

To the best of our knowledge, the related work in the domain of Linked Open Data where other aspects of serendipity than mere semantic path-finding are addressed, is quite scarce. The closest to our work is [3] which is based on SPARQL querying perspective where authors propose a query modification process to support serendipity features F_{11}: analogy, F_1: surprising observation, F_3: inversion, and F_4: disturbance. There are also similar querying-based approaches in the domain of data mining [17] to enhance the expressiveness of query languages to allow queries like "Find all the customers with deviant transactions." Or to offer meta-query languages ("Find me a pattern that connects something about writers" backgrounds and the characters in their novels"). What distinguishes our approach from the above work is our more comprehensive investigation of serendipity design features and their implications on linked data faceted browsing environments for fostering serendipity on LOD.

6   Conclusions and Future Work

In this paper we presented a novel faceted browsing environment on Linked Data called FERASAT which aims to foster accidental knowledge discovery while browsing data scattered over multiple knowledge graphs. We reviewed the related work and showcased the applicability of FERASAT in the domain of science, technology and innovation by describing two relevant use cases.

As future work, we plan to implement more serendipity-fostering strategies within our faceted browser environment, in particular for detecting successful errors and performing cross-domain analogical reasoning. We also envisage to evaluate the usability of our implementation using a rigorous evaluation framework and also to extend its application to other domains such as life sciences. Another important direction for future work is handling access control when combining public and private datasets in an integrated way as well as potential privacy issues entailed by our proposed Linked Data-based faceted browser.

Acknowledgement. We would like to thank our colleagues from the Knowledge Representation and Reasoning research group at Vrije Universiteit Amsterdam for their helpful comments during the development of our Linked Data-based faceted browser. This work was supported by a grant from the European Union's 7th Framework Programme provided for the project RISIS (GA no. 313082).

References

1. Arenas, M., Grau, B.C., Kharlamov, E., Marciuska, S., Zheleznyakov, D., Jiménez-Ruiz, E.: SemFacet: semantic faceted search over yago. In: 23rd International World Wide Web Conference, WWW 2014, Seoul, Republic of Korea, 7–11 April 2014, Companion Volume, pp. 123–126 (2014)
2. De Vocht, L., Coppens, S., Verborgh, R., Vander Sande, M., Mannens, E., Van de Walle, R.: Discovering meaningful connections between resources in the web of data. In: LDOW (2013)
3. Eichler, J.S.A., et al.: Searching linked data with a twist of serendipity. In: Dubois, E., Pohl, K. (eds.) CAiSE 2017. LNCS, vol. 10253, pp. 495–510. Springer, Cham (2017). https://doi.org/10.1007/978-3-319-59536-8_31
4. Ferré, S.: Expressive and scalable query-based faceted search over SPARQL endpoints. In: Mika, P., Tudorache, T., Bernstein, A., Welty, C., Knoblock, C., Vrandečić, D., Groth, P., Noy, N., Janowicz, K., Goble, C. (eds.) ISWC 2014. LNCS, vol. 8797, pp. 438–453. Springer, Cham (2014). https://doi.org/10.1007/978-3-319-11915-1_28
5. Harth, A.: VisiNav: a system for visual search and navigation on web data. Web Semant. Sci. Serv. Agents World Wide Web 8(4), 348–354 (2010)
6. Heim, P., Ertl, T., Ziegler, J.: Facet graphs: complex semantic querying made easy. In: Aroyo, L., Antoniou, G., Hyvönen, E., ten Teije, A., Stuckenschmidt, H., Cabral, L., Tudorache, T. (eds.) ESWC 2010. LNCS, vol. 6088, pp. 288–302. Springer, Heidelberg (2010). https://doi.org/10.1007/978-3-642-13486-9_20
7. Hildebrand, M., van Ossenbruggen, J., Hardman, L.: /facet: a browser for heterogeneous semantic web repositories. In: Cruz, I., Decker, S., Allemang, D., Preist, C., Schwabe, D., Mika, P., Uschold, M., Aroyo, L.M. (eds.) ISWC 2006. LNCS, vol. 4273, pp. 272–285. Springer, Heidelberg (2006). https://doi.org/10.1007/11926078_20
8. Hoefler, P., Granitzer, M., Veas, E.E., Seifert, C.: Linked data query wizard: a novel interface for accessing SPARQL endpoints. In: LDOW (2014)
9. Karger, D., Schraefel, M.: The pathetic fallacy of RDF. In: SWUI (2006)
10. Khalili, A., de Graaf, K.A.: Linked data reactor: towards data-aware user interfaces. In: 2017 SEMANTiCS. ACM (2017)
11. Khalili, A., Loizou, A., van Harmelen, F.: Adaptive linked data-driven web components: building flexible and reusable semantic web interfaces. In: Sack, H., Blomqvist, E., d'Aquin, M., Ghidini, C., Ponzetto, S.P., Lange, C. (eds.) ESWC 2016. LNCS, vol. 9678, pp. 677–692. Springer, Cham (2016). https://doi.org/10.1007/978-3-319-34129-3_41
12. Khalili, A., Meroño-Peñuela, A.: WYSIWYQ - what you see is what you query. In: Ivanova, V., Lambrix, P., Lohmann, S., Pesquita, C. (eds.) Proceedings of the Third International Workshop on Visualization and Interaction for Ontologies and Linked Data Co-located with the 16th International Semantic Web Conference (ISWC 2017). CEUR Workshop Proceedings, Vienna, Austria, 22 October 2017, vol. 1947, pp. 123–130. CEUR-WS.org (2017)
13. Khalili, A., van Andel, P., den Besselaar, P.V., de Graaf, K.A.: Fostering serendipitous knowledge discovery using an adaptive multigraph-based faceted browser. In: Corcho, Ó., Janowicz, K., Rizzo, G., Tiddi, I., Garijo, D. (eds.) Proceedings of the Knowledge Capture Conference, K-CAP 2017, Austin, TX, USA, 4–6 December 2017, pp. 15:1–15:4. ACM (2017)

14. Maccatrozzo, V., Terstall, M., Aroyo, L., Schreiber, G.: SIRUP: serendipity in recommendations via user perceptions. In: IUI 2017, pp. 35–44. ACM (2017)
15. Norman, D.A.: The Design of Everyday Things: Revised and Expanded Edition. Basic Books Inc., New York (2013)
16. Nunes, T., Schwabe, D.: Towards the design of expressive data exploration environments. In: Proceedings of the Third International Workshop on Visualization and Interaction for Ontologies and Linked Data Co-located with the 16th International Semantic Web Conference (ISWC 2017), Vienna, Austria, 22 October 2017, pp. 60–74 (2017)
17. Ramakrishnan, N., Grama, A.Y.: Data mining: from serendipity to science. Computer 32(8), 34–37 (1999)
18. Saleem, M., Kamdar, M.R., Iqbal, A., Sampath, S., Deus, H.F., Ngonga, A.-C.: Fostering serendipity through big linked data. In: ISWC SemWeb Challenge (2013)
19. van Andel, P.: Anatomy of the unsought finding. serendipity: origin, history, domains, traditions, appearances, patterns and programmability. Br. J. Philos. Sci. 45(2), 631–648 (1994)

Classifying Crises-Information Relevancy with Semantics

Prashant Khare[✉][iD], Grégoire Burel[✉], and Harith Alani[✉][iD]

Knowledge Media Institute, The Open University, Milton Keynes, UK
{prashant.khare,g.burel,h.alani}@open.ac.uk

Abstract. Social media platforms have become key portals for sharing and consuming information during crisis situations. However, humanitarian organisations and affected communities often struggle to sieve through the large volumes of data that are typically shared on such platforms during crises to determine which posts are truly relevant to the crisis, and which are not. Previous work on automatically classifying crisis information was mostly focused on using statistical features. However, such approaches tend to be inappropriate when processing data on a type of crisis that the model was not trained on, such as processing information about a *train crash*, whereas the classifier was trained on *floods, earthquakes, and typhoons*. In such cases, the model will need to be retrained, which is costly and time-consuming. In this paper, we explore the impact of semantics in classifying Twitter posts across same, and different, types of crises. We experiment with 26 crisis events, using a hybrid system that combines statistical features with various semantic features extracted from external knowledge bases. We show that adding semantic features has no noticeable benefit over statistical features when classifying same-type crises, whereas it enhances the classifier performance by up to 7.2% when classifying information about a new type of crisis.

Keywords: Semantics · Crisis informatics · Tweet classification

1 Introduction

The 2017 World Humanitarian Data and Trends report by UNOCHA[1] indicated that in 2016 alone, there were 324 natural disaster, affecting 204 million people, from 105 countries, causing an overall damage cost of $147 billion. During the course of natural disasters, large amounts of content are typically published in real time on various social media outlets. For instance, over 20 million tweets with the words #sandy and #hurricane were posted in just a few days during the Hurricane Sandy disaster[2].

---

[1] UNOCHA, https://data.humdata.org/dataset/world-humanitarian-data-and-tren ds.

[2] Mashable: Sandy Sparks 20 Million Tweets, http://mashable.com/2012/11/02/ hurricane-sandy-twitter.

© Springer International Publishing AG, part of Springer Nature 2018
A. Gangemi et al. (Eds.): ESWC 2018, LNCS 10843, pp. 367–383, 2018.
https://doi.org/10.1007/978-3-319-93417-4_24

Although these messages act as critical information sources for various communities and relief teams, the sheer volume of data generated on social media platforms during crises makes it extremely difficult to manually process such streams in order to filter relevant pieces of information quickly [7]. Automatically identifying crisis-information relevancy is not trivial, especially given the characteristics of social media posts such as colloquialisms, short post length, nonstandard acronyms, and syntactic variations in the text. Furthermore, many posts that carry the crisis hashtag/s can be irrelevant, hence hashtags are inadequate filters of relevancy.

Various works explored classification methods of crisis-data from social media platforms, to automatically categorise them into *crisis-related* or *not related*. These classification methods include both supervised [11,14,20,25] and unsupervised [18] machine learning approaches. Most of these methods are based on statistical features of the text, such as n-grams, text length, POS, and Hashtags. Although statistical models have shown to be efficient in classifying relevancy of crisis-information, their accuracy naturally drops when applied to information that were not included in the training sets. The typical approach to remedy this problem, is to retrain the model on new datasets or apply complex domain adaptation techniques, which are costly and time consuming, and thus are inadequate for crisis situations which typically require immediate reaction.

This work aims to bridge this gap by adding semantic features for the identification of crisis-related tweets on seen and unseen crises types. We hypothesise that adding concepts and properties (e.g., *type, label, category*) improves the identification of crisis information content across crisis domains, by creating a non-specific crisis contextual semantic abstraction of crisis-related content. The main contributions of this paper can be summarised as follow:

1. Build a statistical-semantic classification model with semantics extracted from BableNet and DBpedia.
2. Experiment with classifying relevancy of tweets from 26 crisis events of various types and in multiple languages.
3. Run relevancy classifiers with multiple feature combinations and when crisis types are included/excluded from training data.
4. Show that adding semantics increase of classification accuracy on unseen crisis types by +7.2% in F1 in comparison to non-semantic models.

The paper is structured as follows: Sect. 2 summarises related work. Sections 3 and 4 describe our approach and experiments on classifying relevancy while using different semantic features and crisis datasets. Results are reported in Sects. 4.2 and 4.3. Discussion and conclusions are in Sects. 5 and 6.

2   Related Work

Large volumes of messages are typically posted across different social media platforms during crisis situations. However, a considerable number of these messages are potentially not related and irrelevant. Olteanu et al. [16] made an observation about the broad categories that crisis reports from social media can be categorised into: *related and informative*, *related but not informative*, and *not related*.

Identifying crisis related content from social media is not a new research area. Most supervised machine learning approaches used in this domain rely on linguistic and other statistical attributes of the post such as part of speech (POS), user mentions, length of the post, and number of hashtags. Supervised machine learning approaches range from traditional classification methods such as Support Vector Machines (SVM), Naive Bayes, Conditional Random Fields [8,17,20] to recent trends of deep learning [3]. In [3,4], word embeddings are applied and semantics are added in the form of extracted entities and their types, but adaptability of the model to unseen types of crisis data is not evaluated.

Complex domain adaptation methods has found its application in the areas of text classification and sentiment analysis [6], but have not been applied to crisis situations. In crisis classification, a closely related work [8] took a step towards domain adaptation by considering crisis data from two disasters, Joplin 2011 tornado and Hurricane Sandy. They trained the model on a part of Joplin tornado, and tested it on Hurricane Sandy and remaining part of Joplin data. However, their work was limited to only two crises; one hurricane and one tornado, which often cast similar types of impact on human life and infrastructure. Additionally, the semantic aspect of the crisis was not taken into consideration, which could have potentially highlighted the applicability of the method in multiple crisis scenario.

Unsupervised methods were also explored, often based on clustering [18] and keyword based processing. Our work in this paper complements and extends the aforementioned studies by investigating the use of semantics, derived from knowledge graphs, such as entities occurring in the tweets, and expanding them to their hypernyms and extended information through DBpedia properties.

Previously, we used hierarchical semantics from knowledge graphs to perform crisis-information classification through a supervised machine learning approach [12]. However, the study was limited to 9 crisis events, and confined to training and testing on the same type of crisis-events (i.e., no cross-crisis evaluation).

Some systems were developed that use semantics extracted with Named Entity Recognition tools on DBpedia and WordNet, to support searching of crisis-related information (e.g., Twitcident [2], Armatweet [23]). These system are focused on search, and do not include machine learning classifiers.

As opposed to previous work, we focus on applying these classifiers to two particular cases. First, when the classification model was trained on the data that contained crisis-event type, and secondly, when the crisis event type was not included in the training set. These two cases are aimed to help us better understand if, and when, adding semantics outperforms purely statistical approaches.

3   Semantic Classification of Crisis-Related Content

The automatic identification of crisis-related content on social media requires the training and validation of a binary text classifier that is able to distinguish between *crisis-related* and *not related* crisis content. In this paper, we focus on generating statistical and semantic features of tweets and then training different machine learning models. In the following sections, we present (i) the dataset used for training our classifiers, (ii) the statistical and semantic set of features used for building the classifiers, and (iii) the classifier selection process.

3.1   Dataset and Data Selection

In this study, we use the CrisisLexT26[3] dataset [16]. It contains annotated datasets of 26 different crisis events, which occurred between 2012 and 2013, with 1000 labeled tweets (*'Related and Informative'*, *'Related but not Informative'*, *'Not Related'* and *'Not Applicable'*) for each event. The search keywords used to collect the original data used hashtags and/or terms that are often paired with the canonical forms of a disaster name and the impacted location (e.g., Queensland floods) or meteorological terms (e.g., Hurricane Sandy). We selected all 26 events, and for each event we combined the *Related and Informative* and *Related but not Informative* into the *Related* class, and combined the *Not Related* and *Not Applicable* into the *Not Related* class. These two classes are then used for distinguishing crisis-related content from unrelated content for creating binary text classifiers.

To reduce content redundancy in the data, we removed replicated instances from the collection of individual events by comparing tweets pairs after removing user-handles (i.e., '@' mentions), URL's, and special characters. This resulted in 21378 documents annotated with the *Related* label and 2965 annotated with the *Not Related* label. For avoiding classification bias towards the majority class, we balanced the data from each event by matching the number of *Related* documents with the *Not Related* ones. This was achieved by randomly selecting the same number of *Related* and *Not Related* tweets in any given event. This resulted in a final overall size of 5931 tweets (2966 *Related* and 2965 *Not Related* documents). Table 1 shows the distribution of selected tweets for each event.

3.2   Features Engineering

In order to assess the advantage of using semantic features compared to more traditional statistical features, we distinguish two different feature sets; (1) *statistical* features, and; (2) *semantic* features. *Statistical* features have widely been used in the literature [8,9,11,14,20,25] and are posed as the baseline approach for our work. They capture quantifiable linguistic features and other statistical properties of a given post. On the other hand, *semantic* features capture more contextual information of documents, such as the named entities emerging in

---

[3] CrisisLexT26 http://crisislex.org/data-collections.html#CrisisLexT26.

Table 1. Crisis events data, balanced between related and not-related classes

Nb.	Id	Event	Category			Nb.	Id	Event	Category		
			Related	Not-related	Total				Related	Not-related	Total
1	CWF	Colorado Wildfire	242	242	484	2	COS	Costa Rica Earthquake	470	470	940
3	GAU	Guatemala Earthquake	103	103	206	4	ITL	Italy Earthquake	56	56	112
5	PHF	Philippines Flood	70	70	140	6	TYP	Typhoon Pablo	88	88	176
7	VNZ	Venezuela Refinery	60	60	120	8	ALB	Alberta Flood	16	16	32
9	ABF	Australia Bushfire	183	183	366	10	BOL	Bohol Earthquake	31	31	62
11	BOB	Boston Bombing	69	69	138	12	BRZ	Brazil Nightclub Fire	44	44	88
13	CFL	Colorado Floods	61	61	122	14	GLW	Glasgow Helicopter Crash	110	110	220
15	LAX	LA Airport Shoot	112	112	224	16	LAM	Lac Megantic Train Crash	34	34	68
17	MNL	Manila Flood	74	74	148	18	NYT	NY Train Crash	2	1	3
19	QFL	Queensland Flood	278	278	556	20	RUS	Russia Meteor	241	241	482
21	SAR	Sardinia Flood	67	67	134	22	SVR	Savar Building	305	305	610
23	SGR	Singapore Haze	54	54	108	24	SPT	Spain Train Crash	8	8	16
25	TPY	Typhoon Yolanda	107	107	214	26	WTX	West Texas Explosion	81	81	162

a given text, as well as their hierarchical semantic information extracted from external knowledge graphs.

Statistical Features: For every tweet in the dataset, the following *statistical* features are extracted:

- *Number of nouns*: nouns generally refer to different entities involved in the crisis event such as locations, actors, or resources involved in the crisis event [8,9,20].
- *Number of verbs*: verbs indicate actions that occur in a crisis event [8,9,20].
- *Number of pronouns*: as with nouns, pronouns may indicate involvement of the actors, locations, or resources.
- *Tweet Length*: number of characters in a post. The length of a post may determine the amount of information contained [8,9,19].
- *Number of words*: number of words may be another indicator of the amount of information contained within a post [8,11].
- *Number of Hashtags*: hashtags reflect the themes of the post and are manually generated by the posts' authors [8,9,11].

- *Unigrams*: The entire data (text of each post) is tokenised and represented as unigrams [8,9,11,14,20,25]

The Part Of Speech (POS) features (e.g., *nouns, verbs, pronouns*) are extracted using the spaCy library.[4] Unigrams are extracted with the regexp tokenizer provided in NLTK.[5] Stop-words are removed using a stop-words list,[6] Stemming is also performed using the Porter Stemmer. Finally, TF-IDF vector normalisation is also applied in order to weigh the importance of words (tokens) in the documents according to their relative importance within the dataset. This resulted in a total number of 10757 unigrams (i.e., vocabulary size) for the entire balanced dataset.

Semantic Features: Semantic features are designed to generalise information representation across crises. They are designed to be less crisis specific compared to *statistical* features. We use the Name Entity Recogniser (NER) service Babelfy,[7] and two different knowledge bases for creating these features: (1) BabelNet,[8] and; (2) DBpedia:[9]

- *Babelfy Entities*: the entities extracted by the BabelNet NER tool (e.g., *news, sadness, terremoto*). Babelfy extracts and disambiguates entities linked to the BabelNet [15] knowledge base.
- *BabelNet Senses (English)*: the English labels associated with the entities returned by Babelfy (e.g., *news → news, sadness → sadness, terremoto → earthquake*).
- *BabelNet Hypernyms (English)*: the direct English hypernyms (at distance-1) of each entities extracted from BableNet. Hypernyms can broaden the context of an entity, and can enhance the semantics of a document [12] (e.g., *broadcasting, communiucation, emotion*).
- *DBpedia Properties*: a list of properties associated with the DBpedia URI returned by Babelfy. The following properties are queried using SPARQL: `dct:subject`, `rdfs:label` (only in English), `rdf:type` (only of the type http://schema.org and http://dbpedia.org/ontology), `dbo:city`, `dbp:state`, `dbo:state`, `dbp:country` and `dbo:country` (the location properties fluctuate between `dbp` and `dbo`) (e.g., `dbc:Grief`, `dbc:Emotions`, `dbr:Sadness`).

Using hypernyms shown to enhance the semantics of a document [12], and can assist the context representation of documents by correlating different entities with a similar context. For instance, the following four entities *fireman, policeman, MP (Military Police)*, and *garda* (an Irish word for police) share a common English hypernym: *defender*. To generalise the semantics for tweets in

---

[4] SpaCy Library, https://spacy.io.

[5] Regexp Tokenizer (NLTK), http://www.nltk.org/_modules/nltk/tokenize/regexp.html.

[6] Stop Words List, https://raw.githubusercontent.com/6/stopwords-json/master/stopwords-all.json.

[7] Babelfy, http://babelfy.org.

[8] BabelNet, http://babelnet.org.

[9] DBpedia, http://dbpedia.org.

different languages, we formulate the semantics in English. As a result, we prevent the sparsity that results from the varying morphological forms of concepts across languages (see Table 2 to see an example). The senses and hypernyms are both derived from the BabelNet, and together form the *BabelNet Semantics*. The semantic expansion of the data-set through *BabelNet Semantics* expands the vocabulary (in comparison to the case with statistical features) by 3057 unigrams.

Table 2. Semantic expansion with BabelNet and DBpedia semantics.

	Post A	Post B
Feature	'Sad news to report from #Guatemala -at least 8 confirmed dead, possibly more, by this morning's major earthquake'	'Terremoto 7, 4 Ricther Guatemala deja 15 fallecidos, casas en el suelo, 100 desaperecidos, 100MIL personas sin luz FO'
Babelfy entities	News, sadness, dead, describe, earthquake	Terremoto, casas, suelo, luz, fallecidos
BabelNet sense (English)	News, sadness, dead, describe, earthquake	Earthquake, house, soil, light, dead
BabelNet hypernyms (English)	Broadcasting, communication, emotion, feeling, people, deceased, inform, natural disaster, geologica phenomenon	Natural disaster, geological phenomenon, building, Structure, residential_building granular material, people, deceased
DBpedia properties	dbc:Grief, dbc:Emotions, dbr:Sadness, dbc:Demography, dbr:Death, dbc:Communication, dbr:News, dbc:Geological_hazards, dbc:Seismology, dbr:Earthquake	dbc:Geological_hazards, dbc:Seismology, dbr:Earthquake, dbc:Home, dbc:Structural_system, dbc:Light, dbr:Death, dbc:Demography

Besides the *BabelNet Semantics*, we also use DBpedia properties to obtain more information about the entity (see Table 2) in the form of subject, label, and location specific properties. Semantic expansion of the dataset through *DBpedia Semantics* increases the vocabulary (in comparison to the vocabulary from statistical features) by 1733 unigrams.

We use both of these semantic features, *BabelNet & DBpedia Semantics*, individually and also in combination with each other, while developing the binary classifiers to identify crisis-related posts from unrelated ones. When both BabelNet Semantics and DBpedia semantics are used, the vocabulary (in comparison to the vocabulary as determined in statistical features) is increased by 3824 unigrams. Our experiments will determine whether or not such vocabulary extensions can be regarded as enhancements.

3.3 Classifier Selection

For our binary classification problem, we took into consideration the high dimensionality generated from unigrams and semantic features, and the need to avoid over fitting. In comparison to the large dimensionality of the features, which is in the range of 10–15k under different feature combinations, the training examples are smaller in size (around 6000). This encouraged us to opt for Support Vector Machine (SVM) with a Linear Kernel as the classification model, since this model has been found effective for such kind of problems.[10] Additionally, we validated the appropriateness of SVM Linear Kernel against RBF kernel, Polynomial kernel, and Logistic Regression. Based on 20 runs of 5 fold cross-validation of different feature combinations, SVM Linear Kernel was found to be more statistically significant, and had a better mean F_1 value of 0.8118 and a p-value of <0.00001 when compared to other classifiers (by performing a t-test followed by calculating p-value).

4   Crisis-Related Content Classification Across Crises

In this section, we detail the experimental set up and create the models based on various criteria. Further, we report the results and discuss how including the expanded semantic features impacted the performance of our classifiers, particularly in the cases when it is applied to cross-crisis scenarios.

4.1 Experimental Setting

The experiments are designed to train and evaluate the classification models on (i) the entire dataset, i.e., on all 26 crisis events, (ii) a selection of train/test crisis event data, based on certain criteria for cross-crisis evaluation.

Crisis Classification Models: For the first experiment, we create different classifiers to compute and compare the performance of various feature combinations. Here, we aim to see when all the 26 events (Sect. 3.1) are merged, whether the inclusion of semantics boosts the binary classification. We create multiple classifiers and evaluate them using 5-fold cross validation. To this end, we used scikit-learn library.[11] The different classifiers are trained based on different features combinations:

---

[10] A Practical Guide to Support Vector Classification, http://www.csie.ntu.edu.tw/~cjlin/papers/guide/guide.pdf.

[11] Scikit-learn, http://scikit-learn.org.

- *SF*: A classifier generated with the statistical features only; our baseline.
- *SF+SemEF_BN*: A classifier generated with the statistical features and the semantic features from *BabelNet Semantics* (entity sense, and their hypernyms).
- *SF+SemEF_DB*: A classifier generated with the statistical features, and the semantic features from *DBpedia Semantics* (label, type, and other DBpedia properties).
- *SF+SemEF_BNDB*: A classifier generated with the statistical features, and the combination of semantic features from *BabelNet and DBpedia Semantics*.

Cross-Crisis Classification: For the second experiment, we aim at evaluating models on event types that are not observed during training (e.g., evaluate models on earthquake data, whereas it was trained on flood events). The models are trained on different combination of features and various types of crisis events. We generate the classifiers for the feature combinations as described in the previous experiment (see above). However, in this case, we divide the data into training and test sets based on 2 different criteria as described below:

1. Identify posts from a crisis event, when the *type* of event is already included in the training data (e.g., process tweets from a new flood incident when tweets from other flood crisis are in the training data).
2. Identify posts from a crisis event, when the *type* of the event is not included in the training data.

Since the criteria are defined on the *types* of the events, we hereby distribute the 26 events broadly in 11 *types* as given in Table 3. This categorisation is based on personal understandings of the nature of different types of crisis events, and how related or discrete they might be based on their effects. For instance, we have assumed the *type* of Flood and Typhoon as highly similar, considering that flood are typical direct outcomes of Typhoons (more about this in Sect. 5).

4.2   Results: Crisis Classification

In this section, we present the results from the first experiment, where the entire data (spread across 26 events and all our 11 event types) is merged. The models are trained using 20 iterations of 5-fold cross validation. The results are presented in Table 4. We report the mean of *Precision* (P_{mean}), *Recall* (R_{mean}), and F_1 score (F_{mean}) from 20 iterations, standard deviation in F_1 score (σ), and percentage change of F_1 score compared to the baseline ($\Delta F/F$).

In general, we observe that there is a very small change against the baseline classifier and that both classifiers are able to achieve $F_{mean} > 81\%$. The most noticeable improvement compared to the baseline can be observed for SF+SemEF_BN (1.39%) and SF+SemEF_BNDB (0.6%), which are both statistically significant ($p < 0.05$) based on a 2-tailed one-sample t-test, where the F_{mean} of SF is treated as the null-hypothesis.

To better understand the impact of semantics on the classifier, we perform feature selection using Information Gain (IG) to determine the most informative

Table 3. Types of events in the dataset.

Event type (Nb.)	Event instances	Event type (Nb.)	Event instances
Wildfire/bushfire (2)	CWF, ABF	Haze (1)	SGR
Earthquake (4)	COS, ITL, BOL, GAU	Helicopter crash (1)	GLW
Flood/typhoon (8)	TPY, TYP, CFL, QFL, ALB, PHF, SAR, MNL	Building collapse (1)	SVR
Terror shooting/bombing (2)	LAX, BOB	Location fire (2)	BRZ, VNZ
Train crash (2)	SPT, LAM[a]	Explosion (1)	WTX
Meteor (1)	RUS		

[a]NYT has only 3 tweets in total.

Table 4. Crisis-related content classification results using 20 iterations of 5-fold cross validation, $\Delta F/F$ (%) showing percentage gain/loss of the statistical semantics classifiers against the statistical baseline classifier.

Model	P_{mean}	R_{mean}	F_{mean}	Std. Dev. (σ)	$\Delta F/F$ (%)	Sig. (p-value)
SF (Baseline)	0.8145	0.8093	0.8118	0.0101	-	-
SF+SemEF_BN	0.8233	0.8231	0.8231	0.0111	1.3919	<0.000 01
SF+SemEF_DB	0.8148	0.8146	0.8145	0.0113	0.3326	0.018 78
SF+SemEF_BNDB	0.8169	0.8167	0.8167	0.0106	0.6036	0.000 011

features and how they vary across the classifiers. In SF model, we observe very event-specific features such as *collapse, terremoto, fire, earthquake, #earthquake, flood, typhoon, injured, quake* (Table 5). Within the top features, we also see 7 hashtags among the top 50 features, which reflects how event specific vocabulary plays a role in our classifier and how it may be an issue when dealing with new crisis types. Also, *No.ofHashTag* appeared as a key statistical feature. We observed that 1334 out of 2966 *Related* tweets had 0 hashtags (45% of related tweets), while 471 out of 2965 (15%) *Not Related* tweets had 0 hashtags.

For SF+SemEF_BN and SF+SemEF_DB models, we observed concepts such as *natural_hazard, structural_integrity_and_failure, conflagration, geological phenomenon, perception, dbo:location, dbo:place, dbc:building_defect, dbc:solid_mechanics* among the top 50 crisis-relatedness predictors (Table 5).

Looking more into the results, we can observe that *Structural_integrity_and_failure* is the annotated entity for terms like *collapse, building collapse* which are frequently occurring terms in the earthquake events, floods events, and Savar Building collapse. This is expected considering the significant number of earthquakes and floods events in the data. The *natural_disaster* hypernym is linked to several crisis events terms in the data such as *flood, landslide, earthquake*. Similarly, SF+SemEF_BNDB reflected a combination of both BabelNet and DBpedia semantics among informative features. These results show that semantics may help when dealing with new crisis types.

Although semantic models do not appear to be highly beneficial compared to purely statistical models when dealing with already seen event types, we observed the potential limitations of statistical features when dealing with new event types. Statistical features appear to be overly tied to event instances whereas semantic features seems to better generalise crisis-related concepts.

4.3   Results: Cross-Crisis Classification

We now evaluate the ability of the classifiers and feature to deal with event types that are not present in training data. We first evaluate the model on new instances of event types that have been already seen (Criteria 1) and then perform a similar task but omit event-types in the training dataset (Criteria 2).

Criteria 1 - Content Relatedness Classification of Already Seen Event Types. For the first sub-task, we evaluate our models on new event instances of event types already included when training the models (e.g., evaluate a new flood event on a model trained on data that include previous floods). We train the classifier on 25 crisis events, and use the 26th event as a test dataset.

As shown in Table 3, 26 crisis events have broadly been categorised under 11 *types*. In order to select the *type* of crisis events to test, we looked for such *types* which had a strong presence in the overall dataset. We opted for such crisis events which had at least 4 or more crisis events under the same type. As a result we consider two event types to evaluate: (1) *Flood/Typhoons* event types, and; (2) *Earthquake* event types.

For evaluating the models, we use following events as test data events: (1) For *Flood/Typhoons* we use *Typhoon Yolanda (TPY), Typhoon Pablo (TYP), Alberta Flood (ALB), Queensland Flood (QFL), Colorado Flood (CFL), Philippines Flood (PHF)* and *Sardinia Flood (SAR)* as evaluation data, and; (2) for *Earthquake*, we use *Guatemala Earthquake (GAU), Italy Earthquake (ITL), Bohol Earthquake (BOL)* and *Costa Rica Earthquake (COS)* as evaluation data. For example, when we evaluate the classifiers for TPY, we train our models on all the other 25 events and use the TPY data for the evaluation.

From the results in Table 6 it can be seen that, when the event *type* is previously seen by the classifier in the training data, the improvement from adding semantic features is small and inconsistent over the test cases. SF+SemEF_BN shows improvement over the baseline in 4 out of 11 evaluation cases, while SF+SemEF_DB shows improvement in 6 out of 11 evaluation cases. The average percentage gain ($\Delta F/F$) varies between +0.52% (SF+SemEF_BN) and +1.67% (SF+SemEF_DB) with a standard deviation varying between 6.89% to 7.78%. It indicates that almost half of the test event cases do not show improvement over the statistical features baseline's F_1 score.

Table 5. IG-Score ranks of features for: SF, SF+SemEF_BN and SF+SemEF_DB.

R.	SF		SF+SemEF_BN		SF+SemEF_DB	
	IG	Feature	IG	Feature	IG	Feature
1	0.106	No.OfHashTag	0.106	No.OfHashTag	0.106	No.OfHashTag
2	0.046	Costa	0.056	Costa	0.044	No.OfNouns
3	0.044	No.OfNoun	0.044	No.OfNouns	0.036	Costa_rica
4	0.044	Rica	0.044	Rica	0.035	dbc:countries_in_central_americ
5	0.035	Collapse	0.036	Costa_rica	0.035	Collapse
6	0.033	Terremoto	0.035	Central_american_country	0.031	Terremoto
7	0.026	TweetLength	0.032	Collapse	0.027	dbo:place
8	0.025	7	0.031	Terremoto	0.026	TweetLength
9	0.024	#earthquake	0.026	TweetLength	0.024	#earthquake
10	0.023	Bangladesh	0.026	Fire	0.024	dbo:location
11	0.022	No.OfVerb	0.024	#earthquake	0.023	dbo:populatedplace
12	0.022	#redoctober	0.023	Structural_integrity_and_failur	0.023	dbc:safes
13	0.021	No.OfWords	0.023	Coastal	0.022	structural_integrity_and_failure
14	0.018	Tsunami	0.022	Information	0.022	dbc:building_defect
15	0.017	Fire	0.022	Financial_condition	0.022	dbc:solid_mechanics
16	0.016	Building	0.022	No.OfVerbs	0.022	dbc:engineering_failure
17	0.016	rt	0.022	#redoctober	0.022	bangladesh
18	0.015	Factory	0.021	No.OfWords	0.022	dbc:flood
19	0.014	Toll	0.020	Shore	0.022	dbr:wealth
20	0.014	Flood	0.020	Building	0.022	No.OfVerbs
21	0.013	#bangladesh	0.019	Anatomical_structure	0.021	No.OfWords
22	0.013	#colorad	0.019	Phenomenon	0.02	dbc:coastal_geography
23	0.012	Alert	0.018	Natural_disaster	0.019	dbc:article_containing_video_clip
24	0.012	Hit	0.018	Failure	0.018	dbc:natural_hazard
25	0.012	Typhoon	0.017	Conflagration	0.017	Fire

Criteria 2 - Content Relatedness Classification of Unseen Crisis Types.
In criteria 1, we considered the classification of new event instances when similar
events already appeared in the classifier training data. In criteria 2 we test the
classifier on types of events that are not seen by the classifier in the training data
types. We select the following events and event types: (1) train the classifiers on
rest of the event *types* except *Terror Shooting/Bombing and Train Crash* and

Table 6. Cross-crisis relatedness classification: criteria 1 (best F_1 score is highlighted for each event).

Test event	Instances		SF			SF+SemEF_BN				SF+SemEF_DB				SF+SemEF_BNDB			
	Train	Test	P	R	F_1	P	R	F_1	ΔF/F (in %)	P	R	F_1	ΔF/F (in %)	P	R	F	ΔF/F (in %)
TPY	5717	214	0.808	0.804	0.803	0.777	0.776	0.776	-3.44	0.772	0.771	0.771	-4.01	0.780	0.780	0.780	-2.83
TYP	5755	176	0.876	0.864	0.863	0.853	0.841	0.840	-2.66	0.831	0.83	0.829	-3.84	0.861	0.852	0.851	-1.29
ALB	5899	32	0.72	0.719	0.718	0.754	0.75	0.749	4.25	0.845	0.844	0.844	17.41	0.845	0.844	0.844	17.41
QFL	5375	556	0.791	0.784	0.783	0.80	0.793	0.792	1.18	0.780	0.772	0.77	-1.66	0.789	0.782	0.781	-0.22
CFL	5809	122	0.82	0.803	0.801	0.835	0.828	0.827	3.28	0.806	0.762	0.754	-5.88	0.796	0.77	0.765	-4.41
PHF	5791	140	0.764	0.764	0.764	0.769	0.764	0.763	-0.13	0.772	0.771	0.771	0.93	0.744	0.743	0.743	-2.83
SAR	5797	134	0.684	0.612	0.570	0.747	0.694	0.677	18.79	0.702	0.664	0.648	13.70	0.696	0.664	0.650	14.10
GAU	5725	206	0.788	0.782	0.780	0.739	0.728	0.725	-7.1	0.798	0.786	0.784	0.51	0.779	0.772	0.770	-1.30
ITL	5819	112	0.595	0.589	0.583	0.619	0.589	0.562	-3.58	0.667	0.634	0.615	5.49	0.659	0.616	0.588	0.98
BOL	5869	62	0.743	0.742	0.742	0.732	0.726	0.724	-2.38	0.758	0.758	0.758	2.20	0.684	0.677	0.674	-9.07
COS	4991	940	0.794	0.790	0.790	0.773	0.770	0.770	-2.56	0.740	0.739	0.739	-6.42	0.751	0.750	0.750	-5.08

evaluate on *Los Angeles Airport Shooting (LAX), Lac Megantic Train Crash (LAM), Boston Bombing (BOB)*, and *Spain Train Crash (SPT)*; (2) train the classifiers on rest of the event *types* except *Flood/Typhoon* and evaluate on *TPY, TYP, ALB, QFL, CFL, PHF*, and *SAR*, and; (3) train the classifiers on rest of the event *types* except *Earthquake* and evaluate on *GAU, ITL, BOL*, and *COS*.

Table 7. Cross-crisis relatedness classification: criteria 2 (best F_1 score is highlighted for each event).

Test event	Instances		SF			SF+SemEF_BN				SF+SemEF_DB				SF+SemEF_BNDB			
	Train	Test	P	R	F_1	P	R	F_1	ΔF/F (in %)	P	R	F_1	ΔF/F (in %)	P	R	F	ΔF/F (in %)
LAX	5407	224	0.664	0.656	0.652	0.681	0.679	0.677	3.90	0.666	0.665	0.665	1.95	0.657	0.656	0.656	0.58
LAM	5844	68	0.655	0.632	0.618	0.642	0.632	0.626	1.2	0.619	0.618	0.616	-0.34	0.638	0.632	0.628	1.62
BOB	5407	138	0.669	0.630	0.608	0.663	0.645	0.635	4.40	0.613	0.609	0.605	-0.56	0.628	0.616	0.607	-0.19
SPT	5844	16	0.573	0.563	0.547	0.690	0.688	0.686	25.56	0.767	0.750	0.746	36.5	0.69	0.688	0.686	25.56
TPY	4409	214	0.714	0.664	0.642	0.715	0.640	0.606	-5.67	0.69	0.664	0.651	1.39	0.676	0.617	0.582	-9.45
TYP	4409	176	0.769	0.699	0.678	0.802	0.705	0.679	0.12	0.742	0.682	0.661	-2.54	0.733	0.642	0.603	-10.99
ALB	4409	32	0.727	0.719	0.716	0.771	0.719	0.705	-1.63	0.833	0.813	0.81	13.02	0.742	0.719	0.712	-0.63
QFL	4409	556	0.734	0.694	0.681	0.728	0.676	0.657	-3.51	0.733	0.707	0.698	2.58	0.741	0.707	0.696	2.23
CFL	4409	122	0.792	0.779	0.776	0.736	0.713	0.7060	-9.04	0.707	0.705	0.704	-9.27	0.755	0.754	0.754	-2.87
PHF	4409	140	0.589	0.564	0.532	0.672	0.607	0.566	6.52	0.662	0.643	0.632	18.9	0.617	0.586	0.556	4.67
SAR	4409	134	0.663	0.590	0.537	0.660	0.597	0.553	2.93	0.658	0.619	0.595	10.69	0.691	0.642	0.617	14.84
GAU	4611	206	0.610	0.553	0.487	0.584	0.549	0.495	1.62	0.692	0.650	0.630	29.39	0.667	0.621	0.593	21.79
ITL	4611	112	0.546	0.536	0.509	0.632	0.571	0.516	1.26	0.633	0.589	0.553	8.54	0.661	0.598	0.555	8.93
BOL	4611	62	0.732	0.726	0.724	0.656	0.645	0.639	-11.73	0.684	0.677	0.674	-6.86	0.606	0.597	0.588	-18.77
COS	4611	940	0.595	0.560	0.515	0.626	0.554	0.480	-6.71	0.618	0.578	0.538	4.56	0.645	0.580	0.527	2.33

From results in Table 7, we observe that the average best performing feature is the DBpedia semantics SF+SemEF_DB as it shows an average percentage gain in F_1 score ($\Delta F/F$) of +7.2% (with a Std. Dev. of 12.83%) and shows improvement over the baseline SF classifier in 10 out of 15 events.

Out of 5 events where it does not show improvement, in 2 events the percentage loss $(\Delta F/F)$ is -0.34% and -0.56%. SF+SemEF_BNDB shows improvement over the baseline in 9 out of 15 events with an average percentage gain of $+2.64\%$ in F_1 score $(\Delta F/F)$ over the SF classifier. When we compare this to criteria 1, it appears that semantic features (particularly from DBpedia) enhances the classification performance over statistical features alone when the *type* of event is not seen by the classifier during training. This result shows that although semantics may not improve relatedness classification when dealing with already seen event types, semantics are useful when dealing with event types not found in training datasets. This makes semantic feature more robust than statistical features.

5 Discussion and Future Work

Our experiments explored the impact of mixing semantic features with statistical features, and created a hybrid model, to classify crisis *related* and *not related* posts. We noticed a significant impact of semantics in the scenario when the *type* of the crisis is new to the classifier. While both the *BabelNet* and *DBpedia semantics* performed better than the statistical features, *DBpedia semantics* was found to be more consistent in its performance while classifying a new *type* of crisis event. This is likely because of the better coverage and semantic depth that DBpedia provides.

To better understand the role of semantics in crisis-related content classification, we randomly picked some tweets that were misclassified by either the baseline classifier or the semantic classifiers in the criteria 1 and 2 evaluations. We observed that: (i) semantics can generalise event specific terms compared to statistical features and consequently adapt to new event types (e.g., `dbc:flood` and `dbc:natural_hazard`), (ii) semantic concept can be sometimes too general and not help the classification of the document (e.g., *desire* and *virtue* hypernyms), and (iii) general automatic semantic extraction tools can extract non-relevant entities and confuse the classifiers (e.g., entities about *Formula 1*).

Although this analysis gives better insights concerning the behaviour of the classifiers, we plan to run a more in depth error analysis in the future by analysing additional misclassified documents. This will help improve our understanding of the scenarios and conditions under which each classification approach prevails, and thus would help us determine a more accurate merge between the two classification approaches.

In this work, we performed experiments across different *types* of crisis events. The event types present in the datasets are not uniformly distributed, where some types are more frequent than others, or have much bigger data than others. (See Table 3). In the view of developing automated classifiers that are able to learn about various crisis situations, such a skewed distribution could lead to learning bias. We designed the experiments in light of this distribution, but in order to create classifier models that are able to adapt to various domains of crisis, we would need to learn from more diverse set of crisis situations.

The type of each crisis in the data is the official type which is determined by official agencies (e.g., typhoon, earthquake, flood). We regarded each type to be different from the others, based solely on their *type* label. However, with regards to content, it is not necessarily the case that different type of crises would produce different type of content (e.g., typhoons and floods have a high overlap). To this end, while we do not add a certain *type* of crisis to the training data, we cannot ignore the possibility of having highly related content in the training data, that was the results of including similar or overlapping crises events. Hence in future work, we will take into account not only the event *type*, but also their *content similarity*. The codebase and data generated in this work is accessible[12].

In this work, we dealt with data originating from different languages, but have not performed a cross-lingual analysis. As an immediate future work, we aim to analyse how the classifiers trained in a certain language can adapt to an entirely new language to detect crisis related content.

6 Conclusion

This work presents a hybrid approach by merging semantic and statistical features to develop classification models that detect crisis related information from social media posts. The main application of this approach is demonstrated in the case of identifying crisis-related content on *new types* of crisis events that have not been directly included in the data used for training the classifier. This proposes a way forward towards developing domain adaptive crisis classification models. Adding semantic features reflected an improvement over the statistical features in classification performance on an average of 7.2% when identifying crisis related content on new event types.

Acknowledgment. This work has received support from the European Union's Horizon 2020 research and innovation programme under grant agreement No. 687847 (COMRADES).

References

1. Abel, F., Celik, I., Houben, G.-J., Siehndel, P.: Leveraging the semantics of tweets for adaptive faceted search on Twitter. In: Aroyo, L., Welty, C., Alani, H., Taylor, J., Bernstein, A., Kagal, L., Noy, N., Blomqvist, E. (eds.) ISWC 2011. LNCS, vol. 7031, pp. 1–17. Springer, Heidelberg (2011). https://doi.org/10.1007/978-3-642-25073-6_1
2. Abel, F., Hauff, C., Houben, G. J., Stronkman, R., Tao, K.: Semantics + filtering + search = twitcident. Exploring information in social web streams. In: Conference on Hypertext and Social Media, Hypertext, WI, USA (2012)
3. Burel, G., Saif, H., Fernandez, M., Alani, H.: On semantics and deep learning for event detection in crisis situations. In: Workshop on Semantic Deep Learning, SemDeep, at ESWC, Portoroz, Slovenia (2017)

---

[12] https://github.com/pkhare/crisc_codebase.

4. Burel, G., Saif, H., Alani, H.: Semantic wide and deep learning for detecting crisis-information categories on social media. In: d'Amato, C., Fernandez, M., Tamma, V., Lecue, F., Cudré-Mauroux, P., Sequeda, J., Lange, C., Heflin, J. (eds.) ISWC 2017. LNCS, vol. 10587, pp. 138–155. Springer, Cham (2017). https://doi.org/10.1007/978-3-319-68288-4_9

5. Cristianini, N., Shawe-Taylor, J.: An Introduction to Support Vector Machines and Other Kernel-Based Learning Methods. Cambridge University Press, Cambridge (2000)

6. Dai, W., Xue, G.R., Yang, Q., Yu, Y.: Transferring Naive Bayes classifiers for text classification. In: AAAI, vol. 7, pp. 540–545, July 2007

7. Gao, H., Barbier, G., Goolsby, R.: Harnessing the crowdsourcing power of social media for disaster relief. IEEE Intell. Syst. **26**(3), 10–14 (2011)

8. Imran, M., Elbassuoni, S., Castillo, C., Diaz, F., Meier, P.: Practical extraction of disaster-relevant information from social media. In: International World Wide Web Conference, WWW, Rio de Janeiro, Brazil (2013)

9. Imran, M., Elbassuoni, S., Castillo, C., Diaz, F., Meier, P.: Extracting information nuggets from disaster-Related messages in social media. In: ISCRAM, May 2013

10. Jadhav, A.S., Purohit, H., Kapanipathi, P., Anantharam, P., Ranabahu, A.H., Nguyen, V., Mendes, P.N., Smith, A.G., Cooney, M., Sheth, A.P.: Twitris 2.0: semantically empowered system for understanding perceptions from social data (2010). http://knoesis.wright.edu/library/download/Twitris_ISWC_2010.pdf

11. Karimi, S., Yin, J., Paris, C.: Classifying microblogs for disasters. In: Australasian Document Computing Symposium, Brisbane, QLD, Australia, December 2013

12. Khare, P., Fernandez, M., Alani, H.: Statistical semantic classification of crisis information. In: Workshop on HSSUES at ISWC, Vienna, Austria (2017)

13. Kogan, M., Palen, L., Anderson, K.M.: Think local, retweet global: retweeting by the geographically-vulnerable during Hurricane Sandy. In: Conference on Computer Supported Cooperative Work & Social Computing, CSCW 2015, Vancouver, Canada, February 2015

14. Li, R., Lei, K.H., Khadiwala, R., Chang, K.C.C.: TEDAS: a twitter-based event detection and analysis system. In: IEEE 28th International Conference on Data Engineering, ICDE, Washington, DC, USA, April 2012

15. Navigli, R., Ponzetto, S.P.: BabelNet: the automatic construction, evaluation and application of a wide-coverage multilingual semantic network. Artif. Intell. **193**, 217–250 (2012)

16. Olteanu, A., Vieweg, S., Castillo, C.: What to expect when the unexpected happens: social media communications across crises. In: Proceedings of the 18th ACM Conference on Computer Supported Cooperative Work & Social Computing, pp. 994–1009. ACM, February 2015

17. Power, R., Robinson, B., Colton, J., Cameron, M.: Emergency situation awareness: Twitter case studies. In: Hanachi, C., Bénaben, F., Charoy, F. (eds.) ISCRAM-med 2014. LNBIP, vol. 196, pp. 218–231. Springer, Cham (2014). https://doi.org/10.1007/978-3-319-11818-5_19

18. Rogstadius, J., Vukovic, M., Teixeira, C.A., Kostakos, V., Karapanos, E., Laredo, J.A.: CrisisTracker: crowdsourced social media curation for disaster awareness. IBM J. Res. Dev. **57**(5), 4:1–4:13 (2013)

19. Sakaki, T., Okazaki, M., Matsuo, Y.: Earthquake shakes Twitter users: real-time event detection by social sensors. In: International Conference on World Wide Web, WWW, Raleigh, North Carolina, USA (2010)

20. Stowe, K., Paul, M., Palmer, M., Palen, L., Anderson, K.: Identifying and categorizing disaster-related tweets. In: Workshop on Natural Language Processing for Social Media, EMNLP, Austin, Texas, USA (2016)
21. Vieweg, S., Hughes, A.L., Starbird, K., Palen, L.: Microblogging during two natural hazards events: what Twitter may contribute to situational awareness. In: Proceedings of SIGCHI Conference on Human Factors in Computing Systems, CHI, GA, USA (2010)
22. Vieweg, S.E.: Situational awareness in mass emergency: a behavioral and linguistic analysis of microblogged communications. Doctoral dissertation. University of Colorado at Boulder (2012). https://works.bepress.com/vieweg/15/
23. Tonon, A., Cudré-Mauroux, P., Blarer, A., Lenders, V., Motik, B.: ArmaTweet: detecting events by semantic tweet analysis. In: Blomqvist, E., Maynard, D., Gangemi, A., Hoekstra, R., Hitzler, P., Hartig, O. (eds.) ESWC 2017. LNCS, vol. 10250, pp. 138–153. Springer, Cham (2017). https://doi.org/10.1007/978-3-319-58451-5_10
24. Yin, J., Lampert, A., Cameron, M., Robinson, B., Power, R.: Using social media to enhance emergency situation awareness. IEEE Intell. Syst. **27**(6), 52–59 (2012)
25. Zhang, S., Vucetic, S.: Semi-supervised discovery of informative tweets during the emerging disasters. arXiv preprint arXiv:1610.03750 (2016)

Efficient Temporal Reasoning on Streams of Events with DOTR

Alessandro Margara[1]([✉])[iD], Gianpaolo Cugola[1][iD], Dario Collavini[1],
and Daniele Dell'Aglio[2][iD]

[1] DEIB, Politecnico di Milano, Milan, Italy
{alessandro.margara,gianpaolo.cugola,dario.collavini}@polimi.it
[2] IFI, University of Zurich, Zurich, Switzerland
dellaglio@ifi.uzh.ch

Abstract. Many ICT applications need to make sense of large volumes of streaming data to detect situations of interest and enable timely reactions. Stream Reasoning (SR) aims to combine the performance of stream/event processing and the reasoning expressiveness of knowledge representation systems by adopting Semantic Web standards to encode streaming elements. We argue that the mainstream SR model is not flexible enough to properly express the temporal relations common in many applications. We show that the model can miss relevant information and lead to inconsistent derivations. Moving from these premises, we introduce a novel SR model that provides expressive ontological and temporal reasoning by neatly decoupling their scope to avoid losses and inconsistencies. We implement the model in the DOTR system that defines ontological reasoning using Datalog rules and temporal reasoning using a Complex Event Processing language that builds on metric temporal logic. We demonstrate the expressiveness of our model through examples and benchmarks, and we show that DOTR outperforms state-of-the-art SR tools, processing data with millisecond latency.

1   Introduction

Many information systems need to make sense of large volumes of data as soon as they are produced to detect relevant situations and enable prompt reactions. Areas of application include smart cities, fraud detection systems, and social media analysis. These scenarios demand for processing abstractions and tools to "reason" on streaming data, both in ontological and temporal terms, while also coping with the volume, velocity, and variety of streaming data. More concretely, they require: (1) flexible data models to integrate heterogeneous data coming from multiple sources; (2) integration with background knowledge that describes the application domain; (3) expressive (temporal) reasoning on both streaming and background data; (4) high throughput and low latency.

Several systems have been developed in the last decade to address this problem, but none of them simultaneously tackles the requirements above [11,12]. Stream Processing (SP) systems [3] focus on continuous query answering: they

© Springer International Publishing AG, part of Springer Nature 2018
A. Gangemi et al. (Eds.): ESWC 2018, LNCS 10843, pp. 384–399, 2018.
https://doi.org/10.1007/978-3-319-93417-4_25

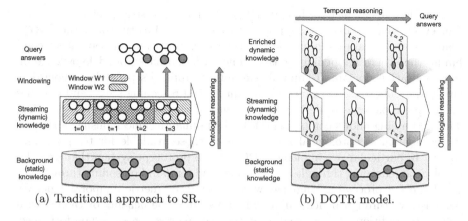

(a) Traditional approach to SR.   (b) DOTR model.

Fig. 1. Comparison of the traditional model to SR and the proposed DOTR model.

use a recent portion of the streaming data to update the results of queries as new data becomes available. They mostly provide a temporal (relational) operations on structured (relational) data. Instead, Complex Event Processing (CEP) systems [14] are specialized in detecting the occurrence of temporal patterns in the stream of input elements. Both SP and CEP systems provide high throughput and low latency, but struggle at integrating heterogeneous data and at exploiting background knowledge on the application domain.

Recently, Stream Reasoning (SR) systems [12,19] addressed these limitations by adopting Semantic Web standards to represent information, thus enabling expressive reasoning on streaming data from heterogeneous sources and static background knowledge. Similar to SP systems, most SR systems continuously update the results of standing SPARQL queries over static background knowledge and dynamic streaming data. They use *window* operators to isolate the recent portion of data to be considered, such as W1 and W2 in Fig. 1(a). Ontological reasoning (when supported) assumes that *all* and *only* the information that is in the current window (plus the background knowledge) holds. SPARQL queries are then applied to both the original and the inferred knowledge, and the process is repeated any time the window content changes [5,8,17].

We claim that this model is not flexible enough to satisfy all the requirements identified above. Although some systems have extended SPARQL with temporal operators [2], the model does not support expressive temporal reasoning. On the other hand, using windows to determine the scope of reasoning and querying can result in information loss or inconsistent derivations (see Sect. 2). In summary, the problem of complementing expressive reasoning on rich ontological knowledge with temporal reasoning in a coherent yet efficient way remains open.

Moving from these premises, we propose a novel approach to SR called DOTR (Decoupled Ontological and Temporal Reasoning). It provides ontological reasoning on streaming and background knowledge, and efficient detection of temporal patterns (temporal reasoning), while keeping the two form of reasoning sharply decoupled. In DOTR (Fig. 1(b)), the incoming stream elements represent events that occur at some point in time, encoded as time-annotated RDF graphs. Ontological reasoning takes place at each point in time separately, combining the events happening at that time with the background knowledge on the application domain. Temporal reasoning is applied separately: it considers enriched events—as determined in the ontological reasoning step—and searches for temporal patterns to derive the relevant consequences of what is happening. This decoupling allows combining established semantics, mechanisms, and tools in the domain of ontological reasoning with those available for temporal reasoning. In particular, we implement DOTR in a prototype system that provides ontological reasoning through Datalog rules and temporal reasoning through the TESLA event processing language, which grounds on metric temporal logic. We demonstrate through benchmarks and case studies the benefits of DOTR with respect to traditional SR approaches in terms of expressiveness and performance. We evaluate DOTR under different workloads and show that it can process input data with a latency of few milliseconds even in the presence of large knowledge bases and complex inference tasks.

The paper is organized as follows. Section 2 presents background information on SR and motivates our work. Sections 3 and 4 present our model and its implementation, while Sect. 5 evaluates its performance. Section 6 discusses related work and Sect. 7 concludes the paper drawing future research directions.

2   Background and Motivations

This section introduces the terminology and concepts that we use in the remainder of the paper and discusses the motivations underneath our work.

We denote a *stream* as a (possibly unbounded) sequence of time-annotated elements ordered according to temporal criteria. Each element brings a unit of information, such as a sensor observation or a stock exchange [11,12]. Individual elements can be represented in different formats: for instance, SP systems often adopt a relational model, whereas SR systems like DOTR promote data integration and expressive reasoning by using the RDF format for stream elements [12,19]. SP, CEP, and SR systems continuously evaluate standing *rules* or *queries* against stream elements. Rule evaluation can be either periodic or triggered by the incoming elements. The dominant approach to SR defines rules as SPARQL queries and adopts *window operators* to determine the scope for evaluating such queries [5,6,8,17]. Window operators create finite views over a stream, namely *windows*, that include the portion of data relevant for the current evaluation of rules. At each evaluation, they produce either the complete results of the processing or the differences—additions/deletions—with respect to the previous evaluation. Although several types of window operators have been defined, the most common are sliding windows, which have a fixed width in terms of time units or data elements and shift (slide) over time, always capturing the most recent part of the stream.

We argue that the processing model based on windows is not adequate to capture temporal relations and can result in undesired (i) duplicate results,

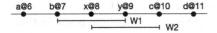

(a) Window of size 3 and slide 1. The pattern (x@8, y@9) is detected twice.

(b) Window of size 3 and slide 3. The pattern (x@8, y@9) remains undetected.

Fig. 2. Processing model based on windows: examples of limitations.

(ii) loss of information, or (iii) inconsistency in reasoning. Figure 2 exemplifies the first two problems. It represents each stream element with a label 1 and its time of occurrence t as 1@t. Imagine we want to detect whenever an element labeled x is followed by an element labeled y after no more than three time units. Figure 2(a) shows that in the presence of sliding windows, the same occurrence might be detected multiple times. For instance, the sequence x@8 and y@9 (denoted x@8, y@9)) is detected both in window W1 and in window W2, requiring additional downstream logic in the case the developer wants to prune duplicate reports of the same occurrence. To avoid this problem, developers can adopt tumbling windows, which partition the input stream in non-overlapping chunks. Unfortunately, this solution might result in missing some occurrences of the pattern of interest. For instance in Fig. 2(b), the sequence (x@8, y@9) is not detected since only x@8 is part of W1 and only y@9 is part of W2. Any intermediate solution based on sliding windows that slide by more than one element at each time would exhibit both problems [23].

Moreover, considering all the facts in the active window as simultaneously true may result in inconsistent derivations [18]. Let us consider a surveillance system that monitors the position of visitors in a building, where sensors deliver a new notification every time a visitor enters a room. In a window of, say, five minutes, a visitor might move through multiple rooms. Thus considering all the notifications in the window as still true would lead to the erroneous conclusion that the visitor is simultaneously in multiple rooms.

Some SR systems partially address the above issues by extending the query language with operators to express temporal relations among the elements in the window [2,23]. However, they do not provide a formal framework to integrate temporal operators and reasoning capabilities, lack a concrete implementation, or do not provide the level of performance required in streaming scenarios.

3   The DOTR Model

We propose a novel DOTR SR model that avoids the issues discussed in Sect. 2 by: (1) performing ontological reasoning at each point in time independently to learn about the state of the application domain at that point in time; (2) correlating information from different point in time in a separate temporal reasoning process.

Figure 1(b) depicts a conceptual view of DOTR. The *background knowledge* contains knowledge about the application domain that holds at any point in time. We assume background knowledge to be encoded in RDF. *Streaming* elements represent dynamic knowledge that only holds at a specific point in time: they indicate the occurrence of events of interest and are represented as time-annotated RDF graphs. At each time t, the state of the environment is represented by the *enriched dynamic knowledge*, comprising the content of any streaming element annotated with time t, any background knowledge about the application domain, and any information that can be derived through ontological reasoning (vertical axis in Fig. 1(b)), expressed using Datalog rules. Temporal reasoning (horizontal axis in Fig. 1(b)) is orthogonal to ontological reasoning and is encoded as patterns that correlate facts that are true at different points in time. In this paper we express patterns using the TESLA CEP language, which grounds on metric temporal logic [9].

The remainder of this section presents the DOTR model in details, starting with an overview of the original TESLA model, and discussing how we integrate Web structured data, background knowledge, and ontological reasoning.

The TESLA Model. In TESLA, each stream element represents an event (notification), having a type, a timestamp, and a set of attribute-value pairs. The type of an event defines the number, name, and type of attributes for that event. TESLA assumes events to occur instantaneously at some point in time and encodes their time of occurrence in the timestamp. For instance, the event `Temperature@10(val = 18.5, room = 'R')` has type `Temperature`, timestamp `10` and two attributes: `val` with float value `18.5`, and `room` with string value `R`.

TESLA models temporal reasoning through rules that define situations of interest—*composite events*—from patterns of events observed in the input stream. As an example, the following `Rule T` defines a composite event of type `Fire` from the observation of `Smoke` and high `Temperature` occurring in the same room within five minutes from each other:

```
Rule T
define      Fire(room: string)
from        Smoke() and last Temperature(val>60, room=Smoke.room) within 5 min. from Smoke
with        Fire.room = Smoke.room
consuming Temperature
```

Patterns of events start from a reference (final) event (`Smoke` in `Rule T`) and specify time ranges in which other events are allowed to occur starting from this reference event. For instance, `Rule T` requires `Temperature` to be within five minutes *before* `Smoke`. Composite events keep the same timestamp as the final event in the pattern: any `Fire` event produced by `Rule T` will have the same timestamp as the `Smoke` event that triggered its production.

Events are selected by *filtering* on their attributes. For instance, `Rule T` requires attribute `val` in `Temperature` to be greater than 60. In addition, attributes of different events can be bound together, as in the case of attribute `room` that must be the same in `Smoke` and `Temperature` events to trigger `Rule T`. The `last` selection modifier indicates that only the last occurrence of an event of type `Temperature` with `val>60` and `room=Smoke.room` must be considered. Other selection modifiers include `first` and `each`. The latter triggers a *different* composite event for each `Temperature` event within five minutes before `Smoke`.

TESLA also supports *negations* and *aggregates*. Both of them operate on the set of events that appear in a given scope, defined with respect to the time of occurrence of other events in the rule. Negations declare events that must *not* occur in the scope, while aggregates compute an aggregation function (such as sum or average) considering the values of an attribute for all the events that occur in the scope. For example, a rule could constrain the *average* val of Temperature events observed in the 5 min before Smoke (aggregate) and could require a Rain event *not* to occur in the same scope (negation).

Finally, the with clause[1] of TESLA rules defines the value of attributes in the composite event, while the consuming clause marks events that are consumed by the rule and cannot be used in subsequent evaluations of the same rule.

The DOTR Data and Rule Model. DOTR abandons the attribute-value format of TESLA and encodes events as time-annotated RDF graphs. For instance, the following graph represents a 25 °C reading from a temperature sensor in location :loc_1 at time 10:

```
{ :reading_1 rdf:type :Temp. :reading_1 :has_val ''25''.
  :reading_1 :is_from_sensor :sensor_1. :sensor_1 :is_at_location :loc_1. } @ 10
```

DOTR couples the temporal knowledge in input streams with atemporal background knowledge encoded as an ontology consisting of an RDF graph and a set of Datalog rules. DOTR rules take time-annotated RDF graphs in input and produce time-annotated RDF graphs as output. They model situations of interest by combining a set of SPARQL queries with TESLA temporal operators. SPARQL queries capture what is happening at each time instant, while TESLA operators combine these facts in temporal patterns. This schema is exemplified by Rule R, which rewrites Rule T from the TESLA model to the DOTR model:

```
Rule R
define    Fire = [dotr_id1 rdf:type :Fire. dotr_id1 :at_room ?room ]
from      Smoke = [SELECT ?read1 ?room1 WHERE
            { ?read1 rdf:type :Smoke. ?read1 :is_from_sensor ?sens1.
              ?sens1 :is_in_room ?room1 }
          ] and last HighTemp = [SELECT ?read2 ?room2 WHERE
            { ?read2 rdf:type :Temp. ?read2 :is_from_sensor ?sens2.
              ?sens2 :is_in_room ?room2. ?read2 :has_val ?v.
              FILTER (?v > 60 && ?room2 = Smoke.?room1). }
          ] within 5 min from Smoke
with      Fire.?room = Smoke.?room1
consuming HighTemp
```

The define clause specifies the RDF graph produced as output. It may include variables, like ?room that will be bound by the with clause, and unique resource identifiers like dotr_id1 that are automatically generated every time a new output graph is produced.

The from clause specifies the temporal pattern that triggers the rule, using the TESLA syntax and semantics. The role of SPARQL in the from clause is to extract the relevant information from the enriched knowledge that holds at each

---

[1] We renamed the original TESLA where clause in with to avoid ambiguities with the WHERE clause used in SPARQL.

time t. In particular, at each time t, SPARQL queries embedded in rules (such as queries Smoke and HighTemp) get re-evaluated to extract flows of (timestamped) *facts of interest*, which TESLA operators combine in patterns.

The (optional) consuming clause retains the TESLA semantics and lists the events unavailable for subsequent triggering of the same rule.

As a concrete example of rule evaluation, consider again Rule R and assume the availability of background knowledge that associates the locations of sensors to rooms: :locA :is_in_room :roomA. :locB :is_in_room :roomA. An inference rule (Datalog) specifies the relation between locations and rooms: :is_in_room(?A,?B) :- :is_at_location(?A,?C), :is_in_room(?C,?B). Upon receiving the time-annotated RDF graph:

```
{ :r1 rdf:type :Temp. :r1 :has_val 70.
  :r1 :is_from_sensor :s1. :s1 :is_at_location :locA. } @ 10
```

DOTR combines it with the background knowledge to derive: :s1 :is_in_room :roomA. Thus the HighTemp SPARQL query produces one result with ?read2=:r1 and ?room2=roomA. Similarly, when receiving the time-annotated RDF graph:

```
{ :r2 rdf:type :Smoke. :r2 :is_from_sensor :s2.
  :s2 :is_at_location :locB. } @ 12
```

DOTR derives: :s2 :is_in_room :roomA. Thus the Smoke SPARQL query produces one result with ?read1=:r2 and ?room1=:roomA. These two facts, derived at time 10 and 12, satisfy all the constraints in Rule R. Thus, DOTR identifies a composite event and generates a timestamped RDF graph as specified by the define clause: { *dotr:id1234* rdf:type :Fire. *dotr:id1234* :at_room :roomA } @ 12, where *dotr:id1234* is a randomly generated unique resource identifier[2].

This example shows how the DOTR rule model sharply separates the role of SPARQL and ontological reasoning from the temporal domain. This approach overcomes the limitations of window-based approaches by enriching individual events independently from their temporal relations. This separation of concerns also simplifies the processing of rules at run-time, enabling the adoption of existing and efficient tools for reasoning and event processing.

The Semantics of DOTR. DOTR inherits the semantics of temporal reasoning from TESLA, which uses the TRIO metric temporal logic to define situations of interest from patterns that predicate on the content and time of input events. The semantics of TESLA encode the occurrence of an event e as a logic predicate that is true when e occurs, and define patterns as a set of logic formulas [9].

DOTR extends TESLA by (i) extracting events from input time-annotated RDF graphs as solution mappings of SPARQL queries evaluated under ontological reasoning regime; (ii) producing output time-annotated RDF graphs. Since ontological reasoning is orthogonal with respect to temporal reasoning, the semantics of TESLA can be extended to capture DOTR by (i) associating each solution mapping produced at time t from a SPARQL query to a logic predicate that is true at time t; (ii) lifting the situations of interest identified by TESLA as RDF graphs with their associated time of occurrence.

---

[2] Alternatively, blank nodes can be used.

4   Implementation

We implemented DOTR in a prototype system[3] that adopts a modular approach to exploit state-of-the-art tools for ontological and temporal reasoning. This provides high performance and simplifies software evolution if better components become available. The prototype uses RDFox [21] to store, query, and reason on background knowledge, and T-Rex [10] for temporal reasoning. Figure 3 shows how the DOTR system operates.

At rule deployment time, a rule parser analyzes the input DOTR rules. For each DOTR rule R, the parser (1) extracts the SPARQL queries embedded in R and submits them to RDFox, (2) translates R into a TESLA rule T by substituting each SPARQL query with the mapping it defines, and submits T to T-Rex, (3) extracts the set of *graph definitions* from the **define** clause of R.

At runtime, upon receiving an RDF graph G with timestamp t, DOTR: (1) enriches G with the background knowledge and derives all the information that holds at t (ontological reasoning); (2) executes the SPARQL queries embedded in rules to extract the facts of interest that hold at t; (3) converts these facts into TESLA events and sends them to T-Rex (temporal reasoning); (4) uses the output generator to convert the composite events produced by T-Rex into time-annotated RDF graphs. Next, we discuss these steps in detail.

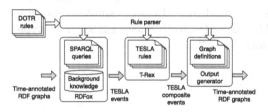

Fig. 3. Architecture of the DOTR system.

Knowledge Inference. The background knowledge is preloaded into RDFox at system initialization time. When a graph G with timestamp t is received, DOTR computes the whole knowledge that holds at t by: (i) removing from RDFox any information Δ^- coming from every graph G' annotated with time $t' < t$; (ii) adding to RDFox all the RDF triples Δ^+ that are in G; (iii) performing ontological reasoning with the available inference rules to remove old information that could be derived *only* in the presence of Δ^- and to add new information that can be derived from Δ^+. This is done in a single inference process by exploiting the incremental materialization of RDFox [20]. After this reasoning step, DOTR determines the facts of interest that are valid at the current time by submitting to RDFox the SPARQL queries extracted from the deployed rules. For each query RDFox generates zero, one, or more facts of interests.

Event Processing. Each fact of interest f gives rise to a new TESLA event. The event type is the label of the query that extracted f and the event attributes are the variables selected by the query. For instance, the example reported at the end of Sect. 3 gives rise to two events: `Smoke@10(read1=':r1',room1=':roomA')` and `HighTemp@12(read2=':r2',room2='roomA')`. T-Rex processes these events trying

---

[3] DOTR is available at https://github.com/margara/DOTR.

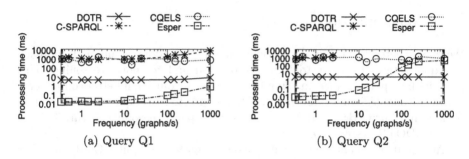

Fig. 4. Performance of DOTR, C-SPARQL, CQELS, and Esper in the CityBench suite.

to detect the temporal patterns expressed within the deployed rules. When a rule is triggered, T-Rex generates one or more composite TESLA events.

Output Translation. The generated events have the type specified in the define clause of the firing rule and one attribute for each variable that appears there. For instance, consider again Rule R in Sect. 3. Each composite event produced by T-Rex has type Fire and a single attribute room, with the same value as the attribute room1 in the Smoke event that triggered the rule. DOTR converts composite events into one or more RDF triples following the graph definition specified in the define clause of the fired rules. In our example, composite event Fire@12(room='roomA') would be converted to: { *dotr:id1234* rdf:type :Fire. *dotr:id1234* :at_room roomA.} @ 12.

5   Evaluation

In this section we measure the performance of DOTR focusing on latency, which is a key requirement for SR, and compare it with state-of-the-art SP, CEP, and SR tools using real data from the CityBench benchmark [1]. We also discuss the differences among these systems in terms of expressiveness and semantics. Furthermore, we use synthetic workloads to study which parameters affect the behavior of DOTR the most.

We perform all the experiments on a Intel Core i7 4850HQ machine with 16 GB of DDR3 RAM, running macOS 10.13.0. We use the processing time per input element as a performance indicator. All the systems under analysis process individual elements from the input stream sequentially and do not overlap the computation of different elements. As a consequence, the inverse of the processing time also represents a good estimate of the maximum rate of input elements that each system supports, that is, its maximum input throughput. In each experiment we submit 30k time-annotated graphs and we compute the average processing time per input element, which includes the time to update the content of the RDFox store, perform reasoning, querying, event processing, and produce output graphs. The input graphs are stored in files on a RAM disk with RDF turtle format. The background knowledge is also stored in RAM by RDFox.

Benchmark. We compare DOTR with the C-SPARQL [5] and CQELS [17] SR systems and with the Esper SP/CEP system, Java version 6.1.0. We rely on the CityBench suite [1], which includes sensor data from the city of Aarhus. We use the vehicle traffic dataset, containing the congestion level between two points over a duration of time, and the weather dataset, with observations on temperature, humidity, and wind. Given the similarities between the benchmark queries, we present the results for queries Q1 and Q2 only. In the case of C-SPARQL and CQELS, we rely on the implementation of the queries provided with the CityBench suite. In the case of Esper, we implement a translator that converts the input RDF elements into Esper events (Java objects). The conversion takes place before the experiments and does not contribute to the time we measure.

We report queries Q1 and Q2 as presented in the original paper on CityBench: (Q1) What is the traffic congestion level on each road of my planned journey? (Q2) What is the traffic congestion level and weather condition on each road of my planned journey? In practice, the implementation of Q1 considers two streams, each containing the congestion of a specific road, and returns all possible pairs of congestion level values, one per stream, that occur in a window of 3 s. The implementation of Q2 considers a stream of congestion readings and a stream of weather readings, and reports congestion level, temperature, humidity, and wind speed notifications that occur in a window of 3 s.

Since DOTR does not distinguish between input elements coming from different streams, we combine RDF triples from all the relevant streams and generate a time-annotated graph for each time instant. Each resulting graph contains 10 triples to represent congestion readings and 5 triples to represent weather readings. In Esper, we encode each sensor reading as a separate event object. In the case of DOTR, C-SPARQL, and CQELS we consider a background knowledge of over 100k triples with the type of property measured by each sensor: congestion or weather reading. In Esper, we encode the property type as an event attribute, thus avoiding the use of a separate background knowledge.

Different engines present different execution models that lead to different results [1,12]. CQELS, Esper, and DOTR operate in a pure reactive way, by producing new results each time they receive an input element. C-SPARQL only supports time-based windows, which produce results periodically, when the window closes. Moreover, C-SPARQL and CQELS rely on the windowing model presented in Sect. 2 and compute *all* the query results that derive from the data in the active window, whereas Esper and DOTR produce only the *new* results at each evaluation, thus automatically removing duplicates.

We implement query Q1 using the `each within` operator that instructs DOTR to always consider *all* the congestion level information contained in the window. This mimics the behavior of C-SPARQL and CQELS, although it avoids producing duplicate results as discussed above. In Esper we select all congestion level events by exploiting the `every` operator offered by the engine. For query Q2, we use the `last within` operator that reports, for each incoming element, only the *last* available information about congestion and weather. This better satisfies the semantics of the query by notifying users about the most recent traffic and weather information when some change occurs. Esper, C-SPARQL, and CQELS do not provide operators to select only the most recent information. This well exemplifies the flexibility of the temporal reasoning offered by DOTR. As we demonstrate later, this flexibility comes with the benefit of a reduced processing time, since temporal reasoning only needs to analyze the latest information.

The processing time of a query depends on the number of events it considers, which depends on the timestamp of events. Accordingly, we measure processing time for different frequencies of event arrival by artificially manipulating the timestamp of input graphs. This is the same approach followed by CityBench.

As Fig. 4 shows, for both query Q1 and Q2 DOTR takes than 4 ms to process each input graph when the frequency of arrival remains below 100 graphs per second. When further increasing the input rate, the latency for Q1 grows up to 7 ms, since the number of congestion elements to consider increases. Instead, the latency of Q2 remains stable below 3 ms, since Q2 only considers the last available notifications.

The latency of C-SPARQL and CQELS is in the order of hundreds or even thousands of milliseconds in the same scenarios, and C-SPARQL often crashes without providing results with a high input rate. The order of magnitude and the trends of these results are in line with those measured in previous studies [1]. The results of C-SPARQL and CQELS are motivated by the nature of the problem, which grows quadratically with the number of elements in each window. C-SPARQL suffers more when the number of elements increases since it recomputes all the results when the window changes, while CQELS indexes and re-uses results from previous window evaluations.

Esper is the winner in Q1 tests, with a processing time always below 0.8 ms. However, Esper does not to use background knowledge, since we encoded all the information within the input events. Also, input events are pre-encoded as plain Java objects in memory, which removes the times of (de)serialization and parsing from our measures. In practice, the time we measure for Esper represents the pure cost of event processing (or temporal reasoning). At high input rates, this processing time is about one tenth of the average processing time of DOTR, in line with the analysis we present in the remainder of this section. CQELS and C-SPARQL exhibit higher processing times for query Q2, since Q2 extracts more input elements and produces more results than Q1. The advantages of the DOTR model become evident: by considering only the last available congestion and weather data, DOTR reduces the amount of elements to process and the amount of results produced. Esper also suffers query Q2, due to the large number of results to produce at each query evaluation. When the input rate grows its processing time grows well above that of DOTR, reaching the level of CQELS.

We may summarize the considerations above by concluding that: (1) under comparable conditions (query Q1), DOTR outperforms C-SPARQL and CQELS by almost two orders of magnitude; (2) thanks to its expressive temporal reasoning, DOTR can better select the results to produce, providing the best performance in query Q2; (3) the use of RDF format, background knowledge, and ontological reasoning increase the expressiveness but come at a cost with respect to traditional event processing, as exemplified by the comparison with Esper.

Sensitivity to Parameters. We study the sensitivity to workload characteristics through synthetic benchmarking, starting from a default scenario and changing one parameter at a time.

Default Scenario. Our default scenario considers ten rules, all having the structure below and differing only for the value X used in the FILTER clause.

```
define  CE = [dotr_id1 :has_val ?num.]
from    A  = [SELECT ?sensorA ?valA ?roomA WHERE
                { ?sensorA :read_valA ?valA. ?sensorA :is_in_room ?roomA.
                  FILTER(?valA>X) } ] and last
        B  = [SELECT ?sensorB ?valB ?roomB WHERE
                { ?sensorB :read_valB ?valB. ?sensorB :is_in_room ?roomB.
                  FILTER(?valB>X && ?roomB=A.?roomA) } ] within 30s from A
with    CE.?num = A.?valA
```

The input time-annotated graphs contain two types of RDF triples: :sensor$K$:read_valA val and :sensor$K$:read_valB val, where K is uniformly distributed in 1..10 and val is a random integer that always satisfies SPARQL filters in rules. Triples of the first type can trigger rules by completing a valid sequence pattern and occur with 20% probability. The timestamps of any two consecutive input graphs differ by one second, simulating an input rate of one graph per second. The background knowledge includes information on the position of sensors, necessary to trigger the rules, in the form: :sensor$S$:equips :object$O$. :object$O$:placed_in :room$X$. :room$R$:number R, where the number of rooms R is uniformly distributed in 1...5 and there are two objects per room. Datalog rule :is_in_room(?S, ?R) :- :equips(?S, ?O), :placed_in(?O, ?R). determines the room each sensor is in. We increase the size and complexity of the background knowledge by adding 10 rules similar to the one above, which contribute in producing triples (albeit not relevant for existing rules). We also add 10k triples to the background knowledge, with additional attributes for each sensor.

In our default scenario each input graph contains a single RDF triple. Table 1 shows the average processing time per input element, together with the absolute and relative cost of each processing phase. DOTR produces results with an average latency of 12.09 ms, spending almost 80% of the time in the processing steps concerned with ontological reasoning. Event processing (temporal reasoning) accounts for about 16% of the overall processing time. Updating the knowledge base by adding new information and removing old one accounts for only 1.65% of the total time. Translating input data from RDF to TESLA native events and back takes about 3% of the total time.

Table 1. Default scenario: processing time.

	Time (ms)	Time (%)
Knowledge update	0.20 ms	1.65%
Ontological reasoning	1.96 ms	16.21%
Query evaluation	7.56 ms	62.53%
Input translation	0.19 ms	1.57%
Event processing	2.01 ms	16.63%
Output translation	0.17 ms	1.41%
Total	12.09 ms	100.00%

Cost of Reasoning. We study the cost of reasoning by increasing the number of Datalog rules in the knowledge store (Fig. 5). The cost of reasoning (and materializing information) is initially small, and the processing time remains almost unchanged from 1 to 1k Datalog rules. After this threshold, the

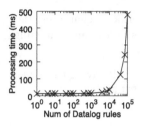
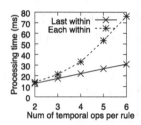
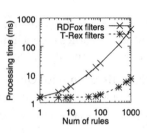

Fig. 5. Datalog rules   **Fig. 6.** Temporal ops.   **Fig. 7.** Rules

impact of reasoning becomes more prominent, and the processing time increases by a factor of 30 from 1k to 100k Datalog rules. Additional experiments, not reported here for space reasons, measure the same level of performance when changing the number of RDF triples in the background store from 1k to 1M.

In general, the cost of reasoning depends not only on the number of rules, but also on their complexity. Given the breadth of the topic and the availability of specialized articles, we do not present a detailed analysis of reasoning. The interested reader can refer to the materialization algorithm of RDFox [20].

Cost of Event Processing. We study the cost of temporal reasoning by adding temporal operators to rules, thus increasing the length of the event patterns to detect (Fig. 6). We consider both patterns with `last within` and with `each within` operators. In the first case, the triggering of a rule generates a single TESLA event, while in the second case it generates as many TESLA events as the number of event bindings that satisfy the pattern. With two to three operators per rule, the two cases are comparable, since the processing time is dominated by reasoning and SPARQL querying. With longer sequences, the `each within` rules cost more, in line with the original results of T-Rex.

Number of Rules. Figure 7 (continuous line) shows the processing time when increasing the number of deployed rules. More rules means more queries to the RDF store, and more results to produce. The processing time remains below 400 ms even in the case of 1k rules, which involves evaluating 2k SPARQL queries for each input graph (one for each of the two events appearing in each rule). To further optimize DOTR, we move from the observation that query processing represents a large fraction of the entire processing time, and we modify DOTR to move data filtering from SPARQL (RDFox) to T-Rex. In this way, SPARQL queries that differ only for their `FILTER` part can be merged together, removing and delegating the filtering step to T-Rex. Our workload represents an optimal setting for the modified system, since all the DOTR rules extract the same two types of events applying different filters (the value X used in the `FILTER` clause). The dashed line in Fig. 7 shows the processing when we enable this optimization. Remarkably, it remains almost constant and below 2 ms with up to 100 rules, and increases to 7 ms only when reaching 1k rules.

6   Related Work

The last decade has seen an increasing interest in techniques and tools to process streaming data. SP systems define abstractions to continuously query streams of (typically relational) data [3], while CEP systems aim to detect situations of interest from streams of low-level event [11,14].

SP and CEP systems are not suited to process Web structured data, to integrate background knowledge, and to perform ontological reasoning [2]. Stream Reasoning (SR) systems address these limitations by adapting stream processing to the RDF data model [12,19].

As discussed in Sect. 2, most SR systems follow the CQL approach and extend SPARQL with windows to support continuous queries over streaming data. C-SPARQL [5], CQELS [17], SPARQL$_{stream}$ [8], and Laser [6] all follow this direction. DL-Lite$_{\mathcal{A}}$ (S, F) [13] extends DL-Lite$_{\mathcal{A}}$ to perform spatial and window-based temporal reasoning over streams. Some proposals investigate the use of Answer Set Programming (ASP) for SR. LARS [7] features model-based semantics by building on ASP enriched with window operators. StreamRule [22] combines a window-based engine, such as CQELS, with an ASP reasoner. INSTANS [23] avoids windows and demonstrates that standard SPARQL queries can express several common forms of ontological and temporal reasoning. Although conceptually interesting, the approach lacks high-level abstractions to express the reasoning tasks. Moreover, it currently does not provide a level of performance comparable with state-of-the-art SP/CEP systems. Perhaps the approach most closely related to ours is EP-SPARQL [2], which extends SPARQL with temporal operators derived from the CEP domain. However, it does not investigate in depth the relation between detection of temporal patterns and semantic inference, as we do in our model.

Some approaches extend RDF with a temporal dimension [15,24]. They differ from DOTR since they do not target on the fly detection of temporal patterns, and they integrate rather than decoupling ontological and temporal reasoning.

Finally, DOTR exploits the recent advances in incremental reasoning: they include the exploitation of time annotations [4], counting algorithms and parallel processing [25], and optimizations for small incremental changes [16].

7   Conclusions

This paper presented a novel model for SR that decouples ontological and temporal reasoning. It grounds ontological reasoning on RDF graphs and Datalog rules, and temporal reasoning on a CEP language that provides an expressive yet computationally efficient subset of a metric temporal logic. We implemented the model by building on state-of-the-art tools for event processing and knowledge storage, query, and inference. The resulting system outperforms existing SR systems, showing that the added expressiveness in terms of temporal reasoning can be beneficial for processing, too. As future work, we will study the usability and expressiveness of the model in greater details, also considering primitives to alter the content of the background knowledge over time.

References

1. Ali, M.I., Gao, F., Mileo, A.: CityBench: a configurable benchmark to evaluate RSP engines using smart city datasets. In: Arenas, M., et al. (eds.) ISWC 2015. LNCS, vol. 9367, pp. 374–389. Springer, Cham (2015). https://doi.org/10.1007/978-3-319-25010-6_25

2. Anicic, D., Fodor, P., Rudolph, S., Stojanovic, N.: EP-SPARQL: a unified language for event processing and stream reasoning. In: International Conference on World Wide Web, WWW (2011)

3. Babcock, B., Babu, S., Datar, M., Motwani, R., Widom, J.: Models and issues in data stream systems. In: Symposium on Principles of Database Systems, PODS (2002)

4. Barbieri, D.F., Braga, D., Ceri, S., Della Valle, E., Grossniklaus, M.: Incremental reasoning on streams and rich background knowledge. In: Aroyo, L., Antoniou, G., Hyvönen, E., ten Teije, A., Stuckenschmidt, H., Cabral, L., Tudorache, T. (eds.) ESWC 2010. LNCS, vol. 6088, pp. 1–15. Springer, Heidelberg (2010). https://doi.org/10.1007/978-3-642-13486-9_1

5. Barbieri, D.F., Braga, D., Ceri, S., Valle, E.D., Grossniklaus, M.: Querying RDF streams with C-SPARQL. SIGMOD Rec. **39**(1), 20–26 (2010)

6. Bazoobandi, H.R., Beck, H., Urbani, J.: Expressive stream reasoning with laser. In: d'Amato, C., Fernandez, M., Tamma, V., Lecue, F., Cudré-Mauroux, P., Sequeda, J., Lange, C., Heflin, J. (eds.) ISWC 2017. LNCS, vol. 10587, pp. 87–103. Springer, Cham (2017). https://doi.org/10.1007/978-3-319-68288-4_6

7. Beck, H., Dao-Tran, M., Eiter, T., Fink, M.: LARS: a logic-based framework for analyzing reasoning over streams. In: Conference on AI, AAAI (2015)

8. Calbimonte, J.P., Jeung, H., Corcho, O., Aberer, K.: Enabling query technologies for the semantic sensor web. Int. J. Sem. Web Inf. Sys. **8**(1), 43–63 (2012)

9. Cugola, G., Margara, A.: TESLA: a formally defined event specification language. In: International Conference on Distributed Event-Based Systems, DEBS (2010)

10. Cugola, G., Margara, A.: Complex event processing with T-REX. J. Sys. Softw. **85**(8), 1709–1728 (2012)

11. Cugola, G., Margara, A.: Processing flows of information: from data stream to complex event processing. ACM Comput. Surv. **44**(3), 15 (2012)

12. Dell'Aglio, D., Della Valle, E., van Harmelen, F., Bernstein, A.: Stream reasoning: a survey and outlook. Data Sci. **1**, 59–83 (2017)

13. Eiter, T., Parreira, J.X., Schneider, P.: Spatial ontology-mediated query answering over mobility streams. In: Blomqvist, E., Maynard, D., Gangemi, A., Hoekstra, R., Hitzler, P., Hartig, O. (eds.) ESWC 2017. LNCS, vol. 10249, pp. 219–237. Springer, Cham (2017). https://doi.org/10.1007/978-3-319-58068-5_14

14. Etzion, O., Niblett, P.: Event Processing in Action. Manning, Shelter Island (2010)

15. Gutierrez, C., Hurtado, C.A., Vaisman, A.: Introducing time into RDF. Trans. Knowl. Data Eng. **19**(2) (2007)

16. Kazakov, Y., Klinov, P.: Incremental reasoning in OWL EL without bookkeeping. In: Alani, H., et al. (eds.) ISWC 2013. LNCS, vol. 8218, pp. 232–247. Springer, Heidelberg (2013). https://doi.org/10.1007/978-3-642-41335-3_15

17. Le-Phuoc, D., Dao-Tran, M., Xavier Parreira, J., Hauswirth, M.: A native and adaptive approach for unified processing of linked streams and linked data. In: Aroyo, L., Welty, C., Alani, H., Taylor, J., Bernstein, A., Kagal, L., Noy, N., Blomqvist, E. (eds.) ISWC 2011. LNCS, vol. 7031, pp. 370–388. Springer, Heidelberg (2011). https://doi.org/10.1007/978-3-642-25073-6_24

18. Margara, A., Dell'Aglio, D., Bernstein, A.: Break the windows: explicit state management for stream processing systems. In: International Conference on Extending Database Technology, EDBT (2017)
19. Margara, A., Urbani, J., van Harmelen, F., Bal, H.: Streaming the web: reasoning over dynamic data. Web Semant. **25**(1), 24–44 (2014)
20. Motik, B., Nenov, Y., Piro, R., Horrocks, I.: Combining rewriting and incremental materialisation maintenance for datalog programs with equality. In: Conference on AI, IJCAI (2015)
21. Nenov, Y., Piro, R., Motik, B., Horrocks, I., Wu, Z., Banerjee, J.: RDFox: a highly-scalable RDF store. In: Arenas, M., et al. (eds.) ISWC 2015. LNCS, vol. 9367, pp. 3–20. Springer, Cham (2015). https://doi.org/10.1007/978-3-319-25010-6_1
22. Pham, T.L., Mileo, A., Ali, M.I.: Towards scalable non-monotonic stream reasoning via input dependency analysis. In: International Conference on Data Engineering, ICDE (2017)
23. Rinne, M., Nuutila, E.: Constructing event processing systems of layered and heterogeneous events with SPARQL. J. Data Semant. **6**(2), 57–69 (2017)
24. Tappolet, J., Bernstein, A.: Applied temporal RDF: efficient temporal querying of RDF data with SPARQL. In: Aroyo, L., et al. (eds.) ESWC 2009. LNCS, vol. 5554, pp. 308–322. Springer, Heidelberg (2009). https://doi.org/10.1007/978-3-642-02121-3_25
25. Urbani, J., Margara, A., Jacobs, C., van Harmelen, F., Bal, H.: DynamiTE: parallel materialization of dynamic RDF data. In: Alani, H., et al. (eds.) ISWC 2013. LNCS, vol. 8218, pp. 657–672. Springer, Heidelberg (2013). https://doi.org/10.1007/978-3-642-41335-3_41

Intelligent Clients for Replicated Triple Pattern Fragments

Thomas Minier[1]([✉]) [iD], Hala Skaf-Molli[1], Pascal Molli[1] [iD],
and Maria-Esther Vidal[2] [iD]

[1] LS2N, University of Nantes, Nantes, France
{thomas.minier,hala.skaf-molli,pascal.molli}@univ-nantes.fr
[2] TIB Leibniz Information Centre for Science and Technology,
University Library & Fraunhofer IAIS, Sankt Augustin, Germany
Maria.Vidal@tib.eu

Abstract. Following the Triple Pattern Fragments (TPF) approach, intelligent clients are able to improve the availability of the Linked Data. However, data availability is still limited by the availability of TPF servers. Although some existing TPF servers belonging to different organizations already replicate the same datasets, existing intelligent clients are not able to take advantage of replicated data to provide fault tolerance and load-balancing. In this paper, we propose ULYSSES, an intelligent TPF client that takes advantage of replicated datasets to provide fault tolerance and load-balancing. By reducing the load on a server, ULYSSES improves the overall Linked Data availability and reduces data hosting cost for organizations. ULYSSES relies on an adaptive client-side load-balancer and a cost-model to distribute the load among heterogeneous replicated TPF servers. Experimentations demonstrate that ULYSSES reduces the load of TPF servers, tolerates failures and improves queries execution time in case of heavy loads on servers.

Keywords: Semantic web · Triple Pattern Fragments
Intelligent client · Load balancing · Fault tolerance · Data replication

1 Introduction

The Triple Pattern Fragments (TPF) [16] approach improves Linked Data availability by shifting costly SPARQL operators from servers to intelligent clients. However, data availability is still dependent on servers' availability, *i.e.*, if a server fails, there is no failover mechanism, and the query execution fails too. Moreover, if a server is heavily loaded, performances can be deteriorated.

The availability of TPF servers can be ensured by cloud providers and consequently servers' availability are depended on the budget of data providers. An alternative solution is to take advantage of datasets replicated by different data providers. In this case, TPF clients can balance the load of queries processing among data providers. Using replicated servers, they can prevent a single point of failure server-side, improves the overall availability of data, and distributes the financial costs of queries execution among data providers.

© Springer International Publishing AG, part of Springer Nature 2018
A. Gangemi et al. (Eds.): ESWC 2018, LNCS 10843, pp. 400–414, 2018.
https://doi.org/10.1007/978-3-319-93417-4_26

Some data providers already replicate RDF datasets produced by other data providers [11]. Replication can be total, *e.g.*, both DBpedia[1] and LANL Linked Data Archive[2] publish the same versions of DBpedia datasets. Replication can also be partial, *e.g.*, LOD-a-lot[3] [4] gathers all LOD Laundromat datasets[4] into a single dataset, hence each LOD Laundromat dataset is a partial replication of LOD-a-lot.

Existing TPF clients allow to process a federated SPARQL query over a federation of TPF servers replicating the same datasets. However, *existing TPF clients do not support replication nor client-side load balancing* [16]. Consequently, the execution time of queries are severely degraded in presence of replication. To illustrate, consider the federated SPARQL query Q_1, given in Fig. 1, and the TPF servers S_1 and S_2 owned respectively by DBpedia and LANL. Both servers host the DBpedia dataset 2015–10. Executing Q_1 on S_1 alone takes **7 s** in average, and returns 222 results. Executing the same query as a federated SPARQL query on both S_1 and S_2 also returns 222 results, but takes **25 s** in average.

```
PREFIX dbo: <http://dbpedia.org/ontology/>
PREFIX rdfs: <http://www.w3.org/2000/01/rdf-schema#>
SELECT DISTINCT ?software ?company WHERE {
    ?software dbo:developer ?company. # tp1
    ?company dbo:locationCountry ?country . # tp2
    ?country rdfs:label "France"@en . # tp3
}
```

Fig. 1. Federated SPARQL query Q_1 finds all software developed by French companies, executed on S_1: http://fragments.dbpedia.org/2015-10/en and S_2: http://fragments.mementodepot.org/dbpedia_201510

Moreover, in the first setting, S_1 received **442 HTTP calls** while, in the federated setting, S_1 received **478 HTTP calls** and S_2 received **470 HTTP calls**. Thus, there was unnecessary transfer of data between the client and servers which increased the global load on servers without producing new results.

Distributing the load of Q_1 processing across S_1 and S_2 requires to know servers capabilities. As TPF servers are heterogeneous, *i.e*, they do not have the same processing capabilities and access latencies, poorly distributed load further deteriorates query processing.

In this paper, we propose ULYSSES, a replication-aware intelligent TPF client providing load balancing and fault tolerance over heterogeneous replicated TPF servers. Managing replication in Linked Data has been already addressed in [10,11,13]. These approaches consider SPARQL endpoints and not TPF servers. Moreover, they focus on minimizing intermediate results and do not address the problems of load-balancing and fault-tolerance. The load balancing problem with

---

[1] http://fragments.dbpedia.org/.

[2] http://fragments.mementodepot.org/.

[3] http://hdt.lod.labs.vu.nl/?graph=LOD-a-lot.

[4] http://lodlaundromat.org/wardrobe/.

replicated datasets is addressed in [9] but without considering heterogeneous servers. The main contributions of this paper are:

- A replication-aware source selection for TPF servers.
- A light-weighted cost-model for accessing heterogeneous TPF servers.
- A client-side load balancer for distributing SPARQL query processing among heterogeneous TPF servers hosting replicated datasets.

The paper is organized as follows. Section 2 summarizes related works. Section 3 presents ULYSSES approach and key contributions. Section 4 presents our experimental setup and details experimental results. Finally, conclusions and future works are outlined in Sect. 5.

2   Related Work

Triple Pattern Fragments. The Triple Pattern Fragments approach (TPF) [16] proposes to shift complex query processing from servers to clients to improve availability and reliability of servers, at the cost of performance. In this approach, SPARQL query processing is distributed between a TPF server and a TPF client: the first only evaluates single triple patterns, issued to the server using HTTP requests, while the latter performs all others SPARQL operations [12]. Queries are evaluated using dynamic Nested Loop Joins that minimize the selectivity of each join, using metadata provided by the TPF server. The evaluation of SPARQL queries by TPF clients could require a great number of HTTP requests. For example, when processing $tp_3 \bowtie tp_2$ (of Q_1 in Fig. 1), each solution mapping of tp_3 is applied to tp_2 to generate subqueries, which are then evaluated against a TPF server. As a TPF server delivers results in several pages, the evaluation of one triple pattern could require several HTTP requests. In our example, the client downloads 429 triples in 5 requests, and generates 429 new subqueries when joining with tp_1.

Federated SPARQL Query Processing with Replication. Federated SPARQL query engines [1,6,7,14] are able to evaluate SPARQL queries over a set of data sources, *i.e.* a federation. However, if the federated query engine is not aware of replicated data, computing complete results will degrade performance: the query engine has to contact every relevant source and will transfer redundant intermediate results. This is an issue for federations of SPARQL endpoints, as pointed in [10,13], and also for federations of TPF servers, as pointed in Sect. 1.

The FEDRA [10] and LILAC [11] approaches address this issue in the context of SPARQL endpoints. Both prune redundant sources and use *data locality* to reduce data transfer during federated query processing. FEDRA is a source selection algorithm that finds as many sub-queries as possible that can be answered by the same endpoint, increasing the number of joins evaluated locally by SPARQL endpoints. LILAC is a replication-aware decomposer that further reduces intermediate results by allocating the same triple patterns to several endpoints. In the context of TPF servers, data locality cannot be exploited and consequently

FEDRA and LILAC are not pertinent. Moreover, FEDRA and LILAC do not address problems of load-balancing and fault tolerance using replicated datasets.

PENELOOP [9] makes available a replication-aware parallel join operator for federated SPARQL queries. PENELOOP parallelizes join processing over SPARQL endpoints or TPF servers hosting replicated data by distributing bindings among available servers. However, PENELOOP approach does not address the issue of heterogeneous servers. As the load of join processing is equally distributed across the federation, servers with poor performance or latency could deteriorate query execution time.

Client-Side Load Balancing with Heterogeneous Servers. Client-side load balancing is well suited for heterogeneous servers [3]. In this context, strategies for selecting servers can be classified into three categories: (i) *random*; (ii) *statistical*, by selecting the server with the lowest estimated latency; (iii) *dynamic*, using probing requests to select the fastest server. Dynamic probes perform better for selecting servers, but they add a communication overhead, as additional messages need to be exchanged between clients and servers. Dynamic probes reduce retrieval time for objects replicated on different servers but are not designed to distribute the cost among servers. Thus, powerful servers could receive all the load, and cost, of query processing. Smart clients [18] provide client-side load balancing and fault tolerance using a weighted random distribution algorithm: the probability of choosing a server is inversely proportional to its response time. Smart clients rely on probing to gather load information about servers but they do not propose an accurate and low-overhead load estimator that can be used to estimate the load of TPF servers.

3   Ulysses Approach

ULYSSES proposes intelligent clients for replicated TPF servers. In order to balance the load on heterogeneous servers hosting replicated datasets, ULYSSES relies on 3 key ideas:

First, it uses a *replication-aware source selection* algorithm to identify which TPF servers can be used to distribute evaluation of triple patterns during SPARQL query processing. The source selection algorithm relies on the replication model introduced in [10,11].

Second, ULYSSES uses each call performed to a TPF server during query processing as a probe to compute the *processing capabilities* of the server. Since triple pattern queries can be resolved in constant time by TPF servers [5], observing HTTP responses times allows to compute an accurate load-estimation of TPF servers. Such estimation is updated in real-time during query processing and allows ULYSSES to dynamically react to failures or heavy load of TPF servers.

Last, ULYSSES uses an *adaptive load-balancer* to perform load balancing among replicated servers. Instead of simply selecting the server with the best access latency, ULYSSES performs its selection using a weighted random algorithm: the probability of selecting a server is proportional to its processing

(a) Replicated fragments

(b) Triple patterns in Q_1 and their relevant fragments and servers

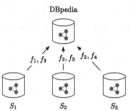

DBpedia

S_1 S_2 S_3

Triple pattern	Relevant fragment	Relevant server(s)
tp_1	f_1	S_1
	f_2	S_2, S_3
tp_2	f_3	S_1, S_2
tp_3	f_4	S_3

$f_1 = \langle$ DBpedia, ?software dbo:developer dbp:Arkane_Studios $\rangle$

$f_2 = \langle$ DBpedia, ?software dbo:developer ?company $\rangle$

$f_3 = \langle$ DBpedia, ?company dbo:locationCountry ?country $\rangle$

$f_4 = \langle$ DBpedia, ?country rdfs:label 'France'@en $\rangle$

Fig. 2. Relevant replicated fragments for query Q_1 (from Fig. 1)

capabilities. Thus, the load of query processing will be distributed across all replicated servers, *minimizing* the individual cost of query processing for each data provider. This load-balancer also provides *fault-tolerance*, by re-scheduling failed HTTP requests using available replicated servers.

3.1   Replication Model

For replication, we follow the approach of replicated fragments introduced in [10,11] and recall related definitions, adapted for TPF servers.

Definition 1 (Fragment). *A fragment is a tuple $f = \langle u, tp_f \rangle$ where u is the authoritative source of the fragment, e.g., DBpedia, and tp_f is the triple pattern met by the fragment's triples.*

Figure 2a shows a federation with three TPF servers S_1, S_2 and S_3, each of them exposing fragments replicated from DBpedia. For example, S_3 replicated the fragment f_4, which correspond to all triples matched by the triple pattern `?country rdfs:label"France"@en`. Notice that a total replication can be easily expressed using a fragment defined by the triple pattern `?s ?p ?o`.

Definition 2 (Fragment mapping). *A fragment mapping is a function $\mathcal{L}$ that maps a fragment to a set of TPF servers.*

For example, in Fig. 2a, the fragment mapping of f_2 is $\mathcal{L}(f_2) = \{S_2, S_3\}$.

Definition 3 (Containment mapping). *A containment mapping is a containment relation $\sqsubseteq$ defined as follows:*

Let $tp(\mathcal{D})$ denote the evaluation of the triple pattern tp over an RDF dataset $\mathcal{D}$. Let tp_1 and tp_2 be two triple patterns. We say that tp_1 is contained in tp_2, denoted by $tp_1 \sqsubseteq tp_2$, if, $\forall$ RDF dataset $\mathcal{D}, tp_1(\mathcal{D}) \subseteq tp_2(\mathcal{D})$.

Computing triple pattern containment has a complexity of $O(1)$, as demonstrated in [10].

Algorithm 1. ULYSSES Source Selection algorithm

Input: Q: SPARQL query, S: set of TPF servers, F: set of fragments
Output: *selection*: map from Triple Pattern to set of set of TPF servers

1 **Function** *SourceSelection(Q, S, C)*:
2   *selection* ← empty map
3   *patterns* ← get triple patterns in Q
4   **for each** $tp \in$ *patterns* **do**
5   *selection*[tp] ← $\emptyset$
6         $R(tp)$ ← *RelevantFragments*(tp, F)
7         $R(tp)$ ← *CheckContainment*$(R(tp), F)$
8   **for each** $f \in R(tp)$ **do**
9             $\mathcal{L}(f)$ ← *FragmentLocations*(f, S)
10   *selection*[tp] ← *selection*[tp] $\cup \{\mathcal{L}(f)\}$

11   **return** *selection*

For example, in Fig. 2a, we have $f_1 \sqsubseteq f_2$, as all triples matching f_1 pattern are included in the triples matching f_2 pattern.

Definition 4 (Fragment relevance). *Let f be a fragment defined by a triple pattern tp_1. Let tp_2 be a triple pattern of a SPARQL query Q. f is relevant to Q if $tp_1 \sqsubseteq tp_2$ or $tp_2 \sqsubseteq tp_1$.*

Figure 2b shows the relevant fragments of query Q_1, from Fig. 1, using the fragments defined in Fig. 2a. For example, f_1 and f_2 are relevant to tp_1, as $tp_{f_1} \sqsubseteq tp_1$ and $tp_{f_2} \sqsubseteq tp_1$.

3.2 Replication-Aware Source Selection for Triple Pattern Fragments

When processing a SPARQL query, ULYSSES loads a *catalog* that describes fragments and the servers that provide access to them, *i.e.*, the fragment localities. In this paper, we made the following assumptions:

- We do not address how the catalog is obtained. It could be provided as an input by the user, any server in the federation or by a dedicated service that record replication between online datasets.
- For simplicity, we consider that replicated fragments are synchronized, *i.e.* there are no updates. Managing consistency between replicated datasets with updates is addressed in [8]. Most TPF servers address this issue by hosting *versioned datasets* [15].

Algorithm 1 presents ULYSSES replication-aware source selection algorithm. This algorithm identifies the TPF servers that can be used to evaluate each triple pattern of a query. The following example illustrates how this algorithm works.

Example 1. Consider Algorithm 1 with the following inputs: the SPARQL query Q_1 from Fig. 1, the set of TPF servers $S = \{S_1, S_2, S_3\}$ and the fragments from Fig. 2. First, relevant fragments are computed for each triple pattern (line 6): $R(tp_1) = \{f_1, f_2\}$, $R(tp_2) = \{f_3\}$ and $R(tp_3) = \{f_4\}$. Notice that triple patterns with more than one relevant fragments require the retrieval of all relevant fragments to get complete results. Next, we compute triple pattern containment to remove redundant fragments (line 7), f_1 is removed because $f_1 \sqsubseteq f_2$, and then fragments are localized on TPF servers (line 9): $L(f_2) = \{S_2, S_3\}$, $L(f_3) = \{S_1, S_2\}$ and $L(f_4) = \{S_3\}$. Finally, the source selection of each triple pattern is computed (line 10): $selection[tp_1] = \{\{S_2, S_3\}\}$, $selection[tp_2] = \{\{S_1, S_2\}\}$ and $selection[tp_3] = \{\{S_3\}\}$.

The results of the source selection algorithm are used to identify the TPF servers that replicate the same relevant fragments. These servers can be used to distribute the evaluation of triple patterns. However, as TPF servers are heterogeneous, *i.e.*, they do not exhibit the same processing capabilities, we must ensure that servers with weaker processing capabilities are less requested in favor of more powerful servers, to maintain good query processing performance. To this end, we define a cost-model to compute and evaluate servers capabilities.

3.3 A Cost-Model for Evaluating TPF Servers Capabilities

The cost model uses server capability factors to evaluate servers capabilities. A *server capability factor* depends on: (i) The access latency of the TPF client for this server. (ii) The processing capabilities of the server, *i.e.*, in terms of CPU, RAM, etc. (iii) The impact of the server loads on its processing capabilities.

As a triple pattern is evaluated in constant time [5], a server capability factor can be deduced from its access time. If an HTTP request is not resolved in the server cache, a *server access time* is the time to receive one page of RDF triples matching a triple pattern from the TPF server[5]. However, as the size of pages could be different among servers, two servers with the same access times do not necessarily produce results at the same rate. Thus, we choose to rely on a *server throughput*, *i.e.*, the number of results served per unit of time, to evaluate more precisely its processing capabilities.

Definition 5 (Server throughput). *Given a set of TPF servers* $S = \{S_1, \ldots, S_n\}$, $\Delta = \{\delta_1, \ldots, \delta_n\}$ *where* δ_i *is the access time of* S_i, *and* $P = \{p_1, \ldots, p_n\}$ *where* p_i *is the number of results served per access to* S_i.

$\forall S_i \in S$, *the server throughput* w_i *of* S_i *is* $w_i = \dfrac{p_i}{\delta_i}$.

Example 2. Consider three TPF servers S_1, S_2 and S_3, with their access times be $\delta_1 = \delta_2 = 100\,\text{ms}$ and $\delta_3 = 500\,\text{ms}$ and the number of results they serve per access be $p_1 = 100$ and $p_2 = p_3 = 400$, respectively. Using Definition 5, we

---

[5] We suppose that an HTTP client is able to detect if an HTTP request has been resolved in the cache.

compute the servers throughput as $w_1 = 1$, $w_2 = 4$ and $w_3 = 0.8$, respectively. Notice that S_1 and S_2 have the same access times, but using their throughput, we observe that S_2 delivers more triples per unit of time than S_1.

Next, we use the throughput of a TPF server to estimate its capability. The capability is normalized with respect to other servers used to evaluate the query.

Definition 6 (Server capability). *Given a set of TPF servers* $S = \{S_1, \ldots, S_n\}$ *and* $W = \{w_1, \ldots, w_n\}$ *where* w_i *is the throughput of* S_i.
$\forall S_i \in S$, the capability ϕ_i of S_i is $\phi_i = \left\lfloor \dfrac{w_i}{\min W} \right\rfloor$.

Example 3. Consider the set of servers $S = \{S_1, S_2, S_3\}$ and their throughputs $W = \{w_1 = 1, w_2 = 4, w_3 = 0.8\}$ from Example 2. Using Definition 6, we compute the capability of S_1, S_2 and S_3 as $\phi_1 = 1$, $\phi_2 = 5$ and $\phi_3 = 1$, respectively. We observe that S_1 and S_3 have similar capabilities, even if S_3 access times is higher than S_1, and that S_2 is five times more powerful than both S_1 and S_3.

3.4 Accessing TPF Servers Based on Capabilities

We follow a load distribution approach similar to Smart Clients [18], with a random algorithm weighted by the servers capabilities. This allows for quick adaptation to variations in server loads: if a server throughput is deteriorated, its capability will decrease and it will be less frequently accessed. Definition 7 states how to access a set of TPF servers in such way.

Definition 7 (Weighted random access). *Given a set of TPF servers* $S = \{S_1, \ldots, S_n\}$ *and* $\Phi = \{\phi_1, \ldots, \phi_n\}$ *where* ϕ_i *is the capability of* S_i.
When selecting a TPF server $S_i \in S$ *to evaluate a triple pattern tp, the probability of selecting S_i is:* $\mathcal{A}(S_i) = \dfrac{\phi_i}{\sum_{j=1}^{n} \phi_j}$, *such as: (i)* $\sum_{S_i \in S} \mathcal{A}(S_i) = 1$; *(ii)*
$\forall S_i \in S, 0 \leqslant \mathcal{A}(S_i) \leqslant 1$.

Example 4. Consider again the set of TPF servers $S = \{S_1, S_2, S_3\}$ and the set of capabilities $\Phi = \{\phi_1 = 1, \phi_2 = 5, \phi_3 = 1\}$ computed in Example 3.
According to Definition 7, the probability of selecting S_1, S_2 and S_3 for evaluating a triple pattern are $\mathcal{A}(S_1) = \dfrac{1}{7}$, $\mathcal{A}(S_2) = \dfrac{5}{7}$ and $\mathcal{A}(S_3) = \dfrac{1}{7}$, respectively.

Next, we define how ULYSSES uses the cost-model to effectively distribute the evaluation of triples patterns across replicated TPF servers.

3.5 Ulysses Adaptive Client-Side Load Balancing with Fault Tolerance

ULYSSES defines an adaptive client-side load balancer that acts as a *transparent component* between the client and the set of replicated TPF servers. When the TPF query engine evaluates a triple pattern, it uses the load balancer to perform

Algorithm 2. ULYSSES Load Balancing algorithm

Data: $S = \{S_1, \ldots, S_n\}$: set of TPF servers, *selection*: map of Triple Pattern
to set of set of TPF servers, $\Phi = \{\phi_1, \ldots, \phi_n\}$: set of servers capabilities.

1 **Function** *EvaluatePattern(tp: triple pattern)*:
2     $\mu \leftarrow \emptyset$
3     $S_{tp} \leftarrow selection[tp]$
4   **for each** $S' \in S_{tp}$ **do**
5   **if** $|S'| > 1$ **then** // `replicated servers available`
6             $s' \leftarrow$ a TPF server selected using Φ, such as $s' \in S'$
7   **else**
8             $s' \leftarrow$ the only server $s' \in S'$
9         $\mu \leftarrow \mu \cup \{$ Evaluate tp at $s' \}$
10   **return** μ

11 **Event** *OnHTTPResponse(S_i: TPF server, δ': request execution time)*:
12   Update access times of S_i and recompute Φ using it

13 **Event** *OnHTTPFailure(q: HTTP request, S_i: TPF server, tp: triple pattern)*:
14     $\forall S' \in selection[tp]$, remove S_i from S'
15   **if** $selection[tp] = \emptyset$ **then** // `all servers have failed`
16         $FailQuery()$
17   Retry q using another relevant TPF server, selected using Φ

---

the evaluation. The load balancer distributes accesses to relevant TPF servers according to servers capabilities as defined in Sect. 3.4.

Algorithm 2 describes the load balancing algorithm used by ULYSSES. First, the sources selected by the source selection algorithm are used to find S_{tp}, a set of set of TPF servers (line 3). Each $S' \in S_{tp}$ is a set of servers that replicates one relevant fragment of tp. ULYSSES has to evaluate tp using at least one server in each S' to get complete results (line 4). For each $S' \in S_{tp}$, if replicated servers are available, the set of servers capabilities is used to select a server to evaluate tp (line 6). Otherwise, the unique server in S' is used to evaluate tp (line 8).

Additionally, ULYSSES load balancer *adapts* to changes in network conditions and provides *fault tolerance*. If a valid HTTP response is received from a server (line 11), its access time is updated in ULYSSES cost-model and the set of servers capabilities is recomputed to be kept up-to-date. Furthermore, if a server has failed to process a request (line 13), it is removed from the cost-model and the request is re-scheduled using an alternative server (lines 14–17).

4 Experimental Study

The goal of the experimental study is to evaluate the effectiveness of ULYSSES: (i) ULYSSES produces complete results and does not deteriorate query execution time; (ii) The load distribution is done conforming to the cost model;

(iii) ULYSSES speed-up query execution when servers are loaded; (iv) ULYSSES is able to tolerate faults and adapts to the load of servers in real time.

We compare the performance of the reference TPF client alone (denoted as TPF) and the same TPF client with the addition of ULYSSES (denoted as ULYSSES)[6].

4.1   Experimental Setup

Dataset and Queries: We use one instance of the Waterloo SPARQL Diversity Test Suite (WatDiv) synthetic dataset [2] with 10^7 triples, encoded in the HDT format [5]. We generate 50,000 DISTINCT queries from 500 templates (STAR, PATH, and SNOWFLAKE shaped queries). Next, we eliminate all duplicated queries, and then pick 100 random queries to be used in our experiments. Queries that failed to deliver an answer due to a query engine internal error with the regular TPF client are excluded from all configurations.

Type of Replication: We consider two types of replication: (i) *total replication*: our WatDiv dataset is replicated by all servers in the experimentation; (ii) *partial replication*: fragments are created from the 100 random queries and are replicated up to two times. Each replica is assigned randomly to a server in the experimentation.

Servers and Client Configurations: We use the Amazon Elastic Compute Cloud (Amazon EC2) to host our WatDiv dataset with the latest version of the TPF server. RDF triples are served per page of 100 triples. Each server use *t2.micro* instances (one core virtual CPU, 1GB of RAM), with 4 workers and no HTTP web cache. HTTP proxies are used to simulate network latencies and special conditions, using two configurations: (i) *Homogeneous*: all servers have access latencies of 300 ms. (ii) *Heterogeneous*: The first server has an access latency of 900 ms, and other servers have access latencies of 300 ms.

The ULYSSES TPF client is hosted on a machine with Intel Core i7-4790S 3.20 GHz and 2 GB of RAM and implemented as an extension of the reference TPF client.

Evaluation Metrics: (i) *Execution time (ET)*: is the elapsed time since the query is posed until a complete answer is produced. (ii) *HTTP response time (HRT)*: is the elapsed time since a HTTP request is submitted by the client to a TPF server until a complete HTTP response is received. (iii) *Number of HTTP requests per server (NHR)*: is the number of HTTP requests performed by the client against each TPF server for a query. Thus, it represents the load that each query injected on each server. (iv) *Answer Completeness (AC)*: is the ratio between the answers produced by the evaluation of a query using the reference TPF client and the evaluation by ULYSSES; values ranges between 0.0 and 1.0.

---

[6] The datasets, queries, code and results relative to the experiment are available the companion web site https://callidon.github.io/ulysses-tpf as long as with an online demo http://ulysses-demo.herokuapp.com.

Results presented for all metrics correspond to the average obtained after three successive evaluation of our queries.

4.2   Experimental Results

Query Execution Time and Answer Completeness: First, we check that ULYSSES preserves answer completeness. We executed our 100 random queries with ULYSSES using one, two and three homogeneous TPF servers. As a baseline, we also executed our queries with the reference TPF client, using one TPF server. In all configurations, ULYSSES is able to produce the same answers as the baseline for all queries.

Next, to confirm that ULYSSES does not deteriorate query execution time, we run a *Wilcoxon signed rank test* [17] for paired non-uniform data for the query execution time results obtained by ULYSSES, using up to three servers, with the following hypothesis: H_0: ULYSSES does not change SPARQL query execution time compared to the reference TPF client; H_1: ULYSSES does change SPARQL query execution time compared to the reference TPF client.

We obtained p-values of $2.83019e^{-17}, 9.0472e^{-12}$ and $5.05541e^{-12}$ for configurations with one, two and three servers, respectively. These low p-values allow for rejecting the null hypothesis and support that ULYSSES do change SPARQL query execution times compared to the reference TPF client.

Next, we validate that ULYSSES is able to distribute the load of query processing according to servers' capabilities both in a total replication settings and in a partial replication settings.

Load Distribution with Total Replication: Figure 3a shows the number of HTTP requests per server (*NHR*) after the evaluation of our workload of 100 queries, with up to four homogeneous servers that totally replicate the dataset. The configuration with one server runs with the reference TPF client, others with ULYSSES. As all servers have the same capabilities according to ULYSSES cost-model, the requests are equally distributed among servers. ULYSSES reduces the number of HTTP requests received per server. Consequently, each server receives fewer loads during query processing and servers availabilities are potentially increased.

Figure 3b shows the same experiment with heterogeneous servers. Again, ULYSSES is able to distribute the load according to servers capabilities: as S_1 is three times slower than other servers, therefore it receives less requests.

Load Distribution with Partial Replication: Figure 3c shows for the five queries (from our 100 queries) that generate the most HTTP requests, the number of HTTP requests per server, grouped by triple patterns in a query. We consider four homogeneous servers and partial replication. Results are similar to those obtained previously: the HTTP requests required to evaluate a triple pattern are distributed across servers that replicate relevant fragments. As the load of a query processing is distributed at triple pattern level, we conclude that the shape of a SPARQL query does not influence the load distribution.

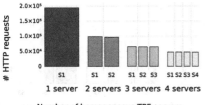

(a) All queries with **homogeneous servers** and **total replication** (All servers have same capabilities)

(b) All queries with **heterogeneous servers** and **total replication** (S_1 is three times slower than the others)

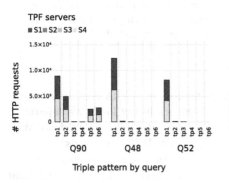

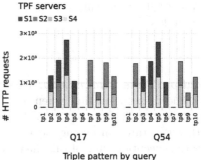

(c) The five queries that generate the most HTTP requests (**Homogeneous servers** and **partial replication**)

Fig. 3. Average number of HTTP requests received by servers after evaluation of Wat-Div queries, using several configurations

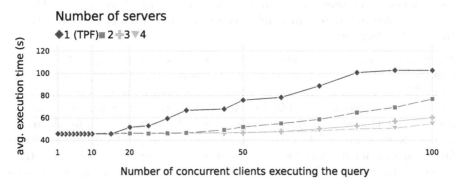

Fig. 4. Average query execution time with an increasing number of concurrent clients and available servers, using ULYSSES client

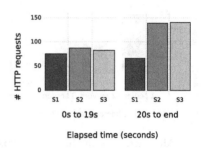

Fig. 5. Average HTTP response time when evaluating query 72 using three homogeneous servers (S_1, S_2, S_3) in presence of failures: S_1 fails at 5s and S_3 fails at 20 s

Fig. 6. Average number of HTTP requests received by servers S_1, S_2, S_3 during evaluation of query 72. Servers start homogeneous, then S_1 access latency is tripled at 20 s

Execution Time Under Load: We study the impact of ULYSSES load balancing on query execution time when servers experience heavy load. We separately study the query 72 (from our set of 100 queries) of the template query from Wat-Div that generates an average load of requests (590 HTTP requests). Figure 4 shows the execution time of this query, using up to twenty homogeneous servers. The servers load is generated using several TPF clients, up to a hundred, that evaluate the same query against the servers.

With only one server, results are similar to those obtained in [16]: as the load increases, the server is less available and the query execution time is deteriorated. Using several replicated servers, ULYSSES distributes the load among servers and improves availablity, so query execution time is significantly improved. This improvement is not proportional to the number of replicated servers available: for example, gains are more important between one and two servers than between three and twenty servers.

Fault Tolerance: We examine how ULYSSES reacts to faults. Figure 5 shows the average HTTP responses times recorded client-side, when ULYSSES evaluates the query 72 using three homogeneous servers S_1, S_2 and S_3 in presence of failure: after 5 s, S_1 becomes unavailable, and after 20 s, S_3 also becomes unavailable. We observe that ULYSSES is able to tolerate servers failure and evaluates the query with 100% answer completeness. When a failure is detected, ULYSSES distributes failed requests among available servers and resumes query execution in less than a second. Tolerating faults involves a slight overhead, as failed requests need to be re-executed.

Load Adaptivity: We examine the evaluation of query 72 in a context where servers load vary during query execution. Figure 6 shows the average number of HTTP requests received by servers S_1, S_2 and S_3 during the evaluation of query 72 by ULYSSES. Replication is total and servers start homogeneous, after 20 s the access latency of S_1 is tripled. Before S_1 becomes loaded, requests are evenly distributed between the three servers, as they have the same processing capabilities. Passed the 20 s, ULYSSES detects that processing capabilities of S_1 have been deteriorated and adapts the load distribution in consequence: S_2 and S_3 receive more requests until the end of the query processing. ULYSSES is able to quickly adapt to changes in servers conditions.

5   Conclusion and Future Works

In this paper, we presented ULYSSES, a replication-aware intelligent TPF client providing load balancing and fault tolerance over heterogeneous replicated TPF servers. ULYSSES accurately evaluates processing capabilities of TPF servers using only HTTP responses times observed during query processing. Experimental results demonstrate that ULYSSES reduces the individual load per server, speeds up query execution time under heavy load, tolerates faults, and adapts to the load of servers in real-time. Moreover, by distributing the load among different data providers, ULYSSES distributes the financial costs of queries execution among data providers without impacting query execution times for end-users.

ULYSSES opens several perspectives. First, we do not address how the catalog of replicated fragments can be acquired. It could be provided by TPF servers as additional metadata or built collaboratively by TPF clients as they evaluate SPARQL queries. Building and maintaining the catalog of replicated data over the web is challenging. Another perspective is to consider divergence over replicated data. Executing queries over weakly-consistent replicated datasets raises interesting issues about the correctness of results.

Acknowledgments. This work is partially supported through the FaBuLA project, part of the AtlanSTIC 2020 program.

References

1. Acosta, M., Vidal, M.-E., Lampo, T., Castillo, J., Ruckhaus, E.: ANAPSID: an adaptive query processing engine for SPARQL endpoints. In: Aroyo, L., Welty, C., Alani, H., Taylor, J., Bernstein, A., Kagal, L., Noy, N., Blomqvist, E. (eds.) ISWC 2011. LNCS, vol. 7031, pp. 18–34. Springer, Heidelberg (2011). https://doi.org/10.1007/978-3-642-25073-6_2
2. Aluç, G., Hartig, O., Özsu, M.T., Daudjee, K.: Diversified stress testing of RDF data management systems. In: Mika, P., et al. (eds.) ISWC 2014. LNCS, vol. 8796, pp. 197–212. Springer, Cham (2014). https://doi.org/10.1007/978-3-319-11964-9_13
3. Dykes, S.G., Robbins, K.A., Jeffery, C.L.: An empirical evaluation of client-side server selection algorithms. In: Proceedings of the Nineteenth Annual Joint Conference of the IEEE Computer and Communications Societies, INFOCOM 2000, vol. 3, pp. 1361–1370. IEEE (2000)
4. Fernández, J.D., Beek, W., Martínez-Prieto, M.A., Arias, M.: LOD-a-lot. In: d'Amato, C., Fernandez, M., Tamma, V., Lecue, F., Cudré-Mauroux, P., Sequeda, J., Lange, C., Heflin, J. (eds.) ISWC 2017. LNCS, vol. 10588, pp. 75–83. Springer, Cham (2017). https://doi.org/10.1007/978-3-319-68204-4_7

5. Fernández, J.D., Martínez-Prieto, M.A., Gutiérrez, C., Polleres, A., Arias, M.: Binary RDF representation for publication and exchange (HDT). Web Semant.: Sci. Serv. Agents World Wide Web **19**, 22–41 (2013)
6. Görlitz, O., Staab, S.: Federated data management and query optimization for linked open data. In: Vakali, A., Jain, L.C. (eds.) New Directions in Web Data Management 1. SCI, vol. 331, pp. 109–137. Springer, Heidelberg (2011). https://doi.org/10.1007/978-3-642-17551-0_5
7. Görlitz, O., Staab, S.: Splendid: SPARQL endpoint federation exploiting void descriptions. In: Proceedings of the Second International Conference on Consuming Linked Data, vol. 782, pp. 13–24. CEUR-WS. org (2011)
8. Ibáñez, L.-D., Skaf-Molli, H., Molli, P., Corby, O.: Col-Graph: towards writable and scalable linked open data. In: Mika, P., et al. (eds.) ISWC 2014. LNCS, vol. 8796, pp. 325–340. Springer, Cham (2014). https://doi.org/10.1007/978-3-319-11964-9_21
9. Minier, T., Montoya, G., Skaf-Molli, H., Molli, P.: Parallelizing federated SPARQL queries in presence of replicated data. In: Blomqvist, E., Hose, K., Paulheim, H., Ławrynowicz, A., Ciravegna, F., Hartig, O. (eds.) ESWC 2017. LNCS, vol. 10577, pp. 181–196. Springer, Cham (2017). https://doi.org/10.1007/978-3-319-70407-4_33
10. Montoya, G., Skaf-Molli, H., Molli, P., Vidal, M.-E.: Federated SPARQL queries processing with replicated fragments. In: Arenas, M., et al. (eds.) ISWC 2015. LNCS, vol. 9366, pp. 36–51. Springer, Cham (2015). https://doi.org/10.1007/978-3-319-25007-6_3
11. Montoya, G., Skaf-Molli, H., Molli, P., Vidal, M.E.: Decomposing federated queries in presence of replicated fragments. Web Semant.: Sci. Serv. Agents World Wide Web **42**, 1–18 (2017)
12. Pérez, J., Arenas, M., Gutierrez, C.: Semantics and complexity of SPARQL. ACM Trans. Database Syst. (TODS) **34**(3), 16 (2009)
13. Saleem, M., Ngonga Ngomo, A.-C., Xavier Parreira, J., Deus, H.F., Hauswirth, M.: DAW: Duplicate-AWare federated query processing over the web of data. In: Alani, H., et al. (eds.) ISWC 2013. LNCS, vol. 8218, pp. 574–590. Springer, Heidelberg (2013). https://doi.org/10.1007/978-3-642-41335-3_36
14. Schwarte, A., Haase, P., Hose, K., Schenkel, R., Schmidt, M.: FedX: optimization techniques for federated query processing on linked data. In: Aroyo, L., Welty, C., Alani, H., Taylor, J., Bernstein, A., Kagal, L., Noy, N., Blomqvist, E. (eds.) ISWC 2011. LNCS, vol. 7031, pp. 601–616. Springer, Heidelberg (2011). https://doi.org/10.1007/978-3-642-25073-6_38
15. Vander Sande, M., Verborgh, R., Hochstenbach, P., Van de Sompel, H.: Toward sustainable publishing and querying of distributed linked data archives. J. Doc. **74**(1), 195–222 (2018)
16. Verborgh, R., Vander Sande, M., Hartig, O., Van Herwegen, J., De Vocht, L., De Meester, B., Haesendonck, G., Colpaert, P.: Triple pattern fragments: a low-cost knowledge graph interface for the web. Web Semant.: Sci. Serv. Agents World Wide Web **37**, 184–206 (2016)
17. Wilcoxon, F.: Individual comparisons by ranking methods. In: Kotz, S., Johnson, N.L. (eds.) Breakthroughs in Statistics. SSS, pp. 196–202. Springer, New York (1992). https://doi.org/10.1007/978-1-4612-4380-9_16
18. Yoshikawa, C., Chun, B., Eastham, P., Vahdat, A., Anderson, T., Culler, D.: Using smart clients to build scalable services. In: Proceedings of the 1997 USENIX Technical Conference, CA, p. 105 (1997)

Knowledge Guided Attention and Inference for Describing Images Containing Unseen Objects

Aditya Mogadala[1]($\boxtimes$)(iD), Umanga Bista[2], Lexing Xie[2], and Achim Rettinger[1](iD)

[1] Institute of Applied Informatics and Formal Description Methods (AIFB),
Karlsruhe Institute for Technology (KIT), Karlsruhe, Germany
{aditya.mogadala,rettinger}@kit.edu
[2] Computational Media Lab, Australian National University (ANU),
Canberra, Australia
{umanga.bista,lexing.xie}@anu.edu.au

Abstract. Images on the Web encapsulate diverse knowledge about varied abstract concepts. They cannot be sufficiently described with models learned from image-caption pairs that mention only a small number of visual object categories. In contrast, large-scale knowledge graphs contain many more concepts that can be detected by image recognition models. Hence, to assist description generation for those images which contain visual objects unseen in image-caption pairs, we propose a two-step process by leveraging large-scale knowledge graphs. In the first step, a multi-entity recognition model is built to annotate images with concepts not mentioned in any caption. In the second step, those annotations are leveraged as external semantic attention and constrained inference in the image description generation model. Evaluations show that our models outperform most of the prior work on out-of-domain MSCOCO image description generation and also scales better to broad domains with more unseen objects.

1 Introduction

Content on the Web is highly heterogeneous and consists mostly of visual and textual information. In most cases, these different modalities complement each other, which complicates the capturing of the full meaning by automated knowledge extraction techniques. An approach for making information in all modalities accessible to automated processing is linking the information represented in the different modalities (e.g., images and text) into a shared conceptualization, like entities in a Knowledge Graph (KG). However, obtaining an expressive formal representation of textual and visual content has remained a research challenge for many years.

Recently, a different approach has shown impressive results, namely the transformation of one unstructured representation into another. Specifically, the task of generating natural language descriptions of images or videos [16] has gained

© Springer International Publishing AG, part of Springer Nature 2018
A. Gangemi et al. (Eds.): ESWC 2018, LNCS 10843, pp. 415–429, 2018.
https://doi.org/10.1007/978-3-319-93417-4_27

much attention. While such approaches are not relying on formal conceptual-izations of the domain to cover, the systems that have been proposed so far are limited by a very small number of objects that they can describe (less than 100). Obviously, such methods – as they need to be trained on manually crafted image-caption parallel data – do not scale to real-world applications, and can't be applied to cross-domain web-scale content.

In contrast, visual object classification techniques have improved consider-ably and they are now scaling to thousands of objects more than the ones covered by caption training data [3]. Also, KGs have grown to cover all of those objects plus millions more accompanied by billions of facts describing relations between those objects. Thus, it appears that those information sources are the miss-ing link to make existing image captioning models scale to a larger number of objects without having to create additional image-caption training pairs with those missing objects. In this paper, we investigate the hypothesis, that con-ceptual relations of entities – as represented in KGs – can provide information to enable caption generation models to generalize to objects that they haven't seen during training in the image-caption parallel data. While there are exist-ing methods that are tackling this task, none of them has exploited any form of conceptual knowledge so far. In our model, we use KG entity embeddings to guide the attention of the caption generator to the correct (unseen) object that is depicted in the image. Our main contributions presented in this paper are summarized as follows:

– We designed a novel approach, called Knowledge Guided Attention (KGA), to improve the task of generating captions for images which contain objects that are not in the training data.
– To achieve it, we created a multi-entity-label image classifier for linking the depicted visual objects to KG entities. Based on that, we introduce the first mechanism that exploits the relational structure of entities in KGs for guiding the attention of a caption generator towards picking the correct KG entity to mention in its descriptions.
– We conducted an extensive experimental evaluation showing the effectiveness of our KGA method. Both, in terms of generating effectual captions and also scaling it to more than 600 visual objects.

The contribution of this work on a broader scope is its progress towards the integration of the visual and textual information available on the Web with KGs.

2   Previous Work on Describing Images with Unseen Objects

Existing methods such as Deep Compositional Captioning (DCC) [4], Novel object Captioner (NOC) [15], Constrained Beam Search (CBS) [2] and LSTM-C [17] address the challenge by transferring information between seen and unseen objects either before inference (i.e. before testing) or by keeping constraints on

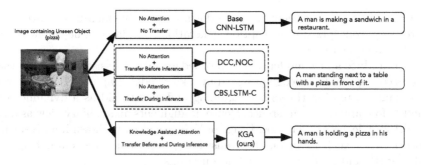

Fig. 1. KGA goal is to describe images containing unseen objects by building on the existing methods i.e. DCC [4], NOC [15], CBS [2] and LSTM-C [17] and going beyond them by adding semantic knowledge assistance. Base refers to our base description generation model built with CNN [13] - LSTM [5].

the generation of caption words during inference (i.e. during testing). Figure 1 provides a broad overview of those approaches.

In DCC, an approach which performs information transfer only before inference, the training of the caption generation model is solely dependent on the corpus constituting words which may appear in the similar context as of unseen objects. Hence, explicit transfer of learned parameters is required between seen and unseen object categories before inference which limits DCC from scaling to a wide variety of unseen objects. NOC tries to overcame such issues by adopting a end-to-end trainable framework which incorporates auxiliary training objectives during training and detaching the need for explicit transfer of parameters between seen and unseen objects before inference. However, NOC training can result in sub-optimal solutions as the additional training attempts to optimize three different loss functions simultaneously. CBS, leverages an approximate search algorithm to guarantee the inclusion of selected words during inference of a caption generation model. These words are however only constrained on the image tags produced by a image classifier. And the vocabulary used to find similar words as candidates for replacement during inference is usually kept very large, hence adding extra computational complexity. LSTM-C avoids the limitation of finding similar words during inference by adding a copying mechanism into caption training. This assists the model during inference to decide whether a word is to be generated or copied from a dictionary. However, LSTM-C suffers from confusion problems since probabilities during word generation tend to get very low.

In general, aforementioned approaches also have the following limitations: (1) The image classifiers used cannot predict abstract meaning, like "hope", as observed in many web images. (2) Visual features extracted from images are confined to the probability of occurrence of a fixed set of labels (i.e. nouns, verbs and adjectives) observed in a restricted dataset and cannot be easily extended to varied categories for large-scale experiments. (3) Since an attention mechanism is missing, important regions in an image are never attended. While, the attention mechanism in our model helps to scale down all possible identified concepts to the relevant concepts during caption generation. For large-scale applications, this plays a crucial role.

We introduce a new model called Knowledge Guided Assistance (KGA) that exploits conceptual knowledge provided by a knowledge graph (KG) [6] as external semantic attention throughout training and also to aid as a dynamic constraint before and during inference. Hence, it augments an auxiliary view as done in multi-view learning scenarios. Usage of KGs has already shown improvements in other tasks, such as in question answering over structured data, language modeling [1], and generation of factoid questions [12].

3   Describing Images with Unseen Objects Using Knowledge Guided Assistance (KGA)

In this section, we present our caption generation model to generate captions for unseen visual object categories with knowledge assistance. KGAs core goal is to introduce external semantic attention (ESA) into the learning and also work as a constraint before and during inference for transferring information between seen words and unseen visual object categories.

3.1   Caption Generation Model

Our image caption generation model (henceforth, KGA-CGM) combines three important components: a language model pre-trained on unpaired textual corpora, external semantic attention (ESA) and image features with a textual (T), semantic (S) and visual (V) layer (i.e. TSV layer) for predicting the next word in the sequence when learned using image-caption pairs. In the following, we present each of these components separately while Fig. 2 presents the overall architecture of KGA-CGM.

Language Model. This component is crucial to transfer the sentence structure for unseen visual object categories. Language model is implemented with two long short-term memory (LSTM) [5] layers to predict the next word given previous words in a sentence. If $\overrightarrow{w_{1:L}}$ represent the input to the forward LSTM of layer-1 for capturing forward input sequences into hidden sequence vectors $(\overrightarrow{h_{1:L}^1} \in \mathcal{R}^H)$, where L is the final time step. Then encoding of input word sequences into hidden layer-1 and then into layer-2 at each time step t is achieved as follows:

$$\overrightarrow{h_t^1} = \text{L1-F}(\overrightarrow{w_t}; \Theta) \tag{1}$$

$$\overrightarrow{h_t^2} = \text{L2-F}(\overrightarrow{h_t^1}; \Theta) \tag{2}$$

where Θ represent hidden layer parameters. The encoded final hidden sequence $(\overrightarrow{h_t^2} \in \mathcal{R}^H)$ at time step t is then used for predicting the probability distribution

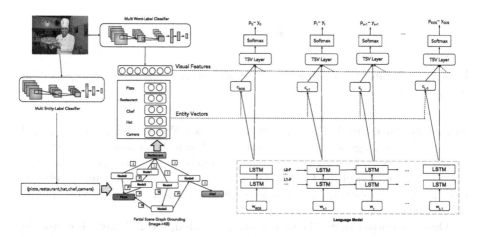

Fig. 2. KGA-CGM is built with three components. A language model built with two-layer forward LSTM (L1-F and L2-F), a multi-word-label classifier to generate image visual features and a multi-entity-label classifier that generates entity-labels linked to a KG serving as a partial image specific scene graph. This information is further leveraged to acquire entity vectors for supporting ESA. w_t represents the input caption word, c_t the semantic attention, p_t the output of probability distribution over all words and y_t the predicted word at each time step t. BOS and EOS represent the special tokens.

of the next word given by $p_{t+1} = softmax(h_t^2)$. The softmax layer is only used while training with unpaired textual corpora and not used when learned with image captions.

External Semantic Attention (ESA). Our objective in ESA is to extract semantic attention from an image by leveraging semantic knowledge in KG as entity-labels obtained using a multi-entity-label image classifier (discussed in the Sect. 4.2). Here, entity-labels are analogous to patches or attributes of an image. In formal terms, if ea_i is an entity-label and $e_i \in \mathcal{R}^E$ the entity-label vector among set of entity-label vectors $(i = 1, .., L)$ and β_i the attention weight of e_i then β_i is calculated at each time step t using Eq. 3.

$$\beta_{ti} = \frac{exp(O_{ti})}{\sum_{j=1}^{L} exp(O_{tj})} \qquad (3)$$

where $O_{ti} = f(e_i, h_t^2)$ represent scoring function which conditions on the layer-2 hidden state (h_t^2) of a caption language model. It can be observed that the scoring function $f(e_i, h_t^2)$ is crucial for deciding attention weights. Also, relevance of the hidden state with each entity-label is calculated using Eq. 4.

$$f(e_i, h_t^2) = tanh((h_t^2)^T W_{he} e_i) \qquad (4)$$

where $W_{he} \in \mathcal{R}^{H \times E}$ is a bilinear parameter matrix. Once the attention weights are calculated, the soft attention weighted vector of the context c, which is a dynamic representation of the caption at time step t is given by Eq. 5.

$$c_t = \sum_{i=1}^{L} \beta_{ti} e_i \qquad (5)$$

Here, $c_t \in \mathcal{R}^E$ and L represent the cardinality of entity-labels per image-caption pair instance.

Image Features and TSV Layer and Next Word Prediction. Visual features for an image are extracted using multi-word-label image classifier (discussed in the Sect. 4.2). To be consistent with other approaches [4, 15] and for a fair comparison, our visual features (I) also have objects that we aim to describe outside of the caption datasets besides having word-labels observed in paired image-caption data.

Once the output from all components is acquired, the TSV layer is employed to integrate their features i.e. textual (T), semantic (S) and visual (V) yielded by language model, ESA and images respectively. Thus, TSV acts as a transformation layer for molding three different feature spaces into a single common space for prediction of next word in the sequence.

If $h_t^2 \in \mathcal{R}^H$, $c_t \in \mathcal{R}^E$ and $I_t \in \mathcal{R}^I$ represent vectors acquired at each time step t from language model, ESA and images respectively. Then the integration at TSV layer of KGA-CGM is provided by Eq. 6.

$$TSV_t = W_{h_t^2} h_t^2 + W_{c_t} c_t + W_{I_t} I_t \qquad (6)$$

where $W_{h_t^2} \in \mathcal{R}^{vs \times H}, W_{c_t} \in \mathcal{R}^{vs \times E}$ and $W_{I_t} \in \mathcal{R}^{vs \times I}$ are linear conversion matrices and vs is the image-caption pair training dataset vocabulary size.

The output from the TSV layer at each time step t is further used for predicting the next word in the sequence using a softmax layer given by $p_{t+1} = softmax(TSV_t)$.

3.2   KGA-CGM Training

To learn parameters of KGA-CGM, first we freeze the parameters of the language model trained using unpaired textual corpora. Thus, enabling only those parameters to be learned with image-caption pairs emerging from ESA and TSV layer such as $W_{he}, W_{h_t^2}, W_{c_t}$ and W_{I_t}. KGA-CGM is now trained to optimize the cost function that minimizes the sum of the negative log likelihood of the appropriate word at each time step given by Eq. 7.

$$\min_{\theta} -\frac{1}{N} \sum_{n=1}^{N} \sum_{t=0}^{L^{(n)}} log(p(y_t^{(n)})) \qquad (7)$$

where $L^{(n)}$ represent the length of sentence (i.e. caption) with beginning of sentence (BOS), end of sentence (EOS) tokens at n-th training sample and N as a number of samples used for training.

3.3   KGA-CGM Constrained Inference

Inference in KGA-CGM refer to the generation of descriptions for test images. Here, inference is not straightforward as in the standard image caption generation approaches [16] because unseen visual object categories have no parallel captions throughout training. Hence they will never be generated in a caption. Thus, unseen visual object categories require guidance either before or during inference from similar seen words that appear in the paired image-caption dataset and likely also from image labels. In our case, we achieve the guidance both before and during inference with varied techniques.

Guidance Before Inference. We first identify the seen words in the paired image-caption dataset similar to the visual object categories unseen in image-caption dataset by estimating the semantic similarity using their Glove embeddings [9] learned using unpaired textual corpora (more details in Sect. 4.1). Furthermore, we utilize this information to perform dynamic transfer between seen words visual features (W_I), language model ($W_{h_t^2}$) and external semantic attention (W_{c_t}) weights and unseen visual object categories. To illustrate, if (v_{unseen}, i_{unseen}) and ($v_{closest}, i_{closest}$) denote the indexes of unseen visual object category "zebra" and its semantically similar known word "giraffe" in a vocabulary (v_s) and visual features (i_s) respectively. Then to describe images with "zebra" in the similar manner as of "giraffe", the transfer of weights is performed between them by assigning $W_{c_t}[v_{unseen},:]$, $W_{h_t^2}[v_{unseen},:]$ and $W_{I_t}[v_{unseen},:]$ to $W_{c_t}[v_{closest},:]$, $W_{h_t^2}[v_{closest},:]$ and $W_{I_t}[v_{closest},:]$ respectively.

    Input: M=$\{W_{he}, W_{h_t^2}, W_{c_t}, W_{I_t}\}$
    Output: M_{new}
1   Initialize List(closest) = cosine_distance(List(unseen),vocabulary) ;
2   Initialize $W_{c_t}[v_{unseen},:]$, $W_{h_t^2}[v_{unseen},:]$, $W_{I_t}[v_{unseen},:] = 0$;
3   **Function** *Before Inference*
4   **forall** *items T in closest and Z in unseen* **do**
5   **if** *T and Z is vocabulary* **then**
6          $W_{c_t}[v_Z,:] = W_{c_t}[v_T,:]$;
7          $W_{h_t^2}[v_Z,:] = W_{h_t^2}[v_T,:]$;
8          $W_{I_t}[v_Z,:] = W_{I_t}[v_T,:]$;
9   **end**
10   **if** *i_T and i_Z in visual features* **then**
11         $W_{I_t}[i_Z,i_T]=0$;
12         $W_{I_t}[i_T,i_Z]=0$;
13   **end**
14   **end**
15      $M_{new} = $ M ;
16   **return** M_{new} ;
17 **end**

Algorithm 1. Constrained Inference Overview (Before)

Input: M_{new}, Im_{labels}, beam-size k, word w
Output: best k successors
1 Initialize $Im_{labels} = $ Top-5 (ea) ;
2 Initialize beam-size k ;
3 Initialize word w=null ;
4 **Function** *During Inference*
5   **forall** *State st of k words* **do**
6   w=st ;
7   **if** *closest[w] in ea* **then**
8           $st = $ closest$[w]$;
9   **end**
10   **else**
11          $st = w$;
12   **end**
13   **end**
14   **return** best k successors ;
15 **end**

Algorithm 2. Constrained Inference Overview (During)

Furthermore, $W_{I_t}[i_{unseen},i_{closest}]$, $W_{I_t}[i_{closest},i_{unseen}]$ is set to zero for removing mutual dependencies of seen and unseen words presence in an image. Hence, aforementioned procedure will update the KGA-CGM trained model before inference to assist the generation of unseen visual object categories during inference as given by Algorithm 1.

Guidance During Inference. The updated KGA-CGM model is used for generating descriptions of unseen visual object categories. However, in the before-inference procedure, the closest words to unseen visual object categories are identified using embeddings that are learned only using textual corpora and are never constrained on images. This obstructs the view from an image leading to spurious results. We resolve such nuances during inference by constraining the beam search used for description generation with image entity-labels (*ea*). In general, beam search is used to consider the best k sentences at time t to identify the sentence at the next time step. Our modification to beam search is achieved by adding a extra constraint to check if a generated unseen visual object category is part of the entity-labels. If it's not, unseen visual object categories are never replaced with their closest seen words. Algorithm 2 presents the overview of KGA-CGM guidance during inference.

4 Experimental Setup

4.1 Resources and Datasets

Our approach is dependent on several resources and datasets.

Knowledge Graphs (KGs) and Unpaired Textual Corpora. There are several openly available KGs such as DBpedia, Wikidata, and YAGO which provide semantic knowledge encapsulated in entities and their relationships. We choose DBpedia as our KG for entity annotation, as it is one of the extensively used resource for semantic annotation and disambiguation [6].

For learning weights of the language model and also Glove word embeddings, we have explored different unpaired textual corpora from out-of-domain sources (i.e. out of image-caption parallel corpora) such as the British National Corpus (BNC)[1], Wikipedia (Wiki) and subset of SBU1M[2]caption text containing 947 categories of ILSVRC12 dataset [11]. NLTK[3] sentence tokenizer is used to extract tokenizations and around 70k+ words vocabulary is extracted with Glove embeddings.

Unseen Objects Description (Out-of-Domain MSCOCO and ImageNet). To evaluate KGA-CGM, we use the subset of MSCOCO dataset [7] proposed by Hendricks et al. [4]. The dataset is obtained by clustering 80 image object category labels into 8 clusters and then selecting one object from each cluster to be held out from the training set. Now the training set does not contain the images and sentences of those 8 objects represented by bottle, bus, couch, microwave, pizza, racket, suitcase and zebra. Thus making the MSCOCO training dataset to constitute 70,194 image-caption pairs. While validation set of 40504 image-caption pairs are again divided into 20252 each for testing and validation. Now, the goal of KGA-CGM is to generate caption for those test images which contain these 8 unseen object categories. Henceforth, we refer this dataset as "out-of-domain MSCOCO".

To evaluate KGA-CGM on more challenging task, we attempt to describe images that contain wide variety of objects as observed on the web. To imitate such a scenario, we collected images from collections containing images with wide variety of objects. First, we used same set of images as earlier approaches [15,17] which are subset of ImageNet [3] constituting 642 object categories used in Hendricks et al. [4] who do not occur in MSCOCO. However, 120 out of those 642 object categories are part of ILSVRC12.

4.2 Multi-label Image Classifiers

The important constituents that influence KGA-CGM are the image entity-labels and visual features. Identified objects/actions etc. in an image are embodied in visual features, while entity-labels capture the semantic knowledge in an image grounded in KG. In this section, we present the approach to extract both visual features and entity-labels.

---

[1] http://www.natcorp.ox.ac.uk/.

[2] http://vision.cs.stonybrook.edu/~vicente/sbucaptions/.

[3] http://www.nltk.org/.

Multi-word-Label Image Classifier. To extract visual features of out-of-domain MSCOCO images, emulating Hendricks et al. [4] a multi-word-label classifier is built using the captions aligned to an image by extracting part-of-speech (POS) tags such as nouns, verbs and adjectives attained for each word in the entire MSCOCO dataset. For example, the caption "A young child brushes his teeth at the sink" contains word-labels such as "young (JJ)", "child (NN)", "teeth (NN)" etc., that represent concepts in an image. An image classifier is trained now with 471 word-labels using a sigmoid cross-entropy loss by fine-tuning VGG-16 [13] pre-trained on the training part of the ILSVRC12. The visual features extracted for a new image represent the probabilities of 471 image labels observed in that image. For extracting visual features from ImageNet images, we replace the multi-word-label classifier with the lexical classifier [4] learned with 642 ImageNet object categories.

Multi-entity-Label Image Classifier. To extract semantic knowledge for out-of-domain MSCOCO images analogous to the word-labels, a multi-entity-label classifier is build with entity-labels attained from a knowledge graph annotation tool such as DBpedia spotlight[4] on training set of MSCOCO constituting 82,783 training image-caption pairs. In total around 812 unique labels are extracted with an average of 3.2 labels annotated per image. To illustrate, considering the caption presented in the aforementioned section, entity labels extracted are "Brush[5]" and "Tooth[6]". An image classifier is now trained with multiple entity-labels using sigmoid cross-entropy loss by fine-tuning VGG-16 [13] pre-trained on the training part of the ILSVRC12. For extracting entity-labels from ImageNet images, we again leveraged lexical classifier [4] learned with 642 ImageNet object categories. However, as all 642 categories denote WordNet synsets, we build a connection between these categories and DBpedia by leveraging BabelNet [8] for multi-entity-label classifier. To illustrate, for visual object category "wombat" (wordnetid: *n1883070*) in ImageNet can be linked to DBpedia Wombat[7]. Hence, this makes our method very modular for building new image classifiers to incorporate semantic knowledge.

4.3 Entity-Label Embeddings

We presented earlier that the acquisition of entity-labels for training multi-entity-label classifiers were obtained using DBpedia spotlight entity annotation and disambiguation tool. Hence, entity-labels are expected to encapsulate semantic knowledge grounded in KG. Further, entities in a KG can be represented with embeddings by capturing their relational information. In our work, we see the efficacy of these embeddings for caption generation. Thus, we leverage entity-label embeddings for computing semantic attention observed in an image

---

[4] https://github.com/dbpedia-spotlight/.
[5] http://dbpedia.org/resource/Brush.
[6] http://dbpedia.org/resource/Tooth.
[7] http://dbpedia.org/page/Wombat.

with respect to the caption as observed from KG. To obtain entity-label embeddings, we adopted the RDF2Vec [10] approach and generated 500 dimensional vector representations for 812 and 642 entity-labels to describe out-of-domain MSCOCO and ImageNet images respectively.

4.4 Evaluation Measures

To evaluate generated descriptions for the unseen MSCOCO visual object categories, we use similar evaluation metrics as earlier approaches [4,15,17] such as METEOR and also SPICE [2]. However, CIDEr [14] metric is not used as it is required to calculate the inverse document frequency used by this metric across the entire test set and not just unseen object subsets. F1 score is also calculated to measure the presence of unseen objects in the generated captions when compared against reference captions. Furthermore, to evaluate ImageNet object categories description generation: we leveraged F1 and also other metrics such as Unseen and Accuracy scores [15,17]. The Unseen score measures the percentage of all novel objects mentioned in generated descriptions, while accuracy measure percentage of image descriptions correctly addressed the unseen objects.

5 Experiments

The experiments are conducted to evaluate the efficacy of KGA-CGM model for describing out-of-domain MSCOCO and ImageNet images.

5.1 Implementation

KGA-CGM model constitutes three important components i.e. language model, visual features and entity-labels. Before learning KGA-CGM model with image-caption pairs, we first learn the weights of language model and keep it fixed during the training of KGA-CGM model. To learn language model, we leverage unpaired textual corpora (e.g. entire MSCOCO set, Wiki, BNC etc.) and provide input word embeddings representing 256 dimensions pre-trained with Glove [9] default settings on the same unpaired textual corpora. Hidden layer dimensions of language model are set to 512. KGM-CGM model is then trained using image-caption pairs with Adam optimizer with gradient clipping having maximum norm of 1.0 for about 15–50 epochs. Validation data is used for model selection and experiments are implemented with Keras + Theano backend[8].

5.2 Describing Out-of-Domain MSCOCO Images

In this section, we evaluate KGA-CGM using out-of-domain MSCOCO dataset.

---

[8] https://github.com/adityamogadala/KGA.

Quantitative Analysis. We compared our complete KGA-CGM model with the other existing models that generate image descriptions on out-of-domain MSCOCO. To have a fair comparison, only those results are compared which used VGG-16 to generate image features. Table 1 shows the comparison of individual and average scores based on METEOR, SPICE and F1 on all 8 unseen visual object categories with beam size 1.

Table 1. Measures for all 8 unseen objects. Underline shows the second best.

F1									
Model	Beam	Microwave	Racket	Bottle	Zebra	Pizza	Couch	Bus	Suitcase	Average
DCC [4]	1	28.1	52.2	4.6	79.9	64.6	<u>45.9</u>	29.8	13.2	39.7
NOC [15]	>1	24.7	55.3	17.7	89.0	69.3	25.5	<u>68.7</u>	39.8	48.8
CBS(T4) [2]	>1	29.7	57.1	16.3	85.7	**77.2**	**48.2**	67.8	**49.9**	54.0
LSTM-C [17]	>1	27.8	<u>70.2</u>	<u>29.6</u>	<u>91.4</u>	68.1	38.7	**74.4**	<u>44.7</u>	**55.6**
KGA-CGM	1	**50.0**	**75.3**	**29.9**	**92.1**	<u>70.6</u>	42.1	54.2	25.6	<u>55.0</u>
METEOR									
DCC [4]	1	22.1	20.3	18.1	22.3	**22.2**	**23.1**	**21.6**	<u>18.3</u>	21.0
NOC [15]	>1	21.5	<u>24.6</u>	21.2	21.8	<u>21.8</u>	21.4	<u>20.4</u>	18.0	21.3
LSTM-C [17]	>1	-	-	-	-	-	-	-	-	23.0
CBS(T4) [2]	>1	-	-	-	-	-	-	-	-	**23.3**
KGA-CGM	1	**22.6**	**25.1**	**21.5**	**22.8**	21.4	<u>23.0</u>	20.3	**18.7**	22.0
SPICE									
DCC [4]	>1	-	-	-	-	-	-	-	-	13.4
CBS(T4) [2]	>1	-	-	-	-	-	-	-	-	**15.9**
KGA-CGM	1	13.3	16.8	13.1	19.6	13.2	14.9	12.6	10.6	<u>14.3</u>

It can be noticed that KGA-CGM with beam size 1 was comparable to other approaches even though it used fixed vocabulary from image-caption pairs. For example, CBS [2] used expanded vocabulary of 21,689 when compared to 8802 by us. Also, our word-labels per image are fixed, while CBS uses a varying size of predicted image tags (T1-4). This makes it non-deterministic and can increase uncertainty, as varying tags will either increase or decrease the performance. Furthermore, we also evaluated KGA-CGM for the rest of seen visual object categories in the Table 2. It can be observed that our KGA-CGM outperforms existing approaches as it did not undermine the in-domain description generation, although it was tuned for out-of-domain description generation.

Qualitative Analysis. In Fig. 3, sample predictions of our best KGA-CGM model is presented. It can be observed that entity-labels has shown an influence for caption generation. Since, entities as image labels are already disambiguated, it attained high similarity in the prediction of a word thus adding useful semantics. Figure 3 presents the example unseen visual objects descriptions.

Table 2. Average measures of MSCOCO seen objects.

Seen objects				
Model	Beam	METEOR	SPICE	F1-score
DCC [4]	1	23.0	15.9	-
CBS(T4) [2]	>1	24.5	18.0	-
KGA-CGM	1	24.1	17.2	-
KGA-CGM	>1	**25.1**	**18.2**	-

Fig. 3. Sample predictions of KGA-CGM on out-of-domain MSCOCO images with beam size 1 when compared against base model and NOC [15]

5.3 Describing ImageNet Images

ImageNet images do not contain any ground-truth captions and contain exactly one unseen visual object category per image. Initially, we first retrain different language models using unpaired textual data (Sect. 4.1) and also the entire MSCOCO training set. Furthermore, the KGA-CGM model is rebuilt for each one of them separately. To describe ImageNet images, image classifiers presented in the Sect. 4.2 are leveraged. Table 3 summarizes the experimental results attained on 634 categories (i.e. not all 642) to have fair comparison with other approaches. By adopting only MSCOCO training data for language model, our KGA-CGM makes the relative improvement over NOC and LSTM-C in all categories i.e. unseen, F1 and accuracy. Figure 4 shows few sample descriptions.

6 Key Findings

The key observations of our research are: (1) The ablation study conducted to understand the influence of different components in KGA-CGM has shown that using external semantic attention and constrained inference has superior performance when compared to using only either of them. Also, increasing the beam size during inference has shown a drop in all measures. This is basically

Table 3. Describing ImageNet images with beam size 1. Results of NOC and LSTM-C (with Glove) are adopted from Yao et al. [17]

Model	Unpaired-text	Unseen	F1	Accuracy
NOC [15]	MSCOCO	69.1	15.6	10.0
	BNC & Wiki	87.7	31.2	22.0
LSTM-C [17]	MSCOCO	72.1	16.4	11.8
	BNC & Wiki	89.1	33.6	31.1
KGA-CGM	MSCOCO	74.1	17.4	12.2
	BNC & Wiki	90.2	34.4	33.1
	BNC & Wiki & SBU1M	**90.8**	**35.8**	**34.2**

Fig. 4. ImageNet images with best KGA-CGM model from Table 3. Guided before inference shows which words are used for transfer between seen and unseen. (Color figure online)

adhered to the influence of multiple words on unseen objects. (2) The performance advantage becomes clearer if the domain of unseen objects is broadened. In other words: KGA-CGM specifically improves over the state-of-the-art in settings that are larger and less controlled. Hereby, KGA-CGM scales to one order of magnitude more unseen objects with moderate performance decreases. (3) The influence of the closest seen words (i.e. observed in image-caption pairs) and the unseen visual object categories played a prominent role for generating descriptions. For example in out-of-domain MSCOCO, words such as "suitcase"/"bag", "bottle"/"glass" and "bus/truck" are semantically similar and are also used in the similar manner in a sentence added excellent value. However, some words usually cooccur such as "racket"/"court" and "pizza"/"plate" played different roles in sentences and lead to few grammatical errors. (4) The decrease in performance have a high correlation with the discrepancy between the domain where seen and unseen objects come from.

7   Conclusion and Future Work

In this paper, we presented an approach to generate captions for images that lack parallel captions during training with the assistance from semantic knowledge encapsulated in KGs. In the future, we plan to expand our models to build multimedia knowledge graphs along with image descriptions which can be used for finding related images or can be searched with long textual queries.

Acknowledgements. First author is grateful to KHYS at KIT for their research travel grant and Computational Media Lab at ANU for providing access to their K40x GPUs.

References

1. Ahn, S., Choi, H., Pärnamaa, T., Bengio, Y.: A neural knowledge language model. arXiv preprint arXiv:1608.00318 (2016)
2. Anderson, P., Fernando, B., Johnson, M., Gould, S.: Guided open vocabulary image captioning with constrained beam search. In: EMNLP (2017)
3. Deng, J., Dong, W., Socher, R., Li, L.J., Li, K., Fei-Fei, L.: ImageNet: a large-scale hierarchical image database. In: IEEE Conference on Computer Vision and Pattern Recognition, CVPR 2009, pp. 248–255. IEEE (2009)
4. Hendricks, L.A., Venugopalan, S., Rohrbach, M., Mooney, R., Saenko, K., Darrell, T.: Deep compositional captioning: describing novel object categories without paired training data. In: CVPR, pp. 1–10 (2016)
5. Hochreiter, S., Schmidhuber, J.: Long short-term memory. Neural Comput. **9**(8), 1735–1780 (1997)
6. Lehmann, J., Isele, R., Jakob, M., Jentzsch, A., Kontokostas, D., Mendes, P.N., et al.: DBpedia-a large-scale, multilingual knowledge base extracted from Wikipedia. Semant. Web **6**, 167–195 (2015)
7. Lin, T.-Y., Maire, M., Belongie, S., Hays, J., Perona, P., Ramanan, D., Dollár, P., Zitnick, C.L.: Microsoft COCO: common objects in context. In: Fleet, D., Pajdla, T., Schiele, B., Tuytelaars, T. (eds.) ECCV 2014. LNCS, vol. 8693, pp. 740–755. Springer, Cham (2014). https://doi.org/10.1007/978-3-319-10602-1_48
8. Navigli, R., Ponzetto, S.P.: BabelNet: the automatic construction, evaluation and application of a wide-coverage multilingual semantic network. Artif. Intell. **193**, 217–250 (2012)
9. Pennington, J., Socher, R., Manning, C.: GloVe: global vectors for word representation. In: EMNLP, pp. 1532–1543 (2014)
10. Ristoski, P., Paulheim, H.: RDF2Vec: RDF graph embeddings for data mining. In: Groth, P., Simperl, E., Gray, A., Sabou, M., Krötzsch, M., Lecue, F., Flöck, F., Gil, Y. (eds.) ISWC 2016. LNCS, vol. 9981, pp. 498–514. Springer, Cham (2016). https://doi.org/10.1007/978-3-319-46523-4_30
11. Russakovsky, O., Deng, J., Su, H., Krause, J., Satheesh, S., Ma, S., Huang, Z., Karpathy, A., Khosla, A., Bernstein, M., et al.: ImageNet large scale visual recognition challenge. Int. J. Comput. Vis. **115**(3), 211–252 (2015)
12. Serban, I.V., García-Durán, A., Gulcehre, C., Ahn, S., Chandar, S., Courville, A., Bengio, Y.: Generating factoid questions with recurrent neural networks: the 30M factoid question-answer corpus. arXiv preprint arXiv:1603.06807 (2016)
13. Simonyan, K., Zisserman, A.: Very deep convolutional networks for large-scale image recognition. arXiv preprint arXiv:1409.1556 (2014)
14. Vedantam, R., Zitnick, L.C., Parikh, D.: CIDEr: consensus-based image description evaluation. In: CVPR, pp. 4566–4575 (2015)
15. Venugopalan, S., Hendricks, L.A., Rohrbach, M., Mooney, R., Darrell, T., Saenko, K.: Captioning images with diverse objects. In: CVPR (2017)
16. Vinyals, O., Toshev, A., Bengio, S., Erhan, D.: Show and tell: lessons learned from the 2015 MSCOCO image captioning challenge. IEEE Trans. Pattern Anal. Mach. Intell. **39**(4), 652–663 (2017)
17. Yao, T., Yingwei, P., Yehao, L., Mei, T.: Incorporating copying mechanism in image captioning for learning novel objects. In: CVPR (2017)

Benchmarking of a Novel POS Tagging Based Semantic Similarity Approach for Job Description Similarity Computation

Joydeep Mondal$^{(\boxtimes)}$, Sarthak Ahuja(iD), Kushal Mukherjee,
Sudhanshu Shekhar Singh, and Gyana Parija

IBM Research Lab, New Delhi, India
jomondal@in.ibm.com

Abstract. Most solutions providing hiring analytics involve mapping provided job descriptions to a standard job framework, thereby requiring computation of a document similarity score between two job descriptions. Finding semantic similarity between a pair of documents is a problem that is yet to be solved satisfactorily over all possible domains/contexts. Most document similarity calculation exercises require a large corpus of data for training the underlying models. In this paper we compare three methods of document similarity for job descriptions - topic modeling (LDA), doc2vec, and a novel part-of-speech tagging based document similarity (POSDC) calculation method. LDA and doc2vec require a large corpus of data to train, while POSDC exploits a domain specific property of descriptive documents (such as job descriptions) that enables us to compare two documents in isolation. POSDC method is based on an action-object-attribute representation of documents, that allows meaningful comparisons. We use stanford Core NLP and NLTK Wordnet to do a multilevel semantic match between the actions and corresponding objects. We use sklearn for topic modeling and gensim for doc2vec. We compare the results from these three methods based on IBM Kenexa Talent frameworks job taxonomy.

1 Introduction

Several contexts require finding similarity between a pair of documents. The problem of finding similarity between a pair of documents also lays groundwork for the problem of clustering similar documents together. Most of the initial research in this domain was based on cosine distance with tf-idf term vectors. Topic modeling based techniques such as LSA and LDA learn an intuitive set of topics from a given corpus of documents, and the topic distribution vectors of documents can be used to find document similarities or cluster documents together. More recently, word2vec and doc2vec based document similarity methods have been gaining popularity.

All the document clustering techniques group similar documents together, while keeping dissimilar documents in different groups. Various document

© Springer International Publishing AG, part of Springer Nature 2018
A. Gangemi et al. (Eds.): ESWC 2018, LNCS 10843, pp. 430–444, 2018.
https://doi.org/10.1007/978-3-319-93417-4_28

similarity measures such as cosine similarity, Dice's coefficient and Jaccard's coefficient [13] have been used in literature to evaluate document similarity. However, the definition of a pair of documents being similar depends on the problem context. For example, finding the same joke [10] told differently is a vastly different problem from finding whether term paper submissions from two students are the same. Irrespective of the clustering technique used, most document similarity learning methods e.g. LDA [17], Doc2Vec [15] etc. require a large corpus of data to learn document features well. No document similarity computation methods work well if the corpus is small, or if only two documents are to be compared.

In our work of enabling hiring solutions via cognitive collaboration, wherein several agents/players such as job match, diversity champion, cultural assessment agent come together to make holistic hiring decision, one problem that we have faced many times is that of identifying which job requisitions are similar. This problem arises in two contexts:

1. Grouping jobs together: A typical application of machine learning in hiring is to learn success models for various jobs. To be meaningful, the models need to be learned at a sufficient level of granularity. Thus, arises the need to cluster jobs together. Grouping jobs together also arises necessity for a cultural assessment agent as similar assessments can be used for alike jobs.
2. Candidates' previous jobs need to be matched with the opening they apply to (or to the openings that will be recommended to them). This requires comparing job description from their previous jobs to the job openings available in the ATS (applicant tracking system).

Job requisitions typically consist of several well defined components: skill and years of experience requirement, job location and a job description. With the rest being structured fields, job title (covered in [8]) and job description, which typically consists of roles and responsibilities the job entails, becomes the primary component that needs to be matched across jobs. RISE [19] proposes a method of job classification followed by similarity establishment processes that leverages both structured and unstructured components of a job.

In this paper, we compare novel part-of-speech tagging based document similarity (POSDC) calculation method with doc2vec and LDA based topic modeling method. POSDC analyzes the actions (verbs), objects of each action (nouns) and attributes of the objects (adjectives) that appear in the two job description to be compared.

This paper is organized as follows. In the next section, we describe the literature on document similarity/clustering. Section 3 describes our job description similarity computation methodology and experimental setup. Section 4 explains the evaluation criteria. Section 5 concludes and discusses some future work.

2   Literature Survey

In typical text document classification and clustering tasks, the definition of a distance or similarity measure is essential. The most common methods employ keyword matching techniques. Methods such TFIDF [9] leverage the frequency of words occurring in a document to infer on similarity. The assumption is that if two documents have a similar distribution of words or have common keywords, then they are similar. Researches have also extended this to N-gram based models [16], where group of consecutive words are taken together to capture the context. With large N gram models, typically large corpus of documents are required to obtain sufficient statistical information.

[16,17] extended these approaches to include a probabilistic generative model that would explain the frequency of occurrence of words. These methods include PLSI (probabilistic latent semantic indexing) and LSA (latent semantic analysis). The assumption is that there are an underlying latent set of topics (with their individual distribution of words describing the topic) and each document is generated from a mixture of these topics. The above described methods fall in the category of bag-of words models. The major limitation of bag-of-words models is that the text is essentially represent as an un-ordered set of words (or n-words, for n gram models). The long-range word relations are not captured leading to loss of information. Another issue with these techniques is that they rely on the surface information of the words and not its semantics. That is, words with two or more meaning (polysemy) are represented in the same way and two or more words with the same meaning (synonymy) are denoted differently.

To alleviate the drawback of bag-of-words model, Le et al. [15] proposed Paragraph to Vector, an unsupervised algorithm that learns feature representations from variable-length pieces of texts, such as paragraphs. The algorithm represents each paragraph by a dense vector which may be used to predict words in the paragraph. Its construction captures semantics and has the potential to overcome the weaknesses of bag-of-words models. Paragraph Vectors outperform bag-of-words models as well as other techniques for text representations and have achieved state-of-the-art results on text classification and sentiment analysis tasks [15].

Another approach to document similarity is via concept modeling (Wikipedia concepts [11], IBM watson natural language understanding service [4]). The main idea is to use many concepts from Wikipedia or any other encyclopedia to construct a reference space, where each document is mapped from a keyword vector to a concept vector. This captures the semantic information contained in the document. [18] have demonstrated the effectiveness of concept matching to overcome the semantic mismatch problem. However, the concepts themselves are not independent. [12] extended Wikipedia matching to document clustering by enriching the feature vector of a text document by using the correlation information between concept articles.

3   Methodology

Our proposed approach to generate a similarity score among two job description D and D' can be divided into four parts as illustrated in Fig. 1. In this section we explain these steps alongside their system implementation in greater detail.

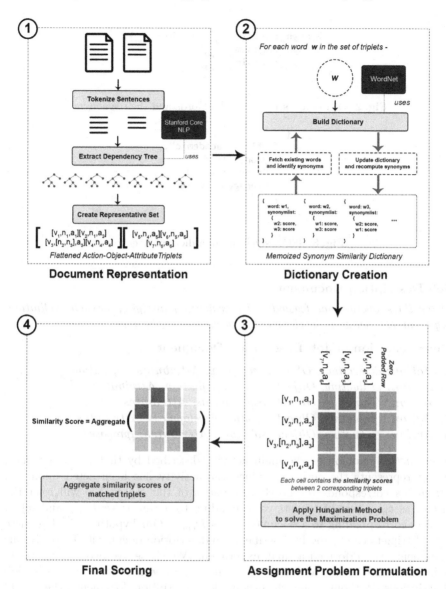

Fig. 1. Main flow describing the four steps for computation of job description similarity

3.1 Document Representation

Each document is treated as a collection of sentences set_{sent}, with each sentence *sent* being further represented as a collection of sets of triplets - **action, object and attributes**. Consider the following illustrative example.

$$
\begin{aligned}
&[\\
&\quad w_1: syn_{w1}:\{w_2:sim_{sem\ w1,w2}, w_3:sim_{sem\ w1,w3}\},\\
&\quad w_2: syn_{w2}:\{w_1:sim_{sem\ w1,w2}\},\\
&\quad w_3: syn_{w3}:\{w_1:sim_{sem\ w1,w3}\}\\
&]
\end{aligned}
$$

Fig. 2. Dictionary structure of keywords and their synonyms

```
{
    "title": "academic",
    "synonymlist":{
        "coach": 0.319
        "managed": 0.316
    }
}
```

Fig. 3. JSON structure of a dictionary entry

Job Description Document

Determines operational feasibility by evaluating analysis, problem definition, requirements, solution development, and proposed solutions.

Representation of Job Description Document

1. **Action**: determines, **Object**: feasibility, **Attributes**: [operational]
2. **Action**: evaluating, **Object**: problem definition, **Attributes**: [ ]
3. **Action**: evaluating, **Object**: requirements, **Attributes**: [ ]
4. **Action**: evaluating, **Object**: solution development, **Attributes**: [ ]
5. **Action**: evaluating, **Object**: solutions, **Attributes**: [proposed]

where *action* symbolizes the main activity described by that particular *sent*, *object* represents the entity on which the activity has been acted upon and *attributes* corresponds to the characteristics of the *object*. We will refer the triplet as t_{POS}, set of triplets corresponding to a *sen* as $sent_{t_{POS}}$ and set of triplets corresponding to a document D as $D_{t_{POS}}$. Our hypothesis is that these sets of triplets can properly describe a job description document. To verify this statement, we performed a small experiment. We chose five people (experts in Job analytics domain) and gave them the generated set of triplets for 10 job descriptions. Without seeing the original job description documents, they could easily extract the actual essence out of these triplet sets.

As all the job description documents were in English, without loss of generality it can be said that the main activity of a *sent* i.e *action* is represented by the non-auxiliary verb v. The entity on which the activity v has been acted upon is generally the object noun corresponding to v in *sent*. Characteristics of an entity are portrayed by the adjectives in English. So, we depicted *attribute* of an *object* as the adjectives corresponding to the object noun present in *sent*. We assume all the sentences in job description documents were in a particular format from which we could extracted the triplet. In cases where an entity of

t_{POS} contains multiple elements, such as in the case of compound nouns, a list of elements is created instead.

For faster computation we used Apache Spark [1] environment to parallalize the sequential loop in Algorithm 1. Apache Spark provides programmers with an application programming interface centered on a data structure called the resilient distributed dataset (RDD), a read-only multiset of data items distributed over a cluster of machines, that is maintained in a fault-tolerant way [2]. We modified Algorithm 1 to Algorithm 3 to incorporate distributed system capabilities.

3.2   Document Parsing and Dictionary Creation

Given a document D, it's corresponding representation discussed in Sect. 3.1 is obtained by parsing the output tree $tree_{dep}$ generated by Stanford Dependency Parser from the NLTK Library [3] for each sentence. Algorithm for creating $D_{t_{POS}}$ is described by below Algorithm 1.

Algorithm 1. Document Representation Algorithm-Sequential

1: **procedure** DocRepSeqProc
2:     **Input:** D
3:     **Output:** $D_{t_{POS}}$
4:     $set_{sent} \leftarrow$ sentence tokenizer (D)
5:     $D_{t_{POS}} \leftarrow null$
6:     **for** each sent of set_{sent} **do**
7:         $sent_{t_{POS}} \leftarrow SenRepProc(sent)$
8:         $D_{t_{POS}} \leftarrow D_{t_{POS}} \cup sent_{t_{POS}}$
9:     **end for**
10: **end procedure**

Algorithm 2. Sentence Representation Algorithm

1: **procedure** SenRepProc
2:     **Input:** $sent$
3:     **Output:** $sent_{t_{POS}}$
4:     $Tree_{dep} \leftarrow$ Stanford POS Dependency Tree $(sent)$
5:     $sent_{t_{POS}} \leftarrow$ modify $Tree_{dep}$ ▷ action, object and attributes are extracted from the tree
6: **end procedure**

After obtaining the D_{tPOS} we used *memoization* and *precomputation* techniques to build a dictionary $Dict$ of words present in the $D_{t_{POS}}$. The structure of the dictionary is depicted as in Fig. 2. In the dictionary, every word w has been stored with its synonym list syn_w. We used Wordnet dictionary from NLTK [5] to get syn_w for a given w. We used cloudant Database to store this dictionary

---

Algorithm 3. Document Representation Algorithm- Parallel

1: **procedure** DocRepParProc
2:     **Input:** D
3:     **Output:** $D_{t_{POS}}$
4:     $set_{sent} \leftarrow sentence\ tokenizer\ (D)$
5:     $D_{t_{POS}} \leftarrow null$
6:     $Map_{set_{sent}}(SenRepProc)$ ▷ it is executed in cluster machines of Spark environment in parallel for each sentence
7: **end procedure**

---

as JSONs. The structure of the JSON is in Fig. 3. syn_w for a w consists of only the words which exist in $Dict$ and cross a threshold of semantic similarity score (sim_{sem}). Algorithm to update the dictionary is given in Algorithm 5.

WordNet is a large lexical database of English language. Nouns, verbs, adjectives and adverbs are grouped into sets of cognitive synonyms which is called *synsets*. Each *synsets* expresses a distinct concept which interlinked by means of conceptual-semantic and lexical relations. Wordnet provides synsets for a given English word [6]. To calculate sim_{sem} between w_1 and w_2 we calculate *wup similarity* score between two synsets corresponding to w_1 and w_2. *Wu Palmer Similarity* or *wup similarity* provides a score denoting how similar two word senses are, based on the depth of the two senses in the taxonomy and that of their Least Common Subsumer (most specific ancestor node) [7]. After getting the scores between each synset we took an average of the scores to get the semantic similarity score between w_1 and w_2 and denoted it as $sim_{sem_{w_1,w_2}}$. Algorithm to find sim_{sem} is described in Algorithm 4.

When $Dict$ is empty and the algorithm encounters a new word it creates $Dict$ and stores an entry corresponding to the word. When $Dict$ exists in the cloudant database and algorithm encounters a w then it first checks whether it is present in $Dict$ or not. If w is not present in $Dict$ then it will create an entry for w and will generate a corresponding syn_w by calculating sim_{sem} with every other words in $Dict$. The sim_{sem} of every other words of $Dict$ will also be updated accordingly. While processing each entry in D_{tPOS}, we precompute the semantic similarity scores among the words and store them in a database. Processing of D_{tPOS} is described in Algorithm 6.

3.3 Assignment Problem Formulation

After document parsing stage, the two documents, D and D', are represented as two sets of triplets, D_{tPOS} and D'_{tPOS}, each with elements t_{POS_1}, t_{POS_2}, ... t_{POS_n} and t'_{POS_1}, t'_{POS_2}, ... t'_{POS_m} respectively. The similarity score between the two job des can be now interpreted as the similarity score between these two sets. The similarity function is explained in detail in the next subsection, and is denoted by **F** for now. To calculate the similarity score between two sets, a naive approach would be to calculate the similarity score between each pair of elements from two sets (S and S'), greedily pick the pair with the highest similarity

Algorithm 4. Semantic Similarity Between Two Words

1: **procedure** SEMSIMPROC
2:     **Input:** w_1, w_2
3:     **Output:** $sim_{sem_{w_1,w_2}}$
4:     $sim_{sem_{w_1,w_2}} \leftarrow 0$
5:     $synSets_{w_1} \leftarrow null$
6:     $synSets_{w_2} \leftarrow null$
7:     $synSets_{w_1} \leftarrow$ synsets from Wordnet for w_1
8:     $synSets_{w_2} \leftarrow$ synsets from Wordnet for w_2
9:     $div \leftarrow 0$
10:     **for** each $synSet_{w_1}$ of $synSets_{w_1}$ **do**
11:         **for** each $synSet_{w_2}$ of $synSets_{w_2}$ **do**
12:             $wup_{score} \leftarrow$ wup similarity between $synSet_{w_1}$ & $synSet_{w_2}$
13:             **if** wup_{score} is not $null$ **then**
14:                 $sim_{sem_{w_1,w_2}} \leftarrow sim_{sem_{w_1,w_2}} + wup_{score}$
15:                 $div \leftarrow div + 1$
16:             **end if**
17:         **end for**
18:     **end for**
19:     $sim_{sem_{w_1,w_2}} \leftarrow \dfrac{sim_{sem_{w_1,w_2}}}{div}$
20: **end procedure**

Algorithm 5. Dictionary Update Algorithm

1: **procedure** DICTUPDATEPROC
2:     **Input:** $w, Dict$
3:     **if** w doesn't exist in $Dict$ **then**
4:         $syn_w \leftarrow null$
5:         **for** every word w_i in $Dict$ **do**
6:             $sim_{sem_{w,w_i}} \leftarrow SemSImProc(w, w_i)$
7:             **if** $sim_{sem_{w,w_i}} > threshold$ **then**
8:                 append w_i to syn_w
9:                 append w to syn_{w_i}
10:             **end if**
11:         **end for**
12:         add w and syn_w to $Dict$
13:     **end if**
14: **end procedure**

score and repeat the process till either one of the sets has no element left. This greedy approach, although simple, does not provide an optimal match between the sets being compared. We assume that there are no repeating descriptions in the descriptive document, hence, the representative set for a document too will not have synonymous elements i.e. no same *action* on the same *object*. This assumption motivates a one-to-one mapping among the two sets being compared for similarity.

Algorithm 6. Document-Triplet-Set Processing Algorithm

1: **procedure** ProcTripProc
2:     **Input:** $D_{t_{POS}}$
3:     **for** each t_{POS} in $D_{t_{POS}}$ **do**
4:         $v \leftarrow action$
5:         $Noun \leftarrow object$
6:         $Adj \leftarrow attribute$
7:         $DictUpdateProc(v, Dict)$
8:         **if** $Noun$ is a compound noun **then**
9:             **for** each noun of $Noun$ **do**
10:                 $DictUpdateProc(noun, Dict)$
11:            **end for**
12:        **else**
13:                $DictUpdateProc(Noun, Dict)$
14:        **end if**
15:        **for** each adj of Adj **do**
16:                $DictUpdateProc(adj, Dict)$
17:        **end for**
18:    **end for**
19: **end procedure**

To find an optimum one-to-one mapping among the aforementioned two sets, we formulate the problem as an assignment problem [14]. In a generic assignment problem, given the cost of assignment among each pair of elements in two sets, the task is to find an optimal one-to-one assignment among the elements that maximizes/minimizes the total cost of assignment. Our problem of finding such a one-to-one mapping among the representative sets of the descriptive documents can be formulated in a similar way - given $\mathbf{F}$ as the cost of assignment function among each pair of elements in the two representative sets, the task is to find an optimal one-to-one assignment among the elements that maximizes the aggregate similarity score. Since the two sets being compared can have unequal number of elements, this is a case of an imbalanced assignment problem.

After formulating the problem as a similarity score maximization assignment problem, we use the *Hungarian Method* [14] to extract out the matches. This method takes as input a $n x n$ square cost matrix and post applying a set of matrix operations, outputs an optimal set of n assignments, one per row and column, which offer a maximum cumulative assignment score. Since ours is a case of an imbalanced assignment problem, given 2 sets with m and n triplets each, we start with a $m x n$ cost matrix, where each cell contains the similarity score between the corresponding row and column elements of the matrix. Without loss of generality, we assume $n > m$, and add zero padding to extend the $m x n$ matrix to a $n x n$ one. Rest of the steps for applying the *Hungarian Method* remain the same, as for a typical score maximization assignment problem. We will refer *Hungarian Method* as $Assign_{Hung.}$ in the rest of the paper.

Post this assignment, the following subsection defines the similarity and aggregation functions.

3.4   Score Calculation

We define four similarity functions for calculating similarity score between two job description documents D and D'. We will refer sim_{sem} function as calculating semantic similarity between two words described in Algorithm 4. The definition of the functions are following,

Definition 1. *If v_1 and v_2 are two single-word verbs and V_{sim} is the similarity function between two verbs then V_{sim} is defined as,*

$$V_{sim}(v_1, v_2) = sim_{sem_{v_1, v_2}} \tag{1}$$

Definition 2. *If N_1 and N_2 are two sets of nouns (nouns can be a set in t_{POS} in case of compound noun) and N_{sim} is the similarity function between two noun sets then N_{sim} is defined as,*

$$N_{sim}(N_1, N_2) = \frac{(1 * |N_1 \cap N_2| + \dfrac{\sum_{i=1}^{n} \sum_{j=1}^{m} sim_{sem_{N'_{1_i}, N'_{2_j}}}}{|N'_1| * |N'_2|})}{(1 + |N_1 \cap N_2|)} \tag{2}$$

where, $N'_1 = N_1 - (N_1 \cap N_2)$ and $N'_2 = N_2 - (N_1 \cap N_2)$.

Definition 3. *If A_1 and A_2 are two sets of adjectives (adjectives can be a set in t_{POS} in case of multiple adjectives corresponding to a noun) and A_{sim} is the similarity function between two adjective sets then A_{sim} is defined as,*

$$A_{sim}(A_1, A_2) = \frac{(1 * |A_1 \cap A_2| + \dfrac{\sum_{i=1}^{n} \sum_{j=1}^{m} sim_{sem_{A'_{1_i}, A'_{2_j}}}}{|A'_1| * |A'_2|})}{(1 + |A_1 \cap A_2|)} \tag{3}$$

where, $A'_1 = A_1 - (A_1 \cap A_2)$ and $A'_2 = A_2 - (A_1 \cap A_2)$.

Definition 4. *If t_{POS_1} and t_{POS_2} are two sets of triplets consisting of (v_1, N_1, A_1) and (v_2, N_2, A_2) respectively. Then, t_{sim} is the similarity function between two triplet sets and t_{sim} is defined as,*

$$t_{sim}(t_{POS_1}, t_{POS_2}) = \frac{1}{(2 + \mathbf{1}_{A_1 \cup A_2 \neq null})} \\ * (V_{sim}(v_1, v_2) * (1 + N_{sim}(N_1, N_2)) \\ * (1 + A_{sim}(A_1, A_2)))) \tag{4}$$

where $\mathbf{1}_{A_1 \cup A_2 \neq null} = 0$, if $A_1 \cup A_2 = null$, 1 otherwise.

Calculating triplet similarity includes finding semantic similarity between *action*, *object* and *attributes*, where *attributes* set can be null but others can't be null. We have already discussed in Sect. 3.1 that *action* are actually nothing but *verbs*, *object* are nothing but *nouns* and *attributes* are nothing but *adjectives*. So, calculating similarity between *action*, *object* and *attributes* boils down to finding semantic similarity between verbs, corresponding nouns and corresponding adjectives. A triplet t_{POS} consists of exactly one *action* or one *verb*, one *object* or a set of *nouns* (in case of compound noun), and a set of *attributes* or a set of adjectives (in case of multiple adjectives). Calculating semantic similarity between two *verbs* is straight forward using $sim_{sem_{w_1,w_2}}$ discussed in Sect. 3.2 and as described in Definition 1. On the other hand, calculating semantic similarity between two noun sets or two adjective sets in (Definitions 2 and 3) is a bit tricky. Both follow the same rule. So, we will discuss about the noun similarity calculation here. We compute the intersection $N_1 \cap N_2$ between two sets N_1 and N_2. We also compute the set difference between both the sets N_1', N_2' as $N_1 - N_1 \cap N_2$ and $N_2 - N_1 \cap N_2$ respectively. Then we compute the pairwise semantic similarity among elements of N_1' and N_2' using $sim_{sem_{w_1,w_2}}$ function. Next, we take the average of these pair wise semantic similarity and treat it as one entity $sim_{sem_{nonIntersec}}$, where

$$sim_{sem_{nonIntersec}} = \frac{\sum_{i=1}^{n} \sum_{j=1}^{m} sim_{sem_{N_{1_i}', N_{2_j}'}}}{|N_1'| * |N_2'|} \tag{5}$$

The other entity is semantic similarity score for $N_1 \cap N_2$ which is 1. Finally, we compute the weighted average of 1 and $sim_{sem_{nonIntersec}}$ where the weights are $|N_1 \cap N_2|$ and 1. After calculating these individual similarity scores we aggregate them to compute the similarity score between two triplets such that *action* gets the highest importance, followed by *object* and *attributes*.

Given two documents D and D' we first compute their corresponding triplet representation $D_{t_{POS}}$ and $D'_{t_{POS}}$. Lets say, $|D_{t_{POS}}| = n$ and $|D'_{t_{POS}}| = m$. Without loss of generality, it can also be stated that $n \geq m$. Then, the similarity matrix Mat_{sim} has been calculated as,

$$Mat_{sim^{i,j}} = t_{sim}(D_{t_{POS}^i}, D'_{t_{POS}^j}) \tag{6}$$

$$\forall i, j \in n, m$$

After Mat_{sim} calculation, it is provided as the input matrix to $Assign_{Hung.}$ algorithm, which returns a unique $1 - 1$ mapping $Map_{D,D'}$. Now the final similarity score between two documents $sim_{D,D'}$ is calculated using the following Eq. 7

$$sim_{D,D'} = \frac{\sum_{k=1}^{m} t_{sim}(D_{t_{POS}^i}, D'_{t_{POS}^j})}{n}$$

$$where\ Map_{D,D'}^k : D_{t_{POS}^i} -> D'_{t_{POS}^j} \tag{7}$$

$$\forall i, j \in n, m$$

Following Algorithm 7 actually describes the procedure to calculate the similarity between two job description documents.

3.5   Experimental Setup and Data-Sets

We used a Spark cluster with 6 executors each having 8 GB of RAM for running our experiments. Apache Spark frame work has been used to incorporate

---

Algorithm 7. Job Description Similarity Calculation Algorithm

---

1: **procedure** DOCSIMCALCPROC
2:       **Input:** D, D'
3:       **Output:** $sim_{D,D'}$
4:       $D_{t_{POS}} \leftarrow DocRepParProc(D)$
5:       $D'_{t_{POS}} \leftarrow DocRepParProc(D')$
6:       $ProcTripProc(D_{t_{POS}})$
7:       $ProcTripProc(D'_{t_{POS}})$
8:       $calculate\ sim_{D,D'}\ by\ equation\ 7$
9: **end procedure**

---

parallelism to carry out the experiments. All the codes have been written in python using pySpark library. Cloudant services have been incorporated as database resource. We also used Stanford Core NLP Parser and Wordnet from NLTK library.

Job description documents from IBM Talent Framework Data have been used to carry out all the experiments. All the sentences in the job description documents are grammatically incomplete in the sense that each of them starts with a verb. Subject noun is missing from each sentence, e.g. "Require analytical skills". So we add "You" or "You are" at the beginning of the each sentence depending upon the form of the verb. If the verb ends with "ing" we added "You are", otherwise we added "You" to make the sentences grammatically correct. In the cases where verbs end with "s" (verb meant to be for third person singular number) "You" has been treated as a name (third person singular number) and thus resolves the grammatical issue. Then these grammatically correct sentences are fed to the Stanford Core NLP Parser for generating dependency tree. As an estimate of the computation time in this setup, the action-object-attribute representation and calculation of job description similarity of 500 cross 500 jobs took 3892.33 s.

4   Evaluation

For testing our method we do Job Family based evaluation. Since we are using IBM Kenexa talent frameworks, we can utilize its default clubbing of jobs into job families. The general expectation is that jobs within a family (intra) will have higher job description similarity scores than those outside the job family (inter). Let

- $F = \{F_1, F_2, ..., F_n\}$ be the set of all job families in the test set.
- $J_i = \{J_{i,1}, J_{i,2}, ..., J_{i,n_i}\}$ be the set of all jobs in family F_i.
- $Intra_i$ be the average similarity between all pairs of jobs within F_i.
- $Inter_i$ be the average similarity between all pairs (A, B) of jobs such that $A \in F_i$ and $B \in F_j$ for all $j \neq i$.
- $R_i = \frac{Intra_i}{Inter_i}$.

Then the gross metric of interest to gauge effectiveness of a document similarity computation method is $S = \frac{\sum_i |F_i| \times R_i}{\sum_i |F_i|}$, computed over a common test set. So, higher S value means better performance of the similarity calculation approach.

Since we intend to benchmark our method against existing state of the art methods, we conduct several experiments with varying corpus of training data with $N_1 = 56$, $N_2 = 129$ and $N_3 = 430$ documents used for training. POSDC does not require any training corpus, therefore the corpus varying experiments are valid only for doc2vec and LDA. Note that the test set consisted of 500 randomly chosen jobs out of the 2344 available in IBM Kenexa talent frameworks, so that there is representation from each job family in the selected test set. The test sets selected did not have any of the jobs on which the models were trained, and were selected separately for the 3 experiments.

As is evident by the bar charts and Table 1, when a large enough corpus is chosen, LDA gives the best overall performance. Otherwise POSDC performs better. When we looked at individual job families, neither LDA nor POSDC completely dominates the other. Doc2vec seems to be consistently inferior to both LDA and POSDC irrespective of the corpus size.

Table 1. Comparison of S value across methods

	N_1	N_2	N_3
POSDC	1.60	1.65	1.59
LDA	1.36	1.37	1.65
DOC2VEC	0.968	0.996	1.01

Total number of job families in IBM Kenexa Talent Frameworks is more than 100. But for the sake of brevity and clarity, we show the bar charts for ten largest job families (in terms of number of jobs included) for all three training corpus sizes.

The comparison of R_i values for ten of the biggest job families corresponding to N_1, N_2 and N_3 can be seen in Figs. 4, 5 and 6 respectively.

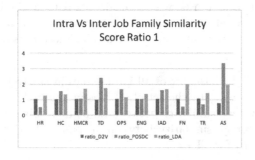

Fig. 4. 10 largest job families' R_i values for N_1

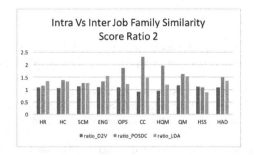

Fig. 5. 10 largest job families' R_i values for N_2

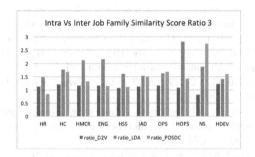

Fig. 6. 10 largest job families' R_i values for N_3

5   Conclusion and Future Work

The core novelty of POSDC is that unlike LDA or doc2vec, it doesn't require any prior training on large corpus. It uses the inherent semantics of job descriptions to find the similarity using available dictionary. As can be seen in our results, it is consistently superior to doc2vec, and even superior to LDA based method when the corpus available to train is smaller. The future work in this direction would be to define similar paradigm(s) for other/generic documents.

In the current approach, we have assumed that there is no duplication or alternate description of the same action-object-attribute triplet within a document. If that is not the case, then effectively the same action-object-attribute triplet in one job may get matched to different ones in another job. This can be overcome by first matching a job description with itself, and removing pairs of action-object-attribute triplets that match with a score above a threshold.

Another possible future direction could be more domain specific rather than being problem specific. Since our motivation to tackle this problem is to find jobs that are similar, we could combine similarity between job title [8] and POSDC to improve upon RISE [19].

References

1. Apache Spark. https://spark.apache.org. Accessed 23 May 2017
2. Apache Spark Wiki. https://en.wikipedia.org/wiki/Apache_Spark. Accessed 23 May 2017
3. NLTK. http://www.nltk.org. Accessed 23 May 2017
4. Watson Natural Language Understanding Service. Accessed 05 Jan 2017
5. Wordnet NLTK. http://www.nltk.org/howto/wordnet.html. Accessed 23 May 2017
6. Wordnet Synsets. https://wordnet.princeton.edu. Accessed 23 May 2017
7. WUP Similarity. http://www.nltk.org/howto/wordnet.html. Accessed 23 May 2017
8. Ahuja, S., Mondal, J., Singh, S.S., George, D.G.: Similarity computation exploiting the semantic and syntactic inherent structure among job titles. In: Maximilien, M., Vallecillo, A., Wang, J., Oriol, M. (eds.) ICSOC 2017. LNCS, vol. 10601, pp. 3–18. Springer, Cham (2017). https://doi.org/10.1007/978-3-319-69035-3_1
9. Aizawa, A.: An information-theoretic perspective of tf-idf measures. Inf. Proces. Manag. **39**(1), 45–65 (2003). http://www.sciencedirect.com/science/article/pii/S0306457302000213
10. Friedland, L., Allan, J.: Joke retrieval: recognizing the same joke told differently. In: Proceedings of the 17th ACM Conference on Information and Knowledge Management, pp. 883–892. ACM (2008)
11. Gabrilovich, E., Markovitch, S.: Computing semantic relatedness using Wikipedia-based explicit semantic analysis. In: IJcAI, vol. 7, pp. 1606–1611 (2007)
12. Hu, J., Fang, L., Cao, Y., Zeng, H.J., Li, H., Yang, Q., Chen, Z.: Enhancing text clustering by leveraging Wikipedia semantics. In: Proceedings of the 31st Annual International ACM SIGIR Conference on Research and Development in Information Retrieval, pp. 179–186. ACM (2008)
13. Huang, A.: Similarity measures for text document clustering. In: Proceedings of the Sixth New Zealand Computer Science Research Student Conference (NZCSRSC 2008), Christchurch, New Zealand, pp. 49–56 (2008)
14. Kuhn, H.W.: The Hungarian method for the assignment problem. Naval Res. Logist. Q. **2**(1–2), 83–97 (1955)
15. Le, Q.V., Mikolov, T.: Distributed representations of sentences and documents. CoRR abs/1405.4053 (2014). http://arxiv.org/abs/1405.4053
16. Manning, C.D., Schütze, H.: Foundations of Statistical Natural Language Processing (1999)
17. Matveeva, I., Levow, G.A., Farahat, A., Royer, C.: Generalized latent semantic analysis for term representation. In: Proceedings of the of RANLP (2005)
18. Pak, A.N., Chung, C.W.: A Wikipedia matching approach to contextual advertising. World Wide Web **13**(3), 251–274 (2010)
19. Pimplikar, R.R., Kannan, K., Mondal, A., Mondal, J., Saxena, S., Parija, G., Devulapalli, C.: RISE: resolution of identity through similarity establishment on unstructured job descriptions. In: Maximilien, M., Vallecillo, A., Wang, J., Oriol, M. (eds.) ICSOC 2017. LNCS, vol. 10601, pp. 19–36. Springer, Cham (2017). https://doi.org/10.1007/978-3-319-69035-3_2

A Tri-Partite Neural Document Language Model for Semantic Information Retrieval

Gia-Hung Nguyen[1]([⊠]) [iD], Lynda Tamine[1] [iD], Laure Soulier[2] [iD],
and Nathalie Souf[1] [iD]

[1] Université de Toulouse, UPS-IRIT, 118 route de Narbonne,
31062 Toulouse, France
gia-hung.nguyen@irit.fr
[2] Sorbonne Université, CNRS - LIP6 UMR 7606, 75005 Paris, France

Abstract. Previous work in information retrieval have shown that using evidence, such as concepts and relations, from external knowledge sources could enhance the retrieval performance. Recently, deep neural approaches have emerged as state-of-the art models for capturing word semantics. This paper presents a new tri-partite neural document language framework that leverages explicit knowledge to jointly constrain word, concept, and document learning representations to tackle a number of issues including polysemy and granularity mismatch. We show the effectiveness of the framework in various IR tasks.

Keywords: Semantic information retrieval · Knowledge source
Deep learning

1 Introduction

The semantic gap is a long-standing research topic in information retrieval (IR) that refers to the difference between the low-level description of document and/or query content (in general bags of words) and the high level of their meanings [30]. The semantic gap inherently hinders the query-document matching which is the crucial step for selecting candidate relevant documents in response to a user's query. The semantic gap commonly originates from the following: (1) *Vocabulary mismatch*, also called *lexical gap*, which means that words with different shapes share the same accepted meaning (senses) (e.g., *car is a synonym of motorcar*); (2) *Granularity mismatch* which means that words with different shapes and senses belong to the same general concept (e.g., *air bag and wheel are both parts of a car*); (3) *Polysemy* which means that a word could cover different senses depending on its surrounding words in the text that represent its context (e.g., *bass* could mean a type of fish or the lowest part of harmony).

To close these gaps, the prominent approaches employed in IR focus on the improvement of query and/or document representations using explicit knowledge provided by external knowledge sources or implicit knowledge inferred from text corpora. A first line of work is based on the use of linguistic sources (e.g., Word-Net) or knowledge graphs (e.g., DBpedia). The key idea of these approaches

© Springer International Publishing AG, part of Springer Nature 2018
A. Gangemi et al. (Eds.): ESWC 2018, LNCS 10843, pp. 445–461, 2018.
https://doi.org/10.1007/978-3-319-93417-4_29

is to inject knowledge about entities/concepts and semantic relations between them (e.g., relations of synonymy or hyperonymy) into query and/or document representations [5,26]. Another line of work particularly tackles the lexical gap in IR through distributional semantics which relies on the assumption that word senses could be inferred from their distribution in the text. Specifically, recent approaches in this category of work aim at projecting word senses in a continuous latent space using neural language models [16] to learn distributed representations of words (also called "word embeddings") using their context. However, authors in [10] have shown that traditional word embeddings are not able to cope with the polysemy problem. Recently, some work [3,15] have tackled this issue. For instance, Cheng et al. [3] propose to extend the skip-gram model [16] to identify the relevant word-concept pairwise given a context by jointly training the corresponding embeddings. The connection between words and concepts is set up based on either implicit senses (corpus-based) or explicit senses (inventoried in a knowledge source).

In this work, we propose a neural network-based model that can jointly cope with the three semantic gap factors mentioned above. The model is based on a semantically-oriented approach of concept/entity, word, and document embeddings which is based on the joint use of raw textual data and knowledge sources within the same embedding space. The model has a high level of generalizability in terms of use in the semantic web since (1) the learned embeddings can be integrated in different tasks such as entity linking [18], semantic annotation of unstructured or structured data [6], ontology matching by estimating levels of alignments between concepts embeddings learned using different ontologies, information extraction from texts by ranking candidate concept/entity embeddings with respect to document embedding, and, word sense disambiguation by using word embeddings as features of a supervised disambiguation method; (2) a wide range of knowledge sources (linguistic, knowledge graphs,...) can be used as evidence in the learning process of the semantic representations. The contributions of the paper are:

- We design a tri-partite neural language model that learns representations of documents, concept/entity and word representations, constrained by the pre-established relations existing in a knowledge source (Sect. 3).
- We experimentally show the quality and effectiveness of the learned representations for semantic IR tasks (Sects. 4 and 5).

2   Related Work

Traditional Neural Approaches for Learning Text Representations.
Building distributed word representations (also called "word embeddings") from large corpora has received increasing attention since the introduction of the probabilistic neural network language model [2]. The *distributional hypothesis* [9] assumes that the representation of words with similar distributions should have similar meanings. For example, two efficient neural network models (i.e.,

word2vec) [16] use the co-occurrence of words to learn word representations. Specifically, the continuous bag-of-word (CBOW) model predicts a target word by maximizing the log-likelihood of its context words in a sliding word window while the second model (skip-gram) tries to predict the context words given the target word. These word representations have attracted lots of research from the IR community these last years with new relevance models [22,29,31]. Going beyond the word level, some work proposes to learn distributed representations of text such as sentences, paragraphs, or documents [25]. A simple but efficient approach consists in inferring the document representation from embeddings of its words. A more complex approach is inspired by neural language models [11,12]. Following the CBOW and the skip-gram frameworks [16] respectively, the Siamese CBOW model [11] and the Skip-thought [12] learn sentence representations by either predicting a sentence from its surrounding sentences or its context sentences from the encoded sentence. As an extension of word2vec, the Paragraph-Vector model [13] jointly learns paragraph (or document) and word representations within the same embedding space. This joint learning relies on the compositional assumption underlying document representation [17,25] leading to a mutual benefit for learning the distributional semantics of both documents and words.

Neural Approaches Empowered by Knowledge Sources for Learning Text Representations. Although distributed representations can efficiently model the semantics of words, using solely the document collection as knowledge evidence source does not allow to cope with three fundamental problems: (1) the readability of the captured word senses since the latter are not easily mappable to lexical sources leading to a limited usefulness [15]; (2) the polysemy problem since neural models fail to discriminate among different senses of a target word [10]; (3) the data sparsity problem since neural approaches based on the distributional hypothesis learn solely on corpus-based cooccurrences of words which prevents the learning of close word representations for semantically close words occurring in different word-based contexts. To tackle these problems, neural approaches investigated the joint use of both corpus-based word distributions and knowledge sources to achieve more accurate text representations [7,14,15,27].

A first line of pioneer work [7,14] have proposed to enhance the readability of the distributed representations of words learned from corpora by leveraging the *relational semantics* expressed in external knowledge sources. The intuition of those work is bring semantically related words (via relations in a knowledge source) closer to each other in the vector space. For instance, the *retrofitting* method [7] leverages lexicon-derived relational information of words by minimizing both (1) the distance of each word with the representation of all connected words in the semantic graph and (2) its distance with the pre-trained word representation, namely its initial distributed representation.

The second and recent line of work aims at refining word embedding using relational constraints to better discriminate word senses by simultaneously learning the concept representations and inferring word senses, and accordingly tackling the polysemy issue [3,4,15,21,27]. Mancini et al. [15] simultaneously learn embeddings for both words and their senses via a semantic network based on the CBOW architecture. The originality of this work relies on the fact that words might be associated with multiple senses, allowing refining embeddings according to the polysemy issue. Unlikely, Cheng et al. [3] assume that polysemy can be captured through context words and therefore propose to compute parallel word-concept skip-grams for each context word by introducing their associated concept in the prediction. In the same mind, Yamada et al. [27] propose a Named Entity disambiguation model that exploits word and concept embeddings learned in a two-step methodology. More particularly, word and concept latent spaces are first learned separately in skip-gram frameworks and then are aligned using word-concept anchors derived from the knowledge source.

There are two key differences between all these close previous work [3,4,15,27] and ours. First, unlike these past approaches, we tackle the readability of word senses and polysemy problems by learning document representations that leverage semantics inventoried in both text corpora and knowledge sources through fine-grained elements including words and concepts in a joint learning process. Moreover, in contrast to [4] that considers the document context as a temporal feature directly injected in the objective function, we assume that there is a mutual benefit to learning simultaneously document, word, and concept embeddings to better capture the semantics at global and local levels. Second, we also tackle the data sparsity problem and show the quality of the learned representations of documents as well as related concepts and words used as auxiliary information to enhance the query-document matching while most of previous work focused on the polysemy problem within NLP tasks.

3   The Tripartite Neural Document Language Model

In this paper, we address the vocabulary mismatch, the granularity mismatch and the polysemy issues through two assumptions:

- *Multi-level context view (A1)*: we conjecture that each word conveys a unique sense within the same document with respect to a relevant concept in a knowledge source; however, a word could convey different senses and being polysemous across documents. Thus, simultaneously learning representations within a multi-level context (namely a global vs. local level for resp. document vs. word and concept contexts) allows embeddings better facing the polysemy issue.
- *Knowledge source-based context view (A2)*: constraining the learning of word-concept pairs with respect to a knowledge source structure allows obtaining close word embeddings for words sharing the same concept even if they occur in different contexts in the document. Thus, granularity mismatch is partially or completely solved based on the knowledge source context.

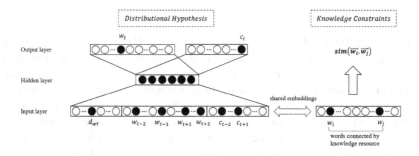

Fig. 1. Model architecture of our tri-partite neural document language model

3.1   Neural Network Architecture

We propose a tri-partite neural document language model that jointly learns the representations of words, concepts, and documents with a prior provided by an external knowledge source. To do so, our model is an extension of the ParagraphVector model [13] which has the same generalizability property with respect to new documents. The objective function fits with: (1) assumption *A1* through component L_C which learns embeddings by making predictions from words and concepts that occur within the multi-level context; (2) assumption *A2* formalized through component L_R which regularizes the embeddings using the relational knowledge constraints. The resulting objective function is:

$$L = L_C + \beta L_R \tag{1}$$

where β is the combination coefficient which is experimentally set to the optimal value according to the validation set (Sect. 4.3). We detail next the training of the embeddings according to the multi-view context (L_C) and their regularization with respect to the knowledge source context (L_R). Formally, the training set consists of the set $\mathcal{S} = \{\mathcal{D}, \mathcal{W}, \mathcal{C}\}$, where $\mathcal{D}$ expresses the collection of documents d, viewed as sequences of ordered words w and ordered associated concepts c within their surrounding contexts; $\mathcal{W}$ is the word-based vocabulary of the document collection $\mathcal{D}$ and $\mathcal{C}$ is the set of concepts in the knowledge source $\mathcal{R}$ that provides knowledge about concepts and relations between concepts. Given document d, we use the automatic annotator TagMe [8] to identify the context-appropriate concept $c_i \in \mathcal{C}$, if any, associated to word $w_i \in d$ according to the mapping of its word-based surrounding context to the knowledge source R. Thus, each window considered in the model training is a sequence of words and their associated concepts (if any). We outline that in this work, we only consider single word-concept mapping within the source R and leave the mapping of multi-word concepts for future work. Figure 1 shows our learning framework on a simple training instance.

3.2 Network Training

Learning the Word, Concept, and Document Representations. In this work, we propose to extend the Distributed Memory version of the *Paragraph Vector* model [13] to learn document embeddings by jointly predicting each word-concept pairwise given their context in the document. In other words, document vectors v_d are learned so they allow predicting its belonging words and concepts, while word vectors v_w and concept vectors v_c are learned so they predict words and concepts in their surrounding context. Specifically, the objective of our joint document-word-concept training is to maximize this log-likelihood:

$$L_C = \sum_{d \in \mathcal{D}} \sum_{w_t \in \mathcal{W}s_d} [\log p(w_t | w_{t \pm k}, c_{t \pm k}, d) + \log p(c_t | w_{t \pm k}, c_{t \pm k}, d) - \frac{\gamma}{|d|} ||v_d||^2]$$

$$(2)$$

where the word sequence of document d is noted $\mathcal{W}s_d$, $w_{t \pm k}$ and $c_{t \pm k}$ refer respectively to word and concept contexts within a context window surrounding term w_t of size k, c_t is the most appropriate concept mapped to word w_t within its context, $\frac{\gamma}{|d|} ||v_d||^2$ is a $L2$ regularizer over the document vector v_d avoiding over-fitting the representation learning of long texts [1] with $|d|$ is the document length and γ is the regularization strength. The probability $p(w_t | w_{t \pm k}, c_{t \pm k}, d)$ of word w_t given its context is defined using a soft-max function:

$$p(w_t | w_{t \pm k}, c_{t \pm k}, d) = \frac{\exp(v_{w_t}^\top \cdot \overline{h}_{w_t})}{\sum_{w' \in \mathcal{W}} \exp(v_{w'}^\top \cdot \overline{h}_{w_t})}$$

$$(3)$$

where $\mathcal{W}$ is the word vocabulary of the collection, $\overline{h}_{w_t}$ is the representation of the context window taken by averaging the input vectors v of the context words $w_{t \pm k}$ and their concepts $c_{t \pm k}$ including document d:

$$\overline{h}_{w_t} = \frac{1}{4k + 1} \left(v_d + \sum_{-k \leq j \leq k, j \neq 0} (v_{w_{t+j}} + v_{c_{t+j}}) \right)$$

$$(4)$$

where the context window of size k includes $2k$ context words. Therefore, $4k + 1$ stands for the number of words and concepts ($+1$ for document d) in the extreme case where each word is mapped to a concept. Similarly, the probability $p(c_t | w_{t \pm k}, c_{t \pm k}, d_{w_t})$ is estimated as:

$$p(c_t | w_{t \pm k}, c_{t \pm k}, d) = \frac{\exp(v_{c_t}^\top \cdot \overline{h}_{c_t})}{\sum_{c' \in \mathcal{C}} \exp(v_{c'}^\top \cdot \overline{h}_{c_t})}$$

$$(5)$$

where $\overline{h}_{c_t}$ is the representation of the context window for concept c_t, estimated similarly to $\overline{h}_{w_t}$ (see Eq. 4). With the large size of $\mathcal{W}$ and $\mathcal{C}$, Eqs. (3) and (5) become impractical. Following [16], we define the alternative objective functions by using the negative sampling strategy for each element $e_t \in \{w_t; c_t\}$:

$$p(e_t | w_{t \pm k}, c_{t \pm k}, d) = \log \sigma(v_{e_t}'^\top \cdot \overline{h}_{e_t}) + \sum_{i=1}^{n} \mathbb{E}_{e_i \sim P_n(e)} \left[\log \sigma(-v_{e_i}'^\top \cdot \overline{h}_{e_t}) \right]$$

$$(6)$$

$\sigma(x)$ is the sigmoid function $\sigma(x) = \frac{1}{1+e^{-x}}$ and $\mathbb{E}_{e_i \sim P_n(e)}$ the expected value of $\log \sigma(-v'^\top_{e_i} \cdot \overline{h}_{e_t})$ when e_i is taken from the unigram distribution $P_n(e)$ [1].

Constraining the Representation Learning with a Knowledge Source Structure. To address the granularity mismatch, we propose to capture relations between words which may not be (sufficiently) learned from the document context in the case where they do not (frequently) occur in the same contexts in documents, which is likely to be explained by data sparsity. Inspired by previous work [28], we equip the objective function with a regularization term which integrates the relational constraints from the knowledge source into word representations. The regularization will simultaneously adjust the word representations with the learning of documents in the training phase such that words that share the same concept or share related concepts have close embeddings. Formally, our objective is to maximize the similarity between any pair of words (w_i, w_j) according to the following objective function:

$$L_R = \sum_{(w_i, w_j) \in W \times W \; \setminus \; linkC(w_i,w_j)=1 \; or \; linkR(w_i,w_j)=1} sim(w_i, w_j) \qquad (7)$$

where $linkC(w_i, w_j) = 1$ if words w_i and w_j are associated to the same concept and $linkR(w_i, w_j) = 1$ if these words are associated to related concepts. $sim(w_i, w_j)$ is the cosine similarity between both word vectors v_{w_i} and v_{w_j}.

4 Experimental Design

The objective of our evaluation is twofold: (1) assessing the quality of document embeddings learned using our neural model and (2) measuring the impact of the learned representations on the effectiveness of IR tasks. The source code of our model and the learned embeddings will be available at https://cloud.irit.fr/index.php/s/NQqk8fgZI7lIIGp.

4.1 Dataset

We use the Robust04 collection[1] which is the standard news dataset used in the standard evaluation challenge TREC Robust Track 2004 including 528,155 documents and 250 topics. The title of each topic has been collected to build the set of queries. To enhance the representations with relational semantics, we exploit DBpedia as knowledge source due to its large coverage. Queries and documents are annotated by *TagMe*[2] [8], a publicly available state-of-the-art annotation tool for linking text to DBpedia entities. We use the names of DBpedia base entities to annotate the queries and documents and exploit the gold:hypernym relation.

---

[1] http://trec.nist.gov/data/robust/04.guidelines.html: the dataset is available for the scientific community under acceptance of a license agreement.

[2] https://tagme.d4science.org/tagme/.

For the sake of simplicity with respect to the model description in Sect. 3, we refer to entities by concepts. The annotation of the Robust04 collection results in 1 to 3 concept-length, with 1 concept in average and documents with 31 concepts in average (over 488 words in average).

4.2   Evaluation Methodology

We evaluate our proposed tri-partite model according to three scenarios:

- **PV:** which refers to the Paragraph-Vector Model [13] from which we build our extended neural model. This scenario learns word and document representations without using any evidence from an external knowledge source.
- **S2DV:** this scenario learns document, word, and concept representations by using concepts from a knowledge source as formulated in the component L_C of the objective function L (Eq. 1). But, this setting ignores the relationships established between concepts, and so, skips the regularization component L_R.
- **S2DVR:** our full proposed learning model that learns document, word, and concept representations by using both concepts and their relationships established in a knowledge source as formulated in the full objective function L.

Moreover, with respect to the experimental objectives mentioned above, we use two evaluation frameworks detailed below.

Evaluating the Quality of Document Embeddings. Considering the primary objective of our model which consists in learning document representations, we first evaluate the quality of the learned document embeddings. To achieve this goal, we use the document similarity task described in the pioneer work of Le and Mikolov [13] which consists in discriminating the similarity of documents with respect to a target query. More specifically, for each query in the dataset, we create a pool of document triplet in which the two first ones are retrieved from a state-of-the IR model according to this query and the third document is randomly sampled from document rankings with respect to other queries. The underlying objective is to measure in which extent the document similarity metric (namely the standard cosine similarity) estimated using learned document representations allows to provide a more important similarity for documents issued from the same target query and a smaller similarity for documents issued from other queries. Similar to [13], we use the error rate over all the queries measuring when representations give smaller similarity for the first two documents than the third one. Obviously, the lower the error rate is, the more effective the document representation is. To evaluate the quality of our document embeddings, we compare the error rates obtained using the embeddings provided by our model to those obtained using the following document representations:

- **TF-IDF** which refers to the traditional document modeling in IR in which documents are represented through a word vector weighted using the Tf-Idf schema. This baseline aims at measuring the effect of using distributional semantics on the quality of the embeddings.

- **AWE** [25] which builds document embeddings by averaging the embedding of its words. The goal behind the comparison with this representation is to evaluate the impact of considering a multi-level context (namely concepts and documents in addition to words) on the quality of the embeddings.

Evaluating the Effectiveness of Embeddings within IR Tasks. To evaluate the effectiveness of the obtained embeddings on IR performance, we propose two types of IR models in which those embeddings are injected. Performance effectiveness of these models is measured using standard metrics: the Mean Average Precision (MAP) and the Recall at rank 1000.

- *Document re-ranking.* This type of model consists in enhancing a basic document relevance score with an additional score based on an external evidence. To inject the learned embeddings, we combine a traditional document relevance score with a similarity score computed between the query and the document embeddings. We specifically use the model proposed in [14]:

$$RSV(Q, D) = \alpha \cdot IRScore(Q, D) + (1 - \alpha) \cdot NeuralScore(Q, D) \quad (8)$$

where α is a combination parameter tuned using a two-fold cross-validation according to the MAP metric, $IRScore$ is the document score obtained using a traditional IR model, namely BM25, and $NeuralScore$ is the cosine similarity between the query and the document representations. While document embeddings are learned using our framework, the query embeddings are considered as "unseen documents" for which the representation is inferred from the learned model, as done in the ParagraphVector model [13].

- *Query expansion.* This type of model consists in rewriting the initial query by exploiting an external evidence. In our setting, we use evidence issued from relevant words and/or concepts based on the assumption that relevance could be captured by computing similarities between query embeddings in one side and word/concept embeddings in the other side. To do so, we rely on the state-of-the art model proposed in [29] in which queries are expanded using each element e (namely words and/or concepts) with the highest neural similarity score $p(e|\hat{q})$:

$$p(e|\hat{q}) = \frac{\sigma(\hat{e}, \hat{q})}{Z} \quad (9)$$

where $\hat{q}$ and $\hat{e}$ are respectively the embeddings of query q (learned as explained above) and word/concept element e, $\sigma(\cdot, \cdot)$ denotes the exponential cosine similarity of two vectors and Z is the normalization factor calculated by summing $\sigma(\hat{e'}, q)$ over all terms e' in the vocabulary (namely all words over all documents or all concepts extracted from all words). Then, this neural probability is linearly interpolated with the maximum likelihood estimation $p_{mle}(e|q)$ of the original query (namely, term-based count probability) as follows:

$$p(e|q*) = \alpha p_{mle}(e|q) + (1 - \alpha)p(e|\hat{q}) \quad (10)$$

The top m elements (words and/or concepts) with the highest probabilities $p(e|q*)$ are used to expand the initial query.

For comparative effectiveness purpose, we inject the learned representation obtained using the PV, S2DV, and S2DVR scenarios within each of the models described above. In addition, we compare the effectiveness of those models to a traditional baseline IR model that does not rely on a neural approach. To keep fair comparison, we choose a semantic baseline IR model, noted **LM-QE** [20]. The latter performs a language-based query expansion with semantically related concepts. Using such baseline additionally ensures the comparability of results with scenarios S2DV and S2DVR since all these models are likely faced to the problem of word sense disambiguation that could degrade retrieval performance as already shown in past work [19].

4.3   Experimental Setting

For the distributional-based model configurations (PV, SD2V, SD2VR), we set the dimension of embeddings to 300 and empirically select the window size $k = 8$. After removing non-alphanumeric words, we only keep words with frequency in the corpus higher than 5. The initial learning rate is set to 0.02 and decreased linearly during the SGD training process. We use the negative sampling technique where the negative sample is set to 5. The β parameter in Eq. 1 is set up to 10^{-5}. We test the regularization strength γ in Eq. 2 from 0.1, 1, and 10 as suggested in [1], the best performance is obtained with $\gamma = 0.1$. In practice, it is worth mentioning that since our model is based on the ParagraphVector learning mechanism, the integration of concepts in the input vector simply increases the training time linearly function of the vocabulary size. The complexity of the model is likely impacted by the regularization term. The inference to new documents or queries is not time-consuming. All the retrieval models are performed using the Indri[3] search engine.

Table 1. Comparative results for the document similarity task measuring the quality of our document embeddings. %Chg: error rate reduction w.r.t. SD2VR.

Model	Error rate	%Chg
TF-IDF	7.2%	−12.5%
Avg-WE	9.6%	−34.37%
PV	7.9%	−20.25%
SD2V	8.3%	−24.09%
SD2VR	6.3%	

5   Results

5.1   Analyzing the Quality of Document Embeddings

We analyze here the quality of document embeddings using the document similarity task described in Sect. 4.2. Table 1 illustrates the obtained results in terms

---

[3] https://www.lemurproject.org/indri.php.

PV   SD2VR

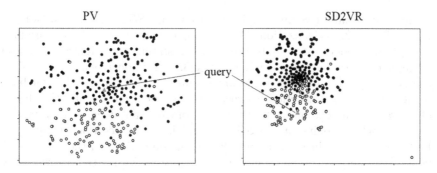

Fig. 2. A t-SNE projection of document embeddings issued from the *PV* (left side) and the *SD2V* models (right side) for the query 443 (yellow triangle). Relevant documents are white, irrelevant documents are black. (Color figure online)

of error rate for each scenario (PV, SD2V, SD2VR) in comparison to each baseline (TF-IDF and AWE). From a general point of view, we could say that our full model *S2DVR* obtains better results than all the scenarios and baselines. We can observe that using relational information between concepts for learning document embeddings lowers the error rate of -24.09% (from 8.3% for the *SD2V* scenario to 6.3% for the *S2DVR* one). One could infer from this observation that there is a synergic effect for representing documents while learning jointly the implicit relations between words in the text and the explicit relations between its associated concepts as inventoried in a knowledge source. This statement clearly argues toward the effectiveness of our model to cope with both the polysemy and granularity mismatch problems. Second, we can see that learning document embedding by leveraging both concepts and relations allows building document representations better suited for capturing the document semantics. Specifically, by comparing our best scenario (*SD2VR*) with respect to the different baselines, we could suggest the following statements:

- Our full model *SD2VR* decreases the error rate of -12.5% with respect to the *TF-IDF* baseline. This result is consistent with previous work [13] that argues toward the benefit behind learning document representations by leveraging the distributional semantics. We can also see that the error rate for the scenario *SD2VR* based on a multi-level of distributional semantics (6.3%) is lower than the one obtained by the *AWE* baseline (9.6%) which estimates document representations at the word level. This result is also consistent with prior work [13]. In this spirit, we show that the error rate obtained by the *PV* baseline (7.9%) is lower than the one obtained by the *AWE* baseline (9.6%).
- In addition to these findings, we can see that our full model *SD2VR* scenario allows to drastically decline the error rate of -20.25% with respect to the *PV* baseline. This confirms our intuition about the benefit of integrating the relational semantics inventoried in knowledge sources while learning distributed representations of documents. We further this quantitative analysis with a

comparative qualitative analysis between *PV* and *SD2VR*. The results highlighted from a 2D-visualization of queries and document embeddings obtained using both models corroborate the previous statements. Figure 2 shows an example of query output, namely query 443, and its document set including the ground truth and other irrelevant documents. We can see that for both models, there is a distinction between two clusters of documents (the cluster of relevant documents in white, the cluster of irrelevant documents in black). However, when looking at the *SD2VR* model, we can see that the query is better located within the relevant cluster, in comparison to the *PV* model, where the query is centered between both clusters with a trend toward the cluster of irrelevant documents.

5.2 Evaluating the Effectiveness of Learned Embeddings in IR Tasks

Table 2 presents the results obtained for document re-ranking and query expansion tasks according to the different scenarios (PV, SD2V, SD2VR) and the retrieval baseline (LM-QE). Below, we discuss the results obtained within each of both tasks and then we conduct a cross-analysis of the main emerging results.

Document Re-ranking. From a general point of view, we can see from Table 2 two main statements:

- Our full model scenario (SD2VR) significantly overpasses the semantic IR model *LM-QE* with an improvement rate reaching +17.73%. This suggests, according to formula 8, that the injection of the neural similarity scores in the relevance document score computation enhances the ranking performance. By comparing to the LM-QE baseline, we can conjecture that this is probably due the use of the deep semantic representation of documents. This is confirmed by the results obtained using the *PV* scenario compared to the LM-QE baseline. However, as we can see, considering additional evidence issued from the knowledge source seems to hinder the document re-ranking performance since the performance results achieved with both *SD2V* and *SD2VR* are lower than the *PV* scenario. A deep analysis of this observation is reported in the cross-analysis.
- The comparison of our both scenarios *SD2V* and *SD2VR* shows that the full version of our model *SD2VR* slightly increases the search effectiveness. Similarly to findings risen from the analysis of the document similarity task, this result suggests that relations in knowledge sources provide useful relational knowledge for enhancing the quality of learned word representations.

Query Expansion Task. Table 2 presents the retrieval performance results obtained within the query expansion task by considering three configurations (See formulas 9–10): expanding with words only, expanding with concepts only, expanding with both words and concepts. As can be seen from

Table 2. Effect of the embeddings on retrieval effectiveness for both IR tasks in terms of MAP and Recall. Bold values express results higher than baselines.

	IR models		MAP	Recall
Semantic IR baseline	LM-QE		0.2110	0.6593
Document re-ranking	PV		0.2507	0.6895
	SD2V		0.2379	**0.6834**
	SD2VR		0.2384	**0.6841**
Query expansion	PV	word	0.2460	0.6804
	SD2V	word	0.2443	**0.6891**
		concept	**0.2497**	**0.6897**
		both	**0.2461**	**0.6894**
	SD2VR	word	0.2451	**0.6886**
		concept	**0.2516**	**0.6892**
		both	0.2489	**0.6890**

Table 2, the comparison of the performance results achieved using our proposed model (either in terms of MAP and Recall) outlines: (1) the superiority of the neural model scenarios (*PV* (0.2460), *SD2V* (0.2497), *SD2VR* (0.2516)) over the semantic baseline IR model *LM-QE* (0.2110) with respect to all query expansion configurations. This result highlights the ability of the word/concept embedding-based similarity to select good expansion elements, likely due to the quality of the embeddings themselves; (2) expanding queries with 'concepts only' seems to be the most successful retrieval scenario. More particularly, we observe that expanding queries with concepts identified on the basis of concept embeddings used in our both scenarios (SD2V, SD2VR) overpasses the *PV* scenario which is the strongest baseline in both evaluation tasks. For instance, the query 683 "Czechoslovakia breakup" is expanded with terms "use_chapel" and "targy" for the *PV* setting while the SD2VR setting allows to extend the query with concepts $#!*Czechoslovak_Socialist_Republic* and $#!*Dissolution_of_Czechoslovakia* which are more related to the query topic. This result could be considered as consistent with previous work [24] that argue toward the joint use of words and concepts to perform effective query expansion since, in our proposed model, concept embeddings are learned in a joint learning process of words and concepts.

Cross-Analysis and Discussion. One general result that we can infer from the above experiments is that retrieval performance depends heavily on the nature of the embeddings exploited and/or the nature of the retrieval task. This finding is consistent with the general feeling in the IR community that points on the variability of performance levels of semantic IR models [23]. More specifically, the analysis of the performance results of document re-ranking and query expansion tasks reveals that the embeddings learned using our tri-partite neural model are likely to be more effective to capture auxiliary knowledge to enhance the query representation than to improve a query-document relevance score. At a first glance, this observation could be explained by the fact that query expansion leverages the complete multi-level context including words, concepts, and documents, while the document re-ranking only leverages document representations. In addition, although document representations are used for both tasks, the document latent space serves to learn the representation of short queries in the query expansion task while this space serves to learn long documents in the document re-ranking task. Our intuition is that the accuracy of the alignment performed by our model between document vectors to both word and concept vectors might be sensitive to the disambiguation error introduced in the concept-based document annotation stage. To get a better insight on this intuition, we studied the relationship between the length of both documents/queries, in terms of concept numbers, and performance. This study revealed that only the document level is significant. More particularly, we performed a qualitative analysis aiming at measuring to what extent documents with higher number of concepts are less likely to be selected by our knowledge-based retrieval model, and most specifically by the document re-ranking model. We first identify query sets for which our best model $SD2VR$ performs worse (Q^-), identically ($Q^=$), or better (Q^+)

Table 3. Qualitative analysis of search effectiveness for the re-ranking task with respect to the document length criteria in terms of concept number.

Query set	#queries	Avg_concept_qrels	Avg_concept_docs
Q^-	117 (46.99%)	78.56	66.80
$Q^=$	7 (2.81%)	69.92	50.24
Q^+	125 (50.20%)	64.77	62.25

Table 4. Examples of top ranked document-query pairs belonging to Q^+ and Q^-. Terms in bold are query terms.

Q+ Q412: airport security	
Document FT941-4175 34 concepts relevant	...In spain $#!Spain, another european union country $#!Nation_state facing terrorist campaign, only armed police $#!Police have responsibility $#!Moral_responsibility for **security** $#!Security in **airports**. In Heathrow $#!Heathrow_Airport, since BAA $#!Heathrow_Airport_Holdings was privatised, [...]
Q- Q314: marine vegetation	
Document LA091189-0098 60 concepts irrelevant	[...] the **marine** $#!Ocean craft, the same color $#!Color as surrounding **vegetation**, was not easy to spot, singley said. [...]Because the plane route was not known and radar $#!Radar was unable to track it, **Marine** officials relied upon civilian reports in the search $#!The_Search_(2014_film) [...]

in terms of MAP than the PV model (with a margin ranging between $+/-5\%$). This baseline is particularly interesting since it does not involve concepts and so, abstracts the problem of word sense disambiguation. Second, we analyze the average number of identified concepts in relevant documents, namely the ground truth, (noted $Avg\_concept\_qrels$) and in top selected documents (noted $Avg\_concept\_docs$). Table 3 presents the obtained results. We can see that for worse queries (Q^-) the number of concepts in documents belonging to the ground truth is higher than the one for other query sets (namely 78.26 vs. 69.92 for $Q^=$ and 64.77 for Q^+). This suggests that our model is less able to catch the semantics of documents including a high number of concepts. To get a better insight on this phenomena, we depict in Table 4 an example of query extracted from both query sets Q^+ and Q^- and one associated top retrieved document obtained using our SD2VR scenario. We can see that the document retrieved by the query extracted from Q^+ is annotated with a few concepts that are semantically close to the query topic than those identified in the document retrieved for the query belonging to Q^- that are less-topically focused ($\$\#!Color$) or erroneously annotated ($\$\#!The\_Search\_(2014\_film)$). This observation corroborates our possible explanation related to the relationship that might exist between (1) the improper alignment of the document representations with word/concept vectors during the representation learning process, and (2) disambiguation error rate; particularly for documents that entail a high number of concepts. However, further investigation is needed.

6   Conclusion

In this paper, we introduce a new neural tri-partite document model powered with evidence issued from external knowledge sources to overcome the crucial semantic gap issue in IR. The key idea is to leverage explicit relational semantics, namely concepts and relations, provided in knowledge sources to enhance distributional-based document representations that could be injected in a retrieval model. The framework extends the ParagraphVector model by jointly learning document, word, and concept representations in a same distributional semantic space. The experimental evaluation shows the effectiveness of our framework for different IR settings. An interesting future work would be the generalization of the representation learning to multi-word concepts through compositional neural representations. The analysis of the sensitivity of these representations to disambiguation errors introduced by word sense disambiguation algorithms would also be worth of interest.

References

1. Ai, Q., Yang, L., Guo, J., Croft, W.B.: Analysis of the paragraph vector model for information retrieval. In: ICTIR, pp. 133–142. ACM (2016)
2. Bengio, Y., Schwenk, H., Senécal, J.S., Morin, F., Gauvain, J.L.: Neural probabilistic language models. In: Innovations in Machine Learning (2006)

3. Cheng, J., Wang, Z., Wen, J.R., Yan, J., Chen, Z.: Contextual text understanding in distributional semantic space. In: CIKM, pp. 133–142 (2015)
4. Choi, E., Bahadori, M.T., Searles, E., Coffey, C., Sun, J.: Multi-layer representation learning for medical concepts. In: KDD, pp. 1495–1504 (2016)
5. Corcoglioniti, F., Dragoni, M., Rospocher, M., Aprosio, A.P.: Knowledge extraction for information retrieval. In: Sack, H., Blomqvist, E., d'Aquin, M., Ghidini, C., Ponzetto, S.P., Lange, C. (eds.) ESWC 2016. LNCS, vol. 9678, pp. 317–333. Springer, Cham (2016). https://doi.org/10.1007/978-3-319-34129-3_20
6. Efthymiou, V., Hassanzadeh, O., Rodriguez-Muro, M., Christophides, V.: Matching web tables with knowledge base entities: from entity lookups to entity embeddings. In: d'Amato, C., Fernandez, M., Tamma, V., Lecue, F., Cudré-Mauroux, P., Sequeda, J., Lange, C., Heflin, J. (eds.) ISWC 2017. LNCS, vol. 10587, pp. 260–277. Springer, Cham (2017). https://doi.org/10.1007/978-3-319-68288-4_16
7. Faruqui, M., Dodge, J., Jauhar, S.K., Dyer, C., Hovy, E., Smith, N.A.: Retrofitting word vectors to semantic lexicons. In: NAACL (2015)
8. Ferragina, P., Scaiella, U.: TAGME: on-the-fly annotation of short text fragments (by Wikipedia entities). In: CIKM, pp. 1625–1628. ACM (2010)
9. Harris, Z.S.: Distributional structure. Word **10**(2–3), 146–162 (1954)
10. Iacobacci, I., Pilehvar, M.T., Navigli, R.: SensEmbed: learning sense embeddings for word and relational similarity. In: ACL, pp. 95–105 (2015)
11. Kenter, T., Borisov, A., de Rijke, M.: Siamese CBOW: Optimizing word embeddings for sentence representations. ACL 2016, pp. 941–951 (2016)
12. Kiros, R., Zhu, Y., Salakhutdinov, R.R., Zemel, R., Urtasun, R., Torralba, A., Fidler, S.: Skip-thought vectors. In: NIPS, pp. 3294–3302 (2015)
13. Le, Q.V., Mikolov, T.: Distributed representations of sentences and documents. In: ICML, pp. 1188–1196 (2014)
14. Liu, X., Nie, J.-Y., Sordoni, A.: Constraining word embeddings by prior knowledge – application to medical information retrieval. In: Ma, S., Wen, J.-R., Liu, Y., Dou, Z., Zhang, M., Chang, Y., Zhao, X. (eds.) AIRS 2016. LNCS, vol. 9994, pp. 155–167. Springer, Cham (2016). https://doi.org/10.1007/978-3-319-48051-0_12
15. Mancini, M., Camacho-Collados, J., Iacobacci, I., Navigli, R.: Embedding words and senses together via joint knowledge-enhanced training. In: CoNLL (2017)
16. Mikolov, T., Chen, K., Corrado, G., Dean, J.: Efficient estimation of word representations in vector space. arXiv preprint arXiv:1301.3781 (2013)
17. Mitchell, J., Lapata, M.: Vector-based models of semantic composition. In: ACL, pp. 236–244 (2008)
18. Moreno, J.G., Besançon, R., Beaumont, R., D'hondt, E., Ligozat, A.-L., Rosset, S., Tannier, X., Grau, B.: Combining word and entity embeddings for entity linking. In: Blomqvist, E., Maynard, D., Gangemi, A., Hoekstra, R., Hitzler, P., Hartig, O. (eds.) ESWC 2017. LNCS, vol. 10249, pp. 337–352. Springer, Cham (2017). https://doi.org/10.1007/978-3-319-58068-5_21
19. Navigli, R.: Word sense disambiguation: a survey. ACM Comput. Surv. **41**(2), 101–1069 (2009)
20. Pal, D., Mitra, M., Datta, K.: Improving query expansion using WordNet. J. Assoc. Inf. Sci. Technol. **65**(12), 2469–2478 (2014)
21. Rastogi, P., Poliak, A., Durme, B.V.: Training relation embeddings under logical constraints. In: KG4IR@SIGIR (2017)
22. Rekabsaz, N., Mitra, B., Lupu, M., Hanbury, A.: Toward incorporation of relevant documents in word2vec. In: Neu-IR@SIGIR (2017)
23. Richardson, R., Smeaton, A.F.: Using WordNet in a knowledge-based approach to information retrieval (1995)

24. Trieschnigg, D.: Proof of concept: concept-based biomedical information retrieval. Ph.D. thesis, University of Twente (2010)
25. Vulić, I., Moens, M.F.: Monolingual and cross-lingual information retrieval models based on (bilingual) word embeddings. In: SIGIR, pp. 363–372. ACM (2015)
26. Xiong, C., Callan, J.: Query expansion with freebase. In: ICTIR. ACM (2015)
27. Yamada, I., Shindo, H., Takeda, H., Takefuji, Y.: Joint learning of the embedding of words and entities for named entity disambiguation, pp. 250–259 (2016)
28. Yu, M., Dredze, M.: Improving lexical embeddings with semantic knowledge. In: ACL, pp. 545–550 (2014)
29. Zamani, H., Croft, W.B.: Estimating embedding vectors for queries. In: ICTIR, pp. 123–132. ACM (2016)
30. Zhao, R., Grosky, W.I.: Narrowing the semantic gap-improved text-based web document retrieval using visual features. IEEE Trans. Multimed. 4(2), 189–200 (2002)
31. Zuccon, G., Koopman, B., Bruza, P., Azzopardi, L.: Integrating and evaluating neural word embeddings in information retrieval. In: ADCS, p. 12. ACM (2015)

Multiple Models for Recommending Temporal Aspects of Entities

Tu Ngoc Nguyen[1(✉)] [iD], Nattiya Kanhabua[2(✉)], and Wolfgang Nejdl[1(✉)]

[1] L3S Research Center/Leibniz Universität Hannover, Hannover, Germany
{tunguyen,nejdl}@L3S.de
[2] NTENT España, Barcelona, Spain
nkanhabua@NTENT.com

Abstract. Entity aspect recommendation is an emerging task in semantic search that helps users discover serendipitous and prominent information with respect to an entity, of which *salience* (e.g., popularity) is the most important factor in previous work. However, entity aspects are temporally dynamic and often driven by events happening over time. For such cases, aspect suggestion based solely on salience features can give unsatisfactory results, for two reasons. First, salience is often accumulated over a long time period and does not account for *recency*. Second, many aspects related to an event entity are strongly time-dependent. In this paper, we study the task of temporal aspect recommendation for a given entity, which aims at recommending the most relevant aspects and takes into account time in order to improve search experience. We propose a novel *event-centric* ensemble ranking method that learns from multiple time and type-dependent models and dynamically trades off salience and recency characteristics. Through extensive experiments on real-world query logs, we demonstrate that our method is robust and achieves better effectiveness than competitive baselines.

1 Introduction

Beyond the traditional "ten blue links", to enhance user experience with entity-aware intents, search engines have started including more semantic information, (1) suggesting related entities [4,9,30,31], or (2) supporting entity-oriented query completion or complex search with additional information or *aspects* [1,22,26]. These aspects cover a wide range of issues and include (but are not limited to) types, attributes/properties, relationships or other entities in general. They can change over time, as *public attention* shifts from some aspects to others. In order to better recommend such entity aspects, this temporal dimension has to be taken into account.

Exploiting collaborative knowledge bases such as Wikipedia and Freebase is common practice in semantic search, by exploiting anchor texts and inter-entity links, category structure, internal link structure or entity types [4]. More recently, researchers have also started to integrate knowledge bases with query logs for *temporal* entity knowledge mining [5,30]. In this work, we address *the*

© Springer International Publishing AG, part of Springer Nature 2018
A. Gangemi et al. (Eds.): ESWC 2018, LNCS 10843, pp. 462–480, 2018.
https://doi.org/10.1007/978-3-319-93417-4_30

temporal dynamics of recommending entity aspects and also utilize query logs, for two reasons. First, query logs are strongly entity related: more than 70% of Web search queries contain entity information [19, 21]. Queries often also contain a short and very specific piece of text that represents users' intents, making it an ideal source for mining entity aspects. Second, different from knowledge-bases, query logs naturally capture temporal dynamics around entities. The intent of entity-centric queries is often triggered by a current event [17, 18], or is related to "what is happening right now".

Previous work do not address the problem of temporal aspect recommendation for entities, often event-driven. The task requires taking into account the impact of temporal aspect dynamics and explicitly considering the relevance of an aspect with respect to the time period of a related event. To demonstrate the characteristics of these entity aspects, we showcase a real search scenario, where entity aspects are suggested in the form of query suggestion/auto-completion, given the entity name as a prior. Figure 1 shows the lists of aspect suggestions generated by a well-known commercial search engine for academy awards 2017 and australia open 2017. These suggestions indicate that the top-ranked aspects are mostly time-sensitive, and as the two events had just ended, the recommended aspects are timeliness-wise irrelevant (e.g., *live, predictions*).

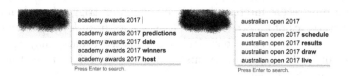

Fig. 1. [Screenshot] Recommendation generated by a commercial search engine for academy awards 2017 and australia open 2017, submitted on March 31th, 2017, on a clean history browser.

Although the exact techniques behind the search engine's recommendation are unknown, the mediocre performance might be caused by the effect of aspect salience (query popularity in this case) and the *rich get richer* phenomenon: the salience of an aspect is accumulated over a long time period. Figure 2 illustrates changes in popularity of relevant searches captured in the AOL (left) and Google (right) query logs (e.g., ncaa printable bracket, ncaa schedule, and ncaa finals) for the NCAA[1] tournament. The basketball event began on March 14, 2006, and concluded on April 3, 2006. In order to better understand this issue, we present two types of popularity changes, namely, (1) frequency or query volume (aggregated daily), and cumulative frequency. Frequencies of pre-event activities like printable bracket and schedule gain increased volume over time, especially in the *before* event period. On the other hand, up-to-date information about the event, such as, ncaa results rises in importance when the event has started

---

[1] A major sports competition in the US held annually by the National Collegiate Athletic Association (NCAA)- https://en.wikipedia.org/wiki/Ncaa.

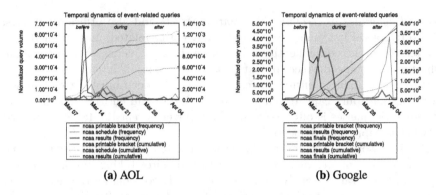

Fig. 2. Dynamic aspect behaviors for entity ncaa in AOL and Google.

(on March 14), with very low query volume before the event. While the popularity of results or finals aspect exceeds that of ncaa printable bracket significantly in the periods *during* and *after* event, the cumulative frequency of the pre-event aspect stays high. We witness similar phenomenon with the same event in 2017 in the Google query logs. We therefore postulate that (1) long-term salience should provide good ranking results for the periods *before* and *during*, whereas (2) short-term or recent interest should be favored on triggers or when the temporal characteristics of an event entity change, e.g., from *before/during* to *after* phase. Different event types (breaking or anticipated events) may vary significantly in term of the impact of events, which entails different treatments with respect to a ranking model.

Our contributions can be summarized as follows.

- We present the first study of temporal entity aspect recommendation that explicitly models triggered event time and type.
- We propose a learning method to identify time period and event type using a set of features that capture temporal dynamics related to event diffusion.
- We propose a novel event-centric ensemble ranking method that relies on multiple time and type-specific models for different event entities.

To this end, we evaluated our proposed approach through experiments using real-world web search logs – in conjunction with Wikipedia as background-knowledge repository.

2   Related Work

Entity aspect identification has been studied in [22,26]. [26] focuses on salient ranking features in microblogs. Reinanda et al. [22] start from the task of mining entity aspects in the query logs, then propose salience-favor methods for ranking and recommending these aspects. When regarding an aspect as an entity, related work connected to temporal IR is [31], where they study the task of time-aware entity recommendation using a probabilistic approach. The method also *implicitly* considers event times as triggering sources of temporal dynamics, yet relies on coarse-grained (monthly) granularity and does not recognize different phases of the event. It is therefore not really suitable for recommending fine-grained, temporal aspects. 'Static' entity recommendation was first introduced by the Spark [4] system developed at Yahoo! They extract several features from a variety of data sources and use a machine learning model to recommend entities to a Web search query. Following Spark, Sundog [9] aims to improve entity recommendation, in particular with respect to freshness, by exploiting Web search log data. The system uses a stream processing based implementation. In addition, Yu et al. [30] leverage user click logs and entity pane logs for global and personalized entity recommendation. These methods are tailored to ranking entities, and face the same problems as [31] when trying to generalize to 'aspects'.

It is also possible to relate these entity aspects to RDF properties/relations in knowledge bases such as FreeBase or Yago. [7,28] propose solutions for ranking these properties based on salience. Hasibi et al. [10] introduce dynamic fact based ranking (property-object pairs towards a sourced entity), also based on *importance* and *relevance*. These properties from traditional Knowledge Bases are often too specific (fact-centric) and temporally static.

3 Background and Problem Statement

3.1 Preliminaries

In this work, we leverage clues from entity-bearing queries. Hence, we first revisit the well-established notions of query logs and query-flow graphs. Then, we introduce necessary terminologies and concepts for entities and aspects. We will employ user log data in the form of queries and clicks.

Our datasets consist of a set of queries Q, a set of URLs U and click-through information S. Each query $q \in Q$ contains query terms $term(q)$, timestamps of queries $time(q)$ (so-called *hitting time*), and an anonymized ID of the user submitted the query. A clicked URL $u \in U_q$ refers to a Web document returned as an answer for a given query q. Click-through information is a transactional record per query for each URL clicked, i.e., an associated query q, a clicked URL u, the position on result page, and its timestamps. A co-clicked query-URL graph is a bipartite graph $G = (V, E)$ with two types of nodes: query nodes V_Q and URL nodes V_U, such that $V = V_Q \cup V_U$ and $E \subseteq V_Q \times V_U$.

3.2 Problem Definitions

We will approach the task of recommending temporal entity aspect as a ranking task. We first define the notions of an *entity query*, a *temporal entity aspect*, developed from the definition of entity aspect in [22], and an *event entity* . We then formulate the task of recommending temporal entity aspects.

Definition 1. *An entity query q_e is a query that is represented by one Wikipedia entity e. We consider q_e as the representation of e.*

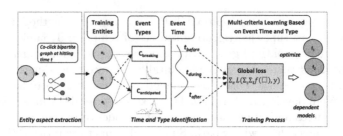

Fig. 3. Learning time and type-specific ranking models.

Definition 2. *Given a "search task" defined as an atomic information need, a temporal "entity aspect" is an entity-oriented search task with time-aware intent.* An entity-oriented search task is a set of queries that represent a common task in the context of an entity, grouped together if they have the same intent [22]. We will use the notion of query q to indicate an entity aspect a interchangeably hereafter.

Definition 3. *An entity that is related to a near event at time t_i is called an event-related entity, or event entity for short.* Relatedness is indicated by the observation that *public attention* of temporal entity aspects is triggered by the event. We can generalize the term *event entity* to represent any entity that is related to or influenced by the event. An event entity e that is associated to the event whose type $\mathscr{C}$ can be either *breaking* or *anticipated*. An event entity is also represented as a query with hitting time t. The association between t and the event time –defines e's time period $\mathscr{T}$– that can be either of the *before, during* or *after* phases of the event. When the entity is no longer event-related, it is considered a "static" entity.

Problem (Temporal Entity-Aspect Recommendation): *Given an event entity e and hitting time t as input, find the ranked list of entity aspects that most relevant with regards to e and t.*

Different from time-aware entity recommendation [27,31], for an entity query with exploratory intent, users are not just interested in related entities, but also entity aspects (which can be a topic, a concept or even an entity); these provide more complete and useful information. These aspects are very time-sensitive especially when the original entity is about an event. In this work, we use the notion of *event entity*, which is generalized to indicated related entities of any trending events. For example, Moonlight and Emma Stone are related entities for the 89th Academy Awards event. We will handle the aspects for such entities in a temporally aware manner.

4   Our Approach

As event entity identification has been well-explored in related work [14–16], we do not suggest a specific method, and just assume the use of an appropriate method. Given an event entity, we then apply our aspect recommendation method, which is composed of three main steps. We summarize the general idea of our approach in Fig. 3. First, we extract suggestion candidates using a bipartite graph of co-clicked query-URLs generated at hitting time. After the aspect extraction, we propose a *two-step* unified framework for our entity aspect ranking problem. The first step is to identify event type and time in a joint learning approach. Based on that, in the second step, we divide the training task to different sub-tasks that correspond to specific event type and time. Our intuition here is that the timeliness (or short-term interest) feature-group might work better for specific subsets such as breaking and after events and vice versa. Dividing the training will avoid timeliness and salience competing with each other and maximize their effectiveness. However, identifying time and type of an event on-the-fly is not a trivial task, and breaking the training data into smaller parts limits the learning power of the individual models. We therefore opt for an ensemble approach that can utilize the whole training data to (1) supplement the uncertainties of the time-and-type classification in the first step and (2) leverage the learning power of the sub-models in step 2. In the rest of this section, we explain our proposed approach in more detail.

4.1 Aspect Extraction

The main idea of our approach for extracting aspects is to find related entity-bearing queries; then group them into different clusters, based on *lexical* and *semantic* similarity, such that each cluster represents a distinct aspect. The click-through information can help identifying related queries [25] by exploiting the assumption that any two queries which share many clicked URLs are likely to be related to each other.

For a given entity query e, we perform the following steps to find aspect candidates. We retrieve a set of URLs U_e that were clicked for e from the beginning of query logs until the hitting time t_e. For each $u_j \in U_e$, we find a set of distinct queries for which u_j has been clicked. We give a weight w to each query-URL by normalizing *click frequency* and *inverse query frequency* (CF-IQF) [6], which calculate the importance of a click, based on click frequency and inverse query frequency. $CF - IQF = cf \cdot log(N/(qf + 1))$, where N is the number of distinct queries. A high weight $CF - IQF$ indicates a high click frequency for the query-URL pair and a low query frequency associated with the URL in the whole query log. To extract aspect candidates from the click bipartite graph, we employ a personalized random walk to consider only one side of the query vertices of the graph (we denote this approach as **RWR**). This results in a set of related queries (aspects) to the source entity e, ranked by click-flow relatedness score. To this end, we refine these extracted aspects by clustering them using Affinity Propagation (AP) on the similarity matrix of *lexical* and *semantic* similarities. For semantic measure, we use a *word2vec* skip-gram model trained with the English Wikipedia corpus from the same time as the query logs. We pick one aspect with highest frequency to represent each cluster, then select top-k aspects by ranking them using RWR relatedness scores[2].

4.2 Time and Type Identification

Our goal is to identify the probability that an event-related entity is of a specific event type, and in what time period of the event. We define these two targets as a joint-learning time-series classification task, that is based on event diffusion. In the following, we first present the feature set for the joint-learning task, then explain the learning model. Last we propose a light-weight clustering approach that leverages the learning features, to integrate with the ranking model in Sect. 4.3.

Features. We propose a set of time series features for our multi-class classification task. *seasonality* and *periodicity* are good features to capture the *anticipated* -recurrent events. In addition, we use additional features to model the temporal dynamics of the entity at studied/hitting time t_e. We leverage query logs and Wikipedia revision edits as the data sources for *short* and *long* span time series construction, denoted as $\psi_Q^{(e)}$ and $\psi_{WE}^{(e)}$ (for seasonal, periodical event signals) respectively[3]. The description of our features follows:

- **Seasonality** is a temporal pattern that indicates how periodic is an observed behavior over time. We leverage this time series decomposition technique for detecting not only seasonal events (e.g., Christmas Eve, US Open) [23] but also more fine-grained periodic ones that recurring on a weekly basis, such as a TV show program.
- **Autocorrelation**, is the cross correlation of a signal with itself or the correlation between its own past and future values at different times. We employ autocorrelation for detecting the trending characteristics of an event, which can be categorized by its predictability. When an event contains strong interday dependencies, the autocorrelation value will be high. Given observed time series values $\psi_1, ..., \psi_N$ and its mean $\bar{\psi}$, autocorrelation is the similarity between observations as a function of the time lag l between them. In this work, we consider autocorrelation at the one time unit lag only (l = 1), which shifts the second time series by one day.
- **Correlation coefficient**, measures the dynamics of two consecutive aspect ranked lists at time t_e and $t_e - 1$, return by **RWR**. We use Goodman and

---

[2] About complexity analysis, the click bipartite graph construction costs $O(m + n)$ and RWR in practice, can be bounded by $O(m + n)$ for top-k proximity nodes. Note that m, n are the number of edges and nodes respectively. AP is quadratic $O(kn^2)$ time, (with k is the number of iterations), of our choice as we aim for a simple and effective algorithm and our aspect candidate sets are not large. A more efficient algorithm such as the Hierarchical AP can be used when candidate sets are large. The cost of constructing the similarity matrix is $O(n^2)$.

[3] Wikipedia page views is an alternative, however it is not publicly available for the time of our query logs, 2006.

Kruskal's gamma to account for possible new or old aspects appear or disappear in the newer list.

- **Level of surprise**, measured by the error margin in prediction of the learned model on the time series. This is a good indicator for detecting the starting time of *breaking* events. We use Holt-Winters as the predictive model.
- **Rising and falling signals.** The intuition behind time identification is to measure whether $\psi_Q^{(e)}$ is going up (*before*) or down (*after*) or stays trending (*during*) at hitting time. Given $\psi_Q^{(e)}$, we adopt an effective parsimonious model called SpikeM [20], which is derived from epidemiology fundamentals to predict the rise and fall of event diffusion. We use the *Levenberg-Marquardt* algorithm to learn the parameter set and use the parameters as features for our classification task.

Learning Model. We assume that there is a semantic relation between the event types and times (e.g., the before phase of *breaking* events are different from *anticipated*). To leverage the dependency between the ground labels of the two classification tasks, we apply a joint learning approach that models the two tasks in a cascaded manner, as a simple version of [11]. Given the same input instance $\mathscr{I}$, the 1st stage of the cascaded model predicts the event type $\mathscr{C}$ with all proposed features. The trained model $\mathscr{M}^1$ is used in the 2nd stage to predict the event time $\mathscr{T}$. We use the logistic regression model $\mathscr{M}^2_{LR}$ for the 2nd stage, which allows us to add additional features from $\mathscr{M}^1$. The feature vector of $\mathscr{M}^2_{LR}$ consists of the same features as $\mathscr{M}^1$, together with the probability distribution of $P(\mathscr{C}_k|e,t)$ (output of $\mathscr{M}^1$) of as additional features.

Ranking-Sensitive Time and Type Distribution. The output of an effective classifier can be directly used for determining a time and type probability distribution of entities; and thus dividing the training entities into subsets for our *divide-and-conquer* ranking approach. However, having a pre-learned model with separate and large training data is expensive and could be detrimental to ranking performance if the training data is biased. We therefore opt for effective on-the-fly *ranking-sensitive* time and type identification, following [3] that utilizes the 'locality property' of feature spaces. We adjust and refine the approach as follows. Each entity is represented as a feature vector, and consists of all proposed features with importance weights learned from a sample of training entities (for ranking). We then employ a Gaussian mixture model to obtain the centroids of training entities. In our case, the number of components for clustering are fixed before hand, as the number of event types multiplied by the number of event times. Hence the probability distribution of entity e at time t belonging to time and type $\mathscr{T}_l, \mathscr{C}_k$, $P(\mathscr{T}_l, \mathscr{C}_k|e,t)$ is calculated as $1 - \frac{\|\mathbf{x}^e - \mathbf{x}^{c_{\mathscr{T}_l, \mathscr{C}_k}}\|^2}{\max_{\forall T,C}\|\mathbf{x}^e - \mathbf{x}^{c_{\mathscr{T}_l, \mathscr{C}_k}}\|^2}$, or the distance between feature vector $\mathbf{x}^e$ and the corresponding centroid $c_{\mathscr{T}_l, \mathscr{C}_k}$.

4.3 Time and Type-Dependent Ranking Models

Learning a single model for ranking event entity aspects is not effective due to the dynamic nature of a real-world event driven by a great variety of multiple factors. We address two major factors that are assumed to have the most influence on the dynamics of events at aspect-level, i.e., time and event type. Thus, we propose an adaptive approach based on the ensemble of multiple ranking models learned from training data, which is partitioned by entities' temporal and type aspects. In more detail, we learn multiple models, which are co-trained using data *soft* partitioning/clustering method in Sect. 4.2, and finally combine the ranking results of different models in an ensemble manner. This approach allows sub-models to learn for different types and times (where feature sets can perform differently), without hurting each other. The adaptive global loss then co-optimizes all sub-models in a unified framework. We describe in details as follows.

Ranking Problem. For aspect ranking context, a typical ranking problem is to find a function f with a set of parameters ω that takes aspect suggestion feature vector $\mathscr{X}$ as input and produce a ranking score $\hat{y}$: $\hat{y} = f(\mathscr{X}, \omega)$. In a learning to rank paradigm, it is aimed at finding the best candidate ranking model f* by minimizing a given loss function $\mathscr{L}$ calculated as: $f^* = \arg\min_f \sum_{\forall a} \mathscr{L}(\hat{y}_a, y_a)$.

Multiple Ranking Models. We learn multiple ranking models trained using data constructed from different time periods and types, simultaneously, thus producing a set of ranking models $\mathbf{M} = \{M_{\mathscr{T}_1, \mathscr{C}_1}, \ldots, M_{\mathscr{T}_m, \mathscr{C}_n}\}$, where $\mathscr{T}_i$ is an event time period, $\in \mathscr{T}$, and $\mathscr{C} = \{\mathscr{C}_1, \mathscr{C}_2, \ldots, \mathscr{C}_n\}$ are the types of an event entity. We use an ensemble method that combines results from different ranking models, each corresponding to an identified ranking-sensitive query time $\mathscr{T}$ and entity type $\mathscr{C}$. The probabilities that an event entity e belongs to time period $\mathscr{T}_l$ and type $\mathscr{C}_k$ given the hitting time t is $P(\mathscr{T}_l, \mathscr{C}_k | e, t)$, and can be computed using the time and type identification method presented in Sect. 4.2.

$$f^* = \arg\min_f \sum_{\forall a} \mathscr{L}\left(\sum_{k=1}^{n} P(\mathscr{C}_k | a, t) \sum_{l=1}^{m} P(\mathscr{T}_l | a, t, \mathscr{C}_k) \hat{y}_a, y_a\right) \tag{1}$$

Multi-criteria Learning. Our task is to minimize the global relevance loss function, which evaluates the overall training error, instead of assuming the independent loss function, that does not consider the correlation and overlap between models. We adapted the L2R RankSVM [12]. The goal of RankSVM is learning a linear model that minimizes the number of discordant pairs in the training data. We modified the objective function of RankSVM following our global loss function, which takes into account the temporal feature specificities of event entities. The temporal and type-dependent ranking model is learned by minimizing the following objective function:

$$\min_{\omega,\xi,e,i,j} \frac{1}{2}||\omega||^2 + C\sum_{e,i,j} \xi_{e,i,j}$$

$$\text{subject to, } \sum_{k=1}^{n} P(\mathscr{C}_k|e,t) \sum_{l=1}^{m} P(\mathscr{T}_l|e,t,\mathscr{C}_k)\omega_{kl}^T X_i^e \qquad (2)$$

$$\geq \sum_{k=1}^{n} P(\mathscr{C}_k|e,t) \sum_{l=1}^{m} P(\mathscr{T}_l|e,t,\mathscr{C}_k)\omega_{kl}^T X_j^e + 1 - \xi_{e,i,j},$$

$$\forall X_i^e \succ X_j^e, \xi_{e,i,j} \geq 0.$$

where $P(\mathscr{C}_k|e,t)$ is the probability the event entity e, at time t, is of type $\mathscr{C}_k$, and $P(\mathscr{T}_l|e,t,\mathscr{C}_k)$ is probability e is in this event time $\mathscr{T}_l$ given the hitting-time t and $\mathscr{C}_k$. The other notions are inherited from the traditional model ($X_i^q \succ X_j^e$ implies that an entity aspect i is ranked ahead of an aspect j with respect to event entity e. C is a trade-off coefficient between the model complexity $||\omega||$ and the training error $\xi_{a,i,j}$.

Ensemble Ranking. After learning all time and type-dependent sub models, we employ an unsupervised ensemble method to produce the final ranking score. Supposed $\bar{a}$ is a testing entity aspect of entity e. We run each of the ranking models in $\mathbf{M}$ against the instance of $\bar{a}$, multiplied by the time and type probabilities of the associated entity e at hitting time t. Finally, we sum all scores produced by all ranking models to obtain the ensemble ranking, $score(\bar{a}) = \sum_{m \in M} P(\mathscr{C}_k|e,t)P(\mathscr{T}_l|e,t,\mathscr{C}_k)\mathsf{f}^*_m(\bar{a})$.

4.4 Ranking Features

We propose two sets of features, namely, (1) *salience* features (taking into account the general importance of candidate aspects) that mainly mined from Wikipedia and (2) *short-term interest* features (capturing a trend or timely change) that mined from the query logs. In addition, we also leverage click-flow relatedness features computed using RWR. The features from the two categories are explained in details as follows.

Salience **features** - or in principle, long-term prominent features.

- **TF.IDF** of an aspect a is the average $TF.IDF(w)$ of all terms $w \in a$; $TF.IDF(w)$ is calculated as $tf(w,D)log\dfrac{N}{df(w)}$, whereas D is a section in the related Wikipedia articles C of entity e. To construct C, we take all in-link articles of the corresponding Wikipedia article of e; $tf(w,D)$ is the term frequency, $df(w)$ denotes the number of sections which w appears.
- **MLE-based**, where we reward the more (cumulated) frequently occurring aspects from the query logs. The maximum likelihood s_{MLE} is $\dfrac{sum_{w \in a} n(w,e)}{\sum_{a'} \sum_{t \in a'} f(w,e)}$, where $f(w,e)$ denotes the frequency a segment (word or phrase) $w \in a$ co-occurs with entity e.

- **Entropy-based**, where we reward the more "stable" aspects over time from the query logs. The entropy is calculated as: $s_E = \sum_{t \in T} P(a|t, e) log P(a|t, e)$, where $P(a|t, e)$ is the probability of observing aspect a in the context of entity e at time t.
- **Language Model-based**, how likely aspects are generated by as statistical LM based on the textual representation of the entity $d(e)$. We model $d(e)$ as the corresponding Wikipedia article text. We use the unigram model with default Dirichlet smoothing.

Short-term interest features, are described as follows.

- **Temporal click entropy.** Click entropy [8] is known as the measurement of how much diversity of clicks to a particular query over time. In detail, the click entropy is measured as the query click variation over a set of URLs for a given query q. In this work, a temporal click entropy accounts for only the number of clicks on the time unit that the entity query is issued. The temporal click entropy TCE_t can be computed as $\sum_{u \in U_q} -P(u|q) \log P(u|q)$ where U_q is a set of clicked URLs for a given query q at time t. The probability of u being clicked among all the clicks of q, $P(u|q)$ is calculated as $\frac{|click(u,q)|}{\sum_{u_i \in U_q} |click(u_i,q)|}$.
- **Trending momentum** measures the trend of an aspect based on the query volume. The trending momentum at time t, Tm_t is calculated using the moving average (Ma) technique, i.e., $Tm_t = Ma(t, i_s) - Ma(t, i_l)$. Whereas, i_s, i_l denotes the short and long time window from the hitting time.
- **Cross correlation** or temporal similarity, is how correlated the aspect _wrt._ the main entity. The more cross-correlated the temporal aspect to the entity, the more influence it brings to the global trend. Given two time series ψ_t^e and ψ_t^a of the entity and aspect at time t, we employ the cross correlation technique to measure such correlation. Cross correlation $CCF(\psi_t^e, \psi_t^a)$ gives the correlation score at lagging times. Lagging time determines the time delay between two time-series. In our case, as we only interest in the hitting time, we take the maximum CCF in a lag interval of $[-1, 1]$.
- **Temporal Language Model-based**, similar to the _salient_ feature, only the textual representation $d(e)$ is the aggregated content of top-k most clicked URLs at time t.

5   Evaluation

In this section, we explain our evaluation for assessing the performance of our proposed approach. We address three main research questions as follows:

RQ1: How good is the classification method in identifying the most relevant event type and period with regards to the hitting time?

RQ2: How do long-term salience and short-term interest features perform at different time periods of different event types?

RQ3: How does the ensemble ranking model perform compared to the single model approaches?

In the following, we first explain our experimental setting including the description of our query logs, relevance assessment, methods and parameters used for the experiments. We then discuss experimental results for each of the main research questions.

5.1   Experimental Setting

Datasets. We use a real-world query log dataset from AOL, which consists of more than 30 million queries covering the period from March 1, to May 31, 2006. Inspired by the taxonomy of event-related queries presented in [13], we manually classified the identified events into two distinct subtypes (i.e., *Breaking* and *Anticipated*). We use Tagme[4] to link queries to the corresponding Wikipedia pages. We use the English Wikipedia dump of June, 2006 with over 2 million articles to temporally align with the query logs. The Wikipedia page edits source is from 2002 up to the studied time, as will be explained later. To count the number of edits, we measure the difference between consecutive revision pairs extracted from the Special:Export[5].

Identifying Event Entities. We reuse the event-related queryset from [14], that contains 837 entity-bearing queries. We removed queries that refer to past and future events and only chose the ones which occured in the period of the AOL dataset, which results in 300 distinct entity queries. Additionally, we construct a more recent dataset which consists of the volume of searches for 500 trending entity queries on Google Trend. The dataset covers the period from March to May, 2017. To extract these event-related queries, we relied on the Wikipedia Portal:Current events[6] as the external indicator, as we only access Google query logs via public APIs. Since the click logs are missing, the Google Trend queryset is used only as a supplementary dataset for *RQ1*.

Dynamic Relevance Assessment. There is no standard ground-truth for this novel task, so we relied on manual annotation to label entity aspects dynamically; with respect to the studied times according to each event period. We put a range of 5 days before the event time as *before* period and analogously for *after*. We randomly picked a day in the 3 time periods for the studied times. In our annotation process, we chose 70 popular and trending event entities focusing on two types of events, i.e., *Breaking* (30 queries) and *Anticipated* (40 queries). For each entity query, we make used of the top-k ranked list of candidate suggestions generated by RWR, cf. Sect. 4.1. Four human experts were asked to evaluate a pair of a given entity and its aspect suggestion (as relevant or non-relevant) with respect to the event period. We defined 4 levels of relevance: 3 (very relevant), 2 (relevant), 1 (irrelevant) and 0 (don't know). Finally, 4 assessors evaluated 1,250 entity/suggestion pairs (approximately 3,750 of triples), with approximately 17

---

[4] https://tagme.d4science.org/tagme/.

[5] https://en.wikipedia.org/wiki/Special:Export.

[6] https://en.wikipedia.org/wiki/Portal:Current_events.

suggestions per trending event on average. The average Cohen's Kappa for the evaluators' pairwise inter-agreement is k = 0.78. Examples of event entities and suggestions with dynamic labels are shown in Table 1. The relevance assessments will be made publicly available.

Table 1. Dynamic relevant assessment examples.

Entity	Suggestion	Dynamic Label		
		Before	During	After
kentucky derby + odds		VR	VR	R
kentucky derby + contenders		VR	R	R
kentucky derby + winner		NR	R	VR
kentucky derby + results		NR	VR	VR

Methods for Comparison. Our baseline method for aspect ranking is RWR, as described in Sect. 4.1. Since we conduct the experiments in a query log context, time-aware query suggestions and auto-completions (QACs) are obvious competitors. We adapted features from state-of-the-art work on time-aware QACs as follows. For the QACs' setting, entity name is given as prior. Instead of making a direct comparison to the linear models in [22] – that are tailored to a different variant of our target – we opt for the supervised-based approach, $SVM_{salient}$, which we consider a fairer and more relevant salient-favored competitor for our research questions.

Most popular completion (**MLE**) [2] is a standard approach in QAC. The model can be regarded as an approximate Maximum Likelihood Estimator (MLE), that ranks the suggestions based on past popularity. Let $P(q)$ be the probability that the next query is q. Given a prefix x, the query candidates that share the prefix $\mathcal{Q}_c$, the most likely suggestion $q \in \mathcal{Q}_c$ is calculated as: $MLE(x) = argmax_{q \in \mathcal{Q}_c} P(q)$. To give a fair comparison, we apply this on top of our aspect extraction cf. Section 4.1, denoted as $RWR + MLE$; analogously with recent MLE.

Recent MLE (**MLE-W**) [24, 29] does not take into account the whole past query log information like the original MLE, but uses only recent days. The popularity of query q in the last n days is aggregated to compute $P(q)$.

Last N query distribution (**LNQ**) [24, 29] differs from MLE and W-MLE and considers the last N queries given the prefix x and time x_t. The approach addresses the weakness of W-MLE in a time-aware context, having to determine the size of the sliding window for prefixes with different popularities. In this approach, only the last N queries are used for ranking, of which N is the trade-off parameter between *robust* (non time-aware bias) and *recency*.

Predicted next N query distribution (**PNQ**) employs the past query popularity as a prior for predicting the query popularity at hitting time, to use this prediction for QAC [24, 29]. We adopt the prediction method proposed in [24].

Table 2. Example entities in May 2006.

Anticipated	may day, da vinci code, cinco de mayo, american idol,
	anna nicole smith, mother's day, danica patrick, emmy rossum,
	triple crown, preakness stakes, belmont stakes kentucky derby, acm awards
Breaking	david blaine, drudge report, halo 3, typhoon chanchu,
	patrick kennedy, indonesia, heather locklear

Table 3. Event type and time classification performance.

	Dataset	Model	Accuracy	Weighted F1
Event-type	AOL	Majority votes	63.7%	57.6%
		SVM	*78.7%*	*89.2%*
	GoogleTrends	Majority votes	60.8%	67.6%
		SVM	*82.7%*	*84.5%*
Event-time	AOL	Logistic regression	67.5%	71.5%
		Cascaded	*72.8%*	*83.4%*
	GoogleTrends	Logistic regression	70.8%	77.5%
		Cascaded	*74.5%*	*81.8%*

Parameters and Settings. The jumping probability for RWR is set to 0.15 (default). For the classification task, we use models implemented in Scikit-learn[7] with default parameters. For learning to rank entity aspects, we modify RankSVM. For each query, the hitting time is the same as used for relevance assessment. Parameters for RankSVM are tuned via grid search using 5-fold cross validation (CV) on training data, trade-off $c = 20$. For W-MLE, we empirically found the sliding window $W = 10$ days. The time series prediction method used for the PNQ baseline and the prediction error is Holt-Winter, available in R. In LNQ and PNQ, the trade-off parameter N is tuned to 200. The short-time window i_s for the trending momentum feature is 1-day and long i_l is 5-days. Top-k in the temporal LM is set to 3. The time granularity for all settings including hitting time and the time series binning is 1 day.

For RQ1, we report the performance on the *rolling* 4-fold CV on the whole dataset. To seperate this with the L2R settings, we explain the evaluating methodology in more details in Sect. 5.2. For the ranking on partitioned data (RQ2), we split *breaking* and *anticipated* dataset into 6 sequential folds, and use the last 4 folds for testing in a rolling manner. To evaluate the ensemble method (RQ3), we use the first two months of AOL for training (50 queries, 150 studied points) and the last month (20 queries as shown in Table 2, 60 studied points) for testing.

---

[7] http://scikit-learn.org/.

Metrics. For assessing the performance of classification methods, we measured accuracy and F1. For the retrieval effectiveness of query ranking models, we used two metrics, i.e., Normalized Discounted Cumulative Gain (NDCG) and $recall@k$ ($r@k$). We measure the retrieval effectiveness of each metric at 3 and 10 ($m@3$ and $m@10$, where $m \in \{NDCG, R\}$). $NDCG$ measures the ranking performance, while $recall@k$ measures the proportion of relevant aspects that are retrieved in the top-k results.

5.2   Cascaded Classification Evaluation

Evaluating methodology. For **RQ1**, given an event entity e, at time t, we need to classify them into either *Breaking* or *Anticipated* class. We select a studied time for each event period randomly in the range of 5 days before and after the event time. In total, our training dataset for AOL consists of 1,740 instances of *breaking* class and 3,050 instances of *anticipated*, with over 300 event entities. For *Google Trends*, there are 2,700 and 4,200 instances respectively. We then bin the entities in the two datasets chronologically into 10 different parts. We set up 4 trials with each of the last 4 bins (using the history bins for training in a *rolling* basic) for testing; and report the results as average of the trials.

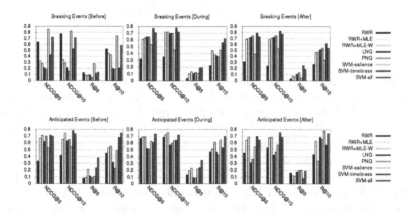

Fig. 4. Performance of different models for event entities of different types.

Results. The baseline and the best results of our 1st stage event-type classification is shown in Table 3-**top**. The accuracy for basic majority vote is high for imbalanced classes, yet it is lower at weighted F1. Our learned model achieves marginally better result at F1 metric.

We further investigate the identification of event time, that is learned on top of the event-type classification. For the gold labels, we gather from the studied times with regards to the event times that is previously mentioned. We compare the result of the cascaded model with non-cascaded logistic regression. The results are shown in Table 3-**bottom**, showing that our cascaded model, with features inherited from the performance of SVM in previous task, substantially improves the single model. However, the overall modest results show the difficulty of this multi-class classification task.

5.3 Ranking Aspect Suggestions

For this part, we first focus on evaluating the performance of single L2R models that are learned from the pre-selected time (before, during and after) and types (*Breaking* and *Anticipate*) set of entity-bearing queries. This allows us to evaluate the feature performance i.e., *salience* and *timeliness*, with time and type specification (RQ2). We then evaluate our ensemble ranking model (results from the cascaded evaluation) and show it robustly improves the baselines for all studied cases (RQ3). Notice that, we do not use the learned classifier in Sect. 5.2 for our ensemble model, since they both use the same time period for training, but opt for the *on-the-fly* ranking-sensitive clustering technique, described in Sect. 4.2.

RQ2. Fig. 4 shows the performance of the aspect ranking models for our event entities at specific times and types. The most right three models in each metric are the models proposed in this work. The overall results show that, the performances of these models, even better than the baselines (for at least one of the three), vary greatly among the cases. In general, $SVM_{salience}$ performs well at the **before** stage of breaking events, and badly at the **after** stage of the same event type. Whereas $SVM_{timeliness}$ gives a contradictory performance for the cases. For anticipated events, $SVM_{timeliness}$ performs well at the **before** and **after** stages, but gives a rather low performance at the **during** stage. For this event type, $SVM_{salience}$ generally performs worse than $SVM_{timeliness}$. Overall, The SVM_{all} with all features combined gives a good and stable performance, but for most cases, are not better than the well-performed single set of features L2R model. In general, these results prove our assumption that *salience* and *timeliness* should be traded-off for different event types, at different event times. For feature importances, we observe regularly, stable performances of *same-group* features across these cases. *Salience* features from knowledge bases tend to perform better than from query logs for *short-duration* or less popular events. We leave the more in-depth analysis of this part for future work.

RQ3. We demonstrate the results of single models and our ensemble model in Table 4. As also witnessed in RQ2, SVM_{all}, will all features, gives a rather stable performance for both NDCG and Recall, improved the baseline, yet not significantly. Our *Ensemble* model, that is learned to trade-off between *salience* and *timeliness* achieves the best results for all metrics, outperforms the baseline significantly. As the testing entity queries in this experiment are at all event times and with all event types, these improvements illustrate the robustness of our model. Overall, we witness the low performance of adapted QAC methods. One reason is as mentioned, QACs, even time-aware generally favor already *salient* queries as follows the *rich-get-richer* phenomenon, and are not ideal for entity queries that are event-related (where aspect relevance can change abruptly).

Table 4. Performance of the baselines (RWR relatedness scores, RWR + MLE, RWR + MLE-W, LNQ, and PNQ) compared with our ranking models; *,†, ∓ indicates statistical improvement over the baseline using t-test with significant at $p < 0.1$, $p < 0.05$, $p < 0.01$ respectively.

Methods	NDCG@3	NDCG@10	R@3	R@10
RWR	0.3208	0.4137	0.1208	0.3749
RWR + MLE	+29.94%	+9.73%	−21.09%	+5.15%*
RWR + MLE-W	+11.56%	+11.46%	−18.93%*	+3.28%
LNQ	+15.39%	−3.75%	−19.74%	−30.31%
PNQ	+13.19%	−9.95%	−23.46%	−33.53%
$SVM_{salience}$	+41.75%*	+9.18%	+23.32%*	+9.93%
$SVM_{timeliness}$	+15.19%	+17.53%	+14.77%	+11.3%
SVM_{all}	+52.65%*	+40.87%*	+9.73%†	+24.3%
Ensemble	**+85.12%∓**	**+45.34%†**	**+42.78%***	**+17.45%***

Time-aware QACs for partially long prefixes like entities often encounter sparse traffic of query volumes, that also contributes to the low results.

6   Conclusion

We studied the temporal aspect suggestion problem for entities in knowledge bases with the aid of real-world query logs. For each entity, we ranked its temporal aspects using our proposed novel time and type-specific ranking method that learns multiple ranking models for different time periods and event types. Through extensive evaluation, we also illustrated that our aspect suggestion approach significantly improves the ranking effectiveness compared to competitive baselines. In this work, we focused on a "global" recommendation based on public attention. The problem is also interesting taking other factors (e.g., *search context*) into account, which will be interesting to investigate in future work.

Acknowledgements. This work was partially funded by the German Federal Ministry of Education and Research (BMBF) under project GlycoRec (16SV7172).

References

1. Balog, K., Dalton, J., Doucet, A., Ibrahim, Y.: Report on esair'15. In: ACM SIGIR Forum
2. Bar-Yossef, Z., Kraus, N.: Context-sensitive query auto-completion. In: WWW 2011 (2011)
3. Bian, J., Li, X., Li, F., Zheng, Z., Zha, H.: Ranking specialization for web search: a divide-and-conquer approach by using topical ranksvm. In: WWW 2010 (2010)

4. Blanco, R., Cambazoglu, B.B., Mika, P., Torzec, N.: Entity recommendations in web search. In: Alani, H., Kagal, L., Fokoue, A., Groth, P., Biemann, C., Parreira, J.X., Aroyo, L., Noy, N., Welty, C., Janowicz, K. (eds.) ISWC 2013. LNCS, vol. 8219, pp. 33–48. Springer, Heidelberg (2013). https://doi.org/10.1007/978-3-642-41338-4_3

5. Chirigati, F., Liu, J., Korn, F., Wu, Y.W., Yu, C., Zhang, H.: Knowledge exploration using tables on the web. In: Proceedings of the VLDB Endowment (2016)

6. Deng, H., King, I., Lyu, M.R.: Entropy-biased models for query representation on the click graph. In: Proceedings of SIGIR 2009 (2009)

7. Dessi, A., Atzori, M.: A machine-learning approach to ranking RDF properties. Future Gener. Comput. Syst. **54**, 366–377 (2016)

8. Dou, Z., Song, R., Wen, J.-R.: A large-scale evaluation and analysis of personalized search strategies. In: Proceedings of WWW 2007 (2007)

9. Fischer, L., Blanco, R., Mika, P., Bernstein, A.: Timely semantics: a study of a stream-based ranking system for entity relationships. In: Arenas, M., Corcho, O., Simperl, E., Strohmaier, M., d'Aquin, M., Srinivas, K., Groth, P., Dumontier, M., Heflin, J., Thirunarayan, K., Staab, S. (eds.) ISWC 2015. LNCS, vol. 9367, pp. 429–445. Springer, Cham (2015). https://doi.org/10.1007/978-3-319-25010-6_28

10. Hasibi, F., Balog, K., Bratsberg, S.E.: Dynamic factual summaries for entity cards. In: SIGIR 2017 (2017)

11. Heitz, G., Gould, S., Saxena, A., Koller, D.: Cascaded classification models: combining models for holistic scene understanding. In: NIPS (2009)

12. Joachims, T.: Training linear svms in linear time. In: Proceedings of KDD 2006 (2006)

13. Kairam, S.R., Morris, M.R., Teevan, J., Liebling, D.J., Dumais, S.T.: Towards supporting search over trending events with social media. In: ICWSM (2013)

14. Kanhabua, N., Ngoc Nguyen, T., Nejdl, W.: Learning to detect event-related queries for web search. In: WWW 2015 Companion. ACM (2015)

15. Kanhabua, N., Ren, H., Moeslund, T.B.: Learning dynamic classes of events using stacked multilayer perceptron networks. CoRR, abs/1606.07219 (2016)

16. Karmaker Santu, S.K., Li, L., Park, D.H., Chang, Y., Zhai, C.: Modeling the influence of popular trending events on user search behavior. In: WWW 2017 (2017)

17. Kong, W., Li, R., Luo, J., Zhang, A., Chang, Y., Allan, J.: Predicting search intent based onl pre-search context. In: SIGIR 2015 (2015)

18. Kulkarni, A., Teevan, J., Svore, K.M., Dumais, S.T.: Understanding temporal query dynamics. In: Proceedings of WSDM 2011 (2011)

19. Lin, T., Pantel, P., Gamon, M., Kannan, A., Fuxman, A.: Active objects: actions for entity-centric search. In: WWW 2012 (2012)

20. Matsubara, Y., Sakurai, Y., Prakash, B.A., Li, L., Faloutsos, C.: Rise and fall patterns of information diffusion: model and implications. In: Proceedings of KDD. ACM (2012)

21. Pound, J., Mika, P., Zaragoza, H.: Ad-hoc object retrieval in the web of data. In: WWW 2010 (2010)

22. Reinanda, R., Meij, E., de Rijke, M.: Mining, ranking and recommending entity aspects. In: Proceedings of SIGIR, pp. 263–272. ACM (2015)

23. Shokouhi, M.: Detecting seasonal queries by time-series analysis. In: SIGIR 2011 (2011)

24. Shokouhi, M., Radinsky, K.: Time-sensitive query auto-completion. In: IGIR 2012 (2012)

25. Silvestri, F.: Mining query logs: turning search usage data into knowledge. Found. Trends Inf. Retrieval **4**(1–2), 1–174 (2010)
26. Spina, D., Meij, E., De Rijke, M., Oghina, A., Bui, M.T., Breuss, M.: Identifying entity aspects in microblog posts. In: SIGIR 2012 (2012)
27. Tran, N.K., Tran, T., Niederée, C.: Beyond time: dynamic context-aware entity recommendation. In: Blomqvist, E., Maynard, D., Gangemi, A., Hoekstra, R., Hitzler, P., Hartig, O. (eds.) ESWC 2017. LNCS, vol. 10249, pp. 353–368. Springer, Cham (2017). https://doi.org/10.1007/978-3-319-58068-5_22
28. Vadrevu, S., Tu, Y., Salvetti, F.: Ranking relevant attributes of entity in structured knowledge base. US Patent 9,229,988, 5 Jan 2016
29. Whiting, S., Jose, J.M.: Recent and robust query auto-completion. In: WWW 2014 (2014)
30. Yu, X., Ma, H., Hsu, B.-J.P., Han, J.: On building entity recommender systems using user click log and freebase knowledge. In: Proceedings of WSDM, pp. 263–272. ACM (2014)
31. Zhang, L., Rettinger, A., Zhang, J.: A probabilistic model for time-aware entity recommendation. In: Groth, P., Simperl, E., Gray, A., Sabou, M., Krötzsch, M., Lecue, F., Flöck, F., Gil, Y. (eds.) ISWC 2016. LNCS, vol. 9981, pp. 598–614. Springer, Cham (2016). https://doi.org/10.1007/978-3-319-46523-4_36

GDPRtEXT - GDPR as a Linked Data Resource

Harshvardhan J. Pandit[1](✉)(ID), Kaniz Fatema[2](ID), Declan O'Sullivan[1](ID), and Dave Lewis[1](ID)

[1] ADAPT Centre, Trinity College Dublin, Dublin, Ireland
{harshvardhan.pandit,declan.osullivan,dave.lewis}@adaptcentre.ie
[2] University of Derby, Derby, United Kingdom
k.fatema@derby.ac.uk

Abstract. The General Data Protection Regulation (GDPR) is the new European data protection law whose compliance affects organisations in several aspects related to the use of consent and personal data. With emerging research and innovation in data management solutions claiming assistance with various provisions of the GDPR, the task of comparing the degree and scope of such solutions is a challenge without a way to consolidate them. With GDPR as a linked data resource, it is possible to link together information and approaches addressing specific articles and thereby compare them. Organisations can take advantage of this by linking queries and results directly to the relevant text, thereby making it possible to record and measure their solutions for compliance towards specific obligations. GDPR text extensions (GDPRtEXT) uses the European Legislation Identifier (ELI) ontology published by the European Publications Office for exposing the GDPR as linked data. The dataset is published using DCAT and includes an online webpage with HTML id attributes for each article and its subpoints. A SKOS vocabulary is provided that links concepts with the relevant text in GDPR. To demonstrate how related legislations can be linked to highlight changes between them for reusing existing approaches, we provide a mapping from Data Protection Directive (DPD), which was the previous data protection law, to GDPR showing the nature of changes between the two legislations. We also discuss in brief the existing corpora of research that can benefit from the adoption of this resource.

Keywords: GDPR · DPD · Linked resource · Regulatory technology
Legal compliance · SKOS · DCAT · e-governance

1 Introduction

The General Data Protection Regulation (GDPR) is the new European data protection legislation that enters into force on 25th May 2018. It is an important legislation in terms of changes to the organisational measures required for compliance. In particular, GDPR focuses on the use of consent and personal

© Springer International Publishing AG, part of Springer Nature 2018
A. Gangemi et al. (Eds.): ESWC 2018, LNCS 10843, pp. 481–495, 2018.
https://doi.org/10.1007/978-3-319-93417-4_31

data and provides the data subject with several rights. These new changes have spurred innovation within the community - both in the industry as well as in academia [3,5,6,21] - that targets compliance with the various obligations of the GDPR. While such solutions claim assistance to the various provisions of the GDPR, comparing and collecting such solutions is a difficult undertaking due to the inability of consolidating them in an efficient manner.

A lack of method to address specific sections of the GDPR prevents related methods from being linked together in a uniform and consistent manner. This creates challenges in the comparison of their degree and scopes, especially regarding metrics of solutions that claim to assist in compliance. This hampers progress as it limits the findability of information related to a particular resource - in this case a concept or a point within the GDPR text.

Since particular points and concepts within a legislation are referred to using a form of numbering system, for example - Article 5(1) refers to the first point within Article 5, this can be used to create URIs that refer to each distinct resource within the GDPR. Using these URIs it is possible to define information targetting or referring to specific points or concepts. In this manner, legal resources and concepts within GDPR can be linked to each other as well to other resources.

Organisations and researchers gain the advantage through this of linking queries and results directly to the relevant text of GDPR, thereby making it possible to record and measure solutions for compliance towards specific obligations. The same approach can also be used in linking related legislations to the GDPR. Such links between associated information offer the benefit of being machine-readable and therefore can be queried and acted upon in an automated manner.

Through this paper and its associated resources, we aim to alleviate the above discussed limitation of legal text and demonstrate the application of FAIR principles to link together information associated with the GDPR and its compliance. To this effect, we present GDPR text extensions (GDPRtEXT), which consists of GDPR text defined as a DCAT catalog containing the official text as well as created RDF resources as datasets, and a SKOS ontology defining concepts related to GDPR. An application of GDPRtEXT is presented in the form of linking GDPR with its predecessor - the Data Protection Directive (DPD) - to facilitate the adoption of existing solutions in addressing GDPR. All resources described are documented and available online[1] under the CC-by-4.0 license[2].

The rest of the paper is structured in the following manner - Sect. 2 discusses the motivation and creation of the GDPR linked data resource and GDPRtEXT ontology. Section 3 contains the mapping between DPD and GDPR obligations. Section 4 describes the related work. Section 5 discusses potential applications and benefits to the community. Section 6 concludes the paper with a discussion of future work.

---

[1] https://openscience.adaptcentre.ie/projects/GDPRtEXT/.

[2] https://creativecommons.org/licenses/by/4.0/.

2   Creation of Resource

2.1   Motivation

In our previous work involving the GDPR [10,13,15,19], we faced challenges in referring to GDPR concepts and obligations as well as in consolidating information referring to particular obligations. In light of this, we initially used the solution of assigning a permanent URI to each point in the text using HTML fragments so as to refer to them as linkable resources. Later, we extended this approach to create a RDF dataset that could be used in other works and queried using SPARQL. In light of its usefulness and benefits to the community, we removed the project specific artefacts to provide it as an open resource.

2.2   Scope

The scope of this work is explicitly limited only to the GDPR. Although other legislations are explicitly mentioned within GDPR, they are not addressed in this resource. At the time of creation of this resource, the GDPR is considered to be final, i.e. published as a complete version as opposed to being a draft. Updates (related legislations or future laws) to the GDPR are published as separate legal documents that can be similarly annotated and added to this dataset, whereby they can then be published together through the DCAT catalog. Where updating the ontology is necessary, it should be approached as incorporating new legal laws into existing knowledge bases.

2.3   GDPR as Linked Data

The GDPR document [7] is structured as three types of statements in the following order - 173 Recitals, 99 Articles, and 21 Citations. The articles are structured within Chapters (numbered from I to X) and Sections, where each Chapter has zero or more sections. An article may contain several points which may have sub-points that may or may not be numbered. Citations appear at the end of the document and are numbered by their order of reference within the text.

To define legal resources, we use the European Legislation Identifier (ELI)[3] ontology published by the European Publications Office. *ELI* allows identification of legislation through URI templates at the European, national and regional levels based on a defined set of related attributes or terms. It provides properties describing each legislative act as a set of metadata definitions and its expression in a formal ontology. Serialisation of *ELI* metadata elements provides integration of metadata into the legislative websites using RDFa.

We use the latest iteration of the ELI OWL ontology (v1.1, released 2016-09-19) to define the classes *Chapter, Section, Article, Point, SubPoint, Recital,* and *Citation* as subclasses of *eli:LegalResourceSubdivision* (*LRS*), which is itself a subclass of *eli:LegalResource* (*LR*). *LR* is used to define resources at the document level, whereas *LRS* is used to define the resources contained within a

---

[3] http://publications.europa.eu/mdr/eli/index.html.

LR. *ELI* defines the properties *has_part* and its inverse *is_part_of* to connect two *LR*s. GDPRtEXT extends these with additional properties to connect the various chapters, sections, articles, and points with each other. As we extend *ELI*, GDPRtEXT can be used in a manner that is compatible with the intended use of *ELI*, including its use in websites as RDFa.

The official text of the GDPR available online[4] as a HTML page was used to extract its text using Javascript[5]. This was then exported as a JSON document with metadata such as resource type (article, chapter, etc.) and numbering (roman, arabic, or unnumbered). The RDF dataset was generated through a python script using rdflib[6] that created the triples iteratively using the ELI extension described above.

DCAT[7] and VOID[8] were used to define the GDPR catalog containing three datasets as described in Table 1. The first dataset describes official documents published by the European Publication Office as distributions with their canonical urls. The second dataset describes distributions containing a copy of the GDPR text hosted by the ADAPT Centre and contains HTML and JSON representations of the GDPR. The HTML version uses the id-attribute to define fragment identifiers for each legal resource within the text. This makes it possible to directly refer (or navigate) to a particular article, point, or sub-point within the text. This is similar to the RDF distribution of the GDPR text where each legal resource has a distinct URI. The third dataset contains RDF serialisations of the GDPR in the Turtle, N-Triples, N3, and JSON-LD formats.

The catalog describes a SPARQL endpoint hosted using the OpenLink Virtuoso[9] triple-store for exposing the RDF dataset containing the GDPR text along with an online front-end using Pubby[10] as shown in Fig. 1. All URIs for the dataset and distributions use the permanent-url (purl.org) scheme to refer to resources.

Table 1. Datasets and distributions in the GDPRtEXT DCAT catalog

Dataset	Distributions	Comment
Canonical_dataset	HTML, PDF, XML	Official distributions
Textid_dataset	HTML, JSON, text	With IDs
Annotated_dataset	XML, N3, NT, Turtle, JSON-LD	RDF datasets

---

[4] http://eur-lex.europa.eu/eli/reg/2016/679/oj.
[5] https://opengogs.adaptcentre.ie/harsh/GDPRtEXT/.
[6] https://rdflib.readthedocs.io/en/stable/.
[7] https://www.w3.org/TR/vocab-dcat/.
[8] https://www.w3.org/TR/void/.
[9] https://virtuoso.openlinksw.com/.
[10] http://wifo5-03.informatik.uni-mannheim.de/pubby/.

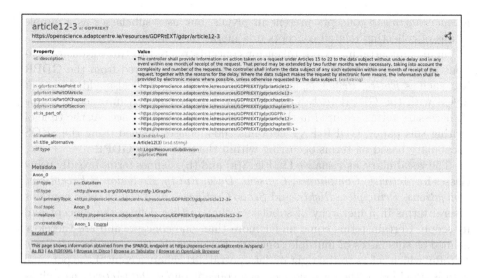

Fig. 1. Article 12(3) in GDPRtEXT as RDF displayed using Pubby

2.4 GDPRtEXT Ontology

The aim of the GDPRtEXT ontology is to provide a way to refer to the concepts and terms expressed within the GDPR. The ontology does not aim to provide an interpretation of compliance obligations using methods such as inference. It is intended to be an open resource for addressing modeling solutions for inter-operability related to GDPR compliance.

The development of the ontology followed the seminal guide *"Ontology Development 101"* [18]. The development started by deciding on the scope which led to the aim of providing a way to refer to the various concepts defined in the GDPR. The SKOS[11] vocabulary was chosen to provide descriptions of GDPR concepts as it is a W3C Recommendation for defining terms.

The defined terms were linked to the relevant points in the GDPR text using the URI scheme described in the previous section through the *rdfs:isDefinedBy* property. Additional links between the terms were created using the additionally created annotation property termed *'involves'*. The development of the ontology was done using the Protégé[12] v5.2.0 ontology development environment.

Following the preliminary collection of terms, additional terms were added to the ontology in order to create a hierarchy of concepts based on the requirements of the GDPR. For example, identified data types such as personal data and anonymous data are defined as subclasses of the common term Data. This allows a representation of the encapsulation of concepts and provides a way to refer to the term in its abstract form. Note that the ontology does not use the

---

[11] https://www.w3.org/TR/skos-reference/.
[12] https://protege.stanford.edu/.

broader/narrower concepts present in SKOS, but uses subclasses as a simple means of collecting related concepts in a hierarchical manner.

Similar undertakings were taken for concepts related to the various obligations and entities. Additional concepts mentioned or inferred from the GDPR text such as *Entity, Principle,* and *Unlawful Processing* were also added but not linked with the GDPR text. The collection was undertaken in order to define all necessary terms required in the documentation of compliance. At the time of writing this paper, GDPRtEXT contains 200+ classes defined using the SKOS vocabulary based on terms occurring within the text of the GDPR.

The vocabulary, as visualised in Fig. 3(a) and (b), defines terms broadly using classes for *Activity, Compliance, Consent, Data, Entity, Exclusion & Exceptions, Obligations, Principles, Rights,* and *Seals/Certifications.* Each of these contains several terms in a hierarchy of subclasses that further defines the concept and its scope. Certain terms come under more than one concept, and are therefore defined as subclasses of multiple concepts. For example, the term *ProvideCopyOfData,* which refers to the right of data portability where a copy of the personal data is provided to the data subject, is a concept under *DataActivity* as well as *RightOfDataPortability.*

Various resources other than the official text of the GDPR were used to understand the terms and concepts. We used the resources made available by official sources such as Data Protection Commissioner of Ireland[13] and Information Commissioner's Office of UK[14] as well as industry-based sources such as Nymity's GDPR handbook[15].

2.5   Documentation

The documentation of the ontology presented a challenge due to the large number of terms. To automate part of the process, we used the Wizard for Documenting Ontologies (Widoco)[16] [12], which uses LODE[17] [20] for generating ontology documentation and WebVOWL[18] [16] for its visualisation. The resulting HTML documentation is available online[19] as depicted in Fig. 2. The documentation groups terms based on core concepts such as *Consent, Data, Activity,* and *Compliance* to make the documentation more readable. Each term in the ontology was defined with the metadata as specified by WIDOCO's best practices document[20] to generate its comprehensive documentation.

The documentation contains two example use-cases of GDPRtEXT. The first shows its use in compliance reporting by linking the relevant tests and results

---

[13] https://www.dataprotection.ie/.
[14] https://ico.org.uk/.
[15] https://www.nymity.com/.
[16] https://doi.org/10.5281/zenodo.591294.
[17] http://www.essepuntato.it/lode.
[18] http://vowl.visualdataweb.org/webvowl.html.
[19] http://purl.org/adaptcentre/openscience/ontologies/GDPRtEXT/docs.
[20] https://dgarijo.github.io/Widoco/doc/bestPractices/index-en.html.

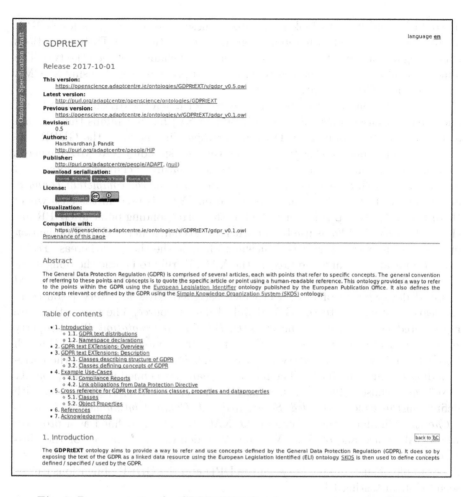

Fig. 2. Documentation for GDPRtEXT Ontology generated using Widoco

with the GDPR articles they represent. This is shown using the EARL[21] vocabulary for expressing test results. The second example shows the linking of GDPR obligations with the previous data protection law, which is described in more detail in the next section. We have also used GDPRtEXT to link provenance terms with their definitions in relevant GDPR articles [19].

3 Linking DPD Obligations with GDPR

The Data Protection Directive (DPD) is the previous data protection legislation which was adopted in 1995 and is superseded by the GDPR. As a large number of solutions and approaches already exist that address compliance with the DPD,

---

[21] https://www.w3.org/TR/EARL10-Schema/.

it would be beneficial to look into reusing these existing solutions for GDPR. To that end, we provide a mapping from DPD obligations to GDPR obligations containing annotations that describe the nature of change between the two. The annotation also describes changes required in our previous work in using XACML rules to model DPD obligations [8,9].

The annotations are available online in the form of a HTML table, a CSV file, and a RDF dataset. Each row (HTML table, CSV) has 5 columns that contain a reference from a point in DPD to its corresponding point in the GDPR, the nature of change between the two, whether the corresponding XACML rule needs to be extended, and a description comment. The nature of change is represented as one of the following - *same, reduced, slightly changed, completely changed*, and *extended*. For XACML rules, the notation '*N/A*' is used in the case where there were no XACML rules for DPD but the corresponding point in GDPR has changed. The value '*No*' is used where there is no change in the GDPR obligation or the existing XACML rule is sufficient to handle the change, whereas '*Yes*' is used to indicate a change required in the XACML rule to handle the obligation.

To model the annotations as a RDF resource using GDPRtEXT, we created a linked data version of the DPD which assigned URIs for every resource in the legislation similar to the GDPR linked data resource. The annotations are represented as instances of the class *DPDToGDPRAnnotation*. The property *resourceInDPD* is used to refer to the particular resource within DPD through its URI. Similarly, the property *resourceInGDPR* is used to refer to the corresponding resource in GDPR. The nature of change is defined using the property *hasChange* whose value is an instances of the class *ChangeInObligation*, with defined instances for *Extended, Same, Reduced, CompletelyChanged*, and *SlightlyChanged*. Similarly, the change in the XACML rules is defined as a property whose values are one of *Yes, No*, and *N/A* defined as instances of the class *ChangeInXACMLRule*. Comments are defined using the *rdfs:comment* property. An example of such linking between the DPD and the GDPR obligations can be seen below in Listing 3-1.

```
@prefix gdpr:
<http://purl.org/adaptcentre/openscience/resources/GDPRtEXT#>.
@prefix dpd:
<http://purl.org/adaptcentre/openscience/resources/DPD#>.
@prefix rdfs: <http://www.w3.org/2000/01/rdf-schema#>.

dpd:mappingrule6 a dpd:DPDToGDPR_Annotation ;
    dpd:hasChange dpd:ChangeExtended ;
    dpd:hasXACMLChange dpd:XACMLNoChange ;
    dpd:resourceInDPD dpd:Article7-a ;
    dpd:resourceInGDPR gdpr:Article6-1-a ;
    rdfs:comment "added consent given to ..." .
```

Listing 3-1. Linking obligation between DPD and GDPR related to processing of personal data and consent

4   Related Work

The creation of the GDPRtEXT vocabulary was influenced by the work done by Bartolini and Muthuri in the creation of their data protection ontology based on the GDPR [2,3]. The purpose of their ontology was to model the requirements and duties of the controller to be compliant with the GDPR. To this end, their ontology defines several properties and 'rules' as well as equivalency of classes for compliance concepts. By contrast, GDPRtEXT does not contain any inference but provides a definition of useful terms using SKOS. This demonstrates the difference of scope between the two approaches and the varying complexities of the work involved.

Bartolini's ontology is based on a draft of the GDPR, and as such, contains some minor inconsistencies with the published (final) version. Additionally, the authors term the ontology to be a preliminary work in its early stages. While their use of classes and inferences can prove to be useful in determining compliance, GDPRtEXT takes a more generic approach of trying to provide a way to refer to specific concepts within the GDPR, making it possible to combine the approaches.

Expressing legal obligations as a set of rules that are machine-processable allows automated systems to be modelled for compliance. One such recent approach models GDPR obligations as machine-readable rules using ODRL[22] [1]. The model is based on using 31 articles to create a graph containing 313 nodes and 810 defined edges to express relations between obligations. The aim of this work is to create a compliance checking tool for GDPR. Using the relations, a hierarchy of obligations is expressed as dependencies between them. The obligations are categorised into core obligations and those depending on them, called as sub-obligations. A total of 48 obligations have been identified in this manner along with 105 dependant sub-obligations. The published paper contains a diagram of the relations between the articles, but does not provide a way to access the data regarding obligations.

The approach of linking GDPR articles together based on obligations is similar in principle to the approach described in this paper, and shows the benefits of creating a linked data version of the GDPR. Using a collection of concepts as provided by GDPRtEXT, the defined obligations can be linked to their respective GDPR text, which allows consolidation of information in the usage and documentation.

5   Applications and Benefit to Community

Example applications of legal ontologies in the areas of information and knowledge systems and compliance solutions are described by [11,14,17]. The publication describing the data protection ontology [3] described in Sect. 4 provides applications in the domains of information retrieval, transition from DPD to GDPR, automated classification and summarisation, question answering, decision support and decision making, and autonomous agent systems.

---

[22] https://www.w3.org/TR/odrl-model/.

The advantages of linked data have been documented before [4,22], and are equally applicable to legislations such as DPD and GDPR. Here, we discuss the benefits provided by GDPRtEXT in consolidating related research with a focus on compliance solutions.

We take the example of the work described in the previous section of modelling the GDPR obligations as machine-processable ODRL rules intended for a compliance based system. The work describes dependencies between the GDPR obligations, which extends to the same dependencies between the ODRL rules modelled from these obligations. This results in a hierarchical model of obligations where compliance of a rule depends on compliance of all of its sub-rules.

Consider an organisation or a researcher that wishes to use these rules to augment the compliance system they have in place. It is more than likely that both solutions in this case refer to the GDPR via text or some internal form of reference. In order to consolidate both approaches such that they are compatible with each other, modifications will have to be made to either or both, the degree and scope of which varies with the complexity of the system. Additionally, comparing the compliance for a particular obligation from different systems again might involve the use of a text-based or internal form of reference which is isolated to that particular system and might not be machine-readable.

If instead, a common form existed that could be used to refer to the required concepts or obligations, then the task of consolidation of information becomes significantly simpler. In the above example use-case, the ODRL rules and other systems can refer to specific GDPR obligations through the same set of URIs as provided by GDPRtEXT. This makes it possible to link related information in a consistent manner between systems that act on the same obligations to provide consolidated compliance results.

This use-case can be extended to communications between entities such as data subjects, data controllers, data processors, and data protection authorities. The nature of information exchanged between these entities becomes increasingly complex due to the involvement of multiple systems that interact with different entities. Consolidating compliance related information between these entities can benefit from adoption of a common baseline for describing the GDPR such as that provided by GDPRtEXT.

GDPRtEXT relates to and exposes GDPR which is an important legal document. Therefore, ensuring the resource stays alive and available is of essence with respect to its use by the community. Currently, the resource is hosted by Trinity College Dublin on its VM cluster which is managed by a dedicated team of system administrators. Additionally, since GDPRtEXT uses permanent urls (via purl.org) for resolving the actual URL of the resource, it is possible to move the resource to a different location without changing how it is exposed to the world. While we plan to continue maintaining the resource, this provides a way to move the resource to another maintainer or a community hosting service such as Github if the need arises in the future. A copy of the resource is mirrored on hosting sites such as Datahub and Zenodo, providing alternate means of access should the need arise.

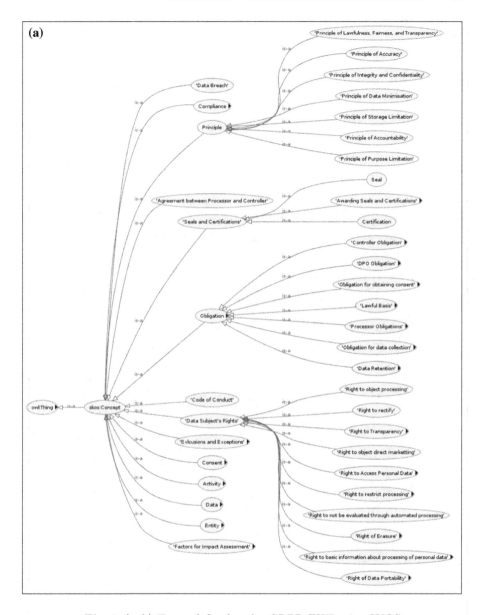

Fig. 3. (a, b) Terms defined under GDPRtEXT using SKOS

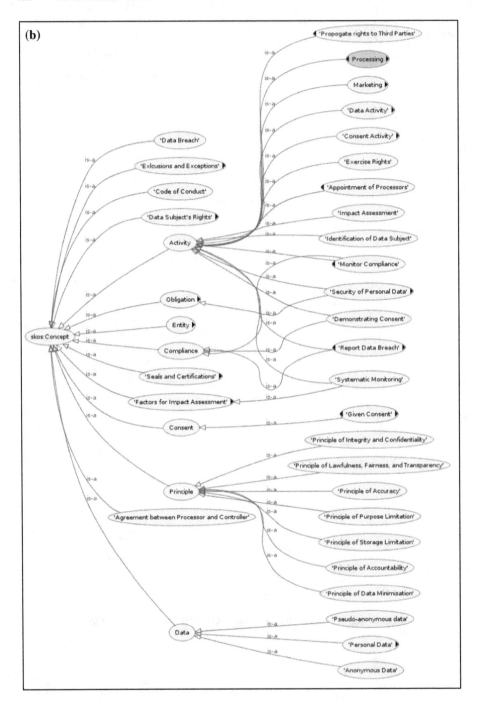

Fig. 3. (*continued*)

6   Conclusion and Future Work

In this paper, we presented GDPR text extensions (GDPRtEXT), which uses the European Legislation Identifier (ELI) ontology published by the European Publications Office for exposing the GDPR as linked data. The resulting dataset is published using DCAT and VOID vocabularies with distributions for official publication, an annotated online copy of the GDPR that uses fragment identifiers to refer to individual points, and its serialisations in several RDF formats. The dataset is published using the CC-by-4.0 license and is available with a DOI at Zenodo[23] and at Datahub[24]. We have submitted GDPRtEXT to *data.gov.ie*[25] as a suggested dataset which would allow it to be indexed by the EU Open Data Portal[26]. The dataset contains a SPARQL endpoint with a front-end using Pubby. GDPRtEXT also provides a SKOS vocabulary for defining terms and concepts in GDPR. An example of linking related legislations was provided using Data Protection Directive (DPD) that reused existing work in modelling obligations using XACML. The applications and benefits of GDPRtEXT to the community were also discussed.

GDPRtEXT is an ongoing effort and we actively seek suggestions as well as support and guidance from the community[27]. In terms of future work, we plan to work on the documentation so as to make it more accessible to the community outside of the semantic web domain. To this end, we are looking into conceptualising a model for the documentation and dissemination of GDPR metadata related to consent, provenance, data sharing, and compliance.

The online webpage displaying the linked data version of GDPR currently only displays its text. Using Javascript along with Web Annotation Data Model[28], it is possible to display additional information associated with particular articles or points. This can be used to create a rich interface for the GDPR that filters or displays information in an interactive manner. Examples of annotations displayed alongside GDPR are compliance status reports and legal notes showing information related to fulfilment of a particular obligation.

The principle of linked data works only when there are links to both (or all) involved resources. Therefore, we plan on using GDPRtEXT with GDPR related work such as European Privacy Seal (EuroPriSe)[29], which is an organisation that provides certifications and seals for GDPR compliance. The criteria used by EuroPriSe is based on translating the requirements of GDPR into questions that can be answered in the context of an audit or a certification. These questions, therefore, are based on obligations specified by the GDPR, and their answers determine compliance to these obligations. This is an area where

---

[23] https://doi.org/10.5281/zenodo.1146351.
[24] https://datahub.ckan.io/dataset/gdprtext.
[25] https://data.gov.ie/dataset/suggest/a5f365f6-719f-4eab-9bfe-4d494aeb31ee.
[26] http://data.europa.eu/euodp/.
[27] https://opengogs.adaptcentre.ie/harsh/GDPRtEXT/issues.
[28] https://www.w3.org/TR/annotation-model/.
[29] https://www.european-privacy-seal.eu.

GDPRtEXT can be used to link the related information in EuroPriSe's certifications and compare them to similar research undertaken in the domain of GDPR compliance.

Acknowledgement. This paper is supported by the ADAPT Centre for Digital Content Technology, which is funded under the SFI Research Centres Programme (Grant 13/RC/2106) and is co-funded under the European Regional Development Fund.

References

1. Agarwal, S., Kirrane, S., Scharf, J.: Modelling the general data protection regulation. In: Internationales Rechtsinformatik Symposion (IRIS 2017) (2017)
2. Bartolini, C., Muthuri, R.: Reconciling data protection rights and obligations: an ontology of the forthcoming EU regulation (2015)
3. Bartolini, C., Muthuri, R., Cristiana, S.: Using ontologies to model data protection requirements in workflows. In: Ninth International Workshop on Juris-Informatics (JURISIN 2015) (2015). http://orbilu.uni.lu/handle/10993/22383
4. Bizer, C., Heath, T., Berners-Lee, T.: Linked data-the story so far. In: Semantic Services, Interoperability and Web Applications: Emerging Concepts, pp. 205–227 (2009)
5. Bonatti, P., Kirrane, S., Polleres, A., Wenning, R.: Transparent personal data processing: the road ahead. In: Tonetta, S., Schoitsch, E., Bitsch, F. (eds.) SAFE-COMP 2017. LNCS, vol. 10489, pp. 337–349. Springer, Cham (2017). https://doi.org/10.1007/978-3-319-66284-8_28
6. Chassang, G.: The impact of the EU general data protection regulation on scientific research. ecancermedicalscience **11**, 709 (2017)
7. Regulation (EU) 2016/679 of the European Parliament and of the Council of 27 April 2016 on the protection of natural persons with regard to the processing of personal data and on the free movement of such data, and repealing Directive 95/46/EC (General Data Protection Regulation). Official J. Eur. Union L119, 1–88 (2016). http://eur-lex.europa.eu/legal-content/EN/TXT/?uri=OJ:L:2016:119:TOC
8. Fatema, K., Chadwick, D.W., Van Alsenoy, B.: Extracting access control and conflict resolution policies from european data protection law. In: Camenisch, J., Crispo, B., Fischer-Hübner, S., Leenes, R., Russello, G. (eds.) Privacy and Identity 2011. IAICT, vol. 375, pp. 59–72. Springer, Heidelberg (2012). https://doi.org/10.1007/978-3-642-31668-5_5
9. Fatema, K., Debruyne, C., Lewis, D., OSullivan, D., Morrison, J.P., Mazed, A.A.: A semi-automated methodology for extracting access control rules from the European data protection directive. In: 2016 IEEE Security and Privacy Workshops (SPW), pp. 25–32. IEEE (2016)
10. Fatema, K., Hadziselimovic, E., Pandit, H.J., Debruyne, C., Lewis, D., O'Sullivan, D.: Compliance through informed consent: semantic based consent permission and data management model. In: 5th Workshop on Society, Privacy and the Semantic Web - Policy and Technology (PrivOn 2017). CEUR Workshop Proceedings, vol. 1951 (2017). http://ceur-ws.org/Vol-1951/#paper-05

11. Gangemi, A., Prisco, A., Sagri, M.-T., Steve, G., Tiscornia, D.: Some ontological tools to support legal regulatory compliance, with a case study. In: Meersman, R., Tari, Z. (eds.) OTM 2003. LNCS, vol. 2889, pp. 607–620. Springer, Heidelberg (2003). https://doi.org/10.1007/978-3-540-39962-9_64

12. Garijo, D.: WIDOCO: a wizard for documenting ontologies. In: d'Amato, C., Fernandez, M., Tamma, V., Lecue, F., Cudré-Mauroux, P., Sequeda, J., Lange, C., Heflin, J. (eds.) ISWC 2017. LNCS, vol. 10588, pp. 94–102. Springer, Cham (2017). https://doi.org/10.1007/978-3-319-68204-4_9

13. Hadziselimovic, E., Fatema, K., Pandit, H.J., Lewis, D.: Linked data contracts to support data protection and data ethics in the sharing of scientific data. In: Proceedings of the First Workshop on Enabling Open Semantic Science (SemSci). CEUR Workshop Proceedings, vol. 1931, pp. 55–62 (2017). http://ceur-ws.org/Vol-1931/#paper-08

14. Hoekstra, R., Breuker, J., Di Bello, M., Boer, A., et al.: The LKIF core ontology of basic legal concepts. LOAIT **321**, 43–63 (2007)

15. Lewis, D., Moorkens, J., Fatema, K.: Integrating the management of personal data protection and open science with research ethics. In: Ethics in NLP Workshop, EACL, pp. 60–65 (2017)

16. Lohmann, S., Link, V., Marbach, E., Negru, S.: WebVOWL: web-based visualization of ontologies. In: Lambrix, P., Hyvönen, E., Blomqvist, E., Presutti, V., Qi, G., Sattler, U., Ding, Y., Ghidini, C. (eds.) EKAW 2014. LNCS (LNAI), vol. 8982, pp. 154–158. Springer, Cham (2015). https://doi.org/10.1007/978-3-319-17966-7_21

17. Mommers, L.: A knowledge-based ontology of the legal domain. In: Second International Workshop on Legal Ontologies, JURIX (2001)

18. Noy, N.F., McGuinness, D.L., et al.: Ontology development 101: a guide to creating your first ontology (2001)

19. Pandit, H.J., Lewis, D.: Modelling provenance for gdpr compliance using linked open data vocabularies. In: 5th Workshop on Society, Privacy and the Semantic Web - Policy and Technology (PrivOn 2017). CEUR Workshop Proceedings, vol. 1951 (2017). http://ceur-ws.org/Vol-1951/#paper-06

20. Peroni, S., Shotton, D., Vitali, F.: The live OWL documentation environment: a tool for the automatic generation of ontology documentation. In: ten Teije, A., Völker, J., Handschuh, S., Stuckenschmidt, H., d'Acquin, M., Nikolov, A., Aussenac-Gilles, N., Hernandez, N. (eds.) EKAW 2012. LNCS (LNAI), vol. 7603, pp. 398–412. Springer, Heidelberg (2012). https://doi.org/10.1007/978-3-642-33876-2_35

21. Steyskal, S., Kirrane, S.: If you can't enforce it, contract it: enforceability in policy-driven (linked) data markets. In: SEMANTiCS (Posters and Demos), pp. 63–66 (2015)

22. Wilkinson, M.D., Dumontier, M., Aalbersberg, I.J., Appleton, G., Axton, M., Baak, A., Blomberg, N., Boiten, J.W., da Silva Santos, L.B., Bourne, P.E., et al.: The fair guiding principles for scientific data management and stewardship. Scientific data **3** (2016). Artical no. 160018

Transfer Learning for Item Recommendations and Knowledge Graph Completion in Item Related Domains via a Co-Factorization Model

Guangyuan Piao[✉][iD] and John G. Breslin

Insight Centre for Data Analytics, Data Science Institute,
National University of Ireland Galway, Galway, Ireland
guangyuan.piao@insight-centre.org, john.breslin@nuigalway.ie

Abstract. With the popularity of Knowledge Graphs (KGs) in recent years, there have been many studies that leverage the abundant background knowledge available in KGs for the task of item recommendations. However, little attention has been paid to the *incompleteness* of KGs when leveraging knowledge from them. In addition, previous studies have mainly focused on exploiting knowledge from a KG for item recommendations, and it is unclear whether we can exploit the knowledge in the other way, i.e, whether *user-item interaction histories* can be used for improving the performance of completing the KG with regard to the domain of items. In this paper, we investigate the effect of knowledge transfer between two tasks: (1) *item recommendations*, and (2) *KG completion*, via a co-factorization model (CoFM) which can be seen as a *transfer learning* model. We evaluate CoFM by comparing it to three competitive baseline methods for each task. Results indicate that considering the *incompleteness* of a KG outperforms a state-of-the-art factorization method leveraging existing knowledge from the KG, and performs better than other baselines. In addition, the results show that exploiting *user-item interaction histories* also improves the performance of completing the KG with regard to the domain of items, which has not been investigated before.

1 Introduction

Knowledge Graphs (KGs) such as DBpedia [16] and Wikidata [33] have received great attention in the past few years. KGs provide a great amount of knowledge which can be used in different applications such as inferring user interest profiles [15], personalization of digital health for individuals [32], and recommender systems [17,20]. For instance, DBpedia provides cross-domain background knowledge about entities/things, and the latest version of this KG describes 4.58 million things including 87,000 movies. Figure 1 shows pieces of information about the entity dbr[1]:Bled_White_(2011_film), which can be retrieved from

---

[1] The prefix dbr denotes http://dbpedia.org/resource/.

© Springer International Publishing AG, part of Springer Nature 2018
A. Gangemi et al. (Eds.): ESWC 2018, LNCS 10843, pp. 496–511, 2018.
https://doi.org/10.1007/978-3-319-93417-4_32

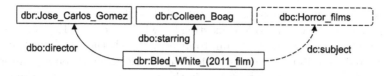

Fig. 1. Pieces of information about the movie `dbr:Bled_White_(2011_film)` from DBpedia. The piece of information with dotted lines denotes missing information from the knowledge graph.

DBpedia using SPARQL[2] queries through the SPARQL endpoint for DBpedia. Each piece of information about an entity in DBpedia is a RDF[3] triple, which consists of a *subject*, *predicate*, and *object* (e.g., `dbr:Bled_White_(2011_film)`, `dbo:starring`, `dbr:Colleen_Boag` in Fig. 1). With the freely accessible knowledge from KGs such as DBpedia, a big effort has been made in order to consume the knowledge for intelligent or adaptive systems such as recommender systems [3,21]. The focus of existing studies leveraging KGs for recommender systems has been on exploiting KG-enabled features for different types of machine learning or graph algorithms. Although previous studies have shown some useful insights about leveraging background knowledge about items from KGs for recommender systems, most of these studies have not considered the *incompleteness* of KGs.

Despite the fact that KGs provide billions of machine-readable facts about entities, they are far from complete [9], and a dedicated line of research has focused on the task of KG completion [6,8]. Indeed, most KGs use the *Open World Assumption*, i.e., it is not necessarily false if a KG does not contain a certain piece of information. The piece of information may be true but is missing from the KG. For example, the piece of information with dotted lines in Fig. 1 shows that the category `dbc`[4]`:Horror_films` is missing for the entity `dbr:Bled_White_(2011_film)` in DBpedia, which is important information in the context of recommending movies. Most previous studies that exploit KG-enabled features for item recommendations were based on the *existing* knowledge of KGs, and did not incorporate the *incompleteness* of KGs. In addition, these studies have focused on leveraging knowledge in one direction, i.e., from KGs to the task of item recommendations. Therefore, it is not clear that whether the knowledge from item recommendations, *user-item interaction histories*, can be transferred to the KG completion task with respect to the domain of items.

In this paper, we leverage a co-factorization model to investigate transfer learning [25] between these two tasks: (1) *item recommendations*, and (2) *KG completion* with respect to the domain of items. Here, *transfer learning* denotes using one task as a "source" task and the other as a "target" task. First, with item recommendations as the target task and KG completion as the source task, we are interested in whether incorporating the *incompleteness* of a KG

---

[2] https://www.w3.org/TR/rdf-sparql-query/.

[3] https://www.w3.org/RDF/.

[4] The prefix `dbc` denotes http://dbpedia.org/resource/Category.

performs better when compared to a state-of-the-art approach using a Factorization Machine (FM) which exploits existing knowledge from the KG, and outperforms other baselines. Second, we aim to investigate whether the knowledge can be transferred from item recommendations to the KG completion and improves the performance when KG completion is the target task. We use DBpedia as our KG in this study, which has been widely used for KG-enabled recommender systems. In summary, our contributions are as follows:

- We study knowledge transfer between two tasks: (1) *item recommendations*, and (2) *KG completion* for the specific domain of items, via a co-factorization model (CoFM). This transfer learning model incorporates the incompleteness of a KG for item recommendations, and incorporates the knowledge from item recommendations for completing the KG (Sect. 3).
- In Sect. 5, we evaluate CoFM with three baselines for each task, and show that incorporating the *incompleteness* of KG outperforms the baselines significantly. In addition, we show that exploiting the knowledge from item recommendations improves the performance of KG completion with respect to the domain of items, which has not been studied in previous studies.

2   Related Work

In this section, we review some related work on (1) exploiting KGs for item recommendations, and (2) KG completion.

Exploiting Knowledge Graph for Item Recommendations. With the popularity of Linked Open Data (LOD), much research work has been done in order to leverage the background knowledge from LOD (mainly from open KGs such as DBpedia) for items with different purposes with respect to recommender systems, e.g., for improving recommendation performance [4,13,17,18,20,21,24,28,35], for explaining recommendations [19], and for cross-domain recommendations [12]. Various approaches have been investigated for LOD-enabled Recommender Systems (LODRecSys) with aims at improving the recommendation performance, such as semantic similarity/distance measures for measuring the similarity/distance of two entities in the same domain [26,27], applying graph-based algorithms by incorporating background knowledge of items from KGs [18,20,21], and feeding KG-enabled features into different types of machine learning approaches [4,24,28]. A detailed review on LODRecSys can be found in [7,10].

More recently, Zhang et al. [35] used the sum of several embeddings of an item with respect to *structural, textual,* and *visual* knowledge from a KG in addition to the item embedding learned from user-item interactions for item recommendations. However, the loss functions for item recommendations and KG completion have the same weight which might not be optimal for the target task, and the knowledge transfer from item recommendations to the KG completion task was not investigated. Piao et al. [28] proposed using a FM with lightweight LOD features which can be directly obtained from the DBpedia SPARQL endpoint such as the *predicate-object lists* and *PageRank scores* of items. In [28], the authors also showed that their approach outperforms baseline methods such as BPRMF [30] and a state-of-the-art approach, which uses *learning-to-rank* algorithms for consuming KG-enabled features [24]. We use the FM approach of [28], which consumes the *existing* knowledge from a KG without considering the incompleteness of the KG, as one of our baselines.

Knowledge Graph Completion. Although KGs provide large amounts of facts about entities/things, they are highly incomplete [9]. For instance, Google observed that 71% of people in Freebase [1] lack a place of birth, and 75% lack a nationality [5]. To tackle the problem, two groups of embedding-based approaches have been proposed. One is using factorization approaches such as tensor factorization [2,6,22,23], and the other is using neural network models [11,14,34]. A typical work is TransE [2], which is a translation-based model for learning embeddings of entities and the relationships between them. The main idea of TransE is based on the assumption that if (s, p, o) is a valid triple, then the sum of embeddings for s and p should be close to the embedding of o. Drumond et al. [6] showed that using PITF (Pairwise Interaction Tensor Factorization) [31] is highly successful in predicting incomplete triples in KGs compared to other *canonical decomposition* approaches such as the one from [8].

Our work differs from previous work on KG completion as we focus on whether the knowledge transferred from *user-item interaction histories* in the task of item recommendations improves the KG completion performance with respect to the specific domain of items.

3 Learning with a Co-Factorization Model

In this section, we first formulate the two tasks - (1) item recommendations, and (2) KG completion, and then describe state-of-the-art approaches for each task in Sects. 3.1 and 3.2, respectively. Finally, we present a co-factorization model (CoFM) for transfer learning between these two tasks in Sect. 3.3.

- *Item recommendations* (task#1): Given user-item interaction histories, i.e., likes or dislikes about items (we consider binary interactions in this study), our goal is to provide the top-N item recommendations for a target user.
- *KG completion* (task#2): This task can be formulated into a top-N recommendations task as well, in the same way as previous studies [6,14]. For a given (*subject, predicate*) pair, the task is providing the top-N *object* recommendations from a set of candidate *objects*. Candidate *objects* are all objects in the *range* of a given *predicate* defined in the DBpedia ontology.

3.1 Factorization Machines for Item Recommendations

We use FMs for item recommendations. It is a state-of-the-art framework for latent factor models, and has been widely used for collaborative filtering tasks. The FM model of order $d = 2$ is defined as:

$$\hat{y}^{FM}(x) = w_0 + \sum_{i=1}^{q} w_i x_i + \sum_{i=1}^{q} \sum_{j>i}^{q} <v_i, v_j> x_i x_j \qquad (1)$$

where $\hat{y}^{FM}(x)$ denotes the predicted score using FMs, w_0 denotes the weight for a bias term, x represents feature values, and v represents the latent factors of each feature. In addition, $w_0 \in \mathbb{R}, x$ and $w \in \mathbb{R}^q, v_i \in \mathbb{R}^m$, m is the dimensionality of the factorization, and q is the number of features. The first part of the FM model is similar to a simple linear regression, which captures the interactions of each input variable x_i. In addition, the second part of the model captures all pairwise interactions of input variables $x_i x_j$ using the latent factors of features. As a general framework, FMs can mimic many state-of-the-art latent factor models such as BPRMF [30] and PITF [31], which has been shown in a previous study [29]. For a more detailed description of FMs, please refer to Rendle [29].

The first task is to provide the top-N item recommendations based on the history of user-item interactions. We focus on a binary response $y_{d_{ui}}$ (e.g., a user u likes or dislikes an item i) of each item in this study. Let β_0 denote the bias, β_i denote the weights of features with respect to i, and θ_i denote a list of latent factors for i, which can be learned through FMs with the training dataset. In addition, $\mathbf{x_{d_{ui}}}$ denotes a list of explicit features in a training example d_{ui}. The simplest case for $\mathbf{x_{d_{ui}}}$ is that it consists of one categorical feature to denote a user u, and the other categorical feature to denote an item i. Following the definition of the FM model (Eq. 1), we can estimate the preference score of an item i based on $\mathbf{x_{d_{ui}}}, \beta$ and Θ as $f(s_{d_{ui}} | \mathbf{x_{d_{ui}}}, \beta, \Theta)$, where

$$s_{d_{ui}} = \beta_0 + \beta_u + \beta_i + <\theta_u, \theta_i> \qquad (2)$$

The task of recommending the top-N items can be formalized as optimizing the Bayesian Personalized Ranking (BPR) [30] loss as follows:

$$\ell(a_1, a_2) = \sum_{a_1 \in \mathcal{D}_{ui}^+} \sum_{a_2 \in \mathcal{D}_{ui}^-} - \log[\delta(s_{a_1} - s_{a_2})] \qquad (3)$$

where δ is a sigmoid function: $\delta(x) = \frac{1}{1+e^{-x}}$, and $\mathcal{D}_{ui}^+$ and $\mathcal{D}_{ui}^-$ denote the set of positive and negative training instances, respectively. In detail, a positive training instance consists of a user and an item which the user liked in the training dataset. On the other hand, a negative instance for the user consists of the user and a randomly chosen item which is not in the list of items the user liked before in the training set. The intuition behind BPR is that a liked item for a user should be ranked higher (with a higher score) compared to a random one in the list of items with which the user has not interacted. In fact, the FM using BPR for optimization with users and items as features, is exactly a biased BPRMF [30], which has been shown in the previous study [29].

3.2   Translating Embeddings for KG Completion

The second task is the KG completion with respect to the domain of items, which can be formulated as *object* recommendations given a *subject* and *predicate* pair

[6]. We use a translation-based embedding model, TransE [2], for the second task. TransE is one of the most popular approaches for KG completion due to its effectiveness despite its simplicity. The intuition behind this model is to learn latent factors for *subjects, predicates,* and *objects,* in order to satisfy $\phi_s + \phi_p \approx \phi_o$ when (s, p, o) is a valid triple in the KG. In other words, for a valid triple (s, p, o), we want to make the embedding of o (ϕ_o) be the nearest neighbor of $\phi_s + \phi_p$ where the distance is measured by a dissimilarity function $d(\phi_s + \phi_p, \phi_o)$ such as L_2-norm. Therefore, the prediction score of a candidate o for given (s, p) can be measured as follows when L_2-norm is used as the dissimilarity function:

$$s'_{d_{spo}} = \sqrt{\sum_{j=1}^{m}(\phi_{s_j} + \phi_{p_j} - \phi_{o_j})^2} \tag{4}$$

where m denotes the dimensionality of the factorization/embedding for s, p, and o. Afterwards, the candidate set of *objects* can be ranked by their prediction scores, where an *object* with a higher distance score should be ranked lower. The loss to be optimized in TransE can be defined as below in our settings [2]:

$$\ell(b_1, b_2) = \sum_{b_1 \in \mathcal{D}^+_{spo}} \sum_{b_2 \in \mathcal{D}^-_{spo}} [\gamma + s'_{b_1} - s'_{b_2}]_+ \tag{5}$$

where $\mathcal{D}^+_{spo}$ and $\mathcal{D}^-_{spo}$ denote the set of positive and negative training instances, respectively. Here, a positive instance denotes a valid triple (s, p, o), which can be found in the training set, and a negative instance consists of s, p, and a randomly chosen *object* o^- which does not exist in the training set. $[x]_+ = 0$ *for* $x < 0$, and x otherwise, and γ is a margin hyperparameter. In the same way as [2], we set γ to 1.0, and use L_2-norm as our dissimilarity function.

3.3 Transfer Learning via a Co-Factorization Model for the Two Tasks

As we can see from Eqs. 2 and 4, we have two related representations for the latent factors of an item i in task#1 (or *subject* s in task#2), i.e., θ_i and ϕ_s, in the context of the two different tasks. In this work, we investigate two strategies for modeling the relationship between the two representations of items/subjects for transfer learning between the two tasks. For the sake of simplicity, we consider simple cases of $\mathbf{x_{d_{ui}}}$, i.e., two categorical features (to denote u and i) for $\mathbf{x_{d_{ui}}}$.

Shared Latent Space (CoFM$_A$). A straightforward approach to model the relationship between two representations for the latent factors of an item/subject in the two tasks is to assume that their latent factors are exactly the same, i.e., $\theta_i = \phi_s = \rho_{is}$, where ρ_{is} is the same latent factor for both. Given this assumption, the preference score functions (Eqs. 2 and 4) for the aforementioned two tasks can then be re-written as:

$$s_{d_{ui}} = \beta_0 + \beta_u + \beta_i + <\theta_u, \underline{\rho_{is}}>, \quad s'_{d_{spo}} = \sqrt{\sum_{j=1}^{m}(\underline{\rho_{is_j}} + \phi_{p_j} - \phi_{o_j})^2} \tag{6}$$

This approach is based on a strong assumption that an item and a subject from the two different tasks have the same latent representation.

Via Latent Space Regularization (CoFM$_R$). An alternative approach to work with the two latent representations of an item/subject is regularizing these representations to make them not reside too far away from each other. We incorporate this intuition into the model by imposing the following regularization:

$$\lambda_{\phi,\theta}\|\phi_s - \theta_i\|_F^2 \tag{7}$$

where $\lambda_{\phi,\theta}$ is a regularization parameter.

Another issue for transfer learning between the two tasks is the different output scales of the two loss functions: Eqs. 3 and 5. Hence, we modify the loss function of the KG completion task (Eq. 5) as follows in order to make both loss functions in the two tasks have the same scale.

$$\ell(b_1, b_2) = \sum_{b_1 \in \mathcal{D}_{spo}^+} \sum_{b_2 \in \mathcal{D}_{spo}^-} -\log[\delta(\gamma + s_{b_1}' - s_{b_2}')]_+ \tag{8}$$

Summary. Putting everything together, our co-factorization model in the view of *transfer learning* can be formulated as follows:

$$Opt(CoFM) : Opt(T) + \epsilon \times Opt(S), \tag{9}$$

$$Opt(T) = \arg\ \min \sum_{d_T \in \mathcal{D}_T} \ell_T(\cdot), \quad Opt(S) = \arg\ \min \sum_{d_S' \in \mathcal{D}_S'} \ell_S(\cdot)$$

where ϵ is a transfer (auxiliary) parameter to denote the importance of the knowledge transfer from the source task (S) to the target task (T). Let $\mathcal{D}_T$ and $\mathcal{D}_S$ denote the original training instances in the target and source tasks, respectively. $\mathcal{D}_S'$ is a set of training instances that is randomly sampled from $\mathcal{D}_S$ in order to match the size of $\mathcal{D}_T$, i.e., $|\mathcal{D}_T| = |\mathcal{D}_S'|$. For each instance $d_T \in \mathcal{D}_T$, we choose an instance d_S' randomly with a replacement from $\mathcal{D}_S$ where the *item* in d_T is the same as the *subject* in d_S', i.e., $d_T(i) = d_S'(s)$. With the same size for both T and S, we then use the well-known Stochastic Gradient Decent (SGD) to learn the parameters in the CoFM. An overview of the algorithm to optimize Eq. 9 using SGD is presented in Algorithm 1 when the target task is item recommendations. Our approach can be seen as a *transfer learning* [25] model as we are transferring knowledge between two different but related tasks in the same domain. It is worth noting that, in contrast to *multi-task learning* which aims to learn both tasks simultaneously, *transfer learning* aims to achieve the best performance for T with the transferred knowledge from S.

4   Experiment Setup

Here we describe our evaluation metrics (Sect. 4.1), the datasets for our experiment (Sect. 4.2), and the methods we compared for evaluating our approach (Sect. 4.3).

Algorithm 1. Main elements of the algorithm to optimize Eq. 9 using SGD when the target task T is item recommendations.

---

input : training datasets $\mathcal{D}_{ui}$ and $\mathcal{D}'_{spo}$ with the same size of $|\mathcal{D}|$, initialized
        parameters for CoFM
output: learned parameters for CoFM
repeat
    for d_{ui} *in* $\mathcal{D}_{ui}$ **do**
        Optimize Opt(T) for $\theta_u, \theta_i, \beta$
          perform SGD for BPR loss function in terms of d_{ui}
        Select d'_{spo} **in** $\mathcal{D}'_{spo}$ **where** $d'_{spo}(s) = d_{ui}(i)$
        Optimize Opt(S) for ϕ_s, ϕ_p, ϕ_o
          perform SGD for BPR loss function in terms of d'_{spo}
until *converged*;

4.1 Evaluation Metrics

The recommendation performance was evaluated via five evaluation metrics that have been widely used in previous studies as below. We describe these metrics in the context of item recommendations for users.

- **MRR**: MRR (Mean Reciprocal Rank) is the average of the reciprocal ranks of relevant items for users. It can be measured as: $MRR = \frac{1}{|U|} \sum_{k=1}^{|U|} \frac{1}{rank_k}$, where U denotes the set of users, and $rank_k$ refers to the rank position where the first *relevant* item with respect to a user $u \in U$ occurs.
- **MAP**: MAP (Mean Average Precision) measures the mean of the average precision scores (AP) of liked items of all users. The average precision of a user u is defined as: $AP_u = \frac{\sum_{n=1}^{N} P@n \times like(n)}{|I|}$, where n is the number of items, $|I|$ is the number of liked items of u, and $like(n)$ is a binary function to indicate whether the user prefers the n-th item or not.
- **P@N**: $P@N = \frac{|\{relevant\ items@N\}|}{N}$ (Precision at rank N) is the proportion of the top-N recommendations that are relevant to the user.
- **R@N**: $R@N = \frac{|\{relevant\ items@N\}|}{|\{relevant\ items\}|}$ (Recall at rank N) represents the mean probability that relevant items are successfully retrieved within the top-N recommendations.
- **nDCG@N**: nDCG (Normalized Discounted Cumulative Gain) takes into account rank positions of the relevant items, and can be computed as follows: $nDCG@N = \frac{1}{IDCG@N} \sum_{k=1}^{N} \frac{2^{\hat{r}_{uk}} - 1}{\log_2(k+1)}$ where $\hat{r}_{uk}$ is the relevance score of the item at position k with respect to a user u in the top-N recommendations, and IDCG@N denotes the score obtained by an ideal top-N ranking.

In the same way as [28], we use the *bootstrapped paired t-test* for testing the significance. The significance level of α is set to 0.05 unless otherwise noted.

4.2   Dataset

We use two datasets in the movie and book domains, which have been widely used in LODRecSys [18, 24, 28].

- **Movielens dataset** [24]. The dataset is a refined Movielens dataset[5] for LODRecSys. It consists of users and their ratings about movies, and each of the items in this dataset has been mapped into DBpedia entities if there is a mapping available[6]. In the same way as previous studies [24, 28], we consider ratings higher than 3 as positive feedback and others as negative ones.
- **DBbook dataset**. The dataset[7] consists of users and their binary feedback (1 for likes, and 0 otherwise), where the items have been mapped to DBpedia entities if there is a mapping available.

Table 1 shows the main details of user-item interactions and RDF triples in the two datasets. There are 3,997 users and 3,082 items with 827,042 ratings in the Movielens dataset. The DBbook dataset consists of 6,181 users and 6,733 items with 72,372 interactions. The sparsity of the DBbook dataset (99.38%) is higher than that of the Movielens dataset (93.27%). For item recommendations, we use 80% and 20% of each dataset for training and test sets where 20% of the training set was used for validation. In addition, all of the items were considered as candidate items for recommendations in the same way as [24] instead of considering only "rated test-one" evaluation. The second part of Table 1 shows the details of extracted triples for items/subjects in the two datasets from the DBpedia SPARQL endpoint. In the Movielens dataset, 2,952 out of 3,082 (95.8%) items have at least one triple. There are 21 distinct predicates and 18,550 objects in the Movielens dataset, which results in 81,835 triples in total. In the case of DBbook dataset, 6,211 out of 6,733 (92.2%) items have at least one triple. There are 36 distinct predicates and 16,476 objects in the DBbook dataset, which results in 72,911 triples in total. For KG completion with respect to the domain of items, we adopt the same splitting strategy as [6] for constructing training and test sets. We randomly choose a *subject* and *predicate* pair (s, p) for a given s, and then use all triples containing the pair to construct the test set. The other triples with the same *subject* were put into the training set.

We repeated five times by sampling new training and test sets for the two tasks using the aforementioned strategies, and applied different methods to them. The results in Sect. 5 are based on the averages over five runs.

4.3   Compared Methods

We use CoFM$_A$ to denote the CoFM which shares latent space with the assumption that two latent factors of an item/subject in the two tasks are exactly the same,

---

[5]   https://grouplens.org/datasets/movielens/1m/.
[6]   http://sisinflab.poliba.it/semanticweb/lod/recsys/datasets/.
[7]   http://challenges.2014.eswc-conferences.org.

Table 1. Statistics of Movielens and DBbook datasets.

		Movielens	DBbook
Statistics of user-item interactions	# of users	3,997	6,181
	# of items	3,082	6,733
	# of ratings	827,042	72,372
	Avg. # of ratings	206	12
	Sparsity	93.27%	99.38%
	% of positive ratings	56%	45.85%
Statistics of RDF triples	# of subjects	2,952 (3,082)	6,211 (6,733)
	# of predicates	21	36
	# of objects	18,550	16,476
	# of triples	81,835	72,911

and use CoFM$_R$ to denote the CoFM which uses regularization for modeling the relationship between the two latent factors of an item/subject in the two tasks.

Parameter Settings of CoFM. The transfer (auxiliary) parameter ϵ was determined by a separate validation set randomly retrieved from 20% of the training set for the first run in terms of the loss on the target task in each dataset. According to the results, ϵ was set to 0.05 for the Movielens dataset when either KG completion or item recommendations is the target task. For the DBbook dataset, ϵ was set to 0.05 and 1.0 when KG completion and item recommendations is the target task, respectively. In addition, we set the same value for all regularization parameters in our approach for the sake of simplicity. $\lambda = 0.01$ when item recommendations is the target task, and $\lambda = 0.001$ when KG completion is the target one. The dimensionally value m was set to 64, which is the same as in [6], for all factorization-based approaches.

We compare CoFM against the following methods for item recommendations.

- kNN-item (kNN): kNN-item is an item-based k-nearest neighbors algorithm. We use a MyMedialiite[8] implementation for this baseline where $k = 80$.
- BPRMF [30]: BPRMF is a matrix factorization approach for learning latent factors with respect to users and items, optimized for BPR. BPRMF can be seen as the model for item recommendations in CoFM, which is a FM model without transferring knowledge from the KG completion task.
- FM$_{LOD}$ [28]: FM$_{LOD}$ exploits *lightweight* KG-enabled features about items from DBpedia, which can be obtained directly from its SPARQL endpoint.

---

[8] http://www.mymedialite.net/.

For the KG completion task, we compare CoFM against the following methods:

- MFPP: Most Frequent Per Predicate (MFPP) is a baseline method which recommends the *objects* that co-occur most frequently with the *predicate p* given a *subject s* and *predicate* pair (s, p).
- PITF [31]: This model has been proposed in [31] for tag recommendations. In [6], the authors applied a PITF model optimized for the BPR criterion, which captures the interactions among *subjects*, *predicates*, and *objects* of RDF triples. We re-implement this approach under the framework of FMs.
- TransE [2]: This is a *translation-based* approach which models relationships by interpreting them as translations operating on the entity embeddings. We re-implemented this approach based on the parameters from [2]. As one might expect, TransE can be seen as the model for the KG completion task in CoFM without transferring knowledge from item recommendations.

We use SGD to learn the parameters in the aforementioned factorization models.

5   Results

Table 2 shows the results of comparing CoFM with the aforementioned methods in each task on the Movielens and DBbook datasets. Overall, CoFM provides the best performance compared to other approaches in item recommendations as well as KG completion in both datasets. As we can see from Table 2(a), $CoFM_R$ provides the best performance, and improves the recommendation performance significantly ($\alpha < 0.01$) compared to kNN and BPRMF for item recommendations on the Movielens dataset. Similarly, $CoFM_R$ outperforms baselines such as MFPP and PITF significantly for KG completion. In detail, a significant improvement of $CoFM_R$ over PITF in MRR (+21%), MAP (+15%), nDCG@5 (+19.8%), P@5 (+31.2%), and R@5 (+8.2%) can be noticed. On the DBbook dataset (Table 2(b)), $CoFM_A$ provides the best performance instead of $CoFM_R$. $CoFM_A$ outperforms kNN and BPRMF significantly for item recommendations, and outperforms MFPP and PITF for the KG completion task ($\alpha < 0.01$). One of the possible explanations for the observation that the best performance is achieved by $CoFM_R$ for the Movielens dataset and by $CoFM_A$ for the DBbook one might be due to the different sparsity levels of the two datasets. As we can see from Table 1, the DBbook dataset has higher sparsities compared to the Movielens dataset for both tasks. $CoFM_A$, which can be seen as having strong knowledge transfer with the assumption that item/subject embeddings in the two tasks are the same, may possibly be more useful for this sparse dataset and leads to better performance.

FM_{LOD} **vs.** CoFM. We observe that $CoFM_R$, which incorporates the *incompleteness* of DBpedia, outperforms FM_{LOD} which leverages *existing* knowledge from DBpedia on the Movielens dataset. A significant difference between the two approaches in terms of all evaluation metrics can be noticed ($\alpha < 0.01$). On the DBbook dataset, $CoFM_A$ also consistently outperforms FM_{LOD} in terms of all evaluation metrics specifically in terms of precision, e.g., +8.3% of P@5, +8% of P@10, and +5.6% of P@20 ($\alpha < 0.01$). The results show that incorporating the incompleteness of the KG improves the performance of item recommendations significantly.

Table 2. Results of *KG completion* and *item recommendations* on the Movielens (a) and DBbook (b) datasets. S denotes source task while T denotes target task. The gray cells denote significant improvement over the best-performing baseline.

(a) Movielens

	S: KG completion T: item recommendations					S: item recommendations T: KG completion				
	kNN	BPRMF	FM_{LOD}	$CoFM_A$	$CoFM_R$	MFPP	PITF	TransE	$CoFM_A$	$CoFM_R$
MRR	0.510	0.594	0.609	0.602	**0.622**	0.183	0.266	0.317	0.302	**0.322**
MAP	0.181	0.218	0.224	0.220	**0.227**	0.090	0.193	0.217	0.208	**0.222**
nDCG@5	0.358	0.425	0.436	0.429	**0.445**	0.149	0.248	0.292	0.279	**0.297**
P@5	0.291	0.355	0.366	0.360	**0.372**	0.070	0.096	0.123	**0.126**	**0.126**
R@5	0.075	0.097	0.100	0.098	**0.102**	0.103	0.230	0.241	0.240	**0.249**
nDCG@10	0.440	0.500	0.510	0.504	**0.518**	0.171	0.273	0.311	0.299	**0.316**
P@10	0.258	0.307	0.314	0.310	**0.318**	0.046	0.064	0.077	**0.081**	0.079
R@10	0.129	0.161	0.165	0.164	**0.170**	0.149	0.271	0.277	0.280	**0.283**
nDCG@20	0.583	0.645	0.653	0.648	**0.660**	0.194	0.297	0.331	0.321	**0.336**
P@20	0.218	0.252	0.257	0.254	**0.259**	0.031	0.042	0.047	**0.051**	0.048
R@20	0.213	0.257	0.261	0.260	**0.265**	0.199	0.311	0.313	0.318	**0.319**

(b) DBbook

	S: KG completion T: item recommendations					S: item recommendations T: KG completion				
	kNN	BPRMF	FM_{LOD}	$CoFM_A$	$CoFM_R$	MFPP	PITF	TransE	$CoFM_A$	$CoFM_R$
MRR	0.015	0.115	0.121	**0.125**	0.100	0.168	0.383	0.408	**0.412**	0.412
MAP	0.011	0.077	0.081	**0.083**	0.065	0.152	0.321	0.340	**0.345**	0.343
nDCG@5	0.008	0.105	0.110	**0.114**	0.091	0.162	0.372	0.399	**0.410**	0.400
P@5	0.003	0.034	0.036	**0.039**	0.031	0.048	0.111	0.117	**0.119**	0.119
R@5	0.010	0.096	0.101	**0.106**	0.085	0.177	0.363	0.377	0.380	**0.381**
nDCG@10	0.014	0.125	0.131	**0.134**	0.108	0.181	0.389	0.416	**0.423**	0.416
P@10	0.004	0.024	0.025	**0.027**	0.022	0.031	0.064	0.067	**0.068**	0.067
R@10	0.023	0.135	0.141	**0.147**	0.116	0.220	0.396	0.406	0.408	**0.408**
nDCG@20	0.022	0.145	0.153	**0.156**	0.126	0.203	0.404	0.428	**0.434**	0.430
P@20	0.004	0.017	0.018	**0.019**	0.015	0.021	0.037	0.037	**0.038**	0.038
R@20	0.043	0.187	0.196	**0.198**	0.138	0.279	0.428	0.433	0.435	**0.436**

With vs. Without Knowledge Transfer. We now look at the results of CoFM with and without transferring knowledge between the two tasks. BPRMF and TransE can be seen as the CoFM without transferring knowledge between these tasks. On the Movielens dataset, $CoFM_R$ improves the performance by 2.3%–5.2% compared to BPRMF for item recommendations ($\alpha < 0.01$). Regarding the KG completion task, $CoFM_R$ outperforms TransE significantly for all evaluation metrics as well. On the DBbook dataset, $CoFM_A$ improves the performance by 5.9%–14.7% compared to BPRMF for item recommendations. For the KG completion task, $CoFM_A$ outperforms TransE significantly in terms of all evaluation metrics

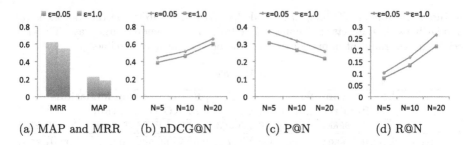

Fig. 2. The performance of item recommendations on the Movielens dataset with $\epsilon = 0.05$ and $\epsilon = 1.0$ using CoFM$_R$.

except R@10. This indicates that transferring knowledge between the two tasks improves the performance on both tasks compared to each single model without transferring knowledge from the other task.

With vs. Without Tuning the Transfer Parameter ϵ. Figure 2 shows the results of item recommendations on the Movielens dataset using CoFM$_R$ with a tuned value for the parameter ϵ ($\epsilon = 0.05$) and without tuning the parameter ($\epsilon = 1.0$). As we can see from the figure, tuning the transfer value ϵ plays an important role in achieving the best performance for the target task.

To sum up, the implications of these results are twofold. With a proper transfer parameter, (1) incorporating the *incompleteness* of a KG can improve the performance of item recommendations, and (2) the knowledge from item recommendations, i.e., *user-item interaction histories* can also be transferred to the task of KG completion with respect to the domain of items, which improves the performance significantly.

6   Conclusions

In this paper, we investigated the effect of transferring knowledge between two tasks: (1) *item recommendations*, and (2) *knowledge graph completion* with respect to the domain of items. Compared to previous approaches, which directly leverage the existing background knowledge in a KG, the transfer learning model CoFM incorporates the incompleteness of a KG into the design of CoFM. The experimental results are promising and suggest that incorporating the incompleteness of a KG improves the recommendation performance significantly compared to a state-of-the-art FM approach, which uses existing knowledge from a KG, and outperforms other baselines as well. In addition, we further explored potential synergies that transfer knowledge from item recommendations, i.e., *user-item interaction histories* to the task of KG completion, which has not been explored in previous studies. Results indicate that the knowledge from *user-item interaction histories* can be transferred to the KG completion task, and improves its performance significantly. As a further step, we plan to investigate other ways to model the relationship between two representations of an item/subject in the two tasks, e.g., using different dimensions for representing items.

Acknowledgments. This publication has emanated from research conducted with the financial support of Science Foundation Ireland (SFI) under Grant Number SFI/12/RC/2289 (Insight Centre for Data Analytics).

References

1. Bollacker, K., Evans, C., Paritosh, P., Sturge, T., Taylor, J.: Freebase: a collaboratively created graph database for structuring human knowledge. In: Proceedings of the 2008 ACM SIGMOD International Conference on Management of Data, pp. 1247–1250. ACM (2008)
2. Bordes, A., Usunier, N., Garcia-Duran, A., Weston, J., Yakhnenko, O.: Translating embeddings for modeling multi-relational data, pp. 2787–2795 (2013)
3. Di Noia, T., Cantador, I., Ostuni, V.C.: Linked open data-enabled recommender systems: ESWC 2014 challenge on book recommendation. In: Presutti, V., Stankovic, M., Cambria, E., Cantador, I., Di Iorio, A., Di Noia, T., Lange, C., Reforgiato Recupero, D., Tordai, A. (eds.) SemWebEval 2014. CCIS, vol. 475, pp. 129–143. Springer, Cham (2014). https://doi.org/10.1007/978-3-319-12024-9_17
4. Di Noia, T., Mirizzi, R., Ostuni, V.C., Romito, D.: Exploiting the web of data in model-based recommender systems. In: Proceedings of the 6th ACM Conference on Recommender Systems, pp. 253–256. ACM (2012)
5. Dong, X.L., Gabrilovich, E., Heitz, G., Horn, W., Lao, N., Murphy, K., Strohmann, T., Sun, S., Zhang, W.: Knowledge vault: a web-scale approach to probabilistic knowledge fusion. In: The 20th SIGKDD, pp. 601–610. ACM (2014)
6. Drumond, L., Rendle, S., Schmidt-Thieme, L.: Predicting RDF triples in incomplete knowledge bases with tensor factorization. In: Proceedings of the 27th Annual ACM Symposium on Applied Computing, pp. 326–331. ACM (2012)
7. Figueroa, C., Vagliano, I., Rodríguez Rocha, O., Morisio, M.: A systematic literature review of linked data-based recommender systems. Concurrency Computation **27**, 4659–4684 (2015)
8. Franz, T., Schultz, A., Sizov, S., Staab, S.: TripleRank: ranking semantic web data by tensor decomposition. In: Bernstein, A., Karger, D.R., Heath, T., Feigenbaum, L., Maynard, D., Motta, E., Thirunarayan, K. (eds.) ISWC 2009. LNCS, vol. 5823, pp. 213–228. Springer, Heidelberg (2009). https://doi.org/10.1007/978-3-642-04930-9_14
9. Galárraga, L., Razniewski, S., Amarilli, A., Suchanek, F.M.: Predicting completeness in knowledge bases. In: Proceedings of the Tenth ACM International Conference on Web Search and Data Mining, pp. 375–383. ACM (2017)
10. de Gemmis, M., Lops, P., Musto, C., Narducci, F., Semeraro, G.: Semantics-aware content-based recommender systems. In: Ricci, F., Rokach, L., Shapira, B. (eds.) Recommender Systems Handbook, pp. 119–159. Springer, Boston (2015). https://doi.org/10.1007/978-1-4899-7637-6_4
11. Guo, S., Wang, Q., Wang, B., Wang, L., Guo, L.: Semantically smooth knowledge graph embedding. In: ACL, vol. 1, pp. 84–94 (2015)
12. Heitmann, B.: An open framework for multi-source, cross-domain personalisation with semantic interest graphs. In: Proceedings of the Sixth ACM Conference on Recommender systems, pp. 313–316. ACM (2012)
13. Heitmann, B., Hayes, C.: Using linked data to build open, collaborative recommender systems. In: AAAI Spring Symposium, pp. 76–81. AAAI (2010)
14. Ji, G., Liu, K., He, S., Zhao, J.: Knowledge graph completion with adaptive sparse transfer matrix. In: Thirtieth AAAI Conference on Artificial Intelligence (2016)

15. Kapanipathi, P., Jain, P., Venkataramani, C., Sheth, A.: User interests identification on Twitter using a hierarchical knowledge base. In: Presutti, V., d'Amato, C., Gandon, F., d'Aquin, M., Staab, S., Tordai, A. (eds.) ESWC 2014. LNCS, vol. 8465, pp. 99–113. Springer, Cham (2014). https://doi.org/10.1007/978-3-319-07443-6_8

16. Lehmann, J., Isele, R., Jakob, M., Jentzsch, A., Kontokostas, D., Mendes, P.N., Hellmann, S., Morsey, M., van Kleef, P., Auer, S.: DBpedia-a Large-scale, multilingual knowledge base extracted from Wikipedia. Semant. Web J. 1, 1–5 (2013)

17. Lu, C., Stankovic, M., Radulovic, F., Laublet, P.: Crowdsourced affinity: a matter of fact or experience. In: Blomqvist, E., Maynard, D., Gangemi, A., Hoekstra, R., Hitzler, P., Hartig, O. (eds.) ESWC 2017. LNCS, vol. 10249, pp. 554–570. Springer, Cham (2017). https://doi.org/10.1007/978-3-319-58068-5_34

18. Musto, C., Lops, P., Basile, P., de Gemmis, M., Semeraro, G.: Semantics-aware graph-based recommender systems exploiting linked open data. In: Proceedings of the 2016 Conference on User Modeling Adaptation and Personalization, pp. 229–237. ACM (2016)

19. Musto, C., Narducci, F., Lops, P., De Gemmis, M., Semeraro, G.: ExpLOD: a framework for explaining recommendations based on the linked open data cloud. In: Proceedings of the 10th ACM Conference on Recommender Systems, pp. 151–154. RecSys 2016. ACM, New York (2016)

20. Musto, C., Semeraro, G., de Gemmis, M., Lops, P.: Tuning personalized pagerank for semantics-aware recommendations based on linked open data. In: Blomqvist, E., Maynard, D., Gangemi, A., Hoekstra, R., Hitzler, P., Hartig, O. (eds.) ESWC 2017. LNCS, vol. 10249, pp. 169–183. Springer, Cham (2017). https://doi.org/10.1007/978-3-319-58068-5_11

21. Nguyen, P., Tomeo, P., Di Noia, T., Di Sciascio, E.: An evaluation of SimRank and personalized PageRank to build a recommender system for the web of data. In: Proceedings of the 24th WWW, pp. 1477–1482. ACM (2015)

22. Nickel, M., Murphy, K., Tresp, V., Gabrilovich, E.: A review of relational machine learning for knowledge graphs. Proc. IEEE 104(1), 11–33 (2016)

23. Nickel, M., Tresp, V., Kriegel, H.P.: Factorizing yago: scalable machine learning for linked data. In: Proceedings of the 21st International Conference on World Wide Web, pp. 271–280. ACM (2012)

24. Noia, T.D., Ostuni, V.C., Tomeo, P., Sciascio, E.D.: Sprank: semantic path-based ranking for top-n recommendations using linked open data. ACM Trans. Intell. Syst. Technol. (TIST) 8(1), 9 (2016)

25. Pan, S.J., Yang, Q.: A survey on transfer learning. IEEE Trans. Knowl. Data Eng. 22(10), 1345–1359 (2010)

26. Passant, A.: dbrec — music recommendations using DBpedia. In: Patel-Schneider, P.F., Pan, Y., Hitzler, P., Mika, P., Zhang, L., Pan, J.Z., Horrocks, I., Glimm, B. (eds.) ISWC 2010. LNCS, vol. 6497, pp. 209–224. Springer, Heidelberg (2010). https://doi.org/10.1007/978-3-642-17749-1_14

27. Piao, G., Breslin, J.G.: Measuring semantic distance for linked open data-enabled recommender systems. In: Proceedings of the 31st Annual ACM Symposium on Applied Computing, pp. 315–320. ACM, Pisa (2016)

28. Piao, G., Breslin, J.G.: Factorization machines leveraging lightweight linked open data-enabled features for top-N recommendations. In: Bouguettaya, A., Gao, Y., Klimenko, A., Chen, L., Zhang, X., Dzerzhinskiy, F., Jia, W., Klimenko, S.V., Li, Q. (eds.) WISE 2017. LNCS, vol. 10570, pp. 420–434. Springer, Cham (2017). https://doi.org/10.1007/978-3-319-68786-5_33

29. Rendle, S.: Factorization machines with libFM. ACM Trans. Intell. Syst. Technol. **3**(3), 57:1–57:22 (2012)
30. Rendle, S., Freudenthaler, C., Gantner, Z., Schmidt-Thieme, L.: BPR: Bayesian personalized ranking from implicit feedback. In: Proceedings of the 25th Conference on Uncertainty in Artificial Intelligence, pp. 452–461. AUAI Press (2009)
31. Rendle, S., Schmidt-Thieme, L.: Pairwise interaction tensor factorization for personalized tag recommendation. In: Proceedings of the Third ACM International Conference on Web Search and Data Mining, pp. 81–90. ACM (2010)
32. Sheth, A., Perera, S., Wijeratne, S., Thirunarayan, K.: Knowledge will propel machine understanding of content: extrapolating from current examples. In: 2017 IEEE/WIC/ACM International Conference on Web Intelligence. ACM (2017)
33. Vrandečić, D., Krötzsch, M.: Wikidata: a free collaborative knowledgebase. Commun. ACM **57**(10), 78–85 (2014)
34. Wang, Z., Zhang, J., Feng, J., Chen, Z.: Knowledge graph embedding by translating on hyperplanes. In: AAAI, pp. 1112–1119 (2014)
35. Zhang, F., Yuan, N.J., Lian, D., Xie, X., Ma, W.Y.: Collaborative knowledge base embedding for recommender systems. In: Proceedings of the 22nd ACM SIGKDD International Conference on Knowledge Discovery and Data Mining, KDD 2016, pp. 353–362. ACM, New York (2016)

Modeling and Summarizing News Events Using Semantic Triples

Radityo Eko Prasojo[(✉)] [ID], Mouna Kacimi[ID], and Werner Nutt[ID]

Free University of Bozen-Bolzano, Piazza Domenicani 3, 39100 Bozen-Bolzano, Italy
{RPrasojo,Mouna.Kacimi,Werner.Nutt}@unibz.it

Abstract. Summarizing news articles is becoming crucial for allowing quick and concise access to information about daily events. This task can be challenging when the same event is reported with various levels of detail or is subject to diverse view points. A well established technique in the area of news summarization consists in modeling events as a set of semantic triples. These triples are weighted, mainly based on their frequencies, and then fused to build summaries. Typically, triples are extracted from main clauses, which might lead to information loss. Moreover, some crucial facets of news, such as reasons or consequences, are mostly reported in subordinate clauses and thus they are not properly handled. In this paper, we focus on an existing work that uses a graph structure to model sentences allowing the access to any triple independently from the clause it belongs to. Summary sentences are then generated by taking the top ranked paths that contain many triples and show grammatical correctness. We further provide several improvements to that approach. First, we leverage node degrees for finding the most important triples and facets shared among sentences. Second, we enhance the process of triple fusion by providing more effective similarity measures that exploit entity linking and predicate similarity. We performed extensive experiments using the DUC'04 and DUC'07 datasets showing that our approach outperforms baseline approaches by a large margin in terms of ROUGE and PYRAMID scores.

1 Introduction

A large amount of news articles is published daily to cover important events. The volume of such content can be overwhelming for news readers compromising their ability to get an overall, but concise, picture of what is happening. To solve this issue, multi-document summarization approaches were developed providing a quick access to essential information [4, 9, 10, 12, 13, 19, 22, 26]. The main challenge of summarizing news articles is how to capture the different perspectives, view points, and levels of detail reported for the same event. Once these differences are captured, their inclusion in the summary is far from being trivial. For example, different news platforms reported the following information about the same event:

© Springer International Publishing AG, part of Springer Nature 2018
A. Gangemi et al. (Eds.): ESWC 2018, LNCS 10843, pp. 512–527, 2018.
https://doi.org/10.1007/978-3-319-93417-4_33

> *S1:* *"President Donald Trump has fired FBI Director James Comey, the White House said in a statement Tuesday evening."* (TIME)
>
> *S2:* *"Donald Trump fired FBI director James Comey in order to stop an investigation which could have potentially ruinous consequences for the administration."* (New York Times)
>
> *S3:* *"Democrats said James Comey was fired because the FBI was investigating alleged links between the Trump campaign and Russia."* (BBC)
>
> *S4:* *"The Trump administration attributed Comey's dismissal to his handling of the investigation into Democratic nominee Hillary Clinton's email server."* (CNN)
>
> *S5:* *"Donald Trump could be forced to leave office over the investigations into his administration's links with Russia."* (INDEPENDENT)

The above sentences put the light on different aspects of the dismissal of the FBI director. They give diverse types of details that we call *facets*, including time, news provenance, and possible reasons for firing the FBI director. Thus, the task of summarization consists in first identifying the main facts and their facets from a set of news articles, and then fusing those facets to have a concise description of each event.

This problem falls into the category of abstractive approaches where sentences of the original text are rephrased to create summaries [1,3,5,6,8–10,12,13,21,22,26,27]. The main idea of abstractive summarization is to leverage fine-grained fact extraction where a fact can be represented as words or semantic triples of the form ⟨Arg1; predicate; Arg2⟩. Most existing approaches rely on similarity between facts to merge information [1,3,6,9,10,13,19,22,26]. In the previous example, sentences *S1* and *S2* contain the same fact ⟨Donald Trump; fired; FBI director⟩ and therefore they can be fused to summarize three facets of information including the source of the news, the time, and the reason. Typically the similarity between sentences is based on facts belonging to main clauses. Thus, if two sentences contain similar facts in subordinate clauses, their fusion is not easily handled. For example, considering the main clause, sentence *S3* talks about firing the FBI director and sentence *S5* talks about "the end of Trump's presidency". By contrast, considering the subordinate clause, they both talk about the "Russian investigation and its consequences". Thus, by fusing *S3* and *S5* we can have different facets of the fact "Russian investigation".

The above problem is best handled using semantic summarization [12,19]. The idea is to extract facts, represented as triples, from text documents and model them as a graph. The nodes of the graph can be either words or word types. Each edge connecting two nodes represents their consecutive occurrence in the same sentence of the original text. Summary sentences are then generated using the top ranked paths in terms of grammaticality and fact coverage. The graph model facilitates the retrieval and the fusion of important triples from both main and subordinate clauses. Additionally, facts are naturally connected along the paths with their facets. So, finding the best paths would automatically lead to finding the most important facets to be included in the summary. The main limitations are related to how this approach was applied to news summarization by Li et al. [12]. First, fact fusion merges triples having similar word types leading, in some cases, to incorrect results. For example, "Trump" and "Obama" both are of type person but they are two different entities and therefore sentences containing them should not be fused together. Second, long paths covering many triples are not necessarily the best since they might concatenate unrelated facts. Third, facts are clustered using predefined themes, which is inflexible for the dynamic nature of news content. In this paper, we aim at tackling the above problems extending the approach proposed by Li et al. [12] to handle news summarization in a more effective way. Our main contributions are as follows:

1. We propose a fact fusion strategy based on entity linking and predicate similarity. We perform entity linking via entity recognition, name normalization, and coreference resolution using Stanford NLP and DBpedia Spotlight, whereas predicate similarity is done using WordNet::Similarity.
2. In addition to the grammaticality and fact coverage, we employ node degrees to rank paths. This results in boosting paths having multiple authoritative nodes and therefore finding important facts to be included in the summary.
3. We propose an alternative to the predefined classification of facts by employing a dynamic grouping using K-means clustering. To this end, we use word2vec [17] trained on the Google News dataset to generate word vectors which are then used to cluster similar facts.
4. We run extensive experiments using the DUC'04 and DUC'07 datasets, showing that our approach outperforms the baseline approaches with a large margin in terms of ROUGE and PYRAMID scores.

2   Related Work

Our work falls into the category of abstractive summarization of news articles. Many previous attempts were based on facts extracted from main clauses [6,10,22,26], in contrast to ours, that aims to enrich summaries with facets obtained from subclauses. Moreover, they did not focus on obtaining new facts by fusing together individual facts, instead they simply merged or clustered similar facts. Nevertheless, some core components of these approaches are related to our work. The first one is a fact extraction technique, which is either done via Open Information Extraction (OIE) such as OLLIE [25] and ClausIE [7], Semantic Role Labeling such as SEMAFOR [11] and SENNA SRL [5], or constituent/grammatical dependency parsing. The second one is a fact merging or clustering technique, which can be adopted for a triple fusion approach. Vanderwende et al. [26] used dependency parsing to extract simple facts, leveraged triple similarity, entity coreference and event coreference for clustering, and then generated summary sentences by unfolding the entity fragments end event fragments. Similarly, D'Aciarno et al. [6] and later Amato et al. [1] leveraged dependency parsing for fact extraction and employed similarity measures based on the subject, predicate, and object for fact merging. Pighin et al. [22] developed their own data-driven pattern extractor for their basic semantic unit, and was able to merge multiple facts expressed in different ways.

Khan et al. [10] developed an approach that exploits SENNA [5] to extract basic semantic unit. They used WordNet::Similarity [21] for SRL unit clustering and then selected their representative fact from each cluster via a scoring function obtained by a genetic algorithm. Summary sentences were generated using SimpleNLG [8] with several heuristics employed. Genest and Lapalme [9] used dependency parsing for fact extraction in the form of INIT (Information Unit), another triple-like structure. Then, they produced summary sentences using a text-to-text generation based on SimpleNLG. Khan et al.'s BSU and Genest & Lapalme's INIT can be annotated with dative or locative information, which makes their representation richer than the other approaches described above. Similarly, Li [13] used a simple BSU parsing to extract simple facts, which later are clustered based on semantic relatedness between concepts, similarity between verbs, and sentence co-occurrence. The sentence generation is a series of subject, predicate, and object unfoldings from the BSUs. Unfolded objects can be in the form of subclauses. However, fine-grained facts from the subclauses are not specifically extracted and merged.

On the other hand, we found fewer attempts that exploit fact extraction from subclauses. Bing et al. [3] used constituent parsing to extract noun phrases (NPs) and verb phrases (VPs), which then, being separately clustered, are combined after checking whether some NPs and VPs together satisfy constraints such as compatibility and validity. As a result, some NPs can be matched to VPs obtained from different sentences, forming new, potentially more informative summary sentences. Additionally, NPs (VPs) appearing in a constituent subtree up to two levels on a path containing only NP (VP) nodes are also taken into account, effectively parsing independent subclauses, but not dependent ones. Moreover, the approach did not address grammaticality when forming new sentences, and the new sentence formation is limited to coreference resolution of entities. The most relevant work to ours is by Li et al. [12], who developed a pattern-based approach to extract abstractive summaries from news articles. In contrast to Bing et al.'s, Li et al.'s approach is orthogonal to the type of subclause (dependent or independent). It also employs a grammaticality score in order to maintain the quality of its summary sentences. In the next section, we will explain in more detail Li et al's work and how our work is built upon it.

3   Background

Our work is based on the approach developed by Li et al. [12]. The main idea is to identify patterns of triples and further build summaries based on sentences having the largest number of patterns. Practically, triples are extracted from news articles, using OLLIE [25], in the form of ⟨arg1; predicate; arg2⟩, for example ⟨Donald Trump; fired; FBI director⟩. Then, a pattern is generated from each triple, annotating the heads of arguments arg1 and arg2 with their types. The annotation is done using Stanford NER [15] and SEMAFOR [11]. For example, annotating the triple ⟨Donald Trump; fired; FBI director⟩ generates the pattern ⟨PROTAGONIST; fired; PERSON⟩. As OLLIE may return clausal arguments, patterns with such arguments do not get their head annotated. For example ⟨PERSON; killed by; a gunman who is on the loose⟩ has only one argument annotated but it is a valid pattern. Further, patterns are clustered into pre-defined themes specific for TAC 2010 guided summarization task. Examples of such themes include, "what happened", "reason", "damages", and "counter-measures". Then, from each cluster, a graph is constructed by fusing together all patterns in the cluster based on their POS and lemma, ignoring stop words. Finally, sentences are generated by traversing all possible paths in the graph, and then ranked based on their grammaticality and pattern coverage. The top ranked path in each cluster is then picked as the representative summary sentence for the cluster.

We observe that the approach by Li et al. [12] has three main problems. The first one is that it uses a predefined list of "themes" to group patterns, which is specific for some, but not all kinds of news articles. Therefore, we need to develop an alternative way to cluster patterns when the themes are unknown. Second, they rely on POS and lemma for pattern fusion. We think that this is prob-lematic because it can potentially fuse unrelated patterns, which consequently generate incorrect sentences. For example, consider the two patterns: ⟨Trump; told; Comey to stop his investigation about Russia⟩ and ⟨Trump; fired; Comey because of his investigation about Hillary Clinton⟩. The graph fusion approach will generate the following result:

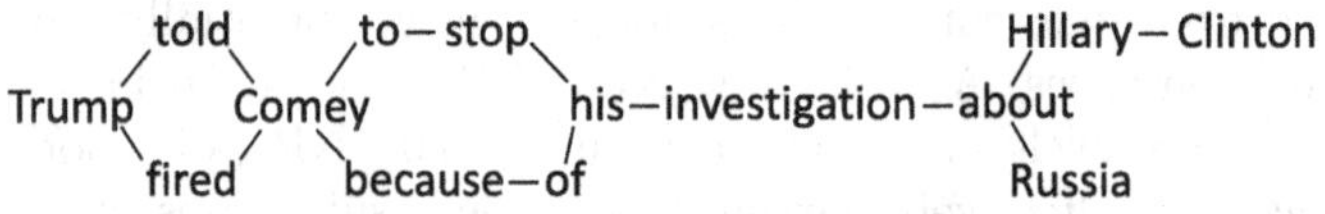

Fig. 1. An example of a fusion graph

Because the sentence ranking is based on pattern coverage and grammaticality, the chosen sentence would be "Trump told Comey to stop his investigation about Hillary Clinton" which is not correct w.r.t. the original news articles. The third problem is that pattern fusion relies on object typings returned by Stanford NER and SEMAFOR. Consider if Trump and Obama both appear in the original text. Both are of type PERSON, so during the fusion they will be merged together, which is not something that should happen because it often leads to incorrect summary sentence generation.

4   Improvements and Extensions

Our summarization approach follows the same line as the work of Li et al. [12], which we consider a baseline solution. Figure 2 shows an overview of our approach. Triple extraction and grouping, graph fusion, and ranking modules indicate the steps that are improved from the baseline. On the other hand, entity and verb linking modules indicate our extensions of the baseline.

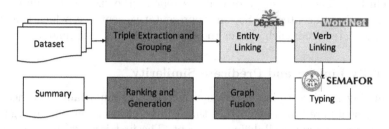

Fig. 2. Improvements and extensions

4.1 Triple Extraction and Grouping

We start by extracting triples from a set of news articles. Similarly to the baseline approach, we use OLLIE [25] to extract triples of the form ⟨arg1; predicate; arg2⟩. The summarization process starts by finding groups of similar triples, as it is crucial to find the sentences that have the same focus of the news. In other words, we aim at finding triples that tackle similar facets. Consider these triples:

> T1: ⟨Donald Trump; fired; FBI director James Comey in order to stop the Russian investigation⟩
>
> T2: ⟨Democrats; said; FBI director James Comey was fired upon his handling of the investigation into Hillary Clinton's email server⟩
>
> T3: ⟨Donald Trump; fired; FBI director James Comey the White House said in a statement Tuesday evening⟩

We observe that *T1* and *T3* have the same first argument, the same predicate, and the same head of the second argument. Thus, they can be considered as most similar triples. However, *T1* and *T2* are more similar because both talk about the reason of the dismissal of Comey. The baseline approach tackled this problem by first grouping triples into predefined themes, such as "consequences" and "reasons", relying on training data. Since this solution does not cover all news article datasets and is not flexible considering the dynamic nature of news, we propose an unsupervised approach to define triple groups (i.e., themes).

Our approach consists of three main steps. First, we use word2vec [17] trained on the Google News dataset to generate word embeddings for each word in each triple. Second, we enhance the generated word vectors by using PCA (Principal Component Analysis) as it was shown by [2] that this weighting improves the effectiveness of textual similarity tasks by 10% to 30%, and outperforms sophisticated supervised methods. Third, we perform K-means clustering, a well established technique in machine learning, to create K clusters of similar triples based on the generated word vectors. The clustering technique starts by selecting randomly K triples as centroids and then maps all triples to the most similar centroid. The centroids then get updated and the process repeats until we obtain stable clusters. The number K of clusters reflects the size of the summary in terms of number of sentences. So, one representative sentence, which is a set of triples, is selected from each cluster to be part of the final summary.

4.2   Entity Linking and Predicate Similarity

When finding similar triples, mentioned entities are important. The heads of triple arguments are typically entities that can be either a person, an organization, a location, or any well-defined concept. The first issue with entity recognition is that existing tools do not have an agreement on what an entity is and therefore they might miss some important entities such as "Crimea". The second issue is that entities are not always mentioned using their full names, but sometimes using abbreviations or only last names of people, which we call aliases. Interestingly, traditional Named Entity Recognition (NER) tools are not always able to recognize entities from aliases. The third issue is that NER approaches are not designed to detect entities that appear as coreferences. This is a problem for our work since we need to find similar triples. For example, there is no way to detect that the triples ⟨Donald Trump; fired; FBI director James Comey⟩ and ⟨He; fired; Comey⟩ have identical meaning because the entities are not resolved.

To overcome the above problems we follow our approach in [23], where we performed entity linking. We start by doing entity recognition, where we exploit DBpedia Spotlight [16], a large-scale knowledge base extracted from Wikipedia. It is a graph database that uses the RDF format. It represents Wikipedia categories as resources and uses the *rdf:type* predicate to state whether a resource is a class or an individual of a class. Using this property, we filter entities by removing all results produced by NER tools that have no property *rdf:type* in DBpedia Spotlight. Then, we introduce a name normalization technique that converts all aliases to normalized names to facilitate entity extraction. To begin, we extract entities from the news article using the entity filtering technique described earlier. For entities of type Person, we set as aliases first names, middle names, and last names. For other types, we find possible aliases using DBpedia Spotlight. As last step, we apply the Stanford Deterministic Coreference Resolution System [24] to map coreferences to their corresponding entities.

Another problem related to triple similarity are predicates. Some predicates, which are typically represented as verbs, have the same meaning. For example, the two triples ⟨Donald Trump; fired; FBI director James Comey⟩ and ⟨Donald Trump; dismissed; FBI director James Comey⟩ are basically the same. However, this cannot be detected if the two predicates are considered as two different words. To solve this problem, we use WordNet::Similarity [21] to detect similar predicates and use only one representative word for them. Since WordNet returns a similarity score for each pair of predicates, we set the similarity threshold high, concretely 90%, so we only fuse verbs (predicates) that have very close meanings.

4.3   Fusion Graph and Strict Merging

As a first step, we follow the baseline approach to build a fusion graph for each group of similar triples or patterns. At the beginning we use patterns since we strictly follow the baseline approach. The graph is constructed by iteratively adding patterns to it, as shown in Algorithm 1. A node is added to the graph for each word (token) in the pattern, where consecutive words are linked with directed edges. When adding a new pattern, a token from the pattern is merged with an existing node in the graph providing that they have the same POS tag and they share the same lemma. An essential observation is that some words such as "he" and "his" have the same POS tag "PRP" and the same lemma, but they should not be merged together. Also, stopwords like "the", "to", and "of" should not be merged together in order to avoid noise. It is important to clarify that without annotation, the core of each pattern is simply a sentence of the original text. The structure of triples is used only to identify their predicates and the arguments, to perform head argument annotation and triple similarity checking.

Algorithm 1. Graph Fusion

Data: P: set of patterns
Result: (V, E): graph of fused patterns

1   **ConstructGraph(P)**
2   **begin**
3     $(V, E) := (\emptyset, \emptyset)$; // `empty graph`
4   **foreach** $p \in P$ **do**
5       $prevV := null$;
6       $ptokens := p.splitToTokens()$;
7   **foreach** $t \in ptokens$ **do**
8   **if** $t \notin V$ **or** $isStopword(t)$ **then**
9           $curV :=$ **new** $Vertex(t)$;
10          $V := V \cup \{curV\}$
11   **else**
12           $curV := G.getV(t)$;
13   **if** $prevVertex \neq null$ **then**
14           $e :=$ **new** $Edge(prevV, curV)$;
15           $E := E \cup \{e\}$;

We enhance the fusion graph by merging triples without annotation taking into account entity linking and predicate similarity when adding nodes. In other words, a token can now be entities or predicates, and therefore their linkings or similarities are involved during the merging process (the $t \notin V$ in line 8–10 in Algorithm 1). We also employ strict merging, where merging is done only for matching entities and predicates, but not for other types of nodes. The idea is to avoid topic drift and concatenating triples that are not compatible. The example in Sect. 3 show that the fusion of the two triples ⟨Trump; told; Comey to stop his investigation about Russia⟩ and ⟨Trump; fired; Comey because of his investigation about Hillary Clinton) might lead to the sentence "Trump told Comey to stop his investigation about Hillary Clinton" which is not correct.

4.4 Summary Sentence Selection

Sentences that compose the final summary are selected from the fusion graph. One path corresponds to one sentence. Paths are ranked based on two criteria: their grammaticality and their triple (or pattern) coverage. So, highly ranked paths should cover many paths which means that they summarize several facets of the same fact. Moreover, they should be grammaticality correct.

We implemented our own grammatical checker based on Stanford NLP and languagetools.org,[1] since the model used by the baseline was not publicly available. We performed a partial grammatical fix, focusing on the dangling verbs, i.e. verbs that are not correctly anchored to a subject, that are results of either OLLIE or the graph fusion. The fix is done by transforming the verb phrase into a well-formed clause using a relative pronoun (which, that, who, where, etc.) or a participle by analyzing the grammatical dependency to detect the occurrence of the dangling verbs and entity typing to determine the correct pronoun. Additionally, we analyze whether a dangling verb should be a passive voice by checking whether there exists a preposition that is connected to the verb as a nominal modifier. Finally, sentences without verbs are discarded.

We further enhanced path ranking exploiting, in addition to pattern coverage and grammaticality, node degrees. A node degree is the total number of both incoming and outgoing edges of the node. The idea is to select a path that has multiple important nodes, which are nodes having high degrees. Practically, our path ranking algorithm is a multi-step pairwise comparison in the following order: (1) pattern coverage, (2) node degree, and (3) grammaticality. For the node degree step, we compare first the average degree then the total degree of two paths. Finally, leveraging our grammaticality checker and fixer model, we set higher precedence in the following order: originally grammatical paths, grammatically fixable paths, and ungrammatical, non-fixable path.

5   Experiments

5.1   Setup

Datasets. For our evaluation, we used the DUC'04[2] and DUC'07[3] datasets, which represent one of the most important English corpora for summarization. The DUC'04 contains 50 news topics while the DUC'07 dataset provides 45 news topics. Each news topic contains 10 news articles and 4 human summaries. We also prepared a dataset for manual assessment of the quality of our

---

[1] https://www.languagetool.org/.
[2] http://duc.nist.gov/duc2004/tasks.html.
[3] http://duc.nist.gov/duc2007/tasks.html.

summaries. The code of our work can be found in https://gitlab.inf.unibz.it/rprasojo/summarization.

Assessment. The results are assessed automatically. We basically compare the summaries generated by the different approaches under comparison with the human summaries. In the case of manual assessment done on the randomly generated 100 summary sentences, we proceeded as follows. We asked 20 students and researchers in our faculty to independently assess the coherence and correctness of the summary sentences on a scale between 1 to 5. After that, we computed the average score of each sentence. The correctness of sentences regards whether the reported information corresponds to what really happened. By contrast, coherence is about the correctness of the sentence structure.

Strategies Under Comparison. We used the approach by Li et al. [12] as the baseline for our experiments. This approach represents the starting point of our work. We performed further improvements and tested the impact of each extension on the results. So, we have the following strategies under comparison:

1. **B**. The baseline approach by Li et al. [12];
2. **B+ EL**. The baseline approach with Entity Linking;
3. **B+ PL**. The baseline approach with Predicate Linking;
4. **B+ EL+ PL**. The baseline approach with Entity and Predicate Linking;
5. **B+ EL+ PL-T**. The baseline approach with Entity and Predicate Linking but without Typing Annotation;
6. **B+ EL+ PL-T+SM**. The baseline approach with Entity and Predicate Linking, without Typing Annotation, and with Strict Merging;
7. **B+ EL+ PL+SM**. The baseline approach with Entity and Predicate Linking and Strict Merging.

Metrics. We have used the following measures in our evaluation:

1. **ROUGE.** The ROUGE measure [14] consists in computing the overlap between automatically produced summaries and human produced summaries, which are considered as ground truth. The overlap between summaries is typically in terms of n-grams, where n is defined by the experiment setting. In our work, we used n-grams of size 1 and 2. The ROUGE metric is represented by two quantitative measures: *Recall* and *Precision*. We compute the *Recall* as the number of overlapping n-grams divided by the total number of n-grams present in the human produced summary. By contrast, the precision is given as the number of overlapping n-grams divided by the total number of n-grams in the automatic summary. In our experiments, we compute the *F1* measure, that combines both precision and recall.
2. **PYRAMID.** PYRAMID scoring [18] involves semantic matching of Summary Content Units (SCUs), so it can recognize semantically synonymous facts. We use the automated version proposed in [20], which leverages a weighted factorization model to transform the n-grams within sentence bounds of the generated summary, and the contributors and label of an SCU

into 100 dimensional vector representation. If the similarity between an n-gram vector of a summary and an SCU exceeds a given threshold, then the SCU is assigned to the summary. We use the same setting described in [3], including the two threshold values 0.6 and 0.65.

5.2   Results

The overall results of our approach are shown in Tables 1 and 2. The ROUGE scores are shown in Table 1 for all strategies and datasets. We observe that our approach improves significantly the precision and F1 measure over the baseline approach. For the DUC'04 dataset we have an increase of precision of 7% and of *F1* measure of 11% considering unigram matching R-1. These values naturally decrease for bigram matching R-2, but we still improve the precision and *F1* measure by 2% and 3% respectively. The same observations hold for DUC'07 with very similar values for unigram matching R-1. We notice that the improvement is a bit higher for bigram matching R-2, where we have an increase of precision and *F1* measure that is no less than 3%. Having a closer look at the results of the different strategies we implemented, we observe that all our extensions improves precision and *F1* measure with respect to the baseline approach. Each added extension increases the precision and *F1* measure with a minimum of 1%. We just note a very slight decrease in *F1* measure for both datasets depending on whether we use typing annotations or not.

Table 1. ROUGE scores in %, where B = Baseline, EL = Entity Linking, PL = Predicate Linking, T = Typing, and SM = Strict Merging

Method	DUC'04				DUC'07			
	R-1		R-2		R-1		R-2	
	R	F1	R	F1	R	F1	R	F1
B	32.65	27.21	8.31	7.12	30.81	26.12	7.01	6.89
B+EL	36.73	36.14	10.11	9.64	34.61	34.23	9.19	8.83
B+PL	34.44	33.89	9.66	8.43	31.55	33.07	8.38	8.12
B+EL+PL	37.36	36.82	10.64	9.77	35.97	36.00	9.63	9.44
B+EL+PL-T	38.21	37.33	10.68	9.89	36.88	36.61	9.70	9.61
B+EL+PL-T+SM	38.76	**38.81**	10.73	**10.01**	37.52	**37.97**	9.77	**9.89**
B+EL+PL+SM	**39.15**	38.77	**10.95**	9.95	**37.91**	37.62	**10.02**	9.80

We further computed the PYRAMID scores for the DUC'07 dataset as shown in Table 2. This dataset was the only one providing a ground truth with semantic annotation for PYRAMID scoring, while DUC'04 does not provide such a ground truth so a PYRAMID evaluation for it is not possible. We observe that our approach provides a significant improvement over the baseline that goes up to 25%.

Besides the ROUGE and PYRAMID score, our evaluation shows how the contentedness of the graph evolves as a result of our improvements. Initially, the

Table 2. PYRAMID (DUC'07 in %)

Method	T:0.6	T:0.65
B	48.12	40.90
B+EL	65.47	56.89
B+VL	61.71	53.75
B+EL+VL	69.94	61.08
B+EL+VL-T	71.22	62.65
B+EL+VL-T+SM	72.66	63.41
B+EL+VL+SM	**73.04**	**63.88**

baseline relies on the typing in the graph fusion, which causes a highly liberal merging. For instance, if a cluster of patterns contain many <PERSON>, even though not referring to the same person, then some of the paths will be long (i.e. high pattern coverage), with many of them potentially resulting in an incorrect merging. By leveraging EL+VL, the typings are replaced with the corresponding entity and verb annotations. This causes less liberal merging. Evidently, after applying EL+VL, the average pattern coverage score goes down from 6.32 to 3.29 with standard deviation down from 3.02 to 0.87, so our graph becomes more compact and less convoluted. Combined with the ROUGE and PYRAMID scores, we can be confident that most paths that are "fixed" from the baseline are bad paths. Less variance on the pattern coverage score also means more usage of node degree ranking tiebreakers. We measured that it rises from 11% (baseline) to 80% (B+EL+VL+SM).

We also give an example of two summaries, one generated by the baseline approach and one by our approach. The summaries are of the news articles talking about Donald Trump firing the FBI director.

> **Baseline.** Donald Trump to leave office over the investigations into his administration's links with Russia, a former National Security Agency said. Comey informing Congress that the FBI didn't find anything and continued to believe Clinton's practices did not merit the pursuance of any criminal charges. Comey was fired now at a time before he made Tuesday's decision. He told the Senate last week it had made him "mildly nauseous" to think his intervention could have affected the election. Senator Richard Burr stopped conducting its own investigation into Russian meddling in the 2016 election. Other congressional committees are investigating a possible Russian connection mostly behind closed doors. Trump's decision means that the bureau is conducting a search for a new director which will begin immediately. White House press secretary Sean Spicer learned of his dismissal from televisions said law enforcement veteran who had been critical of the Justice Department under former President George W. Bush to the top domestic investigative and surveillance organization.

B+EL+VL+SM. The US President Donald Trump was to face an indictment over allegations his campaign team colluded with Russia to disrupt the presidential election, which could put an end to his presidency. Today President Donald J. Trump informed FBI Director James Comey that he has been terminated and removed from office said in a statement Tuesday evening. The White House said that the impetus for the firing of Comey came from Rosenstein, who accused Comey of attempting to "usurp the attorney general 's authority" by publicly announcing why he felt the case should be closed without prosecution. Comey learned of his dismissal from televisions said law enforcement sources. Mrs Clinton lays part of the blame for her shock election defeat last November on Mr Comey. Mr. Comey's bungling of the investigation into Hillary Clinton's private email server violated longstanding Justice Department policy. He told the Senate last week it had made him "mildly nauseous" to think his intervention could have affected the election. The House of Representatives and Senate intelligence committees are looking into the same allegations.

We observe that the summary provided by our approach has more correct sentences than the one by the baseline. More importantly, we can see a logical flow with our approach. The summary starts with the risks related to the Russian inverstigation, then moves smoothly to the consequence which is the dismissal of the FBI director. Then, it talks about the claimed motivation which is Clinton inverstigation, how Comey got the notification and how he felt. By contrast, the baseline summary talks about most of these issues but in almost random order.

5.3   Manual Evaluation

We manually assessed the coherence and correctness of our summary. These two metrics are best illustrated in the examples shown above. We can see that the sentence from the baseline "Comey was fired now at a time before he made Tuesday's decision" is incorrect. Also the sentence "Donald Trump to leave office over the investigations into his administration's links with Russian." is incoherent. We ran our manual assessment on randomly selected 200 summary sentences, 100 for each approach (B and B+EL+VL+SM). Table 3 shows that our approach has a slightly better coherence and highly better correctness than the baseline.

Table 3. Manual evaluation result

Method	Coherence	Correctness
Baseline	4.08	2.61
B+EL+VL+SM	4.33	4.69

The assessors have a high degree of agreement, with an average standard deviation of 0.87 per sentence. There are very few instances of polar differences, totaling 6 out of 200 sentences. The high coherence score for both approach shows that the graph fusion is able to keep coherence during the pattern merging process, even for the baseline. The assessors seem to give penalty to the coherence score when the sentence is less grammatical, which suggests that the partial grammatical fixer in our ranking model has some impact in increasing the coherence of the improved approach. On the other hand, the high increase in correctness suggests that the graph fusion is much more effective in correctly merging facts when leveraging entity and predicate linkings rather than typing.

6   Conclusions and Lessons Learned

We have proposed in this paper a summarization technique based on semantic triples and graph models starting from an existing baseline approach. We have proposed a series of improvements that help finding important facts mentioned in news articles together with their facets. We have shown that our linking techniques increase both the recall and F-measure. This suggests that our entity linking and predicate linking are more effective than the typing annotation used by the baseline in the graph fusion. Most of the entities and predicates were originally annotated with their types, causing incorrect merging during the fusion step. Our entity and predicate linking "replace" this annotation, which helps fixing incorrect merging. Removing the typing entirely seems to further increase the recall. However, adding strict merging on top of the typing annotation produces the best recall at the expense of the precision (and $F1$ measure). This suggests that if entity and predicate linking are employed, merging based on typing annotation is still better in terms of recall than merging non-annotated tokens. In terms of PYRAMID scores, our approach produces more Summary Content Units than the baseline. This strengthens the ROUGE results, showing that our improvements help producing summaries with more informative content. We can also see from the manual assessment that our approach has high coherence and correctness scores.

Acknowledgment. This work has been partially supported by the project TaDaQua, funded by the Free University of Bozen-Bolzano.

References

1. Amato, F., d'Acierno, A., Colace, F., Moscato, V., Penta, A., Picariello, A.: Semantic summarization of news from heterogeneous sources. Advances on P2P, Parallel, Grid, Cloud and Internet Computing. LNDECT, vol. 1, pp. 305–314. Springer, Cham (2017). https://doi.org/10.1007/978-3-319-49109-7_29
2. Arora, S., Liang, Y., Ma, T.: A simple but tough-to-beat baseline for sentence embeddings (2016)
3. Bing, L., Li, P., Liao, Y., Lam, W., Guo, W., Passonneau, R.: Abstractive multi-document summarization via phrase selection and merging. In: Proceedings of the 53rd Annual Meeting of the Association for Computational Linguistics and the 7th International Joint Conference on Natural Language Processing, vol. 1, pp. 1587–1597 (2015). (Volume 1: Long Papers)

4. Christensen, J., Soderland, S., Bansal, G., Mausam: Hierarchical summarization: scaling up multi-document summarization. In: Proceedings of the 52nd Annual Meeting of the Association for Computlational Linguistics, pp. 902–912 (2014)

5. Collobert, R., Weston, J., Bottou, L., Karlen, M., Kavukcuoglu, K., Kuksa, P.: Natural language processing (almost) from scratch. J. Mach. Learn. Res. **12**(Aug), 2493–2537 (2011)

6. d'Acierno, A., Moscato, V., Persia, F., Picariello, A., Penta, A.: Semantic summarization of web documents. In: 2010 IEEE Fourth International Conference on Semantic Computing (ICSC), pp. 430–435. IEEE (2010)

7. Del Corro, L., Gemulla, R.: ClausIE: Clause-based open information extraction. In: Proceedings of the 22nd International Conference on World Wide Web, pp. 355–366. ACM (2013)

8. Gatt, A., Reiter, E.: SimpleNLG: A realisation engine for practical applications. In: Proceedings of the 12th European Workshop on Natural Language Generation, pp. 90–93. Association for Computational Linguistics (2009)

9. Genest, P.-E., Lapalme, G.: Framework for abstractive summarization using text-to-text generation. In: Proceedings of the Workshop on Monolingual Text-To-Text Generation, pp. 64–73. Association for Computational Linguistics (2011)

10. Khan, A., Salim, N., Kumar, Y.J.: A framework for multi-document abstractive summarization based on semantic role labelling. Appl. Soft Comput. **30**, 737–747 (2015)

11. Kshirsagar, M., Thomson, S., Schneider, N., Carbonell, J., Smith, N.A., Dyer, C.: Frame-semantic role labeling with heterogeneous annotations. In: ACL, vol. 2, pp. 218–224 (2015)

12. Li, P., Cai, W., Huang, H.: Weakly supervised natural language processing framework for abstractive multi-document summarization: weakly supervised abstractive multi-document summarization. In: Proceedings of the 24th CIKM, pp. 1401–1410. ACM (2015)

13. Li, W.: Abstractive multi-document summarization with semantic information extraction. In: EMNLP, pp. 1908–1913 (2015)

14. Lin, C.-Y., Hovy, E.: Automatic evaluation of summaries using n-gram co-occurrence statistics. In: Proceedings of the 2003 NAACL, vol. 1, pp. 71–78. Association for Computational Linguistics (2003)

15. Manning, C.D., Surdeanu, M., Bauer, J., Finkel, J.R., Bethard, S., McClosky, D.:. The Stanford coreNLP natural language processing toolkit. In: ACL (System Demonstrations), pp. 55–60 (2014)

16. Mendes, P.N., Jakob, M., García-Silva, A., Bizer, C.: DBpedia spotlight: shedding light on the web of documents. In: Proceedings of the 7th International Conference on Semantic Systems, pp. 1–8. ACM (2011)

17. Mikolov, T., Sutskever, I., Chen, K., Corrado, G.S., Dean, J.: Distributed representations of words and phrases and their compositionality. In: Advances in Neural Information Processing Systems, pp. 3111–3119 (2013)

18. Nenkova, A., Passonneau, R.J.: Evaluating content selection in summarization: The Pyramid method. In: HLT-NAACL, vol. 4, pp. 145–152 (2004)

19. Oya, T., Mehdad, Y., Carenini, G., Ng, R.: A template-based abstractive meeting summarization: leveraging summary and source text relationships. In: Proceedings of the 8th International Natural Language Generation Conference (INLG), pp. 45–53. Association for Computational Linguistics, Philadelphia, June 2014

20. Passonneau, R.J., Chen, E., Guo, W., Perin, D.: Automated pyramid scoring of summaries using distributional semantics. In: ACL, vol. 2, pp. 143–147 (2013)

21. Pedersen, T., Patwardhan, S., Michelizzi, J.: WordNet::Similarity: Measuring the relatedness of concepts. In: Demonstration Papers at HLT-NAACL 2004, pp. 38–41. Association for Computational Linguistics (2004)
22. Pighin, D., Cornolti, M., Alfonseca, E., Filippova, K.: Modelling events through memory-based, open-IE patterns for abstractive summarization. In: ACL, vol. 1, pp. 892–901 (2014)
23. Prasojo, R.E., Kacimi, M., Nutt, W.: Entity and aspect extraction for organizing news comments. In: Proceedings of the 24th ACM International on Conference on Information and Knowledge Management, CIKM 2015, pp. 233–242. ACM, New York (2015)
24. Raghunathan, K., Lee, H., Rangarajan, S., Chambers, N., Surdeanu, M., Jurafsky, D., Manning, C.: A multi-pass sieve for coreference resolution. In: Proceedings of the 2010 Conference on Empirical Methods in Natural Language Processing, EMNLP 2010, pp. 492–501. Association for Computational Linguistics, Stroudsburg (2010)
25. Schmitz, M., Bart, R., Soderland, S., Etzioni, O., et al.: Open language learning for information extraction. In: Proceedings of the 2012 Joint Conference on Empirical Methods in Natural Language Processing and Computational Natural Language Learning, pp. 523–534. Association for Computational Linguistics (2012)
26. Vanderwende, L., Banko, M., Menezes, A.: Event-centric summary generation. In: Working Notes of DUC, pp. 127–132 (2004)
27. Wang, L., Raghavan, H., Castelli, V., Florian, R., Cardie, C.: A sentence compression based framework to query-focused multi-document summarization. arXiv preprint arXiv:1606.07548 (2016)

GNIS-LD: Serving and Visualizing the Geographic Names Information System Gazetteer as Linked Data

Blake Regalia[1]([✉]), Krzysztof Janowicz[1]([✉]), Gengchen Mai[1], Dalia Varanka[2], and E. Lynn Usery[2]

[1] STKO Lab, University of California, Santa Barbara, USA
{blake,gengchen.mai}@geog.ucsb.edu, janowicz@ucsb.edu
[2] U.S. Geological Survey, Reston, USA
{dvaranka,usery}@usgs.gov

Abstract. In this dataset description paper we introduce the GNIS-LD, an authoritative and public domain Linked Dataset derived from the Geographic Names Information System (GNIS) which was developed by the U.S. Geological Survey (USGS) and the U.S. Board on Geographic Names. GNIS provides data about current, as well as historical, physical, and cultural geographic features in the United States. We describe the dataset, introduce an ontology for geographic feature types, and demonstrate the utility of recent linked geographic data contributions made in conjunction with the development of this resource. Co-reference resolution links to GeoNames.org and DBpedia are provided in the form of `owl:sameAs` relations. Finally, we point out how the adapted workflow is foundational for complex Digital Line Graph (DLG) data from the USGS National Map and how the GNIS-LD data can be integrated with DLG and other data sources such as sensor observations.

Keywords: Linked data gazetteer
Geographic Names Information System · Geospatial semantics
Feature type ontology

Resource type: Dataset
Permanent URL: http://w3-id.org/usgs

1 Introduction and Motivation

Linked Data and Semantic Web technologies are very popular in the broader Geosciences as they address several key challenges [12] within those domains such as improving interoperability across heterogeneous datasets, e.g., spanning physical and human geography, easing the publishing and retrieval of datasets, support co-reference resolution without enforcing global consistency, and so forth. However, similar to many technologies before, the early Linked Data cloud faced

© Springer International Publishing AG, part of Springer Nature 2018
A. Gangemi et al. (Eds.): ESWC 2018, LNCS 10843, pp. 528–540, 2018.
https://doi.org/10.1007/978-3-319-93417-4_34

a chicken-and-egg problem. The value proposition of Linked Data and Semantic Web technologies became evident to industry, government agencies, and end users, only after a substantial number of datasets were deployed, interlinked, and made accessible using query endpoints, graphical user interfaces, and services, such as question answering. To overcome this challenge, the early Linked Data cloud was driven by Semantic Web researchers triplifying popular, third-party datasets. While this rapidly growing size of data sources helped fuel the initial enthusiasm for Linked Data and showcase interesting applications, it was not without its own shortcomings.

For instance, datasets were triplified, and ontologies were created without substantial domain expertise, and the published datasets and their endpoints were not maintained [9]. At one point, according to http://sparqles.ai.wu.ac.at/, 54% of monitored endpoints had an uptime of 0–5%. This is not surprising as university projects are often not well suited for long-term maintenance, quality control, end-user support, and other tasks that do not align with the research and innovation focus of universities. The original data providers, such as government agencies, research centers, and the industry, however, did not yet have the interest and expertise to deploy their data as Linked Data. Nonetheless, these early datasets (and vocabularies) served their purpose, namely showcasing the potential of Linked Data and overcoming the chicken-and-egg problem.

Thanks to these initial datasets, we are currently witnessing a second wave of Linked Data publishing, namely one driven by the providers themselves such as research libraries, government agencies, large-scale data infrastructures, e.g., in the context of NSF's EarthCube effort, and industry. These efforts often require specific strategies, workflows, and tools to ensure long-term maintenance and support for their specific target audience. In contrast to individual research projects, these larger endeavors are only launched when the responsible organizations are convinced that they can be kept alive on the long term. Among many other factors, this requires technology transfer between research, industry, and government agencies [6], customization of (open source) software to internal workflows, strategies for long-term maintenance and (continuous) release cycles, as well as administration and support. The resulting linked datasets are not meant to replace existing linked datasets but to complement them by providing an authoritative alternative.

Example of domains in which this second wave of Linked Data publishing is currently ongoing are the Earth Sciences and Geography. To give a concrete example, the GeoNames gazetteer is one of the most interlinked datahubs on the Linked Data cloud. GeoNames ingests several data sources and mixes authoritative data (e.g., from Geographic Names Information System) with volunteered geographic information (VGI). However, it does not maintain a SPARQL endpoint, does not make use of `rdf:type` predicates but uses its own `gn:featureCode` property instead, introduces its own feature type catalog that is not used by any other geographic data set, and only contains a subset of the data made available by GNIS. It does, however, introduce a vast variety of geographic features from other (volunteered) resources. Consequently, it is desirable to complement GeoNames with authoritative data sources that are produced and maintained by the organizations responsible for the data. This way, different target audiences can prioritize their needs, e.g., in terms of endpoint availability, update intervals, coverage, accuracy, and so forth.

The GNIS gazetteer is an essential, authoritative dataset across domains and tasks as places in general act as nexuses that connect actors, events, and objects. To give but a few examples, exhibits such as photographs and paintings can depict a location and are taken at a location. Specimen and samples more generally are collected at a specific location and stored at another one. Agencies and news organizations need to make sure that they refer to the same location despite multiple places sharing the same name or using different spelling variants.

In this paper, we will introduce GNIS-LD, an authoritative Linked Data version of the Geographic Names Information System[1]. We will discuss its value as a testbed for future linked geographic data aimed at supporting the scale and geometric complexity of very large geographic information repositories. We will discuss the need for complementing GeoSPARQL with dereferenceable URIs and geometric metadata [19] and for serving the dataset in a client-sided, extensible Semantic Web Browser [18]. As for describing the dataset itself, we will also introduce an ontology for geographic feature types based on the Enhanced Digital Line Graph Design specs [8] used in the GNIS and the USGS National Map as well as a co-reference resolution graph between GNIS, DBpedia, and GeoNames. Finally, we will show an example for integrating GNIS-LD with Digital Line Graph data about waterbody segments with sensor stations that measure properties such as flow velocity. Our work follows the tradition of other geographic data source providers such as [1].

2   Geometry and the Linked Data Web

Answering the need to store and query geospatial data on the Semantic Web, OGC's GeoSPARQL [16] addressed the most pertinent issues surrounding alternative approaches at the time. While the proposed standard has been foundational in establishing Linked Data as a compatible publishing mechanism for traditional Geographic Information Systems (GIS), it has also revealed major limitations in practice [2]. Most notably, the need to serialize complex geometries as RDF literals has bogged down the storage, transmission, and query potential that traditional GIS have been refining for decades.

More recently, there has been interest in mitigating the considerable storage and query impact that accompanies implementations of the GeoSPARQL standard. For instance, Debruyne et al. [7] curbs geospatial processing demands by storing several copies of a feature's geometry at different levels of polygon simplification. Bereta et al. [3] avoid the need to store geometry data in a hefty serialization format that normally persists in a triplestore's RDF literal bank by instead bridging relational spatial databases with SPARQL engines, allowing

---

[1] Throughout the paper, we will use prefixed names for IRIs and provide the mappings here: http://phuzzy.link/context/gnis-ld.

geometry to persist in their native GIS (which internally is stored in some binary geospatial format) while virtualizing the existence of a GeoSPARQL-compatible serialization format such as Well Known Text (WKT) to the end user.

Our approach is to complement GeoSPARQL's strengths and overcome its limitations by rethinking the need for storing or virtualizing geometry data in the triplestore entirely, especially considering that GeoSPARQL implementations *already* depend on auxiliary binary geometry objects for geospatial query processing. As previously described [19], it is important to recognize that the main explanation for retaining a human-readable serialization of complex geometries in a triplestore (over the alternative) is so that SPARQL query results may transmit geometry data. However, complex geometries are not human-readable anyway as they consist of hundreds or thousands of coordinate pairs. Therefore, we suggest that geographic linked data publishers use dereferenceable URIs to represent complex geometric objects instead. Using a named node in this capacity means that each geometric object has its own URI as opposed to the common blank-node approach often used in the wild with GeoSPARQL objects. It's important to note that we also encourage adding triples to each geometric object to describe it, such as the feature's centroid, its bounding box, digitizing scale, and so forth. The contents of the geometry are then accessible by dereferencing the URI, allowing the data to persist in a native GIS on the host, or even remotely on another source which greatly improves the reusability of geometry data on the Linked Data Web as a whole.

This approach has been instrumental in meeting the storage, transmission, and query demands seen at the scale of the USGS datasets from the National Map, which includes a comprehensive coverage of the topography and water features throughout the entire United States. These datasets contain hundreds of thousands of complex geometries such as high-resolution polylines and polygons. In Listing 1, we show an excerpt from the extended dataset for two features that have a geometry. The first feature's geometry is a point which is accompanied by its complete WKT literal, while the second feature's geometry is a *linestring* with a WKT literal for its bounding box. Both geometry URIs can be dereferenced to obtain their full, encapsulated geometry data in a serialization format determined by the client via content negotiation. Together with the dereferencing functionality provided by the server, GNIS-LD passes all tests on Vafu (and other Linked Data validators)[2, 3].

The client may use content negotiation on a dereferenceable URI to download a feature's geometry data in a serialization format that suits their needs. For our particular implementation, these HTTP requests are handled by the server[4] that queries a local geodatabase in order to extract and convert a feature's geometry into the format given by the request's 'Accept' header. A few example requests are shown in Listing 2.

---

[2] See, for instance, https://bit.ly/2G7anvR.

[3] http://phuzzy.link/browse/gnis-ld.org/sparql/select#usgeo-multipolygon:nhdf.4456 0536.

[4] https://github.com/blake-regalia/gnis-ld.org/blob/master/lib/server/server.js.

```
# GNIS features have point geometries. Geometry URIs dereference to their coordinate data
gnisf:430  ago:geometry  usgeo-point:gnisf.430 .

# The named node for a geometry also has triples, such as its WKT serialization
usgeo-point:gnisf.430  geosparql:asWKT
        "<http://www.opengis.net/def/crs/OGC/1.3/CRS84>POINT(-113.667433
        34.38335)"^^geosparql:wktLiteral .

# NHD features have complex geometries. They can also be dereferenced
nhd:44560536  ago:geometry  usgeo-multipolygon:nhdf.44560536 .

# A geometry includes triples such as how many points it has, its bounding box, and so forth
usgeo-multipolygon:nhdf.44560536 rdf:type ago:MultiPolygon ;
    ago:pointCount 9059 ;  ago:ringCount 225 ;
    ago:centroid "<http://www.opengis.net/def/crs/EPSG/0/4326>POINT(-120.033432894877
        39.0959954262897)"^^geosparql:wktLiteral ;
    ago:boundingBox  "<http://www.opengis.net/def/crs/EPSG/0/4326>POLYGON((-120.164012990588
        38.9283332062421,-120.164012990588 38.2489710724111,-119.926092324291
        39.2489710724111,-119.926092324291 38.9283332062421,-120.164012990588
        38.9283332062421))"^^geosparql:wktLiteral ;  # and more ...
```

Listing 1 Two geographic features (one located by a point, the other by a linestring) and the triples describing their geometric representations.

```
#!/bin/bash
feature="http://gnis-ld.org/lod/geometry/multipolygon/nhdf.44560536"

# request geometry as GeoJSON
curl "$feature" -H "Accept: application/vnd.geo+json"
## {"type":"MultiPolygon","coordinates":[[[[-119.989951524192,...]]]]}

# request geometry as Well-Known Text
curl "$feature" -H "Accept: text/plain"
## MULTIPOLYGON(((-119.989951524192 39.2487662057447,...)))
```

Listing 2 Example curl requests demonstrating content negotiation for various serialization formats when downloading a geometry's data.

3   Converting GNIS to Linked Data

USGS/BGN maintains the official GNIS in several relational database tables which get published regularly in data dumps as flat CSV files[5]. The contents of the GNIS include national features and topical gazetteers, which primarily contain records that represent the naming of physical or cultural places on the surface of the Earth. Each entry has various attributes such as the type of geographic feature it represents, its WGS84 point coordinate, the city, county and state it belongs to, the elevation above sea level, the date the entry was created, the original map source, alternative names, historical records, and an official citation.

Our process begins at these data dumps, which we feed through a collection of scripts[6] that transform the CSV files into RDF by following steps derived from the GNIS topical gazetteer schema[7]. We introduce a simple vocabulary[8] to

---

[5] https://geonames.usgs.gov/domestic/download_data.htm.
[6] https://github.com/blake-regalia/usgs-triplifier/tree/master/lib/gnis.
[7] https://geonames.usgs.gov/domestic/gaz_fileformat.htm.
[8] http://gnis-ld.org/lod/gnis/ontology/.

Table 1. Dataset statistics

Quantity	Attribute
37,170,932	triples
6,743,075	named subject nodes
2,276,454	GNIS features
2,014,638	sameAs relations to GeoNames
503,171	sameAs relations to DBpedia
494,757	alternative names
66	feature types
2,537 MiB	worth of Turtle files

(a) General statistics about the GNIS-LD dataset.

Instance Count	Feature Type
231,967	Church
231,508	Stream
216,473	School
201,066	Populated Place
162,509	Locale
160,298	Building
145,534	Cemetery
74,282	Reservoir
70,619	Summit

(b) Top 10 GNIS feature types by instance counts.

describe GNIS feature attributes and a revised USGS ontology[9] to describe the feature type class hierarchy and to support the linking of features across datasets, such as those datasets found in The National Map[10]. Furthermore, metrics such as elevation above sea level, and length or area of geometric objects, are encoded as XSD-datatyped QUDT[11] objects.

URIs are minted according to the ID fields that act as foreign keys in relational joins, e.g., a reference to a GNIS feature with ID 1654975 becomes 'gnisf:1654975'. These URIs reflect the *permanent identifiers* assigned by the USGS and so they are guaranteed to always reference the same feature in all versions, i.e., past, present and future, of the GNIS. We also provide owl:sameAs links[12] to GeoNames.org, which includes the GNIS as one of its sources (more on that in Sect. 4). However, GeoNames.org does not track the provenance of its features, such as by storing the source id along with a feature's attributes, so we resort to aligning the GNIS-LD with GeoNames.org by matching exact names, comparing their alternative names, and testing that their locations exist within some distance threshold[13]. This approach may miss matches that have undergone name changes between the two versions of the GNIS. To this end, future work will employ spatial signatures [21] to improve the alignment with GeoNames. Out of the 2.23 million US features on GeoNames.org, we are able to match 90.1% of these records to the GNIS-LD. Alignment with DBpedia also uses exact name string matching but it additionally compares attributes such as the county, state, and place type for each feature. We then use the results from the GeoNames.org matching process to enhance our alignment with DBpedia via owl:sameAs transitivity. The number of matches can be seen in Table 1.

---

[9] http://gnis-ld.org/lod/usgs/ontology/.
[10] https://viewer.nationalmap.gov/basic/.
[11] http://www.qudt.org/release2/qudt-catalog.html.
[12] http://gnis-ld.org/resource/gnis-sameas-geonames.ttl.
[13] https://github.com/blake-regalia/usgs-triplifier/tree/master/lib/align.

4   The Dataset

The GNIS and other USGS products are public domain datasets[14] that are maintained, updated, and supported by the U.S. Federal Government. We created the GNIS-LD as a 5-star linked open dataset version of the GNIS for USGS to maintain. The GNIS dataset as of February 1, 2018 contains over 2.27 million features for the United States (see Table 1a) together with their geometries, alternative names, types, containment relations, elevations, historic notes, and so forth. It contains man-made features such as cities as well as natural features such as mountain peaks and ranges across different scales from single buildings to entire states. Our Linked Data triplification process yields 37 million triples for the GNIS dataset alone. These features are made up of 66 distinct types, with the top 10 feature types shown in Table 1b.

It is worth putting the GNIS-LD into context by describing its relation to GeoNames.org[15] and LinkedGeoData[16]. Most importantly, these two resources either directly imported or indirectly inherited a significant portion of their US data from the GNIS at one point in time. However, they do not necessarily reflect the current version of the GNIS and also allow for volunteered contributions from the community. GNIS-LD is an authoritative, comprehensive, triplified version of the most up-to-date dataset for the names of places in the US. Furthermore, whereas GeoNames is not 5-star Linked Data and has no SPARQL endpoint, and LinkedGeoData supports only a subset[17] of the SQL MM spatial specification (via non-standard Extensible Value Testing filter functions under the `bif:` prefix in SPARQL), GNIS-LD offers a 5-star Linked Dataset with full GeoSPARQL support[18]. Finally, our dataset is designed to be compatible with high-resolution, complex geometries provided by USGS. We show some preliminary work integrating one of these datasets with the GNIS-LD in Fig. 1. In this example, the `nhd:gnisFeature` predicate links the sole geometry of Lake Tahoe to its GNIS feature which represents the naming of the water body.

The GNIS gazetteer is particularly important as it acts as a nexus between other datasets and to support interaction and workflows of human users (as compared to software agents) which is most often done using place names instead of geometries. For instance, and as depicted in Fig. 2, a USGS station from the WaterWatch program is located inside/at a segment of Tobesofkee Creek near the city of Macon, GA; thereby linking measurement results to the creek and city. As the city record from GNIS is linked to DBpedia via an `owl:sameAs` relation, one can get additional information e.g., demographic data, about the city.

---

[14]   https://www2.usgs.gov/laws/info_policies.html#copyrights.
[15]   https://old.datahub.io/dataset/geonames-semantic-web.
[16]   http://linkedgeodata.org/About.
[17]   http://docs.openlinksw.com/virtuoso/sqlrefgeospatial/.
[18]   https://wiki.apache.org/marmotta/GSoC/2015/MARMOTTA-584.

```
# see <http://phuzzy.link/context/gnis-ld> for prefix mappings

# how many lakes are there in California? result: 73,497
select (count(?lake) as ?lakes) {
    ?lake a nhd:Reservoir ;
          gnis:state gnisf:California .
}

# what is the total length of the Truckee River? result: 148.3 km
select (sum(?segment_length) as ?river_length) {
    ?river nhd:gnisFeature/rdfs:label "Truckee River"@en ;
           ago:geometry ?geometryUri .

    ?geometryUri ago:boundingBox ?boundingBox ;
        ago:length [
            qudt:numericValue ?segment_length ;
            qudt:unit unit:M ;
        ] .
}
```

Listing 3 Showcasing a few sample queries on the GNIS-LD and NHD geometries.

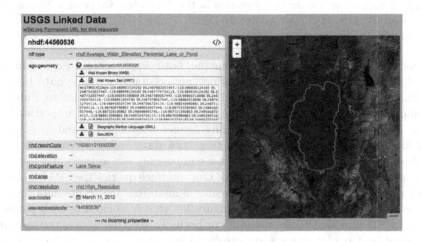

Fig. 1. A geographic feature with polygon geometry converted to linked data and linked to its GNIS record, as displayed in our web interface.

5   User Interface

When it comes to choosing a Linked Data front-end interface that supports the display of and interaction with geospatial data, one can select from a small number of existing solutions. GeoLink [11,14], Sextant [4,15], and SPEX [20] each take a unique approach to exploring geographic data, which can have many possible modes of interaction depending on the nature of the dataset, e.g., trajectories, time series, complex geometries, and so on, as well as browsing paradigms, i.e., whether to use an interactive map, faceted browser, graph-view, or something in between. Other, non geo-specific, approaches focus on modularity. Among these, Linked Data Reactor [10], Uduvudu [13], LodLive [5], and Fresnel [17] unite under the common goal of building Linked Data interfaces out of reusable components.

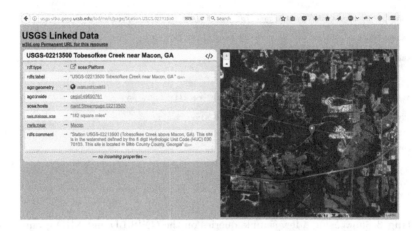

Fig. 2. A streamgage measurement station in the Tobesofkee Creek near Macon, CA annotated using the SOSA/SSN ontology.

For GNIS-LD we decided to combine both approaches by maximizing reusability and at the same time offering support for geographic data beyond points. The resulting interface named Phuzzy.link [18], is similar to Pubby[19] insofar that it describes each resource by showing its outgoing properties in a tabular format with hyperlinks for locally dereferenceable URIs and special formatting for certain datatyped literals (e.g., xsd:date values). Where our approach differs from previous works is how components are sourced and how the content-agnostic interfaces is generated. Our interface queries the SPARQL endpoint directly from the client and creates human-readable representations of the resource using a customizable configuration that is tailored to each dataset, either by the provider, the community, or both. To keep displays between pages consistent and readable, rows are displayed in order according to the priority assigned to each predicate by the data provider. For example, rdf:type is among our highest priority for outgoing predicates, so it will be displayed as the first row for each resource that has an rdf:type triple, followed by its rdfs:label, and so forth.

The text for hyperlinks that point to adjacent resources will also be substituted by their rdfs:label if one was returned in the initialization SPARQL query used by the interface. For incoming triples, the interface also asks for a subject's rdf:type if it is available so that the interface can organize the results into collapsible groups as shown in Fig. 3. This helps reduce the clutter on the screen for common objects that are linked to by many triples, such as counties and states.

We designed the interface to embed special interactive features for select resource types. Namely, we support: unit conversion for quantities such as elevation values, display format toggling for date and time literals, interactive map

---

[19] http://wifo5-03.informatik.uni-mannheim.de/pubby/.

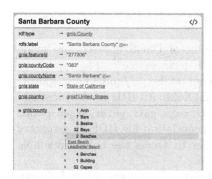

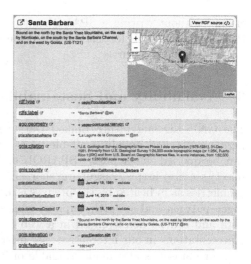

Fig. 3. Santa Barbara county is the gnis:county of many GNIS features, which are grouped and collapsed together by their rdf:type in the incoming properties section.

Fig. 4. The interface showing GNIS data about Santa Barbara, CA including its location on a map, available at https://bit.ly/2DPZGM4.

plotting for places with geometries, and the option to download a feature's source geometry data in a variety of serialization formats. With the exception of the last feature, all interactivity is handled in-browser by the client so that the endpoint's resources can be reserved for executing SPARQL queries. We discuss these features in greater detail below.

GNIS survey data for elevation above sea level are recorded in imperial units (ft). Since many users will encounter the need to convert these quantities to meters or kilometers, we approached unit conversion as the need for a modular feature within the user interface that can be adapted to any quantity types. By utilizing the QUDT ontology[20], we preemptively download conversion rates to a quantity's possible units given in the QUDT vocabularies. A user can then select from a dropdown menu of available units to convert a quantity entirely in-browser, i.e., without additional queries to the server.

To make geometry data available from within the user interface, an interactive element can be expanded by clicking the globe icon that appears next to a geometry's URI, shown in Fig. 1. From there, a list of possible serialization formats is shown with download options next to each item. Clicking the option to display the geometry as text or to download it as a file both trigger an asynchronous HTTP request set with the appropriate 'Accept' headers.

Users who explore Linked Data through a front-end are not always interested in high-level views that encapsulate the underlying RDF. For those who want to see how an ontology is being utilized or to simply access a resource's RDF

---

[20] http://www.qudt.org/release2/qudt-catalog.html.

closure without writing a SPARQL query, we provide a display toggle ($</>$) that shows the RDF for the current resource's outgoing triples in a textbox of syntax-highlighted Turtle.

6 Availability and Sustainability

The GNIS-LD and future Linked Data versions of USGS datasets are made permanently and openly available as a public data service[21]. The repository can be queried via a public SPARQL endpoint at http://gnis-ld.org/sparql/ select; see also http://yasgui.org/short/H130H1XcM. All IRIs for features and geometries as indicated by the prefixes nhd, nhdf, usgs, gnis, gnisf, usgeo-point, usgeo-polygon and so forth, support content-negotiation for RDF or geometry data and can be dereferenced in a web browser to access the human-readable representations in our interactive user interface.

Our dataset is also made available on datahub.io[22] as part of the US Geological Survey organization. The datahub.io entry includes references for:

- **VoID description**—Machine readable metadata about the dataset.
- **GNIS feature definitions**—Feature type vocabulary for GNIS.
- **GNIS-LD RDF dump**—The entire GNIS dataset as RDF.
- **USGS-LD SPARQL endpoint**—The SPARQL endpoint for live data.
- **USGS-LD SPARQL service description**—Machine readable metadata about the SPARQL endpoint.

Updates to the underlying source data will subsequently trigger updates to the endpoint's triple store and RDF data dumps.

7 Summary and Future Work

In this resource paper, we presented an authoritative Linked Dataset for the Geographic Names Information (GNIS) System that complements existing crowd-sourced and non-authoritative resources. The datasource contains millions of places in the United States together with their geometries, alternative names, types, containment relations, elevations, historic notes, and so forth. The data contains places across more than 60 feature types and across different scales ranking from places of worships to rivers. Accompanying the dataset, we also provide an ontology, a SPARQL endpoint, metadata about the dataset and endpoint, RDF data dumps, and a dereferencing web interface with content negotiation for RDF and geometry data. Co-reference resolution links to GeoNames and DBpedia are provided as owl:sameAs relations. GNIS-LD is a milestone for the linked geodata community as it is among the first and few authoritative geographic datasets released in direct collaboration with the US government

---

[21] https://www2.usgs.gov/publishing/policies.html.
[22] https://old.datahub.io/dataset/geographic-names-information-system-gnis.

agencies that created and maintained these data, and it is important for the Semantic Web because places in general act as nexuses that connect actors, events, and objects.

We presented preliminary work for how this resource aligns with upcoming datasets such as the DLGs[23] and National Map data more broadly as well as with other authoritative data sources such as USGS WaterWatch sensor data. In the future, we will aim at providing further links to other Linked Data sources such as Getty's TGN as well as integration with other types of sensor data.

References

1. Atemezing, G.A., Abadie, N., Troncy, R., Bucher, B.: Publishing reference geodata on the web: opportunities and challenges for IGN France. In: TC/SSN at ISWC, pp. 9–20 (2014)
2. Atemezing, G.A., Troncy, R.: Comparing vocabularies for representing geographical features and their geometry. In: Terra Cognita 2012 Workshop, vol. 3 (2012)
3. Bereta, K., Koubarakis, M.: Ontop of geospatial databases. In: Groth, P., Simperl, E., Gray, A., Sabou, M., Krötzsch, M., Lecue, F., Flöck, F., Gil, Y. (eds.) ISWC 2016. LNCS, vol. 9981, pp. 37–52. Springer, Cham (2016). https://doi.org/10.1007/978-3-319-46523-4_3
4. Bereta, K., Nikolaou, C., Karpathiotakis, M., Kyzirakos, K., Koubarakis, M.: Sextant: visualizing time-evolving linked geospatial data. In: Proceedings of the 2013th International Conference on Posters and Demonstrations Track, vol. 1035, pp. 177–180. CEUR-WS. org (2013)
5. Camarda, D.V., Mazzini, S., Antonuccio, A.: LodLive, exploring the web of data. In: Proceedings of the 8th International Conference on Semantic Systems, pp. 197–200. ACM (2012)
6. Varanka, D.E., Wendel, J., Janowicz, K.: Technology transfer to incorporate linked geospatial data for national mapping (under review)
7. Debruyne, C., Clinton, É., McNerney, L., Nautiyal, A., O'Sullivan, D.: Serving Ireland's geospatial information as linked data. In: International Semantic Web Conference (Posters and Demos) (2016)
8. Guptill, S.C.: An enhanced digital line graph design. Technical report, USGPO; Books and Open-File Reports Section, US Geological Survey (1990)
9. Hogan, A., Hitzler, P., Janowicz, K.: Linked dataset description papers at the semantic web journal: a critical assessment. Semant. Web 7(2), 105–116 (2016)
10. Khalili, A., de Graaf, K.A.: Linked data reactor: towards data-aware user interfaces. In: Proceedings of the 13th International Conference on Semantic Systems, SEMANTiCS (2017)
11. Krisnadhi, A., et al.: The GeoLink modular oceanography ontology. In: Arenas, M., et al. (eds.) ISWC 2015. LNCS, vol. 9367, pp. 301–309. Springer, Cham (2015). https://doi.org/10.1007/978-3-319-25010-6_19
12. Kuhn, W., Kauppinen, T., Janowicz, K.: Linked data - a paradigm shift for geographic information science. In: Duckham, M., Pebesma, E., Stewart, K., Frank, A.U. (eds.) GIScience 2014. LNCS, vol. 8728, pp. 173–186. Springer, Cham (2014). https://doi.org/10.1007/978-3-319-11593-1_12

---

[23] https://lta.cr.usgs.gov/DLGs.

13. Luggen, M., Gschwend, A., Anrig, B., Cudré-Mauroux, P.: Uduvudu: a graph-aware and adaptive UI engine for linked data. In: LDOW@ WWW (2015)
14. Mai, G., Janowicz, K., Hu, Y., McKenzie, G.: A linked data driven visual interface for the multi-perspective exploration of data across repositories. In: VOILA@ ISWC, pp. 93–101 (2016)
15. Nikolaou, C., Dogani, K., Kyzirakos, K., Koubarakis, M.: Sextant: browsing and mapping the ocean of linked geospatial data. In: Cimiano, P., Fernández, M., Lopez, V., Schlobach, S., Völker, J. (eds.) ESWC 2013. LNCS, vol. 7955, pp. 209–213. Springer, Heidelberg (2013). https://doi.org/10.1007/978-3-642-41242-4_26
16. Perry, M., Herring, J.: OGC GeoSPARQL-A geographic query language for RDF data. OGC Implementation Standard, September 2012
17. Pietriga, E., Bizer, C., Karger, D., Lee, R.: Fresnel: a browser-independent presentation vocabulary for RDF. In: Cruz, I., Decker, S., Allemang, D., Preist, C., Schwabe, D., Mika, P., Uschold, M., Aroyo, L.M. (eds.) ISWC 2006. LNCS, vol. 4273, pp. 158–171. Springer, Heidelberg (2006). https://doi.org/10.1007/11926078_12
18. Regalia, B., Janowicz, K., Mai, G.: Phuzzy.link: A SPARQL-powered client-sided extensible semantic web browser
19. Regalia, B., Janowicz, K., McKenzie, G.: Revisiting the representation of and need for raw geometries on the linked data web. In: Proceedings of the Workshop on Linked Data on the Web (LDOW), CEUR Workshop Proceedings (2017)
20. Scheider, S., Degbelo, A., Lemmens, R., van Elzakker, C., Zimmerhof, P., Kostic, N., Jones, J., Banhatti, G.: Exploratory querying of SPARQL endpoints in space and time. Semant. Web 8(1), 65–86 (2017)
21. Zhu, R., Hu, Y., Janowicz, K., McKenzie, G.: Spatial signatures for geographic feature types: Examining gazetteer ontologies using spatial statistics. Trans. GIS 20(3), 333–355 (2016)

Event-Enhanced Learning for KG Completion

Martin Ringsquandl[1,2]([✉]), Evgeny Kharlamov[3], Daria Stepanova[4],
Marcel Hildebrandt[1], Steffen Lamparter[2], Raffaello Lepratti[5], Ian Horrocks[3][iD],
and Peer Kröger[1]

[1] Ludwig-Maximilians University, Munich, Germany
martin.ringsquandl@siemens.com
[2] Siemens AG CT, Munich, Germany
[3] University of Oxford, Oxford, UK
[4] Max-Planck Institut für Informatik, Saarbrücken, Germany
[5] Digital Factory, Siemens PLM Software, Plano, USA

Abstract. Statistical learning of relations between entities is a popular
approach to address the problem of missing data in Knowledge Graphs.
In this work we study how relational learning can be enhanced with
background of a special kind: event logs, that are sequences of entities
that may occur in the graph. Events naturally appear in many important
applications as background. We propose various embedding models that
combine entities of a Knowledge Graph and event logs. Our evaluation
shows that our approach outperforms state-of-the-art baselines on real-
world manufacturing and road traffic Knowledge Graphs, as well as in a
controlled scenario that mimics manufacturing processes.

1 Introduction

Knowledge Graphs (KGs) nowadays power many important applications including Web search[1], question answering [3], machine learning [19], data integration [10], entity disambiguation and linking [5,8]. A KG is typically defined as a
collection of triples $\langle entity, predicate, entity \rangle$ that form a directed graph where
nodes are entities and edges are labeled with binary predicates (relations). Examples of large-scale KGs range from general-purpose such as Yago [24] and DBPedia [12] to domain specific ones such as Siemens [10] and Statoil [9] corporate
KGs.

Large-scale KGs are often automatically constructed and highly incomplete [6] in the sense that they are missing certain triples. Due to their size
and the speed of growth, manual completion of such KGs is infeasible. In order
to address this issue, a number of relational learning approaches for *automatic
KG completion* have been recently proposed, see [6,16] for an overview. Many of
these approaches are based on learning representations, or *embeddings*, of entities and relations [4,17,22]. It was shown that the quality of embeddings can

---

[1] https://en.wikipedia.org/wiki/Knowledge_Graph.

© Springer International Publishing AG, part of Springer Nature 2018
A. Gangemi et al. (Eds.): ESWC 2018, LNCS 10843, pp. 541–559, 2018.
https://doi.org/10.1007/978-3-319-93417-4_35

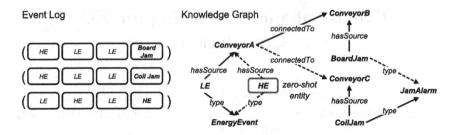

Fig. 1. Excerpt of a manufacturing KG and an event log. (Color figure online)

be significantly improved if the embedding's vector space is enriched with additional information from an *external source*, such as a corpora of natural language text [27] or structural knowledge such as rules [25] or type constraints [11].

An important type of external knowledge that is common in practice and to the best of our knowledge has not been explicitly considered so far is *event log* data. Events naturally appear in many applications including social networks, smart cities, and manufacturing. In social networks the nodes of a KG can be people and locations, and edges can be friendship relations and places of birth [30], while an event log for a person can be a sequence of (possibly repetitive) places that the person has visited. In smart cities a KG can model traffic [21] by representing cameras, traffic lights, and road topology, while an event log for one day can be a sequence of traffic signals where jams or accidents have occurred. In smart manufacturing an event log can be a sequence of possible states, e.g., overheating or low power of machines such as conveyors, and these logs can be emitted during a manufacturing process.

In this work we define an event log for a KG as a set of sequences constituted of entities (possibly with repetitions) that may occur in the KG as nodes. Moreover, we assume that not every entity from a KG, but only what we call *event entities* can occur in logs. In the above: visited cities, traffic signals, and alarms are event entities. As we see later in the paper this separation of entities in a KG into event and non-event is important and practically motivated. We now illustrate an industrial KG and event log.

Example 1. Consider an industrial KG that is inspired by a Siemens automated factory, that we will use later on for experiments, and that contains information about factory equipment, products, as well as materials and processes to produce the products. The KG was semi-automatically generated by parsing heterogeneous spreadsheets and other semi-structured data repositories and it is incomplete. In Fig. 1 we depict a small excerpt from this KG where solid lines denote relations that are in the KG while dashed – the missing relations. The KG contains the topology of the conveyors A, B, and C and says that two of them (A and B) are connected to each other: ⟨*ConveyorA, connectedTo, ConveyorB*⟩. The KG also stores operator control specifications, in particular, event entities that the equipment can emit during operation. For example, *CoilJam*, is an event entity and it can be emitted by conveyor C, i.e., $\langle CoilJam, hasSource, ConveyorC \rangle$. Event entities have further semantics described by the typing, e.g. $CoilJam$ is of type $JamAlarm$, severity levels, and possible emitting source locations. At the same time, the KG misses the facts that the conveyors A and C are connected in the factory; that $BoardJam$ is of type $JamAlarm$, and $HighEnergy$ (HE) has the source $ConveyorA$ and is of type $EnergyEvent$.

Additionally, in the example, we assume that an event log recorded during the operation of the factory consists of three following sequences over event entities:

$$(HE, LE, LE, BoardJam), (HE, LE, LE, CoilJam), (LE, HE, LE, HE).$$

Observe that the event log suggests that a jam typically occurs after a sequence of two consecutive low energy consumption (LE) events.   □

An event log gives external knowledge to the KG by specifying frequent sequential patterns on the KG's entities. These patterns capture some processes that the nodes of a KG can be involved in, i.e., manufacturing with machines described by the KG, traveling by a person mentioned in the KG, or traffic around traffic signals. This type of external knowledge has conceptual differences from text corpora where KG entities are typically described in a natural language and where occurrences of KG entities do not necessarily correspond to any process. Events are also different from rules or constraints that introduce formal restrictions on some relations.

The goal of this work is to understand how event logs can enhance relational learning for KGs. We address this problem by proposing an *Event-enhanced Knowledge Learning* (*EKL*) approach for KG completion that intuitively has two sub–steps:

1. *Event alignment*, where event entities are aligned in a low-dimensional vector space that reflects sequential similarity, and
2. *KG completion*, where the KG is extended with missing edges that can be either event-specific, e.g., such as the *type* edge between $BoardJam$ and $JamAlarm$ in Example 1, or not event-specific, e.g., such as *connectedTo* between $ConveyorA$ and $ConveyorC$ in Example 1.

Observe, the event logs *directly* influence the first step while also *indirectly* the second step of EKL. Hence, we expect a collective learning effect in a sense that the overall KG completion can benefit from event alignment, and vice versa.

Example 2. During the first step EKL will align $BoardJam$ and $CoilJam$ to be similar. In the second step EKL will accordingly adjust entities $ConveyorC$ and $ConveyorB$ and then predict that $ConveyorA$ is likely to also be connected to $ConveyorC$. Intuitively the missing link between the conveyors can be inferred from the sequential pattern in the event log: the log tells us that both $BoardJam$ and $CoilJam$ occur as a consequence of two consecutive LE events and therefore exhibit similar semantics. This similarity is carried to conveyor entities B and C, which leads to an increased likelihood that they both follow the same entity $ConveyorA$.   □

Note that the prediction of event-specific missing links is not the standard task for relational learning since we are predicting links *within* the background. Moreover, our approach can address the *zero-shot scenario*, where some event entities only appear in the event log, but they are novel to the KG (it is marked with red in Fig. 1). E.g., *HE* in Example 1 corresponds to an entity that is missing in the KG, that has to be aligned during the first step of EKL and then linked to *ConveyorA* as well as to its type during the second step of EKL. Thus, EKL can also populate a KG with new (unseen) entities.

The contributions of our work are as follows:

- Several EKL approaches to KG completion that comprise
  - two model architectures that allow to combine (representations of) a KG and an event log for simultaneous training of both representations;
  - three models for event logs that reflect different notions of event context.
- An extensive evaluation of our approach and comparison to a state-of-the-art baseline on real-world data from a factory, on smart city traffic data, and controlled experiment data. Our results show that we significantly outperform two state-of-the-art baselines and the advantages are most visible for predicting links between entities that reflect the sequential process nature within the KG.

Finally, note that we presented a very preliminary version of this work as a short in-use paper [20]. Here we are significantly different from [20] and extend it, since [20] does not describe our EKL models and it only focusses on several simple KG extension scenarios that we do not study here.

2   Existing Methods for KG Completion

We now review the problem of KG completion and the existing methods to address it, following the standard problem definition, c.f. [4,22,26]. Let $\mathcal{E}$ be a finite set of (all possible) entities and $\mathcal{R}$ a finite set of relations. A KG $\mathcal{K}$ is a set of triples $\langle h, r, t \rangle$, where $h, t \in \mathcal{E}$ and $r \in \mathcal{R}$. Given a KG $\mathcal{K}$ and a triple $\langle h, r, \_ \rangle$ (resp. $\langle \_, r, t \rangle$) where '$\_$' denotes a missing entity, the *KG completion* problem is to predict the missing t (resp. h) by computing for each $e \in \mathcal{E}$ a score $f(\langle h, r, e \rangle)$ (resp. $f(\langle e, r, t \rangle)$) that reflects the likelihood of the triple $\langle h, r, e \rangle$ (resp. $\langle e, r, t \rangle$) being in the KG.

Statistical Relational Learning for KG Completion. Statistical relational learning has gained a lot of attention by the research community, including translation-based models [4,26], latent tensor factorization [18], neural tensor networks [23] and others (see e.g., [16] for an overview). In this work we focus on translation-based models. They address the KG completion problem by reducing it to a representation learning task where the main goal is to represent entities h, t and relations r occurring in $\mathcal{K}$ in a low-dimensional, say d-dimensional, vector space $\mathbf{h}, \mathbf{t}, \mathbf{r} \in \mathbb{R}^d$, which define the model parameter matrices $\mathbf{W}_{\mathcal{E}} \in \mathbb{R}^{|\mathcal{E}| \times d}$ and

$\mathbf{W}_{\mathcal{R}} \in \mathbb{R}^{|\mathcal{R}| \times d}$ respectively. These parameters are typically referred to as *latent representations* or simply *embeddings*.

Such KG representations have been shown to be effectively learned by using a ranking loss with the objective that true triples should be ranked before false/unknown ones according to the scoring function. This learning objective is formulated as minimizing a margin-based ranking loss:

$$\mathcal{L}_{\mathcal{K}} = \sum_{(h,r,t) \in \mathcal{K}} \sum_{(h',r,t') \in N} max(0, \gamma + f(\mathbf{h}, \mathbf{r}, \mathbf{t}) - f(\mathbf{h}', \mathbf{r}, \mathbf{t}')), \tag{1}$$

where $f(\cdot)$ is some scoring function that operates on the entity and relation embeddings $\mathbf{h}, \mathbf{r}, \mathbf{t}$ and $\mathbf{h}', \mathbf{r}, \mathbf{t}'$ from N, which is a set of negative examples, i.e. presumably false triples not contained in $\mathcal{K}$. This loss is minimized when the true triples outscore the false ones by a constant margin γ. In practice the training is done using mini-batches of $\mathcal{K}$, instead of iterating over all triples, together with stochastic-gradient descent (SGD), since this introduces more variance in the embedding parameter updates and can prevent early convergence in local optima.

For example, in the TransE model [4], given $\mathcal{K}$ such f relies on distance or similarity between vectors. Intuitively, TransE follows the intuition that there is a linear relation for triples $\mathbf{h} + \mathbf{r} \approx \mathbf{t}$, hence the scoring function is defined as a dissimilarity measure (e.g. ℓ^2-norm) $f(\mathbf{h}, \mathbf{r}, \mathbf{t}) = \|\mathbf{h} + \mathbf{r} - \mathbf{t}\|_2^2$. This means that *translating* entity h with relation r should end up close to its tail entity t in the latent d-dimensional space. In order to prevent overfitting, the magnitudes of parameters in TransE are normalized after each mini-batch to unit-norm vectors, i.e. $\forall e \in \mathcal{E} : \|\mathbf{e}\| = 1$.

Enhancing KG Learning with Background Knowledge. It was shown that traditional representation learning can be improved using background knowledge. Most prominently, external text corpora can be used as background [27–29,31]. The main approaches follow the idea of computing two separate representations of entities: a text-based and a KG-based one. There are two proposals to combine both representations:

1. include a linear combination layer to directly modify $\mathbf{h}$, $\mathbf{r}$, and $\mathbf{t}$ in $\mathcal{L}_{\mathcal{K}}$ of Eq. 1, or
2. add a dedicated learning objective for text-based representations to $\mathcal{L}_{\mathcal{K}}$.

The TEKE model [27] follows the first proposal, by incorporating textual context of entities into a KG by exploiting a co-occurrence network of entities and words in the text thus defining a combination between pre-trained language model word embeddings and KG entities. It includes $\mathbf{n}(h)$ as the weight-averaged neighborhood word vector representation of an entity h and then applies a linear combination $\hat{\mathbf{h}} = \mathbf{A}\mathbf{n}(h) + \mathbf{h}$ to make up the final entity representation used in triple scoring. Furthermore, TEKE uses a weighted average of the merged neighborhood word embeddings for pairs of entities h, t in the text as $\mathbf{n}(h, t)$ to transform the relation embeddings $\hat{\mathbf{r}} = \mathbf{B}\mathbf{n}(h, t) + \mathbf{r}$.

The DKRL [29] follows the second proposal and adds three $\mathcal{L}_\mathcal{K}^i$ to the objective for text-based representations, where $\mathcal{L}_\mathcal{K}^1$ uses a translation objective within text-based representations, $\mathcal{L}_\mathcal{K}^2$ is a mixed translation from text-based to KG-based and $\mathcal{L}_\mathcal{K}^3$ from KG-based to text-based. Intuitively, DKRL considers correlation between entities within $\mathcal{K}$, between $\mathcal{K}$ and the text and within the text. The text embeddings are learned using a continuous bag of words or a deep convolutional neural network. The KG and the text-based representations are then jointly optimized.

SSP [28,31] also follow the second proposal and exploit the semantic information about KG's entities given in the form of textual entity descriptions. The SSP method strengthens the effect of text descriptions by performing the embedding process in the semantic subspace and a topic model for entity text descriptions. They combine the objective of KG embeddings $\mathcal{L}_\mathcal{K}$ and of text embeddings $\mathcal{L}_\mathcal{S}$ using the joint formulation:

$$\mathcal{L}_{joint} = \mathcal{L}_\mathcal{K} + \alpha \mathcal{L}_\mathcal{S}, \tag{2}$$

where, α is a hyper-parameter used as a weighting factor. The main advantage of this approach is that the simultaneous training of both objective functions within an aggregated objective allows both models to influence each other.

3   Event-Enhanced KG Completion

In this section we present our approach to KG completion enhanced with event logs: we start with the problem definition, proceed to limitations of existing approaches to address the problem, propose our adaptation of the joint model formulation to the event-based setting based on $\mathcal{L}_\mathcal{K}$ and $\mathcal{L}_\mathcal{S}$, and define several ways to combine $\mathcal{L}_\mathcal{K}$ and $\mathcal{L}_\mathcal{S}$.

3.1   Problem Definition

Let $\mathcal{X} \subseteq \mathcal{E}$ be a set of *event* entities. An *event log s* is a finite sequence $(e_1, \ldots, e_m)$ of entities from $\mathcal{X}$ and a sequence dataset $\mathcal{S}$ a set $\{s_1, \ldots, s_n\}$ of event logs. E.g., an event log $(LE, HE, BoardJam, ShutdownA)$ is generated by machines during operation.

The *event-enhanced KG completion* problem is, given a KG $\mathcal{K}$, a sequence dataset $\mathcal{S}$, and a triple $\langle h, r, \_ \rangle$ (resp. $\langle \_, r, t \rangle$), to predict the missing t (resp. h) by exploiting both $\mathcal{K}$ and $\mathcal{S}$ for the computation of a score $f(\langle h, r, e \rangle)$ (resp. $f(\langle e, r, t \rangle)$) for each $e \in \mathcal{E}$. We consider three variations of the event-enhanced completion problem with respect to the entities h, t in the given/predicted triple: the first setting corresponds to the standard KG completion problem, while the other two are specific for our scenario.

1. *non-event entities*: neither given nor predicted entities of $\langle h, r, \_ \rangle$ (resp. $\langle \_, r, t \rangle$) are from $\mathcal{X}$, as in $\langle ConveyorA, connectedTo, ConveyorB \rangle$ from Example 1,
2. *event entities known by KG*: each given or predicted event entity of $\langle h, r, \_ \rangle$ (resp. $\langle \_, r, t \rangle$) is in $\mathcal{K}$, as in $\langle BoardJam, type, JamAlarm \rangle$ from Example 1,
3. *event entities unknown by KG*: either given or predicted event entity of $\langle h, r, \_ \rangle$ (resp. $\langle \_, r, t \rangle$), does not appear in $\mathcal{K}$, as for HE from Example 1. This corresponds to the problem of *zero-shot learning*.

3.2   Limitation of Existing Methods

We now discuss why the existing background-enhanced learning approaches are insufficient or cannot be naturally applied at all to our setting. Approaches of the first kind such as TEKE rely on the assumption that all entities of the KG should also appear in the background. This assumption is critical to TEKE's enhancement of $\mathbf{Bn}(h, t)$, which is undefined if either h or t have no text representation. In our setting only the event entities occur in the background and in applications such as manufacturing only a small fragment of KG entities are actually event entities. Moreover, TEKE relies only on mere co-occurrences of words and KG entities in the text corpora and ignores the sequential correlation among entity occurrences. Approaches of the second kind including DKRL and SSP require that a dedicated piece of background, that is, a text corpus, is attached to each individual entity of the KG, while in our setting all event entities share a single event log, i.e. the same background is attached to every event entity. Although the convolutional version of DKRL is able to respect sequential correlation between the words in the entity description, it can not be directly applied to sequences of event entities, since this requires a different embedding objective. Instead of using the final output of the last convolutional layer as representation of the entity, we need to learn representations of the actual tokens in the sequence. The same limitations hold for the topic model of SSP, which also requires a dedicated background for each entity in the KG.

We note that that is a body of work on Business Process Mining that we see as relevant to our work since manufacturing can be seen as a business process. The exact nature of relation requires further study and it as a future work.

3.3   Adaptation of Joint Model Formulation

Observe that in our setting the KG embedding objective function is dominated by non-event entities, i.e., pre-trained event embeddings would be continuously marginalized during training. Thus, we see the joint training objective in Eq. 2 for SSP where there is an explicit definition of the background for learning as the most natural approach for our context and adapt to the idea of simultaneous training of both objective functions.

At the same time, adaptation of Eq. 2 to our setting is a non-trivial task that requires to carefully design three ingredients: *(i)* an embedding model $\mathcal{L}_{\mathcal{K}}$ *(ii)*

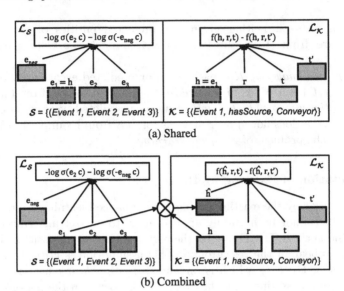

Fig. 2. Architectures: (a) shared entity embeddings (b) combination of separated entity embeddings.

an embedding model $\mathcal{L}_S$ *(iii)* a way to connect the two models for simultaneous training. In our work we do not develop a new $\mathcal{L}_K$ and exploit TransE as $\mathcal{L}_K$. The reason is that for our setting it is a good compromise between computational efficiency and quality of prediction.

In the remaining part of the section we start with our novel proposal on how to combine the embeddings of $\mathcal{L}_K$ and $\mathcal{L}_S$, and then present our new models for event embeddings $\mathcal{L}_S$ that we refer to as *event-enhanced knowledge learning (EKL)*.

3.4   Combining $\mathcal{L}_K$ and $\mathcal{L}_S$

We now propose two architectures to combine $\mathcal{L}_K$ and $\mathcal{L}_S$. The first, *shared*, is specific for our setting and different from what was used for text enhanced learning, while the second, *combined*, is inspired by TEKE.

Shared Architecture. In contrast to text-enhanced KG embeddings, in our setting both the KG and the background contain exclusively entities from $\mathcal{E}$. Hence, we can directly employ an architecture that uses a *single shared entity representation* for both $\mathcal{L}_K$ and $\mathcal{L}_S$. In such a shared architecture one can define an identity connection between event entity embeddings $\mathbf{e}$ and $\mathbf{h}, \mathbf{t}$, the entity embeddings in the KG, i.e. the event embedding matrix $\mathbf{W}_{\mathcal{X}}$ is the $|\mathcal{X}|$-by-d submatrix of $\mathbf{W}_{\mathcal{E}}$. During training, the gradients of both objective functions are averaged and therefore simultaneously updated.

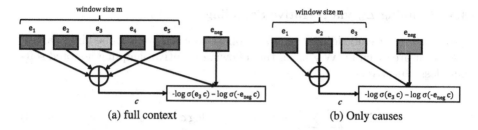

Fig. 3. Context models to predict target: (a) from causes and effects (b) from causes only

Figure 2a illustrates this approach on a simplistic example. Starting at the bottom, given an event sequence and a KG we simultaneously proceed with both objectives $\mathcal{L}_{\mathcal{K}}$ and $\mathcal{L}_{\mathcal{S}}$ as follows: The event entities of the event sequence are directed to the event embedding model using a shared entity representation. In the example the input event *Event1* uses the vector representation $\mathbf{e_1}$. In parallel, head and tail entities h, t of the input triples from the KG on the right-hand side are also taken from the shared entity embedding matrix resulting in $\mathbf{h}$ and $\mathbf{t}$ respectively. The shared aspect is further indicated with the dashed representations stating that $\mathbf{h} = \mathbf{e_1}$. Note that the representation of the relation r in the input triple is not affected, since relation embeddings are used exclusively in the KG embedding model in $f(\mathbf{h}, \mathbf{r}, \mathbf{t})$. On top of each embedding model the calculation of the actual objective function $\mathcal{L}_{\mathcal{S}}$ and $\mathcal{L}_{\mathcal{K}}$ is carried out and combined according to $\mathcal{L}_{joint}$ with negative event sample $\mathbf{e_{neg}}$ and negative entity sample $\mathbf{t'}$.

Combined Architecture. The shared architecture proposes a very compact and efficient model with only few parameters. In correspondence to TEKE, we also propose a more flexible *combined* architecture that allows two separate representations of $\mathbf{W}_{\mathcal{X}}$ and $\mathbf{W}_{\mathcal{E}}$, however, without relying on the co-occurrence of head and tail entity. More precisely, given $\mathbf{e}$ from $\mathbf{W}_{\mathcal{X}}$ and $\mathbf{h}$ from $\mathbf{W}_{\mathcal{E}}$, we define $\hat{\mathbf{h}}$ with a custom combination operator denoted as $\mathbf{h} \otimes \mathbf{e}$ as follows:

$$\hat{\mathbf{h}} = \mathbf{h} \otimes \mathbf{e} := \mathbf{h} \odot \mathbf{a_r} + \mathbf{e} \odot \mathbf{b_r},$$

where $\mathbf{a_r}$ and $\mathbf{b_r}$ are trainable weighting vectors for each relation r and $\odot$ is the Hadamard product. Intuitively, this allows the model to adjust the influence of event embeddings on the KG entity embeddings specifically for each relation in a weighted average fashion. Figure 2b shows this combination leading to $\hat{\mathbf{h}}$ being fed into the triple scoring functions.

Note that both of the above proposed architectures are very general, as in fact any KG embedding model, e.g. factorization-based, can be 'plugged' in them.

3.5   Defining $\mathcal{L}_S$ via Negative Sampling

As for the event embeddings, we first propose to learn event embedding parameters that are given by $\mathbf{W}_\mathcal{X}$ using the following negative sampling adapted softmax loss objective:

$$\mathcal{L}_S = \sum_{s \in \mathcal{S}} \sum_{e_i \in s} -\log \sigma(\mathbf{e_i}^\top \mathbf{c_i}) - \log \sigma(-\mathbf{e_{neg}}^\top \mathbf{c_i}), \tag{3}$$

where σ is the sigmoid function, $\mathbf{e}, \mathbf{e_{neg}}$ are the vector representations of the target event and a negative sample event of an additional parameter matrix for the softmax prediction respectively, whereas $\mathbf{c}$ is the representation of the *context* of the target event, i.e. some of its predecessors and successors in the event log. Intuitively, this loss is minimized when the context representations consistently have higher similarity to the actual target compared to the negative sample. The notion of context is critical for such definition of $\mathcal{L}_S$ and we propose two models of context where we assume that the further an event appears from a given one, the lower is their dependency. We model this assumption by selecting a sliding window of size m, which stores only those events that potentially can have effect on each other.

EKL$_{Full}$ Model. In the full model, we define the context as the target's predecessors and successors in a sliding window. This is conceptually shown in Fig. 3a, where a sliding window contains a target event entity in the center and its neighboring events (i.e., *context*) are the center event's possible causes and effects. The goal is to predict the target event based on the representations of its causes and effects. Following this intuition, we define the context operation for a given context target e_i in a window of size m:

$$\mathbf{c_i} = \bigoplus_{j=1}^{\lfloor \frac{m}{2} \rfloor} \mathbf{e}_{i-j} \oplus \bigoplus_{j=1}^{\lfloor \frac{m}{2} \rfloor} \mathbf{e}_{i+j},$$

where $\oplus$ represents the vector concatenation operation. Since the resulting vector from the concatenation is of size $\mathbb{R}^{(m-1)\cdot d}$, the size of the vector that represents the target entity $\mathbf{e}$ for classification in the softmax has to be adapted as well, i.e., $\mathbf{e} \in \mathbb{R}^{(m-1)\cdot d}$. Note that the actual entity representations preserve their original size in the d-dimensional space, hence the only additional parameters are needed for the prediction of each $\mathbf{e}$. Therefore, we can still ensure the efficient training of event sequence embeddings. The window size m is added as an additional hyper-parameter.

EKL$_{Cause}$ Model. Further we also address the case where only the causing events may have influence on the target. In order to preserve the predictive information that a sequence of events inherently possesses, we propose to concatenate the representation of the $m-1$ event predecessors to predict a given target event, i.e. the m-th event in the window. Formally this can be denoted as

$c_i = \bigoplus_{j=1}^{m-1} e_{i-j}$. In Fig. 3b we illustrate this idea again for a generic sequence window of event entities. Observe that the target event here is always the last one in the window.

Note that negative sampling in EKL_{Full} and EKL_{Cause} should be done with care. In order to avoid an accidental inclusion of dependent events as negatives, we make sure that the negative sample is always taken from outside of the complete sequence, i.e. after a certain time threshold before and after the target event.

3.6 Defining $\mathcal{L}_{\mathcal{S}}$ via Autoencoders: EKL_{Auto} Model

Sequence modeling is usually closely related to Recurrent Neural Networks (RNNs). Based on previous experiments it was known that RNNs do not yield good representations of the events for our datasets. Another natural way to learn representations of event sequences is to resort to the family of autoencoder models. The goal here is to encode the sequence s to a latent representation and then to try decoding this back, hence, the latent encoding needs to conserve the sequential information within a low-dimensional vector. Formally, our event embedding objective is the mean-squared error of the original sequence and its decoding:

$$\mathcal{L}_{\mathcal{S}} = \sum_{s \in \mathcal{S}} (\mathbf{s} - \phi(\omega(\mathbf{s})))^2, \tag{4}$$

where $\mathbf{s} = [\mathbf{e_1}, \mathbf{e_2}, \cdots, \mathbf{e_m}]$ is the stacked vector representation of s and $\phi \circ \omega$ is the encoder-decoder function chain. In this work we use a convolutional autoencoder [13] with different filter sizes (adapted to the window size) on the stacked vectors of the sequence, i.e. for one filter $\mathbf{W}_f$ we have: $\omega(\mathbf{s}) = \sigma(\mathbf{s} \star \mathbf{W}_f + b)$ and $\phi(\mathbf{h}) = \sigma(\mathbf{h} \star \tilde{\mathbf{W}}_f + c)$, where $\star$ is the convolution operator, σ is the sigmoid activation function, $\tilde{\mathbf{W}}_f$ is the flipped filter matrix, and b and c are bias terms.

4   Evaluation

We have implemented both of our architectures for event-enhanced KG completion into a system prototype[2] employing the TransE model with the original max-margin objective and negative sampling techniques in TensorFlow [1]. In contrast to the original implementation provided by the authors, our TensorFlow models use a more efficient training technique from [15] exploiting the AdaGrad variant of stochastic gradient-descent [7], which has been shown to yield good quality of prediction for other relational learning models, due to its frequency-adaptive weighting of updates [17].

The AdaGrad technique is beneficial for parameter updates of entities that are only sparsely connected in the KG, and on the other hand, it prevents overfitting for densely connected entities. As suggested for TransE [4], all embeddings

---

[2] Source code of EKL: http://github.com/NetherNova/event-kge.

Table 1. Characteristics of two domain-specific datasets

Dataset	$|\mathcal{K}|$	$|\mathcal{S}|$	$|\mathcal{E}|$	$|\mathcal{R}|$
Manufacturing	6, 791	56, 000	3,180 (728)	10
Traffic	11, 000	157, 000	13,113 (4,000)	5

were initialized by sampling from a uniform distribution $U[-\frac{6}{\sqrt{d}}, \frac{6}{\sqrt{d}}]$. In terms of negative sampling we employ the random replacement of head or tail entities relying on the closed-world assumption and the Bernoulli sampling proposed in [26].

4.1   Evaluation Protocol

We evaluated our three novel approaches for event representations, i.e., EKL_{Auto}, EKL_{Full} and EKL_{Cause}, together with the two architectures (shared and combined) for KG completion by comparing them to plain TransE and the state-of-the-art TEKE model, precisely the TransE-based TEKE_E version, as a baseline for incorporating events, which are in the TEKE case treated as common text corpus and pre-trained using the word2vec skipgram model [14]. In each of the experiments, the original KG is split into a training (70% of the original KG), validation (10%) and test (20%) sets. Final results on quality of prediction are calculated based on the test set, for which we report two commonly-used evaluation metrics:

- **Mean Rank:** the average rank of the entities (head and tail) that would have been the correct ones;
- **Hits@N:** the portion of ranks within N highest ranked entities for $N \in \{1, 3, 10\}$.

The mean rank in our experiments corresponds to the *filtered* version that has been originally proposed in [4], i.e. in the test set when ranking a particular triple $\langle h, r, t \rangle$, all $\langle h, r, t' \rangle$ triples with $t \neq t'$ are removed. Employing grid search through the hyper-parameters we determine the best configuration by mean rank on the validation set with early stopping over a maximum of 100 epochs.

4.2   Dataset Descriptions

Our experiments were performed on two real-world datasets enriched with event sequences: *manufacturing* and *traffic*. The statistical details of these datasets are presented in Table 1, where we report the total number of triples $|\mathcal{K}|$, the number of sequences $|\mathcal{S}|$, the total number of entities $|\mathcal{E}|$ with the number of event entities stated in brackets and the number of relations $|\mathcal{R}|$. We made both datasets and the corresponding sequences available online, see the Github link above.

Manufacturing Dataset. The first dataset is an excerpt of a real-world manufacturing KG from an automated factory that stores data about production equipment, product-part descriptions, and production processes. It models several automated production lines and contains entities corresponding to equipments, products, material, and processes connected via different domain-specific relations, e.g. *connectedTo, madeOf, follows*. The events are messages collected from a subset of the production machines, i.e. machine event logs. These are mostly alarms and warnings reporting about critical states of the production process, e.g. alarms about jams at the material intake of a machine. Some event sequences were known not to influence each other; these bring noise to the embeddings. To avoid this situation, we pre-processed the raw sequences of events by splitting them into multiple disjoint ones based on a maximum time gap that was given by domain experts. This does not bias the embeddings to any of the models, since it just removes spurious correlations. Then, we set the following parameters: mini-batch size to 32 samples; $d \in \{40, 60, 80\}$ as embedding size; and $\eta \in \{0.01, 0.05, 0.1\}$ as learning rate. For the event embeddings, we set the context window size $m \in \{2, 3, 4, 5\}$ for EKL_{Cause} and EKL_{Auto}, $m \in \{3, 5, 7, 9\}$ for EKL_{Full} and $\alpha \in \{0.1, 0.5, 1.0\}$. The number of negative samples for all event embedding models was empirically set to 8.

Traffic Dataset. Here we took a fragment of the *CityPulse* data collection[3] that was used in the smart city applications [2] for monitoring traffic with sensors placed on several locations in the area of Aarhus in Denmark. From this dataset we engineered a KG consisting of the sensor locations, streets, routes, and point of interest locations with typing information crawled from the Google places API[4]. The event data is based on the observed vehicle counts for different routes, e.g. *IncreasedTrafficEvent* between two streets. Since connected streets as well as similar localities (e.g., schools) should intuitively exhibit a similar traffic pattern, the events may be used to complete the data about street connections and locality information. This dataset is particularly challenging and interesting, as the number of entities is *higher* than the number of overall facts, witnessing the KG sparsity. To cope with the large number of entities and triples in the KG, we set the mini-batch size to 64 samples and the embedding size d from $\{60, 80, 100\}$, while keeping the rest of the hyper-parameters the same as in the previous scenario.

4.3   Evaluation Results

Overall KG Completion. In Table 2 we report the results for the variations (1) and (2) of the event-enhanced KG completion problem from Sect. 3.1. As expected, our EKL models significantly outperform TEKE and TransE in both settings. We report that EKL_{Cause} in the shared architecture shows the best

---

[3] iot.ee.surrey.ac.uk:8080/datasets.html.

[4] developers.google.com/maps/documentation/javascript/places.

Table 2. KG completion results for EKL and baselines, where m/n denotes completion results for shared/combined architecture.

Model	Mean rank	Hits@10	Hits@3	Hits@1
Dataset: Manufacturing				
TransE	317	36.1	23.2	7.5
TEKE_E	596	24.5	10.8	3.6
EKL$_{Full}$	285/663	37.9/23.5	25.0/12.3	8.0/4.8
EKL$_{Cause}$	**280**/691	**38.1**/21.4	**25.8**/11.5	7.4/5.2
EKL$_{Auto}$	302/692	34.5/22.5	23.6/10.1	**9.6**/2.7
Dataset: Traffic				
TransE	4126	26.8	24.6	9.5
TEKE_E	897	25.3	22.6	18.9
EKL$_{Full}$	1118/**758**	27.0/27.3	**25.3**/24.5	21.1/20.6
EKL$_{Cause}$	999/783	27.2/27.0	24.7/24.4	20.0/20.5
EKL$_{Auto}$	944/840	27.5/**27.7**	24.8/24.8	**22.2**/20.6

results in terms of mean rank and the first two hits metrics in the manufacturing case. The shared entity embeddings are highly beneficial for the other EKL models as well and show significant improvements compared to the TEKE_E model. In this case, TEKE_E performs even worse than default TransE, confirming that mere co-occurrence between events does not contribute to the completion. However, in the traffic scenario TEKE_E shows much stronger results compared to TransE, but using our combined architecture achieves consistently better results, as in terms of mean rank EKL$_{Full}$ outperforms the rest. On the other hand, the EKL$_{Auto}$ model has highest hits@1 for both datasets using the shared embeddings, therefore it is the most specific model, but cannot generalize as well as EKL$_{Full}$ and EKL$_{Cause}$.

Impact on Relations. Table 3 (top right and left) contains the mean rank for every KG relation achieved by the best EKL and TEKE_E model on the manufacturing and traffic data. For the manufacturing scenario the relations that are semantically closer to events benefit from the sequential embeddings more than others and we expected this effect. E.g., the improvement for the *connectedTo* relation that links equipments to each other is more evident than for other relations like materials partonomy *isPartOf*. The additional knowledge given by the sequences also propagates to the process-oriented *follows* relation, for which the significant improvement over TEKE is observed. Similar conclusions can be made about the traffic scenario. Here, again the EKL$_{Cause}$ model performs exceptionally well on the *hasStartPoint* relation, while for less event-dependent relations such as *locatedAt* the difference of EKL compared to TEKE is less apparent.

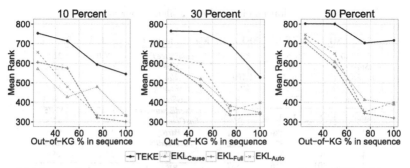

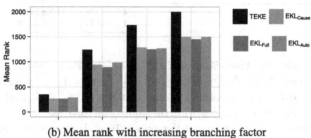

(a) Mean rank on zero shot test sets with increasing portion of out-of-KG entities

(b) Mean rank with increasing branching factor

Fig. 4. Meanrank evaluation: (a) zero shot test sets, (b) with increasing branching factor

Further evaluation is focused on the manufacturing scenario, since this dataset has richer semantics in terms of relations and typing of event entities.

Impact of Window Size. In Table 3 (bottom, left) we examine the impact of the window size on the overall mean rank performance of our models. One can observe that capturing the sequential nature of the event entities is sensitive to the window size parameter. In our manufacturing scenario the EKL_{Cause} model performs very well for small window sizes, and the results deteriorate after the window size of 4. In the preparation of EKL_{Full} the window size must always be an odd number, therefore the window size here is increased by two. It can be observed that EKL_{Full} needs a slightly larger window to capture the context, and shows best performance at a window size of 7. In case of EKL_{Auto} we see a deterioration after window size 3.

Zero-Shot Learning. The zero-shot learning (variation (3) of the event-enhanced KG completion problem in Sect. 3.1) addresses the case when triples about event entities present in the test set are not in the training KG, hence their links to known entities in the KG can only be inferred through their sequential occurrence.

Table 3. Evaluation results and controlled experiment statistics

Traffic Rel	TEKE_E	EKL$_{Full}$	Manufacturing Rel	TEKE_E	EKL$_{Cause}$
hasSource	868	**837**	connectedTo	674.0	**28.5**
hasStartingPoint	970	**350**	type	807.9	**163.9**
hasEndPoint	1,627	**1,104**	follows	16.1	**7.8**
locatedAt	**214**	291	isMadeOf	29.5	**12.5**
type	**788**	829	hasSource	289.7	**169.9**

|Window|	EKL$_{Full}$	EKL$_{Cause}$	EKL$_{Auto}$
2	-	**280**	361
3	293	322	**302**
4	-	**306**	328
5	301	356	337
7	**285**	-	-
9	287	-	-

involvedEquipment	37.15	**17.75**
hasComponent	234.1	**47.3**
isPartOf	**15.4**	64.8
observedBy	525.8	**769.9**
hasSkill	22.2	**14.4**

BF	$|\mathcal{K}|$	$|\mathcal{E}|$
2	3,459	2,005 (549)
3	11,925	7,102 (2,180)
4	16,578	9,097 (2,155)
5	24,835	15,252 (4,809)

To evaluate the effectiveness of our EKL models in a zero-shot learning setting, we have accordingly designed tailored KG test sets, by varying the percentage of the *out-of-KG* event entities in the test set (10%, 30%, and 50% of the overall set of event entity triples). Furthermore, we also vary the percentage of out-of-KG event entities in the event log, where 100% indicates that every out-of-KG entity of the test set has been observed *at least once* in one of the sequences. The results of our experiments are reported in Fig. 4a. Note that in the setting on the right, when 50% of all event entities are solely present in the test set, the EKL$_{Full}$ model consistently outperforms all other approaches w.r.t. mean rank. In other settings, as the sequence dataset proportion is increased, EKL$_{Full}$ shows best improvement and ends up with the lowest mean rank eventually.

It appears that EKL$_{Full}$ is more stable at capturing typing and location of events, due to its incorporation of future context, compared to EKL$_{Cause}$ and EKL$_{Auto}$. On the other hand, all EKL models significantly outperform TEKE in all zero-shot settings and seem to converge with less data. We argue that this is due to their ability to capture sequential correlations inside the event logs and the joint optimization.

Controlled Topology of Processes. In our real-world manufacturing scenario the process entities reflect the *topology* of physical equipment in the factory. Since our experiments witness that EKL does the best predictions for relations that reflect this topology, we designed a controlled scenario where we can validate how the changes in topology affect quality of prediction.

To this end we chose six relations that naturally determine manufacturing topology: *follows, isA, hasSource, involvedEquipment, hasComponent,* and *connectsTo*. We scaled the topology in two dimensions: *structure of the processes* and *number of events*. This gave us four KGs, each describing a complex tree-shaped manufacturing process, where one concrete piece of manufacturing equipment is attached to each node of the tree and multiple events are attached to each piece of equipment. These KGs are described in Table 3 (bottom right), where **BF** stands for branching factor.

We now describe the concrete procedure that we followed to generate these KGs. First, we set the branching factor of the process varying from 2 to 5 and the depth of the process. The intuition behind the branching factor is that, starting from a root process step, the successor steps can be partly executed in parallel and the branching controls this degree of parallelism, which is a common characteristic of real-world processes in manufacturing, road traffic, etc. E.g., in a manufacturing case a particular preparation process may have a fixed set of three successor process steps (branching factor three) each performing a different operation in parallel to the others. Second, for each process we iteratively constructed the process-tree starting from the root, until the process depth, by randomly selecting the number of children in each node to be at most the branching factor. Using the process-tree, we generate corresponding equipment entities participating in the process. Then, using multiple random walks through the process-tree (with restart) we simulated $50,000$ ($|\mathcal{S}| = 50,000$) event occurrences that are linked to the equipment of the process. Each random walk follows successor process entities from the root to the end with uniform probability for all successors and a small probability of staying in the current process. Hence, we end up with multiple cause and effect event patterns in the sequence data instead of having a purely linear chaining. Note that the relative amount of event entities to overall entities in the KG stays roughly at 30%.

Again, we compared our three event-enhanced KG embedding models to TEKE_E. The results are presented in Fig. 4b. Observe that, as the branching increases, the more all EKL models outperform TEKE_E, since the alignment of process and machine entities no longer follows a linear sequence, which is hard to capture without considering sequential correlations. In general, EKL_{Full} seems to be the most effective event embedding model in terms of adapting to the non-linear process chains, while we conjecture that EKL_{Auto} might be more prone to overfit to linear sequences.

5   Conclusions

We proposed EKL, a novel method for event-enhanced learning of knowledge graph embeddings by jointly modeling representations of KGs and event logs consisting of sequences of event entities. Our approach has many applications across domains such as manufacturing, smart cities, and social networks. More specifically, we proposed two different architectures, using a single shared entity embedding layer and another one using combined embeddings for joint optimization. Furthermore, we presented several event embedding models with various notions of context concatenation and an event sequence Autoencoder model. Evaluation on two real-world scenarios and a controlled experiment showed the effectiveness of our approach compared to the state-of-the-art TEKE model. Especially process-oriented parts of KGs exhibit significantly improved completion performance when provided with event embeddings. Our EKL models are also capable of zero-shot learning, in which event entities are not linked to the KG. The scaled zero-shot experiments showed that EKL models significantly improve handling of zero-shot event entities in the KG completion.

Acknowledgements. This work was partially supported by the EPSRC projects DBOnto,MaSI[3] and ED[3].

References

1. Abadi, M., Barham, P., Chen, J., Chen, Z., et al.: TensorFlow : a system for large-scale machine learning. In: OSDI (2016)
2. Ali, M.I., Gao, F., Mileo, A.: CityBench: a configurable benchmark to evaluate RSP engines using smart city datasets. In: Arenas, M., et al. (eds.) ISWC 2015. LNCS, vol. 9367, pp. 374–389. Springer, Cham (2015). https://doi.org/10.1007/978-3-319-25010-6_25
3. Bordes, A., Chopra, S., Weston, J.: Question answering with subgraph embeddings. In: EMNLP, pp. 615–620 (2014)
4. Bordes, A., Usunier, N., García-Durán, A., Weston, J., Yakhnenko, O.: Translating embeddings for modeling multi-relational data. In: NIPS, pp. 2787–2795 (2013)
5. Cucerzan, S.: Large-scale named entity disambiguation based on Wikipedia data. In: EMNLP-CoNLL, pp. 708–716 (2007)
6. Dong, X., Gabrilovich, E., Heitz, G., Horn, W., Lao, N., Murphy, K., Strohmann, T., Sun, S., Zhang, W.: Knowledge vault: a web-scale approach to probabilistic knowledge fusion. In: ACM SIGKDD, pp. 601–610 (2014)
7. Duchi, J.C., Hazan, E., Singer, Y.: Adaptive subgradient methods for online learning and stochastic optimization. J. Mach. Learn. Res. **12**, 2121–2159 (2011)
8. Hachey, B., Radford, W., Nothman, J., Honnibal, M., Curran, J.R.: Evaluating entity linking with Wikipedia. Artif. Intell. **194**, 130–150 (2013)
9. Kharlamov, E., Hovland, D., Skjæveland, M.G., Bilidas, D., Jiménez-Ruiz, E., Xiao, G., Soylu, A., Lanti, D., Rezk, M., Zheleznyakov, D., Giese, M., Lie, H., Ioannidis, Y.E., Kotidis, Y., Koubarakis, M., Waaler, A.: Ontology based data access in Statoil. JWS **44**, 3–36 (2017)
10. Kharlamov, E., Mailis, T., Mehdi, G., Neuenstadt, C., Özçep, Ö.L., Roshchin, M., Solomakhina, N., Soylu, A., Svingos, C., Brandt, S., Giese, M., Ioannidis, Y.E., Lamparter, S., Möller, R., Kotidis, Y., Waaler, A.: Semantic access to streaming and static data at Siemens. JWS **44**, 54–74 (2017)
11. Krompaß, D., Baier, S., Tresp, V.: Type-constrained representation learning in knowledge graphs. In: Arenas, M., et al. (eds.) ISWC 2015. LNCS, vol. 9366, pp. 640–655. Springer, Cham (2015). https://doi.org/10.1007/978-3-319-25007-6_37
12. Lehmann, J., Isele, R., Jakob, M., Jentzsch, A., Kontokostas, D., Mendes, P.N., Hellmann, S., Morsey, M., van Kleef, P., Auer, S., Bizer, C.: Dbpedia - a large-scale, multilingual knowledge base extracted from Wikipedia. Semant. Web **6**(2), 167–195 (2015)
13. Masci, J., Meier, U., Cireşan, D., Schmidhuber, J.: Stacked convolutional auto-encoders for hierarchical feature extraction. In: Honkela, T., Duch, W., Girolami, M., Kaski, S. (eds.) ICANN 2011. LNCS, vol. 6791, pp. 52–59. Springer, Heidelberg (2011). https://doi.org/10.1007/978-3-642-21735-7_7
14. Mikolov, T., Chen, K., Corrado, G., Dean, J.: Distributed representations of words and phrases and their compositionality. In: NIPS, pp. 1–9 (2013)

15. Minervini, P., Fanizzi, N., D'Amato, C., Esposito, F.: Scalable learning of entity and predicate embeddings for knowledge graph completion. In: ICMLA, pp. 162–167 (2015)
16. Nickel, M., Murphy, K., Tresp, V., Gabrilovich, E.: A review of relational machine learning for knowledge graphs. Proc. IEEE **104**(1), 11–33 (2016)
17. Nickel, M., Rosasco, L., Poggio, T.A.: Holographic embeddings of knowledge graphs. In: AAAI, pp. 1955–1961 (2016)
18. Nickel, M., Tresp, V., Kriegel, H.P.: A three-way model for collective learning on multi-relational data. In: ICML (2011)
19. Ringsquandl, M., Lamparter, S., Brandt, S., Hubauer, T., Lepratti, R.: Semantic-guided feature selection for industrial automation systems. In: Arenas, M., et al. (eds.) ISWC 2015. LNCS, vol. 9367, pp. 225–240. Springer, Cham (2015). https://doi.org/10.1007/978-3-319-25010-6_13
20. Ringsquandl, M., Lamparter, S., Kharlamov, E., Lepratti, R., Stepanova, D., Kroeger, P., Horrocks, I.: On event-driven learning of knowledge in smart factories: the case of siemens. In: IEEE Big Data (2017)
21. Santos, H., Dantas, V., Furtado, V., Pinheiro, P., McGuinness, D.L.: From data to city indicators: a knowledge graph for supporting automatic generation of dashboards. In: Blomqvist, E., Maynard, D., Gangemi, A., Hoekstra, R., Hitzler, P., Hartig, O. (eds.) ESWC 2017. LNCS, vol. 10250, pp. 94–108. Springer, Cham (2017). https://doi.org/10.1007/978-3-319-58451-5_7
22. Shi, B., Weninger, T.: ProjE : embedding projection for knowledge graph completion. In: AAAI 2017, pp. 1–14 (2017)
23. Socher, R., Chen, D., Manning, C.D., Ng, A.Y.: Reasoning with neural tensor networks for knowledge base completion. In: NIPS, pp. 1–10 (2013)
24. Suchanek, F.M., Kasneci, G., Weikum, G.: YAGO: a core of semantic knowledge. In: Proceedings of WWW, pp. 697–706 (2007)
25. Wang, Q., Wang, B., Guo, L.: Knowledge base completion using embeddings and rules. In: IJCAI, pp. 1859–1866 (2015)
26. Wang, Z., Zhang, J., Feng, J., Chen, Z.: Knowledge graph embedding by translating on hyperplanes. In: AAAI, pp. 1112–1119 (2014)
27. Wang, Z., Li, J.Z.J.: Text-enhanced representation learning for knowledge graph. In: IJCAI, pp. 1293–1299 (2016)
28. Xiao, H., Huang, M., Meng, L., Zhu, X.: SSP: semantic space projection for knowledge graph embedding with text descriptions. In: AAAI, pp. 1–10 (2017)
29. Xie, R., Liu, Z., Jia, J., Luan, H., Sun, M.: Representation learning of knowledge graphs with entity descriptions. In: IJCAI, pp. 2659–2665 (2016)
30. Yang, Z., Tang, J., Cohen, W.W.: Multi-modal bayesian embeddings for learning social knowledge graphs. In: IJCAI, pp. 2287–2293 (2016)
31. Zhong, H., Zhang, J., Wang, Z., Wan, H., Chen, Z.: Aligning knowledge and text embeddings by entity descriptions. In: EMNLP, pp. 267–272 (2015)

Exploring Enterprise Knowledge Graphs: A Use Case in Software Engineering

Marta Sabou[1](✉)[iD], Fajar J. Ekaputra[1][iD], Tudor Ionescu[2], Juergen Musil[1][iD],
Daniel Schall[2], Kevin Haller[1][iD], Armin Friedl[1], and Stefan Biffl[1]

[1] Technical University of Vienna, Vienna, Austria
{marta.sabou,fajar.ekaputra,juergen.musil,kevin.haller,armin.friedl,
stefan.biffl}@tuwien.ac.at
[2] Siemens AG Vienna, Vienna, Austria
{tudor.ionescu,daniel.schall}@siemens.com

Abstract. When reusing software architectural knowledge, such as design patterns or design decisions, software architects need support for exploring architectural knowledge collections, e.g., for finding related items. While semantic-based architectural knowledge management tools are limited to supporting lookup-based tasks through faceted search and fall short of enabling exploration, semantic-based exploratory search systems primarily focus on web-scale knowledge graphs without having been adapted to enterprise-scale knowledge graphs (EKG). We investigate how and to what extent exploratory search can be supported on EKGs of architectural knowledge. We propose an approach for building exploratory search systems on EKGs and demonstrate its use within Siemens, which resulted in the STAR system used in practice by 200–300 software architects. We found that the EKG's ontology allows making previously implicit organisational knowledge explicit and this knowledge informs the design of suitable relatedness metrics to support exploration. Yet, the performance of these metrics heavily depends on the characteristics of the EKG's data. Therefore both statistical and user-based evaluations can be used to select the right metric before system implementation.

Keywords: Software engineering · Software architectural knowledge
Enterprise knowledge graph · Exploratory search

1 Introduction

In the area of software engineering, software documentation in general [9] and software architectural knowledge (AK) in particular [3] are important assets throughout the software engineering life-cycle. AK encompasses software design patterns, architecture descriptions, reference architecture models (i.e., the outcome of the software architecture design process) as well as the design decisions taken by the software architects during the design process itself [13]. AK has considerable value as it enables reusing already validated design solutions. Therefore,

© Springer International Publishing AG, part of Springer Nature 2018
A. Gangemi et al. (Eds.): ESWC 2018, LNCS 10843, pp. 560–575, 2018.
https://doi.org/10.1007/978-3-319-93417-4_36

its management is crucial as it affects the effectiveness of architecture decision making processes that steer the evolution of a software platform.

Therefore, researchers investigate for more than a decade approaches and systems to support software engineers and architects with AK management [3]. Some of these approaches are based on Semantic Web techniques, with ontology-based semantic data enabling intuitive, graphical navigation of AK [4,14] or acting as backbones for wiki-based systems offering browsing, faceted-search and querying capabilities [5–7,10,15,22]. Some ontology enabled faceted search systems were shown to improve the effectiveness and efficiency of AK retrieval [5,15]. Yet, recent studies indicate that architects still mostly rely on ad-hoc decisions to address architectural quality attributes (e.g., scalability) and that they have limited awareness of available alternatives when making architectural decisions to address quality attributes [1,2]. Therefore, a challenge is providing search mechanisms that go beyond information lookup, such as achievable with faceted-search, and support software architects in *exploring the space of available AK elements, especially plausible alternatives.* This challenge also exists at Siemens AG, a large organization with a key focus on software engineering. Siemens software architects need support to intuitively search for and explore architectural knowledge but are currently poorly supported in this task by legacy technologies which rely primarily on databases and wikis.

A promising approach to support software architects who need to sieve through and make sense of AK repositories is *exploratory search* which enables open-ended, weakly-defined information seeking tasks such as learning and sense-making [23]. Previous evidence shows that semantic structures can support exploration, e.g., by improving search performance and decreasing frustration levels [8]. And indeed, several semantics-based exploratory search systems were proposed [16]. Typically, these systems support exploration by presenting new knowledge derived from the underlying semantic structure *algorithmically* (e.g., through relatedness and similarity metrics) and they primarily focus on enabling the exploration of large knowledge graphs (e.g., DBpedia) [16].

Although enterprises increasingly create their own *Enterprise Knowledge Graphs (EKG)* to represent expert knowledge [19], adapting exploratory search to such graphs has received limited attention. Expert knowledge has been characterised as domain specific and constrained in its scope [20] as well as highly structured, detailed and interconnected [11]. Therefore we define EKGs as (1) *highly specific*, often encoding a single, narrowly defined domain; (2) comparatively *small* (compared to e.g., general knowledge graphs such as DBpedia) and (3) *deeply structured with detailed interconnections* between their concepts.

Our goal is to implement and exploratory search system of architectural knowledge at Siemens. Therefore, we investigate the following research questions:

RQ1: How to implement exploratory search on EKGs? What is a suitable approach? What main steps need to be followed?

RQ2: How to identify suitable relatedness metrics? Our hypothesis is that relatedness metrics supporting exploration could be derived based on domain knowledge from the EKG's ontology. We investigate methods to select the most suitable metric that minimise the need for expensive user studies.

RQ3: Are explanations derived from the EKG helpful? Based on [17], our hypothesis is that relatedness explanations which can be derived based on domain-specific relatedness metrics are helpful to support exploration.

We investigate these research questions in the context of Siemens. Since previous studies have positively evaluated semantics-based faceted-search AK management systems [5,15], we designed, implemented and deployed the Semantic Search for Architectural Knowledge (STAR) prototype, a system that enables faceted search of AK. Additionally, we extended this system with *exploratory search* that takes advantage of the underlying EKG. STAR is novel in the AK management system landscape because it goes beyond faceted search based on the ontology structure, such as in [5–7,10,15,22], and introduces exploratory search by recommending related AK, derived from the underlying EKG by semantic relatedness metrics. From the perspective of exploratory search research, we propose an approach for implementing this paradigm on an EKG and report on its concrete use in practice. STAR has been integrated into the current use case setting in a way that augments rather than replaces legacy solutions, and, as a result, is being used for accessing AK by cca. 200–300 Siemens software architects. Although we report work in the context of Siemens, our approach and lessons learned are of interest to other companies that need exploratory AK management, or, more broadly, enterprises with an EKG which could enable exploratory search.

Next, we describe the Siemens use case (Sect. 2) and present our approach to implement exploratory search (Sect. 3) as well as its main steps: the creation of the STAR EKG (Sect. 4), the definition and evaluation of relatedness metrics (Sects. 5, 6) and the actual system implementation (Sect. 7). We overview related work (Sect. 8) and conclude with lessons learned, benefits and challenges (Sect. 9).

2   Use Case

Siemens AG is the largest manufacturing and electronics company in Europe. Its central research and development unit, Siemens Corporate Technology, shapes innovation activities in the company and provides solutions to the company's Business Units, e.g., through the creation of software by some 4800 software engineers across the globe.

A portion of this workforce (i.e., software and system architects, technical project managers, senior developers, research group leaders) focuses on designing software architecture. On a daily basis, these employees take several architectural design decisions [13] carefully selecting the most appropriate architectural elements (e.g., design patterns and tactics) to employ and weighing the effects of these elements on the desired architectural qualities of the created system (e.g., scalability, reliability, accessibility). In their decisions, they also consider specific characteristics and requirements of the domain for which the software is designed (e.g., cloud computing, smart cities, cyber-physical systems).

A key task in designing software architecture is finding and reusing AK. For example, an architect wants to design a system that has the *qualities* of being *configurable* and *expressive*. He knows that the *façade* pattern enables designing systems with these characteristics, but would like to know about other patterns with similar effects, which he can consider for reuse. This reuse of already validated architectural solutions not only makes the design process faster but also ensures a better outcome, i.e., a well-designed software product. To enable such knowledge reuse, architectural knowledge is documented and during the years, this activity has led to several collections of semi-structured documents describing AK elements and their use within Siemens projects. The corpus of our use case contained about 600 AK entities (e.g., design patterns and tactics).

Siemens employs a wide range of advanced methods and platforms to manage AK, relying primarily on wiki-based systems and on databases (see Sect. 7). The search functionalities of these approaches rely primarily on organizational metadata such as the project where the AK was applied or the group/person that developed it. It is *difficult to search for AK based on meaningful features* such as e.g., its effect on architectural qualities or the (fine-grained) relations between architectural elements. There is therefore a need for sophisticated AK search capabilities to intuitively search and easily find AK. Going beyond simply organizing and accessing AK, the search system should support discovering new knowledge in a serendipitous fashion, i.e., learning something relevant but unexpected. One instance of serendipitous learning is finding related AK elements: for example, two design patterns might be considered as related when they have comparable effects on architectural qualities. We implement an exploratory search system in this context as described next.

3   Implementing Exploratory Search: Approach

Our approach for implementing exploratory search on an EKG, assumes a green-field context where the EKG itself needs to be created. Recently, knowledge graphs were defined as *"a set of interconnected typed entities and their attributes"*, where an ontology defines the vocabulary of the graph [19]. Therefore, our approach covers both ontology and EKG construction among other steps:

Create ontology to capture the relevant domain knowledge. While any of the existing ontology creation methodologies can be followed, in an enterprise setting at least the following three stages apply: **1. Scoping** clarifies the purpose of the system as well as the use cases and competency questions to be supported; **2. Definition** creates the first version of the ontology taking into account organization internal and external data sources; **3. Refinement** of the ontology with respect to the use case, data to be represented in the EKG and actual usage during system implementation.

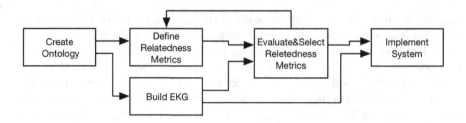

Fig. 1. STAR approach for creating an exploratory search system.

Build EKG. To create the EKG entities based on the defined ontology, several methods can be used to transfer relevant data into a semantic representation.

Define relatedness metrics. Taking the view of exploratory search as recommending related entities, at this step suitable relatedness metrics are define, for example, by relying on domain specific heuristics.

Evaluate and select relatedness metrics. Before implementing relatedness metrics in a concrete exploratory search system, it is vital to test these. A combination of statistical comparison techniques and user studies is recommended. Evaluation results can be taken into account to refine the metrics.

Implement system with the selected metric(s).

The next sections describe the application of the approach within our use case.

4   Creating the STAR EKG of Architectural Knowledge

Creating the STAR EKG entailed ontology construction and its population. To construct the STAR ontology, in an initial **scoping** workshop system purpose, use cases, and competency questions were clarified. To create an ontology that could play the role of a common denominator on architectural knowledge terminology within the company, it was decided to build on widely adopted AK models and extend these with domain and organizational specific concepts. The main standard for documenting software architectures is the ISO/IEC/IEEE 42010:2010 [12]. It comprises the meta models used to derive standard-conform viewpoints, architecture frameworks and architecture description languages.

During ontology **definition**, the project team, including a knowledge engineer and a software engineering researcher, identified a list of relevant concepts based on: (1) the datamodel of the legacy database for storing AK; (2) ISO/IEC/IEEE 42010 and (3) other AK ontologies proposed in the literature [7,22]. Next, the relations that hold between these concepts were identified, thus making explicit the information encoded implicitly in the database schema. To **refine** the ontology, several iterations were performed with Siemens partners to validate the relevance and usefulness of these concepts for the use case. As part of these iterations, the AK corpus was transformed into the ontology in order to check coverage. A stakeholder workshop closed the development process, where

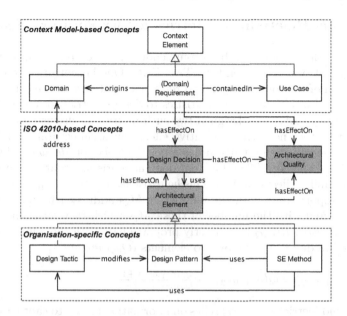

Fig. 2. STAR ontology: main concepts and their relations.

the first draft version of the ontology was approved. Smaller, implementation specific adaptations happened during the ontology's use in system development.

The STAR EKG consists of the STAR ontology[1] (Fig. 2) with 20 concepts, 30 properties and around 1000 entities that are instances of the ontology classes and were extracted from legacy databases as discussed in Sect. 7. Because design decisions play a key role in the work of software architects, these are modeled as a core concept in the STAR ontology, i.e., *DesignDecision* (90 entities). They have effects on *ArchitecturalQualities* (95), which refer to desired characteristics of the designed system such as accuracy, accessibility, autonomy or usability. Design decisions rely for their realization on (i.e., use) *ArchitectureElements (AE)*. These three concepts and their relations emerge as a core modeling pattern in the software architecture domain. Types of architectural elements interesting for the context of Siemens are *DesignPatterns* (301), *DesignTactics* (137) and *SEMethods* (43). The design process and its elements are affected by and address a set of *ContextElements*. Relevant for Siemens are context elements such as *Domain* (107), *UseCase* and *Requirement*. Finally, a set of concepts have been introduced to capture the provenance of the information (such as the *Author* that added it) or relevance for a certain *Project* (18), *ProjectRole* (e.g., test architect, requirements engineer) or *ProjectPhase* (e.g., design, testing).

---

[1] The STAR ontology is available at: http://data.ifs.tuwien.ac.at/star/.

5   Defining Relatedness Metrics for Exploratory Search

We achieve exploratory search by recommending related architectural elements (e.g., design patterns) based on the STAR EKG. One benefit of the ontological representation of the core concepts and relations of interest to the company was that it provided intuitions about heuristics to design metrics for computing the relatedness of two AEs. We designed two such metrics, as discussed next.

AEs have either negative or positive effects on architectural qualities. For example, the *façade* design pattern has a positive effect on *flexibility*, but negatively affects *accessibility*. Therefore, one domain heuristic is that AEs are related if they have similar effects on AQs. This heuristic lead to the Rel_{AQ} metric which is directly proportionate with the number of AQs addressed by both elements ($Q(ae_1, ae_2)$) and with the number of those AQs which they affect in the same way ($Q_a(ae_1, ae_2)$). Rel_{AQ} is indirectly proportionate with the number of qualities affected in different ways by two elements ($Q_{da}(ae_1, ae_2)$).

$$Rel_{AQ}(ae_1, ae_2) = Q(ae_1, ae_2) * \frac{|Q_a(ae_1,ae_2)|+1}{|Q_{da}(ae_1,ae_2)|+1}$$

Our second metric (Rel_{DOM}) relies on information theory to capture the relation between architectural elements and the domains that they address. For each domain (e.g., "smart cities"), its information content is computed ($IC(d)$). A domain addressed by many elements has a lower IC than a domain addressed only by a few elements. Rel_{DOM} is the average information content of the domains that both architectural elements address ($D(ae_1, ae_2)$).

$$IC(d) = -log \frac{count(ae_i.address.d)}{\sum_{i,j} count(ae_i.address.d_j)}; Rel_{DOM}(ae_1, ae_2) = \frac{\sum_{d_i \in D} IC(d_i)}{|D(ae_1,ae_2)|}$$

Generating explanations. For Rel_{AQ}, explanations of AE relatedness list the AQs on which the two AEs have the same effect and those AQs which are affected differently. For Rel_{DOM}, we list the domains that both elements address.

6   Evaluation of Relatedness Metrics

After designing the relatedness metrics we perform an evaluation to select the metric to be integrated into the exploratory search system. Our approach is to first perform a comparative evaluation of the overall behaviour of the metrics over the entire EKG, and based on the findings to select the most promising metric (Sect. 6.1) which is then evaluated in a user study (Sect. 6.2).

6.1   Comparative Evaluation of Relatedness Metrics

We use statistical methods to compare the overall behaviour of the two metrics over the entire EKG. The box-plots and the relative frequency histograms displayed in Fig. 3 show that Rel_{AQ} leads to a variety of values and has a good discriminative power among related architectural elements while Rel_{DOM} returns similar values for most element pairs, thus only weakly supporting relatedness identification. Indeed, although over 100 domains are defined in the EKG, 68% of the architectural elements address only the domain "abstract" and therefore the applicability of the information content inspired metric on this data is not optimal. Therefore, our user evaluation focuses on Rel_{AQ} alone.

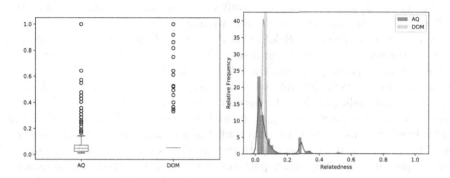

Fig. 3. Comparison of the overall behaviour of the relatedness metrics.

6.2   User Based Evaluation

The task of determining architectural element relatedness received limited attention in the literature so far. Therefore, the main goals of the user based evaluations were: (Q1) to assess how difficult this task is for human raters; (Q2) to determine the quality of ratings derived by the relatedness metric Rel_{AQ} and (Q3) to investigate whether explanations derived from the EKG support users in understanding relatedness among architectural elements.

Experimental Data. We focus the evaluation on design patterns as the largest group of architectural elements in our collection. The relatedness metric supports an exploratory search interface, in which only patterns related above a certain threshold are shown. Our interest therefore is to evaluate how well the metric works for highly related pattern pairs. We computed the weighted Rel_{AQ} values for all patterns in the dataset and chose five patterns for which relatedness pairs ranked highest (e.g., façade, proxy). For each pattern, we selected the top 5 related patterns recommended by Rel_{AQ}. The evaluation dataset therefore consisted in 25 pattern pairs and the explanations for deriving their relatedness (e.g., the qualities on which the patterns had/did not have the same effect).

The study population consisted in 8 participants (6 from Siemens, 2 from the university), all with a software engineering background and with education ranging from undergraduate (2), to graduate (1), doctoral (2) and post-doc (3) levels. Industrial experience with software architecture ranged from 1 year (2), to 5–7 years (4) and 10 years (2). In terms of experience with software design patterns the population included 2 experts, 5 advanced and 1 intermediate participant. Participants were divided in two groups, Gr1 and Gr2.

Study Task. Participants were shown pattern pairs, their descriptions and (for half of the dataset) an explanation of how their relatedness was derived.

They were asked to rank the pairs relatedness on a 5-point scale (1 completely unrelated; 5 very related) considering a broad notion of relatedness that one would expect in the context of an exploratory search system. Gr1 evaluated the first half of the pair set without explanation and the second half with explanation, while Gr2 did the opposite. A post-study survey collected background information and opinions about the study task as qualitative data. Based on the collected data the following *conclusions* were drawn.

Q1: Difficulty of Pattern Relatedness Judgement. Based on the data collected through the survey to the question *How challenging was the task of comparing the patterns?*, most participants considered the task of average difficulty (avg:3.25 on a scale from 1-very difficult to 5-very easy). Main issues encountered were: (1) the understanding of the patterns was hampered when the quality of pattern descriptions was suboptimal (e.g., too short, too generic); (2) it was difficult to judge how patterns relate without considering a concrete context such as a use case; (3) generally, the notion of pattern relatedness was perceived as challenging to quantify especially when patterns shared some common characteristics but differed in others (e.g., when patterns had: different intentions but similar realization/different realization but similar intention). Interpreting the actual rankings made by the participants in terms of Fleiss Kappa, we obtained an overall agreement of 34%, with a fixed marginal Kappa of 0.16. This shows only a slight agreement among human raters and suggests that the task is more challenging than perceived by our participants in the qualitative questionnaire.

Q2: Quality of Relatedness Ratings. In the post-study survey, participants rated the plausibility of the reviewed pattern pairs as moderate, avg. 2.15 on a scale from 1 (not plausible) to 4 (very plausible). This perception correlates with the interpretation of the experimental data. We considered as successful recommendation all pairs that had an average rating score of 3 or above derived from the 8 raters. We obtained an overall precision value of 52%, a reasonable result considering the inherent difficulty of the task. Looking at pair sets returned for each of the 5 patterns, precision at three (Prec@3) had an average value of 60% across the five pair sets corresponding to the seed patterns.

Q3. Usefulness of Relatedness Explanations. Based on the survey results, explanations of pattern relatedness as currently provided were considered moderately helpful, avg. 2 on a scale from 1 (not helpful) to 4 (very helpful). Main factors that lowered the usefulness of the explanations were: (1) too many architectural qualities were shown, thus increasing confusion; (2) AQs were not sufficiently clear, an explanatory sentence would have helped; (3) some AQs were perceived as not specific enough to be meaningful (e.g., maintainability can include both error handling and complexity management). As a result of these findings, explanations are not included in the current user interface.

Useful suggestions were collected for improving explanations, most of them (e.g., (2), (4) in the following list) revealing the need for more sophisticated semantic analysis on more detailed semantic annotations. Suggestions included: (1) provide more context information; (2) use more selective qualities that describe relations more appropriately; (3) reduce the number of the displayed

AQs; (4) explanations should be more detailed and based on a multitude of criteria (e.g., pattern domain, functionality, the problems solved); (5) recommend more refined relations between patterns (e.g., complements, refines, occurs with).

7   System Implementation

We implemented a faceted and exploratory search solution by *augmenting the legacy search solution* (top-half of Fig. 4) already in place at Siemens. In that solution, architectural knowledge was *acquired* through crawling mechanisms from both organization external and internal sources (e.g., project and domain-specific Wikis and databases of AK). As part of the acquisition phase, AK elements were enriched with information about experiences with their use in Siemens specific projects/domains and with their effect on system qualities. These metadata elements were added as key-value pairs and stored in a NoSQL database (i.e., MongoDB) as part of the *synthesis* stage of the system. A *keyword-based search interface* retrieves the architectural elements relevant for a given keyword and displays these in a search-engine style. The search interface proved helpful for users (i.e., software architects and engineers) to find relevant information about particular AKs and their application at Siemens. However, the solution lacked more detailed information about the relation between architectural elements and therefore provided limited support to explore the AK collection in more depth.

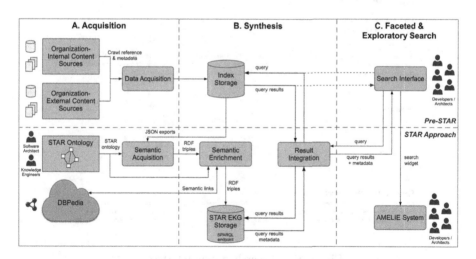

Fig. 4. System overview without (top-half) and with the STAR approach (lower-half).

We extended the legacy search solution with components for acquiring, storing and exploring semantic information (lower-half of Fig. 4). *Semantic Acquisition* focuses on ontology population. Ontology instances were created from the information stored in MongoDB in a two-step process: (1) GSON and Apache Jena libraries were used to convert the JSON export from MongoDB into a temporary RDF file reflecting the databases key-value pair structure; (2) SPARQL construct queries were developed to transform the temporary RDF data into instances of the STAR ontology, thus creating the STAR EKG. The *Semantic Enrichment* component includes modules for data linking and computing additional semantic links between architectural elements. As some of the design patterns are not company specific, 66 were linked to the equivalent pages in DBpedia by defining linkage rules based on the $rdfs : label$ values through the SILK framework. Furthermore, during semantic enrichment an "is related to" relation is added between the architectural element pairs related above a threshold according to Rel_{AQ}. The resulting EKG is stored in a Sesame repository.

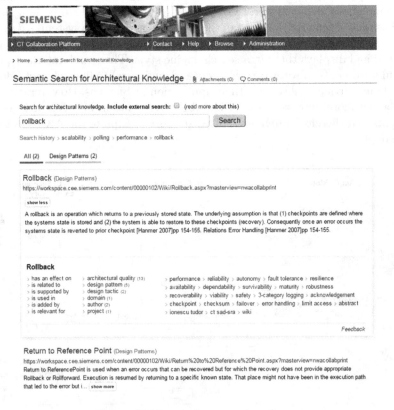

Fig. 5. STAR search system interface.

The *search mechanism* extends the search workflow of the legacy system. For a given search term, the MongoDB keyword search is used to locate all relevant resources. These results are used by the *Result Integration* component to retrieve relevant metadata from the EKG thus enhancing the MongoDB results with additional semantic information. The *Search Interface* component contains tabs for all results as well as tabs dedicated to results of key types (e.g., Design Patterns, Architectural Qualities) as shown in Fig. 5. The detailed information about one search result (e.g., the "rollback" design pattern) contains the full-text description of that result. An extension of this legacy interface consists in displaying the semantic information relevant for a result and allowing its inspection through faceted-search. In this interface, the first column lists all relevant semantic relations for the current entity; the second column shows all semantic entity types relevant to the current entity (e.g., "architecture quality") and how many instances of each type are semantically related to the result; the third column contains a collection of all entities (of all types) connected to the current result through semantic relations (i.e., a semantic entity-cloud).

The interface supports two modes of result inspection. Firstly, users get an overview of semantically relevant entities through the semantic entity cloud and can directly access those that they know and are interested in. Secondly, inspection can also be performed at schema element level. Clicking on a relation in the first column (e.g., "has an effect on"), will update the second column to contain only those entity types that are connected through this relation (e.g., "architectural quality") and reduce the entities in the third column to the entities of the current type and related to the result with the selected semantic relation (i.e., all architectural qualities on which rollback has an effect on). Similarly, by selecting a concept in column two, only the relations that exist between that concept and the result are maintained and the semantic entity cloud is updated accordingly. Exploratory search of related entities is enabled by "is related to", which connects the AEs that are related to the current entity according to Rel_{AQ}.

System Adoption. The STAR system is currently used by about 200–300 Siemens experts world-wide. The main user categories include software and system architects, technical project managers, senior developers, and research group leaders. The tool is also embedded as a search widget in Amelie - the state of the art Siemens tool for AK management. Amelie integrates various architectural artifacts from the entire development lifecycle of different software-intensive Siemens products. STAR helps by providing contextualized search capabilities depending on the current system view (i.e., what the user currently sees on the screen) by using the inputs and the navigation history of the user.

8 Related Work

We position our work in the landscape of *Architecture Knowledge Management* and *Exploratory Search* research. Semantic Web technologies have been used as a basis for several AK management tools [3]. Some tools exploit ontologies as a basis for more intuitive visualisation of AK, thus supporting the overview and analysis of AK collections [14] or, allowing a better understanding of the dependency between architectural design decisions [4]. Other tools use light-weight ontologies as backbones for wiki-based systems to enable browsing, faceted-search and querying: (1) for managing the documentation of service-oriented architectures [10]; (2) for AK search [22]; (3) for finding AK through structured navigation and faceted search based on concept properties, and the execution of pre-defined SPARQL queries in ArchiMind [5–7]; or (4) to manage software design rationales [15]. As ontology-based faceted search was shown to improve the effectiveness and efficiency AK retrieval compared to file-based approaches [5,15], our work also adopts a faceted-search approach but aims to advance the state of the art with an approach to implement exploratory search strategies.

Although *exploratory search* is a rather broad and evolving concept [18], in the Semantic Web area a common approach to exploration is to suggest entities related to the current search result [16]. The majority of efforts focus on exploration of large KGs, e.g., DBpedia or Freebase, with the adoption of this concept to more restrained enterprise KGs receiving limited attention. The evaluation of exploratory search systems is a critical issue firstly because user-based evaluations are costly to conduct and secondly, because novel evaluation approaches are sought that go beyond Information Retrieval style assessment [18]. In this landscape, we propose and illustrate the concrete application of an approach for adapting the exploratory search paradigm to EKGs. We propose using statistical evaluation and comparison of metrics to reduce the need for user studies.

9   Conclusions and Lessons Learned

Adequate AK management is a prerequisite to making software architecture design more efficient and effective. Yet, software architects are only weakly supported in their exploration of AK, both in general and in the context of Siemens in particular. In this paper, we investigate implementing exploratory search on an architectural knowledge EKG, thus going beyond current faceted-search tools and illustrating exploratory search on an enterprise-wide rather than generic KG. We propose an approach to build such systems and demonstrate its application at Siemens, resulting in a faceted and exploratory search system impacting the work of 200–300 software architects. The main conclusions to our research questions in the terms of lessons learned, benefits and challenges are as follows.

Concerning **RQ1**, related to *implementing exploratory search on EKGs*, we presented our overall approach and demonstrated its use in the context of Siemens. This approach considers the EKG's ontology as key for informing the design of relatedness metrics and puts special emphasis on the evaluation and selection of these metrics before system implementation (see conclusions to RQ2).

During EKG creation, the *ontology engineering process* was beneficial in several ways. First, it led to the identification of a *core ontology* meaningful to a heterogeneous population of software architects within Siemens. To that end, alignment with other ontologies and standards in the domain *revealed key concepts and relations in the domain*. For example, the relation between design decisions, architectural qualities and architectural elements emerged as a recurring ontology design pattern in this domain. Second, in this phase we *made explicit semantic relations* which were only implicitly present in previous non-semantic solutions (e.g., databases). Third, we *identified missing concepts* from the organizational specific model, such as the *Rationale* concept from ISO/IEC/IEEE 42010:2010 which would be a natural extension of the STAR ontology. A challenge was that ontology creation and data migration required several iterations and took *longer than expected* by the industry partner.

Best practices from system development were (1) the *lightweight integration of semantic technologies with legacy infrastructure*, which lead to lower development costs and facilitated technology acceptance; and (2) *including exploratory search elements into faceted search* systems which were known to be effective.

In line with our hypothesis for **RQ2**, the EKG's ontology captured essential domain knowledge beneficial for *informing the design of relatedness metrics*. Yet, a key challenge was that *metric performance depends on the EKG data characteristics*. A lesson learned is that distributional statistics can give insights into which metrics are viable on the data of a given EKG early into the system development process. In our use case, we excluded information content metrics based on such evaluations. User studies, although expensive, are beneficial to assess the actual performance of the metrics but also to provide further insights into the details of the exploration task. In our use case, through a user study, we found that the task of pattern relatedness assessment itself is challenging even for human raters, and at the same time collected feedback to better define the pattern relatedness notion. The study showed that the performance of relatedness identification with Rel_{AQ} was reasonable (Prec $= 52\%$; Prec@3 $= 60\%$). As the evaluation focuses on the relatedness metrics, it is limited in providing feedback on how the actual task of AK search has been improved. Such evaluation is left for future work.

Our hypothesis for **RQ3** was that relatedness explanations derived from the underlying EKG could support exploration. Yet we could not verify this hypothesis in the current setting with explanations being rated as only moderately helpful. Nevertheless, user feedback suggests possible improvements of explanations if these would be based on more detailed semantic annotations, which are missing from the current model. In fact, lack of more fine-grained semantic relations might have had a negative influence on the evaluation results.

Future work will focus on improving the AK collections quality through (semi-) automatic mechanisms for data acquisition and cleansing similar to [15, 21]. In particular, we aim to extract more refined semantic relations between architectural elements as a pre-requisite to a better performance of exploratory search. On the improved data, we will investigate more sophisticated relatedness metrics to support exploratory search, taking also into account the characteristics of the underlying EKG when defining them. More generically, we are interested in further investigating the notion of exploratory search in EKGs, including (1) testing our approach in other settings and (2) comparing the performance of domain-dependent with domain-independent relatedness metrics.

References

1. Ameller, D., Galster, M., Avgeriou, P., Franch, X.: A survey on quality attributes in service-based systems. Softw. Q. J. **24**(2), 271–299 (2016)
2. Bagheri, H., Garcia, J., Sadeghi, A., Malek, S., Medvidovic, N.: Software architectural principles in contemporary mobile software: from conception to practice. J. Syst. Softw. **119**, 31–44 (2016)
3. Capilla, R., Jansen, A., Tang, A., Avgeriou, P., Ali, M.: 10 years of software architecture knowledge management : practice and future. J. Syst. Softw. **116**, 191–205 (2016)
4. De Boer, R.C., Lago, P., Telea, A., van Vliet, H.: Ontology-driven visualization of architectural design decisions. In: Joint Working IEEE/IFIP Conference on Software Architecture and European Conference on Software Architecture (WICSA/ECSA), pp. 51–60 (2009)
5. De Graaf, K.A., Liang, P., Tang, A., van Vliet, H.: How organisation of architecture documentation affects architectural knowledge retrieval. Sci. Comput. Program. **121**, 75–99 (2016)
6. De Graaf, K.A., Tang, A., Liang, P., Khalili, A.: Querying software architecture knowledge as linked open data. In: IEEE International Conference on Software Architecture Workshops (ICSAW), pp. 272–277 (2017)
7. De Graaf, K.A., Tang, A., Liang, P., van Vliet, H.: Ontology-based software architecture documentation. In: Proceedings of Joint Working Conference on Software Architecture and European Conference on Software Architecture (WICSA/ECSA), pp. 121–130 (2012)
8. Dimitrova, V., Lau, L., Thakker, D., Yang-Turner, F., Despotakis, D.: Exploring exploratory search: a user study with linked semantic data. In: International Workshop on Intelligent Exploration of Semantic Data, pp. 1–8 (2013)
9. Ding, W., Liang, P., Tang, A., van Vliet, H.: Knowledge-based approaches in software documentation: a systematic literature review. Inf. Softw. Technol. **56**(6), 545–567 (2014)
10. Happel, H.-J., Seedorf, S., Schader, M.: Ontology-enabled documentation of service-oriented architectures with ontobrowse semantic Wiki. In: PRIMIUM - Process Innovation for Enterprise Software, pp. 61–80 (2009)
11. Hoffman, R.R.: How can expertise be defined? Implications of research from cognitive psychology. In: Williams, R., Faulkner, W., Fleck, J. (eds.) Exploring Expertise, pp. 81–100. Palgrave Macmillan UK, London (1998). https://doi.org/10.1007/978-1-349-13693-3_4
12. ISO/IEC/IEEE: ISO/IEC/IEEE 42010:2010 systems and software engineering architecture description. Technical report. ISO/IEC/IEEE (2010)
13. Jansen, A., Netherlands, T., Bosch, J.: Software architecture as a set of architectural design decisions. In: Joint Working IEEE/IFIP Conference on Software Architecture (WICSA), pp. 109–120 (2005)
14. Kruchten, P., Lago, P., van Vliet, H.: Building up and reasoning about architectural knowledge. In: Hofmeister, C., Crnkovic, I., Reussner, R. (eds.) QoSA 2006. LNCS, vol. 4214, pp. 43–58. Springer, Heidelberg (2006). https://doi.org/10.1007/11921998_8
15. López, C., Codocedo, V., Astudillo, H., Cysneiros, L.M.: Bridging the gap between software architecture rationale formalisms and actual architecture documents: an ontology-driven approach. Sci. Comput. Program. **77**(1), 66–80 (2012)

16. Marie, N., Gandon, F.: Survey of linked data based exploration systems. In: International Conference on Intelligent Exploration of Semantic Data, pp. 66–77 (2014)
17. Marie, N., Gandon, F., Ribière, M., Rodio, F.: Discovery hub: on-the-fly linked data exploratory search. In: International Conference on Semantic Systems, pp. 17–24 (2013)
18. Palagi, E., Gandon, F., Giboin, A., Troncy, R.: A survey of definitions and models of exploratory search. In: Workshop on Exploratory Search and Interactive Data Analytics, pp. 3–8. ACM, New York (2017)
19. Pan, J.Z., Vetere, G., Gomez-Perez, J.M., Wu, H.: Exploiting Linked Data and Knowledge Graphs in Large Organisations, 1st edn. Springer, Heidelberg (2017). https://doi.org/10.1007/978-3-319-45654-6
20. Shanteau, J.: The psychology of experts: an alternative view. In: Wright, G., Bolger, F. (eds.) Expertise and Decision Support, pp. 11–23. Springer, Boston (1992). https://doi.org/10.1007/978-0-585-34290-0_2
21. Soliman, M., Galster, M., Riebisch, M.: Developing an ontology for architecture knowledge from developer communities. In: IEEE International Conference on Software Architecture (ICSA), pp. 89–92 (2017)
22. Tang, A., Liang, P., van Vliet, H.: Software architecture documentation: the road ahead. In: Working IEEE/IFIP Conference on Software Architecture, pp. 252–255 (2011)
23. White, R.W., Roth, R.A.: Exploratory Search: Beyond the Query Response Paradigm. Morgan & Claypool, San Rafael (2009)

Using Link Features for Entity Clustering in Knowledge Graphs

Alieh Saeedi$^{(\boxtimes)}$, Eric Peukert , and Erhard Rahm

University of Leipzig and ScaDS Dresden/Leipzig, Leipzig, Germany
saeedi@informatik.uni-leipzig.de

Abstract. Knowledge graphs holistically integrate information about entities from multiple sources. A key step in the construction and maintenance of knowledge graphs is the clustering of equivalent entities from different sources. Previous approaches for such an entity clustering suffer from several problems, e.g., the creation of overlapping clusters or the inclusion of several entities from the same source within clusters. We therefore propose a new entity clustering algorithm CLIP that can be applied both to create entity clusters and to repair entity clusters determined with another clustering scheme. In contrast to previous approaches, CLIP not only uses the similarity between entities for clustering but also further features of entity links such as the so-called link strength. To achieve a good scalability we provide a parallel implementation of CLIP based on Apache Flink. Our evaluation for different datasets shows that the new approach can achieve substantially higher cluster quality than previous approaches.

1 Introduction

Knowledge graphs physically integrate entities from multiple sources with their properties, relationships and concepts in a graph-like structure [14,16]. Popular knowledge graphs in the Web of Data include DBpedia and Yago that combine information about millions of real-world entities (such as persons or locations) of different domains from Wikipedia and other sources. Web search engines such as Google or Bing also integrate information from web pages into their knowledge graphs and use this information to enhance the search results for web queries. The automatic construction and maintenance of such large knowledge graphs faces substantial challenges regarding data quality [5]. One main task is entity resolution to identify different representations referring to the same real-world entity in order to fuse the knowledge about such an entity within the knowledge graph.

While entity resolution and the corresponding problems such as link discovery are intensely investigated research topics (see related work), this problem is still not sufficiently solved for the large-scale integration of data from many sources as needed for knowledge graphs. For more than two sources a binary linking of entities is not sufficient but all matches of the same entity should be clustered

© Springer International Publishing AG, part of Springer Nature 2018
A. Gangemi et al. (Eds.): ESWC 2018, LNCS 10843, pp. 576–592, 2018.
https://doi.org/10.1007/978-3-319-93417-4_37

together to derive a fused entity representation in the knowledge graph. There are several known approaches for such an entity clustering [8]. At the University of Leipzig, we have recently developed a scalable tool called FAMER (FAst Multi-source Entity Resolution system) [18] that integrates parallel implementations of six such clustering schemes, including Connected Components as the baseline, Correlation Clustering and Star clustering [1]. Clustering is applied on a *similarity graph* where entities are represented as vertices and edges link pairs of entities with a similarity above a predefined threshold. FAMER can construct such similarity graphs for entities of multiple sources based on different linking schemes; existing links from the Web of Data could also be used to build the similarity graph. The clustering schemes use this graph (with the similarity values) to determine groups of matching entities aiming at maximizing the similarity between entities within a cluster and minimizing the similarity between entities of different clusters. We have also developed a tool to visually analyze the similarity graphs and clusters determined by FAMER [17].

Analyzing the clusters determined by the different clustering schemes, we observed some common problems in particular overlapping clusters and so-called source-inconsistent clusters. Algorithms like Star clustering can associate entities to more than one cluster leading to cluster overlaps and thus wrong clusters. For cleaned data sources without duplicates as assumed in FAMER[1] each cluster should contain at most one entity per source. We call clusters violating this restriction *source-inconsistent*. While the similarity graphs determined by FAMER never link entities from the same source the transitive clustering of linked entities, e.g., with the baseline approach Connected Components, can easily lead to source-inconsistent clusters which should be avoided or repaired.

In this paper, we propose and evaluate new algorithms to create high-quality entity clusters or to repair clusters determined by other approaches so that the observed cluster problems are avoided. Specifically, we make the following contributions:

- We propose a new clustering approach called CLIP (Clustering based on LInk Priority) to determine high quality, overlap-free and source-consistent entity clusters. Its cluster decisions are based on a link prioritization considering not only link similarities but also the so-called link strength and link degree.
- We propose an approach called RLIP (cluster Repair based on LInk Priority) to repair entity clusters such that the overlap and source inconsistency problems are resolved. It includes a component to resolve overlapping clusters and uses CLIP to produce source-consistent clusters.
- We develop parallel implementations for both approaches based on Apache Flink and integrate them into the FAMER framework for multi-source entity resolution.
- We comprehensively evaluate the cluster quality and scalability of the new approaches for different datasets and compare them with previously proposed clustering schemes.

---

[1] If necessary, the individual sources could be deduplicated before the entity resolution with other sources.

In the next section we discuss related work. Section 3 provides an overview of FAMER and the new approaches. In Sect. 4 we define concepts and describe the new algorithms. Section 5 is the evaluation. Finally, we conclude in Sect. 6.

2 Related Work

Entity resolution and link discovery have been the subject of much research and several surveys and books provide overviews about the main methods, e.g., [4,6,12]. Most of these previous approaches focus on finding duplicates in a single source or matching entities in only two data sources. Scalability is mainly supported by blocking techniques to reduce the search space for finding possible matches. Some tools also support parallel matching, but mainly for MapReduce (e.g., [10,12]) and not yet for newer execution platforms based on Apache Spark or Apache Flink.

There is already a substantial number of entity clustering schemes, mainly to group duplicates in a single data source [4]. Hassanzadeh and colleagues comparatively evaluated several of these entity clustering algorithms in [7]. Our FAMER tool [18] includes distributed versions for a subset of the best algorithms from [7] and supports their use for clustering entities from multiple sources. While the problem of cluster overlaps was already observed in [7], considering multiple sources also leads to the problem of source-inconsistent clusters that we address in this paper. Clustering entities from multiple sources of course leads to increased difficulties to achieve high performance and effectiveness compared to considering only one or two data sources. We are aiming at supporting scalability and efficiency by applying both blocking and parallel processing. Furthermore we are proposing advanced clustering methods that avoid the problems of previous clustering schemes and achieve a better match and cluster quality. We are not aware of other tools supporting a parallel entity clustering for multiple sources.

Repair was already studied in pairwise ontology matching, e.g., to ensure that mappings only contain 1:1 matches (which can be achieved by computing stable marriages) or to correct other mapping-induced inconsistencies [2,15]. However, repair for multiple source mappings was not covered. For entity resolution, [13,19] already investigated repair techniques mainly by exploiting the transitive closure of matches to add or remove match links. The repair of entity clusters proposed in [19] depends on manual user feedback which is difficult to provide for very large datasets. Ngonga Ngomo et al. are not concerned with entity clusters but focus on finding missing/wrong links and also try to repair entities replicated in different sources [13]. By contrast, CLIP and RLIP avoid/repair overlapping and source-inconsistent clusters in multi-source entity resolution utilizing different link features. Moreover, CLIP and RLIP are implemented as parallel algorithms on Apache Flink to allow for large-scale entity resolution.

3 Overview

Figure 1 illustrates the main components of the FAMER framework for holistic entity clustering. The input are entities from multiple sources and the output

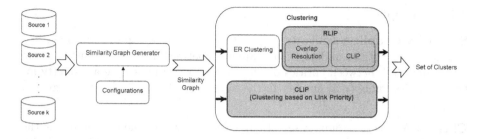

Fig. 1. FAMER workflow for multi-source entity clustering (new components in gray)

is a set of clusters containing matching entities. The first part is a configurable component to generate a similarity graph where similar entities are linked pairwise with each other. As outlined in [18], this phase starts with blocking, e.g. using Standard Blocking on a specific property, so that only entities of the same block need to be compared with each other. Pairwise matching is typically based on the combined similarity of several properties and a threshold for the minimal similarity. A future version of FAMER will also support the use of learned models for binary match classification. In this paper, we focus on the second part of FAMER to use the similarity graph to determine entity clusters. In the initial version, we support six approaches that will also be considered for comparison in this paper: connected components, correlation clustering (CCPivot) [3], Center [8], Merge Center [8] and two variations of star clustering [1] that can lead to overlapping clusters. There is also a specific clustering method based on already existing links from the Web of Data as input [11] which is not further considered here. To this system we add the components shown in gray in Fig. 1. First, we provide a new clustering scheme CLIP as an alternative to the previous clustering schemes that avoids both overlapping and source-inconsistent clusters. Second, we provide the RLIP approach to repair clusters determined by one of the previous clustering schemes. RLIP first resolves overlapping clusters, if necessary, and then applies CLIP to eliminate source-inconsistent clusters.

FAMER is implemented using Apache Flink so that the calculation of similarity graphs and the clustering approaches can be executed in parallel on clusters of variable size. For the implementation of the parallel clustering schemes we also use the Gelly library of Flink supporting a so-called vertex-centric programming of graph algorithms to iteratively execute a user-defined program in parallel over all vertices of a graph [9]. The vertex functions are executed by a configurable number of worker nodes among which the graph data is partitioned, e.g., according to a hash partitioning on vertex ids.

4 Approach

We first define the main concepts and then describe the CLIP and RLIP algorithms.

4.1   Concepts

Similarity Graph: A similarity graph $SG = (V, E)$ is a graph in which vertices of V represent entities and edges of E are links between matching entities. There is no direct link between entities of the same source. Edges have a property for the similarity value (real number in the interval $[0, 1]$) indicating the degree of similarity.

Cluster: A cluster groups a set of entities that are assumed to represent the same real-world entity. In our implementation, we also include the similarity links between cluster members from the originating similarity graph. Hence a cluster C_i is represented by a *cluster graph* $C_i = (V_i, E_i)$ with the clustered entities in V_i and intra-cluster similarity links in E_i.

Maximum Link: An entity from a *source A* may have several links to entities of a *source B*. From these links, the one with the highest similarity value is called maximum link. For example, for entity a_1 in Fig. 2-a the maximum link with respect to source B is the one with similarity 0.95 to entity b_1.

Based on this concept we define the strength of links and classify links into *strong, normal,* and *weak* links. Considering a link ℓ between entity e_i from source A and entity e_j from another source B we define these link types as follows:

Strong Link: Link ℓ is classified as a *strong* link, if it is the maximum link from both sides, i.e. for e_i to source B and for e_j to source A. In Fig. 2-a, entity a_1 from source A has a strong link, colored in green, to b_1 in source B. Note that an entity can have several strong links to different sources; e.g., a_1 is also strongly linked to c_2 from source C.

Normal Link: Link ℓ is called a *normal* link, if it is the maximum link for only one of the two sides. In Fig. 2-a, the link between a_1 and b_2 is a normal link (colored in blue) as it is the maximum link from b_2 to source A, but not the maximum link from a_1 to source B.

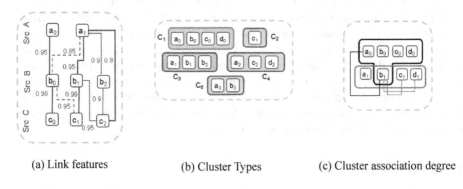

(a) Link features   (b) Cluster Types   (c) Cluster association degree

Fig. 2. Clustering concepts (Color figure online)

Weak Link: Link ℓ is a *weak* link, if it is not the maximum link for any of the two sides. In Fig. 2-a, the link between a_1 and b_0 is such a weak link and shown with a red dashed line.

Link Degree: The link degree is the minimum vertex degree of its two end point vertices. In Fig. 2-a, the vertex degree of a_1 is 4 and the vertex degree of b_1 is 3, so that the link degree between a_1 and b_1 is $min(4,3) = 3$.

Link Prioritization: Our clustering approach is based on the introduced link features to prioritize links based on their link similarity value, link strength (strong, normal, weak), and link degree. Links with higher similarity value, higher strength and lower degree have priority over links with lower similarity, lower strength and higher degree.

Source-Consistent Cluster: A cluster that contains at most one entity per source is called a *source-consistent* cluster. In Fig. 2-b, the red-colored cluster is source-inconsistent since it contains two entities (b_1 and b_2) from source B. The other clusters colored in blue and green are source-consistent.

Complete Cluster: A source-consistent cluster that contains entities from all sources is called a *complete* cluster. The green-colored cluster in Fig. 2-b is a complete cluster for four sources A, B, C, and D as it contains one entity from each source.

Cluster Association Degree: An entity e that is shared between two or more clusters will be in some cases assigned to the cluster with the highest association degree. The association degree of e for cluster C of size k corresponds to the average similarity of e to the $k-1$ other entities e_i in C, i.e., it is determined by the ratio of the sum of similarity values of the intra-cluster links involving e and $k-1$. In Fig. 2-c, entity b_1 is member of the gray and black clusters of sizes 4 and 5, respectively. Assuming a link similarity of 1 for the shown links, the association degree for b_1 is 2/3 for the gray cluster and 1/4 for the black cluster. Hence, b_1 will be preferably assigned to the gray cluster.

4.2 Entity Clustering with CLIP

The proposed CLIP algorithm favors strong links for finding clusters while weak links will be ignored. This helps to find good clusters even when the similarity graph contains many links with lower similarity values. The approach works in two main phases. In the first phase, CLIP determines all complete clusters based on strong links between entities from all sources. The second phase also considers normal links and iteratively clusters the remaining entities based on link priorities such that no source-inconsistent or overlapping clusters are generated.

The pseudocode of CLIP is shown in Algorithm 1. Its input is a similarity graph SG and the output is the cluster set CS. Figure 3 illustrates the algorithm for entities from four data sources A, B, C, and D. Entities with the same index are assumed to belong to the same cluster, e.g. entity a_0 from source A and b_0 from source B. The sample similarity graph in the example already

Algorithm 1. CLIP

Input : $SG = (V, E)$
Output: *Cluster set* $CS = \{\}$
/* PHASE 1   */
1 *DetermineLinkStrength(E)*
   /* Links are classified so that $E = E_{Strong} \cup E_{Normal} \cup E_{Weak}$ */
2 $G' = (V, E_{Strong})$
3 *Cluster set* $CS' \leftarrow ConnectedComponents(G')$
4 $CS \leftarrow getCompleteClusters(CS')$
   /* PHASE 2   */
5 $V' \leftarrow V - V_{Complete}, \ E' \leftarrow (E_{Strong} - E_{Complete}) \cup E_{Normal}$
6 $G' = (V', E')$
   /* Vertices and links of the complete clusters are removed from the current
      graph G'   */
7 $CS' \leftarrow ConnectedComponents(G')$
8 **for** *(Cluster$_i$ $\in CS'$) in Parallel* **do**
9   **if** *(IsSourceConsistent(Cluster$_i$))* **then**
10         $CS \leftarrow CS \cup Cluster_i$
11   **else**
12   *Assume* $v_t \in V_{Cluster_i}$ *as a cluster* $t = 1, 2, ..., n$
13   *Cluster set* $CS_i \leftarrow \{C_1, C_2, ..., C_n\}$
14   *IntraLinks* $\leftarrow E_{Cluster_i}$
15   **repeat**
16            $\ell_{Ci,Cj} \leftarrow getMaxPriority(IntraLinks)$
17            $MergeClusters(C_i, C_j)$
18            $UpdateClusterSet(CS_i)$
19   *RemovedLinks* $\leftarrow RemoveConflictingLinks(IntraLinks)$
20   *IntraLinks* $\leftarrow IntraLinks - RemovedLinks$
21   **until** *(IntraLinks* $\neq \{\}$)
22 $CS \leftarrow CS \cup \bigcup_{i=1}^{m} CS_i$

---

links most matching entities but also contains wrong links, e.g. (b_0, c_1). In phase 1, we start with determining the strength of all links (line 1 of Algorithm 1). Then we only use strong links to determine graph G' (line 2). We then apply *ConnectedComponents* on G' to identify complete clusters and add these to the output (lines 3–4). In the example of Fig. 3, the second graph in the upper half differentiates between strong, normal, and weak links by showing them as green, blue and dashed lines, respectively. Focussing on strong links, we obtain four connected components in the example, one of which (for index 0) results in a complete cluster that is added to the output of phase 1.

For phase 2, we remove the vertices and edges from the complete clusters. Furthermore, we ignore weak links and only consider strong and normal links in the updated graph G' (lines 5–6 of Algorithm 1). Again we use *ConnectedComponents* to consider the resulting connected components as

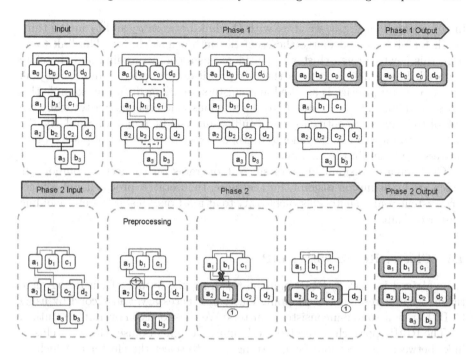

Fig. 3. CLIP example (Color figure online)

possible clusters (line 7). Afterwards these components $Cluster_i$ are processed in parallel (line 8). If the cluster $Cluster_i$ is already a source-consistent cluster, it is directly added to the CLIP output (lines 9–10). Otherwise the component/cluster is source-inconsistent and will be iteratively processed as outlined below. In the example of Fig. 3, phase 2 is illustrated in the lower part which starts with a reduced similarity graph that has no longer the entities from the complete cluster determined in phase 1 and that only contains strong and normal links. We then obtain two connected components one of which (with index 3) is already a source-consistent cluster that is thus added to the output. The remaining source-inconsistent component/cluster needs further processing.

In the processing of source-inconsistent clusters/components we initially consider each entity of component $Cluster_i$ as a cluster C_i of its own (lines 12–13). We then iteratively process the intra-component links (lines 15–21) in the order of their maximal link priority and merge linked entity pairs from different sources into larger clusters such that no source inconsistency is created (line 17). For merged clusters, the cluster set is updated accordingly (line 18). Links from the newly formed cluster to entities of the same sources already present in the formed cluster (conflicting links) are removed from the intra-component link set (lines 19–20). The process for each component terminates when the corresponding intra-component link set is empty (line 21). The union of all cluster sets CS_i determined in this way for the different components combined with the previously determined clusters in phase 1 form the final output of CLIP (line 22).

In the example of Fig. 3, we start with the link between a_2 and b_2 in the third graph for phase 2 and merge these entities into a new cluster. The link to a_1 from this newly formed cluster is considered as a conflicting link and therefore removed. In the next iterations the link priorities are updated and a new link with maximum priority is selected and clusters are merged. In the example this leads to adding entities c_2 and d_2 to the previously determined cluster while the link of this cluster to entity a_1 is in conflict and will be removed. Similarly, the cluster with index 1 can be generated. Together with the output of phase 1, four clusters are found in the example.

CLIP creates disjoint clusters since it operates on connected components which are by definition disjoint. Furthermore, the iterative processing of source-inconsistent components adds each entity to at most one cluster thereby avoiding cluster overlaps.

4.3   Cluster Repair with RLIP

As explained in Sect. 3, RLIP aims at repairing the output of clustering algorithms by first resolving overlapping clusters, if necessary, and second by using CLIP to repair source-inconsistent clusters. We thus focus on overlap resolution.

The RLIP approach to resolve overlapping clusters also uses the intra-cluster links between entities[2] and favors strong links to select the cluster to which an overlapped entity should be assigned. In particular, overlapped entities that have only strong links to one cluster are assigned to this cluster and for overlapped entities with strong links to several clusters we choose the cluster with the highest association degree for this entity. Overlapped entities with no strong link are kept as singletons. The cluster decision cannot be made directly if an overlapped entity is only strongly linked to another overlapped entity since the best result will depend on the cluster decision for the other overlapped entity. We therefore treat such cases in a second iteration of the algorithm. If in the second iteration the entity still is linked to only overlapped entities, all of them will become singletons.

Algorithm 2 outlines overlap resolution in more detail. The input is a set of cluster graphs CS and the output is a set of disjoint clusters $outputCS$. The cluster graphs in the output can be merged into a similarity graph as input for the subsequent execution of CLIP. In line 1, we first determine and store the strength of links in the input cluster graphs. Then, we determine the overlapped entities and process them in parallel in one or two iterations. For overlapped entity v, we store all strongly linked entities in $adjacentVertices$ (line 5). If there is no such entity, the overlapped entity is kept as a singleton (lines 6–8). Otherwise, the clusters of non-overlapped entities (line 11) of $adjacentVertices$ are determined and stored in the set $associatedClusters$ (lines 10–13). If there is no such cluster, i.e., all strongly linked entities are overlapped entities, and we are in the first iteration we wait and this entity will become a singleton in the second iteration

---

[2] RLIP could also repair cluster results determined outside FAMER by computing the similarity links between entities within clusters beforehand.

Algorithm 2. Overlap Resolution

Input : *Cluster set* $CS = \bigcup\limits_{i=1}^{m} CS_i(V_i, E_i)$

Output: *Cluster set outputCS*

1   $outputCS \leftarrow DetermineLinkStrength(CS)$

    /* Links are classified so that $E_i = E_{i(Strong)} \cup E_{i(Normal)} \cup E_{i(Weak)}$ */

2   **for** *(iterationNo := 1 **to** 2)* **do**

3      $OV \leftarrow getOverlappedVertices(outputCS)$

        /* OV : Vertices that belong to more than one cluster   */

4   **for** $v \in OV$ **in Parallel do**

5         $adjacentVertices \leftarrow StronglyLinkedPairs(v)$

6   **if** $(adjacentVertices.Size() = 0)$ **then**

7            $UpdateClusterSet(outputCS, v)$

            /* remove v and its associating links from all clusters.   */

8            $outputClusterset \leftarrow outputClusterset \cup (newCluster(v))$

            /* v is a singleton.   */

9   **else**

10           $associatedClusters \leftarrow \{\}$

11   **for** $(v_n \in adjacentVertices)$ **do**

12   **if** $(v_n \notin OV)$ **then**

13                $associatedClusters \leftarrow associatedClusters \cup getCluster(v_n)$

14   **if** $(associatedClusters.Size() = 0 \wedge iterationNo > 1)$ **then**

15             $UpdateClusterSet(v)$

16             $outputClusterset \leftarrow outputClusterset \cup (newCluster(v))$

17   **else**

18             $resolvedCluster \leftarrow \underset{associatedClusters}{argmax} \; (association(cluster_i, v))$

19             $UpdateClusterSet(v)$

20     $iterationNo + +$

21 **return** $outputCS$

(lines 14–16). Otherwise, the cluster association degree of the overlapped entity v to all members of *associatedClusters* is determined and v is assigned to the cluster with the maximal association degree (lines 17–19). Obviously, if there is only one element in *associatedClusters*, v will go to this cluster.

Figure 4 illustrates overlap resolution for four input clusters (C_1, C_2, C_3, and C_4) where entities a_0, a_5 and d_4 belong to two clusters and entity b_2 even to three clusters. The algorithm starts by determining the strength of the links. In the second box of Fig. 4, strong, normal and weak links are shown by green, blue and dashed red lines. The output of the first iteration (third box) shows that entity a_5 is considered as a singleton because it is not strongly linked to any other entity. Entity a_0 is assigned to cluster C_1 because of a higher association degree to C_1 than to C_2. Entity d_4 is strongly linked only to the overlapped entity b_2 so we do not decide about d_4 in this iteration. Entity b_2 has strong links to non-overlapped entities only to cluster C_3 so it is removed from clusters C_2 and C_4. In the second iteration (last box), the remaining overlapped entity d_4 is also resolved. It is linked to entity b_2 which has been assigned to cluster C_3 in the previous iteration, so d_4 is now also assigned to C_3 and removed from cluster C_4. We have thus resolved all overlaps although the resulting clusters are not necessarily source-consistent (e.g., cluster C_3 has two entities from source D). So the output of overlap resolution is then processed by CLIP to obtain both disjoint and source-consistent clusters.

5   Evaluation

We now evaluate the effectiveness and efficiency of the proposed clustering and repair algorithms CLIP and RLIP in comparison to the previous clustering schemes of FAMER. We first describe the used datasets from three domains. We then analyze comparatively the effectiveness of the proposed algorithms. Finally, we evaluate runtime performance and scalability.

5.1   Datasets and Similarity Graphs

We use the same evaluation datasets as in [18] to facilitate the comparison with the previously studied clustering schemes. Table 1 summarizes the main characteristics of these datasets as well as their properties and functions used for blocking and calculating the similarity links. The smallest dataset DS1 is a real dataset with geographical entities of type 'settlement' from four sources (DBpedia, Geonames, Freebase, NYTimes). The perfect clusters for DS1 are manually determined. The two larger datasets are based on the real data from the MusicBrainz database (DS2) and the North-Carolina voter registry (DS3) but apply synthetic data generators to create duplicates and corruptions of property values to make entity resolution harder. The DS2 dataset is heavily corrupted and consists of five sources with duplicates for 50% of the original records in two to five sources. The DS3 dataset consists of five sources with 1 million entities per source such that 50% of the entities are replicated in all sources without any corruption. Moreover, 25% of the entities are corrupted and replicated in all sources, and the remaining 25% are corrupted but present in only some sources. The degree of corruption is moderate so that matches are easier to find than for DS2. For determining the similarity graphs with FAMER, we first apply a standard blocking based on the prefix of a specific property (specified in Table 1) so that only entities with the same prefix value need to be compared. Pairwise similarity between entities is determined based on the string similarity (JaroWinkler or trigram) of selected properties and, for DS1, the geographical distance between settlements and a variable minimal similarity threshold θ.

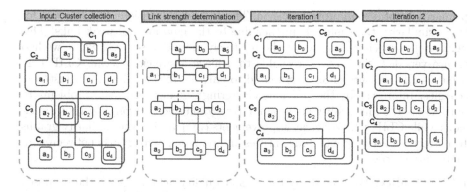

Fig. 4. Overlap resolution (example) (Color figure online)

Table 1. Dataset characteristics and linking details

-	Data sets			Similarity graph configuration	
Domain	#entities	#sources	#clusters	Blocking key	Sim functions
DS1 (geographical)	3,054	4	820	PreLen1 (label)	JW (label), distance
DS2 (music)	20,000	5	10,000	PreLen1 (album)	Trigram (title)
DS3 (person)	5,000,000	5	3,500,840	PreLen3 (surname)	JW (name), JW (surname), JW (suburb), JW(postcode)

5.2 Cluster Quality

CLIP Quality: We first evaluate the cluster quality achieved with the new CLIP clustering scheme in comparison with six known clustering schemes for the three datasets. For this purpose we assume that all entities in the determined clusters match with each other and determine the precision, recall and F-measure compared to the matches of the perfect cluster result. Figure 5 shows the achieved results for these metrics and different similarity thresholds θ for the seven clustering schemes (CLIP, Connected Components, CCPivot, Center, MergeCenter, Star-1, Star-2) as well as for the similarity graph used as input to the clustering schemes (although this graph has only links but no clusters). The results for the six previous approaches correspond to those reported in [18].

We observe that CLIP achieves an excellent quality result and outperforms all previous algorithms in terms of precision and F-measure for all three datasets. Recall is comparable to the best approaches and only slightly worse compared to approaches such as Connected Components achieving the best possible recall (albeit at the expense of the poorest precision). A closer inspection of the CLIP behavior showed that its good recall is already achieved by determining the connected components for finding complete clusters and source-consistent clusters involving only strong and normal links. By contrast, the CLIP iterations to split source-inconsistent components into several source-consistent clusters is primarily helpful to improve precision. The excellent precision of CLIP, even for lower similarity thresholds, is further due to the ignorance of weak links. This behavior is especially helpful for the relatively dirty dataset DS2 where we had to use very low similarity thresholds to achieve a sufficient recall. CLIP here achieves a F-Measure of 82% compared to only 65–75% for the other clustering schemes. Interestingly, the previous clustering schemes had even problems to outperform the link quality of the similarity graph due to wrong clustering decisions while CLIP achieves clear improvements compared to the similarity graphs by correctly clustering matching entities and removing wrong links between non-matching entities.

RLIP Quality: We now study the cluster quality achieved with the proposed repair approach RLIP when applied to the cluster results of the six previous clustering schemes. Figure 6 summarizes the achieved F-Measure results (averages

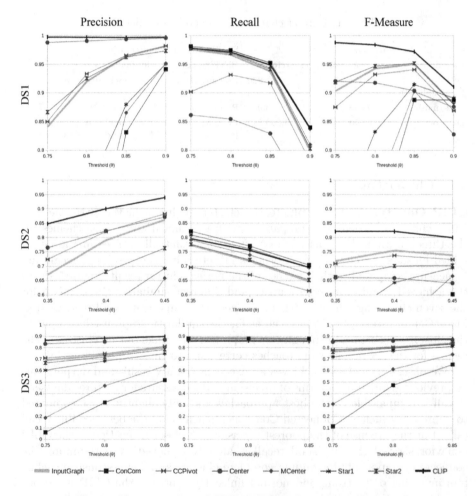

Fig. 5. Cluster quality of CLIP vs other clustering approaches

over all considered values for similarity threshold θ) for the three datasets with
the original clustering schemes only (blue bars on the left) and with additionally
applying RLIP (red bars on the right). On the right we also show the average
F-measure results for CLIP. We observe that RLIP can improve F-measure for
all algorithms indicating an excellent effectiveness of the proposed cluster repair.
The biggest improvements are achieved for the two poorest performing clustering schemes, Connected Component and MergeCenter, that both achieve a high
recall but low precision. Here the CLIP component of RLIP achieves a substantial improvement in precision; the already high recall of the input enables that
the repaired results for ConnectedComponent and MergeCenter are among the
best overall. In fact, the repaired results for ConnectedComponent are essentially
identical to the CLIP results. Overlap resolution is only applied to the results of
Star-1 and Star-2 and helps to also achieve very good quality for their repaired
clusters. The clusters determined with CCPivot and Center can be improved to
a lesser degree since these algorithms remove already many links thus hurting
recall. The only exception is DS3 for which all clustering schemes achieve a similarly high recall so that the repaired results after applying RLIP are also close
together for all algorithms.

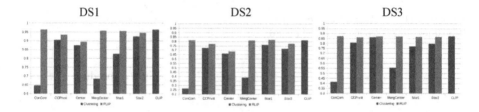

Fig. 6. Cluster quality without and with repair using RLIP (Color figure online)

5.3   Runtimes and Speedup

The runtimes of the clustering algorithms are determined on a Hadoop cluster
with 16 worker nodes, each consisting of an E5-2430 6(12) 2.5 GHz CPU, 48 GB
RAM and two 4 TB SATA disks. The nodes are connected via 1 Gigabit Ethernet.
The used software versions are Flink 1.1.2, Hadoop 2.6.0 and openSUSE 13.2.
We run Apache Flink with 6 threads and 40 GB memory per worker.

Table 2 shows the runtimes of CLIP for the biggest dataset DS3 with similarity threshold $\theta = 0.8$; Fig. 7 depicts the corresponding speedup curve varying
the number of workers from 1 to 16. We observe that the parallel execution of
CLIP achieves an optimal speedup for up to 8 workers, while the speedup for
16 workers is 11.2 indicating that the dataset DS3 might not be big enough
for 16 workers. Comparing the execution times of CLIP with those of the other
algorithms (shown in the left part of Table 3), we see that CLIP is relatively
slow with the second highest runtimes. Most of the CLIP execution time is
spent for the iterative processing of source-inconsistent components in phase 2

of the algorithm. While we process different components in parallel the runtime is determined by the biggest such component which thus becomes a bottleneck.

Table 3 also includes runtimes of repairing clusters with RLIP (middle part) as well as the sum of the execution times for clustering and repair (right part). The shown RLIP execution times include both the times for overlap resolution (for Star-1 and Star-2) and for the CLIP component. We observe that the RLIP runtimes are dominated by the CLIP component while overlap resolution is much faster. The runtimes for the CLIP component of RLIP differ for the different clustering schemes and are the highest for ConnectedComponent and MergeCenter where precision is improved most by the iterative processing of large components. Interestingly, the combined execution time for the previous clustering schemes and their repair is in several cases lower than only applying CLIP while achieving similar cluster quality, especially for the two Star clustering schemes.

Table 2. CLIP runtimes for DS3 (seconds)

#workers	1	2	4	8	16
Runtimes	5477	2696	1303	711	486

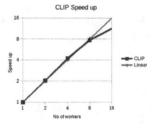

Fig. 7. Speedup

Table 3. DS3 runtimes for clustering schemes and RLIP (seconds)

Method	ER clustering			RLIP						Sum		
#workers	4	8	16	4		8		16		4	8	16
				OV	CLP	OV	CLP	OV	CLP			
ConCom	51	57	55	-	1303	-	711	-	486	1354	768	541
CCPivot	1530	1008	688	-	651	-	361	-	223	2181	1369	911
Center	390	208	117	-	440	-	228	-	144	830	436	261
MCenter	640	349	194	-	882	-	472	-	306	1522	821	500
Star-1	288	149	85	178	489	94	249	55	209	955	492	349
Star-2	214	124	67	202	424	97	236	61	283	840	457	411

6   Conclusion and Outlook

We have proposed a new method called CLIP to cluster matching entities from multiple sources as well as a repair method called RLIP to improve entity clusters determined by other clustering schemes. The approaches avoid or resolve overlapping and source-inconsistent clusters and utilize several features of similarity links in a new way, in particular the link strength. Our evaluation for three datasets shows that the new approaches achieve excellent cluster quality and outperform previous clustering schemes to a large degree. The RLIP repair approach could improve the quality for all considered clustering schemes and achieve comparable quality than applying CLIP alone, in some cases with even lower execution times. The parallel implementations for CLIP and RLIP achieved good speedup values thereby supporting scalability to larger datasets.

In future work, we will investigate further performance optimizations in the iterative portion of the CLIP algorithm. We further plan to make the FAMER tool with the proposed clustering schemes publicly available and apply it in several applications, in particular to build large, high quality knowledge graphs.

Acknowledgements. This work is partially funded by the German Federal Ministry of Education and Research under project ScaDS Dresden/Leipzig (BMBF 01IS14014B).

References

1. Aslam, J.A., Pelekhov, E., Rus, D.: The star clustering algorithm for static and dynamic information organization. Graph Algorithms Appl. **5**, 95–129 (2006)
2. Calì, A., Lukasiewicz, T., Predoiu, L., Stuckenschmidt, H.: A framework for representing ontology mappings under probabilities and inconsistency. In: Proceedings URSW (2007)
3. Chierichetti, F., Dalvi, N., Kumar, R.: Correlation clustering in mapreduce. In: Proceedings KDD, pp. 641–650. ACM (2014)
4. Christen, P.: Data Matching. Springer, Heidelberg (2012). https://doi.org/10.1007/978-3-642-31164-2
5. Dong, X., et al. Knowledge vault: a web-scale approach to probabilistic knowledge fusion. In: Proceedings KDD, pp. 601–610 (2014)
6. Elmagarmid, A.K., Ipeirotis, P.G., Verykios, V.S.: Duplicate record detection: a survey. IEEE Trans. Knowl. Data Eng. **19**(1), 1–16 (2007)
7. Hassanzadeh, O., Chiang, F., Lee, H.C., Miller, R.J.: Framework for evaluating clustering algorithms in duplicate detection. PVLDB **2**(1), 1282–1293 (2009)
8. Hassanzadeh, O., Miller, R.J.: Creating probabilistic databases from duplicated data. VLDB J. **18**(5), 1141–1166 (2009)
9. Junghanns, M., Petermann, A., Neumann, M., Rahm, E.: Management and analysis of big graph data: current systems and open challenges. In: Zomaya, A.Y., Sakr, S. (eds.) Handbook of Big Data Technologies, pp. 457–505. Springer, Cham (2017). https://doi.org/10.1007/978-3-319-49340-4_14
10. Kolb, L., Thor, A., Rahm, E.: Dedoop: efficient deduplication with hadoop. PVLDB **5**(12), 1878–1881 (2012)
11. Nentwig, M., Groß, A., Rahm, E.: Holistic entity clustering for linked data. In: Proceedings ICDMW, pp. 194–201. IEEE (2016)
12. Nentwig, M., Hartung, M., Ngonga Ngomo, A.-C., Rahm, E.: A survey of current link discovery frameworks. Semant. Web **8**(3), 419–436 (2017)
13. Ngonga Ngomo, A.-C., Sherif, M.A., Lyko, K.: Unsupervised link discovery through knowledge base repair. In: Presutti, V., d'Amato, C., Gandon, F., d'Aquin, M., Staab, S., Tordai, A. (eds.) ESWC 2014. LNCS, vol. 8465, pp. 380–394. Springer, Cham (2014). https://doi.org/10.1007/978-3-319-07443-6_26

14. Paulheim, H.: Knowledge graph refinement: a survey of approaches and evaluation methods. Semant. web **8**(3), 489–508 (2017)
15. Pesquita, C., Faria, D., Santos, E., Couto, F.M.: To repair or not to repair: reconciling correctness and coherence in ontology reference alignments. In: Proceedings of the 8th International Conference on Ontology Matching, pp. 13–24 (2013)
16. Rahm, E.: The case for holistic data integration. In: Pokorný, J., Ivanović, M., Thalheim, B., Šaloun, P. (eds.) ADBIS 2016. LNCS, vol. 9809, pp. 11–27. Springer, Cham (2016). https://doi.org/10.1007/978-3-319-44039-2_2
17. Rostami, M.A., Saeedi, A., Peukert, E., Rahm, E.: Interactive visualization of large similarity graphs and entity resolution clusters. In: Proceedings EDBT (2018)
18. Saeedi, A., Peukert, E., Rahm, E.: Comparative evaluation of distributed clustering schemes for multi-source entity resolution. In: Kirikova, M., Nørvåg, K., Papadopoulos, G.A. (eds.) ADBIS 2017. LNCS, vol. 10509, pp. 278–293. Springer, Cham (2017). https://doi.org/10.1007/978-3-319-66917-5_19
19. Wang, Q., Gao, J., Christen, P.: A clustering-based framework for incrementally repairing entity resolution. In: Bailey, J., Khan, L., Washio, T., Dobbie, G., Huang, J.Z., Wang, R. (eds.) PAKDD 2016. LNCS (LNAI), vol. 9652, pp. 283–295. Springer, Cham (2016). https://doi.org/10.1007/978-3-319-31750-2_23

Modeling Relational Data with Graph Convolutional Networks

Michael Schlichtkrull[1], Thomas N. Kipf[1(✉)], Peter Bloem[2],
Rianne van den Berg[1], Ivan Titov[1,3], and Max Welling[1,4]

[1] University of Amsterdam, Amsterdam, The Netherlands
{m.s.schlichtkrull,t.n.kipf,r.vandenberg,titov,m.welling}@uva.nl
[2] Vrije Universiteit Amsterdam, Amsterdam, The Netherlands
p.bloem@vu.nl
[3] University of Edinburgh, Edinburgh, UK
[4] Canadian Institute for Advanced Research, Toronto, Canada

Abstract. Knowledge graphs enable a wide variety of applications, including question answering and information retrieval. Despite the great effort invested in their creation and maintenance, even the largest (e.g., Yago, DBPedia or Wikidata) remain incomplete. We introduce Relational Graph Convolutional Networks (R-GCNs) and apply them to two standard knowledge base completion tasks: Link prediction (recovery of missing facts, i.e. subject-predicate-object triples) and entity classification (recovery of missing entity attributes). R-GCNs are related to a recent class of neural networks operating on graphs, and are developed specifically to handle the highly multi-relational data characteristic of realistic knowledge bases. We demonstrate the effectiveness of R-GCNs as a stand-alone model for entity classification. We further show that factorization models for link prediction such as DistMult can be significantly improved through the use of an R-GCN encoder model to accumulate evidence over multiple inference steps in the graph, demonstrating a large improvement of 29.8% on FB15k-237 over a decoder-only baseline.

1 Introduction

Knowledge bases organize and store factual knowledge, enabling a multitude of applications including question answering [1–6] and information retrieval [7–10]. Even the largest knowledge bases (e.g. DBPedia, Wikidata or Yago), despite enormous effort invested in their maintenance, are incomplete, and the lack of coverage harms downstream applications. Predicting missing information in knowledge bases is the main focus of statistical relational learning (SRL).

We consider two fundamental SRL tasks: link prediction (recovery of missing triples) and entity classification (assigning types or categorical properties to entities). In both cases, many missing pieces of information can be expected to reside within the graph encoded through the neighborhood structure. Following

---

M. Schlichtkrull and T. N. Kipf—Equal contribution.

© Springer International Publishing AG, part of Springer Nature 2018
A. Gangemi et al. (Eds.): ESWC 2018, LNCS 10843, pp. 593–607, 2018.
https://doi.org/10.1007/978-3-319-93417-4_38

this intuition, we develop an encoder model for entities in the relational graph and apply it to both tasks.

Our entity classification model uses softmax classifiers at each node in the graph. The classifiers take node representations supplied by a relational graph convolutional network (R-GCN) and predict the labels. The model, including R-GCN parameters, is learned by optimizing the cross-entropy loss.

Our link prediction model can be regarded as an autoencoder consisting of (1) an encoder: an R-GCN producing latent feature representations of entities, and (2) a decoder: a tensor factorization model exploiting these representations to predict labeled edges. Though in principle the decoder can rely on any type of factorization (or generally any scoring function), we use one of the simplest and most effective factorization methods: DistMult [11]. We observe that our method achieves significant improvements on the challenging FB15k-237 dataset [12], as well as competitive performance on FB15k and WN18. Among other baselines, our model outperforms direct optimization of the factorization (i.e. vanilla DistMult). This result demonstrates that explicit modeling of neighborhoods in R-GCNs is beneficial for recovering missing facts in knowledge bases.

Our main contributions are as follows: To the best of our knowledge, we are the first to show that the GCN framework can be applied to modeling relational data, specifically to link prediction and entity classification tasks. Secondly, we introduce techniques for parameter sharing and to enforce sparsity constraints, and use them to apply R-GCNs to multigraphs with large numbers of relations. Lastly, we show that the performance of factorization models, at the example of DistMult, can be significantly improved by enriching them with an encoder model that performs multiple steps of information propagation in the relational graph.

2 Neural Relational Modeling

We introduce the following notation: we denote directed and labeled multi-graphs as $G = (\mathcal{V}, \mathcal{E}, \mathcal{R})$ with nodes (entities) $v_i \in \mathcal{V}$ and labeled edges (relations) $(v_i, r, v_j) \in \mathcal{E}$, where $r \in \mathcal{R}$ is a relation type.[1]

2.1 Relational Graph Convolutional Networks

Our model is primarily motivated as an extension of GCNs that operate on local graph neighborhoods [13,14] to large-scale relational data. These and related methods such as graph neural networks [15] can be understood as special cases of a simple differentiable message-passing framework [16]:

$$h_i^{(l+1)} = \sigma \left(\sum_{m \in \mathcal{M}_i} g_m(h_i^{(l)}, h_j^{(l)}) \right),$$

(1)

---

[1] $\mathcal{R}$ contains relations both in canonical direction (e.g. *born_in*) and in inverse direction (e.g. *born_in_inv*).

where $h_i^{(l)} \in \mathbb{R}^{d^{(l)}}$ is the hidden state of node v_i in the l-th layer of the neural network, with $d^{(l)}$ being the dimensionality of this layer's representations. Incoming messages of the form $g_m(\cdot, \cdot)$ are accumulated and passed through an element-wise activation function $\sigma(\cdot)$, such as the $\text{ReLU}(\cdot) = \max(0, \cdot)$.[2] $\mathcal{M}_i$ denotes the set of incoming messages for node v_i and is often chosen to be identical to the set of incoming edges. $g_m(\cdot, \cdot)$ is typically chosen to be a (message-specific) neural network-like function or simply a linear transformation $g_m(h_i, h_j) = W h_j$ with a weight matrix W such as in [14]. This type of transformation has been shown to be very effective at accumulating and encoding features from local, structured neighborhoods, and has led to significant improvements in areas such as graph classification [13] and graph-based semi-supervised learning [14].

Motivated by these architectures, we define the following simple propagation model for calculating the forward-pass update of an entity or node denoted by v_i in a relational (directed and labeled) multi-graph:

$$h_i^{(l+1)} = \sigma \left(\sum_{r \in \mathcal{R}} \sum_{j \in \mathcal{N}_i^r} \frac{1}{c_{i,r}} W_r^{(l)} h_j^{(l)} + W_0^{(l)} h_i^{(l)} \right), \tag{2}$$

where $\mathcal{N}_i^r$ denotes the set of neighbor indices of node i under relation $r \in \mathcal{R}$. $c_{i,r}$ is a problem-specific normalization constant that can either be learned or chosen in advance (such as $c_{i,r} = |\mathcal{N}_i^r|$).

Intuitively, (2) accumulates transformed feature vectors of neighboring nodes through a normalized sum. Choosing linear transformations of the form $W h_j$ that only depend on the neighboring node has crucial computational benefits: (1) we do not need to store intermediate edge-based representations which could require a significant amount of memory, and (2) it allows us to implement Eq. 2 in vectorized form using efficient sparse-dense $\mathcal{O}(|\mathcal{E}|)$ matrix multiplications, similar to [14]. Different from regular GCNs, we introduce relation-specific transformations, i.e. depending on the type and direction of an edge. To ensure that the representation of a node at layer $l+1$ can also be informed by the corresponding representation at layer l, we add a single self-connection of a special relation type to each node in the data.

A neural network layer update consists of evaluating (2) in parallel for every node in the graph. Multiple layers can be stacked to allow for dependencies across several relational steps. We refer to this graph encoder model as a relational graph convolutional network (R-GCN). The computation graph for a single node update in the R-GCN model is depicted in Fig. 1.

2.2   Regularization

A central issue with applying (2) to highly multi-relational data is the rapid growth in number of parameters with the number of relations in the graph. In practice this can easily lead to overfitting on rare relations and to models of very

---

[2] Note that this represents a simplification of the message passing neural network proposed in [16] that suffices to include the aforementioned models as special cases.

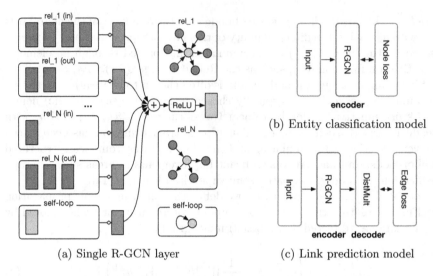

(a) Single R-GCN layer

(b) Entity classification model

(c) Link prediction model

Fig. 1. Diagram for computing the update of a single graph node/entity (red) in the R-GCN model. Activations (d-dimensional vectors) from neighboring nodes (dark blue) are gathered and then transformed for each relation type individually (for both in- and outgoing edges). The resulting representation (green) is accumulated in a (normalized) sum and passed through an activation function (such as the ReLU). This per-node update can be computed in parallel with shared parameters across the whole graph. (b) Depiction of an R-GCN model for entity classification with a per-node loss function. (c) Link prediction model with an R-GCN encoder (interspersed with fully-connected/dense layers) and a DistMult decoder. (Color figure online)

large size. Two intuitive strategies to address such issues is to share parameters between weight matrices, and to enforce sparsity in weight matrices so as to limit the total number of parameters.

Corresponding to these two strategies, we introduce two separate methods for regularizing the weights of R-GCN-layers: *basis-* and *block-diagonal-* decomposition. With the basis decomposition, each $W_r^{(l)}$ is defined as follows:

$$W_r^{(l)} = \sum_{b=1}^{B} a_{rb}^{(l)} V_b^{(l)}, \qquad (3)$$

i.e. as a linear combination of basis transformations $V_b^{(l)} \in \mathbb{R}^{d^{(l+1)} \times d^{(l)}}$ with coefficients $a_{rb}^{(l)}$ such that only the coefficients depend on r.

In the block-diagonal decomposition, we let each $W_r^{(l)}$ be defined through the direct sum over a set of low-dimensional matrices:

$$W_r^{(l)} = \bigoplus_{b=1}^{B} Q_{br}^{(l)}. \qquad (4)$$

Thereby, $W_r^{(l)}$ are block-diagonal matrices:

$$\text{diag}(Q_{1r}^{(l)}, \ldots, Q_{Br}^{(l)}) \quad \text{with} \quad Q_{br}^{(l)} \in \mathbb{R}^{(d^{(l+1)}/B) \times (d^{(l)}/B)}. \tag{5}$$

Note that for $B = d$, each Q has dimension 1 and W_r becomes a diagonal matrix. The block-diagonal decomposition is as such a generalization of the diagonal sparsity constraint used in the decoder in e.g. DistMult [11].

The basis function decomposition (3) can be seen as a form of effective weight sharing between different relation types, while the block decomposition (4) can be seen as a sparsity constraint on the weight matrices for each relation type. The block decomposition structure encodes an intuition that latent features can be grouped into sets of variables which are more tightly coupled within groups than across groups. Both decompositions reduce the number of parameters needed to learn for highly multi-relational data (such as realistic knowledge bases).

The overall R-GCN model then takes the following form: We stack L layers as defined in (2) – the output of the previous layer being the input to the next layer. The input to the first layer can be chosen as a unique one-hot vector for each node in the graph if no other features are present. For the block representation, we map this one-hot vector to a dense representation through a single linear transformation. While in this work we only consider the featureless approach, we note that GCN-type models can incorporate predefined feature vectors [14].

3   Entity Classification

For (semi-)supervised classification of nodes (entities), we simply stack R-GCN layers of the form (2), with a softmax($\cdot$) activation (per node) on the output of the last layer. We minimize the following cross-entropy loss on all labeled nodes (while ignoring unlabeled nodes):

$$\mathcal{L} = -\sum_{i \in \mathcal{Y}} \sum_{k=1}^{K} t_{ik} \ln h_{ik}^{(L)}, \tag{6}$$

where $\mathcal{Y}$ is the set of node indices that have labels and $h_{ik}^{(L)}$ is the k-th entry of the network output for the i-th labeled node. t_{ik} denotes its respective ground truth label. In practice, we train the model using (full-batch) gradient descent techniques. A schematic depiction of the model is given in Fig. 1b.

4   Link Prediction

Link prediction deals with prediction of new facts (i.e. triples *(subject, relation, object)*). Formally, the knowledge base is represented by a directed, labeled graph $G = (\mathcal{V}, \mathcal{E}, \mathcal{R})$. Rather than the full set of edges $\mathcal{E}$, we are given only an incomplete subset $\hat{\mathcal{E}}$. The task is to assign scores $f(s, r, o)$ to possible edges (s, r, o) in order to determine how likely those edges are to belong to $\mathcal{E}$.

In order to tackle this problem, we introduce a graph auto-encoder model (see Fig. 1c), comprised of an entity encoder and a scoring function (decoder). The encoder maps each entity $v_i \in \mathcal{V}$ to a real-valued vector $e_i \in \mathbb{R}^d$. The decoder reconstructs edges of the graph relying on the vertex representations; in other words, it scores *(subject, relation, object)*-triples through a function $s : \mathbb{R}^d \times \mathcal{R} \times \mathbb{R}^d \to \mathbb{R}$. Most existing approaches to link prediction (for example, tensor and neural factorization methods [11,17–20]) can be interpreted under this framework. The crucial distinguishing characteristic of our work is the reliance on an encoder. Whereas most previous approaches use a single, real-valued vector e_i for every $v_i \in \mathcal{V}$ optimized directly in training, we compute representations through an R-GCN encoder with $e_i = h_i^{(L)}$, similar to the graph auto-encoder model introduced in [21] for unlabeled undirected graphs.

In our experiments, we use the DistMult factorization [11] as the scoring function, which is known to perform well on standard link prediction benchmarks when used on its own. In DistMult, every relation r is associated with a diagonal matrix $R_r \in \mathbb{R}^{d \times d}$ and a triple (s, r, o) is scored as

$$f(s, r, o) = e_s^T R_r e_o. \tag{7}$$

As in previous work on factorization [11,20], we train the model with negative sampling. For each observed example we sample ω negative ones. We sample by randomly corrupting either the subject or the object of each positive example. We optimize for cross-entropy loss to push the model to score observable triples higher than the negative ones:

$$\mathcal{L} = -\frac{1}{(1+\omega)|\hat{\mathcal{E}}|} \sum_{(s,r,o,y) \in \mathcal{T}} y \log l\big(f(s, r, o)\big) + \\ (1-y) \log\big(1 - l\big(f(s, r, o)\big)\big), \tag{8}$$

where $\mathcal{T}$ is the total set of real and corrupted triples, l is the logistic sigmoid function, and y is an indicator set to $y = 1$ for positive triples and $y = 0$ for negative ones.

5   Empirical Evaluation

5.1   Entity Classification Experiments

Here, we consider the task of classifying entities in a knowledge base. In order to infer, for example, the type of an entity (e.g. person or company), a successful model needs to reason about the relations with other entities that this entity is involved in.

Datasets. We evaluate our model on four datasets[3] in Resource Description Framework (RDF) format [22]: AIFB, MUTAG, BGS, and AM. Relations in

---

[3] http://dws.informatik.uni-mannheim.de/en/research/a-collection-of-benchmark-datasets-for-ml.

these datasets need not necessarily encode directed subject-object relations, but are also used to encode the presence, or absence, of a specific feature for a given entity. In each dataset, the targets to be classified are properties of a group of entities represented as nodes. The exact statistics of the datasets can be found in Table 1. For a more detailed description of the datasets the reader is referred to [22]. We remove relations that were used to create entity labels: *employs* and *affiliation* for AIFB, *isMutagenic* for MUTAG, *hasLithogenesis* for BGS, and *objectCategory* and *material* for AM.

For the entity classification benchmarks described in our paper, the evaluation process differs subtly between publications. To eliminate these differences, we repeated the baselines in a uniform manner, using the canonical test/train split from [22]. We performed hyperparameter optimization on only the training set, running a single evaluation on the test set after hyperparameters were chosen for each baseline. This explains why the numbers we report differ slightly from those in the original publications (where cross-validation accuracy was reported).

Table 1. Number of entities, relations, edges and classes along with the number of labeled entities for each of the datasets. *Labeled* denotes the subset of entities that have labels and that are to be classified.

Dataset	AIFB	MUTAG	BGS	AM
Entities	8,285	23,644	333,845	1,666,764
Relations	45	23	103	133
Edges	29,043	74,227	916,199	5,988,321
Labeled	176	340	146	1,000
Classes	4	2	2	11

Baselines. As a baseline for our experiments, we compare against recent state-of-the-art classification results from RDF2Vec embeddings [23], Weisfeiler-Lehman kernels (WL) [24,25], and hand-designed feature extractors (Feat) [26]. Feat assembles a feature vector from the in- and out-degree (per relation) of every labeled entity. RDF2Vec extracts walks on labeled graphs which are then processed using the Skipgram [27] model to generate entity embeddings, used for subsequent classification. See [23] for an in-depth description and discussion of these baseline approaches. All entity classification experiments were run on CPU nodes with 64 GB of memory.

For WL, we use the *tree* variant of the Weisfeiler-Lehman subtree kernel from the Mustard library.[4] For RDF2Vec, we use an implementation provided by the authors of [23] which builds on Mustard. In both cases, we extract explicit feature vectors for the instance nodes, which are classified by a linear SVM. For

---

[4] https://github.com/Data2Semantics/mustard.

the MUTAG task, our preprocessing differs from that used in [23, 25] where for a given target relation (s, r, o) all triples connecting s to o are removed. Since o is a boolean value in the MUTAG data, one can infer the label after processing from other boolean relations that are still present. This issue is now mentioned in the Mustard documentation. In our preprocessing, we remove only the specific triples encoding the target relation.

Results. All results in Table 2 are reported on the train/test benchmark splits from [22]. We further set aside 20% of the training set as a validation set for hyperparameter tuning. For R-GCN, we report performance of a 2-layer model with 16 hidden units (10 for AM), basis function decomposition (Eq. 3), and trained with Adam [28] for 50 epochs using a learning rate of 0.01. The normalization constant is chosen as $c_{i,r} = |\mathcal{N}_i^r|$.

Hyperparameters for baselines are chosen according to the best model performance in [23], i.e. WL: 2 (tree depth), 3 (number of iterations); RDF2Vec: 2 (WL tree depth), 4 (WL iterations), 500 (embedding size), 5 (window size), 10 (SkipGram iterations), 25 (number of negative samples). We optimize the SVM regularization constant $C \in \{0.001, 0.01, 0.1, 1, 10, 100, 1000\}$ based on performance on a 80/20 train/validation split (of the original training set).

For R-GCN, we choose an $l2$ penalty on first layer weights $C_{l2} \in \{0, 5 \cdot 10^{-4}\}$ and the number of basis functions $B \in \{0, 10, 20, 30, 40\}$ based on validation set performance, where $B = 0$ refers to no basis decomposition. Block decomposition did not improve results. Otherwise, hyperparameters are chosen as follows: 50 (number of epochs), 16 (number of hidden units), and $c_{i,r} = |\mathcal{N}_i^r|$ (normalization constant). We do not use dropout. For AM, we use a reduced number of 10 hidden units for R-GCN to reduce the memory footprint. All entity classification experiments were run on CPU nodes with 64 GB of memory.

Table 2. Entity classification results in accuracy (average and standard error over 10 runs) for a feature-based baseline (see main text for details), WL [24, 25], RDF2Vec [23], and R-GCN (this work). Test performance is reported on the train/test set splits provided by [22].

Model	AIFB	MUTAG	BGS	AM
Feat	55.55 ± 0.00	77.94 ± 0.00	72.41 ± 0.00	66.66 ± 0.00
WL	80.55 ± 0.00	**80.88 ± 0.00**	86.20 ± 0.00	87.37 ± 0.00
RDF2Vec	88.88 ± 0.00	67.20 ± 1.24	**87.24 ± 0.89**	88.33 ± 0.61
R-GCN (Ours)	**95.83 ± 0.62**	73.23 ± 0.48	83.10 ± 0.80	**89.29 ± 0.35**

Our model achieves state-of-the-art results on AIFB and AM. To explain the gap in performance on MUTAG and BGS it is important to understand the nature of these datasets. MUTAG is a dataset of molecular graphs, which was later converted to RDF format, where relations either indicate atomic bonds or merely the presence of a certain feature. BGS is a dataset of rock types with hierarchical feature descriptions which was similarly converted to RDF format, where relations encode the presence of a certain feature or feature hierarchy. Labeled entities in MUTAG and BGS are only connected via high-degree hub nodes that encode a certain feature.

We conjecture that the fixed choice of normalization constant for the aggregation of messages from neighboring nodes is partly to blame for this behavior, which can be particularly problematic for nodes of high degree. A potentially promising way to overcome this limitation in future work is to introduce an attention mechanism, i.e. to replace the normalization constant $1/c_{i,r}$ with data-dependent attention weights $a_{ij,r}$, where $\sum_{j,r} a_{ij,r} = 1$.

5.2 Link Prediction Experiments

As shown in the previous section, R-GCNs serve as an effective encoder for relational data. We now combine our encoder model with a scoring function (which we refer to as a decoder, see Fig. 1c) to score candidate triples for link prediction in knowledge bases.

Datasets. Link prediction algorithms are commonly evaluated on FB15k, a subset of the relational database Freebase, and WN18, a subset of WordNet. In [12], a serious flaw was observed in both datasets: The presence of inverse triplet pairs $t = (e_1, r, e_2)$ and $t' = (e_2, r^{-1}, e_1)$ with t in the training set and t' in the test set. This reduces a large part of the prediction task to memorization of affected triplet pairs, and a simple baseline LinkFeat employing a linear classifier and features of observed training relations was shown to outperform existing systems by a large margin. Toutanova and Chen proposed a reduced dataset FB15k-237 with all such inverse triplet pairs removed. We therefore choose FB15k-237 as our primary evaluation dataset. Since FB15k and WN18 are still widely used, we also include results on these datasets using the splits introduced in [29] (Table 3).

Table 3. Number of entities and relation types along with the number of edges per split for the three datasets.

Dataset	WN18	FB15K	FB15k-237
Entities	40,943	14,951	14,541
Relations	18	1,345	237
Train edges	141,442	483,142	272,115
Val. edges	5,000	50,000	17,535
Test edges	5,000	59,071	20,466

Baselines. A common baseline for both experiments is direct optimization of *DistMult* [11]. This factorization strategy is known to perform well on standard datasets, and furthermore corresponds to a version of our model with fixed entity embeddings in place of the R-GCN encoder as described in Sect. 4. As a second baseline, we add the simple neighbor-based LinkFeat algorithm proposed in [12].

We further compare to ComplEx [20] and HolE [30], two state-of-the-art link prediction models for FB15k and WN18. ComplEx facilitates modeling of asymmetric relations by generalizing DistMult to the complex domain, while HolE replaces the vector-matrix product with circular correlation. Finally, we include comparisons with two classic algorithms – CP [31] and TransE [29].

Table 4. Results on FB15k-237, a reduced version of FB15k with problematic inverse relation pairs removed. CP, TransE, and ComplEx were evaluated using the code published for [20], while HolE was evaluated using the code published for [30]. R-GCN+ denotes an ensemble between R-GCN and DistMult.

| Model | MRR | | Hits @ | | |
	Raw	Filtered	1	3	10
LinkFeat		0.063			0.079
DistMult	0.100	0.191	0.106	0.207	0.376
R-GCN	**0.158**	0.248	**0.153**	0.258	0.414
R-GCN+	0.156	**0.249**	0.151	**0.264**	**0.417**
CP	0.080	0.182	0.101	0.197	0.357
TransE	0.144	0.233	0.147	0.263	0.398
HolE	0.124	0.222	0.133	0.253	0.391
ComplEx	0.109	0.201	0.112	0.213	0.388

Results. We provide results using two commonly used evaluation metrics: *mean reciprocal rank* (MRR) and *Hits at n* (H@n). Following [29], both metrics can be computed in a raw and a filtered setting. We report filtered and raw MRR, and filtered Hits at 1, 3, and 10.

We evaluate hyperparameter choices on the respective validation splits. We found a normalization constant defined as $c_{i,r} = c_i = \sum_r |\mathcal{N}_i^r|$, i.e. applied across relation types, to work best. For FB15k and WN18, we report results using basis decomposition (Eq. 3) with two basis functions, and a single encoding layer with 200-dimensional embeddings. For FB15k-237, we found block decomposition (Eq. 4) to perform best, using two layers with block dimension 5 × 5 and 500-dimensional embeddings. We regularize the encoder via edge dropout applied before normalization, with dropout rate 0.2 for self-loops and 0.4 for other edges. We apply $l2$ regularization to the decoder with a penalty of 0.01.

We use the Adam optimizer [28] with a learning rate of 0.01. For the baseline and the other factorizations, we found the parameters from [20] – apart from the dimensionality on FB15k-237 – to work best, though to make the systems comparable we maintain the same number of negative samples (i.e. $\omega = 1$). We use full-batch optimization for both the baselines and our model.

On FB15k, local context in the form of inverse relations is expected to dominate the performance of the factorizations, contrasting with the design of the R-GCN model. Preliminary experiments revealed that R-GCN still improved performance on high-degree vertices, where contextual knowledge is abundant. Since the two models for this dataset appear complementary, we attempt to combine the strengths of both into a single model R-GCN+: $f(s,r,t)_{\text{R-GCN+}} = \alpha f(s,r,t)_{\text{R-GCN}} + (1-\alpha)f(s,r,t)_{\text{DistMult}}$, with $\alpha = 0.4$ selected on FB15k development data. To facilitate a fair comparison to R-GCN, we use half-size embeddings for each component of R-GCN+. On FB15k and WN18 where local and long-distance information can both provide strong solutions, we expect R-GCN+ to outperform each individual model. On FB15k-237 where local information is less salient, we do not expect the combination model to outperform a pure R-GCN model significantly.

In Table 4, we show results for FB15k-237 where (as previously discussed) inverse relation pairs have been removed and the LinkFeat baseline fails to generalize[5]. Here, our R-GCN model outperforms the DistMult baseline by a large margin of 29.8%, highlighting the importance of a separate encoder model. As expected from our earlier analysis, R-GCN and R-GCN+ show similar performance on this dataset.

The R-GCN model further compares favorably against other factorization methods, despite relying on a DistMult decoder which shows comparatively weak performance when used without an encoder. The high variance between different decoder-only models suggests that performance could be improved by combining R-GCN with a task-specific decoder selected through validation. As decoder choice is orthogonal to the development of our encoder model, we leave this as a promising avenue for future work.

In Table 5, we evaluate the R-GCN model and the combination model on FB15k and WN18. On the FB15k and WN18 datasets, R-GCN and R-GCN+ both outperform the DistMult baseline, but like all other systems underperform on these two datasets compared to the LinkFeat algorithm. The strong result from this baseline highlights the contribution of inverse relation pairs to high-performance solutions on these datasets.

6   Related Work

6.1   Relational Modeling

Our encoder-decoder approach to link prediction relies on DistMult [11] in the decoder, a special and simpler case of the RESCAL factorization [32], more

---

[5] Our numbers are not directly comparable to those reported in [12], as they use pruning both for training and testing (see their Sects. 3.3.1 and 4.2). Since their pruning schema is not fully specified (values of the relation-specific parameter t are not given) and the code is not available, it is not possible to replicate their set-up.

Table 5. Results on the FB15k and WN18 datasets. Results marked (*) taken from [20]. Results marks (**) taken from [30].

Model	FB15k					WN18				
	MRR		Hits @			MRR		Hits @		
	Raw	Filtered	1	3	10	Raw	Filtered	1	3	10
LinkFeat		0.779			0.804		0.938			0.939
DistMult	0.248	0.634	0.522	0.718	0.814	0.526	0.813	0.701	0.921	0.943
R-GCN	0.251	0.651	0.541	0.736	0.825	0.553	0.814	0.686	0.928	0.955
R-GCN+	**0.262**	**0.696**	**0.601**	**0.760**	**0.842**	0.561	0.819	0.697	0.929	**0.964**
CP*	0.152	0.326	0.219	0.376	0.532	0.075	0.058	0.049	0.080	0.125
TransE*	0.221	0.380	0.231	0.472	0.641	0.335	0.454	0.089	0.823	0.934
HolE**	0.232	0.524	0.402	0.613	0.739	**0.616**	0.938	0.930	**0.945**	0.949
ComplEx*	0.242	0.692	0.599	0.759	0.840	0.587	**0.941**	**0.936**	**0.945**	0.947

effective than the original RESCAL in the context of multi-relational knowledge bases. Numerous alternative factorizations have been proposed and studied in the context of SRL, including both (bi-)linear and nonlinear ones (e.g., [17,20, 29,30,33,34]). Many of these approaches can be regarded as modifications or special cases of classic tensor decomposition methods such as CP or Tucker; for an overview of tensor decomposition literature we refer the reader to [35].

Incorporation of paths between entities in knowledge bases has recently received considerable attention. We can roughly classify previous work into (1) methods creating auxiliary triples, which are then added to the learning objective of a factorization model [36,37]; (2) approaches using paths (or walks) as features when predicting edges [18]; or (3) doing both at the same time [19,38]. The first direction is largely orthogonal to ours, as we would also expect improvements from adding similar terms to our loss (in other words, extending our decoder). The second research line is more comparable; R-GCNs provide a computationally cheaper alternative to these path-based models. Direct comparison is somewhat complicated as path-based methods used different datasets (e.g. sub-sampled sets of walks from a knowledge base).

6.2 Neural Networks on Graphs

Our R-GCN encoder model is closely related to a number of works in the area of neural networks on graphs. It is primarily motivated as an adaption of previous work on GCNs [13,14,39,40] for large-scale and highly multi-relational data, characteristic of realistic knowledge bases.

Early work in this area includes the graph neural network (GNN) [15]. A number of extensions to the original GNN have been proposed, most notably [41,42], both of which use gating mechanisms to facilitate optimization.

R-GCNs can further be seen as a sub-class of message passing neural networks [16], which encompass a number of previous neural models for graphs, including GCNs, under a differentiable message passing interpretation.

As mentioned in Sect. 5, we do not in this paper experiment with subsampling of neighborhoods, a choice which limits our training algorithm to full-batch descent. Recent work including [43–45] have experimented with various subsampling strategies for graph-based neural networks, demonstrating promising results.

7   Conclusions

We have introduced relational graph convolutional networks (R-GCNs) and demonstrated their effectiveness in the context of two standard statistical relation modeling problems: link prediction and entity classification. For the entity classification problem, we have demonstrated that the R-GCN model can act as a competitive, end-to-end trainable graph-based encoder. For link prediction, the R-GCN model with DistMult factorization as decoder outperformed direct optimization of the factorization model, and achieved competitive results on standard link prediction benchmarks. Enriching the factorization model with an R-GCN encoder proved especially valuable for the challenging FB15k-237 dataset, yielding a 29.8% improvement over the decoder-only baseline.

There are several ways in which our work could be extended. For example, the graph autoencoder model could be considered in combination with other factorization models, such as ConvE [34], which can be better suited for modeling asymmetric relations. It is also straightforward to integrate entity features in R-GCNs, which would be beneficial both for link prediction and entity classification problems. To address the scalability of our method, it would be worthwhile to explore subsampling techniques, such as in [43]. Lastly, it would be promising to replace the current form of summation over neighboring nodes and relation types with a data-dependent attention mechanism. Beyond modeling knowledge bases, R-GCNs can be generalized to other applications where relation factorization models have been shown effective (e.g. relation extraction).

Acknowledgements. We would like to thank Diego Marcheggiani, Ethan Fetaya, and Christos Louizos for helpful discussions and comments. This project is supported by the European Research Council (ERC StG BroadSem 678254), the SAP Innovation Center Network and the Dutch National Science Foundation (NWO VIDI 639.022.518).

References

1. Yao, X., Van Durme, B.: Information extraction over structured data: question answering with freebase. In: ACL (2014)
2. Bao, J., Duan, N., Zhou, M., Zhao, T.: Knowledge-based question answering as machine translation. In: ACL (2014)

3. Seyler, D., Yahya, M., Berberich, K.: Generating quiz questions from knowledge graphs. In: Proceedings of the 24th International Conference on World Wide Web (2015)
4. Hixon, B., Clark, P., Hajishirzi, H.: Learning knowledge graphs for question answering through conversational dialog. In: Proceedings of NAACL HLT, pp. 851–861 (2015)
5. Bordes, A., Usunier, N., Chopra, S., Weston, J.: Large-scale simple question answering with memory networks. arXiv preprint arXiv:1506.02075 (2015)
6. Dong, L., Wei, F., Zhou, M., Xu, K.: Question answering over freebase with multi-column convolutional neural networks. In: ACL (2015)
7. Kotov, A., Zhai, C.: Tapping into knowledge base for concept feedback: leveraging conceptnet to improve search results for difficult queries. In: WSDM (2012)
8. Dalton, J., Dietz, L., Allan, J.: Entity query feature expansion using knowledge base links. In: ACM SIGIR (2014)
9. Xiong, C., Callan, J.: Query expansion with freebase. In: Proceedings of the 2015 International Conference on The Theory of Information Retrieval, pp. 111–120 (2015)
10. Xiong, C., Callan, J.: Esdrank: connecting query and documents through external semi-structured data. In: CIKM (2015)
11. Yang, B., Yih, W., He, X., Gao, J., Deng, L.: Embedding entities and relations for learning and inference in knowledge bases. arXiv preprint arXiv:1412.6575 (2014)
12. Toutanova, K., Chen, D.: Observed versus latent features for knowledge base and text inference. In: Proceedings of the 3rd Workshop on Continuous Vector Space Models and their Compositionality, pp. 57–66 (2015)
13. Duvenaud, D.K., Maclaurin, D., Iparraguirre, J., Bombarell, R., Hirzel, T., Aspuru-Guzik, A., Adams, R.P.: Convolutional networks on graphs for learning molecular fingerprints. In: NIPS (2015)
14. Kipf, T.N., Welling, M.: Semi-supervised classification with graph convolutional networks. In: ICLR (2017)
15. Scarselli, F., Gori, M., Tsoi, A.C., Hagenbuchner, M., Monfardini, G.: The graph neural network model. IEEE Trans. Neural Netw. 20(1), 61–80 (2009)
16. Gilmer, J., Schoenholz, S.S., Riley, P.F., Vinyals, O., Dahl, G.E.: Neural message passing for quantum chemistry. In: ICML (2017)
17. Socher, R., Chen, D., Manning, C.D., Ng, A.: Reasoning with neural tensor networks for knowledge base completion. In: NIPS (2013)
18. Lin, Y., Liu, Z., Luan, H., Sun, M., Rao, S., Liu, S.: Modeling relation paths for representation learning of knowledge bases. In: EMNLP (2015)
19. Toutanova, K., Lin, V., Yih, W., Poon, H., Quirk, C.: Compositional learning of embeddings for relation paths in knowledge base and text. In: ACL (2016)
20. Trouillon, T., Welbl, J., Riedel, S., Gaussier, E., Bouchard, G.: Complex embeddings for simple link prediction. In: ICML (2016)
21. Kipf, T.N., Welling, M.: Variational graph auto-encoders. arXiv preprint arXiv:1611.07308 (2016)
22. Ristoski, P., de Vries, G.K.D., Paulheim, H.: A collection of benchmark datasets for systematic evaluations of machine learning on the semantic web. In: Groth, P., Simperl, E., Gray, A., Sabou, M., Krötzsch, M., Lecue, F., Flöck, F., Gil, Y. (eds.) ISWC 2016. LNCS, vol. 9982, pp. 186–194. Springer, Cham (2016). https://doi.org/10.1007/978-3-319-46547-0_20

23. Ristoski, P., Paulheim, H.: RDF2Vec: RDF Graph embeddings for data mining. In: Groth, P., Simperl, E., Gray, A., Sabou, M., Krötzsch, M., Lecue, F., Flöck, F., Gil, Y. (eds.) ISWC 2016. LNCS, vol. 9981, pp. 498–514. Springer, Cham (2016). https://doi.org/10.1007/978-3-319-46523-4_30

24. Shervashidze, N., Schweitzer, P., Leeuwen, E.J., Mehlhorn, K., Borgwardt, K.M.: Weisfeiler-lehman graph kernels. J. Mach. Learn. Res. 12(Sep), 2539–2561 (2011)

25. de Vries, G.K.D., de Rooij, S.: Substructure counting graph kernels for machine learning from rdf data. Web Semant. Sci. Serv. Agents World Wide Web 35, 71–84 (2015)

26. Paulheim, H., Fümkranz, J.: Unsupervised generation of data mining features from linked open data. In: Proceedings of the 2nd International Conference on Web Intelligence, Mining And Semantics, p. 31 (2012)

27. Mikolov, T., Sutskever, I., Chen, K., Corrado, G.S., Dean, J.: Distributed representations of words and phrases and their compositionality. In: NIPS (2013)

28. Kingma, D., Ba, J.: Adam: a method for stochastic optimization. arXiv preprint arXiv:1412.6980 (2014)

29. Bordes, A., Usunier, N., Garcia-Duran, A., Weston, J., Yakhnenko, O.: Translating embeddings for modeling multi-relational data. In: NIPS (2013)

30. Nickel, M., Rosasco, L., Poggio, T.: Holographic embeddings of knowledge graphs. In: AAAI (2016)

31. Hitchcock, F.L.: The expression of a tensor or a polyadic as a sum of products. Stud. Appl. Math. 6(1–4), 164–189 (1927)

32. Nickel, M., Tresp, V., Kriegel, H.P.: A three-way model for collective learning on multi-relational data. In: ICML (2011)

33. Chang, K.W., Yih, W., Yang, B., Meek, C.: Typed tensor decomposition of knowledge bases for relation extraction. In: EMNLP (2014)

34. Dettmers, T., Minervini, P., Stenetorp, P., Riedel, S.: Convolutional 2D knowledge graph embeddings. In: AAAI (2018)

35. Kolda, T.G., Bader, B.W.: Tensor decompositions and applications. SIAM Rev. 51(3), 455–500 (2009)

36. Guu, K., Miller, J., Liang, P.: Traversing knowledge graphs in vector space. In: EMNLP (2015)

37. Garcia-Duran, A., Bordes, A., Usunier, N.: Composing relationships with translations. Technical report. CNRS, Heudiasyc (2015)

38. Neelakantan, A., Roth, B., McCallum, A.: Compositional vector space models for knowledge base completion. In: ACL (2015)

39. Bruna, J., Zaremba, W., Szlam, A., LeCun, Y.: Spectral networks and locally connected networks on graphs. In: ICLR (2014)

40. Defferrard, M., Bresson, X., Vandergheynst, P.: Convolutional neural networks on graphs with fast localized spectral filtering. In: NIPS (2016)

41. Li, Y., Tarlow, D., Brockschmidt, M., Zemel, R.: Gated graph sequence neural networks. In: ICLR (2016)

42. Pham, T., Tran, T., Phung, D., Venkatesh, S.: Column networks for collective classification. In: AAAI (2017)

43. Hamilton, W.L., Ying, R., Leskovec, J.: Inductive representation learning on large graphs. In: NIPS (2017)

44. Chen, J., Zhu, J.: Stochastic training of graph convolutional networks. arXiv preprint arXiv:1710.10568 (2017)

45. Chen, J., Ma, T., Xiao, C.: FastGCN: fast learning with graph convolutional networks via importance sampling. In: ICLR (2018)

Ontology-Driven Sentiment Analysis
of Product and Service Aspects

Kim Schouten and Flavius Frasincar[✉] [iD]

Erasmus University Rotterdam, P.O. Box 1738,
3000 DR Rotterdam, The Netherlands
{schouten,frasincar}@ese.eur.nl

Abstract. With so much opinionated, but unstructured, data available
on the Web, sentiment analysis has become popular with both companies and researchers. Aspect-based sentiment analysis goes one step
further by relating the expressed sentiment in a text to the topic, or
aspect, the sentiment is expressed on. This enables a detailed analysis of
the sentiment expressed in, for example, reviews of products or services.
In this paper we propose a knowledge-driven approach to aspect sentiment analysis that complements traditional machine learning methods.
By utilizing common domain knowledge, as encoded in an ontology, we
improve the sentiment analysis of a given aspect. The domain knowledge
is used to determine which words are expressing sentiment on the given
aspect as well as to disambiguate sentiment carrying words or phrases.
The proposed method has a highly competitive performance of over 80%
accuracy on both SemEval-2015 and SemEval-2016 data, significantly
outperforming the considered baselines.

1 Introduction

With so much opinionated, but unstructured, data available on the Web, sentiment analysis has become popular with both companies and researchers. Its goal
is to extract the sentiment of content creators, such as the writers of consumer
reviews, and to aggregate this information into easy to digest overviews, info-
graphics, or dashboards. Depending on the specific scenario, sentiment can be
modeled as a set of emotions, or, more commonly, as a point on a polarity scale
ranging from positive to negative. Polarity can be binary with just the positive
and negative value, or it can be modeled as a 5-star score, or even as a real
number within a given interval (e.g., between -1.0 and 1.0).

Since reviews often go into detail about certain characteristics of the entity
under review, it is useful to go one step further and perform aspect-based sentiment analysis. Here, instead of computing a sentiment score for the whole review,
or even per sentence, the goal is to locate the different characteristics, or aspects,
the reviewer writes about, and then compute a sentiment score for each of the
mentioned aspects. This yields more in-depth results, as people are often not
positive (or negative) about every aspect of the product or service they bought.

© Springer International Publishing AG, part of Springer Nature 2018
A. Gangemi et al. (Eds.): ESWC 2018, LNCS 10843, pp. 608–623, 2018.
https://doi.org/10.1007/978-3-319-93417-4_39

In general, aspect-based sentiment analysis methods can be classified as knowledge-based or as machine learning based [13]. This is of course not a perfect classification, as machine learning methods often incorporate information from dictionaries, such as sentiment lexicons. Nevertheless, it is a useful distinction as machine learning methods require a sufficient amount of training data to perform well, while knowledge-based methods do not. In the pursuit of high performance, machine learning classifiers have become very popular at the expense of knowledge-based systems. In this paper we hypothesize that both have their use and that the two methods are in fact complementary. Using both statistical learning and rules with a knowledge repository is thus hypothesized to work best. To that end, we have designed an ontology in the restaurant domain with rules to decide what sentiment to assign in which situation, as well as a bag-of-words model, with additional features, such as a sentiment value of the sentence, based on a Support Vector Machine classifier. With the focus being solely on the sentiment analysis of aspects, the aspect detection phase is not considered in this paper, and hence, the aspect annotations in the data are used as a starting point.

In the next section, some related work is discussed, followed by the problem definition and overview of the used data sets in Sect. 3. In Sect. 4, the employed domain ontology is explained, as well as the rules to predict a sentiment value for a given aspect. It also contains a short overview of the used bag-of-words model. The base models and the hybrid combinations are evaluated in Sect. 5, and in Sect. 6, conclusions are given and directions for future research are provided. The developed ontology and source code can be found at https://github.com/KSchouten/Heracles.

2   Related Work

A short overview of the field of affective computing, which encompasses sentiment analysis, is presented in [3]. The author argues that hybrid methods, combining the intuitive nature and explanatory power of knowledge-driven approaches and the high performance of statistical methods, are the most promising way to improve the effectiveness of affective algorithms. This forms the research hypothesis of this work as well, as we combine both approaches in a way that is similar to [1]. In that work, statistical methods are combined with a set of linguistic patterns based on SenticNet [2]. Each sentence is processed in order to find the concepts expressed in it. The discovered concepts are linked to the SenticNet knowledge repository, which enables the inference of the sentiment value associated to the sentence. If there are no concepts expressed in this sentence or if the found concepts are not in the knowledge base, then a deep learning, bag-of-words method is employed to determine the sentiment for that sentence. Note that this is a sentence-level approach and not an aspect-based approach, like we consider here. Our work has a similar setup in that it first tries to use the knowledge-driven approach to make a prediction, using the statistical method as a backup when the knowledge-base is insufficient.

A multi-domain approach to sentence-level sentiment analysis is presented in [4]. While sentiment is assigned to sentences instead of aspects, the sentences can come from different domains, so the proposed method needs to disambiguate sentiment words based on the domain the sentence is from. This is similar to our approach where sentiment words are disambiguated based on the aspect they are about. Differently from [4], our ontology does not feature a strict separation of semantic information and sentiment information. Furthermore, [4] uses fuzzy membership functions to describe the relations between concepts, sentiment, and domains, and while this gives more modeling flexibility, it makes it harder to reason over the knowledge graph, which is one of the things we want to explore in this work. Other work that uses fuzzy ontologies includes [8], where an ontology is used to aid in aspect-based sentiment analysis. However, the used ontology is automatically generated and only captures a concept taxonomy, missing out on the more advanced options such as using axioms for context-dependent sentiment words.

In [16], a method is presented that predicts the sentiment value for sentiment-bearing words based on the context they are in. For this task, a Bayesian model is created that uses the words surrounding a sentiment-bearing word, including the words that denote the aspect, to predict the actual sentiment value of the word given the context. Similar to our approach, it uses a two-stage setup, where a backup method is used when the first method cannot make a decision. In this case, if the Bayesian model cannot make a decision about the sentiment value of the word, the previous opinion in the text is checked and if there is a conjunction between the two (i.e., no contrasting or negation words), it will assign the same sentiment value to the current word.

The methods presented in this work improve on our previous approach for ontology-enhanced sentiment analysis, presented in [14], in two major ways. First, the ontology is designed more effectively, being able to support both aspect detection and sentiment analysis better, although this work only focuses on sentiment analysis. This is achieved by clearly distinguishing between three types of sentiment words: generic sentiment words that always have the same sentiment value regardless of the context, aspect-specific sentiment words that infer the presence of a single aspect and are only applicable to that aspect (e.g., "rude" for the service aspect), and context-dependent sentiment words that are applicable to more than one aspect, but not necessarily all of them, and that may have different sentiment values for different aspects (e.g., "small" being generally negative for portions, but usually positive for price). Our previous work, while designating the generic sentiment words as such, does not distinguish between the second and third type of sentiment words, which leads to mistakes.

Last, our previous approach utilized the ontology-derived information in the form of additional input features for the Support Vector Machine (SVM) model, while in the current work we use a two-stage approach. In the primary stage, the ontology is used to find and infer sentiment for the current aspect, and if successful, that becomes the prediction of the method. Only when the ontology either finds both positive and negative signals, or none at all, we employ an SVM model to predict the sentiment. This secondary, or backup, model is a slightly improved bag-of-words model that does not use ontology features. For improved comparison, the performance comparison in Sect. 5 includes an SVM model with additional ontology features, similar to [14].

3   Specification of Data and Tasks

For this research, the widely used set of restaurant reviews from SemEval-2015 Task 12 [12] and SemEval-2016 Task 5 Subtask 1 [11] is employed. The SemEval-2016 data contains the SemEval-2015 data and consists of a training set of 350 reviews with in total 2506 sentiment-labeled aspects and a test set of 90 reviews with in total 859 sentiment-labeled aspects. Given that the SemEval-2015 data is a subset of SemEval-2016, it has similar properties, which are therefore not discussed separately.

An excerpt of the raw data is given in Fig. 1. The provided annotations already split the dataset into reviews and sentences, and each sentence can be labeled with zero or more opinions, which is an aspect together with the expressed sentiment related to that aspect.

```
<sentence id="1032695:1">
<text>Everything is always cooked to perfection, the
    service is excellent, the decor cool and understated.</
    text>
<Opinions>
<Opinion target="NULL" category="FOOD#QUALITY" polarity="
    positive" from="0" to="0"/>
<Opinion target="service" category="SERVICE#GENERAL"
    polarity="positive" from="47" to="54"/>
<Opinion target="decor" category="AMBIENCE#GENERAL"
    polarity="positive" from="73" to="78"/>
</Opinions>
</sentence>
```

Fig. 1. A snippet from the used dataset showing an annotated sentence from a restaurant review.

Some aspects are explicit, which means that there is a specific text segment that expresses that aspect, called the target expression, while others are implicit meaning that there is no such target expression. The target expression, if available, is part of the provided annotations. Some statistics related to aspects and sentiment can be found in Fig. 2. In Fig. 2a, the number of times each category label appears is presented and in Fig. 2b, the proportion of aspects that have a sentiment value that is different from the majority within the same textual unit is shown. This gives the minimum error rate for a sentence-level or review-level sentiment analysis system, respectively, as these systems are not able to assign

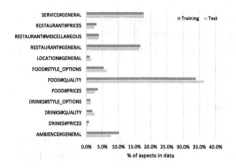

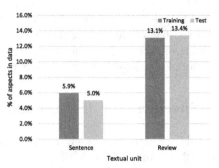

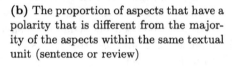

(a) Relative frequencies of each aspect category label

(b) The proportion of aspects that have a polarity that is different from the majority of the aspects within the same textual unit (sentence or review)

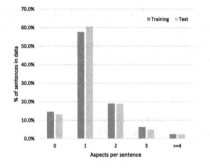

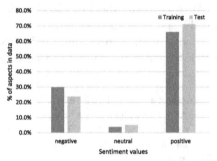

(c) The distribution of aspects per sentence

(d) Relative frequencies of each sentiment label

Fig. 2. Some statistics related to the used data set

different sentiment values to aspects within the same textual unit. Figure 2c shows that while most have just one aspect, a significant number of sentences contain more than one aspect. This complicates the sentiment analysis as it is not always clear to which aspect a certain sentiment expression pertains. Figure 2d presents the distribution of sentiment values over aspects, showing that this data set is unbalanced with respect to sentiment.

The task of aspect sentiment classification is to give the sentiment value for each aspect, where the aspects are already provided. Thus, all annotations, like the ones given in Fig. 1, are provided, except the values of the `polarity` fields. The accuracy of the classifier is simply the number of correct classifications over the total number of aspects to be classified.

4   Method

All review sentences are preprocessed using the Stanford CoreNLP package [9], performing basic operations such as tokenization, part-of-speech tagging, lemmatization, syntactic analysis, as well as sentiment analysis. The latter is an already trained neural network that assigns a numeric sentiment score to each syntactic constituent in a parse tree.

For the machine learning backup method, we opted for a Support Vector Machine (SVM) with a radial basis function kernel, given that SVMs have proven to be very effective for text classification problems [10]. Since the `polarity` field can have three sentiment values, a multi-class SVM is trained that is able to classify an aspect into one of three sentiment values: positive, neutral, or negative. For this work, the Weka [5] implementation of the multiclass SVM is utilized, which internally performs 1-vs-1 pairwise classifications.

4.1   Ontology Design

For the ontology, the aim is to limit the number of asserted facts and to use the reasoner to infer the sentiment of a given expression. The ontology consists of three main classes: *AspectMention*, *SentimentMention*, and *SentimentValue*. The latter simply has *Positive* and *Negative* as its subclasses, and the setup is such that if a certain concept is positive, it is a subclass of *Positive* and if it expresses a negative sentiment, that concept is modeled as a subclass of *Negative*. The *AspectMention* class models the mentions of aspects and *SentimentMention* models the expressions of sentiment. A schematic overview of the ontology is shown in Fig. 3.

The *SentimentMention*s can be divided into three types. The first group is formed by type-1 *SentimentMention*s, which always denote a positive (negative) sentiment, regardless of which aspect they are about. In Fig. 3, these are denoted with hexagons. These subclasses of *SentimentMention* are also a subclass of the sentiment class they express. Hence, *Good* is a subclass of both *SentimentMention* and *Positive*. Type-2 *SentimentMention*s are those expressions that are exclusively used for a certain category of aspects, meaning that the presence of the aspect category can be inferred from the occurrence of the *SentimentMention*. In Fig. 3, these classes are denoted with rounded squares. For instance, *Delicious* is a subclass of *SentimentMention*, but also of both *SustenanceMention* and *Positive*, where *SustenanceMention* encompasses concepts related to food and drinks. This means that if we want to predict the sentiment value of an aspect in the service category, we will ignore the word "delicious" if it is encountered, because it cannot possibly be about the current aspect. The third type (type-3) of *SentimentMention*s contains context-dependent sentiment expressions, and this group is shown as an ellipse in Fig. 3. Here, the inferred sentiment depends on the aspect category. For instance, *Small* when combined with *Price* is a subclass of *Positive*, while when it is combined with *Portion* it is a subclass of *Negative*. Some of the words in this group are not ambiguous per se, but are simply not indicative of any particular aspect category while at the same time not being generally applicable. An example is the concept *Fresh*, which is always positive, but can only be combined with certain aspects: it matches well with subclasses of *SustenanceMention* (e.g., "fresh ingredients") and *Ambience-Mention* (e.g., "a fresh decor"), but not with subclasses of, e.g., *PriceMention* or *LocationMention*.

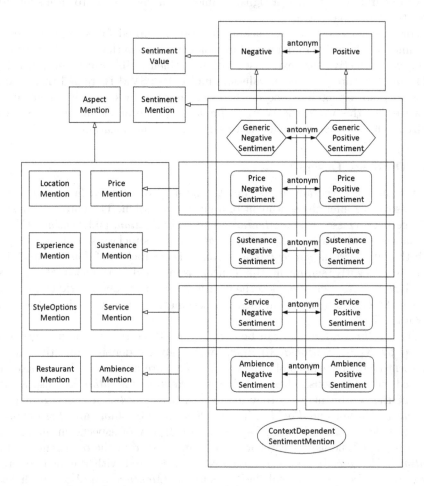

Fig. 3. A schematic overview of the main ontology classes

When a type-1 `SentimentMention` is encountered, its sentiment value is used for the classification of all aspects within scope (i.e., the sentence). While the scope of the complete sentence can be considered too broad, as generic sentiment words usually apply to just one aspect, not all of them, in preliminary experiments, it was shown that limiting the scope to a word window or to steps over the grammatical graph is sub-optimal. A type-2 `SentimentMention` is only used for the classification of aspects that belong to the implied aspect category. For type-3 `SentimentMentions`, a new class is created that is a subclass of both the property class and the aspect class. If the ontology provides any information on that combination, its sentiment value can be inferred. Otherwise, the ontology does not provide any sentiment information for that combination of aspect and property.

The ontology is lexicalized by attaching annotations of type *lex* to each concept. A concept can have multiple lexicalizations, and since this ontology is designed to work within a single domain, there are not many ambiguous words that would point to more than one concept in the ontology. Furthermore, some concepts have one or more *aspect* properties, which link a concept to one of the aspect categories in the data annotations. This means that such a concept, and all of its subclasses fit within that aspect category. For instance, the `Ambience` concept has an *aspect* property with the value "AMBIENCE#GENERAL". Last, concepts that are a subclass of `SentimentValue` have an *antonym* property that links that concept to its antonym (e.g., `Positive` has antonym `Negative`). This is used when found ontology concepts are subject to negation.

For this research, a domain ontology is manually constructed using the Onto-Clean methodology [6], and represented in OWL. To demonstrate the usefulness of ontologies, a choice is made for a relatively small, but focused ontology. Hence, it contains about 365 concepts, predominantly *AspectMentions*, but also including 53 type-1 *SentimentMentions*, 38 type-2 *SentimentMentions*, and 15 type-3 *SentimentMentions*. The maximum depth of the class hierarchy, not counting *owl:Thing* at the top, is 7.

4.2 Sentiment Computation

An overview of the sentiment computation method is shown in Algorithm 1, outlining the three cases for type-1, type-2, and type-3 sentiment expressions, respectively. The input for sentiment prediction is an ontology, an aspect, and whether or not a bag-of-words model is used as a backup method in case the ontology does not specify a single sentiment value for this aspect. The PRE-DICTSENTIMENT method starts by retrieving all the words that are linked to the ontology with a URI and that are in the sentence containing the aspect. It also checks whether the current word is negated or not. For this we look for the existence of a *neg* relation in the dependency graph, or the existence of a negation word in a window of three words preceding the current word [7].

In the next step, the type of the concept is retrieved from the ontology and, depending on its type, the algorithm executes one of three cases. As mentioned before, if the concept is a type-2 sentiment expression, then its inferred aspect category has to match with the current aspect, otherwise it is ignored. For example, when encountering the word "delicious", it leads to the concept `Delicious` due to the lexical property, which is a subclass of `SustenancePositiveProperty`.

1. `Delicious` $\equiv$ $\exists lex.\{$"delicious"$\}$
2. `Delicious` $\sqsubseteq$ `SustenancePositiveProperty`

3. SustenancePositiveProperty ⊑ Sustenance ⊓ Positive

Furthermore, the Sustenance concept is linked to several aspect categories that exist in the annotated dataset by means of an *aspect* property.

4. Sustenance ≡ ∃*aspect*.{"FOOD#QUALITY"}
5. Sustenance ≡ ∃*aspect*.{"FOOD#STYLE_OPTIONS"}

Hence, when the current aspect for which we want to compute the sentiment is annotated with either one of those two categories, the word "delicious" is considered to be of positive sentiment. For aspects with a different category, the same word is considered to be neutral.

Algorithm 1. Pseudocode for computing aspect sentiment

```
 1: function PREDICTSENTIMENT(Ontology o, Aspect a, boolean useBOW) : SentimentValue
 2:     Set<String> foundURIs = ⊥
 3:     Set<Word> words = GETWORDSWITHURI(GETSENTENCE(a))
 4:     for all Word w ∈ words do
 5:         boolean negated = ISNEGATED(w)
 6:         String URI = GETURI(o, w)
 7:         if ISTYPE1(o, URI) then
 8:             foundURIs = foundURIs ∪ GETSUPERCLASSES(o, URI, negated)
 9:         end if
10:         if ISTYPE2(o, URI) ∧ CATEGORYMATCHES(a, URI) then
11:             foundURIs = foundURIs ∪ GETSUPERCLASSES(o, URI, negated)
12:         end if
13:         if ISTYPE3(o, URI) then
14:             for all String relURI ∈ GETRELATEDASPECTMENTIONS(w) do
15:                 String newURI = ADDSUBCLASS(o, URI, relURI)
16:                 foundURIs = foundURIs ∪ GETSUPERCLASSES(o, newURI, negated)
17:             end for
18:         end if
19:     end for
20:     boolean foundPositive = (PositiveSentimentURI ∈ foundURIs)
21:     boolean foundNegative = (NegativeSentimentURI ∈ foundURIs)
22:     if foundPositive ∧ ¬ foundNegative then
23:         return Positive
24:     else if ¬ foundPositive ∧ foundNegative then
25:         return Negative
26:     else if useBOW then
27:         return GETBOWPREDICTION(a)
28:     else
29:         return GETMAJORITYCLASS // this is Positive in our data sets
30:     end if
31: end function
```

If the current SentimentMention is generic (type-1) or matching aspect-specific (type-2), then all superclasses are added to the set of *foundURIs*. If the current concept is a type-3, or context-dependent, SentimentMention, we need to check if it is related to an AspectMention and whether the combination of those two triggers a class axiom or not. Hence, we create a subclass with both the SentimentMention and the AspectMention as its direct superclasses, and add all (inferred) superclasses to the set of $foundURIs$. If there is a class axiom covering this combination, then the set of all inferred superclasses of this new subclass will include either Positive or Negative. When the current word was determined to be negated, the GETSUPERCLASSES method will add the antonym of each superclass instead, provided the ontology has an antonym for that class.

A good example of a Type-3 SentimentMention is Small, for which the ontology contains two sentiment-defining class axioms in the ontology, as well as a property that links the concept to the lexical representation "small".

1. Small $\equiv \exists lex.\{$ "small" $\}$
2. Small $\sqcap$ Price $\sqsubseteq$ Positive
3. Small $\sqcap$ Serving $\sqsubseteq$ Negative

Furthermore, Portion $\sqsubseteq$ Serving and we assume the review text contains a phrase like "small portions", "portions are small", or something similar. First, the words "small" and "portions" are linked to their respective ontology concepts by means of the lex attribute. Then, since, Small is neither a generic type-1 SentimentMention, nor an aspect-specific type-2 SentimentMention, it is paired with related words in the sentence to see if there are any class axioms to take advantage of. In this case, *small* is directly related to *portions*, so a new class is created called SmallPortion, that is a direct subclass of Small and Portion:

4. SmallPortion $\sqsubseteq$ Small $\sqcap$ Portion

This triggers the class axiom defined earlier, leading to

5. SmallPortion $\sqsubseteq$ Negative

Hence, Negative is added to the list of found classes, as all the other superclasses were already known as superclasses from the two individual classes.

The last step is to check whether the previous inferences have resulted in finding Positive or Negative. If we find one but not the other, the aspect is determined to have the found sentiment value. If either no sentiment value is found, or both sentiment values are found, the ontology does not give a definitive answer. In that case, if we opt to use a bag-of-words backup model, then it is used here. If bag-of-words is not used, we default to predicting Positive as that is the majority class.

4.3   Bag-of-Words Model

The bag-of-words model is used both as a baseline, and as a backup model in case the ontology cannot decide which sentiment to assign. For the most part, it is a classical bag-of-words model with binary features for each lemma in the review that contains the current aspect. In preliminary experiments, this gave better results than using the lemmas from the sentence only. We hypothesize that this might be due to the fact that with more words, it is easier to get the

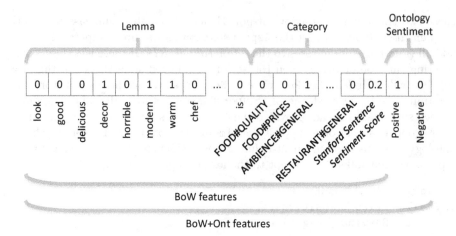

Fig. 4. Feature vector example for BoW+Ont model

overall sentiment of the review correctly, while for sentences, being a lot smaller, this would be harder. Given that the majority of the aspects follow the overall sentiment of the review, the effect of having more words to work with is larger than the effect of missing out on those aspects with a sentiment value different from the overall review. Furthermore, there is a set of dummy features to encode the aspect category as well as a numerical feature denoting the sentiment of the sentence. This sentiment score is computed by a sentiment component [15] in the Stanford CoreNLP package and falls roughly in the range of $[-1, 1]$. The model is trained as a multi-class Support Vector Machine that is able to predict positive, negative, and neutral. These last two features are aspect-specific and sentence-specific, so the model is technically not bound to predict the same sentiment for all aspects within the same review. The feature vector is illustrated in Fig. 4.

4.4   Bag-of-Words Model with Ontology Features

Besides the rule-based ontology method using the bag-of-words model as a backup, it also makes sense to use the bag-of-words model as the leading model and add ontology information in the form of additional features. Hence, we add two binary features to the bag-of-words model, one to denote that the presence of the Positive concept and one to denote the presence of the Negative concept (see Fig. 4). Furthermore, to keep it in line with the rule-based ontology method, when both Positive and Negative are present, this is regarded as having no information so both features will be zero.

5   Evaluation

To evaluate the performance of the proposed method and the baselines, all methods are trained on the training data and tested on the official test data. To determine the required (hyper)parameters, such as C and *gamma* for the SVM, about

20% of the training data is reserved as a validation set. After the optimal values have been found, the model is trained using those settings on the whole training data. This is done for both the 2015 and 2016 editions of Restaurant data set from the SemEval ABSA task and the results are shown in Tables 1 and 2, respectively. From the results, we can conclude that the ontology method on its own is not sufficient, which is caused by the fact that it only works for roughly 50% of the aspects and defaults to predicting the majority class for the other half. However, as evidenced by the increased performance for both hybrid methods, the ontology method is able to provide information that is complementary to the information contained in the bag-of-words.

Table 1. Comparison of the four methods on the 2015 data, using out-of-sample, in-sample, and 10-fold cross-validation performance.

| | Out-of-sample | In-sample | Cross-validation | | Paired two-sided t-test | | |
	Accuracy	Accuracy	Accuracy	St.dev	Ont	BoW	Ont+BoW
Ont	63.3%	79.4%	79.3%	0.0508			
BoW	80.0%	91.1%	81.9%	0.0510	5.98E−05		
Ont+BoW	82.5%	89.9%	84.2%	0.0444	4.67E−14	3.70E−09	
BoW+Ont	81.5%	91.7%	83.9%	0.0453	6.74E−09	2.95E−05	0.453

Table 2. Comparison of the four methods on the 2016 data, using out-of-sample, in-sample, and 10-fold cross-validation performance.

| | Out-of-sample | In-sample | Cross-validation | | Paired two-sided t-test | | |
	Accuracy	Accuracy	Accuracy	St.dev	Ont	BoW	Ont+BoW
Ont	76.1%	73.9%	74.2%	0.0527			
BoW	82.0%	90.0%	81.9%	0.0332	4.96E−14		
Ont+BoW	86.0%	89.3%	84.3%	0.0319	3.52E−20	1.83E−11	
BoW+Ont	85.7%	90.4%	83.7%	0.0370	7.63E−17	5.37E−06	0.0304

Since the results on the official test data sets are comparable with previous SemEval submissions, an overview of the top 6 best performing systems is given in Table 3 with our proposed system listed in bold. Note that the proposed system did not participate in SemEval together with these systems, so the sole function of Table 3 is to provide context for the listed performances.

For various amounts of training data, the accuracies of all four methods are plotted in Figs. 5 and 6. Since the Ont method does not depend on training data, its performance remains constant. However, we can see that both hybrid methods consistently outperform the BoW baseline and that the difference in performance widens with less training data, especially on the 2015 data. Since

Table 3. Ranks of the proposed method in top of SemEval-2015 and SemEval-2016 ranking

2015		2016	
Team	Accuracy	Team	Accuracy
Ont+BoW	82.49	XRCE	88.1%
sentiue	78.7%	IIT-T	86.7%
ECNU	78.1%	**Ont+BoW**	86.0%
Isislif	75.5%	NileT	85.5%
LT3	75.0%	IHS-R	83.9%
UFRGS	71.7%	ECNU	83.6%
wnlp	71.4%	AUEB	83.2%

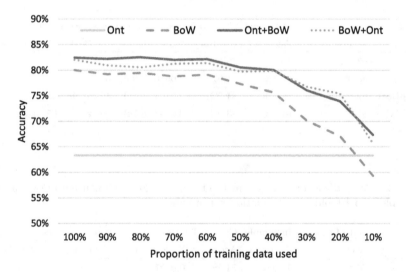

Fig. 5. The accuracy of all four methods at different amounts of training data (SemEval-2015)

the performance of both methods would depend on which part of the training data is randomly selected, the reported numbers are the average of 5 runs.

Because the ontology-based method so clearly distinguishes between different choices based on whether the positive and/or negative class is detected in the sentence, an overview is given in Table 4 of the performance of the ontology-based method (without BoW backup) as well as the bag-of-words model (without Ont features), split out per scenario. From this, it is evident that the knowledge-based approach complements the traditional machine learning method. When able to make a decision, the ontology-based method performs better than the bag-of-words model (top two lines in Table 4), but the reverse is true when the ontology does not have the information to come to a conclusion (bottom two

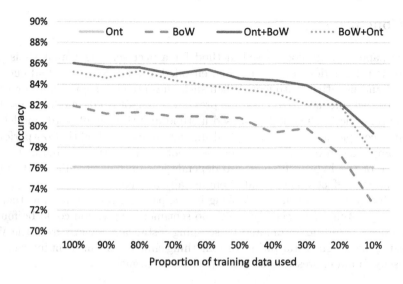

Fig. 6. The accuracy of all four methods at different amounts of training data (SemEval-2016)

lines in Table 4). In that case, it is better to use the bag-of-words model than to default to the majority class, which is the default behavior of the ontology-based method without BoW backup. Interestingly, the aspects for which both a positive and a negative sentiment is detected in the sentence are harder for the bag-of-words model to predict the sentiment for than sentences where the ontology did not find any sentiment expressions. The fact that the bag-of-words model does relatively well on the latter suggests omissions in the ontology. Clearly, the bag-of-words model is able to find some clues as to what sentiment to predict, even though these are not present in the ontology.

Table 4. The performance of the ontology and bag-of-words based on whether the Positive and/or Negative concept from the ontology was found or inferred for an aspect.

	Out-of-sample 2015 data			Out-of-sample 2016 data		
	Size	Acc. ontology	Acc. BoW	Size	Acc. ontology	Acc. BoW
Found only Positive	42.7%	**88.1%**	83.7%	55.3%	**93.1%**	87.6%
Found only Negative	9.8%	**94.0%**	85.5%	8.4%	**73.2%**	62.0%
Found both	4.3%	47.2%	**52.8%**	4.1%	62.9%	**68.6%**
Found none	43.2%	33.4%	**77.3%**	33.8%	50.7%	**79.7%**

6   Conclusion

In this paper, an ontology-based method for aspect sentiment analysis is presented. It utilizes domain information, encoded in an ontology, to find cues for positive and negative sentiment. When such cues are either not found, or when both positive and negative cues are present, a bag-of-words model is used as a backup method. The ontology-based method and the bag-of-words model are shown to complement each other, resulting in a hybrid method that outperforms both. Since the ontology-based model does not need any training data, the performance of the hybrid method also depends less on having sufficient training data, and this effect was illustrated empirically as well.

For future work, we suggest looking into expanding the ontology, as there is still a large group of aspects for which no sentiment expression could be found. This process could be automated by scraping restaurant reviews from the Web and using the assigned star rating, or something similar, as sentiment information to classify found expressions as being positive or negative.

References

1. Cambria, E., Hussain, A.: Sentic Computing: A Common-Sense-Based Framework for Concept-Level Sentiment Analysis. SC, vol. 1. Springer, Cham (2015). https://doi.org/10.1007/978-3-319-23654-4
2. Cambria, E., Olsher, D., Rajagopal, D.: SenticNet 3: a common and common-sense knowledge base for cognition-driven sentiment analysis. In: Proceedings of the 28th AAAI Conference on Artificial Intelligence (AAAI 2014), pp. 1515–1521. AAAI (2014)
3. Cambria, E.: Affective computing and sentiment analysis. IEEE Intell. Syst. **31**(2), 102–107 (2016)
4. Dragoni, M., Tettamanzi, A.G.B., da Costa Pereira, C.: A fuzzy system for concept-level sentiment analysis. In: Presutti, V., et al. (eds.) SemWebEval 2014. CCIS, vol. 475, pp. 21–27. Springer, Cham (2014). https://doi.org/10.1007/978-3-319-12024-9_2
5. Frank, E., Hall, M.A., Witten, I.H.: The WEKA Workbench. Online Appendix for "Data Mining: Practical Machine Learning Tools and Techniques", 4th edn. Morgan Kaufmann, Burlington (2016)
6. Guarino, N., Welty, C.: Evaluating ontological decisions with OntoClean. Commun. ACM **45**(2), 61–65 (2002)
7. Hogenboom, A., van Iterson, P., Heerschop, B., Frasincar, F., Kaymak, U.: Determining negation scope and strength in sentiment analysis. In: 2011 IEEE International Conference on Systems, Man, and Cybernetics (SMC 2011), pp. 2589–2594. IEEE (2011)
8. Lau, R.Y., Li, C., Liao, S.S.: Social analytics: learning fuzzy product ontologies for aspect-oriented sentiment analysis. Decis. Support Syst. **65**(C), 80–94 (2014)
9. Manning, C.D., Surdeanu, M., Bauer, J., Finkel, J., Bethard, S.J., McClosky, D.: The Stanford CoreNLP natural language processing toolkit. In: Proceedings of 52nd Annual Meeting of the ACL: System Demonstrations, pp. 55–60. ACL (2014)

10. Mullen, T., Collier, N.: Sentiment analysis using support vector machines with diverse information sources. In: Proceedings of the 2004 Conference on Empirical Methods in Natural Language Processing (EMNLP 2004), vol. 4, pp. 412–418. ACL (2004)

11. Pontiki, M., Galanis, D., Papageorgiou, H., Androutsopoulos, I., Manandhar, S., Al-Smadi, M., Al-Ayyoub, M., Zhao, Y., Qin, B., Clercq, O.D., Hoste, V., Apidianaki, M., Tannier, X., Loukachevitch, N., Kotelnikov, E., Bel, N., Jiménez-Zafra, S.M., Eryiğit, G.: SemEval-2016 task 5: aspect based sentiment analysis. In: Proceedings of the 10th International Workshop on Semantic Evaluation (SemEval 2016). ACL (2016)

12. Pontiki, M., Galanis, D., Papageorgiou, H., Manandhar, S., Androutsopoulos, I.: SemEval-2015 task 12: aspect based sentiment analysis. In: Proceedings of the Ninth International Workshop on Semantic Evaluation (SemEval 2015), pp. 486–495. ACL (2015)

13. Schouten, K., Frasincar, F.: Survey on aspect-level sentiment analysis. IEEE Trans. Knowl. Data Eng. **28**(3), 813–830 (2016)

14. Schouten, K., Frasincar, F., de Jong, F.: Ontology-enhanced aspect-based sentiment analysis. In: Cabot, J., De Virgilio, R., Torlone, R. (eds.) ICWE 2017. LNCS, vol. 10360, pp. 302–320. Springer, Cham (2017). https://doi.org/10.1007/978-3-319-60131-1_17

15. Socher, R., Perelygin, A., Wu, J.Y., Chuang, J., Manning, C.D., Ng, A.Y., Potts, C.P.: Recursive deep models for semantic compositionality over a sentiment treebank. In: Proceedings of the 2013 Conference on Empirical Methods on Natural Language Processing (EMNLP 2013), pp. 1631–1642. ACL (2013)

16. Xia, Y., Cambria, E., Hussain, A., Zhao, H.: Word polarity disambiguation using Bayesian model and opinion-level features. Cogn. Comput. **7**(3), 369–380 (2015)

Frankenstein: A Platform Enabling Reuse of Question Answering Components

Kuldeep Singh[1][(✉)], Andreas Both[2], Arun Sethupat[3], and Saeedeh Shekarpour[4]

[1] Fraunhofer IAIS, Sankt Augustin, Germany
`kuldeep.singh@iais.fraunhofer.de`
[2] DATEV eG, Nuremberg, Germany
`contact@andreasboth.de`
[3] University of Minnesota, Minneapolis, USA
`sethu021@umn.edu`
[4] University of Dayton, Dayton, USA
`sshekarpour1@udayton.edu`

Abstract. Recently remarkable trials of the question answering (QA) community yielded in developing core components accomplishing QA tasks. However, implementing a QA system still was costly. While aiming at providing an efficient way for the collaborative development of QA systems, the Frankenstein framework was developed that allows dynamic composition of question answering pipelines based on the input question. In this paper, we are providing a full range of reusable components as independent modules of Frankenstein populating the ecosystem leading to the option of creating many different components and QA systems. Just by using the components described here, 380 different QA systems can be created offering the QA community many new insights. Additionally, we are providing resources which support the performance analyses of QA tasks, QA components, and complete QA systems. Hence, Frankenstein is dedicated to improving the efficiency of the research process w.r.t. QA.

Keywords: Question answering · Reusability · Integration
Annotation model · Evaluation · Pipeline

Resource Type: Software Framework
Repository: https://github.com/WDAqua/Frankenstein
License: GNU General Public License v3.0

1 Introduction

Our research vision lies in *building up an infrastructure in which the state-of-the-art question answering (QA) core components can be easily integrated, run, and evaluated.* This vision was triggered by the fact that so far QA community

© Springer International Publishing AG, part of Springer Nature 2018
A. Gangemi et al. (Eds.): ESWC 2018, LNCS 10843, pp. 624–638, 2018.
https://doi.org/10.1007/978-3-319-93417-4_40

has released a considerable body of research as well as valuable running components accomplishing various QA tasks. To achieve our goal vision, we recently published foundations [3, 22, 25] being essential to solve the interoperability, integration and reusability issues. Initially, we published the qa vocabulary [22] as a flexible and extensible data model for annotating outputs of QA components. Thereafter, we proposed Qanary [3], a methodology for integrating components of QA systems which (i) utilises qa vocabulary for annotation, (ii) is independent of programming languages, (iii) is agnostic to domains and datasets, (iv) integrates components on different granularity levels. Lately, we published the Frankenstein [25], which is concerned with (1) a prediction mechanism to predict the performance of a component given a question and a required task; (2) an approach for composing performance-optimised pipelines[1] by integrating the most accurate components for the current QA tasks (i.e. the user's question). Frankenstein uses Qanary methodology to integrate state-of-the-art QA components within its architecture. However, we disregarded implementation details, reusability, configuration details, integration advantages of Frankenstein in [25], while this paper introduces Frankenstein as an application/platform addressing (a) how to build a new QA pipeline using 29 integrated components (b) how each component can be reused independently (c) how to evaluate the questions/texts. Hence, we *disassemble* the Frankenstein implementation to present a large set of reusable components from the QA community which can be run, evaluated and compared using the additional tools Frankenstein is offering. In other words, by decoupling Frankenstein architecture, the overall architecture becomes collection of 29 components as reusable resources, which can be either used to build QA pipeline or text analysis. We introduce major modules of Frankenstein which not only enable detecting optimum pipelines but also enable us to easily *run, evaluate* and *compare* any configured QA system. Frankenstein integrates 29 QA components by developing an individual wrapper for each component. Thus, end-user does not need to get involved in configuration and implementation details of components. In fact, these components can be directly reused to build QA systems. Consequently, just by using the QA components described in this paper 380 reasonable QA pipelines can be created with little effort. Hence, many new insights w.r.t. the performance of QA might be derived using these components and pipelines which also providing support for analytics as well as adopting additional components.

The contribution of this paper is to release the Frankenstein modules containing two kinds of open-source resources namely (i) reusable components as well as (ii) component-wise runners and evaluators. These resources are briefly described in the following:

[R1] **Reusable QA Components:** We collected 29 QA components accomplishing various QA tasks, i.e. named entity identification/recognition (NER), Named Entity Disambiguation (NED), Relation Linking (RL), Class Linking (CL), and Query Builder (QB). Then, we implemented a wrapper for every

---

[1] Please be noted that a full QA pipeline is composed of all the necessary tasks to transform a user-supplied textual question into a formal query.

included component which enables these popular tools to be easily integrated and reused in the Frankenstein framework. Therefore, these components can be used for building modular question answering systems which might analyse text, provide knowledge extraction etc. Furthermore, the wrapper annotates the output of the components using the qa vocabulary to provide machine readability and homogeneity among outputs of all components.

R2 **Evaluators for components and benchmarks:** We have automatised the process of running and evaluating any component integrated within Frankenstein. Thus, it enables evaluating and comparing QA components for individual stages of QA pipeline. Consequently, it is possible to analyse the performance of each QA component as well as of the whole QA systems which lead to completely new insights on the performance of particular QA tasks. Hence, researchers are enabled to easily uncover quality flaws and improve the performance while aiming at existing or novel fields of applicability. The evaluator components are independent of the input benchmark, and it is configurable in easy steps based on the requirement of the user.

This work is substantially impactful for QA and NLP communities because (1) it facilitates comparison of NED, NER, CL, and QB components w.r.t. any given gold standard; (2) it can easily integrate new and upcoming components at any stage of QA pipeline to ensure scalability. Thus, by this platform, the research community will be empowered to an automatic approach which easily reuses the core components and facilitates running and comparing the performance of components over any given benchmarks.

The rest of this paper is organised as follows. Section 2 presents the importance and impact of this work for the research community. Section 3 lists all of the components integrated so far along with their characteristics. The major modules of Frankenstein are presented in Sect. 4. Section 5 presents our plan for availability and sustainability of resources. Section 6 reviews the state-of-the-art and we close with the conclusion and future work in Sect. 7.

2   Broader Impact

Impact on QA Community. Recently, QA community was supported by the modular approaches such as openQA [14], Qanary [3,23], OKBQA [12], QALL-ME [7], and Frankenstein [25] aiming at integrating and reusing the existing QA core components. Frankenstein is a smart solution on top of Qanary to the limitations observed in the prior approaches. For example, openQA expects Java implementation of the components which is not possible in most of the cases. Also, openQA and QALL-ME have configuration difficulties and its components are not directly reusable in other approaches. More importantly these frameworks do not support a dynamic pipeline methodology. Moreover, the distinguished features united within Frankenstein makes it scalable, user-friendly and fully automatic which are rare in the prior approaches. Apart from these general characteristics, Frankenstein resources make the researchers needless of developing a QA full pipeline. In fact, researchers can focus on improving individual stages of QA pipelines while reusing $\boxed{\text{R1}}$ for other QA tasks to complete their pipeline.

For example, recent work on query builder component [33] has reused results of components for building and evaluating QA pipeline for its empirical study. In this way, QA researchers can focus on independent stages to make it more accurate and intelligent. Furthermore, using the automated process of evaluation (i.e. $\boxed{\text{R2}}$) within Frankenstein assists researchers to easily integrate their newly developed component and evaluate its performance against the-state-of-the-art components over any given benchmark.

Impact Beyond QA Community. Although the primary contribution of our work targets the QA community, other disciplines – particularly information extraction (IE) and Natural language processing (NLP) communities – are beneficial of Frankenstein because of the common tasks such as NED, RL, and CL. For example, 11 of NER components and 9 of NER components are integrated into Frankenstein and coupled with tools (i.e. $\boxed{\text{R1}}$ and $\boxed{\text{R2}}$). These components are also utilised in information retrieval and social media analytics for entity recognition and disambiguation on large textual corpora or a tweet corpus. Any given benchmark can be uploaded to $\boxed{\text{R2}}$ therefore possibly, a domain-specific evaluation of performance is published. Enabling these communities to reuse the existing components opens new perspectives for the future steps. For example, there is no meticulous study about the performance details as for where each component is well-performed or what is its pitfalls.

3   Reusable Components and Characteristics

Named Entity Recognition and Disambiguation Components. The aim of the named entity recognition (NER) task is to recognise the entities present in the question and the aim of named entity disambiguation is to link these spotted entities to its knowledge base mentions (e.g. for DBpedia [1]). For instance, in the example question "Who is the mayor of Berlin?", an ideal component performing NER task recognises `Berlin` as entity and components for NED task link it to its DBpedia mention `dbr:Berlin`[2]. The following NER and NED components are now available as reusable resources within Frankenstein.

1. **Entity Classifier** uses rule base grammar to extract entities in a text [5]. Its REST endpoint is available for wider use for NER task.
2. **Stanford NLP Tool:** Stanford named entity recogniser is an open source tool that uses Gibbs sampling for information extraction to spot entities in a text [8].
3. The **Babelfy** is a multilingual, graph-based approach that uses random walks and the densest subgraph algorithm to identify and disambiguate entities

---

[2] `dbr` corresponds to http://dbpedia.org/resource/.

present in a text [16]. We have used public API[3] of Babelfy for NER and NED task as separate components.

4. **AGDISTIS** is a graph based disambiguation tool that couples the HITS algorithm with label expansion strategies and string similarity measures to disambiguate entities in a given text [30]. The code is publicly available[4].

5. **DBpedia Spotlight** is a web service[5] that uses vector-space representation of entities and using the cosine similarity, recognise and disambiguate the entities [15].

6. **Tag Me** matches terms in a given text with Wikipedia, i.e. links text to recognise named entities. Furthermore, it uses the in-link graph and the page dataset to disambiguate recognised entities to its Wikipedia URls [6]. Tag Me is open source, and its REST API endpoint[6] is available for further (re-)use.

7. **Other APIs:** Besides the open-source available components, there are many commercial APIs that also provides open access for the research community. We have used such APIs for NER and NED tasks. Aylien API[7] is one of such APIs that uses natural language processing and machine learning for text analysis. Its text analysis module also consists of spotting and disambiguation entities. TextRazor[8], Dandelion[9], Ontotext[10] [13], Ambiverse[11], and MeaningCloud[12] are other APIs that have been used by us for NER and NED tasks.

Relation Linking Components. Relation Linking (RL) task aims to disambiguate the natural language (NL) relations present in a question to its corresponding mention in a knowledge base (KB). Considering our example question "Who is the mayor of Berlin?" a relation linker component would correctly link the text "mayor of" to `dbo:leader`[13]. For Relation Linking (RL), we rely on following open source components:

1. **ReMatch** maps natural language relations to knowledge graph properties by using dependency parsing characteristics with adjustment rules [18]. It then carries out a match against knowledge base properties, enhanced with word lexicon Wordnet via a set of similarity measures. It is an open source tool, and the code is available for reuse as RESTful service[14].

---

[3] http://babelfy.org/guide.

[4] https://github.com/dice-group/AGDISTIS.

[5] https://github.com/dbpedia-spotlight/dbpedia-spotlight.

[6] https://services.d4science.org/web/TagMe/documentation.

[7] http://docs.aylien.com/docs/introduction.

[8] https://www.textrazor.com/docs/rest.

[9] https://dandelion.eu/docs/api/datatxt/nex/getting-started/.

[10] http://docs.s4.ontotext.com/display/S4docs/REST+APIs.

[11] https://developer.ambiverse.com/.

[12] https://www.meaningcloud.com/developer.

[13] i.e. http://dbpedia.org/ontology/leader.

[14] https://github.com/mulangonando/ReMatch.

2. **RelationMatcher:** This component [24] devise semantic-index based representation of PATTY [19] (a knowledge corpus of linguistic patterns and its associated properties in DBpedia) and a search mechanism over this index with the purpose of enhancing relation linking task. We call this component RelationMatcher in Frankenstein. The main idea of this component to (1) improve linguistic similarity with cosine similarity by converting PATTY into vector space, (2) address the problem of PATTY patterns not being uniform by introducing some penalty function.

3. **RelMatch:** The disambiguation module (DM) of OKBQA framework [12] provides disambiguation of entities, classes, and relations present in a natural language question [12]. This module is the combination of AGDISTIS and disambiguation module of AutoSPARQL project [27]. We name it as RelMatch. The DM module is an independent component in OKBQA framework and available for reuse[15]. We name this component as "OKBQA relation Disambiguator".

4. **RNLIWOD:** Natural Language Interfaces for the Web of Data ((NLIWOD) community group[16] provides reusable components for enhancing the performance of QA systems. We utilise one of its components to build similar relation linking component[17]. We call this component "RNLIWOD relation linker".

5. **Spot Property:** This component is the combination of RNLIWOD and OKBQA disambiguation module [12] for relation linking task. We call this component Spot Property.

Components for Class Linking. To correctly generate a SPARQL query for a NL query, it is necessary to also disambiguate classes against the ontology.[18] For example, considering the question "Which river flow through Seoul" the word "river" needs to be mapped to `dbo:River`[19]. In Frankenstein, we deployed two components for this task:

1. **NLIWOD CLS:** NLIWOD Class Identifier is one among the several other tools provided by NLIWOD community for reuse. The code for class identifier is available on GitHub (see footnote 17).

2. **OKBQA Class Identifier:** This component is part of OKBQA disambiguation module (see footnote 15). We reused it for specific task of class linking.

Components for Query Builder. A query builder generates SPARQL queries using disambiguated entities, relations and classes which can serve as input from previous steps in QA pipeline. We have used two components for this task:

1. **NLIWOD QB:** Template based query builders are widely used in QA community for SPARQL query construction (e.g. HAWK [29], TBSL [27] etc).

---

[15] http://repository.okbqa.org/components/7.

[16] see also https://www.w3.org/community/nli/.

[17] https://github.com/dice-group/NLIWOD.

[18] https://www.w3.org/TR/rdf-schema/#ch_class.

[19] i.e. http://dbpedia.org/ontology/River.

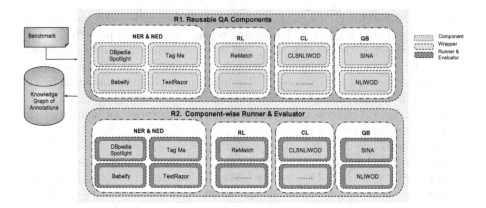

Fig. 1. Modules of Frankenstein (i) Reusable QA component wrappers and (ii) Evaluators.

We build a template based SPARQL query construction based on NLIWOD reusable resources (see footnote 17).

2. **SINA Query Builder:** SINA is a keyword and natural language query search engine that is based on Hidden Markov Models for choosing the correct dataset to query [21]. We decoupled the existing SINA implementation to use its Query builder as independent component.

The complete list of components, their expected input and output can be found in our public GitHub repository[20].

4   Approach for Building Reusable QA Components Within Frankenstein

Figure 1 represents the resource-wise (module-wise) architecture of Frankenstein. It is decoupled into two independent categories, (i) R1 which provides an individual wrapper for each component, and (ii) R2 which provides an individual runner & evaluator for every integrated component. In the following, these two sets of resources are described in more details.

4.1   Integration Approach and Its Challenges

Here, we present the integration approach and its associated challenges for integrating components accomplishing tasks of NER, NED, RL, CL, and QB using Qanary methodology applied in Frankenstein.

---

[20] The components are listed with file name Component_List.csv in https://github.com/WDAqua/Frankenstein.

Employing Qanary Methodology and qa ***Vocabulary.*** Qanary follows a micro service-based architecture where all components are accessible as RESTful services [3] to be possibly integrated into a Qanary QA process. A QA process within Qanary is a knowledge-driven process where input/output about *question, answer, annotations* generated in different steps of QA pipeline is conceptualized and annotated by the qa vocabulary. Each component integrated into a QA pipeline populates a local knowledge graph (typically its output is annotated by qa vocabulary) shared with other components within Qanary. This way establishes a standard communication between the components to be a foundation for exchangeability and composability.

In order to be able to annotate outputs generated by all the QA tasks, we had to extend the original version of qa vocabulary [22] by adding new concepts for RL, CL, and QB tasks, and reuse annotations of NER and NED s from [4]. E.g., to describe relations appeared in the natural language question, we introduce the annotation:

```
PREFIX rdf:   <http://www.w3.org/1999/02/22-rdf-syntax-ns#>
PREFIX rdfs:  <http://www.w3.org/2000/01/rdf-schema#>
qa:AnnotationOfRelation   rdf:type           owl:Class ;
                          rdfs:subClassOf    qa:AnnotationOfQuestion .
```

For instance, for the given question Who is the mayor of Berlin?, the annotated output of RNLIWOD component for RL task is shown below[21]. There, the output i.e., http://dbpedia.org/ontology/leaderName is annotated by the qa vocabulary. However w.r.t. qa extension, we also introduce further annotations qa:AnnotationOfClass and qa:AnnotationOfAnswerSPARQL for CL and QB tasks. We reused qa:AnnotationOfSpotInstance and qa:AnnotationOfInstance for NER and NED tasks from [4].

```
<tag:stardog:api:0.9278702836234858>
  a <http://www.wdaqua.eu/qa#AnnotationOfRelation>;
  oa:core/hasTarget _:bnode_5daa0259_7cbe_4e6c_8504_3f73463e0fd8_69;
  oa:hasBody <http://dbpedia.org/ontology/leaderName>;
  oa:annotatedBy <http://RNLIWOD.com>;
  oa:AnnotatedAt "2017-10-02T13:04:21.27"^^xsd:dateTime.
```

Alignment of QA Component Annotations. To ensure interoperability of a new component with existing ones, it has to express the semantics of its generated information using the qa vocabulary. We call this the *alignment* of the component to qa. There are at least three ways to align the knowledge of a component about the given question. (1) SPARQL queries: A component can execute SPARQL INSERTs in the knowledge base to generate new annotations expressed using the qa vocabulary, (2) OWL axioms: When a component already generates information in a specific vocabulary like the NIF vocabulary used by DBpedia Spotlight [15] OWL axioms might express the semantic relation to the specific vocabulary to the qa vocabulary (e.g. by defining owl:sameAs rules), (3) Distributed Ontology Language (DOL): It enables heterogeneous combinations

---

[21] Where oa is identified as http://www.w3.org/ns/openannotation/core/.

of ontologies written in different languages and logics [17]. We presented alignments of some existing components using the Qanary approach in [3] and reused similar alignments in this paper.

Wrapping Components and Challenges. During the development of Qanary wrappers in Frankenstein for different components, we encountered several challenges. The first challenge was to deal with interoperability issues among the components. For instance, a number of components were available as RESTful service, while a few ones [18,24] had the only open source code. Thus, we implemented a RESTful service on top of their source codes to make them easily reusable. The second challenge was associated with the heterogeneous output formats of the components. While some just provide output in JSON (e.g. [6,16]), some provide output in their own specific vocabulary (e.g. OntoText [13]). A more challenging case was decoupling SINA from its monolithic implementation required to change the complete package structure, dependencies, input format etc. of the original code to make it reusable.

4.2   Integrating Evaluation Module

Another set of valuable resources in Frankenstein is its evaluation modules. These modules have three configurations (1) benchmark creation, (2) pipeline configuration, and (3) evaluators. The configurations are briefly described below:

Creating Benchmarks for QA Tasks. We follow the methodology provided in [4,24] to create benchmarks for each individual stage of QA pipeline. For our running example Who is the mayor of Berlin? the corresponding SPARQL query in QALD-5[22] is:

```
PREFIX dbo: <http:/dbpedia.org/ontology/>
PREFIX res: <http:/dbpedia.org/resource/>
SELECT DISTINCT ?uri WHERE {
    res:Berlin dbo:leader ?uri.
}
```

For NED and RL tasks, our modules compare the detected named entities and relations by the components with the entities or relations mentioned in the corresponding SPARQL query (e.g. res:Berlin for NED and dbo:leader for RL). For class linking (CL) components, a similar approach is applied when questions contain class references. To assess the performance of QB components, we run the generated SPARQL query and the benchmark SPARQL query, then we compare the return answers. For our running question a query builder's performance is evaluated by For evaluating the complete pipeline, answers of the pipeline can be compared with the gold standard answers. In future, we plan to provide a simple configuration that directs the SPARQL results to GERBIL [31] which is an evaluation platform for complete QA processes.

---

[22] https://qald.sebastianwalter.org/index.php?x=home&q=5.

Pipeline Configuration and Runner. To ease the process of composing pipelines, we have automatised the whole process of configuring and running them using Bash scripts. Based on the required task, the users can choose the components, update the script and automatically run the pipeline in three different modes- (1) Frankenstein static, (2) Frankenstein dynamic, and (3) Frankenstein improved [25]. Below a sample Bash command is represented:

```
(a) ../serverUpdateAndRun.sh stanfordNER
(b) ../serverUpdateAndRun.sh Babefly AGDISTIS
```

The first command i.e., (a), runs a single component i.e., `stanfordNER` and the second command simultaneously run the two components `Babefly` and `AGDISTIS`. These scripts are very useful when the user want to evaluate 1000 s of questions at bulk. However, Frankenstein is provided with an in-built UI from Qanary for executing pipeline with a single input question.

Pipeline Execution. We implemented an independent module called LC-Evaluator within Frankenstein for executing pipelines. This module is customised in an automatic way for evaluating every individual component of the pipeline. This module obtains questions from a text file (supports csv and txt formats). A user can run a single component or a pipeline containing multiple components. However, the pipeline executor automatically passes the questions sequentially to the associated components. Relying on Qanary methodology, the outputs of components (annotations) are stored in a knowledge graph (i.e., Stardog v4.1.3[23]). Then, the pipeline executor reads the annotations of a particular question from the triplestore and creates an independent file using the turtle format (TTL) for the given input question with the label "questionID_component.ttl". This process is efficient in case of a large number of questions or text. The user can upload the text file containing annotations of a question, then execute the LC-Evaluator component, and all the output is automatically generated in form of `.ttl` extension for each question.

Pipeline Evaluator. We developed individual benchmarks for each step of QA pipeline used in evaluation module. Currently, since LC-QuAD [26] and QALD-5 [28] are the most popular and largest state-of-the-art gold standards, thus we developed individual benchmarks out of them for each separate QA task. In the future, we plan to provide additional benchmark files (e.g. for other QALD series). For NED task and for full pipeline evaluation, we plan to integrate pipeline evaluator to GERBIL platform [32]. Using these benchmarks, users are enabled to evaluate the performance of their components for any step of QA pipeline w.r.t. other QA components in Frankenstein.

5   Availability and Sustainability

In this section, we describe the accessibility of resources and our plan for its sustainability. We have published the source code of all the reusable components

---

[23] https://www.stardog.com/.

integrated in Frankenstein at our public GitHub repository[24] under GPL 3.0[25]. The GitHub repository includes following files:

- $\boxed{\text{R1}}$ in the Qanary folder. Detailed instructions have been provided how to install and use these components integrated using Qanary.
- $\boxed{\text{R2}}$ and detailed instructions to use are present in Evaluation folder.
- A complete component list of 29 integrated components of $\boxed{\text{R1}}$ with its input, output, API restriction is provided.

Regarding the sustainability, the resources are currently maintained by WDAqua project[26]. Once project ends in December 2018, the repository will be transferred to AskNow[27], an initiative to bring all the question answering tools and techniques under a single repository.

6   Related Work

A large number of QA systems were developed in the last years. This can be inferred from the number of QA systems (>38 in the last 5 years) that were evaluated against QALD[28], a popular benchmark for QA systems. Unfortunately, most QA systems follow a monolithic approach, not only at an implementation level but also conceptually. Hence, there is limited reusability for further research. As a consequence creating new QA systems is cumbersome and inefficient. On the other hand, many QA systems reuse existing components. For example, there are services for named entity identification (NEI) and disambiguation (NED) like DBpedia Spotlight [15] and AIDA [11] that are already reused across several QA systems. We are aware of at least three frameworks attempting to provide a reusable architecture for QA systems besides Frankenstein. QALL-ME [7] provides a reusable architecture skeleton for building multilingual QA systems. The main disadvantages are that it proposes a fixed pipeline that cannot be changed. openQA [1] allows combining multiple QA systems. The main downside is that it does not offer modularisation of QA systems and requires the QA systems to be implemented in Java using the provided interfaces. OKBQA [12] is a recent and effective attempt to develop question answering systems with a collaborative effort. OKBQA has 24 components whereas Frankenstein has 29 components. The limitation of OKBQA is that it divides the components into four tasks, namely template generation, disambiguation, query generation, and answer generation and follow strict input/output format. However, in Frankenstein and its resources, the number of tasks is not fixed. When a new component performing a new task needs to be integrated into Frankenstein, it can be done just be extending qa vocabulary which is not the case in OKBQA. Frankenstein is built on top of Qanary ecosystem that also provides entity annotation benchmarking

---

[24] https://github.com/WDAqua/Frankenstein.
[25] https://www.gnu.org/licenses/gpl.html.
[26] http://wdaqua.eu/.
[27] https://github.com/AskNowQA.
[28] https://qald.sebastianwalter.org.

and benchmark 6 QA components [4]. Combining efforts of Frankenstein, Qanary ecosystem and OKBQA will benefit the QA community, as we have reused many independently available QA components from OKBQA repository[29] and plan to provide Frankenstein components for OKBQA.

Besides the QA frameworks, evaluation frameworks like GERBIL [32] have emerged over the last years. GERBIL provides means to benchmark several QA systems on multiple datasets in a comparable and repeatable way fostering the open science methodology. Using GERBIL, many entity disambiguation components can be evaluated using different datasets. However, GERBIL does not provide support for other stages of QA pipeline besides entity annotation and linking. Very recently, this framework is further extended for benchmarking the complete QA pipelines [31]. We plan to integrate some of the reusable components of [R2] along with the possibility to benchmark complete QA pipeline in GERBIL.

Besides the question answering community, reusability of components has been a long trend in software engineering [2,10,20]. For example, Rainbow is a popular framework that uses reusable infrastructure to support the self adaptation of software systems [9]. Apache UIMA[30] is another open source project that supports reusable framework, tools, annotators to build software systems for knowledge extraction and information analysis.

7 Conclusion and Future Work

In this paper, we decoupled the Frankenstein architecture and presented reusable resources as an extension to the Qanary. Frankenstein is dedicated to extending the Qanary ecosystem by the following contributions:

[R1] It contributes a large set of new components to the ecosystem of reusable components initiated by the Qanary. Consequently, researchers and practitioners are now enabled to create a large set of different QA systems out-of-the-box due to the composability features inherited from the Qanary. We calculated that only by using the components directly provided by Frankenstein/Qanary 380 different ready-to-use QA pipelines can be created with small invest on time.

[R2] It provides additional evaluators and intermediate data representations as well as corresponding tools which enables researchers and practitioners to evaluate the tasks within the current QA process. Using these new data sources it is possible to establish quality improving operations on particular QA components or the whole QA process while aiming at improving the QA process for particular fields of applicability. Our recent publication (cf., [25]) already proved possible impact but the additional potential for the QA community is significant.

---

[29] http://repository.okbqa.org/components/.
[30] https://uima.apache.org/.

Hence, by using the resources provided by Frankenstein the efficiency for building and evaluating QA systems increased significantly for academics and industry which might lead to a boost of new research results.

Frankenstein is contributing to our broader research agenda of offering the QA community an efficient way of applying their research to a research field which is driven by many different fields, consequently requiring a collaborative approach to achieve significant progress.

In the future, we will add even more resources to Frankenstein and its environment, particularly data from evaluations on-top of well-known benchmarks (e.g. the QALD series) leading to new insights on the strengths and flaws of the QA components available in the community as well as machine learning tools enabling optimisation of QA systems with less manual efforts.

Acknowledgements. Parts of this work received funding from the European Union's Horizon 2020 research and innovation programme under the Marie Sklodowska-Curie grant agreement No. 642795, project: Answering Questions using Web Data (WDAqua). We thank Maria Esther Vidal for her valuable inputs.

References

1. Auer, S., Bizer, C., Kobilarov, G., Lehmann, J., Cyganiak, R., Ives, Z.: DBpedia: a nucleus for a web of open data. In: Aberer, K., Choi, K.-S., Noy, N., Allemang, D., Lee, K.-I., Nixon, L., Golbeck, J., Mika, P., Maynard, D., Mizoguchi, R., Schreiber, G., Cudré-Mauroux, P. (eds.) ASWC/ISWC -2007. LNCS, vol. 4825, pp. 722–735. Springer, Heidelberg (2007). https://doi.org/10.1007/978-3-540-76298-0_52

2. Batory, D.S., O'Malley, S.W.: The design and implementation of hierarchical software systems with reusable components. ACM Trans. Softw. Eng. Methodol. **1**, 355–398 (1992)

3. Both, A., Diefenbach, D., Singh, K., Shekarpour, S., Cherix, D., Lange, C.: Qanary – a methodology for vocabulary-driven open question answering systems. In: Sack, H., Blomqvist, E., d'Aquin, M., Ghidini, C., Ponzetto, S.P., Lange, C. (eds.) ESWC 2016. LNCS, vol. 9678, pp. 625–641. Springer, Cham (2016). https://doi.org/10.1007/978-3-319-34129-3_38

4. Diefenbach, D., Singh, K., Both, A., Cherix, D., Lange, C., Auer, S.: The qanary ecosystem: getting new insights by composing question answering pipelines. In: Cabot, J., De Virgilio, R., Torlone, R. (eds.) ICWE 2017. LNCS, vol. 10360, pp. 171–189. Springer, Cham (2017). https://doi.org/10.1007/978-3-319-60131-1_10

5. Dojchinovski, M., Kliegr, T.: Entityclassifier.eu: real-time classification of entities in text with Wikipedia. In: Blockeel, H., Kersting, K., Nijssen, S., Železný, F. (eds.) ECML PKDD 2013. LNCS (LNAI), vol. 8190, pp. 654–658. Springer, Heidelberg (2013). https://doi.org/10.1007/978-3-642-40994-3_48

6. Ferragina, P., Scaiella, U.: Fast and accurate annotation of short texts with Wikipedia pages. IEEE Softw. **29**(1), 70–75 (2012)

7. Ferrández, Ó., Spurk, C., Kouylekov, M., Dornescu, I., Ferrández, S., Negri, M., Izquierdo, R., Tomás, D., Orasan, C., Neumann, G., Magnini, B., González, J.L.V.: The QALL-ME framework: a specifiable-domain multilingual question answering architecture. J. Web Sem. **9**(2), 137–145 (2011)

8. Finkel, J.R., Grenager, T., Manning, C.D.: Incorporating non-local information into information extraction systems by Gibbs sampling. In: Proceedings of the Conference of 43rd Annual Meeting of the Association for Computational Linguistics, ACL 2005, 25–30 June 2005. University of Michigan, USA (2005)
9. Garlan, D., Cheng, S.-W., Huang, A.-C., Schmerl, B., Steenkiste, P.: Rainbow: architecture-based self-adaptation with reusable infrastructure. Computer **37**(10), 46–54 (2004)
10. Heineman, G.T., Councill, W.T.: Component-Based Software Engineering. Putting the Pieces Together, p. 5. Addison-Wesley, Boston (2001)
11. Ibrahim, Y., Amir Yosef, M., Weikum, G.: AIDA-social: entity linking on the social stream. In: Exploiting Semantic Annotations in Information Retrieval (2014)
12. Kim, J.-D., Unger, C., Ngonga Ngomo, A.-C., Freitas, A., Hahm, Y.-G., Kim, J., Nam, S., Choi, G.-H., Kim, J.-U., Usbeck, R., et al.: OKBQA framework for collaboration on developing natural language question answering systems (2017)
13. Kiryakov, A., Popov, B., Terziev, I., Manov, D., Ognyanoff, D.: Semantic annotation, indexing, and retrieval. J. Web Sem., 49–79 (2004)
14. Marx, E., Usbeck, R., Ngonga Ngomo, A.-C., Höffner, K., Lehmann, J., Auer, S.: Towards an open question answering architecture. In: Proceedings of the 10th International Conference on Semantic Systems, SEMANTICS 2014, Leipzig, Germany, 4–5 September 2014, pp. 57–60. ACM (2014)
15. Mendes, P.N., Jakob, M., García-Silva, A., Bizer, C.: DBpedia spotlight: shedding light on the web of documents. In: I-SEMANTICS (2011)
16. Moro, A., Raganato, A., Navigli, R.: Entity linking meets word sense disambiguation: a unified approach. TACL **2**, 231–244 (2014)
17. Mossakowski, T., Kutz, O., Lange, C.: Three semantics for the core of the distributed ontology language. In: Formal Ontology in Information Systems (2012)
18. Mulang, I.O., Singh, K., Orlandi, F.: Matching natural language relations to knowledge graph properties for question answering. In: Semantics 2017 (2017)
19. Nakashole, N., Weikum, G., Suchanek, F.M.: PATTY: a taxonomy of relational patterns with semantic types. In: EMNLP-CoNLL (2012)
20. Neighbors, J.M.: The Draco approach to constructing software from reusable components. IEEE Trans. Softw. Eng. **5**, 564–574 (1984)
21. Shekarpour, S., Marx, E., Ngonga Ngomo, A.-C., Auer, S.: SINA: semantic interpretation of user queries for question answering on interlinked data. J. Web Sem. **30**, 39–51 (2015)
22. Singh, K., Both, A., Diefenbach, D., Shekarpour, S.: Towards a message-driven vocabulary for promoting the interoperability of question answering systems. In: ICSC 2016, CA, USA, pp. 386–389 (2016)
23. Singh, K., Both, A., Diefenbach, D., Shekarpour, S., Cherix, D., Lange, C.: Qanary - the fast track to creating a question answering system with linked data technology. In: ESWC 2016 Satellite Events, Crete, Greece, pp. 183–188 (2016)
24. Singh, K., Mulang, I.O., Lytra, I., Jaradeh, M.Y., Sakor, A., Vidal, M.-E., Lange, C., Auer, S.: Capturing knowledge in semantically-typed relational patterns to enhance relation linking. In: Proceedings of the Knowledge Capture Conference, K-CAP 2017, Austin, TX, USA (2017)
25. Singh, K., Radhakrishna, A.S., Both, A., Shekarpour, S., Lytra, I., Usbeck, R., Vyas, A., Khikmatullaev, A., Punjani, D., Lange, C., Vidal, M.E., Lehmann, J., Auer, S.: Why reinvent the wheel-let's build question answering systems together. In: The Web Conference (WWW 2018) (2018, to appear)

26. Trivedi, P., Maheshwari, G., Dubey, M., Lehmann, J.: LC-QuAD: a corpus for complex question answering over knowledge graphs. In: d'Amato, C., Fernandez, M., Tamma, V., Lecue, F., Cudré-Mauroux, P., Sequeda, J., Lange, C., Heflin, J. (eds.) ISWC 2017. LNCS, vol. 10588, pp. 210–218. Springer, Cham (2017). https://doi.org/10.1007/978-3-319-68204-4_22

27. Unger, C., Bühmann, L., Lehmann, J., Ngonga Ngomo, A.-C., Gerber, D., Cimiano, P.: Template-based question answering over RDF data. In: WWW (2012)

28. Unger, C., Forascu, C., López, V., Ngonga Ngomo, A.-C., Cabrio, E., Cimiano, P., Walter, S.: Question answering over linked data (QALD-5). In: Working Notes of CLEF 2015 - Conference and Labs of the Evaluation forum, Toulouse, France, 8–11 September 2015. CEUR-WS.org (2015)

29. Usbeck, R., Ngonga Ngomo, A.-C., Bühmann, L., Unger, C.: HAWK-hybrid question answering using linked data. In: Proceedings of The Semantic Web. Latest Advances and New Domains - 12th European Semantic Web Conference, ESWC 2015, Portoroz, Slovenia, 31 May -4 June 2015 (2015)

30. Usbeck, R., Ngonga Ngomo, A.-C., Röder, M., Gerber, D., Coelho, S.A., Auer, S., Both, A.: AGDISTIS - graph-based disambiguation of named entities using linked data. In: Mika, P., Tudorache, T., Bernstein, A., Welty, C., Knoblock, C., Vrandečić, D., Groth, P., Noy, N., Janowicz, K., Goble, C. (eds.) ISWC 2014. LNCS, vol. 8796, pp. 457–471. Springer, Cham (2014). https://doi.org/10.1007/978-3-319-11964-9_29

31. Usbeck, R. Röder, M., Hoffmann, M., Conrads, F., Huthmann, J., Ngonga Ngomo, A.-C., Demmler, C., Unger, C.: Benchmarking question answering systems. Semant. Web J. (to be published)

32. Usbeck, R., Röder, M., Ngonga Ngomo, A.-C., Baron, C., Both, A., Brümmer, M., Ceccarelli, D., Cornolti, M., Cherix, D., Eickmann, B., Ferragina, P., Lemke, C., Moro, A., Navigli, R., Piccinno, F., Rizzo, G., Sack, H., Speck, R., Troncy, R., Waitelonis, J., Wesemann, L.: GERBIL: general entity annotator benchmarking framework. In: Proceedings of the 24th International Conference on World Wide Web, WWW 2015, Florence, Italy, 18–22 May 2015 (2015)

33. Zafar, H., Napolitano, G., Lehmann, J.: Formal query generation for question answering over knowledge bases. In: ESWC 2018 (2018, to Appear)

Querying APIs with SPARQL: Language and Worst-Case Optimal Algorithms

Matthieu Mosser, Fernando Pieressa⬤, Juan Reutter, Adrián Soto(✉)⬤,
and Domagoj Vrgoč⬤

Pontificia Universidad Católica de Chile, Santiago, Chile
assoto@uc.cl

Abstract. Although the amount of RDF data has been steadily increasing over the years, the majority of information on the Web is still residing in other formats, and is often not accessible to Semantic Web services. A lot of this data is available through APIs serving JSON documents. In this work we propose a way of extending SPARQL with the option to consume JSON APIs and integrate the obtained information into SPARQL query answers, thus obtaining a query language allowing to bring data from the "traditional" Web to the Semantic Web. Looking to evaluate these queries as efficiently as possible, we show that the main bottleneck is the amount of API requests, and present an algorithm that produces "worst-case optimal" query plans that reduce the number of requests as much as possible. We also do a set of experiments that empirically confirm the optimality of our approach.

1 Introduction

The Semantic Web provides a platform for publishing data on the Web via the Resource Description Framework (RDF). Having a common format for data dissemination allows for applications of increasing complexity since it enables them to access data obtained from different sources, or describing different entities. The most common way of accessing this information is through SPARQL endpoints; SPARQL is the standard language for accessing data on the Semantic Web [20], and a SPARQL endpoint is a simple interface where users can obtain the RDF data available on the server by executing a SPARQL query.

In the Web context it is rarely the case that one can obtain all the needed information from a single data source, and therefore it is necessary to draw the data from multiple servers or endpoints. In order to address this, a specific operator that allows parts of the query to access different SPARQL endpoints, called SERVICE, was included into the latest version of the language [30].

However, the majority of the data available on the Web today is still not published as RDF, which makes it difficult to connect it to Semantic Web services. A huge amount of this data is made available through Web APIs which use a variety of different formats to provide data to the users. It is therefore important to make all of this data available to Semantic Web technologies,

© Springer International Publishing AG, part of Springer Nature 2018
A. Gangemi et al. (Eds.): ESWC 2018, LNCS 10843, pp. 639–654, 2018.
https://doi.org/10.1007/978-3-319-93417-4_41

in order to create a truly connected Web. One way of achieving this is to extend the SERVICE operator of SPARQL with the ability to connect to Web APIs in the same way as it connects to other SPARQL endpoints. In this paper we make a first step in this direction by extending SERVICE with the option to connect to JSON APIs and incorporate their data into SPARQL query answers. We picked JSON because it is currently one of the most popular data formats used in Web APIs, but the results presented in the paper can easily be extended to any API format.

By allowing SPARQL to connect to an API we can extend the query answer with data obtained from a Web service, in real time and without any setup. Use cases for such an extension are numerous and can be particularly practical when the data obtained from the API changes very often (such as weather conditions, state of the traffic, etc.). To illustrate this let us consider the following example.

Example 1. We find ourselves in Scotland in order to do some hiking. We obtain a list of all Scottish mountains using the WikiData SPARQL endpoint, but we would prefer to hike in a place that is sunny. This information is not in WikiData, but is available through a weather service API called weather.api. This API implements HTTP requests, so for example to retrieve the weather on Ben Nevis, the highest mountain in the UK, we can issue a GET request with the IRI:

```
http://weather.api/request?q=Ben_Nevis
```

The API responds with a JSON document containing weather information, say of the form

```
{"timestamp": "24/10/2017 11:59:07",
 "temperature": 3, "description": "clear sky",
 "coord": {"lat": 56.79, "long": -5.02}}
```

Therefore, to obtain all Scottish mountains with a favourable weather all we need to do is call the API for each mountain on our list, keeping only those records where the weather condition is "clear sky". One can do this manually, but this quickly become cumbersome, particularly when the number of API calls is large. Instead, we propose to extend the functionality of SPARQL SERVICE, allowing it to communicate with JSON APIs such as the weather service above. For our example we can use the following (extended) query:

```
SELECT ?x ?l WHERE {
    ?x wdt:instanceOf wd:mountain.
    ?x wdt:locatedIn wd:Scotland.
    ?x rdfs:label ?l.
    SERVICE <http://weather.api/request?q={?l}>{(["description"]) AS (?d)}
    FILTER (?d = "clear sky")
}
```

The first part of our query is meant to retrieve the IRI and label of the mountain in WikiData. The extended SERVICE operator then takes the (instantiated)

URI template where the variable ?l is replaced with the label of the mountain, and upon executing the API call processes the received JSON document using an expression ["description"], which extracts from this document the value under the key description, and binds it to the variable ?d. Finally, we filter out those locations with undesirable weather conditions.   □

With the ability of querying endpoints and APIs in real time we face an even more challenging task: How do we evaluate such queries? Connecting to APIs poses an interesting new problem from a database perspective, as the bottleneck shifts from disk access to the amount of API calls. For example, when evaluating the query in Example 1, about 80% of the time is spent in API calls. This is mostly because HTTP requests are slower that disk access, something we cannot control. To gauge the time taken for APIs to respond to a GET request we did a quick study of five popular Web APIs. The results presented in Table 1 show us the minimum, the maximum, and the average time over our calls for each API.

Table 1. Min, max, and average response time (in seconds) of popular Web APIs based on ten typical calls they support.

	Yelp!	Twitter	Open weather	Wikipedia	StackOverflow	All
Min	0.4	0.4	0.4	0.8	0.3	0.3
Max	1.3	0.8	1.4	1.3	1.5	1.5
Avg	1.1	0.5	0.6	1.0	0.6	0.76

Hence, to evaluate these queries efficiently we need to understand how to produce a query plan for them that minimizes the number of calls to the API.

Contributions. Our main contributions can be summarized as follows:

– *Formalization.* We formalize the syntax and the semantics of the SERVICE extension which supports communication with JSON APIs. This is done in a modular way, similar to the SPARQL formalization of [28], making it easy to incorporate this extension into the language standard.
– *Implementation.* We provide a fully functional implementation of the extended SERVICE operator within the Apache Jena framework, and test its functionality on a range of queries over real world and synthetic data sources. We also set up a demo at [2] for trying out the new functionality.
– *Optimization.* Given that the most likely bottleneck for our queries is the number of API calls, we design, implement and test a series of optimizations based on the AGM bound [8,27] for estimating the number of intermediate results in relational joins, resulting in a worst case optimal algorithm for evaluating a large fragment of SPARQL patterns that uses remote SERVICE calls.

Related Work. Standard SERVICE that connects to SPARQL endpoints has been extensively studied in the literature [5–7,24,25]. The main conclusions regarding efficiency in this context resonate with our argument that the amount of calls to external endpoints is the main bottleneck for evaluation. For standard SERVICE there are several techniques we can use to alleviate this issue (see e.g. [6,7]), and for our implementation we opt for the one that minimizes the database load. In terms of bringing arbitrary API information into SPARQL most of the works [14,23,26,31] are based on the idea of building RDF wrappers for other formats. This is somewhat orthogonal to our approach and can be prohibitively expensive when the API data changes often (like in Example 1). The most similar to our work are the approaches of [9,15,16] that incorporate API data directly into SPARQL, but do not provide a worst-case optimal implementation, nor formal semantics of the extended SERVICE operation. Our paper is a continuation of the demo presentation [22].

Organization. We recall standard notions in Sect. 2. The formal definition and examples of the extended SERVICE are given in Sect. 3. The worst-case optimal algorithm for evaluating queries that use SERVICE is presented in Sect. 4. Experimental evaluation is given in Sect. 5. For space reasons detailed proofs can be found in our online appendix [1], and further examples at [2].

2   Preliminaries

RDF Graphs. Let $\mathbf{I}$, $\mathbf{L}$, and $\mathbf{B}$ be infinite disjoint sets of *IRIs*, *literals*, and *blank nodes*, respectively. The set of *RDF terms* $\mathbf{T}$ is $\mathbf{I} \cup \mathbf{L} \cup \mathbf{B}$. An *RDF triple* is a triple (s, p, o) from $\mathbf{T} \times \mathbf{I} \times \mathbf{T}$, where s is called *subject*, p *predicate*, and o *object*. An *(RDF) graph* is a finite set of RDF triples. For simplicity we assume that RDF databases consist of a single RDF graph, although our proposal can easily be extended to deal with datasets with multiple graphs.

SPARQL Queries. We assume the reader is familiar with the syntax and semantics of SPARQL 1.1 query language [20], as well as the abstraction proposed in [28]. We use this abstraction for our theoretical work, but examples are stated in the standard syntax.

Following [28], we define queries via *graph patterns*. Graph patterns are defined over terms $\mathbf{T}$ and an infinite set $\mathbf{V} = \{?x, ?y, \ldots\}$ of *variables*. The basic graph pattern is called a *triple pattern*, and is a tuple $t \in (\mathbf{I} \cup \mathbf{V}) \times (\mathbf{I} \cup \mathbf{V}) \times (\mathbf{I} \cup \mathbf{V} \cup \mathbf{L})$. All other graph patterns are defined recursively, using triple patterns, and operators AND, OPT, UNION, FILTER and SERVICE. We consider SERVICE patterns of the form $(P_1$ SERVICE a $P_2)$, with $a \in (\mathbf{I} \cup \mathbf{V})$ and P_1, P_2 graph patterns. If P is a graph pattern we denote the set of variables appearing in P by var(P). Finally, we define *SPARQL queries* as expressions of the form SELECT W WHERE $\{ P \}$, where P is a graph pattern, and W a set of variables.

We use the usual semantics of SPARQL, defined in terms of *mappings* [20,28]; that is, partial functions from the set of variables $\mathbf{V}$ to IRIs. The *domain* dom(μ) of a mapping μ is the set of variables on which μ is defined. Two mappings μ_1 and μ_2 are *compatible* (written as $\mu_1 \sim \mu_2$) if $\mu_1(?x) = \mu_2(?x)$ for all variables $?x$ in $\mathsf{dom}(\mu_1) \cap \mathsf{dom}(\mu_2)$. If $\mu_1 \sim \mu_2$, then we write $\mu_1 \cup \mu_2$ for the mapping obtained by extending μ_1 according to μ_2 on all the variables in $\mathsf{dom}(\mu_2)\backslash\mathsf{dom}(\mu_1)$. Note that if two mappings μ_1 and μ_2 have no variables in common they are always compatible, and that the empty mapping $\mu_\emptyset$ is compatible with any other mapping. For sets M_1 and M_2 of mappings we define their join as $M_1 \bowtie M_2 = \{\mu_1 \cup \mu_2 : \mu_1 \in M_1, \mu_2 \in M_2 \text{ and } \mu_1 \sim \mu_2\}$. Given a graph G and a pattern P, we denote the *evaluation* of a graph pattern P over G as the set of mappings $[\![P]\!]_G$. We refer to [20] for a full specification of the semantics.

3   Enabling SPARQL to Make JSON Calls

While theoretically one can use our ideas to connect SPARQL to any Web API, we concentrate on the so-called REST Web APIs, which communicate via HTTP requests, and we only consider requests of type GET. Of course, any implementation needs to take care of many other details when connecting to APIs (e.g. authentication). Our implementation takes this into consideration, but for space reasons here we just focus on the problem of evaluating these queries. An endpoint allowing the users to try the SERVICE-to-API functionality can be found at [2], and the source code of our implementation can be found at [3].

We assume that all API responses are JSON documents, and we use JSON *navigation conditions* to navigate and retrieve certain pieces of a JSON document, analogous to the way JSON documents are navigated in programming languages. For example, if we denote by J the JSON received in Example 1, we use $J[\texttt{"temperature"}]$ to obtain the temperature and $J[\texttt{"coord"}][\texttt{"lat"}]$ to obtain the latitude. We always assume that the general structure of the JSON response is known by users; this can be achieved, for example, by including the schema of the response in the documentation of the API (see e.g. [17,29]). This is a common assumption when one works with Web APIs.

3.1   Syntax and Semantics of the Extended SERVICE Operator

A *URI Template* [21] is an URI in which the query part may contain substrings of the form $\{?x\}$, for $?x$ in **V**. For example, the following is a URI template:

`http://weather.api/request?q={?city},{?country}`

The elements inside brackets are replaced by concrete values in order to make a request. In what follows, we will refer to the variables in such substrings of a URI template U as the variables of U, and denote them with $var(U)$.

Here is how we propose to extend SERVICE to enable calls to APIs. Let P_1 be a SPARQL pattern, U a URI template using only variables that appear in P_1, $?x_1, \ldots, ?x_m$ a sequence of pairwise distinct variables that do *not* appear in P_1, and $N_1, \ldots, N_m$ a sequence of JSON navigation instructions. Then the following is a SPARQL pattern, that we call a SERVICE-to-API pattern:

$$P_1 \text{ SERVICE } U\{(N_1, N_2, \ldots, N_m) \text{ AS } (?x_1, ?x_2, \ldots, ?x_m)\} \tag{1}$$

The intuition behind the evaluation of this operator over a graph G is the following. For each mapping μ in the evaluation $[\![P_1]\!]_G$ we instantiate every variable $?y$ in the URI template U with the value $\mu(?y)$, thus obtaining an IRI which is a valid API call[1]. We call the API with this instantiated IRI, obtaining a JSON document, say J. We then apply the navigation instruction N_1 to J and, assuming the instruction returns a basic JSON value, store this value into $?x_1$. Similarly, the value of N_2 applied to J is stored into $?x_2$, and so on. The mapping μ is then extended with the new variables $?x_1, \ldots, ?x_m$, which have been assigned values according to J and N_i. Notice that in (1) the pattern P_1 can again be an overloaded SERVICE pattern connecting to another JSON API, thus allowing us to obtain results from one or more APIs inside a single query.

Semantics. The semantics of a SERVICE-to-API pattern is defined in terms of the *instantiation* of an URI template U with respect to a mapping μ (denoted $\mu(U)$), which is simply the IRI that results by replacing each construct $\{?x\}$ in U with $\mu(?x)$. If there is some $?x \in \text{var}(U)$ such that $\mu(?x)$ is not defined, we define $\mu(U)$ as an invalid IRI that will result in an error when invoked.

Thus, every mapping produces an IRI, which we then use to execute an HTTP request to the API in the body of the IRI. Formally, given an URI template U and a mapping μ, we denote by $\text{call}(U, \mu)$ the result of the following process:

1. Instantiate U with respect to μ, obtaining the IRI $\mu(U)$.
2. Produce a request to the API signed by $(\mu(U))$, obtaining either a JSON document (in case the call is successful) or an error.

Informally, we refer to this process as the call to U with respect to the mapping μ. We adopt the convention that HTTP requests that do not give back a JSON document result in an error, that is, $\text{call}(U, \mu) = \text{error}$ whenever the request using U does not result in a valid JSON document.

For instance, if μ is a mapping, such that $\mu(?y) = \text{Ben\_Nevis}$, and $U = $ <http://weather.api/request?q={?y}> is a URI template, then $\mu(U) = $ <http://weather.api/request?q=Ben_Nevis>. When this request is executed against the weather API in the IRI, the answer result is either a JSON document similar to the one from Example 1, or it is an error.

To define the evaluation we need some more notation. First, if $?x$ is a variable and $t \in \mathbf{T}$, we use $?x \mapsto t$ to denote the mapping that assigns t to $?x$ and does not assign values to any other variable. Next, given a JSON document J, a navigation expression N, and a variable $?x$, we define the set $M_{?x \mapsto J[N]}$ that contains the single mapping $?x \mapsto J[N]$, when $J[N]$ is a basic JSON value (integer, string, or boolean), and is equal to the empty set $\emptyset$ otherwise. We also assume that $M_{?x \mapsto J[N]} = \emptyset$ when J is not a valid JSON document, or $J = \text{error}$.

The semantics of a SERVICE-to-API pattern P of the form (1) is then:

$$[\![P]\!]_G = \bigcup_{\mu \in [\![P_1]\!]_G} \{\mu\} \bowtie M_{?x_1 \mapsto \text{call}(U,\mu)[N_1]} \bowtie \cdots \bowtie M_{?x_m \mapsto \text{call}(U,\mu)[N_m]}$$

---

[1] Note that replacing $?y$ in a URI template with $\mu(?y)$ may result in a IRI, and not a URI, since some of the characters in $\mu(?y)$ need not be ASCII. To stress this, we use the term IRI for any instantiation of the variables in a URI template.

Therefore, a mapping in $\llbracket P \rrbracket_G$ is obtained by extending a mapping $\mu \in \llbracket P_1 \rrbracket_G$ by binding each $?x_i$ to $\mathrm{call}(U, \mu)[N_i]$. In the case that $\mathrm{call}(U, \mu) = \texttt{error}$ (e.g. when $\mu(?x)$ is not defined for some $?x \in \mathrm{var}(U)$), or that $\mathrm{call}(U, \mu)[N_i]$ is not a basic JSON value, the mapping μ will not be extended to the variables $?x_i$, and will not be part of $\llbracket P \rrbracket_G$. This is consistent with the default behaviour of SPARQL SERVICE [30] which makes the entire query fail if the SERVICE call results in an error. In the case that we want to implement the SILENT option for SERVICE which makes the latter behave as an OPTIONAL (see [30]), we would need to change the $\emptyset$ in the definition of $M_{?x \mapsto J[N]}$ to the empty mapping $\mu_\emptyset$, since this mapping can be joined with any other mapping.

For example, if $P_1 = \{?\texttt{x wdt:P131 wd:Q22 . ?x rdfs:label ?y}\}$ is a pattern, and $U = $ `<http://weather.api/request?q={?y}>` a URI template. Let

$$P = P_1 \text{ SERVICE } U\{([\texttt{"temperature"}]) \text{ AS } (?\texttt{t})\}$$

be the pattern we are evaluating over some RDF graph G, and assume that $\llbracket P_1 \rrbracket_G$ contains the following mappings.

	$?x$	$?y$
μ_1	wd:London	London
μ_2	wd:Berlin	Berlin

The evaluation of P over G is then obtained by extending mappings in $\llbracket P_1 \rrbracket_G$ using U. That is, we iterate over $\mu \in \llbracket P_1 \rrbracket_G$ one by one, execute the call $\mathrm{call}(U, \mu)$, and store the value $\mathrm{call}(U, \mu)[\texttt{"temperature"}]$ into the variable $?\texttt{t}$, in case that the obtained JSON value is a string, a number, or a boolean value, and discard μ otherwise. For example, if we assume that the calls are as follows,

$$\mathrm{call}(\mu_1, U) = \{\texttt{"temperature"}: 22\}, \ \mathrm{call}(\mu_2, U) = \texttt{error}$$

then the evaluation $\llbracket P \rrbracket_G$ will contain the following mapping

	$?x$	$?y$	$?t$
μ_1	wd:London	London	22

Since $\mathrm{call}(U, \mu_2)$ returns an error, the mapping μ_2 can not be extended, so it will not form a part of the output. In the case that the "SILENT semantic" is triggered, we would actually output μ_2 where $?t$ would not be bound.

3.2   A Basic Implementation

We propose a way to implement the overloaded SERVICE operation on top of any existing SPARQL engine without the need to modify its inner workings. To do so, we partition each query using this operator into smaller pieces, and evaluate these using the original engine whenever possible. More precisely, whenever we find a pattern of the form:

$$P \equiv P_1 \text{ SERVICE } U\{(N_1, N_2, \ldots, N_m) \text{ AS } (?x_1, ?x_2, \ldots, ?x_m)\}$$

in our query, we process it over a local database G using the following algorithm:

1. Compute $[\![P_1]\!]_G$ (recursively if P_1 contains a SERVICE-to-API pattern).
2. Define $M = \emptyset$.
3. For each $\mu \in [\![P_1]\!]_G$ do:
   - Execute call(U, μ); if an error is returned, start step 3 with the next μ;
   - For $1 \leq i \leq m$, compute $M_i = M_{?x_i \mapsto \text{call}(U,\mu)[N_i]}$; if there was an error, start step 3 with the next μ;
   - Let $M = M \cup (\{\mu\} \bowtie M_1 \bowtie \cdots \bowtie M_m)$.
4. Finally, to compute $[\![P]\!]_G$, serialize the set of mappings M using the VALUES operator, as in [7], to allow it to be used by the next graph pattern inside the WHERE clause in which it appears.

Regarding the final step, the obtained mappings need to be serialized in case P is followed by another graph pattern P_2. In particular, if we are processing a query of the form SELECT * WHERE $\{P . P_2\}$, with P as above, then P_2 needs to be able to access the values from the mappings matched to P.

With this implementation, the natural question is whether this basic implementation can be optimized. As we have mentioned, the bottleneck in our case is API calls, so if we want to evaluate queries as efficiently as possible we need to do the least amount of API calls as possible. There are a number of optimisations we can immediately implement in our basic implementation that will reduce the number of calls, and we try some of them in Sect. 5. However, next we consider a rather different question, for a broad subclass of patterns: Can we reformulate query plans to make sure we are making as few calls as possible?

4   A Worst-Case Optimal Algorithm

Our goal is to evaluate SERVICE-to-API queries as efficiently as possible, which implies minimising the number of API calls we issue when evaluating queries. This takes us to the following question: what is the minimal amount of API calls that need to be issued to answer a given query? Ideally, we would like to issue a number of calls that is linear in the size of the output of the query: for each tuple in the output we issue only those calls that are directly relevant for returning that particular tuple. But in general this is not possible. Consider the pattern

$$(?x_0, p, ?x_1) \text{ AND} \ldots \text{ AND } (?x_{m-1}, p, ?x_m) \text{ SERVICE } U\{(N) \text{ AS } ?y\},$$

where U uses variables $?x_1, \ldots, ?x_m$. Then the number of calls we would need to issue could be of order $|G|^m$ (e.g. when all triples in G are of the form (a, p, b)), but depending on the API data the output of this query may even be empty!

What we can do is aim to be optimal in the worst case, making sure that we do not make more calls than the number we would need in the worst case over all graphs and APIs of a given size. We can devise an algorithm that realises this bound if we focus on the smaller class of SPARQL queries made just from AND, FILTER and SERVICE-to-API operators, which we denote as *conjunctive patterns*. This is the federated analogue of conjunctive queries, which amount to roughly two thirds of the queries issued on the most popular endpoints on the Web, according to [12].

As we shall see, bounding the number of API calls for this fragment is intimately related to bounding the number of tuples in the output of a relational query, a subject that has received considerable attention in the past few years in the database community (see e.g. [8,18,27]). To illustrate this, let P be a conjunctive SERVICE-to-API pattern of the form:

$$(\ldots (((((P_1 \; S_1) \; \text{AND} \; P_2) \; S_2) \; \text{AND} \; P_3) \; S_3) \; \ldots \; P_n) \; S_n,$$

where each P_i is a SPARQL pattern (not using SERVICE) and each S_i is of the form SERVICE U $\{(N_1, N_2, \ldots, N_m)$ AS $(?x_1, ?x_2, \ldots, ?x_m)\}$, with U, m, and each of the N_js and $?x_j$s possibly different for different S_i.

We can now cast the problem of processing the query P over an RDF graph G as the problem of answering a join query over a relational database as follows. First, we simulate each SPARQL pattern P_i as a relation R_i with attributes corresponding to the variables of P_i (i.e. we project out the constants from each pattern in P_i since they do not contribute to an output). Second, we view an API U in each SERVICE call S_i described above as a relation T_i with *access methods* (see e.g. [10,13]), that has *output attributes* $?x_1, \ldots, ?x_m$ and input attributes var(U). Intuitively, an access method prevents arbitrary access to a relation; the only way to retrieve the tuples of a relation T with input attributes $A_1, \ldots, A_k$ is to provide appropriate values for $A_1, \ldots, A_k$, after which we are given all the tuples in T that match these input values.

It is now easy to see that answering P over G is the same as answering the following relational query[2]:

$$Q_P = R_1 \bowtie T_1 \bowtie R_2 \bowtie T_2 \bowtie \ldots \bowtie R_n \bowtie T_n, \tag{2}$$

over the relational instance that has the result of $[\![P_i]\!]_G$ stored in R_i, and the API data in T_i, for $i = 1 \ldots n$. Queries of the form (2) are known as *join queries*. Generally, join queries that do not use access methods are one of a few classes of queries for which we know tight bounds for the size of their outputs [8]. In what follows, we show that this bound can be extended even for queries that use access methods, such as (2), thus allowing us to solve the problem of evaluating SERVICE-to-API patterns.

We say that every action of matching values for the input attributes of one of the T_i's is a *call* operation, and we are able to offer a tight bound on the number of calls needed to answer a join query with access method such as Q_P. The main result we show in this section is the following. Take any feasible[3] join query Q, and a database D. Denote by $M_{Q,D}$ the maximum size of the projection of any relation appearing in Q over a single attribute in the database D. Furthermore, let $2^{\rho^*(Q,D)}$ be the AGM bound [8] of the query Q over D, i.e. the maximum

---

[2] We abuse the notation and denote relational joins using the same symbol that we use for mappings; the two operators are always distinguished by the context.

[3] Some queries with access methods may not be answerable, e.g. a query with only input attributes. We call queries that can be answered feasible (see Subsect. 4.1).

size of the output of Q over any relational database having the same number of tuples in each relation as D^4. Then we can prove the following:

Theorem 1. *Any feasible join query under access methods Q can be evaluated over any database instance D using a number of calls in*

$$O(M_{Q,D} \times 2^{\rho^*(Q,D)}).$$

To show this proposition we provide an algorithm that, given a query Q_P obtained from a conjunctive SERVICE-to-API pattern as described above, constructs a query plan for Q_P that is guaranteed to make a number of calls satisfying the bound. We also show that this bound is tight: one can construct a family of patterns and instances of growing size where one actually needs that amount of API calls. We then show that the query plan for Q_P can be used to construct a query plan for P that is worst-case optimal.

4.1   API Calls as Relational Access Methods

Our shift into the relational setting is to facilitate the presentation when merging all the different data paradigms involved in the evaluation of SERVICE-to-API patterns. In the following we assume familiarity with relational databases and schemas, and relational algebra. For a quick reference see [4].

We denote access methods with the same symbol as relations, but making explicit which of the attributes are input attributes, and which are output attributes. For example, an access method for a relation $R(A, B, C)$ with attributes A, B and C and where A and C are input attributes is denoted by $R(A^i, B^o, C^i)$ (letter i is a shorthand for *input* and o for *output*).

Access methods impose a restriction on the way queries are to be evaluated, as there are queries that cannot be evaluated at all. To formalise the intuition that access methods impose a restriction on the way queries are to be evaluated, we say that a relation R_i in a join query $R_1 \bowtie R_2 \bowtie \ldots \bowtie R_m$ is *covered* if all of its input attributes appear as an output in any of the relations $R_1, \ldots, R_{i-1}$. Then such a join query is said to be *feasible* when all its relations are covered. For example, consider a schema with relations $R(A^i, B^o)$, $S(A^o, B^o)$ and $T(B^i, C^o)$. Then $S \bowtie R \bowtie T$ is feasible: the input for R is an output of S and likewise for T. But $R \bowtie T$ is not feasible, as we do not have a source for the input of R. Naturally, a join query can only be answered if it is equivalent to a feasible query, so without loss of generality we focus on feasible queries. This is also enough for our purposes, as all queries we produce out of conjunctive SERVICE-to-API patterns are feasible.

We adopt the convention that, for a relation T with input attributes $A_1, \ldots, A_k$ and a set R of tuples having all attributes $A_1, \ldots, A_k$, the number of calls required to answer $R \bowtie T$ corresponds to the size of $\pi_{A_1,\ldots,A_k}(R)$.

---

[4] The bound is obtained by solving a specific linear program that depends on the query and the arity of the relations in D. We do not have space to formally state this result or this program, but refer to [19] for an excellent summary.

Intuitively, this means that we answer $R \bowtie T$ by selecting all different inputs coming from the tuples of R, and issue one call for each of these inputs.

We can then analyse the number of calls for the naive left-deep join plan for $Q = R_1 \bowtie R_2 \bowtie \ldots \bowtie R_m$, which corresponds to setting $\phi_1 = R_1$ and iteratively computing $\phi_{i+1} = \phi_i \bowtie R_{i+1}$ until we obtain ϕ_n, which corresponds to the answers of Q. How many calls do we issue? In the worst case where all except R_1 are relations representing APIs, we would need to issue a number of calls corresponding to the sum of the tuples in R_1, $R_1 \bowtie R_2$, and so on until $R_1 \bowtie \ldots \bowtie R_{n-1}$.

It turns out that we can provide a much better bound for the number of calls required, as well as an algorithm fulfilling this bound. In the following section we show an algorithm that produces a reformulation of Q whose left-deep plan issues a number of calls that agrees with the bound in Theorem 1. We also show that the algorithm is as good as it gets for arbitrary feasible join queries.

4.2   The Algorithm

Let $Q = R_1 \bowtie R_2 \bowtie \ldots \bowtie R_m$ be a feasible join query under some access methods, and let $A_1, \ldots, A_n$ be an enumeration of all attributes involved in Q, in order of their appearance. Without loss of generality, we assume that there is exactly one access method per relation in Q (if not one can construct two different relations, the worst case analysis does not change). We use $Input(R)$ to denote the set of all input attributes of the access method for R.

Our algorithm is inspired by the optimal plan exhibited in [8,19] for conjunctive queries without access methods. Starting from Q, we construct a query $Q^* = \Delta_n$, where the sequence $\Delta_1, \ldots, \Delta_n$ is defined as:

1. For Δ_1, let $S_1^1, \ldots, S_{k_1}^1$ be all relations in $\{R_1, \ldots, R_n\}$ whose set $Input(S_\ell^1)$ of input attributes is contained in $\{A_1\}$ (including relations with only output attributes). Then

$$\Delta_1 = \pi_{A_1}(S_1^1) \bowtie \ldots \bowtie \pi_{A_1}(S_{k_1}^1).$$

2. For Δ_i, let again $S_1^i, \ldots, S_{k_i}^i$ be all relations such that $Input(S_\ell^i)$ is contained in $\{A_1, \ldots, A_i\}$. Then

$$\Delta_i = \Delta_{i-1} \bowtie \pi_{A_1, \ldots, A_i}(S_1^i) \bowtie \ldots \bowtie \pi_{A_1, \ldots, A_i}(S_{k_i}^i).$$

The feasibility of Q^* follows from the fact that Q is feasible, so every relation with inputs $A_1, \ldots, A_i$ appears after all these attributes are outputs of previous relations, and we order attributes in the order of appearance. According to the construction above, we can write Q^* as a natural join $Q^* = E_1 \bowtie \ldots \bowtie E_r$ of expressions E_i which are join free. We then evaluate Q^* using a left-deep join plan: we start with the leftmost expression $\phi_1 = E_1 = \pi_{A_1}(R)$ in Q^*, where R is some relation, and then keep computing $\phi_t = \phi_{t-1} \bowtie E_t$, for $t = 2, \ldots, r$. The relation ϕ_r contains our output. Part of our plan involves caching the results of all relations R with $Input(R) \neq \emptyset$ the first time they are requested, and before we compute any projection over them. This only imposes a memory requirement that is at most as big as what we would need with the basic implementation.

Analysis. Recall that for a query Q and instance D, $M_{Q,D}$ is the maximum size of the projection of any relation in Q over a single attribute, and $2^{\rho^*(Q,D)}$ is the AGM bound of the query. Theorem 1 now follows from the following proposition.

Proposition 1. *Let Q be a feasible join query over a schema with access methods and D a relational instance of this schema. Let Q^* be the query constructed from Q by the algorithm above. Then the number of calls required to evaluate Q^* over D using a left-deep plan is in*

$$O(M_{Q,D} \times 2^{\rho^*(Q,D)}).$$

Let m be the number of relations in Q and n the total number of attributes. If we are considering combined complexity (i.e. Q is part of the input), the bound above raises to $O(m \times M_{Q,D} \times 2^{\rho^*(Q,D)})$ for the algorithm that does caching. Likewise, the number of calls is in $O(n \times m \times M_{Q,D} \times 2^{\rho^*(Q,D)})$ if we rule out the possibility of caching.

For the worst case optimality we show queries realising the upper bound.

Proposition 2. *There is a schema S, a query Q and a family of instances $(D_n)_{n \geq 1}$ such that: (i) The maximum size of the projection of a relation in D over one attribute is n, (ii) The AGM bound is n^2, and (iii) Any algorithm evaluating Q must make at least n^3 calls to a relation with access methods.*

SERVICE-to-API Patterns. To create optimal plans for SERVICE-to-API patterns, we need to show that (1) our translation from patterns to relational queries is sound and creates feasible queries, and (2) how to devise an optimal plan for the SERVICE pattern when given a plan for the relational query.

For (1), let P be a SERVICE-to-API pattern and Q_P the constructed join query, and consider an RDF graph G. Then the instance $I_{P,G}$ in which Q_P should be evaluated is defined next, and the correctness lemma follows.

- Each relation R_i in $I_{P,G}$ with attributes $?x_1, \ldots, ?x_m$ contains the set of tuples $\{(\mu(?x_1), \ldots, \mu(?x_n)) \mid \mu \in [\![P]\!]_G\}$.
- Each relation T_i in $I_{P,G}$ with input attributes $?z_1, \ldots, ?z_k$ and output attributes $?y_1, \ldots, ?y_p$ contains the set of tuples $\{(\mu(?z_1), \ldots, \mu(?z_k), \mu(?y_1), \ldots, \mu(?y_p)) \mid \mu \in [\![P]\!]_G\}$.

Lemma 1. *Let P be a conjunctive SERVICE-to-API pattern using variables $\{?x_1, \ldots, ?x_\ell\}$. A tuple $(a_1, \ldots, a_\ell)$ is in the evaluation of Q_P over $I_{P,G}$ if and only if there is a mapping $\mu \in [\![P]\!]_G$ such that $(a_1, \ldots, a_\ell) = (\mu(?x_1), \ldots, \mu(?x_\ell))$.*

While not obvious, this lemma also shows that the query is feasible, as long as P is not trivially unanswerable (i.e., as long as there is a graph G for which $[\![P]\!]_G$ is nonempty). Note that for finding the worst-case optimal plan for Q_P we do not need to construct the instance $I_{P,G}$, as this would amount to pre-computing the answer $[\![P]\!]_G$. Next, for (2): we show how the optimal plan for Q_P gives us an optimal plan for P:

Proposition 3. *Let P be SERVICE-to-API pattern, G an RDF graph and Q_P, $I_{P,G}$ the corresponding relational query with access methods and instance as constructed above. Then any optimal query plan Q^* for Q_P over an instance $I_{P,G}$ can be transformed (in polynomial time) into a query plan for P that evaluates P over G using the same amount of API calls as the evaluation of Q^*.*

Proof. The plan for P mimics step-by-step the plan for Q_P. That is, assume that $Q^* = E_1 \bowtie \cdots \bowtie E_r$ is the reformulation of Q_P from Sect. 4.2. Starting with $\phi_1 = E_1$, we iteratively compute the the set $[\![\phi_i]\!]_G = [\![\phi_{i-1}]\!]_G \bowtie E_i$ of mappings for each $i = 2 \cdots r$. This is done in the following way. Whenever $E_i = \pi_{?x_1, \ldots, ?x_p} R_i$, we evaluate the query SELECT $?x_1, \ldots, ?x_p$ WHERE P_i over G. On the other hand, if E_i is a relation using T_j for the first time, we call the API (because Q_P is feasible we will have all the needed input parameters), cache all the API results and then only retrieve the attributes that are not projected out in E_i. All subsequent appearances of T_j are evaluated directly on the cached JSON file. (If we are not using caching, then we need to call the API for each E_k, where $k > i$, that uses T_j.) Since the query ϕ_r is equivalent to Q^*, it is also equivalent to Q_P. Thus the output of this query plan correctly computes $[\![P]\!]_G$ by Lemma 1. The number of calls is worst-case optimal by Propositions 1 and 2.

5   Experiments

The goal of this section is to give empirical evidence that the worst-case optimal algorithm of Sect. 4 is indeed a superior evaluation strategy for executing queries that use API calls. We also constructed several real world use cases, for space reasons we defer them to the appendix [1] and the online demo [2].

Experimental Setup. To construct a benchmark for SERVICE-to-API patterns we reformulate the queries from the Berlin benchmark [11] by designating certain patterns in a query to act as an API call. We then run a battery of tests that simulate real-world APIs by sampling from the distributions of the response times presented in the introduction. The experiments where run on a 64-bit Windows 10 machine, with 8 GB of RAM, and Intel Core i5 7400 @ 3.0 GHz processor. Experiments were repeated five times, reporting the average value.

Adapting the Berlin Benchmark to Include API Calls. The Berlin benchmark dataset [11] is inspired by an e-commerce use case. It has products that are offered by vendors and are reviewed by users. Each one of those entities has properties related with them (such as labels, prices, etc.). The size of the dataset is specified by the user. To test our implementation we created a database of 5000 products consisting of 1959874 triples.

The benchmark itself is composed of 12 queries. Our adaptation consists of exposing the data of five recurrent patterns we find in the benchmark queries as APIs that return JSON documents. For instance, {?x bsbm:productPropertyNumericZ ?y} is one such pattern, where Z is a number between 1 and 5. This pattern is used to return the value of some numeric property of a product with the label ?x, so we created a (local) API route api/numeric-properties/{label}, that will give us all the values of numeric properties of an object. For instance, if a product with the IRI bsbm:Product1 has a label "Product 1", and its numerics properties are PropertyNumeric1 = 3, PropertyNumeric2 = 10, the request api/numeric-properties/Product_1 returns the JSON: "p1": 3, "p2": 10. The other API routes we implemented are similar (details can be found in [1]).

Next, we transform the original benchmark queries by replacing each pattern used when creating the APIs by a SERVICE call to the corresponding API. For instance, in the case of the "numeric properties API" described above, we replace each pattern of the form: {?product bsbm:productPropertyNumericX ?valueX}, by the following API call:

```
SERVICE <api/numeric-properties/{label}>{ ([``pX'']) AS (?valueX) }
```

We did a similar transformation for each pattern including entities served by our APIs. We ran all the queries of the Berlin Benchmark except Q6, Q9, and Q11, because they were too short to include API calls in their patterns. Also, we change the OPTIONAL operator in each query by AND, because the two are the same in terms of worst case optimal analysis.

Implementation. Our implementation of SERVICE-to-API patterns is done on top of Jena TBD 3.4.0 using Java 8 update 144. We differentiate three evaluation algorithms for SERVICE-to-API patterns: (1) *Vanilla*, the base implementation described in Sect. 3; (2) *Without duplicates*, the base algorithm that uses caching to avoid doing the same API call more than once; and (3) *WCO*, the worst-case optimal algorithm of Sect. 4.

Results. The number of API calls done for each of the three versions of our algorithm are shown in Table 2. As we see, avoiding duplicate calls reduces the number of calls to some extent, but the best results are obtained when we use the worst-case optimal algorithm. We also measured the total time taken for the evaluation of these queries. Query times range from over 8000 s to just 0.7 s for the Vanilla version, and in average the use of *WCO* reduces by 40% the running times of the queries. Full details in [1].

Table 2. The number of API call per query for each algorithm. WCO plans average 53% reduction in API calls.

	Q1	Q2	Q3	Q4	Q5	Q7	Q8	Q10	Q12	AVG
Vanilla	5332	77	5000	5066	2254	15	1	7	1	0%
W/O duplicates	4990	3	4990	4990	608	15	1	7	1	20%
WCO	2971	0	3284	4571	608	13	0	0	1	53%

6   Conclusion

In this paper we propose a way to allow SPARQL queries to connect to HTTP APIs returning JSON. We describe the syntax and the semantics of this extension, show how it can be implemented on top of existing SPARQL engines, provide a worst-case optimal algorithm for processing these queries, and demonstrate the usefulness of this algorithm both formally and in practice.

In future work, we plan to support formats other than JSON, and explore how to support it in public endpoints. It would be also interesting to test how issuing API calls in parallel affects the running times of different algorithms. Another line of work we plan to pursue is to support automatic entity resolution based on an API answer, thus allowing us to transform API information back into IRIs to be used again by SPARQL, instead of just literals.

Acknowledgements. Work funded by the Millennium Nucleus Center for Semantic Web Research under Grant NC120004.

References

1. Online Appendix. http://dvrgoc.ing.puc.cl/APIs/SPARQLAPI.pdf
2. Online demo of SERVICE-to-API. http://67.205.159.121/query/#/
3. SERVICE-to-API implementation. http://67.205.159.121/query/code/
4. Abiteboul, S., Hull, R., Vianu, V.: Foundations of Databases. Addison-Wesley, Boston (1995)
5. Buil-Aranda, C., Arenas, M., Corcho, O.: Semantics and optimization of the SPARQL 1.1 federation extension. In: Antoniou, G., Grobelnik, M., Simperl, E., Parsia, B., Plexousakis, D., De Leenheer, P., Pan, J. (eds.) ESWC 2011. LNCS, vol. 6644, pp. 1–15. Springer, Heidelberg (2011). https://doi.org/10.1007/978-3-642-21064-8_1
6. Aranda, C.B., Arenas, M., Corcho, Ó., Polleres, A.: Federating queries in SPARQL 1.1: syntax, semantics and evaluation. J. Web Sem. **18**(1), 1–17 (2013)
7. Buil-Aranda, C., Polleres, A., Umbrich, J.: Strategies for executing federated queries in SPARQL1.1. In: Mika, P., et al. (eds.) ISWC 2014. LNCS, vol. 8797, pp. 390–405. Springer, Cham (2014). https://doi.org/10.1007/978-3-319-11915-1_25
8. Atserias, A., Grohe, M., Marx, D.: Size bounds and query plans for relational joins. SIAM J. Comput. **42**(4), 1737–1767 (2013)
9. Battle, R., Benson, E.: Bridging the semantic web and web 2.0 with representational state transfer (REST). J. Web Sem. **6**(1), 61–69 (2008)
10. Benedikt, M., Leblay, J., Tsamoura, E.: Querying with access patterns and integrity constraints. PVLDB **8**(6), 690–701 (2015)
11. Bizer, C., Schultz, A.: The Berlin SPARQL benchmark. Int. J. Semant. Web Inf. Syst. **5**(2), 1–24 (2009)
12. Bonifati, A., Martens, W., Timm, T.: An analytical study of large SPARQL query logs. CoRR, abs/1708.00363 (2017)
13. Calì, A., Martinenghi, D.: Querying data under access limitations. In: ICDE 2008, pp. 50–59 (2008)
14. Dimou, A., Sande, M.V., Colpaert, P., Verborgh, R., Mannens, E., de Walle, R.V.: RML: A generic language for integrated RDF mappings of heterogeneous data. In: LDOW (2014)

15. Fafalios, P., Tzitzikas, Y.: SPARQL-LD: a SPARQL extension for fetching and querying linked data. In: ISWC Demos (2015)
16. Fafalios, P., Yannakis, T., Tzitzikas, Y.: Querying the web of data with SPARQL-LD. In: Fuhr, N., Kovács, L., Risse, T., Nejdl, W. (eds.) TPDL 2016. LNCS, vol. 9819, pp. 175–187. Springer, Cham (2016). https://doi.org/10.1007/978-3-319-43997-6_14
17. Galiegue, F., Zyp, K.: JSON schema: core definitions and terminology. Internet Eng. Task Force (IETF) (2013)
18. Gottlob, G., Lee, S.T., Valiant, G., Valiant, P.: Size and treewidth bounds for conjunctive queries. J. ACM **59**(3), 16:1–16:35 (2012)
19. Grohe, M.: Bounds and algorithms for joins via fractional edge covers. In: Tannen, V., Wong, L., Libkin, L., Fan, W., Tan, W.-C., Fourman, M. (eds.) In Search of Elegance in the Theory and Practice of Computation. LNCS, vol. 8000, pp. 321–338. Springer, Heidelberg (2013). https://doi.org/10.1007/978-3-642-41660-6_17
20. Harris, S., Seaborne, A.: SPARQL 1.1 query language. W3C (2013)
21. IETF: URI Template (2012). https://tools.ietf.org/html/rfc6570
22. Junemann, M., Reutter, J.L., Soto, A., Vrgoč, D.: Incorporating API data into SPARQL query answers. In: ISWC 2016 Posters and Demos (2016)
23. Kobayashi, N., Ishii, M., Takahashi, S., Mochizuki, Y., Matsushima, A., Toyoda, T.: Semantic-JSON. Nucleic Acids Res. **39**, 533–540 (2011)
24. Montoya, G., Vidal, M., Acosta, M.: A heuristic-based approach for planning federated SPARQL queries. In: COLD 2012 (2012)
25. Montoya, G., Vidal, M.-E., Corcho, O., Ruckhaus, E., Buil-Aranda, C.: Benchmarking federated SPARQL query engines: are existing testbeds enough? In: Cudré-Mauroux, P., et al. (eds.) ISWC 2012. LNCS, vol. 7650, pp. 313–324. Springer, Heidelberg (2012). https://doi.org/10.1007/978-3-642-35173-0_21
26. Müller, H., Cabral, L., Morshed, A., Shu, Y.: From restful to SPARQL: a case study on generating semantic sensor data. In: ISWC 2013, pp. 51–66 (2013)
27. Ngo, H.Q., Porat, E., Ré, C., Rudra, A.: Worst-case optimal join algorithms. In: PODS 2012, pp. 37–48 (2012)
28. Pérez, J., Arenas, M., Gutierrez, C.: nSPARQL: a navigational language for RDF. J. Web Sem. **8**(4), 255–270 (2010)
29. Pezoa, F., Reutter, J.L., Suarez, F., Ugarte, M., Vrgoč, D.: Foundations of JSON Schema. In: WWW 2016, pp. 263–273 (2016)
30. Prud'hommeaux, E., Buil-Aranda, C.: SPARQL 1.1 Federated Query. W3C Recommendation, 21, 113 (2013)
31. Rietveld, L., Hoekstra, R.: YASGUI: not just another SPARQL client. In: Cimiano, P., Fernández, M., Lopez, V., Schlobach, S., Völker, J. (eds.) ESWC 2013. LNCS, vol. 7955, pp. 78–86. Springer, Heidelberg (2013). https://doi.org/10.1007/978-3-642-41242-4_7

Task-Oriented Complex Ontology Alignment: Two Alignment Evaluation Sets

Élodie Thiéblin$^{(\boxtimes)}$ ⓘ, Ollivier Haemmerlé, Nathalie Hernandez ⓘ, and Cassia Trojahn ⓘ

Institut de Recherche Informatique de Toulouse, Toulouse, France
{elodie.thieblin,ollivier.haemmerle,nathalie.hernandez,
cassia.trojahn}@irit.fr

Abstract. Simple ontology alignments, largely studied, link one entity of a source ontology to one entity of a target ontology. One of the limitations of these alignments is, however, their lack of expressiveness which can be overcome by complex alignments. Although different complex matching approaches have emerged in the literature, there is a lack of complex reference alignments on which these approaches can be systematically evaluated. This paper proposes two sets of complex alignments between 10 pairs of ontologies from the well-known OAEI conference simple alignment dataset.

The methodology for creating the alignment sets is described and takes into account the use of the alignments for two tasks: ontology merging and query rewriting. The ontology merging alignment set contains 313 correspondences and the query rewriting one 431. We report an evaluation of state-of-the art complex matchers on the proposed alignment sets.

1 Introduction

Ontology matching is an essential task for the management of the semantic heterogeneity in open environments. The matching process aims at generating a set of correspondences (i.e., an alignment) between the entities of different ontologies. Two 'paradigms' organise the field. While approaches generating simple correspondences are limited in expressiveness by linking single entities, complex matching approaches are able to generate correspondences which better express the relationships between entities of different ontologies. Earlier works have introduced the need for complex alignments [15,35]. Different approaches for generating such complex alignments have been proposed in the literature. While the proposal of [23,24] relies on correspondence patterns, the one in [13] uses knowledge-rules in Markov-Logic Networks. Those in [20,21,36] rely on statistical methods and correspondence patterns and the one in [18] deals with genetic programming. Finally, the approach in [22] uses path-finding algorithms combined with statistical techniques. Despite the progress in the field, there is a

© Springer International Publishing AG, part of Springer Nature 2018
A. Gangemi et al. (Eds.): ESWC 2018, LNCS 10843, pp. 655–670, 2018.
https://doi.org/10.1007/978-3-319-93417-4_42

lack of reference alignment sets on which the complex approaches can be systematically evaluated. Most efforts on evaluation are still dedicated to the matching approaches dealing with simple alignments. Systematic evaluation of them has been carried out over the last fifteen years in the context of the Ontology Alignment Evaluation Campaigns (OAEI)[1]. Even though this well-known campaign proposes a task-oriented benchmark (the OA4QA track [28]), it does not propose a complex alignment benchmark.

This paper proposes two alignment sets to extend the OAEI conference track dataset [3,37] with complex alignments for two task purposes: ontology merging and query rewriting. The methodology for creating the alignment sets is described and takes into account the use of the alignments for the two targeted tasks. Here we extend the work presented in [31,33] by enriching the alignment sets with new pairs of ontologies and by considering the task for which the alignment is needed. We also extend the work in [33] and by adding an evaluation of three systems [13,23,24]. We extend the evaluation of the work in [31] by adding a new system described in [13] and by evaluating all the three systems on the ten pairs of ontologies for each alignment set.

The paper is organised as follows. After giving the background on ontology matching (Sect. 2) and discussing related work (Sect. 3), we describe the methodology to create the alignments (Sect. 4), the alignments themselves and their use for the evaluation of approaches (Sect. 5). We conclude with a discussion on the proposal.

2   Background

In this paper, the complex correspondences are described using the $\mathcal{DL}$ syntax and the ontologies are graphically represented using the diagrammatic logic formalism defined in [29].

2.1   Complex Alignments

Ontology matching [8] is the process of generating an alignment A between two ontologies: a source ontology o_1 and a target ontology o_2. A is directional, denoted $A_{o_1 \rightarrow o_2}$. $A_{o_1 \rightarrow o_2}$ is a set of correspondences. Each correspondence is a triple $\langle e_{o_1}, e_{o_2}, r \rangle$. e_{o_1} and e_{o_2} are the members of the correspondence: they can be single ontology entities (classes, object properties, data properties, instances, values) of respectively o_1 and o_2 or constructions of these entities using constructors or transformation functions. r is a relation, e.g., equivalence ($\equiv$), subsumption ($\sqsubseteq$, $\sqsupseteq$), or disjointedness ($\perp$) between e_{o_1} and e_{o_2}.

The ontologies used in the following examples are illustrated in Fig. 1. We consider two types of correspondences depending on the type of their members:

- if the correspondence is **simple**, both e_{o_1} and e_{o_2} are atomic entities: one single entity is matched with another single entity, e.g., o_1:*Person* $\equiv$ o_2:*Human* is a simple correspondence.

---

[1] http://oaei.ontologymatching.org/.

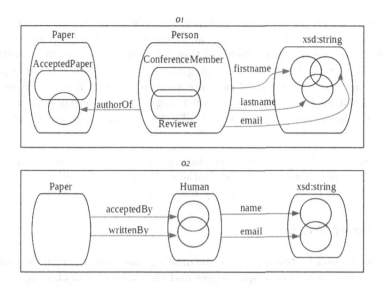

Fig. 1. Fragment of two heterogeneous ontologies.

- if the correspondence is **complex**, at least one of e_{o_1} or e_{o_2} involves a constructor or a transformation function. For example,
    1. o_1:$authorOf \equiv o_2$:$writtenBy^-$ is a complex correspondence with the *inverseOf* constructor.
    2. o_1:$AcceptedPaper \equiv \exists\, o_2$:$acceptedBy.\top$ is a complex correspondence with the *existential* constructor.
    3. o_2:$name$ is the concatenation of the o_1:$firstname$ and o_1:$lastname$ is a complex correspondence with a transformation function[2].

A complex alignment contains at least one complex correspondence. We will refer to approaches that generate simple alignments as *simple matchers* and to approaches that generate complex alignments as *complex matchers*.

2.2 Tasks Involving Complex Ontology Alignments

Ontology alignments are the basis for various tasks, from data translation, query rewriting, ontology merging to ontology versioning. These tasks all serve the purpose of interoperability. Here, we assume that the different tasks may have different correspondence expressiveness needs. We chose to focus this study on two tasks:

- **Ontology merging** is the process of creating a new ontology from two aligned ontologies (e.g., o_1 and o_2). The correspondences of the alignment are transformed into axioms of the resulting ontology. For decidability reasons, the expressiveness of the correspondences for ontology merging has to

---

[2] Transformation functions can not be formalised into DL.

be $\mathcal{SROIQ}$ [11]. For ontology merging, the Alignment API [5] can deal with complex alignments by translating an alignment into OWL axioms.

– **Query rewriting** is the process of transforming a query expressed with the terms of o_1 with the terms of o_2 using an alignment between o_1 and o_2. The correspondences of the alignment are used as rules to rewrite the original query (written for o_1). For query rewriting, there is no expressiveness constraint. Various systems such as [4,16,30] deal with complex correspondences for SPARQL query rewriting.

For example, the correspondence stating that o_2:*name* is equivalent to the concatenation of o_1:*firstname* and o_1:*lastname* (Fig. 1) is not applicable for ontology merging but is adequate for query rewriting.

3   Related Work

This paper focuses on two aspects of the ontology matching field, the approaches for generating complex correspondences and the evaluation of these approaches (on complex correspondences and task-oriented). We discuss state-of-the-art approaches on these two aspects leaving besides matching of other kind of schemata.

3.1   Complex Ontology Matchers

The complex matchers can be classified according to use of ontology-level or instance-level knowledge. A second axis of classification is whether the matchers rely on correspondence patterns, defined by Scharffe [25] as "templates of ontology correspondences that occur quite often". We classify the complex matchers on these two axis. In the first group, the approaches rely on correspondence patterns and on ontology-level knowledge only. The approaches in [23,24] propose a set of matching conditions to detect correspondences that fit a set of patterns, The conditions are based on the labels of the ontologies entities, the structures of these ontologies and the compatibility of the data-types of data-properties.Both approaches take a simple reference alignment as input. The approach in [24] uses linguistic evidence whereas the one in [23] mostly relies on string similarity.

In the second group, the approaches do not rely on correspondence patterns and do not require instance-level knowledge: KAOM (Knowledge-Aware Ontology Matching) [13] is a system which uses Markov Logic Networks as a probabilistic framework for ontology matching. The Markov Logic formulae use the entities of the two ontologies (source and target) as *constants*, the relations between entities and the input *knowledge rules* as *evidence*. The *knowledge rules* can be axioms of an ontology or they can be specified by the user.

Approaches which rely on correspondence patterns and require instance-level knowledge are: the ones in [20,21,36] which use statistical information based on the linked instances to find *class by attribute-value* correspondences [36], conjunctions of *attribute-value* pairs [20] or *attribute-value = attribute-set-of-values* correspondences [21].

Approaches not relying on correspondence patterns and require instance-level knowledge are: the one in [18] which uses genetic programming on instances to find correspondences with transformation functions between two knowledge bases. The one in [22] uses a path-finding algorithm to find correspondences between two knowledge bases with common instances. The correspondences found by this approach are of the form *property path = property path*.

The different approaches discussed above are generic in the sense that they generate alignments regardless to a specific task.

3.2 Evaluation of Matchers

Alignments generated by matchers can be evaluated in different ways [6]. One way consists in comparing alignments to reference ones (gold standard). However, constructing such references is a time-consuming task. In the lack of such resources, alternatives include manual labelling on sample alignments, alignment coherence measurements [17] and checking the conservativity principle violation of alignments [27]. Furthermore, the quality of a matcher can be assessed regarding its suitability for a specific task or application [10,12,28]. Finally, alternative approaches for validating alignments consider the generation of natural language questions to support end-users in the validation task [1] or validation of correspondences using graph-based algorithms in a semi-automatic way [26].

While matching evaluation has been focused on simple alignments, complex evaluation has been addressed to a lesser extent. Although a large spectrum of matching cases are proposed in the OAEI, e.g., involving synthetically generated or real case datasets with large or domain-specific ontologies, these datasets are limited to alignments with simple correspondences.

A notable alignment set has been proposed between biology ontologies in [19]. In opposite to "classical" alignments, the correspondences of these alignments, called "compound alignments" involve entities from more than two ontologies. For example, $o_1{:}A \equiv o_2{:}B \sqcap o_3{:}C$ is a compound correspondence. We consider these correspondences as complex since one of its member contains a constructor but it is out of the scope of our study.

In the context of complex ontology matching where reference alignments are scarce, the evaluation of most approaches is done by manually calculating the precision of the correspondences generated by the systems. The approaches in [21,23,24,36] manually classified the output correspondences (or a subset of them) into true positives and false positives to calculate the precision. The approaches in [23,24] were tested on the ontologies of the OAEI conference and benchmark tracks (the simple reference alignment being used as input). The approaches in [21,36] were tested on Linked Open Data (LOD) repositories with large amounts of linked instances such as Yago, DBpedia, Geonames, etc.

With respect to the few complex alignment sets, most of them have been created to evaluate specific complex matching approaches. In order to evaluate the recall of his approach [36] proposed an algorithm to create an evaluation data set. This data set is composed of a synthetic ontology containing 50 classes with known *Class-by-attribute-value* (a correspondence pattern) correspondences with DBpedia and 50 classes with no known correspondences with DBpedia. Both ontologies are populated with the same instances. The approach of [21] estimated their recall based on the recurring pattern between DBpedia and Geonames: $\exists dbpedia{:}country.\{theCountryInstance\}$ $\equiv \exists geonames{:}countryCode.\{theCountryCode\}$ where $theCountryInstance$ is a country instance of DBpedia such as $dbpedia{:}Spain$ and $theCountryCode$ is a country code such as *"ES"*. They estimated the number of occurrences of this pattern between these ontologies and calculated the recall based on this estimation. The approach of [22] manually created a set of reference correspondences between two ontologies on which their approach was evaluated. On the nine reference correspondences, only two can not be expressed with simple correspondences. The closer approach to ours is from [13] who extended the conference dataset with complex alignments to evaluate their knowledge-rule based approach. However, the methodology used for the construction of the dataset is not specified and the dataset is not available online.

In order to evaluate and compare alignment approaches, we need evaluation alignment sets. As discussed above, complex matchers have been evaluated on custom evaluation alignment sets. When the evaluation used a reference alignment, manually or automatically created, it usually contained correspondences which match only one pattern (*Class by attribute-value* for [36], *attribute-value = attribute-value* for [21]).

Approaches using complex correspondences for a given purpose (query rewriting for example), also propose alignment sets created for their needs, even though they have not been used for matcher evaluation. For instance, the authors of [16] present a set of complex correspondences used for query rewriting[3]. However, they are not in a reusable format and only concern a pair of ontologies. In [32], complex correspondences between agronomic ontologies were manually created for query rewriting on the LOD.

Regarding task-oriented evaluation, the authors of [12] propose ontology alignment evaluation methods for different task purposes: thesaurus merging, and data translation. The OA4QA track[4] of the OAEI [28] evaluate the suitability of an alignment for the task of query answering. This evaluation dataset consists in the conference track ontologies populated with DBLP, 18 queries over these ontologies and simple reference alignments. The evaluation approach for query rewriting proposed by [10] is very similar. The evaluation data set they propose is also composed of queries, populated instances and simple reference alignments.

Summing up, there is no complex alignment set for systematic evaluation. Moreover, complex alignments are not considered in task-oriented alignment evaluation.

---

[3] http://www.music.tuc.gr/projects/sw/sparql-rw/.

[4] http://www.cs.ox.ac.uk/isg/projects/Optique/oaei/oa4qa/index.html.

4   Methodology

In this section, we introduce the methodology that we have followed to create the complex alignment sets. As we focus on the purpose of an alignment to create it, we describe a general methodology followed by the variants for the generation of complex alignments dedicated to the ontology merging and query rewriting tasks. As this methodology has been manually applied, it is not suitable for large scale ontologies. Its purpose is to translate each entity of the source ontology o_1 using entities of the target ontology o_2 when possible for a given task.

The methodology focuses on finding as many complex correspondences as possible with an equivalence relation according to the task purpose of the alignment.

The methodology is articulated in the following steps:

1. Find simple equivalence correspondences between o_1 and o_2. If such an alignment is not available, state-of-the-art approaches [2] may provide a good base which can be manually enriched.
2. Create the complex correspondences based on the simple correspondences so that the complex correspondences fit the purpose of the alignment.
3. Express the correspondences in a reusable format (e.g., EDOAL).

Methodology to Create an Alignment for Ontology Merging. The first requirement for ontology merging is that the resulting ontology must be coherent; in other words, the reasoning on the resulting ontology must be decidable. Therefore, the alignment should follow the $\mathcal{SROIQ}$ expressiveness and should not bring any incoherence. In order to create the ontology merging alignment, we have followed this methodology. It relies on a reasoner to verify the coherence of the merged ontology.

1. Create a new ontology importing o_1 and o_2.
2. Express the simple correspondences obtained at the first step of the global methodology in OWL. Check coherence of the merged ontology (e.g., run a reasoner).
3. For each entity of o_1 not in a simple equivalence correspondence, find an equivalent construction with entities from o_2. This step is done by descending the ontology hierarchy (start by the most general to the most specific).
   - if a construction is found, add the new axiom to the merged ontology and verify the coherence of the merged ontology (e.g., run a reasoner).
   - if no equivalent construction if found, look for the closest super entity or construction from o_2 entities. If this axiom is not already entailed by the reasoner, add it to the merged ontology.
4. Repeat previous step but for each entity of o_2.

We chose this top-down approach because if an axiom is defined on an entity e_1, the reasoner will be able to make inferences on the entities subsumed by e_1 [14].

Methodology to Create an Alignment for Query Rewriting. For query rewriting, the expressiveness of the correspondences is not limited. Transformation functions can be used as well as "complex roles" (which are limited in $\mathcal{SROIQ}$). Therefore, the coherence of an alignment can not be verified because a reasoning task is not decidable given its expressiveness.

1. For each entity e_1 of o_1 not in a simple equivalence correspondence, find a semantically equivalent construction from o_2 entities.
   - if no equivalence can be found, look for the closest entity or construction from o_2 subsumed by e_1.
2. Repeat previous step for each entity of o_2 (constructions from o_1 entities).

We chose this subsumption entity substitute as for each entity, we wish to get the closest interpretation possible without errors: therefore the biggest subset of the interpretation of e_1.

5   Complex Alignment Set

The alignment sets are available at https://doi.org/10.6084/m9.figshare. 4986368.v7 under CC-BY license. They are expressed in first-order logic (FOL), EDOAL [5], and OWL for the ontology merging alignment set. EDOAL can express transformations as well as logical relations between entities. We have considered this language instead of others (SWRL, etc.) as it is integrated in the Alignment API and extends the Alignment Format (*standard de facto* in OAEI campaigns). Before describing the proposed alignment sets, we introduce the Conference dataset from which our dataset have been built.

5.1   The Conference Dataset

The conference dataset[5] was proposed in [34]. It has been widely used [37], especially in the OAEI where it is a reference evaluation track. This dataset is composed of 16 ontologies on the conference organisation domain and simple reference alignments between 7 of these ontologies. These ontologies were developed individually. The motivation for the extension of this dataset is that the ontologies are real ontologies (as opposed to synthetic ones), they are expressive and largely used for evaluation in the field. Moreover, the reference alignments of simple correspondences between these ontologies are available.

   We chose five ontologies among the ones in the reference simple alignment for their different number of classes (c.f. Table 1): *cmt*, *conference* (Sofsem), *confOf* (confTool), *edas* and *ekaw*.

   The reference simple alignment set was modified during the first step of the methodology. The modifications made to the reference simple alignment set are specified in the FOL alignments on the repository.

---

[5] http://oaei.ontologymatching.org/2016/conference/index.html and http://owl.vse. cz:8080/ontofarm/.

Table 1. Number of entities by type of each ontology

	cmt	conference	confOf	edas	ekaw
Classes	30	60	39	104	74
Object properties	49	46	13	30	33
Data properties	10	18	23	20	0

5.2 Conference Complex Alignment Sets

We detail in the following the two created alignment sets. The methodology was manually applied by one expert to all ten pairs of ontologies involving the five ontologies.The number of entities of these ontologies is detailed in Table 1. The merged ontologies were checked for coherence with the HermiT reasoner [9].

The **ontology merging set** is composed of 313 correspondences with 54 complex correspondences from 9 different patterns (some patterns are composite). The **query rewriting set** is composed of 431 correspondences with 191 complex correspondences from 17 different patterns (some patterns are composite). The patterns are used *a posteriori* for analysing the alignments, not as a basis for the correspondence creation. An extensive list of the patterns can be found in [25]. The meaning of the abbreviations used in the following tables is: CAT: $A \equiv \exists b.C$, CAE: $A \equiv \exists b.\top$, $CIAE$: $A \equiv \exists b^-.\top$, CAV: $A \equiv \exists b.\{v\}$, *neg*: not exists, *dom*: domain restriction, *range*: range restriction, *dom/range*: domain and range restriction, *transfo*: transformation function on data properties, *c*: class, *rel*: object property, *prop*: data property, *chain*: a chain of properties (object properties and/or data properties), *IP*: inverse of an object property, *composite* or *compo*: different patterns in same correspondence. The domain restriction and range restriction patterns are correspondence patterns from [25] and not OWL axiom primitives.

Figure 2 details the number of correspondences per pattern per alignment set. Table 2 presents examples of correspondences from the alignment sets and their type. The ontology merging alignment set has no correspondences implementing domain or range restrictions, transformation functions, inverse properties, union of object or data properties, or negation. Indeed, these correspondences are either not in $\mathcal{SROIQ}$ (domain restriction, range restriction, union of properties) or were already entailed by previous correspondences (inverse property, negation). The number of subsumptions also differs in both alignment sets because of the adopted methodology (*top-down* subsumption in ontology merging and *bottom-up* subsumption in query rewriting). Nevertheless, the subsumption correspondences are frequent in both sets. As above, we argue that complex correspondences come as a complement to simple correspondences. Their need may be different depending on the task purpose of the alignment. For query rewriting for instance, complex correspondences represent 44% of all correspondences whereas they only represent 17% of all correspondences for ontology merging.

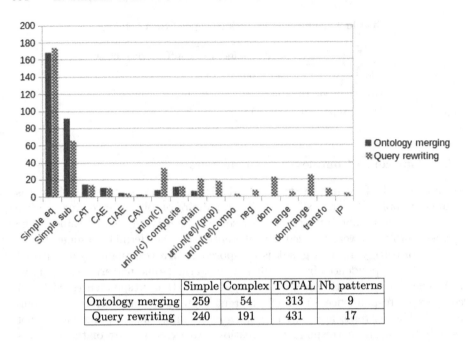

	Simple	Complex	TOTAL	Nb patterns
Ontology merging	259	54	313	9
Query rewriting	240	191	431	17

Fig. 2. Number of correspondences per pattern per alignment set.

6   Evaluation of Complex Matchers

As populating the ontologies to match with common instances would add new considerations for the evaluation dataset (e.g., choice and quantity of the instances), we chose to evaluate the available approaches that do not need common instances, as those described in [13,23,24].

We evaluated the matchers on the correspondences they output. Here we only evaluate the complex correspondences output as simple correspondences are taken as input by the approaches. For ontology merging, we only consider the $\mathcal{SROIQ}$ compliant correspondences output by the approaches. The correspondences output by the matchers were classified into true positive or false positive by comparison with each reference alignment set. A true positive is semantically equivalent to a correspondence in the reference alignment. The number of true and false positive are presented in Table 3. The knowledge rules needed for [13] were the one used in the evaluation section of the paper.

Precision, recall and F-measure have been computed for both alignment sets as shown in Fig. 3. For both purposes, Ritze2010 [24] has the best precision but its recall is the lowest. For the purpose of ontology merging, Ritze2009 [23] has a slightly better F-measure than the others. For query rewriting, Jiang2016 (KAOM) [13] is better than the other approaches. The precision of KAOM is better on the query rewriting alignment set than on the ontology merging set because most of its output correspondences are of the form o_1:role $\equiv$ o_2:otherRole.o_2:Domain.o_2:Range. Such correspondences are not expressible in

Table 2. Example of correspondences of the query rewriting alignment set and their type (correspondence pattern)

Source entity	rel.	Target construction	Type
cmt:ConferenceMember	≡	∃ edas:isMemberOf.⊤	CAE
edas:AcceptedPaper	≡	∃cmt:hasDecision.cmt: Acceptance ⊔ ∃cmt:acceptedBy.⊤	union(c) composite
conference:Submitted_ contribution	≡	∃cmt:submitPaper⁻.⊤	CIAE
conference:Reviewed_ contribution	≡	edas:RejectedPaper ⊔ edas:AcceptedPaper	union(c)
cmt:ProgramCommittee Member	≡	∃conference:was_a_member_of. conference:Program_committee	CAT
edas:paperDueOn	≡	conference:has_important_dates ∘ conference:is_a_date_of_full_paper_ submission	chain
ekaw:Early- Registered_Participant	≡	∃confOf:earlyRegistration.{true}	CAV
cmt:AuthorNotReviewer	≡	confOf:Author ⊓ ¬∃confOf:reviewes.⊤	neg
cmt:hasProgram CommitteeMember	≡	conference:has_members. conference:Program_committee.⊤	dom
edas:isReviewedBy	≡	confOf:reviewes⁻	IP

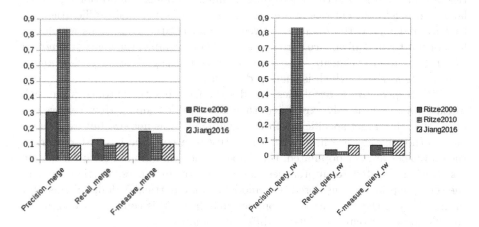

Fig. 3. Precision, Recall and F-measure of the three evaluated approaches

$\mathcal{SROIQ}$ therefore we did not consider them during the evaluation on the ontology merging alignment set.

Table 3. True positive (TP) and false positive (FP) complex correspondences of the three evaluated approaches. $\mathcal{SROIQ}$ and *All* correspondences compared to the number of complex correspondences in the reference alignment sets

Approach	TP (SROIQ)	TP+FP (SROIQ)	Ontology merging	TP (All)	TP + FP (All)	Query Rewriting
Ritze2009 [23]	7	23	54	7	23	191
Ritze2010 [24]	5	6	54	5	6	191
KAOM [13]	5	53	54	15	101	191

We also note that some correspondences in both alignment sets whose pattern detecting conditions were described in Ritze2009 [23] and Ritze2010 [24] were not retrieved by these two approaches because of the too restrictive conditions.

7   Discussion

In this section, we discuss the limitations and ways to improve the alignment sets, the evaluation and the potential reusability of these sets.

First of all, some difficulties were met with respect to the creation of the complex correspondences. Even though a real effort was made to grasp the semantics of every ontology entity based on its context (axioms, annotations, pseudo-labelling, neighbour entities and entity usage), one of the main difficulties was to fully understand the nuances between similar entities definitions which can lead or not to an equivalence correspondence. For example, the concept *reviewer of a paper* can either mean "*a person who reviews a paper*" or "*a person who is assigned to a paper*" which is slightly different.

With respect to the ontologies, besides the fact that the ontologies are real-world ones and relatively expressive, they are relatively small. However, we can argue that the target specificity of these alignments was not size but expressiveness (although they are limited to one entity to a construction). Moreover, as the ontologies are not populated, this impacts the evaluation of complex matchers which is limited to approaches not relying on instances. Furthermore, as the set of ontologies considered here model a same particular domain, this may bring a bias in the evaluation of complex matchers. This could be overcome by considering other ontology sets on different domains.

Regarding the (reference) generated alignments, they have been manually created based on one domain expert's interpretation of each ontology given the specific task scenario. Thus, they are not absolute. We have also made the assumption that the task impacts the alignment's expressiveness. However, we do not consider the final application for which the alignment is used (e.g., conference paper management, conference attendees management, etc.). Taking into account the specific application purpose for an alignment would may impact not only the expressiveness of the alignment but also its content.

With respect the evaluation, the metrics used here are the classical precision, recall and f-measure. Applied to complex correspondences, they present some limits. First, the relation of the correspondence is not taken into account. Second, the same correspondence can be expressed in different ways: in this evaluation, we manually compared two expressions. Third, we could consider the confidence of correspondences (here we assume that all generated correspondences by matchers are 1.0). Finally, the evaluation is not task-centered in the sense that the alignments generated by the approaches were not applied to query rewriting or ontology merging.

Nevertheless, the evaluation of the matchers shows that there is room for improvements in complex alignment generation. In our evaluation, we could observe that a good precision is often achieved in detriment of recall. The approaches [23,24] globally perform better for the task of ontology merging due to the set of correspondence patterns guiding their detection. The approach of [13] is the only one from the three approaches that considers object property restrictions, needed for query rewriting. In case the ontologies were populated with linked instances, the *Class-by-attribute-value (CAV)* correspondences of the alignment set could be detected by the approaches of [20,21,36], the correspondences with transformation functions such as string concatenation could be detected by the approaches of [18], and property chains could be detected by the approach of [22].

Summing up, as future directions in the field, some aspects have to be better addressed. Regarding the use of these alignment sets in complex ontology matching evaluation, population of the ontologies and consensus version (currently in work) should be taken into account. Regarding the evaluation process, automatising the process and finding better metrics seem compulsory. For example, semantic precision and recall [7] could be applied on the deductive closure set of axioms for ontology merging. An other metric could also take into account the conservativity [27], coherence and decidability of the merged ontology. Gold standard queries, as for the OA4QA campaign [28] could be a solution for query rewriting.

8   Conclusion and Perspectives

This paper has presented two task-oriented complex ontology alignment sets. Our work outlines two main points: the first one is that complex alignments are necessary to tightly align two ontologies. The second one is that two alignments can differ according to their task purpose. As the evaluation has shown, these alignment sets are rather challenging.

As discussed in the previous section, the proposed alignment sets can be improved in different directions. Therefore, we plan to address the points mentioned in the discussion and to extend the alignments with construction to construction correspondences. The evaluation of complex matchers is a problem that has not yet been addressed. We hope that this first rudimentary evaluation will pave the way towards a more complete benchmark for complex alignment evaluation.

References

1. Abacha, A.B., Zweigenbaum, P.: Means: une approche sémantique pour la recherche de réponses aux questions médicales. TAL **55**(1), 71–104 (2014)
2. Achichi, M., Cheatham, M., Dragisic, Z., Euzenat, J., Faria, D., Ferrara, A., Flouris, G., Fundulaki, I., Harrow, I., Ivanova, V., et al.: Results of the ontology alignment evaluation initiative 2017. In: 12th ISWC workshop on ontology matching, OM 2017, Wien, Austria, pp. 61–113 October 2017
3. Cheatham, M., Hitzler, P.: Conference v2.0: an uncertain version of the OAEI conference benchmark. In: Mika, P., et al. (eds.) ISWC 2014. LNCS, vol. 8797, pp. 33–48. Springer, Cham (2014). https://doi.org/10.1007/978-3-319-11915-1_3
4. Correndo, G., Shadbolt, N.: Translating expressive ontology mappings into rewriting rules to implement query rewriting. In: 6th Workshop on Ontology Matching (2011)
5. David, J., Euzenat, J., Scharffe, F., Trojahn dos Santos, C.: The alignment API 4.0. Semant. Web **2**(1), 3–10 (2011)
6. Do, H.-H., Melnik, S., Rahm, E.: Comparison of schema matching evaluations. In: Chaudhri, A.B., Jeckle, M., Rahm, E., Unland, R. (eds.) NODe 2002. LNCS, vol. 2593, pp. 221–237. Springer, Heidelberg (2003). https://doi.org/10.1007/3-540-36560-5_17
7. Euzenat, J.: Semantic precision and recall for ontology alignment evaluation. In: IJCAI (2007)
8. Euzenat, J., Shvaiko, P.: Ontology Matching. Springer, Heidelberg (2013). https://doi.org/10.1007/978-3-642-38721-0
9. Glimm, B., Horrocks, I., Motik, B., Stoilos, G., Wang, Z.: HermiT: an OWL 2 reasoner. J. Autom. Reason. **53**(3), 245–269 (2014)
10. Hollink, L., van Assem, M., Wang, S., Isaac, A., Schreiber, G.: Two variations on ontology alignment evaluation: methodological issues. In: Bechhofer, S., Hauswirth, M., Hoffmann, J., Koubarakis, M. (eds.) ESWC 2008. LNCS, vol. 5021, pp. 388–401. Springer, Heidelberg (2008). https://doi.org/10.1007/978-3-540-68234-9_30
11. Horrocks, I., Kutz, O., Sattler, U.: The even more irresistible SROIQ. Kr **6**, 57–67 (2006)
12. Isaac, A., Matthezing, H., van der Meij, L., Schlobach, S., Wang, S., Zinn, C.: Putting ontology alignment in context: usage scenarios, deployment and evaluation in a library case. In: Bechhofer, S., Hauswirth, M., Hoffmann, J., Koubarakis, M. (eds.) ESWC 2008. LNCS, vol. 5021, pp. 402–417. Springer, Heidelberg (2008). https://doi.org/10.1007/978-3-540-68234-9_31
13. Jiang, S., Lowd, D., Kafle, S., Dou, D.: Ontology matching with knowledge rules. In: Hameurlain, A., Küng, J., Wagner, R., Chen, Q. (eds.) Transactions on Large-Scale Data- and Knowledge-Centered Systems XXVIII. LNCS, vol. 9940, pp. 75–95. Springer, Heidelberg (2016). https://doi.org/10.1007/978-3-662-53455-7_4
14. Jiménez-Ruiz, E., Cuenca Grau, B., Horrocks, I., Berlanga, R.: Ontology integration using mappings: towards getting the right logical consequences. In: Aroyo, L., et al. (eds.) ESWC 2009. LNCS, vol. 5554, pp. 173–187. Springer, Heidelberg (2009). https://doi.org/10.1007/978-3-642-02121-3_16

15. Maedche, A., Motik, B., Silva, N., Volz, R.: MAFRA—a MApping FRAmework for distributed ontologies. In: Gómez-Pérez, A., Benjamins, V.R. (eds.) EKAW 2002. LNCS (LNAI), vol. 2473, pp. 235–250. Springer, Heidelberg (2002). https://doi.org/10.1007/3-540-45810-7_23

16. Makris, K., Bikakis, N., Gioldasis, N., Christodoulakis, S.: SPARQL-RW: transparent query access over mapped RDF data sources. In: 15th International Conference on Extending Database Technology, pp. 610–613. ACM (2012)

17. Meilicke, C., Stuckenschmidt, H.: Incoherence as a basis for measuring the quality of ontology mappings. In: 3rd International Conference on Ontology Matching, vol. 431, pp. 1–12 (2008)

18. Nunes, B.P., Mera, A., Casanova, M.A., Breitman, K.K., Leme, L.A.P.: Complex matching of RDF datatype properties. In: 6th ISWC Workshop on Ontology Matching(2011)

19. Oliveira, D., Pesquita, C.: Improving the interoperability of biomedical ontologies with compound alignments. J. Biomed. Semant. **9**(1) (2018)

20. Parundekar, R., Knoblock, C.A., Ambite, J.L.: Linking and building ontologies of linked data. In: Patel-Schneider, P.F., Pan, Y., Hitzler, P., Mika, P., Zhang, L., Pan, J.Z., Horrocks, I., Glimm, B. (eds.) ISWC 2010. LNCS, vol. 6496, pp. 598–614. Springer, Heidelberg (2010). https://doi.org/10.1007/978-3-642-17746-0_38

21. Parundekar, R., Knoblock, C.A., Ambite, J.L.: Discovering concept coverings in ontologies of linked data sources. In: Cudré-Mauroux, P., et al. (eds.) ISWC 2012. LNCS, vol. 7649, pp. 427–443. Springer, Heidelberg (2012). https://doi.org/10.1007/978-3-642-35176-1_27

22. Qin, H., Dou, D., LePendu, P.: Discovering executable semantic mappings between ontologies. In: Meersman, R., Tari, Z. (eds.) OTM 2007. LNCS, vol. 4803, pp. 832–849. Springer, Heidelberg (2007). https://doi.org/10.1007/978-3-540-76848-7_56

23. Ritze, D., Meilicke, C., Šváb Zamazal, O., Stuckenschmidt, H.: A pattern-based ontology matching approach for detecting complex correspondences. In: 4th ISWC Workshop on Ontology Matching, pp. 25–36 (2009)

24. Ritze, D., Völker, J., Meilicke, C., Šváb Zamazal, O.: Linguistic analysis for complex ontology matching. In: 5th Workshop on Ontology Matching, pp. 1–12 (2010)

25. Scharffe, F.: Correspondence patterns representation. Ph.D. thesis, Faculty of Mathematics, Computer Science and University of Innsbruck (2009)

26. Serpeloni, F., Moraes, R., Bonacin, R.: Ontology mapping validation. Int. J. Web Portals **3**(3), 1–11 (2011)

27. Solimando, A., Jiménez-Ruiz, E., Guerrini, G.: Minimizing conservativity violations in ontology alignments: algorithms and evaluation. Knowl. Inf. Syst. **51**(3), 775–819 (2017)

28. Solimando, A., Jiménez-Ruiz, E., Pinkel, C.: Evaluating ontology alignment systems in query answering tasks. In: ISWC 2014 International Conference on Posters and Demonstrations, pp. 301–304 (2014)

29. Stapleton, G., Howse, J., Bonnington, A., Burton, J.: A vision for diagrammatic ontology engineering. In: International Workshop on Visualizations and User Interfaces for Knowledge Engineering and Linked Data Analytics, pp. 1–13 (2014)

30. Thiéblin, É., Amarger, F., Haemmerlé, O., Hernandez, N., Trojahn, C.: Rewriting SELECT SPARQL queries from 1:n complex correspondences. In: 11th ISWC Workshop on Ontology Matching, pp. 49–60 (2016)

31. Thiéblin, É., Haemmerlé, O., Hernandez, N., Trojahn, C.: Un jeu de données d'é valuation de correspondances complexes entre ontologies. In: 28es Journées francophones d'Ingénierie des Connaissances IC 2017, pp. 68–79 (2017)

32. Thiéblin, É., Amarger, F., Hernandez, N., Roussey, C., Trojahn dos Santos, C.: Cross-querying LOD datasets using complex alignments: an application to agronomic taxa. In: Garoufallou, E., Virkus, S., Siatri, R., Koutsomiha, D. (eds.) MTSR 2017. CCIS, vol. 755, pp. 25–37. Springer, Cham (2017). https://doi.org/10.1007/978-3-319-70863-8_3
33. Thiéblin, É., Haemmerlé, O., Hernandez, N., Trojahn, C.: Towards a complex alignment evaluation dataset (poster). In: 12th ISWC Workshop on Ontology Matching, pp. 217–218 (2017)
34. Šváb, O., Svátek, V., Berka, P., Rak, D., Tomášek, P.: Ontofarm: towards an experimental collection of parallel ontologies. In: Poster Track of ISWC 2005 (2005)
35. Visser, P.R., Jones, D.M., Bench-Capon, T.J., Shave, M.: An analysis of ontology mismatches; heterogeneity versus interoperability. In: AAAI 1997 Spring Symposium on Ontological Engineering, Stanford, CA, USA, pp. 164–72 (1997)
36. Walshe, B., Brennan, R., O'Sullivan, D.: Bayes-ReCCE: a Bayesian model for detecting restriction class correspondences in linked open data knowledge bases. Int. J. Semant. Web Inf. Syst. (IJSWIS) 12(2), 25–52 (2016)
37. Zamazal, O., Svátek, V.: The ten-year ontofarm and its fertilization within the onto-sphere. Web Semant.: Sci. Serv. Agents World Wide Web 43, 46–53 (2017)

Where is My URI?

Andre Valdestilhas[1]([✉])(iD), Tommaso Soru[1](iD), Markus Nentwig[2](iD),
Edgard Marx[3], Muhammad Saleem[1], and Axel-Cyrille Ngonga Ngomo[4]

[1] AKSW Group, University of Leipzig, Leipzig, Germany
{valdestilhas,tsoru,saleem}@informatik.uni-leipzig.de
[2] Database Group, University of Leipzig, Leipzig, Germany
nentwig@informatik.uni-leipzig.de
[3] Leipzig University of Applied Sciences, Leipzig, Germany
edgard.marx@htwk-leipzig.de
[4] Data Science Group, Paderborn University, Paderborn, Germany
axel.ngonga@upb.de

Abstract. One of the Semantic Web foundations is the possibility to
dereference URIs to let applications negotiate their semantic content.
However, this exploitation is often infeasible as the availability of such
information depends on the reliability of networks, services, and human
factors. Moreover, it has been shown that around 90% of the information
published as Linked Open Data is available as data dumps and more than
60% of endpoints are offline. To this end, we propose a Web service called
Where is my URI?. Our service aims at indexing URIs and their use in
order to let Linked Data consumers find the respective RDF data source,
in case such information cannot be retrieved from the URI alone. We
rank the corresponding datasets by following the rationale upon which
a dataset contributes to the definition of a URI proportionally to the
number of literals. We finally describe potential use-cases of applications
that can immediately benefit from our simple yet useful service.

Keywords: Link discovery · Linked data · Endpoints · URI
Dereferencing

Resource type: Web Service Index
Permanent URL: https://w3id.org/where-is-my-uri/.

1 Introduction

In the Web of Data, applications such as Link Discovery or Data Integration
frameworks need to know where a specific URI is located. However, due to decentralized architecture of the Web of data, reliability and availability of Linked
Data services, locating such URIs is not a trivial task. Locating the URIs from
a well-known data dump might be easy. For example, it is trivial to know that
the URI http://dbpedia.org/resource/Leipzig belongs to the DBpedia dataset.

© Springer International Publishing AG, part of Springer Nature 2018
A. Gangemi et al. (Eds.): ESWC 2018, LNCS 10843, pp. 671–681, 2018.
https://doi.org/10.1007/978-3-319-93417-4_43

However, locating the dataset where the URI http://citeseer.rkbexplorer.com/id/resource-CS116606 was first defined is a time-consuming task. Consequently, this can greatly affect the scalable and time-efficient deployment of many Semantic Web applications such as link discovery, Linked Data enrichment, and federated query processing. On the other hand, such provenance information about URIs can lead to regenerate and validate the links across datasets.

The availability of the current available services to provide such information is unfortunately one of the key issues in Semantic Web and Linked Data. It has been shown that around 90% of the information published as Linked Open Data is available as data dumps only and more than 60% of endpoints are offline [14]. The availability problem is mostly due to cost associated with storing and providing querying services.

To this end, we propose *Where is my URI?* (WIMU), a low-cost Semantic Web service to determine the RDF data source of URIs along with their use. We also rank the data sources in case a single URI is provided by multiple data sources. The ranking is based-on a scoring function. Currently, our service processed more than 58 billion unique triples from more than 660,000 datasets obtained from LODStats [1] and LOD Laundromat [2]. For each URI, our service provides the corresponding datasets and the number of literals in the datasets having this URI. The service is both available from a web interface as well as can be queried from a client application using the standard HTTP protocol. We believe our service can be used in multiple Linked Data related problems such as devising fast link discovery frameworks, efficient source selection, and distributed query processing.

Our main contributions are as follows:

- We provide a regularly updated[1] database index of more than 660K datasets from LODStats and LOD Laundromat.
- We provide an efficient, low cost and scalable service on the web that shows which dataset most likely defines a URI.
- We provide various statistics of datasets indexed from LODStats and LOD Laundromat.

The service is available from https://w3id.org/where-is-my-uri/ under GNU Affero public license 3.0 and the source code is available online[2].

The rest of the paper is organized as follows: We first provide a brief overview of the state-of-the-art. We then discuss the proposed approach in detail, including the index creation, the web interface, and the data processing. We finally present our evaluation results and conclude.

2   Related Work

The work presented in [4] shows how to set up a Linked Data repository called *DataTank* and publish data as turtle files or through a SPARQL endpoint. The

---

[1] Updated monthly due to the huge size of data processed.

[2] https://github.com/dice-group/wimu.

difference with WIMU is that we provide a RESTful service instead of a setup to configure a Linked Data repository.

The work in [7] is based on an approach developed for the *3store* RDF triple store and describes a technique for indexing RDF documents allowing the rank and retrieval of their contents. Their index contained 10^7 triples, which was remarkable for the early years of the Semantic Web. Moreover, their system is not available for tests anymore. A similar point here is that the authors claim that for a given URI from an RDF document, the system will retrieve the URLs of documents containing that URI.

In the approach called LOD-A-LOT [5] which is a queryable dump file of the LOD Cloud[3], there are some differences with WIMU. The first, it is not possible to know the provenance of the URI in order to know which dataset the URI was defined. They provide a huge dump file[4] containing all the data from LOD Laundromat[5]. LOD Laundromat itself provides an endpoint to an inverted index of their data[6]. However, finding the original document a URI was defined in is not trivial, as the returned metadata only describe the datasets themselves [2]. Moreover, as the primary aim of LOD Laundromat is to "clean" Linked Data, most dumps are possibly not continuously monitored, once cleaned.

Comparing with all the approaches above, the main advantage of WIMU is that the datasets a URI likely belongs to are ranked using a score. Our index has also a larger coverage, as it includes data from the two largest Linked Data hubs, i.e., LODStats [1] and LOD Laundromat [2], and the most updated SPARQL endpoints. Finally, WIMU is able to process RDF files containing more than one URI at the same time[7].

3   The Approach

WIMU uses the number of literals as a heuristic to identify the dataset which most likely defines a URI. The intuition behind this can be explained in two points: (1) Literal values are the raw data that can disambiguate a URI node in the most direct way and (2) The Semantic Web architecture expects that datasets reusing a URI only refer to it without defining more literal values. One more reason for point (1) is that: it is straightforward to understand whether two literal values are different, whereas disambiguating URIs usually requires more effort.

We store the collected data in an Apache Lucene[8] index. Due to runtime performance and complexity reasons, we found that storing the information into

---

[3] http://lod-cloud.net/.

[4] A HDT file with more than 500 GB which requires more than 16 GB RAM to process.

[5] http://lodlaundromat.org/.

[6] http://index.lodlaundromat.org/.

[7] For   example: https://w3id.org/where-is-my-uri/Find?link=http://www.linklion. org/download/mapping/citeseer.rkbexplorer.com---ibm.rkbexplorer.com.nt.

[8] https://lucene.apache.org/.

Lucene was more convenient than a traditional triple store such as Virtuoso[9]. The rationale behind this choice is that a tuple such as *(URI, Dataset, Score)* would be expressed using at least three triples; for instance:

```
:R001 :hasURI :URI001
:R001 :hasDataset :Dataset001
:R001 :hasScore "20"^^http://www.w3.org/2001/XMLSchema#Integer
```

where :R001 is an index record URI. Therefore, materializing all records would have substantially increased the space complexity of our index.

3.1   The Index Creation

The index creation, the core of our work, is shown in Fig. 1 and consists in the following four steps:

1. Retrieve list of datasets from sources (i.e., LOD Stats and LOD Laundromat).
2. Retrieve data from datasets (i.e., dump files, endpoints, and HDT files).
3. Build three indexes from dump files, endpoints, and HDT files.
4. Merge the indexes into one.
5. Make the index available and browsable via a web application and an API service.

Fig. 1. Creation workflow of the WIMU index.

For each processed dataset, we keep its URI as provenance. After we have downloaded and extracted a dump file, we process it by counting the literals as objects for each subject. For endpoints and HDT files, we use a SPARQL query:

```
SELECT ?s (count(?o) as ?c) WHERE {
    ?s [] ?o . FILTER(isliteral(?o))
} GROUP BY ?s
```

We process the data in parallel, distributing the datasets among the CPUs. If a dataset is too large for a CPU, we split it into smaller chunks. To preserve space, dump files are deleted after being processed. The index was generated using an Intel Xeon Core i7 processor with 64 cores, 128 GB RAM on an Ubuntu 14.04.5 LTS with Java SE Development Kit 8.

---

[9] https://virtuoso.openlinksw.com/.

3.2   The Web Interface and the API Service

In order to simplify the access to our service, we create a web interface where it is possible to visualize all the data from the service, as Fig. 2 shows.

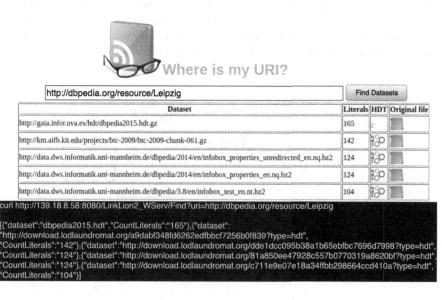

Fig. 2. Web interface.

The web interface allows the user to query a URI and see the results in a HTML web browser; the API service allows the user to work with an output in JSON format. In Fig. 2, we can see an example of usage of the service, where WIMU is requested for the dataset in which the URI dbpedia:Leipzig was defined. Figure 4 shows the generic usage of WIMU.

4   Use Cases

In this section, we present three use-cases to show that our hypothesis works on the proposed tasks.

4.1   Data Quality in Link Repositories

The first use-case is about quality assurance in a link repository by re-applying link discovery algorithms on the stored links. This task concerns important steps of the Linked Data Lifecycle, in particular *Data Interlinking* and *Quality*. Link repositories contain sets of links that connect resources belonging to different datasets. Unfortunately, the subject and the object URIs of a link often do not have metadata available, hence their Concise Bounded Descriptions (CBDs) are hard to obtain. In Sect. 4.1, $(D_1, ..., D_n|x) : D_n$ represent the datasets and x is the quantity of literals. The **input** for our service in this use-case is S; the **output** is $\{(D_1, 3), (D_2, 1), (D_3, 2)\}$, where $D1$ most likely defines S due to the highest number of literal. In the same way, the dataset that most likely defines T is D_4 with 7 literals. Once we have this information, the entire CBD of the two resources S and T can be extracted and a Link Discovery algorithm can check whether the `owl:sameAs` link among them should subsist (Fig. 3).

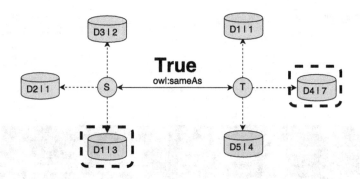

Fig. 3. First use-case.

4.2   Finding Class Axioms for Link Discovery

A class axiom is needed by the link discovery algorithm to reduce the number of comparisons. Here, the aim is to find two class axioms for each mapping in the link repository.

To this end, we use real data including a mapping[10] from the LinkLion repository [9] between http://citeseer.rkbexplorer.com/id/resource-CS65161 (S) and http://citeseer.rkbexplorer.com/id/resource-CS65161 (T). Our service shows that S was defined in four datasets, whereas the dataset with more literals was http://km.aifb.kit.edu/projects/btc-2009/btc-2009-chunk-039.gz[11]. Thus, we can deduce where the URI S was most likely defined. Knowing the datasets allows us to extract the axioms of the classes our URIs belong to. The techniques to decrease the complexity vary from choosing the most specific class to using an ontology learning tool such as DL-Learner [8].

---

[10] http://www.linklion.org/download/mapping/citeseer.rkbexplorer.com---ibm.rkbexp lorer.com.nt.

[11] Also available in HDT file from http://download.lodlaundromat.org/15b06d92ae 660ffdcff9690c3d6f5185?type=hdt.

Fig. 4. Usage.

4.3 Federated Query Processing

Federated queries, which aim to collect information from more than one datasets is of central importance for many semantic web and linked data applications [11,12]. One of the key step in federated query processing is the *source selection*. The goal of the source selection is to find relevant sources (i.e., datasets) for the given user query. In the next step, the federated query processing engine makes use of the source selection information to generate an optimized query execution plan. WIMU can be used by the federated SPARQL engines to find the relevant sources against the individual triple patterns of the given SPARQL query. In particular, our service can be helpful during the source selection and query planning in cost-based SPARQL federation engines such SPLENDID [6], SemaGrow [3], HiBISCuS [13], CostFed [10], etc.

4.4 Usage Examples

The service API provides a JSON as output, allowing users to use WIMU with some programming language compatible with JSON. Here we give examples, for more details please check the manual[12].

Service: https://w3id.org/where-is-my-uri/Find.
Parameters Table 1:

Table 1. Parameters

Parameter	Default	Description
Top	0	Top ocurrences of the datasets where the URI was defined
URI	-	URI expected to search

Input (Single URI example):
    https://w3id.org/where-is-my-uri/Find?top=5&uri=http://dbpedia.org/resource/Leipzig.

---

[12] More examples such as many URIs, linksets, and generation of Concise Bounded Description (CBD) check https://dice-group.github.io/wimu/.

Output:

```
[
 {
  "dataset":
  "http://downloads.dbpedia.org/2016-10/core-i18n/en/infobox_properties_en.ttl.bz2",
  "CountLiteral": "236"
 },
 {
  "dataset": "http://gaia.infor.uva.es/hdt/dbpedia2015.hdt.gz",
  "CountLiteral": "165"
 },
 {
  "dataset":
  "http://download.lodlaundromat.org/a9dabf348fd6262edfbbcf7256b0f839?type=hdt",
  "CountLiteral": "142"
 },
 {
  "dataset":
  "http://download.lodlaundromat.org/dde1dcc095b38a1b65ebfbc7696d7998?type=hdt",
  "CountLiteral": "124"
 }
]
```

Java and the API Gson[13]:

```
private void exampleJson() throws Exception {
  String service = "https://w3id.org/where-is-my-uri/Find?uri=";
  String uri = "http://dbpedia.org/resource/Leipzig";
  URL url = new URL(service + uri);
  InputStreamReader reader = new InputStreamReader(url.openStream());
  WIMUDataset wData = new Gson().fromJson(reader, WIMUDataset[].class)[0];
  System.out.println("Dataset:" + wData.getDataset());
  System.out.println("Dataset(HDT):" + wData.getHdt());
}
```

5   Statistics About the Datasets

To the best of our knowledge, LODStats [1] is the only project oriented to monitoring dump files; however, its last update dates back to 2016. Observing Table 2, we are able to say that from LODStats, not all datasets are ready to use. Especially, more than 58% are off-line, 14% are empty datasets, 8% of the triples that have literals as objects are blank nodes and 35% of the online datasets present some error using the Apache Jena parser[14]. A large part of those data was processed and cleaned by LOD Laundromat [2].

The algorithm took three days and seven hours to complete the task. Thus, we will create a scheduled job to update our database index once a month. With respect to the information present in the Fig. 5, we can observe that the majority of files from LODStats are in RDF/XML format. Moreover, the endpoints are represented in greater numbers (78.6%), the dominant file format is RDF with 84.1% of the cases, and 56.2% of errors occurred because Apache Jena was not

---

[13] https://github.com/google/gson.
[14] See https://github.com/dice-group/wimu/blob/master/ErrorJenaParser.tsv.

Table 2. Datasets.

	LOD laundromat	LODStats	Total
URIs indexed	4,185,133,445	31,121,342	4,216,254,787
Datasets checked	658,206	9,960	668,166
Triples processed	19,891,702,202	38,606,408,854	58,498,111,056

able to perform SPARQL queries. Among the HDT files from LOD Laundromat, 2.3% of them could not be processed due to parsing errors. Another relevant point is that 99.2% of the URIs indexed with WIMU come from LOD Laundromat, due to 69.8% of datasets from LODstats contain parser errors in which WIMU was not able to process the data.

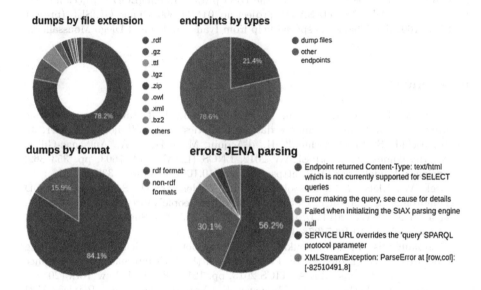

Fig. 5. Dump files and Apache Jena parsing error.

Finally, we validated our heuristic assessing if the URI really belongs to the dataset with more literals. To this end, we took a sample of 100 URIs[15] that belong to at least two datasets, where we assess manually the data in order to check if the results are really correct. As a result, the dataset containing the correct information was found as first result in 90% of the URIs and among the top three in 95% of the URIs.

---

[15] https://github.com/dice-group/wimu/blob/master/result100.csv.

6 Conclusion and Future Work

We provide a database index of URIs and their respective datasets built upon large Linked Data hubs such as LODStats and LOD Laundromat. In order to make this data available and easy to use, we developed a semantic web service. For a given URI, it is possible to know the dataset the URI likely was defined in using a heuristic based on the number of literals. We showed two use-cases and carried out a preliminary evaluation to facilitate the understanding of our work. As future work, we will integrate the service into the version 2.0 of the LinkLion repository, so as to perform linkset quality assurance with the application of link discovery algorithms on the stored links.

Acknowledgments. This research has been partially supported by CNPq Brazil under grants No. 201536/2014-5 and H2020 projects SLIPO (GA no. 731581) and HOBBIT (GA no. 688227) as well as the DFG project LinkingLOD (project no. NG 105/3-2), the BMWI Projects SAKE (project no. 01MD15006E) and GEISER (project no. 01MD16014E). Thanks to special help from Ivan Ermilov and Diego Moussallem.

References

1. Auer, S., Demter, J., Martin, M., Lehmann, J.: LODStats – an extensible framework for high-performance dataset analytics. In: ten Teije, A., Völker, J., Handschuh, S., Stuckenschmidt, H., d'Acquin, M., Nikolov, A., Aussenac-Gilles, N., Hernandez, N. (eds.) EKAW 2012. LNCS (LNAI), vol. 7603, pp. 353–362. Springer, Heidelberg (2012). https://doi.org/10.1007/978-3-642-33876-2_31
2. Beek, W., Rietveld, L., Bazoobandi, H.R., Wielemaker, J., Schlobach, S.: LOD laundromat: a uniform way of publishing other people's dirty data. In: Mika, P., et al. (eds.) ISWC 2014. LNCS, vol. 8796, pp. 213–228. Springer, Cham (2014). https://doi.org/10.1007/978-3-319-11964-9_14
3. Charalambidis, A., Troumpoukis, A., Konstantopoulos, S.: SemaGrow: optimizing federated SPARQL queries. In: Proceedings of the 11th International Conference on Semantic Systems, SEMANTICS 2015, pp. 121–128. ACM, New York (2015)
4. Colpaert, P., Verborgh, R., Mannens, E., Van de Walle, R.: Painless URI dereferencing using the DataTank. In: Presutti, V., Blomqvist, E., Troncy, R., Sack, H., Papadakis, I., Tordai, A. (eds.) ESWC 2014. LNCS, vol. 8798, pp. 304–309. Springer, Cham (2014). https://doi.org/10.1007/978-3-319-11955-7_39
5. Fernández, J.D., Beek, W., Martínez-Prieto, M.A. Arias, M.: LOD-a-lot: A queryable dump of the LOD cloud (2017)
6. Görlitz, O., Staab, S.: SPLENDID: SPARQL endpoint federation exploiting VoID descriptions. In: Hartig, O., Harth, A., Sequeda, J. F. (eds.) 2nd International Workshop on Consuming Linked Data (COLD 2011) in CEUR Workshop Proceedings, vol. 782, October 2011
7. Harris, S., Gibbins, N., Payne, T.R.: SemIndex: preliminary results from semantic web indexing (2004)
8. Lehmann, J.: DL-Learner: learning concepts in description logics. J. Mach. Learn. Res. **10**(Nov), 2639–2642 (2009)

9. Nentwig, M., Soru, T., Ngonga Ngomo, A.-C., Rahm, E.: LinkLion: a link repository for the web of data. In: Presutti, V., Blomqvist, E., Troncy, R., Sack, H., Papadakis, I., Tordai, A. (eds.) ESWC 2014. LNCS, vol. 8798, pp. 439–443. Springer, Cham (2014). https://doi.org/10.1007/978-3-319-11955-7_63

10. Potocki, A., Saleem, M., Soru, T., Hartig, O., Voigt, M., Ngomo, A.-C.N.: Federated SPARQL query processing via CostFed (2017)

11. Saleem, M., Kamdar, M.R., Iqbal, A., Sampath, S., Deus, H.F., Ngomo, A.-C.N.: Big linked cancer data: integrating linked TCGA and PubMed. J. Web Semant. Sci. Serv. Agents World Wide Web **27–28**, 34–41 (2014). Semantic Web Challenge 2013

12. Saleem, M., Kamdar, M.R., Iqbal, A., Sampath, S., Deus, H.F., Ngonga, A.-C.: Fostering serendipity through big linked data. In: Semantic Web Challenge at ISWC (2013)

13. Saleem, M., Ngonga Ngomo, A.-C.: HiBISCuS: hypergraph-based source selection for SPARQL endpoint federation. In: Presutti, V., d'Amato, C., Gandon, F., d'Aquin, M., Staab, S., Tordai, A. (eds.) ESWC 2014. LNCS, vol. 8465, pp. 176–191. Springer, Cham (2014). https://doi.org/10.1007/978-3-319-07443-6_13

14. Vandenbussche, P.-Y., Umbrich, J., Matteis, L., Hogan, A., Buil-Aranda, C.: SPARQLES: monitoring public SPARQL endpoints. Semant. Web **8**(6), 1049–1065 (2017)

Optimizing Semantic Reasoning
on Memory-Constrained Platforms Using
the RETE Algorithm

William Van Woensel[(✉)] ⓘ and Syed Sibte Raza Abidi ⓘ

Faculty of Computer Science, Dalhousie University, Halifax, Canada
{william.van.woensel, raza.abidi}@dal.ca

Abstract. Mobile hardware improvements have opened the door for deploying rule systems on ubiquitous, mobile platforms. By executing rule-based tasks locally, less remote (cloud) resources are needed, bandwidth usage is reduced, and local, time-sensitive tasks are no longer influenced by network conditions. Further, with data being increasingly published in semantic format, an opportunity arises for rule systems to leverage the embedded semantics of semantic, ontology-based data. To support this kind of ontology-based reasoning in rule systems, rule-based axiomatizations of ontology semantics can be utilized (e.g., OWL 2 RL). Nonetheless, recent benchmarks have found that any kind of semantic reasoning on mobile platforms still lacks scalability, at least when directly re-using existing (PC- or server-based) technologies. To create a tailored solution for resource-constrained platforms, we propose changes to RETE, the mainstay algorithm for production rule systems. In particular, we present an adapted algorithm that, by selectively pooling RETE memories, aims to better balance memory usage with performance. We show that this algorithm is well-suited towards many typical Semantic Web scenarios. Using our custom algorithm, we perform an extensive evaluation of semantic, ontology-based reasoning, using our custom RETE algorithm and an OWL2 RL ruleset, both on the PC and mobile platform.

Keywords: RETE · OWL2 RL · Rule-based reasoning · OWL reasoning
Reasoning optimization

1 Introduction

Using structured domain knowledge, production rule systems realize a diversity of tasks in domains such as business, science and healthcare. Knowledge is formulated as a set of productions (i.e., if-then rules) together with a set of assertions. In the healthcare domain, production rule systems are often at the core of Clinical Decision Support Systems (CDSS), which aid in diagnosis, prognosis and treatment tasks [1, 2]. To semantically structure health data, a variety of biomedical ontologies (e.g., see BioPortal [3]) and clinical health terminologies (e.g., SNOMED-CT [4]) are available. In order to improve decision support accuracy, a CDSS can leverage the embedded semantics of semantic health data, such as subclass, transitive and symmetric relations between drugs, illnesses and treatments. Performing this kind of ontology-based,

© Springer International Publishing AG, part of Springer Nature 2018
A. Gangemi et al. (Eds.): ESWC 2018, LNCS 10843, pp. 682–696, 2018.
https://doi.org/10.1007/978-3-319-93417-4_44

semantic reasoning in (production) rule systems requires a rule-based axiomatization of ontology semantics. The W3C OWL2 RL profile [5] is highly relevant, since it partially axiomatizes the OWL2 RDF-based semantics as a set of high-level, abstract IF-THEN rules.

There is a growing demand to deploy production rule systems, such as clinical decision support systems, directly on mobile, resource-constrained platforms. Examples include clinical, time-sensitive tasks to be performed directly on mobile consumer devices [6], and sensor networks pushing reasoning down to the device layer to cope with unstable communication [7]. However, recent benchmarks [8] show that the mobile performance of existing, desktop- or server-based reasoners still leaves much to be desired. It may be noted that, although modern mobile consumer devices are outfitted with 2 GB of RAM or more, single apps are only assigned max. 192 MB on Android; whereas devices in sensor networks may even feature much less memory.

To optimize semantic, ontology-based reasoning in rule systems, we propose a novel version of the RETE algorithm, a well-known algorithm for production rule systems, which aims to better balance memory usage with performance. The RETE algorithm uses *alpha nodes* to represent rule premises, with *alpha memories* keeping matching premise facts (tokens). Our proposed $RETE_{pool}$ algorithm is based on the observation that generic rule premises, which occur frequently in OWL2 RL, result in a large duplication of data in alpha memories. For instance, the same set of tokens can match OWL2 RL premises *<?x ?p ?y>*, *<?c owl:unionOf ?x>* and *<?c rdf:type owl:Class>*. An extreme example is a "wildcard" premise, i.e., with variables at all positions, which will effectively duplicate the data from all other premises. By pooling a selection of alpha memories into a single shared memory, the $RETE_{pool}$ algorithm aims to reduce duplication of data in RETE. We note that $RETE_{pool}$ is well-suited towards Semantic Web settings that typically involve an existing, multi-purpose RDF store. We integrated this algorithm into Apache Jena [9] and AndroJena [10], a port of Apache Jena for mobile (Android) platforms. We present an extensive evaluation of semantic reasoning, using a rule system featuring the $RETE_{pool}$ algorithm and an OWL2 RL ruleset, both on PC and mobile platform (Android). This work is motivated by our previous work, where we (1) developed a mobile patient diary with built-in local decision support [6] based on rule-based reasoning; and (2) presented a set of mobile benchmarks, together with a mobile benchmark framework, using existing reasoners [11].

The paper is structured as follows. First, Sect. 2 summarizes our OWL2 RL ruleset, which implements the OWL2 RL specification and is used to realize semantic reasoning. In Sect. 3, we summarize and exemplify the RETE algorithm. Section 4 presents the $RETE_{pool}$ algorithm. In Sect. 5, we extensively evaluate semantic reasoning using $RETE_{pool}$ and our OWL2 RL ruleset. In Sect. 6, we discuss relevant state of the art, and Sect. 7 presents conclusions and future work.

2 OWL2 RL Ruleset

To realize semantic reasoning on mobile, resource-constrained platforms, we rely on the W3C OWL2 RL profile. The OWL2 Web Ontology Language Profiles document [5] introduces three distinct OWL2 profiles, which are optimized to handle specific application scenarios. The OWL2 RL profile is aimed at balancing expressivity with reasoning scalability, and presents a partial, rule-based axiomatization of OWL2 RDF-Based Semantics [12]. As only a partial axiomatization, OWL2 RL guarantees completeness for ABox reasoning but not for TBox reasoning [13]; and places syntactic restrictions on ontologies to ensure all correct inferences. Nevertheless, this trade-off seems acceptable when targeting scalable reasoning on resource-constrained platforms.

Based on the OWL2 RL specification, we created a concrete OWL2 RL ruleset that is re-usable by any arbitrary rule engine, which means no particular internal support (e.g., for datatypes or lists) was assumed. Below, we focus on 3 non-trivial issues that occur when attempting to create an OWL2 RL ruleset:

(1) A pair of rules (*#dt-type2* and *#dt-not-type*) support RDF datatype semantics by inferring datatypes (e.g., typing integer "42" with *xsd:int*) and flagging datatype inconsistencies. Two other rules (*#dt-eq* and *#dt-diff*) infer equality and inequality of literals, which requires differentiating literals from URIs (to avoid these rules firing for URI resources as well). As such, these rules require built-in support for RDF datatypes and literals, which cannot be assumed for arbitrary systems; hence, we chose to leave out these rules. We note that related work, including DLEJena [14] and the SPIN [15] and OWLIM [16] OWL2 RL rulesets, also do not include datatype rules. Others opted to leave out datatype rules due to their significant performance issues [17].

(2) Another set of rules lacks an antecedent and are thus always applicable. Some of these rules lack variables (e.g., specifying that *owl:Thing* has type *owl:Class*), and were represented as axiomatic triples accompanying the ruleset. Other rules comprise "quantified" variables in the consequent; e.g., stating that each annotation property has type *owl:AnnotationProperty*. Similarly, these were implemented by creating an axiom for each annotation (OWL2 [18]) and datatype property (OWL2 RL [5]).

(3) *N-ary rules* refer to a finite list of elements. A first subset **(L1)** places restrictions on a limited number of list elements; e.g., *#eq-diff2* flags an inconsistency if *two* members of an *owl:AllDifferent* instance are defined as equivalent. A second subset **(L2)** places restrictions on all elements; e.g., *#cls-int1* will type a resource with an intersection class only when the resource is typed by *all* of the intersection member classes. A third ruleset **(L3)** yields inferences for all list elements; e.g., *#scm-uni* will infer subclass relations for all classes that are members of a union class.

Rulesets **(L1)** and **(L3)** can be supported by adding two auxiliary list-membership rules (Rule 1), which link each list element to all preceding list cells; meaning the first cell will be directly linked to all elements.

$$T(?\,l, first, ?\,m) \rightarrow T(?\,l, hasMember, ?\,m)$$
$$T(?\,l_1, rest, ?\,l_2), T(?\,l_2, hasMember, ?\,m) \rightarrow T(?\,l_1, hasMember, ?\,m)$$

Rule 1. Two rules for inferring list membership.

E.g., using these rules, *#scm-uni* (**L3**) may be formulated as follows (Rule 2; note that Rule 3 similarly belongs to (L3)):

$$T(?\,c, unionOf, ?\,l), T(?\,l, hasMember, ?\,cl) \rightarrow T(?\,cl, subClassOf, ?\,c)$$

Rule 2. Rule inferring subclasses based on union membership (*#scm-uni*).

Multiple solutions are possible for n-ary rules from (**L2**). We chose a solution that *replaces* each (L2) rule by a set of auxiliary rules [16], which infer intermediary assertions for each list cell $i(0 \leq i < n)$, and, based on these inferences, finally generates the n-ary inference if the first cell is related to an (L2) assertion. We note that this is the only solution that does not require pre-processing the ruleset or ontology for per ontology update, compared to e.g., instantiating (L2) rules based on n-ary assertions [19], or "binarizing" (i.e., converting all n-ary assertions to binary ones). For details on these solutions, we refer to the online documentation [20].

Based on these considerations, we created an OWL2 RL ruleset written in the SPARQL Inferencing Notation (SPIN) based on an initial ruleset created by Knublauch [15]. This initial ruleset did not specify axioms, and relied on built-in Apache Jena functions to implement n-ary rules. Our final ruleset contains 78 rules and 43 supporting axioms, and can be found online [20]. We checked the conformance of the OWL2 RL ruleset using the OWL2 RL conformance test suite by Schneider and Mainzer [21]. We note that some of these tests had to be left out, either due to the limitations of our OWL2 RL ruleset or difficulties testing conformance. We detail these cases online [20].

3   Using RETE for Reasoning on RDF

Production rule systems operate by matching production conditions to a set of assertions, and then adding/removing assertions based on the production's actions [22]. For this purpose, the RETE algorithm sets up a network consisting of *alpha nodes* for each condition (i.e., intra-condition check), and *beta nodes* to join shared variables between these conditions (i.e., inter-condition check). Each alpha node, and all but the last beta node, is linked to a *memory* keeping the results of these checks. A rule ends with a *terminal node*, which represents the actions. To create a RETE network, the *right input* of each beta node is linked to an alpha node, and its *left input* to the previous beta node, or if none exists, the first alpha node (cfr. Ishida [23]). When reasoning over RDF data, an intra-condition check matches a triple pattern (or FILTER expression) to an RDF triple token [7, 24]. Below, we show the RETE network for the *#cls-int2* OWL2 RL rule to be applied on an RDF dataset described using an OWL2 RL ontology; and describe the reasoning process when new facts (tokens) enter the network.

$$T(?\,c, intersectionOf, ?\,x), T(?\,x, hasMember, ?\,c_i), T(?\,y, type, ?\,c) \rightarrow T(?\,y, type, ?\,c_i)$$

Rule 3. Rule inferring resource types based on intersection members (#cls-int2).

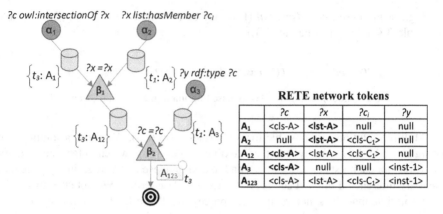

Fig. 1. Example RETE structure (rule #cls-int2).

At time t_1, triple tokens A_2 and A_3 enter the network, which are matched by alpha nodes α_2 and α_3 and inserted into their memories. At time t_2, incoming token A_1 is matched to alpha node α_1, and inserted into its memory. Since nodes α_1 and α_2 are connected by beta node β_1, the new token triggers a join attempt between the left-input A_1 token and the right-input A_2 token. As shown in the token table, tokens A_1 and A_2 have the same value for shared variable ?x (i.e., <lst-A>), leading to a successfully joined token A_{12} that is added to the β_1 memory. With this new token at its left input, node β_2 attempts a join with right input token A_3. Both tokens have the same value for shared variable ?c (i.e., <cls-A>), leading to a successfully joined token A_{123}. This token reaches the terminal node, which will use the instantiated variables to infer a new fact, i.e., <inst-1> rdf:type <cls-C_1>.

A standard RETE optimization is to re-use alpha nodes (and memories) when the same premise occurs multiple times, and beta nodes in case rules share the first two or more premises (else, the contents of the beta memories may differ). Re-using nodes and memories reduces the number of match and join operations, and avoids duplicate storage of tokens. To speed up the joining process, the most restrictive conditions (i.e., alpha nodes) are often placed first, and Cartesian products are avoided [7, 23]. Alpha and beta memories are typically indexed to allow for hashed joins [9, 25].

4 The RETE$_{pool}$ Algorithm

A default RETE optimization involves re-using alpha memories for identical premises (Sect. 3), which reduces data duplication. Nevertheless, we observe that generic rule premises (i.e., with more than 1 variable) typically still lead to large duplications of data in alpha memories. For instance, the memory related to premise <?x ?p ?y> will effectively duplicate all data from the memory of <?p rdf:type owl:ObjectProperty>; and both memories will overlap with the memory of <?y rdf:type ?c>. This is especially apparent in the OWL2 RL ruleset with its many generic premises. An extreme example are wildcard premises, which are found in the OWL2 RL ruleset and match all tokens. As such, they effectively duplicate data from all other alpha memories. Furthermore, we note that many Semantic Web applications involve an existing RDF store, which is used to load data into the rule system but for other purposes as well (e.g., querying). Alpha memories will always duplicate (parts of) this RDF store, thus presenting a second, orthogonal level of data duplication.

We present the *RETE_pool* algorithm, which pools alpha memories into a single shared memory. As a result, duplicate tokens, i.e., tokens occurring in multiple alpha memories, are only stored once in a single memory. In doing so, data duplication in alpha memories is effectively avoided. In scenarios with an existing RDF datastore, *RETE_pool* can directly re-use this store as the shared memory; thus avoiding both internal duplication, as well as duplication between the RETE structure and RDF store. Below, we discuss the implementation of the *RETE_pool* algorithm.

4.1   Implementation of RETE_pool

The *RETE_pool* algorithm utilizes *virtual* alpha memories (cfr. Hanson [26]) in the RETE network, which keep a mask on the single, shared memory that represents the related premise (e.g., $<?c\ rdf{:}type\ ?t>$). For instance, an RDF store may be used as the shared memory, as is done in our evaluation (Sect. 5).

New tokens are added to the shared memory, and injected at suitable alpha nodes into the network (see Fig. 1). In this process, a beta node will attempt to join the new token with other tokens from its input alpha memory. Joining two tokens implies they have the same value(s) for the shared variable(s). Hence, join operations can be performed by searching the alpha memory for tokens matching the shared variable(s) value(s). In our case, the virtual memory's mask is extended with these values, and then used as a search constraint on the shared memory. By extending the mask, only tokens that match the alpha node premise will be returned. This is illustrated in Fig. 2. At time t_3, token A_{12} is used to extend the virtual memory mask with the token's value of shared variable $?c$, leading to search constraint $S = ?, P = rdf{:}type, O = <cls\text{-}A>$.

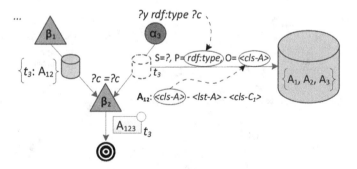

Fig. 2. Usage of the shared memory in RETE_pool.

Since each join involves accessing a (very) large shared memory, instead of a relatively small alpha memory, it is clear that this algorithm optimizes memory at the cost of performance. This is confirmed by our evaluation (Sect. 5). We note that the issue that $RETE_{pool}$ aims to solve, i.e., data duplication in alpha memories, clearly depends on premise selectivity. By only utilizing a virtual alpha memory for overly generic, non-restrictive premises, we may thus better balance memory usage with runtime performance. To that end, $RETE_{pool}$ allows configuring a selectivity threshold $t_s (0 < t_s \leq 1)$. In case the premise selectivity (i.e., number of matching facts) equals or exceeds t_s, a virtual memory will be utilized, otherwise a regular memory. Our evaluation studies the effects of different values for t_s on memory and performance.

Below, we discuss an additional issue that arises when an existing, pre-loaded RDF store is being re-used.

4.2 Reciprocal Join Issue

Many Semantic Web applications will start out with a pre-loaded RDF datastore, which will be used to inject data into the rule system. When utilizing $RETE_{pool}$, an opportunity exists to re-use this datastore as a single shared memory. In this case, each virtual alpha memory will initially be fully "populated", since it references the pre-loaded RDF dataset (Sect. 4.1). This is illustrated in Fig. 3.

At time t_0, token A_1 is injected into the network, and joins with token A_2 from node α_2 (already present in its virtual memory). At time t_1, token A_2 is injected and similarly joins with token A_1 (also present) – thus performing a second, redundant ("reciprocal") join. Later on, in case token A_{12} was stored twice in memory β_1, four joins with token A_3 would take place: one for each of the two A_{12} tokens at times t_0 and t_1; and when token A_3 is injected at time t_2, again once for each A_{12} token. A single successful rule firing requires an exponential $2^{(|\mathcal{A}_r|-1)}$ joins, with $\mathcal{A}_r = \{ \alpha_i \in \mathcal{R}_r \}$ the set of alpha nodes in network $\mathcal{R}_r$ (for any rule r). In case duplicate tokens are not stored (e.g., duplicate checking takes place), a single rule firing would still require $(|\mathcal{A}| - 1) \times 2$ joins. Without reciprocal joins, a single successful rule firing requires only $|\mathcal{A}_r| - 1$ joins.

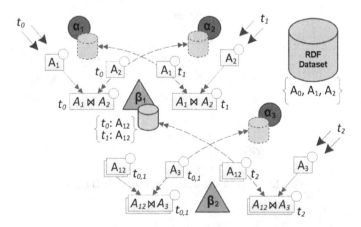

Fig. 3. Example where the reciprocal-join issue occurs in $RETE_{pool}$.

Since this issue only occurs during the first reasoning cycle, we introduced a custom reasoning process for this cycle. In this process, only tokens are injected that match the first alpha node α_1. As the token travels through the network, all possible joins will be attempted, since all tokens are already at their virtual alpha memories – while avoiding reciprocal joins. In Fig. 3, by only injecting token A_1, a second, redundant join with A_2 will be avoided, which in turn avoids redundant joins later on in the network.

5   Semantic Reasoning Benchmarks

This section presents benchmark results for ontology-based reasoning, using a rule system and an OWL2 RL ruleset. For the rule system, we benchmarked multiple configurations of the $RETE_{pool}$ algorithm, and compared the results to a baseline RETE algorithm. To test the performance impact on resource-constrained platforms, we ran each benchmark on a PC as well as on a mobile device.

Below, we discuss the setup (Sect. 5.1) and present the benchmarks (Sect. 5.2).

5.1   Benchmark Setup

5.1.1   Baseline System
We extended the original Apache Jena RETE implementation [27] with standard optimizations, including the re-use of RETE nodes and memories, memory indexing and join ordering (see Sect. 3). These optimizations are considered standard-practice in modern RETE systems [7, 25, 28], making the extended system an appropriate baseline. We also copied these extensions to Jena's Android port, i.e., AndroJena [10]. In the benchmark results, this baseline system is referred to as $RETE_{base}$. We implemented the $RETE_{pool}$ algorithm on top of this baseline implementation.

5.1.2   OWL2 RL Ontologies and Ruleset
Our benchmarks were executed on the BioPortal ontologies from the OWL 2 RL Benchmark Corpus [29]. On PC, reasoning over 3 of the 45 ontologies took longer than 10 min (our cut-off time) for any configuration, so these were left out. For the 42 remaining ontologies, the number of statements range from 246 to 57310 (avg. 6684), and their file sizes (N3 format) range from 24 KB to 5852 KB (avg. 642 KB). For the mobile benchmarks, we considered a subset of 34 BioPortal ontologies, since the other 11 ontologies either caused out-of-memory exceptions, or ran longer than 10 min. For these ontologies, the number of statements range from 246 to 7291 (avg. 2199) and their file sizes (N3 format) from 24 KB to 838 KB (avg. 210 KB). As a result, we note that average performance times for PC and mobile are not directly comparable. We detail each set of ontologies in our online documentation [20]).

As the benchmark ruleset, we utilized the OWL2 RL ruleset introduced in Sect. 2. This ruleset contains 78 rules and 43 supporting axioms, and can be found online [20]. As mentioned, we checked the conformance of this ruleset using the OWL2 RL conformance test suite by Schneider and Mainzer [21], and detail the results online [20].

5.1.3 Benchmark Platforms

Benchmarks were performed on two platforms:

(1) *PC*: Lenovo ThinkPad T530, with a dual-core Intel Core i7-3520 M CPU (2.9 Ghz), 8 GB RAM and a 64 bit infrastructure, running Windows 7.0 (Service Pack 1).
(2) *Mobile*: LG Nexus 5 (model LG-D820), with a 2.26 GHz Quad-Core Processor and 2 GB RAM. This device runs Android 6, which grants apps 192 MB of heap space.

During the benchmarks, both devices were connected to a power supply.

5.1.4 RETE$_{pool}$ Configurations

We benchmarked the following algorithms and configurations (regular memories are utilized for beta nodes).

(A.i) *RETE$_{base}$*: a regular memory is utilized for each alpha node.
(A.ii) *RETE$_{full-pool}$*: a virtual alpha memory is utilized for each alpha node.
(A.iii) *RETE$_{part-pool}$*: a virtual alpha memory is only utilized in case its premise selectivity exceeds the configured threshold: $0.1 - 0.25 - 0.5 - 0.75 - 1$.

Further, we consider two orthogonal scenarios for *RETE$_{pool}$*:

(S.i) A shared memory is introduced for the sole purpose of supporting *RETE$_{pool}$*;
(S.ii) An existing RDF store is re-used as the shared memory pool.

We utilized the Apache Jena RDF store as the shared memory. Each configuration was benchmarked in a one-shot reasoning scenario, i.e., with a single reasoning cycle over each of the benchmark ontologies. For *RETE$_{X-pool}$* configurations, the shared RDF store was pre-loaded with the ontology, after which a custom reasoning process took place (see Sect. 4.2). This allowed us to estimate premise selectivity by using the number of matched tokens from the actual benchmark ontology.

5.1.5 Benchmark Metrics

We measure the following performance metrics:

(P.1) *Network compilation time*: time needed to compile the network, including selecting memory indices and deciding the best join order.
(P.2) *Reading time*: time needed for the system to read and parse the data.
(P.3) *Reasoning time*: time needed to complete the first reasoning cycle.
(P.4) *Initialization time*: time needed to load the ontology into the shared memory. As mentioned, for *RETE$_{X-pool}$* configurations, the shared memory was pre-loaded with the ontology, after which reasoning took place (Sect. 5.1.4).

In addition, we collect the following memory-related metrics:

(M.1) *Number of alpha memories*: the total number of alpha memories, differentiating between different types (i.e., regular vs. virtual memories).
(M.2) *Alpha memory size*: the total size (KB) taken up by the set of alpha memories.

(M.3) *Total memory size*: the total size (KB) taken up by the set of alpha memories and the shared memory pool.

(M.4) *RDF nodes size*: the total size (KB) taken up by RDF node data. The contents of an RDF graph are kept in RDF node objects. By considering this memory size separately, these are not accidentally counted towards only (M.2) or (M.3).

(M.5) *Shared memory size*: the total size (KB) taken up by the shared memory, if any.

For evaluating the (Z.ii) *shared memory pool* setup, we also measure the following:

(M.6) *Memory operations*: the number and performance overhead of memory operations, including updating the shared memory and individual RETE memories.

To obtain actual memory usage (KB), we performed heap dumps on PC and Android. Per configuration, a heap dump was taken after reasoning over the ontology that yielded the min., median and max. number of alpha memory tokens, respectively.

5.2 Benchmark Results

Table 1 shows the memory usage for $RETE_{base}$ (i.e., the baseline system) and the $RETE_{pool}$ configurations. In particular, it shows the memory usage for the min., median and max. ontology (see Sect. 5.1.5). The table lists the number of alpha memories (M.1), alpha memory sizes (M.2), and (for ease of reference) the total memory size, which includes alpha memories and the shared memory (if any) (M.3). Further, the table shows the reasoning performances (P.3).

The following memory metrics are identical for all configurations (KB): (M.4) *RDF nodes size*: 5.1.5 median: 800 (min: 203 – max: 26760); (M.5) *Shared memory size*: median: 562 (min: 98 – max: 26070). Further, the following performance metrics (ms) are identical: (P.1) *Network compilation time*: avg. ca. 5 (PC), 71 (mobile); (P.2) *Reading time*: avg. ca. 73 (PC), 696 (mobile). As mentioned, a separate data loading step took place for $RETE_{X-pool}$ configurations (P.4). This amounts to 11 ms for median (min: 3 ms – max: 670 ms) on PC, and 99 ms for median (min: 15 ms – max: 1034 ms).

Note that $RETE_{part-pool}$ configurations with $t_s = 0.1$ and $t_s = 0.25$; and $t_s = 0.75$ and $t_s = 1$ are pairwise identical, so we only present $t_s = 0.1$ and $t_s = 1$.

We first observe that only 46 alpha memories are required for a total of 78 OWL2 RL rules, due to the re-use of alpha (and beta) nodes and memories where possible (Sect. 3). Memory savings for $RETE_{pool}$ depend on the concrete application scenario: i.e., whether (S.i) a separate shared memory needs to be introduced, or (S.ii) an existing, multi-purpose RDF store can be re-used for this purpose.

Scenario (S.i)

Even in scenario (S.i), we expect significant memory savings since duplication of data in alpha memories is either avoided entirely ($RETE_{full-pool}$) or partially ($RETE_{part-pool}$). Indeed, memory savings for $RETE_{full-pool}$ are huge, with a ca. 60% for the median ontology (min: 55%, max: 50%). As expected, the number of regular alpha memories

Table 1. Memory usage (KB) and reasoning performance (ms) *: $RETE_{part\text{-}pool}$ (t_s), †: r = regular, v = virtual, **: median (min – max), ***: average (min – max).

Version*	Memory usage (KB)**			Reasoning performance*** (ms) (P.3)	
	# α mem. (M.1)†	α mem. size (M.2)	Total mem. size (M.3)	PC	Mobile
$RETE_{base}$	#**r**: 46 #**v**: 0	1487 (263–52789)	1487 (263–52789)	15705 (18–322352)	24968 (1051–199974)
$RETE_{full\text{-}pool}$	#**r**: 0 #**v**: 46	20 (20–20)	582 (118–26090)	51905 (51–1187570)	69573 (2903–542670)
$RETE_{part\text{-}pool}$ (0.1)	#**r**: 42 #**v**: 4	482 (100–13757)	1044 (198–39874)	16303 (27–340194)	29287 (1526–212573)
$RETE_{part\text{-}pool}$ (0.5)	#**r**: 43 #**v**: 3	859 (161–14675)	1421 (259–40745)	16475 (23–338109)	26444 (1145–202646)
$RETE_{part\text{-}pool}$ (1)	#**r**: 44 #**v**: 2	891 (166–30067)	1453 (264–56137)	17715 (25–365843)	25203 (1115–198404)

(M.1) increases together with threshold t_s. This causes data duplication among individual memories, as well as with the shared memory; thus increasing the total memory usage (M.3). For $RETE_{part\text{-}pool}$ (0.1), memory savings drop to ca. 30% for median (min: 25%, max: 25%); for $RETE_{part\text{-}pool}$ (0.5), ca. 4% (min: 1%, max: 23%); and for $RETE_{part\text{-}pool}$ (1), memory usage is similar for median and min., and increases for max.

At the same time, we observe that $RETE_{full\text{-}pool}$ greatly reduces performance; by factors of avg. ca. 3,3 and 2,8 for PC and mobile, respectively[1]. We expect $RETE_{part\text{-}pool}$ to strike a better memory/performance balance, with performance improving as threshold t_s increases. Indeed, performance improves greatly on mobile (e.g., $t_s = 0.1$: avg. ca. 58%), and approaches $RETE_{base}$ as t_s increases. On PC, we observe the same effect (e.g., $t_s = 0.1$: avg. ca. 69%) at least until $t_s \geq 0.5$, after which performance (slightly) worsens. This is likely due to excessive garbage collection; when leaving out the 7 most memory-intensive ontologies, $RETE_{part\text{-}pool}$ performance is constant for all t_s at avg. ca. 1,25 s ($RETE_{base} = 1.15$ s, $RETE_{full\text{-}pool} = 3.3$ s).

We conclude that $RETE_{part\text{-}pool}$ (0.1) effects the best memory/performance balance. Compared to $RETE_{base}$, its saves memory by 30% for median (min: 25%, max: 25%) whereas it is ca. 4.3 s slower on mobile and 0.6 s slower on PC. While $RETE_{part\text{-}pool}$ (0.5) only incurs a penalty of ca. 1.5 s on mobile and 0.8 s on PC, its memory savings are significantly lower, i.e., 4% for median (min: 1%, max: 23%). At the same time, we note that an extra initialization time is incurred for all $RETE_{X\text{-}pool}$ configurations (P.4).

---

[1] Note that performance times for PC and mobile are not directly comparable (Sect. 5.1.2).

Scenario (S.ii)

In scenario (S.ii), since we are re-using an RDF store that is utilized for other purposes as well, the size of the shared memory is not counted towards our total memory usage. In that case, memory savings by $RETE_{full\text{-}pool}$ are tremendous, using only ca. 0,04% (max) to ca. 7,6% (min) compared to $RETE_{base}$. In fact, $RETE_{part\text{-}pool}$ (1), which utilizes the most memory, still only takes up avg. ca. 57% of $RETE_{base}$.

For $RETE_{part\text{-}pool}$ (0.1): memory savings include 68% for median (min: 62%, max: 74%); for $RETE_{part\text{-}pool}$ (0.5), savings constitute 42% for median (min: 39%, max: 72%); for $RETE_{part\text{-}pool}$ (1), savings include 40% for median (min: 37%, max: 43%).

In this case, we conclude that $RETE_{part\text{-}pool}$ (0.5) is preferable: it greatly improves performance (ca. 65%) on mobile (PC is only slightly slower), while, in this scenario, memory savings are significant as well. Further, the performance gains by $RETE_{part\text{-}pool}$ (1) do not seem comparable to its increased memory usage. As before, we note that any $RETE_{x\text{-}pool}$ configuration also incurs an extra initialization time (P.4).

6 Related Work

To realize ontology-based reasoning, many mobile reasoners, i.e., targeting resource-constrained platforms, utilize rule-based OWL axiomatizations; such as custom entailment rulesets [30, 31] or OWL2 RL rulesets [7, 13]. For instance, MiRE4OWL [32] and μOR [31] apply a custom entailment ruleset; Seitz et al. [17] load the CLIPS engine with the OWL2 RL ruleset; and Tai et al. [7] and BaseVISor [33] rely on rules implementing pD* semantics. In general, by focusing on subsets of rule axioms, rule-based axiomatizations allow easily adjusting reasoning complexity to the application scenario [7], or avoiding resource-heavy inferences [16, 17]. In contrast, transformation rules used in tableau-based DL reasoning are often hardcoded, making it hard to de-select them at runtime [7]. Also, most classic DL optimizations improve performance at the cost of memory, which is limited in mobile devices [8].

To deal with data duplication caused by generic rule premises in OWL2 RL, we presented the $RETE_{pool}$ algorithm, which utilizes virtual alpha memories that act as masks (or views) on a large, shared dataset. This concept was first introduced by Hanson for the Ariel system [26]. Later on, Hanson et al. [34] presented a set of optimizers that choose an efficient Gator network (see below), possibly including virtual alpha memories, based on database size, predicate selectivity and update frequency distribution, among others. In this paper, we implemented this concept to realize more memory-efficient, semantic ontology-based reasoning on mobile platforms. We further consider typical Semantic Web scenarios, where an RDF store is already available and possibly pre-loaded with data, as well as the issues ensuing from such a setup. As opposed to Hanson et al., our evaluation focuses in particular on how memory and performance may be balanced by using different selectivity thresholds t_s.

Some approaches [13, 14] support a different solution for dealing with generic rule premises, as they occur in rule-based axiomatizations such as OWL2 RL. In these solutions, a first step materializes all schema-related inferences in the ontology (e.g., using a separate OWL reasoner), which is then followed by a rule instantiation step. Based on the materialized schema, the second step creates multiple concrete rules for each generic rule by replacing schema variables by concrete schema references. This kind of approach deals poorly with ontology schema updates, and is thus only suitable for scenarios where such updates do not occur (or occur very infrequently). As a different solution to optimizing mobile, semantic reasoning, Tai et al. [7] present a selective rule loading algorithm, which composes a pD* ruleset based on ontology expressivity; and a two-phase RETE construction process, which utilizes selectivity information from the first phase to optimize join sequences in the second phase. Komazec and Cerri [35] integrated a special ε network into RETE to optimize RDFS entailments.

We note that other production rule algorithms aside from RETE exist. Miranker [22] proposed the TREAT algorithm, which, instead of storing join results, re-calculates results of intermediate joins when required. In doing so, TREAT avoids the memory and maintenance overhead of beta memories. The Gator [36] and RETE* [37] algorithms generalize RETE and TREAT, treating both as special cases. The more recent PHREAK algorithm, introduced by the well-known Drools production system [25], is based on RETE but incorporates lazy and goal-oriented aspects. As our work focuses on reducing data duplication in alpha memories, which is an issue that, to the best of our knowledge, potentially affects all these approaches and algorithms, it can be considered complementary to these efforts.

7 Conclusions and Future Work

In this paper, we presented the $RETE_{pool}$ algorithm which, by pooling a particular selection of RETE alpha memories, aims to balance memory usage with performance. We illustrated how this algorithm is well-suited for many typical Semantic Web scenarios, which typically utilize an existing, multi-purpose RDF store. We performed an extensive set of benchmarks, which evaluated semantic, ontology-based reasoning using our OWL2 RL ruleset and multiple configurations of the algorithm, both on PC and mobile platforms. In line with expectations, the $RETE_{pool}$ algorithm drastically reduces memory usage. By configuring selectivity thresholds, i.e., where virtual alpha memories are only used in case estimated selectivity exceeds a threshold, we were better able to balance memory savings with performance overhead.

Our evaluation has a number of limitations. Firstly, our solution and evaluation focuses specifically on semantic reasoning using the OWL2 RL ruleset, which includes many generic rule premises. For other rulesets with more concrete premises, utilizing $RETE_{pool}$ will likely lead to smaller memory savings. Hence, future work includes running additional benchmarks to test the usefulness of this approach for other types of rulesets. Secondly, premise selectivity was estimated based on the actual number of tokens matched from the benchmark ontology. Clearly, this will not be possible in incremental reasoning scenarios, where only a very limited amount of initial data is available. As a result, future work involves utilizing other kinds of selectivity estimates (e.g., based on SPO position). Thirdly, our goal was to establish to what extent the proposed optimization reduces memory usage and impacts performance – which can only be done by comparisons with the baseline system. When we arrive at a more mature, fully-fledged rule system, future work will involve comparisons to other rule systems. Finally, to avoid the main pitfall of $RETE_{pool}$ – i.e., accessing a large shared memory for each join attempt – future work involves creating a more fine-grained memory strategy. We observe that alpha memories will often completely subsume other memories, depending on premise structure: e.g., premise $<?c\ rdf{:}type\ ?t>$ subsumes premise $<?c\ rdf{:}type\ owl{:}Class>$. By constructing a nested memory structure, a subsuming memory could directly access the data of subsumed memories, while still reducing duplication.

References

1. Maghsoud-Lou, E., Christie, S., Abidi, S.R., Abidi, S.S.R.: Protocol-driven decision support within e-referral systems to streamline patient consultation, triaging and referrals from primary care to specialist clinics. J. Med. Syst. **41**, 139 (2017)
2. Jafarpour, B., Abidi, S.S.R., Abidi, S.R.: Exploiting semantic web technologies to develop owl-based clinical practice guideline execution engines. IEEE J. Biomed. Heal. Inform. **20**, 388–398 (2014)
3. The National Center for Biomedical Ontology: BioPortal. http://bioportal.bioontology.org/
4. SNOMED International: SNOMED-CT. http://www.snomed.org/snomed-ct
5. Calvanese, D., Carroll, J., De Giacomo, G., Hendler, J., Herman, I., Parsia, B., Patel-Schneider, P.F., Ruttenberg, A., Sattler, U., Schneider, M.: OWL2 Web Ontology Language Profiles, 2nd edn. http://www.w3.org/TR/owl2-profiles/#OWL_2_RL
6. Van Woensel, W., Roy, P.C., Abidi, S.R., Abidi, S.S.R.: A mobile and intelligent patient diary for chronic disease self-management. In: Studies in Health Technology and Informatics, pp. 118–122 (2015)
7. Tai, W., Keeney, J., O'Sullivan, D.: Resource-constrained reasoning using a reasoner composition approach. Semant. Web. **6**, 35–59 (2015)
8. Bobed, C., Yus, R., Bobillo, F., Mena, E.: Semantic reasoning on mobile devices: do androids dream of efficient reasoners? Web Semant. Sci. Serv. Agents World Wide Web **35**, 167–183 (2015)
9. Apache: Apache Jena. https://jena.apache.org/
10. AndroJena. https://github.com/lencinhaus/androjena
11. Van Woensel, W., Al Haider, N., Ahmad, A., Abidi, S.S.R.: A cross-platform benchmark framework for mobile semantic web reasoning engines. In: Mika, P., et al. (eds.) ISWC 2014. LNCS, vol. 8796, pp. 389–408. Springer, Cham (2014). https://doi.org/10.1007/978-3-319-11964-9_25
12. Carroll, J., Herman, I., Patel-Schneider, P.F.: OWL 2 Web Ontology Language RDF-Based Semantics, 2nd edn. https://www.w3.org/TR/owl2-rdf-based-semantics/
13. Motik, B., Horrocks, I., Kim, S.M.: Delta-reasoner: a semantic web reasoner for an intelligent mobile platform. In: Proceedings of the 21st International Conference Companion on World Wide Web, pp. 63–72. ACM, New York (2012)
14. Meditskos, G., Bassiliades, N.: DLEJena: a practical forward-chaining OWL 2 RL reasoner combining Jena and Pellet. Web Semant. **8**, 89–94 (2010)
15. Knublauch, H.: OWL 2 RL in SPARQL using SPIN. http://composing-the-semantic-web.blogspot.ca/2009/01/owl-2-rl-in-sparql-using-spin.html
16. Bishop, B., Bojanov, S.: Implementing OWL 2 RL and OWL 2 QL rule-sets for OWLIM. In: Dumontier, M., Courtot, M. (eds.) OWLED. CEUR-WS.org (2011)

17. Seitz, C., Schönfelder, R.: Rule-based OWL reasoning for specific embedded devices. In: Aroyo, L., et al. (eds.) ISWC 2011. LNCS, vol. 7032, pp. 237–252. Springer, Heidelberg (2011). https://doi.org/10.1007/978-3-642-25093-4_16

18. Hitzler, P., Krötzsch, M., Parsia, B., Patel-Schneider, P.F., Rudolph, S.: OWL 2 Web Ontology Language Primer, 2nd edn. http://www.w3.org/TR/owl2-primer/

19. O'Connor, M., Das, A.: A pair of OWL 2 RL reasoners. In: OWL: Experiences and Directions Workshop 2012 (2012)

20. Documentation: Shared RETE Memory. https://niche.cs.dal.ca/materials/rete-shared-mem/

21. Schneider, M., Mainzer, K.: A conformance test suite for the OWL 2 RL RDF rules language and the OWL 2 RDF-based semantics. In: 6th International Workshop on OWL: Experiences and Directions (2009)

22. Miranker, D.P.: TREAT: A Better Match Algorithm for AI Production Systems (Long Version). University of Texas at Austin, Austin (1987)

23. Ishida, T.: An optimization algorithm for production systems. IEEE Trans. Knowl. Data Eng. **6**, 549–558 (1994)

24. Miranker, D., Depena, R., Jung, H., Sequeda, J.F., Reyna, C.: Diamond: a SPARQL query engine, for linked data based on the rete match. In: Artificial Intelligence Meets the Web of Data Workshop, Co-located at ECAI (2012)

25. Red Hat: Drools - RETE Algorithm. https://docs.jboss.org/drools/release/latest/drools-docs/html_single/#_reteoo

26. Hanson, E.N.: The design and implementation of the ariel active database rule system. IEEE Trans. Knowl. Data Eng. **8**, 157–172 (1996)

27. Apache Jena Inference Support. https://jena.apache.org/documentation/inference/

28. Friedman-Hill, E.J.: Jess - RETE Algorithm. http://www.jessrules.com/docs/71/rete.html

29. Matentzoglu, N., Bail, S., Parsia, B.: A snapshot of the OWL web. In: Alani, H., et al. (eds.) ISWC 2013. LNCS, vol. 8218, pp. 331–346. Springer, Heidelberg (2013). https://doi.org/10.1007/978-3-642-41335-3_21

30. Kim, T., Park, I., Hyun, S.J., Lee, D.: MiRE4OWL: mobile rule engine for OWL. In: Proceedings of the 2010 IEEE 34th Annual Computer Software and Applications Conference Workshops, pp. 317–322. IEEE Computer Society, Washington, D.C. (2010)

31. Ali, S., Kiefer, S.: μOR – a micro OWL DL reasoner for ambient intelligent devices. In: Abdennadher, N., Petcu, D. (eds.) GPC 2009. LNCS, vol. 5529, pp. 305–316. Springer, Heidelberg (2009). https://doi.org/10.1007/978-3-642-01671-4_28

32. Kim, T., Park, I., Hyun, S.J., Lee, D.: MiRE4OWL: mobile rule engine for OWL. In: 2010 IEEE 34th Annual Computer Software and Applications Conference Workshops, pp. 317–322. IEEE (2010)

33. Matheus, C.J., Baclawski, K., Kokar, M.M.: BaseVISor: a triples-based inference engine outfitted to process RuleML and R-Entailment rules. In: Second International Conference on Rules and Rule Markup Languages for the Semantic Web, pp. 67–74 (2006)

34. Hanson, E.N., Bodagala, S., Chadaga, U.: Trigger condition testing and view maintenance using optimized discrimination networks. IEEE Trans. Knowl. Data Eng. **14**, 261–280 (2002)

35. Komazec, S., Cerri, D.: Towards efficient schema-enhanced pattern matching over RDF data streams. In: 1st International Workshop on Ordering and Reasoning (OrdRing 2011) (2011)

36. Hanson, E., Hasan, M.S.: Gator: an optimized discrimination network for active database rule condition testing. Technical report TR-93-036, University of Florida, December 1993

37. Wright, I., Marshall, J.: The execution kernel of RC++: RETE*, a faster RETE with TREAT as a special case. Int. J. Intell. Games Simul. **2**(1), 36–48 (2003)

Efficient Ontology-Based Data Integration
with Canonical IRIs

Guohui Xiao[1]([⊠])(iD), Dag Hovland[2](iD), Dimitris Bilidas[3](iD), Martin Rezk[4],
Martin Giese[2](iD), and Diego Calvanese[1](iD)

[1] Faculty of Computer Science, Free-University of Bozen-Bolzano, Bolzano, Italy
{xiao,calvanese}@inf.unibz.it
[2] Department of Informatics, University of Oslo, Oslo, Norway
{hovland,martingi}@ifi.uio.no
[3] National and Kapodistrian University of Athens, Athens, Greece
d.bilidas@di.uoa.gr
[4] Rakuten, Tokyo, Japan
martin.rezk@rakuten.com

Abstract. In this paper, we study how to efficiently integrate multiple relational databases using an ontology-based approach. In ontology-based data integration (OBDI) an ontology provides a coherent view of multiple databases, and SPARQL queries over the ontology are rewritten into (federated) SQL queries over the underlying databases. Specifically, we address the scenario where records with different identifiers in different databases can represent the same entity. The standard approach in this case is to use sameAs to model the equivalence between entities. However, the standard semantics of sameAs may cause an exponential blow up of query results, since all possible combinations of equivalent identifiers have to be included in the answers. The large number of answers is not only detrimental to the performance of query evaluation, but also makes the answers difficult to understand due to the redundancy they introduce. This motivates us to propose an alternative approach, which is based on assigning canonical IRIs to entities in order to avoid redundancy. Formally, we present our approach as a new SPARQL entailment regime and compare it with the sameAs approach. We provide a prototype implementation and evaluate it in two experiments: in a real-world data integration scenario in Statoil and in an experiment extending the Wisconsin benchmark. The experimental results show that the canonical IRI approach is significantly more scalable.

1 Introduction

Large organizations, both public and private, typically need to manage, in multiple information systems, large amounts of data stored across multiple heterogeneous data sources. To support decision making in such settings, there is the need to access in an integrated way the data managed by the different systems, which in general are stored in different databases. A key challenge for data integration

© Springer International Publishing AG, part of Springer Nature 2018
A. Gangemi et al. (Eds.): ESWC 2018, LNCS 10843, pp. 697–713, 2018.
https://doi.org/10.1007/978-3-319-93417-4_45

in such settings is that the different systems have often been designed separately serving different purposes, and thus lack a coherent view of the underlying data.

Ontology-based data access (OBDA) [24] is a successful paradigm that addresses this challenge by relying on semantic technologies to provide a uniform conceptual view over heterogeneous data. Specifically, an ontology describing the domain of interest is connected to a data source through a declarative specification, given in terms of *mappings* [8] that relate symbols (i.e., classes and properties) in the ontology to (SQL) views over the data. The ontology layer can be queried using SPARQL, and queries are automatically rewritten by an OBDA engine into SQL queries expressed over the underlying database. Thus, users no longer need an understanding of the structure and organization of the data in the source. *Ontology-based data integration* (OBDI) is an extension of OBDA in which the data is not stored in a single database, but in a multitude of databases that need to be queried in an integrated way, while still maintaining the same conceptual architecture based on mappings [3]. OBDI has been successfully deployed in several domains, such as oil and gas [18], maritime security [1], and cultural heritage [2].

An important aspect in OBDI is the fact that the same conceptual entity may be stored in different databases but represented by different identifiers. Consider e.g., the same person, represented in one database through name, surname, and date of birth, in a second database through the social security number, and in a third database through the taxcode. In order to combine the information coming from different systems so as to produce coherent results to queries, we need a way to relate different representations so that they can be recognized as representing the same entity. This is challenging both from the theoretical and from the practical points of view.

The standard approach in the Semantic Web to modeling the fact that different IRIs actually represent the same entity is to use owl:sameAs[1], which defines an equivalence relation between entities. In our previous work [5], we have shown how an approach based on the use of sameAs can be adopted also for OBDI. A serious drawback of this approach is that the semantics of sameAs may cause an exponential blowup of query results, since all possible combinations of equivalent identifiers have to be included in the answer to a query. The large number of answers is detrimental to the performance of query evaluation, and also introduces redundancy making answers difficult to understand.

To address this problem, we propose here an alternative approach, based on assigning to each entity a *canonical IRI*. Such canonical IRI is the one of choice for relating occurrences of the entity that are identified differently in different data sources, and also for returning the entity to the user. The idea of exploiting a canonical representation of IRIs internally, for optimization purposes, has already been used in some reasoning engines. E.g., RDFox [22] uses an optimized approach for rule evaluation by forward chaining based on propagating a canonical representation for entities. Also Stardog adopts a similar strategy in query

---

[1] For space reasons, from now on we will use sameAs as an abbreviation for owl:sameAs.

answering, by only returning a canonical representation of equivalent entities, to avoid the combinatorial explosion in query results[2].

However, lifting this idea to the OBDI scenario is non-trivial. On the one hand, the choice on which source should provide the canonical IRI for an entity depends on the actual (type of) entity, and on the data sources in which it appears. A more critical issue is due to the fact that in OBDI, entities with the corresponding IRIs are not materialized but kept *virtual*, since they are generated dynamically at query answering time from the data in the sources through the mappings. Hence it is not really feasible to explicitly substitute the entities by canonical ones. Instead our proposal is based on embedding such information in the mapping specification, while delegating to the designer of the OBDI system the responsibility of choosing which canonical IRIs to adopt.

For such a setting, we provide the following contributions:

- We formally define the *canonical IRI semantics* as a SPARQL entailment regime. We show that such semantics is equivalent to the sameAs semantics (taking into account equivalence of IRIs), thus guaranteeing soundness and completeness of the associated query answering algorithm (see Sect. 3).
- We show that query answering and the canonical IRI semantics can be reduced to a simple entailment regime by means of query rewriting. However, this query rewriting step is only of theoretical interest since the rewritten query is not efficiently executable (see Sect. 4).
- We propose an alternative practical *mapping rewriting-based* technique for query answering, inspired by algorithms for mapping saturation [2] (see Sect. 5).
- We provide a prototype implementation of our technique and evaluate it in two experiments. The first experiment is based on a real-world data integration scenario in the oil company Statoil [18]. The second experiment is based on the Wisconsin benchmark [9]. The experimental results show that the canonical IRI approach is significantly more scalable (see Sect. 6).

We start our technical development by introducing in Sect. 2 the necessary background.

2   Preliminaries

We present now the preliminary notions on RDF graphs, SPARQL, and ontology-based data access on which we build in the rest of the paper.

2.1   RDF and SPARQL

SPARQL [14] is the W3C standard language designed to query RDF graphs. We consider a vocabulary of three pairwise disjoint and countably infinite sets of symbols: **I** for *IRIs*, **L** for *RDF literals*, and **V** for *variables*. In line with

---

[2] https://www.stardog.com/docs/#_same_as_reasoning.

previous work on ontology-based data access, we do not consider blank nodes. The elements of $\mathbf{T} = \mathbf{I} \cup \mathbf{L}$ are called *RDF terms*, and those of $\mathbf{T} \times \mathbf{I} \times \mathbf{T}$ are called *(RDF) triples*. An *(RDF) graph* is a set of triples. A *triple pattern* is an element of $(\mathbf{T} \cup \mathbf{V}) \times (\mathbf{I} \cup \mathbf{V}) \times (\mathbf{T} \cup \mathbf{V})$. A *basic graph pattern* (*BGP*) is a finite set of triple patterns. We consider the fragment of SPARQL queries defined by Q in the following EBNF grammar[3]:

$$P ::= B \mid Q \mid P \text{ FILTER } F \mid P \text{ UNION } P \mid (P, P) \mid P \text{ OPT } P$$
$$Q ::= \text{SELECT } \{ \mathbf{V} \text{ AS } \mathbf{V} \} \text{ WHERE } P$$

where B is a BGP and F is a *filter expression* (we refer to [14] for details). An expression $\{?y_1 \text{ AS } ?x_1, \ldots, ?y_n \text{ AS } ?x_n\}$ is called a *projection* with *answer variables* $\{?x_1, \ldots, ?x_n\}$. We abbreviate "$?x$ AS $?x$" with $?x$. For a SPARQL query $Q = \text{SELECT } R \text{ WHERE } Q_1$, we use $sig(Q)$ to denote the answer variables of R.

The semantics of SPARQL queries is given in terms of *solution mappings*, which are *partial* maps $s \colon \mathbf{V} \to \mathbf{T}$ with (possibly empty) domain $dom(s)$. Here, following [20,23,25], we use the set-based semantics for SPARQL (rather than the bag-based one, as in the W3C specification). More specifically, for a BGP B, the *answer* $[\![B]\!]_G$ to B over a graph G is $[\![B]\!]_G = \{s \colon var(B) \to \mathbf{T} \mid s(B) \subseteq G\}$, where $var(B)$ is the set of variables occurring in B and $s(B)$ is the result of substituting each variable u in B by $s(u)$. Then, the *answer* to a SPARQL query Q over a graph G is the set $[\![Q]\!]_G$ of solution mappings defined by induction using the SPARQL algebra operators (filter, join, union, optional, and projection) starting from BGPs; cf. [17]. This semantics is known as *simple entailment*.

2.2 SPARQL Entailment Regimes

SPARQL entailment regimes allow for querying RDF graphs with richer reasoning capabilities [12]. Specifically, an entailment regime E specifies how to obtain from an RDF graph G an entailed graph $eg^E(G)$. Then, the answer $[\![B]\!]_G^E$ to a BGP B under the entailment regime E is defined as $[\![B]\!]_{eg^E(G)}$. Similarly, The answer $[\![Q]\!]_G^E$ to a SPARQL query Q under the entailment regime E is defined as $[\![Q]\!]_{eg^E(G)}$. Note that entailment regimes only modify the evaluation of BGPs but not that of other SPARQL operators.

We present now the standard W3C semantics for SPARQL queries over OWL 2 ontologies under different entailment regimes. Under the *OWL 2 direct semantics entailment regime*, one can query an RDF graph G that consist of two parts: the *intensional* sub-graph (i.e., TBox or ontology) $\mathcal{T}$ representing the background knowledge in terms of class and property axioms, and an *extensional* sub-graph (i.e., ABox) $\mathcal{A}$ representing the data as class and property assertions. We write such a graph G, which represents a *knowledge base*, as $(\mathcal{T}, \mathcal{A})$ to emphasize the partitioning when necessary. Moreover, for convenience, we use the triple notations $(s, \mathtt{rdf\!:\!type}, C)$ and (s, p, o) and the ABox assertion notations $C(s)$ and $p(s, o)$ interchangeably.

---

[3] Recall that in EBNF "{A}" means any number of repetitions of A.

We work with ontologies expressed in the OWL 2 QL profile [21] of OWL 2. Such profile induces the *OWL 2 QL* (or simply, *QL*) *entailment regime* in which, for an OWL 2 QL knowledge base G we have $eg^{QL}(G) = \{t \mid G \models_{DL} t\}$, where $\models_{DL}$ denotes the standard OWL 2 entailment, defined in terms of description logics semantics, cf. [27]. Under the QL entailment regime, a SPARQL query Q formulated over an ontology $\mathcal{T}$ is *first-order rewritable*, i.e., Q can be rewritten into a query $Q_{\mathcal{T}}$ such that for every ABox $\mathcal{A}$, evaluating Q over $(\mathcal{T}, \mathcal{A})$ (under the QL entailment regime) is equivalent to evaluating $Q_{\mathcal{T}}$ over $\mathcal{A}$ (under the simple entailment regime) [4, 20].

2.3   SPARQL Entailment Regimes for sameAs

In addition to the input graph $G = (\mathcal{T}, \mathcal{A})$, we consider now a set $\mathcal{A}^s$ of sameAs triples of the form sameAs(a, b), specifying the equivalence between individuals a and b.

We now define an entailment regime that interprets sameAs as the equivalence closure (i.e., the reflexive, transitive, and symmetric closure) of $\mathcal{A}^s$. For a set $\mathcal{A}^s$ of sameAs assertions, we denote by $(\mathcal{A}^s)^*$ the equivalence closure of $\mathcal{A}^s$. Given an RDF graph $\mathcal{A}$ and a set $\mathcal{A}^s$ of sameAs assertions, we define the *sameAs entailed graph* $sag(\mathcal{A}, \mathcal{A}^s)$ of $\mathcal{A}$ with respect to $\mathcal{A}^s$ as

$$\mathcal{A} \cup \{C(o') \mid C(o) \in G, \text{sameAs}(o, o') \in (\mathcal{A}^s)^*\}$$
$$\cup \{R(o_1', o_2') \mid R(o_1, o_2) \in G, \text{sameAs}(o_1, o_1') \in (\mathcal{A}^s)^*, \text{sameAs}(o_2, o_2') \in (\mathcal{A}^s)^*\}.$$

Given an entailment regime E, we can derive an extended entailment regime $E+sameAs$, which takes into account equivalences between entities inferred through sameAs statements, as follows:

$$eg^{E+sameAs}(\mathcal{T}, \mathcal{A} \cup \mathcal{A}^s) = eg^E(\mathcal{T}, sag(\mathcal{A}, \mathcal{A}^s))$$

In this paper, we are mostly interested in the SPARQL entailment regimes QL and $QL+sameAs$, but our results also apply to other entailment regimes E in which sameAs is treated as a standard object property, and new sameAs triples *cannot* be inferred.

2.4   Ontology-Based Data Access and Integration

In ontology-based data access (OBDA), we start from an *OBDA specification* $\mathcal{P} = (\mathcal{T}, \mathcal{M}, \mathcal{S})$, consisting of a set $\mathcal{T}$ of OWL 2 axioms, a set $\mathcal{M}$ of *mapping assertions*, and a relational database schema $\mathcal{S}$. An *OBDA instance* $(\mathcal{P}, D)$ is given by an OBDA specification $\mathcal{P}$ and a relational database instance D compliant with $\mathcal{S}$.

Mapping assertions allow one to define how an ABox should be populated with values retrieved by means of SQL queries. Each mapping assertion has one of the forms

$$C(f(\boldsymbol{x})) \leftarrow sql(\boldsymbol{y}) \qquad\qquad P(f(\boldsymbol{x}), f'(\boldsymbol{x'})) \leftarrow sql(\boldsymbol{y})$$

such that $x \subseteq y$ and $x' \subseteq y$, sql is an arbitrary SQL query over $\mathcal{S}$ projecting columns y, and f and f' are functions constructing RDF terms out of values retrieved from the database. In a concrete mapping language like R2RML [8], these functions are specified as templates for IRIs and literals. For example, <http://statoil.com/wellbore/{id}> is an IRI template where "{id}" is a place-holder, and it generates, e.g., the IRI <http://statoil.com/wellbore/25> when {id} is instantiated with "25". In practice, it is desired that each IRI can be constructed by at most one IRI template, and we make such assumption here; formally, the union of all the IRI templates occurring in an OBDA specification is an injective function. By applying all mapping assertions in $\mathcal{M}$ to D, one can derive a (virtual) RDF graph $\mathcal{A}_{\mathcal{M},D}$ [24]. Then, SPARQL query answering over an OBDA instance $(\mathcal{P}, D)$ is defined as query answering over $(\mathcal{T}, \mathcal{A}_{\mathcal{M},D})$.

We recall that, ontology-based data integration (OBDI) considers a set of data sources instead of a single one, but otherwise the formal treatment is identical to that of OBDA.

The inspiration for working with equality in OBDI came from problems we encountered in the context of the EU-funded project Optique [11], when query-ing data in the Norwegian oil company Statoil. This is also the background of the *real world* experiments in Sect. 6.1. In the following, we present our run-ning example, which provides a simplified version of the experimental setting of Optique. The content of the tables below is real data from the Norwegian Petroleum Directorate FactPages[4].

Example 1. Assume two databases `national` and `corporate` with one table each:

national.wellbore				corporate.drillingops		
name	opPurp	wlbFld		name	driStDt	reason
1/3-1	WILDCAT			NO_1/3-1	06-07-1968	WILDCAT
2/4-2	WILDCAT	EKOFISK		NO_2/4-2	18-09-1969	
1/3-10	APPRAISAL	OSELVAR		NO_1/2-1	20-03-1989	WILDCAT
1/2-1	WILDCAT	BLANE		NO_1/3-A-1_H	22-07-2011	PRODUCTION

In both tables, the column `name` is the only key (i.e., names are unique within each table). These columns have almost the same values in the two databases, except that in the `corporate` database they are prefixed with "NO_" (country code for Norway). An example set of mapping assertions is:

```
:NationalWellbore/{name} :inField {wlbFld} ; :purpose {opPurp} .
← SELECT name, wlbFld, opPurp FROM national.wellbore

:CorporateWellbore/{name} :drillingStarted {driStDt} ; :purpose {reason} .
← SELECT name, driStDt, reason FROM corporate.drillingops
```

---

[4] http://factpages.npd.no.

Examples of triples in the ABox defined by this OBDA scenario are[5]

```
(:NationalWellbore/1/2-1,         :inField,        BLANE),
(:CorporateWellbore/NO_1/3-A-1_H, :drillingStarted, 22-07-2011),
(:NationalWellbore/1/3-10,        :purpose,        APPRAISAL),
(:CorporateWellbore/NO_1/2-1,     :purpose,        WILDCAT).
```

Compare the property :purpose, which is mapped to several databases, with the properties :inField and :drillingStarted, which are mapped to a single database each. Properties like :purpose may or may not have values for the same entity in different datasets. So the SPARQL query $(?w, \texttt{:purpose}, ?p)$ returns both $\{?w \mapsto \texttt{:NationalWellbore/1/3-1}, ?p \mapsto \texttt{WILDCAT}\}$ and $\{?w \mapsto \texttt{:CorporateWellbore/NO\_1/3-1}, ?p \mapsto \texttt{WILDCAT}\}$ as answers, while the query $((?w, \texttt{:inField}, ?f), (?w, \texttt{:drillingStarted}, ?d))$ has no answers.

There are different ways of improving this situation. Perhaps the most obvious and direct one is to just change the mapping set such that the wellbores are mapped into equal IRIs. This is not always possible, as a data source may not be under the control of the mapping author; consider, e.g., Linked Open Data. Moreover, when integrating two OBDA systems where there already are IRIs defined, instead of modifying existing mapping sets, it is in general more convenient to add mappings stating the equivalences between IRIs, so as to virtually generate the sameAs relation, e.g., (:NationalWellbore/1/3-1, sameAs, :CorporateWellbore/NO_1/3-1). Such mappings also serve as a documentation for the way the data is linked. ∎

3   Canonical IRI Semantics

We observe that the standard sameAs semantics is not scalable for query answering in general. Suppose that $\mu = \{?x_1 \mapsto a_1, \ldots, ?x_n \mapsto a_n\}$ is a solution mapping of a SPARQL query q over an ABox that includes assertions $\{\texttt{sameAs}(a_i, b_i) \mid 1 \leq i \leq n\}$. Then one can replace any a_i by b_i in μ, resulting in a semantically equivalent solution mapping, which is still a valid answer to q. In this case, there are 2^n such possibilities. This example shows that in general, sameAs could cause an exponential blowup of query results. Such large numbers of answers are not only detrimental to the performance of query evaluation, but also make the query answers difficult to understand due to the redundancy they introduce. Indeed, our motivation is to integrate multiple datasets, and what we care most are the entities, not the IRIs that represent them. This motivates us to propose an alternative approach, which is based on assigning *canonical IRIs* to entities.

We assume that, in addition to $\mathcal{A}$, we have a set $\mathcal{A}^c$ of *canonical IRI assertions* using the property canIriOf. We make the following assumption on $\mathcal{A}^c$, which states that one IRI cannot have more than two canonical representations:

---

[5] The IRI encoding of special symbols like "/" is omitted for readability.

Assumption 1. *The property* `canIriOf` *is inverse functional in* $\mathcal{A}^c$, *i.e.,:*

$$\{\texttt{canIriOf}(c_1, i),\ \texttt{canIriOf}(c_2, i)\} \subseteq \mathcal{A}^c \quad \text{implies} \quad c_1 = c_2.$$

Definition 1 (Canonical IRI and Canonical Graph). *For an IRI o, the canonical IRI* $can_{\mathcal{A}^c}(o)$ *of o is c_o, if* $\texttt{canIriOf}(c_o, o) \in \mathcal{A}^c$ *for some c_o, and o otherwise. Given $\mathcal{A}$ and $\mathcal{A}^c$, the canonical graph* $cg(\mathcal{A}, \mathcal{A}^c)$ *is*

$$\{C(can_{\mathcal{A}^c}(o)) \mid C(o) \in \mathcal{A}\} \cup \{P(can_{\mathcal{A}^c}(o_1), can_{\mathcal{A}^c}(o_2)) \mid P(o_1, o_2) \in \mathcal{A}\}.$$

Given an entailment regime E without special treatments of canonical IRI assertions, we can now define the *canonical IRI entailment regime* $E{+}can$ as:

$$eg^{E+can}(\mathcal{T}, \mathcal{A} \cup \mathcal{A}^c) \;=\; eg^E(\mathcal{T}, cg(\mathcal{A}, \mathcal{A}^c))$$

Now we study the relationship between the canonical IRI semantics and the `sameAs` semantics. To do so, we first define the correspondence between $\mathcal{A}^c$ and $\mathcal{A}^s$.

Definition 2. *We say that $\mathcal{A}^c$ is compliant with $\mathcal{A}^s$ if the following two conditions hold:*

1. *if* $\texttt{canIriOf}(o_1, o_2) \in \mathcal{A}^c$, *then* $\texttt{sameAs}(o_1, o_2) \in (\mathcal{A}^s)^*$;
2. *if* $\texttt{sameAs}(o_1, o_2) \in (\mathcal{A}^s)^*$, *then* $can_{\mathcal{A}^c}(o_1) = can_{\mathcal{A}^c}(o_2)$.

Next, we extend canonical graphs to SPARQL queries. More precisely, given a SPARQL query Q, we obtain $cg(Q, \mathcal{A}^c)$ by replacing each IRI o in Q by $can_{\mathcal{A}^c}(o)$.

In the following, we assume that SPARQL queries contain neither `sameAs` nor `canIriOf`. The next proposition shows that query answering under the canonical IRI and the `sameAs` entailment regimes are equivalent in the following sense:

Theorem 1. *Let $(\mathcal{T}, \mathcal{A})$ be a KB, $\mathcal{A}^c$ compliant with $\mathcal{A}^s$, Q a SPARQL query, $sig(Q) = \{?x_1, \ldots, ?x_n\}$, and E an entailment regime that does not imply new* `sameAs` *or* `canIriOf` *assertions. It holds that*

- *if* $\{?x_1 \mapsto o_1, \ldots, ?x_n \mapsto o_n\} \in [\![Q]\!]_{\mathcal{T}, \mathcal{A} \cup \mathcal{A}^s}^{E+sameAs}$, *then*

$$\{?x_1 \mapsto can_{\mathcal{A}^c}(o_1), \ldots, ?x_n \mapsto can_{\mathcal{A}^c}(o_n)\} \in [\![cg(Q, \mathcal{A}^c)]\!]_{\mathcal{T}, \mathcal{A} \cup \mathcal{A}^c}^{E+can};$$

- *if* $\{?x_1 \mapsto o_1, \ldots, ?x_n \mapsto o_n\} \in [\![Q]\!]_{\mathcal{T}, \mathcal{A} \cup \mathcal{A}^c}^{E+can}$, *and* $\texttt{sameAs}(o_j, o_j') \in (\mathcal{A}^s)^*$, *for* $j \in J \subseteq \{1, \ldots, n\}$, *then*

$$\{?x_j \mapsto o_j \mid j \notin J\} \cup \{?x_j \mapsto o_j' \mid j \in J\} \in [\![Q]\!]_{\mathcal{T}, \mathcal{A} \cup \mathcal{A}^s}^{E+sameAs}.$$

Example 2. Referring to Example 1, a possible set $\mathcal{A}_c$ of canonical IRI assertions (satisfying Assumption 1) is:

$$\{\,(\texttt{:Wellbore/1},\ \texttt{canIriOf},\ \texttt{:NationalWellbore/1/3-1}),$$
$$(\texttt{:Wellbore/1},\ \texttt{canIriOf},\ \texttt{:CorporateWellbore/NO\_1/3-1}),$$
$$(\texttt{:Wellbore/2},\ \texttt{canIriOf},\ \texttt{:NationalWellbore/2/4-2}),$$
$$(\texttt{:Wellbore/2},\ \texttt{canIriOf},\ \texttt{:CorporateWellbore/NO\_2/4-2})\,\}$$

An example of a set $\mathcal{A}_s$ such that $\mathcal{A}_c$ is compliant with $\mathcal{A}_s$ is:

{ (:NationalWellbore/1, sameAs, :CorporateWellbore/1),
  (:NationalWellbore/2, sameAs, :CorporateWellbore/2) }

Here we have chosen the canonical representative to always be of the (new) form :Wellbore/$\{id\}$. This is a choice made by the mapping author, and the canonical representative could also have been one of the existing IRIs. If we let D be the database and $\mathcal{M}$ the mappings from Example 1, the query

$$Q = \texttt{SELECT } ?w, ?f, ?d \texttt{ WHERE } ((?w, \texttt{:inField}, ?f), (?w, \texttt{:drillingStarted}, ?d))$$

has a non-empty answer set over the canonical graph $cg(\mathcal{A}_{\mathcal{M},D}, \mathcal{A}_c)$, including the answer $\{?w \mapsto \texttt{:Wellbore/1}, ?f \mapsto \texttt{EKOFISK}, ?d \mapsto \texttt{06-07-1968}\}$. In Sect. 5 we will see mapping assertions that populate this ABox. ∎

4   Handling Canonical IRI Semantics by Query Rewriting

In this section, we develop a query rewriting algorithm for canonical IRI semantics so that the canonical graph does not need to be materialized. This rewriting algorithm is mostly of theoretical interest but not meant to be implemented, since the structure of rewritten queries is too complex.

We recall that BGP queries under the simple entailment regime are monotonic (in the input graph G): if $s \in [\![Q]\!]_G$ then $s \in [\![Q]\!]_{G \cup \Delta G}$. However, observe that BGP queries under canonical IRI semantics are non-monotonic: for example let $G = \{(a, \texttt{rdf:type}, C)\}$, $\Delta G = \{(c_a, \texttt{canIriOf}, a)\}$, and $Q = (?x, \texttt{rdf:type}, C)$; then $\{?x \mapsto a\} \in [\![Q]\!]_G^{can}$ but $\{?x \mapsto a\} \notin [\![Q]\!]_{G \cup \Delta G}^{can}$. This means that for some (and actually for every) BGPs Q, there is no union of BGPs Q' such that for all RDF graphs G, $[\![Q]\!]_G^{can} = [\![Q']\!]_G$. The reason is that $[\![Q]\!]_G^{can}$ is always non-monotonic in G, while $[\![Q']\!]_G$ is always monotonic in G. Thus we cannot rewrite a BGP under the canonical IRI semantics to a union of BGPs under the standard SPARQL semantics and expect to obtain the same answers. In the following, we show that query answering under the $E+can$ entailment regime can be reduced to query answering under the E entailment regime, by using non-monotonic SPARQL construct like NOT EXISTS.

To define such a translation, we first introduce a subquery, denoted $qc[?xc, ?x]$, that returns $can_{\mathcal{A}^c}(?x)$ for $?xc$. This is achieved by encoding the two cases of Definition 1:

$$qc[?xc, ?x] = \texttt{SELECT } ?xc, ?x \texttt{ WHERE } ((?xc, \texttt{canIriOf}, ?x) \texttt{ UNION}$$
$$(\texttt{SELECT } ?x \texttt{ AS } ?xc, ?x \texttt{ WHERE } ((?x, ?p_1, ?o) \texttt{ UNION } (?s, ?p_2, ?x))$$
$$\texttt{FILTER NOT EXISTS } (?y, \texttt{canIriOf}, ?x)))$$

Lemma 1. *Let $\mathcal{A}$ and $\mathcal{A}^c$ be as above and a an individual occurring in $\mathcal{A}$. Then*

$$\{?xc \mapsto c_a, ?x \mapsto a\} \in [\![qc[?xc, ?x]]\!]_{\mathcal{A} \cup \mathcal{A}^c} \quad iff \quad c_a = can_{\mathcal{A}^c}(a).$$

Definition 3. *The* canonical-iri *rewriting* $\psi(Q)$ *of a SPARQL query* Q *is obtained from* Q *by replacing each triple pattern* t *with the sub-query* $\psi(t)$ *obtained from* t *as follows:*

(1) for each variable $?x$, *introduce a fresh variable* $?x_c$,
(2) for each occurrence of a variable $?x$, *introduce a fresh variable* $?x_o$, *change* $?x$ *to* $?x_o$, *and join with* $qc[?x_c, ?x_o]$, *and*
(3) for each variable $?x$, *add a projection* $?x_c$ *AS* $?x$.

Example 3. Consider Example 1 and the query
$Q =$ SELECT $?w$, $?f$, $?d$ WHERE $((?w, :\text{inField}, ?f), (?w, :\text{drillingStarted}, ?d))$.
Then
$\psi(Q) =$ SELECT $?w$, $?f$, $?d$ WHERE (
       (SELECT $?wc1$ AS $?w$, $?fc$ AS $?f$ WHERE
         $((?wo1, :\text{inField}, ?fo), qc[?wc1, ?wo1], qc[?fc, ?fo]))$,
       (SELECT $?wc2$ AS $?w$, $?dc$ AS $?d$ WHERE
         $((?wo2, :\text{drillingStarted}, ?d), qc[?wc2, ?wo2], qc[?dc, ?do])))$ ∎

We note that Step 2 in Definition 3 is necessary to deal with each *occurrence* of a variable separately, as shown in the following example:

Example 4. Let $\mathcal{A} = \{(a, \text{P}, b)\}$, $\mathcal{A}^c = \{(c, \text{canIriOf}, a), (c, \text{canIriOf}, b)\}$, and $B = (?x, \text{P}, ?x)$ a BGP. It is easy to see that the following query returns the expected answers:

   $\psi(B) =$ SELECT $?xc$ AS $?x$ WHERE $((?x', \text{P}, ?x''), qc[?xc, ?x'], qc[?xc, ?x''])$. ∎

Theorem 2. *For any* E, $\mathcal{T}$, $\mathcal{A}$, $\mathcal{A}^c$, *and* Q, $[\![Q]\!]_{\mathcal{T}, \mathcal{A} \cup \mathcal{A}^c}^{E+can} = [\![\psi(Q)]\!]_{\mathcal{T}, \mathcal{A} \cup \mathcal{A}^c}^{E}$.

We observe that although the size of the rewritten query is linear in the size of the original one, the approach is impractical. Intuitively, the number of variables in the NOT EXISTS clauses and in the inner UNION clauses is linear in the number of variables in the original query, and a (naive) query execution engine would need to enumerate over all individuals in the ABox for each such variable. Hence, the query execution time would essentially grow exponentially in the number of variables in the query.

5   Handling Canonical IRI Statements in OBDA

We now propose a practical approach to supporting canonical IRI semantics for ontology-based integration of cross-linked datasets. We assume that the mapping set $\mathcal{M}$ may include a subset $\mathcal{M}^c$ consisting of all mapping assertions populating canIriOf triples.

central.aliasTable		
id	nationalName	corporateName
1	NO_1/3-1	1/3-1
2	NO_2/4-2	2/4-2
3	NO_1/2-1	1/2-1
4	NO_1/3-A-1_H	
5		1/3-10

```
:Wellbore/{id} canIriOf
   :NationalWellbore/{nationalName} .
← SELECT id, nationalName FROM central.aliasTable

:Wellbore/{id} canIriOf
   :CorporateWellbore/{corporateName} .
← SELECT id, corporateName FROM central.aliasTable
```

Fig. 1. Table and mappings for Example 5

Example 5. We extend the OBDA scenario from Example 1 with mappings for canIriOf into tables in a database central, both shown in Fig. 1. The canonical IRI mapping assertions relate wellbores in databases national and corporate by employing an existing aliasing table in database central. By materializing these mappings and the database, we obtain the assertions in Example 2. *Master tables* like central are available in the Statoil use case, and are typical in corporate scenarios.

The canonical IRI mappings do not depend on the existence of such master tables, as arbitrary SQL queries in the source part of mappings can be used. However, regarding both maintainability and performance, our experience is that materializing the resolution of equality into a master table is a better choice. ∎

In an OBDA setting, we propose a practical method based on compiling the consequences of canonical IRI semantics into mappings. This method is inspired by the mapping saturation algorithm used for classical OBDA [20,26].

In order to make sure that the RDF graph constructed from the mappings satisfies Assumption 1, we state a stronger assumption on the mappings:

Assumption 2. *For each IRI template iri, there is at most one mapping assertion of the form: $iri_c(a)$ canIriOf $iri(b) \leftarrow sql(a, b)$.*

Lemma 2. *If $\mathcal{M}^c$ is a set of mapping assertions satisfying Assumption 2, then $\mathcal{A}_{\mathcal{M}^c, D}$ satisfies Assumption 1 for every database instance D.*

Now we are ready to present the mapping rewriting algorithm. Intuitively, it replaces all the individuals and IRI-templates in the mapping by their canonical representation.

Definition 4. *Let $\mathcal{M} = \mathcal{M}' \cup \mathcal{M}^c$ be a set of mapping assertions. The canonical-iri rewriting $cm(\mathcal{M}', \mathcal{M}^c)$ of $\mathcal{M}$ is obtained by processing each $m \in \mathcal{M}'$ as follows:*

- *for each IRI template $iri(a)$ occurring in m, if $\mathcal{M}^c$ contains a mapping*

$$iri_c(b_0) \text{ canIriOf } iri(b_1) \leftarrow sql(b_0, b_1)$$

then we replace $iri(a)$ in the target of m by $iri_c(b_0)$ and join the source query with $sql(b_0, b_1), a = b_1$.
- *for each occurrence of an IRI o, if $o = iri(a)$ for some IRI template iri, then we process it as in the IRI template case.*

Example 6. Let $\mathcal{M}'$ be the mappings in Example 1 and $\mathcal{M}_c$ the mappings in Example 5. Then $cm(\mathcal{M}', \mathcal{M}_c)$ obtained according to Definition 4 is as follows:

```
:Wellbore/{id} :inField {wlbField} ; :purpose {opPurp} .
← SELECT wlbFld, opPurp, id FROM national.wellbore, central.aliasTable
  WHERE name = nationalName

:Wellbore/{id} :drillingStarted {driStDt} ; :purpose {reason} .
← SELECT driStDt, reason, id FROM corporate.drillingops, central.aliasTable
  WHERE name = corporateName                                                ∎
```

It is easy to see that the algorithm described in Definition 4 has the same effect as applying cg to the RDF graph:

Lemma 3. *Let $\mathcal{M} = \mathcal{M}' \cup \mathcal{M}^c$ be a set of mapping assertions, and D a database instance. Then $cg(\mathcal{A}_{\mathcal{M}',D}, \mathcal{A}_{\mathcal{M}^c,D}) = \mathcal{A}_{cm(\mathcal{M}',\mathcal{M}^c),D}$.*

It follows that the mapping rewriting algorithm is sound and complete.

Theorem 3. *Let E be an entailment regime, $\mathcal{P} = (\mathcal{T}, \mathcal{M}, \mathcal{S})$ an OBDA specification where $\mathcal{M} = \mathcal{M}' \cup \mathcal{M}^c$, $(\mathcal{P}, D)$ an OBDA instance, and Q a SPARQL query. Then $[\![Q]\!]_{\mathcal{T},\mathcal{A}_{\mathcal{M},D}}^{E+can} = [\![Q]\!]_{\mathcal{T},\mathcal{A}_{cm(\mathcal{M}',\mathcal{M}^c),D}}^{E}$.*

This theorem shows that the support for canonical IRI semantics in OBDA can be implemented by simply adding a canonical-iri rewriting step into the existing workflow during the startup of an OBDA system.

The canonical IRI approach shown above shifts effort from the rewriting to the mapping construction. That is, compared with the approach using sameAs triples, more information must be encoded in the mappings. Specifically, one must encode transitivity, and choose a representative for each equivalence class. An important question is therefore if this is applicable in practical scenarios. Our experience from the Statoil use case is that one can exploit existing *master tables* correlating the names used for objects in different databases. The mappings for canonical IRIs are simple mappings into these tables.

6   Implementation and Experiments

The canonical IRI approach described above has been implemented in *Ontop* [2], which now supports both sameAs and canonical IRI semantics. Observe that *Ontop* does not perform SQL federation, therefore it usually relies on systems such as Teiid[6] or Exareme [7] to integrate multiple databases. These systems act as *mediators* and expose to *Ontop* a set of tables coming from the different databases. In particular, *Ontop* has been tested with Exareme intensively. Exareme was initially developed as an engine for complex dataflow processing on elastic clouds [19], and was subsequently enriched with data federation capabilities. As a result, the Exareme SQL federation engine is able to decompose complex relational queries, use common sub-expression identification techniques

---

[6] http://teiid.jboss.org.

in order to save processing costs (e.g., to process only once identical query fragments coming from different subqueries of a union query), and decide which query fragment should be sent to each external database. Exareme then processes intermediate results coming from different databases in parallel in order to produce the final results.

We now present two sets of experiments evaluating the performance of queries over crossed-linked datasets. One experiment was conducted on a production environment of databases in Statoil, based on queries from geoscientists at the company. Since all the data sources are on production servers with confidential data, the load changes, and the OBDA setting is too complex to isolate different features of this approach, we also created a controlled OBDA environment in our own server to study our technique.

6.1   Real-World Experiments

We integrated 7 data sources (relational databases) used in Statoil, extending an existing ontology and the set of mappings, and creating the tables necessary for `sameAs` and `canIriOf`. The queries and ontology are published in [15] and a description of the corporate use case is given in [18]. One of the data sources is the *slegge* database, which is also described in [15] together with the mappings toward this database.

The experiments in Statoil were run with a catalogue of 76 SPARQL queries constructed from information needs written down by geologists and geoscientists in the company. The domain of the queries is that of subsurface exploration, with a focus on wellbore information. The most complex query had 23 triple patterns, using object and data properties coming from 5 data sources. The queries were executed with a 20 min timeout, both with sameAs approach and with the canonical IRI approach.

The *Ontop* rewriting engine and Exareme SQL federation engine all run on virtual machines deployed on the company intranet, as the data cannot be moved out. *Ontop* ran on a single machine, while the Exareme SQL federation ran on 8 other machines. The oracle databases are version 10g, and run on separate machines.[7]

We realize that this setup does not comply with the normal *clean* setup of a database experiment. However, the complexity (7 datasources) and realism (real questions and production databases) of the setup means the results have great value, although their precision is sub-optimal. Compare this with biology, where the *in vivo* experiments on live creatures, dealing with the full complexity of the organisms, may lead to results that cannot be seen in the *in vitro* experiments, and therefore are considered superior.

The total query execution times, for both the sameAs and canonical IRI approaches are shown in Fig. 2. The improvement from sameAs to canonical IRI

---

[7] Typical machine: HP ProLiant Server, 24 Intel Xeon CPUs (X560@2.67 GHz), 283 GB RAM.

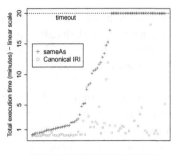

Queries ordered by execution time with sameas

	sameAs	Canonical IRI
Total queries	76	76
Timeouts	31	11
Min exec. time	12s	0.50s
Mean exec. time	11m	4.3m
Median exec. time	11m	0.77m

Fig. 2. Execution time and statistics for the queries in the federated setting at Statoil

is drastic. With the canonical IRI approach all queries, with three exceptions, are faster, there are fewer timeouts, and the majority of the queries execute within 3 min.

6.2   Controlled Experiments Using Wisconsin Benchmark

We also evaluated the canonical IRI approach in a more controlled setting. All files needed to reproduce this example are provided online[8]. This example is a simulated federated scenario with a single database consisting of 4 Wisconsin tables [9], representing different datasets, and 6 *linking tables*, see [5]. We reused the Wisconsin Benchmark tables, each of them containing 100M rows, and we created 3 new *canonical IRI tables* out of existing linking tables. We added the columns for provenance and canonical id, so that the mappings can generate canIriOf relations out of these 3 tables.

To evaluate the overhead of equality reasoning when answering SPARQL queries, we considered the following three parameters: *(1)* number of linked datasets (2–3); *(2)* selectivity of the query (returning 0.001%, 0.01%, 0.1% of the dataset); *(3)* number of equal objects between datasets (10%, 30%, 60%). In total, we ran 1332 queries, grouped in 9 groups: (G1) no properties, (G2) 1 data property and 0 object properties, (G3) 0 data properties and 1 object property, ..., (G9) 2 data properties and 2 object properties.

The results confirm an improvement, reducing the high cost of execution of the queries. In the previous setting based on sameAs, with the 6 linking tables and 2 linked-datasets scenario, with 120M equal objects (60%), in the worst case, most of the queries ran in around 3 min, while with the new canonical IRI approach, all queries can be executed in around 1 min. The query that performed worst in the previous setting (4 joins, 2 data properties, 2 object properties) returned 480 000 results and took around 6 min. In the new setting, for the same query, the number of results reduced to 60 000, avoiding duplicates. The resulting SQL query is simpler, and can be executed in only 50 s. In the

---

[8] https://github.com/ontop/ontop-examples/tree/master/eswc-2018-canonical-iri.

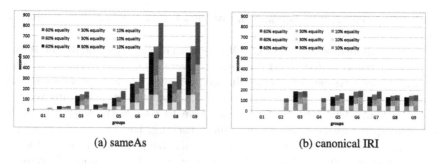

(a) sameAs   (b) canonical IRI

Fig. 3. Execution times of most expensive queries with 2 datasets

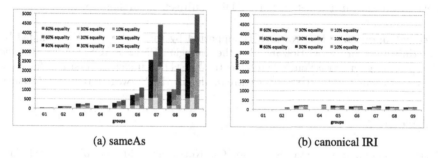

(a) sameAs   (b) canonical IRI

Fig. 4. Execution times of most expensive queries with 3 datasets

3 linked-datasets scenario, the improvement is even more visible: the slowest executions took around 9 min in the previous setting, and less than 1.5 min in the new setting. The worst query in the previous setting took around 1.5 h, and returned 1 620 000 results. This query can now be executed in 53 s, and the number of results returned is significantly reduced to 60 000. The number of linked datasets is the variable that has most impact on query performance, but it is less influential in the canonical IRI setting. Another observation is that compared to the sameAs setting, the optimization for canonical IRI semantics is done only in the off-line phase and additional startup time is negligible. In fact, the startup time is only around 5 s.

In Figs. 3 and 4, we visualize the comparison of the execution times in these two settings. For each group, we show the execution times of the most expensive queries. The results confirm that under the canonical IRI semantics, we are able to run the queries significantly faster and the query answering times are more uniform.

7   Conclusions

This work is a natural continuation of [5], which was the first work to study the issue of equivalence of IRIs in OBDI and used the standard sameAs construct to model equivalence between entities. Our proposal based on canonical IRIs improves on such an approach in terms of efficiency, and avoids the drawback of redundant answers.

Another important aspect in OBDI is how to efficiently evaluate the rewritten SQL queries over federated databases. Several federated database systems and prototypes have been presented in the literature. Early approaches include TSIMMIS [6], Garlic [13], and Tukwila [16]. Unpredictability regarding processing is the main issue that these systems have to cope with, using techniques such as adaptive query planning and query caching. BigDAWG [10] is a more recent approach that lays emphasis on the "one size does not fit all" principle, by trying to take advantage of specialized engines used as endpoints in order to efficiently process different types of data. How to natively deal with federated query evaluation in the setting of OBDI is subject of further work.

Acknowledgement. This research is supported by the project OBATS, funded by Free University of Bozen-Bolzano, by the Euregio IPN12 KAOS, funded by the "European Region Tyrol-South Tyrol-Trentino" (EGTC) under the first call for basic research projects, and by the Sirius Centre funded by the Norwegian Research Council.

References

1. Brüggemann, S., Bereta, K., Xiao, G., Koubarakis, M.: Ontology-based data access for maritime security. In: Sack, H., Blomqvist, E., d'Aquin, M., Ghidini, C., Ponzetto, S.P., Lange, C. (eds.) ESWC 2016. LNCS, vol. 9678, pp. 741–757. Springer, Cham (2016). https://doi.org/10.1007/978-3-319-34129-3_45
2. Calvanese, D., Cogrel, B., Komla-Ebri, S., Kontchakov, R., Lanti, D., Rezk, M., Rodriguez-Muro, M., Xiao, G.: Ontop: answering SPARQL queries over relational databases. Semant. Web J. **8**(3), 471–487 (2017)
3. Calvanese, D., De Giacomo, G., Lembo, D., Lenzerini, M., Poggi, A., Rosati, R., Ruzzi, M.: Data integration through $DL-Lite_{\mathcal{A}}$ ontologies. In: Schewe, K.-D., Thalheim, B. (eds.) SDKB 2008. LNCS, vol. 4925, pp. 26–47. Springer, Heidelberg (2008). https://doi.org/10.1007/978-3-540-88594-8_2
4. Calvanese, D., De Giacomo, G., Lembo, D., Lenzerini, M., Rosati, R.: Tractable reasoning and efficient query answering in description logics: the DL-$Lite$ family. J. Autom. Reason. **39**(3), 385–429 (2007)
5. Calvanese, D., Giese, M., Hovland, D., Rezk, M.: Ontology-based integration of cross-linked datasets. In: Arenas, M., Corcho, O., Simperl, E., Strohmaier, M., d'Aquin, M., Srinivas, K., Groth, P., Dumontier, M., Heflin, J., Thirunarayan, K., Staab, S. (eds.) ISWC 2015. LNCS, vol. 9366, pp. 199–216. Springer, Cham (2015). https://doi.org/10.1007/978-3-319-25007-6_12
6. Chawathe, S.S., Garcia-Molina, H., Hammer, J., Ireland, K., Papakonstantinou, Y., Ullman, J.D., Widom, J.: The TSIMMIS project: integration of heterogeneous information sources. In: Proceedings of the 10th Meeting of the International Proceedings Society of Japan (IPSJ 1994), pp. 7–18 (1994)
7. Chronis, Y., Foufoulas, Y., Nikolopoulos, V., Papadopoulos, A., Stamatogiannakis, L., Svingos, C., Ioannidis, Y.E.: A relational approach to complex dataflows. In: Proceedings of the EDBT/ICDT Workshops. CEUR, vol. 1558. ceur-ws.org (2016)
8. Das, S., Sundara, S., Cyganiak, R.: R2RML: RDB to RDF mapping language. W3C Recommendation, W3C, September 2012. http://www.w3.org/TR/r2rml/

9. DeWitt, D.J.: The Wisconsin benchmark: past, present, and future. In: Gray, J. (ed.) The Benchmark Handbook. Morgan Kaufmann, Burlington (1992)
10. Duggan, J., Elmore, A.J., Stonebraker, M., Balazinska, M., Howe, B., Kepner, J., Madden, S., Maier, D., Mattson, T., Zdonik, S.: The BigDAWG polystore system. SIGMOD Rec. **44**(2), 11–16 (2015)
11. Giese, M., Soylu, A., Vega-Gorgojo, G., Waaler, A., Haase, P., Jiménez-Ruiz, E., Lanti, D., Rezk, M., Xiao, G., Özçep, Ö.L., Rosati, R.: Optique: zooming in on big data. IEEE Comput. **48**(3), 60–67 (2015)
12. Glimm, B., Ogbuji, C.: SPARQL 1.1 entailment regimes. W3C Recommendation, W3C, March 2013. http://www.w3.org/TR/sparql11-entailment/
13. Haas, L.M., Kossmann, D., Wimmers, E.L., Yang, J.: Optimizing queries across diverse data sources. In: Proceedings of the VLDB 1997, pp. 276–285 (1997)
14. Harris, S., Seaborne, A.: SPARQL 1.1 query language. W3C Recommendation, W3C, March 2013. http://www.w3.org/TR/sparql11-query
15. Hovland, D., Kontchakov, R., Skjæveland, M.G., Waaler, A., Zakharyaschev, M.: Ontology-based data access to slegge. In: d'Amato, C., Fernandez, M., Tamma, V., Lecue, F., Cudré-Mauroux, P., Sequeda, J., Lange, C., Heflin, J. (eds.) ISWC 2017. LNCS, vol. 10588, pp. 120–129. Springer, Cham (2017). https://doi.org/10.1007/978-3-319-68204-4_12
16. Ives, Z.G., Florescu, D., Friedman, M., Levy, A., Weld, D.S.: An adaptive query execution system for data integration. SIGMOD Rec. **28**(2), 299–310 (1999)
17. Kaminski, M., Kostylev, E.V., Cuenca Grau, B.: Query nesting, assignment, and aggregation in SPARQL 1.1. ACM Trans. Database Syst. **42**(3), 17:1–17:46 (2017)
18. Kharlamov, E., Hovland, D., Skjæveland, M.G., Bilidas, D., Jiménez-Ruiz, E., Xiao, G., Soylu, A., Lanti, D., Rezk, M., Zheleznyakov, D., Giese, M., Lie, H., Ioannidis, Y.E., Kotidis, Y., Koubarakis, M., Waaler, A.: Ontology based data access in Statoil. J. Web Semant. **44**, 3–36 (2017)
19. Kllapi, H., Sitaridi, E., Tsangaris, M.M., Ioannidis, Y.: Schedule optimization for data processing flows on the cloud. In: Proceeding ACM SIGMOD 2011, pp. 289–300 (2011)
20. Kontchakov, R., Rezk, M., Rodríguez-Muro, M., Xiao, G., Zakharyaschev, M.: Answering SPARQL queries over databases under OWL 2 QL entailment regime. In: Mika, P., et al. (eds.) ISWC 2014. LNCS, vol. 8796, pp. 552–567. Springer, Cham (2014). https://doi.org/10.1007/978-3-319-11964-9_35
21. Motik, B., Cuenca Grau, B., Horrocks, I., Wu, Z., Fokoue, A., Lutz, C.: OWL 2 Web Ontology Language Profiles, 2nd edn. W3C Recommendation, W3C, December 2012
22. Motik, B., Nenov, Y., Piro, R.E.F., Horrocks, I.: Handling owl:sameAs via rewriting. In: Proceedings of AAAI 2015, pp. 231–237. AAAI Press (2015)
23. Pérez, J., Arenas, M., Gutierrez, C.: Semantics and complexity of SPARQL. ACM Trans. Database Syst. **34**(3), 16:1–16:45 (2009)
24. Poggi, A., Lembo, D., Calvanese, D., De Giacomo, G., Lenzerini, M., Rosati, R.: Linking data to ontologies. J. Data Semant. **10**, 133–173 (2008)
25. Rodriguez-Muro, M., Rezk, M.: Efficient SPARQL-to-SQL with R2RML mappings. J. Web Semant. **33**, 141–169 (2015)
26. Sequeda, J.F., Arenas, M., Miranker, D.P.: OBDA: query rewriting or materialization? In practice, both! In: Mika, P., et al. (eds.) ISWC 2014. LNCS, vol. 8796, pp. 535–551. Springer, Cham (2014). https://doi.org/10.1007/978-3-319-11964-9_34
27. W3C OWL Working Group. OWL 2 Web Ontology Language document overview, 2nd edn. W3C Recommendation, W3C, December 2012

Formal Query Generation for Question Answering over Knowledge Bases

Hamid Zafar[1]([⊠])(ID), Giulio Napolitano[2](ID), and Jens Lehmann[1,2](ID)

[1] Computer Science Institute, University of Bonn, Bonn, Germany
{hzafarta,jens.lehmann}@cs.uni-bonn.de
[2] Fraunhofer IAIS, Sankt Augustin, Germany
{giulio.napolitano,jens.lehmann}@iais.fraunhofer.de

Abstract. Question answering (QA) systems often consist of several components such as Named Entity Disambiguation (NED), Relation Extraction (RE), and Query Generation (QG). In this paper, we focus on the QG process of a QA pipeline on a large-scale Knowledge Base (KB), with noisy annotations and complex sentence structures. We therefore propose SQG, a SPARQL Query Generator with modular architecture, enabling easy integration with other components for the construction of a fully functional QA pipeline. SQG can be used on large open-domain KBs and handle noisy inputs by discovering a minimal subgraph based on uncertain inputs, that it receives from the NED and RE components. This ability allows SQG to consider a set of candidate entities/relations, as opposed to the most probable ones, which leads to a significant boost in the performance of the QG component. The captured subgraph covers multiple candidate walks, which correspond to SPARQL queries. To enhance the accuracy, we present a ranking model based on Tree-LSTM that takes into account the syntactical structure of the question and the tree representation of the candidate queries to find the one representing the correct intention behind the question. SQG outperforms the baseline systems and achieves a macro F1-measure of 75% on the LC-QuAD dataset.

1 Introduction

Extensive progress has been made in recent years by systems using Knowledge Graphs (KGs) as their source of information. As the complexity of such systems may be considerable, it is common practice to segment the whole task into various subtasks usually performed sequentially, including Named Entity Disambiguation (NED), Relation Extraction (RE) and Query Generation (QG) among others [1]. This segmentation, however, rarely corresponds to true modularity in the architecture of implemented systems, which results in the general inability by the wider community to successfully and efficiently build upon the efforts of past achievements. To tackle this problem, researchers introduced QA modular frameworks for reusable components such as OKBQA [2,3] but little attention has been given to query generation. For instance, OKBQA includes 24

© Springer International Publishing AG, part of Springer Nature 2018
A. Gangemi et al. (Eds.): ESWC 2018, LNCS 10843, pp. 714–728, 2018.
https://doi.org/10.1007/978-3-319-93417-4_46

reusable QA components of which only one is a query generator. Nonetheless, the increasing complexity of questions leads to the following challenges for the query generation task [1,4]:

1. Coping with large-scale knowledge bases: Due the very large size of existing open-domain knowledge bases such as DBpedia [5] and Freebase [6], special consideration is required.
2. Question type identification: For instance the question might be a boolean one, thus the query construction should be carried out accordingly to generate desired answer.
3. Managing noisy annotations: The capability to handle a set of annotations including several incorrect ones might increase the chance of QG to construct the correct query.
4. Support for more complex question which requires specific query features such as aggregation, sort as well as comparison.
5. Syntactic ambiguity of the input question: For example, "Who is the father of X?" might be interpreted as "X is the father of who?" if the syntactical structure of the question is ignored.

To the best of our knowledge, none of the existing works can deal with all these challenges. Thereby, we present SPARQL Query Generator (SQG), a modular query builder for QA pipelines which goes beyond the state-of-the-art. SQG is able to process noisy input and employs a ranking mechanism of candidate queries based on Tree-LSTM. The model overcomes the limitations of linear solutions [7,8] by exploiting the structural similarity of the candidate queries with the dependency of the utterance. We also considered scalability aspects, which enables us to evaluate SGQ on a large Q/A dataset based on DBpedia [5].

2 Related Work

Diefenbach et al. [1] studied more than 25 QA systems and discussed the different techniques these used for each component, including the query generation component. They show that in most QA systems the query generation component is highly mixed with components performing other tasks, such as segmentation or relation extraction. Furthermore, their work mainly focused the analysis on the overall performance of the QA systems, as only a few systems and publications provided deep analysis of the performance of their query generation component. For instance, CASIA [9], AskNow [10] and Sina [11] each have a SPARQL generation module, but do not provide an evaluation on it. [4] is a very comprehensive survey of question answering over knowledge graphs, analyzing 72 publications and describing 62 question answering systems for RDF knowledge graphs. In particular, they argue that it may not be beneficial that a wide range of research articles and prototypes repeatedly attempt to solve the same challenges: better performance may be obtained by providing sophisticated and mature solutions for individual challenges. An alternative approach to QA pipelines is end-to-end systems such as [12], which directly construct SPARQL queries from training data. However, those are currently mostly restricted to simple questions with a single relation and entity in which case query generation is straightforward. While those systems are an interesting area of research and may be extensible to more complex questions, they are unlikely to completely replace QA pipelines due to the large amount of training data required.

To the best of our knowledge, there is a very limited number of working query builders in the question answering community which can be used independently and out of the box. Recent studies [2,3] explored the possibility of using independent QA components to form a fully functional QA system. Singh et al. [3] introduced Frankenstein, a QA framework which can dynamically choose QA components to create a complete QA pipeline, depending on the features of the input question. The framework includes two query building components: Sina and NLIWOD QB. NLIWOD is a simple, template-based QB, which does not include any kind of query ranking. Given correct inputs, NLIWOD compares the pattern based on a number of input entity and relation to build the output query. Sina [11] was originally a monolithic QA system, which did not provide a reusable query builder. However, Singh et al. [3] decoupled the query building component to make it reusable. Its approach consists in the generation of minimal sets of triple patterns containing all resources identified in the question and select the most probable pattern, minimizing the number of triples and of free variables. Another approach not far from ours is presented by Abujabal et al. [8]. In contrast to approaches such as [7,13,14] which rely on handcrafted utterance-query templates, they provided a learning model to generate the the template set. Furthermore, [7,8] rely on ranking methodologies for choosing among candidate queries. However they rely on question-query templates, previously learned by distant supervision, which are ranked on several manually engineered features by a preference function learned via random forest classification. By contrast, our ranking approach is based on the similarity between candidate walks in a minimal subgraph and the sentence structure of question.

3   Approach

We formally describe knowledge graphs and the query generation problem as a subproblem for question answering over knowledge graphs. Within the scope of this paper, we define a *knowledge graph* as a labelled directed multi-graph: a tuple $K = (E, R, T)$ where E is a set called entities, R is a set of relation labels and $T \subseteq V \times R \times V$ is a set of ordered triples. The definition captures the basic structure of, e.g., RDF datasets and property graphs.

We define *query generation* as follows: We assume that a question string s and a knowledge graph K are given. In previous steps of the QA pipeline, entity and relation linking have already been performed, i.e. we have a set of mappings M from substrings (utterances) of s to elements of E and R, respectively. The task of query generation is to use s, D and M to generate a SPARQL query.

This definition completely decouples the query generation task from the NED and RE tasks. However, in a realistic setting, the NED and RE modules produce a list of candidates per utterance in the question. As a result, we relax the constraint on the utterance annotation to have a list of candidates per each utterance. Formally, we define the task of *advanced query generation* based on the definition of query generation, where each substring of s is mapped to a non-empty subset of E or R respectively, i.e. there are several candidates for entities and relations. For instance, Fig. 1 illustrates that for the question "What are some artists on the show whose opening theme is Send It On?", the annotation for the "artists" might be *dbo:Artist* or *dbo:artists* and so on. In Sect. 4.2, we show that considering multiple candidates leads to a better performance, in comparison to the case where only the top candidate is considered by the query generator.

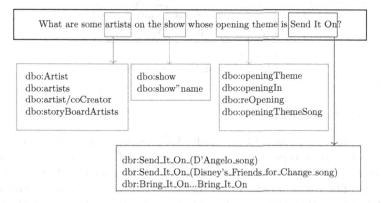

Fig. 1. A sample question annotated with output from NED and RE components. There is a list of candidates for each spotted utterance in the question ranked based on their confidence score.

Our hypothesis is that the formal interpretation of the question is a walk w in the KG which only contains the target entities E and relations R of the input question s plus the answer nodes. The definition of a (valid) walk is as follows:

Definition 1 (Walk). *A walk in a knowledge graph $K = (E, R, T)$ is a sequence of edges along the nodes they connect:* $W = (e_0, r_0, e_1, r_1, e_2, \ldots, e_{k-1}, r_{k-1}, e_k)$ *with* $(e_i, r_i, e_{i+1}) \in T$ *for* $0 \leq i \leq k - 1$.

Definition 2 (Valid Walk). *A walk W is valid with respect to a set of entities E' and relations R', if and only if it contains all of them, i.e. :*

$$\forall e \in E' : e \in W \text{ and } \forall r \in R' : r \in W$$

A node e with $e \in W$ and $e \notin E'$ is *unbound*. An *unbound node* is an abstract node which is used to connect the other nodes in the walk. This node, however, can be related later to one or a set of specific nodes in the KG.

We carry out the task of capturing the valid walks in two steps: First, we establish a type for the question (e.g. boolean or count). Depending on the type, a number of valid walks are extracted from the KG, however, most of them may be an incorrect mapping of the input question, in the sense that they do not capture the correct intention behind the question. Thus, we sort the candidate walks with respect to their similarity to the input question. The overall architecture of SQG is shown in Fig. 2 and in the following sections we discuss each step in more detail.

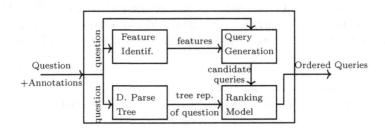

Fig. 2. The architecture of SQG

3.1 Query Generation

In order to find candidate walks in the KG, we need to start from a linked entity $e \in E$ and traverse the KG. Given the size of the existing KGs such as DBpedia [15] or Freebase [6], however, it is very time-consuming to enumerate all valid walks. Thus, we restrict to the subgraph consisting of all the linked entities and relations. In this subgraph, we can then enumerate the candidate walks, which can be directly mapped to SPARQL queries. Yet, the type of question is a crucial feature that has to be identified in order to create the candidate queries with correct structure from the valid walks.

Capture the Subgraph. We start with an empty subgraph, which is populated with the linked entities E as its nodes. Then, we augment the nodes with edges that correspond to the linked relations R, if such connections exist in the KG. This is illustrated in Fig. 3, if only the solid lines are considered. In this step, we consider every possible direct way of connecting the entity(s) and the relation(s) to enrich the subgraph: a relation might connect two existing nodes in the subgraph, or it may connect an entity to a new unbound node. Thus, this subgraph might contain several valid walks but the correct one, since the intention of the question might require to include nodes in the two-hop distance. For instance, in Fig. 3, the answer node ("*unbound*$_1$") is in the two-hop distance from the entity "dbr:Send_it_on" and is not included in the current subgraph. Consequently, we need to expand the subgraph with the set of candidate relations R. Depending on the question, such expansion might correspond to a very large portion of the underlying KG, which may not be even useful to create the final list of candidate walks. Instead of expanding the subgraph, we expand the existing edges of the subgraph with the set of candidate relations excluding the relation that the existing edge represents. As a result, the search space in the underlying KG is greatly reduced (see Fig. 3, where the dashed lines represent the edge expansions). Algorithm 1 summarize the process of capturing the subgraph.

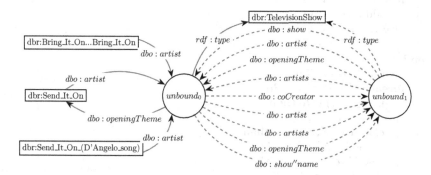

Fig. 3. The captured subgraph for the given question, annotated with candidate entities and relations; solid lines are the one that are in one hop distance; dashed line means more than one hop distance; circles represent unbound nodes, rectangles are the linked entities and edges are the relations in the KG.

Enumerate Candidate Walks. At this point, we have a subgraph that covers all the entities and the relations in the question. We consider every unbound node as a potential answer node, therefore we look for valid walks according to Definition 2. For our example, Fig. 4 reveals four valid walks. In case there is only one valid walk in the subgraph, we map the walk to a SPARQL query and report it as the corresponding query for the given question. Note that further augmentations might be required to support different types of questions, such as those requiring counts or returning boolean values. If there is more than one valid walk, then ranking (as described below) needs to be performed in order to find the most similar query to the input question.

Feature Identification. SQG supports simple and compound questions. In order to support questions such as boolean and count questions, we first need to identify the type of question. Furthermore, there are questions where a relation is required to be used twice. For instance in question *What awards have been awarded both to Ingmar bergman and James O'Brien?* the relation *award* needs to be used twice in order to create the desired query. In some works, predefined patterns were used for similar purposes [10, 16, 17]. However, we train an *SVM* and *Naive Bayes* model for each tasks: one to classify the questions into boolean, count or list questions; and one to decide whether to use a relation twice; based on their *TF-IDF* representation.

Although TF-IDF is a simple representation, the results in Sect. 4.2 reveal that it is strong enough for the purpose. Given the class of the question, the

Data: E', R', K
Result: G: Minimal covering subgraph
Initialize G as an empty graph;
Add $\forall e \in E'$ to G as nodes;
foreach $e \in E', r \in R'$ **do**
    if $(e, r, ?) \in K$ **then**
        | add $(e, r, ?)$ to G ;
    else if $(?, r, e) \in K$ **then**
        | add $(?, r, e)$ to G ;
end
foreach $(e_1, r, e_2) \in G$ **do**
    foreach $r' \in R', r' \neq r$ **do**
        if $(e_2, r', ?) \in K$ **then**
            | add $(e_2, r', ?)$ to G ;
        else if $(?, r', e_2) \in K$ **then**
            | add $(?, r', e_2)$ to G ;
        else if $(e_1, r', ?) \in K$ **then**
            | add $(e_1, r', ?)$ to G ;
        else if $(?, r', e_1) \in K$ **then**
            | add $(?, r', e_1)$ to G ;
    end
end

Algorithm 1. Capture the subgraph

query generator will format the query accordingly. In the case of a count query, for instance, the query generator adds the corresponding function to the output variable of the SPARQL query. Moreover, Based on the predication of the classifier to use a relation twice, an artificial relation will be added to the input of query generator which contains all the candidate relations.

3.2 Query Ranking

There might be more than one valid walk, due to the uncertainty in the linked entities/relations and complexity of the KGs. As a result, we need a way to rank them with respect to the intention of the input question. Yih et al. [16] proposed a model based on convolutional neural networks to represent the input questions and the core-chains in a latent semantic space and compute the cosine similarity. Although the order of the words is captured to some extent in the model, the overall structure of the input question and candidate core-chains is not taken into account. Considering the fact that the walks consist of many shared entities/relations, our hypothesis for the ranking model is that the structure of the walks is a distinctive feature to distinguish the similarity between the candidate walks and the input question. For instance, four walks are generated for our running example, which have distinct structures (see Fig. 6). Therefore, the desired model should be able to incorporate the structure of the input. Tai et al. [18] presented Tree-LSTM, an enhanced version of the vanilla LSTM, which

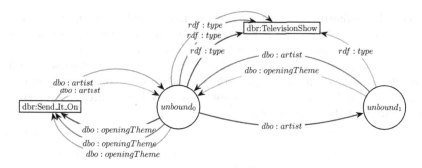

Fig. 4. Four candidate walks are found which are shown in different colors (Color figure online)

considers the tree representation of the input rather than just the sequence of input tokens. They applied the model to the semantic relatedness of natural language sentences and sentiment classification. We present a ranking model based on Tree-LSTM. It considers the tree representation of the candidate walks with respect to the syntactical structure of the question in order to compute their similarity. In the following, we shortly introduce LSTM and Tree-LSTM, subsequently we discuss the final model to fulfill the task.

Preliminaries. As opposed to the vanilla neural networks, where the inputs at different steps are assumed to be independent, Recurrent Neural Networks (RNN) have a hidden state h_t at each step t, which depends not only on the current input but also the previous hidden state h_{t-1}. This formulation enables RNNs to memorize the previous computations for an arbitrarily long sequence of inputs. In practice, however, it has been pointed out that the memory functionality of the RNNs is limited to a few steps back [19]. As a remedy to this issue, RNNs with Long-Short Term Memory (LSTM) units were introduced [20]. They are empowered by a memory cell which is able to keep the state for a longer period of time.

Tree-LSTM RNNs and LSTMs consume the input in a sequential manner. However, when the structure of the input is not simply sequential, special treatment is required. Tai et al. altered the architecture of LSTM to support tree-structured input [18]. Tree-LSTMs aim to incorporate information that rests in the child nodes, whilst LSTM support only sequential propagation. Tree-LSTM units take into account the state of its child nodes to compute its internal state and the output. This architecture enables Tree-LSTMs to easily incorporate the tree structure of our input.

Ranking Model. The ranking model consists of two Tree-LSTMs which are used to map the input walks and question into a latent vectorized representation. We will later apply a similarity function to rank the candidate queries based on the similarity score. In the preparation phase for the input question to the *Question Tree-LSTM*, we substitute the surface mentions of the entities in the question with a placeholder. Then the dependency parse tree is created (see Fig. 5). Furthermore, the *Query Tree-LSTM* receives the tree representation of the candidate walks. Figure 6 depicts the candidate walks of the running example. While all of the candidate walks are valid, only Fig. 6a provides the correct interpretation of the input question.

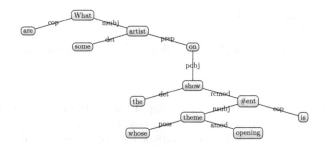

Fig. 5. Dependency parse tree of the running example

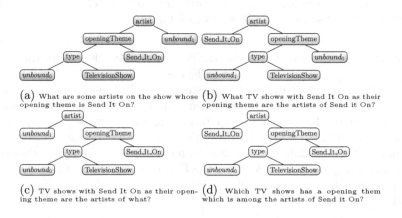

(a) What are some artists on the show whose opening theme is Send It On?

(b) What TV shows with Send It On as their opening theme are the artists of Send it On?

(c) TV shows with Send It On as their opening theme are the artists of what?

(d) Which TV shows has a opening them which is among the artists of Send it On?

Fig. 6. Tree representation of the candidate walks along with their NL meaning

4   Empirical Study

In this section, we discuss the benchmark dataset and compare the result of SQG with two baseline systems. We further provide an extensive analysis of SQG on its different sub-modules such as an evaluation of question type classification, query generation, and ranking model.

SQG is implemented using Python/pytorch. Additionally, we use Glove word embedding [21] as the word representation in the ranking model. The source code of SQG is published on our GitHub page https://github.com/AskNowQA/SQG.

4.1   Datasets

We use the *LC-QuAD* [22] dataset in our experiments. The dataset consists of 5,000 question-answer pairs that cover different complexity and types of questions, such as simple and compound, boolean and count. Each pair is also annotated with the corresponding SPARQL query, target entities, and relations. The annotations are compatible with DBpedia [5] (version 2016-04).

4.2   Performance Evaluation

Some QA systems use a pipeline approach, but are not modular, hence it would require a major engineering effort to extract their query building components in order to compare against them. However, Singh et al. [3] reported the performance of Sina QB and NLIWOD QB in terms of precision, recall and F1-measure on a subset of LC-QuAD containing 3,200 questions. We compare the performance of SQG on the same subset of LC-QuAD with the same metrics. Table 1 demonstrates that SQG significantly outperforms the baseline systems.

Table 1. The comparison of SQG with existing works

Approach	Precision	Recall	F1-measure
Sina*	0.23	0.25	0.24
NLIWOD*	0.48	0.49	0.48
SQG	0.76	0.74	0.75

* Result of the baseline systems are taken from [3]

There are three shortcomings in the baseline systems. First, they require the correct entity/relation as input as NLIWOD does not support multiple candidates and Sina fails when there are more than three candidates. Second, the query augmentation ability is limited in both systems, and third, they lack a ranking mechanism, which is required to reorder the list of candidate queries with respect to the question. We have addressed these problems in our approach and, in the next section, we first evaluate the feature identification in SQG. Afterwards, we define different scenarios, in which the input of the query generator varies from only target entity/relations to the list of candidates per utterance. Finally, we examine the performance of Tree-LSTM as the ranking mechanism.

Feature Identification. First, we assess the accuracy of two different classifiers. Note that the results are independent of the entity/relation linking module, as they take no additional input from it. We perform a 10-fold cross validation on 50% of the dataset to train the model and find the optimal parameter values. We then evaluate the classifiers using the optimal parameter values on the test set (See Table 2). A large amount of diverse training data ensures that the models, albeit simple, perform satisfactorily. Avoiding a manually crafted set of patterns enables SQG to be more applicable in different settings without further manual intervention.

Table 2. The accuracy of feature identification on the LC-QuAD dataset

	Model	Precision	Recall	F1-measure
Question type	Naive Bayes	0.92	0.92	0.91
	SVM	0.99	0.99	0.99
Duplicate relation	Naive Bayes	0.87	0.90	0.88
	SVM	0.90	0.91	0.89

Query Generator Evaluation. In order to provide the input for the query generator, we uses two set of tools: TagMe [23] for entity linking along with RNLIWOD[1] for relation linking; and EARL [24] a joint entity/relation linking tool. The performance of EARL was superior on the evaluation dataset and for brevity we report the results using EARL. Below we introduce three scenarios to evaluate the query generator as well as the ranking model in various settings:

Top-1 correct. We supply only the correct target linked entity/relation to provide an upper-bound estimation of our performance.

Top-5 EARL+correct. We consider a more realistic setting where a list of 5-candidates per entity/relation from EARL [24] is provided. In order to evaluate SQG independent of the linker system, we insert the correct target linked entity/relation if it does not already exist on the list. The purpose of this scenario is to assess the robustness of SQG when the input annotations include several incorrect links as well as the correct ones.

Top-5 EARL. We use the output of EARL [24] to evaluate the QG component in a fully functional QA system.

The evaluation results of query generation for all three scenarios are summarized in Table 3. In *Top-1 correct*, the query generator failed once to generate any candidate query, while in six other cases none of the candidate query(s) returns the desired answer. In this scenario, the ratio of generated queries per question is close to one, because only the true target entities/relations were given to the query generator. Consequently, the number of valid walks is very low.

In the second row of Table 3, which corresponds to *Top-5 EARL+correct*, we observe that the query generator is able to process the noisy inputs and cover 98% of the questions. Furthermore, the average number of generated query per question has increased to 2.25. In the next section, we study how this increase in the average number of generated query affects the ranking model.

The performance in *Top-5 EARL* has dropped dramatically in comparison to the first two scenarios. The main reason is that for 85% of the questions,

---

[1] https://github.com/dice-group/NLIWOD.

EARL provided partially correct annotations, which means that either there are utterance(s) in the question which are annotated with an incorrect set of entities/relations, or there are utterance(s) in the question which should not be annotated, while EARL incorrectly annotates them with a set of entities/relations. However, if we consider only the questions where EARL manages to include all the correct target links to SQG, the coverage is again 98%, which is consistent with the result of the artificial injection experiment from *Top-5 EARL+correct*.

Table 3. Evaluation metrics of query generator

Scenario	Incorrect (%)	No walk (%)	Covered (%)	Avg. #query
Top-1 correct	0.01	0.0	0.99	1.18
Top-5 EARL+correct	0.02	0.0	0.98	2.25
Top-5 EARL	0.12	0.72	0.16	3.28

Ranking Model Evaluation. Before we analyze the ranking model, we examine the dataset that is prepared for it. We employ the Stanford Parser [25] to generate the dependency parse tree of the input questions and the generated candidate queries from the output of the query generator to create the dataset for the ranking model. We split the dataset into 70%/20%/10% for the train set, development set, and test set, respectively. Table 4 provides some insights on the dataset, on which the ranking model is evaluated.

In the *Top-1 correct* scenario, the number of generated queries per question is 1.18, because there are not many possible ways to connect the linked entity/relations. Moreover, the first row of Table 4 demonstrates that the number of incorrect items in the dataset is not proportional to the number of correct items. As a result, the ranking model is given an unbalanced dataset, since the dataset mostly contains positive examples. In *Top-5 EARL+correct*, the number of generated queries is higher, which leads to not only more training data for the ranking model but also more diverse data such that we would not face the same problem as in the previous scenario. The second row of Table 4 shows that the distribution of incorrect and correct data is almost equal, which leads to an increase in the performance of the ranking model, as it provides the model enough data on both classes to learn the set of parameters that perform well. In *Top-5 EARL*, the distribution of correct and incorrect instances in the datasets is not balanced, though the average number of generated queries is higher than in the other scenarios. Note that in this scenario, the total number of generated queries is far lower than in the other scenarios, because the 72% of cases no walk is generated. The peak in the number of incorrect instances is caused by wrong annotations, which were provided by the NED and RE component.

We have used two similarity functions in the ranking model: Cosine similarity and a neural network-based function analogous the approach presented in [18].

Table 4. The distribution of incorrect and correct data per scenario

Scenario	Size	Train		Dev		Test	
		Correct	Incorrect	Correct	Incorrect	Correct	Incorrect
Top-1 correct	5,930	0.85	0.15	0.84	0.16	0.87	0.13
Top-5 EARL+correct	11,257	0.46	0.54	0.46	0.53	0.48	0.52
Top-5 EARL	4,519	0.20	0.80	0.19	0.81	0.22	0.78

The neural network computes the distance and the angle between the two latent representations of the query. However, the neural network-based approach had superior performance compared to the cosine similarity function. Thus, in the following, we provide the result of the ranking model using the neural network as the similarity function. Note that for every scenario, the parameters of the similarity network was tuned on the development set. In the interest of comparing the Tree-LSTM ranking model to a simpler model such as LSTM, Deep LSTM siamese network for text similarity [26] using word-level embedding and the same similarity function. Table 5 demonstrates the superiority of Tree-LSTM over LSTM in all three scenarios.

In the *Top-1 correct*, despite the unbalanced distribution of the dataset, the ranking model achieves an F1 measure of 74%. This, however, does not accurately reflect the performance results for the ranking model as the average number of generated queries in this scenario is 1.18, which means that mostly there is only one candidate query per question.

As the second row of the Table 5 reveals, the F1-measure increases from 75% in *Top-1 correct* to 84% in *Top-5 EARL+correct*. In contrast to the Top-1 correct, the average number of generated queries in *Top-5 EARL+correct* is almost double to 2.25 and the distribution of correct/incorrect example is almost balanced. This results show that the model performs better in comparison to *Top-1 correct* when it is given a bigger and balanced dataset.

A micro F1-measure of 74% was achieved the *Top-5 EARL*. Further analysis reveals that there are two main factors for the drop in the performance: first, the input dataset is highly unbalanced towards incorrect instances; Additionally, the size of the is considerably smaller than the one in *Top-5 EARL+correct*.

Table 5. Micro accuracy of the ranking model using the top ranked item

Scenario	LSTM	Tree-LSTM		
	F1 (%)	Precision (%)	Recall (%)	F1 (%)
Top-1 correct	0.54	0.77	0.74	0.75
Top-5 EARL+correct	0.41	0.84	0.84	0.84
Top-5 EARL	0.32	0.73	0.75	0.74

5   Conclusions and Future Works

We discussed the challenges of query generation in QA systems and introduced SQG, a two-step SPARQL query generator as a reusable component that can be easily integrated into QA pipelines. In the first step, a set of candidate queries are generated, which is followed by a ranking step that arranges the candidate queries based on their structural similarity with respect to the dependency parse tree of the input question. We provide a detailed analysis of the effect of different factors on the performance of QG component such as question type detection, noisy input and ranking the candidate queries. In our experiments, SQG outperformed current query generation approaches. In future work, we plan to add support for more question types, which requires union, sorting, comparison or other aggregation functions e.g. min and max. Also, we will investigate the accuracy of SQG on other QA datasets that might shed light on unseen weaknesses.

Acknowledgment. This research was supported by EU H2020 grants for the projects HOBBIT (GA no. 688227) and WDAqua (GA no. 642795) as well as by German Federal Ministry of Education and Research (BMBF) funding for the project SOLIDE (no. 13N14456).

References

1. Diefenbach, D., Lopez, V., Singh, K., Maret, P.: Core techniques of question answering systems over knowledge bases: a survey. Knowl. Inf. Syst. **55**, 1–41 (2017)
2. Kim, J.-D., Unger, C., Ngomo, A.-C.N., Freitas, A., Hahm, Y.-G., Kim, J., Nam, S., Choi, G.-H., Kim, J.-U., Usbeck, R., et al.: OKBQA framework for collaboration on developing natural language question answering systems (2017)
3. Singh, K., Radhakrishna, A.S., Both, A., Shekarpour, S., Lytra, I., Usbeck, R., Vyas, A., Khikmatullaev, A., Punjani, D., Lange, C., Vidal, M.E., Lehmann, J., Auer, S.: Why reinvent the wheel–lets build question answering systems together. In: The Web Conference (WWW 2018) (2018, to appear)
4. Höffner, K., Walter, S., Marx, E., Usbeck, R., Lehmann, J., Ngomo, A.-C.N.: Survey on challenges of question answering in the semantic web. Semant. Web **8**(6), 895–920 (2017)
5. Auer, S., Bizer, C., Kobilarov, G., Lehmann, J., Cyganiak, R., Ives, Z.: DBpedia: a nucleus for a web of open data. In: Nixon, L., et al. (eds.) ASWC/ISWC -2007. LNCS, vol. 4825, pp. 722–735. Springer, Heidelberg (2007). https://doi.org/10. 1007/978-3-540-76298-0_52
6. Bollacker, K., Evans, C., Paritosh, P., Sturge, T., Taylor, J.: Freebase: a collaboratively created graph database for structuring human knowledge. In: Proceedings of the 2008 ACM SIGMOD International Conference on Management of Data, pp. 1247–1250. ACM (2008)
7. Bast, H., Haussmann, E.: More accurate question answering on freebase. In: Proceedings of the 24th ACM International on Conference on Information and Knowledge Management, pp. 1431–1440. ACM (2015)
8. Abujabal, A., Yahya, M., Riedewald, M., Weikum, G.: Automated template generation for question answering over knowledge graphs. In: Proceedings of the 26th International Conference on World Wide Web, pp. 1191–1200 (2017)

9. He, S., Zhang, Y., Liu, K., Zhao, J.: CASIA@ V2: a MLN-based question answering system over linked data (2014)
10. Dubey, M., Dasgupta, S., Sharma, A., Höffner, K., Lehmann, J.: AskNow: a framework for natural language query formalization in SPARQL. In: Sack, H., Blomqvist, E., d'Aquin, M., Ghidini, C., Ponzetto, S.P., Lange, C. (eds.) ESWC 2016. LNCS, vol. 9678, pp. 300–316. Springer, Cham (2016). https://doi.org/10.1007/978-3-319-34129-3_19
11. Shekarpour, S., Marx, E., Ngomo, A.-C.N., Auer, S.: SINA: semantic interpretation of user queries for question answering on interlinked data. Web Semant. Sci. Serv. Agents World Wide Web 30, 39–51 (2015)
12. Lukovnikov, D., Fischer, A., Lehmann, J., Auer, S.: Neural network-based question answering over knowledge graphs on word and character level. In: Proceedings of the 26th International Conference on World Wide Web, pp. 1211–1220. International World Wide Web Conferences Steering Committee (2017)
13. Fader, A., Zettlemoyer, L., Etzioni, O.: Paraphrase-driven learning for open question answering. In: Proceedings of the 51st Annual Meeting of the Association for Computational Linguistics, vol. 1, pp. 1608–1618 (2013)
14. Berant, J., Chou, A., Frostig, R., Liang, P.: Semantic parsing on freebase from question-answer pairs. In: Proceedings of the 2013 Conference on Empirical Methods in Natural Language Processing, pp. 1533–1544 (2013)
15. Lehmann, J., Isele, R., Jakob, M., Jentzsch, A., Kontokostas, D., Mendes, P., Hellmann, S., Morsey, M., van Kleef, P., Auer, S., Bizer, C.: DBpedia - a large-scale, multilingual knowledge base extracted from wikipedia. Semant. Web J. 6(2), 167–195 (2015)
16. Yih, S.W., Chang, M.-W., He, X., Gao, J.: Semantic parsing via staged query graph generation: question answering with knowledge base (2015)
17. Lopez, V., Fernández, M., Motta, E., Stieler, N.: PowerAqua: supporting users in querying and exploring the semantic web. Semant. Web 3, 249–265 (2012)
18. Tai, K.S., Socher, R., Manning, C.D.: Improved semantic representations from tree-structured long short-term memory networks. In: Long Papers ACL 2015, Beijing, China, July 26–31 2015, vol. 1, pp. 1556–1566 (2015)
19. Bengio, Y., Simard, P., Frasconi, P.: Learning long-term dependencies with gradient descent is difficult. IEEE Trans. Neural Netw. 5, 157–166 (1994)
20. Hochreiter, S., Schmidhuber, J.: Long short-term memory. Neural Comput. 9(8), 1735–1780 (1997)
21. Pennington, J., Socher, R., Manning, C.: Glove: global vectors for word representation. In: Proceedings of the 2014 Conference on Empirical Methods in Natural Language Processing (EMNLP), pp. 1532–1543 (2014)
22. Trivedi, P., Dubey, M.: A corpus for complex question answering over knowledge graphs. In: 16th International Semantic Web Conference (2017)
23. Ferragina, P., Scaiella, U.: Fast and accurate annotation of short texts with wikipedia pages. IEEE Softw. 29(1), 70–75 (2012)
24. Dubey, M., Banerjee, D., Chaudhuri, D., Lehmann, J.: EARL: joint entity and relation linking for question answering over knowledge graphs (2018)
25. Chen, D., Manning, C.: A fast and accurate dependency parser using neural networks. In: Proceedings of the 2014 Conference on Empirical Methods in Natural Language Processing (EMNLP), pp. 740–750 (2014)
26. Mueller, J., Thyagarajan, A.: Siamese recurrent architectures for learning sentence similarity (2016)

A LOD Backend Infrastructure
for Scientific Search Portals

Benjamin Zapilko[(⊠)] [iD], Katarina Boland[iD], and Dagmar Kern[iD]

GESIS - Leibniz-Institute for the Social Sciences, Cologne, Germany
{benjamin.zapilko,katarina.boland,dagmar.kern}@gesis.org

Abstract. In recent years, Linked Data became a key technology for organizations in order to publish their data collections on the web and to connect it with other data sources on the web. With the ongoing change in the research infrastructure landscape where an integrated search for comprehensive research information gains importance, organizations are challenged to connect their historically unconnected databases with each other. In this article, we present a Linked Open Data based backend infrastructure for a scientific search portal which is set as an additional layer between unconnected non-RDF data collections and makes the links between datasets visible and usable for retrieval. In addition, Linked Data technologies are used in order to organize different versions and aggregations of datasets. We evaluate the in-use application of our approach in a scientific search portal for the social sciences by investigating the benefit of links between different data sources in a user study.

1 Introduction

The landscape of research infrastructures like libraries, archives and research data centers is undergoing significant changes [5,9,13], which is also reflected in the research agendas of international and national funding agencies. Were data collections and databases providing scientific information and research data originally unconnected due to historically grown organizational structures, there is now a demand for an integrated and connected provision of this information which is also justified through the ongoing Open Science discussion. In an online survey with 337 social science researchers in Germany, we found evidence that researchers are interested in links between information of different types and from different sources. As a result, not only data collections should be connected with each other, but there is also a need for integrated search functionalities.

However, in current scientific portals these user needs are often not yet reflected. For example, publications and research data are typically held in separate data collections, represented in different metadata schemas and different data formats. They have to be accessed differently, e.g. via different search portals. Even when pushing these data collections into one single database with a search functionality on top, the challenge of connecting datasets of different collections with each other remains. This problem does not only involve the identification of links, but also the treatment of vague links, i.e. if the identifier of a

© Springer International Publishing AG, part of Springer Nature 2018
A. Gangemi et al. (Eds.): ESWC 2018, LNCS 10843, pp. 729–744, 2018.
https://doi.org/10.1007/978-3-319-93417-4_47

linked dataset is unknown and several similar datasets as candidates exist. It is also necessary to keep track of provenance information, i.e. where the datasets come from and how the link has been created. Additionally, there is a problem of disambiguation, since different data collections may contain duplicates. Finally, it has to be decided whether new infrastructures should be built or whether historically grown infrastructures can be reused and extended.

For publishing and connecting data on the Web, Linked Open Data (LOD) [8] has become a popular method in recent years [17,20]. Numerous institutions have started with efforts into that direction like several libraries (e.g. German National Library[1], the French National Library [19], Library of Congress[2], Europeana [10]) but also archives and museums[3], or organizations which hold statistical data like Eurostat[4], World Bank[5], and smaller data providers. Especially in the library sector, Linked Open Data has become a popular technique for publishing bibliographic metadata on the Web and connect it to other Linked Datasets [21] like authority data and persistent identifiers like VIAF[6].

In this article, we present a Linked Open Data based backend infrastructure for scientific search portals which is set as an additional layer between unconnected data collections and makes the links between datasets visible and searchable. Historically built infrastructures are kept running. In this approach, Linked Data serves as backbone for connecting datasets of different data collections. Metadata of the original non-RDF data collections (including information about links to other datasets) is imported into a link database where connections between datasets are identified. The links between datasets are stored as a graph and made available in an Elasticsearch index for an efficient integration into search portals. In order to address occurring heterogeneity with vague links between datasets, a research data ontology is used for representing different versions and aggregations of research datasets. In contrast to existing approaches, our approach covers the full workflow from heterogeneous non-RDF data collections up to the provision in an efficient search index with the integrated and interlinked data. We evaluated the implementation of this approach in a real world scenario, a scientific search portal by conducting a user study where the benefit of links between different datasets is investigated.

The rest of the paper is structured as follows. In Sect. 2, we give an overview of the use case. We present concept and implementation of the LOD backend infrastructure in Sect. 3 and present an evaluation through a user study in Sect. 4. In Sect. 5, we provide an overview of related work and similar approaches. Finally, in Sect. 6, we conclude and give an outlook on future work.

---

[1] http://www.dnb.de/EN/Service/DigitaleDienste/LinkedData/linkeddata.html.
[2] http://id.loc.gov/.
[3] http://americanart.si.edu/collections/search/lod/about/.
[4] http://ec.europa.eu/eurostat/de.
[5] http://www.worldbank.org/.
[6] https://viaf.org/.

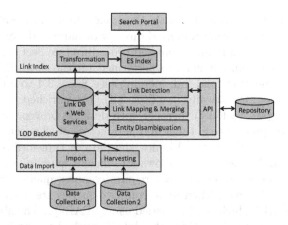

Fig. 1. Architecture of the LOD backend infrastructure

2 Use Case

The use case in this paper is centered on a research infrastructure organization, GESIS - Leibniz-Institute for the Social Sciences. GESIS offers a wide range of information and data, e.g. publications, research data, projects, and others, in various specialized portals. These portals are characterized by a high degree of heterogeneity in terms of architecture, data management, technical implementation, and the data itself. The data in these portals are poorly interlinked.

In a survey, we collected information needs of 337 social science researchers in Germany with an online questionnaire. We found that researchers are interested in links between information of different types and from different sources. For example, about 40% of the participants stated that "I'm looking for research data mentioned in a paper" is one of their own information needs. Therefore, the individual information objects in these data collections need to be integrated and interlinked.

3 Linked Open Data Backend Infrastructure

In this section, we present our approach for a LOD backend infrastructure. We describe the architecture and its components in detail and explain how the datasets of the original data collections are imported, linked, enriched and provided for the search portals via an Elasticsearch index.

3.1 Architecture

The architecture of our approach is set up additionally to existing infrastructures, i.e. original databases and portals as well as attached workflows remain the same. In Fig. 1, an overview of the architecture is shown.

Depending on the accessibility of the data (e.g. through a search index or as a dump file), the data is either imported directly or harvested from the different data sources and updated in an automated procedure (see Sect. 3.2). At import, several steps of data enrichment are performed on the data like mapping of IDs, entity disambiguation and link merging (see Sects. 3.4 to 3.6). Additional links are generated automatically (see Sect. 3.4). The enriched data is stored in the link database (see Sect. 3.7) together with detailed provenance information about the creation process (e.g. times and parameters of all executed algorithms creating or modifying the data). Finally, the data is transformed and pushed into an Elasticsearch index, which allows for efficient querying of the data (see Sect. 3.8). Since our use case does not require complex queries, we decided to use Elasticsearch. However, when more complex queries are desired we provide RDF through an API which can be queried using SPARQL. The above described processes are executed offline. Once the data is pushed to the index, no other processes are slowing down the search system's performance. Currently, the index holds 108435 documents with 277678 links between them.

Parts of this infrastructure have been developed in the DFG-funded projects InFoLiS I and II[7] and have been extended for our purposes. The overall architecture is generalized, i.e. the infrastructure can be reused for different use cases. Only the import and possibly required mappings of IDs have to be adjusted when including different data sources. Some components are using GESIS portals to lookup metadata or IDs[8]. However, for a general applicability of the infrastructure these portals can be replaced with others depending on the data sources and domains (see Repository in Fig. 1).

3.2 Data Sources

The infrastructure uses easily extendible JAVA routines for harvesting and import to allow processing of different data formats. We imported a variety of sources relevant for our use case. These include publications, research data, research projects, institutions and scales (survey instruments) as interlinked entities. The data is partly provided by the scientific community, partly created by GESIS staff; it is provided in different data formats either via dumps or via a Solr interface. Figure 2 gives a more structured overview of this heterogeneous input data. All data is transformed into the InFoLiS link format on import (this format is described in more detail in Sect. 3.3). Additionally, we use the embedded InFoLiS web service framework for automatically detecting links to research data in full texts of scientific publications.

---

[7] www.infolis.gesis.org.

[8] https://dbk.gesis.org/dbksearch/,   http://zis.gesis.org/,   https://www.da-ra.de/, http://datasearch.gesis.org/,   http://sowiport.gesis.org/   and   http://www.ssoar. info/.

Name	Description	Format
GESIS Bibliographies	Bibliographies for research data	BibTeX
ZIS	Bibliographies for scales	BibTeX
SOFISWiki	projects, publications, data, institutions	custom (Solr index)
GESIS Data Catalog	Research data to literature links	custom (Solr index)
GESIS Library	Research data to literature links	custom (Solr index)
automatically created links	Research data to literature links	native

Fig. 2. Overview of data sources

3.3   Data Format

Figure 3 illustrates how entities and links are stored in the database using the respective InFoLiS format. As an entity may represent a publication, dataset, research project, institution, scale or data reference (here: citedData), the format includes a wealth of different bibliographic metadata fields such as collection titles, editors or versioning information. For better comprehensiveness, the list of bibliographic metadata is abbreviated here[9].

For entity links, the fields fromEntity and toEntity of a link specify the URIs of the origin and target entity of the link relation. The field linkReason gives the URI to a TextualReference, an entity containing a text snippet taken from the fromEntity containing the reference to the toEntity, i.e. it constitutes the reason why a link was established between the two entities. For automatically created links, this is the text snippet extracted using an extraction pattern. Some manually created links also feature a text snippet explaining the relationship between the linked entities. The linkView shows the reference to the toEntity. For automatically created links, this is the reference extracted from the text snippet in the linkReason field. For manually created links, this is the name of the linked entity, if given in the source data. The field entityRelations specifies the relation of the reference in linkView to the toEntity. When the fromEntity is of type publication and the toEntity of type citedData, the entityRelation typically is "references". When the fromEntity is of type citedData and the toEntity of type dataset, the entityRelations specifies the match of granularity of citation and linked dataset, i.e. whether the linked dataset holds exactly the cited data or only a subset or a superset of it.

It is important to note the structure of the links: given a publication which references a dataset and a dataset being described by that reference, these relations are represented using two links: one link from a publication entity to a citedData entity plus one link from the citedData entity to a dataset entity. This way of modelling relations has the advantage that matchings from references to actual datasets can be updated easily, e.g. when new datasets are entered in the

---

[9] For a full overview of the format, see https://github.com/infolis/infolis-web/blob/master/data/infolis.tson.

entityType	entityView	entityProvenance	name	year	authors	...	entityReliability
*Type of the entity	Citation string	Source of the entity	bibliographic metadata: Title	bibliographic metadata: Year	bibliographic metadata: Authors	further bibliographic metadata	Reliability score: 1 for manually created entities, <1 for automatically generated data
dataset	Schupp, Jürgen; Goebel, Jan; Kroh, Martin et. al. (2017): Sozio-oekonomisches Panel (SOEP), Daten der Jahre 1984-2015 (internationale Version) Version: 32i.1. Dataset. http://doi.org/10.5684/soep.v32i.1	datasearch	Sozio-oekonomisch es Panel (SOEP), Daten der Jahre 1984-2015 (internationale Version)	2017	Schupp, Jürgen; Goebel, Jan; Kroh, Martin; Schröder, Carsten; Bartels, Charlotte; Erhardt, Klaudia; Fedorets, Alexandra; (...)	...	1
citedData	Mikrozensus 1982	InfoLink	Mikrozensus	1982	(empty)	(empty)	0.3

* information type: publication | dataset | project | institution | instrument | citedData

EntityLink

fromEntity	toEntity	entityRelations	provenance	linkView	linkReason	confidence
URI of entity1	URI of entity2	+*Relation of entity2 to the cited entity	Source of the link	*Reference of entity2 used for creating the link	**URI of the Textual Reference entity representing a text snippet containing the reference to entity2	Reliability score: 1 for manually created links, <1 for automatically generated data
http://example.foo/en tity/150a5a30-16321 1e7-bd8a-3010	http://example.foo/en tity/0037e2a0-e418- 11e7-bd8a-87c3	part_of_temporal	InfoLink	SOEP 1995	http://example.foo/textualReference/ 0132e2a1-e573-12d7-ba8a-88a0	0.53
http://example.foo/en tity/150e5301-37760 0d9-ad0b-5389	http://example.foo/en tity/97321a70-990f-1 1e7-9c5b-d59d	references	InfoLink	Mikrozensus 1982	http://example.foo/textualReference/ b1ee4260-98cb-11e7-91ad-2742	0.3
http://example.foo/en tity/295e0a01-67591 0c9-da2a-3409	http://example.foo/en tity/0735e790-a957- 03d6-2d3a-439e	(empty)	DBK	USIA, Washington (1960): Internationale Beziehungen (Februar 1960)	(empty)	1

+   used values: references | part_of_temporal | superset_of_temporal | same-as_temporal
*   available for automatically generated links
** available for all automatically and some of the manually generated links

Fig. 3. Format of entities and links in the link database

repository used for matching. However, this model makes querying links from publications to datasets more costly as more queries are required.

3.4   Link Detection

We employ the following mechanisms for link detection: 1. extraction and lookup of DOIs; 2. pattern-based reference extraction and linking; 3. term-based reference extraction and linking. All of them are implemented as extensions to the InFoLiS framework and are thus executable as web services.

Extraction and lookup of DOIs. DOIs are extracted from full texts and looked up in a research data repository (da|ra in our case) to retrieve further metadata. Any DOI not found in the repository is ignored as DOIs can be used to identify other entities such as publications that are not of interest here.

Pattern-based reference extraction and linking. Many research data citations to date lack persistent identifiers. Instead, often a more colloquial way of referencing research data is followed [1]. To identify these research data references, we use a method based on the semi-automatic generation of extraction patterns which is included in the InFoLiS framework as an enhanced version of the algorithm described in [1].

Term-based reference extraction and linking. The aforementioned algorithm yields a list of research data citations. From this list, we compiled a set of names used to refer to research datasets. We curated this list to remove any false entries and enhance them with additional relevant dataset names. This list cannot directly be extracted by crawling a research data repository such as da|ra because the exact titles given in the metadata are rarely cited in publications. Authors prefer a more colloquial representation of the titles in their citations [1]. Each term in this list is searched in all available full texts of publications. The extracted references are then linked to research data records by mapping them to records in a research data repository. While this leads to duplicate links when used in addition to the pattern-based approach, this procedure generates additional links and increases the recall of the overall approach.

We applied the introduced link detection on all documents in the Open Access repository SSOAR and saved all resulting links directly in our database. Furthermore, we developed an automated workflow to apply automatic link detection on any new documents uploaded to SSOAR as an extension to the InFoLiS infrastructure. Any links created by this procedure are incorporated into the link database automatically. Finally, the link detection mechanism can be activated at any time to process any document and store the resulting links in the link database by using the respective web service.

Full texts of the manually linked publications are often not publicly available. Using SSOAR documents, we focus on a distinct set of publications for automatic link creation. Thus, the overlap between the manually and automatically created links is low which means that we gain valuable new information by our automated methods but at the same time cannot easily evaluate the full system's precision and recall. We are currently implementing a manual review phase for all links generated at document upload in SSOAR.

3.5   Entity Disambiguation and Link Merging

The links imported from the different sources come with varying metadata and varying degrees of granularity and exactness. Also, the input data may contain duplicates, both within and across sources and both on entity level and on link level: multiple data sources may contain the same entity, e.g. publication, with equal or diverging metadata and with equal or diverging links.

ID matching. In the ideal case, the linked entities in the source data are represented by IDs. However, different sources use different types of identifiers, e.g. DOIs, URNs, URLs or handles. In order to link information items inside a repository, the identifiers of the source dataset have to be matched with the identifiers used in that repository. Matching of IDs is also required for entity disambiguation. Thus, we perform a lookup in repositories for research data and for publications respectively. When a matching record is found, an entity is created in the link database representing this record/the linked entity. This entity is reused when a matching reference occurs again in the same or in another data source, i.e. at this step, publication and dataset entities are disambiguated.

Disambiguation. Some links in the source data, however, are only vague: they contain a reference to an object (e.g. a citation string or the referenced objects metadata) rather than to an ID. These references are mapped to an ID by querying repositories using the available metadata, a publication repository if the cited entity is a publication or a research data repository if the entity is a dataset. References that cannot be mapped to any record are assigned a URI as their distinct ID. In order to disambiguate such entities, we use normalized versions of titles, years and author names. Entities lacking any of these fields are ignored to minimize matching errors.

Merging. When a duplicate entity is found, the links of all copies are merged. For this, the link database is searched for all ingoing and outgoing links of the entity already present in the database. For every entity, there must be at least one link or else the entity would not have been included in database in the first place. Thus, for every found link, the following cases may occur:

1. the new entity shares the same link, i.e. it is linked to the same entity
2. the new entity does not have this link
3. the new entity is linked to the same entity but on a lower level of granularity
4. the new entity is linked to the same entity but on a higher level of granularity

Likewise, the new entity may contain new links hitherto not present in the database.

   At this point, all entities are disambiguated including sources and targets of known and new links. With this information, we can determine whether links are equal, i.e. whether they link the same entities. For our use case, the direction of a link does not hold any meaning, all links are being treated as bidirectional because in information systems, it is usually desired to show links between resources for the title views of each resource involved, not just for one of them. Hence, links are considered equal when the linked entities are equal regardless of which of these entities is the source or the target of the link.

1. When the link already exists, provenance information of the new link is added to the provenance information of the known link. The confidence value is updated to the higher confidence value of both links. In case of conflicting metadata, the metadata with the higher confidence is kept. The new link is discarded and only the updated link remains in the database.
2. When the new entity does not have the current link, no action is required.
3. When the new link is the more coarse-grained version of a known link, the known link is kept and the new link is discarded.
4. When the new link is the more fine-grained version of a known link, the new link is added to the database with the disambiguated entity as source/target entity. The known link is deleted.
5. When the link is not yet known, it is added to the database with the disambiguated entity as source/target entity.

Whether a link is a more coarse- or fine-grained version of another is determined using the research data ontology described in Sect. 3.6. Lookup of the entities in the ontology is performed automatically while the ontology has been created manually.

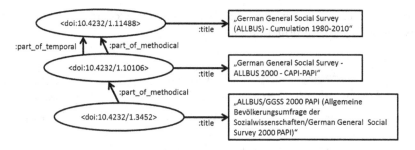

Fig. 4. Example of the research data ontology with different granularities

3.6 Research Data Ontology

There is often a mismatch between the granularity in which data is cited and the granularity in which data is registered in data repositories [14]. In order to address this problem, we developed a research data ontology that captures the relationships between many of the datasets relevant to our use case. The ontology models hierarchical relationships between research datasets, i.e. a dataset may consist of different data collections (e.g. taken place in different years) which may also include different versions of the dataset (e.g. different samples or with errata). In Fig. 4, an example of the research data ontology is shown which illustrates different granularities of research datasets. For comparing the granularity of links, the linked research data entities are compared. If the first link points to a higher level in the research data ontology, e.g. a cumulated data file, while the second points to a lower level of the same dataset, e.g. a specific subset of the cumulated data file, the first link is seen as being more coarse-grained than the second. Beside using the ontology for merging, it is also accessible in the link database so that for every research data entity in the database, its relations to other datasets can be retrieved.

3.7 Link Database

As described in Sect. 3.1, we reuse the InFoLiS infrastructure consisting of a Node.js based API backend which provides RESTful web services and an LOD representation of the data. Since we work with heterogeneous document-like data, we use a MongoDB for storage. Storing the data in graphs allows for easy representation of the links between items and storing additional, necessary information like provenance information. This is highly important in order to comprehend how and on which basis links have been generated. The infrastructure has been modularized and deployed in Docker containers which allows an execution with moderate resources.

3.8 Elasticsearch Index

For a fast and efficient search, the link database is pushed into an Elasticsearch index. While the link database features indirect links for facilitating updates regarding reference matching (see Sect. 3.3), indirect links are not desired in the index queried by the information portals.

Fig. 5. Links before and after transformation

Thus, we implemented an algorithm to flatten links when necessary and push all links to the search index in a simplified format. Figure 5 illustrates a set of links before and after transformation. In this example, a publication holds two dataset references which are matched to one or more datasets. After flattening (right side of the figure), the publication is now linked to the datasets directly. Note that an entity can still be linked to a citedData entity if the latter is not linked to a dataset. Information on the data citations is not lost but instead added to the links' metadata. The algorithms for transforming the links and pushing them to the index are implemented as an enhancement to the InFoLiS framework and can be invoked via the web service.

fromID	toID	fromType	fromView	toType	toView	linkReason
ID of entity1	ID of entity2	Information type+ of entity1	Citation string of entity1	Information type+ of entity2	Citation string of entity2	**Text snippet containing the reference to entity2
gesis-sso ar-6762	datasearch-ht tpwww-da-ra-deoaip--oaioa i-da-ra-de557 591	publication	Erwerbsarbeit und Erwerbsbevölkerung im Wandel: Anpassungsprobleme einer alternden Gesellschaft. Frankfurt am Main, Campus Verl., 1998, 281 S., (Veröffentlichung aus dem Verbund Arbeits- und Innovationspotentiale im Wandel)	dataset	Schupp, Jürgen; Goebel, Jan; Kroh, Martin et. al. (2017): Sozio-oekonomisches Panel (SOEP), Daten der Jahre 1984-2015 (internationale Version) Version: 32i.1. Dataset. http://doi.org/10.5684/soep.v3 2i.1	Datenbasis ist das Sozio-oekonomische Panel (SOEP) (Projektgruppe Panel 1995).
gesis-sso ar-20988	literaturpool-5 7321a70-990f -11e7-9c5b-d 59dcbf11d82	publication	Hartmann, Peter H. (1990): Wie repräsentativ sind Bevölkerungsumfragen? Ein Vergleich des ALLBUS und des Mikrozensus	citedData	Mikrozensus 1982	Verwendet wurden Daten des Mikrozensus 1982
ZA2125	wzb-bib-b000 028159	dataset	USIA, Washington (1960): Internationale Beziehungen (Februar 1960)	publication	Merritt, Richard L.; Puchala, Donald J. (Hrsg.): Western European Perspectives on International Affairs: Public Opinion Studies and Evaluations. New York: Praeger 1968.	(empty)

+   information type: publication | dataset | project | institution | instrument | citedData
*   available for automatically generated links
** available for all automatically and some of the manually generated links

Fig. 6. Additional or different fields of links in the Elasticsearch index

In Fig. 6, additional fields added to the links before pushing to the index and fields with different content are displayed. In addition to the fields shown in

Fig. 3, the links in the index feature the fields fromID and toID, which contain the persistent identifiers of the respective entities instead of the entities' URIs. The fromEntity and toEntity fields are, however, still present so that every entity in the index is connected to the respective entity in the link database. The fields fromView and toView contain the content of the entities' entityView fields and fromType and toType their entityType field content. The field linkReason contains the text snippet as a string instead of the URI of the TextualReference entry. Hereby, each link instance contains all information needed to display the link in an search portal's result list without needing additional queries to the index. The metadata in the link database and index can be used to enhance the presentation of the information in the portals. For example, the linkView field can be used to group links by their name. By displaying the linkReason text snippets, users can get a glimpse on how an entity is referenced in the linked entity, i.e. in what relation precisely they stand. The entityRelations can be used to improve ranking, i.e. to give priority to exact matches over partly matching dataset records. Information about the source of an entity or link in the field provenance can be used to filter searches. Figure 7 shows how the fields linkView and linkReason are displayed in the GESIS search portal.

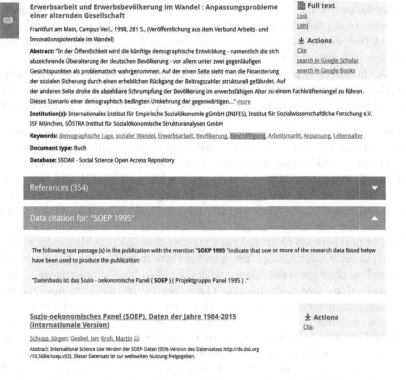

Fig. 7. Presentation of linkView and linkReason in the GESIS search

4   Evaluation

The LOD infrastructure is used productively in the new GESIS search portal that provides access to a range of different linked social science information in an integrated way. To evaluate the user experience of linked information between different information types, we performed a user study with 17 participants (7 female, 10 male, average age 33.35 years (SD = 10.04)). All participants work at German universities, three as a professors, four as postdocs, nine as research associates, and one as a student assistant. They were recruited by email invitations. To date of the user study, the portal included publications, scales, projects, and institutions. The study is based on our use case introduced in Sect. 2. It was conducted in two steps: (1) a prescribed evaluation scenario to familiarize participants with interlinked information and (2) a free exploration phase were participants had time to use the prototype in the context of their own research interests.

In the evaluation scenario the users had to perform the following actions:

1. They were provided with a detailed information view of a literature entry (as shown in Fig. 7) as a starting point and were asked to find information about the research data that are cited in the paper.
2. After following the link to one of the research data sets and getting to the corresponding detailed information view, they were asked to find information about the project in which context the data set was created and which other studies had also applied the same survey instrument.
3. After checking the project information, they clicked on the corresponding link to the survey instrument entry and saw on the detailed information view a list of other research data that have also applied this survey instrument.

We encouraged the participants to think-aloud during both steps to get their direct feedback and asked at the end for their assessments regarding usefulness, trust in the provided links and completeness of the linked information.

12 participants found the links very useful, four useful and one found it neither useful nor not useful (collected through a Likert-scale ranging from 1 "not useful at all" to 5 "very useful", mean = 4.65, SD = 0.5). One participant stated that she was enabled to get connections that otherwise would be very hard to find. 14 participants indicated they trusted that the provided links would lead them to the right information. Yet, some of them mentioned that their confidence was based on their good experience with GESIS so far. Completeness of the links was expected by five participants. The other twelve subjects appreciated the additional information provided but didn't expect any system developed with a reasonable amount of effort to be able to show all connections. At the end, we asked participants if knowledge about the origin of the links is important for them, especially whether they have been created manually or automatically. For 14 participants the origin of the links was not important. 5 persons added that it was more important that the links lead to the correct information than how the link was created. However, three participants indicated they liked to know

the origin of the links. Two of them said it would increase their confidence in the information provided.

Besides the mostly positive feedback, there are also some challenges that arise on the user interaction side. The chance to get lost after following a couple of links is high. We observed this especially in the free exploration task. Participants had problems to get back to their starting point. We are currently exploring visualization techniques that should help to keep the overview. Furthermore, after following a couple of links, the relation to the original information need gets lower: participants had problems to understand that all publications of a project were listed and not only those that were related to their initial search query. In this case, a ranking of the linked information items according to the information need or an appropriate labelling might be helpful.

5   Related Work

There are similar approaches considering the integration and linking of heterogeneous Linked Data. The tool Karma [12] allows data integration from a variety of data formats, their conversion and mapping as well as to push them into a search index. However, Karma does not address data enrichment tasks like entity disambiguation and link merging which was necessary for our use case. Built on Karma is the approach of [7] which uses Karma in order to allow an on-the-fly integration of static and dynamic Linked Datasets. The framework LDIF [18] converts heterogeneous Linked Data sources into one representation which can then be further processed. When the original data is not RDF, it has to be converted beforehand. The output is either N-Quads or N-Triples which needs to be transformed again in order to push them into a search index.

Established linking tools like Limes [15] and Silk [22] enable to find links between Linked Datasets. In contrast, our approach currently focuses on already existing, manually created links between datasets or on identification of implicit links between datasets by parsing pdf documents. In our approach, linking tools could be used in order to find links to additional Linked Datasets in the LOD cloud.

The Open PHACTS Discovery Platform [6] allow users to perform complex queries over a variety of integrated and linked RDF sources of the pharmacological and physiochemical domain. Once the data is available in RDF format it can be integrated and is linked by the Large Knowledge Collider (LarKC) [3] using its Identity Mapping Service and ConceptWiki. The data is available via an API for further use, e.g. in search platforms. A similar approach was developed for educational resources [4]. In this approach education resources available on the web and datasets from the LOD cloud have been integrated and linked and made available via an API. However, no data enrichments tasks comparable to our use case have been conducted. Similar approaches for other domains have been developed in [2,11]. The Semantic Web index Sindice [16] was a lookup index for Semantic Web documents which allowed for searching over different, even unconnected Linked Datasets. Being a pure index, the challenges of data integration, linking and enrichment were not addressed.

None of the of the mentioned approaches covers the full workflow from non-Linked Data sources via integration and linking up to a provision via an efficient and searchable index.

6 Conclusion and Outlook

The presented LOD backend infrastructure has been developed for research information of the social sciences. However, although presented among the use case of GESIS, it can be applied and adjusted for similar use cases, since all components have been developed independently of any specific portal or metadata schema. The source code of the underlying InFoLiS infrastructure is available via GitHub[10] for further reuse.

When integrating datasets from different data collections of a domain, one will most likely face the occurrence of equivalent person names in different collections. This problem can be solved with author disambiguation algorithms. Our basic entity disambiguation methods do not yet make use of these. Another potential extension is the linking to external Linked Datasets, e.g. in the LOD cloud. In the context of research information, thesauri and authority data with persistent identifiers may lead to a benefit for users and improved retrieval. Moreover, they can serve as a linking hub in order to find related datasets.

Acknowledgements. Parts of the approach presented in this paper have been developed in the InFoLiS project funded by DFG (SU 647/2-1 and MA 5334/1-2). The concept of the LOD backend infrastructure has been created by Benjamin Zapilko and Katarina Boland in the internally funded project LOD infrastructure. All extensions have been developed by Katarina Boland. The user study has been conducted during the development of the GESIS search by Dagmar Kern. The GESIS search portal has been developed by Daniel Hienert.

References

1. Boland, K., Ritze, D., Eckert, K., Mathiak, B.: Identifying references to datasets in publications. In: Zaphiris, P., Buchanan, G., Rasmussen, E., Loizides, F. (eds.) TPDL 2012. LNCS, vol. 7489, pp. 150–161. Springer, Heidelberg (2012). https://doi.org/10.1007/978-3-642-33290-6_17
2. Celli, F., Keizer, J., Jaques, Y., Konstantopoulos, S., Vudragovic, D.: Discovering, indexing and interlinking information resources. F1000Research **4**, 432 (2015). [version 2; referees: 3 approved]
3. Cheptsov, A., Assel, M., Gallizo, G., Celino, I., DellAglio, D., Bradesko, L., Witbrock, M., Della Valle, E.: Targe knowledge collider. A service-oriented platform for large-scale semantic reasoning. In: Proceedings of the International Conference on Web Intelligence, Mining and Semantics (WIMS 2011), ACM International Conference Proceedings Series, Sogndal, Norway (2011)

---

[10] https://github.com/infolis/.

4. Dietze, S., Yu, H.Q., Giordano, D., Kaldoudi, E., Dovrolis, N., Taibi, D.: Linked education: interlinking educational resources and the web of data. In: The 27th ACM Symposium on Applied Computing (SAC-2012), Special Track on Semantic Web and Applications, 25–29 March 2012, Trento, Italy (2012)
5. Dua, A., Nelle, D., Stock, G., Wagner, G.G.: Facing the future: European research infrastructures for the humanities and social sciences (2014)
6. Gray, A.J.G., Groth, P., Loizou, A., Askjaer, S., Brenninkmeijer, C., Burger, K., Chichester, C., Evelo, C.T., Goble, C., Harland, L., Pettifer, S., Thompson, M., Waagmeester, A., Williams, A.J.: Applying linked data approaches to pharmacology: architectural decisions and implementation. Semant. Web 5(2), 101–113 (2014)
7. Harth, A., Knoblock, C., Stadtmller, S., Studer, R., Szekely, P.: On-the-fly integration of static and dynamic sources. In: Proceedings of the Fourth International Workshop on Consuming Linked Data (COLD 2013) (2013)
8. Heath, T., Bizer, C.: Linked Data: Evolving the Web into a Global Data Space. Synthesis Lectures on the Semantic Web Theory and Technology, 1st edn, pp. 1–136. Morgan & Claypool, San Rafael (2011)
9. Hey, T., Tansley, S., Tolle, K.M.: The Fourth Paradigm: Data-Intensive Scientific Discovery, vol. 1. Microsoft Research, Redmond (2009)
10. Isaac, A., Haslhofer, B.: Europeana linked open data-data.europeana.eu. Semant. Web 4, 2917 (2013)
11. Jupp, S., Malone, J., Bolleman, J., Brandizi, M., Davies, M., Garcia, L., Gaulton, A., Gehant, S., Laibe, C., Redaschi, N., Wimalaratne, S.M., Martin, M., Le Novere, N., Parkinson, H., Birney, E., Jenkinson, A.M.: The EBI RDF platform: linked open data for the life sciences. Bioinformatics 30(9), 13381339 (2014)
12. Knoblock, C.A., Szekely, P., Ambite, J.L., Gupta, S., Goel, A., Muslea, M., Lerman, K., Taheriyan, M., Mallick, P.: Semi-automatically mapping structured sources into the semantic web. In: Proceedings of the Extended Semantic Web Conference, Crete, Greece (2012)
13. Lyon, L.: The informatics transform: re-engineering libraries for the data decade. Int. J. Digit. Curation 7(1), 126–138 (2012)
14. Mathiak, B., Boland, K.: Challenges in matching dataset citation strings to datasets in social science. D-Lib Mag. 21(1/2), 23–28 (2015)
15. Ngonga Ngomo, A.C., Auer, S.: LIMES: a time-efficient approach for large-scale link discovery on the web of data. In: Proceedings of the Twenty-Second International Joint Conference on Artificial Intelligence (IJCAI 2011), vol. 3, pp. 2312–2317. AAAI Press (2011)
16. Oren, E., Delbru, R., Catasta, M., Cyganiak, R., Stenzhorn, H., Tummarello, G.: Sindice.com: a document-oriented lookup index for open linked data. IJMSO 3, 37–52 (2008)
17. Schmachtenberg, M., Bizer, C., Paulheim, H.: Adoption of the linked data best practices in different topical domains. In: Mika, P., et al. (eds.) ISWC 2014. LNCS, vol. 8796, pp. 245–260. Springer, Cham (2014). https://doi.org/10.1007/978-3-319-11964-9_16
18. Schultz, A., Matteini, A., Isele, R., Mendes, P., Bizer, C., Becker, C.: LDIF - a framework for large-scale linked data integration. In: 21st International World Wide Web Conference (WWW 2012), Developers Track, Lyon, France (2012)

19. Simon, A., Wenz, R., Michel, V., Di Mascio, A.: Publishing bibliographic records on the web of data: opportunities for the BnF (French National Library). In: Cimiano, P., Corcho, O., Presutti, V., Hollink, L., Rudolph, S. (eds.) ESWC 2013. LNCS, vol. 7882, pp. 563–577. Springer, Heidelberg (2013). https://doi.org/10.1007/978-3-642-38288-8_38
20. Smith-Yoshimura, K.: Analysis of international linked data survey for implementers. D-Lib Mag. 22(7/8), 110 (2016)
21. Van Hooland, S., Verborgh, R.: Linked Data for Libraries, Archives and Museums: How to Clean, Link and Publish Your Metadata. Facet Publishing, Croydon (2014)
22. Volz, J., Bizer, C., Gaedke, M., Kobilarov, G.: Discovering and maintaining links on the web of data. In: Bernstein, A., Karger, D.R., Heath, T., Feigenbaum, L., Maynard, D., Motta, E., Thirunarayan, K. (eds.) ISWC 2009. LNCS, vol. 5823, pp. 650–665. Springer, Heidelberg (2009). https://doi.org/10.1007/978-3-642-04930-9_41

Detecting Hate Speech on Twitter Using a Convolution-GRU Based Deep Neural Network

Ziqi Zhang[1]([✉])[ID], David Robinson[2][ID], and Jonathan Tepper[2]

[1] University of Sheffield, Sheffield, UK
ziqi.zhang@sheffield.ac.uk
[2] Nottingham Trent University, Nottingham, UK
david.robinson2015@my.ntu.ac.uk, jonathan.tepper@ntu.ac.uk

Abstract. In recent years, the increasing propagation of hate speech on social media and the urgent need for effective counter-measures have drawn significant investment from governments, companies, and empirical research. Despite a large number of emerging scientific studies to address the problem, a major limitation of existing work is the lack of comparative evaluations, which makes it difficult to assess the contribution of individual works. This paper introduces a new method based on a deep neural network combining convolutional and gated recurrent networks. We conduct an extensive evaluation of the method against several baselines and state of the art on the largest collection of publicly available Twitter datasets to date, and show that compared to previously reported results on these datasets, our proposed method is able to capture both word sequence and order information in short texts, and it sets new benchmark by outperforming on 6 out of 7 datasets by between 1 and 13% in F1. We also extend the existing dataset collection on this task by creating a new dataset covering different topics.

1 Introduction

In recent years, the exponential growth of social media such as Twitter and community forums has been increasingly exploited for the propagation of hate speech and the organisation of hate based activities [1, 4]. The anonymity and mobility afforded by such media has made the breeding and spread of hate speech - eventually leading to hate crime - effortless in a virtual landscape beyond the realms of traditional law enforcement. In the UK, there has been significant increase of hate speech towards the migrant and Muslim communities following recent events including leaving the EU, and the Manchester and the London attacks [12]. This correlates to record spikes of hate crimes, and cases of threats to public safety due to its nature of inciting hate crimes, such as that followed the Finsbury van attack [3]. Surveys and reports also show the rise of hate speech

---

Z. Zhang—The work was carried out when the author was at the Nottingham Trent University.

© Springer International Publishing AG, part of Springer Nature 2018
A. Gangemi et al. (Eds.): ESWC 2018, LNCS 10843, pp. 745–760, 2018.
https://doi.org/10.1007/978-3-319-93417-4_48

and related crime in the US following the Trump election [18], and the EU where 80% of young people have encountered hate speech online and 40% felt attacked or threatened [2].

Social media companies (e.g., Twitter, Facebook) have come under pressure to address this issue [13], and it has been estimated that hundreds of millions of euros are invested every year [10]. However, they are still being criticised for not doing enough. This is largely because standard measures involve manually reviewing online contents to identify and delete offensive materials. The process is labour intensive, time consuming, and not sustainable in reality [10, 26].

The pressing need for scalable, automated methods of hate speech detection has attracted significant research using semantic content analysis technologies based on Natural Language Processing (NLP) and Machine Learning (ML) [4, 7, 9, 10, 16, 17, 20, 23–27]. Despite this large amount of work, it remains difficult to compare their performance [21], largely due to the use of different datasets by each work and the lack of comparative evaluations. This work makes three contributions to this area of work. First, we use a CNN+GRU (convolutional neural network, gated recurrent unit network) neural network model optimised with dropout and pooling layers, and elastic net regularisation for better learning accuracy. Compared to existing deep learning models that use only CNNs, the GRU layer also captures sequence orders that are useful for this task. Second, we create a public dataset of hate speech by collecting thousands of tweets on the subjects of religion and refugees, which extends currently available datasets [7, 25, 26] by both quantity and subject coverage. Third, we test our model against several baselines and also previously reported results on all existing public datasets, and set new benchmark as we show that our model outperforms on 6 out of 7 datasets by as much as 13% in F1. We also undertake error analysis to identify the challenges in hate speech detection on social media.

The remainder of this paper is structured as follows. Section 2 reviews related work; Sect. 3 introduces the CNN+GRU model; Sect. 4 describes our datasets, followed by experiments in Sect. 5 and conclusion in Sect. 6.

2   Related Work

2.1   Terminology

Recent years have seen an increasing number of research on hate speech detection as well as other related areas. As a result, the term 'hate speech' is often seen mixed with other terms such as 'offensive', 'profane', and 'abusive languages', and 'cyber bullying'. To distinguish them, we identify that hate speech (1) targets individual or groups on the basis of their characteristics (targeting characteristics); (2) demonstrates a clear intention to incite harm, or to promote hatred; (3) may or may not use offensive or profane words. For example:

'Assimilate? No they all need to go back to their own countries. #BanMuslims Sorry if someone disagrees too bad.'

In contrast, 'All you perverts (other than me) who posted today, needs to leave the O Board. Dfasdfdasfadfs' is an example of abusive language, which often bears the purpose of insulting individuals or groups, and can include hate speech, derogatory and offensive language [17]. 'i spend my money how i want bitch its my business' is an example of offensive or profane language, which is typically characterised by the use of swearing or curse words. 'Our class prom night just got ruined because u showed up. Who invited u anyway?' is an example of bullying, which has the purpose to harass, threaten or intimidate typically individuals rather than groups.

In the following, we cover state of the art in all these areas with a focus on hate speech. Our experiments will only involve hate speech, due to both dataset availability and the focus of this work.

2.2 State of the Art

State of the art primarily casts the problem as a supervised document classification task [21]. These methods can be divided into two categories: one relies on manual feature engineering that are then consumed by algorithms such as SVM, Naive Bayes, and Logistic Regression [4,7,9,16,24–27] (**classic methods**); the other represents the more recent deep learning paradigm that employs neural networks to automatically learn multi-layers of abstract features from raw data [10,17,20,23] (**deep learning methods**).

Classic Methods. [21] summarised several types of features used in the state of the art. *Simple surface features* such as bag of words, word and character n-grams have shown to be highly predictive in hate speech detection [4,16,23–26], as well as other related tasks [17,28]. Other surface features can include URL mentions, hashtags, punctuations, word and document lengths, capitalisation, etc. [7,17]. *Word generalisation* includes the use of word clusters [24], and techniques such as topic modelling [27,28] and word embedding learning [9,17,23] that learn low-dimensional, dense feature vectors for words from unlabelled corpora. Such word vectors are then used to construct feature vectors of messages. *Sentiment analysis* makes use of the degree of polarity expressed in a message [4,7,11,23]. *Lexical resources* are often used to look up specific negative words (such as slurs, insults, etc.) in messages as their presence can be predictive features [4,11,17,27]. *Linguistic features* utilise syntactic information such as Part of Speech (PoS) and certain dependency relations as features [4,7,11,28]. For example, [4] noted that 'othering phrases' denoting a 'we v.s. them' stance are common in hate speech. *Meta-information* refers to data about messages, such as gender identity of a user associated with a message [25,26], or high frequency of profane words in a user's post history [27]. In addition, *Knowledge-Based features* such as messages mapped to stereotypical concepts in a knowledge base [8] and *multimodal information* such as image captions and pixel features [28] were used in cyber bully detection but only in very confined context [21].

In terms of the classification algorithms, Support Vector Machines (SVM) is the most popular algorithm [4,7,16,24,27]. Others can include as Naive Bayes [7,16], Logistic Regression [7,9,16,25,26], and Random Forest [7,27].

Deep learning based methods employ Deep artificial Neural Networks (DNN) to learn abstract feature representations from input data through its multiple stacked layers for the classification of hate speech. The input can take various forms of feature encoding, including many of those used in the classic methods. However, the input features are not directly used for classification. Instead, the multi-layer structure learns new abstract feature representations that are used for learning. For this reason, deep learning based methods focus on the design of the network topology, which automatically extracts useful features from a simple input feature representation. Note that this excludes those methods [9,16] that use DNN to learn word or text embeddings and subsequently apply another classifier (e.g., SVM) to use such embeddings as features for classification. Instead, we focus on DNN methods that perform the classification task itself.

To the best of our knowledge, methods belonging to this category include [1, 10,20,23], all of which use simple word and/or character based one-hot encoding as input features to their models, while [23] also use word polarity. The most popular network architectures are Convolutional Neural Network (CNN) and Recurrent Neural Networks (RNN), typically Long Short-Term Memory network (LSTM). In the literature, CNN is well known as an effective network to act as 'feature extractors', whereas RNN is good for modelling orderly sequence learning problems [19]. In the context of hate speech classification, intuitively, CNN extracts word or character combinations [1,10,20] (e.g., phrases, n-grams), RNN learns word or character dependencies (order information) in tweets [1,23].

While each type of network has been used for hate speech classification, no work has explored combining both structures for this task. In theory, CNN+RNN networks are powerful structures to capture order information between features extracted by CNNs. In practice, they are found to be more effective than structures solely based on CNNs or RNNs in tasks such as gesture [22] and activity recognition [19], and Named Entity Recognition [5]. In hate speech classification, we hypothesise that a CNN+RNN type of structure can be more effective as it may capture co-occurring word n-grams as useful patterns for classification, such as the pairs (muslim refugees, deported) and (muslim refugees, not welcome) in the sentence 'These muslim refugees are not welcome in my Country they should all be deported...'. However, practically, it remains a question as to what extent such orderly information is present in short messages, and how can we optimise such a network for classification accuracy.

2.3   Datasets

It is widely recognised that a major limitation in this area of work is the lack of comparative evaluation [21]. The large majority of existing works were evaluated on privately collected datasets for different problems. [17] claimed to have created the largest datasets for abusive language by annotating comments posted on Yahoo! Finance and News. The datasets were later used by [16]. However, they are not publicly available. Also, as we illustrated before, abusive language can be different from hate speech. Currently, the only publicly available hate speech datasets include those reported in [7, 10, 20, 25, 26], which are all Twitter-based. [26] annotated 16,914 tweets into 'sexism', 'racism' and 'neither'. The corpus was collected by searching for tweets containing frequently occurring terms (based on some manual analysis) in tweets that contain hate speech and references to specific entities. It was then annotated by crowd-sourcing over 600 users. The dataset was later expanded in [25], with about 4,000 as new addition to their previous dataset. This dataset was then annotated by two groups of users to create two different versions: domain experts who are either feminist or anti-racism activist; and amateurs that are crowd-sourced. Later in [10], the authors merged both expert and amateur annotations in this dataset by using majority vote; and in [20], the dataset of [26] was merged with the expert annotations in [25] to create a single dataset. [7] annotated some 24,000 tweets for 'hate speech', 'offensive language but not hate', and 'neither'. These were sampled from tweets filtered using a hate speech lexicon from Hatebase.org.

3 Methodology

3.1 Pre-processing

Given a tweet, we start by applying a light pre-processing procedure described below based on that reported in [7] to normalise its content. This includes: (1) removing the characters | : , ; & ! ? \; (2) applying lowercase and stemming, to reduce word inflections; and (3) removing any tokens with a document frequency less than 5, which reduces sparse features that are not informative for learning. Empirically, this was found to lead to better classification accuracy.

Further, we also normalise hashtags into words, so '#refugeesnotwelcome' becomes 'refugees not welcome'. This is because such hashtags are often used to compose sentences. We use dictionary based look up to split such hashtags.

3.2 The CNN+GRU Architecture

Our CNN+GRU network is illustrated in Fig. 1. The first layer is a word embedding layer, which maps each text message (in generic terms, a 'sequence') into a real vector domain. To do so, we map each word onto a fixed dimensional real valued vector, where each element is the weight for that dimension for that word. In this work, we use the word embeddings with 300 dimensions pre-trained on the 3-billion-word Google News corpus with a skip-gram model[1] to set the weights of our embedding layer. We also constrain each sequence to be 100 words which is long enough to encode tweets of any length, truncating long messages and pad the shorter messages with zero values.

The embedding layer passes an input feature space with a shape of 100×300 to a drop-out layer with a rate of 0.2, the purpose of which is to regularise learning to avoid overfitting. Intuitively, this can be thought of as randomly removing a word in sentences and forcing the classification not to rely on any individual

---

[1] https://github.com/mmihaltz/word2vec-GoogleNews-vectors.

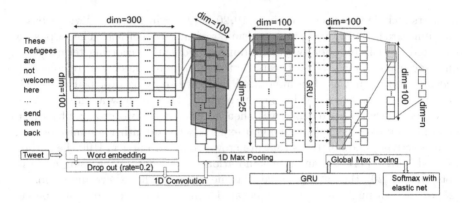

Fig. 1. The CNN+GRU network architecture. This diagram is best viewed in colour. (Color figure online)

words. The output feeds into a 1D convolutional layer with 100 filters with a window size of 4, padding the input such that the output has the same length as the original input. The rectified linear unit function is used for activation. This convolves the input feature space into a 100 × 100 representation, which is then further down-sampled by a 1D max pooling layer with a pool size of 4 along the word dimension, producing an output of shape 25 × 100. Each of the 25 dimensions can be considered an 'extracted feature'.

These extracted features then feed into the GRU layer, which treats the feature dimension as timesteps and outputs 100 hidden units per timestep. The key difference between a GRU and an LSTM is that a GRU has two gates (reset and update gates) whereas an LSTM has three gates (namely input, output and forget gates). Thus GRU is a simpler structure with fewer parameters to train. In theory, this makes it faster to train and generalise better on small data; while empirically it is shown to achieve comparable results to LSTM [6]. Next, a global max pooling layer 'flattens' the output space by taking the highest value in each timestep dimension, producing a 1 × 100 vector. Intuitively, this selects the highest scoring features to represent a tweet. Finally, a softmax layer takes this vector as input to predict probability distribution over all possible classes (n), which will depend on individual datasets. The softmax activation is also regularised using the elastic net regularisation that linearly combines the L_1 and L_2 norms, but is designed to solve the limitations of both [29].

We use the categorical cross entropy loss function and the Adam optimiser to train the model. The first is empirically found to be more effective on classification tasks than other loss functions including classification error and mean squared error [15], and the second is designed to improve the classic stochastic gradient descent (SGD) optimiser and in theory combines the advantages of two other common extensions of SGD (AdaGrad and RMSProp) [14].

Model Parameters. As described above, many of our model parameters are based on empirical findings reported previously, default values or anecdotal evidence, except the batch size and epoches for training which we derive from developmental data (to be detailed later). Arguably, these may not be the best settings for optimal results, which are always data-dependent. However, we show later in experiments that the model already obtains promising results even without extensive data-driven parameter tuning.

Comparison Against Similar DNNs. Our network architecture is similar to those in [5, 19, 22]. The differences include: (1) we use a GRU instead of an LSTM for the reasons stated before; (2) we add a drop-out layer to regularise learning and a global max pooling layer to extract features from the GRU; (3) we use elastic net to regularise the output from the softmax layer. [5] also used bidirectional LSTM in the Named Entity Classification task, while [19, 22] stacked multiple convolutional layers to extract hierarchical features in image processing. We do not use such complex models as we show that our simple CNN+GRU is already performing well in this task and is able to benefit from both convolutional features and order information captured by GRU, which confirms our hypothesis. For the same reason, we build our model on only word embeddings although many suggest that character-level features can be more effective. We show later in experiments that such a structure is very powerful that it even outperforms DNN models based on character embeddings.

4 Dataset Creation

As introduced before, the only publicly available hate speech datasets include that of [7], and [25, 26] that are also used to create variants used in [10, 20]. While [7] classify hate speech in general without identifying the targeting characteristics, [25, 26] collected data for sexism and racism. In this work, we create a different dataset by collecting tweets discussing refugees and Muslims, which were media focus during the time of writing due to various recent incidents [3, 12]. All tweets are annotated for two classes: hate and non-hate, firstly by a computational linguistic researcher and then cross-checked by a student researcher. Disputed annotations were then discussed and corrected to ensure both agree with the correction. The general annotation guideline in [26] were followed.

To collect the data, we follow the mainstream approach [26] starting with an initial search for tweets containing common slurs and terms used pertaining to targeting characteristics, then manually identify frequently occurring terms in tweets that contain hate speech and references to specific entities (frequent keywords), then further filter the tweets with these frequent keywords.

Specifically, we started with using the Twitter Streaming API to collect tweets containing any of the following words for a period of 7 days: `muslim, islam, islamic, immigration, migrant, immigrant, refugee, asylum`. This created a corpus of over 300,000 tweets (duplicates and retweets removed), from which we randomly sampled 1,000 for annotation (batch 1). However, it was found that tweets annotated as hate speech were extremely rare (<1%). Therefore, we manually inspected the annotations and further filtered the remaining tweets (disjoint with batch 1) by the following words found to be frequent for hate speech: `ban, kill, die, back, evil,` hate, attack, terrorist, terrorism, threat, deport. We then sampled another 1,000 tweets (batch 2) from this collection for annotation. However, the amount of true positives was still very low (1.1%). Therefore we created another batch (batch 3) by using the Twitter Search API to retrieve another 1,500 tweets with the following hashtags considered to be strong indicators of hate speech: #refugeesnotwelcome, #DeportallMuslims, #banislam, #banmuslims, #destroyislam, #norefugees, #nomuslims. The dataset however, contains over 400 tweets after removing duplicates, and about 75% were annotated as hate speech. Finally we merge all three batches to create a single dataset, which we make public to encourage future comparative evaluation[2].

5   Experiment

5.1   Datasets

We use a total of 7 public datasets including ours for evaluation, as shown in Table 1. To our knowledge, this is by far the most comprehensive collection of hate speech datasets used in any studies.

Table 1. Statistics of datasets used in the experiment

Dataset	#Tweets	Classes (#tweets)	Targeting characteristics
WZ-L	16,093	Racism (1,934) sexism (3,149) neither (11,010)	Racism, sexism
WZ-S.amt	6,594	Racism (123) sexism (1,073) both (15) neither (5,383)	Racism, sexism
WZ-S.exp	6,594	Racism (85) sexism (777) both (35) neither (5,697)	Racism, sexism
WZ-S.gb	6,594	Racism (90) sexism (911) both (27) neither (5,564)	Racism, sexism
WZ-LS	18,625	Racism (2,012) sexism (3,769) both (30) neither (12,810)	Racism, sexism
DT	24,783	Hate (1,430) non-hate (23,353)	General
RM	2,435	Hate (414) non-hate (2,021)	Refugee, Muslim

WZ-L is the larger dataset created in [26]. **WZ-S.amt** is the smaller dataset created in [25], annotated by amateurs; while **WZ-S.exp** is the same dataset annotated by experts. In [10], the authors took the WZ-S.amt and WZ-S.exp datasets to create a new version by taking the majority vote from both amateur and expert annotations where the expert was given double weights. We follow the same practice and in case of tie, we take the expert annotation. We refer to this

---

[2] Find out at: https://github.com/ziqizhang/chase/tree/master/data.

dataset as **WZ-S.gb**. Note that although WZ-S.amt, WZ-S.exp and WZ-S.gb datasets contain the same set of tweets, state of the art results are found to be quite different on some of them (see Sect. 5.4), suggesting that the annotations can be different. Further, [20] combined the WZ-L and the WZ-S.exp datasets into a single dataset and in case of duplicates, we take the annotation from WZ-L. We refer to this dataset as **WZ-LS**. All datasets only contain the tweet IDs, some of which have been deleted or made private at the time of writing and therefore, the numbers in Table 1 may be different from the original studies.

DT refers to the dataset created in [7]. It also contains tweets annotated as 'abusive (but non-hate)'. In this work, we set such annotations to be 'non-hate' so the dataset contains only two classes. Finally, our dataset on refugees and Muslims is referred to as **RM**.

5.2 Baseline and Comparative Models

Baselines. We create a number of baselines. **First**, we use the SVM model described in [7][3]. Each tweet is firstly pre-processed using the procedure described in Sect. 3.1. Next, following the original work, a number of different types of features are used as below. We refer to these as the **Basic** feature set:

- Surface features: word unigram, bigram and trigram each weighted by TF-IDF; number of mentions, and hashtags[4]; number of characters, and words;
- Linguistic features: Part-of-Speech (PoS) tag unigrams, bigrams, and trigrams, weighted by their TF-IDF and removing any candidates with a document frequency lower than 5; number of syllables; Flesch-Kincaid Grade Level and Flesch Reading Ease scores that to measure the 'readability' of a document;
- Sentiment features: sentiment polarity scores of the tweet, calculated using a public API[5].

Extending on this, we add additional surface based features as follows and refer to these as the **Enhanced** feature set:

- number of misspellings within a tweet: we check the pre-processed tweet against both a UK and US English dictionaries, then calculate the ratio between the number of misspelled words and the number of all words.
- number of emoji's uses regular expression to find tokens matching the format of an emoji from an original tweet and return a number.
- number of special punctuations uses regular expression to count the numbers of question and exclamation marks as they can be used as an expletive.
- percentage of capitalisation computes the percentage of characters that are capitalised within the tweet.
- hashtags: the lowercase hashtags from tweets.

---

[3] Code: https://github.com/t-davidson/hate-speech-and-offensive-language.

[4] Extracted from the original tweet before pre-processing which splits hashtags.

[5] https://github.com/cjhutto/vaderSentiment.

We use **SVM** to refer to the model using all Basic features identified above, and **SVM+** as the one using the Enhance feature set. Notice that the SVM baseline is also the model used in [7].

Second, we create another two baseline by modifying our CNN+GRU network. First, we remove the drop-out and the global max pooling layers and the elastic net regularisation, to create **CNN+GRU$_B$**; second, we further remove the GRU layer to create a CNN only network **CNN**. While the first allows us to evaluate the effect of the modifications on a basic CNN+GRU structure, the second allows us to evaluate whether GRU does capture useful order information from short messages such as tweets. We apply all these baselines on all seven datasets and compare the results against our model, **CNN+GRU**.

State of the Art. In addition to the baselines, we also compare our results against those reported figures in [10, 20, 25, 26] on the corresponding datasets.

5.3 Implementation, Parameter Tuning, and Evaluation Metrics

We used the Python Keras[6] with Theano backend[7] and the scikit-learn[8] library to implement all models[9]. For each dataset, we split it into 75:25 to use 75% in a grid-search to tune batch size and learning epoches using 5-fold cross-validation experiments, and test the optimised model on the 25% held-out data. We report results using the standard Precision (P), Recall (R), and F1-measures.

5.4 Results and Discussion

Table 2 compares our model against the baselines as well as state of the art on F1[10] (on an 'as-is' basis where available, indicated by citations) on each of the seven datasets. The highest figures are highlighted in **bold**.

Baselines Performance. Among the four baselines, neural network based methods consistently outperformed SVM and SVM+, by as much as 9% on the WZ-LS dataset. For SVM+, adding enhanced features leads to incremental improvement over SVM, as we notice increase in F1 on 6 out of 7 datasets. Comparing CNN+GRU$_B$ against CNN, it shows that adding the GRU recurrent layer does bring further improvement as we notice a 1% improvement on five out of seven datasets. While the relatively small improvement could be due to the short text nature of tweets, the consistent gain in F1 suggests that GRU still captures useful order information in addition to CNNs.

CNN+GRU Performance. Compared against baselines, our CNN+GRU model achieves the highest F1 on all datasets. Compared against CNN+GRU$_B$, the improved model sees further incremental improvement on 5 datasets by

---

[6] https://keras.io/.

[7] http://deeplearning.net/software/theano/.

[8] http://scikit-learn.org/.

[9] Code available at https://github.com/ziqizhang/chase.

[10] We use micro-average to be comparable to previously reported results.

Table 2. F1 result of the proposed method against baselines and state of the art. The best figures are highlighted in **bold**. The 'Best features' is a setting reported in [25], where their method used the combination of the best performing features.

Dataset	SVM	SVM+	CNN	CNN+GRU$_B$	CNN+GRU	State of the art	
WZ-L	0.74	0.74	0.80	0.81	**0.82**	0.74	Waseem [26], best F1
WZ-S.amt	0.86	0.87	0.91	**0.92**	**0.92**	0.84	Waseem [25], best features
WZ-S.exp	0.89	0.90	0.90	0.91	**0.92**	0.91	Waseem [25], best features
WZ-S.gb	0.86	0.87	0.91	0.92	**0.93**	0.90	Gamback [10], best F1
WZ-LS	0.72	0.73	0.81	0.81	0.82	0.82	Park [20], WordCNN
						0.81	Park [20], Character-CNN
						0.83	Park [20], HybridCNN
DT	0.87	0.89	**0.94**	**0.94**	**0.94**	0.87	SVM, Davidson [7]
RM	0.86	0.89	0.90	0.91	**0.92**	0.86	SVM, Davidson [7]

adding dropout, max pooling and elastic net regularisation. Compared against SVM and SVM+ baselines, CNN+GRU makes an improvement between 2 and 9%. Compared to previously reported results in the state of the art, our CNN+GRU model obtained an improvement of: 7% on WZ-L, 1% on WZ-S.exp, 8% on WZ-S.exp, 13% on WZ-S.gb, 7% on DT, and 6% on RM. On the WS-LS dataset, our model outperforms [20] on their character-only CNN models, losing 1% to their hybrid model that combines both word and character features. Similarly, [10] also used character features in their CNN model. As discussed before, the literature generally acknowledges that character-based features are more effective than word-based. Hence taking into account the above results, we argue that the better results obtained by our CNN+GRU models using only word-based features is due to the superiority in the network architecture.

5.5   Error Analysis

We carry out further studies to analyse the errors made by the classifiers to understand the challenges for this task. To do so, on each dataset and for each class, we identify the tweets where all three neural network models (CNN+GRU, CNN+GRU$_B$, CNN) predicted incorrectly. Then in Table 3 we show the distribution of such errors across all classes for each dataset. The figures show that, on the WZ-S.amt, WZ-LS and WZ-L datasets, the classifiers make about the same number of errors on the 'racism' and 'non-hate' tweets, and twice the errors on the 'sexism' tweets. If we factor in the number of tweets per class on these datasets (see Table 1), it is obvious that the classifiers make relatively more errors on predicting any categories of hate tweets than non-hate. The situation is similar on the WZ-S.exp and WZ-S.gb datasets, and intensifies on the DT and RM datasets where only 'hate' and 'non-hate' are considered. Interestingly, increasing training data does not always reduce errors proportionally. For example, comparing the WZ-S.amt against the WZ-L datasets in Table 1, the number of 'sexism' tweets increases from 16% of all instances to 20% and the number of 'racism' tweets increases from 2% to 12%. However, the classifiers did not seem to benefit very much as errors have increased by 8% on 'sexism' tweets and dropped only 3% on 'racism' tweets (Table 3).

Table 3. Distribution of errors over all classes in each dataset.

	Racism	Sexism	Both	Non-hate	Hate
WZ-S.amt	25%	46%	3%	26%	N/A
WZ-S.exp	12%	52%	8%	28%	N/A
WZ-S.gb	14%	50%	7%	29%	N/A
WZ-LS	23%	52%	1%	23%	N/A
WZ-L	22%	54%	N/A	24%	N/A
DT	N/A	N/A	N/A	6%	94%
RM	N/A	N/A	N/A	30%	70%

We further analyse the vocabularies of each class on each dataset. For each class, we calculate two statistics. **Instance-2-Uwords, I2U** ratio divides the number of instances (tweets) of the class by the number of unique words found in that class. This measures on average, the number of instances sharing at least one word. Intuitively, a higher number suggests that instances of the class are more likely to have overlap in words. We hypothesise that this translates to overlap in features, i.e., the features of instances of this class are dense; and therefore, these instances may be easier to classify. **Uwords-2-Class, U2C** ratio divides the number of unique words found *only* in that class (i.e., the words must not be present in other classes) by the number of unique words in that class (i.e., the words can be present in other classes at the same time). Intuitively, if a class has a lot of words that are unique to itself, it may have many unique features that makes it easier to classify. Table 4 shows the two ratios for different datasets.

Firstly, comparing 'non-hate' against any other classes of hate tweets, 'non-hate' tweets have much higher I2U and U2C scores. For example, on the DT dataset, on average, more than 6 tweets will share at least one word (I2U = 6.3), and 'non-hate' tweets have 45% of words that are unique to that class. Comparatively the figures are much lower for the 'hate' tweets on this dataset.

Table 4. Analysis of Instance-2-Uwords (I2U) and Uwords-2-Class (U2C) ratios.

	Racism		Sexism		Both		Non-hate		Hate	
	I2U	U2C	I2U	U2C	I2U	U2C	I2U	U2C	I2U	U2C
WZ-S.amt	.25	0	.84	0	.12	0	3.1	.22	-	-
WZ-S.exp	.26	.003	.70	.006	.19	0	3.3	.32	-	-
WZ-S.gb	.28	.003	.77	.008	.19	0	3.2	.29	-	-
WZ-LS	1.0	.004	1.4	.008	.16	0	3.8	.11	-	-
WZ-L	1.1	.004	1.3	.008	-	-	3.5	.11	-	-
DT	-	-	-	-	-	-	6.3	.45	.71	0
RM	-	-	-	-	-	-	2.2	.31	.65	.009

Intuitively, this may mean that 'non-hate' tweets have much higher overlap in their features and they also have much more unique features compared to 'hate'. Both make 'non-hate' easier to predict, hence explaining the significantly higher errors on the 'hate' class on this dataset. Again the situation is similar on other datasets. On WZ based datasets, the relatively lower I2U and U2C values for 'racism' than 'sexism' also suggests that the first is a harder class to predict. This may explain the observation before that the increase in data on this class did not proportionally translate to improvement in classification accuracy.

We manually analysed a sample of 200 tweets from the WZ-S.amt, DT and RM datasets, covering all classes to identify tweets that are difficult to classify. **Non-distinctive features** appear to be the majority of cases. For example, one would assume that the presence of the phrase `'white trash'` or pattern `'* trash'` is more likely to be a strong indicator of hate speech than not, such as in `'White bus drivers are all white trash...'`. However, our analysis shows that such seemingly 'obvious' features are also prevalent in non-hate tweets such as `'... I'm a piece of white trash I say it proudly'`. As we show previously in Table 4, hate tweets in our datasets lack unique features to distinguish themselves from non-hate tweets. The second example does not qualify as hate speech since it does not 'target individual or groups' or 'has the intention to incite harm', which is indeed often very subtle to identify from lexical or syntactic levels. Similarly, **subtle metaphors** are often commonly found in false negatives such as `'expecting gender equality is the same as genocide'`. **Out of embedding vocabulary (OOV) words** are words that are frequent in hate tweets, but are not included in the word embedding model we used. For example, `'faggot'` in the hate tweet `'I'm just upset they got faggots on this show'` is an OOV word in the Google embedding model. This raises the question whether using a different or multiple word embedding models to reduce OOV can further improve learning accuracy. **Questioning or negation** is often found in false positives such as `'I honestly hate the term 'feminazi' so much. Stop it'`. Further, expression of **Stereotypical views** such as in `'... these same girls ... didn't cook that well and aren't very nice'` is also common in false negative sexism tweets. These are difficult to capture because they require understanding of the implications of the language.

6   Conclusion and Future Work

The propagation of hate speech on social media has been increasing significantly in recent years and it is recognised that effective counter-measures rely on automated data mining techniques. This work makes several contributions to this problem. First, we introduced a method for automatically classifying hate speech on Twitter using a deep neural network model combining CNN and GRU that are found to empirically improve classification accuracy. Second, we conducted comparative evaluation on the largest collection of public datasets and show that the proposed method outperformed baselines as well as state of the art in most cases. Our results make new reference for future comparative studies. Third, we created and published another hate speech dataset, complementing existing ones by focusing on religion (Muslim) and refugees. Finally, our analysis shows that the presence of abstract concepts such as 'sexism', 'racism' or 'hate' is very difficult to detect if solely based on textual content. But the task may potentially benefit from knowledge about social groups and communication modes.

We will explore future work in a number of ways, such as other network structures to extracting different features; explore different word embeddings' effect on learning; and integrate user-centric features, such as the frequency of a user detected for posting hate speech and the user's interaction with others.

Acknowledgement. Part of this work was conducted during the SPUR project funded by the Nottingham Trent University. We also thank Qian Wang, a student funded by the Nuffield Foundation for data analysis in this work.

References

1. Badjatiya, P., Gupta, S., Gupta, M., Varma, V.: Deep learning for hate speech detection in tweets. In: Proceedings of the 26th International Conference on World Wide Web Companion, pp. 759–760 (2017)
2. BBCNews: Countering hate speech online. http://eeagrants.org/News/2012/. Accessed July 2017
3. BBCNews: Finsbury park attack: son of hire boss held over Facebook post. http://www.bbc.co.uk/news/uk-wales-40347813. Accessed May 2017
4. Burnap, P., Williams, M.L.: Cyber hate speech on Twitter: an application of machine classification and statistical modeling for policy and decision making. Policy Internet **7**(2), 223–242 (2015)
5. Chiu, J.P., Nichols, E.: Named entity recognition with bidirectional LSTM-CNNs. Trans. Assoc. Comput. Linguist. **4**, 357–370 (2016)
6. Chung, J., Gulcehre, C., Cho, K., Bengio, Y.: Empirical evaluation of gated recurrent neural networks on sequence modeling. In: NIPS 2014 Deep Learning and Representation Learning Workshop (2014)

7. Davidson, T., Warmsley, D., Macy, M., Weber, I.: Automated hate speech detection and the problem of offensive language. In: Proceedings of the 11th Conference on Web and Social Media. AAAI (2017)
8. Dinakar, K., Jones, B., Havasi, C., Lieberman, H., Picard, R.: Common sense reasoning for detection, prevention, and mitigation of cyberbullying. ACM Trans. Interact. Intell. Syst. **2**(3), 18:1–18:30 (2012)
9. Djuric, N., Zhou, J., Morris, R., Grbovic, M., Radosavljevic, V., Bhamidipati, N.: Hate speech detection with comment embeddings. In: Proceedings of the 24th International Conference on World Wide Web, pp. 29–30. ACM (2015)
10. Gambäck, B., Sikdar, U.K.: Using convolutional neural networks to classify hate-speech. In: Proceedings of the First Workshop on Abusive Language Online, pp. 85–90. Association for Computational Linguistics (2017)
11. Gitari, N.D., Zuping, Z., Damien, H., Long, J.: A lexicon-based approach for hate speech detection. Int. J. Multimed. Ubiquit. Eng. **10**(10), 215–230 (2015)
12. Guardian: Anti-muslim hate crime surges after Manchester and London Bridge attacks. https://www.theguardian.com. Accessed July 2017
13. Guardian: Zuckerberg on refugee crisis: 'hate speech has no place on Facebook'. https://www.theguardian.com. Accessed July 2017
14. Kingma, D.P., Ba, J.: Adam: a method for stochastic optimization. In: Proceedings of the 3rd International Conference for Learning Representations (2015)
15. McCaffrey, J.D.: Why you should use cross-entropy error instead of classification error or mean squared error for neural network classifier training. https://jamesmccaffrey.wordpress.com. Accessed Jan 2018
16. Mehdad, Y., Tetreault, J.: Do characters abuse more than words? In: Proceedings of the SIGDIAL 2016 Conference, Los Angeles, USA, pp. 299–303. Association for Computational Linguistics (2016)
17. Nobata, C., Tetreault, J., Thomas, A., Mehdad, Y., Chang, Y.: Abusive language detection in online user content. In: Proceedings of the 25th International Conference on World Wide Web, pp. 145–153 (2016)
18. Okeowo, A.: Hate on the rise after Trump's election. http://www.newyorker.com/. Accessed July 2017
19. Ordóñez, F.J., Roggen, D.: Deep convolutional and LSTM recurrent neural networks for multimodal wearable activity recognition. Sensors **16**(1), 115 (2016)
20. Park, J.H., Fung, P.: One-step and two-step classification for abusive language detection on Twitter. In: ALW1: 1st Workshop on Abusive Language Online, Vancouver, Canada. Association for Computational Linguistics (2017)
21. Schmidt, A., Wiegand, M.: A survey on hate speech detection using natural language processing. In: International Workshop on Natural Language Processing for Social Media, pp. 1–10. Association for Computational Linguistics (2017)
22. Tsironi, E., Barros, P., Weber, C., Wermter, S.: An analysis of convolutional long short-term memory recurrent neural networks for gesture recognition. Neurocomputing **268**(C), 76–86 (2017)
23. Vigna, F.D., Cimino, A., Dell'Orletta, F., Petrocchi, M., Tesconi, M.: Hate me, hate me not: hate speech detection on Facebook. In: Proceedings of the First Italian Conference on Cybersecurity, pp. 86–95 (2017)
24. Warner, W., Hirschberg, J.: Detecting hate speech on the world wide web. In: Proceedings of the Second Workshop on Language in Social Media, LSM 2012, pp. 19–26. Association for Computational Linguistics (2012)

25. Waseem, Z.: Are you a racist or am i seeing things? Annotator influence on hate speech detection on Twitter. In: Proceedings of the Workshop on NLP and Computational Social Science, pp. 138–142. Association for Computational Linguistics (2016)
26. Waseem, Z., Hovy, D.: Hateful symbols or hateful people? Predictive features for hate speech detection on Twitter. In: Proceedings of the NAACL Student Research Workshop, pp. 88–93. Association for Computational Linguistics (2016)
27. Xiang, G., Fan, B., Wang, L., Hong, J., Rose, C.: Detecting offensive tweets via topical feature discovery over a large scale Twitter corpus. In: Conference on Information and Knowledge Management, pp. 1980–1984. ACM (2012)
28. Zhong, H., Li, H., Squicciarini, A., Rajtmajer, S., Griffin, C., Miller, D., Caragea, C.: Content-driven detection of cyberbullying on the Instagram social network. In: Proceedings of the Twenty-Fifth International Joint Conference on Artificial Intelligence, IJCAI 2016, pp. 3952–3958. AAAI Press (2016)
29. Zou, H., Hastie, T.: Regularization and variable selection via the elastic net. J. Roy. Stat. Soc. Ser. B Stat. Methodol. 67(2), 301–320 (2005)

Author Index

Printed in the United States
by Baker & Taylor

Printed in the United States
By Bookmasters